Islam in Historical Perspective

Islam in Historical Perspective provides readers with an introduction to Islam, Islamic history and societies with carefully selected historical and scriptural evidence that enables them to form a comprehensive and balanced vision of Islam's rise and evolution across the centuries and up to the present day. Combining historical and chronological approaches, the book examines intellectual dialogues and socio-political struggles within the extraordinarily rich Islamic tradition. Treating Islam as a social and political force, the book also addresses Muslim devotional practices, artistic creativity and the structures of everyday existence. *Islam in Historical Perspective* is designed to help readers to develop personal empathy for the subject by relating it to their own experiences and the burning issues of today. It contains a wealth of historical anecdotes and quotations from original sources that are intended to emphasize its principal points in a memorable way.

This new edition features a thoroughly revised and updated text, new illustrations, expanded study questions and chapter summaries.

Alexander Knysh is Professor of Islamic Studies in the Department of Near Eastern Studies at the University of Michigan and Academic Project Director at St. Petersburg State University, Russian Federation.

Islam in Historical Perspective

Second Edition

Alexander Knysh

Routledge
Taylor & Francis Group

NEW YORK AND LONDON

First published 2017
by Routledge
711 Third Avenue, New York, NY 10017

and by Routledge
2 Park Square, Milton Park, Abingdon, Oxon OX14 4RN

Routledge is an imprint of the Taylor & Francis Group, an informa business

Library of Congress Cataloging in Publication Data
Names: Knysh, Alexander D.
Title: Islam in historical perspective / by Alexander Knysh.
Description: 2nd. edition. | New York ; London : Routledge, 2017. |
   Includes bibliographical references and index.
Identifiers: LCCN 2016015658 | ISBN 9781138193697 (alk. paper)
Subjects: LCSH: Islam—Historiography. | Islam—History.
Classification: LCC BP49 .K69 2017 | DDC 297—dc23
LC record available at https://lccn.loc.gov/2016015658

ISBN: 978-1-138-19369-7 (hbk)
ISBN: 978-1-138-19370-3 (pbk)
ISBN: 978-1-315-63922-2 (ebk)

Typeset in Times New Roman
by Apex CoVantage, LLC

To Snezhana with gratitude and affection

Contents

Preface   xv
Acknowledgments   xvi
Note on Transliteration and Dates   xvii

Introduction   1

What Is Islam? 1
Multiplicity of Approaches to the Study of Islam 1
Islam as an Object of Interpretation and a Source of Meaning 3
Notes 6

1   Arabia: The Cradle of Islam   7

Geography 7
The Arabs 8
Bedouin Lifestyle 9
Social Structures 10
Raiding and Warfare 10
Mecca: A Trade Hub 11
Mecca: A Religious Center 11
Other Religious Communities of Arabia 15
Conclusions 16
Questions to Ponder 16
Summary 17
Notes 17

**2   Muhammad and the Beginnings of Islam: The Making
of the Muslim Community**   19

Muhammad's Background and Early Life 19
The First Revelations 20
Muhammad's Public Preaching and Opposition to It 22
Migration (Híjra) *and the Formation of the Islamic* Umma 26
Muhammad as Political and Religious Leader and Private Individual 29
The Battle of Úhud 31
The Battle of the Ditch 32

Muhammad and the Bedouin Tribes of Arabia 32
The Conquest of Mecca and Beyond 33
Conclusions 35
Question to Ponder 35
Summary 36
Notes 37

3   After Muhammad: The Rightly Guided Caliphs and the Conquests   **40**

The Muslim Conquests Under 'Umar 42
The Conquest of Syria and Palestine 44
The Conquest of Iraq 46
The Conquest of Egypt 48
The Conquests Continue: The Fall of the Sasanid Empire 48
The Death of 'Umar and the Succession of 'Uthman 49
Conclusions 49
Question to Ponder 50
Summary 50
Notes 51

**4   The Murder of 'Uthman, the *Fitna* Wars, and the Rise and
    Consolidation of the Umayyad Dynasty**   **53**

Who's "Right" and Who's "Wrong"? 53
The Election of 'Uthman 53
Grievances Against 'Uthman 54
The Accession of 'Ali and the Battle of the Camel 57
The Struggle Between 'Ali and Mu'awiya 60
The Battle of Siffin 61
The Kharijites 63
The Last Years of 'Ali's Caliphate 64
Mu'awiya Becomes Caliph 64
The Death of Mu'awiya, the Accession of Yazíd, and the Tragedy at Karbala' 65
The Caliphate of 'Abdallah b. al-Zubayr 66
The Rebellion of Mukhtár 67
The End of 'Abdallah b. al-Zubayr's Caliphate and the Triumph of the Marwánids 68
The Consolidation of Umayyad Power Under 'Abd al-Malik and His Successors 69
Conclusions 70
Questions to Ponder 71
Summary 72
Notes 73

5   The Principal Source of Islam: The Qur'an   **76**

The Qur'an as Revelation and Sacred Book 76
The Name and Structure 77
The Language of the Qur'an 79

The Mysterious Letters 80
The Collection of the Qur'an 81
The Central Theme of the Qur'an: God 83
The Prophets and Messengers 84
The Judgment Day, Paradise, and Hell 87
Conclusions 88
Questions to Ponder 89
Summary 89
Notes 90

6   **The Prophetic *Hadíth* and Sunna and the Emergence of the Shari'a**   **92**

Hadíth *as the Muslim Gospel? 92*
The Importance of Hadíth *93*
The Types of Hadíth *93*
The Transmission and Collection of Hadíth *95*
The Writing Down of Hadíth *and the Elevation of the*
    Status of the Prophet's Sunna 96
The Six Sunni Hadíth *Collections 98*
The Shi'ite Hadíth *98*
Sacred or Holy Hadíth (Hadíth Qúdsi) *100*
The Emergence of the Shari'a Law 101
Questions to Ponder 102
Summary 102
Notes 103

7   **The Problem of the Just Ruler and the First Divisions**
    Within the Community   **105**

Opposition to the Umayyads 105
The Rise of the Mawáli 106
The Kharijites 106
'Ali's Party 109
The Uneasy Loyalists 111
Some Early Theological Concepts 112
Conclusions 114
Questions to Ponder 115
Summary 115
Notes 116

8   **The 'Abbásid Revolution and Beyond**   **118**

The Theological Underpinnings 118
The Sources of Discontent 119
The Turn of the Wheel: 'Abbásid Propaganda and
    the Beginning of the Third Fitna *120*
The Triumph of the 'Abbásid Cause 123

The Consolidation of 'Abbásid Power 124
The Rearticulation of the Doctrine of the Imamate 125
Conclusion: The 'Abbásid Empire at Its Prime 128
Questions to Ponder 128
Summary 129
Notes 129

9   **Islamic Scholarship Under the 'Abbásids: The Rise and
    Development of the Schools of Law**   **131**

Introduction 131
The Major Stages of the Evolution of Islamic Legal Thought 131
The Qur'anic Roots of Islamic Law 134
Qur'anic Legislation Pertaining to Marriage, Divorce, and Inheritance 135
Qur'anic Punishments for Homicide 136
Fiqh, the Fuqahá', the Muftis, and the Judges 136
The Abrogation Theory 138
The "Qur'anic Commands" That Are Not in the Qur'an 138
The Formation of the Regional Schools of Law 139
*Muhammad al-Sháfi'i (d. 820) and the Crystallization
    of the Islamic Legal Theory 140*
The Four Roots of Islamic Jurisprudence 141
Later Developments 143
Parallel Systems of Justice Under the 'Abbásids 144
Conclusions 144
Questions to Ponder 145
Summary 145
Notes 146

10   **Islamic Scholarship Under the 'Abbásids: Theological
     Debates and Schools of Thought**   **148**

*The Qur'an as the Foundation of Islamic Faith and Cult
    and an Object of Disputation 148*
The Beginnings of Theological Reasoning in Islam 148
Divine Predestination Versus Human Free Will 151
The Doctrine of Postponement and the Problem of Faith 153
The Emergence of Mu'tazilism 154
The Supporters of Hadíth and Their Theological Creed 158
Ibn Hánbal and the Inquisition 160
The Theological "Middle Way": Ash'arism 161
Ash'arism, Maturidism, and the Hadíth Party 163
Conclusions 164
Questions to Ponder 164
Summary 164
Notes 165

11 Twelver Shi'ism and Zaydism 167

The Crystallization of the Shi'ite Creed in Opposition to Sunnism 167
The Divergence of the Shi'ite and Sunni Visions of Islam 171
The Vicissitudes of the Shi'ite Imamate Under the 'Abbásids 172
The Shi'ite Community in the Absence of the Divinely Ordained Guide 175
The Political and Social Aspects of the Doctrine of Occultation 177
"The Shi'ite Century" (946–1055): Political and Social Aspects 178
The Blossoming of Shi'ite Theology and Jurisprudence 180
Shi'ite Views of the Qur'an 183
Zaydism 184
Conclusions 186
Questions to Ponder 187
Summary 187
Notes 188

12 Shi'ism as a Revolutionary Movement: The Isma'ilis 193

Who Are the Isma'ilis? 193
The Rise and Spread of Revolutionary Isma'ilism 195
The Teaching and the Mission 195
The Proclamation of 'Abdallah ('Ubaydallah) the Máhdi,
    and the Qarmati–Fatimid Split 199
The Rise of the Fatimids 200
The Conquest of Egypt and the Consolidation of Fatimid Power 202
Another Split: Al-Hákim and the Druzes 204
The Crisis Over Al-Mustánsir's Succession and the Rise of the Nizári Community 207
The Principal Articles of the Nizári Creed 209
The Collapse of the Fatimid Caliphate 211
The Háfizi-Táyyibi Split and Its Impact on the Fortunes of Later Isma'ilism 211
The Qarmati Revolt and the Rise and Fall of the Qarmati State in Bahrain 212
Conclusions 214
Questions to Ponder 215
Summary 215
Notes 216

13 Ascetic and Mystical Movement in Islam: Sufism 220

Introduction 220
The Name and the Beginnings 221
Basic Ideas and Goals 221
The Archetypal "Sufi": Al-Hásan al-Basri and His Followers 222
Regional Manifestations 223
The Formation of the Baghdadi School of Sufism 224
The Systematization of the Sufi Tradition 227
The Maturity of Sufi Science: Al-Ghazali the Conciliator 229
Sufism as Literature 229

Sufi Metaphysics: The Impact of Ibn 'Arabi 232
Major Intellectual and Practical Trends in Later Sufism 233
The Rise and Spread of Sufi Brotherhoods (Tariqas) *234*
Sufism and the Cult of "Friends of God" (Saints) 237
Sufism and Shi'ism 238
Sufism Today 240
Conclusions 242
Questions to Ponder 243
Summary 243
Notes 245

14 Intellectual Struggles in Premodern Islam: Philosophy Versus Theology **248**

Fálsafa *as a Rational Discipline 248*
Fálsafa *and* Kalám *249*
Fálsafa *as an Elaboration of Neoplatonic Doctrines 250*
The Beginnings of Fálsafa *251*
Al-Kindi, the Philosopher of the Arabs 251
Abu Bakr al-Razi, the Physician and Freethinker 253
Al-Farábi, the Second Teacher 254
Ibn Sina (Avicenna) 256
Al-Ghazali, the Proof of Islam 261
Ibn Rushd (Averroes), the Commentator 265
Conclusions 268
Questions to Ponder 269
Summary 270
Notes 271

15 Transmission and Conservation of Knowledge:
   'Ulamá', *Mádrasas*, and Sufi Lodges **274**

The Status, Venues, and Bearers of Learning in Muslim Societies 274
Elementary Education: The Kuttáb *275*
The Muslim College: Mádrasa *277*
The Economic Foundations of Mádrasa *Education 278*
Methods and Curricula of Mádrasa *Education 279*
Sufi Lodges 281
Conclusions 283
Questions to Ponder 284
Summary 284
Notes 284

16 The Basic Beliefs and Practices of Islam: Islamic Life Cycle **286**

Islamic Ethos and the Five Pillars 286
Visiting the Prophet's Tomb at Medina 301
How Religion Shapes the Lives of Individual Muslims 301
Conclusions 305
Questions to Ponder 305

Summary 305
Notes 306

17   Islamic Art and Religious Architecture (Mosque)   **309**

The Qur'an as the Focus of Devotion 309
Scriptural Evidence Against Figural Arts 310
How Did Artists Respond to the Restrictions? 311
The Mosque: Architectural and Devotional Aspects 316
Conclusions 320
Questions to Ponder 320
Summary 320
Notes 321

18   Women in Islamic Societies   **323**

The Controversial Topic 323
Women in the Qur'an 324
Women in Hadíth *and* Fiqh *329*
Theorizing the Muslim Woman 332
Conclusions 336
Questions to Ponder 336
Summary 337
Notes 338

19   Islam and the West   **341**

The Arab Conquests of Christian Lands 341
The Beginnings of the Crusader Movement in Europe 343
God's Wars: The First Crusades and the Muslim Response 344
The Muslims Strike Back 350
The Legacy of the Crusades 352
The Founder of Islam and His Message in the Eyes of
*   His Followers and Through the Christian Looking Glass 353*
The Scandinavian Caricatures of Muhammad and
*   the Resurgence of Old Prejudices 359*
Islamic Influences on European Culture 360
The Curious (and Inexplicable) Rise of the West 361
Questions to Ponder 362
Summary 363
Notes 364

20   Islam in the Gunpowder Empires: The World of Islam Faces
Modernity and European Colonialism   **367**

The Gunpowder Empires 367
What Is Modernity? 379
The Beginnings of European Colonial Expansion 380
Muslim Responses: Economic and Social 383

Questions to Ponder 385
Summary 386
Notes 387

**21   Renewal and Reform in Islam: The Emergence
      of Islamic Modernism and Reformism**   389

Different Reformers and Different Reforms 389
The Fundamentalist Reform of Muhammad b. 'Abd al-Wahháb (d. 1792) 392
The Modernist Reforms of al-Afgháni and 'Abdo 395
Muhammad Rashíd Ridá (d. 1935) and al-Manár 406
By Way of Conclusion: A Summary of the Major Precepts of Islamic Reform 409
Questions to Ponder 410
Summary 411
Notes 412

22   Islam as a Political Force and Vehicle of Opposition   415

Major Stages of the Movement for Reform and Renewal of Islam 415
The Complicated Issue of Terminology 415
The Latest Stages of the Evolution of Islamic Activism 417
Ayatollah Khomeini (d. 1989) and the Iranian Revolution 435
Conclusions 441
Questions to Ponder 442
Summary 442
Notes 444

23   Islam Reinterpreted: Major Trends in Islamic Thought Today   448

In Quest of Liberal Islam 448
The Principal Themes of Islamic Liberalism 449
The Geopolitical Roots of Liberal Islam 452
Conclusions 467
Questions to Ponder 468
Summary 468
Notes 470

24   The Ideology and Practice of Globalized Jihadism   475

The Afghan War, 'Abdallah 'Azzám, and the Rise of Transnational Jihadism 476
*Changing the Target and Means: al-Qa'ida, Usáma bin
    Ládin, and Áyman al-Zawáhiri 481*
Instead of a Conclusion: Does the Islamist Project Have a Future? 491
Conclusions 491
Questions to Ponder 493
Summary 493
Notes 495

Bibliography   500
Index   511

Preface

Books about Islam are legion. They take a wide range of approaches to the subject, some of which are outlined in the Introduction. It is difficult to write something fresh and original on the subject, unless one decides to boldly demolish the academic wisdom about Islam accumulated over the past decades and to come up with a totally novel theory of its teachings and practices and their implementation by various Muslim communities the world over. However, this book does not attempt to do this. Instead, it provides factual evidence for readers with little or no prior knowledge of Islamic religion that should enable them to form their own opinion of the vicissitudes of Islam across time and space. The author has sought to avoid broad generalizations about Muslim beliefs and practices, paying special attention to the truly astounding diversity of their interpretation by Muslims living in different historical epochs and sociopolitical conditions. The author makes no attempt to extract and postulate a transhistorical and immutable essence of Islamic faith and practice. His goal is to present, to the extent this is possible, a balanced and historically grounded view of the Islamic tradition. The author addresses a number of controversial and emotionally charged topics, as the status of women in Islam, the often negative portrayal of its founder in the Western media, the Crusades, the possibility and viability of "liberal Islam," the multifarious and often controversial consequences of the Western colonization of the Muslim world, neocolonialism and state-building in the Middle East, "Islamic terrorism," especially the jihadism of al-Qa'ida and Islamic State, and so on. In discussing doctrinal and political disagreements within Islam, special attention is paid to non-Sunni communities (the Kharijites, the Twelver Shi'ites, the Isma'ilis, the Druze, and the Zaydis) that are often overlooked in general overviews of Islam and Islamic history. While the geographical and chronological scope of this book is very broad and the historical evidence presented rather detailed, they are essential to convey to the reader the complexity of Islam and its interpretations by its practitioners. In short, the author designed his book for "a people who reflect" (Q 16:10).[1] They are his intended audience.

Note

1 Here and everywhere "Q" stands for Qur'an.

Acknowledgments

This book has taken a long time to be written. It has benefited from the suggestions and insights of many individuals.

My special thanks goes to Dr. Victoria (Vika) Gardner and Dr. Erik Ohlander, whose corrections and suggestions have served me in good stead in preparing the final version of the text for publication. I owe a great debt of gratitude to the Woodrow Wilson International Center for Scholars in Washington, D.C., whose yearlong fellowship (2007–2008) allowed me to revise and finalize the text of the first edition of the book. In preparing the second edition, I benefited from the suggestions of my colleagues at St. Petersburg State University, especially Dr. Anna Matochkina, Professor Oleg Redkin, Dr. Olga Bernikova, Vladimir Rozov, and Oleg Sokolov, who are members of a research team devoted to the study of the vicissitudes of the concept of Islamic state. Last but not least, I am grateful to my family for their understanding and support, without which this book would have never been completed. As the author, I bear full responsibility for any factual or printing errors that may have crept into my text.

Note on Transliteration and Dates

The author has used a simplified transliteration of Arabic, Persian, and Turkish names and terms that makes no distinction between emphatic and nonemphatic consonants (usually conveyed in specialized academic books by Latin letters with dots underneath). Macrons (short stroke marks above Latin vowels) to differentiate between long and short vowels of the Arabic alphabet have not been used either. The simplified transliteration was adopted to facilitate the reception of the book by the reader with no prior knowledge of academic transcription conventions. Some exceptions apart, the author has adhered to the spelling of Muslim names and terms that is current in the English-speaking media. The accented letters (á, í, and ú) are occasionally used in the transliteration of some names and terms to indicate where the stress falls. The dates are given according to the Common Era calendar (c.e.) with no Muslim, or Hijra(h), calendar equivalents.

Introduction

What Is Islam?

Before examining any given phenomenon, we must first ask ourselves what the object of our examination will be. In our case, we need to provide a definition—tentative as it may be—of the phenomenon called "Islam." Our ability to furnish such a definition implies that we have at least a general notion of what belongs to this category and what should be excluded from it. For instance, we may ask ourselves whether it is appropriate to talk about "Islamic feminism" as an integral part of modern Islam or dismiss it as a Western product arbitrarily grafted onto it from outside. A similar question arises in regard to some modern religious movements that have emerged out of Islam, for example, the Baha'iyya (Baha'ism) and the Ahmadiyya, whose relationship with mainstream Islam, either Sunni or Shi'ite, remains a hotly disputed issue. Excluding or including these and other groups or intellectual trends inevitably compels us to draw on our personal understanding of what is or is not Islam. In other words, as investigators of the phenomenon called "Islam" we are consciously or unconsciously constructing our subject by selecting and emphasizing some of its aspects, while neglecting, deemphasizing, or even deliberately excluding others. As a result, any portrayal of Islam, including ours, is inevitably selective, incomplete, and potentially biased to boot.

Such regrettable deficiencies notwithstanding, we should not be deterred from the noble task of intellectual exploration, for we can say more or less the same about any object of human knowledge, especially in the field of the humanities and social sciences. As investigators, we inevitably have our own preformed convictions, prejudices, and blind spots. But we also have our insights that assist us in our task.

Multiplicity of Approaches to the Study of Islam

Like any religion, Islam can be examined from a variety of angles. For instance, it can be studied as a sacred tradition with its distinct mythology, history, sacred figures, sacred landscape, sacred time, as well as its peculiar vision of the cosmos. This approach is characteristic of the discipline known as "history of religions" that is being taught at many colleges and universities across North America.

This "macro" approach to Islam, which emphasizes its general, universal characteristics, coexists with "micro" studies of Muslim societies. Its practitioners are interested in how Islam is believed and observed by a particular community or an ethnic group in a specific geographical locality. For instance, they may focus on the life cycle of the members of this community, namely, their trajectory from cradle to grave and the role of Islam in this existential journey. Adherents of the micro approach may also choose to investigate how the general precepts and practices of Islamic faith are debated and contested by various social and religious groups within this community. This approach to Islam is usually pursued by social and cultural anthropologists.

Another possible approach to Islam treats it first and foremost as a social and political force closely associated with certain distinctive political and social structures. Practitioners of this approach tend to focus on Islam's role as an ideology of political legitimization (e.g., for the rule of a given statesman or dynasty) or see it as a means of mass mobilization that allows Muslim rulers and the religious elites loyal to them to rally the Muslim masses around a certain objective, such as war, whether defensive or offensive, or against internal opposition. Obviously, those who find themselves at odds with powers-that-be no less readily avail themselves of the mobilizing potency of Islam to challenge the status quo and its stalwarts.

Other investigators approach Islam as, primarily, a system of educational practices supported by a network of religious schools and colleges. Still others are interested in Islam's function as a social and psychological safety net that assists Muslims living in different historical epochs and localities and in coping with poverty, social inequality, and the psychological problems (desperation, despondency) resulting therefrom.

Although the exact objects of the academic approaches just outlined may vary, their adherents have certain things in common. First, they tend to view Islam primarily as a political and institutional structure and social force; second, they stress Muslims' ability to adapt their faith to the changing political, economic, and social conditions of their existence. Studies of Islam based on such general assumptions are commonly practiced by social and institutional historians of the Muslim world, anthropologists, and students of so-called Islamic politics. What they usually neglect is the fact that, in addition to everything else, Islam also constitutes a source of the strong devotional and emotional commitment that we call "religious faith."

Scholars of Islam who seek to overcome the shortcomings of the aforementioned "functional" or "pragmatic" approaches to Islam are usually based in religious studies programs and departments. They pay more attention than their social science colleagues to how Islam shapes the cultural and psychological life of Muslim societies or Muslim minority communities in non-Muslim countries. Religious studies scholars often approach Islam as a progressive unfolding in space and time of certain foundational ideas that manifest themselves in all spheres of the lives of its followers—from their sociopolitical actions to theological and philosophical thought, to artistic self-expression (e.g., Islamic music, Islamic architecture, Islamic literature, and so on). This approach, which in American academy is most vividly represented by Marshall G.S. Hodgson (1922–1968), can be described as "civilizational," namely, one that presents disparate Muslim societies as part of a larger Islamic civilization. It pays special attention to Islam's spiritual dimensions by showing how Muslim faith encourages the faithful to embark on a mystical or intellectual quest for the absolute truth or how it prompts them to strive to rebuild the world on Islamic principles. The advocates of the civilizational approach consider diverse implementations of Islam's foundational ideas by different Muslims to be their respective reactions to a pivotal historical phenomenon—the revelation, in the seventh century, of the divine will to the prophet Muhammad, the founder of Islam. The present book is inspired in part by this approach, because, despite its inevitable drawbacks, it is best suited for the task of providing a comprehensive account of Islam's rise and development in time and space.

Our brief survey of possible approaches to the study of Islam would be incomplete without mentioning the so-called insider approach, namely one that presents Islam from within the Islamic tradition, as it were. It is often adopted by those who have a deep personal commitment to Islam's teachings, rituals, and values. The advantage of the insider approach lies in the fact that it strives to bridge the cognitive gap between the observer and his or her object and thereby to provide a view of Islam as held by its followers, not outsiders. Its potential drawback is that it inevitably (and naturally) tends to privilege a particular interpretation of the Islamic religion (out of many possible ones), to present it as the only true and authentic one, and then to use it as a yardstick to measure the "correctness" or "deviance" of alternative interpretations. Only recently has there emerged among some liberal-progressive Muslim intellectuals a tendency to consider all diverse trends in Islam as equally valid and worthy of appreciation. Unfortunately, it still has little traction outside the rather narrow circle of Muslim liberals in the Muslim world and in the West.[1]

All these approaches are equally legitimate and complementary insofar as they highlight the different facets of the extraordinarily rich and variegated phenomenon that we call "Islam." The fact that this book has adopted a modified version of the civilizational approach does not mean that it is objectively "better" than the other approaches just outlined. On the contrary, readers of this book are invited to acquaint themselves with the alternative perspectives on Islam that are mentioned in the endnotes to each chapter.

Islam as an Object of Interpretation and a Source of Meaning

As with any religious tradition or philosophical doctrine, Islam, for its followers, constitutes a world-orientational framework that allows them to face the chaotic reality around them in order to invest it with meaning so as to make it familiar, "livable," and predictable. Religion, which ostensibly is all about otherworldly beings and realities,[2] serves a thoroughly this-worldly purpose.[3] It endows everyday human activities with a meaning that transcends the narrow confines of the here and now. Put differently, religion links the individual lives of believers to what they perceive to be an eternal and universal source of truth and goodness. No less important, it also holds promise for salvation and moral restitution in the hereafter. In and of itself, a religion or religious doctrine is neither inherently good nor inherently evil. It acquires a concrete, practicable meaning in the course of its appropriation and interpretation by its adherents. It is these adherents who endow religion with ever new meaning(s) and who derive from it certain practical conclusions that they then implement in real life. As a set of ideas, symbols, images, and values, religions are not very different from secular world-orientational ideologies, such as socialism, nationalism, secularism, liberalism, and so on.[4] Like any of these, religions are subject to a wide variety of different, sometimes diametrically opposed understandings and interpretations.

Thus, the same religious tradition can be interpreted as preaching both peace and war. For example, many Christians consider Christianity to be a religion of peace and nonviolence founded on the principle of "Love thy neighbor." Yet, looking back on its history, we find such violent episodes as the Crusades, during which Jews and Muslims were indiscriminately slaughtered in the name of Christ, or the long and bloody wars between the Catholics and the Protestants in sixteenth- and seventeenth-century Europe, as well as the notorious Spanish inquisition. Likewise, Jewish history, as presented in the foundational writings of Judaism, abounds in acts of violence against non-Israelites, be they Midianites, Philistines, Amalekites, Hittites, Amorites, Perizzites, Hivites, Jebusites, or Canaanites (see, for instance, Numbers 31; Samuel 1:27–31; the entire book of Joshua, and so on), while at the same time educating Jews in ways to live a pious and godly life.

Such contradictions are not necessarily the exclusive peculiarity of religions. Secular ideologies—insofar as we can distinguish them from religions—carry diametrically opposed messages. While nationalism inculcates in its adherents pride in the nation's cultural and social achievements, it may also promote xenophobia, that is, hatred of other nations, and, as a consequence, violence against them.

Islam is not an exception to this rule. Its rich legacy contains different, occasionally conflicting messages that are, moreover, liable to different, oftentimes incompatible interpretations. Whereas some Muslims set great store by the so-called internal jihad, that is, a spiritual struggle against one's base passions and carnal appetites,[5] others see in the same Qur'anic injunctions first and foremost a command to fight against "infidels," namely those who refuse to embrace the basic tenets of the Islamic religion (see, for example, Q 5:9 and 2:193). They may even interpret these verses as a call to warfare not only against non-Muslims but also against those Muslims with whom they disagree. In short, no religious tradition is inherently militant or, on the contrary, peaceful. Religions, like secular ideologies, are what their followers take them to be.

Thus, as with any religious tradition, Islam means different things to different individuals who practice it according to their understanding. Interpretations of Islam are always contextual, namely, they are shaped by the personal conditions and convictions of the interpreter(s); furthermore, their respective interpretations may depart substantially, sometimes drastically, from the original intent of the Muslim scriptures. In order to legitimize their understanding of Islam, many of its interpreters claim to be "restoring" or "rediscovering" its original meaning that has somehow become "obscured" or "distorted" over time. This persistent return to the original sources of a religious tradition with a view to restoring it to its original purity is called "fundamentalism."[6]

In conclusion, this book seeks to present Islam as a product of dialogues among different, often quite dissimilar, interpretations of its original tenets by its followers living under different historical conditions. On the other hand, it depicts Islam as the response of its followers to challenges posed by its non-Muslim critics. Interpretations of Islam that result from such internal debates and external challenges pertain to ritual and devotional practices, concepts of God and his attributes, the status of the divine revelation, patterns of social organization and political legitimacy, the nature of faith, social justice, and so on. The book's goal is to show how Islam is being continually reshaped and readjusted to reflect the needs and aspirations of its followers in any given age. This continual interpretation and reinterpretation of Islam by Muslims across the globe (see Map I.1) is a collective effort. In the end, it is aimed at providing Muslims with a comprehensive and detailed guide to personal fulfillment in this life and to salvation in the hereafter.

Basing ourselves on this premise, we encourage the reader not to see Islam as a self-sufficient and independent historical agent, as it is often presented in some popular accounts of its doctrines and practices. In and of itself, Islam does not "teach," "conquer," "embrace," or "reject" cultures, practices, and values. Rather, it is Muslims who interpret what Islam should or should not be, and it is Muslims who endeavor to implement their diverse understandings of their faith in real life. They are then *the true agents of history*. Their interpretations are inevitably shaped by their varying sociopolitical circumstances and life experiences. In other words, their understandings of Islam are always historically and socially conditioned. Bearing these considerations in mind should help us to avoid blanket generalizations about Islam—generalizations that claim to capture and represent its transhistorical, immutable essence. Islam is always the product of an encounter between the believer or a group of believers and the object of their belief. As such, interpretations of Islam are always unique and unrepeatable in their detail, although some general interpretative patterns tend to persist across the centuries. Finally, if we grant that Islam's interpretations by its followers are always conditioned by the sociopolitical and cultural circumstances prevailing in their societies, we simply cannot study Islam in isolation from these conditions. This general consideration has determined the historical framework within which Islam is presented in this book.

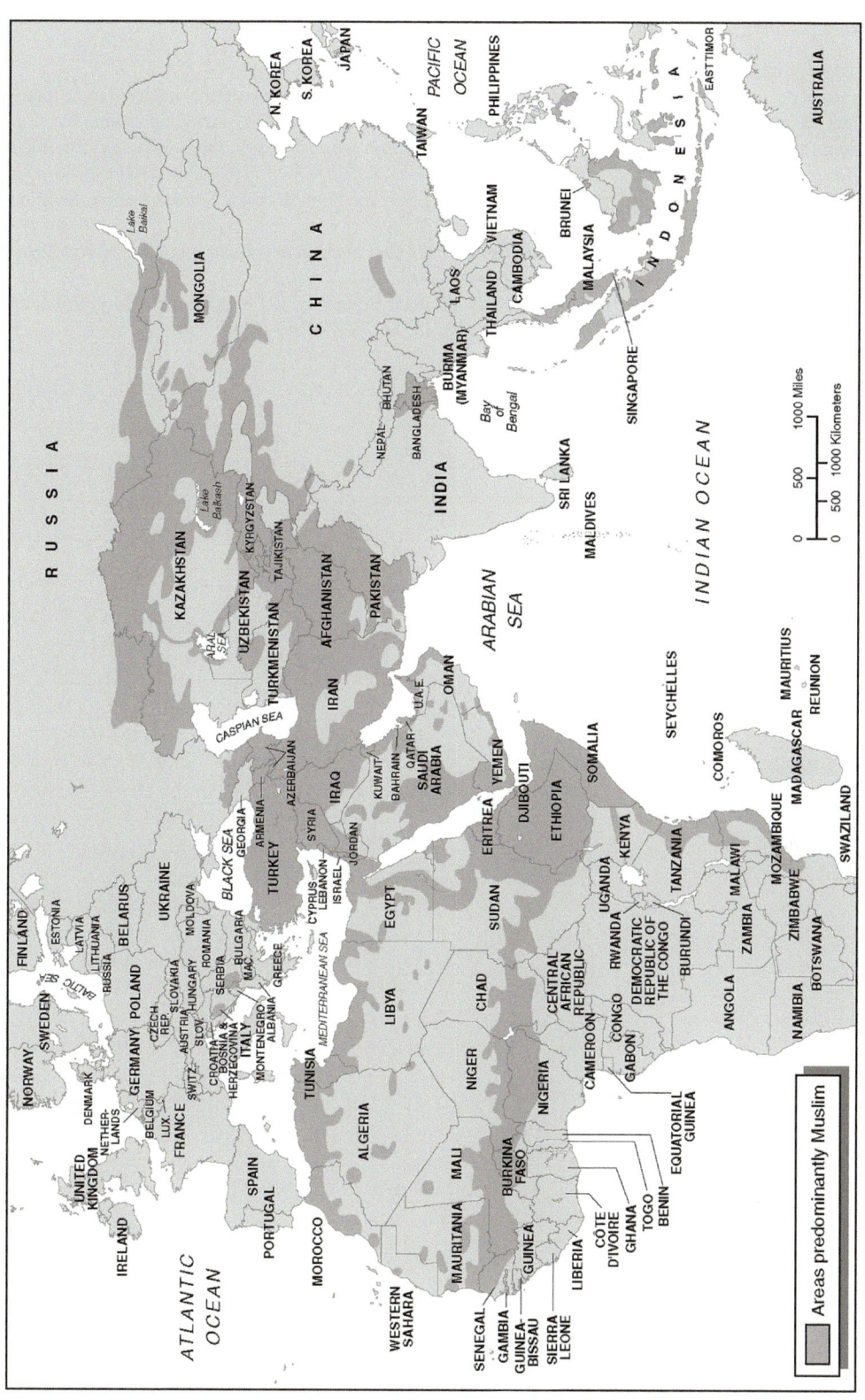

Map 1.1 The Muslim World Today: Areas with Predominantly Muslim Population

Notes

1 For some prominent representatives of liberal Islam, see Chapter 23.
2 This is not necessarily true of all world religions. For example, Buddhism is often considered to be totally distinct from the monotheistic religions that originated in the Middle East, including Islam; see, e.g., Patricia Crone, *Pre-Industrial Societies: Anatomy of the Pre-Modern World*, Oneworld, Oxford, 2003, p. 132.
3 For a concise summary of Western approaches to religions, see Ivan Strenski, *Thinking About Religion*, Blackwell Publishing, Oxford, 2006.
4 See, e.g., Richard King, *Orientalism and Religion: Post-Colonial Theory, India and "the Mystic East,"* Routledge, London and New York, 1999, pp. 13–14.
5 Based on a prophetic statement to this effect; cf. Michael Bonner, *Jihad in Islamic History*, Princeton University Press, Princeton, NJ, 2006, pp. 11–14, 22, 45, 51, 78–79, 169–170.
6 As discussed in Chapter 22 of this book.

Chapter 1

Arabia
The Cradle of Islam

Geography

The Arabian Peninsula is known in Arabic as *jazírat al-'árab*, literally "the island of the Arabs." It has the shape of a rectangle spanning 1,200 by 900 miles at its extreme measurements. Its territory occupies a little over one million square miles. The Peninsula is separated from the neighboring world by natural barriers: water on three sides (Persian Gulf, Arabian Sea, Indian Ocean, and Red Sea) and the Syrian Desert on the fourth. The land consists of barren deserts, mountains and plateaus (especially in the west), and steppes. The Peninsula's southernmost part is affected by the Indian Ocean's monsoons that bring in a limited amount of rainfall. This area and the mountainous areas of North Yemen receive enough rainfall to allow local populations to grow wheat, millet, sorghum, and palm trees. The sandy desert, called al-Rub' al-Khali (the "Empty Place"), in the southeast and the Nufud desert in the north have almost no water (see Figure 1.1).

Figure 1.1 Arabian Desert Landscape
Paul D. Smith/Shutterstock

The principal centers of Islam, Mecca and Medina, are located in the rugged, inhospitable area in the central western part of the Arabian Peninsula known as the Hijáz. As in the rest of Arabia, rains in the Hijáz are very rare, but when they come they may bring devastating flash floods that leave widespread destruction in their wake. After an abundant rainfall, the water that was not used for irrigation by the local population is stored in specially built reservoirs or in water holes. Amidst this barren, inhospitable terrain, we find a small number of oases with springs and wells, where agriculture is possible. Yáthrib, later to be renamed as Medina, the "City [of the Prophet]," was one such agricultural oasis. Mecca, the native town of the founder of Islam, had no major source of water and had to sustain itself by caravan trade and proceeds from the annual pilgrimage to its shrines.

The Arabs

The main population of Arabia is Arabs, from the Hebrew for "steppe" or "desert"—hence, "steppe/desert (people)." According to the Bible, the Arabs descend from Noah's eldest son Shem (Sem). Together with Phoenicians, Arameans, and Jews, they form a separate linguistic group known as "Semitic," that is, the descendants of Shem/Sem. Arabs trace their genealogy back to Ishmael (Arab., Isma'il), son of Abraham (Ibrahim) by his slave girl Hagar. Hence their Latin nickname *Hagareni* (from the Greek *Hagarenoi*). In medieval Europe, they were also known as "Saracens"—a word of obscure provenance that was also borrowed by Latin authors from Greeks.

The Arabs are divided into two major groups: Yamani, residing in the south of the Arabian Peninsula, and Mudari, who occupied its northern part. Before Islam, the Yamani southerners spoke Sabaean (South Semitic) and the Mudari northerners various dialects of Arabic. Southern Arabia had a developed agriculture that sustained a relatively sophisticated civilization known as Sabaean or Himyarite. It was represented by several kingdoms that shared a common religious culture and engaged in both trade and war with one another. The well-being of this civilization, which stood apart from the predominantly nomadic and seminomadic tribal culture of northern and central Arabia, rested on agricultural produce (dates, wheat, and millet) and long-distance trade in frankincense, myrrh, and other aromatic gum resins. South Arabian caravan traders sold their goods to their imperial neighbors in the north, the Byzantines, and the Persians. The rest of the Arabian population also traded, albeit in less valuable items such as dates and animal skins. It has been argued that they may have also exported silver and gold extracted locally.[1] The inhabitants of South Arabia served as intermediaries in the trade between the Mediterranean world in the West and the Indian Ocean in the East. Somewhat paradoxically, in Latin sources this barren and inhospitable region was often referred to as *Arabia Felix* ("Happy Arabia"). This name seems to have been based on the belief, among the Greek and Latin populations of the Mediterranean basin, that its inhabitants possessed an enormous wealth that they had acquired through their trade in the precious aromatic substances previously enumerated. The developed agriculture of South Arabia was supported by complex irrigation systems of which the famous Marib Dam, located in present-day Yemen, was definitely the most spectacular example. The dam was breached around 535, never to be restored. Its destruction symbolized the progressive decline of the settled culture of the south vis-à-vis the warlike, nomadic, and seminomadic tribes of central Arabia. The exact reasons for the collapse of the South Arabian kingdoms are not quite clear. It is occasionally attributed to climatic factors (e.g., the progressive desiccation of the area), which allegedly forced its settled population to give up their agricultural pursuits and revert to nomadism and cattle herding. Some other cataclysms are also cited, such as the gradual but inexorable expansion into the area of the nomadic tribes of central Arabia, which eventually undermined the settled civilization of the South Arabian kingdoms.[2]

Bedouin Lifestyle

The majority of Arabian nomads were organized in clans, tribes, and tribal confederations. They were and still are often collectively called "Bedouin(s)," from the Arabic *badw* or *bédu* ("steppe or desert people"). The Bedouin nomadic and seminomadic lifestyle determined their ethical values, which were different from those of the neighboring Byzantine and Sasanian Empires, which were settled agrarian societies. Life in the desert was a constant struggle for survival with no state institution or central authority to regulate and protect it (see Figure 1.2). Since individual Bedouins simply could not survive on their own, they had to rely on kinsfolk for protection. All members of the kinship group derived their descent from one and the same ancestor, which made for their strong sense of loyalty to one another, especially in time of adversity.[3] Another vivid characteristic feature of Bedouin life was hospitality, which could occasionally be excessive or even ruinous for the hosts. A story has it that a renowned tribal poet felt obligated to slaughter his family's camels to entertain unexpected visitors[4]—an act that, in our time, would be similar to someone dismantling his family cars and selling their parts in order to feed his guests. Such gestures, costly as they may have been for the host, were essential for him to command respect among his fellow Arabs. Alongside loyalty to one's kin, the lack of state and legal structures encouraged the development in the Bedouin milieu of a cult of fierce individualism, personal valor, and prowess. This, in turn, encouraged Bedouins to test their mettle by raiding neighbors' camps and flocks. In addition to demonstrating their personal bravery, raiding helped the Bedouins to supplement their meager livelihood.

Bedouin clans and tribes were characterized by a very high degree of mobility. They journeyed long distances on camels in search of pastures and water holes for their livestock, mostly goats

Figure 1.2 A Bedouin Encampment, Dating Between 1841 and 1851

John Frederick Lewis, 1804-1876, British. Yale Center for British Art, Paul Mellon Collection. Public Domain: Wikimedia Commons.

and sheep. Their diet consisted of milk, dates, camel flesh; wheat or millet were usually purchased from the settled populations of Arabian oases. Nomadic Bedouins resided in tents made of camel or goat hair. Bedouin dependence on the camel is captured in an oft cited adage: "The Bedouin is the parasite of the camel." Crude and ungenerous as this statement may sound, it is impossible to deny that it was the domestication of the camel that made the Bedouin lifestyle possible at all, as it helped human beings to inhabit such an inhospitable and rugged environment as the Arabian deserts.[5] The mobility of the Bedouin tribes could give them a temporary advantage in warfare against their sedentary and agriculturist neighbors, who had large armies that were not always easy to mobilize and deploy.

Social Structures

A typical tribe consisted of the chief (*shaykh,* literally "elder") and his family (a tribal nobility of sorts), a number of other free families, client clans not related by blood, and slaves. The dire conditions of life in the desert made for a strong "democratic" spirit among its inhabitants whose behavior was characterized by self-reliance, independence, tenacity, and endurance. Tribesmen resented any authority or subordination and treated their *shaykh* as first among equals. They expected him to consult them on any issues pertaining to the tribe's or clan's fortunes. This lack of social hierarchy stood in sharp contrast to the organization of the neighboring Byzantine (Greek) and Sasanian (Persian) Empires, which had an elaborate hierarchy of social classes or estates, namely, the emperor and his court, the military landowning aristocracy, the priests/clergy, the craftsmen and merchants, and, at the very bottom of the social pyramid, the peasants and slaves. Whereas the populations of the empires were subject to elaborate legal codes, in Arabian society blood ties substituted for law. Kinship was the primary mark of citizenship and the entitlement to protection by relatives. The Bedouins took great pride in their lineage and eulogized their ancestors in spirited poetry, which was recited and transmitted orally. Although the inhabitants of central and northern Arabia lived in oases and towns as well as in the desert, there was no clear-cut boundary between the Bedouin of the desert and the dweller of an Arabian urban center. They often intermingled during annual fairs and intermarried among themselves, thereby forging and reinforcing alliances between semisettled and seminomadic groups. During such Arabian fairs, not only material goods exchanged hands but also cultural commodities, especially poetry, witticisms, and stories. In short, tribal ties among settled populations of Arabia were almost as strong as they were among the nomadic Bedouins.

Raiding and Warfare

In the absence of a stable source of livelihood and faced with a scarcity of food and other necessities, the Bedouin, as mentioned, occasionally resorted to raiding and robbery. Raiding neighboring tribes for booty and captives was a common feature of life in Arabia before Islam. Raids frequently resulted in blood feuds between clans and tribes that lasted for decades. Feats of glory and perseverance exhibited by individual tribal warriors and tribes as a whole were glorified in the epic narratives called the "Days of the Arabs." They recounted details of tribal conflicts and eulogized fallen and surviving heroes. Apart from the epic tales, poetry in particular was the supreme cultural expression of the harsh experiences and vicissitudes of tribal life. It is not accidental that poetry is often called the "register of the Arabs." Composed in a special poetic language that was distinct from the vernacular dialects of various Bedouin tribes, it was understood and appreciated by all of them.[6] Poets were held in high regard for their poetic skills. As in the "Days of the Arabs," poetic compositions glorified feats of bravery and bemoaned the death of heroes. Poets exalted the martial and moral virtues (especially generosity) of their tribe or clan, while ridiculing the depravity and cowardice of its rivals. As spokesmen and advocates for their tribes, poets enjoyed a special status among their kin. In general, oratory—the art of eloquent speech—was highly valued by all Arabs. Moreover, they believed that words possessed magical qualities: They could bring fortune and misfortune and even hurt like arrows or other weapons. Common were poetic competitions between poets representing different tribes that took place during annual fairs in towns and oases. Each successful poem delivered at such gathering of tribes was quickly memorized and carried across Arabia by professional "rhapsodes" (Arab. *ruwa*; sing. *rawi*), that is, transmitters and performers of oral poetry. One can thus say that poetry was the common cultural glue that held together the fractious Arabian tribes and that instilled in them a sense of common ethnic identity above and beyond narrow tribal and clannish loyalties and peculiarities. Thanks to their poetry and epic tales, as well as the similar physical conditions of their existence, Arabs shared a common world outlook as well as a common code of honorable behavior.

Mecca: A Trade Hub

Northern and central Arabia did not benefit from the rain-bringing monsoons that made agriculture possible in the southern areas of the Peninsula. Therefore, in addition to cattle herding, its inhabitants had to rely on either brigandage or trade to secure their livelihood. In the north, the major trade hub was Palmyra (in present-day Syria), while in west-central Arabia (the Hijáz), commercial activities were centered on the town of Mecca. Around the year 400, Mecca became home to the Arab tribe named Quraysh. Muhammad, the future prophet of Islam, was a member of the Hashim clan of that tribe. While the majority of the Quraysh were nominally town dwellers, they nevertheless retained their tribal organization and ethos, which they shared with their tribal allies who lived in and around Mecca and in the Hijáz generally. Qurayshi merchants organized and sent trade caravans to Syria and Persia (Iran), as well as to Axum, also known as Abyssinia (present-day Ethiopia). Axum was a Christian kingdom that nominally recognized the tutelage of the Byzantine (or Eastern Roman) Empire with the capital in Constantinople (see Map 1.1).

Mecca: A Religious Center

Mecca and its environs appear to have been a site of the annual poetic contests discussed in the previous section. Although in Western academic literature, Mecca is often called a "city," in the decades preceding the rise of Islam, it was probably only a cluster of mud-brick houses that looked more like a village by today's standards. At the same time, thanks to its being the site of a pagan sanctuary frequented by the nearby Bedouin tribes, it enjoyed a special status in their eyes. Hostilities, hunting, and the settling of tribal scores were strictly prohibited on its territory. One can describe it as a sacred enclave of sorts amidst the territory in which violent intertribal conflicts and warfare were the order of the day. Mecca had no municipal authority recognized by all of its inhabitants. Rather, it was an assemblage of different clans of the Quraysh tribe, their retainers (including slaves), and, possibly, some non-Quraysh groupings. However, the overwhelming majority of Meccans were members of the Quraysh tribe.

As mentioned, Mecca enjoyed a special status in the eyes of central and western Arabian Bedouin tribes due to its being the site of a pagan sanctuary. Pre-Islamic Arabs had a pantheon of gods and goddesses associated with their sanctuaries. They were scattered across the breadth and width of Arabia. Thus, we are told of the fertility goddess al-Lat, whose sanctuary was located in the town of Ta'if, southeast of Mecca; the fortune goddess Manat near Medina;[7] and the fertility and motherhood goddess al-'Uzza, who was worshiped by the Quraysh and

Map 1.1 Arabia on the Eve of Islam (sixth–seventh centuries)

other tribes in a valley near Mecca.[8] A humanlike statue of Húbal, a stellar deity associated with human fate and fortune, was installed in the middle of the Meccan sanctuary.[9] Apart from gods and goddesses, the Arabian lore of the age featured a number of supernatural beings: the *jinn* and *'ifríts* (spirits), the evil female demon called *ghul* (hence the English "ghoul" and its derivatives), and all manner of hobgoblins. The latter were believed to be able to sneak into people's houses by night to annoy them by overturning pots, turning milk in the jug or even in the udder sour, upsetting lamps, and, on occasion, causing more serious damage, injury, or even loss of life. To placate them, one had to recite certain charms or make small sacrifices.[10] If this did not help, in the tribal society of Arabia there were religious specialists, known as *kāhin*s (soothsayers), who claimed to be able to communicate with these invisible and potentially troublesome creatures. Ordinary tribesmen and tribeswomen often solicited the help of such specialists in order to protect themselves from the machinations of evil spirits, usually for a fee.

Religion, that is, belief in the presence of invisible but powerful beings, was important insofar as it was relevant to the Bedouins' everyday life. While they had faith in their tribal gods and goddesses, the Bedouins apparently had no notion of the hereafter. In their view, upon their death, human beings simply ceased to be. Once in the grave, mortal human bodies turned into rotting bones and, eventually, into dust indistinguishable from the soil in which they had been buried. The pagan Arabs knew this fact through empirical observation. The Qur'an (45:24) quotes them as saying: "There is nothing but our present life; we live and we die, and nothing but Time (*dahr*) destroys us." Hard-nosed observers, they had no compelling reason to believe otherwise. In line with their disenchanted, fatalistic perception of the world, the Arabs believed that the best men and women could do under the circumstances was to try to avoid the numerous dangers awaiting them and to make their lives as comfortable and safe as possible here and now. In this endeavor, each tribe was assisted by a host of tribal protectors or gods, who were often represented by inanimate objects, such as stones and rocks, crude statues, trees, or even springs. Acknowledgment of these patron gods by the members of a tribe implicitly sanctified their sense of kinship and belonging to the same collectivity. At the same time, the gods were expendable and could be replaced if found ineffective. Muslim sources recount a story about a tribal god made of dates mixed with clarified butter that was allegedly eaten by its disaffected worshipers during a famine.[11]

The pagan Arab worldview rested on the concept of *dahr* that was just mentioned in the Qur'anic verse. An infinite and relentless extension of time, *dahr* was roughly identical with the notion of fate. Like the desert wind that erases footprints in the sand stretching to the horizon, *dahr* erases the lives, possessions, and deeds of human beings.[12] Pre-Islamic Arab poets portrayed *dahr* as a formidable and inscrutable mythical being that relentlessly devoured human life and destroyed human endeavors, plans, and undertakings. It could cause earthly happiness and bliss, but more often it caused misery and grief. *Dahr* was thus identified with the doom of death and with the inexorable working of an indifferent, impersonal, and faceless force that we usually call "fate." Pre-Islamic Arabs saw this time-fate as an all-powerful entity: It changes everything, and nothing can resist it. In the Arab tribal mentality, time symbolized the transience and impermanence of everything; it could bring good fortune to a tribe or an individual household, but it could also randomly cause the death of a relative, a loved one, or a friend. Like a sure arrow, *dahr* never missed the mark—an image that figures prominently in pre-Islamic poetry.[13]

Yet, despite their overall fatalism, the pagan Arabs still believed that human beings could set their marks on time by punctuating it with the days of vengeance and military glory. Battles were events that allowed human beings to transcend time in an act of courage and defiance, even if this act cost them their lives. Such memorable acts were used as markers of time because, unlike transitory human beings, the days of martial glory continued to live in the memory of the tribes long after the event. Years were often named after the battles that took place during them.

Probably the most potent symbol of Arab paganism was the Ka'ba (literally, "cube"). Located in Mecca, it constituted the center of the pagan cult and the destination of the annual ritual pilgrimage by Bedouin tribes. It also served as an important sanctuary and repository of the tribal gods and goddesses. They were represented by crude statues, sacred stones, wooden effigies, and so on. Before it was cleansed of its pagan paraphernalia by the prophet Muhammad, the black cubic structure of the Ka'ba is said to have housed three hundred sixty-seven such pagan idols. In spite of their commitment to their tribal gods and goddesses, the Arab pagans believed in the existence of a chief deity that stood above all other gods and goddesses. He was called *rabb* ("Lord") of the Ka'ba and was considered by the Arabs to be the creator god and the supreme deity of the Meccan sanctuary. Sometimes the Arabs referred to him simply as "the god," in Arabic *allah*. However, Allah did not enjoy any special cult or play a significant role during the ritual visits of the Bedouin tribes to the Meccan sanctuary (see Figure 1.3).

When the Bedouins came to Mecca to visit their gods, they were hosted by the members of the Quraysh tribe, who derived their prestige and special status in Arabian society from their

Figure 1.3 Muslim Pilgrims in Prayer at the Sacred Shrine of Islam in the Courtyard of Masjid al-Haram (Sacred Mosque) in Mecca, Saudi Arabia

stewardship of the Meccan sanctuary. A legend has it that the Quraysh had wrested this prestigious function from its previous owners several generations before the birth of the prophet Muhammad. The task of the Quraysh as the custodians of the Meccan sanctuary (*háram*) was to organize and supervise annual pilgrimages to their native town. The Quraysh had agreements and treaties with the neighboring Bedouin tribes who visited their gods deposed in the *háram*. As wealthy traders, some Quraysh clans lent the visitors money, thereby becoming their creditors.

According to some Western historians of Islam,[14] the relative prosperity of the Meccan population led to the transformation of their traditional tribal values. In this view, the growing inequality within the Quraysh tribe—especially between the rich clans of Umayyads and Makhzumis and the poorer ones, such as Banu Háshim, the native clan of the prophet Muhammad—led to the tensions that were resolved through the emergence of a new religion that called for a more equitable social order.

Whether we accept this interpretation or not, it is impossible to deny that Islam (literally, "submission to [the will of one] God") introduced a new form of social solidarity that was aimed at supplanting kinship ties and replacing them with loyalty to the new religious community, called *umma*. Built on the common belief in the one and only God, Allah, the rise of this new community completed the process of the rejection of the old pagan cults and of the tribal values associated with them.

Other Religious Communities of Arabia

While pagans probably constituted the majority of Arabia's population, it was also home to two monotheistic communities—Jewish and Christian. Their followers resided in a number of centers scattered across the Peninsula. There were also a few Zoroastrian communities in eastern Arabia (Oman and Bahrain) and also in Yemen, which maintained ties with the Sasanid Empire of Iran. However, the presence of Zoroastrians was insignificant numerically and ideologically compared to that of the Jews and Christians.[15]

The Jews of Yáthrib—the name of Medina before Islam[16]—and other oasis towns seem to have been the descendants of the Jewish tribes that had fled from Palestine in the aftermath of the Jewish rebellions against Roman rule in the first and second centuries of the Common Era (C.E.). These Jewish settlers became thoroughly Arabized and spoke a local variant of the Arabic language. Organized in tribal units similar to those of their pagan neighbors, they enjoyed relative prosperity. They may have professed a peculiar or "sectarian" version of Judaism, as some Qur'anic references to Judaic faith occasionally seem to indicate (e.g., Q 9:30). However, in the absence of any historical documentation, we can say no more.

In the second decade of the sixth century, the Jewish king of Yemen, Dhu Nuwás ("He of the Curls"), launched a campaign of forceful conversion of local Christians to Judaism. His ruthless persecutions of the Christian communities of South Arabia led to its invasion by the Negus (king) of Christian Abyssinia (Ethiopia) and the subsequent spread of Christianity in that region and beyond. Again, as in the case with Arabian Judaism, we can only speculate over the kind of Christianity professed by the Arabian Christians. It seems feasible that Arabia served as a refuge to those who had rejected the orthodox creed supported by the Church authorities and the Emperor of Constantinople. At that time, such heterodox versions of Christianity were Monophysitism—a teaching that asserted that in the incarnate Christ there is only one nature (divine), not two—and Nestorianism, which maintained the opposite stance, namely, that the two natures of Christ are self-subsisting and therefore cannot be physically united in the person of the God-man. Whether or not the Christians of South Arabia were indeed followers of any of these doctrines is impossible to determine.

Mentions of the vicissitudes of Arabian Christianity in local inscriptions allow us to conclude that there were several major centers of Christian faith in South Arabia (present-day Saudi Arabia and Yemen), which became the chief targets of Dhu Nuwás's missionary zeal.[17]

Despite the presence of the enclaves of monotheistic faith in Arabia, Arabs in general and Meccans in particular were not eager to convert to either Judaism or Christianity. The triumph of the Abyssinian expeditionary force over Dhu Nuwás did not lead to mass conversions to Christianity among the Bedouins of central and western Arabia. They realized that by embracing Christianity they were likely to become subjects of the Christian Emperor of Byzantium, much like their northern neighbors, the Christian Arabs of the Ghassan tribe. Conversion, the Arabs of the Hijáz quite reasonably assumed, would force them to give up their treasured independence and submit to an outside political power. The unsuccessful military expedition against Mecca—the mainstay of Arabian paganism—by a Christianizing Ethiopian ruler of Yemen around 570 may have been a result of such an apprehension. In any event, its failure, possibly reflected in *sura* (chapter) 105 of the Qur'an, further convinced the Arabs of the validity of their pagan faith. However, their tenacious loyalty to the beliefs of their ancestors did not prevent them from being exposed to the monotheistic tenets of Judaism and Christianity, thereby preparing at least some of them for the preaching of monotheism by one of their own. It was into this world that the prophet of Islam was born.

Conclusions

As we have seen, Islam originates in a complex religious environment that is characterized by the presence in central and western Arabia of pagan (polytheistic) beliefs, Judaism, Christianity, and, in South Arabia, Zoroastrianism, although the latter's impact on the local Arab tribes seems to have been relatively minor. One should not, however, assume that the tenets of Islam as articulated in the Qur'an is a simple mixture of these religious traditions. First, as we shall soon see, elements of these religions acquired different weight and importance at different stages of Muhammad's prophetic mission. Second, their integration into the new system of belief and practice called "Islam" was a highly complex process in the course of which they were drastically readjusted to fit the emerging Islamic worldview articulated in the Qur'an and the teachings of the prophet Muhammad. Third, thanks to their prior exposure to these diverse religious traditions, Muhammad's pagan listeners were able to understand, if not necessarily accept the meaning of his message. To make his preaching more effective, the images and narratives of the prior religions had to be couched in their own language and recast so as to resonate with the realities and experiences of tribal life in Arabia.

Questions to Ponder

Some scholars of Islam have argued that, although all of the aforementioned strands of religious thought (Jewish, Christian, and Zoroastrian) played a role in Muhammad's preaching of the new religion, it was first and foremost the tribal/Bedouin and pagan beliefs and practices that served as Islam's frame of reference. If we accept this view, then Islam at the time of its appearance was primarily an Arabian religion. Critics of this thesis point out that Islam was a product of urban environment (first Mecca and later Yáthrib/Medina), which, they argue, was already impregnated with Near Eastern religious ideas, images, and symbols. Hence, Islam was essentially a product of Near Eastern antiquity, and thus akin to Judaism and Christianity, with the Arabian pagan beliefs occupying a relatively marginal place in its composition. Keep these two explanations in mind while reading the next chapter and try to articulate and justify your own approach to this complex issue.

Summary

- Geography is destiny. The Arabian Peninsula is a combination of deserts, rough terrain, mountains, and oases. The central-western areas of the Peninsula are occupied by stateless nomadic cattle-breeders.
- The Peninsula's human landscape consists of the settled agrarian and trade societies of South Arabia and the Bedouin tribes of central and northern Arabia. Tribal democracy is the predominant pattern of life among the Bedouins ("steppe-people"). Raiding and cattle breeding are the major sources of tribal livelihood. Poets are held in high regard as spokesmen of the tribe and defenders of tribal honor.
- The importance of Mecca is determined by its strategic position as a major way station along the trade route between the southern and northern parts of Arabia and, by extension, between the Indian Ocean and the Mediterranean basin.
- Religious beliefs of the Arabian populations range from tribal paganism/polytheism to enclaves of Judaism, Christianity, and a very limited presence of Zoroastrianism. These religions are seen by the Bedouin as "foreign imports" and, in the case of Zoroastrianism and Christianity, potential conduits of foreign (imperial) influence and eventually domination.
- On the religious plane, Mecca's importance springs from its being a repository of tribal idols and a major center of pagan cult in the Hijáz. Arabs before Islam do not care much about the afterlife. Preoccupied with this-worldly affairs, they see time-fate (*dahr*) as an irresistible, all-destructive, and self-sufficient force. The supreme god of the pagan Arabian pantheon (*allah*) is conceived as the "lord of the Ka'ba"—the black cubic structure in the center of Mecca that is the object of an annual pagan pilgrimage (*hajj*). Allah has no cult among the pagan Arabs; their primary loyalty is to their tribal gods and goddesses.
- The Quraysh tribesmen are the stewards or custodians of the Meccan shrine (*háram*) and organizers of the annual *hajj* performed by the local Bedouin tribes. Their allegiance to the pagan religion is driven by economic and social factors (concern for their *hajj*-based income and their privileged social and religious status among the Arabian tribes).
- The nonpagan religions of Arabia are Christianity, Judaism, and Zoroastrianism. Attempts to impose one or the other religion on the Arabs by outside actors met with limited success. The Arabian Peninsula remained predominantly pagan/polytheist until the advent of Islam.

Notes

1 Gene Heck, *Islam, Inc.: An Early Business History*, King Faisal Center for Research and Islamic Studies, Riyadh, 2004, pp. 1–78.
2 Greg Fisher (ed.), *Arabs and Empires Before Islam*, Oxford University Press, Oxford, 2015.
3 Montgomery Watt and Richard Bell, *Introduction to the Qur'an*, Edinburgh University Press, Edinburgh, 1994, pp. 5–6.
4 Reynold Nicholson, *A Literary History of the Arabs*, Charles Scribner, New York, 1907, pp. 85–86.
5 Richard Bulliet, *The Camel and the Wheel*, Columbia University Press, New York, 1990, pp. 28–56.
6 As argued by some, but by no means all, linguists, see, e.g., Kees Versteegh, *The Arabic Language*, Columbia University Press, New York, 2001, pp. 46–47.
7 Before Islam, this town was named Yáthrib.
8 These three goddesses were occasionally called "daughters of Allah" in Islamic sources that quote pre-Islamic Bedouin lore.

9 For the pre-Islamic Arabian pantheon, see Nabih Amin Faris (trans.), *The Book of Idols: Being a Translation from the Arabic of the Kitab al-asnam*, Princeton University Press, Princeton, NJ, 1952.

10 John Burton, *An Introduction to the Hadith*, Edinburgh University Press, Edinburgh, 1994, pp. 2–3.

11 Patricia Crone, *Meccan Trade and the Rise of Islam*, Princeton University Press, Princeton, NJ, 1987, p. 238.

12 What follows is a summary of Gerhard Böwering's article, "Ideas of Time in Persian Mysticism," in Richard Hovannisian and Georges Sabagh (eds.), *The Persian Presence in the Islamic World*, Cambridge University Press, Cambridge, 1998, pp. 172–198.

13 See, e.g., Julia Ashtiany, T. M. Johnstone, J. D. Latham, and R. B. Serjeant (eds.), *The 'Abbasid Belles-Lettres*, Cambridge University Press, Cambridge, 1990, pp. 288–289.

14 For instance, Montgomery Watt (1909–2006) in his influential monographs *Muhammad at Mecca*, Clarendon Press, Oxford, 1953 and *Muhammad at Medina*. Clarendon Press, Oxford, 1956.

15 Watt and Bell, *Introduction*, pp. 8–9.

16 It is located some 270 miles north of Mecca.

17 For details, see Irfan Shahid, *Byzantium and the Arabs in the Sixth Century*, 2 vols., Dumbarton Oaks Research Library and Collection, Washington, DC, 1995.

Chapter 2

Muhammad and the Beginnings of Islam

The Making of the Muslim Community

Muhammad's Background and Early Life

Muhammad b. 'Abdállah, the founder of Islam, was born in Mecca in 570 in the clan of Banu Háshim, which was part of the Quraysh tribe based in central-western Arabia.[1] Although respected by their fellow tribesmen, the Banu Háshim lacked the wealth of the more prosperous clans of the Quraysh, such as the Banu Umáyya and Banu Makhzúm. Muhammad's father died before the birth of his son. When he was six or seven years of age, Muhammad's mother also died, leaving him in the care of his grandfather 'Abd al-Muttálib (see Table 2.1). His orphanage, mentioned in the Qur'an (93:6–8), was a major disadvantage in a tribal society in which man's worth was often measured by the strength and numbers of his male relatives. After the death of his grandfather, Muhammad was brought up by his uncle Abú Tálib, who trained him as a caravan driver.[2] As legend has it, while in Syria with a Meccan caravan, a Christian monk reportedly recognized in Muhammad the future prophet predicted by the Judeo-Christian scriptures.[3]

At some point in his life, Muhammad was recommended to a well-to-do widow named Khadíja, who employed him to trade for her in Syria. After some time, Khadíja, encouraged by her Christian cousin Wáraqa, proposed marriage to Muhammad. Khadíja gave birth to several female children. One of their daughters, Fátima, who later married Muhammad's cousin 'Ali, is by far the best known and revered, especially among the Shi'ites.

Until he turned forty, Muhammad seems to have shared the pagan beliefs of his people: He took part in the Meccan pilgrimage rituals and, at the age of thirty-five, participated in the restoration of the Ka'ba, which was at that time a pagan sanctuary.[4] However, new religious ideas were already in the air. Many Arabs—Khadíja's cousin, Wáraqa, who had converted to Christianity, being one—were no longer satisfied with the old Arab polytheism. One possible evidence of this dissatisfaction is the mention in Muslim sources of the *hanífs*, a group of "spontaneous" monotheists who entertained some monotheistic ideas without committing themselves to either Judaism or Christianity. Wáraqa may have been one of them before converting to Christianity. The *hanífs* seem to have worked out, perhaps each for himself, some sort of private faith of a monotheistic slant. Muhammad with his inquisitive mind could not keep aloof from such new spiritual and intellectual currents of the age. When he turned forty, he began to seclude himself in a cave on Mount Hirá' outside Mecca to engage in meditation over his personal condition and the meaning of human existence in general. Some Western scholars attributed Muhammad's propensity for introspection to the fact that he had no male children—all of them had died in infancy. In the male-oriented environment of tribal Arabia, in which the number of male children often determined the worth of their father, this was not only a major disadvantage but also a stigma of sorts. If we accept this line of argument, then Muhammad's response to his predicament was definitely an overreaction. Many Arabs in general and Meccans in particular must have had the same problem, but none of them endeavored to resolve it by introducing a new religion.

Table 2.1 Ahl al-Bayt: The People of [the Prophet's] House

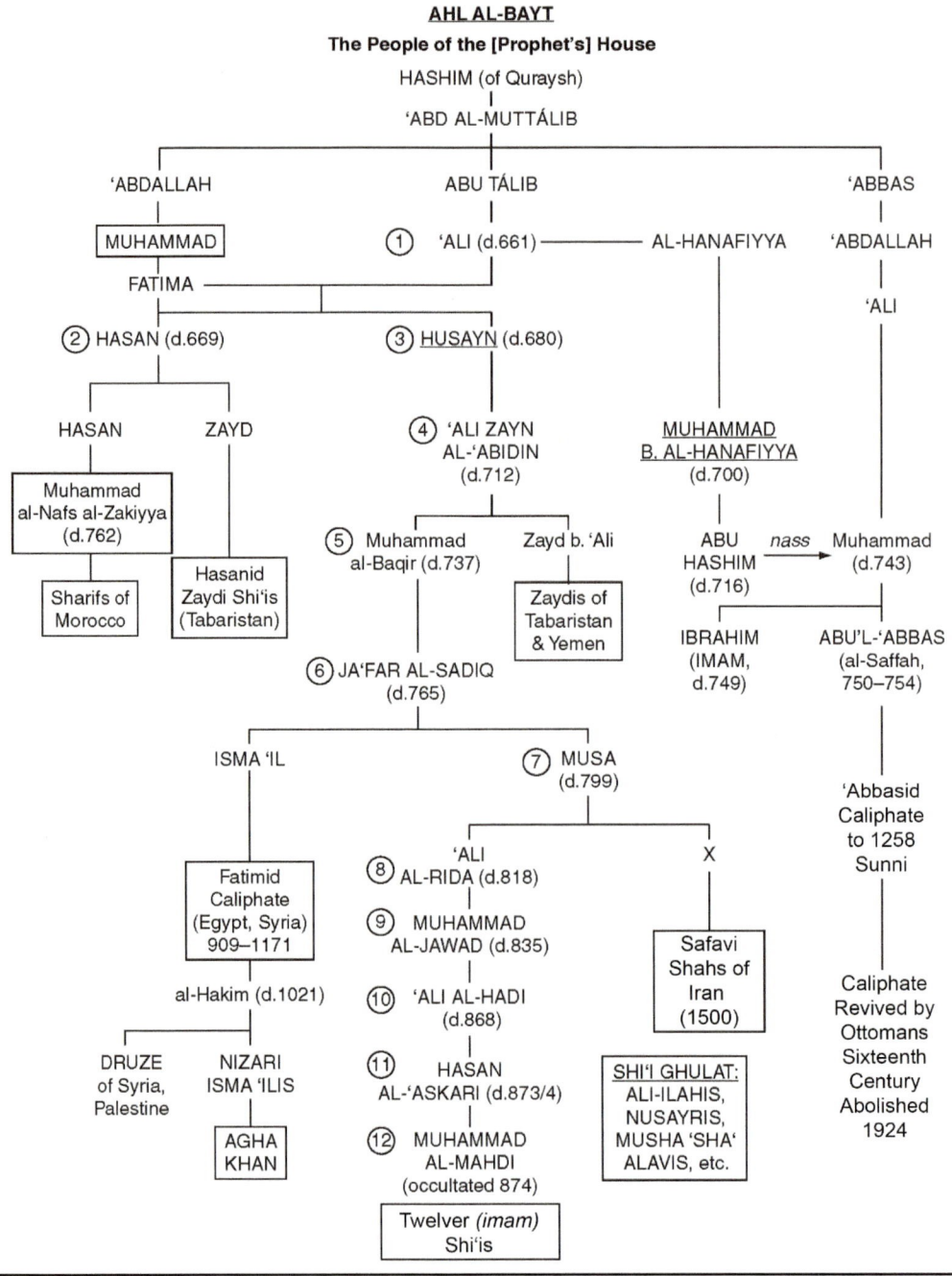

Courtesy of Alexander Knysh

The First Revelations

During one of his retreats to the cave on Mount Hirá' outside Mecca, Muhammad heard a voice and saw a vision in which a mysterious creature summoned him to offer worship to God the creator, the God of the monotheist communities. This God was Allah.[5] The pagan Arabs of Mecca and its environs were apparently aware of Allah's existence but had no cult specifically dedicated to him. The Qur'an describes Muhammad's encounter with the promulgator of the first revelation as follows (Q 96:1–5):

> Read[6] in the name of thy Lord who created,
> Who created man of blood coagulated.
> Read! Thy Lord is the most beneficent,
> Who taught by the pen,
> Taught that which they knew not onto men.[7]

According to a standard Muslim account, Muhammad identified the mysterious visitor as the angel Gabriel (see Figure 2.1). Their next encounter took place either immediately after

Figure 2.1 The Archangel Gabriel Commands Muhammad to Begin His Prophetic Mission (Western picture dated 1847)

Theodor Hosemann/Public Domain/Wikimedia Commons

the first revelation or a few days later when Muhammad observed Gabriel who, according to Q 53:6–10:

> Stood poised, being on the higher horizon, then drew near and suspended hung; two bows'-lengths away, or nearer, then revealed to his servant what he has revealed.[8]

The Muslim tradition says that these first encounters with the mysterious force left Muhammad terrified. However, after having been reassured by his wife Khadíja and her Christian cousin Wáraqa, he accepted the summons as coming from God himself. After that Muhammad continued to receive further messages that he interpreted as divine revelations. They usually came in an aural form but occasionally also in ocular manifestations, as in the verse we have just mentioned. Later on, these messages collectively came to be known as "al-Qur'an," that is "reading, or recitation [of the divine word]." For the first three years of his prophetic career, only Muhammad's wife and a few close relatives, including his young cousin 'Ali and his adopted son and freedman Zayd b. Háritha, were inducted into his mystery and shared the cult of the one God with him.[9] They were followed by Abu Bakr and 'Uthman, both of whom would succeed the Prophet at the head of the Muslim community after the latter's death in 632.[10] This cult involved the ritual worship of God, according to the rules that were revealed to Muhammad by Gabriel.

Muhammad's Public Preaching and Opposition to It

After three years had elapsed, divine messages demanded that Muhammad summon his fellow Quraysh to worship his God, warning them of the terrible calamities that would befall those who refused (see Q 15:94–96).[11] Muhammad's revelations identified the pagan attachment to multiple divinities as *shirk*, that is "giving partners to God," a phenomenon that we today call "polytheism." Closely associated with *shirk* was *kufr*—a willful and haughty rejection of the truth revealed by God to Muhammad.[12] Muhammad's preaching condemned both *shirk* and *kufr* as capital sins that God will never pardon.[13]

Muhammad's early public sermons dictated to him by God (Allah) were extremely intense and eloquent. They called upon his listeners to obey their Lord by doing good works and showing gratitude to their creator for his boundless mercy and benevolence. The sermons also encouraged God's human servants to think constantly of the resurrection of bodies on the Day of Judgment over which God will preside as the supreme judge of humankind. Muhammad's revelations depict these dramatic events, as well as the subsequent human suffering and bliss in the hereafter, in striking, memorable images that were supposed to strike fear and awe into the hearts of his listeners. The last twenty-five chapters of the Qur'an convey well the fervor and intensity of Muhammad's early message. They contain descriptions of the horrors of Judgment Day, of the subsequent tortures of the damned in the hellfire, and of the pleasures experienced by the true believers in paradisiacal gardens. Reworked to express the specifically Islamic vision of the state of affairs in the world and the hereafter, these common Biblical pictures and concepts[14] were deemed to demonstrate the enormity of the human condition and the importance for human beings to make the right choice in this earthly life. This choice, according to Muhammad's revelations, entailed a full and unquestioning submission to God, or *islám*. No amount of wealth or healthy, strong sons would save humans from divine punishment, for they are but God's temporal gifts to his servants.[15] As such, they require that their human recipients show gratitude to God by worshiping him and fulfilling his commandments. Moral transgressions, such as excessive pride, defiant self-reliance, greed, oppression of the poor, and, of course, the mockery and rejection of the truth of the divine message brought by Muhammad, were vigorously condemned.[16] They were bound to bring severe punishment upon those guilty of them in the hereafter.[17]

All these ideas were presented in Muhammad's sermons not as something new and unprecedented but as a restoration of the primordial monotheism of Abraham and the Hebrew prophets who had followed in his wake, including John the Baptist and Jesus.[18] Abraham was portrayed in the Qur'an not as a Jew or a Christian (3:67–68) but as one who had "surrendered" himself (*áslama*; hence *islám*—submission [to the divine will]) and practiced pure monotheism. As for Muhammad, he was nothing but a "warner" (*nadhír*) and a messenger (*rasúl*)[19] whom God had charged with the task of informing his fellow Arabs about his will in their own, "clear Arabic" language (Q 12:2; 14:4; 34:43; 36:1–5; 42:7; 43:3; 44:58). The Qur'an refers to this divine messenger to the Arabs as *úmmi* (7:157), that is, "illiterate," probably in the sense that he had not previously been given a divine scripture. Now God gave him one, the Qur'an, and commanded him to convey it to a people who, like him, had not yet been recipients of a divine revelation.

Initially, many Meccans dismissed Muhammad's preaching as the grandiloquence of a poet seeking fame or mundane advantage (Q 37:37; 50:30–32; 52:30) or the senseless incantations of a man possessed by demons (26:221–223 and 34:43–45).[20] Some derided his claims to prophethood and demanded a supernatural demonstration of the divine provenance of his message (Q 6:37; 7:204; and 29:48).[21] Others accused him of rehashing "the fairy-tales of the ancients" (Q 6:25; 8:31; 16:24; 25:6; 46:17; and 68:15), that is, the biblical stories of the Jews and the Christians, in order to frighten his audience into doing his will.

To those Qurayshi tribesmen who at first had dismissed Muhammad's spirited orations as mere "ravings" of a poet or a soothsayer, their full consequence became clear when he started to attack the gods and customs of the Meccan pagans and to claim that their ancestors, much revered in the tribal society of Arabia, had been laboring under a delusion.[22] Unsurprisingly they were annoyed by Muhammad's demand that they abandon the time-tested "way" (*sunna*) of their ancestors and adopt the "ways of God" as described in Muhammad's revelations (Q 5:103; 31:21; etc.). Apart from being upset over the Prophet's moral condemnation of the Meccan beliefs and customs, a number of wealthy Meccan merchants also felt that their mercantile interests would suffer as a result of his preaching. In particular, they feared that Muhammad's monotheistic message might dissuade Arab pagans from visiting Mecca during the pilgrimage season and participating in the annual fair associated with it. Furthermore, his message of a one and only God undermined the position of the Quraysh as the stewards of the polytheistic sanctuary and the substantial material advantages and social prestige that came with it.

At first, the mercantile aristocracy of Mecca tried to persuade Muhammad to give up his preaching by offering him wealth and power.[23] When this stratagem proved to be ineffective, they organized a boycott of his clan, Banu Háshim, in the hopes that its leaders would either silence Muhammad or disavow him.[24] His followers within other clans were ostracized and pressured to recant, while those who were not protected by kinship ties (especially, slaves) were physically tortured.[25] These persecutions and ill treatment forced a group of eighty-three Muslims and their families to seek refuge in Abyssinia (Ethiopia), where they were well received by the Christian Negus (king), who recognized in them fellow monotheists.[26] The death in 619 of Muhammad's loyal supporters, Abu Tálib, who had stood by his nephew without embracing his teaching, and Khadíja, dealt a severe blow to Muhammad's cause.[27] Faced with the boycott and day-to-day hostility of the Quraysh, he reportedly tried to make his message acceptable to his polytheist adversaries by admitting the high status of the "daughters of Allah," the female goddesses mentioned in Chapter 1.[28] This episode has given rise to the story of the so-called Satanic verses allegedly inserted into chapter (*sura*) 53 of the Qur'an, which was later reported by some Muslim historians and Qur'an commentators (such as Ibn Ishaq, d. 768, and al-Tábari, d. 923).[29] Whether real or invented, this story aptly captures Muhammad's frustration at his inability to win over his Meccan audience. At about the same time, Muhammad's attempt to propagate his monotheist teaching at the nearby oasis town of al-Tá'if came to naught; he was ridiculed and driven away by its inhabitants, who remained loyal to their deity, the goddess al-Lat.[30] Although in 619 the boycott of the Banu Háshim by the rest of the Quraysh was finally lifted,[31] Muhammad's situation did not get much better. His uncle Abu Láhab, the "Flame Man," who was now head of the Banu Háshim clan, was convinced by a few leading Meccan power brokers to withdraw his support from Muhammad. As a consequence, the Prophet was left face-to-face with his numerous powerful adversaries. The episode of his disavowal by Abu Láhab is reflected in *sura* 111 of the Qur'an, which threatens Abu Láhab and his wife a humiliating punishment in the hellfire.[32]

Around that time, although the exact chronology of this legendary event is uncertain, Muhammad was taken by archangel Gabriel on the night journey to Jerusalem,[33] which is generally believed to be mentioned in Q 17:1: "Glory be to Him, Who carried His servant by night from the Holy Mosque to the Further Mosque, the precincts of which We [God] have blessed." Gabriel and Muhammad ascended through the seven heavens into the presence of God, paying visits to the inhabitants of each heaven—the prophets of the Judeo-Christian scriptures. The Prophet conversed with Adam in the first heaven, Jesus and his cousin John the Baptist in the second, Joseph in the third, Idrís (identified by Muslim scholars as either Enoch or Elijah) in the fourth, Aaron in the fifth, Moses in the sixth, and Abraham in the seventh. This legend may be interpreted as symbolizing Muhammad's induction into the ranks of the major monotheistic prophets of the Judeo-Christian tradition. The same subtext can be discerned behind the legend of the opening of the Prophet's breast (alluded to in Q 94: 1–3), according to which the angels Gabriel and Michael visited him in his sleep to cleanse his heart with snow or the water of the well of Zamzam so as to remove from it any mundane faults and aspirations.[34]

In the meantime, Muhammad took to preaching his cause among the Arabs who came to Mecca for the spring and fall fairs, as well as among the pilgrims to the Meccan shrine (see Figure 2.2). He succeeded in making a few converts from among visitors from Yáthrib, an oasis town some 270 miles north of Mecca (later to be called Medina). The next year, they brought with them their friends and relatives to collectively pledge full support to Muhammad should he and his Meccan followers decide to settle in Yáthrib.[35] The invitation from Yathrib was prompted by several factors, the internal strife among the tribal population of the city being the most important. For more than a decade, Yáthrib had been torn apart by a bloody feud between two Arab tribes, Aws and Khazraj. Concerned leaders of both tribes hoped that the arrival of a man with religious credentials coming from the respected Quraysh tribe would help them to broker reconciliation. In 622, faced with the unrelenting opposition to his mission on the part of his countrymen, Muhammad decided to emigrate to Yáthrib. He started by sending his followers there in small groups. Eventually, he and his close friend and early convert Abu Bakr were also forced to leave. To be more exact, they had to flee Mecca when they got the wind of an assassination plot against them contrived by the Meccan headmen. The two men escaped under the cover of night and hid in a cave, an episode that, according to Muslim historians and exegetes, is alluded to in Q 9:40. Legend has it that the fugitives were concealed from their enemies by a cob-web miraculously woven by a spider over a short period of time to cover the entrance to the cave. On seeing the unbroken cobweb, the pursuers reportedly decided not to search the cave and left.[36]

Figure 2.2 The Archangel Gabriel Bringing the Prophet the Demand from God to Leave Mecca and Go to Yáthrib/Medina

Granger, NYC

Migration (*Híjra*) and the Formation of the Islamic *Umma*

Muhammad's migration to Yáthrib/Medina is called *híjra* in Arabic. The year in which it took place (622 C.E.) has become the first year of the Muslim era. It was a momentous event, which, in addition to the physical relocation of the first Muslim community to a new place of residence, had a broad range of symbolic and practical ramifications. On the practical level, it meant the abandonment by the "emigrants" (*muhájirún*) of their material possessions in Mecca, thereby placing themselves under the full protection and provision of their new hosts, the Muslims of Medina, who came to be known as "helpers" (*ansár*). On the symbolic level, the *híjra* marked the decisive rupture of kinship ties—ties that were so central to the functioning of Meccan society. As a result, a new type of solidarity was established, one based on the allegiance to the same religious faith and its enunciator, the prophet Muhammad. The tribal structure based on kinship and loyalty to one's clan was abandoned in principle, although, as we shall soon see, kinship continued to matter. Muslim historical sources have referred to the pre-Islamic past as the "Age of Ignorance" (*jáhiliyya*), that is, the time characterized by all the negative features associated with the tribal code of behavior—proud individualism, recklessness, vengefulness, disregard for the needy and downtrodden, in addition to a gamut of other moral/ethical vices, such as fornication, drunkenness, gambling, and the like.[37]

For the prophet Muhammad, the move to Medina was a unique opportunity to build a new social order from scratch or, rather, on the basis of the principles that were revealed to him in the Qur'an. His message was adjusted accordingly. It now required of the Prophet's followers not just personal devotion and worship of the one and only deity but also observance of a set of rules of social and ethical behavior. The Qur'anic passages from the Medinan period of the Prophet's mission laid the stress on social etiquette, rules of decency, dietary prohibitions, family relations, and each Muslim's responsibilities toward the community at large. The Muslims were to show compassion to the weak and to restrict the license of the strong. Understandably, such goals were best achieved in a polity of like-minded individuals who shared the same basic beliefs and values. This polity was *umma*[38]—an Arabic word that came to designate the group of people who responded to the Prophet's preaching, formed a new religious community with him, and pledged to obey him and God, on whose behalf he was speaking. The system of values shared by the members of the Islamic *umma* stood in direct opposition to the values of the pagan Bedouin society: It inculcated in the believers such virtues as humility, generosity, brotherhood, mercifulness, and unquestioning obedience to the will of God as expressed in the Qur'an and the Prophet's teachings. A rigid borderline was drawn between the adherents of polytheism (*mushrikun*) and the monotheists (*muslimun*). There could be no compromise between the two. Should the former refuse to acknowledge the sovereignty of the latter, they should be fought by all means necessary.

Upon his arrival in Medina, the Prophet had to deal with four major categories of its population: (1) the "helpers" (*ansár*), namely the members of the Aws and Khazraj tribes who had invited him to arbitrate in their feuds; (2) his Meccan supporters who had emigrated with him from Mecca to Medina (*muhájirún*); (3) the three tribes that professed Judaism; and (4) those members of the Aws and Khazraj tribes who rejected his teaching and resented his role as the new ruler of the city. Of the latter, some pretended to have embraced Islam in the hopes of reaping the benefits of being the dominant group now headed by the Prophet. However, their commitment to Islam was superficial, a pure expediency. The Qur'an repeatedly brands them as "hypocrites" or "turncoats" (*munáfiqún*)[39] because they recognized the Prophet's authority only nominally, without believing in his prophetic mission in their heart of hearts, and were therefore prepared to withdraw their allegiance to him at the first reversal of fortunes. After having been accepted as judge and ruler by all the major groups of Medina's population, Muhammad declared Medina a sacred enclave under the tutelage of God and his prophet, in which any hostile action or settling of tribal scores was strictly prohibited. Eventually, he drafted the document known in Western scholarship as the "constitution of Medina." It stipulated Muhammad's role as the final recourse and arbitrator in conflicts between any factions of the city population:

> If any dispute or controversy likely to cause trouble should arise, it must be referred to God and to Muhammad, the Messenger (*rasúl*) of God.[40]

Special provisions were made for some Jewish factions of Medina allied with Muhammad's followers in the city. They were obligated to contribute to the cost of war, fight alongside the Muslims, be loyal to the Muslim state, and seek mutual advice and consultation with the Muslims and their leader, while preserving their religion.[41] The formation of the new Muslim polity in Yáthrib (Medina) with Muhammad as its political and military leader inevitably created tensions between the Muslims and the Meccan pagans on the one hand and, gradually, also between the Muslims and the Jewish tribes of Medina on the other. The latter had their own reasons to mistrust Muhammad. First, their faith prevented them from accepting Muhammad's claim to be a new monotheistic prophet. He lacked the prerequisite qualities of a prophet explicated in their scriptures. Besides, he was not a Jew and therefore could not have been the messiah promised to the Jews. Furthermore, the Jewish tribes of Medina interpreted Muhammad's renditions of the contents of the Bible as evidence of his poor knowledge of their religion and ridiculed him.[42] Some Jewish opponents of Muhammad and the "hypocrites" formed a league against him and his community.[43] In response, Muhammad accused them of "distorting" or "misunderstanding" the true meaning of their scriptures and thereby relapsing into polytheism, as their ancestors had done before them.[44] After failing to win the Jews of Medina over to his side, Muhammad, who had initially viewed them as his natural allies, turned against his Jewish detractors.

Muhammad's attitude toward the pagans of Mecca was much more personal, since they not only had derided his teaching but also expelled him and his companions from their native town, depriving them of property and livelihood. Indeed, the Meccan emigrants to Medina had no property in that city and were therefore entirely dependent on the rather meager resources of their hosts, the *ansár*. As a consequence, the Muslims were left with no option but to begin raiding Meccan caravans in order to seize booty. In other words, raiding became an economic necessity for the fledgling Muslim community.[45] This aggressive course of action was justified by the old grievances against the erstwhile persecutors. The Meccans were proclaimed to be the enemies of God and his *umma*, and their possessions were fair game for the Muslims:

> Leave is given to those who fight because they were wronged—surely God is able to help them—who were expelled from their habitations without right, except that they say "Our Lord is God."[46]

As is evident from this and similar passages, the Qur'an portrays the Meccans as being actively and maliciously opposed to the divine will, while also persecuting those who strove to do it. For this they had deserved punishment that was to be inflicted on them not by God himself (as the revelations from the Meccan period seem to have indicated) but by his newly established Muslim community in Medina. This idea became an important new motif of the revelations that Muhammad was receiving in that city. They indicate that God had helped Muhammad to found the first Muslim community in Medina for a purpose. It was to serve as an instrument of divine wrath to be directed against those who had willfully and stubbornly chosen to ignore his commands. While the revelations from the Meccan period of Muhammad's preaching had, for the most part, deferred the punishment of the unbelievers to the Day of Judgment and the hereafter, in Medina Muhammad's revelations explicitly called for the divine punishment to be administered by the Muslim community here and now. Implementing this new injunction became the principal task of the *umma*.

The first attack against the Meccans by a small detachment of Muslims occurred at a locale named Nakhla in 624. It took place during a sacred month of the Arabian lunar calendar—a time when, according to the religion of pagan Arabs, aggression and warfare were strictly prohibited. One Meccan was killed and some booty taken. Because the Prophet did not explicitly sanction the raid, he had the option of disavowing it.[47] However, after some hesitation, he accepted the booty and distributed it among his followers, citing the following revelation from God:

> They will question you concerning the holy month, and fighting in it. Say: "Fighting in it is a heinous thing, but to bar from God's way, and disbelief in Him, and the Holy Mosque,[48] and to expel people from it—that is more heinous in God's sight; and persecution is more heinous than slaying."[49]

The die was cast, and an all-out conflict with the Meccan leadership became inevitable. Indeed, the raid at Nakhla deepened the breach between the Quraysh of Mecca and the Muslims of Medina and resulted in a series of hostilities between them that were to last for six years. As one can see, Muhammad's revelations now unequivocally asserted the primacy of Islam over the customs and values of pagan society; the process of severing tribal and kinship ties that had started with the *hijra* was brought to a logical conclusion by the declaration of an all-out war against the pagans of Mecca and their allies. The moral independence of Islam from pagan values and conventions was now final and unequivocal.

The success of the Nakhla raid encouraged Muslims from Medina to undertake another expedition against Meccan trade activities in 624. This time, the target was a Meccan caravan from Syria. It managed to avoid the Muslim attack by deviating from its expected route. Instead of the caravan, at the wells of Badr, southwest of Medina, the Muslim detachment of 313 or 314 men encountered a Meccan force twice or even thrice their size. It had been dispatched by the Meccan leadership to protect its trade interests. The Muslims had no option but to fight. And fight they did. Led and encouraged by Muhammad, they showed good discipline, valor, and superior organization. At the end of the day, they were victorious. The success of the outnumbered Muslims was such that the Qur'an deemed it necessary to explain it by a miraculous intervention of an angelic host that joined forces with the Muslim contingent (Q 8:9). Several leading men of the Quraysh were killed in battle, including the leader of the expedition, an archenemy of Islam, nicknamed Abu Jahl (literally, "Father of Ignorance"). Many Meccan warriors were captured to be later exchanged for ransom.[50]

The Battle of Badr represents the first military triumph of Islam as a newly founded political formation. It was the beginning of a series of military victories against the Meccans and their tribal allies. From that time on, the Muslim raiding activity continued unabated, and in the following year an entire Meccan caravan was captured by a Muslim raiding party. Muslim successes reinforced the position of Muhammad as leader of the new Arabian state. More and more Arabs were eager to embrace Islam in order to become part of its success. Muhammad used his newly won political capital to settle accounts with his monotheistic critics, the Jews, who, as mentioned, had refused to recognize him as a prophet. He ordered the Jewish tribe of Banu Qaynuqa' to be expelled from Medina, citing their hostility toward the Muslim community and their plot to join forces with his Meccan enemies. The Banu Qaynuqa' (some two thousand adults) left Medina for a Jewish settlement farther north.

Muhammad's decisive rupture with the Jews of Medina was reflected in a series of new revelations that commanded the Muslims to change the direction of prayer from Jerusalem to Mecca and its principal sanctuary, the Ka'ba:

> The fools among the people will say, "What has turned them from the direction they were facing in their prayers aforetime?" Say: "To God belong the East and the West; He guides whomever He will to a straight path . . . and We[51] did not appoint the direction you were facing, except that We might know who followed the Messenger from him who turned on his heels."[52]

Simultaneously, the sacred status of the Ka'ba was forcefully reasserted. It was proclaimed to be the first house of worship built by Abraham and his son Ishmael and thus firmly linked to Islam's sacred history.[53] Abraham's status as neither a Jew nor a Christian but the first "submitter" (*múslim*) to the will of God and the herald of the monotheistic faith (*islám*) was forcefully accentuated (Q 2:125–129).[54] The *hajj* (pilgrimage) to the Meccan sanctuary was declared to be part and parcel of the Muslim faith and ritual. The Muslim fast of Ramadán—the month in which the Qur'an was first revealed to Muhammad and in which the Battle of Badr was won—now replaced the time of the Jewish fast of Atonement in the month of [al-]Muharram.[55] Although the remaining two Jewish tribes of Medina were allowed to practice their religion, they had to acknowledge the primacy of Islam and its messenger and to defer to him in case of conflict with another section of Medina's population. This situation was fraught with tensions that were bound to come into the open during moments of crisis.

In addition to the external opposition instigated by the Jews, Muhammad found himself facing an internal opposition on the part of the so-called "hypocrites" (*munáfiqún*), the pagans of Medina who, as has already been mentioned, had adopted Islam out of expediency after the initial successes of the *umma*. Led by one Ibn Ubáyy,[56] the "hypocrites" were stridently condemned in the Qur'an as a fifth column of sorts—dissenters and doubters who had refused to join the fight against the enemies of the Muslim community:

> They have taken their oaths as a covering, then they have barred [others] from the way of God. Surely, evil are the things that they have been doing . . .
>
> That is because they have believed, then they have disbelieved; therefore a seal has been set on their hearts, and they do not understand . . . God assail them! How perverted they are![57]

Despite the plotting of internal and external adversaries, the building of the new state proceeded apace. Muhammad's enemies proved to be incapable of decisively challenging his authority or undermining his cause.

Muhammad as Political and Religious Leader and Private Individual

As mentioned, Muhammad's prestige not only as a religious preacher but also as an astute statesman and diplomat grew by the day. He became a respected military leader, who received one-fifth of the booty captured during raids against Meccan caravans and in the battlefield (see Figure 2.3).[58] His special status was confirmed by the revelation that allowed him to have many simultaneous wives beyond the four allowed to his followers.[59] It has been argued, however, that Muhammad used his marriages with women from different clans and tribes to cement his political alliances.[60] Indeed, only one wife, 'A'isha, daughter of his future successor Abu Bakr, was a virgin when Muhammad married her.[61] As wives of the leader of the *umma*, they were entitled to tokens

Figure 2.3 The Prophet Muhammad in the Circle of His Companions (Ottoman Turkish painted miniature)

Dresden, Saxon State Library/akg-images Turkish painted miniature, c. 1559/1600

of special respect from the rest of the Muslims. The Qur'an stipulated that they were to live in seclusion, not engage in any frivolity, and receive male visitors only from behind a curtain or veil (*hijáb*).[62]

Although Muhammad tried to spread his affection equally among his wives, 'A'isha, a vivacious and fun-loving young woman, was definitely Muhammad's best loved (after Khadíja). He stood by her in an episode when she was accused of adultery by the "hypocrite" Ibn Ubáyy, after having been accidentally left behind by her companions and found by a young man during the night. At that time, even the Prophet's closest companion and male relative, 'Ali, was inclined to accept this accusation at face value. However, Muhammad remained firm in his denial, and 'A'isha was soon vindicated by a special revelation, which was later to become part of the Islamic law pertaining to a false accusation of adultery:

> Why, when you heard it, did the believing men and women not of their own account think good thoughts, and say, "This is a manifest calumny"? Why did they not [demand of the accusers that they] bring four witnesses to prove their allegation. But since they [the accusers] did not bring the witnesses, in God's sight they are liars.[63]

Muhammad retained his affection for 'A'isha until the very end of his life and is said to have died in her lap.[64]

Despite his newly acquired prestige and high social status, Muhammad continued to live a simple and modest life without any luxury. He ate frugally and shared his food with the needy. He even washed his own clothes. Responding to his community's need for guidance and instruction, he made available himself to numerous visitors and eagerly answered their endless queries about the new faith and new ways to do things.[65] His oral instructions on various issues of Islamic etiquette and morals, as well as theological questions, worship, and communal life, were to become an indispensable source of Islamic religion alongside the Qur'an. They came to be known as the "[exemplary] Way of the Prophet" (*sunnat al-nabi*).

The Battle of Úhud

Following the Battle of Badr, the Quraysh became seriously alarmed at Muhammad's growing prestige not only in Medina but also among the Arab tribes of the Hijáz. Since he had emigrated to Medina three years earlier, he acquired sufficient military strength and political clout to undermine their trade with Syria and to discredit them in the eyes of their tribal allies. In 625, the Quraysh decided to deal a decisive blow to Muhammad and his new polity. They equipped a major military expedition against Medina that consisted of a three-thousand-strong force of mounted fighters headed by Abú Sufyán b. Harb, the leader of the powerful Umayyad clan.[66] Initially, Muhammad's comrades advised him against confronting the superior Meccan army outside the city. However, by cutting date palms and destroying the new harvest, the Meccans forced the Muslims to abandon their fortified positions and meet the enemy and its tribal allies at Úhud, a flat-topped mountain located at the distance of three miles north of Medina. Although at first outnumbered—reportedly one to three—the Muslims, led by Muhammad, were successful in beating off the Meccan charge. However, at the sight of the retreating Meccan force, some of Muhammad's men abandoned their positions on the flank to join in the plundering of the Meccans' wagon train. Khálid b. al-Walíd, a talented military commander of the Meccan force, saw the opening in the Muslim ranks and led his men into it. Surprised by this unexpected attack, the Muslims retreated in disarray. Many of them—up to seventy, according to some accounts, including Muhammad's uncle Hamza—were killed. Muhammad sustained a wound on the face, but he held his ground, saving his followers from an impending annihilation. The Quraysh were overjoyed by their victory. Their women, who had accompanied the Meccan army, desecrated the bodies of fallen Muslim warriors. Hind, the wife of the Meccan leader Abu Sufyan, tore the liver from the body of Muhammad's fallen uncle Hamza and ate it raw. This was her way to exact revenge on Hamza for killing her father at the Battle of Badr one year earlier. To mark the Meccan victory, Hind made a necklace of the ears and noses of the fallen Muslim warriors.[67] Flush with the excitement of the victory, the Meccan commanders, however, neglected to finish the job. They either did not feel strong enough or were reluctant to sacrifice their lives storming Medina's strongholds and engaging in hand-to-hand combat in its narrow alleys. Thus, although the prestige of the Quraysh was repaired, the victors did not accomplish their goal of dealing a fatal blow to the Muslim *umma*. In the aftermath of this defeat, Muhammad turned against another Jewish tribe, the Banu Nadír, whom he accused of secretly plotting to strike the Muslims in the back during that recent bout of conflict. On his orders, the Muslims expelled the Jews from the city and seized their quarters and palm groves.[68] Whereas the Prophet also received revelations condemning the "hypocrites" and other "doubters" among the Arab inhabitants of Medina for their vacillation during the Battle of Úhud,[69] they contained no specific sanctions against the culprits. So they were left alone.

The Battle of the Ditch

In 627, two years after the Battle of Úhud, it became clear to the Meccans that Muhammad's new polity was growing stronger rather than weaker. In fact, it had become the principal threat to Quraysh authority in the Hijáz and beyond. The Quraysh leaders of Mecca decided to crush their Muslim enemy once and for all. To this end, they invited their numerous Bedouin allies to join them for an all-out attack on Medina. In April 627, the ten-thousand-strong army of the Quraysh and their tribal confederates laid siege to the Medinan oasis. To neutralize the Bedouin cavalry of the Meccan army, the Muslims of Medina dug moats and ditches around the most vulnerable parts of the city. This stratagem gave the name to the entire campaign, which went down in history as the Battle of the Ditch.[70] For about a month, the city's population successfully defended themselves. Faced with a lack of military success and unable to provision their mounts, the motley confederacy began to disintegrate. As the Bedouin allies started to return to their tribal territories and families, the Quraysh had no option but to lift the siege and withdraw to Mecca, where they were greeted with the dejection and despondency of its population.

The Muslims followed the Meccan withdrawal by the massacre of some 600 male members of the Jewish tribe Banu Qurayza, whom the Muslims accused of negotiating a peaceful surrender to the Meccans. The Prophet reportedly received the order to attack his Jewish neighbors from the angel Gabriel, who, in his turn, was sent to him by God.[71] Muhammad's rage was aggravated by the fact that the previously exiled Jewish tribes had been actively supporting the Quraysh coalition. Hence the harsh punishment meted to the remaining Jews by the Muslims: The men of the Banu Qurayza, between six hundred and seven hundred in number, were brought to the marketplace of Medina, beheaded, and buried in specially dug trenches.[72]

Muhammad and the Bedouin Tribes of Arabia

In the aftermath of the Battle of the Ditch and the destruction of the last Jewish tribe of Medina, Muhammad no longer faced any real opposition in the city. Whatever Jewish or pagan population that remained in the city unquestionably accepted his authority as the head of the city and its environs. The task now was to build alliances with the Bedouin tribes of Arabia with a view to creating a robust political entity that would rival the Meccan state. This goal was accomplished partly by the voluntary conversion of the tribes and partly by diplomacy, such as, for example, playing on the traditional rivalries among them. This process had started already before the Battle of Úhud and continued in the years that followed. To secure the goodwill of Bedouin tribes of Arabia, Muhammad often acted as a neutral arbitrator in their conflicts, which had been a major drain on the tribes' meager resources. His arbitration no doubt contributed to his growing standing in the eyes of the Bedouins. An astute diplomat, Muhammad was ready to allow the tribes to practice any faith they wanted as long as they agreed to enter into a military alliance with the Medinan *umma*. Such alliances of friendship and cooperation were established not only with the pagans but also with the powerful Christian Arab tribes along the Arabian-Byzantine border.[73] Simultaneously, envoys were dispatched from Medina to the tribes of western and southern Arabia to teach them the fundamentals of Islam and to ensure the collection of a tax (*zakát*) for the community's treasury. The Jewish tribes of Arabia, as we have already seen, were subjected to a different treatment. They were not seen as worthy and reliable partners by the Muslim leadership and had to unconditionally submit to Muslim rule in return for a special tribute called *jizya*.[74] In the case of Medina's tribal Arab allies, the tax was called *sádaqa* or *zakát*. Refusal by a tribe to pay the *zakát* tax would be punished by the dispatch of a Muslim force to its territory. As an incentive, the allied tribes were offered an opportunity to participate in the raiding activity and conquests of the Muslims, which had been quite successful and therefore attractive to the resource-strapped tribesmen.

The Conquest of Mecca and Beyond

The coalition carefully assembled by Muhammad and his closest lieutenants during their stay in Medina could not survive without subjugating its main rival, Mecca, and taking control of the vital trade routes to Yemen and Syria. Consistent with the Prophet's policies previously described, this goal, too, was achieved by a combination of diplomatic and military means.

In 628, Muhammad announced his intention to perform a pilgrimage to the Meccan sanctuary in a gesture that can be interpreted both as a veiled message to the Meccan leaders of the inevitability of the Muslim triumph and the Prophet's desire to demonstrate his continual commitment to the sacred status of the Meccan sanctuary—a major concern for its Qurayshi overlords. Accompanied by a force of some fourteen hundred men and a herd of camels to be offered as sacrifice, Muhammad arrived in the vicinity of Mecca in March 628 and set up a camp at the place called [al-]Hudaybiyya.[75] The would-be successor ("caliph")[76] to the Prophet, 'Uthman, entered Mecca on his behalf but was detained there. The Meccans then sent out a negotiator to the Muslim camp to persuade the Prophet not to enter the holy city this year.[77] The Meccan leadership felt that after the debacle they had suffered at Medina one year earlier, Muhammad's entry would deprive them of whatever prestige they were still enjoying among their Bedouin allies. Muhammad's comrades, especially the future second caliph 'Umar, urged him to launch an attack against Mecca. After some hesitation, Muhammad chose to negotiate a deal with the Meccan representatives and eventually signed a treaty with them that came to be known as the Treaty of [al-]Hudaybiyya.[78] The treaty stipulated that in the coming year, the Meccans would evacuate the sanctuary to allow the Muslims of Medina to perform the *hajj* unmolested. It also gave permission to the Bedouin tribes of the Hijáz to join any side (either Meccan or Muslim) without fearing any retaliation on the part of their former ally. Although the Muslims also had to make some concessions (namely, to return members of the Quraysh—presumably minors and women—who had emigrated to Medina without the permission of their guardians), overall the Treaty was favorable to the Muslim side. It once again demonstrated the growing prestige of the Prophet and his followers to the tribes of central Arabia and beyond. As a result, Muhammad was able to win over to his side many of Mecca's former allies.

In the middle of the negotiations with the Meccan leadership, an important symbolic act took place in the Muslim camp. After learning about the alleged murder of 'Uthman by the Meccans—it later turned out to be a false rumor—Muhammad called upon his followers to take an oath of allegiance to him.[79] This oath, which was symbolized by the handclasp known as *bay'a*, was to become a highly significant, paradigmatic element of Muslim religious and political life in the subsequent decades and centuries. When reading Muslim historical chronicles, one finds the act of *bay'a* repeated over and over again. This could be pledges of allegiance by Muslims to a new caliph, to an incoming governor, or to a military commander (*amir*). The most spectacular outcome of the Treaty of [al-]Hudaybiyya was the so-called fulfilled pilgrimage to Mecca that Muhammad and some two thousand of his followers performed in 629. After seven years of exile, the Prophet finally returned to his hometown—and with a vengeance.[80]

Upon his return to Medina from [al-]Hudaybiyya, Muhammad had to face the criticism of those of his followers who thought that he should have attacked Mecca. However, the successful conquest of the rich oasis of Kháybar six weeks later helped to allay this discontent. Kháybar was inhabited by several wealthy Jewish tribes and Hebraized Arabs, who had earlier given refuge to some Jewish exiles from Medina. After a long and difficult siege, Kháybar fell to the attackers, partly due to the internal discord among its Jewish defenders. A considerable amount of booty was captured by the Muslims, including a substantial cache of fine armory.[81]

In 630, a skirmish between some Bedouin allies of the Quraysh and the Muslims gave the latter a pretext to annul the [al-]Hudaybiyya Treaty. Muhammad assembled all of his—by now numerous—Bedouin allies and besieged Mecca. The Meccans, weakened by the desertion of their allies and faced with the military superiority of the Medinan troops, chose to surrender without a fight. Their leader, Abu Sufyan of the Umayyad clan of Quraysh, came to Muhammad's camp and pledged his allegiance to Islam and Muhammad.[82] In return for the city's peaceful surrender, the Prophet granted a general amnesty to all of its inhabitants, including his former persecutors. Muhammad now entered his hometown not as a pilgrim but as its new master. The Meccan sanctuary was cleansed of its idols and sacred stones, except, according to some reports, for two pictures of Jesus ('Isa) and his mother Mary (Maryam).[83] It is on this momentous occasion that the Prophet reportedly recited the famous Qur'anic verse: "The truth has come and falsehood has vanished away."[84]

The Quraysh leaders submitted and began to take part, together with the Muslims, in raids against some Bedouin tribes that still refused to acknowledge Medina's authority. Their participation was rewarded so lavishly as to cause some disgruntlement among Muhammad's Medinan followers.[85] A Qur'anic passage indicates that the Muslim victories over several pagan Arab tribes were due in part to a direct divine assistance.[86] Thus, during the Battle of Hunayn[87] in 630, shortly after the conquest of Mecca, God bestowed upon the Prophet the [gift] of "inner tranquility"[88] and assisted the Muslim fighters with "the legions [of angels] you could not see."[89] The oasis of al-Ta'if, a trading rival to Mecca, was captured after a protracted siege.[90] Although Mecca had become part of the Islamic polity, Muhammad's headquarters remained in Medina, the city that had welcomed him and his followers at the time of hardship. The Prophet always returned to Medina after his military campaigns. In the summer of 630, Muhammad set out on a military expedition toward the Syrian-Byzantine border. He had already tried to advance in that direction in 629, when a three-thousand-strong Muslim force he had dispatched to the north was routed by a large Byzantine army near the town of Mu'ta in present-day Jordan.[91] This time, the Muslim military expedition, led by Muhammad and marked by the miracles he performed en route,[92] reached the town of Tabúk in northwest Arabia. Although the Muslims never made contact with an enemy force, the local Arab chieftains were impressed enough to offer their allegiance to the Prophet.[93] This and a few other military expeditions up north were intended to expand Medina's sphere of influence, primarily onto the lands of the Arab tribal allies of the Byzantine and Sasanid Empires. This trend would continue under Muhammad's successors, eventually resulting in the partial, in the case of Byzantium, and total, in the case of Sasanid Iran, annexation of imperial lands by the Muslim state.

In the tenth year after the *hijra* (632), the rites of the Muslim pilgrimage (*hajj*) were thoroughly Islamicized in the course of what came to be known as the Prophet's "Farewell Pilgrimage."[94] During his famous speech on the plain of 'Arafat in the vicinity of Mecca, the Prophet exhorted all Muslims to be brethren and to treat each other and their womenfolk with kindness and respect, to observe God's commands, to abolish usury, and not to use the Jewish custom of adding an extra month to the lunar calendar to synchronize it with the seasonal, solar calendar.[95] The status of the Ka'ba as the first place of worship founded by Abraham and Ishmael was once again forcefully reasserted. Those Arabs who still remained pagan were proscribed from taking part in the pilgrimage. In 632, upon his return to Medina, Muhammad fell ill and soon died in the arms of 'A'isha,[96] apparently without explicitly appointing a successor.[97] According to a famous story, 'Umar, the Prophet's close friend and companion, refused to come to terms with his death, saying that, like Moses before him, Muhammad "went and was hidden from his people for forty days, returning to them after it was said that he had died."[98] The more experienced Abu Bakr restrained 'Umar and, having confirmed that the Prophet had indeed passed away, announced the news to the assembled Muslims, saying: "O men, if anyone worships Muhammad, Muhammad is dead: if anyone worships God, God is alive, immortal!"[99]

It was only on hearing Abu Bakr's solemn admonition that both 'Umar and the rest of the Muslims finally realized that the Prophet was no longer with them.[100] Muhammad was buried in the house where he died. A new, postprophetic era in the life of the Muslim community, established and cemented by Muhammad, was dawning.

Conclusions

The religious revolution initiated and accomplished by the prophet Muhammad and his closest followers is often seen as a truly unique event in the history of humankind. Within one decade, the entire pagan society of Arabia was totally transformed, and the foundations of a new religion, society, and culture were firmly established. Within the next decade and a half, the whole of the Middle East was drastically transformed as the lands of the great powers of the age, Byzantium and Sasanid Iran, were overrun and subjugated by the victorious Muslim armies. The victors brought with them ideas and values that constituted the foundations of a new civilization that kept expanding dramatically for decades to come. The Muslims in the past and today have explained the rise and growth of the Muslim state by divine intervention: Their *umma* was selected by God to serve as an irresistible instrument of his will. God granted the Muslims victory as a reward for their loyalty to the true religion of Abraham and all those prophets who had tried to restore his monotheistic message over the ages until it had achieved its final and purest expression in the message of Muhammad. While this explanation may strike us as partisan and apologetic, one does not necessarily have to be a Muslim to adopt it. Many Christians who had witnessed the Muslim triumph considered it to be a divinely ordained punishment inflicted on them by God for their moral sins, disunity, and doctrinal transgressions. The idea of divine intervention (or providence) is still present in the Christian explanation, but the reasons given are different.

Question to Ponder

If one refuses to accept the idea of divine intervention (or divine providence), one must offer an alternative explanation. Please formulate your own understanding of the astounding success of the Muslim state and try to defend it by making use of the evidence found in the first two chapters of this book or any additional materials you choose to consult. In your explanation, you are welcome to draw on your prior knowledge of theories of religious, social, and political change, such as Marxism, Weberianism, Malthusianism (demographics), geographical determinism (as represented by Jared Diamond, among others), and so on.

Summary

- Before his prophetic mission, Muhammad went from orphan to merchant. The Prophet's wife Khadíja played a pivotal role in his life and in his decision to disseminate his religious teaching.
- Khadíja's cousin Wáraqa explains Muhammad's message as coming from God via an angel of revelation (Gabriel). The message emphasizes the oneness and uniqueness of God and condemns Arabian polytheism (*shirk*). Muhammad's revelations depict him as the restorer of Abraham's (Ibrahim's) monotheistic message, a warner of his people, a new messenger (*rasúl*) dispatched to humankind by the God of Abraham and of other Hebrew and Christian prophets.
- Among the Quraysh's reasons for opposition to Muhammad is their fear that it will deprive them of their privileged status and the proceeds of the *hajj* and of the trans-Arabian trade in which they are major players. The Qurayshi elite dismiss Muhammad as a troublemaker bent on self-aggrandizement or a tool of outside powers.
- Muhammad's rejection by the Quraysh compels him to look for allies outside Mecca. He finds them in the tribal population of the oasis town of Yáthrib, who invite him to arbitrate in their conflicts. Faced by mounting persecutions, Muhammad and his followers move to Yáthrib/Medina (*híjra*) and form the first Muslim community (*umma*) there.
- The nascent Muslim community of Yáthrib (to be subsequently called Medina) consists of two groups: the emigrants (*muhájirún*) from Mecca and the local helpers (*ansár*). The economic difficulties faced by the Muslim *umma* in Yáthrib/Medina in the aftermath of the *híjra* cause them to begin raiding Meccan trade caravans.
- The conflict with the Meccans leads to the Battle of Badr (624). The Muslims' resounding victory allows Muhammad to consolidate his authority and become the town's uncontested religious and political leader. His new status is confirmed by the so-called Constitution of Medina.
- Many Jewish leaders of Medina refuse to recognize Muhammad as a new monotheistic prophet and cast doubt on the authenticity of his revelations. Muhammad's consequent rupture with the Jewish community of Medina is symbolized by the change of the direction of the canonical prayer from Jerusalem to Mecca and the establishment of the uniquely Islamic fast during the month of Ramadán. The three Jewish tribes of Medina suffer varying fates under Muhammad's rule.
- Muhammad becomes a statesman. In his family life, he defends his youngest wife 'A'isha and receives a Qur'anic injunction confirming his position. The Prophet's behavior is increasingly perceived as the "[exemplary] prophetic custom" (*súnnat al-nabi*), to be implemented by Muslims in their private and public life.
- The consequences of the battles of Úhud and the Ditch (625 and 627): the defeat of the Muslims at Úhud is inconclusive—the Meccans fail to "finish the job." The Meccan siege of Medina unravels two years later, further enhancing the Prophet's prestige among the Arabian tribes.
- The *zakát* (tax) imposed on the Arabian tribes becomes a material symbol of their allegiance to the Prophet's *umma*. The majority of the tribes submit to the Prophet's authority.
- Amid Muhammad's military campaigns and victories, the conquest of Mecca in 630 caps the last years of the Prophet's ministry (628–632). Muhammad's principal

adversaries in Mecca, the leaders of the Umayyad clan, pledge their allegiance to the Prophet and accept Islam. With the Islamization of the *hajj* rituals, Mecca becomes the spiritual and ritual center of the new religion.

- The first Muslim attempts at conquering the lands of the neighboring empires (with their long-term repercussions) precede Muhammad's death in 632 and the beginning of the postprophetic era.

Notes

1 What follows is based for the most part on Alfred Guillaume's translation of Ibn Ishaq's (d. 768) "The Life of the Messenger of God" (*sirat rasul Allah*); see Alfred Guillaume (trans.), *The Life of Muhammad*, Oxford University Press, Oxford and Karachi, 1982.
2 Ibid., p. 79.
3 Ibid., pp. 79–81.
4 Whether or not Muhammad shared the views of his pagan tribesmen is a moot point. Standard Muslim accounts of his life describe him as a monotheist from his birth; see, e.g., Guillaume (trans.), *Life*, pp. 80–81. According to this view, he participated in the rituals associated with the Meccan sanctuary as a believer in a one and only God. This view, in turn, is consistent with the Muslim belief that the sanctuary itself had been monotheistic long before the Quraysh settled there, its monotheistic origins having been later obscured by Arabian paganism.
5 Literally, "the god": the generic Arabic/Semitic word for "deity" (*ilah*) with the Arabic definite article "al-" attached to it.
6 The Arabic verb *qara'* used here can be rendered into English as both "read" and "recite."
7 The poetic translation is Guillaume's; see Guillaume (trans.), *Life*, p. 106.
8 Here and in what follows, we use the English translation of the Qur'an by Arthur J. Arberry, *The Koran Interpreted*, Touchstone, New York, 1996, with occasional modifications; in cases when the numbering of Qur'anic verses in Arberry's translation is different from that of the standard Egyptian edition of 1924, references to Arberry's translation are given in parentheses.
9 Guillaume (trans.), *Life*, pp. 111–117.
10 Ibid., p. 115.
11 Ibid., p. 117.
12 Montgomery Watt and Richard Bell, *Introduction to the Qur'an*, Edinburgh University Press, Edinburgh, 1994, p. 150.
13 Walter Björkman, "Kafir," in *Encyclopedia of Islam*, 2nd ed.; online edition: http://referenceworks.brillonline.com; Daniel Gimaret, "Shirk," in *Encyclopedia of Islam*, 2nd ed.; online edition: http://referenceworks.brillonline.com.
14 Marshall Hodgson, *The Venture of Islam*, University of Chicago Press, Chicago, 1974, vol. 1, pp. 163–165.
15 See, e.g., Q 19:76–80.
16 See Q 107:1–7 and 2:86.
17 Hodgson, *The Venture*, vol. 1, pp. 163–166.
18 Ibid., p. 163.
19 See, e.g., Q 13:8.
20 Guillaume (trans.), *Life*, p. 121.
21 As described in Guillaume (trans.), *Life*, p. 181.
22 Ibid., p. 119.
23 Ibid., pp. 133–134.
24 Ibid., pp. 159–160 and Hodgson, *The Venture*, vol. 1, p. 156.
25 Guillaume (trans.), *Life*, pp. 143–146.
26 Ibid., pp. 150–153.
27 Ibid., pp. 191–192.

28 Regarding the cult of "the daughters of Allah" among the Quraysh see Guillaume (trans.), *Life*, pp. 80, 137, and 165–167.

29 For a standard account see Guillaume (trans.), *Life*, pp. 165–167.

30 Ibid., pp. 192–194.

31 Ibid., pp. 172–175.

32 Ibid., p. 161.

33 The earliest extant biography of the prophet Muhammad by Ibn Ishaq (read: Is'haq; d. 768) treats his "night journey and ascension to Heaven" (*al-isra' wa 'l-mi'raj*) as a real historical episode that took place at that particular juncture of the Prophet's life; see Guillaume (trans.), *Life*, pp. 181–187. I follow this tradition without questioning its historicity and with the understanding that what matters here is not what "really happened" but rather how Muslims have constructed their sacred history—a process in which historical fact is intricately interwoven with historical imagination.

34 Guillaume (trans.), *Life*, p. 72 and Muhammad Asad (trans.), *The Message of the Qur'an* (translated and explained by Muhammad Asad), Dar al-Andalus, Gibraltar, 1980, p. 960, notes 1 and 2.

35 Guillaume (trans.), *Life*, pp. 197–199.

36 The story is frequently related, but its exact origin is elusive; see, e.g., http://www.musalla.org/Articles/Seerah/seerah21.htm; the *hadith* of the spider's web mentioned in the *al-Musnad* of Ibn Hanbal (d. 855) is considered by many Muslim scholars to be "weak"; see http://islamqa.info/en/27224.

37 For details see Toshihiko Isutsu, *Ethico-Religious Concepts in the Qur'an*, McGill University Press, Montreal, 1966, passim.

38 Literally "nation" or "people."

39 A whole chapter (*sura*) of the Qur'an detailing their misdeeds is named after them; see Q 63.

40 Guillaume (trans.), *Life*, p. 233; for the entire text, see ibid., pp. 231–233.

41 Ibid., pp. 232–233.

42 Ibid., pp. 246 and 254–258.

43 Ibid., pp. 242–246.

44 For details of the debates between Muhammad and his Jewish opponents, see ibid., pp. 246–270.

45 For a list of the first raids, see ibid., pp. 281–289.

46 Q 22:40–41.

47 Hodgson, *The Venture*, vol. 1, pp. 175–176.

48 Namely, the Meccan sanctuary.

49 Q 2:217.

50 Guillaume (trans.), *Life*, pp. 295–314.

51 That is, God, who here speaks of himself in the plural using the so-called majestic or royal 'we.'

52 Q 2:142–143; Guillaume (trans.), *Life*, pp. 258–259, 289.

53 Guillaume (trans.), *Life*, pp. 84–89, 268, 552–553, 628, 691, and 774; Gerald Hawting, "Ka'ba," in *Encyclopedia of the Qur'an*. General Editor: Jane Dammen McAuliffe; online edition: http://referenceworks.brillonline.com.

54 Guillaume (trans.), *Life*, p. 260.

55 Angelika Neuwirth, "Ramadan," in *Encyclopedia of the Qur'an*. General Editor: Jane Dammen McAuliffe; online edition: http://referenceworks.brillonline.com.

56 His full name was 'Abdallah b. Ubayy b. Salul al-'Awfi (d. 631); see Guillaume (trans.), *Life*, pp. 277–279.

57 Q 63:2–4.

58 Q 8:1 and 41.

59 Q 33:50 is often interpreted to this effect; see Barbara Stowasser, "Wives of the Prophet," in *Encyclopedia of the Qur'an*. General Editor: Jane Dammen McAuliffe; online edition: http://referenceworks.brillonline.com.

60 Stowasser, "Wives."

61 Ibid.

62 Q 33:53; cf. 33:32; regarding the new meaning later acquired by this term, see Asma Barlas, "Women's Readings of the Qur'an," in Jane McAuliffe (ed.), *The Cambridge Companion to the Qur'an*, Cambridge University Press, Cambridge, 2006, pp. 267–268.

63 Q 24:12–13; I have amended Arberry's translation by providing some contextual details missing in the original; for a detailed account of the "lie that was uttered," as this episode is called in Muhammad's biography, see Guillaume (trans.), *Life*, pp. 493–499.

64 Ibid., p. 682; for 'A'isha's life and role in the early Muslim community, see Denise Spellberg, *Politics, Gender and the Islamic Past: The Legacy of 'A'isha bint Abi Bakr*, Columbia University Press, New York, 1994.

65 As detailed in his biography; see Guillaume (trans.), *Life*, passim.

66 For a standard account of the Battle of Úhud, see Guillaume (trans.), *Life*, pp. 370–391; for the Qur'anic references to this fateful event, see ibid., pp. 391–401.

67 Ibid., p. 385.

68 Ibid., pp. 437–445.

69 See, e.g., Q 3:118–123.

70 As described in Guillaume (trans.), *Life*, pp. 450–460.

71 Ibid., p. 461.

72 Ibid., p. 464.

73 For the latest study of Arab tribes before Islam, see Greg Fisher (ed.), *Arabs and Empires Before Islam*, Oxford University Press, Oxford, 2015, esp. chapters 4, 5, and 6.

74 Based on Q 9:29.

75 Guillaume (trans.), *Life*, pp. 499–501.

76 From the Arabic *khalifa*, one who comes after, i.e., "successor" or "lieutenant."

77 Ibid., pp. 503–504.

78 Ibid., p. 504.

79 Ibid., p. 503.

80 Ibid., pp. 530–531.

81 Ibid., pp. 510–519.

82 Ibid., pp. 546–547.

83 Ibid., pp. 552–553.

84 Q 17:81 (17:84 in Arberry's translation); for this interpretation see, e.g., http://www.qtafsir.com/index. php?option=com_content&task=view&id=2793&Itemid=72.

85 Guillaume (trans.), *Life*, pp. 592–597.

86 Q 9:25–26.

87 A valley between Mecca and the al-Ta'if oasis.

88 In Arabic, *sakína*; some Western scholars derive this word from the Hebrew *shechina* or *shekhina* ("divine presence"); see, e.g., Rudi Paret, *Der Koran: Kommentar und Konkordanz*, Verlag W. Kohlhammer, Stuttgart, 1971, p. 52 and the literature cited there.

89 According to one Muslim fighter, "I saw the like of a black garment coming from heaven until it fell between us and the enemy. I looked, and lo black ants everywhere filled the valley. I had no doubt that they were angels. Then the enemy fled," Guillaume (trans.), *Life*, p. 572.

90 Guillaume (trans.), *Life*, pp. 587–592

91 Ibid., pp. 531–540; see also Frants Buhl, "Mu'ta," in *Encyclopedia of Islam*, 2nd ed.; online edition: http://referenceworks.brillonline.com.

92 See, e.g., ibid., p. 608.

93 Ibid., pp. 602–609.

94 Ibid., pp. 649–652.

95 Ibid., pp. 650–651; for the practice of adjusting the solar and lunar calendars through the intercalation of an extra month every three years, see Alexander Knysh, "Months in the Qur'an," in *Encyclopedia of the Qur'an*. General Editor: Jane Dammen McAuliffe; online edition: http://referenceworks.brillonline.com.

96 Guillaume (trans.), *Life*, p. 682.

97 The Shi'ites came to insist that the Prophet appointed his cousin 'Ali as his successor at the Pond of Khumm.

98 Guillaume (trans.), *Life*, p. 682.

99 Ibid., p. 683; cf. Q 3:144.

100 Guillaume (trans.), *Life*, p. 683.

Chapter 3

After Muhammad
The Rightly Guided Caliphs and the Conquests

After the death of its founder, the Islamic community was faced with a number of internal and external challenges. Its very existence depended on the ability of its members to cope with them by rallying around one leader. The most dangerous scenario was a potential conflict over the leadership of the *umma* between the helpers (*ansár*) of Medina and the emigrants (*muhájirún*), the first Meccan Muslims who had accompanied Muhammad to Medina after he had to flee from his native city. This rift could have led to the election of two rival leaders and, as a result, to the inevitable split of the community into Meccan and Medinan "branches." Were this to have happened, Muslim unity would have been fatally ruptured.[1]

The other challenges were external. Upon the news of Muhammad's death, there appeared in different parts of Arabia a number of individuals claiming divine guidance and prophetic status. Their preaching of their own religious messages threatened to undermine the hard-won position of Islam as the religion of if not all the Arabs, then at least the majority of them.[2] Finally, many Bedouin allies of Mecca and Medina, who had made their pacts with Muhammad, no longer felt obligated to maintain loyalty to his successor. In practice, this meant their refusal to contribute the obligatory *zakát* tax to the Muslim communal treasury. While some tribes canceled their agreements with the Muslim state in Medina altogether, others pledged to remain within the coalition as long as they were exempt from the *zakát*. This disloyalty on the part of the Bedouin tribes was fueled by their deeply ingrained desire to be independent of outside political control. In refusing to render the *zakát* to the new head of the *umma*, Bedouin tribal leaders hoped to regain their treasured independence, especially in the light of appearance in various corners of Arabia of several new prophets, who preached a message similar to Muhammad's.

The potentially fatal rift between the Meccans and the Medinans was prevented by the bold actions of Abu Bakr and 'Umar, who called for the unity of the Muslims in the face of a crisis.[3] While the body of the Prophet was being prepared for burial, they rushed to a spontaneous meeting of the *ansár*, who had assembled to elect one of their own as their new leader. During the heated altercations that ensued, 'Umar pledged his loyalty to Abu Bakr. His disarming ardor and commitment to Muslim unity persuaded the *ansár* to follow suit. The religious prestige of the Quraysh as the custodians of the Meccan sanctuary may have also played a role in the *ansár*'s decision. The new Muslim leader came to be known as *khalífa* (rendered as "caliph" in English), namely, "successor" or "deputy" of the Prophet. The external challenges took some time to overcome. To prevent their former allies from seceding, the Muslims launched a series of military expeditions that have come to be known as "wars on apostasy" (*ridda*). They lasted from 632 until 634 and ended with the decisive triumph of the Muslim state. The credit for this victory largely goes to Khálid b. al-Walíd, a commander of genius, who, as we remember, had distinguished himself at the Battle of Úhud, albeit on the Meccan side. He had later converted to Islam and served the Muslim community with loyalty and distinction—deserving the honorary title "Sword of God"—until he was dismissed from his office by 'Umar, following the Muslim occupation of Syria.

Khálid b. al-Walíd led several successful campaigns against the secessionist tribes and was able to reduce them to obedience, which meant first and foremost the resumption of the payment of the *zakát* tax. Khálid's greatest success was the destruction of the movement launched by a "false prophet" named Musaylima in the district of Yamáma, in central Arabia. The decisive battle took place in the Garden of Death—so-called because of the high number of casualties on both sides. Thanks to the valor of the Muslim fighters, Musaylima's force was vanquished, and he himself was killed in the hand-to-hand melee. Musaylima's rebellion was probably the gravest challenge to the Muslim community because it came not from a disloyal tribal leader seeking independence but from a claimant to a prophetic inspiration similar to that of Muhammad; furthermore, Musaylima had a scripture and laws of his own,[4] as well as the economic and logistical wherewithal to challenge the recently established Muslim control over the Arabian Peninsula.[5]

When Abu Bakr died, all of Arabia was firmly under Muslim sway (see Map 3.1). The rebellious tribes were forced to pay the *zakát* to the Muslim treasury in Medina and to render a number of their men to be held hostage in the city. This was done to deter the tribes from rebelling again against the Muslim state. As a leading American scholar of early Arabian society has aptly remarked:

> The *ridda* wars thus represent the culmination of that general process of political consolidation begun by Muhammad by which an Islamic ruling elite established full control over the tribal population of the whole Arabian peninsula. They represent, too, the culmination of that process by which the new state, run by sedentary tribesmen, attained virtually complete control over the nomadic sector of the Arabian peninsula, which had traditionally been able to avoid such domination.[6]

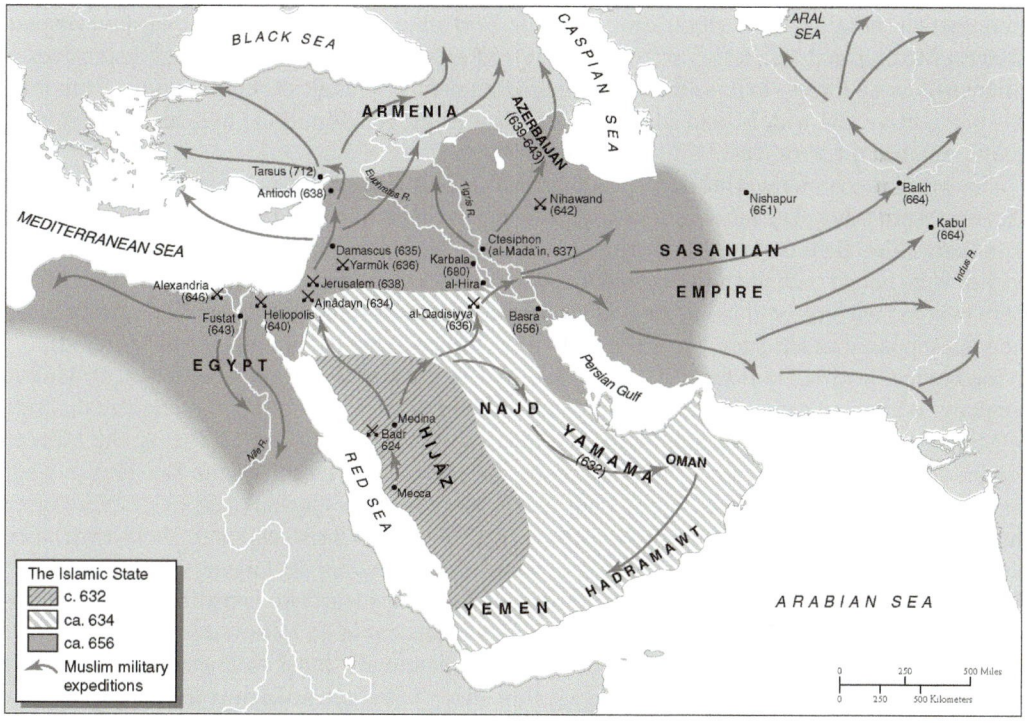

Map 3.1 Arabia at the Time of the Rightly Guided Caliphs and the Arab Conquests, 632–700

The consolidation of authority in the hands of the new ruling elite—the Quraysh, the *ansár*, and several close tribal allies of the Quraysh—provided them with the manpower and material resources to undertake the conquest of the neighboring lands to the north, namely Syria and Iraq. By seizing these lands, the Muslim community acquired the necessary springboard for the subjugation of the entire Near East, North Africa, the Iberian Peninsula, Iran, and Central Asia.

The Muslim Conquests Under 'Umar

The success of the Muslim conquest of the Near East and beyond has been variously attributed to demographic, economic, political, and military factors. Some scholars cite Arabia's inability to sustain its growing population and the resultant push for their massive migration to the nearby territories. Others point out the fortuitous (from the Arab point of view) combination of the newly acquired Arab military strength and the weakness of the Byzantine and Sasanian Empires in the aftermath of a protracted war between them. Many observers acknowledge the motivating and consolidating role of the Islamic religion in uniting Arabia's mutually hostile tribes around the common goal and inspiring them to spread their religion, which they considered to be God's final revelation to humankind, beyond its borders. In the final analysis, it appears that these and perhaps a few other factors "conspired" to propel the newly converted Arabs from their barren hinterland to the center stage of Near Eastern civilization that they inherited from the empires they had vanquished. Be this as it may, the fact remains that, despite their cultural, logistical, and organizational inferiority, the Arab-Muslim armies managed to triumph decisively over their seemingly invincible imperial neighbors that can rightfully be viewed as the two "superpowers" of that age.[7]

As suggested in the previous section, the Arab-Muslim expansion into the lands beyond Arabia was the logical outcome of the earlier trend that pushed all Arabs to unify under the leadership of a new elite that based its legitimacy on the fact that one of its own had given the world a new monotheistic religion. It is significant that this new elite came from the urban environment (Mecca, Medina, and, to a lesser extent, al-Ta'if), whereas the tribes that submitted themselves—voluntarily or by force—to its authority were predominantly nomadic or seminomadic. Seen from this perspective, the widely held stereotype of Islam as the religion of the nomads appears to be questionable at the very least.[8]

The Muslim commonwealth under Muhammad and his successors included both Muslim and Christian Arab tribes. The latter were treated as subjects of the Muslim state and, occasionally, also as military allies. Because many Arab tribes of the north lived in the lands of Arabia's imperial neighbors or were bound with them by contractual agreements, any attempt by the Muslim Arabs to win them over to their side or to invite them to convert to Islam was fraught with conflict, since it inevitably presupposed an intrusion into the spheres of influence of the Byzantines and the Sasanids.

Ideological justifications for warfare against Arabia's imperial neighbors were not difficult to come by. While numerous Qur'anic injunctions to fight those who refused to recognize the truth of Muhammad's message and submit to God's will were originally directed against the Meccan pagans and the Jews of Medina,[9] they could now be interpreted as a call on the Muslims to wage war on any non-Muslim enemy within their reach. Moreover, the Qur'an itself (33:27) promised the faithful victory over the People of the Book (i.e., Jews and Christians) and "their lands, their habitations, and their possessions, and a land where you [Muslims] had never set foot before."[10] Furthermore, as we remember, Muhammad himself had sent at least two expeditions to the southern borders of Syria and Palestine, thereby setting a precedent to be followed by his successors.

On his deathbed, Abu Bakr appointed 'Umar, Muhammad's loyal follower and formidable warrior as his successor at the head of the Muslim state. 'Umar presided over the earliest and the most critical stages of the Muslim conquests of nearby territories (see Figure 3.1). His capacity as the commander-in-chief of the conquering Arab armies was reflected in his new title. While Abu Bakr had been styled simply as *khalífa* ("caliph"), 'Umar became both the *khalífa* and the *amír al-mu'minín*, namely, the "[military] commander of the faithful" (see Figure 3.2).

Figure 3.1 Illustration of the Entry of the Caliph 'Umar into Jerusalem

Getty Images/Bettmann. Drawn by O. Fikentsher

Figure 3.2 Muhammad (Veiled), Accompanied by Abu Bakr and 'Ali

Baldwin H. Ward & Kathryn C. Ward/CORBIS Rights Managed

Unlike the Prophet, 'Umar could not claim to be a recipient of revelations from God, since they ceased with the death of the founder of Islam. However, as an early convert and a right-hand man of the Prophet, 'Umar spent much time by his side and was intimately familiar with his habits, mentality, and decision making. 'Umar's familiarity with the Prophet's "ways" gave him the authority to speak on the Prophet's behalf and even to interpret God's will. This situation was accepted by the vast majority of Muslims—at least, during 'Umar's tenure his authority was never directly questioned or called into doubt. In addition to his close association with the Prophet, 'Umar's leadership rested on his formidable personal stature as a warrior and a staunch defender of Islam, especially at the time when it was still the religion of a persecuted minority in Mecca. However, 'Umar's personality and prestige alone were insufficient to deal with the numerous problems faced by the quickly expanding Islamic state and the growing number of Muslims. New administrative structures and system of taxation had to be established. The latter was introduced already at the earliest stages of the conquest, as we shall see in our discussion of the conquest of Syria. Administrative needs of the young Muslim polity led to the establishment of the *diwán*, the register of all Muslims, in which they were ranked according to their seniority in Islam and their proximity to the Prophet. The amount of their pensions was determined by their respective position in the *diwán* registry. The resources that were distributed through the *diwán* accrued through revenues generated by immovable property of the state, that is, arable lands, grain mills, irrigation works, and so on. In addition, all participants in military operations were entitled to a share of booty seized on the battlefield and the *jizya* poll tax imposed on the subjugated non-Muslim population, who came to be styled "protected people" (*ahl al-dhimma*).[11]

Outside Arabia, 'Umar ordered that Arab warriors and their families be settled in special garrison towns to prevent them from mixing with the local populations. This was done to maintain their combat readiness, which was absolutely essential for the success of the conquests. Initially, Arab warriors (*muqatila*) in such towns tended to settle in separate quarters according to their tribal affiliations. An overarching ideology was necessary to cement these disparate and occasionally mutually hostile tribal groupings. Islam became the unifying ideology of the Arab *muqatila*. Mosques, where communal worship and preaching took place on Fridays and where state edicts were announced, became the foci of social, political, and devotional life of the Arab garrison towns. Friday sermons contained extensive citations from Muhammad's revelations that now circulated in both oral and written form. These revelations, collectively known as the Qur'an (literally, "reading" or "recitation" [of the divine revelation]), and the Islamic ritual (five daily prayers, fasting, almsgiving, and the *hajj* pilgrimage) became the ideological and devotional glue that kept the assorted assemblage of Arab tribes together and infused them with the sense of a common identity and purpose. Each garrison town had a commander, who was charged with leading the Friday prayer service, mobilizing the fighters for military campaigns, settling disputes and administering justice (preferably in accordance with the spirit of the Qur'an and the prophetic precedent), and distributing the revenues. The majority of these commanders and high-level administrators were drawn from the ranks of the Quraysh, the native tribe of the Prophet, and to a lesser extent, the tribe al-Thaqif of the al-Ta'if oasis, as well as the *ansár* of Medina. On the whole, however, the Quraysh, or rather its more powerful clans, became the ruling elite of the fledgling Muslim empire (see Map 3.2).

The Conquest of Syria and Palestine

Already under Abu Bakr, the Muslim military commander Khálid b. al-Walíd launched a series of raids against the Byzantine and Sasanid Empires that had been exhausted by the decades of mutual hostilities and internal upheavals. These initial raids proved successful and yielded much booty. In 635, under the new caliph 'Umar, the Medinan leaders made the important decision to embark on

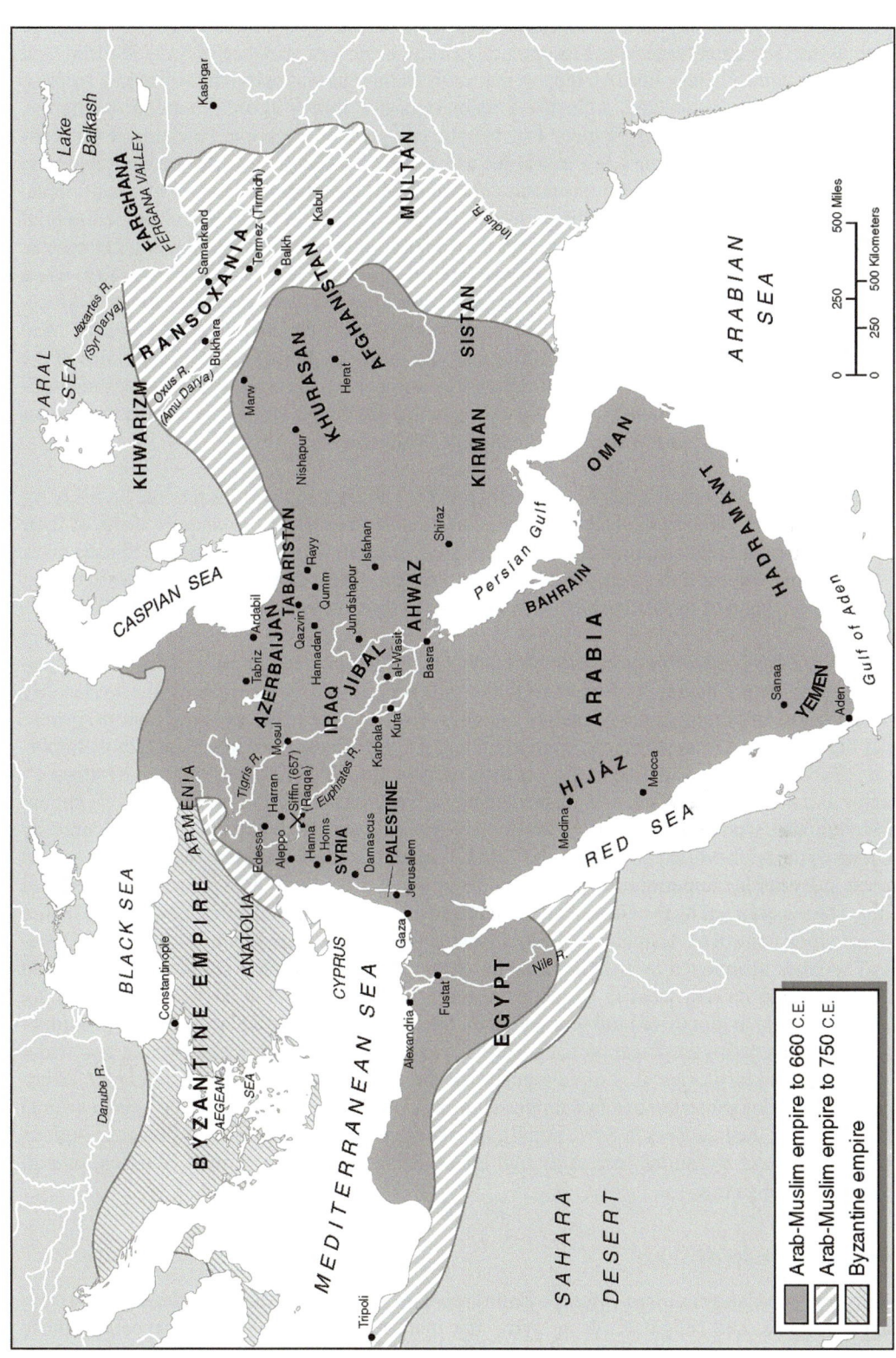

Map 3.2 The Expansion of the Caliphate

a systematic conquest of Syria and Palestine,[12] a province of the Byzantine Empire with the capital in Damascus. The other target was Mesopotamia (Iraq), a western province of Sasanian Iran, and the seat of its capital, Ctesiphon. Already in that year, Damascus was seized by Arabs in a surprise attack but was soon evacuated. After these reconnaissance forays into the imperial territories, 'Umar's generals set about carrying out a systematic conquest. In Syria and Palestine, it was conducted in several stages. After a few initial incursions, in 634–636 the Muslims fought and won several major battles against Byzantine armies dispatched by the emperor based in Constantinople. After the decisive defeat of a Byzantine army at the river Yarmuk in 636, the Byzantine imperial hold on Syria and Palestine was broken, and their major cities, including Jerusalem, Damascus, and Antioch, fell to the Arabs one after another with little struggle. Emperor Heraclius tried to wrest the Holy City from the "Ishmaelites" and landed some troops by sea near the city of Antioch. However, they were driven back by an Arab force led by Abu 'Ubayda. Syria and Palestine were now firmly under Arab-Muslim rule. In most cases, the lives and property of the inhabitants of the surrendered cities were protected by capitulation treaties between the city elders and the Arab military commander. The conditions of such treaties were usually rather lenient. Typical in this regard is Khálid b. al-Walíd's treaty with the population of Damascus:

> This is the treaty which Khalid b. al-Walid makes with the people of Damascus, on his entry into the town. He assures them their lives and goods, their churches and the walls of their town. No house will be pulled down or taken away from its owner. To guarantee this, he takes God as his witness and promises them the protection of the Prophet, of his successors [i.e., the caliphs] and of the faithful. He will do no ill to them as long as they pay the tribute.[13]

Thus, the Arab conquerors gave their new subjects full internal autonomy and military protection in return for the payment of a tribute and a poll tax (*jizya*). In many cases, the Syrian city dwellers (most of whom spoke Aramaic) found themselves in a better position than they were under the intrusive, Greek-speaking Byzantine bureaucracy. Taxes were lower, and, most importantly, the Syrians were now free to profess their own version of Christianity (Monophysitism),[14] which was considered heretical and persecuted by the religious authorities of the empire's capital Constantinople, who adhered to the so-called Dyophysitist or Chalcedonian creed.[15] Scared by the news of the Arab-Muslim invasion, the Greek-speaking landowning class, which had a vested interest in Byzantine imperial rule, had fled to Anatolia in the face of the Arab advance, never to return. The vacuum left by the Greek landowners and officials was filled by the new Arab-Muslim elite who took control of Aramaic-speaking Christian and Jewish populations of Syria and Palestine. The lands abandoned by the Greek landowners were treated as the domain of the Muslim state (*fay'*), and its rent went to the state treasury. In the countryside, a regular property tax (*kharáj*), payable in money or kind was levied on the owners of fields, according to their productivity. The same or similar fiscal policies were implemented across the entire breadth and width of the conquered territories. It is often argued that the Arab Muslims' religious tolerance, even-handedness, and noninterference in the internal affairs of the local communities played a critical role in securing their success in Syria and Egypt, whose Christians had suffered severe religious persecutions under Byzantine rule. Although the situation was no doubt more complex, overall this argument rings true.

The Conquest of Iraq

The diverse populations of Iraq (Mesopotamia) represented a wide variety of ethnic groups, languages, cultures, and religions. As in Syria, the majority of the population, especially those inhabiting the alluvial plains of Iraq, spoke a dialect of Aramaic. There were also Persian and

Arabic speakers. The linguistic diversity of Iraq was matched by its religious diversity. Zoroastrianism was the official religion of the Persian-speaking elite, whereas Nestorian Christianity represented the denomination of the largest single religious community in Iraq, followed by the Jews. There were other religious communities as well (e.g., Manichaeans and Mazdakites), but they were numerically insignificant.

Iraq was ruled by the Persian-speaking ruling class—military aristocracy and priests—that professed Zoroastrianism. In addition to the Zoroastrian Persian-speaking administrators and soldiers, there were numerous seminomadic Arab irregulars who were employed by the Sasanid rulers to guard the empire's western borders. By the time of the Arab conquest (633), the Sasanid Empire had been severely exhausted by years of war and the subsequent internecine struggle within the ruling house. Furthermore, the empire's most productive agricultural lands and irrigation systems were devastated by the invading Byzantine armies and the disastrous floods in the years directly preceding the Arab-Muslim conquest. Finally, its Arab retainers had been discontented by the decision of the Sasanid rulers to terminate their long-standing employment agreements, depriving them of a vital source of livelihood. Which of these factors proved decisive or, rather, all "conspired" to secure the success of the Arab-Muslim armies is hard to tell. What matters is that Iraq and, after a few decades, also the Iranian highlands became a Muslim domain, whereas the great and seemingly invincible Sasanid Empire ceased to exist.

As in Syria, the conquest of Iraq was spearheaded by the military detachments of the brilliant Muslim commander Khálid b. al-Walíd in 633–634 who had already distinguished himself under Abu Bakr. They subjugated the Arab nomadic groups and Arabized towns west of the river Euphrates. With Khálid's subsequent departure to Syria, the first stage of the conquest came to an end. It resumed under the caliph 'Umar, who, as mentioned, had made a decision to pursue a systematic conquest of the imperial lands lying northeast of Arabia with the goal of incorporating them permanently into the Muslim state. The initial push was unsuccessful. The Sasanid forces not only contained the Arab advance but also soundly defeated the invading Arab army during the so-called Battle of the Bridge. The next and final stage of the conquest was conducted by an able general Sa'd b. Abi Waqqas of the Quraysh tribe. In 637, he led the Muslims to victory in the famous Battle of al-Qadisiyya in central Iraq (near the town of al-Hira). This victory is even more remarkable as the Muslims were outnumbered and poorly equipped, whereas Persians had all they needed, including fighting elephants, to defeat their Arab-Muslim adversary. Yet the Persians failed to take advantage of their military superiority and were vanquished. Building upon their success at al-Qadisiyya, the Arab-Muslim troops subjugated the rest of Iraq. The remains of the Sasanid military force at first retreated to their capital at Ctesiphon (Arab., "al-Madá'in"), whereupon the Sasanid leadership decided to abandon the city and seek refuge in the Zagros Mountains of Iran in the hopes that they could regroup while the rugged terrain impeded the Muslims' victorious advance. At Ctesiphon, one of the richest cities of Asia, the Arab-Muslim warriors discovered treasures they had not even dreamed of. They could not even fathom the true wealth of the treasure, assembled for many centuries by one of the most powerful dynasties of the Near East and the chief rivals to the Roman emperors. The astonishment of the victors is described by a Western historian as follows:

> The untutored Bedouins reveled in a fairy-land of riches, gold, and silver, silks and jewels; in their ignorance they mistook sacks of camphor for salt and were astonished at its bitter taste, and the story goes that a tribesman who sold a jacinth [a type of sapphire] for a thousand *dirham*s, on being asked why he did not demand more for it, replied that he was unaware that there was a bigger number than a thousand.[16]

The riches of Ctesiphon did not divert Sa'd b. Abi Waqqas and his army from their main objective. They continued to pursue the retreating Sasanid force led by Emperor Yazdagird III. A reformed Persian force was again soundly routed by the Arabs at the Battle of Jalúla' at the foothills of the Zagros Mountains. With Iraq now firmly under his control, Sa'd b. Abi Waqqas was poised to follow the retreating Sasanian forces farther east beyond the confines of Iraq but was overruled by a prudent 'Umar, who was reluctant to send the Muslim force deep into a rugged terrain with a hostile Persian-speaking population. In the southern part of Iraq, where no major Persian force was deployed, the Arab-Muslim troops were confronted with a scattering of Persian garrisons that they quickly overran. After the remainder of the Persian army retreated to Iran, the lands of southern Iraq fell under Muslim rule.

When hostilities in Iraq finally came to an end, the caliph 'Umar ordered Muslim troops to settle in the newly founded garrison towns of Kufa (central Iraq) and Basra (lower Iraq). They were to become the seats of Arab power in Iraq and the bases of military operations against Sasanid Iran that resumed in 641, following the Arab occupation of Egypt.

The Conquest of Egypt

The situation in Egypt on the eve of the Arab-Muslim conquest was similar to that in Syria. The Egyptians were recovering from a devastating invasion by a Sasanid army that lasted from 617 to 627 and that was part of the long war between the Sasanids and the Byzantines. The majority of the country's population were Copts, who adhered to the Monophysitic version of Christianity and were therefore viewed by the imperial Byzantine church as heretics. The Byzantium viceroy of Egypt, patriarch Cyrus, was an ardent enforcer of the imperial orthodoxy who zealously persecuted the Copts. Floggings, tortures, and executions of "heretical" leaders of the Monophysite Coptic church were common across the land. The Egyptian peasants, heavily taxed by the Byzantium Greek-speaking landlords, had little reason to give their lives defending Constantinople's rule.

The conquest of Egypt was executed by an able Qurayshi military commander and statesman 'Amr b. al-'As (d. 663). He is said to have urged 'Umar to initiate the conquest of Egypt following the successful occupation of Syria in 639. Some sources say that he had started the invasion of Egypt on his own accord, then presented 'Umar with a fait accompli.[17] Be this as it may, after launching a reconnaissance raid in the Delta of the Nile in late 639, he received reinforcements from Syria[18] and in July 640 routed the main Byzantine force in Egypt at the Battle of Heliopolis. The death in 641 of the Byzantine emperor Heraclius and the weak and ineffective regency that followed hastened the loss of Egypt by the Byzantine Empire. In the same year, the Arab-Muslim armies completed the occupation of the country, and in 642 Alexandria, the main Byzantine stronghold in Egypt, was evacuated by its defenders. With the conquest successfully accomplished, 'Amr b. al-'As turned his attention to the business of governing the country, administering justice, and regulating taxation. He excelled in these tasks as he did in the conquest. As in Iraq, a permanent military settlement for the conquering army was established. Named Fustat, it served as the headquarters of Muslim governors of Egypt for several centuries and was eventually integrated into the neighboring city of Cairo that was founded in the tenth century.

The Conquests Continue: The Fall of the Sasanid Empire

After the conquest of Egypt had been successfully accomplished, 'Umar ordered the Muslim armies of Syria and Iraq to resume their advance into Cilicia (Greater Armenia), Anatolia, and Iran. In Anatolia, the Muslim force led by Mu'awiya b. Abi Sufyan, the son of Muhammad's archenemy and, later, the first caliph of the Umayyad dynasty, had only a limited success. The local Greek-speaking population was hostile to the invaders and, unlike the Aramaic-speaking Syrian Monophysites or the Egyptian Copts, had little reason to believe that they would be better off under the new rulers. The Byzantine capital in Constantinople was able to defend itself successfully from the Arab-Muslim invasion.

In Sasanid Persia—or what had remained of it after the loss of Iraq—the situation was both similar and different from that in Anatolia. The local population of the Iranian highlands was committed to the Persian ruling house, but the latter itself was greatly weakened by the loss of its capital and of the vital material resources of Iraq. Yazdagird III, the last Sasanid emperor, had retired to Rayy, a holy city of Zoroastrianism, and had tried to regroup his forces and to expel the advancing Arab-Muslim forces. The two armies met at Nihawánd, a town in the Zagros Mountains of western Persia, in 641 or 642. The Arab warriors led by the able military commander al-Nu'man, who died on the battlefield, demolished the Sasanid force.[19] The remains of the once proud and powerful Sasanid Empire now lay open to the Arab-Muslim conquest. One by one, the major Persian cities of the Iranian plateau fell to the conquerors, although it took the Arabs many years of intensive military operations to reach the eastern-most areas of the Sasanid empire at the river Oxus, in present-day Central Asia. By that time, Yazdagird III had been treacherously murdered by a miller while hiding near the city of Marw/Merv (651).[20] The spirit of Persian resistance was now totally broken.

The strategic importance of the subjugation of the Sasanid lands by the Arab-Muslim armies is difficult to overestimate. The Muslim state now acquired the enormous economic resources of Iraq and Iran, which enabled it to continue to expand in all directions. It used the rich Sasanian administrative experience to build a powerful and lasting government structure that, in its turn, became the foundation of what came to be known as the Arab-Islamic caliphate. It is no accident that the capital of this state at the peak of its power was located in Iraq.

The Death of 'Umar and the Succession of 'Uthman

One unexpected outcome of the conquest was the assassination of the caliph 'Umar by a Persian Zoroastrian, who had been taken prisoner after the battle of Nihawánd. Some modern historians have argued that the assassin was motivated "with the shame for his country and with hatred for her victorious conquerors."[21] Others insist that his attack was prompted by the man's personal grievance against his master, a companion of the Prophet named al-Mughira.[22] All we know for sure is that the assassin was a carpenter by profession. It is somewhat ironic that throughout his tenure 'Umar himself was strongly opposed to the presence of non-Arabs (al-'ulúj) and non-Muslims in Medina, the birthplace of the Muslim state. Yet some exceptions to this rule were occasionally made, and one of them was to cost the caliph his life. It should be noted that 'Umar's pro-Arab bias—he considered the Arabs to be the "[elect] people of God"—was always tempered by his even deeper commitment to the cause of Islam.[23] In any event, on his deathbed, 'Umar reportedly expressed satisfaction that at least he was not killed by an Arab.

Conclusions

Under 'Umar's able rule, the foundations of the caliphate, the state ruled by a deputy or successor to the Prophet, were firmly established. 'Umar achieved this goal by enforcing strict and occasionally brutal discipline in the garrison cities. In return for their obedience and military service, the Arab-Muslim warriors and their families were provided with generous stipends and a share in the war booty. Islam constituted the ideological glue that kept the motley arrangement of Arab tribes together and motivated them in their conquests. Western and Muslim scholars often stress the fact that in his statesmanship and decision making, 'Umar consistently applied the principle of consultation (*shúra*) that the Qur'an (3:153)[24] commanded the Prophet to implement in "matters of public concern." In this way, 'Umar "succeeded in imposing his will on the Muslim community and in directing the Arab armies in their extensive conquests without the means of coercion and repression available to later despotic rulers."[25] His impact on the fortunes of Islam was second only to that of the Prophet himself. However, in the final account, 'Umar's attempts to administer the caliphate according to the principles of consultation, seniority in Islam, and personal merit (this last principle was, of course, applied exclusively to the Arabs) proved ephemeral. Within less than two decades the principle of consultation was replaced with authoritarian dynastic rule and succession within the ruling family. In the meantime, the presence in the young Muslim state of a vast mass of ordinary Arabs and non-Arab converts to Islam subjugated to the Quraysh elite became a major destabilizing factor. The stage was set for the first conflict within the Muslim polity that erupted under 'Umar's successor, the caliph 'Uthman.

Question to Ponder

Some Western writers have compared the role of caliph 'Umar in promoting the cause of Islam and establishing its doctrinal and institutional foundations to that of St. Paul for Christianity. Discuss the appropriateness of this parallel.

Summary

- The death of the Prophet in 632 created a potential split between the emigrants (*muhájirún*) and the helpers (*ansár*).
- The first caliph ("successor"/"deputy" [of the Prophet]) Abu Bakr (632–634) is elected and rules during the so-called wars on apostasy (*ridda*). The *zakát* is reimposed on the recalcitrant tribes. The favorable outcome of the wars for the Muslims of Medina concludes the political consolidation of Arabia begun by Muhammad. The Muslim leadership establishes full control over the tribal population of the Arabian Peninsula.
- Under the rule of the caliph 'Umar (634–644), Arab-Islamic forces conquer the lands of the Sasanid and Byzantine Empires (Syria and Palestine, Iraq, Iran, Egypt, and North Africa). 'Umar's new title of *amír al-mu'minín* ("commander of the faithful") is a symbolic acknowledgment of his status as the commander in chief of the Muslim conquests. 'Umar's policies in the conquered territories include the establishment of garrison cities to keep the Arab warriors separate from the local population and the use of Islam to cement the often mutually hostile Arab tribal detachments.
- The status of the non-Muslim communities (primarily the Jews and Christians) under Muslim rule entail the payment of the poll tax (*jizya*) in return for protection and some degree of autonomy within their respective communities.
- Factors that contribute to the success of the Arab-Muslim arms in the Byzantine provinces are religious persecution of the local population by the imperial church of Constantinople and the relatively lenient policies of the Arab conquerors, as well as the tensions between the Greek-speaking elites and their Syriac- and Coptic-speaking

subjects. The Battle of Yarmuk in 636 becomes the turning point in the Arab-Muslim conquest of Syria.

- The reasons for Muslim military success in the war against the Sasanid Empire include its military and economic exhaustion after several decades of incessant warfare with the Byzantine Empire, the power struggle within the ruling dynasty, natural disasters, and the disloyalty of the Sasanids' Arab allies in Iraq. The Battle of al-Qadisiyya in 637 leads to the fall of the Sasanian capital Ctesiphon.
- Egypt is conquered by the army of 'Amr b. al-As in 642, and the Sasanid Empire finally falls around 650.
- 'Umar dies at the hands of a Persian slave in 644.

Notes

1 Marshall Hodgson, *The Venture of Islam*, Chicago University Press, Chicago, 1974, vol. 1, p. 197; for a Muslim version of this event, see Alfred Guillaume (trans.), *The Life of Muhammad*, Oxford University Press, Oxford, 1982, pp. 683–687.
2 Guillaume (trans.), *Life*, pp. 648–649.
3 Ibid., pp. 685–687.
4 Among other things, he prescribed his followers formal prayers three times a day, fasting, and abstinence from wine.
5 Montgomery Watt, "Musaylima," in *Encyclopedia of Islam*, 2nd ed.; online edition: http://referenceworks.brillonline.com.
6 Fred Donner, *The Early Islamic Conquests*, Princeton University Press, Princeton, NJ, 1981, p. 89.
7 Montgomery Watt and Richard Bell, *Introduction to the Qur'an*, Edinburgh University Press, Edinburgh, 1994, pp. 2–3.
8 See, e.g., "Nomadic Life and the Expansion of Islam," at http://people.opposingviews.com/nomadic-life-expansion-islam-9461.html.
9 See, e.g., Reuven Firestone, *Jihad: The Origin of Holy War in Islam*, Oxford University Press, Oxford, 1999, pp. 77–91 and 127–134.
10 Michael Bonner, *Jihad in Islamic History: Doctrines and Practice*, Princeton University Press, Princeton, NJ, 2006, pp. 60–61.
11 For details, see Yohanan Friedmann, "Dhimma," in *Encyclopedia of Islam*, 3rd ed.; online edition: http://referenceworks.brillonline.com.
12 In Muslim geography, "Syria" (Arab. "al-Sha'm") included the territories of present-day Syria, Palestine, Israel, Jordan, and South Turkey.
13 John Joseph Saunders, *A History of Medieval Islam*, Routledge, London and New York, reprint, 1990, p. 46.
14 The doctrine that teaches that in the incarnate Christ there was only one nature (divine), not two (namely, human and divine); in recent academic and Christian literature, this term is often replaced by "Miaphysitism," considered to be more neutral and less polemical but, in the end, also problematic; see, e.g., Greg Fisher (ed.), *Arabs and Empires Before Islam*, Oxford University Press, Oxford, 2015, pp. 279–283 and "General Index" under "Miaphysites."
15 Christ is conceived of having two natures in one person; ibid., p. 279.
16 Saunders, *A History of Medieval Islam*, p. 51.
17 Arent Wensinck, "'Amr b. al-'As," in *Encyclopedia of Islam*, 2nd ed.; online edition: http://reference works.brillonline.com.
18 Which may indicate that 'Umar was aware and fully supported his initiative; ibid.

19 For details, see Oleg Bolshakov, *Istoriia Khalifata. Tom II: Epokha velikikh zavoevanii 633–656*, Nauka, Moscow, 1993, pp. 98–100.

20 Ibid., pp. 185–186.

21 Saunders, *A History of Medieval Islam*, p. 57.

22 Bolshakov, *Istoriia. II*, p. 155.

23 Wilferd Madelung, *The Succession to Muhammad: A Study of the Early Caliphate*, Cambridge University Press, Cambridge, 1997, pp. 75–76.

24 According to Arberry's translation; in the majority of other translations of the Qur'an, this passage corresponds to Q 3:159.

25 Madelung, *The Succession*, p. 76.

Chapter 4

The Murder of 'Uthman, the *Fitna* Wars, and the Rise and Consolidation of the Umayyad Dynasty

Who's "Right" and Who's "Wrong"?

Before we discuss the tragic events of the first civil wars in Islam that were triggered by the assassination of the caliph 'Uthman, several remarks are in order. We should keep in mind that after the death of the Prophet, his followers found themselves at a loss as how to proceed and who should be their rightful leader in religious and sociopolitical actions. As we saw, 'Umar's decisions regarding civil, administrative, military, and religious matters rested on his personal prestige and his intimate knowledge of the Prophet's ways. However, the boundaries of what was religiously correct or incorrect, as well as the notions of Islamic legitimacy (for instance, of the Muslim ruler) at that time, were still in flux and shifted with the perspective of the individual viewer. The terms "heresy" and "orthodoxy" that are being frequently invoked in relation to early Christianity can be misleading when applied to the fledgling Muslim community in the postprophetic epoch. From the outset, in church councils, Christianity had a relatively efficient mechanism of separating those in the right from those in the wrong. No such structure existed in early Islam, which has no church in the first place. This is not to say that early Muslims did not denounce each other as "deviators" from what they considered to be the correct Islam of the Qur'an and the Prophet. In fact, their disagreements were almost always couched in religious terminology, since religion was the dominant, if not the only, expressive idiom of the age. What was different from Christianity was the absence of one uniformly acknowledged center of religious authority.

Seen from this perspective, those early Muslims who were dissatisfied with 'Uthman's rule, perceived it as his willful departure from the Qur'anic and prophetic statements emphasizing the equality of all Muslims regardless of their tribal or family ties.[1] This is not how 'Uthman's relatives, the Umayyads, saw the situation. Taking pride in their affiliation with the most powerful and noble clan of the Quraysh, they considered themselves to be the only legitimate heirs to the Prophet's state and religious teaching.[2] Furthermore, they also viewed themselves as indispensable guarantors of the unity of all Muslims in the face of external and internal challenges. The vilification of the Umayyads in later Islamic sources penned by their opponents should be treated with caution. It reflects the position of either the supporters of 'Ali b. Abi Talib's rights to the caliphate or the rulers of the 'Abbásid dynasty who had overthrown the Umayyads in 750. For both, Umayyad rule constituted a major deviation from the divinely foreordained course of events that, in their view, should have led to the rise of a just and legitimate Muslim state under the leadership of the members of the Prophet's clan, the Hashimites.

The Election of 'Uthman

On his deathbed, 'Umar appointed a consultative council (*al-shúra*) of six members whom he entrusted with the task of electing his successor. It consisted of the closest companions of the Prophet: 'Uthman, 'Ali, Sa'd b. Abi Waqqás, 'Abd al-Rahman b. 'Awf, al-Zubayr, and Talha.[3] In theory, all members of the council were eligible to be elected. In reality, however, this was the contest between 'Ali and 'Uthman. Despite 'Ali's credentials as the first (or second) male convert to Islam, the closest male relative of the Prophet, and his son-in-law, the major clans of the Quraysh had vigorously supported 'Uthman's candidature in the run-up to the election. 'Ali, on the other hand, had no partisans either on the electoral council or among the most influential members of the Qurayshi elite. He did enjoy a wide popular support, but this factor had little impact on the deliberations of the electoral council. Just the opposite, as potential candidates for the caliph's post, the members of the council were apprehensive of 'Ali's popularity with the masses. Some scholars even have argued that "jealous of each other . . . [they] chose the weakest among them."[4] This opinion is not quite accurate. 'Uthman, who was a wealthy merchant and a prominent member of the Qurayshi aristocracy, was highly regarded by the Prophet. The latter even had given him two of his daughters in marriage. This alone places 'Uthman above the two previous caliphs—although Abu Bakr's and 'Umar's daughters were married to Muhammad, the Prophet did not reciprocate by giving any of them his daughters in marriage.[5] An astute and well connected diplomat, 'Uthman was seen by the Qurayshi elite as the only serious alternative to the unpredictable and impetuous 'Ali, whom, they feared, it would be difficult if not impossible to control once elected.

Grievances Against 'Uthman

It seems likely that it was this important consideration rather than 'Uthman's personal deficiencies that determined the outcome of the election. This is not to say that 'Uthman had none. Unlike the other members of the council and his predecessor 'Umar, 'Uthman had never been entrusted with a position of authority in the administration of the Muslim state. For example, he had never led a raid or an army. His military and administrative inexperience may explain why from the outset he chose to rely almost exclusively on the men of his own clan, the Umayyads, who received positions of authority under 'Uthman's rule.[6] They replaced many prominent commanders and governors who had led the Muslim troops during the initial stages of Islamic conquests under 'Umar.[7] The third caliph consolidated the governorship of the important province of Syria/Palestine, which had initially been divided among three governors, by giving it over to his relative Mu'awiya of the Umayyad clan of Quraysh. Similar kinship-based appointments were made in Egypt and Iraq. No wonder that his "unabashed favoritism towards his close kin"[8] caused much resentment among Muslims outside the Umayyd clan. In particular, the malcontents resented 'Uthman's propensity to distribute the best agricultural lands captured during the conquests among his relatives or cronies, while prohibiting the rest of the Muslims from purchasing any such lands at all. As an example, one should mention the fact that 'Uthman assigned the most fertile and profitable lands of Iraq to his relatives and supporters—a practice that caused some to call this part of Iraq the "garden of Quraysh."[9] 'Uthman's actions stood in direct opposition to 'Umar's, who, on the contrary, refused to allocate the conquered lands to anyone including members of his own clan.[10] If anything, 'Umar seems to have discriminated against his own relatives in order to avoid accusations of nepotism.[11] Against this background, 'Uthman's lavish favors to his relatives in money and kind caused a great deal of uneasiness among many Muslims.[12]

While, on the face of it, the uneasiness was caused by 'Uthman's social and economic policies, his critics almost uniformly tended to express it in religious terms. 'Uthman may have been justified in trusting his own kin over outsiders, however, in the eyes of his detractors, his favoritism was a grave violation of the principle of equality of all Muslims, and as such, a transgression against the will of God as manifested in the Qur'an and the actions of the Prophet and his two successors, Abu Bakr and 'Umar. In addition to 'Uthman's predilection for his kin, perhaps exaggerated,[13] there were other reasons for widespread disaffection with his rule. Again, in contrast to 'Umar who was relentless in applying penalties to violators, as prescribed by the Qur'an and the Prophet, 'Uthman was reluctant to do so, especially in cases that involved his relatives or friends. For example, he reportedly had refused to punish the governor of Kufa, his uterine brother, who, in a drunken stupor, vomited on the pulpit while conducting the Friday prayer.[14] This was an egregious violation of the Qur'anic prohibition on the consumption of alcohol by a person who was supposed to uphold the standards of Islamic behavior. Despite the gravity of the offence, 'Uthman refused to punish his appointee, thereby alienating the people of Kufa, who would later become ardent supports of 'Ali. Even more controversial was 'Uthman's favorable treatment of the Prophet's former enemies among the Qurayshi elite, whom he had not only pardoned but also showered with expensive gifts and sinecures. Such actions could not but enrage the Muslim veterans, who still vividly remembered the relentless enmity that 'Uthman's favorites had shown toward the Prophet and his teaching at the dawn of Islam.[15]

To sum up, by treating the wealth and property of the Muslim state as his own possessions[16] and by setting the interests of his clan above the Islamic precept that all Muslims are equal before God, 'Uthman steered the caliphate, probably unwittingly, in the direction of an autocratic state.[17] Such states were quite normal around the Mediterranean basin at that age, but the Muslim state, founded on the principle of equality of the faithful before God, was supposed to be different. Naturally, many Muslims deeply resented the unwelcome changes under 'Uthman's rule. These and other grievances were cited by later Muslim historians, mostly hostile to the Umayyads, to explain why some members of the *umma* would go as far as to murder the legitimately chosen successor to the Prophet. Whether these grievances were real, exaggerated, or even unfounded is not that important. What matters is the outcome.

In the meantime, broad popular indignation with 'Uthman's rule had come to a head. It found a prominent spokesman in 'Amr b. al-'As, the conqueror and later governor of Egypt. Dismissed from his gubernatorial post under 'Uthman's nepotistic policies, 'Amr began to agitate against the caliph among the people of Medina. About the same time, in Egypt a riot broke out against the governor appointed by 'Uthman. A group of mutineers arrived in Medina to submit their grievances directly to the caliph. Assured of a quick redress, they embarked on a journey back to Egypt. En route, they intercepted 'Uthman's messenger with a letter instructing the governor of Egypt to punish the leaders of the delegation upon their return. It is not quite clear whether the letter was indeed 'Uthman's or it was dispatched by his first cousin and later caliph, Marwán, unbeknown to 'Uthman. Both 'Uthman and Marwán denied involvement in this matter.[18] We shall probably never know the truth. For the Egyptian mutineers, the provenance of the letter was of little import. All they knew was that they had been double-crossed by the caliph or his secretary. Enraged, they besieged the caliph's house that had no protection but a wall. At that point, 'Uthman seems to have lost any support he might have had among the *ansár* of Medina and even among those Qurayshi leaders who were not members of his clan. Both 'A'isha and 'Ali, despite their long-standing hostility to each other,[19] were critical of 'Uthman's conduct of state affairs. In short, the caliph's actions alienated him from practically all of the Prophet's companions in Medina, including some prominent members of the Quraysh tribe.[20] 'Ali's attempts at mediation between the embattled caliph and the rebels bore no fruit. He was subsequently accused of not trying hard enough or even of being in league with them, which was probably not true.[21] 'Ali did enjoy high prestige among the rebels, but his main power base was in Kufa, not in Egypt, and the Kufan detachment loyal to him that was in town during the siege of 'Uthman's headquarters did not take part in the rebellion. In any event, the Egyptian rebels, who now had nothing to lose but their heads, demanded that the caliph resign from his post and inform all his appointed governors in the provinces of his resignation. In the course of negotiations, various Qur'anic verses were invoked by both sides to justify their respective actions. Averse to the spilling of Muslim blood,

'Uthman procrastinated. More importantly, he refused to ask his loyal governors to dispatch their troops to Medina to suppress the rebellion. At the same time, he adamantly rejected the demand by the rebels to abdicate his office. As rumors of approaching rescue armies from the provinces started to circulate among the malcontents, they grew desperate and, on June 16, 656, the fighting began. Abandoned by his kin and allies,[22] 'Uthman was left face-to-face with his enemies, among whom was Muhammad, son of the first caliph Abu Bakr.[23] As his house was being stormed by the rebels, he hid in his wife's chamber. According to a standard account of this event, he was reading the Qur'an when the rebels entered the room and murdered him (see Figure 4.1). Some bloodied pages of 'Uthman's copy of the Qur'an have survived until today and are cherished by Muslims as a tragic symbol of the community's loss of innocence. The era of civil wars and conflict, later to be known as *fitna* ("trial" or "temptation"), was dawning.

Figure 4.1 The Caliph 'Uthman Murdered by a Group of Mutineers in 656 (Western drawing)

The Murder of Othman, the Third Successor of Mohammed (litho), Burton, H.M. (20th century) / Private Collection / The Stapleton Collection / Bridgeman Images

The Accession of 'Ali and the Battle of the Camel

The murder of 'Uthman in the summer of 656 precipitated a chain of events that are still being seen as pivotal for the fortunes of the young Muslim *umma*. Interest in these events among Muslims goes beyond a mere quest for historical truth. This seminal age was dominated by the strong personalities with which many of today's Muslims still identify themselves. Wittingly or not, they also embrace religious and political agendas of the Islamic factions that emerged in the course of these momentous upheavals. No wonder that the perception of this period and its actors by today's Muslims varies according to the ideals of the faction or personality they identify themselves with. This factor should be borne in mind by every scrupulous observer trying to make sense of these dramatic events, although, in the final account, their "real course is impossible to reconstruct."[24]

Although 'Ali was eventually acknowledged as caliph by the majority, his entire tenure was plagued by the accusations of illegitimacy leveled against him by several oppositional groups. Generally, 'Ali's opponents professed their continual loyalty to the murdered caliph, questioned the process of his accession to power, and demanded that either 'Ali himself or the relatives of 'Uthman should punish the killers.[25] Since for various reasons 'Ali was unwilling or unable to meet their demands, the opponents had a convenient pretext to regard his leadership of the *umma* as illegitimate and to demand his resignation. Furthermore, 'Ali's candidacy was not proposed or approved by an electoral council (*shúra*), which 'Umar, the founder of this institution, considered to be an essential precondition for legitimate succession.[26] Most importantly, 'Ali lacked the support of the majority of the Quraysh, who, under the first three caliphs, had become the ruling elite and power brokers of the Islamic state.[27] No wonder that his supporters came for the most part from the ranks of the *ansár*, many of whom were disgusted by the pro-Qurayshi policies of 'Uthman. So those who had pledged allegiance to 'Ali were either the *ansár* or his close relatives from the Háshim clan of Quraysh. The rebels who had killed 'Uthman and those who sympathized with their cause were also 'Ali's natural allies. For them, 'Ali was the only person capable of protecting them from the vengeance of the powerful Umayyad clan.

As opposition to 'Ali's rule began to take shape, many of the Quraysh who had made fealty to him earlier on disavowed him and joined ranks of his enemies.[28] In a way, 'Ali himself contributed to the formation of such oppositional factions. His idealism prompted him to make a clear break with the perceived or real injustices of 'Uthman's rule by confiscating the latter's property, distributing it among the people of Medina,[29] and removing from their posts all the powerful provincial governors appointed by his predecessor.[30] The disgruntled (dis)appointees and their retainers flocked to Mecca, which quickly became the major seat of the anti-'Ali opposition. In his noble-minded desire to redress the past wrongs committed by 'Uthman, 'Ali had given a number of important posts to the leaders of the Medinan *ansár*. This gesture confirmed many of the Quraysh in their fears that 'Ali's rule would usher in the domination of the state apparatus by the families of *ansár*, whom they rightly viewed as their rivals. In short, 'Ali's sincere and wholehearted pursuit of equity and justice made him many powerful enemies. With the benefit of hindsight and citing 'Umar's comment regarding 'Ali's "light-mindedness," some Western historians have construed his behavior following his accession to power and later during the civil war as evidence of his "political naiveté" and "lack of prudence and calculation."[31] This, certainly, is a matter of perspective.

The Meccan opposition to 'Ali's rule was led by 'A'isha, a widow of the Prophet, who had wielded a considerable influence among the Quraysh and their tribal allies.[32] Although critical of 'Uthman's administrative practices and decisions during his reign,[33] she had a much stronger and long-standing animosity toward 'Ali, whom she, in her own words, did not consider worth "a single finger of 'Uthman."[34] The reasons for this animosity are variously explained, the most frequently mentioned being 'Ali's publicly declared suspicions of her infidelity to her husband in the episode when she spent a night with a young man after having been left behind by her caravan.[35] Be this as it may, 'Ali's demands for allegiance were rejected by many Meccans; when his letter arrived in Mecca, it was contemptuously chewed up and spit out by a young Meccan aristocrat.[36]

The revolt against 'Ali was declared by the powerful Meccan clans in the name of revenge for 'Uthman's murder.[37] Significantly, as opposition to 'Ali's rule grew stronger, his foes accused him of not just harboring the perpetrators but also of actually engineering the murder of the third caliph.[38] The leaders of the opposition included, apart from 'A'isha, two early converts to Islam and companions of the Prophet, Talha and al-Zubayr, who, as we remember, were contenders for the caliphate as members of the electoral council (shúra) appointed by 'Umar on the eve of his death. The chief demand of the trio was the convocation of another shúra to nominate the new caliph. Naturally, both Talha and al-Zubayr entertained the hope of being the nominee. How these three principal opponents of 'Ali planned to share the leadership of the umma among themselves is not quite clear.

By the time of the first fitna, the caliphate's military power was centered on the provinces, where the war-hardened Arab tribal contingents were quartered at the time of the conquests. This fact explains why the major hostilities took place outside Arabia, first in Iraq and later in the territories between Iraq and Syria. 'Ali's base of support was in Kufa (Iraq), which was to become the seat of his caliphate (656–661). The strategic importance of the provinces was not lost on 'A'isha, al-Zubayr, and Talha. The rebellious trio and their followers left Mecca and marched across the Arabian deserts to Basra in the hopes of securing the support of the Arab tribal detachments stationed there. After several skirmishes, they managed to overcome the resistance of the local forces loyal to 'Ali and take full control of the city. In the meantime, 'Ali and his Meccan followers also marched out from Medina to Iraq. 'Ali's letter to the people of Kufa called upon them to join in his fight against the rebels based in Basra. When 'Ali's troops approached that city, some tribes that had originally sided with the rebellious triumvirate defected to him, giving him strategic advantage. The rest, however, stood by the rebels, inspired by the slogan of revenge for 'Uthman and defense of 'A'isha, whom they reverently styled as the "Mother of the Faithful."[39] The fact that she participated in the final battle between the two factions, while sitting on her camel, is eloquent evidence of her pivotal role in this momentous event in the history of the umma.[40] After three days of fruitless negotiations, the decisive battle was fought and won by 'Ali and his supporters. The rebel force was soundly defeated and dispersed.[41] Speaking about a religious dimension of the conflict, the Western scholar Wilferd Madelung (b. 1930) emphasizes the fact that 'Ali's followers kept invoking their allegiance to what they called the "religion of 'Ali" (din 'Ali). This may have meant their recognition of his legitimacy as the legatee (wasi) of the Prophet and, consequently, his exclusive right to lead the Muslim community to salvation. 'Ali, however, reportedly protested against the use of this term, stressing that his religion is nothing but the "religion of Muhammad."[42] Nevertheless, the seeds of a vision of Islam focused on the preeminence of 'Ali as champion of Islam after the death of the Prophet were already sown. They would grow into a full-fledged theology and ritual practice based on it, as will be shown later in this book.

Two of the three leaders of the rebellion lost their lives. Al-Zubayr seems to have deserted the battle shortly after it had started. Some sources say that he had lost heart, while others argue that he had lost confidence in the justice of his cause. Be this as it may, on his way back to the Hijáz, he was ambushed and killed by a few Bedouins, who, though neutral, were disgusted by his desertion because it egregiously violated the Arab code of honor. Talha was killed on the battlefield, although not by his foes but by an ally, the future caliph Marwán. The latter had long suspected Talha of secretly instigating the murder of 'Uthman[43] and took the opportunity to exact revenge on him by shooting the fatal arrow that caused Talha to bleed to death.

The fiercest fight occurred around 'A'isha's camel. She sat on top of it in an armored litter or howdah.[44] Dozens of pious Muslims, both Qurayshi aristocrats and ordinary tribesmen, were massacred by 'Ali's troops as they were trying to protect the "Mother of the Faithful" from being captured by the enemy. The camel was finally hamstrung and fell down. 'A'isha was captured,

Figure 4.2 'Ali's Victory over 'A'isha and Her Supporters at the Battle of the Camel in 656 ('Ali is depicted
           here as a flame)

akg-images/British Library

and the battle came to an end. It left at least three thousand Muslims dead: twenty-five hundred on the rebel side and between four hundred and five hundred on 'Ali's side.[45] 'A'isha was soon pardoned by 'Ali and sent back to Medina, where she spent the rest of her life. Her political career came to an end after she was taken prisoner by 'Ali's supporters. Some reports indicate that she might have been haunted by the memory of the horrible carnage around her camel in which so many men close to her lost their lives (see Figure 4.2). After all, as Mother of the Faithful, she must have felt responsible for "driving Muslims to kill Muslims."[46]

The Struggle Between 'Ali and Mu'awiya

After 'Ali's victory in the Battle of the Camel, many of his former opponents pledged allegiance to him but not for long. Some soon retracted their pledge and went over to Mu'awiya, 'Ali's most serious opponent based in Syria.[47] Mu'awiya, the governor of Syria under 'Uthman, had rather little to show in the way of Islamic credentials. He was a son—one of two—of Abu Sufyán of the Umayyad clan of Quraysh, who had accepted Islam only on the eve of Muhammad's conquest of Mecca, when all other options were closed for him and his family. Moreover, it was his mother who ate the liver of the Prophet's uncle Hamza raw after the Battle of Úhud in retaliation for his killing of her father. Hence, Mu'awiya's derogatory nickname, "Son of the Liver Eater." Nevertheless, after the triumph of Islam and surrender of Mecca to Muhammad, Abu Sufyán and his two sons partici- pated in the conquest of Syria and reaped from it rich material benefits.[48] At the time, Mu'awiya distinguished himself as an astute diplomat and administrator, who managed to unite under his leadership the diverse and often mutually hostile tribal factions stationed in Syria.[49] By the time of his conflict with 'Ali, he had secured the unquestioning loyalty of his Syrian troops—the most disciplined and effective fighting force in the entire Muslim realm. After 'Ali's triumph in Iraq, Mu'awiya was prepared to hold on to his governorship at all costs.[50] Although he had failed to come to 'Uthman's rescue at the time of the trouble in Medina, he now declared himself the principal avenger of his murder. Since he indeed came from the same clan as 'Uthman, the Umayyads, his claim was taken seriously by many. To infuse his followers with avenging zeal, the bloodstained shirt worn by 'Uthman at the time of his death was displayed on the pulpit of the main mosque of Damascus, together with several fingers of his wife, Na'ila, which had been cut off by the rebels as she was trying to protect his fallen body from desecration. According to a Muslim chronicle:

> The people kept on coming and crying over it [the shirt] as it hung on the *minbar*[51] with the fingers attached to it, for a whole year. The Syrian soldiers swore an oath that they would not make love to women . . . or sleep on beds until they had killed the killers of 'Uthman and anyone who might prevent them in any way . . . They remained around the shirt for a year.[52]

In his opposition to 'Ali, Mu'awiya decided to form a league—albeit after some hesitation— with an unlikely ally, 'Amr b. al-'As. The latter, as we might remember, vigorously agitated against 'Uthman after the caliph had dismissed him from his office of the governor of Egypt. Some sources even allege that 'Amr's anti-'Uthman propaganda was largely responsible for the arrival of the Egyptian mutineers in Medina with the demand to redress their grievances against 'Amr's successor, an 'Uthman appointee.[53] Nevertheless, Mu'awiya and 'Amr managed to put aside whatever grievances they had against each other and made a deal: 'Amr would support Mu'awiya's bid for power against 'Ali. In return, Mu'awiya would help him regain Egypt, which was then ruled by a governor appointed by 'Ali. For Mu'awiya, 'Amr, who had retained the loy- alty of his former troops in Egypt, was a valuable, even indispensable, ally. In addition, he was a better military strategist than Mu'awiya; after all, it was owing in large part to 'Amr's military genius that the Muslims were able to conquer Egypt, the "granary of the Middle East." After the two men had become allies, 'Amr advised his partner to rally the military commanders of Syria to his cause by deliberately dramatizing for them the dreadfulness of 'Ali's alleged role in the assassination of the caliph 'Uthman. Simultaneously, Mu'awiya called upon the commanders to fight for justice. The goal of this fight was, apart from punishing 'Uthman's killers, to establish a new electoral council (*shúra*), which, in accordance with the precedent set by 'Umar, should decide who the legitimate caliph should be.

Initially, Mu'awiya was proclaimed the military commander (*amír*) of the newly created coalition of his and 'Amr's supporters. However, before long, his aspirations to become caliph became evident, among other things through his correspondence with 'Ali, whom he effectively treated as an usurper of the caliphate. Furthermore, he kept hinting at 'Ali's alleged role in the murder of 'Uthman[54] and quoted the Qur'anic verse 17:33[55] to claim the role of the rightful avenger for the third caliph's blood.[56] Provoked by Mu'awiya's words and actions, 'Ali had no choice but launch an attack on the challenger. Convincing the Iraqis, primarily those of Kufa, to once again go to war against those who had refused to offer him allegiance was not an easy task. Like rank-and-file soldiers in any society, supporters of 'Ali (now referred to as his "party"—al-shi'a, or shi'at 'Ali, a term that has later come to denote all supporters of the rights of 'Ali and his progeny, the 'Alids) were aware that they were fighting the battles of their leaders, in which they had no personal stake. Conceivably, Mu'awiya's confederates among the Arab tribal levies stationed in Syria felt the same way. Not surprisingly, therefore, many men in Syria and Iraq refused to take sides and remained neutral throughout the conflict between the two contenders.

The Battle of Siffin

After 'Ali's force was assembled in Iraq, he led it to Syria. In June 657, he met Mu'awiya's army at Siffin on the Upper Euphrates river, near the present-day city of Raqqa. After his repeated demands that Mu'awiya recognize his caliphal authority had been rejected, a battle between the two Arab-Muslim armies became inevitable. It was preceded by several weeks of skirmishes interspersed with fruitless negotiations, during which both sides appealed to the Book of God, the Qur'an. Finally, on June 18, 657, 'Ali sent the Syrians a final ultimatum demanding that they recognize his authority, which, in his words, was confirmed by the Qur'an, or face extermination. An entire week was spent in what can be described as dueling: Each army dispatched a small detachment to the battlefield, which would engage the enemy, then return to its respective camp after several hours of fighting. The final battle began on July 26, after more than a month of desultory hostilities and continued for three days. Both sides sustained heavy casualties and had to seek strength in the Qur'an, as is evident from the following prefight exhortation by a Kufan Qur'an-reciter, a follower of 'Ali:

> Unite together, and let us march against our enemy with deliberation and purpose. Then stand firm, help one another, remember God, let no man ask his brother for anything, do not keep turning around, be valiant in the face of their [the Syrians'] courage, and make *jihad* against them in expectation of your divine reward "until God decides between us and them, for He is the best of judges."[57]

Exasperated by the stalemate, 'Ali proposed to Mu'awiya that they fight a duel in order to prevent further bloodshed. Mu'awiya, who, according to Muslim sources was an astute diplomat, not a fighter, flatly rejected the proposal. So the fighting continued unabated day and night with the tide slowly turning in 'Ali's favor (see Figure 4.3). It was then that 'Amr b. al-'As, with his usual shrewdness, advised Mu'awiya to attach scrolls of the Qur'an to the lances of his warriors and raise them high. According to 'Amr b. al-'As, this gesture was deemed to encourage the two sides to submit themselves to arbitration based on the Book of God. A chronicle describes this fateful event as follows:

> So they [the supporters of Mu'awiya] raised the *masáhif*[58] on lances and said: "This is the Book of God between us and you. Who will protect the frontier districts of the Syrians [from the Byzantine Christians], if they all perish, and who those of the Iraqis if they all perish?" When the men [of 'Ali] saw that the *masáhif* had been raised, they said: "We respond to the Book of God, and we turn in repentance to it."[59]

Figure 4.3 'Ali and His Supporters Fight Against the Army of the Syrian Governor Mu'awiya in 657
akg-images/British Library

'Ali's attempts to dissuade his followers from abandoning fighting proved futile. His arguments that the leaders of the opposing side were cunning and that the copies of the Qur'an on their lances were but a ruse on their part fell on deaf ears.[60] The fighters were exhausted by several weeks of hostilities and longing for respite. Besides, many of 'Ali's most loyal supporters were extremely pious; some, as the one whose speech was previously cited, belonged to the category of the so-called Qur'an-reciters (*qurrá'*), who held its words to be sacred and final. They petitioned 'Ali:

> 'Ali, respond to the Book of God when you are called to it. Otherwise we shall deliver you up entirely to the enemy or do what we did to ['Uthman] Ibn 'Affan. It is our duty to act in accordance with what is in The Book of God.[61]

Faced with widespread discontent and insubordination, 'Ali recalled the troops from the battle-field and sent a messenger to Mu'awiya, asking for his conditions. The conditions, Mu'awiya replied, were as follows: Each side was to send a representative to resolve the issue according to the Qur'an. Once the arbiters had made their decision, each side was to abide by the verdict. While the majority of 'Ali's men accepted this arrangement, a group of about four thousand men, prob-ably the most pious and uncompromising, rejected it and demanded the resumption of hostilities in order to find out whose side God was on. 'Ali ignored their plea. In seeking to prevent further bloodshed, he chose to follow the opinion of the majority, thereby irrevocably alienating the bel-ligerents.[62] Disgusted, they hastily left his camp and headed to Kufa. This disgruntled group became 'Ali's enemies and fought against him and his followers upon their return to Iraq. Many historians, today as before, view 'Ali's deference to the majority at Siffin as his grave mistake and the principal cause of his undoing.[63]

The Syrians appointed 'Amr b. al-'As as their representative, while the Iraqis, after much bickering and against 'Ali's best judgment, opted for the former governor of Kufa, Abu Musa al-Ash'ari, who was not a friend of 'Ali and who had warned him against spilling Muslim blood on the eve of departure for Syria. The arbitrators were given seven months to arrive at a decision and to deliver it to the warring parties.

The Kharijites

By even the basic standards of political pragmatism, 'Ali's acceptance of arbitration on Mu'awiya's terms was a grave mistake. He paid dearly for it. Many of 'Ali's former followers both inside and outside his camp were infuriated by his vacillation and the resultant inconclusive outcome of the Battle of Siffin. As 'Ali's army was marching back to Kufa, there developed a deep rift in the ranks of his followers between the supporters and the opponents of the arbitration. The opponents adopted the phrase "No judgment but God's" as their slogan. Their leaders argued that resorting to human arbitrators instead of allowing God's will to manifest itself in the outcome of the battle was a grave sin or even infidelity on the part of 'Ali.[64] After 'Ali had reached Kufa, around twelve thousand of his critics withdrew to a place outside the city. They announced that they no longer recognized 'Ali as their leader (imam). Their withdrawal or secession (khuruj) gave the name to their movement, that of the khawarij, or, in an Anglicized form, "Kharijites."[65] 'Ali managed to placate some of them, but the radicals, who had joined forces with the belligerents who had left 'Ali's camp at Siffin, remained adamant that the war should be resumed before the end of the term set for the arbitration. For the irredentist Kharijites, allegiance was not owed to a person, be it 'Ali or Mu'awiya, but to the Qur'an and the exemplary custom of the righteous, that is, the Prophet, Abu Bakr, and 'Umar.[66] They chose a leader among themselves, arguing that 'Ali's credentials as the commander of the faithful were annulled by his acceptance of the "sinful" human arbitration proposed by Mu'awiya. The lead-ers of the most irreconcilable Kharijites insisted that loyalty is due only to the leader (imam) as long as he remains faithful to the Book of God and the custom of the pious members of the first Muslim community in Medina. In accordance with this doctrinal position, by committing a grievous sin (i.e., agreeing to the arbitration), 'Ali had forfeited his status as the successor to the Prophet and the commander of the faithful. So true Muslims owed him no loyalty.[67]

In the meantime, the arbitrators could agree on one thing only: 'Uthman's murder was wrongful and unjust, which, of course, was what Mu'awiya had claimed all along. Thus, although not explic-itly stated, their decision undermined 'Ali's position as the head of the Muslim state. The arbitrators had failed to agree on anything else. They refused to confirm 'Ali's position as the rightful caliph or to decide whether it was necessary to convene a new shura in order to elect the new one. In the end, their verdict was rejected by the majority of 'Ali's supporters in Kufa. In the meantime, Mu'awiya was proclaimed caliph by his followers, which made another war between the Muslims of Syria and Iraq inevitable because there could not be two caliphs at the head of the umma. How-ever, before setting out on another military expedition, 'Ali had to deal with his former allies-turned-enemies, the Kharijites. Not only had they agitated against him, but they also started to kill those of his supporters who refused to join their rebel force because they viewed those Muslims who had not accepted their creed as apostates or infidels.[68] In May 658, 'Ali's army met the main Kharijite force at the Nahrawán Canal in Iraq and massacred as many as six hundred Kharijite warriors, losing just a few of its own.[69] The massacre of his former supporters consolidated the divide between the Muslims of Iraq loyal to 'Ali (the Shi'ites) and his new enemies who had emerged from his own ranks (the Kharijites). It also severely undermined 'Ali's ability to recruit troops for his impending campaign against Mu'awiya's supporters in Syria.[70]

The Last Years of 'Ali's Caliphate

After the debacle at Siffín, Mu'awiya's forces took to raiding 'Ali's partisans in Iraq and intercepting pilgrimage caravans.[71] Simultaneously, Mu'awiya dispatched 'Amr b. al-'As to wrest Egypt from the governor appointed by 'Ali, which 'Amr successfully accomplished in July–August 658. Heartened by this success, Mu'awiya continued to send raiding parties to Arabia and western Iraq in an effort to further undermine 'Ali's authority by showing his subjects that their leader was no longer capable of protecting them. In his own domain in Iraq, 'Ali also had to deal with Kharijite bands operating in various parts of the country. Highly motivated, the Kharijites were a dangerous enemy: many of them were prepared to meet martyrdom in defending their cause and punishing 'Ali for the death of their comrades at Nahrawán.

In 660, Mu'awiya dispatched a major military force to Arabia. Its depredations there helped to invigorate 'Ali's efforts to recruit fighters for another campaign against his Syrian rival. He planned to launch it in the winter of 661, but his plans soon unraveled. As 'Ali was entering the congregational mosque of Kufa on January 26, 661, he was attacked by a Kharijite named Ibn Múljam, who struck him with a poisoned sword on the crown of the head. As he rushed toward 'Ali, Ibn Múljam shouted the Kharijite slogan: "The judgment is God's, not yours, 'Ali, nor your men with swords!"[72] Mortally wounded, 'Ali died two days later. According to Muslim historians, the Kharijites intended to simultaneously assassinate all three men whom they had held responsible for deviating from the Book of God: 'Ali in Kufa, Mu'awiya in Damascus, and 'Amr b. al-'As in Fustat. 'Ali was killed, Mu'awiya was wounded on his buttocks but survived, and a wrong person was assassinated instead of 'Amr in Egypt.[73] The troubled caliphate of 'Ali b. Abi Talib, the first male convert to Islam as well as the Prophet's cousin and son-in-law, came to an end, leaving the door open for the accession of the Umayyad family led by Mu'awiya. Summarizing these events, a Western scholar sympathetic to 'Ali has argued that:

> Umayyad highhandedness, misrule and repression were gradually to turn the minority of 'Ali's admirers into a majority. In the memory of later generations 'Ali became the ideal Commander of the Faithful.[74]

This, of course, was the view of 'Ali's supporters. Mu'awiya's family and followers had a totally different view of his personality and legacy.

Mu'awiya Becomes Caliph

Upon the death of 'Ali, his elder son, al-Hásan, was declared caliph by his father's supporters. A pious pacifist with little political acumen who had opposed his father's militant policy,[75] he was no match for the cunning Mu'awiya steeped in political maneuvering.[76] Pressed by a militant faction of 'Ali's supporters, al-Hásan attempted to organize a military campaign against the Umayyad caliph. However, he soon succumbed to Mu'awiya's cajoling and pleaded with his followers to stop hostilities. In return for Mu'awiya's promise to nominate him as his successor, al-Hásan abdicated in favor of his Umayyad rival. It is clear that Mu'awiya shrewdly played on al-Hásan's desire to preserve the unity of the Muslim *umma* and his reluctance to spill Muslim blood.[77] Be this as it may, al-Hásan then retired with a great fortune to Medina, where he lived a quiet family life surrounded by wives,[78] children, and concubines. He died in 670, either of a prolonged illness or, possibly, of a poison administered by one of his wives on the orders of Mu'awiya.[79]

By that time, Mu'awiya's caliphal authority was fully established. With his Syrian troops and governors in the provinces loyal to him, there simply was no viable rival to challenge his authority. Besides, the majority of Muslims were apparently exhausted by six years of the fratricidal violence and thus prepared to accept any powerful ruler capable of preventing another civil war. Since the Umayyad rulers' Islamic legitimacy and primacy in Islam were questionable in the eyes of many Muslims,[80] Mu'awiya and his successors spared no effort in asserting their role as avengers of the blood of the murdered caliph 'Uthman. 'Ali and his followers were reviled as dissenters and occasionally cursed from the pulpits of the mosques.[81] When implemented in Kufa,[82] this practice may have been a deliberate strategy to provoke 'Ali's partisans and then have them punished for their disloyalty. Similar anti-'Alid statements were made in the public speeches of the Umayyad caliphs during their annual pilgrimages to Mecca. However, on the whole, massive persecutions of 'Ali followers were discontinued, stability was restored, and popular discontent subsided. This is not to say that there was no opposition to Mu'awiya's rule. The old grievances and slights still rankled, and the imposition of strict centralized rule and discipline on the freedom-loving and independent Bedouins fed resentment among the rank-and-file members of the Muslim military units. The Kharijites remained active in Iraq, Iran, and parts of Arabia. Many Quraysh families in Medina and Mecca were also disturbed by what they perceived as Mu'awiya's high-handedness in treating the Quraysh nobility and his favoritism toward certain families to the exclusion of others. The caliph also had a formidable rival in the person of Marwán, the former advisor to the caliph 'Uthman and an erstwhile ally of Mu'awiya's against 'Ali, who now served as governor of Medina. Marwán, who belonged to a different branch of the Umayyad clan, considered himself and his descendants to be more worthy of the caliphate than the descendants of Abu Sufyán headed by Mu'awiya. Finally, in the Hijáz, there emerged several claimants to the caliphate. One of them was al-Husayn, the younger son of 'Ali, the other 'Abdallah b. al-Zubayr, a son of the Prophet's companion al-Zubayr, who, as we remember, had participated in the rebellion against 'Ali's rule and was murdered after the Battle of the Camel in 656. 'Abdallah b. al-Zubayr's bid for the caliphate would prove a serious challenge to Umayyad authority, as we shall soon see. As it became clear that Mu'awiya was grooming his only son Yazíd as his successor,[83] the anti-Umayyad opposition grew stronger and more vocal. Seeing that so far no caliph had been succeeded by his son, Mu'awiya's intention was interpreted by many as a gross violation of the principles of succession established by the first two caliphs. The critics justly considered Mu'awiya's designs to enthrone his son without election by the *shúra* council to be an attempt on his part to institute a hereditary monarchy.

The Death of Mu'awiya, the Accession of Yazíd, and the Tragedy at Karbala'

For as long as Mu'awiya was still alive, he was able to keep all his potential opponents in check by a combination of raw force, bribery, tireless cunning, and fulsome flattery, for which he was famous.[84] However, in spite of his efforts, upon his death many Muslim leaders refused to recognize his son Yazíd as caliph, citing his unsuitability for the office; in addition to his lack of religious knowledge, he was fond of hunting and drinking wine with his boon companions.[85] To anticipate our discussion of the events that followed, we should say that the second round of civil wars, or the so-called second *fitna*, was precipitated initially by the refusal of the leading Muslim families of the Hijáz to accept Yazíd's candidacy and, following the latter's death in 683, the inability of the Sufyanid branch of the Umayyad family to furnish suitable candidates for the caliphate.[86]

The first challenge to Yazíd's caliphate came from al-Husayn, the younger son of 'Ali and Fátima—a daughter of the Prophet by his first wife Khadíja. The only living grandson of the Prophet, al-Husayn was seen by many as the natural candidate for the leadership of the *umma*. Yazíd was desperate to have him pledge allegiance; however, al-Husayn and the other claimant to the caliphate, 'Abdallah b. al-Zubayr, refused to acknowledge his authority and escaped from Medina to Mecca, where they took refuge in the Meccan sanctuary.[87] The leading families of Medina persuaded al-Husayn, now in his mid-fifties, to make a bid for power. Messengers arrived from Kufa, promising al-Husayn massive support in that city, which, as we remember, was the main power base of his late father.[88] Al-Husayn sent his own messenger, a son of 'Ali's brother named Muslim, to Kufa to rally support for his bid for the caliphate. The messenger was apprehended by the troops loyal to the ruthlessly efficient Umayyad governor of Iraq, 'Ubaydallah b. Ziyád, who had him and a few of his companions decapitated.[89] 'Ubaydallah's cruel suppression of the budding rebellion cowed the majority of Kufa's population into submission. In the meantime, al-Husayn was marching across the desert with a small band of relatives and followers, some fifty fighters and twenty or so women and children. The promises of an all-out insurrection given to him by the Kufans did not materialize. Al-Husayn and his companions never reached Kufa. They were intercepted by an Umayyad detachment at a place known as Karbalá/Kerbelá (some 60 miles southwest of Baghdad), surrounded, and exterminated. 'Ali, later to be known as 'Ali Zayn al-'Abidín (i.e., "'Ali, the Ornament of the Worshippers"), who would become the fourth *imam* of the Shi'ites (after 'Ali, al-Hasan, and al-Husayn), was the only son of al-Husayn to survive the ordeal. In all, twenty-six of his relatives were killed, including three sons and seven brothers. Two or three sons of his late elder brother al-Hasan also perished during the massacre.[90] Al-Husayn's head was cut off and sent first to Iraq's governor 'Ubaydallah, who reportedly spat on and kicked it, then had it sent to the caliph Yazíd in Damascus.[91] The day of al-Husayn's cruel death, the 10th of the month Muhárram/October 10, 680, became a major Shi'ite holiday. For the Shi'ites, the murder of the Prophet's younger grandson has come to symbolize the injustices inflicted upon the Prophet's family by the illegitimate caliphs of first the Umayyad and later also of the 'Abbásid dynasty. In al-Husayn, Shi'ism, the movement of the partisans of 'Ali and his descendants, acquired its greatest martyr. The accounts of his and his family's sufferings at the hands of Umayyad soldiers have been dramatized ever since to discredit Umayyad rule. Al-Husayn's rebellion was not, however, the only challenge faced by the Umayyads.

The Caliphate of 'Abdallah b. al-Zubayr

Shortly after the death of al-Husayn, Yazíd found himself confronted with another opponent, the Qurayshi nobleman 'Abdallah b. al-Zubayr. 'Abdallah's Islamic credentials were solid compared to those of Yazíd's. His father, al-Zubayr, was a brother of the Prophet's first wife Khadíja on his father's side and a cousin of the Prophet on his mother's side. He himself was the first child born to the Muslim community in Medina two years after the emigration (*híjra*).[92] The grandson of Abu Bakr but also the nephew of 'A'isha, who treated him almost as her son,[93] he was seen by many as a perfect candidate for the caliphate, especially after the tragic death of al-Husayn.[94] When he and al-Husayn were invited to acknowledge the caliphal authority of Yazíd, they refused and took refuge in the Meccan sanctuary. As al-Husayn was marching toward Kufa at the head of a small band of his supporters, 'Abdallah had secretly begun to recruit supporters among the Meccan and Medinan families and their tribal allies. Yazíd responded by sending 'Abdallah's own brother to Mecca to arrest him on charges of sedition. The brother's force was defeated by

'Abdallah's followers, and he himself was captured and executed.[95] The triumphant 'Abdallah declared Yazíd deposed and called for the election of a new caliph by the *shúra* council. His call was supported by the *ansár* of Medina, who seized this opportunity to throw off their allegiance to Yazíd. The Umayyads dispatched a large Syrian army to deal with the rebels in Arabia. After defeating the opponents of Yazíd at Medina, the Syrians laid siege to Mecca. The Syrian commander al-Husayn b. Numayr ordered the bombardment of the holy city with catapults from the top of the nearby mountain Abu Qubays.[96] Projectiles hurled at the city from several catapults badly damaged and set on fire the Meccan sanctuary and the Ka'ba itself. However, in 683, when news came about the untimely death of Yazíd,[97] the army lifted the siege and headed back for Syria. After he had been declared caliph, Ibn al-Zubayr took it upon himself to rebuild, expand, and embellish the Ka'ba, an action for which he is remembered to this day.[98]

The succession crisis in Syria—the new Umayyad caliph Mu'awiya II was sickly and died several weeks after his inauguration—encouraged 'Abdallah b. al-Zubayr to declare himself commander of the faithful and to lay claim to the caliphate publically and unequivocally. Initially he was very successful: Due to the chaos in the Umayyad house, many Muslims saw him as the most deserving caliph available.[99] 'Abdallah b. al-Zubayr and his relatives and supporters secured the allegiance of the key provinces of the Muslim Empire—Egypt, Iraq, Iran, and Arabia—whose governors recognized his authority, albeit only nominally. He had supporters even in Syria/Palestine, but the loyalties of the Arab tribes stationed there were divided between him and Marwán, 'Uthman's former secretary and a major political and military player under Mu'awiya and Yazíd.

An Umayyad who belonged to a different branch of the family than Mu'awiya, Marwán harbored his own caliphal ambitions, which he made public after the death of Mu'awiya II. The Syrian troops loyal to him recognized him as caliph on the condition that he should be succeeded by Yazíd's son Khálid, then thirteen, when the latter would come of age. Marwán later reneged on this agreement and appointed his own son as his successor.[100] Marwán's decisive achievement was his defeat of the Syrian tribal supporters of 'Abdallah in a pitched and bloody battle near Damascus in 684.[101] Thanks to this victory, Marwán was able to consolidate his grip on Syria/Palestine and proceeded to dislodge 'Abdallah's supporters from Egypt. Upon his death in 685, Marwán's son 'Abd al-Malik, not Khálid b. Yazíd, took over as his successor. He had to fight hard for almost a decade to secure the ascendancy of the new branch of the Umayyad dynasty, the Marwánids.[102]

The Rebellion of Mukhtár

In Iraq, 'Abdallah b. al-Zubayr's authority was challenged by a rebellion in the name of 'Ali's son by a woman of the Hanifa tribe, Muhammad b. al-Hanafiyya (d. 700).[103] The driving force behind this rebellion, which lasted from 685 through 687, was a profound remorse felt by many inhabitants in Kufa over their failure to come to the rescue of al-Husayn during his uneven battle with the Umayyads at Karbalá. Overcome by this remorse, some of these "penitents" (*tawwábún*), as they are called in Muslim sources, launched a suicidal attack against the vastly superior Umayyad army and were massacred to the last man, thereby expiating their sin. Others turned their attention to Muhammad b. al-Hanafiyya, who, though not a descendant of 'Ali and Fátima, was seen by many as 'Ali's legitimate heir. This movement was spearheaded by one Mukhtár al-Tháqafi, who had suffered at the hands of the Umayyad governor of Iraq, 'Ubaydallah, during al-Husayn's rebellion and who was full of hatred for those who had deprived the 'Alids of their rights. Mukhtar's enemies were not only the Umayyad "usurpers" but also those Muslims in Iraq who had pledged allegiance to the newly declared Meccan caliph 'Abdallah b. al-Zubayr, thereby, once again, ignoring the rights of the descendants of 'Ali. Therefore, his first adversary was not an Umayyad ruler, as one might have expected, but the governor of Iraq appointed by 'Abdallah

b. al-Zubayr. Mukhtár's main slogans were revenge for the death of al-Husayn and his relatives at Karbalá and a pledge of allegiance to Muhammad b. al-Hanafiyya as the only legitimate leader (*imam*) of the Muslims. This was Mukhtár's personal understanding of justice, as annunciated in the Qur'an. Mukhtár presented himself to his audience as an agent acting on behalf of the would-be *imam*. Whether such claims were supported by Muhammad b. al-Hanafiyya himself, who at that time resided in the Hijáz, is not quite clear. At least, Muhammad did not explicitly disavow him. In his absence and with his tacit approval, Mukhtár could present his "master" not only as the next caliph but also as a messianic divinely guided redeemer (*máhdi*), whom God had entrusted with the mission of setting right the wrongs of this world and of restoring justice, especially with regard to 'Ali's family. Thus, it appears that Mukhtár can be considered the first in the history of Islam to publicly announce and act on behalf of this messianic idea, which, as we will soon see, was to become so prominent in practically all subsequent Shi'ite movements.

Initially, Mukhtár's preaching won him many followers among the leaders of the Kufan community, who wanted to be independent of 'Abdallah b. al-Zubayr's governor in Basra. After securing their support, Mukhtár started a rebellion against 'Abdallah b. al-Zubayr's appointees and succeeded in expelling them from Kufa to Basra, which remained firmly under the control of 'Abdallah b. al-Zubayr's lieutenants. Fulfilling his vow to avenge the death of al-Husayn, Mukhtár sought out and punished those whom he considered directly or indirectly involved in the murder of 'Ali's younger son. Before long, Mukhtár learned about an Umayyad army advancing toward Iraq in order to bring it back into the Umayyad fold. Mukhtár's troops routed the Umayyads in Upper Iraq and killed their commander 'Ubaydallah, the former governor of Iraq who was, as we remember, directly responsible for al-Husayn's death. One interesting fact about Mukhtár's movement is his heavy reliance on the non-Arab elements of Iraq's population (mostly of Persian descent), who were brought there as prisoners of war, and their descendants, many of whom had already converted to Islam. Mukhtár is said to have treated thcm in the same way as he did Arab Muslims by allocating to them an equal share of war booty. This attitude seems to have created ill will between him and the Arab tribal leaders of Kufa, most of whom later deserted him, rending his movement much weaker militarily.[104] The non-Arab elements who joined Mukhtar's rebellion were known as "clients" of the Arabs, or *mawáli*. They were to play an important and occasionally critical role in the subsequent history of the Muslim state.[105] Despite its initial success, Mukhtár's pro-'Alid polity in Kufa was short-lived. In the spring of 687, it was destroyed by the forces of the governor of Basra, aided by the Arab tribal leaders of Kufa, who, as mentioned, had abandoned Mukhtár earlier. In an attempt to besmirch the reputation of Mukhtár in the eyes of the masses generally sympathetic to his cause, his wives were forced to testify that he pretended to be a prophet and thus placed himself beyond the pale of Islam.[106] However, this defamation campaign failed to suppress his most consequential legacy, namely, his allegiance to the 'Alid cause generally and to Muhammad b. al-Hanafiyya in particular.[107] The latter remained a major focus of pro-'Alid hopes for decades to come.

The End of 'Abdallah b. al-Zubayr's Caliphate and the Triumph of the Marwánids

Even without Mukhtár, 'Abdallah b. al-Zubayr's hold on Iraq remained precarious because of the constant fighting between various tribal factions based there and the incessant troubles in northwest Arabia and western Iran caused by roaming Kharijite bands that left a trail of devastation in their wake. The Kharijites effectively cut off 'Abdallah's brother Mus'ab and his followers in Iraq from their leader's headquarters in Mecca, making it difficult for the caliph to coordinate their activities. The two principal rivals for power remained on the scene: 'Abdallah

b. al-Zubayr in the Hijáz and 'Abd al-Malik, son of the caliph Marwán, in Syria. An able military leader and politician, 'Abd al-Malik was busy consolidating his hold on Syria and preparing for the invasion of Iraq. In 691, he personally led a Syrian tribal army to Iraq, where he decisively defeated the Iraqi force headed by Mus'ab. He then entered Kufa to receive the homage of its population as the new caliph.

Following this victory, 'Abd al-Malik dispatched his trusted lieutenant al-Hajjáj to deal a final blow to 'Abdallah b. al-Zubayr holed up in Mecca. The siege of the sacred city of Islam began in March 692 and lasted for six months, during which time the city and its sanctuary were again subjected to bombardment with fiery projectiles, which continued even during the pilgrimage season.[108] Eventually, most of 'Abdallah's supporters lost heart and capitulated. The caliph,[109] however, refused to give himself up and was killed in action near the Ka'ba. His body was cruci-fied and his head sent to 'Abd al-Malik. The Umayyads were victorious again, although this time a different branch of the family, the Marwánids, ended up holding the reins of power.

Despite the general hostility to the Umayyads that dominates later Muslim sources, especially those from the 'Abbásid period, the success of the dynasty in reestablishing the unity of the Mus-lim *umma* was directly or indirectly acknowledged by Muslim historians. The year in which the remaining opponents of Umayyad rule were vanquished (692) has come to be known as "the year of [the reestablishment of] the community." Reassembling the *umma* after decades of the devastat-ing and seemingly incessant civil strife was no small feat.[110]

The Consolidation of Umayyad Power Under 'Abd al-Malik and His Successors

The rule of 'Abd al-Malik (685–705) and his son al-Walíd (705–715) witnessed the consolida-tion of Umayyad authority and the unprecedented centralization of power in the hands of the caliph. In their efforts to strengthen their dynastic rule, the early Umayyad rulers were lucky to have by their side the towering figure of al-Hajjáj, the governor of Iraq and viceroy of the eastern lands of the Caliphate in 694–714. A statesman of genius, al-Hajjáj served under both caliphs with ruthless efficiency and was largely responsible for the continuity of state politics during their reigns. Under 'Abd al-Malik and al-Hajjáj, numerous administrative reforms were intro-duced, including the adoption of Arabic as the language of administration and coinage (instead of Persian in Iran and Iraq and Greek in Syria and Egypt), as well as the deployment of the Syrian troops to the faraway provinces. These loyal and seasoned troops became the mainstay of Umayyad military might. Thanks to their military skills and his own strategic acumen, al-Hajjáj managed to suppress several major rebellions against Umayyad rule in both Iran and Iraq, seeing that, under the previous rulers, Iraq's two garrison cities remained the hotbeds of opposition—often couched in a religious idiom—to Syrian rule. Al-Hajjáj's inaugural speech before the people of Kufa captures the intensity of the confrontation between the authoritarian Umayyad state and the freedom-loving Iraqis:

> By God! I take full accounting, match it in return, and pay it back in kind! I see heads ripe and ready for harvest, and blood ready to flow between turbans and beards! . . . By God, O people of Iraq, I cannot be squeezed like a fig . . . I have been proven to be at the height of my vigor and have run the longest races. The Commander of the Faithful, 'Abd al-Malik, has emptied his quiver and tested the wood of his arrows; he found me the strongest and least likely to break, and thus aimed me at you. Long have you pursued the course of faction and followed the way of waywardness; but now, by God, I will bark you as one does a tree, hack you as one does mimosa, and beat you as one does a camel not of the herd at the watering-hole.[111]

This intimidating rhetoric is indicative of the lengths to which the Umayyad agents were prepared to go in order to secure their hold on the restive eastern provinces. Centralization and control had to be achieved at all costs, even if this meant trampling underfoot the traditional freedoms and sensibilities of the Arab tribesmen. Tribal anarchy and tribal diplomacy had to give way to the unquestioning obedience characteristic of an absolutist monarchy toward which the Umayyads were inexorably steering a reluctant and defiant *umma*.[112]

No wonder that, in Islamic sources from the 'Abbásid period, the rulers of the Umayyad dynasty are routinely portrayed as irreligious, despotic monarchs, who had ruled their subjects with an iron fist and who cared little about Islamic values. Only one exception to this overall pattern is granted by such ideologically motivated, hostile narratives. This exception is the short rule of 'Umar b. 'Abd al-'Aziz, or 'Umar II (717–720), who was generally seen as a God-fearing, pious individual in contrast to his "impious" and "worldly" predecessors and successors.[113] His tomb was the only one spared by the 'Abbásids in the aftermath of their victory over the Umayyad dynasty in 750.

This unfavorable portrait of the first dynasty of Islam should be taken with caution. It stands to reason that the 'Abbásids had a vested interest in vilifying their predecessors, whom they had dislodged from power, as cruel despots and imperfect Muslims. An objective examination of historical facts shows that the Umayyads were anxious to maintain their religious credentials, viewing Islam as the essential glue to hold together the fractious and mutually hostile Arab tribal levies that constituted the military foundation of their power.

Conclusions

As we have seen, Umayyad legitimacy was based on their role as the unifiers of the community fractured in the aftermath of 'Uthman's assassination. However, this claim alone was not enough to justify their reign. They had to show their subjects that they were indeed genuinely Islamic rulers whose rule was the fulfillment of the will of God as conveyed by the Qur'an. The Umayyads sought to achieve this goal by maintaining the supremacy of Islam as the religion of their state in opposition to all other religious denominations in their domain. With this goal in mind, they undertook a number of reforms, substituting, for instance, newly minted coins with Arabic-Islamic slogans for the "infidel" Byzantine and Sasanian coins that had been in circulation at the beginning of their reign. A legend has it that the new coinage with statements of Islamic creed was introduced by 'Abd al-Malik (d. 705) in response to the threat by a Byzantine emperor to issue coins with anti-Muslim inscriptions.[114] Apart from the creedal statements and the name of the caliph, the coins generally featured no portraits of rulers or any other figural representations—in contradistinction to the Byzantine and Sasanian coins that usually carried both.[115] This "fear of images" was to become a distinguishing characteristic of Islam in a conscious retort to Christianity, whose followers made extensive use of figural iconography in their cultic practices.

In another symbolic act to separate Islam from its monotheistic predecessors, Christianity and Judaism, which were professed by the majority of the new subjects of the Muslim state, the caliph 'Abd al-Malik ordered the construction in 692 of the monument that came to be known as the "Dome of the Rock" on the Temple Mount in Jerusalem. This imposing building, which was architecturally different from the traditional Muslim mosque, was deemed to serve as "a graphic statement of the identity and superiority of Arab faith"[116] in relation to its monotheistic rivals. The same applies to the construction under the caliph al-Walíd (r. 705–715) of the so-called Mosque of the Umayyads in Damascus, which incorporated the former Christian church of St. John. The ideological intent of these acts is obvious and requires no further elaboration.

Less visibly but no less importantly, the Umayyads endeavored to regulate and control their subjects' everyday life within their large realm. The most obvious way to do this was to

Islamize it. Alongside governors and military commanders, they now also appointed religious judges (*qadi*s) to the garrison towns of Syria, Iraq, and Egypt. These religious functionaries were responsible for administering justice in accordance with the precepts of the Qur'an and the Sunna (exemplary custom) of the Prophet.[117] Simultaneously, they were charged with cracking down on various manifestations of non-Islamic behavior, such as gambling, commercial and fiscal fraud, capital crimes, prostitution, drinking of wine, and so on. As for the caliphs themselves, they made it their duty to lead Muslims on an annual *hajj* and to mete out justice during public audiences. All these and other measures were deemed to maintain their image as proper and observant Muslim rulers in the eyes of their subjects. Last but not least, the Umayyads were expected by their subjects to expand and protect the "Abode of Islam" by waging an offensive or defensive jihad against their non-Muslim neighbors. As a result of this constant military expansion, a giant Islamic Empire emerged that stretched from North Africa and the Iberian Peninsula in the west to Central Asia and northern India in the east.[118] The convergence of imperial and Islamic symbolism in the person of the Umayyad ruler is quite telling. He embodied, on the one hand, the role of Islam as the theological foundation of the Umayyad state, and, on the other, his conscious desire to imitate his imperial predecessors, the Roman/Byzantine emperors and the shahs of Iran.[119]

Yet, for all its apparent might, the foundations of the Umayyad Empire were not without structural flaws. Its control over the restive Muslims of the garrison cities of Iraq and further east remained precarious; driven by various religious agendas (especially pro-'Alid and Kharijite), these constituencies were staunchly opposed to Umayyad rule. The factional struggle among the tribal confederations that constituted the military foundation of the Umayyad Empire continued to produce instability throughout the dynasty's reign.[120] It was exacerbated by the favoritism toward the loyal Syrian troops exhibited by the caliphs and the struggle for power within the royal household, whose members relied on the support of one or the other military-tribal faction. Last but not least, the growing number of converts to Islam (*mawáli*; sing. *máwla*) and their treatment as "second-class" citizens of the community by the Arab elite created tensions that threatened to develop into an open conflict along ethnic lines. 'Umar II's attempts to alleviate this problem by making the non-Arab Muslims equal to the Arabs came to an abrupt end after his early death in 720. Eventually, the combination of these structural flaws would lead to the unraveling of Umayyad rule. Given the multitude of problems faced by the Umayyads, their undeniable achievements in the field of administration, Islamizing the life of their subjects, and establishing the foundations of Islamic culture seem even more remarkable in retrospect.

Questions to Ponder

1   After considering the vicissitudes of Islam's early history, how would you account for the eventual triumph of the Umayyad family, whose Islamic credentials were probably the weakest of all contenders? Focus in particular on the conflict between 'Ali and Mu'awiya and, later on, on that of Yazíd /Marwán/'Abd al-Malik and their 'Alid and Zubayrid opponents.

2   Did 'Ali stand a chance to win in his struggle against Mu'awiya and his allies (such as 'Amr b. al-'As)?

3   What were the causes of his undoing other than bad luck?

4   Were both civil wars (*fitnas*) avoidable, or was conflict built into the very structure of the early Muslim state?

Summary

- Given the fluid notions of rightful and wrongful rule in early Islam, will any objective criteria or authority define the Umayyad state as "Islamic" or "un-Islamic"?
- The controversial election of 'Uthman (644) by the electoral council (*shúra*) becomes the triumph of the Qurayshi nobility.
- Among the reasons for popular discontent with 'Uthman's rule is his habit of distributing the best agricultural lands captured during the conquests and the most lucrative posts in the state apparatus among his relatives or cronies. His reluctance to punish his relatives for corruption and transgressions against Islamic law becomes another cause for popular discontent.
- The siege of 'Uthman's house in Medina precedes his subsequent murder by a group of rebels (656). 'Ali is accused of complicity in his murder or, at the very least, of failing to punish its perpetrators.
- The declaration of 'Ali's caliphate is rejected as illegitimate by many, especially the Qurayshi nobles.
- The first civil war, or "trial" (*fitna*), begins in the Muslim state. The principal parties to the conflict are 'Ali and his followers, based primarily in Kufa (Iraq), against 'A'isha, Talha, and al-Zubayr, whose followers come from Mecca, Medina, and Basra. At the Battle of the Camel (656), 'A'isha's party is defeated.
- 'Ali and Mu'awiya confront each other at the Battle of Siffín (657).
- 'Ali's indecision leads to arbitration with dubious results. His most uncompromising former followers secede and turn against him, marking the beginning of the radical Kharijite ("secessionist") movement opposed to both 'Ali and Mu'awiya.
- 'Ali's murder by a Kharijite assassin in 661 leaves the door open to the accession of Mu'awiya.
- The Umayyad dynasty is begun. Mu'awiya becomes caliph by default and grooms his son Yazíd as his successor in 680, causing a great deal of discontent among both the Quraysh and other Muslims.
- The 'Alid opposition to Mu'awiya and his son (appointed as his successor) leads to the uprising and subsequent death at Karbalá/Kerbela (Iraq) of al-Husayn, the younger son of 'Ali in 680.
- The initially successful claim to the caliphate of 'Abdallah b. al-Zubayr leads to the pro-'Alid uprising of Mukhtár in Kufa. 'Ali's son Muhammad b. al-Hanafiyya, seen by his partisans as the "divinely guided one" (*máhdi*), becomes the reluctant symbol and rallying cry of Mukhtár's rebellion.
- The triumph of the Marwánid branch of the Umayyad family (692), named after Marwán, personal secretary to 'Uthman and a major political figure, becomes controversial in early Islam.
- The civil strife ends with the consolidation of Umayyad/Marwánid power under the caliph 'Abd al-Malik and his son Walíd (692–715).
- The Umayyad/Marwánid caliphate is transformed into a dynastic absolutist state.
- The structural flaws of the Umayyad state become apparent as it faces opposition from the pro-'Alid party (Shi'ites), the discontented non-Arab Muslims (*mawáli*), and the Kharijites.

Notes

1 See, e.g., Q 49:13; for a detailed discussion of the meaning of this verse, see William Chittick, *In Search of the Lost Heart: Explorations in Islamic Thought*, SUNY Press, Albany, NY, 2012, p. 3.

2 Wilferd Madelung, *The Succession to Muhammad: A Study of the Early Caliphate*, Cambridge University Press, Cambridge, 1997, p. 81.

3 Madelung, *The Succession*, pp. 70–71; Oleg Bolshakov, *Istoriia Khalifata. T. II. Epokha velikikh zavoievanii: 633–656*, Nauka, Moscow, 1993, p. 156.

4 Marshall Hodgson, *The Venture of Islam*, University of Chicago Press, Chicago, 1974, vol. 1, p. 212.

5 Madelung, *The Succession*, p. 79.

6 Bolshakov, *Istoriia. II*, pp. 190–191.

7 Among them was the conqueror of Egypt 'Amr b. al-'As (d. 662 or 664); see Khaled Keshk, "'Amr b. al-'As," in *Encyclopedia of Islam*, 3rd ed.; online edition: http://referenceworks.brillonline.com.

8 Madelung, *The Succession*, p. 81.

9 Bolshakov, *Istoriia. II*, p. 206.

10 Ibid., pp. 196–201.

11 Madelung, *The Succession*, p. 81 and Bolshakov, *Istoriia. II*, pp. 202–205.

12 Madelung, *The Succession*, p. 81.

13 Bolshakov, *Istoriia. II*, pp. 203–205.

14 Ibid., pp. 179–181, 200, 202–203, 205, and 259, note 60.

15 Ibid., pp. 202 and 204.

16 Ibid., pp. 204–205.

17 Madelung, *The Succession*, p. 102.

18 For a detailed discussion of the provenance of the letter, see ibid., pp. 125–127; cf. Bolshakov, *Istoriia. II*, pp. 212–213; at that time, Marwán served as 'Uthman's secretary.

19 It went back to the accusations of adultery leveled against 'A'isha by a group of the Prophet's companions that apparently included 'Ali; for 'A'isha's involvement in these dramatic events leading up to the assassination of 'Uthman, see Madelung, *The Succession*, pp. 100–103.

20 Ibid., p. 96.

21 Ibid., pp. 126–127 and 133–134.

22 It is true, however, that many of 'Uthman's supporters tarried at his own request, for until his hour of death, he remained reluctant to spill Muslim blood in a fratricidal strife; see Madelung, *The Succession*, p. 139.

23 Ibid., p. 138 and Bolshakov, *Istoriia. II*, p. 214.

24 Gernot Rotter (1941–2010) quoted in Oleg Bolshakov, *Istoriia Khalifata. III. Mezhdu dvukh grazhdanskikh voin: 656–696*, Vostochnaia literatura, Moscow, 1998, p. 9.

25 Madelung, *The Succession*, p. 141 and Bolshakov, *Istoriia. III*, p. 20.

26 Madelung, *The Succession*, p. 141 and Bolshakov, *Istoriia. III*, pp. 15 and 23.

27 Madelung, *The Succession*, pp. 141 and 146–147 and Bolshakov, *Istoriia. III*, p. 24.

28 Madelung, *The Succession*, pp. 146–149.

29 Ibid., pp. 149–150 and Bolshakov, *Istoriia. III*, pp. 19–20 and 23.

30 Madelung, *The Succession*, p. 151.

31 Ibid., p. 149.

32 Bolshakov, *Istoriia. III*, pp. 24 and 30; cf. ibid., p. 91.

33 Ibid., pp. 26–27 and Madelung, *The Succession*, p. 147.

34 Madelung, *The Succession*, p. 147.

35 Robert Gleave, "'Ali b. Abi Talib," in *Encyclopedia of Islam*, 3rd ed., E. J. Brill, Leiden and Boston, 2008, fascicle 2, p. 65; for details, see Oleg Bolshakov, *Istoriia Khalifata. T. I. Islam v Aravii*, Nauka, Moscow, 1989, pp. 128–130; cf. Bolshakov, *Istoriia. III*, p. 91.

36 Madelung, *The Succession*, p. 155.

37 Ibid.

38 Ibid., pp. 156–157; Bolshakov, *Istoriia. III*, pp. 24–25.
39 Adrian Brockett (trans.), *The History of al-Tabari,* vol. 16: *The Community Divided*, SUNY Press, Albany, 1997, pp. 114–199.
40 Bolshakov, *Istoriia. III*, pp. 25–26.
41 As detailed in ibid., pp. 29–42 and Madelung, *The Succession*, pp. 166–178.
42 Madelung, *The Succession*, pp. 178–179.
43 Gleave, "'Ali b. Abi Talib," p. 66.
44 Brockett (trans.), *The History of al-Tabari*, pp. 131–158; Bolshakov, *Istoriia. III*, p. 39.
45 Madelung, *The Succession*, p. 177; according to the Muslim chronicles cited by Oleg Bolshakov, both sides lost five thousand warriors with casualties split more or less evenly; *Istoriia. III*, p. 40 and pp. 293–294, note 119.
46 Madelung, *The Succession*, p. 176.
47 Ibid., p. 184.
48 Bolshakov, *Istoriia. I*, pp. 157–163.
49 At that time, the notion of "Syria" (al-Sha'm) included present-day Syria, Palestine/Israel, Lebanon, and Jordan.
50 Madelung, *The Succession*, p. 186.
51 The stepped pulpit of a mosque.
52 Brockett (trans.), *The History of al-Tabari*, pp. 196–197.
53 Madelung, *The Succession*, p. 187.
54 Ibid., pp. 194–195.
55 "Whosoever is slain unjustly, We [i.e., God] have appointed his next-of-kin [to exact revenge]."
56 Madelung, *The Succession*, p. 195.
57 Q 7:87; G.R. Hawting (trans.), *The History of al-Tabari,* vol. 17: *The First Civil War*, SUNY Press, Albany, 1996, p. 71.
58 Namely, scrolls of the Qur'an.
59 Hawting (trans.), *The History of al-Tabari*, p. 78; cf. Madelung, *The Succession*, p. 238.
60 Madelung, *The Succession*, p. 238.
61 Hawting (trans.), *The History of al-Tabari*, p. 79.
62 Madelung, *The Succession*, p. 239.
63 Ibid., pp. 243–244.
64 Ibid., p. 249.
65 Literally, "those who have left or marched out," that is, "seceders" or "rebels."
66 Madelung, *The Succession*, p. 253.
67 Ibid., pp. 251–253.
68 Ibid., p. 261.
69 Ibid., p. 260.
70 Ibid., p. 262.
71 Ibid., p. 263.
72 Bolshakov, *Istoriia. III*, p. 88 and Madelung, *The Succession*, p. 308.
73 Bolshakov, *Istoriia. III*, p. 88.
74 Madelung, *The Succession*, p. 309.
75 Ibid., p. 312.
76 For an attempt to reconstruct Mu'awiya's character, see Bolshakov, *Istoriia. III*, pp. 110–117.
77 For details, see ibid., pp. 97–104.
78 Accounts of the number of his divorced and actual wives vary depending on the sources' pro- or anti-'Alid agenda from seven to seventy; he reportedly fathered seven to eight sons and six daughters, Madelung, *The Succession*, pp. 330 and 380–387.
79 Ibid., p. 331; Bolshakov, on the other hand, treats the story of al-Hasan's poisoning as part of anti-Umayyad propaganda, *Istoriia. III*, p. 146.
80 Most Muslim sources indicate that the Umayyad clan accepted Islam "at the point of the sword" after leading the Meccan opposition to its founder for almost two decades; nevertheless, Mu'awiya's service as a secretary of the Prophet (for two years) who wrote down both his revelations (the Qur'an) and sayings (*hadith*) should not be forgotten, Bolshakov, *Istoriia. III*, p. 110.

81 Oleg Bolshakov, however, doubts this was a regular, officially sanctioned practice; see *Istoriia. III*, p. 115.

82 Ibid.

83 Ibid., p. 113 and pp. 155–156.

84 Ibid., pp. 113–114.

85 Madelung, *The Succession*, p. 348; Bolshakov, *Istoriia. III*, p. 113 and pp. 158–160; note that Bolshakov calls in doubt the widely held opinion of Yazíd's alleged lack of knowledge of Islam.

86 G. R. Hawting, *The First Dynasty of Islam*, Southern Illinois University Press, Carbondale and Edwardsville, 1987, p. 46.

87 Bolshakov, *Istoriia. III*, p. 184.

88 Ibid., p. 186.

89 On the governor, see ibid., pp. 187–189.

90 Ibid., p. 203; Bolshakov mentions three, whereas Madelung says two; see Madelung, *The Succession*, p. 384.

91 Bolshakov, *Istoriia. III*, p. 203.

92 Sandra Campbell, "'Abdallah b. al-Zubayr," in *Encyclopedia of Islam*, 3rd ed.; online edition: http:// referenceworks.brillonline.com.

93 Ibid.

94 Bolshakov, *Istoriia. III*, pp. 206–208.

95 Ibid., p. 207.

96 Ibid., pp. 217–218.

97 He apparently died of injuries sustained after falling off a horse during a hunting trip; see ibid., p. 218.

98 Campbell, "'Abdallah."

99 Ibid.

100 Madelung, *The Succession*, p. 349 and Bolshakov, *Istoriia. III*, p. 229.

101 Campbell, "'Abdallah" and Bolshakov, *Istoriia. III*, pp. 229–230.

102 For details see Bolshakov, *Istoriia. III*, pp. 235–274.

103 In all, according to Oleg Bolshakov's calculations, 'Ali had nine sons by eight wives and about fifteen daughters; ibid., p. 18.

104 Bolshakov, *Istoriia. III*, p. 250.

105 Hawting, *The First Dynasty of Islam*, pp. 51–53.

106 Bolshakov, *Istoriia. III*, p. 254.

107 Ibid.

108 Ibid., p. 267.

109 In Western literature 'Abdallah b. al-Zubayr is frequently referred to as "anti-caliph"; this is hardly accurate, since his claim to the caliphal office was much more widely accepted than that of the Marwánids, whose legitimacy was quite tenuous during the second civil war. This fact, however, was forgotten once he had lost to his rival, 'Abd al-Malik, whom the sources now came to present as "the caliph"; see Bolshakov, *Istoriia. III*, pp. 267–268.

110 Hodgson, *The Venture*, vol. 1, pp. 218–219 and 223; Hawting, *The First Dynasty of Islam*, p. 14.

111 Everett Rowson (trans.), *The History of al-Tabari*, vol. 22: *The Marwanid Restoration*, SUNY Press, Albany, NY, 1989, p. 14.

112 Hodgson, *The Venture*, vol. 1, pp. 241–247.

113 Hugh Kennedy, *The Prophet and the Age of the Caliphates*, Longman, London and New York, 1986, pp. 106–107.

114 Hawting, *The First Dynasty of Islam*, p. 65.

115 Ibid. During the transitional period, however, some Umayyad coins featured the image of the standing caliph with a broad sword. This imagery later disappeared and was replaced by Islamic creedal statements.

116 Jonathan Berkey, *The Formation of Islam*, Cambridge University Press, Cambridge, 2003, p. 81.

117 Hodgson, *The Venture*, vol. 1, p. 226.

118 See, e.g., Khalid Blankenship, *The End of the Jihad State*, SUNY Press, Albany, NY, 1994.

119 See, e.g., Richard Frye, *Ibn Fadlan's Journey to Russia*, Markus Wiener, Princeton, NJ, 2nd ed., 2006, pp. 135–136.

120 See, e.g., Bolshakov, *Istoriia. III*, pp. 222–233.

Chapter 5

The Principal Source of Islam
The Qur'an

The Qur'an as Revelation and Sacred Book

The Qur'an speaks of itself as "guidance to the people," which was sent to humankind to confirm the veracity of the Torah and the Gospel (Q 3:3–4 and 84; see also 2:87, 5:43–44, 48, and 61:6). It was revealed to Muhammad over some twenty-two years of his prophetic ministry, hence the Qur'an's other common name: the "sending down" or "revelation." The content of the Qur'an is not static; it reflects not only the dynamic character of the Prophet's relationship with his Lord, but also the changing conditions and exigencies of the Muslim community under his leadership. Muhammad communicated his revelations to his followers, some of whom probably served as his secretaries. They seem to have committed the text of Muhammad's revelations to writing already during his lifetime.[1] There is no reason to doubt, however, that initially Qur'anic revelations circulated primarily in an oral form. Verses of the Qur'an were memorized by some members of the first Muslim community and recited on such occasions as the five daily prayers, supplications, public sermons, births, funerals, and so on. It has been argued that many of them exhibit the structure of a sermon with a number of distinctive thematic clusters meant for an oral annunciation and aural reception for listeners. These clusters were identified as eschatological prophesies, references to divine signs manifested in nature and history, narratives of salvation history, debates with skeptics and rejecters, and discussions of contemporary events.[2] We should therefore bear in mind that the ways in which the Qur'an was received and appreciated by its followers during the first decades of Islam are quite distinct from its reception by the modern reader, for whom it is first and foremost a book.[3]

The overwhelming majority of Muslims believe the Qur'an to be God's literal and unmediated word. This belief constitutes part of the Muslim creed. The prophet Muhammad was a messenger whom God had selected for delivery of his message to humankind. God communicated his word to Muhammad either directly in a waking state or sleep or, more commonly, via an intermediary, the angel Gabriel (Jibril). For the first Muslims of Mecca and Medina, as for the believers ever since, the Qur'an, revealed to the Arabs via the prophet Muhammad, was a means of accessing and worshipping God. This being the case, the Qur'an is absolutely central to Muslim devotional, intellectual, and cultural life that is virtually permeated and animated by the spirit and letter of the divine word. One can safely argue that the Qur'an constitutes the very foundation of Islamic identity and the singular focus of Muslim devotional life.

The Qur'an is not easy to comprehend because it does not furnish an uninterrupted and chronologically structured narrative that we find in many books of the Hebrew Bible. Nor is there a unifying plot, although several major themes can be discerned, as discussed later in this chapter. Because the Qur'an repeatedly refers to itself as a "book," it will be best to start with a description of its internal structure and characteristics and then try to elucidate the major points of its content by placing it in the historical context of its formation. In so doing, we should keep in mind that

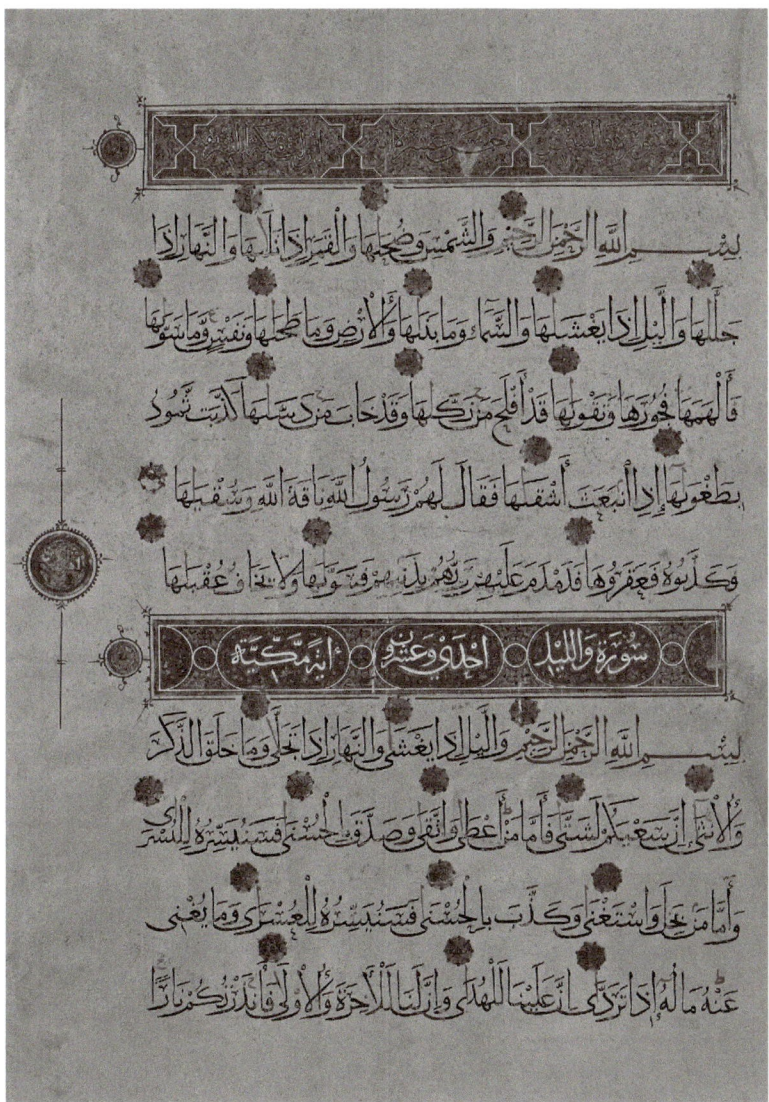

Figure 5.1 Illuminated Page From the Qur'an, *Suras* 91 ("The Sun") and 92 ("The Night")

V&A Images, London / Art Resource, NY

the Qur'anic text that we know today took several decades to acquire its current shape and status as the Muslim scripture (see Figure 5.1).

The Name and Structure

Some Western scholars derive the word *al-qur'an*—its most common Latinized forms are "Alcoran," "Koran," and "Coran"—from the Syriac/Aramaic word *qeryana*, which means "scripture reading; or recitation of a passage from the holy book."[4] This may well be the case, but, on the face of it, there is no need to look beyond the Arabic language to identify its etymology. The

Arabic verb *qara'a*, from which the name "al-Qur'an" is apparently derived, denotes an act of reading or recitation. This etymology is upheld by most Muslim scholars, although some argue that the Qur'an is a proper name that is not related to any word or root. The word "Qur'an" occurs in the text of the Qur'an itself about seventy times. Its most common synonyms, apart from "revelation," are the "Book [of God]," "Reminder," "Wisdom," and "Discernment" or "Separation" (namely, of believers from unbelievers or of good from evil).[5]

The length of the Qur'an is approximately the same as that of the New Testament. It is divided into thirty equal portions (parts) corresponding to the number of days in the month of fasting, Ramadán, when one part is read during the night. These parts are used for liturgical purposes only and have no correspondence whatsoever to the division of the Qur'an into chapters and verses. The chapters and verses are called *sura*s and *áya*s, respectively. The word *sura* has two possible etymologies: either from the Hebrew *shurah,* "a row of bricks in a wall or a row of vines," or from the Syriac/Aramaic *surtha*, "[sacred] writing, text of scripture."[6] The *sura*s number 114. The first *sura*, *al-Fátiha* (the "Opening"), is a short prayer, widely used in Islamic ritual practices. It brings home several roles of God, namely, as the sovereign ruler of the universe, the supreme judge of human beings and their guide to either salvation or perdition:

> In the name of God, the Merciful, the Compassionate
> Praise belongs to God, the Lord of all Being,
> The All-Merciful, the All-Compassionate,
> The Master of the Day of Doom.
> Thee only we serve; to Thee alone we pray for succor.
> Guide us in the straight path, the path of those
> whom Thou hast blessed, not of those against whom Thou
> art wrathful, nor those who are astray.[7]

The style of the last two *sura*s resemble short charms and are used as such by Muslims in their daily life, for instance, in order to ward off evil or when in distress. The *sura*s are arranged roughly in order of length, which varies from dozens of pages to a line or two. Thus, *sura* 2, titled "The Cow," is the longest of all. It occupies 715 lines or 60 printed pages in a standard Egyptian edition, whereas *sura*s near the end of the Qur'an sometimes occupy two lines or less (see, for instance, 108 and 112), *sura* 108 being the shortest of all. However, there is a number of deviations from this rule, as a few longer *sura*s are placed after the shorter ones or vice versa. The reasons behind such deviations are a subject of academic debate.

The contents of a *sura* are usually very diverse. For instance, *sura* 4, "Women," deals with such topics as laws of inheritance, permission/prohibition of marriage within certain degrees of consanguinity, marital relations, problems of peace and war, Muhammad's role as God's representative and, as such, the supreme arbiter of all legal cases and quarrels in Medina, relations of unbelievers with believers, and the status of the so-called "hypocrites" (namely, Muslims in name only, who pretend to be believers), the errors of the Jews and the Christians, and so on. This *sura*, like the majority of longer *sura*s, was revealed after Muhammad's emigration from Mecca to Medina. It thus belongs to the category of "Medinan" *sura*s. Shorter *sura*s were usually but not always revealed during the Meccan period.

In the Muslim tradition, each *sura* has a name of its own and is not usually referred to by its number, as is the case with the majority of Western discourses about Islam and the Qur'an. As a rule, the name of a *sura* has no direct reference to its most important subject matter but is taken from a prominent or unusual word in it. Thus *sura* 16 is known as "Bee" because this insect is mentioned in it, albeit only once in verse 68. In *sura* 26, "Poets," these individuals are mentioned only in verse 224, at the very end of the chapter. In many but not all copies of the Qur'an, both written and printed, the commencement of each *sura* is marked by a heading—first comes the name of the *sura*, followed by a statement about its dating (Meccan or Medinan), and finally the number of its verses. Western and Muslim scholars not only divide the *sura*s into Meccan and Medinan but also agree that some *sura*s may be composite, namely, a *sura* marked as Meccan may contain several Medinan passages and vice versa. Notes about Meccan or Medinan insertions in a *sura* attributed to one or the other period are common in commentaries of the Qur'an. After the heading of the *sura* comes the so-called *basmala*, that is the phrase *bismi'lláhi 'l-rahmán al-rahím,* which means "In the name of God the Merciful, the Compassionate." The exception is *sura* 9, which has no *basmala*. This introductory formula belongs to the original form of the Qur'an because it precedes some documents mentioned in the Qur'anic text, for instance, Solomon's letter to the Queen of Sheba (27:30).

The *sura*s are divided into verses, *ayat*. The meaning of this term is usually conveyed into English as "sign," "marvel," or "wonder," which implies its supernatural, divine origin. Divisions of *sura*s into verses differ depending on the edition of the text. In some, two verses are subsumed under one number; in others, they are divided. Therefore, the number of verses in different editions of the Qur'an may vary from 6,204 to 6,236. This does not mean that there are different verses in different editions; the content of the text and its length are the same in all modern editions.

The Language of the Qur'an

The Qur'an was revealed to humankind in a "clear Arabic language" (Q 16:103; 12:2, and 26:192–195), which, according to Muslim commentators, was the language of the Quraysh, the native tribe of the Prophet. Western scholars have argued that it was similar to the language of pre-Islamic tribal poetry, which had a higher status than the everyday speech of different Arab tribes and that was understood by all of them regardless of their tribal affiliation and native dialect.[8]

From the literary viewpoint, the Qur'an is said to have been articulated in rhyming prose, which makes it neither poetry nor prose strictly speaking. Unlike poetry, it does not have a fixed internal meter, and the rhyming effect is achieved by the use of the same endings throughout the whole *sura* or throughout some of its parts, for example, *an*, *in*, *im*, and so on. Typical in this respect is *sura* 55, titled *al-rahmán* ("The All-Merciful"), which in Arabic sounds as follows:

> *Ar-rahmán/'allama l-qurán/khalqa l-insán/'allámahu l-bayán/ash-shamsu wa-l-qamaru bi-husbán/wa-n-najmu wa-sh-shajaru yasjudán/wa-s-samá rafá'aha wa wada' l-mizán.* (The All-Merciful has taught the Qur'an. He created man and taught him the Explanation.[9] [He also created] the sun and the moon to a reckoning, and the stars and the trees bow themselves; and heaven—He raised it up, and set the Balance.)[10]

In this passage, the rhyming effect is achieved by the use of the Arabic ending *án* that is repeated throughout this *sura*, making for an energetic and occasionally solemn rhythmic flow of its text. Thanks to this aural effect and repetition, the message is imprinted in the memory of the listener. In the longer *sura*s from the Medinan period, the rhyming effect and rhythmic flow are frequently produced by attaching a set of formulas to the end of the otherwise prosaic lines. These formulas usually contain verbs and participles in the plural, such as *kafirín* or *kafirún* ("unbelievers"); *yafhamún* ("they understand"); *ya'lamún* ("they know"); *yaf'alun* ("they do"),[11] or divine epithets, such as *al-hakím* ("The [All-]Wise"); *al-samí'* ("The [All-]Hearing"); *al-'alím* ("The [All-]Knowing"); *al-rahím* ("The [All-]Compassionate"), *al-'azíz* ("All-Mighty"); *al-ghafúr* ("The [All-]Forgiving"), and so on.

Also common is the use of a rhetorical question with the same ending, which produces a rhyming effect throughout the *sura*. For instance, in the already mentioned *sura* 55, the refrain "O which of your Lord's bounties will you [two] deny?" (*fa-bi-ayyi ala'i rabbikúma tukadhdhibáni*) is repeated after almost every other verse. A similar rhetorical device is used in *sura* 77, where the repetition of the phrase "Woe on that Day onto those who give the lie to the truth!" (*waylun yawmaidhin li-l-mukadhdhibína*) serves a dual function: to drive the message home and to create the rhyming effect throughout the *sura*.

Of the other rhetorical features employed in the Qur'an, one should mention the oaths that are characteristic of the earliest layer of revelations. Verses with oaths contain dark predictions and energetic incantations that were meant to produce a deep psychological impact on the listeners and make them recant their errors. Typical of this rhetorical device is *sura* 91, which opens with the following incantation:

> By the sun and his morning brightness and by the moon when she follows him, and by the day when it displays him and by the night when it enshrouds him! By the heaven and that which built it and by the earth and that which extended it! By the soul and that which shaped it and inspired it to both lewdness and fear of God! Prosperous is he who purifies it, and failed is he who is seduced by it.

When recited in Arabic, the oath produces a cadence of sorts that culminates in a forceful assertion that captures the attention of the listener because it does not rhyme with the preceding lines of the *sura*.[12]

In a similar vein, verses containing dark predictions of the horrendous calamities of the Judgment Day are designed to inspire awe and humility in the listeners. They are usually introduced by either "when" or "the day when," as in *sura* 82:

> When the heaven is split open, **when** the stars are scattered, **when** the seas swarm over, **when** the tombs are overthrown, **then** a soul shall know its works, the former and the latter.

Many passages elucidating the import of the Qur'anic message are introduced by the imperative verb "Say!", as in *sura* 6, 12–13, where this rhetorical feature is used extensively to make a memorable creedal statement:

> **Say:** "To whom belongs what is in the heavens and in the earth?" **Say**: "It is God's. He has prescribed for Himself mercy. He will surely gather you to the Resurrection Day, of which there is no doubt."

In other instances, the "say passages" serve as answers to questions from Muhammad's followers as well as "retorts to the arguments or jeers of his opponents, and clarifications of Muhammad's own position,"[13] as in *sura* 3:12, 15, 26, 29, 31, and 32 or *sura* 6:145, 147–151, 158, 161–164.

The Mysterious Letters

Twenty-nine *sura*s are preceded, apart from the usual *basmala*, by a letter or a group of letters, called in Arabic the "openers of the *sura*s," for instance, *alif-lam-mim* (*alm*), *alif-lam-mim-ra* (*almr*), *sad* (*s*), *ha-mim* (*hm*), *ta-sin* (*ts*), *ta-ha* (*th*), *ya-sin* (*ys*), *qaf* (*q*), *nun* (*n*), and so on. Some *sura*s are named after these letters, for example, "TaHa" (20), "YaSin" (36), "Sad" (38), "Nun" (50), "Qaf" (68). They are recited as ordinary letters of the Arabic alphabet, and for the fourteen centuries since the revelation of the Qur'an, their meaning has intrigued and baffled scholars of the Islamic scripture. Some of them consider the "detached letters," as they are called in the Muslim exegetical tradition, to be abbreviations of the words and names that feature in the *sura*s in question. Thus, it has been suggested that *alr* stands for *al-rahmán*, "The All-Merciful"; *almr* for *al-rahím*, "The [All-]Compassionate"; *yásín* for *sayyid al-mursalín*, "The Lord of the [Divine] Messengers"; and so on. Modern scholars have rejected this explanation, arguing that these were but meaningless sounds deemed either to arouse the Prophet's attention to what was about to be revealed or to captivate his audience. In this view, these sounds or interjections some-how inaugurated divine word and separated it from Muhammad's own, human speech, so that the two would not be confused. Still others have suggested that the letters were mystical signs with symbolic meaning that is based on the numerical value of the Arabic letters (for instance, the letter *alif* stands for "one"; *ba* stands for "two"; *lam* for "thirty"; *nun* for "fifty"; *sad* for "ninety"; and so on). Shi'ite scholars treat some letters, especially *ha* and *mim*, as hidden allusions to their *imam*s. Muslim mystics (Sufis) in particular have spilled much ink trying to unravel the signifi-cance of the mysterious letters.[14]

As for modern Western scholars, they have proposed that the so-called mysterious letters sim-ply marked separation between *sura*s before they were given their present titles and numbers. It has also been argued that the letters are abbreviations of the names of the first collectors or memo-rizers of the *sura*s before which they appear, namely *alrz* = al-Zubayr; *almr* = al-Mughira; *hm* = 'Abd al-Rahman; *h* = Hudhayfa; and so on.

Scholars have observed that the letters may be somehow connected to the mention of the scrip-tures and holy books in the *sura*s in question. They appear only in front of those *sura*s that refer to one or the other type of holy scripture either explicitly or implicitly. For instance, in *sura* 20 ("TaHa"), named after the letters *ta* and *ha*, which precede it, the word "Qur'an" appears in the first line of the *sura*, immediately following these two letters. The same is true of *sura*s 27, 28, 31, 32, 36, 38, and a few others. One can mention more theories trying to make sense of the mysterious letters, but the ones already cited should be sufficient to demonstrate that the problem has not yet been resolved to everyone's satisfaction. The standard Muslim view is that the opening letters are a mystery that is known fully only to God, so fallible human beings should not wreck their brains trying to unravel it.

The Collection of the Qur'an

According to standard Muslim accounts, the collection of the Qur'an started already during the caliphate of Abu Bakr (632–634).[15] His right-hand man and would-be successor 'Umar is said to have been concerned by the fact that during the wars of apostasy many readers of the Qur'an, who had learned its content by heart, were killed in battles against the rebellious Arab tribes that seceded from the Muslim community in Medina following the death of the Prophet. 'Umar feared that if more of them were to die, some parts of the Qur'an would be irretrievably lost. He therefore counseled Abu Bakr to undertake the first compilation of the Qur'anic text. After some hesitation, so goes the story, Abu Bakr commissioned Muhammad's former scribe, Zayd b. Thabit,[16] to col-lect the Qur'an from "pieces of papyrus, flat stones, shoulder-blades and ribs of animals, pieces of leather and wooden boards, as well as from the hearts of men." Zayd wrote down what he collected on sheets (*súhuf*) of equal size and then submitted them to Abu Bakr. On Abu Bakr's death, they were passed to 'Umar, and on 'Umar's death to his daughter Hafsa, a widow of the Prophet. This account is open to criticism on a number of grounds. First, it says that it was the battle of the Garden of Death in Yamama, during which many Qur'an readers are said to have fallen, that prompted 'Umar to initiate the collection of the Qur'an.[17] However, if looking at the lists of those who fell in the campaign against the "false prophet" Musaylima, we will find very few of those who were likely to have known much of the Qur'an by heart. So the reasons for collecting and standardizing the text of the Muslim scripture may lie elsewhere.

Despite Abu Bakr's and 'Umar's efforts to preserve the Qur'an, at the accession of 'Uthman there was still no single official collection, or codex, of the Qur'anic text. It is reported that 'Uthman's decision to produce such a canonical text was prompted by the news about disputes concerning the correct reading of certain Qur'anic passages among the Muslim troops deployed on the eastern fringes of the empire, in Armenia and Azerbaijan. The disputes were serious enough to lead the military commander of a Muslim expeditionary force, Hudhayfa, to lay the matter before the caliph. The latter commissioned Zayd b. Thabit and a group of the companions of the Prophet, including 'Abdallah b. al-Zubayr, to compile a standard codex of the Qur'an. When it was ready, 'Uthman ordered it to be sent to garrison towns in the provinces, such as Basra, Kufa, Damascus, Fustat, as well as Mecca.[18]

Although 'Uthman's effort to achieve the uniformity of the Qur'anic text was, on the whole, successful, the pre-'Uthmanic variant readings were by no means forgotten. Most of the standard commentaries on the Qur'an mention such noncanonical readings and their advocates, especially 'Abdallah b. Mas'ud in Kufa (d. 653) and Ubayy b. Ka'b (d. 656) in Syria.[19] The variant readings in the codices of these individuals chiefly affect vowels and punctuation, but occasionally there are different versions of the canonical text. Furthermore, the lists of *sura*s in the noncanonical codices differ from each other and also from the Uthmanic text. For example, 'Abdallah b. Mas'ud omitted the last two *sura*s (113 and 114) because he regarded them as charms or supplications that were not part of the original revelation. It is also doubtful that he included the first *sura*, "The Opening," on the same grounds. Ubayy b. Ka'b, on the contrary, included all these *sura*s in his codex. Furthermore, it contained two additional *sura*s that were not part of the standard text of the Qur'an that we know today. They are short prayers introduced by the verb "say."[20] Later Islamic groups and movements had their own codices. For instance, the Kharijites denied that *sura* 12, "Joseph," was part of the original revelation because of its allegedly "frivolous" nature.

Interestingly, tradition claims that several verses that were not included in the canonical text of the Qur'an were part of the original revelation. The most famous, or infamous, of them is the verse that prescribes death by stoning as punishment for mature adults guilty of fornication. This verse is said to have been part of either *sura* 24 or *sura* 33. It contradicts *sura* 24:2, which stipulates flogging (one hundred lashes) for this crime without specifying the marital status or the age of the perpetrators. It also contradicts Q 4:15, which orders that the fornicators be confined in their home until death or until "God makes a way for them."[21] To resolve the contradiction, Muslim jurists came to argue that these two punishments are restricted to unmarried young men and women, whereas married adults should be stoned. The "stoning verse" was "remembered" by 'Umar, who claimed to have heard it from the Prophet. However, even 'Umar's prestige was not sufficient to convince the drafters of the canonical text to insert it into their codex, so it is not there.[22] Some Western scholars have argued that 'Umar's "remembrance" of the "stoning verse" was occasioned by his strenuous efforts to tighten up discipline in the Arab garrison towns at the time of the conquests.[23] It may not be accidental that about the same time a severe punishment for alcohol consumption (also not stipulated in the Qur'an) was introduced in the garrison towns of Iraq to keep their inhabitants under control. Muslim religious authorities argue that regardless of the presence or absence of the "stoning verse" in the Qur'an, there was enough evidence in the Sunna (custom) of the Prophet, which will be the subject of the next chapter, to justify this type of punishment. The same argument was used to justify the punishment of eighty lashes for wine drinking.

To a similar but also different category belong what later came to be known as the "Satanic verses." They are said to have been placed between Q 53:19 and 53:20, when they were originally annunciated by the Prophet to an audience of both Muslims and pagans in the precincts of the

Ka'ba at Mecca. According to the great Qur'an interpreter al-Tabari (d. 923), who reproduced the controversial verses in his giant commentary on the Qur'an, they said: "Have you considered al-Lat and al-'Uzza and Manat, the third, the other? These are the high-flying cranes, whose intercession is to be hoped for, such as they do not forget."[24] As mentioned in Chapter 1 of this book, these names refer to the three pagan goddesses—commonly known as the "daughters of God"—who were worshipped by some pagan Arab tribes of the Hijáz. The verses are believed to have been "cast upon" the Prophet's tongue by Satan at a time when he was desperate to attract new followers to his monotheistic teaching. Later, so the story goes, Muhammad realized the real source of these verses and received an amended revelation that omitted the praise of the daughters of God and denied their very existence, saying, "They are naught but names yourselves have made, and your fathers" (Q 53:22).[25] This relatively little known fact was discovered by a British fiction writer of Indian descent named Salman Rushdie (b. 1947), who made use of it in his novel "Satanic Verses." In Rushdie's interpretation, the existence of these verses casts doubt on the integrity and provenance of the entire Qur'anic text—an idea that scandalized many Muslims and provoked *imam* Khomeini's famous legal ruling (*fátwa*), issued in 1989 and calling for his execution by believers. Subsequently the book was banned in more than a dozen countries.[26]

The Central Theme of the Qur'an: God

As one might expect, God in his various capacities and manifestations, constitutes the main theme of the Qur'an. The Arabic word "Allah" means "the God," that is "god" (*iláh*) with the definite article (*al-*). According to the Qur'an, it is the same God that is confessed to and worshiped in the two other monotheistic traditions of the Middle East. God's centrality to the Qur'anic worldview and narrative is attested by the frequency of its use in the Muslim scripture. The proper name of God occurs 2,500 times in the Qur'anic text, not to count his numerous epithets or "most beautiful names," as they are called in the Islamic tradition, such as "The Lord" (*al-rabb*), "The All-Glorious" (*al-jalíl*), "The All-Merciful" (*al-rahmán*), "The All-Forgiving" (*al-ghafúr*), "The All-Knowing" (*al-alím*), and so on.

The God of the Qur'an is first and foremost the creator. He has brought this world into being by his creative command "Be!" for the benefit of his creatures. After providing them with sustenance, clothing, and a hospitable living environment, he dispatched to them a succession of messengers and prophets to guide them in the way of living most befitting to them as servants of their creator. The messengers and the prophets have taught their followers the law of God by which they should live. This law reached its perfection and completion in Islam, which is the God's latest and final message to his human servants. God's revelation presents human beings with a fundamental choice: to obey his will and to worship him out of gratitude for his boundless beneficence or to disobey his commands and, as a consequence, face his wrath and punishment in the afterlife.[27] Eventually, God will bring about the end of this world on a day known only to him. This will also be the Day of Judgment of humankind according to their deeds in their earthly life. In other words, the picture of God in the Qur'an is quite similar to one found in the Judeo-Christian scriptures.

The Qur'an never tires of emphasizing the absolute oneness of God. This idea is presented in opposition to the Jewish and Christian religions, whose followers the Qur'an accuses of compromising divine oneness by admitting other objects of worship alongside God. This is clearly stated in *sura* 9:30–31:

Jews say: "Ezra is the Son of God," while Christians say: "Christ is the Son of God." That is the utterance of their mouths, imitating what those who disbelieved before them have said. God assail them! How perverted they are! They have adopted their rabbis and their monks as lords apart from God, and [also] the Messiah, Mary's son. Yet they have been commanded to serve but One God; there is no deity except Him.

While the charge that Ezra was the son of God remains a mystery (some commentators argue that the belief in the divinity of Ezra may have been an oddity confined to the Jewish community of Medina),[28] the overall emphasis of this passage is clear: the Qur'an seeks to cleanse God from any association with his creatures or any other potential objects of veneration. This assertion is in line with the overall message of the Qur'an that consistently and relentlessly emphasizes divine oneness and rejects any attempts to compromise it:

They ascribe to God, as associates, the jinn, though He created them; and they impute to Him sons and daughters without any knowledge. Glory be to Him! High be He exalted above what they ascribe [to Him]! The Creator of the heavens and the earth—how should He have a son, seeing that He has no consort, and He created all things, and He has knowledge of everything?[29]

To summarize, God in the Qur'an possesses the following principal features: He is one, unique, and self-sufficient, whereas everything else is dependent on him as the creator and sustainer; he is omnipotent (all-mighty) and omniscient (all-knowing); he is merciful toward his creatures whom he has provided with everything they need; and he is also the supreme and just judge of their acts. The only proper relationship between God and human beings is that of the master and servant. All these qualities of God are summarized in Q 42:9–11:

God—He is the protector. He quickens the dead, and He is powerful over everything. And whatever you are at variance on, the judgement thereof belongs to God. That then is God, my Lord; in Him I have put my trust and to Him I return penitent. The Originator of the heaven and the earth, He has appointed for you, of yourselves, pairs and pairs also of the cattle therein multiplying you. Like Him there is naught. He is All-hearing, All-seeing. To Him belong the keys of the heavens and the earth. He outspreads and withdraws His provision to whom and from whom He wills. Surely, He has knowledge of everything.

These Qur'anic verses are remarkable in that they describe God as both absolutely transcendent (otherworldly) and, at the same time, possessed of such admittedly humanlike faculties as hearing and seeing. It fell to Muslim scholars of the later generations to try to resolve this apparent paradox. Their efforts will be discussed later on in this book.

The Prophets and Messengers

The prophets and messengers dispatched by God to humankind is another major theme of the Qur'an.[30] They were selected by God to deliver his messages to his servants. Some were given their own scriptures and laws, while others were commissioned by God to remind the believers of the earlier revelations. The lawgiving prophets in the Qur'an are—apart from Muhammad—Abraham, Moses, David, and Jesus. The rest are "warning prophets," who, according to the Qur'an, were dispatched to every nation or community (Q 10:48). They are Isaac (Is'haq), Ishmael (Isma'il), Idris (identified with either Enoch or Elijah), Zechariah (Zakariyya), John the Baptist (Yahya), and a number of other individuals who are identical with the prophets of the Judeo-Christian scriptures. A total of twenty-eight prophets are mentioned in the Qur'anic text.[31] Their prophetic careers are described in the so-called punishment stories[32] in a rather standardized and succinct manner. The usual plot is as follows: a prophet attempts to deliver a divine message to his people. He is rejected and ridiculed by his listeners, who stubbornly adhere to their errone-ous (polytheistic) beliefs. When the deniers attempt to persecute or kill the prophet, God inter-venes, afflicting the persecutors with a terrible calamity, which is meant to demonstrate the ephemeral nature of the prosperity that is not based on a sound religious faith and practice. The guilty community is destroyed, and its pitiful fate becomes a lesson to future generations.[33] However, this lesson is soon forgotten and the subsequent generations make exactly the same mistake.[34] The Qur'an often lays the blame for this on their leaders. The moral of the prophetic and punishment stories in the Qur'an is not difficult to deduce: The rejection of the prophet Muhammad by the Quraysh leaders and rank-and-file is the latest episode in the long chain of similar rejections of prophets by their people (see Figure 5.2).[35]

Figure 5.2 The Ascent of Muhammad to Heaven

Jon Thompson, Sheila R. Canby (eds)., Hunt for paradise, court art of Safavid Iran, 1501-1576. Public Doman/Wikimedia Commons

The story of Jesus ('Isa), son of Mary (Maryam), and his mother constitutes a substantial part of the Qur'anic narrative. Jesus is presented as a forerunner of Muhammad, who, together with his mother, were deified by his misguided followers. In the Qur'an, Jesus explicitly disavows them (Q 5:116–118), and his human nature is forcefully and unequivocally asserted on many occasions, such as this one: "The messiah (*masíh*), son of Mary, was only a messenger; messengers before him passed away; his mother was a just woman; they both ate food" (Q 5:75). At the same time, Jesus is not an ordinary warning prophet. God granted him a scripture, *Injíl* ("The Gospel") that contains a law and valuable lessons for humankind. The Qur'an repeatedly states that, confirmed in his mission with the Holy Spirit, Jesus brought humankind "the clear signs" (2:87 and 253). His miraculous birth and his speech from the cradle (19:28–34 and 3:46) were two instances of such signs. His other supernatural "sign" was his ability to give life to inanimate objects and to restore life in the dead (3:43 and 49). In addition, God gave Jesus the extraordinary ability to cure the blind and the leper (3:49 and 5:110). Moreover, he once asked God to send down a table prepared with food to his apostles, as a proof of his mission, and his request was granted (5:111–114). This episode may refer either to the Last Supper or to the miracle of loaves and fishes.

While the Qur'an constantly asserts Jesus's humanity, it also states that, unlike an ordinary human being, he did not die on the cross but was taken alive to heaven: "They [the Jews] did not slay him, nor crucify him, only a likeness of that was shown to them" (Q 4:157).[36] This puts him in a league of his own, especially because several Qur'anic references link him to the signs and knowledge of "the [final] hour" (Q 43:61–64 and 4:159).[37]

Although the Qur'an emphasizes the importance of all prophets who preceded Muhammad, it unequivocally gives the Muslim prophet pride of place. No wonder that belief in his prophetic mission constitutes the second part of the Muslim profession of faith, known as *shaháda*: "There is no deity but God, and Muhammad is His messenger." Muhammad's role as the indispensable guide of his community to truth and salvation is emphasized throughout the text of the Muslim scriptures, as, for instance, in *sura* 48:28–29: "It is He who has sent His Messenger with the guidance and the Religion of Truth, that He may uplift it above every religion . . . Muhammad is the Messenger of God, and those who are with him are hard against the unbelievers, merciful to one another."

On occasion, the Qur'an invokes the details of Muhammad's prophetic career and the special care bestowed upon him by his Lord. God found him an orphan and sheltered him; God found him erring and guided him; God found him needy and gave him enough sustenance (Q 93:6–11). When God chose Muhammad as the bearer of his message ("chant the Qur'an very distinctly," *sura* 73:4), the Qur'an, he perfected him (94:1–4) and installed him as a perfect example for all believers to follow (Q 33:21 and 48:8). The phrase "Obey God and his Messenger" runs like a red thread through the entire text of the Qur'an (Q 4:59; 8:46, and 3:152–153). At the same time, Muhammad's mortality is repeatedly asserted in order to prevent his followers from exaggerating his significance and distracting them from the worship of the one and only entity worthy of worship—God:

> **Say:** "I am only mortal, like you are. To me it has been revealed that your God is One God; so go straight to Him and ask for His forgiveness."
>
> (Q 41:5)

In the subsequent epochs, Muhammad's statements and actions, as recorded in the prophetic reports (*hadíth*), were to become the exemplary code of behavior incumbent on every Muslim. This code, named the Prophet's "custom" (*sunna*), constitutes the foundation of ethics, morals, and legal practice in Islam. As we shall see in the next chapter, in its importance, the Sunna of the Prophet is second only to the Qur'an itself.

The Judgment Day, Paradise, and Hell

The events of the Judgment Day and the fates of individual human beings are described in dramatic detail in many passages of the Qur'an, as in the following dialogue between God the Judge and the two punishing angels, who are holding God's unfaithful servant before hurling him into the hellfire:

> Death's agony comes in truth; this is what you were shunning!
> And the Trumpet shall be blown; that is the Day of the Threat.
> And every soul shall come and with it a driver and a witness.
> "You were heedless of this; therefore We[38] have now removed
> from you your covering." "Cast, you twain, into Gehenna every
> stubborn unbeliever, every hinderer of the good, transgressor,
> and inciter of distrust, who has set up with God another god."[39]

Divine judgment will separate the sinners from the righteous, whereupon, as we have just seen, the former will be confined to Hell, to be tormented there by ferocious angels, while the latter will be enjoying the delights of paradise, which the Qur'an describes in vivid detail (Q 39:70–75, 41:19–25; 48:5–6; 51:11–27, 56:88–94, 66:6–8, and so on) (see Figure 5.3). The Qur'an abounds

Figure 5.3 The Prophet Muhammad on His Visit to Hell Observes Demons Torturing Slanderers, Oppressors, and Sowers of Discord in the Muslim Community

Granger, NYC

in chilling descriptions of the terrors of the Judgment Day that are designed to emphasize the "immensity of the human situation"[40] in the face of God's justice, as is evident from the following passage from Q 81:1–14:

> When the sun shall be darkened, when the stars shall be thrown down, when the mountains shall be set moving, when the pregnant camels shall be neglected, when the savage beasts shall be stampeded, when the seas shall be set boiling, when the souls shall be coupled, when the buried infant shall be asked for what sin she was slain,[41] when the scrolls shall be unrolled, when heaven shall be stripped off, when Hell shall be set blazing, when Paradise shall be brought nigh, then shall a soul know what it has produced.

In this striking tableaux of horrors, the condemnation of female infanticide practiced by the pagan Arabs in their savage ignorance *jahilíyya*) goes side by side with the portrayal of she-camels neglected by their owners—an unthinkable disregard in a Bedouin society so heavily dependent on these beasts.

While the Qur'an repeatedly threatens unbelievers and idolaters with a painful chastisement, it also shows God's human servants the path to salvation. One must worship God as prescribed by the Qur'an and uphold the following essential beliefs: (1) to declare God to be one and only; (2) to recognize Muhammad as his prophet; (3) to have faith in the prophets who had preceded Muhammad and in the books that they had delivered; (4) to believe in God's angels; (5) to believe in the last day and divine predestination of all events.[42] The closest the Qur'an comes to the biblical Ten Commandments is in a passage from *sura* 17:22–39. Here the believers are enjoined not to set up other deities with God, to treat their parents kindly, to give various categories of people (kinsmen, travelers, and the needy) their due, to be thrifty, not to slay children for fear of poverty, not to commit murder, and to avoid indecency and fornication. However, unlike the Ten Commandments, it is in no sense "the pivotal or focal point of the text; nor is it portrayed in Muslim tradition as central within the context of Muhammad's career."[43]

Conclusions

Even from this cursory and incomplete review of the principal themes of the Qur'an, it is clear that it provided Muslims with only general guidelines to salvation. To be applied to concrete situations and the ever changing conditions of the life of the Muslim *umma,* the Qur'anic text had to be constantly explicated and reinterpreted. This task fell to Muslims who lived in the centuries following the Prophet's death. They started with collecting and discussing ambiguous or obscure passages of the Qur'anic text,[44] difficult words, and apparently incompatible statements found in it. By the end of the eighth century, they created a large body of Qur'an interpretation known as *tafsír*. Its major representative was al-Tabari (d. 923), a scholar whose name is already familiar to us in connection with the so-called "Satanic verses." Al-Tabari produced a massive *tafsír*,[45] titled "Collection of Explication and Interpretation of Verses of the Qur'an," that contained interpretations of the Qur'an produced by Muslim scholars over the three centuries since its first revelation. This commentary meticulously examined philological, prosodic, legal, historical, and literary aspects of the Muslim Holy Scripture. To clarify the circumstances under which each verse or *sura* of the Qur'an was revealed, al-Tabari relied heavily on the prophetic reports and the biographies (*síra*) of the Prophet. To make sense out of numerous biblical figures and events mentioned in the Qur'anic text, al-Tabari and his learned colleagues had to familiarize themselves with the scriptures and mythology of their monotheistic cousins, the Jews and the Christians. Almost simultaneously with the appearance of the aforementioned types of *tafsír*, there emerged allegorical and mystical commentaries that tended to focus on the spiritual and esoteric[46] aspects of the revelation and their resonance with the subtle life of the human spirit. This type of interpretation was practiced primarily by Muslim mystics, or Sufis. As time went on, every major movement or school of thought in Islam developed its own *tafsir* tradition. Thus, we can speak of Sunni, Shi'ite, Kharijite, Mu'tazilite, and Isma'ili *tafsir*s. Representatives of these and other intellectual and political movements and schools of thought used the Qur'anic text to justify their doctrines, ritual practices, and political actions. As we shall see, disagreements over the nature of the Qur'an (namely, whether it was "created" or "uncreated") led to the formation of several distinct theological schools that flourished in the eighth through eleventh centuries. In the end, the overwhelming majority of Muslims have accepted the Qur'an's sacred status and declared it to be "inimitable."[47] This view of the Qur'an implies that no human being or spirit is capable of producing a text of the same excellence and perfection. The Qur'an's uniqueness is, for the majority of the Muslims, the clearest and most incontrovertible evidence of its divine provenance. By virtue of its central importance for Muslim faith and practice, the Qur'an has become the foremost symbol of Islam. This being the case, any attack on its sacredness or veracity is perceived as an attack on Islam itself.

Questions to Ponder

1. How is the Qur'an different from or similar to the other scriptures you are familiar with? What, in your view, is/are its most distinctive characteristic(s)?
2. How does the Qur'an position itself in regard to the other revealed texts? How does it explain the necessity of its revelation, while at the same time acknowledging the revealed nature of the Judeo-Christian scriptures?
3. Why do you think the overwhelming majority of Muslim scholars until today continue to insist that the Qur'an cannot be adequately translated into any foreign language?

Summary

- The Qur'an is the literal word of God that confirms the veracity of the Torah and the Gospel.
- The name of the Qur'an comes from an either Aramaic or Arabic root with basically the same meaning: "recitation or reading" [of a scripture]. The structural units are chapters (*sura*s) and verses (*ayat*s). The first *sura* ("The Opening"), which is seen by Muslims as the epitome of the Qur'anic message, is widely used in Muslim devotional practice. Each of the 114 *sura*s has its name in the Muslim tradition. The Meccan and Medinan *sura*s differ in their lengths and tenors. The opening phrase of each *sura* (*basmala*: "In the name of God the Merciful, the Compassionate") is the same, *sura* 9 being the only exception.
- The Qur'an is articulated in rhyming prose (i.e., neither poetry nor prose, strictly speaking). Rhyming endings are used to achieve sonority and poetic effect. The rhetorical features of the Qur'an consist of rhetorical questions, oaths, incantations, striking pictures of the Judgment Day, and "say" passages; there are also passages that defend the Prophet against his accusers and clarify certain points of the Muslim creed.
- The letters at the beginning of some Qur'anic chapters (*sura*s) are mysterious. Their exact meaning and purpose are still unknown, although explanations and theories abound.

- The text of the Qur'an is collected and canonized. The first records are probably made by the Prophet's private secretaries, whose notes are then collected and arranged roughly in order of their length by the scholar Zayd b. Thabit (around 649–650) on the orders of the caliph 'Uthman. Alternative variants assembled by the Prophet's companions, such as 'Abdallah b. Mas'ud in Kufa (d. 653) and Ubayy b. Ka'b (d. 656) in Syria, are destroyed or declared noncanonical (apocryphal).
- The verses that are not in the Qur'an are the stoning verse, remembered by 'Umar, and the Satanic verses, which were allegedly part of *sura* 53.
- The principal themes of the Qur'an are God and his "most beautiful names" (epithets), the prophets and divine messengers (the Israeli and Christian prophets, the story of Jesus and his mother), and the Day of Judgment and the afterlife (Paradise and Hell).
- The interpretation of the Qur'an (*tafsir*) entails a diversity of exegetical approaches.

Notes

1 This is a hotly disputed issue. Some scholars argue that the text of the Qur'an was recorded at a much later stage, while others insist that it was written down and edited by the Prophet already during his lifetime; for details, see Jane McAuliffe (ed.), *The Cambridge Companion to the Qur'an*, Cambridge University Press, Cambridge, 2006, Chapters 2, 3, and 7; Andrew Rippin (ed.), *The Blackwell Companion to the Qur'an*, Blackwell, Malden, MA, 2006, Chapters 9–13.

2 Angelika Neuwirth, "Structural, Linguistic and Literary Features," in Jane McAuliffe (ed.), *The Cambridge Companion to the Qur'an*, Cambridge University Press, Cambridge, 2006, pp. 104–110; whether the *suras* were liturgies, sermons, or homilies, as argued by some investigators and denied by others, is, in the final account, not that important; see Gabriel Said Reynolds, *The Qur'an and Its Biblical Subtext*, Routledge, New York, 2010, pp. 243–244.

3 Michael Sells, *Approaching the Qur'an: The Early Revelations*, White Cloud Press, Ashland, OR, 1999, pp. 11–13.

4 Montgomery Watt and Richard Bell, *Introduction to the Qur'an*, Edinburgh University Press, Edinburgh, 1994, p. 136; cf. Kees Versteegh, *The Arabic Language*, Columbia University Press, New York, 1997, p. 55.

5 Watt and Bell, *Introduction*, pp. 121–147.

6 Ibid., p. 58.

7 Translated by Arthur J. Arberry.

8 Versteegh, *The Arabic Language*, pp. 46–52.

9 Or "articulate speech."

10 *Sura* 55 verses 1–6 in Arberry's translation.

11 See, e.g., the rhyming structure of *sura*s 2 and 3.

12 Watt and Bell, *Introduction*, p. 78.

13 Ibid., p. 76.

14 See my article "Sufism and the Qur'an," in *Encyclopedia of the Qur'an*. General Editor: Jane Dammen McAuliffe; online edition: http://referenceworks.brillonline.com.

15 For details see McAuliffe (ed.), *The Cambridge Companion* and Rippin (ed.), *The Blackwell Companion*, as well as the relevant articles in *Encyclopedia of the Qur'an*. General Editor: Jane Dammen McAuliffe, especially John Burton, "The Collection of the Qur'an" and Harald Motzki, "Mushaf."

16 His date of death is uncertain and is placed between 662 and 676; see Michael Lecker, "Zayd b. Thabit," in *Encyclopedia of Islam*, 2nd ed.; online edition: http://referenceworks.brillonline.com.

17 Burton, "The Collection" and Motzki, "Mushaf"; see also Oleg Bolshakov, *Istoriia Khalifata. I. Islam v Aravii*, Nauka, Moscow, 1989, pp. 198–199 and Bolshakov, *Istoriia Khalifata. II: Epokha velikikh zavoevanii*, Nauka, Moscow, 1993, p. 192.

18 See the preceding references and Versteegh, *The Arabic Language*, p. 55.

19 Bolshakov, *Istoriia. II*, p. 193, who relies on the fundamental study of the Qur'anic codices by Arthur Jeffery in his *Materials for the History of the Text of the Qur'an*, E. J. Brill, Leiden, 1937.

20 See the study by Arthur Jeffery quoted in the previous note.

21 Nadia Abu-Zahra, "Adultery and Fornication," in *Encyclopedia of the Qur'an*. General Editor: Jane Dammen McAuliffe; online edition: http://referenceworks.brillonline.com.

22 John Burton, "Abrogation," in *Encyclopedia of the Qur'an*. General Editor: Jane Dammen McAuliffe; online edition: http://referenceworks.brillonline.com.

23 Marshall Hodgson, *The Venture of Islam*, Chicago University Press, Chicago, 1974, vol. 1, pp. 209–211.

24 Watt and Bell, *Introduction*, pp. 55–56.

25 Shahab Ahmed, "Satanic Verses," in *Encyclopedia of the Qur'an*. General Editor: Jane Dammen McAuliffe; online edition: http://referenceworks.brillonline.com.

26 For details see Abdulrazak Gurnah (ed.), *The Cambridge Companion to Salman Rushdie*, Cambridge University Press, Cambridge, 2007.

27 Hodgson, *The Venture*, vol. 1, p. 163.

28 Ibrahim Abu-Rabi', "Ezra," in *Encyclopedia of the Qur'an*. General Editor: Jane Dammen McAuliffe; online edition: http://referenceworks.brillonline.com.

29 Q 6:100–101.

30 For comparisons between Qur'anic and Biblical prophetology, see Reynolds, *The Qur'an*, Chapter 2; for a standard Muslim perspective, see Fazlur Rahman, *Major Themes of the Qur'an*, 2nd ed., Bibliotheca Islamic, Minneapolis, MN, 1989, Chapter 8.

31 Andrew Rippin, *Muslims: Their Religious Beliefs and Practices*, Routledge, London and New York, 1990, p. 17.

32 David Marshall, "Punishment Stories," in *Encyclopedia of the Qur'an*. General Editor: Jane Dammen McAuliffe; online edition: http://referenceworks.brillonline.com.

33 Rippin, *Muslims*, p.17.

34 Q 2:87; 50:12–14.

35 Q 5:67–81.

36 Richard Bell, *The Origin of Islam in Its Christian Environment*, Cass, London, reprint, 1968, pp. 153–155.

37 Rudi Paret, *Der Koran: Kommentar und Konkordanz*, Kohlhammer, Stuttgart, 1971, p. 441.

38 Here and throughout the Qur'an, God often speaks of himself in the plural, using the so-called majestic or royal "we".

39 Q 50:19–25.

40 Hodgson, *The Venture*, vol. 1, p. 163.

41 This phrase refers to the pagan Arab practice of burying alive newly born female children "for fear of poverty"; it was prohibited by the Qur'an (17:31).

42 See, for instance, Q 2:285 and 4:136; for a more expanded version of the creed, see 2:177.

43 Rippin, *Muslims*, p. 22.

44 Mentioned in the Qur'an itself, see 3:7.

45 Jane McAuliffe, "The Tasks and Traditions of Interpretation," in idem (ed.), *The Cambridge Companion to the Qur'an*, Cambridge University Press, Cambridge, 2006, pp. 191–193 and 198.

46 Namely, accessible only to the elect few endowed with special, divinely bestowed knowledge or insight.

47 The doctrine of the Qur'an's inimitability is called *i'jaz*.

Chapter 6

The Prophetic *Hadíth* and Sunna and the Emergence of the Shari'a

Hadíth as the Muslim Gospel?

Like its monotheistic cousins, Islam is a religion of the divine revelation. For the Christians, the divine revelation is embodied in the personality of Christ, who is nothing less than the divine word made flesh. The Christian holy book, the Gospel, is based on personal reminiscences, albeit divinely inspired, of its human creators. They document the life, words, and acts of the founder of the Christian movement. The authors of these accounts are clearly identified by the Christian scripture as Mark, Luke, John, and Matthew.[1] By the fourth century of the Christian era, it had been decided which of these accounts should be included in the authentic, or canonical, scripture, while others were dismissed as noncanonical, or apocryphal.[2] In Islam, as we remember, the canonical version of the Qur'anic text was established early on the orders of the caliph 'Uthman, and its noncanonical versions were destroyed.

For the Muslims, the revelation is embodied in their holy book, the Qur'an, which is the literal word of God revealed to human beings via a messenger. The Qur'an portrays the messenger as a mere mortal who was chosen by God to serve as the transmitter of the divine commands, which he, in turn, received either directly from his Lord or through the angel Gabriel.

What the Christians find in the Gospels—accounts of the birth and life of its founder, reports about the miracles he performed, instructions for his followers, the record of his behavior to be emulated by his followers—the Muslims find outside the text of the Qur'an.[3] This source of information about the life and teachings of Islam's founder is called the "custom of the Prophet" or, in Arabic, the *sunnat al-nabi*. The *sunna*,[4] in its turn, consists of individual reports (*hadíth*) of Muhammad's followers which recount his sayings or describe his behavior throughout the twenty-two years of his prophetic career. The word *hadíth* in Arabic literally means "news" or "report." In its original sense, it is singular in Arabic but, in its technical meaning, is used as a collective plural, denoting "news about or reports from the Prophet." Although the words *sunna* and *hadíth* are often treated as synonyms and rendered into European languages as "Islamic tradition," one can differentiate between them: individual reports about the Prophet's actions and words (*hadíth*) can be seen as the building blocks of the edifice called Sunna, that is the systematized classification of the Prophet's instructions and actions rubricated according to topics.

The word *hadíth* may occasionally apply to the sayings or actions of a companion of the Prophet, especially Abu Bakr and 'Umar. However, such *hadíth* are not as numerous, nor do they enjoy the same prestige among the Sunnis as the prophetic *hadíth* that are highly esteemed and transmitted exactly as they were received from their first eyewitness and listener to their last recipient. For the Shi'ites, as we shall see, the *hadíth* attributed to 'Ali and his descendants play almost as important a role as the prophetic *hadíth*.

The Importance of *Hadíth*

Why did the prophetic *hadíth* become so important for the Muslim community already at the earliest stages of its existence? The explanation lies at least in part in the personality of the Prophet that made a great impression on his contemporaries. Not only was he the recipient of the divine word chosen by God, but he also founded a new religious community and state. As a consequence, his message won numerous followers far beyond the confines of Arabia, eventually rendering Islam a universal religion. It is only natural that those of his Arabian companions who had known the Prophet personally were eager to share their reminiscences of him with new converts and the younger generations of Muslims who could not interact with him or observe him directly. The new generations of Muslims, in their turn, were anxious to learn from the eyewitnesses what they could about the Prophet in order to imitate his actions, all the more so since Muhammad's status as the model for his followers is confirmed by the Qur'an itself: "You have a good example in the Messenger of God for whosoever hopes for God and the Last Day and remembers God often."[5] Finally, and no less importantly, the prophetic *hadíth* clarify the meaning of many general Qur'anic commandments, such as those that order the believers to give alms, pray, make ablutions before the prayer, or go on a pilgrimage, without specifying how exactly this should be done. The *hadíth* supply these vital details.

The Types of *Hadíth*

Gradually, there emerged a vast body of accounts, originally, almost exclusively oral, of "Muhammad's every act, his orders, prohibitions, recommendations, approval and disapproval." These narratives, which were soon to acquire normative status, "cover all conceivable aspects of personal, private, domestic, commercial, military, fiscal, and administrative activity undertaken during the twenty two years of Muhammad's public ministry."[6] The *hadíth* can classified according to their contents and themes as ethical or moral, prescriptive or proscriptive, instructional, exegetical, and so on. As an example of an ethical-moral *hadíth* we can cite the following: "A man who had ten children said to him [the Prophet] once: 'I have never kissed any of them.' . . . The Prophet said: 'He who does not treat others gently cannot expect to be treated gently himself, when the time comes.'"[7] This *hadíth* stipulates no sanction for a dispassionate or callous treatment of one's offspring. It simply warns that the insensitive parent should expect the same treatment from his children when the time comes.

A typical *hadíth* of prescriptive/proscriptive kind, in this case pertaining to marriage, is as follows:

> 'Uqba b. al-Harith said that he had married the daughter of Abu Ihab b. 'Aziz. Later on a woman came to him and said: "I have suckled (nursed) 'Uqba and the woman whom he married (his wife) at my breast." 'Uqba said to her: "Neither did I know that you had suckled (nursed) me nor did you tell me." He then rode to see the Messenger of God at Medina, and asked him about this matter. The Messenger said: "How can you keep her as a wife when it has been said [that she is your foster-sister]?" Then 'Uqba divorced her, and she married another man.[8]

Unlike the previous *hadíth*, this one prescribes a clear course of action for 'Uqba to take, while at the same time prohibiting all Muslims to take their foster siblings as their spouses.

A *hadíth* related from the Prophet by a son of the caliph ʻUmar provides instructions on Ramadán fasting, thereby specifying the general Qurʼanic requirement that Muslims should observe a fast during this holy month:

> I heard the Messenger of God saying: "When you see the crescent [of the month of Ramadán], start fasting, and when you see the crescent [of the month of Shawwál, which comes after Ramadan], stop fasting; and if the sky is overcast [and you can't see it], then regard the month of Ramadan as being of thirty days."[9]

This *hadíth* sets clear time limits for the fasting period during the month of Ramadán and can be classified as prescriptive in regard to a particular ritual practice.

Alongside ethical and prescriptive/proscriptive *hadíth*, we find the so-called exegetical (i.e., interpretative) ones that were uttered by the Prophet in order to clarify the meaning of Qurʼanic verses or explain events only briefly cited in the scripture. For instance, a very brief and cryptic Qurʼanic reference to the splitting of the moon in Q 54:1 is elaborated in considerable detail in a group of *hadíth* that describe the exact circumstances of this miraculous occurrence and the names of those who witnessed it. These narratives depict the Prophet as cleaving the moon in the presence of his followers to confirm his prophetic mission—a miracle granted to him by God. Without this additional information provided by these narratives, the passage in question would have been unintelligible to later generations of Muslims.[10] The same applies to many obscure or ambiguous passages in the Qurʼan. The role of exegetical *hadíth* was to supply the missing context by describing the exact historical circumstances in response to which certain verses of the Qurʼan were revealed. This being the case, such exegetical *hadíth* can also be labeled "historical," or, rather, pertaining to the sacred history of Islam. They provide a wealth of information about the events surrounding the revelation, as well as the changing fortunes of the Prophet and his community in Mecca and Medina. Some *hadíth* combine historical information with religious instruction, rendering the latter more credible and memorable. Typical in this regard is the widely quoted *hadíth* that describes the Prophet's encounter with the angel Gabriel disguised as a human being:

> [Angel] Gabriel came to the Prophet—may God bless and greet him—in the image of a man and asked: "Muhammad, what is faith (*imán*)?" He answered: "To believe in God and His angels, His books, His messengers, and His decree—be it good or bad, sweet or bitter for you." The man said: "You have spoken the truth." He [that is, the transmitter of the *hadíth*] said: "We were surprised that someone would declare the Prophet—may God bless and greet him—to be truthful, for he [the visitor] first asked him a question, [then] declared his answer to be truthful." The [strange] man then said: "Tell me, what is Islam?" The Prophet answered: "Islam is to perform your prayer(s), give alms, fast [during the month of] Ramadan, and to perform the pilgrimage to the House [of God]." The man said: "You have spoken the truth." He then said: "Tell me what does doing the beautiful (*ihsán*)[11] mean?" The Prophet answered: "To worship God as if you see Him, for even though you may not see Him, He [always] sees you."[12]

On the one hand, the *hadíth* in question describes a concrete, if miraculous episode from Muhammad's prophetic career. On the other, it teaches his followers an essential lesson about the Islamic religion (*din*), placing special emphasis on its inner dimension, namely on the necessity for the believer to always act as if he or she is being constantly watched by God. In other words, this historical *hadíth* contains an all-important moral-ethical message, while also unequivocally defining the obligations of God's servants vis-à-vis their Maker.

Another example of a historical *hadíth* is the report first recounted by the Prophet's companion Ánas b. Malik (d. 712),[13] a prolific transmitter of prophetic narratives:

> One of the Prophet's expeditions found us at the time of the prayer without water for the ritual ablution. The Prophet was brought a small dish with some water in it and ordered the troops to perform their ablutions from that dish. I could see water gushing up from under his fingers until the entire force had performed their ablution. They totaled seventy men.[14]

This *hadíth* is historical in its external form, although the time and goal of the expedition are not explicitly mentioned because they do not really matter. The true purpose of this narrative is to demonstrate the Prophet's miraculous powers, which, according to the Muslim creed, God granted him in confirmation of his divinely ordained mission.

The numerous *hadíth* that predict the events of the final days before the end of the world are classified as eschatological.[15] Here's one typical example:

> The Messenger of God said, "The Hour will not be established till the sun rises from the west, and when it rises [there] and the people see it, then all of them will believe [in God]. But that will be the time when "No good it will do to a soul to believe then, if it never believed before . . ."[16] The Hour will be established [so suddenly] that two persons spreading a garment between them will not be able to finish their bargain, nor will they be able to fold it up. The Hour will be established while a man is carrying the milk of his she-camel, but cannot drink it; and the Hour will be established when someone is not able to prepare the tank to water his livestock from it; and the Hour will be established when some of you has raised his food to his mouth but cannot eat it.[17]

One can provide many more examples of various types of prophetic *hadíth*, but those already mentioned are indicative of the breadth of subjects they cover as well as their importance for the articulation and codification of the teachings and practices of Islam.

The Transmission and Collection of *Hadíth*

By the early decades of the eighth century, *hadíth* were memorized, preserved, and handed down to upcoming generations of Muslims. The first transmitters of the prophetic reports were members of Muhammad's inner circle, such as his wife 'A'isha (d. 678), the first caliphs Abu Bakr, 'Umar, 'Uthman, 'Ali and their sons, as well as the Prophet's other companions, such as the aforementioned Ánas b. Malik (d. 712) and Abu Huráyra (d. 681), the latter a man with a prodigious memory who is said to have memorized and transmitted some 5,347 *hadíth*.[18]

As more and more *hadíth* reports were circulating within the Muslim community, learned individuals and groups in various regions of the Muslim world began to collect and classify them. This task often involved travels across the length and breadth of the Muslim Empire in search of knowledgeable bearers of these valuable narratives. The collectors were usually men and women of exemplary piety and prodigious memory, who viewed their activity as a special type of service to God or even worship. Originally the *hadíth* circulated largely in an oral form and were transmitted in face-to-face encounters between the transmitter and the collector. The process of reporting was very important, as was the process of documenting and authenticating the transmitted material. Since the *hadíth* were increasingly being used by Muslims to validate certain practices, values, and legal decisions, proving their authenticity was absolutely essential for the Muslim community. A practice, a doctrine, or a decision based on forged prophetic reports not only was faulty but also, in the long term, effectively prevented those who had adopted it from achieving salvation by causing them to stray from the true religion. What consequence could have possibly been graver than that?

The emphasis on the documentation and authentication of the material traced back to the Prophet and his close companions is evident from the division of each *hadíth* into two principal parts: *isnád* and *matn*. The *isnád* ("prop or support") was a chain of transmitters of a report from the Prophet or his companion to the last narrator. The *matn* was the main body or content of the *hadíth* that recorded what the Prophet or one of his companions had said or done. A typical *hadíth* with a complete, uninterrupted *isnád* would look like this:

> 'Ali b. Ahmad al-Ahwazi informed us: Ahmad b. 'Ubayd al-Basri informed us: Ahmad b. 'Ali al-Kharraz informed us: Usayd b. Zayd told us: Mas'ud b. Sa'd told us on the authority of al-Zayyat, on the authority of Abu Hurayra, on the authority of 'A'isha—may God be pleased with her—who recounted the following words of the Messenger of God—may God bless and greet him: "Patience is to be exercised at the first shock."[19]

As we can see, in this *hadíth* the content, or *matn*, is much shorter than the *isnád*. Thus, one can say that the role of *isnád* was to certify the accuracy of the transmission of a *hadíth* from the first listener to the last reporter.

Amidst concerns about the authenticity of the prophetic tradition, the screening of the personal background of the individuals engaged in the transmission of the *hadíth* became an important scholarly activity under the rubric of the "science of the *hadíth*." This screening and validating procedure focused on the personalities of the transmitters, especially their integrity, piety, and the strength or weakness of their memories. As time went on, the doyens of the science of *hadíth* began to classify transmitters according to the following categories—"trustworthy," "truthful," and "weak." Correspondingly, the *hadíth* they transmitted were categorized as "sound" (*sahíh*), "fair" (*hásan*), and "weak" (*da'íf*).[20] Some weak *hadíth* might occasionally have been used in preaching, but they were generally considered unsuitable as bases for legal decisions and rulings. To a special category belonged the so-called fabricated *hadíth*. As blatant forgeries, they were totally unsuitable as guidance for the faithful and were to be suppressed or ignored. Experts on the science of *hadíth* considered it their duty to carefully examine the circumstances under which a given *hadíth* was transmitted, in particular whether or not the individuals mentioned in the *isnád* lived in the same epoch and locality and thus could actually have met one another.

The Writing Down of *Hadíth* and the Elevation of the Status of the Prophet's Sunna

At the outset, the companions of the Prophet were reportedly opposed to the writing down of the *hadíth* out of fear that, once recorded, they might somehow get confused with the text of the Qur'an. To justify their reluctance to record the *hadíth*, they quoted the Prophet as commanding them not to write down anything from him except the Qur'an. In other words, they used a prophetic *hadíth* to disallow the recording of the *hadíth*. However, after the written text of the Qur'an had been collected and canonized under the caliph 'Uthman around 650, this concern was no longer relevant, and the recording of *hadíth* became widespread. By the end of the first Islamic century (720), individual descendants of the Prophet's companions began to collect their fathers' and mothers' reports about the actions and sayings of the Prophet and commit them to writing in the so-called scrolls, or folios (*súhuf*). Some of these earliest collections were arranged around such topics as ritual purity, prayer, pilgrimage, almsgiving, sacrifices, commentary on Qur'anic verses (exegesis), eschatology, commercial transactions and contracts, gifts and bequests, treatment of slaves, capital crimes, family matters (marriage, divorce, support of dependents), division of property and inheritance, good manners, and so on. These topical or thematic collections came to be known as *musánnaf*.[21] An alternative type of these early collections was called *músnad*.[22] Here *hadíth* reports were organized according to the names of their first transmitters, for instance, Abu Huráyra, 'A'isha, Ánas b. Malik, and so on. To find a needed *hadíth* in such a compilation, one had to remember the name of the person who first put it into circulation, which was far beyond the capacity of the overwhelming majority of the believers, including religious professionals. This type of *hadíth* collection, being far less user-friendly, was gradually abandoned in favor of the topically arranged one.

As time went on, the authority of *hadíth* grew steadily due in large part to the efforts of their collectors and memorizers, known collectively as "*hadíth* folk" (*ahl al-hadíth*).[23] It is in their midst that there developed the notion that the *hadíth* and the custom (*sunna*) of the Prophet, which the *hadíth* documented, constituted a source of Islamic doctrine, practice, and legal theory second only to the Qur'an itself (see Figure 6.1). The *hadíth* folk supported their position by references to the Qur'anic verses that portray the Prophet as the infallible legislator for his followers, for example, "Whatsoever the Messenger gives you, accept; whatsoever he forbids you, refrain from."[24] Similar statements about the special status of *hadíth* can be found in *hadíth* themselves. One of them quotes Muhammad as saying: "I have been granted the Book and along with it its equal." The "equal" mentioned here was interpreted as a reference to the Prophet's Sunna.[25] Such an interpretation effectively put the Sunna almost on the same footing with the Qur'an.

In the early ninth century, this nascent idea was brought to fruition by an influential legal scholar and founder of a major juridical school in Sunni Islam named Muhammad al-Shafi'i

Figure 6.1 An Illuminated Manuscript of a Canonical *Hadíth* Collection (Ottoman period, ca. 1500)

(d. 820). He argued that when the Qur'an spoke of the "book and the wisdom" (2:151 and 3:164), it meant the Qur'an and the Sunna of the Prophet. Thus the Sunna as a whole and by implication its individual "building bricks," the *hadíth*, acquired the status of Islam's second revelation. Though not the eternal and sacred word of God, the *hadíth* and the Sunna contain divine guidance as expressed in the words and acts of Islam's founder, whom his followers considered to be infallible. Whatever he said or did was now perceived as a direct product of divine inspiration. Seen from this perspective, the Sunna can rightfully be considered the second source of Islamic faith.

The Six Sunni *Hadíth* Collections

The six collections of the *hadíth* (*al-kútub al-sitta*) have eventually acquired canonical status in Sunni Islam. The two most authoritative of them are called *sahíh* ("authentic" or "sound"). They were compiled by al-Bukhári (d. 870) and Muslim (d. 875),[26] both of whom hailed from the eastern lands of the caliphate: the former from Bukhara in Central Asia and the latter from Khurasán in present-day eastern Iran. Both authors traveled widely in search of *hadíth*, of which al-Bukhári is said to have amassed a stupendous 600,000 and Muslim half that number. Out of this vast sea of narrative material, al-Bukhári selected 9,082, which he considered to be authentic. Muslim's collection contained around 10,000 authentic *hadíth*. If we discount repetitions, which are quite numerous in both collections, the number of individual, nonrepetitive *hadíth* in the *Sahíh*s is 2,762 (al-Bukhári) and a little over 3,000 (Muslim). In al-Bukhári's collection, the *hadíth* are divided into ninety-seven books with three thousand four hundred fifty chapters.[27] Muslim's *Sahíh* contains forty-three books with further subdivisions. The *Sahíh*s cover an astounding range of topics—theological doctrine, eschatology, legal rulings, moral and ethical norms, eating and drinking etiquette, dress codes, dietary restrictions, Qur'anic commentary, the history of the first Muslim community and biography of the Prophet, rules of travel, the merits and virtues of the Prophet and his companions, ritual requirements (prayer, pilgrimage, fasting), almsgiving, contract law, warfare, crimes and punishments, and so on. Although later authorities were able to identify some flawed or suspicious *hadíth* in both collections, they have retained their canonical status up to this day. While in most areas of the Muslim world where Sunnism is predominant, al-Bukhári's collection is given pride of place, in North Africa Muslim's *Sahíh* has been preferred by local Muslims due, in part, to its superior organization.[28]

The other four standard collections are known as "[exemplary] customs or codes [of behavior]" (*súnan*; pl. of *sunna*). Most of them were also compiled by Muslim scholars hailing from the territories of present-day Iran. The *Súnan* of Abu Dawúd al-Sijistáni (d. 889), al-Nasá'i (d. 915), and al-Tírmidhi (d. 892) contain 4,800, 5,000, and 3,956 *hadíth* respectively. The last collection, that of Ibn Mája (d. 887), contains some 4,000 *hadíth*. It was not recognized as canonical until the twelfth century, although in North Africa its authority is not accepted even today. The *Súnan* have catered primarily to the needs of Muslim jurists. They include a disproportionate number of legal *hadíth* concerning the division of property, marriage and divorce, dowry, contracts and mercantile transactions, crimes and punishments, and so on. Some of them, for instance, the collection of al-Nasa'i, omit *hadíth* dealing with Qur'an commentary, eschatology, and the virtues of the Prophet and his companions, focusing instead on legal or juridical reports. The six Sunni canonical collections of *hadíth* are often reverently called "The Six Mothers" to emphasize their importance for Muslim creed and practice.

The Shi'ite *Hadíth*

The great importance of the *hadíth* as a foundation—along with the Qur'an—of Islamic faith and practice is recognized by Sunnis and Shi'ites alike. Whereas the Sunni scholars were busy collecting countless sayings of the Prophet, screening them for authenticity, and arranging them according to their contents, their Shi'ite counterparts focused on the prophetic traditions transmitted by 'Ali and his descendants. Although the contents of Shi'ite and Sunni *hadíth* are often the same or similar (they were uttered by the Prophet), the Shi'ite belief in the primacy and special status of 'Ali and his descendants caused the learned men of the Shi'ite community to collect almost exclusively the prophetic lore transmitted by the members of 'Ali's family. Whereas the Sunnis took stock in the *hadíth* transmitted by the first three caliphs and companions of the Prophet, the Shi'ites rejected them out of hand because, in their view, the three caliphs and those who accepted their authority were sinners, as they failed to recognize 'Ali as the only legitimate successor to the Prophet and usurped his right to lead the community. As a result, the Shi'ite collections feature exclusively the *hadíth* approved and reported by 'Ali and his descendants, the *imam*s. In addition, the sayings and teachings of the *imam*s themselves were included in the Shi'ite variant of the Sunna because they, like the Prophet and 'Ali, were considered by the Shi'ites to be divinely inspired and protected from any error (at least in matters of religion). Shi'ite collections contain chapters of the *hadíth* that emphasize the special, divinely ordained status of the members of the Prophet's family and their right to lead and guide the community of the faithful to the exclusion of other pretenders.

The Shi'ite collections of *hadíth* appeared somewhat later than their Sunnite counterparts, in the tenth century, and may have been a response to them. The first such collection was composed by an Iranian scholar named al-Kulayni (d. 941) under the title *al-Káfi* ("That Which Is Sufficient [in the Knowledge of Religion]"). It was divided into the following sections: the "roots" (theology, prophesy, the right to and requirements for the leader of the Muslim community, and prayers); the "branches" (legal issues and jurisprudence); and the "garden," which contained the didactic and edifying lore. In all, *al-Káfi* comprised 16,199 *hadíth*, which Shi'ites prefer to call "news" (Arabic *khábar*; pl. *akhbár*) in order to differentiate them from the Sunni traditions. The *akhbár* were arranged according to such topics as the creeds, belief and unbelief, ritual purity, burial, prayer, alms tax, fasting, pilgrimage, warfare, legal earnings and marriage, slavery, divorce, and so on.[29] The other Shi'ite collections were produced by Ibn Babawayh (d. 991) and al-Tusi (d. 1067), whose massive *Tahdhíb al-ahkám* ("The Refinement of Legal Rulings") contained 13,590 reports. These three collections, along with al-Tusi's smaller book containing 5,551 *hadíth*, constitute the foundation of the Shi'ite theology, exegesis, belief, ritual practice, ethics, and legal theory.

Among the authorities cited in these four books, the most prominent are the fifth and the sixth Shi'ite *imam*s, Muhammad al-Báqir (d. 735) and Ja'far al-Sádiq (d. 765). Shi'ite *hadíth* experts employed a more-or-less similar system of evaluating reports: the "sound" (*sahíh*) *hadíth*, namely one that can be traced back to 'Ali or the *imam*s; the "authenticated" (*muwáththaq*) *hadíth* reported by a companion of an *imam*, whose trustworthiness was beyond suspicion; the "fair" (*hásan*) *hadíth*, that is, one reported by a transmitter whose integrity was not uniformly recognized but whose authority was enough to use his report as a basis of legal ruling; the "weak" (*da'if*) *hadíth*, namely, one that did not meet any of these criteria. Accordingly, their transmitters were labeled as "reliable," "weak," and "exaggerating."[30] This last category included those who supported the rights of 'Ali and his descendants in principle but who had somehow deviated from the doctrine of the Twelver Shi'ites, which by the tenth century had come to represent the views of the majority of those who supported the rights of 'Ali's family to be the leaders of the *umma*.

An example of a Shi'ite report transmitted on the authority of 'Ali is the following: "Humankind has turned to three types [of leaders]: the scholar,[31] the one who learns [from him], and the trash. We [the family of the Prophet] are the scholars, our party[32] are those who learn [from us], and the rest of humankind who are but trash."[33]

This *hadíth* articulates clearly and unambiguously the central Shi'ite belief that the community of the followers of 'Ali is the only one destined to be saved; its salvation will occur through the sacred knowledge vested in the 'Alid *imam*s. We shall revisit this idea in the following chapters. The identity of the leaders who possess this salutary knowledge is specified in the following Shi'ite *hadíth*, recounted by a companion of the Prophet who was friendly to 'Ali:

> I came to Fátima[34]: I [saw] before her a tablet with the names of the best of her offspring. I counted twelve of them, the last of whom was the Riser (*al-qa'im*).[35] Three of them [bore the name] Muhammad and three of them [bore the name] 'Ali.[36]

An example of a moral-ethical Shi'ite *hadíth* recommends how the family of a deceased person should treat their neighbors. It was transmitted on the authority of the sixth Shi'ite *imam*, Ja'far al-Sádiq, who, we have mentioned, was a major source of Shi'ite learning: "It is required that the neighbors of the person who was afflicted [by the death of a relative] be fed by him for three days."

Sacred or Holy *Hadíth* (*Hadíth Qúdsi*)

In addition to the prophetic *hadíth*, in which the Prophet is the speaker or, more rarely, the *hadíth* attributed to one of his close companions, we find a special class of *hadíth* that quote the words of God communicated to the Prophet by means of inspiration or a dream. They are called "sacred" or "holy" (*qúdsi*). Although such *hadíth* quote God speaking in the first person singular or plural, they do not enjoy the same status as the Qur'an, which was revealed to the Prophet *verbatim* either directly or through the angel Gabriel, is inimitable, and must be used by the Muslims in their five canonical prayers. According to Muslim scholars, unlike the Qur'an, *hadíth qúdsi* do not convey God's exact words but rather their general meaning. Therefore, they cannot be used in the canonical prayers, and the belief in their veracity does not constitute an article of Muslim faith.[37]

When one quotes the Qur'an, one says: "God Most High said this or that." When one quotes a sacred/holy *hadíth*, one says: "The Messenger of God related from Him this or that." Sacred/holy *hadíth* are scattered throughout the canonical as well as noncanonical *hadíth* collections. They were occasionally assembled by scholars under one cover. Naturally, their number is by far smaller than that of prophetic *hadíth*. The most comprehensive collection of *hadíth qúdsi* compiled in the fifteenth century contains 858 such traditions.[38] Other collections are much shorter and usually list around one hundred *hadíth qúdsi*. This type of *hadíth* was and still is particularly popular with Muslim mystics (Sufis), who were fascinated by the possibility of receiving similar communications from God in a flash of inspiration or in a dream.

One *hadíth qúdsi* often quoted in mystical treatises has God say: "I was a hidden treasure and I longed to be known, so I created humans and spirits (*jinn*), so that they would know me."[39] In the mind of Muslim mystics, this divine saying furnishes clear evidence that God can and should be known by his human servants—contrary to the position of mainstream Islamic theology that emphasized God's absolute transcendence and the resultant inability of his human servants to comprehend him or relate to him personally. Another famous *hadíth qúdsi* portrays God as descending each night to the "nearest heaven" and saying: "Who entreats Me, that I may answer him? Who asks [something] of Me, that I may give [it to] him? Who asks my forgiveness, that I may forgive?"[40] This *hadíth* accentuates God's compassion and loving kindness toward his creatures—an idea that both Muslim mystics and ordinary Muslims hold dear. Some divine sayings cited by *hadíth qúdsi* bear close resemblance to passages from the Judeo-Christian scriptures. As an example, one can cite a *hadíth qúdsi* that quotes God as complaining: "O son of Adam, I was hungry, but you did not feed Me; I was thirsty, but you did not give Me a drink; I was ill, but you did not visit Me."[41] Naturally, in the Islamic context where God's incarnation is ruled out, this statement should be understood allegorically, as an allusion to God's always being with the hungry, thirsty, or sick of his servants.

The Emergence of the Shari'a Law

The period between the death of the Prophet and the beginning of the ninth century witnessed the emergence and codification of the two principal sources of Islamic faith, practice, and law: the Qur'an and the Sunna of the Prophet. It is on these two foundations that the Muslim scholars of the period constructed what came to be known as the "divine path" or the *shari'a*. In Western literature, this word is often translated as "law," which is acceptable in principle but can occasionally be misleading since the Shari'a contains norms and precepts that normally fall outside Western legal systems. Whereas in the subsequent narrative the Shari'a is sometimes translated as "Islamic law," this peculiarity should be always kept in mind by the reader. In a nutshell, the scope of the Shari'a is much broader than that of any Western legal code. The Shari'a is the divinely revealed path to salvation that has governed the life of the Muslim communities world-wide up to modern times, at which point it was relegated to a secondary position or totally replaced by secular laws patterned on Western legal codes. However, in some Muslim countries, the precepts of the Shari'a are still being applied in matters pertaining to family and personal law.

As with the Jewish Halakhá, the scope of the Shari'a is much broader than that of Western secular law. It is deemed to serve as the comprehensive guide for the faithful to a pious and religiously correct life and therefore contains moral and ethical precepts, rules pertaining to the conduct of war, devotional rituals, and personal hygiene and daily life. All this runs alongside the norms and regulations that secular-minded Westerners commonly regard as being part of the legal sphere proper (e.g., commercial and contract laws, criminal justice). The precepts of the Shari'a are divided into two large domains: acts of worship (*'ibadát*) and interactions (*mu'amalat*), that is, various types of intercourse among the members of a Muslim society. The former category comprises the rules of worship of God (e.g., prayer, ablutions, fasting, pilgrimage, and so on), whereas the latter deal with the issues that Muslims encounter in their everyday lives, such as marriage, divorce, inheritance, child support, trade, gifts and bequests, commerce, criminal justice, and so on. Any practice that is not explicitly or implicitly sanctioned by the Qur'an or a sound *hadíth* traced back to the Prophet is looked upon with suspicion or can even be dismissed by the learned elite of a Muslim community as a blameworthy innovation, or *bid'a*.

In many respects—and this is implicitly acknowledged by many Muslim jurists—the Shari'a is a human product.[42] It is a sum total of juridical and moral-ethical wisdom accumulated by the brightest lights of the Muslim community since its inception up to the present time. The expertise that allows believers to interpret the Qur'an and the Sunna and to derive practical conclusions from the sometimes contradictory statements found in these sources has come to be known as *fiqh* ("knowledge" or "expertise"). The scholars who are qualified to interpret and apply the divine law to concrete cases are called *fuqahá'*, that is, practitioners of *fiqh*. It is from among these individuals that Muslim rulers have chosen and appointed judges, or *qadis*. While scholars of law may agree on the basic principles of deriving practical norms and judgements from the body of sacred texts and legal precedents established by the first successors to the Prophet, they occasionally disagree on certain relatively minor issues related to acts of worship and quotidian interactions among the Muslims.

By the late ninth and early tenth centuries, such disagreements led to the emergence of four legal schools of Sunni Islam that still bear the names of their founders: the Maliki (after Málik b. Ánas; d. 795), the Hanafi (after Abu Hanífa; d. 767), the Shafi'i (after Muhammad al-Shafi'i, d. 820), and the Hanbali (after Ibn Hanbal, d. 855). The two other medieval Sunni schools of law, the Awza'i (after 'Abd al-Rahman al-Awza'i; d. 774) and the Zahiri (after Dawud al-Zahiri; d. 883) gradually disappeared or became integrated into the other four.[43] The Twelver Shi'ites, as we shall see, developed their own Ja'fari school of *fiqh* (after the sixth Shi'ite *imam* Ja'far al-Sádiq; d. 765). These developments will be discussed in greater detail in the chapters that follow.

Questions to Ponder

1   What factors drove Muslim scholars to collect and transmit the *hadíth*? Why was this practice seen by many Muslims as a meritorious deed or even a religious obligation?
2   Discuss the complex relationship between the *hadíth* reports and the Prophet's Sunna, bearing in mind that in some contexts they may be used as synonyms, whereas in others they may refer to different concepts.
3   How and by whom can the authenticity of *hadíth* be established? Were the methods of verification adopted by *hadíth* specialists effective? What would, in your opinion, be an alternative way to ascertain the narrative material attributed to the Prophet?
4   How are the Shiʻite *hadíth* different from or similar to their Sunni counterparts? Explain the doctrinal foundations of the differences.

Summary

- *Hadíth* consist of "reports" or "news" from and about the Prophet.
- Because the prophetic *hadíth* depict the founder of Islam at various stages of his life and mission, they might be seen as the Muslim equivalent of the Christian Gospels.
- *Hadíth* are normative in character. The Qurʼan (33:21) assures the faithful: "You have a good example in the Messenger of God for whosoever hopes for God and the Last Day and remembers God often." This and similar Qurʼanic statements have determined the importance of *hadíth* for Muslim faith and practice.
- The *hadíth* cover all aspects of Muhammad's ministry, from the personal and domestic to commercial, military, and administrative. *Hadíth* are classified according to their contents: ethical-moral, prescriptive or proscriptive, instructional, exegetical, eschatological, historical, and so on.
- Among the earliest collectors and transmitters of the *hadíth* are ʻAʼisha, the four rightly guided caliphs, Abu Huráyra, Ánas b. Malik.
- The two principal elements of a *hadíth* report are the "body" (*matn*) and the "support" (*isnád*).
- As *hadíth* science and *hadíth* specialists (*ahl al-hadíth*) emerge, the criteria for establishing the authenticity of a *hadíth* are established, with a focus on the *isnád*.
- An individual *hadíth* is related to the custom of the Prophet (*sunna*) that it describes. The *hadíth* become the so-called building blocks of the Sunna.
- The status of the *hadíth* and Sunna become progressively elevated until they become almost equal to the Qurʼan itself and a major source of Muslim juridical theory and practice, as well as being guidelines for Muslim life as a whole.
- Of the classical Sunni collections of *hadíth* ("The Six Mothers"), the most important are the two *sahíh* ("authentic" or "sound") ones by al-Bukhári (d. 870) and Muslim (d. 875).
- The Shiʻite *hadíth* collections differ from their Sunni counterparts, as exemplified by Al-Kulayni (d. 941) in his "That Which Is Sufficient" (*al-Káfi*). The teachings of the Shiʻite *imam*s are of central importance for the formation of a distinctive Shiʻite theology, normal-ethical praxis, and legal theory.
- The scope and uses of the "sacred or "holy" *hadíth*, as quotations of God's direct speech by the Prophet, weigh heavily in the Muslim tradition.

- The *hadīth* are the all-important foundation of the Islamic law (*al-sharí'a*). In premodern Islamic societies, they serve as the comprehensive guide to a pious and religiously correct life. The Shari'a is the repository of moral and ethical precepts, as well as of rules pertaining to practical matters of daily life, the conduct of war, devotional rituals, and personal hygiene, in addition to issues that secular-minded Westerners commonly regard as being part of the legal sphere proper (e.g., commercial and contractual laws, criminal justice).

Notes

1 John Burton, *An Introduction to the Hadith*, Edinburgh University Press, Edinburgh, 1994, p. 17.

2 Ibid.

3 Ibid.

4 From this point on we shall spell the word *sunna* with the capital "S" to underline its foundational status for Islam (alongside the Qur'an); another common spelling in Western literature is "Sunnah."

5 Q 33:21.

6 Burton, *An Introduction to the Hadith*, p. 19.

7 Ibid., p. 100.

8 http://theonlyquran.com/hadith/Sahih-Bukhari/?chapter=3&hadith=76&pagesize=20; *hadith* # 88. I have slightly modified the translation.

9 http://theonlyquran.com/hadith/Sahih-Bukhari/?volume=3&chapter=31&hadith=124; I have slightly modified the translation.

10 For the *hadīth* describing the miracle of the splitting of the moon see, e.g., http://theonlyquran.com/hadith/Sahih-Muslim/?volume=39&chapter=8.

11 This word is also translated into English as "doing something good" or "perfecting something."

12 For a full version of the *hadīth* and its analysis, see Sachiko Murata and William Chittick, *The Vision of Islam*, Paragon House, New York, 1994, pp. xxv–xxviii.

13 On his role in the transmission of *hadīth*, see G. H. A. Juynboll, "Anas b. Malik," in *Encyclopedia of Islam*, 3rd ed.; online edition: http://referenceworks.brillonline.com.

14 Burton, *An Introduction to the Hadith*, p. 98.

15 That is, pertaining to the knowledge and signs of the end of time and the world.

16 Q 6:158.

17 http://theonlyquran.com/hadith/Sahih-Bukhari/?volume=8&chapter=76&hadith=513. I have slightly modified the original translation.

18 Frederick Denny, *An Introduction to Islam*, 3rd ed., Pearson and Prentice Hall, Upper Saddle River, NJ, 2006, p. 152.

19 Quoted in Alexander Knysh (trans.), *Al-Qushayri's Epistle on Sufism*, Garnet Publishing, Reading, 2007, p. 197.

20 James Robson, "Hadith," in *Encyclopedia of Islam*, 2nd ed.; online edition: http://referenceworks.brillonline.com.

21 Lit. "collected" or "arranged."

22 Lit. "supported" or "propped."

23 On their disagreement with the supporters of "sound" or "considered" reasoning (*ahl al-ra'y*) see Peter Hennigan, "Ahl al-ra'y," in *Encyclopedia of Islam*, 3rd ed.; online edition: http://referenceworks.brillonline.com.

24 Q 59:7.

25 Burton, *An Introduction to the Hadith*, p. 115.

26 His full name is Muslim b. al-Hajjáj.

27 James Robson, "al-Bukhari," in *Encyclopedia of Islam*, 2nd ed.; online edition: http://referenceworks.brillonline.com.

28 G.H.A. Juynboll, "Muslim b. al-Hadjdjadj," in *Encyclopedia of Islam*, 2nd ed.; online edition: http://referenceworks.brillonline.com.

29 Heinz Halm, *Shiism*, Edinburgh University Press, Edinburgh, 1991, pp. 42–43.

30 Ibid., p. 43.

31 This word in Arabic means "possessor of knowledge" (*'álim*); the knowledge implied here is the sacred knowledge (*'ilm*) that God has bestowed on the Prophet and his offspring.

32 *Shi'a*, that is, the Shi'ites, literally "the party of 'Ali."

33 al-Kulayni (al-Kulini), *Al-Kafi fi 'ilm al-din*, 7 vols., Maṭba'at al-Ḥaydarī, Tehran, 1955-1961, vol. 1, p. 34.

34 Daughter of the prophet Muhammad by his marriage to Khadíja and a wife of 'Ali. Fátima enjoyed a special place in Shi'ite piety due to her being the mother of two of the *imam*s, al-Hásan and al-Husayn.

35 A name for the Shi'ite messiah who is usually identified with the hidden (twelfth) *imam*.

36 Al-Kulayni, *Usul*, vol. 1, p. 532.

37 James Robson, "Hadith kudsi," in *Encyclopedia of Islam*, 2nd ed.; online edition: http://referenceworks.brillonline.com.

38 Ibid.

39 Many Muslim scholars consider it to be a forgery; see William Chittick, *The Sufi Path of Knowledge*, SUNY Press, Albany, NY, 1989, pp. 66 and 391, note 14.

40 William Graham, *Divine Word and Prophetic Word in Early Islam*, Mouton, The Hague, 1977, Saying 53.

41 Chittick, *The Sufi Path of Knowledge*, pp. 72 and 392; compare Gospel of Matthew, 25:41–45.

42 See, e.g., Norman Calder, "Shari'a," in *Encyclopedia of Islam*, 2nd ed.; online edition: http://referenceworks.brillonline.com.

43 For details see Wael Hallaq, *A History of Islamic Legal Theories*, Cambridge University Press, Cambridge, 1997; Wael Hallaq, *Shari'a: Theory, Practice, Transformations*, Cambridge University Press, Cambridge, 2009; and Christopher Melchert, *The Formation of the Sunni Schools of Law, 9th–10th Centuries C.E.*, E. J. Brill, Leiden, 1997.

Chapter 7

The Problem of the Just Ruler and the First Divisions Within the Community

Opposition to the Umayyads

In trying to make sense of the events of the first and second *fitna* wars, some historians emphasize the role played by social and economic factors in setting in motion and sustaining movements against the rule of the Umayyad clan of the Quraysh. They argue, for example, that opposition to 'Uthman's policies and methods of rule was motivated primarily by economic inequities that had developed in the early Muslim state at the time of the conquests. If we accept this point of view, then we should admit that the opponents of 'Uthman were motivated by resentment toward his policy of distributing the best agricultural lands among his relatives or cronies, while prohibiting the rest of the Muslims from purchasing any land at all.[1] The underlying reasons for this opposition can be described as economic or materialistic. However, it was couched in a religious idiom, because 'Uthman's critics presented his behavior as a deliberate departure from the precedents established by the Prophet and the first and second caliphs. Seen from this vantage point, 'Uthman's actions constituted a grave sin, which effectively deprived him of the right to lead the Muslim community to salvation. How could the leader of the Muslims be a man guilty of a grave sin? In a similar way, 'Uthman's propensity to award the most important and lucrative posts (e.g., governorships) to the men of his own clan[2] was also seen by his critics as a transgression against the Qur'anic injunction that the most worthy members of the community were its most pious.[3] These and other grievances, couched in religious rhetoric, were frequently invoked by later Muslim historians to explain the third caliph's tragic downfall.[4]

In addition to invoking the socioeconomic aspects of the popular discontent with 'Uthman's rule, Western historians of Islam have also mentioned the dramatic and rapid changes in the life of the Arab tribes following the conquest of the new lands and settlement in the garrison towns of Iraq, Syria, and Egypt. The formerly independent nomads suddenly found themselves the subjects of a powerful, wealthy, and increasingly intrusive state. Ruled by a small, clan-based elite, this state demanded of them a new form of loyalty and, even more importantly, strict obedience to the rulers' edicts. The freedom-loving men and women of the desert were now governed by a mighty centralized bureaucracy that rested on the military might of the caliphal state and that brooked no dissent. Many Arabs and their clients, the *mawáli*,[5] felt that they were caught up in the workings of a vast and relentless administrative machine from which there was no escape. Poetry from that era evinces a strong feeling of nostalgia for the good old days of tribal freedom and democracy, when things were simple, and decisions were made by the entire tribe or at least by its free male members. Under 'Uthman and, later on, the Umayyads, the innocence of that free life in the desert and oases was lost forever. Several clans of the Quraysh now lorded it over the rest of the Arabs, including the Prophet's "helpers" from Medina. This situation was fraught with conflict. It was not long in erupting into a full-fledged civil war that resulted in the fragmentation of the Muslim community into three warring factions: the supporters of the Umayyads, the pro-'Alid party, and the Kharijites. This, in a nutshell, is the most common explanation of these dramatic events in Western academic literature. In the words of a Western scholar: "Almost all Muslims of the Umayyad period regretted the loss of the old ways, and almost all were looking for a solution to the problem of how tyranny could be avoided."[6]

The Rise of the Mawáli

Another source of opposition to Umayyad rule was the growing tensions between the Arab-dominated state and the new non-Arab converts to Islam. The latter constituted a class of their own called *mawáli* (sing. *máwla*), which can be rendered into English as "clients" or "dependents." This name reflected the pre-Islamic custom of the "adoption" of an unrelated individual by an Arab tribe. This practice persisted after the religious revolution in Arabia, only now the "clients" were predominantly non-Arab converts to Islam. Without this symbolic adoption, non-Arab Muslims had practically no rights. The *mawáli* could be speakers of Persian, Turkic, Berber, Coptic, or Aramaic. Although they took an active part in the Muslim conquests, suffering substantial losses and deprivations in the process, learned Arabic and the Qur'an, and maintained high standards of Islamic piety, they were still considered by the Arab ruling elite to be second-class citizens of the Muslim community. As such, they were subject to additional taxation and humiliation to the extent that some Arabs considered them to be "the most miserable persons ever to walk on earth." On the practical level, they were regarded by the Arab Muslims as unsuitable for positions of authority such as those of provincial governors, judges, or prayer leaders. Naturally, the discontented *mawáli*, who now resided alongside Arab tribes-in-arms in the garrison cities of Iraq, Syria, and Egypt, turned out to be a fertile recruitment material for various antigovernment movements, whose leaders promised them equality with the Arabs. The resentment of Arab domination among the *mawáli* masses became a major cause of the 'Abbásid revolution, as we shall find out in the next chapter.

While the majority of the opponents of Umayyad rule felt that the Umayyad caliphs were nothing but unjust and illegitimate usurpers,[7] they, for their part, could not agree on a single candidate to replace them. In the Prophet's time, things were straightforward: He was the one who was vested by God with the exclusive authority to lead the community in war and peace; he was the undisputed leader of all faithful, their *imam*, a word that in Arabic denoted "the person who stands in front," either as the prayer leader of a religious congregation or as the ruler of a state. With time, the Muslim community generated several notions of legitimate leadership (or imamate). The first divisions within the Muslim community were occasioned by the disagreement over who can be considered the rightful leader (*imam*) of the Muslims (see Table 7.1).

The Kharijites

The most implacable opponents of the Umayyad regime, the Kharijites ("rebels" or "seceders"),[8] maintained that the community was to be led by its most pious and upright member. To substantiate this idea, the Kharijites quoted the Qur'anic verse describing the most pious member of the community as being the noblest and worthiest "in the sight of God" (49:13). For the Kharijites, only such a religiously impeccable individual had the exclusive right to lead his followers to salvation. The practical implications of this doctrine were rather drastic: It was up to each believer to identify the most pious individual around, to pledge allegiance to him, and to join others who acknowledged that individual's status as the legitimate leader of the newly formed congregation.[9] The next step was for the pious followers of the "most pious" leader to separate themselves from the majority of self-styled Muslims who had irresponsibly accepted an unworthy man as their *imam*. The Kharijites agreed with many supporters of 'Ali that it was right to kill this unworthy

Table 7.1 Parties and Schools of Thought in Islam

Parties and Schools of Thought in Islam

ISLAM

The Problem of Power and Leadership (*imama, khilafa*)

The Problem of Faith (*din and Iman*)

The Problem of Human Free Will vs. Divine Predestination (*al-qadar*)

The Problem of the Divine Essence (*al-dhat*) and the **Divine Attributes** (*sifat*)

The Problem of Legal Theory (*fiqh*)

Seventh Century

- Kharijis
- Sunnis
- Shi'is
- Kharijis
- Jabris
- Qadaris

Eight Century

- Murji'is ("postponers")
- Sunnis
- Mu'tazilis
- Murji'is ("postponers")
- Jahmis
- Mu'tazilis
- Mu'tazilis ("negators")
- Jahmis
- Mushabbihis ("anthropo-morphists")
- Awza'is

Ninth Century

- Hanbalis
- Hanbalis
- Zahiris
- Karramis
- Sifatis ("atttributionists")
- Hanbalis
- Hanafis
- Shafi'is
- Malikis

Tenth Century

- Ash'aris
- Ash'aris
- Zahiris
- Zaydis
- Isma'ilis
- Ja'faris

Eleventh Century

Courtesy of Alexander Knysh

ruler (read the Umayyad caliph), especially if he actively resisted his deposition by the faithful.[10] Fighting the illegitimate ruler was, in fact, the ultimate expression of obedience to God. Unlike the 'Ali's party (*shi'at 'Ali*), which had elevated him to an almost superhuman position, the Kharijites considered 'Ali to be an erring sinner since he had submitted to human arbitration during his encounter with Mu'awiya at Siffin, whereas it was up to God and God alone to determine the outcome of the struggle.

For the Kharijites, any Muslim leader, be it Mu'awiya, 'Ali, or anyone else who had shown himself to be a sinner by making wrong decisions and failing to meet the criteria of Islamic justice as they understood it, was unworthy of rule over other Muslims. Those Muslims who had submitted themselves to his unjust and illegitimate rule effectively placed themselves outside the pale of true Islam. As apostates, they deserved capital punishment or, at the very least, excommunication. The Kharijites believed that the sinful rulers of the Muslim state (i.e., the Umayyads) had forfeited their status as Muslims and lingered in the state of grave sin, which had effectively rendered them unbelievers.[11]

This stringent concept of membership in the community of the righteous was rejected by the majority of Muslims who believed that a Muslim in the state of grave sin was still a Muslim, albeit an impure and erring one. This kind of leniency was not good enough for the radical wing of the Kharijite movement. Based in Iraq, Iran, and Arabia, the radicals claimed that their own small war bands were the only islands of true Islam in the sea of unbelief. The world outside their camp was declared to be the abode of war and infidelity.[12] Its inhabitants were to be treated as unbelievers and fought "until they return to God's command."[13] If they desist, their life, family members, and property were "licit" for the true believers.[14] By their continual and conscious display of camaraderie and equality, the Kharijites sought to recreate the devout atmosphere and fraternal solidarity of the Medinan state when it was guided by the prophet Muhammad. Furthermore, they considered themselves to be the only genuine Muslims left on the face of earth. In line with this belief, they regarded their return from raiding expeditions to their camps as an act of *hijra*, that is, "emigration" from the abode of injustice and unbelief to the Abode of Islam in the same way as the Prophet's move from Mecca to Medina symbolized his decisive break with the pagan society of his native town.[15] In short, they purchased their freedom from oppression and unbelief by opting out of Muslim society at large and setting up small polities or communes outside the reach of the imperial state.[16]

The right of the Kharijite leader to lead his followers in war and peace depended directly on his acceptance by all of his followers and on his competence as military commander. He was subject to deposition by his community for the slightest of sins, although he would retain his position once he had repented and mended his ways.[17] According to the Kharijites, the Muslim community consisted of two groups: the "people of paradise," that is, the members of the Kharijite community, and the "people of hell," who were identified as those who had refused to join their struggle for justice and the triumph of God's will. Non-Muslims were to be tolerated as long as they accepted the protection of a Kharijite band. Women and slaves who embraced Kharijism enjoyed equal rights with free men of the movement and took an active part in jihad against the Kharijites' numerous enemies.[18]

While some Kharijite ideals of justice and equality resonated with the egalitarian aspirations of the Bedouin tribes and the oppressed peasantry of Iraq, in the end their program proved to be too radical for the majority of those who, for one reason or the other, opposed the Umayyad regime.[19] The most radical Kharijite communities, which initially concentrated in Kufa and Basra, gradually became isolated from the main body of the Muslims and were either exterminated or expelled to remote mountains and deserts.[20] Some of them have survived until today in Oman and Algeria, although over time they have lost their militancy and found an accommodation with the non-Kharijite majority. Those who were reluctant to compromise died out. The egalitarian and liberating potential of the Kharijite doctrine remained unrealized or had little impact outside their small communities.[21] At the same, time, their radicalism and militancy have found imitators among the subsequent generations of Muslims, including those who live in our own age.

'Ali's Party

The supporters of 'Ali,[22] who later came to be known as Shi'ites, were especially numerous in the city of Kufa in Iraq. They held 'Ali to be the only legitimate ruler, who had been wrongly deprived of his right to rule (i.e., of the caliphate) by three "interlopers"—Abu Bakr, 'Umar, and 'Uthman. Those of the Prophet's companions who had accepted them as their leaders instead of 'Ali were erring sinners.[23] Their sin was even more grievous because the Prophet had publicly designated 'Ali as his successor[24]—a fact that the supporters of the first three caliphs energetically denied.[25] Initially, the partisans of 'Ali and his family constituted a more or less unified movement. However, like the Kharijites, the pro-Alid party often found it impossible to agree on a single candidate. As a result, they formed several separate communities, each of which derived its distinct identity from the 'Alid candidate it had chosen to support. The largest of these groups, the so-called "Imamis,"[26] restricted the right to lead the community of the faithful to 'Ali and his descendants by his wife Fátima (d. 632), a daughter of the Prophet.[27] Somewhat later they further restricted this right to 'Ali's younger son, al-Husayn, thereby excluding the descendants of his elder brother al-Hásan. A separate branch of the pro-'Alid movement, the Zaydis, held all of 'Ali's descendants by Fátima, including the offspring of al-Hásan, to be eligible for the imamate (see Table 2.1).[28]

The Umayyad period (661–750) witnessed the rise of several 'Alid candidates, each of whom had a loyal following. To justify their insistence that the right to the imamate should be restricted to the Prophet's male progeny, scholars of the 'Ali's party came to argue that the descendants of 'Ali, whom they called "The People of the House" (*ahl al-bayl*), were carriers of a special divinely inspired knowledge (*'ilm*). This notion was unambiguously expressed in the Shi'ite *hadíth* cited in the previous chapter. The sacred knowledge of the Shi'ite leaders (*imam*s), made them, in the eyes of their followers, the only infallible interpreters of God's will and dispensers of right guidance (*húda*) to humankind. This concept effectively deprived all Muslims who were not part of the Prophet's family of the right to lead the Muslim community to salvation. The fact that, apart from 'Ali, the possessors of the sacred *'ilm* were barred from political authority and even killed as they attempted to exercise their right to it was seen by the partisans of 'Ali and his family as a gross injustice.[29] They looked to the moment in the future when the accession to power of 'Ali's offspring would usher in the era of justice and truth, when the ruling usurpers and their misguided followers, who had accepted the unworthy Umayyads as their leaders, would be humbled and punished. In the meantime, no epoch should be devoid of its own leader (*imam*) of 'Alid descent. Some 'Alid groups maintained the view that before his death, the incumbent *imam* should always designate his own successor through the process that came to be known as "bequest" (*nass*, lit. "text").[30] It was the responsibility of every believer to identify the true 'Alid *imam* of his epoch, to abide by the *imam*'s rulings, and, if necessary, to sacrifice his life defending him. Until the moment when God had chosen to grant the *imam* political power, his followers were expected to continue to live under the unjust rule of the Umayyad dynasty and, if necessary, conceal their true beliefs from its agents to avoid persecution (see Figure 7.1).[31]

By the middle of the eighth century, there emerged two principal lines of 'Alid *imam*s. One was represented by Ja'far al-Sádiq (d. 765), a great-grandson of 'Ali's son al-Husayn. Ja'far was an accomplished Muslim scholar (*'álim*), highly regarded by both the pro-'Alid party and the Sunnis. He is credited with the development of a theological teaching that formed the foundation of the Imami-Shi'ite creed in the subsequent centuries. Ja'far's descendants came to be viewed by their

Figure 7.1 Meccan Slave-Girl Delivers a Letter to 'Ali (depicted here as a flame) from the Leaders of the Quraysh Tribe (nineteenth-century miniature painting from Kashmir)

akg-images/British Library

followers as the only legitimate leaders of the Muslim community. Their belief in the uninterrupted succession of the *imam*s from 'Ali down to the latest, twelfth *imam*, who went into what came to be known as "occultation," has earned them the name "Twelvers" or "Twelver Shi'ites."

The second 'Alid line that produced candidates for the Shi'ite imamate was that of Muhammad b. al-Hanafiyya (d. 700), 'Ali's son by a woman of the Hanifa tribe. Muhammad b. al-Hanafiyya's son Abu Háshim, who died without male offspring, allegedly passed on his authority to the family of the Prophet's uncle 'Abbás.[32] Supporters of these Shi'ite candidates came to be known collectively as the "Hashimiyya." This title goes back to the clan of the Quraysh that was established by Háshim, the great-grandfather of the Prophet. The Hashimiyya took active part in a series of revolts against the Umayyads in the 740s, which eventually led to the collapse of this dynasty in 750.[33]

With the emergence of the concept of sacred knowledge and unerring guidance residing in 'Ali's descendants, the 'Alid opposition to Umayyad rule acquired a robust theological dimension. This powerful concept seized the imagination of many Muslims who threw in their lot with the 'Alid party and staked their lives on its cause. They came to treat their 'Alid leaders as superhuman heroes and occasionally even as messiahs. Heady enthusiasm resulted. Some extremist pro-'Alid groups went as far as to hold certain descendants of 'Ali to be living manifestations of God.

Mukhtár, the leader of a revolt in the name of Muhammad b. al-Hanafiyya in Kufa in 685–687,[34] declared him the "rightly guided" leader (*máhdi*),[35] a messianic figure sent by God to remove injustice from this world and to lead his followers to a final triumph over the forces of evil in this world. The rebellion was put down, but the messianic expectations persisted to become a characteristic feature of the internally diverse Shi'ite (pro-'Alid) movement. After the death of Muhammad b. al-Hanafiyya in 700, the messianic expectations of his followers focused on his son, Abu Háshim. Others refused to accept Muhammad b. al-Hanafiyya's death and declared that he was temporarily in hiding, waiting for a propitious moment to make his glorious appearance as the *máhdi*.[36]

Whether they shared such messianic expectations or not, the majority of pro-'Alid Muslims believed that the descendants of 'Ali were recipients of guidance directly from God in more or less the same way Muhammad himself had. Although they were not destined to bring a new law, they were entrusted by God to guide the community to salvation. This conviction helped the pro-'Alid party to deal with what they perceived as the wanton injustices of Umayyad rule. Many Muslims loyal to 'Ali and his descendants began to read the Qur'an in the hopes of discovering in it hidden references to and predictions of the pivotal role of the 'Alid *imam*s and other members of the Prophet's "House" in the postprophetic age. Some pro-'Alid scholars went even further, arguing that behind the "external" (*záhir*) meaning of the revelation there lies its "true," "interior" (*bátin*) aspect that can be brought out only by the 'Alid *imam*s by virtue of the privileged knowledge (*'ilm*) bestowed upon them by God. With time, this idea led to the emergence of a special inwardly oriented reading of the scripture, which treated its text as an assemblage of symbols and subtle allusions whose meaning is accessible only to divinely inspired individuals.

The Uneasy Loyalists

The majority of Muslims chose to maintain at least a semblance of loyalty to the Umayyads on the understanding that a bad peace was still better than a good war. They came to be known as "the supporters of the [Prophet's] Custom and Community/Consensus" (*ahl al-sunna wa 'l-jamá'a*).[37] The first part of this designation was meant to stress their commitment to the authority of prophetic precedents and customs (*sunna*), which they treated as the embodiment, along with the Qur'an, of divine will and guidance. Its second part emphasized their desire for the unity of the faithful under one ruler.[38] The necessity for the faithful to preserve unity at all costs explains why the supporters of the [Prophet's] Custom and Community/Consensus discouraged any public discussion as to who was right or wrong in the first and second *fitna* wars. They knew all too well how divisive such discussions may turn out to be and relegated to God the judgment of the actions of the participants in these fateful events, thereby effectively deferring it until the Day of Judgment. Most of them refused to excommunicate those Muslims who disagreed with their teachings, arguing that only God had the right to judge and punish his servants. This position was the exact opposite of that of the Kharijites, who considered themselves to be the judges of other Muslims (and their executioners, when their faith was found to be "weak" or "incorrect").

On the political plane, the supporters of the Sunna and Consensus took a sober position with regard to the legitimacy of the leader of the community. Although imperfect, the Umayyads had emerged as the winners from the bloody civil wars and, for better or worse, had become unifiers of the Muslim community. This was good enough for the supporters of the Sunna and Consensus: As guarantors of unity, the Umayyads had not only to be tolerated but also humbly obeyed. The alternative was the continuation of the civil strife, which would result in even greater divisions within the community of the faithful. At the same time, some popular spokespersons on behalf of the *ahl al-sunna wa 'l-jama‘a* reserved the right to censure the incumbent Umayyad rulers for what they considered to be violations of the divine law. Unlike the Shi‘ites, the supporters of the Sunna and Consensus did not expect the Muslim leader (*imam*) to be infallible or possess some sort of supernatural knowledge or qualities. The *imam*'s primary task was to maintain public order, defend the borders of the Abode of Islam, and implement the rulings of the divine law as articulated in the Qur'an and the Sunna. The *imam* was, in a sense, an ordinary Muslim upon whom God had, for some unknown reason, chosen to bestow the position of political supreme authority.[39] Unlike the Kharijites and the Shi‘ites who wanted their *imam* to be respectively the most pious of the lot or a direct male descendant of the Prophet, the *imam* of the supporters of the Sunna and Consensus had to meet relatively minimal qualifications, such as descent from a clan of the Quraysh tribe and a modicum of knowledge of the Qur'an and the Sunna. This knowledge was necessary for the *imam* to make religiously sound decisions, but in practice he deferred them to the learned representatives of the *ahl al-sunna wa 'l-jama‘a*. The latter took great pride in being custodians of the Qur'an and the Prophet's Sunna and the sciences pertaining to both. In their opinion, this expertise set them apart from the herd of ordinary believers. As a Kufan *hadíth* scholar once said:

> If I were a bean-seller, you would think nothing of me—without these *hadíth* we would be no better than greengrocers.[40]

The uneducated commoners were expected to submit to the guidance of the intellectual elite of the supporters of the Sunna and Consensus. In return, they were promised collective salvation through participation in the rightly guided community led by the religious experts. The supporters of the Sunna and Consensus viewed both the Kharijites and the ‘Alid party as "extremists" and "deviators" from the correct Islam of the Prophet and his companions. As such, they were doomed to perdition.

Some Early Theological Concepts

Some conscientious leaders of the Sunna and Consensus party were not quite comfortable with their inability to raise their voice against the injustices and excesses of Umayyad rule. To alleviate their feeling of guilt, they justified their passivity by arguing that God, being the sole omnipotent creator and agent in the universe, controlled human destinies, not humans themselves.[41] Destinies were predetermined by God from eternity, and his human servants were not in a position to deviate from the courses prescribed to them by the Maker. This deterministic, or fatalistic, position was espoused by the group of thinkers known as Jabrites, or the supporters of the doctrine of divine "compulsion" (*jabr*). In Western academic literature, they are sometimes also referred to as "predestinarians." Implicitly, the predestinarian position justified the rule of the Umayyads because their victory over their opponents could be interpreted as a fulfillment of God's pre-eternal decree with regard to creation. This position gained currency for the most part among the Muslims loyal to or at least tolerant of the Umayyad state.[42] They were criticized not only by the Kharijites and the partisans of ‘Ali, who advocated active resistance against the Umayyad regime, but also by their fellow Sunnis known as Qadarites,[43] or the supporters of human free will. The Qadarites came from a variety of backgrounds. Although not all of them actively opposed the Umayyad dynasty, the Qadarites criticized its misdeeds, especially whenever they felt that Umayyad rulers had violated the sacred precepts of the Qur'an and the Sunna. By emphasizing human responsibility for the condition of this world, the Qadarite position implicitly justified active involvement of individual Muslims in its affairs. Sunni activists, whether openly Qadarite or not, considered it their religious duty to command what is right and forbid what is wrong because it was enjoined by the Qur'an.[44] At the same time, this group of pious critics of Umayyads remained loyal to their regime, seeing it as a better alternative to rebellion and civil war (see Figure 7.2).

Figure 7.2 'Ali (depicted here as a flame) Cleaves the Leader of the Kharijites with One Blow at the Battle of Nahrawán in Iraq (nineteenth-century miniature painting from Kashmir)

Al-Hásan al-Basri (d. 728), a pious preacher who is commonly regarded as the founding father of Islamic theology, tried to steer a middle course between the predestinarians and the supporters of human free will. He courageously criticized the Umayyad caliphs for their excesses, while at the same time refusing to join those who wanted to rebel against them.[45] His position in regard to the Jabrite–Qadarite debate was ambiguous (perhaps deliberately so). On the one hand, al-Hásan al-Basri considered tyrannical rule to be a punishment inflicted by God upon his servants for their sins and lack of righteousness. As such, it had to be endured with patience and fortitude. On the other hand, he judged sinners harshly and considered them to be fully responsible for their actions. His attempts to steer a middle course between the positions of the two theological parties exposed him to the criticism of both. The dispute between the Jabrites and the Qadarites continued in the following centuries, although their positions grew more sophisticated as time progressed.

Conclusions

If we compare the religio-political agendas—at that time still rather fluid and unformed—of the three Muslim communities just discussed, we can conclude that each of them was motivated by its own distinct concept of justice in this world and of attaining salvation in the next one. The Kharijites considered justice and salvation to be a matter of conscious personal choice and individual self-exertion in the attainment of the goal. To be saved, one must join the group of likeminded individuals, choose the most pious and apt among them as the leader, and take up arms against the unjust and illegitimate rulers of the age. The identity of that leader was not that important for the Kharijites. They did not expect him to have any supernatural qualities, divinely inspired knowledge, or any other form of special access to God. On the contrary, he could and should be replaced by a more suitable one once it was established that he had strayed from the divine law or sinned. Salvation was to be achieved by fighting injustices of this world and striving to implement divine commands to the letter. Because injustices were so obviously rampant in this imperfect world and divine commands so egregiously ignored by the overwhelming majority of Muslims, the Kharijites had to fight against each and every Muslim who refused to join the ranks of their movement. The movement itself having been fragmented into small and often mutually hostile groups, the Kharijites proved to be no match for the more disciplined and professional fighting units of the Umayyad caliph. As a result, martyrdom on the battlefield was the ultimate fate of the majority of the early Kharijite communes. Those who survived repression eventually abandoned the movement's original radicalism and adopted a more accommodating stance toward other Muslims and the Muslim states around them.

The 'Alid party put its faith in the divinely inspired and infallible leader whose right to guide his followers rested on his kinship with the Prophet's family. This principle implied that 'Ali and his descendants were in possession of an infallible, supernatural knowledge of God's will as expressed in the Muslim scripture. Salvation was to be achieved by identifying and following the infallible guide from among the descendants of the Prophet's cousin 'Ali. Pro-'Alid slogans proved to be extremely popular, especially in the eastern provinces of the Muslim Empire. The broad pro-'Alid movement that originated there spearheaded the revolution that swept aside the Umayyad dynasty for the benefit of the 'Abbásids.

Finally, according to the view upheld by the supporters of the Prophet's Sunna and Community/ Consensus, salvation was to be secured collectively through joining and participating in the community guided by the divine word (the Qur'an) and the divinely inspired and inerrant actions and sayings of the Prophet (the Sunna). The religious and political agenda of this community turned out to be the most realistic and durable because the Muslims who threw in their lot with it were ready to tolerate any authority that was capable of assuring public order and the fulfillment, however imperfect, of the principles of the Qur'an and the Sunna. If the incumbent powers-that-be showed themselves to be "impious" and "unjust," they should be admonished by the learned custodians of the divine revelation and the prophetic lore but still tolerated in anticipation of God's justice in the hereafter. The supporters of the Prophet's Sunna and Consensus/Community, or simply the Sunnis, have remained in the majority until today. They constitute between 87% and 90% of the world's Muslim population.

Questions to Ponder

1   Given the fact that the Kharijites insisted on the election of their leader from among the most righteous members of their community, can they be considered harbingers of "Islamic democracy"?
2   Why have their "democratic principles" been rejected by the majority of Muslims?

Summary

- 'Uthman's rule and that of his Umayyad successors are seen by many Muslims as a drastic departure from the precedents established by the Prophet and his first two successors, Abu Bakr and 'Umar, and therefore illegitimate and "un-Islamic."
- Deeper reasons (both economic and political) sustain wider opposition to 'Uthman's rule: the *mawáli* ("clients), that is, non-Arab converts to Islam, the Kharijites ("seceders" or "rebels"), and Shi'ites ('Ali's party). For the *mawáli* and the Kharijites, the agenda is the equality of all Muslims before God. They view only the most pious Muslim, regardless of social background and genealogy, as the rightful leader of the *umma*. The Shi'ites, on the other hand, adopt the strictly genealogical principle of determining the leader's legitimacy: only direct male descendants of 'Ali are qualified to lead the community to salvation.
- Despite the egalitarian agenda of the Kharijite movement, its radicalism entails, in particular, the excommunication of Muslims who disagree with them. The specifically Shi'ite concept emerges of the unerring leader (*imam*) possessed of divinely bestowed knowledge (*'ilm*) and the resultant ability to guide the faithful.
- The Umayyad dynasty's unwilling supporters are the members of the Prophet's Custom and Consensus/Community. They insist that securing the unity of the community and preserving peace should take precedence over all other goals, no matter how lofty and noble. Hasty excommunication of Muslims perceived as "wrongdoers," "deviators," or "heretics" should be avoided. The prophetic traditions (*hadíth*), transmitted and interpreted by knowledgeable scholars, should be the principal source of right guidance for the *umma* (alongside the Qur'an).
- The question of human free will versus the divine predestination of all events becomes an issue. The Jabrite–Qadarite debate has its implications for Umayyad claims to the caliphate. According to the Jabrites, humans are somehow "compelled" by God to act in a certain manner, and their free will has nothing to do with this. According to the Qadarites, human beings have some level of control over their actions and thereby incur responsibility for them. Al-Hásan al-Basri's (d. 728) attempts to articulate a "golden mean" between these two positions in order to safeguard human responsibility for their actions without undermining the notion of divine omnipotence. Grounds are laid for later theological discussions of this critical issue in subsequent centuries.

Notes

1 See, e.g., Oleg Bolshakov, *Istoriia Khalifata. II: Epokha velikikh zavoevanii*, Nauka, Moscow, 1993, Chapter 7 and Wilferd Madelung, *The Succession to Muhammad*, Cambridge University Press, Cambridge, 1997, pp. 81–85.
2 Madelung, *The Succession*, pp. 86–90.
3 "Surely, the noblest among you in the sight of God is the most pious of you" (Q 49:13).
4 From the viewpoint of the followers of 'Ali, 'Uthman's designation as caliph was illegitimate from the outset because he was inferior in his religious credentials to their candidate.
5 On them, see "The Rise of the Mawali."
6 Patricia Crone, *Medieval Islamic Political Thought*, Edinburgh University Press, Edinburgh, 2004, p. 59.
7 Gerald Hawting, *The First Dynasty of Islam*, Southern Illinois University Press, Carbondale and Illinois, 1987, pp. 11–15 and Chapters 7 and 8.
8 See Chapter 4 of this book.
9 Crone, *Medieval*, Chapter 5.
10 Ibid., p. 55.
11 Marshall Hodgson, *The Venture of Islam*, Chicago University Press, Chicago, 1974, vol. 1, pp. 256–258.
12 Crone, *Medieval*, pp. 56–61 and 287–288.
13 Q 49:9.
14 Crone, *Medieval*, pp. 56 and 386–387.
15 Ibid., p. 288.
16 Ibid., pp. 64 and 287–288.
17 Ibid., p. 58.
18 Ibid., p. 363.
19 Hodgson, *The Venture*, vol. 1, pp. 222 and 245.
20 Ibid., p. 313 and Crone, *Medieval*, pp. 320–321.
21 Crone, *Medieval*, pp. 61–62.
22 Arab. *shi'at 'Ali*.
23 For further details see Crone, *Medieval*, Chapters 7 and 8.
24 Ibid., pp. 73 and 74.
25 Mohammad Ali Amir-Moezzi, "Ghadir Khumm," in *Encyclopedia of Islam*, 3rd ed.; online edition: http://referenceworks.brillonline.com.
26 On them see Crone, *Medieval*, Chapter 10.
27 See above Table 2.1. "Ahl al-Bayt," p. 20.
28 Crone, *Medieval*, Chapter 9.
29 Hodgson, *The Venture*, vol. 1, pp. 259–260.
30 Ibid. and Amir-Moezzi, "Ghadir Khumm."
31 This practice is known as *taqiya*, i.e., "pious dissimulation."
32 Crone, *Medieval*, pp. 77–80 and Chapter 8 of this book.
33 Ibid., pp. 89–92.
34 See Chapter 4 and Crone, *Medieval*, pp. 77–79.
35 Ibid., "Index" under "Mahdi."
36 Ibid., pp. 79–80.
37 Hodgson, *The Venture*, vol. 1, pp. 276–279 and Crone, *Medieval*, Chapter 11; both authors call this group the "Hadith Party" or "Hadith Folk," emphasizing their allegiance to the prophetic precedent as recorded in the *hadith*.
38 Crone, *Medieval*, pp. 125–126.
39 Ibid., Chapter 16.
40 Ibid., p. 126.

41 Montgomery Watt, *The Formative Period of Islamic Thought*, Oneworld, Oxford, 1998, pp. 112–116 and Crone, *Medieval*, pp. 135–139.

42 Crone, *Medieval*, p. 137.

43 From the Arabic *qadar*, "[divine] decree/command."

44 E.g., in Q 3:110 and 9:112; for the history and application of this precept in Islamic societies, see Michael Cook, *Commanding Right and Forbidding Wrong in Islamic Thought*, Cambridge University Press, Cambridge, 2000.

45 Watt, *The Formative Period*, pp. 99–104.

Chapter 8

The 'Abbásid Revolution and Beyond

The Theological Underpinnings

As we already know, at the outset, the Umayyads justified their claim to be the legitimate leaders of the Muslim community by presenting themselves as avengers for the blood of the caliph 'Uthman, who was assassinated by a group of Egyptian mutineers. The Umayyads and their supporters argued that by failing to punish 'Uthman's murderers, 'Ali, who was recognized by many as successor to 'Uthman, forfeited his right to the caliphate. Mu'awiya, a relative of 'Uthman, albeit from a different branch of the Umayyad clan, positioned himself as the leader of the avenging faction. After the first civil war (*fitna*) and the death of 'Ali in 656, he was declared caliph (*khalífa*), that is the "successor or deputy of the Prophet" and the "commander of the faithful" (*amír al-mu'minín*).[1]

With time, the Umayyads began to claim a religious authority of their own, arguing that their triumph over their numerous opponents in the first and second civil wars was an unmistakable sign of God's favor toward their house. In other words, their victory was predetermined and made possible by God, who thus vindicated their status as the only rightful leaders of the Muslim community. What more evidence did one need to confirm their legitimacy?[2] After a while, the Umayyads began to style themselves not simply as the successors or deputies of the Prophet but also as the representatives of God himself.[3] This concept of Umayyad legitimacy is finely captured in the following praise of the caliph Mu'awiya by a court poet:

> The earth is God's; He has entrusted it to His *khalífa*.
> God has adorned you with the caliphate and guidance; for what God has decreed there is no change.

Although definitely a piece of flattery, this passage seems to indicate that the idea of the Umayyads being deputies of God had appeared very early on.[4] Taken seriously, this idea implied that the failure of the believers to obey the Umayyad ruler or his agents was tantamount to contradicting the will of God himself. In their capacity as God's vicegerents, the Umayyads made every effort to impose a more or less uniform theological doctrine on their subjects. Those who refused to adhere to it were branded as heretics and persecuted. The principal enemies of the Umayyad state were the Kharijites and the supporters of the rights of 'Ali's family. The adherents of the doctrine of human free will, who advocated the duty of the Muslims to be actively involved in the life of the Muslim community with a view to bringing it closer to the ideals of primeval Islam, also opposed Umayyad rule, albeit passively. Although all these groups advanced compelling religious arguments in support of their positions, "they still lacked the [Umayyad] regime's capacity to imprison, torture, or kill those who disagreed with them."[5] Thus, while the Umayyad rulers would occasionally have 'Ali cursed during the congregational prayers,[6] their 'Alid opponents could not reciprocate by cursing Mu'awiya or 'Uthman without risking their lives. The religiopolitical precepts and agendas of the Umayyads' opponents were described in the previous chapter and need not be repeated here. Faced with the Umayyads' efforts to establish monopoly on the definition of religious orthodoxy, their opponents had two options: to maintain prudent silence or to try to defend their ideals in disputation or on the battlefield. Only when the Umayyad state began to disintegrate after the death of its last powerful ruler, Hishám (743), were the malcontents able to declare vocally and unequivocally their disagreements with the Umayyad understanding of orthodoxy.

The Sources of Discontent

Although they may have disagreed with each other on religious and political alternatives to Umayyad rule, the oppositional forces just mentioned were united in their condemnation of the Umayyads as illegitimate and oppressive "usurpers." The fact that the rule of the Umayyads soon acquired all the trappings of an absolutist monarchical rule similar to that of Byzantine or Sasanid emperors caused further discontent among many of their Muslim subjects. In the hostile historical sources from the 'Abbásid epoch, the Umayyad rulers were consistently referred to not as caliphs but as "kings" (*mulúk;* sing. *málik*)—a title that was supposed to stress the authoritarian nature of their rule and the lack of religious legitimacy.[7]

One major center of opposition to the Umayyads was in the eastern provinces of the empire, especially the eastern Iranian province of Khurasan. The Arab tribal contingents stationed there were jealous of the privileges enjoyed by the elite Syrian troops that constituted the military backbone of the Umayyad regime. Those provincial contingents were often sent on military campaigns that lasted from five months to an entire year, during which time they were separated from their families and were exposed to the hardships of a life on the move and to mortal danger in the battlefield without receiving, in their view, sufficient compensation.

The other discontented group was the *mawáli*, converts to Islam of a non-Arab (for the most part Persian) background. Many of them were now second- or third-generation Muslims who had participated in the Muslim military campaigns alongside Arabs. Despite the attempts to redress their grievances undertaken by the "good" Umayyad caliph 'Umar II (717–720), they effectively remained second-class citizens of the Muslim community. The *mawáli* wanted to be judged not by their ethnic origins but by their faith and their contributions to the well-being and military success of the Muslim state. It is hardly surprising that they proved to be susceptible to anti-Umayyad propaganda.

The external pressures on the Umayyad state were compounded by internal divisions within the Umayyad ruling family that was considerably weakened as a result of this internal disunity. The last decade of the dynasty witnessed a devastating internecine struggle among several Umayyad contenders. During this struggle, at least one of the caliphs, Walíd II, was murdered in 744 by his own Syrian troops in an episode that had further eroded the legitimacy of the Umayyad state.[8] Another major source of weakness was the Umayyad policy of perpetual conquest, which resulted in the overextension of its logistic and financial resources and manpower. Pacifying and controlling the newly conquered lands stretching as far as India in the east and Gaul (France) in the west was a costly proposition. The Umayyad caliphs had to finance their perpetual military ventures by levying ever heavier taxes on their subjects in the countryside and in towns. Even more importantly, their loyal Syrian tribal contingents were decimated by constant warfare in the far-flung provinces of the empire, whose inhabitants frequently rebelled against Umayyad governors. The surviving Syrians troops gradually relinquished their erstwhile loyalty to their Umayyad patrons and became susceptible to anti-Umayyad agitation in the provinces and even in Syria itself.[9] In the meantime, long-standing animosities between different tribal blocks (especially, the "southern" Arab tribes versus the "northerners") kept breaking out, further undermining the Umayyad state's ability to defend itself against its numerous internal and external enemies.

All these weaknesses became evident in the 740s, which witnessed an almost uninterrupted series of popular revolts against Umayyad rule. They were launched by the Kharijites and a broad coalition of advocates of the rights of the Prophet's family, who, as we remember from the previous chapter, were known as the Hashimiyya after the name of the ancestor of the Prophet's native clan, Háshim of the Quraysh tribe. One faction of the Hashimiyya, the 'Abbásids, eventually succeeded in overthrowing the Umayyad dynasty and declared themselves the new caliphs.

The Turn of the Wheel: 'Abbásid Propaganda and the Beginning of the Third *Fitna*

The series of anti-Umayyad revolts that came to be known as the "third *fitna*" lasted from 743 through 750. It led to the downfall of the Umayyad caliphate at the hands of a rebel army from Khurasan, which acted in the name of the 'Abbásid clan of the Quraysh. Because the 'Abbásids were not part of 'Ali's family—they were descendants neither of 'Ali and Fátima (i.e., the 'Alids proper) nor of 'Ali and the woman of the Hanifa tribe (i.e., the offspring of Muhammad b. al-Hanafiyya)—their role in the overthrow of the Umayyads calls for an explanation.

The 'Abbásid family derived its name from Muhammad's uncle 'Abbás (d. 653), who initially rejected his nephew's monotheistic message, fought against the Muslim army at Badr in 624, was captured and later ransomed. While pro-'Abbasid sources claimed that he converted to Islam during his captivity in Medina, most probably he became Muslim either shortly before (629) or after the conquest of Mecca (630) by the Muslims, along with the other leaders of the Quraysh.[10] At the death of the Prophet, 'Abbás was his eldest male relative—a fact that was later emphasized by the supporters of the 'Abbásid family to justify its special role in relation to the other claimants to the caliphate.[11] The Islamic credentials of 'Abbás's son, 'Abdallah b. 'Abbas (d. 688), were much more solid. He was a highly respected scholar and collector of prophetic traditions who is also considered to be the first expert on and interpreter of the Qur'an. 'Abdallah's son 'Ali was also renowned for his piety and humility. In the second decade of the eighth century, the great-grandson of 'Abbás, Muhammad b. 'Ali, decided to throw in his lot with the broad opposition movement against the Umayyads, which had been gaining momentum at that time. He apparently did so in the hopes of deposing the "godless" Umayyads and installing a member of his family as caliph. Initially, the members of the 'Abbásid clan, who resided in a small town in present-day Jordan, did not publicly disclose their true aspirations. Instead, they pretended to be acting on behalf of an unnamed member of the Prophet's house, whom they designated, rather vaguely, as the "one agreed upon (or chosen) from Muhammad's family" (*al-ridá*).[12] Since the 'Abbásids were part of the Prophet's clan (the Hashimites), their claim to the caliphate was not totally unfounded. At that stage, it seems that the movement for the rights of the Prophet's family was still in flux, and it was not entirely clear how the leader would be chosen from among many candidates claiming kinship with the founder of Islam.[13] However, the majority of the opponents of the Umayyad regime, including many of those who sided with the 'Abbásid party, were convinced that the future caliph should be a descendant of the Prophet's cousin 'Ali, either through his marriage to Fátima or to the woman of the Hanifa tribe—that is, an offspring of Muhammad b. al-Hanafiyya. There were also descendants of 'Ali's brothers 'Aqil and Ja'far, who, too, were considered viable candidates for the imamate.[14] This could not have been otherwise, since the core of the anti-Umayyad movement consisted of the supporters of the rights of the 'Alids. Most of them resided in Kufa, waiting for an opportune moment to install a descendant of 'Ali as the rightful leader of the Muslim community. The concealment of the name of the future leader (*imam*) made perfect sense for the members of the opposition movement at that time.[15] For one thing, the disclosure of his identity would expose him to the wrath of the Umayyad rulers, who, as history had finely demonstrated, had no compunctions about knocking rebellious 'Alid candidates out of the way. Because the exact date on which the Umayyad dynasty was to be overthrown was predetermined by God, the partisans of 'Ali's family had no way of knowing whom God would designate as leader when such a time should come. All that was understood beyond doubt was that at a time known only to God, the wheel of history would turn full circle (*dawla*), ushering in the return to the blissful epoch of primeval Islam when the community was led by the Prophet with the only difference that it would now be guided by his direct male descendant.[16] This belief became the basis of the anti-Umayyad agitation in Iraq and in the other provinces of the caliphate. The agitation having been conducted clandestinely, keeping the name of the future *imam* secret made perfect sense to both the rank-and-file and the leaders of the anti-Umayyad movement. As we shall see, in the end, the 'Abbásids managed to use this secrecy to their advantage. When the wheel of history had finally made its full revolution and the time had come for the "one agreed upon" to step into the limelight, they were the ones who were able to outflank all other pretenders to the imamate.[17]

In a movement inspired and sustained largely by the pro-'Alid sentiment, the legitimacy of the 'Abbásid candidate, who came from a different branch of the Háshim clan, was shaky at best. It had to somehow be linked to the pro-'Alid aspirations of the majority of the movement's members. By a quirk of fate, Abu Háshim, the heirless son of Muhammad b. al-Hanafiyya[18] who died in 716, chose to bequeath his 'Alid authority to the head of the 'Abbásid clan, Muhammad b. 'Ali. This episode, which some modern historians have dismissed as 'Abbásid propaganda, is described in a medieval chronicle as follows:

> Abu Háshim . . . went to Syria and met Muhammad b. 'Ali b. 'Abdallah b. 'Abbas. He said: "Cousin, I have the [divinely inspired] Knowledge (*'ilm*) which I shall leave to you by default. Do not divulge it to anyone; this authority which men long for will be in your family." He [Muhammad b. 'Ali] said: "I knew it already; by no means let anyone hear it from you!"[19]

This bequest—which may or may not have taken place but which was vigorously asserted by the leaders of the 'Abbásid clan—allowed its members to secure the allegiance of those who had previously advocated the rights of Muhammad b. al-Hanafiyya and his offspring and to add them to the ranks of their own supporters. The majority of those new allies believed that they were acting on behalf of an 'Alid candidate, whereas in reality they were advancing the cause of the house of 'Abbás, which had no relation to 'Ali's family, except that they belonged to the same branch of the Quraysh tribe. Throughout what came to be known as the "third *fitna*," the 'Abbásid leaders remained deliberately vague as to the precise identity of the *imam* on whose behalf they were waging struggle against the Umayyads. In conversations with ordinary members of their movement they obliquely referred to him either the "one agreed upon from Muhammad's family" or "one of the house [of the Prophet]" (*ahl al-bayl*).[20]

As mentioned, one major center of the 'Alid movement was in Kufa, the traditional hotbed of pro-'Alid sentiment. Simultaneously, pro-'Alid propaganda was actively, if covertly, waged in the eastern provinces of the empire. After the death of Abu Háshim, the 'Abbásids inherited his numerous supporters in the wealthy and populous province of Khurasan (present-day eastern Iran and western Central Asia). The propaganda campaign on behalf of "one of the [Prophet's] family" targeted recently converted Persians and the Arab fighters stationed in the province. By that time, there was considerable integration between these two ethnic groups, since the Arabs often took Persian wives, and their descendants used Persian as their household language.

The message of the anti-Umayyad propaganda campaign was simple. The Umayyads had distorted Islam by departing from the sacred precepts of the Book of God and the Sunna of his

Prophet. The purity of Islam should be restored by installing a member of the Prophet's family at the head of the community. He would then implement the law of God, as taught by the Qur'an and the Prophet, and justice will triumph over oppression and injustice. The wrongs of Umayyad rule should be put right; the rulers themselves must be deposed, and their crimes against the legitimate candidates for the leadership of the community must be avenged. This message proved to be particularly effective among the disenfranchised and disgruntled elements of the Khurasani population. The Persian converts longed for equality with the Arabs, while many, albeit not all, Arab tribal contingents in Iran there were dissatisfied with their underprivileged position compared to the tribal supporters of the Umayyads in Syria, as well as with the harsh conditions of their life in military encampments.

The 'Abbásid propaganda campaign, called *da'wa* ("call [to the truth]"), had started before the death of Abu Háshim and continued with growing intensity under the supervision of Muhammad b. 'Ali the 'Abbasid, who, from his base in what is now Jordan, maintained secret contacts with malcontents in both Iraq and Khurasan. After his death in 743, the leadership of the 'Abbásid clan devolved on his son Ibrahim (743). In 747, when the Umayyads began to lose their grip on power following a series of revolts and internecine struggle within the ruling family, Ibrahim dispatched his Persian-speaking client Abu Múslim to Khurasan with the orders to intensify anti-Umayyad propaganda there and, when the moment was ripe, to raise a revolt in the name of his 'Abbasid master. Abu Múslim's anti-Umayyad, propaganda waged from the city of Marw/Merv (in present-day Turkmenistan, Central Asia), attracted a motley army of supporters. It included both the discontented Arabs warriors stationed in Khurasan (who constituted around 18–20% of the entire movement) and the local Persian-speaking population of different social, ethnic and religious backgrounds, such as the second- and third-generation Muslim *mawáli* (mostly Persians) and more recent Persian-speaking converts from Zoroastrianism. Although the majority of Abu Múslim's followers were non-Arabs, Arabs held the disproportionate number of command posts in his army. Abu Múslim managed to outwit all other local partisans of the 'Alid cause—whom he viewed as his rivals—by keeping secret the identity of the candidate for the caliph's post. When he had grown strong enough, he eliminated his pro-'Alid rivals and took control of all the anti-Umayyad forces in the province. In the summer of 747, in a village near the garrison city of Marw, Abu Múslim unfurled black banners. Together with the black garments worn by the participants in the movement, the black color became a potent symbol of the rebellion. It was meant to symbolize the mourning for the 'Alid leaders murdered by the Umayyad regime. Here is how the beginning of the 'Abbásid revolution is described in a historical chronicle:

> On Wednesday night, the twenty-fifth of Ramadán (May 17, 747), he [Abu Múslim] unfurled the banner, sent to him by the Imam [Ibrahim the 'Abbásid] and called "The Shadow," on a lance fourteen cubits high,[21] and fastened the flag, sent by the Imam and called "The Clouds," on a lance thirteen cubits high,[22] reciting the verse: "Leave is given to those who fight because they were wronged—surely God is able to help them."[23] . . . The interpretation of the two names "The Shadow" and "The Clouds" was: As the clouds cover the earth, so would the 'Abbasid preaching, and as the earth is never without a shadow, so it would never be without an 'Abbasid caliph to the end of time.[24]

The identity of the future caliph probably remained undisclosed in order to prevent the numerous partisans of the 'Alid family from abandoning the movement. Be this as it may, as had been predicted, the wheel of history (*dawla*) had made full turn, and the redressing of the wrongs done to the primeval Islam of the Prophet and the rights of his progeny was about to begin.[25] The Qur'anic verse cited in Abu Múslim's speech was deemed to furnish a scriptural justification for the impending attack on the "ungodly" regime of the Umayyads.

The Triumph of the 'Abbásid Cause

As Abu Múslim's revolutionary levies were preparing for a decisive march on Iraq, the ruling Umayyad caliph Marwán II discovered the connection of the 'Abbásid leader Ibrahim to the revolt in Khurasan and had him assassinated, adding one more name to Abu Múslim's long list of martyrs murdered by the Umayyad regime.[26] In September 749, Abu Múslim felt strong enough to take the field against the Umayyad troops stationed in Iraq. He sent his armed followers to Kufa, where they joined the pro-'Alid faction headed by Abu Sálama, Abu Múslim's confederate in the *da'wa* movement. Abu Sálama, an enthusiastic advocate for the rights of 'Ali's family, approached several potential 'Alid candidates, including the Shi'ite *imam* Ja'far al-Sádiq (d. 765), and invited them to become the "chosen one from the House of the Prophet." They all seem to have declined his solicitations.[27] The most politically active descendants of the 'Ali–Fátima family, such as Zayd b. 'Ali (d. 740), had been killed during the previous decades, while trying to wrest power from the Umayyads. As a result, the pool of eligible individuals was rather slim, and, moreover, none of them seems to have been particularly anxious to risk his life by assuming the leadership of a rebellion, whose outcome was dubious at best. While Abu Sálama was desperately searching for a willing 'Alid leader, the Khurasani troops arrived in Kufa with the explicit orders from Abu Múslim to install a member of the 'Abbásid family as the *imam*. In November 749, a secret meeting of fourteen leading members of the 'Abbásid movement took place in Kufa. Because Ibrahim was no longer alive, they decided to proclaim Ibrahim's surviving brother Abu 'l-'Abbás, a relatively little-known figure,[28] as "the chosen and agreed upon one from the house of Muhammad." Surrounded by the determined Khurasani followers of Abu Múslim, Abu Sálama had no choice but to accept this non-'Alid candidacy.

In the meantime, Abu Múslim and his rebel army had reached Upper Iraq. After a series of engagements, the rebels finally dealt a fatal blow to the army of the caliph Marwán II on the banks of a tributary of the Greater Zab River (750). The caliph managed to escape first to Syria, then to Palestine, from which he made his way to Egypt. There the fugitive caliph was tracked down and killed by a party of Persian-speaking 'Abbásid rebels, whose leader, an Arab, described this episode as follows:

> Then I broke the sheath of my sword, and my companions broke theirs. And I cried out [in Persian]: "Give it to them, bullies!" (*dahíd ya juvánkashán*). It had the effect of molten fire poured on them [the opponents], and they fled. Then a man attacked Marwán and struck him with his sword, killing him.[29]

The death of Marwán II was the last nail in the coffin of the first dynasty of Islam. The caliph's head was cut off and dispatched, together with his staff and ring, to the first 'Abbásid holder of the caliph's office, Abu 'l-'Abbas. The latter's ascension to the caliphal throne ushered in a brutal campaign against surviving members of the Umayyad dynasty. Even the Umayyad dead were not spared the spite of the victors. The graves of the Umayyad caliphs were broken open and their corpses torn out and burned. Soon after the 'Abbásid victory, according to a popular legend, Abu 'l-'Abbas invited eighty princes of the fallen ruling house to a banquet, giving them a solemn promise of immunity. At his signal, a band of executioners entered the room and clubbed the princes to death. Then leather covers were spread over their bodies, and the caliph and his retainers feasted while seated upon their fallen enemies to the accompaniment of their victims' dying groans.[30] Whether truth or legend, this story reflects a widespread perception of the 'Abbásids as ruthless and unscrupulous rulers. One Umayyad prince named 'Abd al-Rahman managed to escape the 'Abbásid terror. He fled to Islamic Spain, where he founded a new Umayyad dynasty that ruled over the Muslim parts of the Iberian Peninsula for more than three hundred years. In the Muslim East, however, Umayyad power was finished for good.

Thus, as predicted by the 'Abbásid propagandists, the wheel of history had turned, crushing one dynasty and propelling the other to the foreground of history.

The Consolidation of 'Abbásid Power

The pro-'Alid forces in Iraq, Arabia, and elsewhere were now rudely awakened to the new political realities they themselves had helped to create. Their goal of overthrowing the Umayyads was successfully achieved, but no descendant of 'Ali was declared caliph as a result. By a cruel quirk of fate, the partisans of 'Ali's family had brought to power another non-'Alid dynasty, whose members had cleverly manipulated to their advantage the idealistic hopes of 'Ali's supporters for restoring truth and justice under the leadership of an 'Alid *imam*.[31] No wonder that the pro-'Alid elements, which had constituted the backbone of anti-Umayyad opposition, came to view the 'Abbásids as just another royal house devoid of Islamic legitimacy. Their hostility toward the 'Abbásids continued unabated until the fall of the dynasty in 1258.

Aware of the frustration of their former allies, the 'Abbásids began to gradually dissociate themselves from 'Ali's family and its representatives. Since the pro-'Alid sympathies of the Kufan leader of the rebellion Abu Sálama were well-known, the new 'Abbásid caliph asked Abu Múslim's permission to get rid of him. Abu Múslim not only granted his request but even sent an assassin to murder his former comrade in arms.

All potential 'Alid claimants to the caliphate were put under close surveillance and occasionally also under house arrest in order to isolate them from their supporters. The subsequent 'Abbásid caliphs attempted to neutralize the 'Alids by granting them all kinds of privileges from tax exemption to special lifetime stipends. However, such measures failed to prevent a string of anti-'Abbásid movements under the 'Alid banners in the next few decades. They were suppressed by raw force.

After the death of Abu 'l-'Abbas, the nascent 'Abbásid state found itself in a precarious position. In 754, the dying caliph appointed his brother Abu Ja'far, later to be known as al-Mansúr ("The Victor"), as his successor. This appointment was rejected by Abu Ja'far's brother 'Abdallah, a popular military commander who had distinguished himself in the critical battles against the Umayyads. He enjoyed a large following among the Khurasani corps, which constituted the military foundation of 'Abbásid power. Abu Ja'far al-Mansúr had to call upon his all-powerful ally Abu Múslim in Khurasan to deal with the challenger. With the arrival of Abu Múslim, many Khurasanian warriors abandoned 'Abdallah in favor of their former chief. Abu Ja'far al-Mansúr knew all too well that Abu Múslim with his loyal Khurasani fighters were the decisive force behind the 'Abbásid revolution. Some modern scholars of Islamic history have even argued that the 'Abbásid victory was largely owed to Abu Múslim and that "the majority of those who appear to have toiled for the 'Abbásid cause were either Abu Múslim loyalists, or were indifferently, passively or grudgingly led in the irresistible direction which Abu Muslim chartered."[32]

For Abu Ja'far al-Mansúr, who aspired to the absolute imperial power similar to that enjoyed by the Persian kings of old, whose realm he had inherited, this situation was intolerable. Taking advantage of Abu Múslim's stay in Iraq, the second 'Abbásid caliph lured him to his camp and had him murdered. The architect of the 'Abbásid victory received a handsome reward from his cunning masters.[33] The caliph hurried to placate Abu Múslim's followers by showering them with various perks, such as grants of land, tax exemptions, and high posts. From then on, the fearsome Khurasanian troops looked on Abu Ja'far al-Mansúr and his son al-Máhdi as legitimate rulers. They remained the military foundation of 'Abbásid power for several decades.[34] The long-standing animosities among the Arab tribal fighters that threatened the stability of the nascent 'Abbásid state were appeased by the caliph al-Mansúr, who showed himself to be an astute diplomat and an able, if ruthless statesman.

As one can see from the ways in which the new caliphs dealt with both their former supporters and opponents, from the outset 'Abbásid rule rested on raw force. However, after their grip on power consolidated to the point of becoming virtually absolutist,[35] the 'Abbásids did make an effort to govern according to the ideals of just rule developed by the learned members of the anti-Umayyad opposition. Whether or not they were successful in positioning themselves as representatives of God and heirs to the Prophet in the eyes of the majority of their subjects, one thing is clear: they brooked no opposition. The power of the Syrian Arabs was drastically reduced, and a new capital was established in the city of Baghdad, which was constructed in 762 not far from the former Sasanid capital Ctesiphon (see Map 8.1).

Early in their rule, the 'Abbásids met the demands of the *mawáli* class for equality with the Muslims of Arab descent. Both Arab and non-Arab Muslims were now treated equally as subjects of the caliphal state.[36] To placate religious scholars who had criticized Umayyad rule as "un-Islamic," the 'Abbásids allowed the learned class a degree of independence and respect and agreed, at least nominally, to listen to their advice and tolerate their criticism. To demonstrate their commitment to Islamic principles of governance, the 'Abbásid rulers selected their religious functionaries, especially judges, from among the most respected and pious Sunni scholars of their realm. Those who refused were left alone and were not molested unless they dared to publicly condemn 'Abbásid rule as un-Islamic.

The Rearticulation of the Doctrine of the Imamate

From the very beginning, the 'Abbásids clearly showed that they had no intention to share their leadership with any members of 'Ali's family. They based their legitimacy on their descent from the Háshim clan of the Quraysh and on the bequest of 'Alid authority they had received from Abu Háshim, the childless son of Muhammad b. al-Hanafiyya. From the viewpoint of the 'Abbásids, the 'Alids' right to lead the community of the faithful to salvation was in no way superior to their own. Like the 'Alids, they were Hashimites, and like the 'Alids they were "a scared lineage elevated above all ethnic, tribal, regional, and local divisions."[37] The 'Abbásids' refusal to acknowledge the primacy of the 'Alids' claims to the imamate and their high-handedness in dealing with 'Alid leaders sparked several revolts led by 'Ali's descendants. One such rebellion was launched in the Hijáz in 762 by Muhammad al-Nafs al-Zakiyya ("The Pure Soul"), a great-grandson of al-Hásan, the elder son of 'Ali. To enhance his bid for power, al-Nafs al-Zakiyya declared himself the "rightly guided one" (*máhdi*) and "studiously imitated the Prophet's behavior."[38] Although he was able to garner broad popular support, his ragtag followers were no match for the seasoned 'Abbásid military. The rebellion of Muhammad's brother Ibrahim in Iraq, although initially successful, was thwarted in 763, marking the end of large-scale 'Alid revolts for the next fifty years or so.[39] Despite these setbacks, the pro-'Alid sentiment would continue to animate movements of protest across the 'Abbásid Empire.

In the meantime, a moderate wing of the pro-'Alid movement, represented first and foremost by the *imam* Ja'far al-Sádiq, a descendant of 'Ali and Fátima via al-Husayn, adopted a pacifist stance toward the 'Abbásid caliphate. Ja'far articulated a distinctive version of allegiance to the 'Alid cause: The legitimate imamate belonged exclusively in the progeny of 'Ali and Fátima, who alone were divinely chosen carriers of the sacred knowledge and divine guidance. All other 'Alid lineages, including that of Muhammad b. al-Hanafiyya, were inferior, so their claims should be ignored. The imamate was to be passed on from father to son within the 'Ali–Fátima lineage, forming an uninterrupted succession of divinely guided and semiholy *imam*s. Although deprived of political power, they were, according to Ja'far and his entourage, the only legitimate spiritual guides for the faithful seeking salvation. Their divinely bestowed status as guides of humankind demanded total obedience from their followers. This doctrine effectively undermined the original

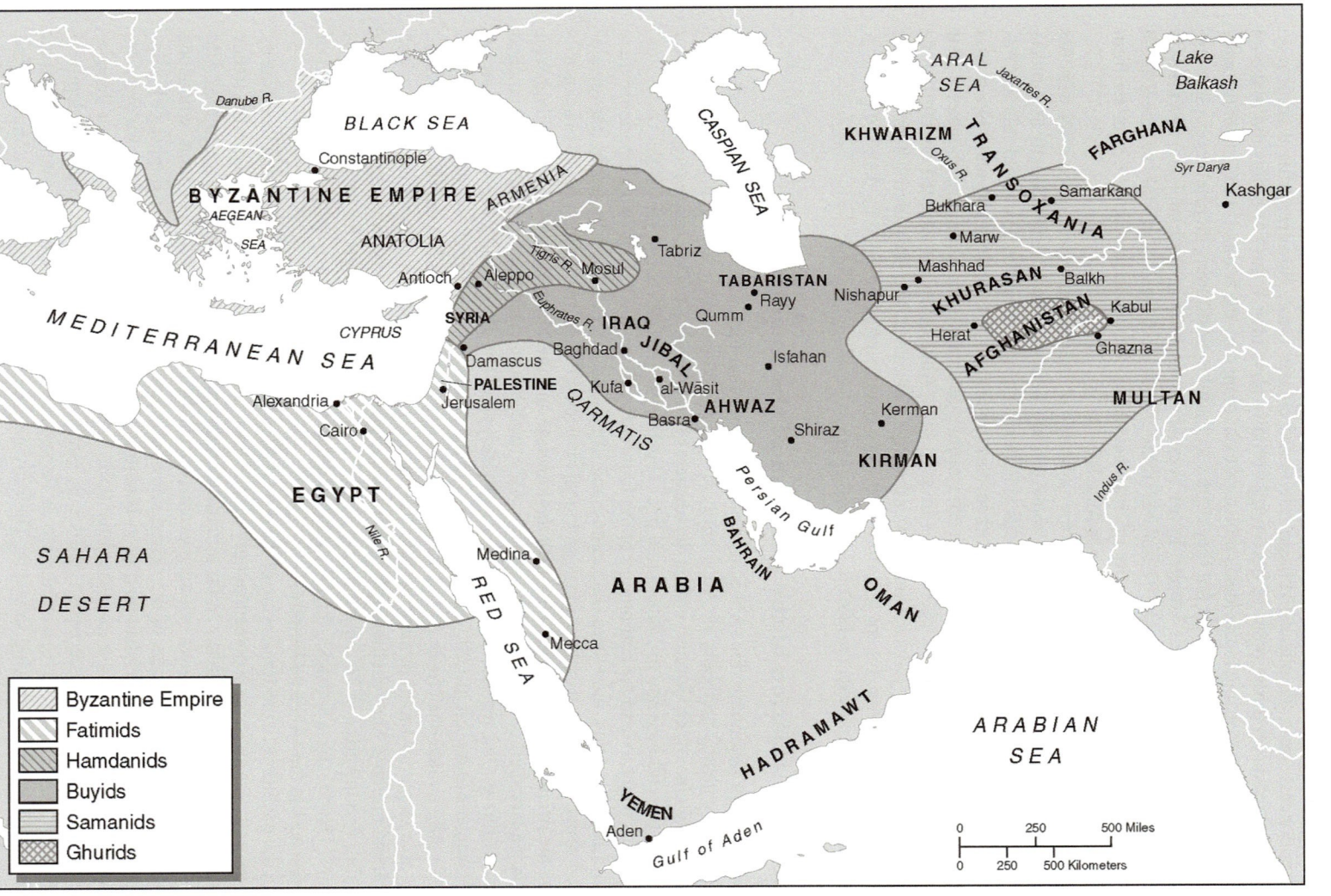

Map 8.1 The 'Abbasid Caliphate and the Successor Dynasties, Tenth–Eleventh Centuries

'Abbásid claim to religious leadership based on the bequest of the 'Alid Muhammad b. al-Hanafiyya. Therefore, the 'Abbásids found it prudent to allow their claim to lapse and began to emphasize instead their descent from the Prophet's uncle 'Abbás and his son 'Abdallah as the decisive proof of the legitimacy of their rule. This ideological shift required a drastic reshaping of the image of 'Abbásid ancestors. Official 'Abbásid historiography now presented the 'Abbásids as ideal Muslims and emphasized their critical contribution to the formation of the Islamic state and Islamic learning.[40] Thus, the political success of the 'Abbásid revolution resulted in the sharpening of the Sunnite and Shi'ite visions of Islam with the 'Abbásids gradually abandoning the original pro-'Alid trappings of their movement to throw in their lot decisively with the Sunni community.[41]

The opponents of 'Abbásid rule were presented with the alternative to continue to fight against the powerful 'Abbásid state or to accept its existence as a necessary evil. As with the Umayyads, the majority eventually chose peace and stability over the continuation of bloodshed, arguing that the unity of the faithful under a less than perfect ruler was better than civil strife and bloodshed. Gradually, despite their apparent faults, the 'Abbásids were able to assert their position as the sole legitimate rulers on behalf of Sunni Islam, leaving the 'Alid party, the *shi'a*, in the minority (see Figure 8.1).[42]

Figure 8.1 The Good Caliph Harun al-Rashid (r. 786–809) Receiving an Embassy from Charles the Great, King of the Franks

Christian Peacemaker Teams/Wikimedia Commons

Conclusion: The 'Abbásid Empire at Its Prime

To govern his sprawling empire, Abu Ja'far al-Mansúr and his successors had to rely on a vast bureaucracy and a broad network of police and spies entrusted with the task of forestalling any conspiracies against 'Abbásid rule. Supervising the day-to-day functioning of this complex imperial machinery was a formidable task that required whole-time commitment. To deal with the nitty-gritty of state administration, the 'Abbásids introduced the post of [prime] minister, or "vizier" (from the Arabic *wazír*, namely "one entrusted with responsibility"). From then on, the caliph performed largely ceremonial functions, which included the prosecution of holy wars against the Byzantine emperor and presiding over the performance of the annual *hajj*. He also participated in the celebrations of the major religious holidays, invested provincial governors, and received foreign envoys. Under al-Mansúr's successors, al-Máhdi (775–785), al-Hádi (785–786), and Harún al-Rashíd (786–809), the 'Abbásid caliphate enjoyed an unprecedented period of peace, prosperity, and cultural and intellectual flowering that is sometimes described in Muslim and Western histories as "The Golden Age of Islam."[43] The cultural richness and dynamism of this period is finely captured in the fanciful tales of "Thousand and One Nights." They reflect an idealistic perception of this momentous epoch by later generations of Muslims. The first half century of 'Abbásid rule was characterized by the growing concentration of power in the hands of the caliph and his retinue. Government-sponsored projects, such as the development of agricultural state lands, the building of hostels and medical facilities, the maintenance of roads and wells, the commercial extraction of salt, and so on, employed dozens of thousands of laborers. The state administration in Baghdad, now run by the all-powerful [prime] minister (vizier), sought to bring all the major activities in its sprawling realm under its control. In the religious sphere, this is evident from the government's practice of appointing Muslim judges (*qadis*). Under the Umayyads, such appointments were made by provincial governors.[44] Now they were handled by the caliph and his viziers. However, despite these centralizing efforts, the 'Abbásids were unable to assert their sway over the religious establishment. The more principled scholars (*'ulamá'*) reserved the right to reject government appointments in order to secure their independence from the powers-that-be so as to be able to criticize the excesses of their rule. In the end, as we shall see, 'Abbásid attempts to establish themselves as the ultimate arbiters in all matters, including religion, failed to bear fruit.

Questions to Ponder

1   Clearly, the supporters of the rights of 'Ali's family failed to achieve their principal goal of installing a caliph of the 'Ali–Fátima lineage. What were the main reasons behind their failure?

2   How was the third *fitna* different from or similar to the previous two? Elaborate.

3   Why did the Kharijite religious ideals and political agenda never stand a chance to be realized on a large scale? Or did they?

4   Is it correct to describe the overthrow of the Umayyads by the 'Abbásids as a "revolution"? If yes, how is it similar to or different from the revolutionary movements with which you are best familiar?

5   Discuss the strategy adopted by the 'Abbásids to legitimize their rule? Was it effective in the end? Why?

Summary

- There are sources of discontent with the dynastic rule of the Umayyads. Their rule is seen by many of their subjects as not only unjust but also outright un-Islamic. They are viewed as dynastic "kings," not as successors to the Prophet. Their commitment to implementing the precepts of true Islam is called into question by their critics. The driving forces of discontent are the *mawáli*, the pro-'Alid party, and some disgruntled Arab tribes stationed in the eastern provinces of the caliphate.
- The 'Abbásid family of the Háshim clan of the Quraysh lay claim to the leadership of the *umma* (a) as members of the Prophet's native clan (via his uncle 'Abbás, d. ca 653) and (b) as recipients of the bequest of the 'Alid Abu Háshim, son of Muhammad b. al-Hanafiyya (d. 700).
- The 'Abbásid propaganda campaign on behalf of the "one agreed upon from the House of the Prophet" is a success in Iraq, Khurasan, and Central Asia.
- The popular revolution of 750 is a complex intertwining of popular aspirations for justice, clannish interests, tribal factionalism, and political cynicism that has resulted in the establishment of the 'Abbásid caliphate based in Iraq and its capital Baghdad.
- Among the revolution's principal actors and beneficiaries, the 'Abbásids snatch the fruits of the victory of the broad anti-Umayyad movement from the supporters of the rights of 'Ali's family.
- The suppression of the pro-'Alid rebellions under the rule of the first 'Abbásid caliphs precede the subsequent rearticulation of the doctrine of the imamate. The 'Abbásids gradually begin to downplay their association with the pro-'Alid cause, focusing instead on their descent from the Prophet's uncle 'Abbás and his learned son 'Abdallah. Simultaneously, the majority of the supporters of the 'Alids, led by the politically powerless *imam*s, reconcile themselves to 'Abbásid rule.
- 'Abbásid power is consolidated under the caliphs al-Máhdi (775–785), al-Hádi (785–786), and Harún al-Rashíd (786–809). The new administrative practices adopted by the caliphs reflect the growing internal complexity of the 'Abbásid Empire.

Notes

1 Gerald Hawting, *The First Dynasty of Islam*, Southern Illinois University Press, Carbondale and Edwardsville, 1987, pp. 26–32; Patricia Crone, *Medieval Islamic Political Thought*, Edinburgh University Press, Edinburgh, 2004, pp. 33–34 and Chapter 4.
2 Crone, *Medieval*, p. 35.
3 Patricia Crone and Martin Hinds, *God's Caliph: Religious Authority in the First Centuries of Islam*, Cambridge University Press, Cambridge, 1986, passim and Crone, *Medieval*, pp. 34–35.
4 Hawting, *The First Dynasty*, pp. 13–14.
5 Steven Judd, "The Third Fitna: Orthodoxy, Heresy and Coercion in Late Umayyad History," an unpublished doctoral dissertation, University of Michigan, Ann Arbor, 1997, p. 282.
6 To what extent the cursing was part of the state policy is a moot point; see Wilferd Madelung, *The Succession to Muhammad*, Cambridge University Press, Cambridge, 1997, p. 344; cf. Oleg Bolshakov, *Istoriia Khalifata. T. III. Mezhdu dvukh grazhdanskikh voin, 656–696*, Vostochnaia literatura, Moscow, 1998, pp. 114–115.
7 Hawting, *The First Dynasty*, pp. 11–18 and Crone, *Medieval*, pp. 44–47.
8 Hawting, *The First Dynasty*, pp. 90–94.

9 See Khalid Y. Blankenship, *The End of the Jihad State*, SUNY Press, Albany, NY, 1994, pp. 230–236.

10 Andreas Görke, "al-'Abbas b. 'Abd al-Muttalib," in *Encyclopedia of Islam*, 3rd ed.; online edition: http://referenceworks.brillonline.com.

11 See Table 2.1. "Ahl al-Bayt: People of [the Prophet's] House"; p. 20.

12 Crone, *Medieval*, pp. 72–73, 87, and 89.

13 Hugh Kennedy, *The Prophet and the Age of the Caliphates*, Longman, London and New York, 1986, p. 24; for a slightly different view, see Crone, *Medieval*, pp. 87 and 89.

14 Crone, *Medieval*, p. 89.

15 Ibid., pp. 72–73.

16 Ibid., p. 79 and Moshe Sharon, *Revolt: The Social and Military Aspects of the 'Abbasid Revolution*, Hebrew University Press, Jerusalem, 1990, pp. 19–20.

17 Crone, *Medieval*, pp. 87–89.

18 See Table 2.1. "Ahl al-Bayt: People of the [Prophet's] House," p. 20.

19 John A. Williams (trans.), *The History of al-Tabari*, vol. 27: *The 'Abbasid Revolution*. SUNY Press, Albany, NY, 1985, p. 147.

20 Crone, *Medieval*, pp. 89–94.

21 Approximately fourteen feet.

22 Approximately thirteen and a half feet.

23 Q 22:39–40.

24 Williams (trans.), *The History of al-Tabari*, vol. 27, pp. 65–66.

25 Crone, *Medieval*, pp. 79, 94, and 97.

26 According to another report, he died of plague in Harran (present-day Turkey).

27 Crone, *Medieval*, p. 87 notes 1 and 2; Marshall Hodgson, *The Venture of Islam*, Chicago University Press, Chicago, 1974, vol. 1, pp. 275–276.

28 Crone, *Medieval*, pp. 87–88.

29 Williams (trans.), *The History of al-Tabari*, vol. 27, p. 174.

30 John Saunders, *A History of Medieval Islam*, Routledge, London and New York, 1990, pp. 102–103.

31 Heinz Halm, *Shiism*, Edinburgh University Press, Edinburgh, 1991, p. 26.

32 Saleh Said Agha, *The Revolution That Toppled the Umayyads*, E. J. Brill, Leiden, 2003, p. 299.

33 Hodgson, *The Venture*, vol. 1, p. 276.

34 Crone, *Medieval*, p. 96; Kennedy, *The Prophet and the Age of the Caliphates*, p. 131 and John Turner, *Inquisition in Early Islam: The Competition for Political and Religious Authority in the Abbasid Empire*. I.B. Tauris, London and New York, 2013, Chapter 1.

35 Hodgson, *The Venture*, vol. 1, pp. 280–281.

36 Ibid., pp. 283–284.

37 Crone, *Medieval*, p. 96.

38 Ibid., p. 79.

39 Kennedy, *The Prophet and the Age of the Caliphates*, p. 132.

40 See, e.g., Görke, "al-'Abbas b. 'Abd al-Muttalib."

41 Jonathan Berkey, *The Formation of Islam*, Cambridge University Press, Cambridge, 2003, p. 109 and Crone, *Medieval*, pp. 89–94 and 96–97.

42 Hodgson, *The Venture*, vol. 1, pp. 275–279.

43 See, e.g., Benson Bobrick, *The Caliph's Splendor: Islam and the West in the Golden Age of Baghdad*, Simon & Schuster, New York, 2012 and Tarif Khalidi, *Classical Arab Islam: The Culture and Heritage of the Golden Age*, Darwin Press, Princeton, NJ, 1985.

44 Kennedy, *The Prophet and the Age of the Caliphates*, p. 134.

Chapter 9

Islamic Scholarship Under the 'Abbásids

The Rise and Development of the Schools of Law

Introduction

As in Judaism, in Islam, religion sanctions and sanctifies law. Because it is annunciated in the scripture, the faithful see it as an expression of divine will, which renders it obligatory for the believer for fear of punishment not just in this life but also (and much more so) in the hereafter. If observed properly, law will lead them to salvation and eternal bliss. Disobeying or neglecting law, on the contrary, will condemn them to eternal damnation and misery in the afterlife. As in premodern Judaic communities, in premodern Islamic societies, law was seen as encompassing legal, moral, ethical, commercial, and ritual norms to be observed by those who are anxious to secure God's pleasure. In medieval Christian Europe, the situation was different due to the simultaneous functioning of both a reformed secular legal code inherited from Imperial Rome and the canon law of the Christian Church.

This said, the Jewish and especially the Muslim scriptures provide only a very general blueprint for the religiously sound way of life. It took time for Jewish and Muslim scholars to work out the ways in which the general and occasionally contradictory injunctions annunciated in their sacred books could be applied to concrete cases and moral and ethical dilemmas that the faithful of either religion encountered in their everyday lives. Seen from this perspective, the Jewish Halakhá and the Muslim Sharí'a, were as much human as divine products, although no doubt inspired by the sacred texts of each religion.

The Major Stages of the Evolution of Islamic Legal Thought

The Qur'an repeatedly enjoins Muslims to obey God and his Prophet. One consequence of this oft repeated injunction was the abolition under Islam of the legal practices peculiar to Arabian tribal paganism. As mentioned in Chapter 1, before the advent of Islam, the tribe as a collective body[1] determined the standards by which its members should live. The tribe relied on a body of unwritten, customary norms and practices that had evolved along with the historical fortunes of the tribe itself. Tribal laws were based primarily on legal precedents that had been accumulated by tribal elders who applied them, in consultation with one another, to new cases as they arose. In the tribal societies of pre-Islamic Arabia, there was neither a generally recognized system of legal authority nor any means to enforce it. Conflicts between individuals and tribal units were resolved either by force of arms or by arbitration. As we remember, it is precisely in the capacity of an outside arbitrator that Muhammad was invited to Yáthrib (Medina) by its mutually hostile tribal factions. Occasionally the role of arbitrators was assumed by Arabian soothsayers and pagan priests, who claimed to be in contact with the spirits of deceased ancestors or with tribal gods and thus able to solicit their advice on matters of disagreement or contestation. Poets, too, would occasionally represent their tribes in legal disputes. Their eloquence rendered them effective advocates for their tribe's rights.

The situation was somewhat different in the urban centers of Arabia. In Mecca, a bustling mercantile center, we find a commercial law of sorts, while in Yathrib (Medina), an agricultural oasis, some elementary legal norms pertaining to land tenure seem to have existed. In Mecca, there were also the rudiments of a system of legal administration represented by a council of the elders delegated by each major clan of the Quraysh tribe.

The year of Muhammad's migration to Yathrib (Medina), 622, ushered in a juridical revolution among the Arabs of the Peninsula. Throughout his stay in that city, the Prophet was receiving divine revelations instructing him how to guide his newly founded community on the right path. Whereas in Mecca he was first and foremost a religious preacher whose pious exhortations were neither obligatory nor enforceable, in Medina Muhammad acted as both legislator and enforcer of divinely inspired rules. Having recognized Muhammad as a prophet of God, the fledgling Muslim state in Medina, which, as we remember, consisted of the Meccan "emigrants" and the local "helpers," accepted his instructions as divinely ordained norms that were obligatory for all Muslims. These rules regulated both relations among the members of the community and between the community and its neighbors, especially the Arabian pagans, Jews, and Christians. They also instructed the first Muslims how to worship God, how to conceive of him, and how to conduct their personal lives.

Muhammad's revelations enshrined in the Qur'an became the foundation of Islamic legal theory and practice. Initially, the Prophet served as the sole legitimate interpreter of the divinely revealed rules. His elucidation of often very general and contradictory Qur'anic injunctions and his own opinions on various legal, moral, and ritual issues constituted the reservoir of normative wisdom upon which his followers came to draw after his death.

When Muhammad died, his successors or deputies, the caliphs, became the principal legislators of the Muslim community. They were actively engaged in adjudication and meted out concrete punishments for the offences that may have been condemned in the Qur'an in general terms but for which no special punishment was stipulated in its text. When faced with cases not explicitly mentioned in the Qur'an or the Sunna of the Prophet, they had to devise new rulings. For instance, 'Umar ruled that the Qur'anic injunction to cut off the hand of the thief "in requital for what they have wrought" (Q 5:38)[2] should be suspended during times of famine. Along with the Qur'an and the Sunna, such newly devised rulings formed the first body of juridical precedent upon which the subsequent generations of Muslim legal experts came to rely.[3]

With the advent of the Umayyads, the caliphs of this dynasty, as well as their provincial governors, judges, and learned advisors, effectively assumed the role of the community's legislators. Their legal decisions were often made on an ad hoc basis and were not grounded in any systematic legal theory.[4] This is not to say that they consciously and deliberately departed from the Qur'anic or prophetic legislation. Many of them were pious individuals who believed that they were executing divine will to the best of their abilities. However, in the final account, their legal decisions were based on their own understanding of revelation, public propriety, common sense, and justice.[5] This situation made for a kind of juridical "free-for-all," in which legislation and adjudication were shaped first and foremost by the legislators' personal propensities, as well as by local conditions and customs that varied substantially from one Muslim province to another.

The task of rendering juridical processes more predictable and uniform was taken up by pious individuals who would often be employed by the Umayyads but who would seek to maintain a certain distance from the rulers by exercising their own sense of justice in legal matters.[6]

When the Umayyad dynasty was overthrown, many of the legislative precedents established during its rule became suspect in the eyes of the 'Abbásid victors. They now looked to scholars unsullied by too close an association with the Umayyad regime to assume the task of articulating and applying the law. The scholars obliged by formulating the foundations of Islamic jurisprudence on the basis of their understanding of the Qur'anic revelation, the prophetic custom (the Sunna), and the local legal precedent. Unlike the more or less ad hoc and pragmatic legal procedures that were predominant under the Umayyads, under the 'Abbásids, juridical theory was articulated by learned individuals who can be characterized as "religious idealists."[7] Although some of these early jurists were employed by the 'Abbásid rulers as judges (qudát; sing. qádi), many of them were anxious to retain their intellectual independence vis-à-vis the state. Some even declined the most lucrative appointments. However, when religious scholars did agree to enter the service of the ruling dynasty as judges, they served it well. As a typical example, one can cite Abu Yúsuf (d. 799) who was appointed as chief qádi of the caliphate by the caliph Harún al-Rashíd (r. 786–809). In this position, Abu Yúsuf generated a substantial body of sophisticated legal devices "by which one might apparently defeat the spirit of the law without disobeying the letter."[8] While such devices may have helped Abu Yúsuf to solve legal problems for his royal employer,[9] they aroused the righteous indignation of the collectors and custodians of prophetic reports (hadíth). The latter cast doubt on the permissibility of using personal discretion by individual judges and insisted that the Prophet's example should be consulted and strictly adhered to in any legal or juridical activity.

Legal theory and practice varied from one region to another—a legacy of the Umayyad period, during which the foundations of several regional schools of law had been laid down by judges residing in different provinces of the caliphate.[10] Such juridical centers were located in Medina, Syria, and Iraq. The Syrian school did not survive the collapse of the Umayyad regime with which it was too closely affiliated. After a period of gestation, in the late eighth century, the disciples of the founders of these regional schools embarked on the task of articulating a comprehensive and sophisticated legal theory. In the process, the personal opinions of the founders of the schools[11] were gradually replaced by references to the actions and sayings of the Prophet that, along with the Qur'an, were declared to be the only legitimate foundations for legal decision making and adjudication. To what extent these juridical precedents and opinions were authentic or were simply ascribed to the Prophet to justify one or the other legal procedure is a hotly debated question.[12] The scholars involved in the process of the alleged ascription were by no means "malicious forgers." They believed that if a given legal opinion met religiously sanctioned standards, the Prophet would not have failed to articulate it when faced with a similar legal issue.[13] According to this view, there was no harm in attributing this opinion to him. Thus, one can say that in the period in question (namely, the second half of the eighth century to the first half of the ninth century), the Muslim legal tradition was "growing backward" as it were—from the legal precedents established by the Umayyad caliphs, as well as the governors and scholars associated with them, back to the legal rulings introduced by the Prophet's companions (particularly, the first four caliphs) and then to the Prophet himself. Understandably, this applies first and foremost to the Sunni legal schools. The Shi'ites, as already mentioned in Chapter 6, looked to 'Ali and his descendants for legal opinions, rulings, and authoritative precedents.

The complex process of juridical theory building culminated in the ninth century[14] with the emergence of four schools of Islamic law in Sunni Islam, each of which appealed to the Qur'an and prophetic precedent. The Twelver Shi'ites, in turn, produced their own version of Islamic law, later named "Ja'fari" (after the sixth imam of the Twelver Shi'ites Ja'far al-Sádiq; d. 765). Some surviving Kharijite communities and, later on, also the Isma'ili and Zaydi Shi'ites developed their own juridical schools.

The subsequent centuries witnessed an ever more sophisticated elaboration of Islamic legal theory. It was flexible enough to accommodate new legal issues as they arose and had served the Muslim community well until the advent of modernity and the colonization of the Muslim world by the European powers in the nineteenth century. The colonial period witnessed the adoption by many Muslim countries of European legal codes (criminal, commercial, and so on) that have remained in force there until today. As a result, Qur'an- and Sunna-based jurisdiction, often substantially modified, is now almost everywhere restricted to the law of personal status and family. Correspondingly, the jurisdiction of traditional Islamic judges (*qadis*) has been drastically curtailed, and legal experts have become largely superfluous.[15] This, in a nutshell, is the history of the formation and functioning of juridical thought in Islam. Let's now discuss some of its aspects in more detail.

The Qur'anic Roots of Islamic Law

The Qur'an constitutes the primary source of the Islamic law (*shari'a;* lit. "path"), which, as mentioned, is much broader in scope than Western secular law, as it governs not only relationships among people but also their religious duties, everyday behavior, ethics, morals, hygiene, and methods of worshipping God. This specificity of Islamic law springs from the Qur'an itself in that the latter does not clearly differentiate among legal norms, ritual duties, morals, and everyday behavior. As a book of religious, moral, and ethical guidance for individual Muslims and the Muslim community as a whole,[16] the Qur'an's legal subject matter is relatively minor and does not exceed four hundred to five hundred verses. Of these, only some eighty verses deal with legal topics in the strict (Western) sense of the word. They are concerned with such issues as division of the spoils of war, homicide, slavery, the prohibition of alcohol and the flesh of the swine, the penalty of flogging for fornication, the responsibilities of parties in marriage and divorce, the division of property within the family, and so on. These regulations often catered to the exigencies of the moment, for example, the prescription of the penalty of eighty lashes for the false accusation of adultery,[17] which was revealed following the episode in which 'A'isha was accused of infidelity after spending a night in the desert with a young Bedouin.

From the very outset, the Qur'an's general, ambiguous, and occasionally self-contradictory legal precepts had to be supplemented by the Prophet's more specific oral instructions as to their real intent and as to how they were to be implemented by his followers in real life. As we already know, these instructions, encapsulated in the Prophet's custom or the Sunna, became an indispensable part of legal theorizing in the early Islamic community. Understandably, the notion of the Prophet as the divinely inspired legislator was based on the carefully selected Qur'anic pronouncements to this effect (e.g., 4:13, 65, etc.).[18]

It has sometimes been argued that the Qur'anic narrative reflects a gradual evolution of Muhammad's self-perception as an admonisher who was sent to instruct his pagan audience in the teachings of the earlier scriptures to that of a legislating prophet in his own right. This transition took place during the Medinan period of the Prophet's career, as evidenced by *sura* 5, which confirms Muhammad's status as the legislator for his community and marshals an impressive array of legal commands concerning diet, hunting, theft, ritual ablutions, purity, retaliation for murder or injury, and so on. This same *sura* also expresses astonishment as to why the Jews of Medina should have recourse to Muhammad,[19] "seeing they have the Torah, wherein is God's judgment" (Q 5:43). Simultaneously, it calls on the Christians to seek guidance and advice in their Gospels (Q 5:46). Thus, the status of the Qur'an as the *Muslim* law is unequivocally articulated in its own text.

At the same time, as mentioned, the Qur'an hardly provides the faithful with an unequivocal and comprehensive legal system. This is evident from its apparently contradictory statements about the status of alcoholic drinks (Q 16:67; 2:219; 4:43, and 5:90–91) and the punishment for adultery (4:15–16 and 24:2). Even when a certain practice is unequivocally condemned, the Qur'an does not necessarily stipulate a concrete, enforceable punishment for the offense. For instance, those who are accused of misappropriating the property of orphans are simply threatened with a painful torment in the hereafter.[20] The Qur'an stipulates no concrete sanctions against them in this life, so it had to be either found in the *hadith* or arrived at through legal reasoning. On the other hand, some issues, such as, marriage and divorce, receive a fairly detailed, if not always unequivocal coverage.

Qur'anic Legislation Pertaining to Marriage, Divorce, and Inheritance

Qur'anic rules concerning marriage and divorce are numerous and variegated. They are aimed at the general improvement of the status of women that was apparently rather low under Arabian customary tribal laws before the advent of Islam. In regard to marriage, the Qur'an commands that the bride herself, not her legal custodian, should receive the dower payable by the husband, or bride-wealth (*mahr*). This was not the case in pre-Islamic times, when marriage was little more than a sale of the woman by her father or other male relative, who received, as vendor, the bride-wealth payable by the husband. The Qur'an made the wife a contracting party to the marriage agreement. In the laws pertaining to divorce, the supreme innovation of the Qur'an seems to be the introduction of the notion of the waiting period (*'idda*). Prior to Islam, the husband could discard his wife at a moment's notice without incurring any postmarital obligations toward her. His oral repudiation of his wife (*taláq*) took effect immediately. The Qur'an suspended the effect of the repudiation until the expiry of the waiting period. It stipulated that this period should last until the repudiated wife had completed three menstrual cycles[21] or, if the woman was pregnant, until delivery of the child. This period is described in the Qur'an as an opportunity for reconciliation, during which the wife was entitled to financial support and, according to some interpretations, also to lodging from her husband.[22] On a more practical level, the waiting period was necessary to determine that the divorced woman was not pregnant and thus to avoid confusion regarding the identity of the child's father should she remarry. This provision was apparently designed to protect the child's right to inheritance by preventing any dispute over its parenthood. For the same reason, the Qur'an stipulated (2:234) that the widow was to wait four months before she could marry again. Alongside such concrete legal regulations, we find general exhortations of a moral nature, such as "retain wives honorably and release them with kindness."

In the Qur'anic verse 4:3, Muslims are permitted to take up to four wives. Historically, this permission seems to have been revealed after the Battle of Úhud in 625, during which, as we remember, many Muslims were killed, leaving their womenfolk without sustenance. The dearth of eligible men was redressed by the revelation that permitted surviving Muslim males to take more than one wife.[23] It can be argued that this permission may have been a temporary measure. Nevertheless, the Islamic legal theory that took shape during the first two centuries of Islam codified this temporary provision and extrapolated it onto all current and future situations. For many centuries, the permission of polygamy had not been called into question, possibly because it was in accord with the predominantly male-centered and patriarchal ethos that prevailed in pre-modern Middle Eastern societies. With the military and political ascendancy of the West in the nineteenth and early twentieth centuries, Western values, including Western views of the role of women in society, were appropriated by some Muslim modernists. As a result, they offered a drastic reconsideration of polygamy, arguing that Q 4:129 effectively precludes Muslim men from taking several wives because it clearly stipulates that a man can take more than one wife only if he is capable of treating them equally. In the view of the Muslim modernists, such equal treatment was impossible in principle because the husband would always give preference to one wife over the other or others. Hence the permission of polygamy should be repealed in favor of monogamous marriage.[24]

Another important legal innovation can be found in the Qur'an's provisions concerning the division of inheritance. In pre-Islamic Arab society, rights of inheritance belonged solely to the male relatives of the deceased on the father's side. Despite some exceptions, the general rule was that females had no rights of succession. The same rule applied to minor children. The Qur'an allotted specific fractions of the deceased's estate to individual relatives, including men and women on both the mother's and the father's side. Simultaneously, both men and women were given full control of their share of inheritance. The Qur'anic ruling did not abolish the old system entirely because women were still entitled to only half of what men received. However, it did modify it with a view to improving the position of female relatives of the deceased as well as some previously excluded categories of relatives.

Qur'anic Punishments for Homicide

On the subject of homicide and physical assaults, the Qur'an stipulates the standard of just retribution that is familiar to us from the Jewish law, namely "an eye for an eye and a life for a life." This Qur'anic rule has replaced the system of indiscriminate blood revenge, under which any member of the guilty party was liable to be murdered by the relatives of the killed. Now, only one life, that of the killer himself, was due for the life of the victim. The relatives of the victim were given the option of demanding retaliation in kind or accepting compensation (one hundred camels or two hundred head of cattle). They could also pardon the offender altogether.

As one can see, the Qur'an has formulated many important legal rules that supersede or modify the rough and unevenly distributed justice characteristic of the life of the Bedouin tribes of Arabia before Islam. These rules, along with the Prophet's instructions inscribed in the Sunna, have become the foundation upon which the edifice of the Islamic law, the Shari'a, was erected in the subsequent centuries.

Fiqh, the *Fuqahá'*, the *Muftis*, and the Judges

Following the death of Muhammad, it fell to his companions and successors to interpret Qur'anic legislation and to develop a clear and noncontradictory legal framework and penal code that, on the one hand, would be firmly rooted in the Qur'an and the Sunna and, on the other, would be flexible enough to respond to new challenges as they arose. To this end, all relevant legal materials were systematically analyzed, and on the basis of this analysis, human actions were classified as forbidden or permitted, disapproved or indifferent, and recommended or obligatory. Of these categories the obligatory and the forbidden fall under the heading of law proper, for law's principal function is to prescribe and to forbid.[25] In other words, the performance or nonperformance of certain actions entail specified legal sanctions. The actions that are recommended or disapproved do not require any sanctions, so they effectively fall outside the legal realm as it is conceived of in modern Western legal theory. Within the context of Islam, such legally nonbinding actions do form an integral part of the Shari'a because it "is as much concerned with recommending and disapproving as it is with prescribing and forbidding."[26] This peculiarity sets the Islamic law apart from Western-style legal codes.

The development and application of such a relatively sophisticated analytical and classificatory system required special expertise, or "[juridical] understanding" (*fiqh*). The individuals possessed of this expertise have come to be known as "practitioners of *fiqh*," or *fuqahá'*.[27] With time, the *fuqahá'*, who originally had been private individuals versed in the Qur'an and Sunna, became professional jurists, who, as has already been mentioned, strove to maintain a certain degree of independence vis-à-vis the imperial dynasties of the Umayyads and 'Abbásids.[28] They were largely responsible for generating "an autonomous body of sacred law" in Islam,[29] which, in theory at least, was supposed to govern all aspects of Muslim personal and communal life. On the practical level, the law developed by the *fuqahá'* on the basis of their expert understanding of the Qur'an and the Sunna was implemented by judges (*qadis*) who were appointed by secular rulers to apply their legal expertise to concrete situations. Unlike the theoretically minded *fuqahá'*, who were less concerned with the law as it actually was than with the law as it ought to be, the judges, in their adjudicatory practices, had to constantly exercise their personal discretion and understanding of the spirit of the divine legislation, while simultaneously availing themselves of the "norms of local custom"[30] and of the administrative practices of the first caliphs. Furthermore, the judges drew heavily on the legal precedents established by the authoritative members of their juridical schools, of which there are four in Sunni Islam and one in Twelver Shi'ism.[31] Periodically, the *fuqahá'* made attempts to restrict the discretionary powers of the judges by demanding that they "return" to the letter of the Qur'an and Sunna. However, for all intents and purposes, the judges remained the primary applicators of the divine will, as they understood it, to concrete legal cases. One can thus say that the entire history of Islamic jurisprudence is characterized by an uneasy coexistence of an abstract juridical ideal formulated by the *fuqahá'* and concrete juridical decisions made by the judges.

One of the major functions of the *fuqahá'* was to deliver nonbinding opinions on certain matters pertaining to the implementation of the Shari'a. These opinions were called *fatwas*. The *fuqahá'* in their capacity of issuers of legal opinions were called *muftis*. For instance, a Muslim who would like to know whether or not it was necessary or meritorious to use a toothpick after meal could seek an advice from a *mufti* (see Figure 9.1). The *mufti* would find a *hadíth* that mentions that the

Figure 9.1 Mufti Reading in His Prayer Stool

Jean-Léon Gérôme. Art Renewal Center: Public Domain: Wikimedia Commons

Prophet was in the habit of using a toothpick. Seeing that following the Prophet's example is meritorious in the eyes of God, the *mufti* would most likely recommend that the inquirer use a toothpick. However, since neither the Qur'an nor the Sunna make the use of a toothpick obligatory for the believer, the *mufti* would rule that the believer is free not to use it, without incurring any punishment.[32]

The Abrogation Theory

Since Qur'anic prescriptions were often mutually contradictory, the *fuqahá'* had to exercise considerable ingenuity to overcome this predicament. With time, they have adopted the theory of abrogation (*naskh*), according to which earlier legal norms were superseded (and canceled) by later revelations. In practice, the latter were those that legal experts considered to be more in line with the prevailing customs and values[33] of the day and thus more acceptable to the community at large. The abrogation theory was justified by references to the Qur'an (such as 2:106, 16:101, and 87:6–7). It had ramifications beyond the strictly juridical field in that it forced Muslim scholars to establish a rigid chronology of "abrogated" and "abrogating" verses. This task required a thorough knowledge of the history of the first Muslim community in Medina so as to determine the time and circumstances in which this or that verse was revealed. Thus, the exigencies of legal interpretation of the Qur'an gave an impetus to the production and accumulation of historical knowledge, creating a fascinating symbiosis of legal, exegetical, and historical expertise. It is exemplified by the work of al-Tabari (d. 923), who was simultaneously a legal expert, an exegete, and an historian. Naturally, the task of interpreting the Qur'an and the Sunna by Muslim jurists required of them, in addition to historical knowledge, a sure grasp of Arabic grammar, semantics, and lexicology. The formation of all these sciences went hand in hand with and was stimulated by the necessity of articulating a coherent and noncontradictory Islamic legal system. In the final account, one can argue that all these Islamic sciences owe their existence to the contemplation of the best minds of the Muslim community over implications of the Qur'an and the Sunna for themselves and their coreligionists.

The abrogation theory achieved great sophistication at the hands of later legal scholars, who, for instance, argued that the famous "sword verse" enjoining the believers to "slay the idolaters wherever you find them" (Q 9:5) abrogates no fewer than 124 other verses commanding "anything less than a total offensive against the non-believers."[34] As time went on the abrogation theory was expanded to include "replacing one legal ruling with another due to the termination of the effective period of the earlier ruling."[35] The expansion of the scope of the abrogation theory has rendered Islamic juridical theory much more flexible and accommodating, despite the fact that some conservative Muslim scholars still had difficulty accepting the system of abrogation as unworthy of an all-wise and all-knowing God. In particular, they could not understand why God had not suppressed the abrogated and thus invalid Qur'anic verses altogether to prevent the faithful from wracking their brains in trying to make sense out of their sequence.[36]

The "Qur'anic Commands" That Are Not in the Qur'an

When, at the early stage of legal theory building, a certain legal practice had to be implemented that the Qur'an was silent about, its proponent would occasionally "remember" that it had originally been in the sacred text but was somehow omitted at a later stage. Naturally, the person who dared to make such claims had to be a highly respected individual with close personal ties to the Prophet. The notorious "stoning verse"[37] remembered by caliph 'Umar and the "suckling verse"[38] remembered by 'A'isha are cases in point. For the Western scholar John Burton, they are eloquent indications of the precedence of the Qur'an over all other sources of juridical or moral authority in Islam with the partial exclusion of the prophetic Sunna.[39] In short, to be legitimate and universally acceptable, a norm or a ruling had to be grounded in the Qur'an.

The Formation of the Regional Schools of Law

When the Prophet was still alive, he served as both the interpreter and enforcer of the divine law as annunciated in the Qur'an. His juridical and executive decisions formed an important resource for later jurists.[40] One Sunni school of law lays special claim to the legal practice of Medina under the Prophet and his first three successors. It was founded by the renowned Medinan jurist Málik b. Ánas (d. 795) and is named after him. Málik worked on the assumption that the legislative legacy of Medina was the most authentic and unadulterated manifestation of divine will. According to Málik, this Medinan legacy should be extrapolated to any new situations as they arise and adopted by all Muslims as their primary legal standard. However, before this could be done, the exemplary practice of the community of Medina had to be described and systematized. To this end, Málik composed a comprehensive juridical treatise entitled "The Leveled Path" (*al-Muwátta'*)—the first legal manual of Islam.[41] "The Leveled Path" is a collection of legal precedents going back to the primeval Muslim community of Medina arranged topically. Only those precedents that were authenticated by the consensus of the leading scholars of Medina passed Málik's muster.[42] Scholars who agreed with Málik's conclusions about the precedence of the Medinan legal practice became known as the followers of Málik's legal method *mádhhab* ("method" or "path"), or the Malikiyya. All actions and legislative decisions described in *al-Muwátta'* were seen by Málik and his followers as sanctioned by God who communicated his will to the Prophet, who in turn passed it on to the foremost scholars in his immediate entourage. Preserved and transmitted to the later generations of Muslim scholars, the Maliki *mádhhab* spread westward to eventually become the primary legal affiliation of the Muslims of North Africa and Spain.

The legal system of the Syrian jurist al-Awzá'i (d. 744) was built on different principles. Al-Awzá'i, a supporter of and advisor to the ruling house of the Umayyads, argued that the tradition of Medina persisted uninterrupted under the Umayyads and their legal advisors, who adjudicated in complete accordance with the spirit and letter of the Qur'an and prophetic legal practice, despite the fact that they were now based in Syria. Hence, the Umayyad juridical lore, which was based on the experiences of the first Muslim community in Medina, constitutes, according to al-Awzá'i, a sound source of legal precedents for the later generations of Muslim jurists to draw on. As mentioned, the Awzá'i school did not survive the overthrow of the Umayyads in 750, although it was still in evidence for another century or so in Islamic Spain (al-Andalus) which by that time was ruled by a fugitive Umayyad prince and his descendants. However, even al-Andalus it was eventually supplanted by the Maliki *mádhhab* that was embraced by the majority of scholars residing in that part of the Muslim world.

Another major regional center of Islamic jurisprudence was located in Iraq. The eponymous founder of this tradition was Abu Hanífa (d. 767). He viewed the juridical theory and practice of the city of Kufa as a faithful reflection and elaboration of the prophetic legal tradition by the leading scholars of the Muslim state who had settled in Iraq at the time of the Arab conquests. The doctrine of the Hánafi school of law, as it has come to be called, took its final shape at the hands of Abu Hanífa's foremost disciples, Abu Yúsuf (d. 799) and al-Shaybáni (d. 805). Abu Yúsuf became the most prominent legist of Iraq after Abu Hanífa and distinguished himself by serving as the legal advisor for the caliph Harún al-Rashíd.[43] From Iraq, the Hánafi *mádhhab* spread to the eastern lands of Islam, to Anatolia, Iran, Central Asia, the Volga region, and India. It has been especially prominent among Turkic-speaking people.

Both the Hánafi and the Maliki schools relied heavily on the received wisdom and legal precedents established by their founding fathers in the second half of the eighth century. Subsequently,

Hánafi and Maliki jurists constantly turned to their authority in legal theorizing and adjudication. This juridical overdependence on fallible human opinion irritated the quickly expanding class of *hadíth* specialists, who considered the statements and actions of the Prophet himself to be the only legitimate source of legal precedent. They dismissed the verdicts and juridical reasoning of Maliki and Hánafi *fuqahá'*, which were not explicitly based on the prophetic *hadíth*, as arbitrary and prone to error. The *hadíth* specialists (*ahl al-hadíth*) insisted that human discretion in legal decision making was to be reduced to a minimum. The decision-making process should be subordinated to the authority of Qur'an and the prophetic *hadíth*, to the exclusion of nonscriptural sources of legislation. For their part, the jurists who were committed to the principles and precedents formulated by the founders of their respective schools considered adherents of *hadíth* to be unfit for making sound legal decisions due to their ignorance of juridical theory and precedent. An attempt to bridge the gap between these two camps of religious experts was undertaken by a scholar who was steeped in the teachings of both the Maliki and the Hánafi schools, while at the same time being a supporter of the use of *hadíth*.

Muhammad al-Sháfi'i (d. 820) and the Crystallization of the Islamic Legal Theory

Born in Syria of a Hashimite family of the Quraysh, Muhammad al-Sháfi'i grew up as an orphan in Mecca. After studying with Málik b. Ánas at Medina, he continued his quest for knowledge in Iraq. There he attended the teaching sessions of Abu Hanífa's disciple named al-Sháybani (d. 805), the author of several authoritative treatises on Hánafi *fiqh.* Eventually, al-Sháfi'i moved to Egypt, where he committed his own juridical ideas to writing. They were formulated on the basis of and in opposition to the teachings of Málik, Abú Hanífa, and al-Sháybani. All things considered, his own legal doctrine seems to be closer in spirit to that of his first teacher, Málik b. Ánas.

Al-Sháfi'i's principal contribution to Islamic jurisprudence lies in his insistence that every human action should correspond to a divine command. The divine commands are either explicitly articulated in the Qur'an and the Sunna or implicit in them and can thus be teased out of them by means of analogical reasoning (*qiyás*).[44] Heedful of the position of the adherents of *hadíth* and seeking to take advantage of the growing number of *hadíth* reports in circulation, al-Sháfi'i suggested that his fellow *fuqahá'* should abandon their excessive reliance on the secondary juridical tradition of one or the other regional school and ground their legislative activity firmly in the Qur'an and the body of the authentic prophetic *hadíth*. In al-Sháfi'i's view, it is the Qur'an and *hadíth* rather than the local legal precedent of a given legal school and its founder that should serve as the primary source of the law.

He justified his new approach as follows: The prophet Muhammad was not only the deliverer of the divine law but also its interpreter. His Sunna was thus nothing but an authoritative interpretation and concretization of the general divine commands contained in the Qur'an. The Prophet's legal decisions and practices, as reported in the *hadíth*, demonstrate how he applied his inspired knowledge of divine will to concrete legal cases. In other words, Muhammad's interpretation of the Qur'an and his juridical decisions are in themselves a vital elaboration of the Qur'anic revelation. Instead of relying on the legal precedents established by fallible human actors, no matter how authoritative, one should seek guidance in Muhammad's personal acts and words because they were divinely guided, inspired, and, as such, inerrant. Implicitly and subtly, al-Sháfi'i's doctrine elevated the *hadíth* as source of juridical theory and practice to almost the same stature as the Qur'an. In line with his teaching, al-Sháfi'i expanded the abrogation theory that had theretofore been restricted to the Qur'anic verses only. While he insisted that a Qur'anic verse could still be abrogated only by another Qur'anic verse, he argued that a *hadíth*, too, can be abrogated only by another *hadíth.* At the same time, the Qur'an cannot abrogate the Sunna.

Figure 9.2 Muslim Judge (*qadi*) Sitting in Judgment of a Legal Case (thirteenth-century book miniature)

If there is a contradiction between the two, it should be due to a human misunderstanding of the true implications of a Qur'anic passage or a *hadíth*. Or else one has simply failed to find a *hadíth* that corroborates the Qur'anic ruling (see Figure 9.2).[45]

Due to the newly found importance of *hadíth*, their provenance from the Prophet acquired special urgency. By al-Sháfi'i's time, Muslim scholars had developed a sophisticated procedure for ascertaining the authenticity of any given *hadíth* through a careful examination of the chain of its transmitters. With the rigorous authentication procedures in place, the possibility of forgery was supposed to have been reduced to a minimum.

The Four Roots of Islamic Jurisprudence

Al-Sháfi'i's system was aimed at reducing the arbitrary element in the process of legal decision making and adjudication. This meant limiting the scope of the jurist's personal discretion (*ra'y*), which was so strongly resented by the experts on *hadíth*. A law that depended on the private opinion of individual lawyers was unacceptable because it was both unpredictable and arbitrary. It seems that the majority of *fuqahá'* agreed with al-Sháfi'i on this issue, although it took them almost half a century after al-Sháfi'i's death to adjust their legal theory so as to subordinate the personal opinion of an individual scholar to the divine will as expressed in the Qur'an or the Sunna. For their part, the adherents of *hadíth* were forced to adapt to the new situation.

Collecting, authenticating, and classifying prophetic reports, commendable as this activity was from the viewpoint of personal piety, was no longer sufficient. If one was to participate in a meaningful legislative and adjudicating activity, one had to master a bare minimum of juridical theory. So, often against their will, the proponents of prophetic *hadíth* had to reinvent themselves as jurists.

Al-Sháfiʻi is credited with the formulation of the basic principles of the legal theory that proved to be acceptable to both the *fuqahá'* and the *hadíth* scholars. He posed the following question: If no answer to a concrete legal case is found in either the Qur'an or the Sunna, how should one go about resolving it? Al-Sháfiʻi proposed that the jurist should draw an analogy between a ruling attested in the Qur'an or the Sunna and the new case at hand. This procedure, which came to be known as "reasoning by analogy" or "analogical reasoning" (*qiyás*), became the third source of Islamic law in al-Sháfiʻi's system. On the one hand, it left some room to human discretion. On the other, it set relatively rigid limits within which it was to be exercised, at least in theory. To al-Shafiʻi thus goes the credit of achieving a compromise between the position of the *fuqahá'* and that of the adherents of *hadíth*. Drawing analogies required of scholars considerable ingenuity as well as a thorough knowledge of the two principal sources of Islamic law. For example, in an attempt to fix the minimal amount of dower or bride-wealth (*mahr*) payable by the husband to his wife on marriage, a parallel was drawn between the loss of virginity by the bride as a result of marriage and the minimal amount of stolen goods that requires the amputation of the hand as the penalty for theft. According to this analogy, in both cases, the end result was a physical loss— virginity in the former and a limb in the latter. On the basis of this analogy, the minimal amount of stolen goods punishable by the loss of limb, which was ten *dirhams*[46] in the Hánafi school and three in the Maliki, was set as the minimal size of the dower or bride-wealth.[47]

Another typical example of reasoning by analogy is the prohibition of all intoxicating beverages, which is derived from the Qur'anic prohibition of grape wine (*khamr*). How does one deal with other beverages that are not explicitly named in the Qur'an? For example, if fermented date juice (*nabídh*) is not mentioned in the sacred text, is it licit for the believers? To resolve this dilemma, jurists drew an analogy between these two beverages on the basis of their common effect on the consumer, namely, both being intoxicants. Hence, the prohibition of the former was construed as the prohibition of the latter and, by extension, of all alcoholic (i.e., intoxicating) beverages and substances, including narcotics. God's command was thus interpreted as the prohibition of the phenomenon of intoxication per se, regardless of the medium.[48]

In addition to the *qiyás*, al-Sháfiʻi identified the fourth source of legal theory—the consensus of the Muslim community (*ijmáʻ*). He declared the authority of *ijmáʻ* to be binding by quoting the widely known prophetic *hadíth*, according to which the Muslim community would never be agreed upon an error. In practice, *ijmáʻ* meant not the agreement of the entire community, which was impossible to achieve in practice especially in the premodern period, but rather that of the community's authoritative experts, who could be presented with a certain problem of law or conscience and then asked to issue a legal ruling in support or rejection of it. The majority answer would then be pronounced to be the community's *ijmáʻ* on the issue at hand and thus applicable by judges to concrete legal cases.

Summarizing al-Sháfiʻi's contributions to the formation of juridical theory, one can say the following:

1 His reform consisted of restricting the weight of legal precedents not sanctified by the authority of the Prophet; whether or not such precedents could now be disguised as prophetic *hadíth* was not that important.
2 His overriding intention was to introduce more uniformity and predictability into the realm of legal theory and practice.

3   Above all, he went far in restricting the sphere of arbitrary opinion, *ra'y*, of an individual judge or jurist on the basis of personal sense of justice.

Al-Sháfi'i's legal reform came at a price. It has made the legal system somewhat more rigid and less accommodating to new situations. Due to its heavy reliance on "sound *hadíth*," it has become closely intertwined with the science of *hadíth* criticism that was discussed in Chapter 6. According to a widely cited allegory of al-Sháfi'i's juridical reform, the production of new legal rulings by Muslim jurists is likened to the harvesting of the fruit from the tree of law that has grown out of its four roots: the Qur'an, the Sunna, *ijmá'*, and *qiyás*.

Later Developments

By and large, al-Sháfi'i's system has become normative in Sunni Islam. Those schools that have rejected some of its elements—such as the Záhiri school of Baghdad, which denied the legitimacy of *qiyás* and insisted on the exclusive and literal reliance of the Qur'an and the Sunna—have gradually withered away. Others (e.g., the Hánafis and the Malikis) have adopted broader, if distinctive, interpretations of *qiyás* than al-Sháfi'i recommended. In the Hánafi and Maliki legal theories, *qiyás* is often but a thinly varnished exercise of personal judgment by the *faqíh*. The Hánafis, for example, have allowed their judges to make use of their personal preference (*istihsán*) in those cases where they could neither find an appropriate Qur'anic/prophetic ruling nor draw an analogy. The Malikis have granted similar discretionary powers to the jurists of their school under the rubric of "consideration of human interest" (*istisláh*).[49] In all Sunni and Shi'ite legal schools, the jurist whose knowledge of the principal sources of Islamic law qualifies him to propose a creative and innovative interpretation (*ijtihád*) of the roots of Islamic jurisprudence is called *mujtáhid*.

Despite its overriding commitment to the authority of the Qur'an and the Sunna, the Hanbali school, named after Ibn Hánbal (d. 855), the leader of the Hadíth-folks party,[50] has eventually allowed its jurists to formulate a legal rule on the basis of a perceived contribution to the common good of the community (*máslaha*). The legitimacy of such concessions has often been the subject of heated debates between those committed to a literal interpretation of the sources of law and those who have sought to render the legal system more flexible in the face of the changing conditions of the community's existence. In the end, the textualist or literalist approach has gained the upper hand, as the Muslim jurists still feel extremely uncomfortable giving the impression that they are articulating the law independently of the scriptures.[51]

The development of Shi'ite *fiqh* was similar to that of the Sunni legal schools. Shi'ite jurists have duly acknowledged the *hadíth*, albeit transmitted through their *imam*s, as the embodiment of the Prophet's Sunna. At the same time, they have taken a broader view of the Sunna by including in it the sayings and teachings of their *imam*s. In contrast to the Sunnis, who believe that direct divine guidance and inspiration ended with the death of the Prophet, the Shi'ites consider the descendants of 'Ali and Fátima to be the natural repositories of the revealed knowledge and, as such, infallible sources of law. The Shi'ite jurists reject the concept of *qiyás* and rely instead on reason (*'aql*) as the fourth source of law. In the absence of the *imam*s, Shi'ite *mujtáhid*s have assumed the task of formulating and developing the positive law for the Shi'ite community. Unlike the Sunnis with their four legal schools, the Twelver Shi'ites adhere to only one *mádhhab*, which, as mentioned, is called "Já'fari," after the name of Ja'far al-Sádiq, the sixth Shi'ite imam. The Zaydi branch of the Shi'ite community, which still exists in the mountainous areas of North Yemen, has developed a distinct system of *fiqh* that is generally closer to the Sunni legal schools than to that of the Twelver Shi'ites. The Kharijites, too, have their own legal school that has survived to this day in Mzab region of North Africa, in Tunisia and in the Sultanate of Oman in southeastern Arabia.

Parallel Systems of Justice Under the 'Abbásids

From the perspective of the 'Abbásid rulers and their ministers (viziers), the *fiqh* legislature developed by legal specialists was too "soft," "convoluted," and thus ineffective for the purposes of absolutist rule. Its main drawback, in their view, was its stringent requirements to base legal verdicts on a clear and incontrovertible evidence—a condition that delayed the exercise of swift justice indispensable for the stability of their monarchical state. To overcome the perceived leniency of Shari'a courts, the 'Abbásids and provincial rulers came to mete out and apply their own penalties from public humiliation to corporal beatings and monetary fines.[52] Thus one can speak of two systems of justice under the 'Abbásids: One was dispensed by the judges in Shari'a courts on the basis of the exact legal norms developed by the *fuqahá'*; the other was the unmediated and swift justice dispensed by the caliphs, their viziers, or military commanders (*amírs*) during special sessions. The latter came to be called "[the courts] for redress of wrongs" (*mazálim*) and were initially established as bulwarks against abuses of power by those in authority. Gradually, all administrative offenses and cases of treason, conspiracy, heresy, and disruption of public order have come under the jurisdiction of the *mazálim* courts. In such courts, the rulers and their officials would act simultaneously as investigators, judges, and jury. Using absolutist powers vested in their office, caliphs would impose any punishment they saw fit without much regard to the niceties of the Shari'a. Torture and corporal punishments were commonly applied in such ad hoc courts to extract confessions, and the Shari'a norms were followed only to the extent that they did not interfere with the overall goal of exercising swift and sure justice. The Shari'a was thus effectively confined to commercial, contractual, ritual, and family matters.[53] The two parallel systems of justice survived the fall of the 'Abbásid dynasty in 1258 and were adopted by the Muslim states and empires that came in its wake: the Ayyubid, the Mamluk, the Ottoman, the Safawid, and the Moghul.

Conclusions

This survey of the evolution of Islamic law and legal theory under the 'Abbásids reflects the transformation of the Muslim community from a state dominated by the Arabs to one in which the Arabs were no longer the majority. Conversions to Islam of non-Arab ethnic groups, primarily but not exclusively Persians, Turks, Slavs, and Berbers, gradually tilted the demographic balance of the Muslim Empire in favor of the new converts. These culturally and ethnically diverse elements had to be accommodated by the system and given equal status under a newly formulated Islamic law. This law was articulated and elaborated by religious specialists belonging to the learned class (*'ulamá'*) of the Muslim community. It is this class that furnished the community with legal experts (*fuqahá'*), who formulated juridical procedures and issued legal rulings (*fatwas*) on issues not explicitly addressed in the foundational texts of Islam—the Qur'an and the Sunna. The carefully assembled edifice called "Shari'a," that is, the "path" to pious living and salvation, was a force that unified the diverse elements of the Muslim imperial state into one community. The precepts of the Shari'a structured the lives of individual Muslims in more or less uniform ways, integrating, accommodating, and eventually transcending vastly disparate local social and cultural customs and legal traditions. The Islamic law provided medieval Muslims with a sense of common identity. Wherever a Muslim went, he was subject to the same law, although, as we have seen, some regional differences persisted within the framework of the four legal schools of Sunni Islam. However, they were not significant enough to fragment the Muslim legal arena. The Shi'ites living in Sunni-dominated lands were in principle subject to their own law and turned to their own jurists for legal advice. However, the differences between the Sunni and Shi'ite legal theory and practice were, in the final account, relatively insignificant as well. Therefore, like the *fuqahá'* of the four Sunni schools, the Sunni and the Shi'ite legal scholars have eventually learned to tolerate each other while acknowledging their differences. When no Shi'ite *fuqahá'* were available, Shi'ites submitted to the jurisdiction of Sunni legal experts. In both communities, their learned representatives (*'ulamá'*) were the principal sources of religious instruction and authority. They transmitted their teachings and their authority through their private networks that, for the most part, lay outside direct state control. The majority of the legal experts were anxious to preserve their independence vis-à-vis the imperial state. Even when they accepted state appointments as judges, their loyalty was first and foremost to their own class and its values. Since the scope of law encompassed "every conceivable arena of social life, from how to pray, to how to structure a business partnership, to how to trim one's beard,"[54] the importance of the *fuqahá'* for the proper functioning of Muslim societies is impossible to overestimate. As we shall see in the next chapter, the rulers would occasionally try to wrest religious authority from the learned class, but, in the end, their attempts have been unsuccessful. Alongside formulating and applying law, the scholars were engaged in theological theorizing. In this field, too, they were unable to achieve unanimity, which led to the articulation of several competing positions regarding the chief articles of Muslim faith.

Questions to Ponder

The Prophet once said that divergence of opinions among Muslims is a blessing to be valued.

1   How is this saying related to disagreements among Muslim legal scholars?
2   Were such disagreements a blessing or a curse for the Muslim community?
3   What were the causes and consequences of such legal disagreements?

Summary

- Islamic law (*shari'a*) presents a comprehensive path to salvation in the hereafter. In that respect, it differs from Western legal codes.
- Muhammad's revelations are the foundation of Islamic legal theory and practice, with the Prophet as the infallible interpreter and enforcer of divine injunctions.
- In the postprophetic epoch, Islamic law evolves under the Umayyads and the 'Abbásids.
- Rooted in the Qur'an, the Shari'a's legal aspects provide for marriage, division of property, commercial transactions, and punishment for homicide.
- Changing conditions of the *umma* necessitate a continual reinterpretation and elaboration of the injunctions of the Qur'an and the Sunna of the Prophet.
- Islamic legal theory, or jurisprudence (*fiqh*), emerges, engaging its learned exponents: the *fuqahá'* (jurisprudents), the *muftis* (issuers of legal rulings), and the *qadis* (judges), the latter of whom apply the legal precepts articulated by the two former groups of legal experts to concrete cases.
- How to deal with the Qur'an's apparent contradictions? Can one verse "cancel" another? The rise of the abrogation theory has its implications for Islamic legal thought.
- Some legal injunctions are not in the Qur'an but are commonly seen as Qur'anic, such as the so-called stoning verse and the suckling verse.
- Regional schools of law are formed in Arabia (Medina), Syria, Iraq, and the Muslim West (North Africa and al-Andalus). The earliest schools are Awza'i (Syria), Maliki (Medina), and Hánafi (Iraq).

- Jurists increasingly rely on authentic *hadíth* in legal theory and practice as a way to avoid an arbitrary and unrestricted use of personal discretion. The four sources ("roots") of Islamic jurisprudence are articulated by al-Sháfi'i (d. 820): the Qur'an, the Sunna, the consensus of the community (*ijmá'*), and reasoning by analogy (*qiyás*).
- Room for human discretion in legal decision making is expanded: "exerting oneself" (*ijtihád*) in an effort to come up with a solution of a new or unprecedented legal problem; exercising personal preference (*istihsán*); and taking into account the notion of the common good of the community (*máslaha*).
- Four legal schools of Sunni Islam crystallize: Maliki, Hánafi, Sháfi'i, and Hánbali, along with their Shi'ite and Kharijite counterparts.
- Under the 'Abbásids, parallel systems of justice develop: administrative courts set by rulers to deal with abuses of power by those in authority and Shari'a courts dealing with matters related to personal status, family, division of property, commercial transactions, debts, and the like.

Notes

1 In reality, it was the tribe's elders and chiefs who articulated and applied the norms by which tribesfolk were supposed to live. Members of a clan of the tribe were free to reject these norms, in which case they would forfeit their tribe's protection. When expelled by their tribe, the insubordinate individual or clan would become fair game to neighboring tribes.

2 Q 5:43, according to Arberry's translation.

3 Wael Hallaq, *A History of Islamic Legal Theories*, Cambridge University Press, Cambridge, 1999, pp. 11–12.

4 Ibid., p. 13.

5 Noel Coulson, *A History of Islamic Law*, Edinburgh University Press, Edinburgh, 1997, pp. 30–31.

6 Steven Judd, *Religious Scholars and the Umayyads*, Routledge, London and New York, 2014.

7 Coulson, *A History*, p. 37.

8 Christopher Melchert, *The Formation of the Sunni Schools of Law, 9th–10th Centuries C.E.*, E. J. Brill, Leiden, 1997, p. 9.

9 Marshall Hodgson, *The Venture of Islam*, Chicago University Press, Chicago, 1974, vol. 1, p. 294.

10 Ibid., pp. 318–322 and 335.

11 See, e.g., Peter Hennigan, "Ahl al-ra'y," in *Encyclopedia of Islam*, 3rd ed.; online edition: http://reference works.brillonline.com.

12 See, e.g., Wael Hallaq, "On Orientalism, Self-Consciousness and History," *Islamic Law and Society*, vol. 18 (2011), pp. 387–439.

13 Melchert, *The Formation*, p. 42.

14 Contemporary academics disagree over the exact period when the Islamic legal theory came to fruition; see Hallaq, *A History*, pp. 30–33.

15 For details, see Wael Hallaq, *Shari'a: Theory, Practice, Transformations*, Cambridge University Press, Cambridge, 2009, Part III.

16 Coulson, *A History of Islamic Law*, p. 11.

17 Q 24:11–17.

18 See Chapter 6.

19 Hallaq, *A History*, pp. 4–5.

20 Coulson, *A History of Islamic Law*, p. 12.

21 Q 2:227–228.

22 Coulson, *A History of Islamic Law*, pp. 14–15.

23 This is a commonly held view of the provenance of this and other Qur'anic injunctions; for a dissenting voice that rejects the reliance by Western and Muslim scholars on Qur'an commentary and the biography

of the Prophet for establishing the origins of Qur'anic legal and moral precepts, see Gabriel Said Reynolds, *The Qur'an in Its Biblical Subtext*, Routledge, London and New York, 2010, pp. 1–36 et passim.

24 J.J. Jansen, *The Interpretation of the Koran in Modern Egypt*, E. J. Brill, Leiden, 1974, pp. 91–93.

25 Bernard Weiss, *The Spirit of Islamic Law*, University of Georgia Press, Athens and London, 1998, p. 18.

26 Ibid., p. 19.

27 Sing. *faqíh*.

28 Weiss, *The Spirit of Islamic Law*, pp. 7–8 and 17.

29 Ibid., p. 3.

30 Ibid., p. 187.

31 As was mentioned, some smaller Muslim communities (e.g., the Isma'ilis, the Zaydis, and the Kharijites) had their own legal systems, but they were by and large similar to those of the Sunnis and the Twelver Shi'ites.

32 Hodgson, *The Venture*, vol. 1, p. 338.

33 Hallaq, *A History*, p. 9.

34 David Powers, "The Exegetical Genre *nasikh al-Qur'an wa mansukhuhu*," in Andrew Rippin (ed.), *Approaches to the History of the Interpretation of the Qur'an*, Clarendon Press, Oxford, 1988, p. 130.

35 Ibid., p. 122.

36 John Burton, "Abrogation," in *Encyclopedia of the Qur'an*. General Editor: Jane Dammen McAuliffe; online edition: http://referenceworks.brillonline.com.

37 That is, one that prescribes stoning to death of married adulterers contrary to the Qur'anic injunctions to either flog them or confine them to their homes; see Dmitry Frolov, "Stoning," in *Encyclopedia of the Qur'an*. General Editor: Jane Dammen McAuliffe; online edition: http://referenceworks.brillonline.com.

38 This verse prohibits marriage between man and woman suckled by the same wet nurse; see Burton, "Abrogation."

39 Ibid.

40 Hodgson, *The Venture*, vol. 1, pp. 318–326.

41 Ibid., p. 321.

42 Coulson, *A History of Islamic Law*, p. 47.

43 Hodgson, *The Venture*, vol. 1, p. 294.

44 Eric Chaumont, "al-Shafi'i," in *Encyclopedia of Islam*, 2nd ed.; online edition: http://referenceworks.brillonline.com.

45 Coulson, *A History of Islamic Law*, p. 58.

46 *Dirham*, from the Greek "drachma," a silver coin whose value fluctuated considerably from one epoch or locality to the other.

47 Coulson, *A History of Islamic Law*, p. 40.

48 For details see Weiss, ibid., pp. 67–68.

49 Weiss, *The Spirit of Islamic Law*, pp. 86–87.

50 It will be discussed in detail in the next chapter.

51 Weiss, *The Spirit of Islamic Law*, p. 86.

52 Hodgson, *The Venture*, vol. 1, p. 339.

53 Ibid., pp. 347–348.

54 Berkey, *The Formation of Islam*, p. 143.

Chapter 10

Islamic Scholarship Under the 'Abbásids
Theological Debates and Schools of Thought

The Qur'an as the Foundation of Islamic Faith and Cult and an Object of Disputation

The Qur'an constitutes the main symbol and source of Muslim faith and practice. It provides Muslims with a means to communicate with God and to worship him in the way he wants to be worshipped. By constantly reciting the Qur'an during their five canonical prayers, believers make it part and parcel of their daily existence. One can say that Qur'anic verses accompany every believer from cradle to grave. On the psychological plane, the all-important event of revelation is being relived by Muslims every time they recite the Qur'an or listen to its recitation. While reciting it, the faithful remind themselves of God's absolute oneness and sovereignty over this world and the practical implications of this truth as manifested in their acts of worship. The Qur'an thus presents itself as the principal object of Muslim devotion and, more generally, intellectual life.[1] Given its critical centrality to the Muslim faith, any alternative means of accessing God can be (and often is) viewed by Muslim scholars as undesirable. According to this view, anything that may potentially be a distraction from the Qur'an (and thus a potential rival to it), such as figurative art, music, or painting, should be rejected by good Muslims, unless those means are harnessed to corroborate or broadcast the message of the Muslim sacred book (see Figure 10.1).[2]

However, as has been demonstrated earlier in this study, the Qur'anic text is not devoid of ambiguity and allows for a wide variety of different interpretations. No wonder, therefore, that understanding the true implications of the Qur'anic message and of the status of the Qur'an itself, namely whether it was created or uncreated, soon became a hotly debated issue among Muslim intellectuals. As time went on, alongside the Qur'an there emerged another important source of Islamic religion, the Prophet's exemplary "custom" (*sunna*). This source of Muslim faith also yielded itself to multiple understandings. The practical legal implications of the Qur'an and the Sunna of the Prophet for the life of their adherents have already been addressed in the previous chapter. Here we will discuss how these sources of Islamic religion have shaped the Muslim belief system, or dogma.

The Beginnings of Theological Reasoning in Islam

Largely the same learned individuals who took it upon themselves to ascertain the implications of the Qur'anic revelation and the Sunna of the Prophet for the believers' everyday lives were also responsible for the articulation of the foundations of Islamic theological doctrines. In fact, the articulation of Islamic theology often went hand in hand with the elaboration of Muslim legal theories. Both these endeavors were part of the growth of Islam as a freestanding devotional tradition and distinctive cosmology. While "theology" in the broad sense of the word addresses the issue of just and legitimate leadership—the principal point of disagreement between the Sunnis,

Figure 10.1 Medieval Qur'an Manuscript (Saljuk period)

Figure 10.2 Muslim Scholars Debating (from a thirteenth-century illuminated manuscript)

Shi'ites, and Kharijites—there were other, less tangible but urgent aspects of the divine revelation that attracted the attention of the community's learned class (see Figure 10.2).

Their line of thinking may be described as follows: While following the rightful leader and fulfilling one's obligations toward God, one's family, and fellow Muslims are essential for one's salvation, these actions may prove to be insufficient for the more demanding believer seeking to formulate and adhere to the correct concept of God and God's relationship with the created world. Whether this realization, as just suggested, indeed motivated the first Muslim theologians or whether they acted spontaneously out of sheer intellectual curiosity or a desire to earn merit in the eyes of God is impossible to determine.

Some Muslim and Western scholars have argued convincingly that Islamic theology emerged in response to the polemic against Islam launched by the representatives of its monotheistic cousins, Judaism and Christianity, and perhaps also by the followers of Zoroastrianism.[3] If we accept this hypothesis, we may argue that the initial goal of Islamic speculative theology was apologetic, that is, to defend Islam against its non-Muslim detractors. To do so, it was not sufficient for the defenders to simply quote the Qur'an, since those who questioned the veracity of its claims simply would not recognize the divine origin and authority of the Muslim holy book. One had to find a neutral polemical ground on which to engage the critics. For this purpose, Greek logic and methods of argumentation—which had gained wide circulation among the educated classes of Mediterranean societies since late antiquity—came in particularly handy.

Greek ideas had entered Islam through the translations of Greek and Syriac (Aramaic) works into Arabic already under the Umayyads. This translation activity grew particularly intense and prolific in the early decades of the ninth century under the caliph al-Ma'mún (813–833), who had established a translation outfit in Baghdad that came to be known as "The House of Wisdom." By "wisdom," al-Ma'mun and the translators he employed understood "Greek wisdom" par excellence. The House of Wisdom was staffed primarily by Arabic-speaking Christians, whom al-Ma'mun charged with translating into Arabic Greek and Aramaic treatises on medicine, logic, philosophy, and astronomy. The attraction of Greek wisdom proved irresistible for many members of the Muslim learned class.[4] Consciously or unconsciously, they had imbibed Greek methods and notions and had begun to deploy them not just against Islam's outside critics but also among themselves in debating their diverse, often incompatible visions of Islam.

These internal and external debates gradually gave rise to a distinctively Islamic theological discourse known as *kalám* ("speech"). It was, in essence, a set of polemical strategies aimed at refuting opponents by driving them into a corner by means of an elaborately constructed logical argumentation. Here is how *kalám* was defined by the great Muslim thinker Ibn Khaldún (d. 1406):

> The science of *kalam* is science that involves arguing with logical proofs in defense of the articles of faith and refuting innovators who deviate in their dogmas from the early Muslims and Muslim orthodoxy. The real core of the articles of faith is the oneness of God.[5]

What were the "articles of faith" that *kalám* was supposed to articulate and defend? According to the majority of Muslim theologians, they included:

1   Belief in the prophets from Adam to Muhammad;
2   Belief in the oneness of God;
3   Belief in the divine origin of the Qur'an and the sacredness of its message;
4   Belief in God's angels;
5   Belief in heaven and hell;
6   Belief in the resurrection of bodies on the Day of Judgment and the final trial of humanity by God.

Some scholars added to this creed the belief in the divine predestination of all events, but this article was not accepted by everyone, as we shall see.[6] Although, with time, *kalám* came to enjoy a fairly wide acceptance among Muslim scholars and to boast a cohort of exceptionally talented exponents, in the final account, it has proved to be less important for Muslim life than *fiqh*. Moreover, *kalám* and its exponents (*mutakállimún;* sing. *mutakállim*) were viewed with suspicion by their conservative and less theoretically savvy colleagues up to the collapse of the 'Abbásid state in 1258 and even beyond. For such conservative scholars with little or no interest in abstract speculations, *kalám* constituted an innovation that found no precedent in the exemplary custom of the Prophet and his companions.[7] Nevertheless, despite their opposition, over time *kalám*'s legitimacy as an "Islamic science" and defender and shaper of the Muslim creed was recognized by the majority of Muslim scholars affiliated with one or the other schools of Sunni *fiqh*.[8] The Shi'ites, in their turn, developed their own version of *kalám*.

In its technical meaning, the word *kalám*, which originally meant "speech," came to denote "a discussion or discourse about God." It is usually rendered into European languages as "discursive, speculative, or rationalist theology." As already mentioned, a practitioner of *kalám* was called *mutakállim*. As an interpreter of the theological aspects of Islamic revelation, the *mutakállim* was different from the exponent of its legal implications (*faqíh*) or from the Muslim judge (*qadi*), who applied the latter's expositions to concrete legal cases. However, in many cases, a Muslim scholar would wear both hats (or, rather, turbans) simultaneously. In other words, theological-speculative and juridical-legal interests were quite often organically combined in one and the same individual. In fact, many, albeit not all, Muslim scholars were both *faqíh*s and *mutakállimún* at one and the same time.

The first Muslim theologians seem to have been based in Basra, where they were associated with a pious moralist al-Hásan al-Basri (d. 728), who is credited with many "firsts" of Islamic culture, including *kalám* and Sufism (Islamic mysticism). Accurately or otherwise, al-Hásan's followers, Wásil b. 'Atá (d. 749) and Dirár b. 'Amr (active in the second part of the eighth century), have been portrayed by Muslim sources as the pioneers of *kalám*. In any event, they seem to have actively propagated some theological ideas and methods among their contemporaries.[9] As a distinctive intellectual trend in Islam based on logical argumentation, *kalám* had crystallized probably during the reign of Harún al-Rashíd (786–809). At that time, it became intimately linked to the nascent school of Islamic thought known as "Mu'tazilism," as we shall discuss shortly.

Divine Predestination Versus Human Free Will

What were the issues discussed within the framework of early Islamic theology? Initially, they seem to have been shaped by the debates over the fateful events and the principal actors of the first civil wars, as well as over the real or perceived injustices of Umayyad rule. Broader existential issues were also addressed, namely how could one account for the pain and suffering experienced by seemingly innocent believers, children, and animals in a world so perfectly designed by an all-powerful, all-knowing, and all-merciful God? This issue, in turn, entailed a host of related questions. How could God in his infinite and perfect wisdom have allowed his chosen community to be ravaged by a series of fratricidal wars? How could he have elevated to power the rulers who were seen by many of their subjects as "impious," "illegitimate," and "tyrannical" to boot? Was this course of events predetermined by God from all eternity, or was it chosen and executed by human actors of their own free will? If the former, how could a just God hold his servants responsible and punish them for actions they were incapable of doing or not doing on their own accord? And how could an all-merciful God, the source of all virtue, have permitted evil to occur and eventually triumph in his realm? If, on the other hand, evil was a result of deliberate human actions how could this be squared with God's omnipotence and control of all things as postulated repeatedly in the Qur'an?

Such questions sparked heated discussions among the community's learned elite, especially because the Qur'an and the Sunna provided conflicting answers to them by asserting God's omnipotence on the one hand and human responsibility on the other. How, for example, should one understand the Qur'anic phrase that says: "God has created you and what you make" (37:96)? Does this mean that God has created all human deeds, be they good or evil? If so, how could this be reconciled with his all-goodness asserted repeatedly by the Qur'an? Discussions of such issues were not simply academic. Answers to them had wide-ranging practical ramifications in that they either implicitly confirmed or called into doubt the legitimacy of the Umayyad caliphs and their suitability as leaders of the Muslim community. For instance, those who viewed the course of earthly life as predetermined by God from all eternity in every single detail would see Umayyad rule as an inexorable execution of the divine will. This being the case, the faithful had no choice but to patiently submit to it. Conversely, those who advocated the ability of the faithful to choose and perform their own actions would argue that by making wrong choices and ignoring the will of God as expressed in the Qur'an Muslims were saddled with unjust rulers as a punishment for their complacency and failure to actively resist evil. In support of their position, the former group would invoke the Qur'anic verses that depicted God as having predetermined all events of this world and the fates of its human inhabitants (such as 37:96, as cited, or 54:49 stating that God "created everything in measure"). Seen in the light of these divine statements, life in this world is nothing but an unfolding of God's primeval divine decree (*qadar*) to which all creatures should obediently submit.

However, an astute polemicist steeped in the Qur'anic narrative would have no trouble finding Qur'anic verses that contradicted this fatalistic conclusion. Moreover, with some ingenuity, this polemicist could interpret the verses advanced by his or her "predestinarian" opponents in such a way as to justify the reality of human free will. For does not God explicitly say in Q 41:17 that some peoples "have [consciously] chosen blindness in preference to guidance"?[10]

This was exactly what al-Hásan al-Basri did in his famous letter to the Umayyad caliph 'Abd al-Malik, when he interpreted Q 7:186 as meaning the opposite of what the "predestinarian" scholars claimed it said.[11] According to al-Hásan al-Basri, the believer could and should actively strive to prevent evil from happening in the same way as merchants and craftsmen take care of their businesses despite being sincere believers in God's predestination of all things. Their failure to take care of their good in hopes that God would do it for them is bound to lead to their ruin. The same, argued al-Hásan al-Basri, applies to ordinary believers who seek to secure salvation in the hereafter. Divine predestination or not, they are required by the divine law to avoid evil and to promote good works. If they are remiss, they will be punished. If it is not in their power to resist evil actively, they should at least make an effort to condemn it by their tongue. In fact, al-Hásan al-Basri chose to do just that: He criticized the Umayyad caliphs for their misdeeds without, however, rallying the believers to rise in rebellion against their rule. When he was invited to take part in an anti-Umayyad uprising, he excused himself, citing the grave danger of fratricidal strife for the well-being of the *umma*.

The supporters of the doctrine of human free came to be known as "Qadarites" after the Arabic *qadar*, which means "[divine] decree" or, perhaps, after *qudra* "[human] ability to perform an action." Their opponents were those Muslims who were anxious to safeguard divine omnipotence that, in their view, would be compromised by the admission that humans could act of their own free will. They can best be described as "fatalists," namely, believers in fate as predetermined by God from all eternity. For them, God created human beings and predestined them to be either in paradise or hell already at the moment of their creation. He then endowed them respectively with either good or evil actions and character traits that would inevitably to take them to their respective destinations. Consequently, humans' noncompliance with God's will was no more possible than altering his or her natural intellectual disposition or physique.[12] The paradox of human free will and divine predestination continued to animate debates among Muslims scholars long after the death of al-Hásan al-Basri and his followers. As we will see, the Mu'tazilite theological school hued close to the former position, whereas their opponents among the adherents of *hadíth* tended to uphold the latter.

The Doctrine of Postponement and the Problem of Faith

The cataclysms of the civil wars, during which the warring factions—the supporters of communal unity (the Sunnis), the pro-'Alid party, and the Kharijites—routinely hurled at each other accusations of "unbelief" or at the very least of "straying from" the Qur'anic message and the Prophet's custom, created a good deal of unease among some pious Muslims. They felt that believers engaging in the mutual excommunications were going too far in that they arrogated the right of God to judge the fidelity and righteousness of his human servants.

It is against this historical background that one should consider the problem of faith and the status of the grave sinner. Initially, it seems that the debates of this sort revolved around the figure of caliph 'Uthman.[13] According to one view, the caliph's sinful, "un-Islamic" actions had effectively rendered him an unbeliever. Therefore, his murder was a religiously justifiable act that entailed no punishment for its perpetrators. This was the view of the pro-'Alid party and the Kharijites. Their opponents, who were not necessarily staunch supporters of the Umayyads but who tolerated them as the necessary evil as long as they were capable of preserving the unity of the faithful, argued that those who took justice into their own hands arrogated God's right to judge and punish his servants.

With time, these two positions were extended beyond the figure of 'Uthman. As discussed, the Kharijites and to a lesser extent the pro-'Alid party viewed their ideological opponents as being beyond the pale of Islam. For the radical Kharijites, those Muslims who disagreed with their religious beliefs deserved to be executed, their families enslaved, and their property confiscated—a treatment that the Islamic law reserved for resisting unbelievers. In the aftermath of the civil wars, some pious Muslims came to realize the detrimental consequence of this radical stance and sought to mitigate it by introducing a more moderate one. It came to be known as the doctrine of postponement (*irjá'*). Those who espoused it argued that fallible human beings were not in a position to pass judgment as to the belief or unbelief of their fellow Muslims, no matter how sinful they may appear to be. Only God knows their true intentions and status in this world and the hereafter.[14] Therefore, only he has the right to judge them. Because the final say regarding a person's belief or unbelief rests with God, so a Muslim seemingly in the state of grave sin should be left alone, and a decision concerning his or her status should be postponed, or rather relegated to God. On the Day of Judgment, God will pass his verdict on the apparent sinner as he sees fit, and justice will be served.

On the practical level, this theory meant that the grave sinner should still be considered a Muslim (with all the rights and privileges this status implied), albeit an impious one. The adherents of the doctrine of postponement (*múrji'a*, that is, the "postponers") classified such a Muslim as an "evildoer" (*fásiq*). The doctrine of postponement was in all likelihood intended to prevent mutual accusations of unbelief that were widespread during the first civil wars and, in so doing, to preserve the unity of the *umma*. To justify their decision to postpone or suspend judgment regarding the status of the evildoer, the postponers appealed to the authority of the Qur'an that repeatedly asserts God's exclusive right to punish or pardon whom he wishes (Q 48:14, 5:118, 33:24, and so on).[15]

For the Shi'ites, the Kharijites, and some factions within the Sunni majority, this approach to the issue of faith versus unbelief was too lax in that it allowed grievous sinners to reside unmolested amidst the true believers. This situation looked even more objectionable when combined with the postponers' doctrine that defined faith only as a verbal assent that may or may not be accompanied by pious deeds. All these issues became the grist for the mill of nascent Islamic theology that evolved within the framework of several influential schools of thought of the age. Mu'tazilism emerged as the most prominent among them.

The Emergence of Mu'tazilism

Early on, the art of *kalám* speculation was associated first and foremost with the so-called Mu'tazilite school of thought, of which Wásil b. 'Atá (d. 748) of Basra is believed to have been the founder. In addition to polemical and argumentative strategies peculiar to *kalám*, the Mu'tazilites espoused a distinct intellectual attitude that emphasized the ability of human reason to unravel the mysteries of divine revelation and to arrive at a complete intellectual clarity with regard to God and the universe. According to Mu'tazilite thinkers, discursive reasoning (*názar*) was given to human beings by God in order for them to know him and to comprehend the nuances of his will. Believers' failure to employ their rational faculty may inadvertently result in their misunderstanding of the nature of God and his will, thereby dooming them to punishment by hellfire.[16] Blind faith and slavish adherence to a prior precedent or opinion were even more repugnant to the Mu'tazilites because they deprived believers of the opportunity to defend their faith against its non-Muslim detractors on rational grounds. To be a good believer, one must be able to defend and justify one's faith effectively by means of *kalám* argumentation. Put differently, for the Mu'tazilites, "he who believed for no good reason was no sound believer."[17] Correct reasoning should be based on four kinds of evidence: rational argumentation, the Qur'an, the Sunna of the Prophet, and the consensus of the Muslim community.[18]

Apart from the confidence in the ability of the human reason to comprehend God, the Mu'tazilites maintained some other distinctive theological views. One such view reportedly has given the name to the entire movement. A legend has it that during a teaching session, Wásil b. 'Atá, a student of al-Hásan al-Basri, asked his teacher about the status of the grave sinner within the community of the faithful. Al-Hásan responded by describing such a person as a "hypocrite" (*munáfiq*) whose status was that of an unbeliever. Apparently dissatisfied with al-Hásan's answer, Wásil and a small group of his followers left al-Hásan's teaching circle in the Basran mosque where they used to assemble, causing al-Hásan to exclaim: "Wásil has isolated (or withdrawn himself—*i'tázala*) from us!" Al-Hásan's indignant remark is said to have given the name to the new school—the Mu'tazilites, or Isolationists.[19] Wásil's argument that the grave sinner is neither a believer nor an unbeliever but rather one who occupies the place between these two positions has become an ideological foundation of this new school of Islamic speculative theology. The ninth and tenth centuries witnessed the emergence of two principal trends within Mu'tazilism—one in Basra and the other in Baghdad. They maintained different intellectual stances on some issues, but their differences were too minor to classify them as two distinct theological schools.

In regard to the issue of the political rule (imamate), the Mu'tazilites were, by and large, staunch adherents of Sunni Islam. As such they were generally loyal to the 'Abbásid caliphal state, although some of them may occasionally have exhibited strong pro-'Alid leanings. Most of the Mu'tazilites were ready to recognize (but not to dramatize) the failings of 'Uthman, Mu'awiyya, and even 'Ali, but preferred to leave it at that without passing judgment on who was right and who was wrong. In this respect, the Mu'tazilites, like the majority of Sunnis, were advocates of the community's solidarity, even if this meant submission to an unjust or even openly sinful ruler.

What set the Mu'tazilites apart from other religious factions and schools of thought of the age was their fascination—their opponents would say infatuation—with Greek logic and syllogistic reasoning. Such reasoning usually involved the application of a logical scheme that consisted of a major premise, a minor premise, and a conclusion. Take, for instance, the following proposition: Every virtue is laudable; kindness is a virtue; therefore, kindness is laudable. Harking back to Aristotle and his Hellenistic followers, this type of argumentation had all the semblance of an incontrovertible means of attaining the truth. Due to their fascination with the power of the human intelligence, the Mu'tazilites considered logical reasoning to be a sure path to religious clarity as well as an effective argumentative tool. Furthermore, they believed in the objective nature of rational reasoning that, in their view, was common to both God and his human creatures. The Mu'tazilites insisted that divine commands and prohibitions, being a product of the rationality that God shares with his human servants, contain an underlying objective, rational meaning that can be unraveled by means of correct intellectual procedures. In line with this view, they rejected the idea that God has arbitrarily designated certain actions as either evil or virtuous and expects human beings to unquestionably avoid or perform them.[20] Put differently, they believed that God marked an action as right because it is right in and of itself, not because he arbitrarily and irrationally declared it to be right.[21] For instance, the divine injunction that believers share wealth with other people by rendering alms (*zakát*) has a valid practical reason behind it. It is designed to prevent the accumulation of wealth in the hands of the fortunate few by spreading it more evenly around the community.[22] Likewise, fasting during the month of Ramadán is prescribed by God because it is objectively good for both one's physical health and one's spiritual well-being. The same applies to ablution, prostrating oneself in prayer, and so on. According to the Mu'tazilites, the Qur'an itself repeatedly and explicitly has invited people to observe the created world and to seek to understand it by using their rational capabilities.[23]

Another characteristic feature of Mu'tazilite thought, as we shall soon see, is its staunch opposition to any anthropomorphic concepts of God that may occasionally be construed from God's descriptions in the Qur'an and the Sunna. They depict God as having arms, eyes, legs, and a face; as any mortal human, God can laugh, rejoice, sit on his throne, descend from heaven, run, and so on. Many members of the Hadíth party insisted that such portrayals should not be explained away but taken literally—no questions asked. Any attempt to allegorize them, in their mind, was an unpardonable neglect of the letter of the revelation that they held to be sacrosanct. The Mu'tazilites dismissed this literalist view as ridiculous and insisted that God was absolutely transcendent and bore no resemblance whatsoever to his creatures—either human or otherwise. For the Mu'tazilites, humanlike accounts of God and his attributes in the Qur'an and the Sunna were mere allegories— his "face" represented his eternal essence, his "eye" his wisdom, his "hand" his power or his "blessing," his "foot" his ability to move or his omnipresence, and so on. These allegories, argued the Mu'tazilites, were designed by God to allow people with undeveloped logical and rational abilities to grasp the gist of the revelation and to revere God as if he were an all-powerful earthly monarch. However, the more accomplished minds understood these references as allegories and conceived of God as an absolutely otherworldly reality that had nothing to do with the created world and inaccessible to the imperfect human senses. On the question of whether God can be visualized by the righteous in the hereafter (in accord with Q 75:22–23 stating, "On that day[24] faces shall be radiant, gazing upon their Lord"), the Mu'tazilites would reply that the word "to see" here meant "to wait" and the word "Lord" meant not "God" but rather "a reward from the Lord." In this way, they sought to safeguard God's transcendence and assert his total difference from the world that he created. God's transcendence, according to the Mu'tazilites, implies that God has no characteristics of a body: color, length, breadth, weight, movement, and so on. Therefore, he can neither be visualized by the human sight nor have any limbs or faculties similar to those of human beings. Furthermore, he cannot be found in any particular direction or in any specific place. Given the fact that anthropomorphic (humanlike) descriptions of God were particularly abundant in the *hadíth*, the Mu'tazilites did not place much value in them and pointed out numerous contradictions and oddities found therein.[25] The adherents of *hadíth* found this Mu'tazilite attitude particularly offensive because they derived their distinct religious identity from the careful study, classification, and preservation of the prophetic lore.

The Mu'tazilites from Basra Abu 'Ali al-Jubbá'i (d. 915) and his son Abu Háshim (d. 933) formulated the five doctrinal propositions that have been the hallmark of this theological school ever since:

1   God's absolute unity (*tawhíd*), which the Mu'tazilites took to mean first and foremost the denial of independence and self-sufficiency of the divine attributes. The latter inhere in the divine essence without introducing any plurality into the Godhead. Hence, God knows things through his essence, not through a freestanding and self-sufficient entity called "knowledge." Likewise, he is alive through his essence, not through an independent attribute of "life," and so on. Admitting plurality within the Godhead, according to the Mu'tazilites, would be tantamount to "giving partners" to him, which the Qur'an condemned as the most grievous of all sins. If we recognize an independent existence of the divine attributes, argued the Mu'tazilites, we will be obligated to admit that they are somehow coeternal with his essence—a clear violation of the critical principle of God's oneness and uniqueness (*tawhíd*). Consequently, the word or speech of God (the Qur'an), which many members of the Hadíth party considered to be eternal and uncreated, are God's creations like everything else in this world. According to the Mu'tazilites, God created the Qur'an; otherwise, it would have been coeternal with God. What some people consider to be God's independent and self-sufficient attributes are, according to the Mu'tazilites, nothing more than the ever changing existential "modes" or "states" of his unique and indivisible essence.[26]

The fact that the Mu'tazilites were adamant about God's absolute oneness and incomparability is finely described by al-Ásh'ari (d. 935), a student of Abu Háshim al-Jubbá'i, who later broke with his teacher to found his own theological school:

> The Mu'tazilites agree that God is one; there is nothing like him; he is . . . not a body, not a form, not flesh and blood, not a person, not substance nor attribute . . . not begetting nor begotten; plurality does not apply to him . . . senses do not attain him; he is not comparable with human beings and does not resemble creatures in any respect . . . he is ceaselessly first, precedent, who appeared before originated things, existent before created things; he is ceaselessly knowing, powerful, living . . . He may not experience benefit or harm, joy, gladness, hurt or pain.[27]

As we can see, this doctrinal position conveys two principal messages: (a) God's essence is unique and indivisible; there is absolutely no trace or hint of plurality in it; (b) God cannot and must not be likened to his creatures; he has no resemblance whatsoever to them.

2   God's absolute justice (*'adl*). God wants only good for his human servants and always does what is best for them. He guides them on the right path and does not compel them to stray from it.[28] Hence any ascription of evil, lie, or injustice to God is to be rejected; human beings alone are responsible for all their acts, be they good or evil. God's justice implies that he will inevitably punish the wrongdoers and reward the righteous. If he fails to do so, he would be an unjust and untrustworthy god, which is absurd. Therefore, God cannot arbitrarily pardon the sinners or punish the righteous, for this would be contrary to his just and truthful nature. Nor can God create sinful or evil actions. This would be beneath him, for, as a rational being, he is subject to the same notions of virtue, justice, and injustice as his human creatures. Moreover, he has endowed human beings with reason in order for them to know what is ethically and morally good and evil, what is just and what is unjust. This means that things can objectively be good or evil not just because they were qualified so by God in

his revealed law. Whether God himself has the power to be unjust was a hotly debated matter within the Mu'tazilite school over which its followers have failed to reach a consensus. In line with their understanding of divine justice, Mu'tazilites downplayed or outright denied the idea of divine predestination. It would be unjust on the part of God to predetermine every human action in advance and to ordain that one Muslim should be arbitrarily saved and the other damned without empowering them to choose their actions. He guides only those who choose to be guided and leads astray only those who choose to be led astray. God creates in believers the power to do or not do certain things and then leaves it to them to exercise it.

3   God's promise [of paradise] and threat [of hell]. According to the Mu'tazilites, each person's acts will determine his or her fate on the Judgment Day. Those who disobeyed him will be sent to hell; those who obeyed him will go to paradise. The Prophet may intercede before God on behalf of some members of his community, but intercession is impossible in the case of people guilty of grave sins (such as denying God, giving "partners" to him, fornication, murder, etc.). The Mu'tazilites stressed that God's justice is consistent with rational laws. God can pardon people but only if they deserve his pardon, for example, by a sincere repentance. Conversely, God is obligated to pardon Muslims who have decided to repent of their sins as long as this repentance is sincere. God cannot punish someone who has not deserved a punishment, such as innocent children or imbeciles, for this would be an instance of injustice that is not befitting him as the Lord of the universe. Nor can he punish the children of idolaters because they were not given a chance to consciously choose the true religion. If he causes innocent creatures (e.g., animals and children) to suffer in this life, in the hereafter he is obligated to grant them a compensation commensurate with the suffering they have experienced.

4   The status of the grave sinner or the "intermediate position." It is over this issue, as we remember, that Wásil b. 'Atá allegedly broke with al-Hásan al-Basri and withdrew from his teaching circle in Basra. According to Wásil and the subsequent generations of the Mu'tazilites, the grave sinner occupies an intermediate position between pure faith and pure unbelief. The person is neither an unbeliever (*káfir*) nor a believer (*mú'min*), as long as he or she professes verbally his or her faith in the oneness of God and in the mission of the prophet Muhammad. However, on the Day of Judgment, that individual will be declared a sinner and be confined to hell to dwell there forever. Contrary to the "lax" position of the advocates of "postponement," the Mu'tazilites insisted that a verbal declaration of faith was insufficient if it is not supported by pious deeds. On this issue, the Mu'tazilites found themselves in agreement with their principal opponents—the adherents of *hadíth*.

5   Commanding the right and forbidding the wrong. This is, according to the Mu'tazilites, a religious obligation incumbent on each Muslim. A Muslim who fails to fulfill it is disobeying God. This obligation must be exercised "where there is opportunity and ability, by tongue, hand, hand and sword, as one may be able."[29] Mu'tazilite thinkers disagreed whether the necessity of this precept can be deduced by logical reasoning or can be known only through revelation.[30] They shared this principle with the majority of Muslims,[31] so it should not be seen as a unique characteristic of the Mu'tazilite school. Whether it implied an armed rebellion against an impious and sinful ruler is a moot point. As we shall see, the critics of Mu'tazilism among the members of the Hadíth party turned out to be more prone to put this precept into practice. Nevertheless, it was included in the Mu'tazilite creed.

On the question of the leadership of the community, the Mu'tazilites refused to condemn any of the parties to the first civil wars, fearing that this might fracture the unity of the Sunni *umma*. Contrary to the position of the Twelver Shi'ites, who considered 'Ali to be the only legitimate caliph, or to the position of the Hadíth party, which judged the excellence of the rightly guided caliphs according to the sequence in which they took the office, the majority of the Mu'tazilites refused to give preference to any of them.

In their theological discussions, the Mu'tazilites made extensive use of foreign (mostly Greek) terms to describe God, his attributes, and his creation: "substance," "atom," "accident," "body," "modes," "existence," "nonexistence," and so on. This brought upon them the ire of the Hadíth party, especially its most vocal representatives, the Hanbalites, who insisted that God could be described only by the names that he applied to himself in his revelation.

As far as their social status is concerned, unlike the Hanbalites whose supporters came from the lower classes, many leaders of the Mu'tazilites, particularly at the later stages of the school's development, were refined intellectuals, often associated with the courtly circles. They looked down upon the illiterate masses, whose crude, literalist beliefs in the physicality of God and the independent existence of his attributes they dismissed as naïve and misguided.

Mu'tazilism, "a tradition of abstract scholastic thought" and "an intellectual technique," was not self-sufficient and had to be combined with other factional and doctrinal allegiances. One could be a [Twelver] Shi'ite Mu'tazilite, a Zaydi [Shi'ite] Mu'tazilite, a Hánafi Mu'tazilite (which was a particularly common combination),[32] or a Shafi'i Mu'tazilite.[33] Even some non-Muslims, especially Jews and, to a lesser extent, also Christians, would adopt some Mu'tazilite argumentative principles without forfeiting their primary religious commitment.[34] This looseness of the school's organizational structure and the lack of support of its followers by state authorities at the later stage of its development led to the gradual decline and eventual demise of Mu'tazilism. After experiencing a period of intellectual vigor and florescence in the ninth and tenth centuries, it began to lose ground to the rival Ash'arite and Maturidite schools of theology and disappeared from the historical scene around or shortly after the Mongol conquest of Baghdad in 1258. It has been argued that the demise of Mu'tazilism was occasioned in part by its close association with ideas and argumentative methods that were perceived by many Muslims as "alien" to the spirit of the Qur'anic revelation.[35] In other words, Mu'tazilite theology probably proved too elitist to secure a broad base of support even among the Muslim scholarly class, not to mention the Muslim masses. Be this as it may, Mu'tazilite ideas, argumentative methods, and overall intellectual attitude have survived the school's dissipation. They were appropriated and creatively reshaped by various streams within the Shi'ite movement (primarily Zaydism and [Twelver] Imamism) and by some Sunni theologians, especially the Ash'arites and the Maturidites.

The Supporters of *Hadíth* and Their Theological Creed

Scholars who led the Hadíth party (*ahl al-hadíth*, lit. the "Hadíth folk")[36] turned out to be the most uncompromising critics of the Mu'tazilite school of thought. It was their strenuous opposition to and criticisms of Mu'tazilite teachings that eventually brought about their disrepute and disappearance. The two scholarly factions disagreed on practically every issue enumerated in the preceding section. Unlike the Mu'tazilites who acknowledged the failings of the protagonists of the first civil wars, the supporters of *hadíth* held them to be immune from any sin. They refrained from passing verdicts on either Mu'awiyya or 'Ali, while recognizing the latter as a rightly guided caliph. At the same time, unlike the Shi'ites, who regarded him as the most excellent of men (after Muhammad) and the only legitimate leader of the Muslim *umma*, or the Mu'tazilites, who viewed all four rightly guided caliphs as equal to one another, the intellectual elite of the *hadíth* party considered 'Ali to be the fourth best in the hierarchy of excellence.[37] They held all companions of the Prophet in high regard if even only by virtue of their being his contemporaries. They insisted that any discussion of their failings and disagreements should be avoided, and the final verdict on their actions be left to God to deliver.

Generally, the adherents of *hadíth* considered the life of the primeval Muslim community under the leadership of Muhammad to be the ideal that all later Muslims should aspire to and emulate to the best of their abilities. To meet this goal, latter-day Muslims should be equipped with a thorough knowledge of the Prophet's life and teachings. This article of the Hadíth party creed explains its members' reverence for the "exemplary custom" (*sunna*) of the individual whom they considered to be "the best of all humankind." Because the Sunna was made up from *hadíth*, they devoted themselves single-mindedly to their collection and preservation. All endeavors and actions of the subsequent generations of Muslims, be they private or public, should be grounded in the *hadíth* and Sunna. For the Hadíth party, any departure from the prophetic example constitutes a blamable "innovation" (*bid'a*) that should not only be avoided by every good Muslim but also be vocally and publicly denounced. The guidance provided by the Qur'an and the Sunna is enough for every observing believer to achieve salvation. Any attempt to understand God and his commands in rational terms alien to the letter of the Scripture is a first step to doubt and eventually unbelief.

Contrary to the Mu'tazilites, who tended to allegorize the sacred text of Islam in order to bring it into compliance with their rationalist, abstract perception of the Creator, the members of the Hadíth party insisted that he should be understood "as is," that is literally. They treasured the word of God too much to allow it to be diluted by an allegorical interpretation. If God has chosen to describe himself as sitting on the throne, this description should be taken at face value and not just a metaphor for his sublimity or might, as the Mu'tazilites would argue. If the Qur'an depicts God as having a hand—a *hadíth* further specifies that he has two hands both of which are right—then he indeed has it (them), even if this hand or these hands may not be identical to human hands. The relationship between the human hand and that of God is a mystery that one should not investigate out of misplaced curiosity. In line with their literalist attitude to the sacred text, the Hadíth party rejected the attempts of the Mu'tazilites to allegorize God by presenting him in abstract metaphysical terms borrowed from the "pagan" Greek philosophical tradition. It stands to reason that, contrary to the Mu'tazilites who were generally skeptical of the validity of *hadíth*, the Hadíth folk considered them the principal source of correct faith and practice alongside the Qur'an.

In sum, the chief disagreement between the Mu'tazilites and the Hadíth folk was over the ability of human reason to discover and explain the nature of God and his attributes. Contrary to the Mu'tazilite confidence in the capability of disciplined human reasoning to unravel the mysteries of divine revelation, the Hadíth folk emphasized its impotence in such matters. They found any rational speculations about God, his attributes, and his relation to this world to be misplaced or even outright blasphemous. Such disputations, in their view, had no basis in the revealed texts of the Qur'an and the Sunna. Because of this conviction, they refused to engage in debates with the Mu'tazilites. They believed such debates to be futile and breeding nothing but doubt and confusion.[38]

Like the Mu'tazilites, the Hadíth folk were Sunnis and, as such, generally loyal to the 'Abbásid state. At the same time, they strove to maintain a certain distance from it by declining official appointments and caliphal favors. Under Harún al-Rashíd (786–809), they were allowed to persecute their opponents. The extreme reverence that the Hadíth folk had toward the Qur'an as the literal and eternal word of God translated into their strongly held conviction that it was not created by God but had existed from all eternity. When they recited its uncreated text, the divine words on their tongues were also in some miraculous way "uncreated."[39] They felt that the Qur'an that they read and held reverently in their hands was something of God himself.[40] In line with this belief, they asserted, illogically from the viewpoint of the Mu'tizilites, that the Qur'an was not creator but not created either. They also believed that, in accordance with a literally understood Qur'anic promise (75:22–23), they will see God with their own eyes in his physical form on the Day of Judgment.

The logically and rationally minded Mu'tazilites were shocked by the Hadíth party's insistence on the uncreated nature of the Qur'anic text and its recitation. They saw it as contrary to the principle of *tawhíd*: There could be no eternal, uncreated entity alongside God's unique, eternal, and uncreated essence, even if the entity was the Qur'an itself.

Another important point of disagreement between the Mu'tazilites and the supporters of *hadíth* lay in the latter's insistence that God should be held above any human understanding of good and evil. God alone is the sole creator of all things, including those that humans consider to be evil. If an act is to be regarded as unjust, it is because God labeled it so, not because of its inherent nature that God must respect. As far as the issue of human free will is concerned, for the Hadíth party, humans cannot be their own masters. Their actions are predetermined by God from eternity, and they are unable to change the destiny prescribed for them by God. Human beings are unfit to judge God as just or unjust, reasonable or unreasonable. It is not the place of human reason to judge God, so any rational speculation about the nature of God and his attributes should be abandoned as futile. Qur'anic statements about God and his attributes should be taken literally, without asking how and why. When God says that he steps down from his throne, humans cannot possibly understand what this means and how this act is related to human actions. It may not be the same as the king's stepping down from his royal throne but in some unfathomable way bears resemblance to it and thus should be taken at face value, not allegorized away.

Ibn Hánbal and the Inquisition

The Hadíth party included many renowned scholars, among whom Ibn Hánbal (d. 855) was the most prominent. A humble and unassuming individual who shunned involvement in the affairs of this world, he was propelled to prominence by the events of the so-called Inquisition (*míhna*). The Inquisition was part of the policy of religious and political consolidation instituted by the caliph al-Ma'mún (r. 813–833), a son of Harún al-Rashíd, who came to power after defeating and killing his brother al-Amín in the bloody civil war of 811–813. An astute and well educated ruler, al-Ma'mún was anxious to expand his base of support among the masses of Baghdad by first trying to co-opt the Shi'ites and later on by empowering the Mu'tazilites and other proponents of *kalám* against the Hadíth party, who, as we have just seen, were strongly opposed to any type of rational inquiry into divine revelation.

Numerous explanations of al-Ma'mún's policies have been offered by Muslim and Western scholars. Most likely, he wanted to assert himself as the final recourse and arbiter in matters of religious dogma. Had he succeeded, he would have united religious authority and temporal power under the aegis of the caliphal office, thereby undercutting the influence of the *'ulamá'* class. Apparently, al-Ma'mún's attempts to formulate an orthodox state creed was accepted by at least some Mu'tazilites but rejected by the supporters of *hadíth*, who did not set much stock by any humanly formulated dogma in principle. The caliph's frustration at their refusal to accept him as a fellow scholar and arbiter in religious disputes is evident from his letter that ushered in the events of the Inquisition:

> The Commander of the Faithful considers that these people [the Hadíth folk] are the worst of the Muslim community and the chief ones in error, the ones who are defective in their belief in the divine unity and who have an imperfect share in the faith. They are vessels of ignorance, banners of mendaciousness, and the tongue of Iblis.[41]

Following this opening salvo, al-Ma'mún proceeds to explain the nature of his opponents' delusion:

By their utterances concerning the Qur'an, these ignorant people have enlarged the breach in their religion and the defect in their trustworthiness; they have made the way easy for the enemy of Islam, and have confessed to perversion of the Qur'anic text and heresy against their own hearts.[42]

Contrary to the Hadíth folk's view of the Qur'an as uncreated and eternal, al-Ma'mún made the doctrine of the created Qur'an the touchstone of the correct belief. His goal was to reestablish the caliph's position as the successor of the prophet Muhammad and the guardian of Islamic law that had largely been lost by his predecessors to the scholarly class (*'ulamá'*).[43] On al-Ma'mún orders, all religious officials in his realm were obliged to declare their allegiance to this creed publicly. Those who refused to publicly pronounce the Qur'an to be created were removed from their posts, flogged, pilloried, and occasionally imprisoned. Ibn Hánbal, a popular religious scholar opposed to the Mu'tazilite thesis of the created Qur'an, was summoned from Baghdad to al-Ma'mún's headquarters on the Muslim-Byzantine border[44] in order to be questioned about his views regarding the Scripture. Luckily for Ibn Hánbal, the caliph died before his arrival. Nevertheless, he was put under house arrest in Baghdad and, one and a half year later (834), summoned to the court of al-Ma'mún's successor, the caliph al-Mu'tasim (r. 833–842) to testify about his beliefs. When the scholar refused to acknowledge the created nature of the Qur'an, he was publicly flogged and thrown into prison.[45] Upon his release, Ibn Hánbal kept a low profile in order not to provoke his persecutors.

Under the caliph al-Mutawakkil (r. 847–861), al-Ma'mún's promotion of the doctrine of the created Qur'an was discontinued. Cognizant of the wide popularity enjoyed by the Hadíth party in the capital, which had grown even wider in the aftermath of the Inquisition, al-Mutawakkil declared its creed of the uncreated Qur'an to be the official doctrine of the 'Abbásid state. Ibn Hánbal was rehabilitated and showered with caliphal favors, most of which he refused to accept. However, the ascendancy of the Hadíth party did not signal the end of speculations among Muslim scholars over the nature of the Qur'an and relationships between the divine essence and the divine attributes more generally. These issues continued to be debated and were among the reasons for the rise of the new theological school known as Ash'arism.

The Theological "Middle Way": Ash'arism

This new trend in theological thinking was introduced by Abu 'l-Hasan al-Ash'ari (d. 936). Born and educated in Basra, he became a zealous supporter of the Mu'tazilites and the favorite pupil of the great Mu'tazilite thinker Abu 'Ali al-Jubbá'i (d. 915), who, together with his son Abu Háshim, had formulated the five pillars of the Mu'tazilite creed.[46] However, at about the age of forty, al-Ash'ari had a dream in which the Prophet commanded him to part ways with the Mu'tazilite school and to embrace the "true religion" of Ibn Hánbal and the Hadíth folk without, however, altogether abandoning the methods of *kalám* speculation. Deeply shaken, al-Ash'ari reportedly broke with his teacher and adopted a much more conservative theological position on many contentious issues debated by the two parties. Although based on the creed of Ibn Hánbal and his followers, al-Ash'ari's approach allowed a limited use of logical reasoning in framing the theological creed. The exact doctrinal positions formulated by al-Ash'ari himself are hard to ascertain. Many views ascribed to him retroactively were actually introduced by his followers. What is clear is that he sought to limit the scope and importance of rational methods in framing the dogma without abandoning them altogether. He thus created what some Western scholars have aptly dubbed the *via media* ("middle way") of Islamic theology.[47]

Let us examine a few examples of al-Ash'ari's middle-of-the-road approach. The Mu'tazilites, as we remember, denied that God has a physical body and argued that he cannot be seen by human beings either in this world or in the next. The Hanbalites insisted that God would be seen by all humans as a physical object ("as a full moon") on the Day of Judgment, since this vision was explicitly promised to them by the Qur'an (Q 75:22–23). Typically, al-Ash'ari took a middle position on this issue: Yes, God will be seen, but the nature of his vision by human beings is beyond human comprehension. On the question of divine attributes, which, according to the Mu'tazilites, were not distinct from God's essence, whereas, according to the Hadith party, they were real and distinct from it, al-Ash'ari maintained that the attributes were indeed real but, at the same time, not other than the divine essence. In other words, God' knowledge is not the same as God's will, while both are somehow not other than God's essence. Likewise, God's humanlike features should not be explained away as mere allegories (the position of the Hadith party), while at the same time they should not to be understood to be similar or equal to the parts of a human body (this was an implicit Ash'ari concession to the strongly anti-anthropomorphic views upheld by the Mu'tazilites). On the issue of faith, al-Ash'ari considered it to be both verbal affirmation and action (the position of the Hadith folk), while insisting that the verbal affirmation, in the end, was primary and essential (a concession to the Mu'tazilite stance). On the issue of the status of the grave sinner, al-Ash'ari rejected the Mu'tazilite thesis of the sinner's "intermediate position" between pure belief and pure unbelief. For him, the grave sinner remained a believer during his lifetime but was destined to be punished in hell in the afterlife.

Contrary to the Mu'tazilites and especially the philosophers who argued that the universe was governed by unchanging and predictable cause–effect relations, al-Ash'ari insisted that God is the only real cause behind all events, although, in his solicitude for his creatures, God allows certain sequences of events to repeat themselves. Every particular event or phenomenon is thus an immediate and unmediated act of God, who is constantly recreating the universe from discrete combinations of individual atoms of matter in accordance with his inscrutable will of the moment.[48] In other words, for al-Ash'ari and his followers, there was no underlying cause behind these ever recreated and reassembled combinations of atoms, except for God's arbitrary will. In this way, God's absolute and arbitrary power over his creation is forcibly and conclusively vindicated. Thus, in the Ash'arite universe, the only dependable knowledge is the knowledge of things and events that have already taken place. Given the absolute arbitrariness of God's will, we cannot predict any future developments. All we can know is how divine will has already manifested itself in concrete historical moments and events. Of these moments, the mission of the Prophet and the revelation of the Qur'an were of particular importance. The fact that they took place is beyond doubt. Therefore, they should be adopted as the foundations of the Muslim community that is destined by God to achieve salvation in the hereafter as long as it remains faithful to the divine will manifested at that historical juncture.[49]

On the issue of divine justice and the relation of God's absolute power to individual human acts, al-Ash'ari found the Mu'tazilite solution simplistic. He is said to have disagreed with his teacher al-Jubbá'i, who advocated the idea that God always rewards humans to the extent they deserve reward, since humans, according to the Mu'tazilite creed, are free to choose their actions as they see fit and incur God's punishment or reward accordingly. Al-Ash'ari's rejection of this concept is cast in the parable of the three brothers. One brother enjoys a high position in Paradise because he has lived a long life and performed many good works. The second brother, who occupies a lower position, complains to God that he died young and was thus unjustly denied the opportunity to do as much good as his brother. A Mu'tazilite rationalist like al-Jubbá'i would explain this conundrum by arguing that God, being omniscient, foresaw that the less rewarded brother would have sinned had he been allowed to live longer. Therefore, God cut him off early to prevent him from becoming a grave sinner. At this point, we learn about the third brother, a sinner being tormented in hell, who asks God why he did not cut him off early too.[50] Here the Mu'tazilites' rationalist logic has reached its limits, for there is no logical way to declare God at once omnipotent, omniscient, and all-just. It is more appropriate to say that all is God's will, and no fallible human explanations and justifications are needed. That was exactly the position of the Hadíth party.

The Ash'arites, however, were not quite comfortable with this kind of absolute fatalism. They believed that a distinction should be made between the actions of a responsible human being and the mechanical motion of a stone when it falls. Although, on the face of it, both are the products of the divine will, the Ash'arites wanted to grant humans at least a modicum of control over their actions. They offered the following solution to this theological conundrum. First, good and evil, indeed the laws of logic itself, are what God has decreed them to be. It is presumptuous of human beings to attempt to judge God or to explain his actions on the basis of the categories that God has arbitrarily established for human beings only. Human responsibility does not spring from independent human actions because this would mean that human beings are capable of creating their own actions. Rather, according to Ash'ari theologians, God creates all human actions directly, while simultaneously giving human agents the power to perform them. By performing certain deed, human beings "acquire" (*kasb*), or partake in, a certain category of actions that was marked by God as either good or evil. In the process of this "acquisition/partaking," human beings become the agents of a given action and thus can be held responsible for it. Although ingenious, the doctrine of acquisition/partaking has failed to convincingly resolve the issue of the ultimate agent of an action (either God or human beings or both). If anything, it has only further obfuscated it.

Ash'arism, Maturidism, and the Hadíth Party

Al-Ash'ari and his followers rejected the basic argument of the Mu'tazilite school that autonomous reason is capable of serving as the unerring judge of what is true in matters pertaining to the revelation. At the same time, after parting ways with his Mu'tazilite teachers, al-Ash'ari continued to make use of the formal language of *kalám* in order to defend the antirationalist and literalist position of the Hadíth party more effectively. As with his Mu'tazilite teachers, he insisted that intellectual inquiry into the revelation is not only commendable but was also decreed by the Qur'an and the Prophet. However, al-Ash'ari's limited and measured use of *kalám* methods still proved to be excessive for the majority of the Hadíth party, who refused to recognize him as one of their own. One of the Hanbalite leaders of Baghdad, al-Barbahári (d. 945), flatly disavowed him. In line with the overall position of the Hadíth party, al-Barbahári considered any rationalist inquiry into the meaning of the revelation to be a blameworthy "innovation" (*bid'a*). Hence the refusal of the majority of the Hanbalites to reconcile themselves to any use of the methods of *kalám*, although some of them have willy-nilly mastered them in order to argue effectively against their theological opponents. Even outside the Hanbalite school, it took several centuries for Ash'arite's *kalám* to acquire the status of official theology primarily among the scholars of the Shafi'i legal school.

In the meantime, the Hanafites in the eastern lands of Islam developed their own version of *kalám* named after its founder, the Central Asian scholar al-Matúridi (d. 944). Like Ash'arism, Maturidism was a compromise between the strictly rationalist attitude of the Mu'tazilites and the "illogical" literalism of the Hadíth folk, although it hewed closer to the Mu'tazilite position on the issues of faith, namely, that a verbal declaration of it is sufficient; divine predestination versus human free will, that is, human beings always have a choice and power to perform two opposite acts, which God creates for them simultaneously, and are thus fully accountable for their actions; and the status of the grave sinner in the hereafter: whereas the Ash'arites insisted that the sinner would stay in hell forever, the Maturidites maintained that he or she would eventually be released and dispatched to paradise.[51]

Conclusions

The beginnings of Islamic rationalist theology can be traced back, on the one hand, to the necessity to defend Islam from its external detractors and, on the other, to the natural human desire to make rational sense out of the divine plan of creation as revealed through the Scriptures. Which of these two factors was primary and which secondary is immaterial. What matters is that the Muslim revelation was subjected to rationalist analysis very early on. This process brought up a host of puzzles that eluded a simple and unequivocal solution. In response to this situation, there emerged two diametrically opposed attitudes to these puzzles within the Muslim learned class ('ulamá'). One was to attack them headlong and through rational argumentation seek such solutions to them that would be consistent with the laws of Greek logic and common sense. This was the approach taken by the Mu'tazilites and some other adherents of *kalám*, including rationally inclined Shi'ites. On the opposite side of the spectrum were those Muslim scholars who considered the application of the alien intellectual methods to the sacrosanct word of the Islamic revelation to be totally inappropriate, even blasphemous. In a similar vein, they considered any theorizing that went beyond the explicit wording of the Qur'an and the Sunna (e.g., allegorized it) to be either suspect or outright heretical. Nevertheless, with time some elements of rational argumentation have become part and parcel of Sunni and Shi'ite theologies, the objections and protests of conservative, unreflecting scholars notwithstanding. At the same time, Islamic rationalist theology (*kalám*) has never attained the same high status and indisputable authority as Islamic legal and juridical theory (*fiqh*).

Questions to Ponder

1   Are we free actors or helpless pawns in the hands of divine predestination? Why was this question so important to medieval Muslim thinkers? What solutions did they offer to this conundrum? Which of them is (are) more convincing and why?
2   Is Ash'arism indeed an ingenious solution to the theological conundrums outlined in this chapter, or is it at best but a rather tenuous compromise between faith and reason?

Summary

- The Qur'an is central to Islamic faith and practice. All Muslims feel it necessary to appeal to the Qur'an's authority to justify their beliefs and actions: hence the abundance of different interpretations of the Qur'anic text over the centuries.
- Islamic theological reasoning begins—from "Greek wisdom" to rational speculation about faith (*kalám*). The so-called translation project is sponsored by the caliph al-Ma'mún (r. 813–833) in making Greek philosophy and logic available to Muslim thinkers. Greek wisdom has a long-ranging and profound impact on Islamic thought.
- The Islamic creed (the six articles of faith) are articulated, the goal of *kalám*, according to Ibn Khaldún (d. 1406).
- The problem of divine justice in this so obviously unjust world of ours is addressed. Where does injustice come from: humans or God? Al-Hásan al-Basri (d. 728) analyzes the apparent contradiction between the divine predestination of all events, on the one hand, and humans' ability to exercise their free will and thus be responsible for their actions, on the other.

- Does the commission of a grave sin by Muslims render them unbelievers? Who has the right to determine his or her status in this world, that is, are sinful individuals inside or outside the community of the faithful?
- The *murji'a* support the doctrine of the postponement of judgment (*irja'*).
- According to their school of discursive theology, the Mu'tazilites attempt to consistently apply rational reasoning and logic to the Islamic revelation. The Mu'tazilite creed includes five articles: (1) Divine unity: There is no plurality within the Godhead, only different existential modes or states of its being. (2) Divine justice: God is just; injustice comes from his human servants. (3) The divine promise of paradise and the threat of the hellfire are absolute and irrevocable: God cannot pardon a grave sinner or condemn a righteous person to hell. (4) The "intermediate position" of the grave sinner: He or she is neither fully within nor fully outside the community of the faithful and thus cannot be decisively excommunicated. (5) Commanding the good and forbidding the wrong, with all its social and political implications.
- Mu'tazilism is a general intellectual attitude and world outlook that is not confined to any one legal school or religious-political party.
- The Hadíth folk (or the Hadíth party) disagree with the Mu'tazilites. God's attributes are real and should be taken literally, not allegorized away. God is free to do as he wills, even though his actions may appear unjust or irrational to us.
- The problem of the created/uncreated Qur'an has its political and social implications. Ibn Hánbal (d. 855) staunchly advocates for the uncreated Qur'an, leading to his public ordeal under the caliph al-Ma'mún and his successors. There are political reasons behind al-Ma'mún's *mihna*.
- With the *via media* ("middle way/road") of al-Ash'ari (d. 936), the Ash'ari theological school in Sunnism is formed in response to both Mu'tazilite rationalism and Hanbalite illogical literalism. The Ash'ari school proposes its own solutions to the problems of human free will versus divine predestination, the nature of the divine attributes, the vision of God by the faithful in the afterlife, and universal causality.

Notes

1 Marshall Hodgson, *The Venture of Islam*, Chicago University Press, Chicago, 1974, vol. 1, pp. 367–369.
2 Ibid., vol. 2, pp. 504–505.
3 Louis Gardet, "'Ilm al-kalam," in *Encyclopedia of Islam*, 2nd ed.; online edition: http://referenceworks.brillonline.com.
4 Montgomery Watt, *Islamic Philosophy and Theology*, Edinburgh University Press, Edinburgh, 1985, Chapter 7 and Majid Fakhry, *A History of Islamic Philosophy*, 3rd ed., Columbia University Press, New York, 2004, pp. 1–19.
5 Ibn Khaldun, *The Muqaddimah: An Introduction to History* (trans. Franz Rosenthal), Columbia University Press, New York, 1958, vol. 3, p. 34.
6 Watt, *Islamic Philosophy*, pp. 25–31.
7 Gardet, "'Ilm al-kalam"; Binyamin Abrahamov, *Islamic Theology: Traditionalism and Rationalism*, Edinburgh University Press, Edinburgh, 1998, p. 9 and Hodgson, *The Venture*, vol. 1, pp. 357–358 and 438–439.
8 Hodgson, *The Venture*, vol. 2, pp. 175–179.
9 Montgomery Watt, *The Formative Period of Islamic Thought*, Oneworld, Oxford, 1998, pp. 209–224.
10 See also Q 7:181–186 and 23:96 and 102–103.
11 See Tilman Nagel, *The History of Islamic Theology* (trans. Thomas Thornton), Markus Wiener Publishers, Princeton, NJ, 2000, p. 39.

12 Ibid., p. 60.

13 For a summary of early debates about the status of 'Uthman, see Watt, *The Formative Period*, pp. 69–77; see also Patricia Crone, *Medieval Islamic Political Thought*, Edinburgh University Press, Edinburgh, 2004, pp. 27–28.

14 Watt, *The Formative Period*, pp. 123–128.

15 Crone, *Medieval*, p. 388.

16 Richard Martin and Mark Woodward, *Defenders of Reason in Islam*, Oneworld, Oxford, 1997, p. 62.

17 Hodgson, *The Venture*, vol. 2, p. 176.

18 Martin and Woodward, *Defenders of Reason in Islam*, p. 63.

19 Watt, *The Formative Period*, p. 209; according to Montgomery Watt, this name was originally applied to those pious Muslims who had refused to pass judgment regarding the actions of the leaders of the first civil war (*fitna*) in an attempt to "stay aloof" (*i'tazal*) from the fray.

20 Oliver Leaman, *An Introduction to Classical Islamic Philosophy*, Cambridge University Press, Cambridge, 2002, p. 14.

21 Ibid., p. 37.

22 Ibid., p. 15.

23 Ibid and Q 2:164, 5:100; 45:5, and 12:2.

24 Namely, the Day of Judgment.

25 Nagel, *The History of Islamic Theology*, p. 119.

26 Richard Frank, *Beings and Their Attributes*, SUNY Press, Albany, NY, 1978, pp. 19–21.

27 Martin and Woodward, *Defenders of Reason in Islam*, p. 68.

28 Ibid., p. 71.

29 Watt, *The Formative Period*, p. 231.

30 Martin and Woodward, *Defenders of Reason in Islam*, p. 82.

31 For details, see Michael Cook, *Commanding Right and Forbidding Wrong in Islamic Thought*, Cambridge University Press, Cambridge, 2000, pp. 469–470 et passim.

32 Nimrod Hurvitz, *The Formation of Hanbalism*, Routledge and Curzon, Oxon and New York, 2002, pp. 123–130.

33 For the Shafi'i, Hánafi, and other legal schools in Islam, see Chapters 6 and 9.

34 Cook, *Commanding Right and Forbidding Wrong*, p. 196 and Harry Wolfson, *The Philosophy of the Kalam*, Harvard University Press, Cambridge, MA, and London, 1976, Chapters 3 and 6.

35 Johann Fueck, "The Role of Traditionalism in Islam," trans. and ed. by Merlin Swartz, *Studies on Islam*, Oxford University Press, Oxford, 1981, p. 107.

36 Hodgson, *The Venture*, vol. 1, p. 386.

37 Nagel, *The History of Islamic Theology*, p. 119.

38 Hurvitz, *The Formation of Hanbalism*, pp. 132–138.

39 Hodgson, *The Venture*, vol. 1, p. 480.

40 Ibid., p. 388.

41 That is, the Devil; Clifford Bosworth (trans.), *The History of al-Tabari*, vol. 32. *Reunification of the 'Abbasid Caliphate*, SUNY Press, Albany, NY, 1987, p. 203.

42 Ibid., p. 208.

43 Livnat Holtzman, "Ahmad b. Hanbal," in *Encyclopedia of Islam*, 3rd ed.; online edition: http://reference works.brillonline.com.

44 In the town of Tarsus, presently in south-central Turkey.

45 According to some Muslim authors, e.g., al-Jahiz (d. 869), he recanted his beliefs under duress; see Holtzman, "Ahmad b. Hanbal."

46 Martin and Woodward, *Defenders of Reason in Islam*, pp. 31–32.

47 See, e.g., Sabine Schmidtke, "Theological Rationalism in the Medieval World of Islam," *al-'Usur al-Wusta*, vol. 20/1 (2008), p. 18.

48 Hodgson, *The Venture*, vol. 1, p. 443.

49 Ibid.

50 Hodgson, *The Venture*, vol. 1, p. 442; cf. Watt, *The Formative Period*, p. 305.

51 Watt, *The Formative Period*, pp. 315–316.

Chapter 11

Twelver Shi'ism and Zaydism

The Crystallization of the Shi'ite Creed in Opposition to Sunnism

Of the numerous movements and theological schools in medieval Islam, only Shi'ism (the "party of 'Ali"; Arab. *shi'at 'Ali*) was able to create a viable and lasting alternative to Sunnism. The success of the Shi'ites came at a cost: as the Shi'ite doctrine grew more sophisticated and its adherents more numerous, politically active, and organized, both the caliphs and the leaders of the Sunni community came to view the Shi'ites as their principal political and religious rivals. As a result, the Sunni ruling elite did their utmost to prevent Shi'ite candidates from gaining political power, whereas Sunni theologians spared no effort to discredit Shi'ism on doctrinal grounds. In sum, throughout the Middle Ages and into the modern period, the Shi'ites have had to defend themselves both politically and ideologically, often against great odds.

The positions of numerous and often mutually hostile political and religious factions within the early Shi'ite movement are quite diverse and rather difficult to summarize. They began to take their final shape only in the aftermath of the 'Abbásid revolution in response to the failure of the pro-'Alid movement to bring to power a member of 'Ali's immediate family. In the process of heated disputes over the meaning and practical implications of being loyal to 'Ali's family, the broad pro-'Alid movement produced multiple branches that disagreed, often irreconcilably, over the identity of the rightful *imam*, the movement's strategic goals, methods to achieve them, as well as some finer theological matters. Among these multiple branches of the movement, the so-called Twelver Shi'ites, or the Imamites, and the Seveners, or Isma'ilis, have proved to be the most consequential. The Zaydi version of 'Alid loyalism also gained a rather broad popular following during the 'Abbásid epoch but later entered a period of contraction and intellectual stagnation. In the end, it has survived only in the mountainous areas of North Yemen that lay beyond the reach of the caliphs' armies and those of their imperial successors.[1] This chapter will address the formation and evolution of Twelver Shi'ism under the 'Abbásids and, briefly, the vicissitudes of its Zaydi version in Yemen.

As we already know, historically, the principal factor that separated the proto-Shi'ites, or the 'Alid party (i.e., the supporters of the caliphate of 'Ali and his descendants), from the proto-Sunnis (the supporters of the caliphate of Abu Bakr, 'Umar, and 'Uthman, who later accepted Umayyad rule as "a lesser evil") was their disagreement over who should be viewed as the rightful leader (*imam*) of the Muslim state. The 'Alid party advocated the genealogical principle of succession, which emphasized the rights of the Prophet's immediate family, especially the descendants of 'Ali, to order the affairs of the Muslim community and to lead its members to salvation. The (proto-)Sunnis, for their part, embraced, at least in theory, the principle of the appointment of a qualified leader[2] (referred to as both "caliph" and "imam") by an electoral council (*shúra*) composed of the leading members of the *umma*.

In real life, following the imposition on the Muslim community of the dynastic rule of the Umayyad family, the incumbent caliph came to simply designate his successor, usually his son or brother. The caliph's decision was then rubber-stamped by an ad hoc electoral council, whose members he had himself handpicked and who hardly ever dared to challenge his designation. One can thus argue that the members of the Sunni community prudently chose to accept the political and military realities of the moment and to submit to the strongest ruler available, namely, one who had the military and political wherewithal to make an effective bid for power and then intimidate or, if necessary, annihilate his competitors. In other words, the Sunnis were prepared to submit to the rule of the strongest political player, no matter how impious or oppressive, as long as he pledged to maintain the norms of the Shari'a law and public order,[3] appoint judges, collect the legal alms, defend the borders of Islam, and, last but not least, preserve the unity of the faithful under his sway. In the opinion of the Sunni majority, life under an unjust but strong leader who met the minimal requirements of the office was better than intracommunal strife that, as the civil wars of the first one and a half centuries of Islam had demonstrated, seemed to be an inevitable consequence of high-minded attempts to bring to power the most just and righteous leader available.

The supporters of 'Ali and his family, who were based mainly in Syria, Iraq, and Iran, refused to put up with this Sunni "pragmatism." They viewed the position of the Sunni majority as unscrupulous and shameful. In their opinion, only the Prophet's biological descendants, who inherited his sinless nature and divinely inspired knowledge, were capable of guiding Muslims to salvation. The learned spokesmen for the 'Alid party never tired of insisting that without this guidance the community was doomed to go astray because ordinary human beings could never govern themselves on their own, without divine intervention. To prove their point, advocates of the 'Alid cause would enumerate the injustices of first the Umayyad and later also of 'Abbásid governments. Justice for all the faithful, great and small, could only be assured by a divinely guided and inspired leader (*imam*) from the 'Alid branch of the Prophet's clan Háshim. This belief was justified by references to the Qur'an (for instance, 33:33)[4] and the numerous prophetic *hadíth* that emphasized the unique virtues of 'Ali and his family or even explicitly asserted his exclusive right to lead the community after the Prophet. Typical in this regard is the prophetic report that presents 'Ali as "the most loved of men" and his wife Fátima, a daughter of the Prophet, as the "most loved of women."[5]

After the triumph of the 'Abbásids—who had come to power on the wave of popular support for 'Ali's direct descendants only to install their own, non-'Alid candidate—the partisans of the 'Alids were forced to furnish a clearer concept of "the chosen one (*al-ridá*) from the Prophet's family," that is, the rightful *imam*. While some supporters of 'Ali's family (for instance, the Zaydis) considered any descendant of 'Ali to be eligible for the imamate, especially if he could assert his right to it by force of arms, the majority gradually restricted the pool of eligible candidates to the progeny of 'Ali and the Prophet's daughter Fátima via their younger son, al-Husayn (d. 680) (see Figure 11.1). According to this belief, those who had barred the descendants of 'Ali and Fátima from becoming the rightful leaders of the Muslim community were but illegitimate and unscrupulous usurpers—a direct affront to the Sunni belief in the rightfulness and unsurpassed excellence of the first three successors (caliphs) to the Prophet. In concert with this logic, the rank-and-file Sunnis who submitted themselves to the authority of these "usurpers" were themselves misguided "renegades": They accepted as their leaders sinful individuals incapable of providing right guidance (*húda*) to the believers. By inserting themselves illicitly into the line of succession to the Prophet, the first Sunni caliphs and their partisans had violated the divine will according to which 'Ali should have become Muhammad's rightful successor (see Figure 11.2).

The majority of pro-'Alid Muslims firmly believed that, already during his lifetime, Muhammad had passed his authority on to 'Ali at the "Pond of Khumm" (*Ghadír Khumm*), a locale

Figure 11.1 Mosque in Karbalá (1932)

approximately halfway between Mecca and Medina.[6] The Sunnis did not deny the meeting of the two but vigorously protested that such an appointment had taken place. For them, the subsequent election of Abu Bakr in Medina was a legitimate, if spontaneous expression of the community's collective will. As time went on, the loyalty to 'Ali and his family upheld by his followers acquired wide-ranging theological and metaphysical dimensions to evolve, eventually, into a distinctive worldview and devotional practice. Thus, 'Ali's partisans came to believe that in addition to the mandate to lead the community of the faithful to salvation, Muhammad also conveyed to his cousin and son-in-law a secret and sacred knowledge (*'ilm*) that allowed him and his descendants to discern the true meaning of the Scripture and thus to become the infallible interpreters of God's will. Naturally, this belief was supported by references to carefully selected Qur'anic passages and the teachings of the Prophet. For example, the learned spokesmen of the 'Alid party were particularly fond of quoting a *hadíth* in which the Prophet described himself as "a city of knowledge" and 'Ali as the "gate" to that city.[7] In another *hadíth*, the function of bearing and preserving the divinely inspired knowledge is extended to 'Ali's family as a whole: "Neither in the East nor in the West will you find true knowledge, except what has its origin in the Prophet's family."[8] This knowledge, according to a Shi'ite *hadíth*, "existed before the creation of the physical world" to be subsequently transmitted "from Adam through the line of prophets" all the way to the "pure ones," namely 'Ali and his male progeny.[9]

The partisans of 'Ali and his family considered this sacred knowledge (*'ilm*) to be inaccessible to ordinary human beings. It was transmitted exclusively from one 'Alid *imam* to the next and was symbolized by the scrolls of sacred books and weapons of the Prophet that, according to the Twelver Shi'ite teaching, were also passed within his family, father to son.[10] The knowledge was a divine gift, often allegorically depicted in Shi'ite sources as "light" (*nur*)—an image that carried

Figure 11.2 The Prophet Muhammad and His Family ('Ali, Hasan and Husayn) on the Ship of Shi'ism That Sails to Salvation (Persian-Safavid miniature from around 1635)

Eric and Edith Matson Photography Collection/Wikimedia Commons

both existential (the 'Alid *imam*s were created thereof) and cognitive (it was a source of their superhuman insight) connotations. Following 'Ali's death, his followers have come to believe that this light resides exclusively in his progeny, upon whom it devolves as a birthright. The *imam*s were thus the only genuine "heirs of the Prophet," the "natural-born" leaders of his community in the postprophetic epoch.[11] All other contenders to this title (for instance, the Sunni caliphs, Sunni scholars, or Sufi masters) were dismissed as illegitimate interlopers or imposters. According to the Shi'ite doctrine, after the death of the Prophet, the Sunni majority misguidedly followed the ordinary and fallible human beings who lacked this divinely inspired knowledge.

In so doing, they have committed a grievous sin and thereby set out on the path of injustice, error, and eventually perdition.

For the pro-'Alid party, 'Ali's historical personality stood as a tragic symbol of the injustices of this world. Although a great and high-minded individual—who was intensely loved by those around him during his lifetime—he, through human weakness and treachery, found himself entangled in the ignoble logic of events, abandoned by his erstwhile supporters and dragged down to a defeat. He may have deserved his fate on the level of real politics, but his personal stature as the Prophet's closest male relative and the first male convert made his defeat and untimely death at the hands of an assassin intolerable for his admirers.[12] According to the Shi'ite version of history, the betrayal of the cause of justice by the majority of Muslims, who had withdrawn their support from 'Ali in favor of the cunning Mu'awiya, was further confirmed by their subsequent complicity in the murder of 'Ali's younger son al-Husayn. Shi'ites believed that God had deliberately dispatched al-Husayn to redeem the wayward community from the sin it had committed by accepting the "illegitimate" rule of the first three caliphs and, later on, of the Umayyad "usurpers" as well. However, God's attempt to lead his servants aright came to nothing once again as the majority of Muslims failed to rise to the occasion. Instead of supporting al-Husayn's rightful bid for the imamate at Karbalá/Kerbelá, they refused to him as their rightful leader (*imam*). This deplorable pattern of behavior on the part of the Sunni majority persisted under the 'Abbásids, who, according to the Shi'ites, had treacherously installed themselves as dynastic despots after having cynically masqueraded as partisans of 'Ali and his descendants.

The Divergence of the Shi'ite and Sunni Visions of Islam

The Shi'ite vision of Muslim history just outlined highlights the profound difference in the world outlooks between the members of the Sunni and Shi'ite communities. For the Sunnis, this world, all its injustices and imperfections notwithstanding, is still the best possible one in that it represents an authentic expression of the divine will. From the Sunni perspective, divine guidance and justice are embodied in the life and practice of the Muslim community that are founded on the Qur'an and the exemplary custom of the Prophet (*sunna*). Membership in this community and a strict adherence to the Shari'a as interpreted and implemented by its leading scholars guarantees the faithful justice in this life and salvation in the hereafter.

The partisans of 'Ali and his family see things in a less optimistic light. For them, the Sunni majority are but misguided and opportunistic renegades, who cared only about their personal well-being and who therefore have traded justice and truth for injustice and falsehood. The sorry state of this world, according to the Shi'ites, can be redressed only by a divinely guided leader (*máhdi*) of the 'Alid stock,[13] whose appearance will usher in the inevitable triumph of truth over falsehood. To support this belief, Shi'ite scholars have often cited 'Ali's prediction that "God will choose the Mahdi . . . from among us, the People of the [Prophet's] House."[14] Since none of the 'Alid candidates—except 'Ali himself (whose caliphate was cut short by an assassin anyway)— was given a chance to implement this bold vision in real life, the arrival of the divinely guided leader has come to be projected into an undefined future in order to alleviate the sufferings of the true believers and to sustain their hopes for a better, more just world. This "futuristic" orientation helps to understand the Shi'ite propensity to *chiliasm* or *millennialism*, namely, an expectation that history will be completed with a blissful millennium, at which point the world as we know it will be put right by a divinely assisted hero, the *máhdi*. Learned exponents of Twelver Shi'ism, many of whom were students of the Shi'ite *imam*s, later identified the *máhdi* with the twelfth descendant of 'Ali and Fátima, who, they claimed, went into "occultation" (*ghayba*) in 874.[15] At a time known only to God, he was expected to make a triumphal appearance before his followers in order to punish the wicked of this world and to reward the true believers who had kept the faith in him against all odds. The Twelver Shi'ite doctrines, which acquired their final shape in the tenth century, described genuine faith as the believer's personal devotion to this divinely guided individual. As their Sunni counterparts, Twelver Shi'ite scholars derived their teachings from the Qur'an and the Sunna of the Prophet. However, they believed that the sacred texts of Islam contained a hidden meaning that could be extracted only by those possessed of divinely revealed knowledge, '*ilm*, that is, the Shi'ite *imam*s and their trusted representatives.

The Vicissitudes of the Shi'ite Imamate Under the 'Abbásids

The foundations of what has come to be known as "Twelver Shi'ism" were articulated by the fifth and sixth Shi'ite *imam*s, Muhammad al-Báqir (d. 733) and his son Ja'far al-Sádiq (d. 765). The former died before the 'Abbásid revolution, the latter fifteen years after it. Both were accomplished scholars whose authority was recognized not only by the party of 'Ali but by many Sunnis as well. Their major achievement was the unification of numerous pro-'Alid factions and disavowing political activism in order to shield their community from the wrath of Sunni rulers. To this end, the *imam*s made a conscious decision to abstain from participation in antigovernment agitation, not to mention armed rebellions. For instance, when the popular 'Alid candidate Muhammad al-Nafs al-Zakiyya ("Muhammad the Pure Soul") rebelled in the Hijáz in 762 during the reign of the second 'Abbásid caliph al-Mansúr (r. 754–775), Ja'far al-Sádiq refused to support this younger cousin of his (who belonged to the Hasanid branch of 'Ali's family) and to recognize him as "the rightly guided one (*máhdi*) of the House of the Prophet"—the title conferred upon the rebel 'Alid by his partisans. Ja'far's prudence was duly acknowledged and rewarded by the caliph al-Mansúr who was otherwise ruthless in his treatment of the 'Alids, viewing them as the main threat to his rule. Not only did the caliph solicit Ja'far's advice, but he also employed some of the *imam*'s closest followers in his service, thereby laying the foundations of 'Alid influence at the caliph's court in Baghdad. With time, this influence had grown quite substantial[16] and served the Twelver Shi'ite community in good stead.

In line with political pacifism, Ja'far sought to strip the Shi'ite doctrine of its most radical and potentially revolutionary elements, such as the belief in the return of the deceased *imam* (*raj'a*) as the enforcer of the true religion and in the *imam*'s semidivine nature. In the past, such "exaggerated" beliefs in the supernatural powers of the 'Alid family had often instigated antigovernment insurgency under millenarian slogans. This form of political activism would inevitably expose the entire Shi'ite community to severe reprisals by the Sunni state. Ja'far's consistent attempts to steer clear of the grand political ambitions entertained by some more radical members of the Shi'ite movement were deemed to allay the suspicions of the Sunni caliphs and protect his followers from their rage. Whereas Ja'far's prudent political stance had not prevented his own sons from joining the rebellion of Muhammad "The Pure Soul," it probably saved their lives after the rebellion had been quashed by the caliphal state.

Ja'far al-Sádiq's community-building efforts were put to a severe test when his elder son and designated successor Isma'il predeceased him. Many of Ja'far's followers refused to believe that the incumbent *imam* could err in such a critical issue as succession. In their opinion, Isma'il's death was but a divine stratagem aimed at protecting him from the murderous designs of the ever suspicious 'Abbásid political authorities. According to the partisans of Isma'il, he and his son Muhammad simply went into hiding in anticipation of a more auspicious moment to make public their bid for the community's leadership. This belief became the ideological basis of the Isma'ili branch of Shi'ism, which will be discussed in the next chapter.[17]

The majority of Ja'far's followers now turned to his eldest surviving son 'Abdallah and accepted him as the *imam*'s successor. Again, their loyalty to the 'Alids was tested, when 'Abdallah died only seventy days after his father. Following a brief period of confusion and soul-searching, the majority pledged their allegiance to another son, Músa al-Kázim (d. 799). Despite his propensity for political activism—Músa had participated in the aborted rebellion of his Hasanid uncle Muhammad "The Pure Soul"—he managed to preserve and consolidate the internal organization of the Twelver Shi'ite community. He did so by dispatching able and loyal agents to different districts of the caliphate and by regularizing the collection of donations on his behalf, which were then sent to his treasury in Medina.[18] Following a string of Shi'ite rebellions in Arabia, North Africa, and Iran in the last two decades of the eighth century, the 'Abbásid caliph Harún al-Rashíd (r. 786–809) had Músa imprisoned. It appears that the caliph's decision was prompted by Músa's claim to be the divinely guided "riser" (al-máhdi al-qá'im), which made him a natural focus of the pro-'Alid party's millenarian expectations. When he died in Baghdad in 799, allegedly poisoned by Harún al-Rashíd's agents, his followers refused to accept his death, arguing that he was still alive and living in "occultation" (ghayba).[19] Following the disappearance of the last imam of the Twelver Shi'ites 175 years later (874), the belief in occultation became central to their doctrine and identity. In the meantime, after some vacillation, the majority of Músa's supporters recognized his son 'Ali as the new imam. The latter was able to regain control of the network of agents established by his father.

During the civil war between Harún al-Rashíd's sons al-Amín and al-Ma'mún (811–813) and the political turmoil that ensued, a number of pro-'Alid factions launched rebellions in the name of one or the other 'Alid candidate. However, the eighth imam 'Ali b. Músa ("al-Ridá") chose to adhere to the quietist, apolitical agenda of his grandfather and refused to join any of them. In 817, after the 'Alid rebellions had been suppressed, al-Ma'mún made a bold decision to declare 'Ali b. Músa "the chosen one of the House of the Prophet" (ridá) and to appoint him as his successor to the office of the caliph. To cement this arrangement, al-Ma'mún gave 'Ali b. Músa one of his daughters in marriage and ordered the black banners of the 'Abbásid dynasty to be replaced by the green ones, which symbolized the house of the Prophet.[20] The exact motives behind al-Ma'mún's actions are an object of academic debates. Clearly, 'Ali al-Ridá's apolitical stance and advanced age played a role in al-Ma'mún's decision, along with the caliph's desire to secure the support of numerous partisans of the 'Alid cause in the aftermath of the fratricidal war between him and his brother Amín. With Baghdad dominated by his brother's followers, al-Ma'mún hoped to win over to his side the powerful Shi'ite organization established by Ja'far al-Sádiq and Músa al-Kázim and further strengthened and expanded under their successor. Some modern historians have cited other reasons for al-Ma'mún's decision, including his desire to placate Shi'ite rebels or the influence of his vizier al-Fadl who had Shi'ite proclivities.[21] Finally, al-Ma'mún may have been driven by the apocalyptic predictions that he would be the last member of the 'Abbásid ruling family and by the resultant desire to unify the 'Alid and 'Abbásid houses in anticipation of the fulfillment of that prophecy.

Be this as it may, al-Ma'mún's designation of 'Ali al-Ridá as his heir apparent contributed to the prestige of the Shi'ite cause and increased the number of its supporters. However, 'Ali al-Ridá's death in 818 near the city of Tus (present-day Meshhed in Iran) seriously dampened their enthusiasm. Shi'ite sources suggest that his death was caused by "the subtlest of poisons" after al-Ma'mún's order. It is not quite clear whether the caliph did this out of jealousy for 'Ali's popularity or because he changed his mind and decided to throw in his lot with the Sunni majority that had apparently been worried by his nomination of an 'Alid imam as his successor.[22] Some historians even doubt that the caliph had a hand in 'Ali al-Ridá's death.[23] The imam's successor, Muhammad al-Taqí ("The God-Fearing"), was a child of seven years who was not in a position to dispense any meaningful guidance to his followers.[24] How could a minor serve as God's decisive "argument" (hujja) for humankind and the carrier of the precious 'ilm that was so important for the salvation of his partisans? To make matters worse, this and the subsequent imams of the Twelver Shi'ites found themselves under close surveillance by the caliph's secret police to prevent them from contacting their supporters in Iraq and the eastern provinces. Under these circumstances, the leadership of the Shi'ite community effectively devolved upon the *imams'* secretaries, disciples, and agents, preparing the ground for the future existence of Shi'ism without an active *imam*.

When this ninth *imam* died at the age of twenty-four, leaving behind another seven-year-old as his successor, the entire future of the Shi'ite project was called into doubt. However, the Shi'ite hierarchy of agents, secretaries, and *imams'* disciples proved to be resilient and effective enough to withstand the crisis that, in the later Shi'ite tradition, came to be known as "confusion" (*hayra*).[25] Now, the rank-and-file Shi'ites had no option but to seek guidance from the community's learned elite, which assumed control over the Twelver Shi'ite network of agents and financial resources.[26] Luckily, the learned men (*rijál*) of the Shi'ite community were able to rise to the occasion. Although they insisted that "since Adam's death, God has never left the earth without an *imam* as a path to God" and that "those who abandon him are bound to perish,"[27] during the *imam*'s minority they acted as his agents (*wukala'*; sing. *wakíl*) or "ambassadors" (*sufara'*; sing. *safír*). In so doing, they effectively replaced him as disseminators and interpreters the *imam*'s sacred *'ilm* among the generality of his followers. Their own legal and doctrinal opinions were now circulated in his name. Simultaneously, the scholars elaborated a distinctly Shi'ite theology and jurisprudence that came to constitute the ideological and legal foundation of Twelver Shi'ite Islam for centuries to come. The crisis of succession was thus successfully averted, and the role of the scholars as intermediaries between the *imam* and his followers became firmly established.

The consolidation of Shi'ism and the growing number of its followers in the capital and provinces throughout the ninth century alarmed the caliph al-Mutawakkil (r. 847–861) enough to cause him to resume the persecution of the Shi'ites. In 848, the tenth *imam* 'Ali al-Hádi ("The Guide [to the Truth]") was brought from Medina to Iraq and placed under house arrest in the caliphate's new capital Samarra, some eighty miles north of Baghdad.[28] In 850, responding to the demands of some powerful Sunnite factions in Baghdad and concerned about the alleged clandestine activities of Shi'ite agents around the tombs of the Shi'ite *imam*s in Iraq, al-Mutawakkil ordered the demolition of the major Shi'ite sanctuary, al-Husayn's tomb at Kerbelá, in an effort to stop the annual Shi'ite pilgrimages to that holy site.[29] The tomb and nearby houses were razed to the ground, whereupon the shrine's site was ploughed over and cultivated.[30] Al-Mutawakkil also removed all known Shi'ites from positions of authority in the state administration and imprisoned those whom he considered to be particularly dangerous.[31] Finally, he curtailed the privileges and pensions of 'Ali's descendants known collectively as *ashráf* (sing. *sharíf*; i.e., "nobleman").

Although al-Mutawakkil's son and successor al-Múntasir (whose rule lasted for less than a year) showed much more tolerance toward the Shi'ites and the *ashráf*,[32] the subsequent *imam*s were forced to reside in Iraq instead of their traditional seat in Medina. As it turned out, this measure on the part of the 'Abbásid caliphs failed to suppress the Shi'ite movement. After living in relative isolation in in Arabia, the *imam*s found themselves closer to the thriving Shi'ite communities of Iraq (Kufa) and Iran (Qumm and Rayy). Ironically, the constant surveillance of 'Abbásid agents notwithstanding, the *imam*s now enjoyed greater freedom of action than the 'Abbásid caliphs of that age, who by that time had been reduced to mere puppets in the hands of their Turkish slave guards.[33]

Upon the death of 'Ali al-Hádi, another succession crisis broke out among the Shi'ite elite as his elder son and heir apparent had predeceased him. Following an intense struggle among several factions within the Shi'ite movement, the majority of Shi'ites accepted the imamate of his middle son, al-Hásan, nicknamed "al-'Askari" because he spent most of his life in the caliph's military camp (*'askar*) of Samarra under the surveillance of 'Abbásid soldiers. His supporters among the Shi'ite scholarly elite prevailed over those of his younger brother Ja'far, whom many Shi'ites saw as better qualified for the office. In particular, they considered al-Hásan's lifestyle as a courtier and his alleged lack of the requisite religious knowledge to be major impediments to his being a proper *imam*. The extent of scrutiny al-Hásan underwent before his confirmation in the office is conveyed by his complaint to his close followers that none of his forebears had been as much doubted by the Shi'ites as he was.[34] The presence of a living *imam* accessible to both his followers and enemies was becoming a liability for the leadership of the Shi'ite community.

Al-Hásan al-'Askari died on January 1, 874, with no known son, at least according to the earliest evidence furnished by Sunni sources.[35] Another succession crisis, or "confusion" (*hayra*), ensued, with the Shi'ite community splintering into at least a dozen factions, each having its own idea of who, if anyone, should be the twelfth *imam*.[36] Some argued that al-Hásan did not die but went into a "temporary occultation" to return triumphantly as the awaited *máhdi*. Others wanted to install al-Hásan's rival brother Ja'far as the next *imam*, which flew in the face of the widely accepted Shi'ite rule that after al-Hásan and al-Husayn, sons of 'Ali, the imamate should never be held by two brothers. Still others insisted that al-Hásan was the last *imam*, although they disagreed as to whether he was also the awaited *máhdi*.[37] A powerful faction led by the influential 'Amri family offered an alternative solution that was subsequently accepted by the majority of the Shi'ites. The 'Amris argued that al-Hásan did have the rightful successor, a son named Muhammad, but this son was concealed by God from human sight in the same way as "the sun is hidden behind clouds."[38] His age at the time of his disappearance, which coincided with the demise of his father (874), was five, so he was supposedly born in 869. This story was eventually adopted by the majority of Shi'ites. In the subsequent Shi'ite tradition, this invisible but miraculously ever present *imam* has come to be known as Muhammad al-Múntazar ("The Awaited").[39]

In retrospect, the disappearance of the twelfth *imam* in Samarra was a logical development of the doctrine of *imam*'s occultation, the beginnings of which can be traced back to the period following the death of the seventh *imam* Músa al-Kázim (799). The latter's followers, too, considered him to be in the state of temporary occultation and for a while waited him to return in glory. Be this as it may, with the occultation of the twelfth *imam* his forthcoming return has become for the majority of Shi'ites the cornerstone of their worldview and self-identity. It preserved the all-important Shi'ite concept of the saving and guiding *imam*, while not demanding that he be physically present among his followers. The site of the twelfth *imam*'s disappearance in Samarra became an object of pilgrimage and is still marked by a memorial mosque attached to the shrine of the last *imam*'s father, al-Hásan al-'Askari. Given its importance for the Shi'ite identity, there is no wonder that its bombing in February 2006 by unidentified assailants outraged the entire Shi'ite community of Iraq, leading to retaliatory violence against Iraq's Sunnis with numerous casualties on both sides.[40] The repercussions of this fateful event are still being felt in the tense and often outright hostile relations between the Shi'ites and Sunnis of Iraq today.

Traditions confirming the soundness of the doctrine of the *imam*'s occultation were diligently assembled by leading Shi'ite scholars of the age including al-Kulayni (d. 941),[41] whose critical contribution to the Shi'ite tradition was mentioned in connection with the Shi'ite *hadíth* in Chapter 6 of this book.

The Shi'ite Community in the Absence of the Divinely Ordained Guide

Although the doctrine of the hidden *imam* offered a compelling solution to the problems posed by his physical presence, it was far from obvious who and how should guide his faithful in anticipation of his impending return. Following the disappearance of the twelfth *imam*, some Shi'ite scholarly families claimed to remain in touch with him and even circulated written decrees on his behalf. In the later Shi'ite tradition, the number of such claimants was restricted to four. Three of them belonged to the powerful 'Amri and Nawbakhti families and one to a Baghdadi scholar named 'Ali al-Samarri.[42] The official Shi'ite doctrine asserts that from 874 (the death of the eleventh imam) to 941, the hidden *imam* stayed in contact with his followers via these four agents, or "ambassadors" as they are known in the Shi'ite tradition.[43] They duly communicated his instructions to his partisans. In return, the "ambassadors" collected a special tax (*khums*; one-fifth of war spoils and profits) on the *imam*'s behalf.[44] The period of the *imam*'s "virtual absence" has come to be known among the Shi'ites as the "Lesser Occultation." On the eve of his death in mid-May 941, the fourth "ambassador" of the hidden *imam*, 'Ali b. Muhammad al-Samarri, received the following missive from his invisible master:

> In the name of God, the Merciful, the Compassionate. O, 'Ali ibn Muhammad al-Samarri . . . you will die in six days. Settle your affairs, and leave no testament in favor of anyone to fill your office after your death. Indeed, the second occultation has occurred, and there will be no [further] appearance save with God's permission.[45]

The document concluded with the warning to the Shi'ites not to heed any "imposters" who would claim to have seen or conversed with the hidden *imam* before the arrival of his archenemy al-Sufyani and the deafening "cry" from the heavens. These two events, according to al-Samarri's testament, would serve as the unmistakable signs of in the *imam*'s triumphal return.[46]

The death of the fourth Shi'ite "ambassador" without a successor inaugurated the beginning of the period of the "Greater Occultation" that, according to the Twelver Shi'ite creed, has continued until this day. As already mentioned, the belief in the eventual advent of the awaited hidden *imam* as the divinely guided redeemer constitutes a cornerstone of the Twelver Shi'ite worldview.[47] The other major articles of the Twelver Shi'ite doctrine were formulated by Shi'ite scholars in the course of the tenth century. They can be summarized as follows:

1 The world cannot exist and properly function without a divinely guided leader, the *imam*[48] of his time who is in possession of sacred knowledge (*'ilm*). This knowledge is confined exclusively to the family of 'Ali and Fátima. Its members (the *imam*s) are divinely appointed to serve as channels of divine guidance and grace to the faithful. Therefore, any denial of their guiding role equals the denial of God's guidance of the faithful, which renders the denier an unbeliever.

2 The presence of the *imam* in this world (even if he is hidden from human sight) is necessary because divine guidance ought to be available to the faithful at all times in order to allow them to live in accordance with the will of God.

3 The true successor of the sixth *imam* (Ja'far al-Sádiq) was neither Isma'il nor 'Abdallah (his elder sons) but his third son Músa al-Kázim.

4 The son of the eleventh *imam*, Muhammad b. al-Hásan, was the only legitimate successor to his father, al-Hásan al-'Askari.

5 After the second and third *imam*s (namely, al-Hásan and al-Husayn, sons of 'Ali b. Abi Talib), the imamate may never belong to two brothers.

6 The twelfth *imam* went into hiding (or, rather, was hidden by God from human sight) in order to avoid persecution. Although he is invisibly present among his followers, his identity remains concealed from them. He will not be recognized until he reappears at a time known only to God.

7 Armed rebellion should be postponed until such time as the hidden *imam* will make his public appearance and call on the faithful to join him in his epic struggle against the forces of evil represented by the wicked (Sunni) rulers and their misguided subjects. Loyalty to the hidden *imam* is the all-important prerequisite for salvation.

8 The successor *imam* cannot be appointed by anyone but God, who communicates his will to the incumbent *imam*; fallible human beings are not in a position to appoint their own *imam* by exercising their free choice.

9 During the Greater Occultation, the learned men of the Shi'ite community serve as its de-facto guides by virtue of their intimate familiarity with the teachings of the Prophet and his *imam*s who are the carriers of the sacred knowledge (*'ilm*) bestowed upon them by God. The scholars serve, as it were, the mouthpieces and executors of the hidden *imam*.

Most of these articles of Shi'ite faith are framed in opposition to the Sunni creed. However, as we shall soon find out, articles 3–5 are also directed against rival Shi'ite groups, especially the Isma'ilis, the Zaydis, and the followers of the brother of the eleventh *imam* named Ja'far. The last article of the Shi'ite creed is particularly remarkable in that it apparently contradicts articles 1 and 2. This contradiction was eventually resolved in the course of intense internal debates and theological ruminations that continued unabated for at least two centuries following the disappearance of the twelfth *imam*. In the end, the leading scholars of the Twelver Shi'ite community were acknowledged by its members as the interpreters of the will of the hidden *imam*, as well as managers of the financial and administrative affairs of the Shi'ite community.[49] Thus, although theoretically the supreme religious authority and guidance were vested exclusively in the *imam*s (either present or absent), in practice they were held by their learned representatives, the Shi'ite men of learning (*rijál*).[50] Due to their minority status under Sunni rule, the *rijál*, being deputies of the hidden *imam*, preferred to stay away from the often hostile and suspicious Sunni rulers and limit their claims to leadership to the religious, moral-ethical, and judicial spheres. This leads us to the question of the political and social circumstances that have occasioned the doctrine of the *imam*'s indefinite occultation.

The Political and Social Aspects of the Doctrine of Occultation

In contemporary Western scholarship, the eventual triumph of the doctrine of the occultation of the twelfth *imam* is often explained by the political and social conditions of the age. By the middle of the ninth century, the formerly all-powerful 'Abbásid caliphs had practically lost their political and military power to their generals and Turkic bodyguards, who became kingmakers, capable of manipulating or even simply replacing their powerless masters as they saw fit. Most of the caliphs of that age (the first half of the tenth century) were mere figureheads, virtual prisoners in their own palaces in Baghdad and later Samarra. Furthermore, the caliphate as a political entity had disintegrated into a host of independent states ruled by local dynasties. These dynasties recognized the caliph as their nominal religious leader and received investiture from him but were otherwise totally independent of Baghdad. Thus, whatever political authority the caliph had was confined to Iraq or even just Baghdad. By the 930s, the real political and military power in Iraq itself effectively passed to the *amír* (commander in chief), who ruled on behalf of the politically impotent caliph.[51]

Under these circumstances, the leaders of the Shi'ite community must have seen no benefit in trying to replace the 'Abbásid caliph with an 'Alid *imam*, since the latter was bound to become a puppet in the hands of his military commanders in the same way as his Sunni counterpart. Shi'ite leaders were much more concerned with preserving the distinctive identity of their religious community, while tacitly cooperating with the incumbent rulers or at least not openly defying them. Their doctrine of the hidden *imam*, whose appearance could be postponed indefinitely, posed no immediate threat to the 'Abbásid ruling elite. Rather, it was "the assertion of a social and political ideal [that] implied a criticism of actual circumstances."[52] In the words of one modern scholar, "[the] Shi'is constituted a community within a community, preserving religious and communal independence from the [Sunni] political structure, and maintaining autonomy from the de facto regime."[53] By rejecting the legitimacy of the first three caliphs and of the companions of the Prophet hostile to 'Ali, the Shi'ites separated themselves from and placed themselves above the "generality" ('amma) of their "misguided" coreligionists (i.e., the Sunnis).[54] As "God's elect" servants (khassa), the Shi'ites were content to remain in a kind of permanent opposition to the "unjust" and "illegitimate" rule of the 'Abbásids without directly challenging it.[55] The most they could hope for was to change it for the better by penetrating the ruling establishment.

To assert their ideological independence from the Sunnis, the Shi'ites had to develop a distinct religious identity, complete with its own theology, jurisprudence, ritual practices, and view of history. The Shi'ite religious elite (rijal) managed to accomplish this task by formulating a distinctive Shi'ite value system, theology, and devotional style. In their endeavors, they were assisted by a historical quirk of fortune that had brought to power in Baghdad a Shi'ite dynasty from the remote Daylam area, south of the Caspian Sea (in present-day Iran).

"The Shi'ite Century" (946–1055): Political and Social Aspects

The so-called Shi'ite century owed its existence to the arrival in Baghdad of the warlords of the Buyid family[56] in January 946. Hailing from the Persian province of Daylam, they had already established control over northwest Iran. Prior to their entry into Baghdad, the office of the chief amír in Iraq changed hands frequently. Its holders, the generals of the 'Abbásid army, enthroned and dethroned caliphs at will. This pattern continued under the Buyids with the only difference that military and political power in Iraq remained within their family for more than a century, providing the country's population with a sense of stability and predictability that they had lost due to the constant fighting among the previous amírs. To underscore their position as the supreme rulers of Iran and Iraq and to distinguish themselves from the previous amírs, the Buyids styled themselves "kings" (Arab. mulúk; sing. málik; Persian shahanshah).[57] Like the amírs before them, they ruled on behalf of the caliphs who, with a few exceptions, were little more than puppets in their hands.[58] In a scathing remark of a Western historian of the 'Abbasid caliphate, the first Buyid ruler of Iraq, Mu'izz al-Dawla (i.e., "Glorifier of the State"; r. 946–967), "son of an obscure Daylami pauper, of a humble family only recently converted to Islam, became the overlord of the 'Abbásid caliph—scion of the Family of the Prophet, the 'Shadow of God on Earth.'"[59]

The Buyids presided over a vigorous cultural efflorescence that some Western historians have dubbed "Islamic renaissance."[60] The remarkable cultural and scientific achievements of this momentous age deserve a separate discussion. What is important for our purpose is that the Buyids from the outset had strong Shi'ite propensities. In all probability, they themselves were adherents of the Zaydi version of Shi'ism that was predominant in their native province of Daylam,[61] and that will be discussed later in this chapter. Despite their openly professed Shi'ite leanings, the Buyids never attempted to depose the Sunni caliph in order to replace him with an 'Alid one. For this there were several reasons. First, the overwhelming majority of their subjects in Iraq and Iran remained Sunni. Therefore, any attempt to institute minority rule under a Shi'ite caliph or imam was fraught with a popular rebellion. Second, although a figurehead, the Sunni caliph was still seen by the majority of Muslims worldwide as their spiritual leader and the primary symbol of Muslim unity.[62] Muslim dynasties that held sway over the provinces of the former caliphate continued to seek his approval at the time of succession. The Buyids themselves, somewhat hypocritically, sought the caliph's endorsement of each incoming ruler. His removal would have pitted them against the broader Sunni world. Third, if the Buyids were to install an 'Alid caliph, they, as Shi'ites, would have owed him a complete and unquestioning allegiance. Naturally, they would rather deal with a Sunni caliph, who, for them as Shi'ites, was illegitimate anyway. In sum, ruling on behalf of a politically impotent but symbolically still significant Sunni caliph seems to have suited the Buyids quite nicely.[63] The goal of replacing him with an 'Alid *imam* remained as remote as it had been under Sunni rulers.

The Buyids' preference for Twelver Shi'ism may have been dictated by similar pragmatic considerations. Although initially adherents of a politically activist form of Shi'ism known as Zaydism,[64] the Buyids opted to cultivate Shi'ism's less militant version, one that relegated the final triumph of truth and justice over falsehood and injustice to an indefinitely postponed arrival of the hidden twelfth *imam*.[65] This doctrine also suited the Twelver Shi'ite leadership in Baghdad and beyond well because it "allowed them to retain allegiance to their hidden *imam* while acceding to the rule of the Buyid emirs."[66] Leaders of the Twelver Shi'ite community definitely benefitted from the Buyids' pro-'Alid sympathies: They were given and accepted high posts in the Buyid administration in the hopes of advancing their cause and reducing the theretofore dominant position of the Sunni scholarly elite. The members of the latter, on the other hand, were not so happy with the Buyid pro-Shi'ite policies generally and the subjugated status that the Buyid "kings" had allotted to their spiritual head, the 'Abbasid caliph, in particular. Their frustration found an expression in their vigorous resentment of any public displays of Shi'ite faith, such as cursing or humiliating the companions of the Prophet whom the Shi'ites considered to be hostile to 'Ali. Frequent clashes between the two communities in Baghdad were reported throughout Buyid rule despite the concerted efforts of the Buyids and their ministers (viziers) to clamp a lid on the Sunni–Shi'ite animosities.[67]

Although the Buyids did their best to maintain neutrality in religious matters in order not to alienate their Sunni subjects, they allowed previously prohibited public displays of Shi'ite devotions, especially the commemoration and mourning of the martyrdom of al-Husayn on the tenth day of the month of Muhárram (known as al-'Ashúra).[68] Thus, on that day in 963:

> The markets [of Baghdad] were closed and commerce ceased. Women, with loosened hair, blackened faces, and rent garments, marched in procession, beating their faces in lamentation.[69]

Another Shi'ite holiday, the day of the Pond of Khumm (*Ghadír Khumm*) on which, according to a Shi'ite tradition, the Prophet designated 'Ali as his successor[70] was also celebrated with a great pomp by Baghdad's Shi'ite population (see Figure 11.3):

> Fires were lit, drums rolled and trumpets were blown, whereupon throngs of Shi'ites proceeded to visit the tombs of the *imam*s and the famous members of 'Ali's family.[71]

In response, the Sunnis of Baghdad instituted their own celebrations, such as the Day of the Cave that commemorated the event in which the Prophet and Abu Bakr (whom the Shi'ites regarded as an interloper and usurper) found refuge from their pagan persecutors in a cave near Mecca on their way to Medina.[72] Such rival public displays of devotion no doubt contributed to the entrenchment of Sunni and Shi'ite positions, leaving little room for reconciliation.[73]

The commitment to Shi'ism on the part of the Buyids found a tangible expression in their effort to restore and adorn the tombs of Shi'ite *imam*s, especially those of 'Ali in Najaf and of al-Husayn in Kerbelá. These and other Shi'ite shrines also received generous endowments from the members of the ruling family.[74]

Figure 11.3 The Prophet Appoints 'Ali as His Successor at the Pond of Khumm

akg-images

The Blossoming of Shi'ite Theology and Jurisprudence

The rule of the Buyid dynasty is sometimes described by Western scholars as "the era of the Twelver Shi'a 'church fathers.'"[75] These seminal Shi'ite scholars benefited from the pro-Shi'ite policies of the Buyids and their ministers, some of whom were important intellectuals in their own right.[76] Among other things, the Buyid state established and funded "a magnificent academy of learning (*dar al-'ilm*)."[77] Located in Karkh, a Shi'ite quarter of Baghdad, it housed a hundred thousand volumes and provided boarding facilities for students.[78]

Among the beneficiaries of the Buyid patronage of Shi'ite learning was Ibn Babawayh (also pronounced Ibn Babuya; d. 991), who is rightly considered to be the most eminent Twelver Shi'ite theologian of the tenth century. While he occasionally visited and taught in Baghdad, he spent most of his life in Qumm, an Iranian city that has produced many Shi'ite scholars and that still remains an important center of Shi'ite learning.[79] Ibn Babawayh also lived in the Iranian city of Rayy as a guest of honor of the local Buyid ruler Rukn al-Dawla.[80] His collection of nine thousand Shi'ite traditions entitled *He Who Is Not Visited by a Faqíh*[81] is considered one of the four canonical books of Twelver Shi'ism. A prolific author, Ibn Babawayh wrote numerous doctrinal treatises that, for the first time, presented Twelver Shi'ite beliefs in a clear and systematic manner.[82] One of his greatest achievements consists in formulating and substantiating the concept of the hidden *imam* and his occultation[83] at a time when "many of the Twelver Shi'ites were gripped with doubt and impatience." This being the case, it was especially important "to restore their [Shi'ites'] confidence and to react to the provocation of their enemies, who doubted even the birth of the [twelfth] *imam* and were asking relentlessly not only for reasons for his occultation but also for the meaning and use this occultation had for [the] Shi'a in general."[84]

Whereas Ibn Babawayh was generally opposed to any attempt to rationalize the Shi'ite belief in the hidden *imam* and his occultation and relied first and foremost on authoritative reports traced to either the *imam*s or their closest followers, the other great Shi'ite scholar of the Buyid epoch, nicknamed al-Shaykh al-Mufíd ("The Beneficial Master"; d. 1022), advocated the use of reason in dealing with theological and juridical issues.[85] Although a student of Ibn Babawayh, he disagreed with his teacher's rejection of rational argumentation in this matter. In his opinion, the existence of the hidden *imam* was consistent with sound reasoning. For instance, in seeking to demonstrate the existence of the hidden *imam* on logical grounds, he would start with the Shi'ite axiom that "the earth can never be devoid of divine proof." He would then proceed to assert that God's proof can only be someone infallible. Since neither the 'Abbásid caliphs nor any other claimants to religious leadership possessed this quality, this meant that the individual in question should be someone else who was currently in hiding.[86] Because no one else was known to be in hiding except the twelfth *imam*, this could not have been anyone other than him. In criticizing Ibn Babawayh for his exclusive reliance on the transmitted tradition, al-Shaykh al-Mufíd argued that "the *imam*s encouraged religious disputation, provided the disputant was firmly rooted in the truth and capable of defending it against heretics and infidels."[87]

Al-Mufíd's exceptional polemical skills and astute use of rational argumentation made him a formidable debater. He is said to have been able to convince any disputants that the wooden column in front of them was actually made of gold.[88] Al-Mufíd's consistent reliance on methods of rationalist argumentation effectively renders him the first Shi'ite *mutakállim*.[89] Indeed, he adopted some theological positions associated with Mu'tazilism by emphasizing divine justice at the expense of divine omnipotence and denying divine predestination of all events in favor of human free will and, as a consequence, human responsibility for their deeds. In so doing, al-Mufíd effectively laid the groundwork for the subsequent integration of Mu'tazilite *kalám* into the Shi'ite dogma.[90]

Al-Mufíd's contributions to the field of Shi'ite jurisprudence were no less significant.[91] He critically examined the teachings of the Sunni schools of law, adopting some of their methods and rejecting or redefining others. For instance, contrary to his Shi'ite predecessors who had flatly denied the consensus (*ijmá'*) of the Muslim community (which was, of course, a predominantly Sunni concept), he was ready to consider it valid as long as it corresponded to the opinion of a Shi'ite *imam*.[92] On the other hand, al-Mufíd vigorously denied reasoning by analogy (*qiyás*), arguing that, unlike the Sunnis, the Shi'ites "had the statements of the *imam*s to guide them."[93] In cases that were not explicitly addressed by the Qur'an, prophetic *hadíth*, or the teachings of the *imam*s, al-Mufíd allowed a limited use of personal reasoning (*'aql*), although, to disassociate himself from the Sunni jurists, he did not call this method *ijtihád*.[94] Finally, al-Mufíd provided a comprehensive description of various intellectual and theological trends and schools of thought in Islam, thereby defining the Twelver Shi'ite position in regard to each of them.[95]

Al-Shaykh al-Mufid's disciples, al-Sharíf al-Múrtada (d. 1044) and Muhammad al-Túsi (d. 1067), proved to be worthy of his vast intellectual legacy. The former, who served as both honorary head of the descendants of 'Ali (*naqíb al-ashráf*) in the capital and director of a Shi'ite academy in Karkh (a district in Baghdad), exhibited an even stronger leaning than his teacher toward Mu'tazilism. He studied under some leading Mu'tazilites of his time and became an enthusiastic advocate of rational methods in both theology and jurisprudence. For him, reason was more than just a tool for defending Shi'ite articles of faith. It was, in and of itself, the starting point of theology.[96] He adopted the allegorical method of the interpretation of the Qur'an and *hadíth*, which was introduced by the Mu'tazilites,[97] in order to explain away the anthropomorphic passages found in the scriptures. If the Qur'an did not explicitly mention the existence of a certain divine attribute but it can be deduced by a sound logical reasoning, then it should still be ascribed to God, despite the absence of scriptural evidence. In a similar vein, al-Sharíf al-Múrtada saw compliance with rational criteria as the chief proof of the authenticity of a transmitted report (*hadíth*), a position that Ibn Babawayh would have almost certainly dismissed as heretical. At the same time, as a convinced Shi'ite, al-Sharíf al-Múrtada condemned the Mu'tazilite (Sunni) concept of the imamate—an issue over which no compromise was possible between the two communities. In the field of juridical decision making, al-Sharíf al-Múrtada allowed the use of independent reasoning, albeit only in matters of secondary importance that were not explicitly addressed in the scriptures and the teachings of the *imam*s.[98] A high-ranking courtier, al-Sharíf al-Múrtada justified his collaboration with the 'Abbásids—who, in the eyes of the Shi'ites, were "tyrants" and "usurpers"—by the necessity to administer justice and provide right guidance to the faithful on behalf of the hidden *imam*. If this implied a temporary compromise with the illegitimate and unjust regime, so be it. In support of his claim, he cited the Qur'anic story of Joseph, who accepted an important post in the Pharaoh's administration (Q 12:55), as well as 'Ali's participation in the election of the "illegitimate" caliph 'Uthman.[99]

Al-Mufid's other disciple, Muhammad al-Túsi (d. 1067), was one of the most consequential Shi'ite thinkers ever, who left a deep imprint on Twelver Shi'ite theology and law. A native of the Iranian city of Tus (near present-day Meshhed/Mashhad, in Iran), he lived in Baghdad until 1056, whereupon he settled near the tomb of *imam* 'Ali in Najaf.[100] His two books *Consideration of the Disputed Reports [from the Imams]* and *Refinement of Legal Rulings* constitute, together with the works of al-Kulayni and Ibn Babawayh, the so-called "four [principal] books" of Twelver Shi'ism,[101] which established the foundations for the functioning of the subsequent generations of Shi'ite doctors of law.[102] Nicknamed "Teacher of the [Shi'ite] Community" (*shaykh al-tá'ifa*) by his admirers, al-Túsi saw his task as refining the methods of separating "sound" *hadíth* from "weak" and "dubious" ones. Unlike al-Sharíf al-Múrtada, he was skeptical of the validity of personal reasoning in theological and juridical matters, although he stopped short of rejecting it altogether. In dealing with the issue of cooperation with and submission to the rule of the "illegitimate" Sunni state in the absence of an *imam*, al-Túsi took a more restrictive position than al-Sharíf al-Múrtada. He considered the Buyids to be "just rulers" and thus be worthy of submission as long as they ruled in accordance with the legal precepts formulated by the leading scholars (*rijál*) of the Twelver Shi'ite community.[103]

This position, which seems to have been shared by the major Twelver Shi'ite luminaries from the Buyid epoch, effectively established the *rijál* as the indispensable shepherds and guides of the Shi'ite community during the *imam*'s occultation. There were disagreements over certain issues, for instance, whether the Shi'ite scholars of a given age had the authority to declare *jihad*, administer legal punishments stipulated by the Qur'an for grave offences, collect taxes on behalf of the hidden *imam*, and declare a certain ruler to be "just" or "unjust."[104] However, these, in a sense, were the questions of the scope of the scholars' authority that did not affect their overall function as the only legitimate representatives of the hidden *imam*. From the Buyid era onward, the majority of Twelver Shi'ites seem to have accepted the guiding role of the *rijál* as the only sure path to righteousness and eventually to salvation in the absence of the hidden *imam*. This acceptance has found its most dramatic and consequential expression in the emergence in the nineteenth century of the institution of the so-called "source of emulation" (*marja'-i taqlíd*). This term designated the supreme Shi'ite scholar of a given epoch whose rulings were mandatory either for the entire Twelver Shi'ite community or, at least, for a large number of its members.[105] Thus, one can say that the theological and legal principles formulated by the leading *rijál* of the "Shi'ite century" have decisively shaped the legal and theological foundations of the Twelver Shi'ite community for centuries to come.

Shi'ite Views of the Qur'an

Given the profound differences between the Sunni and Shi'ite interpretations of Islam, it is only natural that each community adopted a distinct attitude toward the Muslim scriptures. The Qur'an and prophetic *hadíth* being the principal source of the "correct faith" in Islam, each community appealed to them to justify its vision of Islam. Each considered its understanding of the meaning of the scriptures to be the only correct one. The Shi'ite position on this important issue is succinctly captured in the following statement attributed to the prophet Muhammad: "There is one among you who will fight for the [correct] interpretation of the Qur'an just as I myself fought for its revelation, and he is 'Ali b. Abi Talib."[106]

The message of this prophetic *hadíth* is corroborated by a saying attributed to the fifth Shi'ite *imam* Muhammad al-Báqir (d. 733):

> The Qur'an was revealed in four parts: One part concerning us [the Shi'ites], one part concerning our enemies, one part commandments and regulations, and one part customs and parables. And the exalted part of the Qur'an refers to us [that is, the *imams*].[107]

To explain why a distinctive Shi'ite interpretation of the Qur'an is necessary, the Shi'ite learned men (*rijál*) offered a number of arguments. Some insisted that the text of the Qur'an was "doctored" by 'Ali's opponents on the orders of the caliph 'Uthman, who, as we remember, was responsible for its collection and codification.[108] As a result, the Qur'an was deliberately and consistently "purged" of explicit references to the special role of the descendants of 'Ali and Fátima in guiding the Muslim community to salvation.[109] The original version of the Qur'an was declared to be in possession of the hidden *imam*. Obviously, this position was fraught with problems, for how could such a "corrupted" Qur'an have been trusted and revered by Shi'ite Muslims? As a result, it was eventually watered down to the notion that the 'Uthmanic text of the Qur'an is somehow "incomplete" and that a "correct" reading of it should fill in the deliberate "omissions" made by Sunni authorities.[110] The other, and most common, explanation was that the Qur'an contains indirect references and subtle allusions to the special role of 'Ali and Fátima's descendants in guiding Muslims to salvation. They should be brought out by means of an allegorical or symbolic interpretation.[111] Thus, "the signs of God" mentioned in Q 49:29, "the Straight Path" (Q 1:6), "the Way" (Q 25:8 and 27; 6:153; 15:41, etc.), "the guides of men" (Q 7:181), "those deeply rooted in knowledge" (Q 3:7), "the inheritors of the Book" (Q 35:32), "the truthful ones" (Q 9:119), "the possessors of authority" (Q 4:59), and so on—all unmistakably refer to the *imams* of the 'Ali-Fatima lineage.[112]

In line with the Shi'ite concept of the hidden messages and references of the Qur'an, the *imams* were seen by the Shi'ites as uniquely qualified to bring them out and explain by exercising their divinely inspired *'ilm*. This is what the Shi'ites have in mind when they sometimes refer to their leaders as "the living and speaking Qur'an."[113]

In practice, the extraction and explication of the hidden meaning of the Qur'anic text fell to Shi'ite scholars, who relied heavily on the exegetical traditions going back to the *imam*s and their circles of disciples, friends, and confidants. Shi'ite exegetes used a variety of methods, of which we shall mention but few. One is already familiar to us from the previous examples. It consists of the addition to the Qur'anic text of words and phrases that were allegedly omitted by the anti-'Alid compilers of the Qur'an. Typical in this respect is the phrase "concerning 'Ali" that was allegedly dropped from the Qur'anic verse 2:91: "Believe in what God has revealed [concerning 'Ali]."[114]

The second method can be defined as giving a "concrete meaning" to certain general expressions. For instance, the common Qur'anic expression "O those who have believed" was explained by Shi'ite authorities as referring first and foremost to 'Ali and his family.[115] Whenever something positive is said in the Qur'an about an unidentified group of people, it was automatically attributed to 'Ali and his companions, as in the phrase: "Those who believe and do righteous things" (Q 38:28). At the same time, the reference to "the workers of corruption in the earth"[116] in the same verse was construed by Shi'ite scholars as an allusion to "Abu Bakr, 'Umar and their companions."[117] In this way, Shi'ite commentators were able to find a panoply of Qur'anic allusions to the special role of the Shi'ite community and its *imam*s in the history of humankind, as well as to the martyrdom of al-Husayn at Kerbelá/Karbalá', to the inequity and injustice of Sunni rulers, and so on.[118] In this way, the Qur'an itself was effectively pressed into service by the learned elite of the Shi'ite community (*rijál*).

Zaydism

The Zaydi Shi'ites derive their name from Zayd b. 'Ali (d. 740), a great-grandson of 'Ali and Fátima and half-brother of the fifth Shi'ite *imam* Muhammad al-Báqir.[119] Unlike al-Báqir, who adopted a pacifistic stance vis-à-vis the Umayyad state and devoted himself to scholarship and maintenance of the semiclandestine networks of 'Alid agents, Zayd advocated armed resistance to the "unjust rule" of the Umayyad caliphs. In accordance with his activist stance, he personally led a rebellion against the Umayyad caliph Hishám in Kufa in 740 but was killed by a stray arrow at its very beginning in a street battle. Deprived of their leader, Zayd's followers dispersed across the width and breadth of the Islamic world, forming small communities in Iraq, Arabia, and the Daylam and Gilan areas south of the Caspian Sea (in present-day Iran).[120] These communities were headed by individuals who either declared themselves *imam*s or posed as their representatives. In 897, a Zaydi missionary made his way to Yemen at the invitation of the local tribes and established a Zaydi imamate in the country's rugged northern mountains. It persisted until 1962, when it was swept away by the revolution led by a group of Yemeni army officers.[121]

The fact that the followers of Zayd b. 'Ali were eager to support his bid for power and the subsequent Zaydi rebellions in the name of various 'Alid candidates in Arabia, Iraq, and Iran has determined the movement's activist character. This political activism has set the Zaydis apart from the Twelver Shi'ites, whose *imam*s reconciled themselves to the "illegitimate" rule of non-'Alid caliphs and discouraged their supporters from challenging them on the battlefield. For the Zaydis, the 'Alid *imam* who chooses to "sit still" (*qu'úd*) instead of fighting "usurpers" and "oppressors" was not an *imam* at all. This much was accepted by all members of the Zaydi movement. On other issues pertaining to the imamate, members of the Zaydi movements held a variety of opinions, often irreconcilable.

The issue of the legitimacy or illegitimacy of the first three caliphs has given rise to the major divisions in the Zaydi ranks. One group named the Jarúdiyya adopted the standard Shi'ite position, according to which the Prophet did indeed consider 'Ali to be his sole legitimate successor. However, contrary to what the Twelver Shi'ites believed, the Jarúdiyya did not believe that the

Prophet's nomination of 'Ali as his successor was explicit and final because, in the end, only God had the exclusive right to choose the rightful *imam*.[122] These niceties notwithstanding, for the Jarúdiyya, Abu Bakr and 'Umar were still illegitimate "usurpers" ('Uthman's "illegitimacy" especially during the later years of his rule went without saying), who knowingly and unscrupulously deprived the most deserving Muslim leader (*áfdal*) of the age (i.e., 'Ali) of what was rightfully his.[123] Both the first two caliphs and those who accepted them were not sinful or misguided. It was a matter of political expediency at that historical moment.[124] The other branch of the Zaydi movement, the Batriyya, disagreed. Its learned spokesmen advanced the original idea of the "imamate of the inferior" (*mafdúl*). In their opinion, the Prophet had not explicitly appointed 'Ali as his successor, although he definitely was the most deserving of the candidates. Nevertheless, the election of Abu Bakr and 'Umar as the Prophet's successors was valid, and they were legitimate leaders (*imam*s), despite their being "inferior" to 'Ali in terms of religious knowledge, proximity to the Prophet, and righteousness. To justify their position, the Batriyya Zaydis referred to 'Ali's own acceptance of their leadership in spite of his awareness of his superiority.[125] Their respective positions on the problem of leadership allow us to classify the Jarúdiyya and the Batriyya respectively as the pro-Shi'ite and pro-Sunni wings of the Zaydi movement.

On the issue of *imam*'s qualifications, the Zaydis also held a broad range of different opinions that can be summarized as follows. While the first three *imam*s were designated (Muhammad designated 'Ali, who designated al-Hásan, who designated al-Husayn), all subsequent *imam*s had to prove themselves by summoning righteous Muslims to allegiance and leading a rebellion against Sunni rulers.[126] Contrary to the Twelver Shi'ites who asserted the exclusive rights of al-Husayn's descendants to lead the community, the Zaydis insisted that no branch of 'Ali's family should claim monopoly on the imamate. Any descendant of 'Ali and Fátima (namely, the Hasanids as well as the Husaynids) was eligible and legitimate as long as he possessed the requisite religious knowledge, moral and physical integrity, and the courage to rise up against injustice. Once he had demonstrated his superior qualities as leader and laid claim to political power, he was entitled to the support and allegiance of the faithful. Those who refused to join the *imam*'s battle for justice were classified as grave sinners. The Twelver Shi'ite pacifists such as Muhammad al-Báqir and Ja'far al-Sádiq, though competent in religious sciences, were thereby disqualified as full-fledged *imam*s. Furthermore, unlike the Twelvers, the Zaydis did not consider the *imam* to be divinely protected from sin or error. Although his religious decisions could occasionally be challenged, it was his duty as leader of the faithful to exercise independent judgment (*ijtihád*) in religious matters on the basis of his knowledge of the Scripture and the legal precedents established by his predecessors.[127] If, after assuming the post, the *imam* had been found to be remiss in any of his duties, "his imamate was forfeit and he was expected to cede it to a more qualified candidate, who in turn would make his 'summons' and 'rise.'"[128]

In theological matters, Zaydi scholars tended to lean to the Mu'tazilite doctrine[129] with its denial of an anthropomorphic God and insistence on divine justice and believers' responsibility for their actions. The latter precept dovetailed neatly with the political activism of the Zaydi leaders. Naturally, the Mu'tazilite concept of the imamate, being Sunni in character, was discarded as erroneous, although we find many instances when Sunni Mu'tazilites embraced its Zaydi interpretation.

Initially, Zaydi political activism and proselytizing zeal seem to have paid off. In 864, a Zaydi missionary succeeded in wresting power from the 'Abbásid governor of Tabaristán (in present-day Iran) and establishing a small state along the southern coast of the Caspian Sea. His successors, mostly descendants of the second *imam* al-Hásan b. 'Ali (i.e., the Hasanids), managed to preserve their communities in the face of the powerful Samanid (Sunni) dynasty of Bukhara that ruled on behalf of the 'Abbásid caliph. The Zaydi imamate of the Caspian region came to an end in 1126, although small Zaydi pockets in the region had survived until the advent of the Safavid dynasty (in the early sixteenth century), whereupon they converted to Twelver Shi'ism adopted by the Safavid rulers.

In Yemen, a distinctive version of Zaydi Shi'ism was disseminated by a Hasanid missionary, Yahya al-Hádi ila 'l-haqq ("Yahya Who Leads on the Path of Truth"). Around 900, he established a Zaydi state in the mountainous areas of North Yemen. It survived until 1962, when the last ruler of the dynasty of Zaydi *imam*s, Muhammad al-Badr, was overthrown by a popular revolution led by Yemeni military officers.

The Zaydi insistence on the juridical and theological competence of the *imam* has resulted in a succession of highly learned Yemeni rulers, who combined scholarship with military action against their Sunni and Isma'ili neighbors. Until 1598, the peculiarity of the Zaydi doctrine of the imamate had effectively precluded the formation of a stable Zaydi dynasty. Each Zaydi *imam*'s state began and ended with himself—any predictable succession process was contrary to the Zaydi principle of "summoning" and "marching out," which, in principle, could be done by any 'Alid candidate who had the courage to prove himself in battle.[130] Although some *imam*s were succeeded by their sons, uncles, and brothers, the issue of succession was for the most part decided on the battlefield. In practice, this meant that the winner often was the most militarily powerful rather than the most religiously competent of the eligible candidates.[131] No wonder, therefore, that in 1635 it was a Zaydi *imam* named al-Mu'ayyad who managed to expel from Yemen the powerful and well armed Ottoman army that had occupied the country a century earlier.

For a long time, the traditional Zaydi doctrine of "permanent revolution" and "marching out" against incumbent Sunni authorities was a source of political instability in the northern parts of Yemen. This situation came to an end with the formation of a dynasty of *imam*s known as the Qasimites (1598–1851). Within this dynasty, the imamate was transmitted from father to son, making it practically indistinguishable from any Sunni ruling house. The Qasimi rulers and scholars associated with them revised the foundations of Zaydi faith along more pragmatic lines. This revision led to what a Western historian of Yemen has described as the "Sunnisation of Zaydism"—a rapprochement between two versions of Islam in the course of which scholars versed in both Zaydi and Sunni theology and legal theory became the upholders and implementers of the Shari'a. The Zaydi *imam*s, on the other hand, have become "sultans in the Sunni tradition: rulers who must, in theory at least, defer to scholars in matters of religion."[132]

Conclusions

In Zaydi Shi'ism, we find yet another religious and political movement animated by loyalty to the 'Ali and Fátima family and driven by an irrepressible human desire to achieve justice and remove injustice. The Caspian wing of Zaydism, initially vibrant and politically successful, dissipated by the early sixteenth century; its Yemeni "franchise" has proved much more resilient, despite outside pressures and infighting among candidates for the imamate. The survival of the Yemeni branch of Zaydism can be attributed at least in part to its out-of-the-way location in the mountains of northern Yemen and its power base among the warlike tribes of the Yemeni highlands. Interestingly, similar factors account for the survival of Zaydism's Sunni counterpart, the Kharijite (Ibadi) communities of Oman and North Africa (Mzab).

At the same time, both Zaydi and Kharijite attempts to establish just and "democratic" political formations have had only a very limited impact on the state of affairs in the Muslim community as a whole. Neither the Kharijites nor the Zaydis have created either a sophisticated high culture or a powerful enough ideology to attract Muslim masses to their respective causes. In the final analysis, the authoritarianism of the 'Abbásid dynasty, camouflaged as it was by its descent from a branch of the Prophet's family (albeit non-'Alid) and legitimized with some reservations by pragmatic Sunni scholars in the name of the unity of the Muslim state, has proved to be more acceptable to the "silent majority." As a Western scholar has aptly put it, "[T]he unpalatable truth was that the price of civilization was submission to tyrants."[133]

The picture that emerges from the foregoing discussion of the vicissitudes of Shi'ite visions of Islam is one of an astounding variety of opinions around the issue of legitimate and just leadership (imamate) and its political and theological implications. Whereas the Sunni community has reconciled themselves to the absence of divine guidance embodied in a living individual possessed of a supernatural and salvific knowledge, the Shi'ites continued to hold on to this idea until the disappearance of the twelfth *imam* (in the case of the Twelver Shi'ites). When the *imam* went into an open-ended "occultation," allegiance to him became an expression of a certain world outlook and a distinctive type of personal devotion. His role was now taken over collectively by his learned representatives, the Shi'ite scholars (*rijál*), who assumed the responsibility for guiding the *imam*'s followers during his indefinite concealment.

Before the disappearance of the last Twelver Shi'ite *imam*, the Zaydis had refused to obey his predecessors because they "merely sat at home, neither commanding or forbidding."[134] After his disappearance, the Zaydi Shi'ites persisted in seeking out and following a living and active (albeit fallible and deposable) *imam* of the 'Alid line for a long time. However, they too eventually had to submit themselves to the relative stability of dynastic rule with its division of labor between the political and military ruler (*sultán, amír*) and the learned custodians of the Shari'a law and theological knowledge.[135] The revolutionary version of Shi'ism to be discussed in the next chapter is both similar to and different from the ones just described.

Questions to Ponder

1 A Western scholar (Marshall Hodgson) once described Shi'ism as a "piety of protest." Do you agree with this assessment? Explain.
2 Having examined the vicissitudes of the Shi'ite movement, how elastic (or otherwise) you think could the boundaries of the Muslim community be in the period under discussion? Why and how were dissent and frustration with the status quo couched in religious language? How was dissent dealt with by the powers-that-be, and why did it persist so tenaciously across the centuries despite persecution?
3 What relevance (if any) do the individuals, values, and ideas/ideals discussed in this chapter have to the events in the Middle East today (in particular, consider Syria, Iran, Iraq, Lebanon, the Gulf States, and Yemen)? Elaborate.

Summary

- Shi'ism is an alternative vision of Islam and Islamic history (versus that of the Sunni majority). The pragmatism and triumphalism of the latter stand in stark contrast to the idealism and pessimism of the former.
- Ideological justification for the necessity of the imamate: it is the sole guarantor of the proper functioning of the world. In Shi'ite Islam, the *imam* of 'Alid descent, armed with the supernatural, revelatory insight (*'ilm*), is the essential guide to salvation. This Shi'ite concept stands in opposition to the Sunni belief in the collective salvation through participation of Muslims in the divinely chosen community whose scholars guide their followers to salvation by means of the Qur'an and the Sunna.

- The vicissitudes of Shi'ism under the 'Abbásids range between rebellion and pacifism. The sixth Shi'ite *imam* Ja'far al-Sádiq (d. 765) plays a role in consolidating the Shi'ite community and in articulating a distinctly Shi'ite view of Islam. The *imam*s and the 'Abbásid caliphs are Ja'far al-Sádiq and al-Mansúr, al-Ma'mún (d. 833) and 'Ali al-Ridá (d. 818).
- The eleventh *imam*, al-Hásan al-'Askari (874), dies, inaugurating the mysterious disappearance ("occultation") of the twelfth *imam*.
- The Twelver Shi'ite community, in the absence of an active and visible *imam*, articulates the doctrine of occultation (*ghayba*). With the *imam* in an indefinite occultation, his followers should retain loyalty to him and prepare for his eventual return that will usher in the redemption of his community and the punishment of its persecutors.
- The so-called Shi'ite century under Buyid rule (946–1055) witnesses cultural blossoming and the promotion by the Buyid rulers of Shi'ite scholars to positions of authority in the caliphate.
- The greatest luminaries of Shi'ite theology and jurisprudence—Ibn Babawayh (Ibn Babuya; d. 991), al-Shaykh al-Mufid ("The Beneficial Master"; d. 1022), al-Sharíf al-Múrtada (d. 1044), and Muhammad al-Túsi (d. 1067)—articulate Shi'ite attitudes toward secular rulers in general and toward the Buyids (as Shi'ites) in particular.
- With the hidden *imam*'s disappearance communication between the *imam* and his community is severed. With the *imam* in permanent occultation, the learned elite of the Shi'ite community (*rijál*) position themselves as the exponents of the will of the hidden *imam* and the moral-ethical guides of the faithful. The institution of *marja' taqlid* is the culmination of the process of the transmission of religious authority from the *imam* to the *rijál*.
- Among the Shi'ite approaches to the Qur'an, emphasis on the allegorical interpretation of the Qur'anic text is aimed at bringing out the special role of the Shi'ite *imam*s.
- As part of the specific features of Zaydi Shi'ism vis-à-vis Sunnism and Twelver Shi'ism, the concept of the "imamate of the inferior" is a way to avoid the flat condemnation of the first three rightly guided caliphs. Zaydi doctrinal "softness" is offset by Zaydi political and military activism: The Zaydi *imam* is obligated to prove his legitimacy by "marching out" against illegitimate rulers and oppression. With time, the Zaydis draw closer and closer to Sunni *fiqh* in juridical matters. In Yemen, the "Sunnization" of the Zaydi state takes place under the later *imam*s. Later Zaydi *imam*s assume political, military, and administrative functions and begin to rely on scholars for religious guidance.

Notes

1 For details, see Patricia Crone, *Medieval Islamic Political Thought*, Edinburgh University Press, Edinburgh, 2004, Chapter 9.
2 His minimal qualifications included mental and physical health, knowledge of the basics of Islamic religion as well as kinship with the Quraysh, the native tribe of the Prophet; for details see Crone, *Medieval*, pp. 36–39.
3 The principle is otherwise known as "commanding good and forbidding wrong"; for details, see Michael Cook, *Commanding Right and Forbidding Wrong in Islam*, Cambridge University Press, Cambridge, 2000.
4 "People of the [Prophet's] House, God only desires to put away from you abomination and to cleanse you"; this verse is usually believed to have been addressed to the Prophet's wives.

5 Andrew Rippin, *Muslims: Their Religious Beliefs and Practices*, 3rd ed., Routledge, London and New York, 2005, p. 122.

6 Mohammad Ali Amir-Moezzi, "Ghadir Khumm," in *Encyclopedia of Islam*, 3rd ed.; online edition: http://referenceworks.brillonline.com.

7 Tilman Nagel, *The History of Islamic Theology*, Marcus Wiener, Princeton, NJ, 2000, p. 52.

8 Ibid.

9 Mohammad Amir-Moezzi, *The Divine Guide in Early Shi'ism* (trans. David Speight), SUNY Press, Albany, NY, 1994, p. 76.

10 Liyakat Takim, *The Heirs to the Prophet: Charisma and Religious Authority in Shi'ite Islam*, SUNY Press, Albany, NY, 2006, pp. 28, 63, 77, and so on.

11 Ibid., pp. 24–30.

12 Marshall Hodgson, *The Venture of Islam*, Chicago University Press, Chicago, 1974, vol. 1, pp. 216–217.

13 He is sometimes referred to as "Fatimi," that is, an offspring of 'Ali and Fátima.

14 Jassim Hussain, *The Occultation of the Twelfth Imam*, The Muhammadi Trust, London, 1982, p. 55.

15 Douglas MacDonald and Marshall Hodgson, "Ghayba," in *Encyclopedia of Islam*, 2nd ed.; online edition: http://referenceworks.brillonline.com.

16 Said A. Arjomand, "The Crisis of the Imamate and the Institution of Occultation in Twelver Shi'ism," in Etan Kohlberg (ed.), *Shi'ism*, Ashgate Variorum Series, Aldershot, Great Britain, 2003, vol. 33, pp. 109–110; for instance, a prominent Shi'ite scholar named 'Abdallah b. Sinán served as a state treasurer under the 'Abbásid caliphs al-Mansúr and al-Mahdi; see Takim, *The Heirs of the Prophet*, p. 134.

17 Hodgson, *The Venture*, vol. 1, p. 376 and Marshall Hodgson, "Dja'far al-Sadik," in *Encyclopedia of Islam*, 2nd ed.; online edition: http://referenceworks.brillonline.com.

18 Arjomand, "The Crisis of the Imamate and the Institution of Occultation in Twelver Shi'ism," p. 112.

19 Heinz Halm, *Shi'ism*, 2nd ed. (trans. J. Watson and M. Hill), Columbia University Press, New York, 2004, p. 32.

20 Ibid.

21 Moojan Momen, *An Introduction to Shi'i Islam*, Yale University Press, New Haven, CT, and London, 1985, p. 41.

22 Ibid., p. 42.

23 Ibid.

24 Ibid., pp. 42–43.

25 Halm, *Shi'ism*, p. 34.

26 For details concerning the formation of this elite and hierarchy of authority associated with it see Chapter 3 in Takim, *The Heirs of the Prophet*.

27 Nagel, *The History of Islamic Theology*, p. 53 and Momen, *An Introduction*, p. 44.

28 Hussain, *The Occultation of the Twelfth Imam*, p. 50.

29 Halm, *Shi'ism*, p. 33.

30 Hussain, *The Occultation of the Twelfth Imam*, p. 50.

31 Ibid., pp. 51–52.

32 Momen, *An Introduction*, p. 44.

33 Ibid. and Arjomand, "The Crisis of the Imamate and the Institution of Occultation in Twelver Shi'ism," p. 117.

34 Ibid., p. 119; however, Hussain in his *Occultation of the Twelfth Imam*, p. 56, argues that he was kept under such a close watch that he had little opportunity to communicate with "the mass of his followers"; see also Momen, *An Introduction*, p. 44

35 Shi'ite sources insist that al-Hasan had a son named Muhammad by his slave-girl named Narjis or Saqil; see, e.g., Momen, *An Introduction*, p. 44.

36 Ibid., pp. 59–60; Hussain, *The Occultation of the Twelfth Imam*, p. 57.

37 Ibid., pp. 56–66.

38 Some argued that it was al-Hasan himself who had hidden his son immediately after his birth in order to protect him from the murderous plotting of the caliph's guards. The concealment was so perfect that even the identity of his mother is in dispute among the Shi'ite scholars until today; see ibid., pp. 67–78.

39 His other titles are "the divinely guided" (*máhdi*), "the proof [of God]" (*hujja*), "the riser" (*qa'im*); see Momen, *An Introduction*, p. 45.

40 See, for example, Robert Worth, "Blast Destroys Shrine in Iraq, Setting Off Sectarian Fury," *New York Times*, February 22, 2006; online: http://www.nytimes.com/2006/02/22/international/middleeast/blast-destroys-shrine-in-iraq-setting-off-sectarian.html?_r=0.

41 Etan Kohlberg, "From Imamiyya to Ithna 'Ashariyya," *Bulletin of the School of Oriental and African Studies*, vol. 39 (1976), pp. 523–524.

42 Etan Kohlberg, "Safir," in *Encyclopedia of Islam*, 2nd ed.; online edition: http://referenceworks.bril lonline.com/.

43 They are also called "gates" (*abwáb*; sing. *bab*); ibid.

44 For details see Abdulaziz Sachedina, *The Just Ruler in Shi'ite Islam*, Oxford University Press, Oxford, 1988, pp. 237–245.

45 Arjomand, "The Crisis of the Imamate and the Institution of Occultation in Twelver Shi'ism," p. 126 (I have slightly amended the translation).

46 Momen, *An Introduction*, p. 164.

47 Ibid., pp. 165–166.

48 In some Shi'ite creeds, he is also called the "Proof" or "Argument" (*hujja*), meaning the proof of God's continual guidance of his servants; see, for instance, Montgomery Watt, *The Formative Period of Islamic Thought*, Oneworld, Oxford, 1998, p. 274.

49 Takim, *The Heirs to the Prophet*, p. 141.

50 Ibid., p. 140.

51 Joel Kraemer, *Humanism in the Renaissance of Islam: The Cultural Revival During the Buyid Age*, E. J. Brill, Leiden, 1992, p. 34.

52 Watt, *The Formative Period*, p. 277; cf. Hodgson, *The Venture*, vol. 1, pp. 372 and 277–278.

53 Takim, *The Heirs to the Prophet*, p. 141.

54 Kraemer, *Humanism*, p. 65 and Hodgson, *The Venture*, vol. 1, pp. 372–373.

55 Watt, *The Formative Period*, p. 278 and Hodgson, *The Venture*, vol. 1, p. 372.

56 The three brothers who founded the dynasty were "soldiers of fortune" who derived their name from their father Buya, a man of humble origins who had earned his living either as a fisherman or as a wood carrier; Kraemer, *Humanism*, p. 33.

57 Crone, *Medieval*, p. 221.

58 Ibid.

59 Kraemer, *Humanism*, p. 35.

60 Joel Kraemer has devoted a book-length study to the analysis of this phenomenon; see Kraemer, *Humanism*, passim.

61 Halm, *Shi'ism*, p. 45; Kraemer, *Humanism*, pp. 39–40; Crone, *Medieval*, p. 220.

62 Crone, *Medieval*, pp. 232–252.

63 Kraemer, *Humanism*, pp. 38 and 41.

64 As we will see later in this chapter, Zaydism encouraged rebellion against "unjust" and "illegitimate" (namely, Sunni) rulers whenever an opportunity presented itself.

65 Momen, *An Introduction*, pp. 75–76.

66 Kraemer, *Humanism*, p. 41.

67 Ibid., p. 40.

68 Momen, *An Introduction*, p. 82.

69 Kraemer, *Humanism*, p. 42.

70 Marked on the eighteenth day of the Muslim month Dhu 'l-Hijja.

71 Halm, *Shi'ism*, p. 47.

72 Kraemer, *Humanism*, p. 42.

73 Momen, *An Introduction*, p. 82.

74 Halm, *Shi'ism*, p. 47.

75 Kraemer, *Humanism*, p. 48 and Momen, *An Introduction*, pp. 75–84.

76 Kraemer, *Humanism*, p. 55.

77 Ibid.

78 Tamima Bayhom-Daou, *Shaykh Mufid*, Oneword, Oxford, 2005, p. 20.

79 Momen, *An Introduction*, pp. 78–79 and 313–314.

80 Kraemer, *Humanism*, p. 49.

81 That is, "he who has to figure out how to behave and live properly in the absence of a learned expert on legal and moral matters"; Ibn Babawah's book was supposed to serve as a substitute for such an expert.

82 Halm, *Shi'ism*, p. 42.

83 Momen, *An Introduction*, pp. 159–160.

84 Verena Klemm, "The Four *Sufara'* of the Twelfth Imam: On the Formative Period of the Twelver Shi'a," in Etan Kohlberg (ed.), *Shi'ism*, Ashgate, Aldershot, UK, 2003, p. 138.

85 Momen, *An Introduction*, p. 79.

86 Bayhom-Daou, *Shaykh Mufid*, p. 77.

87 Kraemer, *Humanism*, p. 69; cf. Momen, *An Introduction*, p. 317

88 Kraemer, *Humanism*, p. 67.

89 Halm, *Shi'ism*, p. 49 and Momen, *An Introduction*, pp. 79, 81, and 317.

90 Halm, *Shi'ism*, pp. 49–50; Kraemer, *Humanism*, p. 68 and Momen, *An Introduction*, pp. 79 and 81.

91 Momen, *An Introduction*, p. 184.

92 Bayhom-Daou, *Shaykh Mufid*, p. 118.

93 Ibid., p. 119.

94 That is, an independent investigation of a given religious issue by a qualified scholar; Bayhom-Daou, *Shaykh Mufid*, pp. 119–120.

95 Halm, *Shi'ism*, p. 50.

96 Momen, *An Introduction*, p. 79.

97 Kraemer, *Humanism*, p. 74.

98 Halm, *Shi'ism*, p. 51.

99 Ibid., p. 54.

100 Ibid., p. 52 and Momen, *An Introduction*, p. 321.

101 Halm, *Shi'ism*, p. 52.

102 Momen, *An Introduction*, p. 81.

103 Halm, *Shi'ism*, p. 54.

104 For details see Sachedina, *The Just Ruler*, pp. 89–118.

105 Jean Calmard, "Mardja'-i taklid," *Encyclopaedia of Islam*, 2nd ed.; online edition: http://reference works.brillonline.com.

106 Meir Bar-Asher, *Scripture and Exegesis in Early Imami Shiism*, E. J. Brill, Leiden, 1999, p. 88.

107 Ibid., pp. 88–89.

108 Momen, *An Introduction*, pp. 81 and 172–173.

109 E.g., Q 3:33, from which the phrase "the family of Muhammad" was allegedly omitted or Q 3:110, in which the phrase "You are the best of the Muslim nation" (*khayr al-umma*) originally read "You are the best of the Imams" (*khayr al-a'imma*); see Momen, *An Introduction*, pp. 172–173.

110 Bar-Asher, *Scripture*, pp. 90–91.

111 Ibid., pp. 91–92.

112 Momen, *An Introduction*, pp. 151–153.

113 Bar-Asher, *Scripture*, pp. 93–101.

114 The same omission, according to Shi'ite exegetes, was made in Q 4:166; Bar-Asher, *Scripture*, p. 103.

115 Bar-Asher, *Scripture*, p. 107.

116 Q 5:64, 28:77, and 38:28.

117 Bar-Asher, *Scripture*, p. 107.

118 Ibid., pp. 111–117.

119 See Table 2.1 on p. 20.

120 Momen, *An Introduction*, pp. 49–50 and Crone, *Medieval*, pp. 99–100.

121 Crone, *Medieval*, p. 105.

122 Bernard Haykel, *Revival and Reform in Islam: The Legacy of Muhammad al-Shawkani*, Cambridge University Press, Cambridge, 2003, p. 6.

123 Crone, *Medieval*, p. 101.

124 Momen, *An Introduction*, p. 49.
125 Watt, *The Formative Period*, p. 163.
126 Crone, *Medieval*, p. 104.
127 Ibid. and Haykel, *Revival and Reform in Islam*, p. 6.
128 Haykel, *Revival and Reform in Islam*, p. 7.
129 Zayd b. 'Ali, the founder of the movement, is said to have studied with the founder of Mu'tzilite kalám Wasil b. 'Ata; see Momen, *An Introduction*, p. 49.
130 Crone, *Medieval*, p. 106.
131 Haykel, *Revival and Reform in Islam*, p. 7.
132 Ibid., p. 231 and Crone, *Medieval*, p. 106.
133 Crone, *Medieval*, p. 109.
134 Ibid., 104; by "commanding and forbidding" Zaydi scholars meant the *imam*'s duty to wage jihad, apply the precepts of the Shari'a, resist oppressors, and provide moral guidance and just governance to his followers; ibid., p. 105.
135 Nevertheless, the Zaydi *imam* seems to have preserved some trappings of sacredness until the very end of the imamate of Yemen. In November 1999, during my visit to a historical museum in the city of Ta'izz, the residence of the Zaydi *imam* Ahmad, I was told that many of his subjects considered him to be immune to bullets and plotting of his enemies—a belief that his tumultuous career eventually proved wrong.

Chapter 12

Shi'ism as a Revolutionary Movement
The Isma'ilis

Who Are the Isma'ilis?

The Isma'ili movement is named after Isma'il, the eldest son of the sixth Shi'ite *imam* Ja'far al-Sádiq (d. 765). Ja'far believed that each new *imam* must be designated in advance by the incumbent *imam*, guided in his decision by divine inspiration.[1] In accordance with this conviction, he publicly declared Isma'il to be his successor. It so happened that Isma'il died before his father, throwing the pro-'Alid party into confusion. How could an infallible and omniscient *imam*, who claimed to receive his knowledge directly from God, err in such a critical matter as designation?[2] After a brief period of soul-searching, the majority of the Shi'ites turned to Ja'far's eldest surviving son, 'Abdallah. However, he too died a few weeks after the nomination. As we have learned from the previous chapter, many, but not all, of the Shi'ites then accepted Ja'far's other son, Músa al-Kázim, as the seventh *imam*. However, this solution turned out to be unacceptable to some members of the pro-'Alid party, who believed in the infallibility of the nominating *imam*, in this case, Ja'far al-Sádiq. Seven being a magic number in the Islamic tradition, some members of the Shi'ite movement decided that Isma'il's apparent demise was a ruse on the part of God to conceal him from the hostile attention of the 'Abbásid authorities, so that the grounds would be prepared by his partisans for his triumphal return as the rightly guided redeemer (*máhdi*) or the "riser" (*al-qá'im*).[3] His followers then expected him to redress the many wrongs of this world rewarding the faithful and punishing the miscreants.

On the issue of the identity of this apocalyptic figure, there was no agreement among the partisans of Isma'il. Some declared Isma'il's son Muhammad to be the next and final *imam*, as well the expected *máhdi*. Others looked to Ja'far's younger son 'Abdallah as his rightful successor.[4] Despite their differences, in the Sunni tradition the partisans of Isma'il and of his descendants are known under the common sobriquet "Seveners" (because they "stopped" at the seventh *imam*, as it were)[5] or, more commonly, the Isma'ilis. They themselves preferred to be styled "people of the Truth" (*ahl al-haqq*), by which they implied the "hidden" (and therefore the only correct) meaning of the revelation.[6] As with the other Shi'ites, they looked down upon the "misguided" majority of Muslims, the Sunnis.[7] However, the followers of Isma'il and his son also dissociated themselves from the Twelver Shi'ites, whose docility before the 'Abbásid "usurpers" and willingness to wait ad infinitum for their absent *imam* the Isma'ilis resented almost as strongly as the opportunism of the Sunnis. The Twelvers repaid them in kind by denigrating Isma'il and calling in question his suitability for the imamate.[8]

The Isma'ili leaders and their followers were activists who wanted to see truth and justice triumph already in their lifetime. This, they believed, could be achieved only under the leadership of an active *imam* of 'Ali and Fátima descent. Apparently, the Isma'ili leadership's major basis for recruitment was among those Twelver Shi'ites who were dissatisfied with the indefinite absence of the hidden *imam* and who wanted a divinely guided, infallible leader to guide them to truth and justice here and now. The Isma'ilis acknowledged, however, that this leader may occasionally conceal his true identity in anticipation of a more propitious time to publically declare his salvific mission. In the meantime, his faithful were expected to pave the way for his impending arrival by tirelessly spreading his message of truth among the uninitiated. This proselytizing activity was called "summon" or "call" (da'wa). Upon his appearance, the secret Isma'ili cells across the Muslim world were expected to spring into action by joining their leader in his epic struggle against the injustices of this world. Their divinely assured victory was to inaugurate a felicitous era of justice and harmony already in this life, when false appearances and corrupt institutions would disappear and the truth would shine in all its glory. The divinely guided leader (máhdi or qá'im), the Isma'ilis hoped, was destined to put an end to all the quarrels and discord that had divided the Muslim community ever since the Prophet's death. In a lightning-fast campaign, the máhdi would seize power, dethrone the false caliphs, and enter into the inheritance of his ancestor, the prophet Muhammad. Isma'ili missionaries predicted that the máhdi or qá'im would seize Baghdad, the seat of the "false" caliphate, and then proceed to conquer Constantinople, the seat of Christian power. His conquests, according to Isma'ili leaders, would complete the triumph of the "true religion" worldwide. After destroying his enemies, the máhdi-qá'im would institute a just and harmonious social order that was promised to the Muslims by an oft cited prophetic hadíth.

The revolutionary enthusiasm of the partisans of Isma'il was akin to that of the Zaydis with the important difference that the former pinned their messianic expectations on the concrete member of 'Ali's family, either Isma'il b. Ja'far or his son Muhammad, whereas the latter thought that he could be any member of the Prophet's house. Like the Twelvers, the Isma'ilis believed that only the children of Fátima and their progeny were endowed with supernatural knowledge, with infallibility, and, on the cosmic scale, with the duty to institute universal justice and lead the faithful to salvation. Unlike the Twelvers who had found accommodation with the Sunni caliphate in Baghdad (which the doctrine of the indefinitely absent, hidden imam helped to justify) and who had thrived under the protection of the Buyids, the Isma'ilis were determined to pursue their struggle for justice to the bitter end, if need be. It is eminently significant that the gestation of the Isma'ili movement goes back to the period immediately following the occultation of the twelfth imam in 874. This fact indicates that some Shi'ites found the Twelver Shi'ite doctrine relegating the imam's return to an indefinite, distant future to be unsatisfactory. "We are not like the stupid Rafida,[9]" stated an Isma'ili preacher, "who call to somebody absent and awaited."[10] Although temporarily absent, the Isma'ilis felt that their imam was somehow active and responsive to their aspirations, not out of human reach and permanently occulated as the hidden imam of the Twelvers.[11] This activist vision of the imamate had appeal even outside Shi'ite circles. The Isma'ili movement's revolutionary demands for justice under the guidance of the active and militant imam attracted those Muslims who were dissatisfied with the social, economic, and political conditions of the age. Such were quite numerous.

The success of the Isma'li movement should be seen against the background of the overall situation in the lands of Islam. Attempts to implement the revolutionary agenda of the Isma'ili leadership were made possible due to the weakening of caliphal control of Iraq and the adjacent lands in the late ninth century, which resulted in a great deal of political and social turmoil. Taking advantage of the power vacuum and disorder brought about by the weakening of the political center, several revolutionary movements under Isma'ili slogans made a bid for political power across the entire Muslim world. Some of them were able to establish enclaves of Isma'ili rule in remote areas of the Muslim world such as northeastern Arabia, Yemen, Iran, and Central Asia. The western branch of the Isma'ili movement, the Fatimids, had succeeded in founding an Isma'ili "anti-caliphate" first in North Africa and then also in Egypt.

The Rise and Spread of Revolutionary Isma'ilism

The beginnings of revolutionary Isma'ilism are usually traced to the town of 'Áskar Múrkam, some thirty miles north of the prosperous city of Ahwáz in southwestern Iran. The true identity of its founder, 'Abdallah b. Maymún nicknamed "al-Qaddáh" ("The Cataract Remover"), remains a matter of debate.[12] Sources hostile to the Isma'ili movement portray him as a Christian priest who sought to undermine Islam by disseminating his subversive teachings among the Muslims under the guise of Isma'ili *da'wa*.[13] Less biased accounts portray him as a descendant of 'Aqíl, a brother of the caliph 'Ali b. Abi Talib,[14] while pro-Isma'ili sources identify him as the elder son of the Isma'ili *imam* Muhammad b. Isma'il.[15] Given the highly hostile or apologetic nature of the sources at our disposal,[16] it is almost impossible to establish the real course of events and the true identity and intensions of the historical actors. This is, for example, how the formation of the movement is presented by a hostile Sunni source that dates back to the time when 'Abdallah made his teaching public at 'Áskar Múkram:

> He made a large amount of money for himself. He disguised himself by pretending to be a Shi'ite sympathizer and a learned man. But when missionaries arose for him, and when the atheism, licentiousness, cunning and deceit of his teaching became apparent, people rose against him, first the Shi'ites, and then the Mu'tazilites and others, and they took his house by storm. Thereupon he fled to Basra.[17]

'Abdallah's sojourn in Basra did not last long either. When the 'Abbásid authorities got wind of his new whereabouts, he had to flee to Syria, where he settled in the town of Salamiyya. A "melting pot" of sorts, Salamiyya was populated by recent settlers who had arrived from all corners of the Muslim world. Posing as "a merchant from Basra," 'Abdallah continued his propaganda of Isma'ili doctrine (*da'wa*) in the hopes of recruiting new followers. Claiming to be the plenipotentiary representative[18] of the hidden *imam,* Muhammad b. Isma'il, the preacher sent out and received emissaries and missives from across the Muslim world, thereby laying the groundwork for a wide clandestine net of Isma'ili agents (*du'at*; sing. *da'i*), who disseminated Isma'ili ideas among the masses. Once the network of Isma'ili cells had been activated, 'Abdallah began to receive substantial monetary donations from his agents, who had levied a fifth on all property and earnings of their followers.[19]

Upon his death (probably in the last decade of the ninth century), 'Abdallah was succeeded by his sons and grandsons, who continued his mission of spreading the Isma'ili teaching and recruiting new members for the fledgling community through the wide network of secret agents. Their efforts paid off handsomely. Under 'Abdallah's successors, the Isma'ili message acquired a large following in practically every area of the Muslim world: Iraq, Iran, Central Asia, Syria, Arabia, North Africa, and Egypt. In 899, 'Abdallah's great-grandson Sa'íd disclosed his true identity to his followers. He asserted that he was not a representative of the *imam* Muhammad b. Isma'il but was himself the awaited *máhdi* and *qá'im* who had concealed his true identity until the time became ripe for an all-out rebellion against the forces of evil. To mark this momentous transformation, Sa'íd assumed the name 'Abdallah, which, he asserted, was his authentic one from the very beginning. We shall examine the long-ranging implications of his claims to be *máhdi* and *qa'im* further on.[20]

The Teaching and the Mission

One wonders what it was in the doctrine of the Isma'ilis that rendered it so attractive to such different constituencies in vastly diverse geographical and cultural areas? A simple answer is that it offered hope for a more just, prosperous, and pious life to Muslims who were dissatisfied with the religious, social, and political status quo of their age and were therefore anxious to change it. In particular, the Isma'ili call for justice must have resonated with the aspirations of various ethnic communities (e.g., the Berbers of North Africa or Persians of Iran) and disenfranchised social groups (e.g., the Bedouins, peasantry, and certain members of the scholarly class). For such disaffected groups, the Isma'ili revolution was a way of achieving empowerment over and against the privileged ethnic and social estates, as well as freedom from the exactions of their rapacious soldiery. No less importantly, the Isma'ili teaching gave a new, nobler meaning to their daily lives by imbuing them with a sense of pride in being an instrument of the divine plan to improve the state of affairs in this world, and, as a reward, to achieve salvation in the next.

The Isma'ili doctrine is characterized by the belief in the existence of an inner, esoteric (*bátin*) aspect of the Islamic revelation. Because of the centrality of this belief to their worldview, the Isma'ilis are often called in medieval sources *bátiniyya*, that is, those who emphasize the esoteric or secret aspect of the Scripture. Hidden behind its outward or exoteric (*záhir*) wording subject to change and abrogation, the *bátin* was believed by the Isma'ilis to be eternal and immutable.[21] According to Isma'ili scholars, the overwhelming majority of ordinary Muslims mindlessly followed the outward requirements of their religion, namely prayer, fasting, almsgiving, and pilgrimage, without understanding their true significance. It can be revealed only by a special allegorical interpretation known as *ta'wíl*. For example, the outward injunction for the faithful to travel to Mecca and to circumambulate the Ka'ba in reality means that "the believers must betake themselves to the *imam*, the true house of God."[22] In a similar vein, every verse, indeed every word of the Qur'an, including all the proper names it contains, conceals a hidden meaning that lies beyond the reach of the uninitiated. The same applies to the apparently random numbers mentioned in the Scripture. The Isma'ili *ta'wil* serves as the essential hermeneutic[23] key to the true meaning of the Qur'an. For instance, the famous Qur'anic reference to the "seven repeated ones" (15:87)[24] should be understood as a veiled allusion to the seven *imam*s of the Isma'ili doctrine.[25] Likewise, the Qur'anic reference to the rolling up of the heaven on the Judgment Day (39:67) alludes to the abrogation of the external religious law (i.e., the Shari'a) and to the subsequent proclamation of the "true religion" by the divinely guided "riser" (*qá'im*).[26]

The fact that such scriptural allusions are concealed by God from ordinary human beings explains why they should follow the *imam*s who are entrusted with the knowledge of the divine will in regard to the created world. Only these divinely enlightened individuals are capable of leading the masses of faithful to salvation. According to an Isma'ili scholar, "mankind would have neither wisdom nor virtue but for the *imam*s."[27] In short, the *imam*s are the indispensable custodians and interpreters of the "true religion" (*din al-haqq*) that alone opens the gate to salvation.

The person who spreads word about the "true religion" among the masses on behalf of the *imam* is named "caller" or "summoner" (*dá'i*). He acts as both a missionary and a political agent. His role compared to the *imam* is that of the moon compared to the sun in that he absorbs and reflects the light of the true religion emanated by the latter.[28] On the practical level, his duty consists of recruiting new members and initiating them piecemeal into the secret teachings of the Isma'ili intellectual elite. Medieval sources provide numerous accounts of recruitment strategies practiced by *da'i*s. The *da'i* always conducts his mission (*da'wa*) secretly, disguising himself as a merchant, a peddler, or a craftsman. He settles down in a village or town and blends in with the environment. Once he has been accepted by the locals, he begins to go around listening to people's conversations and disputes in order to identify potential recruits. He would then draw them into a conversation, during which he would allude darkly to some secret knowledge that is hidden from everyone, except the initiated. As an example of this recruitment strategy, one can mention the story in which the *da'i* claimed to possess "a sack . . . which contains the knowledge of one of God's secrets." Questioned by the listener or listeners about its nature, the *da'i* would assure them that it had the capacity "to make them rich, to save them, and to take the kingdoms of the world out of the hands of those who now control them, and to place them under their [i.e., the listeners'] rule."[29]

Many found such awe-inspiring promises irresistible and begged the *da'i* to initiate them into this secret knowledge. In such cases, they would be sworn to secrecy by the *da'i*, who would then disclose to them some elements of the Isma'ili teaching, placing special emphasis on the imminent arrival of the *imam* who would reveal the "true religion" in all its majestic glory. Once the recruitment was complete, the convert would be entrusted with the task of converting his relatives and neighbors to the Isma'ili cause. New converts were apparently required to pay a onetime fee upon the initiation, whereupon they would become regular taxpayers who rendered one-fifth of all their property and earnings to the *imam*'s local representative. According to one account, "[E]very woman paid a fifth of what she had spun, and every man a fifth on what he had earned."[30] Success or failure of recruitment being dependent so much on the skills of individual missionaries, their own selection and preparation was a subtle and multistaged process. It was not done during public sermons but through a careful and protracted quest by *da'i*s of spiritually and intellectually suitable individuals who would embrace the Isma'ili teaching and commit wholeheartedly to spreading it among the populace. According to an apt observation of a Western historian of Islam:

> The young men join[ed] a spiritual brotherhood, not a community. Communal demands and family obligations [were] precisely what they left behind.[31]

Once recruited the younger *da'i*s were inducted into the Isma'ili hierarchy of the initiated that oversaw the dissemination of the Isma'ili "call" (*da'wa*) among the masses.

The Isma'ili recruitment strategy just described proved highly effective. Whole villages and Bedouin tribes would quickly become loyal followers of a *da'i*. Initially, the *da'i*s reported directly to the supreme head of the movement (*hujja*), who, as we remember, resided in the Syrian town of Salimiyya. After the proclamation of 'Abdallah as the *qá'im* and the subsequent rise of the Fatimid state first in North Africa, then in Egypt, the *da'wa* organization grew exponentially. The whole Abode of Islam was now divided into "islands" (*jazá'ir*; sing. *jazíra*), each of which was presided over by the regional *hujja*, who, in his turn, supervised the activities of numerous *da'i*s. The latter, in turn, had lieutenants who exerted control over local Isma'ili organizations.[32] The converts formed close-knit communities (cells) in which property and income were distributed equally among the members, so that, in the words of an outside observer, "[T]here were no poor, needy and weak among them."[33] "All became equal," adds the observer, "no one surpassed his comrade and brother through possessions of any kind," and "no one owned anything other than his sword or his other weapons."[34] The weapons were, of course, necessary for the impending rebellion against the 'Abbásid caliph and his armies or against provincial rulers loyal to him, when the time was ripe for the *qá'im* to make his triumphal appearance (see Table 12.1).

In matters of doctrine, the Isma'ilis espoused a distinctive teaching about the origination of the universe (cosmology) and the role of prophets and Shi'ite *imam*s in its functioning. This teaching underwent considerable changes over time. Furthermore, the eastern and western branches of the Isma'ili movement, which we shall be discussing shortly, developed different versions of this teaching. Due to considerations of space, we will provide here only the gist of the original Isma'ili doctrine, omitting numerous important details concerning its historical evolution. The Isma'ili cosmology elaborately combines elements of Hellenistic Gnosticism (a system of occult teachings about ways and means to achieve salvation) and the Neoplatonic doctrine of emanation. Both teachings had enjoyed wide currency among the intellectual elites of the Middle East and North Africa prior to the arrival of Islam. The former teaching emphasized that salvation could be achieved only through an initiation into a secret, divine knowledge ("gnosis" in Greek) and acting

Table 12.1 Isma'Ili Imams

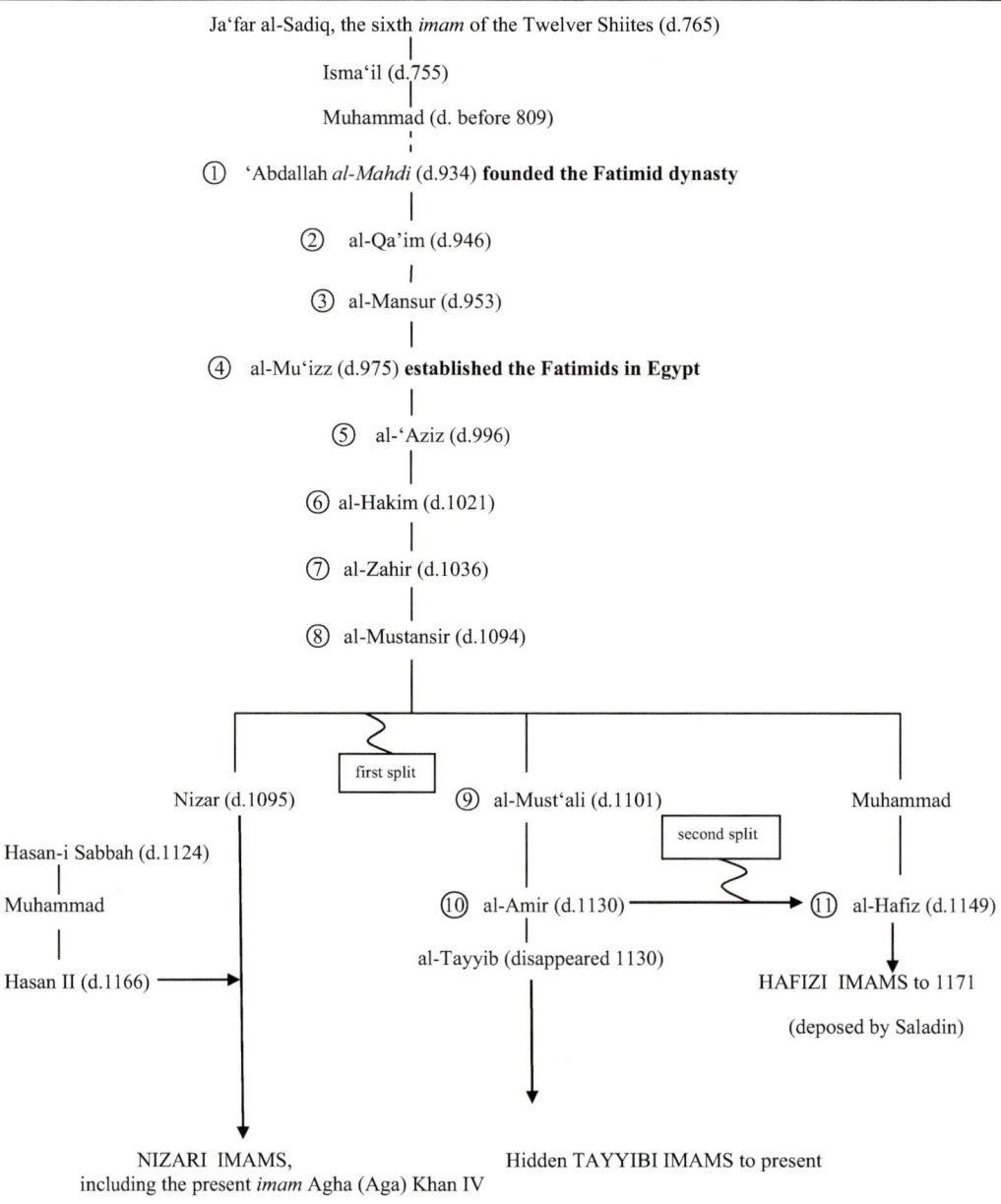

Courtesy of Alexander Knysh

in accordance with it. The latter described the origination of this world from the source of all being, a transcendent divine absolute, through a number of stages.

The Isma'ili version of Neoplatonic cosmology postulates seven stages through which the emanation of existence from the transcendent divine source takes place. These stages are reflected in seven prophetic eras. Each era is inaugurated by an enunciating or speaking prophet (*nátiq*). By his side there always is a silent prophet (*sámit*),[35] who is entrusted by God with the secret meaning of the message brought by the speaking prophet and who is capable of interpreting it to the initiated. The first six "speaking" or "enunciating" prophets were Adam, Noah, Abraham, Moses, Jesus, and Muhammad. Each introduced a religious dispensation of his own. Yet these dispensations were, according to Isma'ili thinkers, but transient outer shells (*zāhir*) of the hidden (*bātin*) truth that represents the immutable and eternal essence of the Torah, the Gospel, and the Qur'an. As mentioned, to each "speaking" prophet, God has assigned a silent companion. Thus, Adam was "accompanied" by Abel, Noah by Shem, Abraham by Ishmael, Moses by Aaron, and Jesus by Simon Peter. When the sixth historical cycle was inaugurated by Muhammad, God designated 'Ali as his silent companion. The period of earthly existence started by the prophet Muhammad's mission is to be followed by the new (and last) cycle. It will be initiated by the *imam* and *māhdi*, Muhammad b. Isma'il, the seventh "enunciating" or "speaking" prophet. Unlike the previous prophets, he will neither open a new cycle of prophecy nor introduce yet another outward (*zāhir*) religious law to replace the one inaugurated by the Prophet of Islam. Instead, he will openly proclaim the "true religion," which until that moment will have been concealed under the veil of the preceding religious dispensations. With the appearance of Muhammad b. Isma'il, all earlier religions will be rendered superfluous, since the truth will no longer need any coverings. Even the law of Islam (Shari'a) will become unnecessary because it will have fulfilled its purpose, which is to conceal the "true religion" until the appointed time. During the *māhdi*'s absence, the teaching that predicts his impending arrival is preserved by his caretakers, the Isma'ili *hujja*s and *da'i*s, whose functions have been described earlier. In this scheme of things, Muhammad b. Isma'il, the awaited redeemer and redresser of wrongs, plays a much more important role than his father, who has given his name to the movement.

The Proclamation of 'Abdallah ('Ubaydallah) the *Māhdi*, and the Qarmati–Fatimid Split

At the initial stages of the movement (the second half of the ninth century), Isma'ili communities were relatively monolithic, unified, as they were, by the belief in the imminent arrival of *imam* and *qā'im* Muhammad b. Isma'il. All Isma'ilis definitely knew who their common enemy was: the "illegitimate" 'Abbásid caliph in Iraq, along with the provincial governors and military commanders loyal to him. Since the Sunni caliph and his lieutenants stood in the way of the divinely preordained course of events, they had to be removed from power by force of arms. The Isma'ilis took a much more nuanced view of the Twelver Shi'ites. On the one hand, they were indignant at what they viewed as the Twelvers' "shameful" accommodation with the 'Abbásid "usurpers." By accepting 'Abbásid rule, the Twelvers "betrayed" the original goal of the 'Alid movement, which was to deliver the imamate to a descendant of the 'Ali and Fátima family. At the same time, from the viewpoint of the Isma'ilis, the Twelvers were not entirely beyond redemption due to their faith in the saving and guiding role of an 'Alid *imam*. No wonder that the Twelvers (and to a lesser extent also Zaydi Shi'ites) were the primary target of Isma'ili propaganda because converting Sunnis, who denied the special role of 'Ali's progeny in the destiny of the *umma*, presented a greater challenge to the propagandists.

By the end of the ninth century, the missionary campaign initiated by the Isma'ili *hujja* 'Abdallah b. Maymún had begun to bear fruit. There was hardly an area of the Muslim world that was not covered by a network of Isma'ili cells. Isma'ili *da'i*s operated in North Africa, southern and eastern Arabia, Iraq, Iran, Central Asia, and even as far as India. From these areas, they sent to Syria caravans loaded with money and all manner of valuables (musk, amber, gems, ornamented weapons, expensive cloth, and so on) that they had collected from their followers on behalf of the *hujja*.[36] The first two *hujja*s after 'Abdallah b. Maymún (i.e., his son and grandson) made every effort to stay in touch with their supporters in different corners of the Muslim world. The *hujja*s' greatest assets were the *da'i* Hamdán Qármat (and his brother-in-law 'Abdán), who had established a base in lower Iraq; the *da'i* Abu Sa'íd al-Jannábi, who was in control of Bahrain in eastern Arabia;[37] two Yemeni *da'is* Ibn Háwshab and 'Ali b. al-Fadl; and Abu 'Abdallah al-Shi'i ("the Shi'ite"), who had managed to secure the loyalty of a powerful Berber tribe in present-day Morocco and Algeria.

By 899, the Isma'ili leaders ensconced in the Syrian trade town of Salamiyya had at their disposal "thousands of loyal believers, tightly organized and furnished with money, weapons and fortified strongholds."[38] The followers were impatiently waiting for the impending appearance of the promised *máhdi*, Muhammad b. Isma'il. It was at that moment that the third *hujja*, a great-grandson of 'Abdallah b. Maymún named Sa'íd, revealed his true identity—he was the awaited *máhdi* and *qá'im* 'Abdallah,[39] who was destined to lead his followers to victory in the epic battle for truth and justice. 'Abdallah's declaration set in motion the vast organization that had been so carefully assembled and prepared by his predecessors and their agents.

The newly announced *máhdi* was faced with a serious problem, though. The fact that Sa'íd-turned-'Abdallah was apparently not the Isma'ili *imam* Muhammad b. Isma'il proved to be a major disadvantage. He tried to overcome it by advancing a series of explanations and alternative genealogies, sometimes contradictory.[40] One may wonder why the leadership of the Isma'ili movement in Salimiyya chose to take such a bold step that could potentially unravel the movement's unity. Some modern historians of Islam have suggested that the head of the movement simply had no choice but to announce his "reincarnation" as the *máhdi* and *qá'im* awaited by the Isma'ilis. According to this opinion, preparations for the Isma'ili rebellion in the provinces of the 'Abbásid Empire had gone too far, and the heady enthusiasm of the followers become very difficult, if not impossible for the leaders to contain. Indeed, spontaneous rebellions in the name of the *máhdi* had already begun to break out in different areas of the Muslim world, exposing the leaders of the organization to retribution by governors loyal to the caliphal state. Further procrastination could have proved fatal.

Unsurprisingly, many Isma'ilis were not convinced by 'Abdallah's/'Ubaydallah's claim to be the awaited *máhdi* and *qa'im*. They ridiculed it and refused to pledge allegiance to the clamant.[41] Among them were the chief *da'i* of Iraq, Hamdán Qármat, and the *da'i* Abu Sa'íd al-Jannábi, who operated in Arabia. The secession of these able leaders and their followers proved to be a severe blow to the Isma'ili uprising. In Iraq, fighting broke out between those who had accepted the *máhdi*'s claims and those who had rejected him as an imposter and continued to wait for the real redeemer, Muhammad b. Isma'il. As a result, both Hamdán Qármat and his brother-in-law 'Abdán were murdered by the *máhdi*'s loyalists. The former gave his name to the eastern branch of the Isma'ili movement, whose members had rejected the *máhdi*'s claims. From then on, they came to be known as "Qarmatis" (Arab. *qarámita*). In medieval Latin sources, they were referred to as "Carmathians." Those Isma'ili communities that accepted the *máhdi*-ship of 'Abdallah/'Ubaydallah came to be known as "Fátimids," a name that emphasized their leaders' claim to be descendants of the Prophet's daughter Fátima, who was married to 'Ali b. Abi Talib, the Prophet's cousin.

The subsequent history of the movement is characterized by hostility and rivalry between its two principal wings. The Qarmatis operated for the most part in Iraq, Arabia, and western Iran, while the Fatimids were active in North Africa, Egypt, Syria, Yemen, and India, where they later on established a durable presence. The greatest achievement of the Fatimid branch of the movement was the conquest of first North Africa and later Egypt. In Egypt, the Fatimids established a cosmopolitan imperial state that became a major geopolitical rival to the 'Abbásid caliphate in Baghdad.

The Rise of the Fatimids

'Abdallah/'Ubaydallah's claim to be the awaited *máhdi* and *qa'im* galvanized some of his Bedouin followers in Syria,[42] who had interpreted it as the signal for an all-out rebellion against the Sunni caliphate. In 902–903, the *máhdi*'s two supporters nicknamed the "Man with the She-

Camel" and the "Man with the Birthmark" led insurrections against the agents of the 'Abbásid state in Syria. Initially successful, their insurgencies were eventually quelled by the more disciplined caliphal troops. The first rebel leader fell in battle; the second was captured and, under torture, revealed the identity of the *máhdi*. 'Abdallah/'Ubaydallah now had no choice but to flee Syria with his family and a handful of supporters. In 904, he found a temporary refuge in Egypt. Since he had few followers there, the *máhdi* was forced to move on. At that juncture, he was faced with a difficult choice of escaping to Yemen or traveling further west to the Maghrib (North Africa). In both regions, the *máhdi* had loyal partisans who had been prepared for his arrival by the local *da'i*s. After some hesitation, the *máhdi* accepted the invitation of the Maghribi *da'i*, Abu 'Abdallah al-Shi'i, and traveled to a remote oasis in present-day Morocco, where he settled down under the guise of a Syrian merchant. Unrecognized, 'Abdallah/'Ubaydallah remained in the oasis from 905 until 909, which gave the *da'i* the opportunity to prepare the grounds for a public declaration of his *máhdi*-ship to the local supporters. They came mainly from the warlike Berber tribe Kutáma, whom Abu 'Abdallah al-Shi'i had managed to rally to the Isma'ili cause. Under his leadership, the Kutáma defeated a local dynasty of Sunni *amír*s loyal to the 'Abbásid caliph and conquered large swathes of land in what is presently eastern Algeria and Tunisia. Abu 'Abdallah al-Shi'i established himself in the expelled *amír*'s capital Qayrawán (Kairouan)[43] and appointed new preachers, ordering them to pray "for Muhammad and his family, for the Commander of the Faithful 'Ali, for al-Hasan and al-Husayn and the resplendent Fatima."[44] He also banned some Sunni practices such as the reading of additional prayers (*tarawíh*) during the nights of Ramadán.[45] These symbolic gestures marked the beginnings of a Shi'ite Isma'ili state in North Africa.

The predominantly Sunni population of Qayrawán was not forced to accept the Isma'ili creed, although they were invited to attend public teaching sessions offered by the Isma'ili *da'i*. The day-to-day affairs of the state (taxation, coinage, army, etc.) were left to competent administrators irrespective of their religious commitments.[46] This modus operandi persisted throughout Isma'ili-Fatimid rule in North Africa and Egypt. Toward the end of the year 909, when Abu 'Abdallah al-Shi'i had secured control over the newly conquered lands, his victorious army marched to the oasis in Morocco in which the *máhdi* had found refuge a few years earlier. When they found out that the *máhdi* had been arrested by a local Sunni ruler, they stormed the oasis, released the *máhdi* from prison, and escorted him and his small entourage, including his son al-Qa'im, to Tunisia. In January 910, the *máhdi*'s advent was officially announced from the pulpits of the major cities of the Maghrib conquered by Abu 'Abdallah al-Shi'i. The reign of the Isma'ili *máhdi* 'Abdallah in that part of the Muslim world was now official.

While among his Berber supporters belief in the *máhdi* was initially unshakable, the Sunni population of Tunisia was skeptical or outright sarcastic.[47] Even for his loyal followers, the appearance of a living and breathing *máhdi* in their midst was something of a shock. An ideal, intangible theological abstraction before his appearance, he could now be observed and scrutinized by those around him. When some of the *máhdi*'s partisans found him to be too human (and thus fallible), disappointment set in. On top of it all, throughout his rule (910–934), the *máhdi* had to contend with a very skeptical public attitude toward his genealogical credentials. Furthermore, even his most devoted partisans, including the architect of his triumph Abu 'Abdallah al-Shi'i, harbored doubts about his Fatimid genealogy. Several Kutáma chieftains eventually prevailed on Abu 'Abdallah al-Shi'i to overthrow the "imposter," but the *máhdi* and his loyal retainers got the wind of the conspiracy and struck first.[48] 'Abdallah/'Ubaydallah sent some influential conspirators away from his capital on various pretexts, whereupon he ordered Abu 'Abdallah al-Shi'i and his brother to be assassinated. Before he was struck down by the assassins, the *da'i* begged them to spare his life only to hear: "[We] kill you at the command of him whom you yourself commanded [us] to obey."[49]

The *da'i*'s murder triggered a series of popular revolts against the *máhdi*. They were put down by his son and successor al-Qa'im,[50] who relied on the support of loyal elements among the Kutáma Berbers. Even more serious was the revolt of the Kharijites of Tahert, a town in present-day Algeria. It was led by one Abu Yazíd (d. 947), nicknamed the "Man of the Donkey." After a long and bloody war, the revolt was put down by the third Fatimid caliph al-Mansúr (r. 946–953).[51] Al-Mansúr's successor al-Mu'ízz managed to expand the Fatimid domain to Cyrenaica (in present-day Libya) and Egypt in the east and all the way to Morocco in the west.

The Conquest of Egypt and the Consolidation of Fatimid Power

Already the second caliph, al-Qa'im, undertook several expeditions to Egypt which proved unsuccessful.[52] Their lessons definitely stood al-Qa'im's successors in good stead. The task of subjugating Egypt to Fatimid rule was finally accomplished under the fourth Fatimid caliph al-Mu'ízz (r. 953–975) in 969. From that time on, Egypt became the main seat of the Fatimid caliphate, whereas the Fatimids' North African possessions lost their strategic importance to the movement and were gradually ceded to the Sunni dynasty of the Zirids.

The conquest of Egypt in 969 was led by the Fatimid general Jawhar ("Diamond"), a military slave of Slavic origin, whose army consisted not only of Berbers but also of Greek and Sicilian mercenary detachments. The Fatimid victory was facilitated by Egypt's economic and political woes. Sources mention mutinies in the army, natural disasters, and squabbles within the ruling class.[53] The conquest of Egypt gave the Fatimid rulers access to the country's enormous resources, which made them a formidable rival to the Sunni caliphs in both Baghdad (the Abbásids) and Cordova (the Umayyads) (see Map 12.1). To commemorate his success, al-Mu'ízz ordered the construction of a new capital, which received the name "Victorious" (*al-qáhira*; hence "Cairo"). The Fatimids soon extended their sway to Palestine and southern Syria. Indirectly, they also

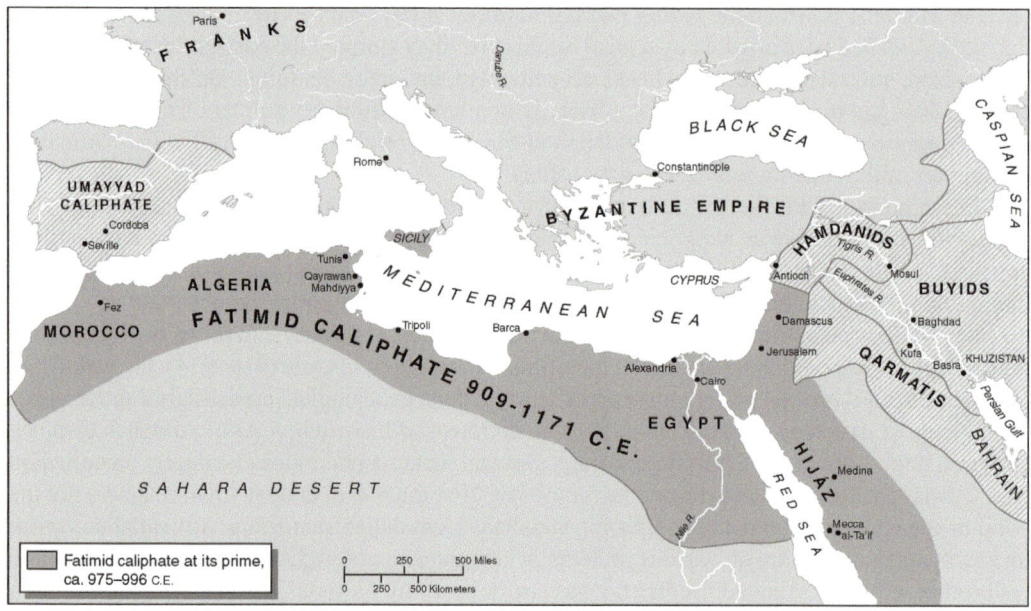

Map 12.1 The Fatimid Empire (909–1171)

controlled the Hijáz with its holy cities Mecca and Medina.[54] Moreover, in 1058, a general loyal to the Fatimids conquered Baghdad, dethroned the Sunni caliph, and had the Friday sermon pronounced in the name of the Fatimid caliph al-Mustánsir (r. 1036–1094). For the first time in history, the Shi'ite version of the call to prayer[55] was heard from the minarets of the 'Abbásid capital. However, one year later, the pro-Fatimid forces were expelled by the Sunni dynasty of Saljuk Turks, who restored the 'Abbásid caliph to power and reintroduced the Sunni call to the prayer. Baghdad was won back to Sunni Islam.

On the doctrinal plane, the radical millenarian and eschatological elements of the Isma'ili teaching, which had animated its adherents for decades, were toned down under the Fatimids. The Fatimid caliph was no longer seen as the final eschatological messiah and harbinger of the Day of Judgment. The messianic age originally promised to the Isma'ilis had not actually come yet, and the final era was still in progress.[56] This being the case, the ruler's role had to be reformulated by the intellectual elite of the Fatimid state. It consisted of unifying the *umma* under a caliph of the Fátima-'Ali stock. This task required the continuation of the Isma'ili propaganda and maintaining close ties between the Fatimids of Egypt and the network of Isma'ili *da'i*s across the width and breadth of the Muslim world.[57]

As far as the creed is concerned, Fatimid scholars continued to pay lip service to the idea of the eventual arrival of the final *imam* (who was now called *al-qá'im* par excellence), who would abolish all previous religious dispensations and laws and who would then inaugurate an age of prosperity and justice. However, much like the Twelver Shi'ites, the Fatimid elite now relegated the appearance of the *imam* and *qá'im* to some indefinite point in the future. The incumbent Fatimid caliph was declared to be the preliminary messiah entrusted by God with the task of preparing the ground for the arrival of the final one. In anticipation of this fateful event, he was to be "succeeded by designation from father to son,"[58] much like the *imam*s of the Twelver Shi'ites were before the occultation of the twelfth *imam*. The Fatimid ruler was "God's deputy (as well as the Mahdi's), the gate to God, a link between Him and mankind, infallible, and endowed with superhuman knowledge."[59] In the meantime, the subjects of the Fatimid caliph were obligated to observe the precepts of Islamic law as interpreted to them by the learned elite of the Fatimid state.

Although the sitting caliph was now demoted to the rank of the preliminary messiah, he was still viewed by his followers as being "rightly guided" by God and thus immune to error. His very body was believed to exude blessing and grace, and being admitted into his presence was a great honor.[60] The caliph's exalted status demanded special rites of acknowledgment, such as the kissing of the earth before his feet. Not everyone was happy with such an ostentatious elevation of the Fatimid ruler. Some of his subjects found this ritual objectionable—a Muslim, they argued, should not kneel before anyone but God. In the end, the issue was left at the individual caliph's discretion. Some caliphs permitted it, others emphatically forbade.[61] In addition to the ritual gestures of humility in the Fatimid caliph's presence, his special status was symbolized by a number of implements such as a crown, the sword of 'Ali, and a canopy over his throne that was replaced by a parasol during his outings. On such public occasions, the Fatimid caliph would often find himself besieged by throngs of petitioners who strove to pass their handwritten requests and complaints on to him. The ruler would grant their requests by writing his decision in the margin or the back of the sheet.[62] However, as with the Sunni caliphate in Baghdad, the day-to-day administration of the state was relegated to the all-powerful "prime minister" or vizier, while the religious affairs of the Fatimid state were handled by the chief Fatimid judge. In administrative matters, the Fatimids exhibited a great deal of pragmatism. Top administrative jobs were given on the basis of merit, not religious affiliation: "four, possibly five, viziers of Fatimid Egypt were Christians, while three were recently converted Jews."[63] In the meantime, the Isma'ili scholarly elite jealously protected their secret theological and cosmological teaching from the "uninitiated" masses, including their own rank-and-file followers. Because, as in North Africa, the majority of

Egypt's population remained Sunni, tensions would occasionally arise between the Isma'ili ruling establishment and their Sunni subjects. The tensions were usually triggered by disagreements over ritual issues. Specifically mentioned in the sources are such matters as the Sunni collective prayers during the nights of Ramadán, the inclusion of a prayer of supplication into the canonical morning prayer (practiced by the Sunnis), the method of determining the end of the Ramadán fast,[64] and the loud and ostentatious mourning of the deceased (practiced by the Sunnis but disallowed by the Shi'ites). When a nephew of the caliph al-Mu'izz asked that female mourners be allowed to publicly weep over his deceased son, his request was emphatically denied by Isma'ili legal experts as being contrary to the Isma'ili law.[65] At the same time and contrary to Sunni sensitivities, al-Mu'izz and his successor al-'Azíz instituted and encouraged public mourning ceremonies commemorating the martyrdom of *imam* al-Husayn at Kerbelá as well as the Shi'ite holiday (*Ghadír Khumm*) commemorating the Prophet's designation of 'Ali as his successor.[66]

Despite the fact that the Fatimids were now masters of a large Mediterranean empire, doubts about their genealogical credentials persisted among their new subjects, the majority of whom, as mentioned, were Sunni Muslims. These doubts are aptly captured in the following anecdote. Soon upon al-Mu'izz's entry into Egypt in 973, he held an audience for the Egyptian notables (including many 'Alids) and wealthy merchants. Some of the attendees mustered enough courage to ask him to produce a proof of his descent from the family of 'Ali and Fátima. In response, so goes the legend, al-Mu'izz drew his sword from its sheath and waved it before the noses of the inquirers, exclaiming: "This is my pedigree!" He then reportedly threw a handful of gold coins toward the assembly, saying: "And this is my noble ancestry!"[67] Apparently his interlocutors found these arguments persuasive.

Another Split: Al-Hákim and the Druzes

The success of the Fatimid state in Egypt rested on three foundations: the agrarian wealth of the Egyptian countryside, the rich proceeds from seafaring and commerce, and the Isma'ili religious doctrine that promised a plenary liberation of Muslims from oppression and injustice.[68] We shall leave the first two foundations for social and economic historians to discuss and focus on the doctrinal foundations of the Fatimid-Isma'ili state that appealed not only to the Egypt-based Isma'ilis but also to their brothers-in-faith across the Muslim world.

The interest that Fatimid rulers and their *da'i*s took in various sciences and traditions of learning led to the creation of a vibrant intellectual atmosphere that was unrivalled by any other Muslim state of that age. Educational institutions enjoyed support at the highest levels. Thus, the Fatimid caliphs al-'Azíz (r. 976–996) and al-Hákim (r. 996–1021) generously endowed the al-Azhar mosque and college (*mádrasa*), which has been one of the greatest centers of Islamic learning ever since. Some modern writers rightly or wrongly consider al-Azhar to be one of the first Muslim universities,[69] in which case it definitely predates its European counterparts in Bologna, Paris, and Oxford. The endowments allotted by the caliphs and their viziers to the al-Azhar complex supported a rich library affiliated with the mosque, as well as salaries for teachers and stipends for students.[70] Crafts and fine arts prospered under these and later rulers of the dynasty. Artifacts from the Fatimid period such as pottery, glassware, furniture, and jewelry continue to amaze us by their beauty and sophistication.

By creatively intertwining ancient Greek and Neoplatonic ideas with their religious convictions, Isma'ili intellectuals produced elegant theories explaining the provenance and subsequent functioning of the universe that dovetailed neatly with the major articles of the Isma'ili doctrine.[71] Isma'ili teachings were disseminated across the Muslim world by *da'i*s, many of whom were now trained at the House of Wisdom in Cairo—an institution founded and endowed by the caliph al-Hákim. The *da'i*s were particularly active and successful in Iraq, Iran, Yemen, and India.[72]

And yet behind this splendid cultural and intellectual veneer always lurked the danger of schism that was present in the Isma'ili community since its very inception. As we have seen, the eastern wing of the Isma'ili movement known as the Qarmatis (Carmathians) flatly rejected the claim of the first Fatimid leader to be the expected *máhdi* and *qá'im*. Their secession deprived the Isma'ili movement of the opportunity to score a decisive victory against the declining 'Abbásid caliphate. Moreover, in subsequent decades, the Qarmatis became avowed enemies of the Fatimid state and waged a series of military campaigns against it in Syria and Egypt, sometimes acting in league with the 'Abbásid caliphs and their generals.[73]

But the Qarmati–Fatimid schism was not the only problem faced by the Isma'ili movement. As we shall see, the problem of succession within the Fatimid family proved no less detrimental to its internal stability. Yet another problem sprang from the close association of the early Isma'ili movement with the so-called extremist wing of the early Shi'ite community. Its representatives were prone to "exaggerate" the status of their leaders to the point of declaring them living manifestations of the Godhead. This trend persisted under Fatimid rule in a latent form until it burst into the open during the reign of the sixth caliph al-Hákim (996–1021).[74]

Al-Hákim was an unusual ruler by any account. He was just eleven years of age when his father, the caliph al-'Azíz, suddenly passed away. At that tender and impressionable age, al-Hákim found himself in the hands of the domineering and occasionally oppressive eunuch Barjawán, a ruthless manipulator, "who treated him not only as a minor but often as a prisoner."[75] The caliph finally managed to get rid of his hated "protector" but not of the traumatic consequences of his custody. From that time on, the caliph remained deeply suspicious of his entourage and was subject to eccentric behavior and "bizarre moods."[76] Some modern scholars have argued that his image may have been gravely distorted by the hostile Sunni historians who "tried to make a real monster out of him" by presenting him as an out-and-out heretic and madman.[77] Whereas the bias of Sunni sources is as logical as it is undeniable, the legends of al-Hákim's erratic and arbitrary rule live on.

We know for sure that the caliph took a deep personal interest in religious matters and led an austere, even ascetic lifestyle. In trying to be a perfect Isma'ili *imam*, al-Hákim generously supported and expanded the Isma'ili missionary project (*da'wa*),[78] built numerous mosques (including one that still stands and bears his name), and personally led the prayer and sermon during the four Fridays of Ramadán (see Figure 12.1). He also purged his administration of venal officials.[79] In response to the popular resentment among Egypt's Muslims over the real or perceived influence of the Christian Copts on the country's administration and economy, al-Hákim imposed severe restrictions on their activities and had many of their churches and monasteries razed to the ground. He then confiscated their estates to pay his army—a measure that was not unprecedented among Egypt's Muslim rulers. Both Christians and Jews living in his realm were then deprived of their autonomous status as religious minorities and obligated to observe Islamic law. Even the country's majority Sunni population was not spared: the caliph gravely offended the Sunnis' religious sensitivities by instituting the practice of a public denunciation of the first three caliphs and some companions of the Prophet hostile to 'Ali.[80]

In retrospect, al-Hákim's policies seem to have lacked consistency and purpose throughout his twenty-five-year-long reign. Thus, after launching the anti-Sunni measures, he then abolished them and, in an attempt to pose as the *imam* of all Muslims (not just the Shi'ites), issued an edict of tolerance to placate his Sunni subjects. Furthermore, he appointed a Hánafi-Sunni scholar to the post of Egypt's chief justice.[81] In a similar way, toward the end of his reign he returned to the Christian Coptic community the churches and monasteries he had confiscated and allowed it to restore the property he had demolished earlier in his rule.[82] In his personal conduct, the caliph held himself to the strictest standards of piety. He avoided luxury and pompous ceremony and "would modestly ride a donkey, clothed like a Sufi in a simple garment of white wool, with

Figure 12.1 The Mosque of the Caliph al-Hákim in Cairo, Egypt
Mohammed Moussa: CC: Wikimedia Commons

sandals on his feet, and his head covered with a cloth in the style of a Bedouin."[83] In the last years of his reign, al-Hákim developed the habit of withdrawing into the desert or to the mountains east of Cairo at night, unaccompanied by bodyguards.

One can only speculate whether it was al-Hákim's unusual behavior or bizarre and inconsistent policies that gave rise to the belief in his divinity among some of his followers. The propaganda campaign launched by these "exaggerators," as they were dubbed by their opponents inside and outside the Isma'ili establishment, sparked a series of riots. The adulation of the quixotic, unpredictable caliph by the "exaggerators" threatened to destabilize the very foundations of the Fatimid state and plunge the whole country into chaos. It is not quite clear whether al-Hákim himself encouraged or condoned this new religious cult centered on his persona. His followers later came to be known as *darziyya* or *durúz* after one of their leaders, Anushtekín al-Dárazi, a Turk from Bukhara. The latter was assassinated—possibly on the orders of al-Hákim himself—in 1019, whereupon the leadership of the movement devolved on al-Dárazi's former rival Hamza b. 'Ali.[84]

The new leader of the "exaggerators" claimed to be no less than the human embodiment of the universal intellect created by al-Hákim, whom he, in turn, presented as a living manifestation of God the Creator.[85] The appearance of a living God riding on a donkey[86] around Cairo proved to be too much for the Fatimid ruling establishment to countenance. Hamza's views were condemned as "extreme," and he was forced to go into hiding. Soon afterward, al-Hákim himself vanished during his one of his donkey rides near the pyramids. Al-Hákim's sudden and mysterious disappearance in the night desert[87] seems to have further confirmed his partisans in their belief in his divine status. Fearful of the impact that their "extremist" preaching could have had on the masses, the Fatimid leadership visited severe reprisals upon the following of Hamza b. 'Ali. Many exaggerators were rounded up and executed; others sought refuge in neighboring regions. As a result of the persecutions, the cult of al-Hákim completely disappeared from Egypt only to reemerge in the highlands of Syria and Lebanon, where it was propagated by Hamza's surviving disciples among the local highlander tribes who sought to "define themselves out of Muslim society."[88] The new religious teaching caught on, winning a substantial number of converts to form a religious community of its own. Impregnable in its mountain fastness, the community, currently known as "Druze," has survived until this day. Its members, some 300,000 men and women, reside in Syria, Lebanon, and Israel. In accordance with the principle of initiation into secret knowledge that they inherited from the Fatimid mission (*da'wa*), the Druze community is divided into two principal classes: the "sages," who are initiated into the secret teachings of the movement's founding fathers and who have the obligation to disseminate them piecemeal among their followers, and the "ignorant," who are expected to obey the "sages" and receive instruction from them. Some tenets of the Druze religion—such as belief in the transmigration of souls, the possibility of incarnation of the divine in certain elect human beings, as well as the impending triumphal return of al-Hákim and Hamza as God and the universal intellect respectively—place it outside not only mainstream Shi'ism but Islam as a whole.[89]

The Crisis Over al-Mustánsir's Succession and the Rise of the Nizári Community

Many modern-day scholars view the long reign of al-Hákim's grandson al-Mustánsir (1036–1094) as the beginning of the unrelenting decline of Fatimid power that culminated in its final destruction by Saláh al-Din (Saladin) in 1171.[90] As with the 'Abbásid caliph, his Fatimid counterpart's major challenge was to control his restive slave soldiers, who constituted the military backbone of the state. In Egypt, the situation was aggravated by the presence in the Fatimid army of several mutually hostile contingents, such as Turks, Berbers, and black Africans (Sudanis). Soon after his ascension to the throne, al-Mustánsir found himself hostage to their violent rivalries. By 1074, the whole country was engulfed in an internecine warfare, forcing the beleaguered caliph to seek the help of the powerful Armenian general Badr al-Jamáli (d. 1094), who had ruled the Syrian city of Acre on behalf of the Fatimids. Badr was able to put down the uprisings of the rebellious Turkish troops, thereby saving the Fatimid caliphate from the imminent collapse. In return, he gained full sway over the state administration and finances to become the real master of Egypt.[91] This pattern of rule persisted under his son al-Áfdal.

In the decades that followed, Fatimid caliphs were reduced to the position of helpless puppets in the hands of the all-powerful vizier and his military commanders. Even more disturbingly for the Fatimid state, these viziers and their generals were prone to tamper with the succession process in order to install on the Egyptian throne the most inept and pliant candidate whom they could easily control. This tampering led to several fateful splits in the movement, many of whose members refused to accept the puppet caliphs arbitrarily installed by their all-powerful viziers.[92]

The succession to al-Mustánsir proved to be a turning point in the history of Fatimid Isma'ilism. Upon his death in 1094, the vizier al-Áfdal put on the throne the caliph's younger son al-Must'ali (who was also the vizier's son-in-law).[93] In so doing, he bypassed the elder son Nizár, whom his father had designated as his only legitimate heir. Nizár fled to Alexandria and revolted but was defeated, captured, and thrown into prison, where he died. Some Isma'ili leaders in Iran, who were waging a bloody and mostly losing battle against the Saljuk Sunni rulers of Iraq and Iran, refused to recognize al-Must'ali as the legitimate caliph. Because of their unswerving commitment to the rights of Nizár, they came to be known as "Nizáris" (*nizáriyya*). Foremost among them was a powerful and popular *da'i* named Hasan-i Sabáh, who had met Nizár in Cairo and who subsequently refused to give allegiance to his younger brother. After a while, Hasan-i Sabáh managed to conquer the eagle's nest of a fortress named Alamút (in the Iranian province of Daylam/Daylaman).[94] It soon became the main seat of the Isma'ili-Nizári mission (da'wa) in western Iran, as well as the military base for Isma'ili-Nizári hostilities against the 'Abbásid caliphate and its Saljuk protectors. An astute and able leader who led an ascetic life and practiced rough justice,[95] Hasan-i Sabáh succeeded in recruiting a considerable number of followers in Daylam(an) and neighboring areas of Iran. As the ranks of his followers swelled, he managed to impose his will on the majority of Isma'ili communities in Iran. Subsequently Hasan-i Sabáh was even able to extend his authority as far as Syria, thereby effectively taking these areas out of the Fatimid sphere of influence.

As mentioned, the Nizári leader also waged war against the powerful Saljuk dynasty of Iraq by using a network of fortified mountain strongholds as his bases of operations. Faced with the overwhelming military might of the Saljuk sultanate, Hasan-i Sabáh and his successors resorted to a more or less systematic use of assassination to advance their political goals.[96] By ambushing and killing their opponents, they sought to avenge the death of their fellow Isma'ilis (Nizáris) or to ward off an impending attack on an Isma'ili-Nizári community by a superior Saljuk fighting force. The targets of such suicidal assassination acts were high-ranking persecutors of the Nizári community. Its militant leaders worked hard to hone the assassination techniques to perfection. They reportedly trained young devotees (fidá'is) who were prepared to kill enemies of the Nizári community even at the cost of their own lives. The would-be assassins "were told that by dying for the cause they purified their souls for the realms of light (Isma'ilis did not believe in bodily resurrection)."[97] In 1092, one such fidá'i succeeded in murdering the powerful Saljuk vizier Nizám al-Mulk, an archenemy of the Isma'ilis.[98] Sunni leaders were not the only targets of Nizári-Isma'ili assassins. Thus, Hasan-i Sabbáh reportedly ordered the assassination of the Fatimid vizier al-Áfdal, whom he held responsible for depriving Nizár of the Fatimid caliphate. When this goal was successfully accomplished by three Syrian fidá'is in 1121, Hásan ordered his followers to celebrate this event for seven days and seven nights.[99]

The Nizári Isma'ilis were definitely not the first to dispose of their enemies by means of assassination, but they resorted to this tactics often enough to become notorious on account of it.[100] According to a Western scholar of the Nizári-Isma'ili movement, "[T]he Isma'ili assassinations were made as public and dramatic as possible, as warnings [to Isma'ilis' enemies], and zealous Isma'ili youths gladly sacrificed their lives in such acts."[101] The tactics of political murder-cum-suicide proved effective (at least in the short term) and continued to be practiced by the Nizáris in the subsequent epochs, striking terror in the hearts of their enemies.[102] Popular fears generated by such politically motivated assassinations led to indiscriminate retaliatory massacres by Sunni rulers of real or suspected Isma'ilis and their sympathizers. Legends began to circulate, according to which these suicidal acts were committed by brainwashed and drugged young men seeking paradise. Among other things, a popular legend had it that Nizári-Isma'ili warriors consumed hashísh, a drug extracted from hemp, before embarking on a suicide mission (allegedly, to suppress the fear of an imminent death). As a result, in hostile Sunni sources, the Nizári-Isma'ili fighters are often called by their derogatory nickname hashíshiyya or hashishiyún. With time, this sobriquet has come to be applied not just to the suicidal attackers proper but also to the Nizári-Isma'ili community as a whole.

The Crusaders, who had encountered a Syrian branch of the Nizári-Isma'ili community in the Levant, gave this word its Latinized form "assassin." In Western Europe and beyond, it has gradually come to denote anyone who is prepared to kill for a political end. Western historians of the Crusades were intrigued by Muslim folklore about bold assassination attacks perpetrated in broad daylight by Isma'ili "assassins." Legends about the fearsome leader of the Syrian Nizáris Rashíd al-Din Sinán (d. 1192), the "Old Man of the Mountain" of the Crusader chronicles, gained wide currency in medieval Europe. According to modern Isma'ili historians, they unwittingly reproduced the hostile and inaccurate stereotypes purveyed by the Sunni enemies of the Isma'ili community.[103] Under Rashíd al-Din's leadership, the Syrian Nizári-Isma'ili community became heavily embroiled in the struggle between the Crusaders and the Syrian Muslims in the Levant. As a rule, the Nizáris sided with the weaker party against the stronger one. Depending on whose side they were on, they would kill either Muslim or Christian rulers (as well as their military commanders). Rival political factions often availed themselves of the services of Nizári *fidá'i*s in order to eliminate their enemies. For instance, the Sunni warlords of Syria, named Zangids, solicited the help of trained Nizári assassins in their struggle against the powerful Sunni sovereign of Egypt Saláh al-Din (Saladin), who had survived several attempts on his life staged by Rashíd al-Din's *fidá'i*s. The Christian knight Marquis Conrad of Montferrat, who was about to ascend the throne of Jerusalem, was less lucky. He was murdered by two *fidá'i*s disguised as Christian monks. The identity of the person who ordered this assassination remains a mystery.[104]

The Principal Articles of the Nizári Creed

We should now say a few words about the internal organization and doctrines of the Nizári-Isma'ili community. In the absence of Nizár, whom his followers in Iran and Syria considered to be the only legitimate *imam*, Hasan-i Sabbáh assumed the role of his representative, or "proof" (*hújja*). Upon his death in 1124, Hasan-i Sabbáh's tomb at Alamut became a Nizári sanctuary (see Figure 12.2). In the eyes of his followers, during his lifetime Hasan-i Sabáh served as the essential link between the family of the vanished Nizár and his followers.[105] Some forty years later, an offspring of Nizár's family reappeared in the fortress of Alamút to claim the imamate.

Figure 12.2 Leader of the Ismaili Order of "Assassins" Giving Orders to Two of His Followers at His Castle in Alamut (fifteenth-century Western book miniature)

This claim was first made by Hasan-i Sabbáh's third successor Hasan II in 1166,[106] then by the latter's son Muhammad, who explicitly declared himself the *imam* destined to preside over the final hour and resurrection of the human race.[107] In this respect, there is a clear parallel between the declarations of Hasan-i Sabbáh's descendants and those made by the first Fatimid *imam* 'Abdallah/'Ubaydallah (alias Sa'íd). All these individuals transformed themselves from the hidden *imam*'s caretakers to the *imam* himself by an act of will.

The exact implications of this transformation, that is, to what extent the Shari'a continued to be observed by the *imam*'s followers, is still a matter of debate.[108] Many Sunni sources indicate that Islam's major injunctions, including the five canonical prayers, were abolished altogether between 1164 and 1210, while Isma'ili writers insist that they continued to be observed, albeit in a more profound, spiritualized manner.[109] Be this as it may, according to the Nizári teaching, the external law becomes redundant in the presence of a living *imam*, whom his partisans believe to be the embodiment of the absolute truth that is no longer hidden behind external religious dispensations.[110] The dynasty of the Nizári *imam*s based in the fortress of Alamút lasted until 1256, when it was wiped out by the army of the Mongol commander Hulagú-khan. One after another, Nizári-Isma'ili strongholds in Iran were overrun by the Mongols and their populations massacred. Several Nizári fortresses in Syria managed to survive the Mongol onslaught only to be conquered by the Mamluks of Egypt under the sultan Baybars (r. 1260–1277). Baybars spared the Nizáris of Syria and treated them as an independent religious community. He occasionally even availed himself of the services of Nizári *fidá'i*s in his struggle against the remnants of the Crusader states in the Levant.

After the fall of Alamút, surviving members of the Nizári-Isma'ili community dispersed across Iran, reaching as far as Azerbaijan. As the other branches of the Isma'ili movement, they experienced several internal splits over succession. Under the Safavid dynasty of Iran, Nizári leaders were actively involved in the political life of the Twelver Shi'ite Empire, while at the same time waging a vigorous propaganda campaign among the Shi'ites of the Indian Subcontinent. The Qajar shahs of Iran (who had succeeded the Safavids) generally treated Nizári-Isma'ili *imam*s leniently and even appointed them to high positions in their administration. The fortunes of Nizári *imam*s in Iran reached their peak under the Qajar ruler Fath 'Ali Shah, who granted the honorific title "Agha (or Aga) Khan" ("Supreme Commander") to the forty-sixth Nizári *imam* Hasan 'Ali Shah (1800–1881), while also giving him his daughter in marriage. The honorific title bestowed upon Hasan 'Ali Shah was inherited by his successors, including the incumbent (forty-ninth) *imam* Karím al-Husayni, known as Aga Khan IV (b. 1936), who currently resides in Switzerland.

Under Fath 'Ali Shah's successor, Aga Khan I fell out of favor and had to seek refuge in western India (first in Bombay/Mumbai and later on in Calcutta/Kolkata). He rendered valuable services to the British Raj during the first Anglo-Afghan War (1839–1842) and the British conquest of Sindh[111] (1842–1843). The British administration rewarded him with a lifetime pension. Aga Khan's three successors have presided over a wide international network of Nizári-Isma'ili communities in Central Asia, India, Pakistan, Malaysia, Singapore, some Arab countries, east Africa, and, more recently, the West (France, Britain, the United States, and Canada). These Nizári communities, which comprise several million members, are now being governed by the constitution of 1986 that was drafted and made official by Aga Khan IV. It affirms some fundamental principles of the Isma'ili doctrine, especially the all-important role of the *imam* in guiding and educating his followers. Simultaneously, it encourages the Isma'ilis to be good citizens of their countries as long as their governments allow them the freedom to practice their religion. At present, the *imam*'s duty to guide and educate his community is interpreted by the incumbent Aga Khan (IV) as a mandate to engage in charitable activities and to sponsor Islamic arts and sciences for the benefit not only of his own followers but also of the societies in which they reside.

The Collapse of the Fatimid Caliphate

Al-Háfiz, the eleventh caliph of the Fatimid dynasty, died in 1149. His reign was marked by the incessant court intrigues and power struggle among his sons, viziers, and military commanders. The caliphs that succeeded al-Háfiz were but helpless "puppets in the hands of their viziers."[112] The already chaotic situation within the country was further aggravated by the constant threat of invasion by the Crusader forces based in Syria and Palestine. Apprehensive of this looming threat, the main Muslim fighter against the Crusaders, Nur al-Din Zangi (Zengi), sent an expeditionary (Sunni) force to Egypt to secure the loyalty of its rulers to his anti-Crusader campaign. Among the military commanders dispatched with that force was a Kurdish officer, Saláh al-Din b. Ayyúb (d. 1193), who is better known in the West under his Latinized name, Saladin. After the death of his superior, general Shirkúh, Saladin was able to impose his will on the last Fatimid *imam,* al-'Ádid, and established himself as the latter's vizier. A fervent Sunni, Saladin set about dismantling the Fatimid state and its ideological foundations. He banned the Shi'ite call to prayer, shut down Isma'ili teaching sessions at the al-Azhar mosque and the House of Wisdom, and appointed a strict Sunni scholar to the position of Egypt's chief justice. In September 1171, he put an end to Fatimid rule in Egypt altogether by publicly proclaiming his allegiance to the 'Abbásid-Sunni caliph in Baghdad.[113] Al-'Ádid, the twenty-fourth (and last) caliph of the Fatimid dynasty, was deposed and died soon afterward. The 262-year rule of the Fatimid caliphs over Egypt came to an end. Several attempts to restore al-'Ádid's descendants to power were crushed by Saladin and his sons, eventually leading to the dissolution of the Háfizi branch of the Isma'ili *da'wa* both in Egypt and other parts of the Muslim world.[114] From that time on, Egypt has been a Sunni state.

The Háfizi-Táyyibi Split and Its Impact on the Fortunes of Later Isma'ilism

As already mentioned, the blatant tampering with succession process within the Fatimid family by the all-powerful vizier al-Áfdal already alienated from it the majority of its followers in the Muslim East, leading to the emergence of the independent Nizári state (and later imamate) in Alamút. Nevertheless, the Isma'ili communities of Egypt, Yemen, western India, and some parts of Syria acknowledged the rights of Nizár's younger brother al-Must'áli and retained their allegiance to the Fatimid state. After a short reign (1094–1101), al-Must'áli was succeeded by his five-year-old son al-Ámir. For the first twenty years of al-Ámir's imamate (1001–1130), his vizier al-Áfdal "remained the effective master of the Fatimid state."[115] Al-Áfdal's assassination by Nizári *fidá'i*s in 1121 (possibly plotted by al-Ámir and his partisans) allowed the caliph to assert his authority for some time, only to be himself murdered by a group of Nizári assassins in 1130.[116] A few months before al-Ámir's assassination, he designated his newborn son, al-Táyyib, as his successor.

Until al-Táyyib came of age, the regency of the caliphate devolved on his cousin 'Abd al-Majíd. However, his regency proved to be short-lived. The reins of power were seized by the vizier al-Áfdal's son Kutayfát, who declared Twelver Shi'ism to be the official religion of the Egyptian state.[117] When Kutayfát, in his turn, was overthrown by a military coup led by the Berber tribes loyal to the Fatimid house, 'Abd al-Majíd was proclaimed first regent and later caliph of the Fatimid state with the title al-Háfiz. This proclamation, which flew in the face of the widely acknowledged Shi'ite principle that the imamate can be transmitted only from father to son (not from brother to brother), rent the branch of the Isma'ili community that had recognized the caliphate of al-Must'áli following the death of his father al-Mustánsir. One important consequence of this split[118] was that the formerly loyal Isma'ili community of Yemen declared its independence from the Egyptian Fatimids in the name of the rights of al-Táyyib, who had mysteriously disappeared during the politically troubled period that followed his father's assassination.

Thus, the western (Fatimid) wing of the Isma'ili movement became split into the rival Nizári, Táyyibi, and Háfizi factions. The Táyyibi community in Yemen was headed by an able queen of the Sulayhid dynasty named Árwa bint[119] Ahmad (d. 1138), who occupied the highest rank in the hierarchy of the Fatimid mission.[120] After the proclamation of al-Háfiz, the queen severed all ties with the Háfizi community of Egypt and formed an independent missionary organization in Yemen. It set about proselytizing in the name of *imam* al-Táyyib among the Muslims and Hindus of western India. In the Subcontinent, the mission was directed by a Táyyibi supreme missionary (*dá'i mútlaq*), who acted on behalf of the *imam* al-Táyyib during the period of his concealment.[121] Much later, in 1539, the position of the supreme *da'i* of the Táyyibi communities in Yemen and India was for the first time assumed by an Indian Isma'ili. Soon afterward, in 1567, the headquarters of the mission itself was transferred from Yemen to the Indian province of Gujarat. These events reflected the growing influence of the Indian Táyyibi community and the decline of its Yemeni homeland. The Indian Táyyibis came to be known as Bóhras (i.e., "merchants," or "traders"), a name that reflected their occupation as traders in and around the Indian Ocean. Upon the death of the twenty-sixth Indian missionary in 1591, the Táyyibi branch of the Isma'ili movement experienced an internal split over the identity of his successor. It led to the formation of two sub-branches, the Da'údis and the Sulaymánis. Their members adhered to different lines of supreme missionaries, whose office, by that time, had become hereditary. Numerically insignificant, the Bóhras have survived until today. They form close-knit communities that pursue trade and keep away from politics and government service.

The Qarmati Revolt and the Rise and Fall of the Qarmati State in Bahrain

We have already mentioned the split between the eastern and western wings of the Isma'ili missionary movement following the declaration in 899 of the *máhdi*-ship of 'Abdallah/'Ubaydallah first in Syria and later in North Africa. Hamdán Qármat and his lieutenant and brother-in-law 'Abdán, as well as many other Isma'ili leaders in western Iran and Arabia, refused to accept the former Syrian *hujja* as their *imam* and continued to wait for the advent of Muhammad b. Isma'il, after whose father the whole movement was named. Following the death of Hamdán and 'Abdán at the hands of the *da'is* loyal to the newly proclaimed Fatimid *máhdi*, the center of Qarmati activities shifted to mainland Bahrain, an area along the northeastern coast of Arabia. This territory had fallen under the sway of 'Abdán's lieutenant named Abu Sa'íd al-Jannábi. Using Bahrain as his base of operations, Abu Sa'íd launched a series of raids against cities and fortresses of lower Iraq. At one point, he even managed to reach the city of Basra.[122] Upon his death in 913, the leadership of his community devolved upon his seven sons, of whom Abu Táhir proved to be the most able and resourceful, despite his young age.[123] In 923, he won his spurs by seizing and pillaging Basra's market in a surprise attack.[124] But this conquest was just the beginning. In the following year, the Qarmatis intercepted a large caravan of pilgrims headed for Mecca and captured valuable treasure, including the caliph's crown, as well as thousands of prisoners. The Qarmatis led by Abu Táhir continued their attacks on pilgrims in Arabia in the subsequent years. They also persisted in raiding the cities of Basra and Kufa in Iraq. While there, they were aided by their local supporters who had up to that point concealed their Isma'ili beliefs.

The dramatic successes and apparent invincibility of the Qarmati movement attracted to it a considerable number of "young men set out to conquer the world for the truth they have found, stirred by the prospect of adventure and heroic deeds."[125] These young revolutionaries "felt that the old way of life was to be swept away, the privileged classes overthrown, and pure justice was to reign."[126] The banners of Bahraini Qarmatis carried the Qur'anic verse (28:5), "We desire to show favor unto those who were deemed weak on earth and to make them imams and their heirs."[127] Driven by a complex combination of motives from heady idealism to a more pragmatic desire to improve their worldly lot, the Qarmati revolutionaries showed no mercy to their opponents, be they the caliph's soldiers or peaceful pilgrims. They, in turn, could expect no leniency once captured. To justify their cruelty and disrespect for religious and social conventions, the Qarmati leaders of Bahrain decided to declare the arrival of the *máhdi* and the end of the Islamic era. In a sermon preached in the central mosque of Kufa, their leader boldly stated:

> The Truth has appeared, and the *máhdi* has risen: the 'Abbasid dynasty is finished, the doctors of law, the Qur'an readers and the experts in the Sunna are finished; now there is nothing more to wait for! We have not come to establish a new dynasty, but rather to put an end to the *shari'a*![128]

After failing to conquer Baghdad in a campaign that shook the 'Abbásid caliphate to its very foundations, the Qarmati levies retreated to their base in Bahrain. In January 930, Abu Táhir and his followers unexpectedly appeared outside the walls of Mecca in the middle of the *hajj* ceremonies. Abu Táhir demanded that he and his followers be allowed to perform the pilgrimage rites in the holy city and gave a solemn pledge that the pilgrims would be given safe conduct. However, once in the city:

> The Qarmatis fell upon the pilgrims, who had just performed the circumambulation (*tawaf*) of the Ka'ba, and created a bloodbath. Many died clinging to the curtain (*kiswa*) with which the Ka'ba was covered every year. The Qarmatis derided the Qur'anic revelation by calling out: "HE is in heaven, and shall his house[129] be on earth?" or they mockingly cited Sura 3:97, where it says about the sanctuary of the Ka'ba: "Whoever enters it is in safety."[130]

As the bodies of slain pilgrims were lying unattended in the streets of Mecca, the Qarmatis looted the treasures of the Ka'ba sanctuary, stripping it of its gold and silver decorations. The sacred Black Stone was removed from a corner of the Ka'ba, put on a camel, and carried off to the Qarmati capital in Bahrain.[131] After such acts of blatant and ostentatious sacrilege, the Qarmatis were no longer able to pretend to be Muslims.[132] The only way for them to justify their actions was to announce the advent of the final *máhdi* and the termination of the era of Islam. Before long, the council of Qarmati leaders indeed "recognized" the *máhdi* in a young Persian lad who was captured during one of their raids and subsequently brought to Bahrain.[133] Abu Táhir and other Qarmati leaders treated the lad as a human manifestation of God and paid obeisance to him. According to Abu Táhir's personal doctor who later defected and fled to Baghdad:

> He [the youth] was around twenty years old, and he wore a yellow turban wound according to the Persian fashion, a yellow robe, and a sash around his waist, and he sat on a grey horse. His name was Abu 'l-Fadl the Zoroastrian.[134]

The doctor describes in graphic detail the acts of sacrilege perpetrated by the newly manifested *máhdi* and his Qarmati followers. They cursed all of the previous prophets, including Muhammad, worshiped fire, encouraged "incest and pederasty," burnt and desecrated copies of the Qur'an, and broke the Black Stone and placed its pieces in a latrine.[135] These and similar acts were deemed to symbolize the abolition of the Shari'a and the arrival of both new and old "Adamic" religion,[136] namely, one that the Qarmatis held to be the ultimate and universal truth. As the hostile account of a defector, the doctor's words should be taken with a grain of salt. However, the fact that the Islamic law was indeed abolished by the Persian youth is confirmed by other sources.

The outrageous actions and demands of the young Persian *máhdi*[137] soon alarmed the Qarmati leaders enough to first persuade Abu Táhir that he was dealing with an imposter and then to have him killed eighty days after the declaration of his advent. The Qarmatis now had to acknowledge grudgingly that the true religion had not yet been revealed. With the true *máhdi*'s appearance delayed, the Islamic rituals were reinstated, and the Black Stone was recovered from the latrine, perfumed, and shown proper reverence. Nevertheless, many of Abu Táhir's Iraqi followers who had joined him in anticipation of the rise of the *mahdi* and the arrival of the era of the sublime truth were demoralized. Some abandoned the Qarmati community in Bahrain and returned to their homes in Iraq. Abu Táhir's Bedouin supporters followed suit and offered their services to 'Abbásid generals and later also to the Buyid rulers of Baghdad. In the subsequent decades, intellectual leaders of the Isma'ili movement had to go to great lengths to downplay or suppress the destructive, antinomian tendencies inherent in the Qarmati interpretation of its teachings. However, as the episode with al-Hákim and his Druze followers has shown, they were not entirely successful. The danger of revolutionary antinomianism continued to lurk in the wings.

The Qarmati state in Bahrain managed to survive the embarrassment of the rise and fall of the false *máhdi*. After the death of Abu Táhir in 944, it was ruled by a council that included his surviving brothers and some leading *da'i*s.[138] The Qarmati leadership concluded a peace treaty with the 'Abbásids and in 951 returned the Black Stone to Mecca for a large ransom paid by the Baghdad caliph. Somewhat paradoxically, their relations with the Fatimid Isma'ilis remained mostly hostile. They deteriorated even further after the Fatimid conquest of Syria and Palestine, which the Qarmatis of Bahrain considered to be their sphere of influence. The second half of the tenth century was marked by the rivalry and occasionally armed conflicts between the Fatimids and their Qarmati opponents. In 971, a Qarmati army succeeded in expelling the Fatimids from Syria and restoring 'Abbásid sovereignty there. In subsequent years, the Qarmatis even managed to invade Egypt and besiege Cairo. They had to be bought off by a large tribute. They were less successful in their attempts to wrest Iraq from the 'Abbásid state, and after several crushing defeats they were forced to retreat to Bahrain permanently. Their troubles did not end there. Throughout the first part of the eleventh century, they had to fight both against the ever more assertive 'Abbásid state and the neighboring Bedouin tribes that rebelled against their rule in the name of the Fatimid *imam*s of Egypt. One such revolt finally led to the fall of the Qarmati state in 1076.

We do not know much about the social and economic foundations of the Qarmati state at its prime, but they were definitely quite unusual. It appears that its free citizens relied heavily on the labor of black slaves imported from Africa. The slaves worked the fields and engaged in various handicrafts. Repairs of houses, wells, and streets and other public works were carried out by black slaves owned by the state. Free residents of the Qarmarti state were not subject to taxation and were eligible to receive state loans in times of need or when they wanted to start a new business. In socioeconomic terms, it was effectively "a welfare state,"[139] at least for its free citizens. In return, the citizens were obligated to participate in the state's military campaigns, which were quite frequent. In the religious sphere, Muslim rituals and dietary laws were not observed, and mosques were kept open only for non-Qarmati visitors.[140]

Conclusions

As we have seen, loyalty to a particular branch of the Prophet's family, especially that of 'Ali and Fátima, has proved to be a powerful means of mobilizing Muslim masses for political and military action against the powers-that-be. This action has often taken the form of either a localized antigovernment rebellion or a broader revolutionary movement in the name of a certain descendant of the 'Ali and Fátima line. Although the overwhelming majority of such rebellions have failed, some have proved to be successful. Of these, the Fatimid conquest of North Africa was by far the most spectacular and consequential, leading to the creation of a stable and prosperous empire on the basis of Isma'ili theological teaching, Mediterranean maritime commerce, and the agrarian wealth of Egypt, the granary of the Middle East. Its Yemeni and Indian outposts, run by *da'i*s, also proved relatively successful and long-lasting. The same applies to the religiopolitical project instituted by Hasan-i Sabáh in the name of the ill-fated Fatimid *imam* Nizár and continued under his successors in Iran and beyond. On the other hand, the Qarmati revolt, with its unbridled radicalism and antinomian tendencies, proved to be quite limited in its geographical scope. Initially violent and devastating and subsequently quixotic in its social and economic practices, it came to an end already in the eleventh century.

In the final account, however, neither the Qarmati nor the Fatimid revolution and the states they had given rise to succeeded in attracting the majority of Muslims to the Isma'ili cause. Furthermore, the Isma'ili movement itself failed to retain its unity in the face of doctrinal dissent and succession crises and, more generally, realpolitik. It eventually disintegrated into a congeries of small self-contained devotional communities in India, the Middle East, and, more recently, the West.

Questions to Ponder

1   Why and how, in your opinion, did medieval Muslims become Shi'is, Isma'ilis, or Sunnis? Was it a free choice on the part of individual Muslims, or were other factors at play?
2   *E pluribus unum*? How elastic (or otherwise) were the boundaries of the Muslim community in the Middle Ages? For example, can the Qarmatis be considered Muslims? And what about the Fatimids and the Nizári followers of Agha Khan?
3   Can Isma'ilism be seen as a precursor of Communism in religious garb, as is sometimes argued in Western and Muslim academic studies and popular accounts?[141] Or was it rather a millenarian, apocalyptic movement along the lines of David Koresh's Branch Davidians or James Warren Jones's Peoples' Temple?
4   Compare and contrast Zaydism and Isma'ilism, bearing in mind their shared commitment to militancy in the name of truth and justice.

Summary

- The specificity of the Isma'ili version of Shi'ism is the belief in an active *imam* as opposed to the indefinitely hidden one of the Twelver Shi'ites.
- In the geopolitical background, the weakening of 'Abbásid power and local misrule encourage radical oppositional movements under religious slogans.
- The beginnings of the Isma'ili movement are associated with 'Abdallah b. Maymún in Iraq and his descendants in Syria. The declaration of the imamate of 'Abdallah ('Ubaydallah) in 899 has long-ranging consequences.
- The network of Isma'ili cells, their propaganda methods, and the movement's internal hierarchy that consists of the "proofs" (*hujja*s), the "summoners"/"preachers" (*da'i*s), and the commoners at various stages of initiation.
- In Isma'ili theology, the Isma'ili hierarchy of the initiated is the reflection of the cosmic order conceived along the lines of the Neoplatonic doctrine of emanation.
- The cyclical movement of time and history is a progressive revelation of the true religion that transcends denominational borders and encompasses all of humankind. The Isma'ilis espouse the concept of "speaking" and "silent" prophets.

- The ultimate revelation of the true religion at the hands of the divinely appointed and directed Isma'ili *máhdi*, or "riser" (*qá'im*), generates millenarian expectations in his followers.
- The split within the Isma'ili movement follows the declaration of 'Abdallah ('Ubaydallah) as *máhdi* and *qa'im* in 899: the Fatimids of the West versus the Qarmatis of the East.
- The Fatimid wing of the movement is successful in Muslim North Africa (among the Berbers). The conquest of Egypt by the *máhdi* and *qa'im* al-Mu'ízz (969) follows, as well as the economic and cultural blossom of the Fatimid state under his successors. Given the economic and doctrinal foundations of the Fatimid caliphate, the doctrine of the true religion needs adjustment to justify the continual absence of the true religion.
- Splits occur within the movement over succession and their long-ranging repercussions for the Fatimid cause. The caliph al-Hákim (1021) disappears, and the Druze movement emerges in the Levant.
- The rise of the Nizári branch of the Isma'ili movement in Syria and Iran follows the death of the caliph al-Mustánsir (1094). Hasan-i Sabbah and his Alamut stronghold play a significant role in the movement. The Nizári use the assassination of political rivals as a means to further their political ambitions and intimidate their enemies.
- The Nizári community evolves from the Middle Ages until today, leadinig to the Aga Khans.
- In 1171, Saladin abolishes the Fatimid caliphate, and the Háfizi branch of the movement dissipates.
- The Táyybi branch of Isma'ilism survives in Yemen and in India in the post-Fatimid epoch and until today.
- The activities of the Qarmati movement in Iraq and northeastern Arabia become extremely violent.
- Qarmati attacks on the Muslim sanctuaries and pilgrimage caravans become a way to expedite the advent of the "true religion."
- The sack of Mecca in 930 and the removal of the Black Stone from the Ka'ba lead to the abolition of the Shari'a by the leadership of the Qarmati state in Bahrain in 931 and its eventual collapse in 1076.
- In Bahrain, the Qarmati "welfare state," with its peculiarities, falls.

Notes

1 Farhad Daftary, *The Isma'ilis: Their History and Doctrines*, Cambridge University Press, Cambridge, 1990, p. 84.
2 Marshall Hodgson, *The Venture of Islam*, Chicago University Press, Chicago, 1974, vol. 1, p. 376; Farhad Daftary, "The Earliest Isma'ilis," in Etan Kohlberg (ed.), *Shi'ism*, Ashgate Variorum, Aldershot, UK, 2003, p. 240.
3 These two terms are basically synonymous in the Shi'ite usage, although the term *al-qa'im* was preferred by the Isma'ilis, especially after the "rise" of the Fatimid *máhdi* 'Ubaydallah or 'Abdallah in 899; Daftary, "The Earliest Isma'ilis," p. 249.
4 Daftary, *The Isma'ilis*, p. 103.
5 According to many Isma'ilis, Muhammad b. Isma'il was *imam* number seven, since 'Ali b. Abi Talib was not an *imam* but the executor (*wasí*) of the prophet Muhammad; Daftary, "Earliest Isma'ilis," p. 250.
6 Patricia Crone, *Medieval Islamic Political Thought*, Edinburgh University Press, Edinburgh, 2004, p. 201.
7 Ibid., p. 215.
8 By labeling him as a drunkard, among other things, see Daftary, *The Isma'ilis*, pp. 94 and 97.
Heinz Halm, *The Empire of the Mahdi* (trans. Michael Bonner), E. J. Brill, Leiden, 1996, pp. 20–21 and 159.

9 A derogatory term for the Twelver Shi'ites among the Sunnis.

10 Quoted in Crone, *Medieval*, p. 198.

11 Ibid.

12 Some sources consider him to be a Christian heretic; see, e.g., Crone, *Medieval*, p. 211.

13 Halm, *The Empire of the Mahdi*, p. 8; cf. Daftary, *The Isma'ilis*, pp. 109–110.

14 Halm, *The Empire of the Mahdi*, pp. 10–11.

15 Daftary, *The Isma'ilis*, pp. 112–113; see Table 12.3. "Isma'ili Imams," p. 198.

16 As succinctly discussed in Farhad Daftary's *Ismailis in Medieval Muslim Societies*, I.B. Taurus, London and New York, 2005, pp. 27–41.

17 Halm, *The Empire of the Mahdi*, p. 6.

18 Literally, "proof" or "argument" (of God), *hujja*.

19 Halm, *The Empire of the Mahdi*, p. 48.

20 Sources hostile to the Isma'ilis invariably call him "'Ubaydallah," meaning, "the little 'Abdallah"; since he was known as 'Abdallah among his followers, we shall use this name rather than 'Ubaydallah.

21 Daftary, *The Isma'ilis*, p. 137; cf. Diana Steigerwald, "Isma'ili ta'wil," in Andrew Rippin (ed.), *The Blackwell Companion to the Qur'an*, Blackwell, Oxford, 2006, p. 387.

22 Crone, *Medieval*, p. 200.

23 That is, one pertaining to understanding and interpretation of (usually) a sacred text.

24 Usually interpreted as a reference to the seven verses of the first *sura* of the Qur'an.

25 Crone, *Medieval*, p. 206.

26 Steigerwald, "Isma'ili ta'wil," p. 392.

27 Crone, *Medieval*, p. 213.

28 Steigerwald, "Isma'ili ta'wil," p. 389.

29 Halm, *The Empire of the Mahdi*, p. 29.

30 Ibid., p. 48.

31 Crone, *Medieval*, p. 217.

32 For details see Daftary, *Ismailis in Medieval Muslim Societies*, pp. 74–76.

33 Halm, *The Empire of the Mahdi*, p. 49.

34 Ibid., pp. 48–49.

35 It has different names in different renditions of the Isma'ili doctrine, such as "foundation" (*asás*), "legatee" or "executor" (*wasí*), etc.

36 Halm, *The Empire of the Mahdi*, pp. 50–51.

37 At that time, this term applied to a much larger coastal area of eastern Arabia than the present-day state of Bahrain.

38 Halm, *The Empire of the Mahdi*, p. 57.

39 As mentioned earlier, he is usually called "'Ubaydallah" (meaning, the "little 'Abdallah") in non-Isma'ili sources.

40 Daftary, *The Isma'ilis*, pp. 128–129.

41 Ibid., pp. 125–126.

42 At that time, the notion "Syria" (al-Sha'm) included the lands of present-day Syria, Jordan, Lebanon, Palestine, and Israel.

43 In present-day Tunisia.

44 Halm, *The Empire of the Mahdi*, p. 124.

45 Ibid., p. 127.

46 Ibid., p. 152.

47 Ibid., p. 160.

48 According to some sources, Abu 'Abdallah al-Shi'i had serious disagreements with the *máhdi* over state policies and resented the latter's attempt to limit his authority.

49 Halm, *The Empire of the Mahdi*, p. 168.

50 Noteworthy are the eschatological connotations of his name—*qa'im*, son of the *máhdi*; both terms refer to the divinely guided messianic figure expected by the Isma'ilis.

51 Daftary, *The Isma'ilis*, pp. 159–160.

52 Halm, *The Empire of the Mahdi*, pp. 168–176.

53 Daftary, *The Isma'ilis*, p. 172.

54 Heinz Halm, *The Fatimids and Their Traditions of Learning*, I.B. Tauris, London, 1997, p. 34.

55 Which added to the Sunni prayer call the phrase "Come to the best of deeds!"; see Halm, *The Empire of the Mahdi*, p. 243.

56 Crone, *Medieval*, p. 205.

57 Ibid., p. 206 and Halm, *The Fatimids*, pp. 56–58.

58 Crone, *Medieval*, p. 207.

59 Ibid.

60 Halm, *The Empire of the Mahdi*, pp. 350–351.

61 Ibid., p. 351.

62 Ibid., p. 354.

63 Crone, *Medieval*, p. 216.

64 The Isma'ilis determine the end of the fast by means of mathematical calculation, as opposed to the empirical observation of the position of the moon by Sunni scholars.

65 Halm, *The Empire of the Mahdi*, p. 244.

66 Daftary, *The Isma'ilis*, p. 185; on *Ghadir Khumm* see the previous chapter.

67 Halm, *The Empire of the Mahdi*, p. 159.

68 Hodgson, *The Venture*, vol. 2, pp. 21–23 and Crone, *Medieval*, p. 216.

69 Alongside the university of al-Qarawiyyin (Karaouine) in Fez, Morocco; see, e.g., http://muslimob server.com/first-university-in-the-world/.

70 Hodgson, *The Venture*, vol. 2, p. 25.

71 Halm, *The Empire of the Mahdi*, pp. 294–297 and 368–372; cf. Halm, *The Fatimids*, pp. 41–55.

72 Daftary, *The Isma'ilis*, p. 192.

73 Ibid., pp. 174–175 and 182.

74 See Table 12.1. "Isma'ili Imams," p. 198.

75 Halm, *The Fatimids*, p. 35.

76 Hodgson, *The Venture*, vol. 2, p. 26; and Daftary, *The Isma'ilis*, p. 188.

77 Halm, *The Fatimids*, p. 35.

78 As was mentioned, he founded the House of [Isma'ili] Wisdom which was responsible for training Isma'ili missionaries.

79 Halm, *The Fatimids*, p. 38.

80 Daftary, *The Isma'ilis*, pp. 188–189.

81 Halm, *The Fatimids*, p. 36; Crone, *Medieval*, p. 216.

82 Halm, *The Fatimids*, p. 37.

83 Ibid., p. 36.

84 Crone, *Medieval*, pp. 210–211.

85 Ibid. and Daftary, *The Isma'ilis*, p. 199.

86 In the Judeo-Christian tradition, donkey is an attribute of the messiah; see Suliman Bashear, "Riding Beasts on Divine Missions: An Examination of the Ass and Camel Traditions," *Journal of Semitic Studies*, vol. 37 (1991), pp. 37–75.

87 His donkey and head covering were reportedly recovered but not his body. Until today, his disappearance remains a mystery. Some argue that he was assassinated on the orders of his sister, Sitt al-Mulk, while others speculate that he may have been devoured by lions. His devotees insist that he went to heaven only to return in triumph at the appointed time.

88 Crone, *Medieval*, p. 211.

89 Daftary, *The Isma'ilis*, pp. 198–199.

90 Crone, *Medieval*, p. 217.

91 Daftary, *The Isma'ilis*, pp. 203–204.

92 Crone, *Medieval*, p. 217.

93 Ibid. and Daftary, *The Isma'ilis*, p. 348.

94 Crone, *Medieval*, p. 211.

95 He executed both his sons, one for alleged murder, the other for drunkenness; see Marshall Hodgson, "Hasan-i Sabbah," in *Encyclopedia of Islam*, 2nd ed.; online edition: http://referenceworks.brillonline.com

 96 Daftary, *The Isma'ilis*, p. 390.
 97 Crone, *Medieval*, p. 211.
 98 Ibid. and Daftary, *The Isma'ilis*, p. 342.
 99 Daftary, *The Isma'ilis*, p. 366.
100 Ibid., pp. 352–353 and Crone, *Medieval*, p. 390.
101 Hodgson, *The Venture*, vol. 2, p. 60.
102 Crone, *Medieval*, pp. 390–391.
103 Daftary, *Ismailis in Medieval Muslim Societies*, pp. 150–151.
104 Ibid., pp. 156–157.
105 Marshall Hodgson, "Hasan-i Sabbah," *Encyclopaedia of Islam*, 2nd. ed., online edition: http://reference
      works.brillonline.com.
106 To make the transition to his new status, the newly announced *imam* broke the fast of Ramadan by eating
      and drinking wine; see Crone, *Medieval*, p. 211.
107 Daftary, *The Isma'ilis*, pp. 390–391.
108 Ibid., p. 388.
109 Crone, *Medieval*, p. 211 and Daftary, *The Isma'ilis*, p. 391.
110 Daftary, *The Isma'ilis*, p. 393.
111 Presently a province of Pakistan.
112 Daftary, *The Isma'ilis*, p. 270.
113 Crone, *Medieval*, p. 217.
114 Daftary, *The Isma'ilis*, pp. 272–274.
115 Ibid., p. 263.
116 Ibid., p. 264.
117 Crone, *Medieval*, p. 217.
118 See Table 12.1. "Isma'ili Imams," p. 198.
119 The Arabic for "daughter."
120 For details, see Samer Traboulsi, "The Queen Was Actually a Man," *Arabica*, vol. 50/1 (2003),
      pp. 96–108.
121 Daftary, *Ismailis in Medieval Muslim Societies*, p. 98.
122 Halm, *The Empire of the Mahdi*, pp. 192 and 250.
123 He was only sixteen when he assumed the leadership of the Bahraini community and led his first military
      campaign against an 'Abbásid force.
124 Daftary, *The Isma'ilis*, p. 161.
125 Crone, *Medieval*, p. 217.
126 Hodgson, *The Venture*, vol. 1, p. 490.
127 Crone, *Medieval*, p. 325.
128 Halm, *The Empire of the Mahdi*, p. 254.
129 Meaning the Ka'ba.
130 Halm, *The Empire of the Mahdi*, p. 256.
131 Crone, *Medieval*, p. 326.
132 As they had done earlier in a letter addressed to an 'Abbásid vizier; see Halm, *The Empire of the Mahdi*,
      p. 251.
133 Crone, *Medieval*, p. 326.
134 Halm, *The Empire of the Mahdi*, p. 258.
135 Daftary, *The Isma'ilis*, p. 163.
136 Halm, *The Empire of the Mahdi*, p. 259 and Crone, *Medieval*, pp. 325–326.
137 It is reported that Abu 'l-Fadl imprudently ordered the execution of some Qarmati chiefs and even rela-
      tives of Abu Táhir himself; see Daftary, *The Isma'ilis*, p. 163.
138 Crone, *Medieval*, p. 326.
139 Ibid.
140 Ibid.
141 See, e.g., ibid., p. 325.

Chapter 13

Ascetic and Mystical Movement in Islam: Sufism

Introduction

The ascetic and mystical element that was implicit in Islam since its very inception grew steadily during the first Islamic centuries (the seventh–ninth centuries), which witnessed the appearance of the first Muslim "devotees"[1] in Mesopotamia, Syria and Iran.[2] By the thirteenth century, they had coalesced into the primitive ascetic communities that spread across the Muslim world and that gradually transformed into the institution called *taríqa*—the mystical "brotherhood" or "order." Each *taríqa* had a distinctive spiritual pedigree stretching back to the prophet Muhammad. It also had its own devotional practices, educational philosophy, head-quarters, and dormitories, as well as a semi-independent economic basis in the form of a pious endowment (either real estate or tracts of land). During the late Middle Ages and the modern period, Islamic mysticism (Sufism) became an important part of the Muslim devotional and intellectual life and social order. Sufism's literature and authorities, its networks of *taríqa* institutions, and its peculiar lifestyles and practices became a spiritual and intellectual "glue" that held together the culturally and ethnically diverse Muslim societies. Unlike Christian mysticism, which was gradually marginalized by the anticlerical and scientific-rationalistic tendencies that were dominant in Western European societies since the Enlightenment, Sufism retained its influence on the spiritual and intellectual life of Muslim societies until the beginning of the twentieth century. At that point, Sufi rituals, values, and doctrines came under critical fire from such dissimilar and often mutually hostile factions of Muslim societies as reformers and modernists, liberal nationalists, religious fundamentalists, and, somewhat later, Muslim socialists. Representatives of all these movements accused Sufis of deliberately cultivating "idle superstitions," of stubbornly resisting the imposition of "progressive" social and intellectual attitudes, and of "exploiting the Muslim masses" to their advantage. Parallel to these ideological attacks, in many countries of the Middle East, the economic foundations of Sufi organizations were undermined by agrarian reforms, secularization of education, and new forms of taxation instituted by Westernized nationalist governments. The extent of Sufism's decline in the first half of twentieth century varied from one country to another. On the whole, however, by the 1950s Sufism had lost much of its former appeal in the eyes of Muslims, and its erstwhile institutional grandeur was reduced to low-key lodges staffed by Sufi masters with little influence outside their immediate coterie of followers. It seemed that in most Middle Eastern and South Asian societies, the very survival of the Sufi tradition was called in question. However, not only has Sufism survived but also has been making a steady comeback of late.[3] Alongside traditional Sufi practices and doctrines, there emerged the so-called "neo-Sufi" movements whose followers seek to bring Sufi values in tune with the spiritual and intellectual needs of modern men and women living in industrialized Western societies.[4]

The Name and the Beginnings

Normative Sufi literature routinely portrays the Prophet and some of his ascetically minded companions as "Sufis" (*sufiyya*). However, this term does not seem to have gained wide currency until the first half of the ninth century, when it came to denote Muslim ascetics and world-renouncers in Iraq, Syria and, possibly, Egypt. More than just fulfilling their religious duties, these pious individuals paid close attention to the underlying motives of their actions and sought to endow them with a deeper spiritual meaning. This goal was achieved through a close reading and meditation on the meaning of the Qur'anic revelation, introspection, imitation of the Prophet's actions, voluntary poverty, and self-mortification. Strenuous spiritual self-exertion was occasionally accompanied by voluntary military service (*ribat wa-jihad*) along the Muslim-Byzantine frontier, where many renowned early devotees flocked in search of "pure life" and martyrdom "in the path of God." Acts of penitence and self-abnegation, which their practitioners justified by references to certain Qur'anic verses and the Prophet's utterances,[5] were, in part, a reaction against the Islamic state's newly acquired wealth and complacency, as well as the "impious" pastimes and conduct of the Umayyad rulers and their officials. For many pious Muslims, these frivolous activities were incompatible with the simple and frugal life of the first Muslim community at Medina. Whereas, as we have seen, some religiopolitical factions, such as the Kharijites and the Shi'ites, tried to topple the "illegitimate" rulers by force of arms, others opted for a passive protest by withdrawing from the corrupt world around them and engaging in supererogatory acts of worship. Even though their meticulous scrupulousness in food and social intercourse were sometimes interpreted as a challenge to secular and military authorities, they were usually left alone as long as they did not agitate against the powers-that-be. As an outward sign of their pietistic flight from "corrupt" mundane life, some early devotees adopted a distinctive dress code—a rough woolen habit that set them apart from the men of the world who preferred more expensive and comfortable silk or cotton. Wittingly or not, the early Muslim devotees thereby came to resemble Christian monks and ascetics, who also donned hair shirts and rough woolen cloaks as a sign of penitence and contempt for worldly luxuries.[6] In view of its pronounced Christian connotations, some early Muslim authorities sometimes frowned upon this custom. In spite of their protests, wearing a woolen robe (*tasawwuf*) was adopted by some piety-minded Muslims in Syria and the Iraq under the early 'Abbasids. By the end of the eighth century, in the central lands of Islam, the nickname *sufiyya* ("wool-people" or "wool-wearers"; sing. *sufi*) had become a self-designation of many individuals given to an ascetic life and mystical contemplation.

Basic Ideas and Goals

While many early Muslims were committed to personal purity, moral uprightness, and strict compliance with the letter of the divine law, some made asceticism and pious meditation their primary vocation. These "proto-Sufis" strove to win God's pleasure through self-imposed deprivations and rules of conduct, such as abstinence from food and sex, self-effacing humility, supererogatory prayers, night vigils, and meditation on the deeper implications of the Qur'an. In their passionate desire to achieve intimacy with God, they drew inspiration from selected Qur'anic verses that stressed God immanent and immediate presence in this world, e.g. 2:115; 2:186; 50:16; etc. They found similar ideas in the prophetic traditions (*hadith*), some of which encouraged the faithful to "serve God as if they see Him," to count themselves among the dead, to be content with the little that they have against the abundance that may distract them from the worship of their Lord, and to remember God constantly.[7] In meditating on such scriptural passages and in imitating the pious behavior ascribed to the first Muslim heroes, the forerunners of the Sufi movement developed a comprehensive set of values and a code of behavior that can be defined as "world-renouncing" or "otherworldly oriented." This attitude to life may have had an implicit political intent, as some early ascetics consciously abandoned gainful professions, avoided any contact with state authorities, or even refused to participate in communal life in protest against perceived or real injustices imposed by the ruling class.[8] With time, the initial world-renouncing impulse of the early ascetic movement in Islam was augmented by the idea of mystical intimacy between the worshiper-lover and his divine beloved. Celebrated in poems and utterances of exceptional beauty and verve, it became a keynote of the nascent Sufi tradition. Another motivation for Islam's ascetics and mystics was the idea of the primordial covenant. Based on the Qur'an (7:172), it focuses on the momentous encounter between God and as yet disembodied humanity drawn from "the loins of the Children of Adam." In the course of this encounter, the human souls bore testimony to God's absolute sovereignty and promised him their undivided devotion. However, once the human souls were placed into their sinful bodies and found themselves in the corrupt world of false idols and appearances, they forgot their primordial promise and succumbed to their drives and passions of the moment. The goal of God's faithful servant, therefore, consists in "recapturing the rapture" of the Day of the Covenant in order to return to the state of primordial purity and faithfulness that characterized the human souls before their descent into the world of materiality and false idols.[9] To this end, the mystic had to work hard to resist not just the corruptive influences of the world but also the egotistic lusts and passions of his own base self (*nafs*). These general tenets manifested themselves in the lives and intellectual legacy of those whom later Sufi literature depicted, somewhat anachronistically, as the first Sufis.

The Archetypal "Sufi": Al-Hásan al-Basri and His Followers

The fame of the early preacher and scholar of Basra, al-Hásan al-Basri (d. 728) rests on the unique uprightness of his personality, which made a deep impression on his contemporaries. He was famous for his fiery sermons in which he warned his fellow citizens against committing sins and urged them to prepare themselves for the Last Judgement by leading pure and frugal lives, as he did himself. He judged sins harshly and considered sinners to be fully responsible for their actions. Respectful of caliphal authority, despite its obvious transgressions against the Muslim morality, he nevertheless criticized its holders for violating the divinely ordained order of things. Al-Hásan's brotherly feeling toward his contemporaries and his self-abnegating altruism were appropriated by later Sufis and formed the foundation of the code of spiritual chivalry (*futuwwa*), which was embraced by Muslim ascetic-mystical associations in the subsequent epochs.

Whether or not al-Hasan was indeed the founding father of the Sufi movement, as he was persistently portrayed in later Sufi literature, his passionate preaching of high moral and ethical standards won him numerous followers from a wide variety of backgrounds—professional Qur'an-reciters, pious warriors of the Muslim–Christian frontier, small-time traders, weavers, and scribes. They enthusiastically embraced al-Hásan al-Basri's spirited rejection of worldly delights and luxury, his criticism of social ills, oppressive rulers and their unscrupulous retainers. The actions and utterances of al-Hásan's followers exhibit their constant fear of divine retribution for the slightest moral lapse and their exaggerated sense of sin, which they sought to alleviate through constant penance, mortification of the flesh, permanent contrition and mourning.[10] This self-denigrating, God-fearing attitude often found an outward expression in constant crying, which earned many early ascetics the name of "weepers" (*bakka'un*). Some of ascetics and mystics came to believe that their almost superhuman piety, moral uprightness, and spiritual fervor placed them above the rank of ordinary believers, who were unable to overcome their simplest passions of the moment, not to mention the complex moral dilemmas faced by God's elect folk. As a result, there emerged among Islam's early ascetics and mystics the concept of "friendship with" God (*walaya* or *wilaya*). They traced it back to several Qur'anic passages suggesting the existence of the category of God's servants enjoying his special favor in this and future life (e.g., 2:62, 165, 262, 274; 8:2–4; 10:62; 18:65; 22:35, 41:30–32; etc.). It is in this relatively narrow circle of early Muslim ascetics and mystics that we witness the emergence of charismatic personalities who enjoyed a special moral-ethical authority among ordinary believers. With time, this spiritual authority developed into a substantial, albeit not immediately obvious social power. Initially, however, the social and political ramifications of this authority were rather limited, confined as it was to the narrow circle of Sufi teachers (*shaykhs*) and their disciples (*muridun*).

The nascent Sufi movement was internally diverse and displayed a variety of devotional styles: The "erotic mysticism" of Rábi'a al-'Adawiyya (d. 801), a preacher of pure, all-consuming, and unselfish love of God, existed side by side with the stern piety of Ibrahim b. Ad'ham (d. 777)—an otherworldly recluse who abstained not only from what was prohibited under the Islamic law but also from that which was permitted. He, in turn, was distinct from both 'Abdallah b. al-Mubarak (d. 797)—an inner-worldly "warrior monk" of the Byzantine–Muslim frontier—or Fudayl Ibn 'Iyad (d. 803), a vocal critic of the rulers and scholarly class of his time, which he accused of departing from the exemplary custom of the Prophet and his first followers. Finally, in Shaqiq al-Balkhi (d. 810), an Iranian ascetic who was killed in action fighting against the "pagan Turks," we find a curious hybrid of Ibrahim b. Ad'ham and 'Abdallah b. al-Mubarak: both a holy warrior and an extreme ascetic who strove to avoid the corruptive influence of the world by completely withdrawing from it. Shaqiq is often described as the earliest exponent, if not the founder, of *tawakkul*—a doctrine of complete trust in and total reliance on God, which entailed absolute fatalism and occasionally abandonment of gainful employment.[11] He is also credited with early theorizing about various levels—or "dwelling stations" (*manazil*)—of the "mystical path" to God.

Regional Manifestations

In the eastern lands of the caliphate, the ascendancy of Iraqi Sufism was delayed by almost one century by the presence of local ascetic groups, notably the Karramiyya of Khurasan (eastern Iran) and Central Asia and the Malamatiyya of Khurasan, whose leaders resisted the imposition of the "foreign" style of ascetic piety. We know relatively little about the values and practices of these groups, which were suppressed by, or incorporated into, the Sufi movement under the dynasty of Turkic-speaking warlords named the Saljuks (r. eleventh–thirteenth centuries).[12]

In the western provinces of the 'Abbásid Empire, we find a few ascetics who studied under al-Hásan al-Basri or his disciples and who taught his ideas to their own students. The most notable of them were Abu Sulayman al-Darani (d. 830) in Syria and Dhu 'l-Nun al-Misri (d. 860) in Egypt. The former emphasized complete reliance on God and unquestioning contentment with his will. Any distraction from God, including marriage, was, for al-Darani, unacceptable. The amount of one's knowledge of God was in direct proportion to one's pious deeds, which al-Darani described as an internal *jihad* and which he valued more than the "external" warfare against an "infidel" enemy. In Egypt, the most distinguished representative of the local ascetic and mystical movement was a Nubian named Dhu 'l-Nun al-Misri, whose involuntary stay in Baghdad on charges of heresy had a profound impact on the local ascetics and mystics. His poetic utterances brim with erotic symbolism that was to become a hallmark of later Sufi poetry. They depict God as the mystic's intimate friend and beloved (*habib*). God, in turn, grants his faithful lover a special, intuitive knowledge of himself, which Dhu 'l-Nun called "gnosis" (*ma'rifa*). This supersensory, esoteric knowledge sets its possessors, God's elect "friends" and "beloved" (*awliyá'*), apart from the generality of the believers.

The activities and teachings of ascetics and mystics, who resided in the caliphate's provinces indicate that the primeval ascetic and mystical movement was not confined to Iraq. However, it was in Iraq and more precisely in Baghdad that it came to fruition as a freestanding ascetic-mystical trend within Islam.

The Formation of the Baghdadi School of Sufism

The ascetic and mystical school of Baghdad—the capital of the 'Abbasid Empire—inherited the ideas and practices of the Muslim devotees from the first Muslim cities of Iraq, Basra and Kufa. However, the beginnings of the Baghdad school proper are associated with several individuals whose teachings decisively shaped its identity. One of them was Ma'ruf al-Karkhi (d. 815), who studied under some prominent members of al-Hásan al-Basri's inner circle. He established himself as an eloquent preacher, who from the pulpit of his own mosque in the Karkh quarter of Baghdad, admonished his audience to practice frugality in food and clothing and be content with God's decree, no matter how adverse. Al-Karkhi took little interest in theological speculation and enjoined deeds, not words. Legends describe his numerous miracles and emphasize in particular the efficacy of his prayers. After his death, his tomb on the Tigris became a site of pious visits and supplicatory prayers. Equally important for the self-identity of the Baghdad school of Sufism is Bishr al-Hafi, "the Barefoot" (d. 842). He started his career as a jurist and *hadíth*-collector but later relinquished his studies and embarked on the life of a pauper because he convinced himself that formal religious knowledge was irrelevant to the all-important goal of salvation. We find a similar career trajectory in the life of another founding father of the Baghdadi school, a learned merchant named Sari al-Saqati (d. 867). His transformation from a well-to-do merchant and respectable *hadíth*-collector to an indigent devotee occurred under the influence of Ma'ruf al-Karkhi's passionate sermons about the transience and pettiness of this-worldly existence as opposed to the glory of the life to come. Like Bishr, Sari declared the collection of prophetic reports, especially when it became a profession and means of livelihood, to be "no provision for the Hereafter." Of the practical virtues requisite of every believer, he emphasized fortitude in adversity, humility, trust in God, and absolute sincerity (*ikhlas*) and warned against complacency, vainglory, and hypocrisy (*riya'*). On these points, Sari's teaching was in agreement with another prominent ascetic-mystic of the age, al-Harith al-Muhasibi (d. 857). Unlike the individuals just mentioned, al-Muhasibi happened to be a prolific writer, whose written legacy reflects his intense and occasionally tortuous quest for truth, purity of thought and deed, and eventually salvation. His emphasis on introspection as a way to bring out the true motives of one's behavior earned him his sobriquet "al-Muhasibi," which means "one who monitors or takes account of oneself." By scrupulously examining the genuine motives of one's actions, argued al-Muhasibi, one can detect and eliminate from them any traces of hypocrisy, self-conceit, and complacency. Although al-Muhasibi's attempts to "theorize" about mystical experience were spurned by some of his Sufi contemporaries as an undesirable "innovation" (*bid'a*), there is little doubt that they contributed in significant ways to the formation of the so-called Sufi science (*'ilm al-tasawwuf*) of the Baghdad school. Moreover, the doyen of the Baghdadi Sufis, Abu 'l-Qasim al-Junayd (d. 910), cultivated a close friendship with al-Muhasibi and was influenced by his Sufi "psychology."

Later Sufi literature portrays al-Junayd as the greatest representative of Baghdad Sufism, who embodied its "sober" strain as opposed to the "intoxicated" one associated with the sayings and actions of Abu Yazid al-Bistami, al-Hallaj, and al-Shibli and their like. Like al-Muhasibi, al-Junayd combined scholarly pursuits with "mystical science," posing as both a legal scholar and a Sufi master (*shaykh*). He was convinced that the most daring aspects of Sufi science should be protected from outsiders who have not themselves "tasted" mystical knowledge and experiences. Hence, his "profoundly subtle, meditated language" that "formed the nucleus of all subsequent elaboration."[13] A popular spiritual master, al-Junayd penned numerous epistles to his disciples, as well as short treatises on mystical themes. Couched in a recondite imagery and arcane technical terminology peculiar to Sufi science, al-Junayd's discourses reiterate the theme, first clearly reasoned by him, that since all things have their origin in God, they are reabsorbed, after their dispersion in the empirical universe, back into the unfathomable mystery of divine unity. On the level of the mystic's personal experience, this dynamic of the reabsorption/dispersion corresponds the state of "passing away" of the human self (*fana'*) in the contemplation of God's absolute oneness, followed by its return to the multiplicity of the world and life in God (*baqa'*). As a result of this experiential "journey," the mystic acquires a new, superior awareness of both God and his creation that cannot be obtained by the study of books or rational reflection. Unlike the "intoxicated" Sufis, who considered *fana'* to be the ultimate goal of the mystic, al-Junayd viewed it as an intermediate (and imperfect) stage of the mystic's spiritual development. On the social plane, al-Junayd preached social responsibility and advised his followers against violating social conventions and public decorum. The accomplished mystic should keep his intimate relations with God to himself and share them only with those who have themselves had similar experiences. He is said to have disavowed his erstwhile disciple Husayn b. Mansur al-Hallaj (d. 922) for making public his intimate interactions with the divine reality. Al-Junayd's prominence as a great, if not the greatest, master of the "classical age" of Sufism (ninth–eleventh centuries) is attested to by the fact that he figures in the spiritual genealogy of practically every Sufi community.

Several individuals in al-Junayd's entourage form a distinct group due to their shared single-minded preoccupation with love of God. One of them was Abu 'l-Husayn al-Nuri (d. 907). Unlike his teacher, al-Nuri shunned any theoretical discussion of the nature of mystical experience and defined Sufism as, first and foremost, "the abandonment of all pleasures of the carnal soul." In seeking to express his intense passion for the divine beloved, al-Nuri frequently availed himself of erotic imagery, which drew upon him the ire of some learned members of the caliph's entourage who charged him and his followers with blasphemy and even attempted to have them executed. Characteristically, in that episode, al-Junayd is said to have avoided arrest by claiming to be a "jurist" (*faqih*), not a Sufi.

A similar, ecstatic type of mysticism was espoused by al-Shibli (d. 946), whose unbridled longing for God manifested itself in bizarre behavior and scandalous public utterances. He indulged in eccentricities, such as burning precious aromatic substances under the tail of his donkey, tearing up expensive garments, tossing gold coins into the crowds, and speaking openly of his identity with the divine.[14] Faced with the prospect of execution on charges of heresy, he affected madness.

Our description of the Baghdad school would be incomplete without a mention of al-Hallaj, whose ecstatic mysticism bears a close resemblance to that of al-Nuri and al-Shibli but who, unlike them, paid with his life for his "intoxication" with divine love. His trial and public execution in Baghdad in 922 on charges of "heresy" demonstrated the dramatic conflict between the spirit of communal solidarity promoted by Sunni scholars (*'ulama'*) and the individualistic, at times antisocial aspirations of lovelorn mystics—a conflict al-Junayd and his "sober" followers sought to overcome by preaching secrecy. Al-Hallaj's trial took place against the background of political intrigues and struggle for power at the caliph's court in Baghdad into which he was drawn, perhaps against his will (see Figure 13.1). His public preaching of the possibility of a loving union between man and God was construed by some religious and state officials as rabble-rousing and sedition. On the other hand, his behavior violated the code of prudence and secrecy advocated by the leaders of the capital's Sufi community, who followed in the footsteps of al-Junayd. Finally, al-Hallaj was also accused of public miracle working with a view to attracting the masses to his message. This too contradicted the ethos of "sober" Sufism requiring that mystics conceal supernatural powers granted to them by God. All this—and perhaps also jealousy of his popularity—lead to his disavowal and condemnation by his fellow Sufis, including al-Junyad and al-Shibli. Whereas the theme of union between the mystic lover and the divine beloved was

Figure 13.1 The Hanging of Husayn Ibn Mansur al-Hallaj
Wikimedia Commons

not unique to al-Hallaj, his speaking about it in public and his desire to achieve it through voluntary martyrdom were unprecedented and scandalous. In the subsequent history of Islamic mysticism, al-Hallaj came to exemplify the "intoxicated" brand of mysticism that was embraced, apart from him, by such Persian mystics as Abu Yazid al-Bistami (d. 875), Ibn Khafif (d. 982), al-Kharaqani (d. 1033), and Ruzbihan al-Baqli (d. 1209).[15]

The age of al-Junayd and al-Hallaj was rich in charismatic and mystical talent. Among their contemporaries Sahl al-Tustari of Basra (d. 896) deserves special mention. He and his followers represented a distinct strain of Sufi piety that assigned a special role to the practice of a constant "recollection" of God (*dhikr*) in order to "imprint" his name in the enunciator's heart. After the mystic has completely internalized *dhikr*, God, according to al-Tustari, begins to effect his own recollection in the heart of his faithful servant. This leads to a loving union between the mystic and his Creator. Al-Tustari's mystical commentary on the Qur'an aimed at plumbing its hidden, esoteric depths with a view to linking Qur'anic images and allusions to the mystic's spiritual and cognitive progress to God.[16]

As mentioned, the Sufism of Iraq and, more specifically, the Baghdad school was not the only ascetic and mystical movement within the confines of the caliphate. In the eastern provinces of the 'Abbasid Empire, it had to compete with its local versions, such as the Malamatiyya and the Karramiyya. The eventual ascendancy of the Iraqi and Baghdadi version of Sufism has not yet found a satisfactory explanation. One reason for its success may lie in "the efficacy of its powerful synthesis of individualist and communalist tendencies," which allowed it to surpass its rivals "by sapping them of their spiritual thrust and absorbing their institutional features."[17] One can also point out the role of powers-that-be in deliberately promoting Baghdadi Sufism against its rivals, which eventually disappeared from the historical scene. If this assumption is correct, the rulers of the age found the loosely structured, urban, middle-class Sufism to be more "manageable" than the lower-class and largely rural Karramiyya or the secretive and independent Malamatiyya.[18] Credit should be given to Sufis of the Baghdad school for aggressively disseminating its teachings and practices among pious publics outside Iraq. This process was accompanied by the emergence in Khurasan and Transoxiana of a considerable body of apologetic Sufi literature that is the subject of the next section.

The Systematization of the Sufi Tradition

The tenth and eleventh centuries witnessed a rapid expansion and growing sophistication of Sufi lore. It was classified and committed to writing by the Sufi authors who can be considered the master architects of Sufi science. They discussed such issues as the exemplary ways of the great Sufi masters of old, Sufi terminology, the nature of miracles, the rules of companionship in Sufi communities, Sufi ritual practices, and so on. Such discussions were accompanied by constant references to the authority of Sufism's "founding fathers," including those whose lives predated its emergence as an independent movement in Islam. In this way, the major paragons of ascetic and mystical piety at the dawn of Islam were declared to be part of the Sufi tradition. This was quite consistent with the apologetic agenda of Sufi writers of the tenth and eleventh centuries—to demonstrate that Sufi teachings and practices were in full agreement with the Sunni creed as laid down by the founding fathers of Islamic legal theory and theology, whose legacy was discussed in Chapters 9 and 10 of this book. By availing themselves of quotations from the Qur'an and the Sunna (such those mentioned earlier in this chapter), they endeavored to prove that Sufism was part and parcel of Islam since its very inception and that the Sufis were true heirs to the Prophet and his closest companions.

The earliest surviving Sufi treatise "That Which is Essential (or Basic) in Sufism" (*Kitab al-luma' fi 'l-tasawwuf*) belongs to Abu Nasr al-Sarraj of Khurasan (d. 988). He associated with the major members of al-Junayd's circle in Baghdad, as well as the followers of Sahl al-Tustari in Basra. Al-Sarraj saw his goal in demonstrating the preeminence of Sufis over all other men of religion. According to al-Sarraj, Sufis and Sufis alone were able to live up to the high standards of personal piety and worship enjoined by the Muslim scripture and the first generations of Muslims. They thus belonged to the spiritual "elite" (*khassa*) of the Muslim community to whom its ordinary members (*'amma*) should turn for guidance. Within this Sufi elite, al-Sarraj identified three categories: the beginners, the accomplished Sufi masters, and the "cream of the cream" of Sufism, whom he called the "people of the true realities" (*ahl al-haqa'iq*). Al-Sarraj's work represents an early attempt by a Sufi to categorize mystical experiences by placing them into a pre-fabricated classificatory system corresponding to the three levels of spiritual attainment just outlined. In addition, al-Sarraj tried to demarcate the limits of Sufi "orthodoxy" in order to cleanse Sufism of what he considered to be the errors and excesses of certain Sufis.

The work of Abu Talib al-Makki (d. 996), "The Nourishment for Hearts" (*Qut al-qulub*), presents the teachings of the Basran school of piety associated al-Tustari and his followers. It is reminiscent of a standard manual of religious jurisprudence in which meticulous discussions of the mainstream Islamic rituals and articles of the Islamic creed are interspersed with quintessential Sufi themes, such as the "states" and "stations" of the mystical path, the permissibility and nature of gainful employment, techniques of pious self-scrutiny and so on. As with al-Sarraj, Abu Talib confidently states that the Sufi teachings and practices reflect the authentic custom of the Prophet and his companions, "transmitted by al-Hasan al-Basri and maintained scrupulously intact by relays of [Sufi] teachers and disciples."[19] Abu Talib's work was highly influential. It formed the foundation of the celebrated "Revivification of Religious Sciences" (*Ihya' 'ulum al-din*) of Abu Hamid al-Ghazali (d. 1111) that will be discussed further on.

To another famous Sufi author of the age, Abu Bakr al-Kalabadhi (d. 990 or 994) of Bukhara in Central Asia, belongs another Sufi textbook.[20] Although it originated in a region located far from Iraq, its author exhibits an intimate knowledge of Iraqi Sufism and its major exponents. As with other advocates of Sufism, al-Kalabadhi saw his main task in demonstrating Sufism's compliance with the principles of Sunni Islam, as represented by both Hanafi and Shafi'i schools of theology and law. Quoting the Sufi authorities of the Baghdad school, al-Kalabadhi meticulously described the principal "stations" of the mystical path: repentance, abstinence, patience, poverty, humility, fear, pious scrupulousness in word and deed, trust in God, contentment with one's earthly portion, recollection of God's name, intimacy, nearness to God, and love of God.[21]

Highly influential expositions of "Sufi science" were written by the Khurasani Sufis Abu 'Abd al-Rahman al-Sulami (d. 1021) and 'Abd al-Karim al-Qushayri (d. 1072). The former is the author of the earliest extant biographical account of Sufi masters entitled "Generations of the Sufis" (*Tabaqat al-sufiyya*) and an influential collection of allegorical and as ascetic-mystical commentaries on the Qur'an.[22] Al-Sulami was intimately familiar and sympathetic with the Malamatiyya ascetic and mystical tradition of Khurasan and included a description of its teachings into his Sufi tracts. Al-Sulami's intellectual legacy became the foundation of all subsequent Sufi literature, including the "Epistle on Sufism" by al-Qushayri (*al-Risala al-qushayriyya fi 'ilm al-tasawwuf*)—admittedly the most widely read and influential treatise on Sufi science that is still being studied in Sufi circles. After providing an account of Sufi biographies, al-Qushayri presented the major concepts and terms of the Sufism of his age, followed by a detailed account of various Sufi practices, including listening to music during "spiritual concerts" (*sama'*), miracles of Sufi saints, rules of companionship and travel, and, finally, "spiritual advice" to Sufi novices (*muridun*). Several other Sufi works were written around that time, including "The Ornament of Saints" (*Hilyat al-awliya'*)—a massive collection of Sufi biographies by Abu Nu'aym al-Isbahani (d. 1038); "The Unveiling of That Which Is Hidden" (*Kash al-mahjub*)—the first Sufi manual in Persian; and the numerous treatises of the Sufi of the Hanbali legal and theological school 'Abdallah al-Ansari (d. 1089) of Herat (Afghanistan). Given the diversity of intellectual backgrounds and scholarly affiliations of these Sufi writers, their literary production displays a surprising uniformity in that they refer to basically the same concepts, individual, terms, anecdotes, precedents, and practices. This fact indicates that by the first half of the eleventh century, the Baghdadi-Iraqi Sufi tradition had already stabilized and spread as far as Central Asia and the Caucasus.[23] These writings show a concerted effort on the part of their authors to bring Sufism into the fold of Sunni Islam by emphasizing its complete consistency with the teachings and practices of Islam's "pious ancestors" (*salaf*). This tendency was brought to fruition in the life and work of the celebrated Sunni theologian Abu Hamid al-Ghazali (d. 1111).

The Maturity of Sufi Science: Al-Ghazali the Conciliator

A naturally gifted man, al-Ghazali, originally from Iran, established himself as the leading Sunni theologian and jurist of his day. After serving as a professor of the prestigious Nizamíyya religious college in Baghdad, he was suddenly afflicted with a nervous illness (1095) and withdrew from public life into an eleven-year spiritual retreat, during which he composed a succession of books including his greatest masterpiece, "The Revivification of Religious Sciences" (*Ihya' 'ulum al-din*) and his autobiography "Deliverance from Error" (*al-Munqidh min al-dalal)*. The latter provides a poignant account of his difficult quest for truth and certainty. Upon examining the most influential systems of thought current his epoch (namely, rationalist theology, the messianic teachings of Isma'ilism and Hellenistic philosophy) al-Ghazali arrived at the idea of the superiority of intuitive, mystical "unveiling" over all other available methods of obtaining certain knowledge. According to al-Ghazali, Sufi morals and spiritual discipline were indispensable in delivering the believer from doubt and self-conceit and in instilling in him intellectual and spiritual serenity, which, in turn, would lead him to salvation in the Hereafter.[24] Concrete ways to achieve this serenity and salvation are detailed in the *Ihya'*—a synthesis and amplification of the ascetic and mystical concepts and practices outlined in the classical Sufi works enumerated above. Al-Ghazali wanted his *Ihya'* to serve as a comprehensive guide for the devout Muslim to every aspect of religious life from daily worship to the purification of the heart and advancement along the personal path to God. Addressed to the general audience, this work highlighted the practical moral and ethical aspects of Sufism, which al-Ghazali presented as being in perfect harmony with the precept of mainstream Sunni Islam. The more esoteric aspects of his thought can be found in his "Niche for the Lights" (*Mishkat al-anwar*), a mystical meditation on the "Light Verse" of the Qur'an (24:35), in which God presents himself simultaneously as the light of truth and existence.[25] Al-Ghazali's "illuminationist" cosmology and sophisticated theory of mystical knowledge received further elaboration in the work of later Sufi thinkers, especially Yahya al-Suhrawardi (d. 1191) and Ibn 'Arabi (d. 1240).

Al-Ghazali undoubtedly performed a great service to devout Muslims of every level of education by presenting obedience to the internalized prescriptions of the Shari'a as a sure and meaningful way to salvation. His Sufi lodge (*khanaqa*) at Tus (near present-day Mashhad, Iran), where he retired toward the end of his life and where he and his disciples lived together, can be seen as an attempt to implement his pious precepts in real life. To what extent al-Ghazali can be considered the ultimate "conciliator" between mainstream Sunni theology and law, on the one hand, and Sufism, on the other, is difficult to ascertain. The success of his *Ihya'* is based more on his imposing reputation as a Sunni scholar "who commanded the respect of all but the narrowest of the orthodox"[26] rather than to his innovative reinterpretation of the Sufi tradition. Nevertheless, there is little doubt that his enthusiastic endorsement of Sufi morals and ethics were of critical importance in making Sufism a respectable and laudable option for both Sunni *'ulamá'* and the rank-and-file members of the Sunni *umma*.

Al-Ghazali's versatility aptly reflects the complexity and sophistication of Islamic culture, in which Sufism was playing an increasingly important role. He was instrumental in fusing elements of various Islamic teachings and practices into a comprehensive worldview and lifestyle that formed the ideological foundation of the nascent Sufi "orders."

Sufism as Literature

Although the goals of poetic expression and mystical experience would seem to be quite distinct (namely, self-assertion as opposed to self-annihilation in the divine or a silent contemplation of God as opposed to a creative verbalization of personal sentiment), under certain conditions they may become complementary, if not identical. Their underlying affinity springs from their common use of symbol and parable as a means to convey subtle experiences that elude conceptualization in a rational discourse. In the same way as poetical vision cannot be captured and dissected by a cut-and-dried rational examination, mystical experience avoids being reduced to a sum total of concrete and noncontradictory statements. Both poetry and mystical experience carry emotional rather than factual content; both depend, in great part, on a stream of subtle, elusive associations for their effect. It is therefore little wonder that mystical experience is often bound intimately with poetic expression. Both the poetry and the experience are couched in the formative symbols of the individual's spiritual and intellectual tradition and shaped by the totality of his or her personal predisposition and intellectual environment.

This being the case, it is only natural, then, for mystical experience to be bound intimately with poetic inspiration and consequently with poetic expression. It is with these general considerations in mind that we should approach the work of Sufism's greatest poets, Farid al-Din 'Attar (d. between 1190 and 1230), Jalal al-Din Rumi (d. 1273), and Jami (d. 1492).

Farid al-Din 'Attar of Nishapur, Iran, is often seen as the greatest mystical poet of Iran after Jalal al-Din Rumi, who learned much from him. The genre of his most important writings is couplet-poems (*mathnawi*), which was to become a trademark of Persian mystical poetry from then on. 'Attar's *mathnawi* usually tell a single frame-story, which, in the course of the narrative, is embellished by numerous incidental stories and narrative vignettes.[27] His more esoteric poems are inward-looking and visionary in character; they show little interest in the events of the external world. Here a few principal ideas are pursued with intensity and great emotion and couched in intricate parables. Among such recurring ideas are the ecstatic annihilation of the mystic in God (*fana'*); the underlying unity of all being (there is nothing other than God, and all things are derived from and return to him); the knowledge of the mystic's own self (giving him the key to the vital mysteries of God and of the universe); the need of every seeker of God for a Sufi master (*shaykh*) to achieve spiritual progress and avoid delusion; and so on. 'Attar's works are full of references to supersensory Sufi realization (*ma'rifa*), which the author presents as superior to all other types of knowing. He availed himself freely of the sayings and stories of earlier Sufi masters, among whom he was particularly fascinated with the tragic figure of al-Hallaj.

Of 'Attar's nonpoetic works, special mention should be made of his "Memorial of the [Sufi] Saints" (*Tadhkirat al-awliyá'*)—a collection of anecdotes about and sayings of the great Muslim mystics before his time. Here 'Attar's literary propensities take precedence over his concern for historical accuracy: he freely embellishes the dry, factual accounts of the older Sufi biographers with fanciful details, entertaining stories, and legends. Whereas such literary additions have rendered 'Attar's Sufi biographies unreliable as sources of historical data, they tell us a great deal about the author's intellectual preferences and religious views, as well his vision of the ideal Sufi master.[28]

The family of Jalal al-Din Rumi, whose followers reverently call "Our Master" (*mawlana*), migrated from Balkh in present-day Afghanistan to Konya in present-day Turkey on the eve of the Mongol invasions (see Figure 13.2). A turning point in Rumi's life was the arrival in Konya in 1244 of the wandering dervish nicknamed "The Sun of Tabriz"[29] (Shams-i Tabriz)—"a wildly unpredictable man who defied all conventions and preached the self-sufficiency of each individual in his search for the divine."[30] In Shams-i Tabriz, Rumi found his muse and an earthly embodiment of divine beauty. Put differently, through Shams Rumi discovered the genuine meaning of his life and art. Rumi's admiration for Shams-i Tabriz transformed him from an ordinary mortal into a divinely inspired poet of great stature. Upon Shams' tragic death in 1247, Rumi suffered a deep psychological crisis, which he tried to overcome by composing poems and participating in Sufi concerts and dances in the hope of finding his friend in his own soul. The real history of the Sufi order founded by Rumi (which came to be known as the Mawlawiyya—after Rumi's honorific title) began with his son Sultan Walad (Sultan Veled; d. 712/1312), whose able

Figure 13.2 The Meeting of Jalal al-Din Rumi and Molla Shams al-Din

Mohammad Tahir Suhravardī/Public Domain/Wikimedia Commons

leadership secured it high prestige and wide acceptance among the Muslims of Anatolia. Although originally recruited from among the craftsmen, the order gradually won over many members of the Anatolian upper class. A distinctive feature of the Mawlawiyya is the preeminent role that its leaders assigned to music and dancing. With time, these performances have been regularized, culminating in the dance of the "whirling dervishes" that is known and admired across the globe. The Mawlawi dancing rituals reflect the highly emotional and spiritualistic world outlook characteristic of the founder and his poetry.

Rumi saw himself as neither a philosopher nor a poet in the usual meaning of these words. Rather, he comes across as a passionate lover of God and his creation, unconcerned about societal conventions and religious stereotypes. In fashioning his own distinctive vision of the world, Rumi drew constantly on the Sufi tradition systematized and elaborated by its major representatives. He viewed all God's creatures as being irresistibly attracted to the source of their existence, their Maker, in the same way as trees rise from the dark soil and extend their branches and leaves toward the sun. As far as God's human creatures are concerned, their inherent longing for their Creator reaches its climax in the state of a mystical annihilation of the human self in the divine essence (*fana'*), which, however, is never complete, except in death. As the flame of a candle continues to exist despite being outshone by the radiance of the sun, so does the mystic's individuality in the overwhelming presence of his Lord. In the state of *fana'*, he becomes both human and divine and, as a consequence, may be tempted to declare his complete identity with God, as al-Hallaj once did. Due the intensely personal and "ecstatic" character of Rumi's style, it found practically no successful imitators in later Persian poetry. In Rumi we find a paragon of Sufi artistic creativity, who harmoniously combined mystical experience with poetic inspiration and literary talent.

'Abd al-Rahman Jami came from the district of Jam near Herat in present-day Afghanistan. As a youth, he developed a deep passion for mysticism and decided to embark on the mystical path. His first spiritual director was Sa'd al-Din Muhammad Kashghari, a foremost disciple of and the organizational successor to the founder of the Naqshbandiyya Sufi brotherhood, Baha' al-Din Naqshband (d. 1389). Later on, Jami made friends with another influential Naqshbandi leader 'Ubaydallah Ahrar (d. 1490), whom he admired and whom he mentioned frequently in his poetical works.[31] Jami spent most of his life in Herat under the patronage of the Timurid sultan Husayn Bayqara (r. 1469–1506), dividing his time between religious studies, poetry, and mystic meditation.

Jami's written legacy in Persian and Arabic includes a giant biographical history of Sufism "The Breaths of Divine Intimacy" (*Nafahat al-uns*) that draws on 'Attar's "Memorial of the Saints" and the works of earlier Sufi writers, such as al-Sulami, al-Ansari, and al-Qushayri. Jami's Arabic treatises on various difficult aspects of Sufi philosophy are masterpieces of lucidity and concision. They reveal his deep indebtedness to Ibn 'Arabi and his philosophically minded followers, whose recondite mystical concepts he sought to make accessible to a less sophisticated audience interested in Sufi cosmology and gnoseology.[32] His writings intricately mingle mystical poetry with didactic, biographical, and metaphysical narratives, providing a helpful summation of various strands of the Sufi tradition current in his age.

Sufi Metaphysics: The Impact of Ibn 'Arabi

As mentioned, Jami was profoundly influenced by Ibn 'Arabi (d. 1240).[33] In this he was not alone; there was hardly a mystical thinker in that age or later on who was not. Although Ibn 'Arabi spent the first half of his life in Islamic Spain (al-Andalus) and North Africa (the Maghrib), his talents came to full bloom in the East, where he composed most of his famous works—including his controversial masterpieces, "The Bezels of Wisdom" (*Fusus al-hikam)* and "The Meccan Revelations" (*al-Futuhat al-makkiyya)*—and trained his most consequential disciple, Sadr al-Din al-Qunawi (d. 1274), who spread his ideas among the Persian-speaking scholars of Anatolia (Turkey), who then disseminated them in Iran.[34]

Ibn 'Arabi's legacy consists of fifty to sixty works, although some modern scholars credit him with a much higher number of writings.[35] Nowhere in these writings did Ibn 'Arabi provide a succinct and final account of his basic tenets. On the contrary, he seems to have been deliberately elusive in presenting his principal ideas and took great care to offset them with numerous disclaimers and often recondite etymological deliberations. In seeking to convey to the reader his personal mystical insights into the nature of religion, God, and the universe, Ibn 'Arabi made skillful use of "symbolic images that evoke emergent associations rather than fixed propositions."[36] Although familiar with the syllogistic methods of reasoning employed by the Muslim philosophers (*falásifa*), he always emphasized that they fell short of capturing the elusive dynamic of oneness and plurality that characterizes the relationship between God and human beings, between human beings and the universe. To communicate this complex dynamic, Ibn 'Arabi availed himself of shocking paradoxes and mindboggling puzzles to awaken his readers to what he regarded as the real state of the universe, namely, the underlying oneness and common source of all of its elements. Oftentimes, his discourses are perceived by the modern reader as a mishmash of seemingly disparate themes and motifs operating on parallel discursive levels from exegesis to poetry and mythology to jurisprudence and speculative theology. Ibn 'Arabi's treatises explored, among other things, such controversial themes as the status of prophecy vis-à-vis sainthood; the concept of the perfect man as an ultimate reflection of God's image in the created world; the relationship between the human "microcosm" and its cosmic counterpart, the "great man"; the elusive and ever changing self-manifestation of the divine absolute in the events and phenomena of the empirical universe; the different aspects and realms of the divine will; and the allegoric and esoteric aspects of the Qur'an and Sunna. He addressed these issues in ways that were "never really repeated or adequately imitated by any subsequent Islamic author."[37] The goal of Ibn 'Arabi's deliberately ambiguous discourses was to "carry the reader outside the work itself into the life and cosmos which it is attempting to interpret."[38] They were "meant to function as a sort of spiritual mirror, reflecting and revealing the inner intentions, assumptions and predilections of each reader . . . with profound clarity."[39] It is, therefore, hardly surprising that each Islamic century produced new interpretations of Ibn 'Arabi's key ideas. Everyone has found something in the Sufi's intellectual legacy that resonated with his or her own personal experiences and world outlook.

It is not the place here to detail Ibn 'Arabi's complex metaphysical and gnoseological doctrines. Suffice it to say that he viewed the world as a product of God's self-reflection that urged his unique and indivisible essence to reveal itself in the constantly changing things and phenomena of the material universe. The created universe (*khalq*) was thus envisioned by Ibn 'Arabi as a giant mirror in which the absolute divine reality (*haqq*) could contemplate its innumerable potentialities. This idea scandalized many medieval *'ulamá'*, who hastened to accuse Ibn 'Arabi of being a proponent of the substantial identity of God and world, which contravened the doctrine of God's absolute transcendence so central to the mainstream Islamic theology of the age. Concerned about the dangerous moral implications of Ibn 'Arabi's ideas for Muslim society,[40] a number of influential *'ulamá'* condemned him as the founder of the heretical doctrine of oneness or unity of being (*wahdat al-wujud*) understood as pantheism pure and simple.[41]

Major Intellectual and Practical Trends in Later Sufism

Al-Ghazali's and Ibn 'Arabi's complex synthesis of Sufi moral and ethical teachings; mystical exegesis; Neoplatonic metaphysics and gnoseology; Gnosticism; and Sunni theological thought aptly captures the internal richness of later Sufism. Thanks to this richness, Sufism was able to meet the intellectual and spiritual needs of a broad variety of potential constituencies—from a humble Qur'an reader or stall keeper of the bazaar to a refined scholar at the ruler's court, as well as various social groups between these two poles. Contrary to a commonly held Orientalist assumption, Sufism's philosophical and metaphysical doctrines were not just "foreign implants" grafted onto the pristine body of Islam. Rather, they were a natural outgrowth of certain tendencies inherent in Muslim beliefs and practices from the very outset. Early Sufi masters already viewed God as the only real agent in this world, to whose will and action the believer should submit unconditionally. In the eleventh–twelfth centuries, this idea evolved—probably not without an influence of Ibn Sina's ontology[42]—into a vision of God as not just the only agent but also the only essence possessed of real and unconditional existence. This vision, which may loosely be defined as unitive or monistic, was rebuffed by the great Hanbali scholar Ibn Taymiyya (d. 1328), who condemned its followers as heretical "unificationists" (*ittihadiyya*) bent on undermining divine transcendence and blurring the all-important borderline between God and his creatures. Nevertheless, Ibn 'Arabi's metaphysics and gnoseology have decidedly shaped Sufi perceptions of God and the cosmos until today.

In addition to predominance of Ibn 'Arabi's teaching, the evolution of Sufism after the twelfth century was characterized by the progressive institutionalization of a number of distinctively Sufi rituals and meditation techniques, including retreat (*khalwa*), collective recollection of God (*dhikr*), and ritualized collective "listening" (*sama '*) to music and mystical poetry. These practices served as means to intensify the relationship between the mystics and God and to open the former to the outpourings of divine grace. During *sama'* sessions, music was played and mystical poetry recited in order to induce in the listeners a heightened perception of God's presence and loving care for his creatures. This, in turn, prompted some sensitive members of the audience to experience ecstatic trances (*wajd*), which could occasionally result in a spontaneous dance, loud shouting, or frantic rhythmical movements. In addition to *sama'*, Sufis could achieve changed states of consciousness and gain supersensory, intuitive insights known as "unveilings" (*mukashafat*), by means of individual meditation on the meaning of Qur'anic verses or frequent, occasionally incessant recitation of Sufi litanies (*awrad*; sing. *wird*).

Drawing on al-Junayd's legacy of prudence and social responsibility, advocates of the "sober" strain of Sufi piety tried to purge it of ecstatic, uncontrollable elements by re-emphasizing moral and ethical behavior and humility as the surest way to God. Compliance with the norms of the Shari'a was seen by the "sober minded" as crucial for the success of the Sufi's efforts to reach proximity with God. This Shari'a-based and community-oriented version of Sufism found eloquent exponents in the famous preachers of Baghdad 'Abd al-Qadir al-Jilani (d. 1166) and Abu Hafs 'Umar al-Suhrawardi (d. 1234). The latter's Sufi manual in Arabic "Gifts of Mystical Knowledge" (*'Awarif al-ma 'arif*), together with its later Persian adaptations, has served as a standard textbook for many generations of Muslim ascetics and mystics.

The Rise and Spread of Sufi Brotherhoods (*Tariqas*)

From the twelfth century onward, the ascetic and mystical lifestyle was increasingly cultivated within Sufi associations or orders (*túruq*; sing. *taríqa*), some of which are still active today. Originally housed in relatively small hostels and lodges (Arab. *zawiya*; Persian *khanaqa*), Sufi communities gradually acquired freestanding complexes of buildings where its members could engage in collective and individual worship undisturbed by the hustle and bustle of daily life. The conduct of members of such Sufi communities was now governed by codes that were enforced by a hierarchically structured leadership. While in the tenth and eleventh centuries, the teacher–disciple relation was relatively informal with the disciple (*murid*) being free to study under several different masters (*shuyukh*; sing. *shaykh*); with the growth and spread of large Sufi orders, it was formalized and strictly regimented. Now, the head of a Sufi *tariqa* was capable of supporting his often quite numerous disciples from pious donations provided by temporal rulers, high-ranking government officials (and their wives), as well as blessing-seeking nobility, wealthy merchants, and members of the military elite. In return, the *shaykh* could demand undivided loyalty of his adherents. The training technique of an individual Sufi master came to be known as his "way" or "method" (*taríq*). Metonymically, it came to be applied to the entire Sufi community established by the founder, which, as a rule, assumed his name. The head of a Sufi order was usually elected from among the deceased leader's closest lieutenants. However, the hereditary principle of succession from father to son was also quite common. After the novice had completed his studies under the guidance of a Sufi master, he was granted a license (*ijaza*) to instruct his own disciples in accordance with the master's spiritual method. His new status as an independent teacher was symbolized by the ritual bestowal—either public or private—of a Sufi robe (*khirqa*) upon the graduate (see Figure 13.3). The typical outfit of a Sufi consisted of a patched cloak (*muraqqa'*), a prayer rug (*sajjada*), a rosary (*misbaha*), and a beggar's bowl (*kashkul*). With time, each Sufi order acquired a distinctive dress code, headgear, and colors that set it apart from other Sufi communities.[43]

Figure 13.3 Itinerant Sufis (dervishes) in Festive Costumes in the City of Tashkent (Central Asia) (nineteenth-century Russian painting)

akg-images

The major early *taríqa*s—the Qadiriyya, Rifaʿiyya, Suhrawardiyya, Chishtiyya, Kubrawi-yya, Naqshbandiyya, and Shadhiliyya were formed in the thirteenth-fourteenth centuries. Each of them had its own character and was initially associated with a particular geographical region. With time, some *taríqa*s spread beyond their places of origin to become part of an international network of Sufi communities. Thus, the Qadiriyya, which originated in Baghdad in the late twelfth century, gradually expanded across the entire Muslim world and is now found from West Africa to India and Indonesia and as far as China. Likewise, the Naqshbandi-yya, founded in Central Asia, thrived in India and the Middle East to become probably the most influential and well organized Sufi community worldwide.[44] Presently, its branches can be found in the Caucasus, the Volga region of Russia, Iraq, Kurdistan, Egypt, and North Africa. The Shadhiliyya emerged in the Maghrib, gained a wide popularity in Egypt and then spread to Yemen and Indonesia. Despite their international outreach, these and other orders have, for the most part, remained decentralized; their regional branches had little in common except for a shared initiatic line, litanies, *dhikr* formulas, and ritual requirements, all of which are usually attributed to the eponymous founder. The political and social roles of the Sufi *túruq* have varied dramatically across time and space and have usually been determined by the per-sonalities of their leaders and the concrete social and geopolitical circumstances of their existence. Therefore, it is very difficult to make any generalizations about any given Sufi order. Nevertheless, such generalizations abound in both popular imagination and literary sources. Thus, the Qadiriyya is famous for its emphasis on the role of its founder, who is believed to be maintaining his guiding and protective presence among his followers in all epochs and locations. Apart from this belief, however, its regional branches have precious little in common. The "loud," energetic *dhikr* and exotic dances of Qadiri dervishes are often con-trasted with the "silent" *dhikr* and emotional restraint of the Naqshbandiyya, which is usually considered by outside observers to be more "sober" and "Shariʿa-abiding." The Rifaʿiyya of Egypt, Iraq, and the Balkans, which is famous for its "howling" *dhikr* and spectacular public performances that involve dervishes walking on live coals, eating glass, and the piercing of their flesh without bleeding (to demonstrate the supernatural spiritual powers of their masters), is viewed as "ecstatic" and even "libertine." Similar generalizations are often made about the orders' stance vis-à-vis state authorities—the Naqshbandiyya being regarded as prone to cooperate with or manipulate them in contrast to the more standoffish attitude of the Chishti-yya and the Shadhiliyya. However, in the end, one and the same order could behave differently under different leaders and in different historical conditions.[45] The distinct identity of each Sufi community is based on the following characteristics:

1   The community's spiritual genealogy (*silsila*),[46] which links its present head to the prophet Muhammad. It may have thirty to forty "rungs." The *silsila* serves as the major source of legitimacy and identity for the community's leader and his or (rarely) her following.
2   The conditions and rituals for admission into the community. Some Sufi orders take men and women, some only men. The novice (*murid*) owes his or her master (*shaykh*) uncon-ditional obedience and is required to seek the master's advice and instruction on all matters of worship, social behavior, and personal life. Initiation rituals differed from one Sufi community to another but are reminiscent of those practiced in medieval artisan guilds with which Sufi orders used to be closely connected.
3   Instructions concerning the methods and formulas of "remembering God" (*dhikr*), which are peculiar to every *taríqa* and which, like the *silsila*, give it a distinctive identity. The instructions stipulate how one should breathe and behave while performing a *dhikr*, as well as the frequency with which *dhikr* formulas should be recited; they also allow or disallow the use of musical instruments and dance during *dhikr* sessions.

4   Instructions regarding the terms and conditions of retreat or seclusion (*khalwa*), that is, the voluntary withdrawal from communal life by the community's members to devote themselves to pious meditation, self-reflection, and silent *dhikr*.

5   Rules of fellowship and communal life that regulate relations among the members of a given Sufi community and between the *shaykh* and his followers.

Unlike the sophisticated metaphysical theories previously discussed, which are usually confined to the intellectual elite of the Sufi community or even deliberately concealed from its rank-and-file members, knowledge of the normative literature of the order is required of all its literate members. The illiterate ones learn the rules of conduct and ritual in the course of oral instruction by the *shaykh* of the order or his deputies.

Sufism and the Cult of "Friends of God" (Saints)

Already during their lifetime, some prominent Sufi masters and heads of Sufi orders were treated as "God's [elect] friends" or "saints" (*awliyá'*) by both their followers and the local non-Sufi population. The exemplary piety and "vaulted spirituality" of the *awliyá'* were perceived by the populace as signs of their special status in the eyes of God. Due to their intimate knowledge of human psychology, which they acquired in the course of training their disciples, as well as their perceived or real lack of self-interest, the *awliyá'* often assumed the role of arbitrators in conflicts between different social and kinship groups or mediators between rulers and their subjects. Their mediatory functions further elevated their stature in the eyes of the masses that came to credit them with supernatural, God-given knowledge and the ability to work miracles (*karamát*). The revered status of the *awliyá'* usually did not cease after their death; their tombs frequently became objects of pious visits and even annual pilgrimages (*ziyarát*), accompanied by special ritual activities and trade fairs (see Figure 13.4). Visitors brought votive gifts to Sufi shrines and

Figure 13.4 Saints' Tombs at a Cemetery in Upper Egypt

A. Knysh

Figure 13.5 A Late Evening View of the Selimiye Mosque in Konya, Turkey, the City of Jalal al-Din Rumi
Zeynel Cebeci: CC: Wikimedia Commons

asked the Sufi masters buried therein for blessing and intercession. Legends were circulated about their miraculous and usually beneficial interference in the lives of their followers during their lifetime and after their death. These miracle narratives were written down in numerous hagiographical collections that constitute a considerable segment of Sufi literature. Devotional activities associated with Sufi shrines were condemned by some puritanically minded scholars, such as Ibn Taymiyya (d. 1328), Ibn 'Abd al-Wahhab (d. 1791), al-Shawkani (d. 1834), and, later on, by numerous nineteenth-century Muslim reformers, as a gross violation of the doctrine of divine oneness, which, according in the opinion of the critics, prohibits the Muslims from seeking the assistance of anyone or anything other than God. It should, however, be pointed out that not all of the "saints" were Sufis and that some Sufi orders, especially in recent times, have discouraged acts of worship and devotion at saints' tombs (see Figure 13.5).

Sufism and Shi'ism

Today, Iran is seen as a predominantly, if not exclusively Shi'ite country. As we will see in Chapter 20, this has not always been the case. Up to the beginning of the sixteenth century, Iran's population had been predominantly Sunni, despite the presence in the country of major Shi'ite centers such as Qumm and Mashhad and a large Shi'ite population. The Iranian population was converted to Shi'ism in the aftermath of the takeover of the country by the Shi'ite dynasty known as Safavids (r. 1501–1722). Of the numerous Sufi orders of Iran before the Safavid takeover in 1501, the most prominent were the Kubrawiyya and the Ni'matullahiyya.[47] The former flourished in Central Asia and Khurasan, only to be displaced by the powerful Naqshbandiyya around the seventeenth century. The Nurbakhshiyya and Dhahabiyya offshoots of the Kubrawiyya Sufi order enjoyed a substantial following among the Iranian Shi'ite population. The founder of the Nurbakhshiyya, Sayyid Muhammad Nurbakhsh (d. 1464), presented himself to his followers as the awaited "divinely guided one" (*máhdi*). This claim set him on a collision course with the Timurid Sunni rulers of eastern Iran and Afghanistan, who feared that he may be plotting a messianic rebellion against them. After they had imprisoned him, he seems to have toned down his claims of being the *máhdi* of the age out of fear of being executed. Nonetheless, the order remained suspect in the eyes of Iran's Safavid Shi'ite rulers, who were, like their Sunni counterparts, concerned that its messianic beginnings might be revived by one of its leaders. After some successes in Kashmir, the order has eventually disappeared from the historical scene.

The Ni'matullahiyya, which started as a Sunni order, embraced Shi'ite Islam under the influence of the Safavids, who had adopted Twelver Shi'ism as the state religion. Initially, the order enjoyed good relations with the Safavid court. They were further cemented by marriages between the Ni'matullahi leadership and the ruling family. The relations soured under Shah 'Abbas (r. 1587–1629), after a Ni'matullahi master took part in an antigovernment rebellion. As a result, the order lost the clout it had had with the earlier Safavids and nearly sank into complete oblivion. It made a surprising comeback in the late eighteenth century, when one of its masters gained a large following among the population of major Iranian cities. The resurgence of the Ni'matullahiyya was greeted with hostility on the part of some influential Shi'ite scholars, who viewed themselves as the only legitimate custodians of the Shi'ite religion and were not prepared to share their authority with the "uncouth" Sufi masters. They accused the leaders of the Ni'matullahiyya of espousing "extremist" views and unleashed a campaign of persecutions against them. A number of leading Ni'matullahi *shaykh*s were assassinated on the orders of the renowned Shi'ite scholar Bihbahaní (d. 1801), who became popularly known as "Sufi-Killer." The fortunes of the brotherhood improved under the Qajar shahs of Iran in the late eighteenth and early twentieth centuries. One of the shahs even joined the ranks of the order. In the first decades of the nineteenth century, the Ni'matullahiyya experienced a severe crisis over succession and disintegrated into a congeries of mutually hostile suborders.[48] Its most influential recent leader, Dr. Javád Nurbakhsh (d. 2008), a psychiatrist by profession, managed to recruit many members of high society in Teheran and to build a chain of Ni'matullahi lodges throughout Iran during the reign of the last shah of Iran Muhammad Reza Pehlevi (d. 1980). When the Iranian revolution of 1978–1979 broke out, Dr. Nurbakhsh emigrated to the West, where he continued to promote the teachings of the Ni'matullahiyya among Iranian refuges and Western converts. A prolific writer, his philosophy is aptly summated by the following statement cited on the Michigan Sufi website:

> The spiritual world is different from the intellectual world both in its aim and method. The aim of the spiritual world is to discover the unity of being on an experiential level, to manifest the Divine nature that lies within us. And the method of the spiritual practice is nothing other than love. Love is the binding principle of the universe and the only reliable guide of humanity in its search for the Truth.[49]

The principal disagreement between the Sufis and the Shi'ites is pretty simple. As we remember, the Shi'ites believe that supernatural knowledge and the resultant ability to guide the faithful to salvation belong exclusively to the Shi'ite leaders of the 'Ali-Fátima family line. Any claimant to these qualities who lacks this all-important genealogical credential is seen by Shi'ite scholars as arrogating the exclusive right of the *imam*s, who are called *awliyá'* in the Shi'ite tradition. This fact alone delegitimizes the Sufi masters, who are also called *awliyá'* by their followers, in the eyes of the Shi'ite religious establishment. Nevertheless, during certain historical periods and among some learned members of Shi'ite societies, various versions of Sufism have been tolerated, albeit grudgingly and with serious caveats.[50] To avoid the impression that they have borrowed certain ideas and theories from "the heretical Sufis," Shi'ite intellectuals prefer to call their version of Sufi metaphysics and theory of knowledge either "gnosis" (*'irfan*) or "wisdom" (*hikma*).[51]

Sufism Today

In today's world, Sufism plays a variety of roles that we can touch upon only briefly. Europeans became acquainted with ascetic-mystical aspects of Islam in the course of their colonial ventures in the Muslim world. Diaries of European travelers to the Middle East, Central and South Asia, and Africa feature vivid descriptions of Sufi dervishes, their lodges, and their behavior. Some of these accounts are positive, stressing Sufis' lofty spirituality, piety, and detachment from mundane concerns, while others ridicule their beliefs and shabby costumes or accuse them of engaging in irrational behavior, charlatanism, venality, superstition, and parasitism (see Figure 13.6). The fact that some Sufi orders were directly or indirectly involved in resistance to the West's "civilizing mission" in the Muslim lands led some colonial officials to believe that they presented a major

Figure 13.6 Whirling Dervishes of the Mawlawiyya Order

Claude Vallet/Wikimedia Commons

military threat to Western colonial rule. As such, they had to be studied and kept under close surveillance. Numerous accounts of Sufi institutions compiled by European colonial administrators and military officers often resemble police reports in that they attempt to determine the numerical strength of the *tarīqa*s, their economic foundations, and their potential to mobilize Muslim masses against Western military and civilian authorities in the colonies. The overall tendency of nineteenth-century European literature devoted to Sufism can be described as attempts to detach it from Islam by portraying it as a foreign implant of sorts that was, in its essence, alien to the spirit and letter of Muslim religion. In line with this logic, Western scholars of Islam spared no effort to trace Sufism's origins back to Christian monasticism, Neoplatonic philosophy, Gnosticism, Buddhism, Shamanism, and so on.[52] Only recently, this Western fixation on the "foreign origins" of Sufi Islam has given way to a more productive approach that emphasizes Sufism's roots in and organic growth from the foundational ideas of Islam itself.[53]

Whereas many Western observers have come to admire the rich literary, intellectual, and spiritual legacy of Sufism, since the end of the nineteenth century, it has found itself under attack from many Muslim reformers and modernizers. They accused Sufi masters of cultivating "idle superstitions" and of manipulating the ignorant masses for selfish political or material gain. Some reform-minded critics of Sufism, who were active in the first half of the twentieth century, went so far as to present Sufism as the principal obstacle to the social and economic progress of their societies. With the spread of leftist ideologies, Sufism became a target of Marxist critique, which has emphasized its role as the "opium of the masses" and the bastion of "retrograde," "medieval" mentality.

At present, the most uncompromising and vocal criticism of Sufism comes from the exponents of so-called Salafi Islam,[54] which we shall discuss in Chapters 22 and 24. Popularly known as "Wahhabis," these puritanically minded Muslims hold Sufism responsible for all manner of heretical "innovations" in Muslim doctrine and practice. In particular, they have railed against the blind obedience of Sufi disciples toward their *shaykh*s, the popular belief in the miracles of Sufi "friends of God," and in the blessings emanating from their tombs. Many Salafi Muslims also condemn the loud remembrance of God (*dhikr*) by Sufis to the accompaniment of music and dance, the construction of sumptuous buildings over the graves of revered Sufi masters, and the mystical idea that chosen Muslims can achieve a loving or cognitive union with God. One contemporary Salafi critic has accused Sufis of violating no fewer than one hundred rulings of the Islamic law, as he understands it.[55] The Salafi vituperations against Sufi "transgressions" are in a sense akin to the Protestant critique of Catholicism with its adulation of saints and their relics, lavish rituals and icons, and popular belief in saintly miracles. Since Salafism is often associated with political activism in the name of Islam and, by association, with "Islamic" militancy or even terrorism, many state authorities in Muslims countries have been deliberately cultivating Sufi institutions to counterbalance what they regard as the "fundamentalist threat" to their rule. This strategy is not without serious pitfalls, as it may discredit Sufi organizations and educational institutions in the eyes of the Muslim masses, who may consequently turn to Salafi groups, either radical or moderate, for support or as means of voicing their social and political grievances. Therefore, contemporary Sufi leaders often have to tread very carefully in order not to be perceived by their coreligionists as stooges of manipulative secular regimes and conduits for their policies.[56]

As already mentioned, Sufi teachings and practices have proven to be attractive to some Western men and women, who are disaffected with Western consumerism, cold rationalism, and lack of spirituality. Over the past forty or fifty years, such individuals have been actively embracing and cultivating various forms of Sufism in Western societies. Many highly educated Westerners have traveled to the Muslim East in order to study under Sufi masters who represent various Sufi brotherhoods and spiritual traditions. Some Sufi *shaykh*s, in their turn, have emigrated to the West, where they established Sufi lodges and acquired a relatively large, diverse, and enthusiastic retinue. Some Westerners interested in spiritual advancement and supersensory enlightenment have attempted to divest Sufism of its Islamic trappings and to present it as yet another expression of the perennial wisdom and spirituality that transcends confessional borders. In the process of this Western reinvention of Sufism, its Shari'a-based aspects and demands have often gone by the wayside. This nondenominational "Sufism lite" has meshed well with New Age religiosity that appeals to Western intellectuals with artistic propensities, as well as psychologists, professionals, academics, office workers, students, and others.

At the same time, many Sufis living in Western societies continue to adhere to the more traditional, time-tested forms of Sufism that emphasize the necessity of strict compliance with the spirit and letter of the Shari'a. These traditionally minded followers of Sufism consider conversion to Islam to be a prerequisite for anyone seeking to join a Sufi community and partake of the blessing of its founder and his successors. Both New Age and traditional Sufi associations can now be found in practically every Western country as well as Russia. Even more importantly, Sufi instruction is no longer confined to Sufi lodges or transmitted by word of mouth in the course of direct contact between the *shaykh* and his followers. In the words of an American academic:

> Now [Sufism] is publicized through mass printing, modern literary genres, and electronic technology—with all the changes in personal relationships that these media entail.[57]

In sum, despite the setbacks it has experienced in recent times and the continuing ascendancy of secularism and scientism in both East and West, Sufi teachings, practices, and institutions are here to stay.

Conclusions

Our survey of the vicissitudes of Sufi institutions across time and space is inevitably cursory and incomplete. A more detailed account would require much more than one chapter of this book. It should be pointed out that Sufi brotherhoods and associations are found in practically every Muslim society. Even in countries such as Turkey and Saudi Arabia where they are officially banned by the state authorities, they continue to operate in semiclandestine manner. As has been demonstrated, the *tariqa*s have played a wide variety of important roles in the social, religious, and cultural life of their countries, although one should be careful about making blanket generalizations about these roles. Some have chosen to steer clear of state authorities, whereas others have actively propagated their teachings among rulers and their courtiers in the hope of influencing their policies in certain directions or securing the financial support of the state. Some Sufi communities have been actively involved in the affairs of this world by helping the poor and needy, while also providing them with spiritual counselling or faith healing. In the premodern era in particular, Sufi individuals and institutions provided much needed social services to their communities that state institutions had often neglected. Sufi hospices for travelers and the homeless and Sufi kitchens for the poor played an important role in allaying the plight of the disadvantaged social classes.

On the other hand, some Sufi brotherhoods we have examined espoused withdrawal from the affairs of this world in quest for personal salvation through constant meditation and renunciation of worldly pleasures. However, even such otherworldly oriented Sufi groups did not remain indifferent to the woes of their societies. Their members served as exemplars of piety and altruistic righteousness, whose prayers were believed to protect ordinary believers from diseases, natural disasters, or exactions of state authorities. After their death, their tombs served as "spiritual clinics" of sorts, which offered hope and consolation to a population who, in premodern times, had little recourse amidst the misery and injustice of everyday existence.

In the political sphere, one and the same order often acted differently under different historical circumstances, as in the case of the Tijaniyya, whose leaders eagerly cooperated with the French colonial authorities in Algeria, while leading a *jihad* against the French in West Africa. Examples of such "inconsistent" or "opportunistic" behavior of Sufi communities are legion, which renders futile any broad generalizations about their past or present social and political roles. What is not in doubt, however, is that, in addition to objective geopolitical conditions, the personalities of *tariqa* leaders have played a major role in determining the course of action that their followers would take.

Even this cursory and incomplete review of Sufism's evolution across time and space shows that it has been inextricably entwined with the overall development of Islamic devotional practices, theology, literature, esthetics, and institutions. Discussing Sufism in isolation from these contexts will result in serious distortions. Sufism's cardinal ideas, practices, and values have been continually reinterpreted, rearticulated, and readjusted in accordance with the changing historical circumstances experienced by its adherents. Attempts to posit an immutable and permanent essence of Sufism are futile.

Questions to Ponder

1   What factors were instrumental in the rise and growth of ascetic-mystical tendencies in early Muslim society? Can or should we separate internal from external factors? How can you explain the focus of Western scholarship on "external origins" of the ascetic-mystical movement in Islam?

2   How and why did Sufism become institutionalized? Was the process of institutionalization inevitable? How can it be reconciled with the oft asserted spontaneity and individuality of mystical experience?

3   Do you see a contradiction between Sufism's oft stated inward orientation and its occasionally active involvement in the political and social life of Muslim societies? What forms did Sufi participation in social and political affairs take?

4   It is often stated that mystical experience is impossible to express (it is ineffable). Why and how have Sufi writers and poets attempted to convey the ineffable to their audiences? Have they been successful?

5   How can the worship of deceased and living "friends of God" be reconciled with the Islamic doctrine of the uniqueness of God as the dispenser of mercy, assistance, and grace? What, in your opinion, are the reasons for the persistence of the cult of God's friends (both living and deceased) in Islamic societies until this day?

6   Discuss the nature of problems faced by followers of Sufi doctrines and practices in Shi'ite societies.

7   Why do you think some modern Western men and women are attracted to Sufi teachings and practices? Is this just a passing fad or a long-term trend that will lead to the flowering of Sufi-inspired spirituality in Western societies?

Summary

*   Islamic mysticism (Sufism) is the product of the rise and development of ascetic and mystical trends in early Muslim society. Ascetic and world-abnegating and world-denigrating elements found in the Muslim scriptures provide justification for aspiring Muslim world renouncers (ascetics).

- The goals of the Muslim mystic are to attain proximity with and better awareness of God and his immediate (immanent) presence in this world. The means to achieving this end by individual Muslims is the rejection of material possessions and worldly pleasures, self-scrutiny, mortification of the flesh, and pious meditation.
- Al-Hásan al-Basri (d. 728) is the prototypical ascetical-mystical teacher. His circle of disciples play a critical role in the dissemination of ascetic and mystical ideas among Muslims at large.
- Rábi'a al-'Adawiyya (d. 801), the greatest female mystic of all time, celebrates a pure, disinterested love of God. The faithful should love God for his own sake, not because of the paradisiacal pleasures and rewards he promises to those who obey his commands.
- The types of ascetic-mystical piety differ in the early Muslim community and among its main advocates.
- The Baghdad school of Sufism emerges and eventually triumphs over other ascetic-mystical movements in the caliphate's provinces. The religiopolitical factors that facilitated this triumph are state sponsorship, class composition, and the wide availability of Sufi manuals of the school in the far-flung corners of the caliphate.
- The chief representatives of the Baghdad school of Sufism are al-Muhásibi (d. 857) and al-Junayd (d. 910).
- Two main trends in Baghdad Sufism are the "sober" versus the "intoxicated" one. Tensions exist between the individualistic (and often ecstatic) quest for and the experience of God and the necessity to maintain public propriety and avoid the hostile attention of state authorities.
- The suppression by religious and state authorities of the intoxicated trend is exemplified by al-Núri (d. 907) and al-Halláj (d. 922). The triumph of the sober and socially responsible asceticism-mysticism is associated with al-Junayd.
- The notion develops of a saintly "friend of God" (*wali*; pl. *awliyá'*) as a divinely chosen individual possessed of a special, revelatory knowledge of God and the world. Sufi friends of God are exponents of the inner, spiritual aspects of the divine revelation (*bátin*).
- Ascetic and mystical lore are systematized and classified in the tenth and eleventh centuries in the Sufi manuals of al-Sarráj (d. 988), al-Súlami (d. 1021), and al-Qushayri (d. 1073).
- Al-Ghazali (d. 1111) attempts s to reconcile and integrate the spiritual aspects of Sufism with the precepts of mainstream Sunni Islam.
- The literary output of Muslim mystics includes the Persian mystical poetry of 'Attar (d. between 1190 and 1230), Jalál al-Din Rumi (d. 1273), and Jami (d. 1492).
- In Sufi metaphysics, the status of the unitive (monistic) cosmology of Ibn 'Arabi (d. 1240) is dubious in the eyes of mainstream Sunni theologians.
- The relationship between the Sufi disciple (*murid*) and his master (*shaykh, murshid, or pir*) is the foundation of Sufi training and communal life, constituting the formation of spiritual "lineages" or "genealogies" (Arab. *silsila*).
- Sufism goes institutional with the rise of Sufi brotherhoods/orders (*taríqa*s). The major Sufi *taríqa*s are the Qadiriyya, Rifa'iyya, Suhrawardiyya, Chishtiyya, Kubrawiyya, Naqshbandiyya, and Shadhiliyya.
- Spiritual "chain" (*silsila*), *murid–shaykh* ties, rules of fellowship, and the commonality of *dhikr* formulas and devotional practices constitute the foundations of Sufi *taríqa* communities worldwide.

- Sufism and sainthood: Sufi masters (*shaykh*s) are seen by their followers and by outsiders as God's elect "friends" or "saints" (*awliyá'*). *Awliyá'* and their tombs, often elaborately built and decorated, become sites of pious visitations (*ziyarát*) and local cults. *Awliyá'* are seen by the populace as workers of saintly miracles (*karamát*), possessors of blessings (*barakát*), mediators between God and ordinary believers, and arbitrators in conflicts among the latter. Some puritanically minded scholars condemn the saints' cult, perceiving it as a serious violation of the principle of *tawhíd* (namely, God being the one and only object of worship and dispenser of grace).
- Sufi brotherhoods enjoy a vast geographical spread from North and Sub-Saharan Africa to Anatolia, Iran, the Caucasus, and Central Asia, as well as from India to the Malaysian Archipelago.
- Sufism and Shi'ism: Sufi orders emerge in Iran. Sufism undergoes changes under the late Safavids and Qajars: the Nurbakhshiyya and the Ni'matullahiyya. Sufi orders are persecuted by some influential Shi'ite leaders (Bihbahaní). Dr. Javád Nurbakhsh (d. 2008) and the Ni'matullahiyya in the West.
- Sufi brotherhoods play variegated roles in premodern and modern Islamic societies: They serve as a social "safety net," centers of education and conflict resolution, "spiritual clinics," and the like. Sufi brotherhoods also interacted with European colonial powers, vacillating between resistance and collaboration.
- In the contemporary world, the quarrel between the Sufis and some Salafi ("fundamentalist") Muslim groups is ongoing. Of the latter, Wahhabis are particularly critical of Sufi beliefs and practices.
- Sufism holds an attraction for the Western populaces, and "neo-Sufi" associations are spreading in Western societies. The two major types of Sufi communities in Western societies are nondenominational and denominational. Sufism is also interpreted as a New Age religion.

Notes

1 Arab. *'ubbad* or *nussak*.
2 What follows is based, in part, on Alexander Knysh, *Islamic Mysticism: A Short History*, E. J. Brill, Leiden and Boston, 2010.
3 Alexander Knysh, "The *tariqa* on a Landcruiser: The Resurgence of Sufism in Yemen," *Middle East Journal*, vol. 3 (2001), pp. 399–414 and Martin van Bruinessen and Julia Day Howell (eds.), *Sufism and the 'Modern' in Islam*, I.B. Tauris, London and New York, 2013.
4 See, e.g., Ron Geaves, Markus Dressler, and Gritt Klinkhammer (eds.), *Sufis in Western Society*, Routledge, London and New York, 2009.
5 Margaret Smith, *Studies in Early Mysticism in the Near and Middle East*, 2nd ed., Oneworld, Oxford, 1995, pp. 125–152; cf. Arthur Arberry, *Sufism: An Account of the Mystics of Islam*, Allen and Unwin, London, 1950, pp. 15–30.
6 Artur Vööbus, *Syriac and Arabic Documents Regarding Legislation Relevant to Syrian Asceticism*, Etse, Stockholm, 1960; cf. Josef van Ess, *Theologie und Gesellschaft im 2. und 3 Jahrhundert Hidschra*, 6 vols., de Gruyter, Berlin and New York, 1991–1995, vol. 2, 1992, pp. 88, 94, 610, etc.
7 Waki' b. al-Jarrah, *Kitab al-zuhd*, ed. by 'Abd al-Rahman al-Faryawani, 2 vols., 2nd ed., Dar al-Sumay'i, Riyadh, 1994, vol. 1, p. 234.
8 Benedikt Reinert, *Die Lehre vom tawakkul in der klassischen Sufik*, de Gruyter, Berlin, 1968, p. 188; van Ess, *Theologie*, vol. 1, pp. 228–229.
9 Gerhard Böwering, *The Mystical Vision of Existence in Classical Islam*, de Gruyter, Berlin, 1980, pp. 145–165.

10 Waki' b. al-Jarrah, *Kitab al-zuhd*, vol. 1, pp. 248–263.

11 Reinert, *Die Lehre*, pp. 172–175.

12 Jacqueline Chabbi, "Réflexions sur le soufisme iranien primitif," *Journal Asiatique*, vol. 266/1–2 (1978), pp. 37–55; Bernd Radtke, "Theologen und Mystiker in Hurasan und Transoxanien," *Zeitschrift der Deutschen Morgenländischen Gesellschaft*, vol. 136/1 (1986), pp. 536–569.

13 Arberry, *Sufism*, pp. 56–57.

14 Reynold Nicholson (ed.), *The Kitab al-luma' fi 'l-tasawwuf of Abu Nasr . . . al-Sarraj*. E. J. Brill, Leiden and London, 1914, pp. 398–406.

15 Knysh, *Islamic Mysticism*, pp. 68–82.

16 For details, see Böwering, *The Mystical Vision*.

17 Ahmet Karamustafa, *God's Unruly Friends*, University of Utah Press, Salt Lake City, 1994, p. 31.

18 Chabbi, "Réflexions," passim.

19 Arberry, *Sufism*, p. 68.

20 Abu Bakr al-Kalabadhi, "Introduction to the Way of the Sufis" (*al-Ta'arruf li-madhhab ahl al-tasawwuf*).

21 Arthur Arberry (trans.), *The Doctrine of the Sufis*, reprint, Cambridge University Press, Cambridge, 1991.

22 Gerhard Böwering (ed.), *The Minor Qur'an Commentary of Abu 'Abd al-Rahman . . . al-Sulami (d. 412/1021)*, Dar al-Mashriq, Beirut, 1995.

23 See, e.g., Alikber Alikberov, *Epokha klassicheskogo islama na Kavkaze*, Vostochnaia literatura, Moscow, 2003.

24 Montgomery Watt, *Faith and Practice of al-Ghazali*, Allen and Unwin, London, 1953.

25 Herman Landolt, "Al-Ghazali and 'Religionswissenschaft,'" *Asiatische Studien*, vol. 55/1 (1991), p. 54; See also Marshall Hodgson, *The Venture of Islam*, 3 vols., University of Chicago Press, Chicago, 1974, vol. 2, p. 314; Peter Heath, *Allegory and Philosophy in Avicenna (Ibn Sina)*, University of Pennsylvania Press, Philadelphia, 1992.

26 Arberry, *Sufism*, p. 83.

27 Hodgson, *The Venture*, vol. 2, p. 305.

28 For details, see Arthur Arberry's "Introduction" to his translation of 'Attar's "Memorial of the Saints"; see Arberry (trans.), *Muslim Saints and Mystics*, reprint, Penguin Books, Arkana, London and New York, 1990.

29 Tabriz is a city in Iranian Azerbaijan (present-day Iran).

30 Hodgson, *The Venture*, vol. 2, p. 245.

31 Nicholas Heer (ed.), *The Precious Pearl: Al-Jami's al-Durrah al-fakhirah*, SUNY Press, Albany, NY, 1979, pp. 1–2.

32 That is, theory of knowledge.

33 His original name was Muhyi al-Din Muhammad Ibn al-'Arabi; however, he is better known today as "Ibn 'Arabi."

34 Henry Corbin, *Creative Imagination in the Sufism of Ibn 'Arabi* (trans. from the French by Ralph Manheim), Princeton University Press, Princeton, NJ, 1969, pp. 69–71 and 224; William Chittick, "Ibn 'Arabi and His School," in S.H. Nasr (ed.), *Islamic Spirituality: Manifestations*, Crossroad, New York, 1991, pp. 49–79; William Chittick, "Rumi and *wahdat al-wujud*," in Amin Banani and Richard Hovannisian (eds.), *Poetry and Mysticism in Islam*, Cambridge University Press, Cambridge, 1994, pp. 77–79.

35 Osman Yahya, *Histoire et classification de l'oeuvre d'Ibn 'Arabi*, 2 vols. Institut français de Damas, Damascus, 1964.

36 Hodgson, *The Venture*, vol. 2, p. 224.

37 James Morris, "How to Study the *Futuhat*," in Stephen Hirtenstein and Michael Tiernan (eds.), *Muhyiddin Ibn 'Arabi: A Commemorative Volume*, Element Books, Brisbane, 1993, pp. 73–89.

38 Hodgson, *The Venture*, vol. 2, p. 315.

39 Morris, "How to Study," p. 73

40 Seeing that human beings are but manifestations of God's essence and, moreover, are indispensable for God's self-knowledge, some may assume themselves to be free from the commandments of the Shari'a and social conventions generally.

41 For details, see Alexander Knysh, *Ibn 'Arabi in the Later Islamic Tradition*, SUNY Press, Albany, NY, 1999.

42 For Ibn Sina's philosophical views, see Chapter 14.

43 For images, see, e.g., John Brown, *The Darvishes or Oriental Mysticism*, 2nd ed., ed. by H.A. Rose, Cass, London, 1968.

44 Itzchak Weismann, *The Naqshbandiyya*, Routledge, London and New York, 2007.

45 Knysh, *Islamic Mysticism*, Chapters 8 and 9.

46 Lit. "chain" (Arab.).

47 This section is a summary of Knysh, *Islamic Mysticism*, pp. 234–244.

48 For further details, see Matthijs van den Bos, *Mystic Regimes: Sufism and State in Iran*, E. J. Brill, Leiden and Boston, 2002.

49 https://michigansufi.wordpress.com/2013/05/26/love-the-path-of-unity/.

50 See, e.g., Alexander Knysh, "Irfan Revisited: Khomeini and the Legacy of Islamic Mystical Philosophy," *Middle East Journal*, vol. 46/4 (Autumn 1992), pp. 631–653.

51 Nasrollah Pourjavady, "Opposition to Sufism in Twelver Shiism," in Frederick de Jong and Bernd Radtke (eds.), *Islamic Mysticism Contested*, E. J. Brill, Leiden and Boston, 1999, pp. 614–623.

52 See, e.g., Carl Ernst, *The Shambhala Guide to Sufism*, Shambhala, Boston, 1997, pp. 8–18.

53 For details, see Alexander Knysh, "Historiography of Sufi Studies in the West," in Youssef Choueiri (ed.), *A Companion for the History of the Middle East*, Blackwell, Oxford, 2005, pp. 106–131.

54 In Western literature and media reportage, this brand of Islam is usually referred to as "Islamic fundamentalism."

55 See, e.g., Alexander Knysh, "Contextualizing the Sufi-Salafi Conflict (from the Northern Caucasus to Hadramawt)," *Middle Eastern Studies*, vol. 43/4 (2007), p. 507.

56 Alexander Knysh, "A Clear and Present Danger: 'Wahhabism' as a Rhetorical Foil," *Die Welt des Islams*, vol. 44/1 (2004), pp. 3–26.

57 Ernst, *The Shambhala Guide*, p. 220.

Chapter 14

Intellectual Struggles in Premodern Islam

Philosophy Versus Theology

Fálsafa as a Rational Discipline

Fálsafa is an Arabic word for the Greek *philosofia*—"love of wisdom." It is a rational discipline that seeks to establish general natural laws governing the universe by means of empirical observation and inductive analysis of results obtained thereby. Once these general laws have been established, all particulars could be construed by the correct application of logical reasoning.[1] Basing oneself on this principle, one can argue that, ideally, *fálsafa* was supposed to give its practitioners a sure, even unmistakable understanding of the true nature of the universe and its functioning.

The question inevitably arises as to what has caused the universe to appear in the first place. By abstracting oneself from the astounding diversity of things and phenomena accessible to the human senses, one can arrive at the ultimate cause and source of all being. One can then proceed to figure out one's own nature and one's role in this general scheme of things. If one accepts the human intellect as the sole guide to truth, one can dispense with the revealed texts or treat them as allegorical statements of rationally obtainable truths that are meant for uncouth minds. In the medieval Muslim world, the individuals who shared these fundamental principles were known as *falásifa* (sing. *faylasúf*), that is adherents of *fálsafa*. The Greek origin of this word indicates that it was a continuation and refinement, on the Muslim soil, of rational and scientific methods of inquiry originating in Ancient Greece.[2]

Despite the "pagan" origins of their preferred method of intellectual inquiry, the *falásifa* were unapologetic. On the contrary, they took great pride in being the custodians and exponents of this age-old rationalist tradition and looked down upon those who were incapable or unwilling to embrace and practice its methods. In many ways, *fálsafa* represented an alternative to Islamic theology and jurisprudence both of which, in the final account, always deferred to the Islamic revelation as manifested in the Qur'an and the Sunna. For the *mutakállimún* and *fuqahá'*, the absolute truth and intellectual certainty could not be found outside and independent of the sacred texts of Islam. Unaided by the revelation, the human intellect was incapable of unraveling the mysteries of divine creation or guiding people to salvation. Whereas the majority of *falásifa* recognized the sacred status and inerrancy of the Qur'an and the Sunna, they believed that *fálsafa*, when understood and practiced correctly, teaches basically the same values and ideas, often in a more streamlined, logically rigorous, and persuasive way. One can say that *fálsafa* exemplified a peculiar worldview and intellectual attitude which, consciously or not, positioned itself as a challenge to the religion-based world outlook that permeated societal and cultural conventions of the premodern age.

Partly for this reason, Muslim philosophy has been a pet subject for Western academic scholars of Islam, steeped as they are in the critical, secularist, and rationalistic attitudes that have prevailed in European societies since the Age of the Enlightenment. They have produced a considerable body of research on *fálsafa* that concentrated on its major representatives whose work is discussed later in this chapter. Seen in a broader historical perspective, however, the influence of *fálsafa* on Muslim societies has been minute in comparison with that of legal scholarship and, to a lesser extent, rationalist theology. To achieve the all-important goal of salvation an ordinary Muslim was obligated to follow the Shari'a, to stay out of trouble, and to strive to be a good member of his or her community in all respects. In the light of such goals, sophisticated rational speculations about the origin and structure of the universe were not just unnecessary but also potentially confusing and detrimental for one's intellectual and spiritual serenity. As we have seen in Chapter 10, even religiously sanctioned discursive theology (*kalám*) was hardly a must for the ordinary believer; one could accept God's existence and fulfill divine commandments without justifying one's faith and actions on rational grounds. The need for *kalám* arises only when the soundness of one's faith has been questioned by outsiders or, as the case may be, when a believer himself or herself has been accosted by doubts about it that he or she tried to dispel.

It is now easy to see why, from the viewpoint of an average educated Muslim, *fálsafa* was much lower on the scale of practical priorities than even *kalám*. Both dealt in abstractions, but the former did so without much regard for the sacred texts, which any believing Muslim would find disturbing, to say the least. No wonder that medieval Muslim opponents of *fálsafa* would argue that it was not only redundant but also outright harmful to the spiritual well-being of the Muslim community. The overwhelming majority of Muslims should therefore do just fine without it. This was the opinion upheld, with a few exceptions, by the learned class. However, in the end, the attraction of Greek wisdom proved to be irresistible for some of its members in the same way as it had for their Christian counterparts several centuries earlier.[3]

Fálsafa and *Kalám*

Although *fálsafa* has much in common with *kalám* (such as the use of logical argumentation and abstract terminology), they apply themselves to different subject matters. The *mutakállim*s were primarily concerned with interpreting revealed texts, formulating the dogma, and defending Islam from its real or imaginary detractors, and, with time, also from those Muslims whom they considered to be heretics. The *falásifa*, on the other hand, were interested, first and foremost, in furnishing a comprehensive and harmonious picture of the universe based on a set of what they considered to be sound and incontrovertible axioms. Interestingly, their abiding fascination with Greek philosophical legacy and unquestioning trust in its veracity was so strong that one may speak of *fálsafa* as a religion of sorts for its adepts. This comparison is even more pertinent given the fact that the scope of *fálsafa* included not just intellectual convictions but also a distinctive social and professional status as well as way of life.

Like the *mutakállim*s, the philosophers availed themselves of Greek terminology such as "essence," "accidents," "substance," "being," "nonbeing," "atoms," "void," "intelligible realities" (as opposed to empirically perceived ones), and so on. Nevertheless, in the final account, the *mutakállim*s recognized the superiority of Arabic as the language of the revelation over the Greek language and intellectual tradition. For them, Aristotelian logic, no matter how refined, was incapable of doing justice to the miracle of the Arabic revelation. The latter's wisdom surpassed even the most sophisticated rational tools.[4] Furthermore, in the versions of *kalám* predominant in the premodern Muslim world (namely, Ash'arism and Maturidism)[5] natural causality, which constitutes the mainstay of *fálsafa*'s vision of the functioning of the universe, is rejected in favor of the belief in God's will being the direct and ultimate cause of all things.[6] In the end, such fundamental differences between *fálsafa* and *kalám* have proved irreconcilable, and the majority of Muslim scholars have come to regard *fálsafa* as "essentially an alien way of thinking"[7] inapplicable to the Islamic belief system. Furthermore, since *fálsafa* addressed basically the same issues as *kalám*, the adherents of the latter considered it to be an unwelcome competitor in the struggle for Muslim minds.[8]

Fálsafa as an Elaboration of Neoplatonic Doctrines

It is important to point out that the *falásifa* did not slavishly follow the Greek philosophical tradition of Aristotle and Plato. Rather, they modified the Greek concepts in an effort to make them consistent with the principal tenets of Muslim religion.[9] As a rule, the Muslim advocates of *fálsafa* did so out of a sincere conviction that the two, if interpreted correctly, could not contradict one another. To effect a happy marriage between the Muslim revelation and Greek philosophy, the *falásifa* had recourse to its later elaboration at the hands of Hellenistic thinkers known collectively as "Neoplatonists."[10] These thinkers viewed the world as a series of progressive emanations from a sublime source of all existence about which, they argued, very little if anything could be positively asserted. The Hellenistic thinker named Plotinus (d. 270), a great admirer of Plato, described this sublime source of all existence simply as the "One." In line with the precepts of Neoplatonic philosophy, the One's realization or reflection in the things and phenomena of the material universe proceeds eternally. The logic of this outflowing, or emanation, of existential possibilities from the One is only vaguely perceived by the majority of human beings. However, a handful of individuals can obtain a sure knowledge of it by means of the superior rational faculties bestowed upon them by the Divine. This initially "pagan" Greek vision of the universe was later appropriated by many Christian theologians who reinterpreted it in such a way as to harmonize it with the articles of Christian faith. For instance, Plotinus's "One" was presented by Christian Neoplatonists as the equivalent of God the Maker of the Christian scriptures, a super being that generates things and phenomena of the empirical world in accordance with a matrix of potentialities inherent in it. In the Christian interpretation in particular, the supreme being of Neoplatonism came to be conceived of as the source not only of all existence but also of all good and grace.

Neoplatonic thinkers presented the emanation of the world from the unfathomable One as a staged process. By reflecting on its own inherent perfections and potentialities, the divine absolute generates the universal reason. The latter, in the process of self-contemplation, produces the universal soul. From the soul's self-contemplation, in turn, there proceeds a succession of heavenly spheres down to the sphere of the moon. It is in this sublunar sphere that intelligible entities emanating from the universal reason and universal soul acquire their material bodies and become accessible to the human perceptions. The emanation proceeds from simpler and purer forms to more composite, complex, and impure forms. Our world is the realm of admixture of spirits and material elements; above it lies a succession of more spiritual, simpler, and purer spheres. Inhabited by intelligences, which could be construed as angels of the holy scriptures, the concentric spheres of the universe are but products of the ceaseless emanation of innumerable existential potentialities inherent in the divine absolute.[11]

This "cosmic drama," as we have seen, was appropriated by some Muslim communities, especially, the Isma'ilis, who creatively integrated it with their theory of the imamate. The Muslim philosophers, too, could not remain immune to the elegant allure of the Neoplatonist theory of emanation. They made it the foundation of their speculations about the origin and structure of the cosmos and the place of human beings in it.[12] In the opinion of Muslim Neoplatonists, the empirical world is but a projection and material embodiment of divine rationality. Hence, God's rational laws can be established by induction from their concrete manifestations in the events and entities of the created universe. In accordance with this general idea, the process of human cognition involves a progressive assent of the continually perfected and active human intellect toward its divine source that encompasses the rational laws governing the process of emanation and thus the universe. In the end, God's creative design achieves its full realization after having been grasped, with the help of an enlightenment of sorts, by the perfected intellects of the elect.

The Beginnings of *Fálsafa*

The beginnings of *fálsafa* are traditionally associated with the translation movement under the early 'Abbásids. It was initiated and sponsored by the caliph al-Ma'mún who ruled from 813 to 833 C.E. Al-Ma'mún established the so-called "House of Wisdom" in Baghdad and employed prominent Syriac/Aramaic-speaking Christian intellectuals to translate major works of Greek sciences, including medicine, astronomy, logic, physics, mathematics, geometry, and, somewhat later, philosophy. The Christian interpreters translated these texts either directly from Greek or from their Syriac/Aramaic renditions.[13] Their translations soon found an enthusiastic audience among certain sophisticated Muslim thinkers, who were fascinated by the rational elegance and persuasiveness of Greek thought. Whereas these intellectuals regarded Plato and Aristotle as the most authoritative exponents of this Greek wisdom, they did not always realize that some philosophical treatises that had circulated in their name were in fact their later renditions by Hellenistic Neoplatonists. For example, they were unaware of the existence of the aforementioned Plotinus (d. 270), who was the first to expound the Neoplatonic doctrine of emanation or of his students and commentators.[14] This ignorance did not prevent the Neoplatonic teachings from having a profound impact on Islamic philosophical thought. The explanation, as already mentioned, lies in the fact that the Neoplatonic theory of emanation was much more amenable to a religious interpretation than pure Aristotelianism or even pure Platonism.

Also popular with Muslim philosophers was the legacy of great Greek physicians, such as Hippocrates and Galen. Their works were studied for more pragmatic reasons, for many Muslim admirers of Greek wisdom earned their livelihood as medical doctors.[15] We will now mention the foremost representatives of *fálsafa* in medieval Islam. Our survey of their lives and teachings is arranged in chronological order. It presents only the major figures and is by no means exhaustive.

Al-Kindi, the Philosopher of the Arabs

Al-Kindi (d. around 870) was an Arab by birth who served as a court physician and the tutor of the caliph's son. It is not quite certain whether he himself knew Greek, but we know for sure that he oversaw the work of some prominent Christian translators of Greek works and borrowed many of his ideas from them. An enthusiastic champion of Greek wisdom, al-Kindi studied logic, arithmetic, music, astronomy, medicine, politics, and alchemy. He also dabbled in some more practical sciences that were of interest to his royal patrons, namely making glass, jewelry, armor, and perfume.[16]

Al-Kindi himself described the ultimate goal of his intellectual pursuits as an attempt "[t]o supply completely what the ancients said . . . and to complete what they did not say comprehensively, in accordance with the custom of language and the practices of the time."[17]

This task required the creation of a new philosophical vocabulary in Arabic, based on Greek philosophical terminology. The introduction of such a vocabulary into Muslim intellectual life is rightly considered to be al-Kindi's major achievement. The terminology he coined on the basis of Greek terms became the staple of later Muslim *fálsafa*.[18]

Al-Kindi was keen to demonstrate the relevance of Greek philosophical ideas to the burning intellectual problems of his age, especially the necessity to develop Islamic rationalist theology, *kalám*. In his famous treatise, "On First Philosophy," he argued that Greek thought should be welcomed by Muslims despite its foreign origins because it is essential for arriving at what he called "the First Truth, which is the cause of all truth." Drawing on the Neoplatonic doctrine of emanation, he described the God of the Qur'an as "the Truly Real One." No final positive affirmation can be made about it except that it is one, which is in total harmony with the Muslim doctrine of *tawhíd*. In this way, al-Kindi, possibly taking his cue from the Mu'tazilite emphasis on the unity and uniqueness of God, absolved God of any hint of multiplicity, which he regarded as a characteristic feature of all creatures. In the words of al-Kindi, "He [God] is the First Cause that has no cause, the Agent that has no agent, the Perfector Who has no perfector, the One Who gives the universe being from non-being, the One Who makes things reasons and causes for others."[19]

This description of the True Real One by al-Kindi demonstrates his desire to justify the Islamic doctrine of divine oneness on philosophical grounds. Elsewhere, al-Kindi made use of Greek logic to demonstrate that God is the only entity or efficient cause that acts without being acted upon. In his opinion, created things can be called "agents" only metaphorically, because all they do is transmit God's underlying agency to other creatures and things. Therefore, all that we consider to be independent causes are, in reality, caused by God, who alone is the uncaused cause. These propositions show that al-Kindi saw his task in availing himself of Greek ideas and logic in order to prove the major articles of the Muslim creed and to assert the existence of one, unique, and uncaused entity—God. This unique entity is the source of all material existence. For al-Kindi, there is no contradiction between the philosophical truths obtained by means of a correct application of the human rational faculty and the divine revelation as transmitted to humankind by prophets and messengers. He was convinced that "the truth must be acquired from whatever source it comes," even though its source may be non-Islamic, as in the case of Greek philosophy. At the same time, like the Mu'tazilites and later the Ash'arites, he advocated the unassailable superiority of the revealed truth over the truths obtained by rational reasoning.[20] In so doing, he indirectly confirmed the validity and necessity of prophethood.

On their own, unaided by prophets, human beings are incapable of attaining the truth. Therefore, God reveals the knowledge of the true reality and purpose of existence to his elect servants (the prophets), who convey it to their followers. Unlike the philosopher who has to exert himself to the limit to obtain sound rational knowledge, the prophet receives his knowledge from God effortlessly, as in a flash of inspiration. At the same time, al-Kindi argues that the knowledge obtained by means of rational reflection is, in its essence, congruent with the divinely inspired messages of the prophets. Like divine revelation, it confirms divine sovereignty and oneness on the one hand, and demonstrates the necessity of the proper morals and ethics on the other. In line with this view, al-Kindi insisted that Muslims should show respect for both philosophy and the revelation and dismissed as ignoramuses those of them who denied the need for a rational apprehension of the revealed truths. Those who reject it cannot do so arbitrarily, he argued, but must prove their position on rational grounds. At the same time, whenever he saw a contradiction between a philosophical postulate and the Muslim revelation, he inevitably opted for the latter.[21] Thus, contrary to the Greek philosophical convention, he recognized the creation of the world out of nothingness and bodily resurrection of human beings on the Judgment Day. Likewise, he admitted the possibility of miracles performed by prophets and saints—a proposition that contradicts the philosophical doctrine of natural causality.[22] In an effort to furnish a rationally sound proof of God's existence, al-Kindi argued that temporal existence must have a beginning and an end; therefore it should have originated at a certain point in time unlike divine existence, which has no beginning and end. In this respect, he differed from some later Muslim philosophers, some of whom implicitly or explicitly recognized the eternity of the material world.

Abu Bakr al-Razi, the Physician and Freethinker

Abu Bakr Ibn Zakariya al-Razi, or "Rhazes" as he was known in Latin Europe, lived in the late ninth and early tenth centuries. Little is known about his life except that he was an accomplished physician who practiced his art in his native city of Rayy (Iran) and in Baghdad. Even the exact date of his death is not known for sure and given as either 925 or 932.[23] Al-Razi occupies a special place in the history of Islamic philosophy. He seems to have started his career as an alchemist, but later he became interested in medicine and excelled in it. He was made head of the hospital in his native city Rayy in Khurasan, where he enjoyed the patronage of the local ruler. Later on he took charge of the hospital in Baghdad.[24]

Al-Razi is generally recognized as "the unsurpassed physician of Islam" superior even to Ibn Sina (Avicenna). His medical works were widely read in medieval Europe as late as the sixteenth century.[25] His philosophical works, however, did not fare as well due to their "heretical" contents. On the personal level, al-Razi was a man of great kindness, generosity, and industry, who was eager to treat ill people no matter how wicked they might be.[26] At the same time, he was a disenchanted man who took a skeptical view of this world and institutionalized religions, especially toward the end of his life. Shortly before his death, he is said to have developed a cataract but refused to have it removed out of fear of pain and unwillingness to see any more of this imperfect and corrupt world.[27]

Al-Razi wrote some two hundred works on various subjects, such as grammar, logic, philosophy, alchemy, astrology, and medicine. In his philosophical treatises, he modified some principles of Aristotle's thought. For instance, he argued against Aristotle's denial of the void.[28] He also disagreed with Aristotle regarding motion, which he considered to be essentially belonging to body, not something added onto it from outside. Building on the ideas of ancient Greeks and anticipating modern physical theories, he argued that bodies are made of individual atoms that are separated by the void. The density or sparsity of the atoms and the magnitude of the void separating them determine, according to al-Razi, the primary qualities of the physical objects made thereof, such as lightness, heaviness, hardness, softness, and so on.[29]

Al-Razi was confident of the power of human intellect. Human beings, he argued, are quite capable of comprehending the real situation in the universe by means of their God-given intellects, which they should constantly cultivate and sharpen through the study of philosophy. Since they have already been given the precious gift of the intellect, human beings can expect no further guidance from God:

> If the multitudes [of human beings], who bring perdition upon themselves and fail to inquire, had contemplated philosophy [even] in the most cursory way, it would have meant their salvation from this turbidity [of earthly existence], even if they comprehended only a small fraction of it.[30]

Thus, according to al-Razi, philosophy is the essential therapy for both soul and body. It allows the human intellect to join with the universal intellect, which contains all laws governing the natural world. All human beings are equally capable of attaining the truth through the proper exercise of their rational faculties. This means that prophetic guidance is not only unnecessary but can be outright detrimental for the well-being of the human race because the conflicting claims of different prophets bring about discord and bloodshed among nations and religious communities. Prophets are nothing but "impostors" misled by the demonic, envious spirits.[31] In one remarkably bold passage al-Razi asserts that:

> [T]he souls of wicked people, who had been transformed into demons, appear to some individuals in the form of angels, and command them: "Go and tell people: 'An angel had

appeared to me and told me: "God has made you an apostle" and [the demon would say] 'I am the angel sent to you.'" This is the reason for the dissemination of discord, and many people have been killed as a result of the machination of these souls-turned-demons.[32]

As already mentioned, unlike Muslim philosophers before and after him, al-Razi believed that ordinary people are fully capable of thinking for themselves and need no guidance from a possessed individual who claims divine inspiration. Human ingenuity, argued al-Razi, is amply evident in the crafts, sciences, and inventions produced by the human race. Asked whether a philosopher should follow a prophetically revealed religion, al-Razi boldly stated: "How can one think philosophically while remaining committed to old wives' tales founded on contradictions, obdurate ignorance, dogmatic stubbornness."[33]

When asked about the numerous contradictions among the philosophers themselves, his answer was: "A philosopher does not slavishly follow the actions and ideas of one master. He learns from his predecessors, but always hopes to surpass them and to improve on their conclusions."[34] Thus, although the philosopher acknowledges the achievements of his intellectual forebears, he should not take their opinions for granted but rather constantly examine and question them. In line with this postulate, al-Razi had no compunctions about criticizing Galen, whom Muslim physicians considered one of the greatest medical geniuses of all times.[35]

In dealing with the problem of the creation of the world in time, al-Razi argued that it was brought into existence by an act of God's free and unrestricted will. He has arbitrarily chosen a moment in time out of all possible and identical moments. If it were not so, then it would follow that his choice was influenced by someone or something outside him, which would belie his oneness, omnipotence, and self-sufficiency. In creating humankind, God bestowed the intellect on each human being, urging his creatures to make use of it as best as they could. Since, in al-Razi's opinion, the human intellect is a direct emanation of God's very essence, it should of necessity strive to reunite with its original source. This reunification, in al-Razi's opinion, is what institutionalized religions allegorically call "salvation." At some point in time, all human souls will reunite with the universal soul and, eventually, with God himself. This reunification will be the end of the world as we know it.[36]

Al-Razi's notion that philosophy should serve as a means of cleansing human souls from turbidity and, as such, the only way to salvation was revolutionary for his time. Furthermore, his blunt denial of the necessity of prophetic guidance for humankind was considered by Muslim religious scholars to be outright blasphemous. It is hardly surprising that he has found no successors of note among later Muslim intellectuals and is still considered by many Muslims familiar with his ideas to be a dangerous freethinker or even atheist. For *fálsafa* to be acceptable to at least some Muslim thinkers, it had to be reconciled with the Abrahamic prophetic tradition that constituted the doctrinal and intellectual foundation of medieval Islamic civilization. Abu Nasr al-Farábi attempted to do just that.

Al-Farábi, the Second Teacher

Born in Central Asia of a Turkic military family, al-Farábi went to study in Baghdad, then moved to Syria, where he attached himself to the court of the local Shi'ite dynasty of the Hamdanids. He died in Damascus around 950. Al-Farábi took interest in logic, metaphysics, the philosophy of language, and political philosophy. He was also an accomplished musician. A prolific commentator and expert on Aristotle, he is often dubbed in Muslim sources as the "second teacher" (the first being Aristotle himself).

Al-Farábi's cosmology is based on a modified version of the Neoplatonic theory of emanation described in a previous section of this chapter. He viewed the world as an eternal emanation of being from the First Principle, God, through ten stages. This emanation, according to al-Farábi, is the consequence of the ten universal intellects contemplating both their own composition (nature) and their Lord. After the first intellect has emanated from the First Principle, it begins to contemplate its Lord. As a result of this contemplation, the body and soul of the first heavenly sphere appear. The same happens at the level of the second intellect, which also generates its body and soul through contemplating both itself and the intellect above it. The rest of the intellects and the bodies and souls of the spheres that they inhabit also emerge according to this tripartite pattern of origination.[37] The loftiest intellects and spheres govern those underneath them, forming a chain of command and control all the way down to the sublunar sphere, which, in al-Farábi's cosmology, is the tenth in this complex hierarchy of emanations. If we ask why such a complex system is needed to explain the origination and structure of the cosmos, the answer would probably be to account for how the undifferentiated unity of divine existence gives rise to the subsequent multiplicity of the empirical universe.[38]

Al-Farábi's cosmos thus presents itself as a series of concentric spheres: the outermost sphere, the first heaven; the sphere of fixed stars; the spheres of Saturn, Jupiter, Mars, the Sun, Venus, Mercury, and finally, the Moon. Each sphere is governed by its own active intellect. Human beings, who inhabit the sphere of the Moon, by properly exercising their rational faculties, are capable of initiating an intellectual ascent back into the presence of the intellect that governs this sublunar sphere. According to al-Farábi, the entire cosmic order thus appears to be completely rational and harmonious, reflecting the rational and harmonious nature of God himself.[39]

So what is the place of human beings in this panrational scheme of things? According to al-Farábi, the ultimate goal of all human beings is happiness:

> Happiness is an end that everyone desires, and everyone who strives to direct himself toward it does so precisely because it is a certain good, which is unquestionably something preferred. Now, while there are many ends that are desired because they are preferred goods, happiness is the most advantageous of the preferred goods. It is thus clear that of all goods, happiness is the greatest.[40]

To achieve happiness, one must constantly improve one's natural disposition—a task that can be fulfilled only "through the discipline of philosophy."[41] Practicing this discipline, in turn, requires a suitable social and political environment modeled on the harmonious structure of the cosmic order. Since the latter is ruled by the all-wise and perfect divine intellect, its earthly equivalent, in al-Farábi's philosophy, is the perfected philosopher who by means of his rational faculty has achieved a certain and precise understanding of the structure of the universe and can now implement his newly found knowledge on the level of human society. Deriving his inspiration from Plato's *Republic*, al-Farábi speaks of this ideal ruler as a "philosopher-king" who presides over a well ordered society, which he refers to, metaphorically, as the "virtuous city." Al-Farábi was perfectly aware that the ideal social order of the virtuous city, which would be conducive to high morality and philosophical meditation, is hard, if not impossible, to implement in real life because of the inferior intellectual qualities and petty material preoccupations of the majority of human beings.[42] To persuade this philosophically illiterate and morally depraved majority to behave properly and to make them think about saving their souls, the universal rational truths of philosophy (al-Farábi refers to them as "intelligibles") must be imparted to them in the form of parables, allegories, and images that the uncouth minds of the populace can easily comprehend. This trade in allegories, parables, and images is the task of the prophets, who are, in their essence, philosophers capable of simultaneously comprehending the philosophical "intelligibles" and "packaging" them for the ignorant masses.

Unlike the philosophers, who are pure rationalists, the prophets are endowed with the imaginative faculty that allows them to transform abstract philosophical truths into vivid and memorable allegorical fables and legends known as "revelation."[43] In this view, the hell of the Qur'anic revelation is but an allegory of the sorry state of those human souls that have refused to improve their natural dispositions by tuning them to the rational harmonies of the cosmic order. The same, according to al-Farábi, applies to paradise, angels, and other articles of the Muslim creed. Thus, the revelation of a prophet is but an approximation and imitation of philosophy designed by God to convey its sublime truths to the average human intelligence in order to save ordinary human beings from the damnation and torment of ignorance.[44] The pure philosopher, who is not entrusted with a prophetic mission, does not need these fanciful fairy tales, because he arrives at the universal truths (or the "intelligibles") directly by properly exercising his rational and contemplative faculties. This point is brought home in an oft quoted passage from al-Farábi's work:

> Both [religion and philosophy] comprise the same subjects and both give an account of the ultimate principles of the beings . . . an account of the ultimate end for the sake of which man is made. If everything of which philosophy gives an account is based on intellectual perception and conception, religion gives an account based on imagination.[45]

How should the philosopher behave in a human society that adheres blindly to an allegorical or mythological representation of truth? According to al-Farábi, for the sake of the well-being of this society, the philosopher is obligated to submit himself voluntarily to the popularized and allegorized religious dispensation that is essential for the proper functioning of social order. To protect this order from unraveling, the philosopher must follow all of this dispensation's conventions, no matter how irrational or naive they might appear to him.[46] The philosophically minded person thus becomes, in the words of al-Farábi, a "solitary plant" in the "desert" of human ignorance and imperfection. Put differently, such a person has no option but to pursue a morally and intellectually sound life within the oppressive, nonphilosophic confines of the "wicked" city (i.e., an imperfect human society). And this, according to al-Farábi, is the best human beings can hope for in this world.

In real life, this pessimistic conclusion has pushed many adherents of Greek wisdom to adopt a kind of intellectual elitism that has become their distinctive trademark. The majority of philosophers looked down upon the ignorant and often hostile populace as well as their learned shepherds, the 'ulamá', and restricted their social intercourse to a small circle of like-minded, intellectually refined individuals. In the face of the obvious impossibility of establishing a "virtuous city" in a clearly unsuitable environment, the intellectual elitism of the falásifa has evolved into the "the internal emigration" of the "isolated wise man" into a life of serene philosophical reflection. Articulated clearly and unequivocally by a sophisticated Andalusian philosopher Ibn Bájja (d. 1139), this idea was shared by the majority of Muslim admirers of Greek wisdom before and after him.[47] Of these, Ibn Sina (Avicenna) deserves special mention.

Ibn Sina (Avicenna)

The complex and multifaceted legacy of Ibn Sina (Avicenna), who is sometimes called the "Preeminent Master" (al-shaykh al-ra'ís) of Islamic philosophy, furnishes ample evidence of the broad dissemination of philosophical knowledge among some members of the Muslim intellectual elite (see Figure 14.1). Firmly convinced that fálsafa offers valuable moral, ethical, and intellectual lessons to the Muslims at large, Ibn Sina invigorated the field of philosophical inquiry in Islam by attempting a comprehensive and systematic exposition of its principles. In accomplishing this task, he relied on the achievements of his intellectual forebears, especially al-Farábi.

Born in 980 near the city of Bukhara in present-day Uzbekistan to a family of a midranking state official, Ibn Sina was a true prodigy by any standard. In his autobiography, he tells us that

Figure 14.1 A Man of Learning (Avicenna) (by a Neapolitan painter, seventeenth century)
Iconographic Collections. Wellcome Images: CC: Wikimedia Commons

he had completed the study of grammar and literature by the age of ten, by which time he had also memorized by heart the entire text of the Qur'an. Ibn Sina quickly surpassed his teachers and embarked on an independent study of those subjects he considered worthwhile. By the age of eighteen, the young man, in his own words, had "devoured libraries" in his reading and acquired all the learning available in his epoch, including *fálsafa*, logic, astronomy, chemistry, mathematics, and medicine.

Ibn Sina began practicing medicine at the age of seventeen when he cured the Samanid ruler of Bukhara of what other doctors had pronounced to be an incurable disease. The ruler appointed him as his court physician and gave him access to his rich library, which Ibn Sina put to good use. He spent the rest of his life serving as a court physician and occasionally also as chief advisor (vizier) to various provincial rulers of western Iran. His position as a courtier exposed him to political intrigue, forcing him to change his masters frequently. He died at the age of fifty-eight of either dysentery or colic. Some scholars suspect that he may have overdosed himself while trying to dull the pain caused by his illness. Ibn Sina's detractors, who were quite numerous, insinuated that he undermined his health by overindulging in drink and sex. According to a popular legend, the original epitaph on his tombstone read: "His philosophy taught him no manners, and his medicine no cures." It seems more likely, however, that he simply overextended himself by trying to handle the affairs of the state and his medical practice during the day, while saving the night for working on his great masterpieces. To keep his mind agile, he confessed to having occasionally "reinforced" himself with a glass of wine. This taxing work schedule left Ibn Sina little time for rest and recuperation, which must have weakened his immune system and made him vulnerable to illness.

Ibn Sina has left behind a rich and variegated intellectual legacy that has contributed to the advancement of many sciences that had currency during his lifetime, including natural history, physics, chemistry, astronomy, mathematics, music, logic, mysticism, and philosophy per se. Of his major works, mention should be made of the "Canon of Medicine." This giant medical encyclopedia deals with such issues as the structure of the human organism, psychology, the nature of sickness and wellness, the general treatment of illnesses, pharmacology, diagnostics, surgery, and various types of diseases. In this enormous book, Ibn Sina makes some remarkable discoveries, suggesting, for the first time it seems, that smallpox is contagious, that diseases are caused by tiny invisible organisms, that cholera is different from plague, and so on. The "Canon's" lucid structure and systematic presentation made it extremely popular with members of the medical profession both in the East and in the West. Its Arabic text was published in Rome in 1593. Latin translations of the "Canon" had appeared much earlier and were studied by such Western luminaries as Thomas Aquinas and Albert the Great.[48] They served as medical textbooks for the students of the oldest European universities in Italy, Belgium, and France up to the eighteenth century, when Ibn Sina's theories and methods were finally superseded by Western experimental medicine. Ibn Sina is also the author of the "Healing of the Soul," which has summarized the ways in which the human soul (i.e., intellect) perceives the world around it, then uses these perceptions to obtain a sure and accurate knowledge of its laws by means of logical reasoning.

While al-Razi and even al-Farábi were relatively independent of Islam as an intellectual force,[49] Ibn Sina saw his task in integrating *fálsafa* more closely with the Muslim creed. He demonstrated much more cogently than al-Farábi the necessity of prophetic guidance and divinely revealed law for the proper functioning of human society. At the same time, like many of his philosophically minded colleagues, he tended to put himself above the commoner, whom he viewed as being incapable of pursuing a determined quest for philosophical knowledge. As already mentioned, contrary to the Shari'a, Ibn Sina allowed himself wine on the grounds that he found it stimulating for his intellectual work. As a refined thinker, he was confident that he knew how to avoid excess, which, in his view, was the main reason for wine's prohibition by the Muslim law.

In his philosophical works, Ibn Sina distinguishes two types of philosophical reasoning: theoretical and practical. The former seeks knowledge of the truth, the latter of the good. Theoretical philosophy, in his view, is the knowledge of things as they are regardless of our choice or action; practical philosophy is the knowledge of things that exist due to our choice and action. The principles of practical philosophy, according to Ibn Sina, are based on the Shari'a. The principles of theoretical philosophy are derived from the contemplation of various existing entities, their properties, and their movements. By correctly exercising his rational faculty, the philosopher rises "above the material nature of [empirical] images until he arrives at concepts that are free of physical features." In the process, the human intellect reunites with the active divine intellect, "which represents the basic structure of reality as emanated from God."[50] This concept, of course, is but yet another variation on the Neoplatonic doctrine of emanation that has been already discussed.

Unlike some earlier Muslim philosophers, who had argued that a monotheistic prophet is none other than a perfect rationalist thinker, Ibn Sina more consistently than any of his predecessors stressed the importance of the prophet's imaginative faculty. Far from being a simple mechanism for converting higher philosophical truths into images and allegories accessible to the philosophically illiterate populace,[51] this faculty allows the prophet to see things that are hidden from even the most perceptive philosopher. According to Ibn Sina, the prophet is somehow attuned to the immediate emanations from the realm of the active divine intellect, which, as mentioned, contains the true realities of all things and phenomena of the empirical world. The revelatory emanations of the active intellect endow the prophet with supersensory intuitions that are more direct and precise than any knowledge obtained through the philosopher's intellectual induction and rational demonstration. The intuitions thus obtained are then translated into persuasive, memorable parables and myths by the prophet's imaginative faculty that the ordinary rationalist philosopher normally lacks.

In dealing with the human condition and purpose in this world, Ibn Sina drew a sharp distinction between the mortal body and the immortal soul that survives the death of human organism. "The soul," he wrote in his "Healing," "does not die with the death of the body" because the latter originates "out of the matter, which is corruptible by its nature," whereas the soul originates from the Universal Soul, which is incorruptible and eternal.[52] This postulate allowed Ibn Sina to justify the Muslim doctrine of resurrection and the afterlife, with which previous philosophers had a serious problem because they adhered to Aristotle's classical notion that the human soul dies with the body.

Ibn Sina's other important contribution to his project of reconciling philosophy and prophetic revelation is his doctrine of existence and its relation to the essence of a thing. Taking his cue from Aristotle, who had pointed out that there is a distinction between what a thing is in itself and the fact that it is (i.e., that it exists), Ibn Sina argued that existence does not necessarily reside in any given essence but is rather superadded onto it as any other quality, such as weight, color, unity, density, and so on. On the basis of this premise, he drew a clear distinction between necessary and possible (or contingent) types of existence. According to Ibn Sina, this distinction sets God apart from his creation insofar as he alone is possessed of an existence that is necessary in itself and does not require any outside existence to sustain it, as all other existing entities do. This critical distinction, in his view, constitutes the ultimate and irrefutable proof of divine existence. Because God's existence is necessary, self-sufficient, and uncaused, it is radically different from that of his creatures. In God, existence inheres in his essence. In all other essences, existence is externally bestowed and therefore possible (contingent); it is a quality borrowed from God, the only real source of all existence. Here is how he describes the critical difference between the two types of existence:[53]

> The necessary existent is the existent, which when posited as not existing, an absurdity results. The possibly existent is the one that, when posited as either existing or not existing, no absurdity results. The necessary existent is the existence that *must be*, whereas the possibly existent is the one that has no "must" about it, whether in terms of its existence or non-existence.[54]

As his predecessors, Ibn Sina had to account for the plurality of the things and phenomena of the empirical universe that somehow emerges from the one, internally undifferentiated source of all being. To resolve this apparent puzzle,[55] Ibn Sina argued that the divine absolute is in and of itself one, simple, and indivisible. However, while being in this unified, undifferentiated state, it is unable to know itself because knowledge logically presupposes a relationship between the knowing subject and its object. It is the inherent desire to know the full range of the potentialities contained within its essence that prompts the First Intellect to emerge from the original oneness of the divine Absolute through the process of self-contemplation. After emerging from this original oneness, the First Intellect proceeds to generate further entities in triads: the intellect itself that governs the body (= heavenly sphere that it inhabits) and the spirit (= soul) that animates it. Our intellects are created from the intellect of the sublunar heavenly sphere, which Ibn Sina called "active intellect" or "form-giver." In occasionally reuniting with it, our intellects receive enlightenment, as a result of which we acquire an accurate and inerrant understanding of the universe and its elements. Seen in historical perspective, Ibn Sina's philosophy can be defined as a synthesis of Aristotelian philosophy, Neoplatonism, and Gnostic tradition. Ibn Sina's refusal to draw a distinction between the revelatory knowledge of the prophet and the rational knowledge of the philosopher appears to be part of his attempt to bridge the divide between prophetic religion and philosophy, while at the same time implicitly asserting the primacy of the latter. A complete reconciliation turned out to be impossible even for this great, if not the greatest mind of Islamic civilization, because some of his conclusions still cannot be reconciled with the Qur'anic teaching, at least if understood literally.

Thus, for instance, Ibn Sina was unable to accept the possibility of the resurrection of physical bodies on the Judgment Day because it was impossible to justify it from the viewpoint of logic, universal laws, and empirical observation. To prove his point, he rejected the idea that the body constitutes part of human being's essence. It is only united with a human essence temporarily, for the duration of its earthly life. In Ibn Sina's view, the existence of body is contingent and temporal; therefore the true essence of any human being is its soul/intellect. Because the soul/intellect is immortal,[56] there is nothing necessary or inevitable about the resurrection of the nonessential human body, once accidentally united with it, at the end of time. The resuscitation of the dead corpse would imply the soul's/intellect's reincarnation in a perishable and corruptible matter—an idea that Ibn Sina found impossible to accept. He also implicitly disagreed with the Qur'anic doctrine of the creation of the world out of nothingness because his understanding of the process of universal emanation implies that God did not choose to create the world at a certain moment in time by an act of free will. Rather, the world emerges out of the oneness of the divine Absolute through that latter's self-contemplation, which Ibn Sina considered to be "an eternal event which does not take place within time."[57] This cosmology logically presupposes that the world is eternal—an incessant effect of God's spontaneous self-meditation, not a necessary and deliberate consequence of God's creative command.[58]

Another point on which Ibn Sina departed from the mainstream theological creed of Islam is the nature of God's knowledge of created things. For Ibn Sina, God's knowledge is limited to universal notions and does not comprise their concrete and tangible manifestations in time and space. After all, the world is nothing but God's knowledge of himself, that is, the existential potentialities and rational laws inherent in his eternal essence.[59] In other words, God has a general knowledge of causes and effects peculiar to the entities that he has created. These causal relations constitute the law that governs the universe. However, God himself is not necessarily aware of each concrete and specific case of the realization of this general law of causality, for in order to do so he would need the humanlike sense perceptions that by their very nature are fallible and imperfect.[60] Being in possession of the fallible knowledge delivered by the sense perceptions would irreparably alter God's perfect essence.[61] This assumption flies in the face of the Qur'anic statements, according to which God knows things in their specific uniqueness, down to the finest points of detail.[62] All these and some other contradictions between Ibn Sina's theories and the revelation were brought up against him by the theologian al-Ghazali, whose critique of Islamic philosophy will be discussed shortly.

To sum up, while Ibn Sina made every possible effort to reconcile prophetically revealed religion with rationalist philosophy, in the final analysis, he implicitly and sometimes explicitly privileged the latter over the former. Had this been otherwise, we would not have classified him as a *faylasúf*. To escape the inevitable contradictions previously enumerated, Ibn Sina confined institutionalized prophetic religion to the political and social sphere of human existence par excellence, while allowing rational inquiry into the objective laws that determine the functioning of the universe. Religion's role, in his view, consists of legitimizing and supporting the existing political and social order with all its merits and drawbacks. *Fálsafa*, on the other hand, serves as the ultimate source of a logically sound and incontrovertible (apodictic) knowledge of the world for those who are capable of comprehending and implementing its sophisticated methods and principles.

Al-Ghazali, the Proof of Islam

Unlike al-Kindi, al-Razi, al-Farábi, and Ibn Sina, al-Ghazali did not consider himself to be a philosopher, nor would he have liked to be considered such. On the contrary, in his famous treatise "The Incoherence of the Philosophers," he mounts a concerted and well argued attack against *fálsafa* in an effort to demonstrate its numerous internal contradictions, as well as the irreconcilable conflict of its principles with the message of the Qur'an. Al-Ghazali's main problem with philosophy was that it was, in his opinion, unable to lead its practitioners to the ultimate goal of human existence. This goal, according to al-Ghazali, is to attain certainty and serenity in preparation for the inevitable death, subsequent resurrection, and the last judgment. This was not what philosophy was all about. On the contrary, in al-Ghazali's opinion, engaging in rational disciplines such as *fálsafa* and *kalám* is likely to breed doubt and disquiet in their adepts. Therefore, al-Ghazali considered philosophy (and to a lesser extent *kalám*) to be not just useless but also outright detrimental for the all-important goal of salvation in the hereafter.

Born in the city of Tus (near present-day Mashhad in Iran), al-Ghazali was left an orphan at an early age.[63] Nevertheless, he received an excellent religious education under the tutelage of the most prominent scholars of his homeland, including the famous Ash'arite theologian al-Juwáyni (d. 1085). His schooling was primarily that of a theologian and jurist, although he did have a Sufi teacher who introduced him to the basics of Sufi theory and practice. A naturally gifted man, al-Ghazali soon established himself as the leading Sunni theologian and jurist of his day. While in Iran, he was patronized by the cultured Saljuk vizier Nizám al-Mulk (d. 1092). At an unspecified date, al-Ghazali moved to Baghdad, where he was appointed professor of the Shafi'i version of Islamic law at the prestigious religious college Nizamíyya, which his patron Nizám al-Mulk had founded and endowed. Al-Ghazali soon distinguished himself as one of the most popular and sought-after scholars of the 'Abbásid capital. In his own words, for four years, he was lecturing to an audience of over three hundred students. Simultaneously, he vigorously pursued the study of philosophy by private reading. He summarized the results of his investigations in several books, including "The Intentions of the Philosophers," a lucid and objective summary of the main philosophical doctrines of his age. Its Latin translations gained a wide circulation in medieval Europe.

In 1095, al-Ghazali suffered a severe nervous breakdown, which incapacitated him so that he could no longer continue his studies and teaching. This psychological crisis was, in his words, precipitated by his thoughts about the ultimate meaning of human life and death, as well as about his personal destiny in the hereafter. Deeply troubled and anxious to overcome his spiritual turmoil, al-Ghazali began to question the intellectual assumptions upon which his whole world outlook had previously rested. In his autobiographical work "Deliverance from Error," he describes his agonizing quest for certainty and his painstaking attempts to rid himself of intellectual doubt and spiritual disquiet:

> Such thoughts as these threatened to shake my reason, and I sought to find an escape from them. But how? In order to disentangle the knot of this difficulty, a proof was necessary. Now a proof must be based on primary assumptions, and it was precisely these of which I was in doubt. This unhappy state lasted about two months. . . .
>
> Coming seriously to consider my state, I found myself bound down on all sides by these trammels. Examining my actions, the most fair-seeming of which were my lecturing and professorial occupations, I found to my surprise that I was engrossed in several studies of little value and profitless as regards my salvation. I probed the motives of my teaching and found that, in place of being sincerely consecrated to God, I was only motivated by a vain desire of honor and reputation. I perceived that I was on the edge of an abyss, and that without an immediate conversion I should be doomed to eternal fire. In these reflections I spent a long time. Still a prey to uncertainty, one day I decided to leave Baghdad and to give up everything; the next day I gave up my resolution. I advanced one step and immediately relapsed. In the morning I was sincerely resolved only to occupy myself with the future life; in the evening a crowd of carnal thoughts assailed and dispersed my resolutions. On the one side the world kept me bound to my post in the chains of covetousness, on the other side the voice of faith cried to me, "Up! Up! Thy life is nearing its end, and thou hast a long journey to make. All thy pretended knowledge is naught but falsehood and fantasy. If thou dost not think now of thy salvation, when wilt thou think of it? If thou dost not break thy chains today, when wilt thou break them?" Then my resolve was strengthened, I wished to give up all and flee; but the Tempter,[64] returning to the attack, said, "You are suffering from a transitory feeling; don't give way to it, for it will soon pass. If you obey it, if you give up this fine position, this honorable post exempt from trouble and rivalry, this seat of authority safe from attack, you will regret it later on without being able to recover it. . . ." Finally, conscious of my weakness and the prostration of my soul, I took refuge in God as a man at the end of himself and without resources.[65]

Having overcome his vacillations, al-Ghazali left Baghdad on the pretext of making a pilgrimage. In reality, he set his mind on abandoning for good his professorship and public career as a jurist and theologian. The exact motives behind al-Ghazali's withdrawal from Baghdad society are obscure. Some Western scholars have suggested that al-Ghazali indeed became dissatisfied with the intellectual and legalistic approach to religion that had been dominant among his fellow scholars and sought to cultivate a more personal experience of God that, he hoped, would lead him to a spiritual rejuvenation.[66] Others have averred that he may have been frightened by a wave of Isma'ili assassinations, especially after his friend and benefactor Nizám al-Mulk had fallen victim to one of them. According to this interpretation, this terrifying event prompted him to seek refuge in Syria. This latter explanation indirectly calls in doubt the spiritual and intellectual reasons for his departure that he himself mentioned in his autobiography.[67]

Be this as it may, al-Ghazali's abandonment of his highly respected and coveted public position in Baghdad allowed him to focus single-mindedly on contemplation and writing. It was during the time of his withdrawal from the life of the imperial court, first to Syria and later on to the Hijáz, that he composed his major works that have made him famous across the Muslim world and beyond. During his retirement, al-Ghazali lived as a poor Sufi, often in solitude, spending his time in meditation and other spiritual and ascetic exercises. This voluntary retirement and incessant meditation on his personal failings helped al-Ghazali to gain a clearer understanding of the validity of the mystic path to God that constituted the centerpiece of Sufi piety and self-discipline. Whether or not he indeed considered himself a full-fledged Sufi master, it was during the last decade of his life that al-Ghazali penned his greatest masterpiece "The Revivification of Religious Sciences." It furnishes a comprehensive and detailed program for the spiritual rejuvenation of Sunni Islam by means of integrating it with some elements of Sufi spirituality and asceticism.

In 1106, Fakhr al-Mulk, son of Nizám al-Mulk and vizier of the Saljuk ruler of Khurasan, pressed al-Ghazali to return to public teaching. He yielded to the pressure, possibly moved by the belief that he was destined to be the "restorer of religion" (*mujáddid*) of the new Islamic century,[68] in accordance with a widely cited prophetic *hadíth*. Be this as it may, in that year al-Ghazali resumed his teaching career at the Nizamíyya college in Nishapur (eastern Iran). Shortly before his death in 1111, he had once again abandoned academic pursuits and retired to his native town of Tus. While there, he had established a Sufi lodge in which he trained young disciples in the theory and practice of Sufi life.

Al-Ghazali's unusual evolution from a successful and highly respected public scholar to a humble recluse is described in his autobiography, "Deliverance from Error," which was quoted earlier in this chapter. The work addresses several major themes. One of them is the intellectual helplessness of the human condition when it is not graced and aided by divine compassion and guidance. The other is the deleterious impact of doubt and skepticism on the believer's faith. Both themes have direct bearing on al-Ghazali's attitude toward philosophy and philosophers as well as some other intellectual and religious movements of the age. In his autobiography, he summarizes the predicament of the philosophers as follows:

> They [philosophers] draw up a list of the conditions to be fulfilled by [rational] demonstration which are known without fail to produce certainty. When, however, they come to treat religious questions, not only are they unable to satisfy these conditions, but they also admit an extreme degree of relaxation.[69]

In sum, according to al-Ghazali, the philosophers have failed to reconcile the knowledge they obtain by means of rational argumentation with the truths enunciated in the Muslim revelation. This point is further explored and brought home in al-Ghazali's earlier treatise entitled "The Incoherence of the Philosophers." Directed primarily against al-Farábi and Ibn Sina, it argues that philosophical doctrines cannot be reconciled with the Qur'anic concepts of bodily resurrection, creation of the world out of nothingness at a certain point in time,[70] and God's knowledge of every individual, contingent event or entity.[71] Since the veracity of none of these teachings can be demonstrated by means of rational argumentation, an irreconcilable contradiction results. It compels the philosophers to either allegorize away the literal meaning of the divine revelation or to bend the rules and logic of their rational argumentation.

Al-Ghazali then proceeds to aver that the relations between the premises and conclusions of a philosophical syllogism[72] cannot persuade both the mind and the heart. The heart demands a different type of conviction, namely, a sincere and unquestioning acceptance of the prophetically revealed truth. This demand contradicts the chief goal of philosophy because every intellectual inquiry into the meaning of revelation (which philosophy encourages) inevitably involves questioning it for consistency. This questioning brings about doubt in the questioner and thereby diverts him or her from the all-important goal of achieving serenity, certainty, and eventually salvation in the hereafter. Seen from this vantage point, philosophy is a useless discipline in that it contains "no provision for the afterlife." Rightly or wrongly, al-Ghazali's incisive critique of the intellectual premises of Islamic philosophy and its incompatibility with Qur'anic teachings is sometimes seen as the principal reason for its progressive decline and eventual paralysis in the subsequent centuries. Although definitely a *fálsafa*'s major nemesis, many more factors were at play there, and al-Ghazali was only one of many factors that led to the fossilization of Muslim philosophical thought in the later Middle Ages and beyond.

For al-Ghazali, the only source of a true knowledge and intellectual certainty is divine inspiration or guidance. It is, in essence, nothing other than the supersensory, intuitive knowledge that Sufi mystics claim to be able to obtain it by means of strict self-discipline, mortification of the flesh, purification of the soul of evil thoughts and traits, and constant meditation on divine majesty and kindness. In regard to religious faith, al-Ghazali found himself in agreement with the Hadíth folk: Believers should concern themselves with living and believing correctly for the sake of divine blessing in this world and salvation in the other; they should not meddle with what does not concern them. Seeking profane knowledge out of idle curiosity or due to spiritual disquiet is the first step to perdition. By studying *fálsafa* (or *kalám* for that matter), the ordinary believer can be easily led astray by its elegant metaphysical constructs and persuasive argumentation. The believer's preoccupation with philosophical argumentation may muddle the original serenity of his or her religious faith, thereby depriving him or her of any hope of salvation in the afterlife. Therefore, only qualified scholars, who through their lifelong study of philosophy have been rendered immune to its allure, are allowed to delve into philosophical inquiry. Thus, al-Ghazali effectively declares *fálsafa* to be a taboo for an average believer because he or she cannot critically evaluate its true import. Nor is it of use to a refined intellectual due to the faulty premises on which it is based and its failure to satisfactorily account for the precepts of prophetic religion. Whereas al-Ghazali's critique of *fálsafa* was itself philosophical in its inspiration and method,[73] he has definitely succeeded in showing the limitations of rational argumentation when confronted with the revealed truths of the Qur'an.

An independent and broad-minded intellectual, al-Ghazali saw his task in breaking away from the narrow confines of Muslim rationalist disciplines—be it philosophy or *kalám*—in order to build a comprehensive foundation for spiritual life in an age when Sunni Islam had found itself under attack from both within (the doctrines of Isma'ili Shi'ism) and without (the Crusades). As a result of a thoroughgoing inquiry into the validity of various intellectual disciplines of his time, al-Ghazali discovered this foundation in Sufism. In his opinion, many aspects of the Sufi tradition were amenable to spiritualizing the religious practice of his coreligionists. By actualizing the inner dimensions of their faith, the believers transform it into their deep-seated and unshakable conviction. In short, for al-Ghazali, Sufism was the only sure way for believers to achieve certitude and serenity that he considered to be essential to their personal salvation.

In dealing with the dangers faced by Islam, al-Ghazali paid special attention to Isma'ilism, which, as we remember from Chapter 12, had achieved extraordinary successes during his lifetime. Most importantly, the Isma'ili Shi'ites had managed to establish the powerful Fatimid Empire that encompassed Egypt, Syria, and North Africa. It posed a mortal threat to the very existence of Sunni Islam. This fact helps to explain al-Ghazali's preoccupation with the Isma'ili "heresy." Did he target Isma'ilism due to its dangerous implications for the Sunni community or rather because of his personal dislike of authoritarian, personality-based ideology? The answer to this question died with him. One may venture a guess that al-Ghazali's strident anti-Isma'ili stance sprang from the fact that he implicitly found some elements of the Isma'ili doctrine to be persuasive. While *kalám* and *fálasafa* were strictly rationalist teachings (the former emphasized dialectical argumentation on the basis of commitment to the revelation; the latter relied on logical demonstration with a view to discovering the timeless norms of nature), the Isma'ilis appealed to a sacred historical institution, the imamate, and the community that had been built around it. Al-Ghazali realized that the secret, esoteric knowledge of the true realities of religion claimed by the Isma'ili leaders could, under favorable circumstances, prove to be irresistibly attractive to the Muslim masses precisely because of the aura of mystery surrounding it. A keen observer, al-Ghazali was aware of the fact that the Isma'ili doctrine of the infallible and divinely guided leader, the *imam*, had served as an effective recruitment tool and the doctrinal foundation of a political and social order established on his behalf. The doctrine's effectiveness was evident from the rise of the powerful Isma'ili state in North Africa, and later also in Egypt, whose agents operated across the width and breadth of the Muslim world. Al-Ghazali saw his task in formulating a viable Sunni alternative to the Isma'ili doctrine of salvation through the guidance of an infallible *imam*.

According to al-Ghazali, the allure of Isma'ilism was determined by the widespread and deeply held popular desire for an uncontested religious authority that by virtue of its purported inerrancy could alone guarantee justice and prosperity to every believer. The Isma'ili *imam*'s claim to be such an authority and thus to be able to guide his followers to justice in this life and to salvation in the hereafter attracted to him a large and enthusiastic following.

After explaining the reasons for the attraction of the Isma'ili doctrine of imamate, al-Ghazali refuted it by arguing that no divinely guided, infallible authority was possible after the death of prophet Muhammad. Any claim to such authority amounted to heresy and unbelief. As a convinced Sunni, he insisted that the Sunni community was the sole beneficiary of God's guidance because, in accordance with a famous prophetic *hadíth,* it was collectively protected by God from error and delusion. Therefore the very membership of this community guaranteed salvation to those believers who kept up faith and were not assailed by doubts about the veracity of their faith. Sufis, who imitated the Prophet meticulously and sought to gain access to the source of divine revelation by cultivating supersensory insight, were ideally positioned to serve as the community's spiritual guides. Despite its importance as a reinvigorating force, argued al-Ghazali, the supersensory knowledge of the true realities of the world and of the Scripture claimed by the Sufis should not be allowed to displace the external religious law (Shari'a) because it is absolutely essential for maintaining a stable social order no matter how imperfect.[74] Nevertheless, the inner aspect of religious faith is of great and abiding importance for the wellbeing of the Muslim community because, in al-Ghazali's opinion, Islam cannot persevere without a continuous reexperiencing of its truths by its elect representatives, that is, the Sufi saints and visionaries. In line with this premise, al-Ghazali assigned the Sufis a pivotal role in preserving the vibrancy of the Muslim faith, as well as in guiding the personal lives and consciousness of all Muslims.

Ibn Rushd (Averroes), the Commentator

In Ibn Rushd, commonly known in the Christian West as "Averroes," we find Islam's greatest defender and promoter of Aristotle. He exemplifies the unique cultural and scientific sophistication of his native country known in Arabic language sources as al-Andalus (Islamic Spain). Born in Cordova (Spain) in 1126 in a family of distinguished Maliki jurists, Ibn Rushd followed the usual trajectory of a Muslim philosopher by combining the study of religious sciences with interests in philology, medicine, mathematics, and astronomy.[75] His outstanding intellectual capacities attracted the attention of the famous Muslim thinker Ibn Tufáyl (d. 1185), who served as court physician to the cultured Almohad sultan Abu Ya'qúb Yúsuf (r. 1163–1184).[76] Ibn Tufáyl, who is famous primarily as the author of the philosophical parable "The Living, Son of the Awake (Hayy b. Yaqzan)," introduced his younger colleague to the sultan in 1169.[77] The latter tested his knowledge of philosophical argumentation and was impressed. Citing Aristotle's "abstruse style," the ruler then commissioned Ibn Rushd to write an exposition of the Greek philosopher's greatest works.[78] Thus began Ibn Rushd's long career as a translator and commentator of Aristotle's works. His Arabic renditions of the Greek philosopher were later translated into Latin to become a major impulse for the rediscovery of his legacy in the Latin West. When Ibn Tufáyl had grown frail, Ibn Rushd succeeded him as the court physician to the sultan. Under the sultan's successor, he also served as chief judge of Seville, the capital of the Almohad state and later also

Figure 14.2 Statue of Averroes in Córdoba, Spain

Saleemzohaib: CC: Wikimedia Commons

of Cordova.[79] In 1195, the new Almohad sultan Abu Yusuf banished him from Marrakesh (in present-day Morocco), possibly because of the jealousy of the Maliki scholars of the city who resented Ibn Rushd's preoccupation with "pagan" Greek philosophy. His books were burned, and an official ban on studying *fálsafa* was circulated by his detractors.[80] Ibn Rushd was eventually restored to favor by the sultan and returned to Marrakesh, only to die there shortly afterward (1198) (see Figure 14.2).

As a judge and state official, Ibn Rushd recognized the necessity of revealed religion for the maintenance of a proper social and political order and prevention of moral vice. At the same time, he advocated the idea of the complementary nature of revealed law (Shari'a) and Greek philosophy, which he called "wisdom" (*hikma*). He justified the necessity of philosophical inquiry into the mysteries of the universe by citing Qur'anic injunctions that encourage believers to "consider the dominion of the heaven and the earth and what things God has created" (7:185 and 45:6) and to "reflect upon the creation of the heavens and the earth" (3:191 and 44:38–39). Ibn Rushd interpreted these verses as God's unequivocal command for his servants to engage in rational contemplation and to investigate the general laws of nature that govern the created world. This is, of course, exactly the object of *fálsafa*, which Ibn Rushd defined as "nothing more than study of existing beings and reflection on them as indications of the Maker."[81]

Like his philosophical forerunners, Ibn Rushd believed that the primary goal of the human race is to seek happiness in this world and in the hereafter. To help them to reach this goal, God created philosophy and religious dispensation (*shar'*). The former is accessible to those few who are capable of a concerted intellectual work and independent investigation; the latter is available to all people regardless of their intellectual capacities.[82] Thus, religious law and philosophy serve essentially the same purpose, but only philosophy is capable of illuminating "the hidden inner meaning of revealed truth."[83] Otherwise, there is a complete harmony between the two, as they "refer to one truth, to one end."[84] For Ibn Rushd, they are just two different routes leading to the same destination.

Since notions of happiness differ from one person to another, there are several levels or kinds of it. The highest one consists of achieving a union with the universal intellect. "Those who are entitled to it," says Ibn Rushd (quoting Galen), "are one in a thousand."[85] This happiness can be defined as the contemplative life of the human intellect, although it should always be complemented by the observance by the philosopher of the ethical and social norms explicated in the Shari'a. The rest of humankind should be content simply with implementing the Shari'a. This guarantees them moral and ethical purity and, as the ultimate reward, felicity in the hereafter. In this way, Islam holds promise of happiness to all categories of people regardless of their level of intellectual attainment, and everyone is entitled to wisdom and happiness in the amount that is appropriate to them. In the words of Ibn Rushd:

> The religions are . . . obligatory, since they lead towards wisdom in a way universal to all human beings, since philosophy only leads a certain number of intelligent people to knowledge of happiness and they therefore have to learn wisdom, while religions seek the education of the masses as a whole.[86]

Thus, whereas a tiny minority of the "intelligent people" seeks higher philosophical knowledge because they are explicitly commanded to do so by the Qur'an, the masses should obediently and unquestioningly follow the literal meaning of the revelation. The shortcomings of their rational faculties account for the fact that the philosophical truths of the revelation are couched in the Qur'an in an allegorical and often anthropomorphic language that is generally alien to philosophical discourse.[87] In their original, pure form, these rational truths would have been incomprehensible to the generality of the believers. The "popular" style of presentation adopted by God in the Qur'an is evidence of God's loving kindness toward his human creatures because it renders "his revelation available to all regardless of their capacity to reason."[88]

As the major representative of Peripatetic (Aristotelian) philosophical thought in his age, Ibn Rushd could not leave unanswered al-Ghazali's attacks against philosophy. On the issue of the eternity of the world, which al-Ghazali imputed to the philosophers, Ibn Rushd argues that if we consider the world to have originated in time, we should admit that time preceded it and is thus eternal. It is much more logical to suppose that both the world and time are part of God's continual generation of existence and existents. Before this process was set in motion, there was nothing in existence but God, or rather the divine Absolute. It was the source of both the world and time. Therefore, al-Ghazali's claim that the philosophers advocate the eternity of the world is misplaced: He poses a logically incorrect question. In dealing with God's knowledge of particulars as opposed to universals, Ibn Rushd dismisses al-Ghazali's accusation that the philosophers deny the former as a nonissue. It is based on the faulty assumption that God's knowledge is somehow similar to human knowledge, which, according to Ibn Rushd, is patently not the case. God's knowledge is different from the regular human knowledge, since it is the *cause* of the object known (because God is its originator), whereas human knowledge is the *effect* of the object known, which exists independently of its human subject. Furthermore, God's knowledge is immutable, whereas human knowledge, applied as it is to mutable and constantly changing entities, is not.[89] As for al-Ghazali's charge that philosophers deny the resurrection of human bodies at the end of time, Ibn Rushd concedes that it cannot be demonstrated on philosophical grounds. He suggests that this and similar dogmas should not be questioned but taken at face value because they serve "as preconditions of happiness and virtue in this world and should be adhered to on moral, social and pragmatic grounds."[90] In general, whenever one encounters an apparent disagreement between the literal meaning of the Scripture and the conclusions reached by syllogistic reasoning, one must resort to an allegorical interpretation (*ta'wil*) of the literal meaning in accordance with the rules of the Arabic language. If practiced correctly, this interpretation is bound to produce an agreement between the text and the conclusions of the philosophical syllogism.[91]

It is interesting to point out that Ibn Rushd's influence on the subsequent history of Islamic intellectual life was rather limited. On the other hand, among medieval European and Jewish scholars, his commentaries on Aristotle's works translated into Latin and Hebrew found a large and eager following.[92] Ibn Rushd's renditions of Aristotle's views, as they were understood by his Christian readers, became part of the theological curricula of major European universities. They caused a series of heated debates in the Christian scholastic circles that involved such Christian luminaries as Hermannus Alemannus (Herman the German; d. 1272), Thomas Aquinas (d. 1274), Bonaventure (d. 1274), Albertus Magnus (d. 1280), Siger of Brabant (d. 1281), Roger Bacon (d. around 1294), and Dante Alighieri (d. 1321).[93] These debates focused on such controversial issues as the eternity of the world and its creation out of nothingness, the scope of divine intervention into the functioning of the universe, and so on.

In Western Christianity, the name of Ibn Rushd (Averroes) has come to be closely associated with the famous theory of "dual truth," according to which religion (faith) and philosophy (reason) have two completely different logics and therefore should not be tested by each other's criteria. Put differently, both are essentially true, each in its own way and in accordance with its own internal logic. This was hardly Ibn Rushd's original view, for, as we have seen, he was an advocate of the harmony of religion and philosophy and was eager to resolve any contradictions between them by means of an allegorical interpretation of the sacred texts. The right to such interpretation, according to Ibn Rushd, should be exercised with care.[94] In practice, this meant that it should be restricted exclusively to the most accomplished philosophers.

Conclusions

In sum, *fálsafa* served as an alternative to the practically unchallenged and dominant religious worldview and moral-ethical values current in medieval Muslim societies. The Muslim *faylasúf* was an individualist who recognized the importance of institutionalized religion for maintaining at least a modicum of social order and justice but who was keen on governing himself by his own intellect in the hopes of attaining the greatest possible intellectual and spiritual perfection and the pleasure attendant to it.[95] He himself determined what was good and what was bad for him personally; he himself was responsible for directing and disciplining his body and soul. Thus, the philosopher effectively created his own personal morality, esthetics, and lifestyle based on his logical conclusions about the universe and on his knowledge of the functioning of human organism. He studied nature in order to discover the uniform logical principles behind the apparent diversity of natural phenomena. Simultaneously, he observed human society around him in order to determine its optimum *modus operandi* and his own place within it. Finally, as already mentioned, he studied his own body with its functions and malfunctions in order to find remedies for its ailments. All this knowledge was supposed to enable the philosopher to achieve the rank of the ideal human individual, who had fully realized his human potential and lived up to the demanding requirements of *philosophia*.

One cannot but notice that on the intellectual and ethical-moral plane, the world of Muslim philosophers stood in striking (and conscious) contrast to the world of the *'ulamá'*. Nevertheless, the majority of *falásifa* considered themselves to be good Muslims and did their utmost to reconcile their philosophical convictions with the predominant religious beliefs of their age. The life stories of the greatest Muslim philosophers examined in this chapter show that they tended to follow certain professions. Most typically, they became doctors, alchemists, and astrologists. In the Middle Ages, these rare professions required specialized training in the fields of anatomy, physiology, psychology, botany, chemistry, mathematics, optics, and astronomy. While the physician was called upon to give advice in case of a dangerous illness or to perform a surgery, the astrologist could give advice to the ruler on certain personal, political, or military matters, for example the propitious time for starting a military campaign, marriage, a political alliance, or the birth of a royal or princely child. Knowledge of chemistry was essential in trying to manufacture the "philosopher's stone," which was believed to be capable of turning base metals into gold or producing the much coveted "elixir" of [eternal] life. The majority of the *'ulamá'* rejected astrology and alchemy as diabolical—a brazen human attempt to arrogate God's exclusive right to create or to know that which is hidden from human sights. The *'ulamá'* were also suspicious of medicine as an illicit interference with the divinely predestined course of events, although in practice they grudgingly recognized its practical necessity. Thanks to the necessity of such rare (and religiously suspect) professions, the philosophers were able to gain access to powerful men of their societies, who protected them from the ignorant masses and from the censure and persecution by the learned guardians of institutionalized religion. One can say that medicine, astrology, and alchemy were the professional niches that allowed the *falásifa* to survive in a commonly hostile intellectual and social environment. Yet, in the final account, their loyalty to religion has always remained suspect in the eyes of both the masses and the religious establishment.

Questions to Ponder

1 To what extent was Islamic philosophy "Islamic" (or otherwise)?
2 Whose views do you find more appealing and convincing: al-Ghazali or Ibn Sina and Ibn Rushd? Can there be a compromise between the worldviews and theories of knowledge they represent?
3 Imagine a polemic between a Muslim scholar (*'álim*) and a *faylasúf*. What arguments are they likely to adduce to justify their respective world outlooks? In particular, what would they say about the divine revelation and its interpretation? About the creation of the world and role of God in it?
4 Can a person be one's own master and guide (per Islamic philosophy), or is one always in need of guidance revealed from above in achieving equilibrium in this life and happiness in the life to come (per Islamic theology)?

Summary

- *Fálsafa* in Islamic societies has Greek/Hellenistic roots. It presents a challenge to the world outlook based on Islamic revelation.
- *Fálsafa* and Islamic speculative theology (*kalám*) have their similarities and differences. The former seeks to furnish a comprehensive and harmonious picture of the universe based on a set of what the philosophers consider to be sound and incontrovertible premises; the latter is primarily concerned with interpreting revealed texts, formulating the dogma, and defending Islam from its real or imaginary detractors. These differences reflect the respective attitudes of these intellectual disciplines toward the scripture and the world as a whole.
- In the Neoplatonic foundations of Islamic cosmology and metaphysics, the world is the result of the emanation of existential possibilities from the divine Absolute in a staged process.
- *Fálsafa* is a product of the so-called translation project initiated by the caliph al-Ma'mún (r. 813–833) in Baghdad. Its place in Muslim societies is different from *fiqh* and *kalám*.
- Al-Kindi (d. ca. 870) is the first Muslim champion of "Greek wisdom." Al-Kindi insists that *fálsafa* is, in its essence, identical with the message of the prophets and therefore should be properly appreciated and studied by Muslims.
- Abu Bakr al-Razi (d. 925 or 935) is an accomplished physician and freethinker. He rejects institutionalized prophetic religions in favor of a rational understanding of the world and its creator by human beings endowed with the rational faculty. Al-Razi considers freedom of intellectual exploration to be the ultimate happiness that human beings can achieve.
- Al-Farábi (d. ca. 950) provides a synthesis of the Neoplatonic doctrine of the emanation of existence from one supreme source, on the one hand, and of Qur'anic cosmology, on the other.
- Al-Farábi believes philosophical thinking to be the surest way to a sound knowledge about the world and its creator; eventually it leads the philosopher to happiness. The prophets "popularize" and disseminate philosophical truths by couching them in accessible parables and allegories.
- In al-Farábi's political theory, the perfect human society is a "virtuous city" ruled by a "philosopher-king," who governs his domain according to rationally sound principles. Most societies of the age are "wicked cities" in which philosophers live as "isolated wise men."
- Ibn Sina (d. 1037) is a great (some say the greatest) Muslim physician, scientist, and philosopher. He draws a distinction between practical and theoretical philosophy. Theoretical philosophy is the knowledge of things as they are regardless of our choice or action; practical philosophy is the knowledge of things that exist due to our choice and action. Ibn Sina sees his task in bridging the divide between prophetic religion and philosophy, while, in the final account, safeguarding the primacy of the latter.
- Ibn Sina's emphasizes the prophet's imaginative faculty (which an ordinary philosopher lacks). Thanks to this rare ability, the prophet can convert higher philosophical truths into images and allegories accessible to the philosophically illiterate populace. Furthermore, his imagination also allows the prophet to see things that are hidden from even the most perceptive philosopher.

- Ibn Sina's doctrine concerns existence and its relation to the essence of a thing. God is the only possessor of existence that is independent and necessary in and of itself, as opposed to the contingent existence of created things bestowed upon them by God.
- Ibn Sina's cosmology is a synthesis of Aristotelian philosophy, Neoplatonism, and Gnosticism. Material existence flows spontaneously from its divine source in a number of stages. Through the correct application of their rational faculties, human beings can trace their origin back to this source of all knowledge and existence and, in so doing, acquire intuitive, supersensory insights into the universal laws that govern the universe.
- Al-Ghazali (d. 1111) searches for truth, serenity, and certainty. He believes that *kalám* and *fálsafa* fall short of this all-important goal. Intuitive Sufi-style knowledge and ascetic self-discipline are the only sure way for the believer to achieve certitude and serenity and, in the final account, salvation in the hereafter.
- Al-Ghazali's vigorous attack against the Isma'ili doctrine of the infallible and divinely guided leader (*imam*) is conditioned by its broad popular appeal to Muslims seeking an unerring guide to truth and salvation. The popularity of the Isma'ili doctrine of the imamate and the strength of the Fatimid Isma'ili state in Egypt pose a grave threat to the very foundations of the Sunni caliphate in Baghdad, which al-Ghazali champions and defends. Al-Ghazali's ultimate goal is to respiritualize and reinvigorate Sunni Islam by imbuing it with Sufi psychology (introspection), humility, and orientation toward the hereafter.
- Ibn Rushd (d. 1198) is the greatest Muslim commentator of Aristotle, treading the path of his Andalusian predecessors Ibn Tufayl and Ibn Bajja.
- Ibn Rushd's definition of *fálsafa* as "nothing more than study of existing beings and reflection on them as indications of the Maker." This study, according to Ibn Rushd, is directly sanctioned by the Qur'an and is therefore incumbent on every good Muslim.
- *Fálsafa* is the preserve of the elect few capable of a concerted intellectual work and independent investigation. On the other hand, religion, with its allegorical language and didactic (educational) parables, is accessible to everyone who is endowed with a modicum of rationality.
- Ibn Rushd rebuts al-Ghazali's critique of *fálsafa*.
- Ibn Rushd's works have a profound influence on Judeo-Christian theology and the intellectual life of medieval Europe as a whole.
- Muslim philosophers hold a tenuous (and unique) position in medieval Muslim societies. Medical professions, alchemy, and astronomy/astrology are "ecological niches" that allow the *falásifa* to escape excommunication and persecution.

Notes

1 Marshall Hodgson, *The Venture of Islam*, University of Chicago Press, Chicago, 1974, vol. 1, p. 422.
2 Jon McGinnis and David Reisman (ed., trans. and annotation), *Classical Arabic Philosophy*, Hackett Publishing, Indianapolis, 2007, p. xvii.
3 Montgomery Watt, *Islamic Philosophy and Theology*, Edinburgh University Press, Edinburgh, 1985, pp. 37–45.
4 Oliver Leaman, *An Introduction to Classical Islamic Philosophy*, Cambridge University Press, Cambridge, 2002, p. 11.
5 See Chapter 10.

6 Hodgson, *The Venture*, vol. 1, pp. 440–441 and Majid Fakhry, *A History of Islamic Philosophy*, 3rd ed., Columbia University Press, New York, 2004, pp. 43–65.

7 Leaman, *An Introduction to Classical Islamic Philosophy*, p. 16.

8 Ibid., p. 13.

9 McGinnis and Reisman (eds.), *Classical Arabic Philosophy*, pp. xviii–xix.

10 Fakhry, *A History*, pp. 21–33.

11 Ibid., pp. 27–32.

12 Ibid., p. 32.

13 Ibid., pp. 10–12.

14 Ibid., pp. 22 and 33.

15 Ibid., pp. 13–14.

16 Ibid., p. 68.

17 Peter Adamson, "al-Kindi," in Peter Adamson and Richard Taylor (eds.), *The Cambridge Companion to Arabic Philosophy*, Cambridge University Press, Cambridge, 2004, p. 33.

18 Fakhry, *A History*, p. 67; McGinnis and Reisman (eds.), *Classical Arabic Philosophy*, p. 1.

19 McGinnis and Reisman (eds.), *Classical Arabic Philosophy*, p. 2.

20 Fakhry, *A History*, pp. 91–94.

21 Ibid.

22 Ibid., pp. 70 and 74–76.

23 Ibid., p. 98.

24 Ibid.

25 McGinnis and Reisman (eds.), *Classical Arabic Philosophy*, p. 36.

26 Ibid., p. 43.

27 Sarah Stroumsa, *Freethinkers of Medieval Islam*, E. J. Brill, Leiden and Boston, 1999, pp. 88–89.

28 McGinnis and Reisman (eds.), *Classical Arabic Philosophy*, p. 46.

29 Fakhry, *A History*, pp. 100–101.

30 Stroumsa, *Freethinkers of Medieval Islam*, p. 115.

31 For the origins of this "impious" legend, see Louis Massignon, "La legende 'De Tribus Impostoribus' et ses origins islamiques," in Louis Massignon and Youakim Moubarac, (eds.), *Opera Minora*, Presses universitaires de France, Paris, 1969, vol. 1, pp. 82–84.

32 Stroumsa, *Freethinkers of Medieval Islam*, p. 106.

33 McGinnis and Reisman (eds.), *Classical Arabic Philosophy*, pp. 41–44.

34 Ibid., pp. 49–53.

35 Ibid., pp. 51–53.

36 Michael Marmura, "Falsafah," in Lindsay Jones (ed.), *Encyclopedia of Religion*, 2nd ed., McMillan Reference, Detroit, 2005, vol. 5, p. 2972.

37 Leaman, *An Introduction to Classical Islamic Philosophy*, pp. 17–18 and Fakhry, *A History*, pp. 122–123.

38 Leaman, *An Introduction to Classical Islamic Philosophy*, p. 18.

39 Fakhry, *A History*, pp. 125–126.

40 McGinnis and Reisman (eds.), *Classical Arabic Philosophy*, p. 104 and Fakhry, *A History*, pp. 130–131.

41 McGinnis and Reisman (eds.), *Classical Arabic Philosophy*, p. 117.

42 Fakhry, *A History*, pp. 129–131.

43 Paul Walker, "Philosophy of Religion in al-Farabi, Ibn Sina and Ibn Tufayl," in Todd Lawson (ed.), *Reason and Inspiration in Islam*, I.B. Taurus, London and New York, 2005, p. 91.

44 Fakhry, *A History*, pp. 131–132.

45 Walker, "Philosophy of Religion in al-Farabi, Ibn Sina and Ibn Tufayl," p. 91.

46 Hodgson, *The Venture*, vol. 1, p. 436.

47 Ibid., vol. 2, p. 317.

48 Leaman, *An Introduction to Classical Islamic Philosophy*, p. 23.

49 When al-Farábi spoke about prophecy, he normally used abstract terms without explicit reference to Islam and the prophet Muhammad.

50 Leaman, *An Introduction to Classical Islamic Philosophy*, p. 22.

51 As argued, for example by al-Farábi, see McGinnis and Reisman (eds.), *Classical Islamic Philosophy*, pp. 114–117.

52 McGinnis and Reisman (eds.), *Classical Arabic Philosophy*, pp. 195–199.

53 This passage gives us a sense of how argument was constructed and presented in philosophical discourses from that age.

54 McGinnis and Reisman (eds.), *Classical Arabic Philosophy*, p. 211.

55 For some reason, medieval Muslim thinkers believed that one can only produce one.

56 See McGinnis and Reisman (eds.), *Classical Islamic Philosophy*, pp. 68–78.

57 Leaman, *An Introduction to Classical Islamic Philosophy*, p. 24.

58 See, for instance, Q 16:40; 36:82; 2:117, according to which God "says to a thing 'Be!' and it is."

59 Nader El-Bizri, "God: Essence and Attributes," in Tim Winter (ed.), *The Cambridge Companion to Classical Islamic Theology*, Cambridge University Press, Cambridge, 2008, p. 133.

60 Leaman, *An Introduction to Classical Islamic Philosophy*, p. 135.

61 El-Bizri, "God," p. 133.

62 For instance, Q 10:61 and 34:3 ("Not even the weight of an atom in the heavens and in the earth escapes His knowledge").

63 What follows is a summary of Knysh, *Islamic Mysticism*, pp. 140–149.

64 That is, the Devil.

65 See http://www.fordham.edu/halsall/basis/1100ghazali-truth.html; I have slightly amended the translation.

66 Arthur Arberry, *Sufism: An Account of the Mystics of Islam*. George Allen and Unwin, London, 1950, p. 79.

67 Hans Küng, *Islam: Past, Present and Future* (trans. John Bowden), Oneworld, Oxford, 2007, p. 346.

68 The year 1106 C.E. corresponded to the year 499 of the Muslim Hijra calendar.

69 Hodgson, *The Venture*, vol. 2, p. 182.

70 As mentioned, both al-Farábi and Ibn Sina espoused various versions of the doctrine of emanation that implies that existence flows eternally and incessantly out of a transcendent source of all being.

71 According to Ibn Sina, God's knowledge comprises only universals, not particulars.

72 In logic, syllogism is an argument that consists of a major premise, a minor premise, and a conclusion. It allows the testing of the truth of premises by showing that what follows from them is true. As an example, one can cite the following simple syllogism: every virtue is laudable (major premise); kindness is a virtue (minor premise); therefore kindness is laudable (conclusion).

73 Leaman, *An Introduction to Classical Islamic Philosophy*, p. 27.

74 Patricia Crone, *Medieval Islamic Political Thought*, Edinburgh University Press, Edinburgh, 2004, pp. 237–247.

75 Fakhry, *A History*, p. 281.

76 Ibid., p. 274.

77 Ibid.

78 Ibid., p. 281.

79 Ibid.

80 Ibid., pp. 281–282.

81 Leaman, *An Introduction to Classical Islamic Philosophy*, p. 180.

82 Fakhry, *A History*, p. 293.

83 Leaman, *An Introduction to Classical Islamic Philosophy*, p. 178.

84 Ibid., p. 180.

85 Ibid., p. 181 and Fakhry, *A History*, p. 302.

86 Leaman, *An Introduction to Classical Islamic Philosophy*, p. 186.

87 Fakhry, *A History*, pp. 287–290.

88 Leaman, *An Introduction to Classical Islamic Philosophy*, p. 186.

89 Fakhry, *A History*, pp. 294–295.

90 Ibid., p. 292 and Majid Fakhry, "Ibn Rushd," in Lindsay Jones (ed.), *Encyclopedia of Religion*, Macmillan, Detroit, 2005, vol. 6, p. 4272.

91 Fakhry, *A History*, pp. 287–290.

92 Ibid., p. 284.

93 Ibid., p. 285.

94 Ibid., pp. 287–292.

95 Ibid., p. 302.

Chapter 15

Transmission and Conservation of Knowledge

'Ulamá', Mádrasas, and Sufi Lodges

The Status, Venues, and Bearers of Learning in Muslim Societies

The Prophet of Islam encouraged his followers to "seek knowledge, even as far away as China"[1] and declared "the quest for knowledge [to be] incumbent upon every Muslim man and Muslim woman."[2] Muslims have taken the advice of the Prophet very seriously: The importance of the pursuit of learning has been emphasized by every major Muslim scholar of the Muslim community.[3] "Knowledge," says one, "is the highest [rank of] nobility, just as love is the highest of ties." "If one is ignorant of knowledge," wrote another, "it is as though he is ignorant of his father. Knowledge for one who seeks it is a father, only better."[4] Books, which together with teachers were the principal carriers of learning at that age, were seen by Muslims as a symbol of power. An early modern Arab scholar wrote:

> A book in a dream means power. He who sees the book in his hand in a dream will acquire power.[5]

Initially, the process of transmission of learning in Islamic societies took place in mosques, as described in the following passage:

> The teacher leaning against a pillar in the court of the mosque with a group of students around him in a semi-circle, side by side with similar groups—this is the typical picture of Muslim education. The teacher dictating, the student taking down his words; or someone reading a text, the teacher's or an older authority's, and the teacher expanding and commenting—this is a typical procedure.[6]

This kind of educational environment determined the subjects that were considered appropriate for study: the Qur'an and its commentary, the *hadíth*, and jurisprudence (*fiqh*), which Abu Hanífa (d. 767), one of the founding fathers of this discipline, defined as "a person's knowledge of his rights and duties."[7] Some elements of medicine and hygiene were also taught, usually within the framework of juridical norms. Secular sciences such as astronomy, calculus, physics, and philosophy were normally excluded from the mosque curriculum, although philology, especially poetry and linguistics, was often offered as a subsidiary discipline to help students to understand the nuances of the text of the Qur'an and the Prophet's Sunna. The study of "foreign" subjects, such as *fálsafa* and medicine, was usually conducted in "academies" along the lines of the House of Wisdom established by the caliph al-Ma'mún, as well as in libraries and hospitals. The institution of the religious "college" (*mádrasa*), which gradually evolved from mosque-based schools to be discussed later in this chapter, did not offer "foreign sciences" due to their non-Islamic provenance.[8] Overall, "foreign sciences" were marginal to the premodern and early modern Muslim educational system, which was dominated by the study of Scripture and divine law.

As Abu Hanífa's statement, previously quoted, eloquently emphasized, the study of these two subjects in mosques and later also in *mádrasa*s had quite concrete practical goals: To instill in students the knowledge of their rights and obligations vis-à-vis God and the Muslim community and, in so doing, to guide them on the path to salvation in the afterlife. This being the case, a minimum amount of this salvific knowledge (namely, the times and methods of prayers, Qur'anic verses to be used in them, the days and times of fasting, the percentage of income or property to be given away as alms, the rites of pilgrimage, and dietary prohibitions) was required of all believers.[9] To learn such basic religious precepts, they could either attend a class at a mosque or learn them from their parents at home. In this way, this sum total of basic religious knowledge was reproduced and transmitted within Muslim societies from the upper classes down to ordinary believers.

Understandably, not every believer was expected to become a religious scholar (*'álim*) or jurist (*faqíh*). However, anyone who had achieved this status by a time-consuming, arduous, and diligent study would become part of the Muslim learned elite referred to collectively as *'ulamá'*. As custodians of the salvific knowledge, the *'ulamá'* in premodern and early modern Muslim societies enjoyed the lofty status of "heirs to the Prophet." In this capacity, they were, according to a famous prophetic saying, the "rulers of kings" in the same way as the latter were the "rulers of [ordinary] people."[10] The teaching, learning, and discussion of Islam's sacred books and their practical legal, ethical, and moral implications for the believers were thus seen by the community at large as a special means of worshiping God and thus a religiously meritorious deed.[11] As one author put it, "[obtaining] knowledge is the prayer of the innermost self, and a worship of the heart."[12] It is, therefore, only natural that initially religious learning was confined to places of prayer.

At the outset, study in circles and groups in the mosque was a rather informal affair. Students would drift from one teacher to another and sample subjects that appealed to them, be it Qur'anic exegesis, *hadíth*, or jurisprudence. Rival circle leaders teaching in the same mosque would occasionally engage in disputations over some finer points of legal theory or Qur'anic pronouncements.[13] In such disputations, scholars with well stocked and prodigious memories, who were able to marshal the greater amount of scriptural evidence in support of their views, usually gained the upper hand. Naturally, they were bound to attract more students than their less gifted rivals. As an anecdote about the rift between al-Hásan al-Basri and Wásil b. 'Atá' demonstrates,[14] students could and did disagree with their teachers and occasionally formed their own study circles in consequence. In sum, during the first Islamic centuries, we find a system of education that was informal, open, and lacking a fixed curriculum. Scholars of different legal schools (Maliki, Hanafi, Shafi'i, and Hanbali) used different juridical manuals (usually those written by the founding fathers of their schools or later commentaries thereon) to teach different versions of Sunni law. Even within one and the same legal school, each scholar was relatively free to choose any manual he liked. Shi'ite scholars had their own educational system with its own textbooks and authorities, either the Shi'ite *imam*s themselves or scholars closely associated with them. Before we proceed to discuss the teaching process at advanced levels, let's have a glimpse of Islamic elementary education in the premodern and early modern era.

Elementary Education: The *Kuttáb*

The process of study at the elementary level started with what we would call "rote learning." Children as young as five–six years old would memorize Qur'anic *sura*s (usually in reverse order, from the shortest to the longer ones), write them down, and recite aloud before their classmates and the teacher. Offspring of caliphs, courtiers, provincial governors, and nobility would normally have private tutors, some of whom were distinguished experts on various religious disciplines. For the rest, the venue of elementary instruction was usually located in a mosque or a room adjacent to it. This room, and later on a freestanding building where children gathered for study, was known as *máktab* or *kuttáb*. It was roughly an equivalent of the Western primary or elementary school. While the principal focus in the *kuttáb* was on memorizing, reading, and writing passages from the Qur'an and *hadíth*, elements of the Arabic language were also taught to help students gain a better understanding of the meaning of the revelation, whose archaic style and vocabulary were "foreign" not just to non-Arab Muslims but also to Arabs speaking their regional vernaculars.[15] Arabic calligraphy and basic religious duties were also taught. Male and female children usually studied in separate rooms. Armed with a reed pen or a piece of chalk and a wooden tablet and squatting on the floor, they would write down the material dictated by the teacher, then read it back to him individually or in chorus. The teacher would then correct their reading and writing mistakes, if any. In larger schools, the teacher was often aided by an assistant or an advanced senior student. In the very beginning, when school buildings were in short supply, lessons were occasionally given in the open air. Thus, a popular eighth-century schoolteacher from Kufa gave classes to a whopping three thousand students as he was riding on his donkey up and down the aisle formed by the rows of sitting children.

Arabic being the language of the revelation, for many centuries instruction at *kuttáb*s was conducted almost exclusively in Arabic regardless of the mother tongue of the student body. This made it extremely difficult for non-Arab students to follow the instructor and acquire any knowledge beyond the ability to mechanically recite several *sura*s. Only in modern times non-Arab students began to receive instruction in their native tongues (Persian, Turkish, Urdu, Malay, and so on). As a norm, all students shared the same room regardless of their level of proficiency, and each was expected to advance at his or her own pace. Whereas practically every Muslim village and town had at least one *kuttáb*, its maintenance was the local community's responsibility until the nineteenth century, when the state finally began to integrate *kuttáb* schools into the statewide educational system modeled on European learning institutions. Prior to that, parents were responsible for meeting maintenance costs and paying the teacher's fees, either in money or kind. Poorer children, who had no money to pay their instructor, would occasionally contribute their labor, doing chores around his household. In general, schoolchildren were encouraged to "glorify and venerate their teacher" and their parents to compensate him generously for his services. As one medieval writer put it:

> It seems to me the greatest duty is that which is due to the teacher, and that which is the most necessary thing for each Muslim to observe.
>
> Indeed it is a duty to offer him a thousand *dirham*s as a sign of honor for his instruction in one single letter of the alphabet.[16]

The command to obey the teacher humbly and unquestionably was strictly observed by all students studying at *kuttáb*s; violators were punished or expelled. Whereas, from the viewpoint of modern-day pedagogy, education in *kuttáb* schools in the Middle Ages and to a lesser extent in modern times has been characterized by mechanical memorization of standard textbooks, blind obedience to the teacher, and lack of any independent and critical intellectual inquiry, these institutions did provide a more or less uniform system of socialization and learning for Muslim children across the Muslim world. They also served as an effective vehicle for integrating the precepts of the Muslim doctrine into their lives. Those schoolchildren who excelled in their studies by mastering the entire text of the Qur'an by heart and acquiring good writing and reading skills were often honored by their communities and could even be granted a stipend to continue their studies at a *mádrasa*.

Figure 15.1 Muslim Students Gathered Around a Teacher
Library of Congress

The Muslim College: *Mádrasa*

As already mentioned, initially religious education was dispensed at mosques and in private houses by learned individuals who may or may not have received remuneration for their services (see Figure 15.1). Those scholars who wanted to teach in the major mosques of the capital had to seek the permission of the caliph himself.[17] Teaching in large city mosques was considered a great privilege. If the teacher happened to be the *imam* and preacher of a mosque, he was usually paid by the state. If not, he would either assess his students a fee or offer classes free of charge. In the latter case, he had to have a source of income, which was not unusual because some early Muslim scholars earned their living as merchants, scribes, or craftsmen. However, as the number of teachers and demand for their services grew, it became necessary to institutionalize what was initially a very informal and loosely structured system of secondary and higher religious education in order to assure its effectiveness and continuity.

In response to this necessity, the institution of *mádrasa* was introduced and funded by some concerned members of the ruling elite. The first *mádrasa*s were probably relatively small lecture halls and libraries attached to a mosque. As already mentioned, the mosque and the religious school were practically indistinguishable due to the underlying commonality of their purpose. This close relationship between the two institutions persisted throughout the subsequent development of Islamic education up until the rise of Western-style schools in the late nineteenth century. As one Western scholar has aptly observed:

> The blurring of the distinction between *madrasa* and mosque should remind us that the transmission of knowledge was, for medieval Muslims, first and foremost an act of piety. Study,

like prayer, was an activity that could only be undertaken effectively in a state of ritual purity. Before attending a class, a scholar must "cleanse himself of ritual impurities and wickedness"; only in this way would he achieve "the glorification of knowledge and the veneration of the holy law."[18]

This intimate tie between mosque and *mádrasa* notwithstanding, with time the latter acquired a freestanding building that consisted of lecture halls, a library, a bathhouse, living quarters of the staff, and a dormitory for students. For the early period, the most vivid example of such a *mádrasa* complex was the Nizamíyya of Baghdad. Endowed and constructed by the cultured Saljuk vizier and patron of al-Ghazali, Nizám al-Mulk (d. 1092), it opened its doors for students and professors in 1067. Even before the Nizamíyya, a few *mádrasa*s had been in existence in eastern Iran.[19] In Egypt and the Maghrib, the Fatimid caliphs also created specialized schools aimed not only at promoting Isma'ili teachings but also, more generally, at encouraging the study of philosophy and logic.[20] However, such Isma'ili institutions were more like academies for the elite than public teaching institutions in the usual meaning of this word. Apart from the Nizamíyya college, the most sumptuous *mádrasa*s of Baghdad were founded and endowed by 'Abbásid caliphs. Of these, the magnificent Mustansiríyya *mádrasa* founded by the 'Abbásid caliph al-Mustánsir in 1234 deserves special mention. It housed professors representing the four schools of Islamic (Sunni) law (each of whom had seventy-five students); several teachers of the Qur'an and *hadíth*; and an associated physician. The facilities of the Mustansiríyya included a large library, baths, a hospital, and a kitchen, as well as a garden with the caliph's pavilion from which he would observe the activities taking place in the educational complex he had established.[21] Although both the Nizamíyya and the Mustansiríyya were destroyed by the Mongols in 1258, the *mádrasa* institution continued to flourish in the subsequent centuries under the generous patronage of the Ayyúbids and the Mamlúks of Egypt, the Rasúlids of Yemen, and numerous local rulers in North Africa, Central Asia, and Iran. By the mid-thirteenth century, Damascus alone boasted sixty *mádrasa*s, while Cairo had over thirty. Under the generous patronage of the Mamlúks, Cairo became probably the largest center of learning in the Muslim world with over seventy *mádrasa*s active at any given time.[22] Its al-Ázhar mosque-*mádrasa* complex, which was mentioned in Chapter 12, still remains a major beacon of traditional Islamic education.

The Economic Foundations of *Mádrasa* Education

In premodern Sunni societies, the economic foundation of the *mádrasa* was a charitable endowment or trust (*waqf*) bequeathed to it by a donor. Usually, donors came from the ruling class—caliphs, viziers, military commanders (and their wives), and, less frequently, wealthy merchants and members of nobility. The *waqf* bequest ordinarily consisted of a tract of land, an orchard, or any rental property or real estate that generated income. In the Muslim East and the central lands of Islam, including Egypt, the donor of a *mádrasa* retained a substantial level of control over its administration as its trustee-administrator. He or, more rarely, she had the right to stipulate the uses of the *mádrasa* property that were acceptable or unacceptable to him or her; appoint and remove professors; set a special fund to support students; and make his or her heirs responsible for its administration. In this capacity, the heirs would be entitled to a special stipend payable from the income of the *waqf* foundation established by its founder. This arrangement allowed the donor to secure the future of his offspring. Being a religious trust fund, the *waqf* could not be arbitrarily confiscated by state authorities or the rapacious military, making it a secure investment.

Not so in the Muslim West. Here the tenets of the Maliki school of law predominant in the region prohibited the donor from exercising control over the trusteeship of the charitable fund once it had been established. This specificity of the Maliki school of law helps to explain why the institution of *mádrasa* was rather late in gaining foothold in Islamic Spain. Here, the first *mádrasa* was established only in the fourteenth century by the ruler (*amír*) of the city of Granada. Prior to that, teaching in this part of the Muslim world was confined to mosques or private houses. In North Africa, too, the first *mádrasas* were established almost exclusively by sultans, who, unlike private individuals, were not as concerned about the financial aspects and subsequent fate of their donations. They were motivated by the desire to enhance their personal prestige as Islamic sovereigns and to present their realms to the outside world as seats of Islamic learning.[23] It stands to reason that the establishment and endowment of *mádrasas* by rulers and their retainers was an important means of legitimizing their rule in the eyes of their subjects and neighbors. Their charitable investments in Islamic education were deemed to assert their prestige as pious Muslim sovereigns eager to support and promote the religion that constituted the doctrinal and legal foundation of their states.[24]

This was not the sole reason for the founding of *mádrasas*. Their royal and princely sponsors were also driven by the desire to secure God's pleasure and benevolence in anticipation of the trials on the Judgment Day. In view of their often oppressive and arbitrary rule, this was a wise precaution to take in anticipation of the final reckoning. Whatever the rulers' hopes and goals may have been, we can confidently say that the institution of *waqf* assured for the proliferation and thriving of *mádrasas* across the Muslim world. In most Muslim countries, the institution of charitable endowments came to an end only in the late nineteenth and early twentieth centuries, when the newly founded nation-states of the Middle East and Central and South Asia launched drastic educational reforms aimed at meeting the challenges posed by modern life and Western political and cultural domination. Ministries of *waqfs* were created in many Muslim states in order for the state to exercise control over the resources of religious endowments and thereby curtail their previous relative independence from the ruler and his administration.

Methods and Curricula of *Mádrasa* Education

The subjects taught in *mádrasas* were in essence the same as those taught in mosque circles that had preceded them. Instruction was focused on the Qur'an, *hadíth*, and their exegesis, with the lion's share of time devoted to legal theory and applied law. Various styles of Qur'an reading and recitation (*tajwíd*) were also taught. Subjects not directly linked to the Islamic tradition were also offered, such as Arabic poetry and grammar, as well as elements of logic. The former two were essential for the proper understanding of the sacred texts, the latter for the conduct of disputations over legal issues, which played an essential role in the pedagogical process.

As with the *kuttáb*, the initial stages of instruction in *mádrasas* consisted of students' learning by heart Qur'anic chapters and as many *hadíth* as they could master. Each *hadíth* was repeated three times to help the students memorize it. With time, the institution called the "house of *hadíth*" emerged as a variant of *mádrasa*. It specialized in the study of prophetic traditions (as opposed to the study of law, which was at the center of the regular *mádrasa* education).

The pedagogical methods of such educational institutions were basically the same. During lecture classes, notes were taken down by students, who would then repeat them numerous times outside the class to allow the material to "sink in." With memorization being the cornerstone of mosque and *mádrasa* education, anything that interfered with it was to be avoided, including, in the words of one medieval author, "reading inscriptions on the tombs, walking between two camels halted together in a line, or flicking away lice." Also to be avoided were memory-dulling foods such as "sour apples, baklava, and vinegar," as well as those food products that took a long time to be digested.[25] Memory was thus the indispensable learning instrument that was to be kept sharp under any circumstances and protected from harmful influences. In preparation for class sessions, students would question one another about the material covered in class in order to determine who had a better mastery of the subject. Those with better understanding of a point would elucidate it to those still "at sea." Lectures of *hadíth* were usually read from standard *hadíth* collections, while lectures on *fiqh* were given by teachers from memory. Apart from lectures, there were reading sessions in the course of which each student would read his or her lecture notes out loud and be corrected by the teacher, if necessary. The lecture notes taken by students during law classes were usually either books of *fiqh* or commentaries on earlier *fiqh* books by renowned jurists of a given juridical school. They could be composed by the students' teacher himself or received by the latter from his own teacher, who may or may not have been its author. In other words, regardless of the authorship, each juridical treatise transmitted in this way would have a "pedigree" stretching from its author to its last possessor, in this case, the teacher of the class. The teacher acknowledged the successful completion of the book's study (or, rather, "reading") by his students by granting each of them a license to transmit it further. Thus, the process of advanced study in the *mádrasa* may be seen as an accumulation of licenses by students with a view to becoming qualified teachers of subjects studied in *mádrasa*s. In this way, the system reproduced itself.

At the advanced stage of their studies, students began to master the art of learned disputation to prepare themselves for debating their colleagues either from their own legal school or representatives of the other schools of Sunni *fiqh*. This art required a thorough knowledge of divergent legal opinions (which were to be learned by heart) and of argumentative strategies employed by jurists in the course of such disputations. In addition, the would-be scholars had to master the niceties of the grammar and style of the Arabic language, which were also taught in *mádrasa*s. On completing their studies, successful students were given licenses to issue legal opinions (*fatwas*) and to teach a large corpus of religious texts. They were now certified religious professionals eligible for employment in a variety of capacities. The licenses (*ijaza*) they received during their *mádrasa* years "served as a credential that established qualification for employment as a judge, deputy judge, professor of law (*mudárris*), deputy professor of law (*ná'ib mudárris*), or repetitor (*mu'íd*)."[26]

Mádrasa graduates were expected to become teachers of the subjects that they had learned and to compose books of their own on law and jurisprudence. Such works were often simple summaries of the books they had studied, which they would use as instructional materials after they had been granted a teaching appointment. Graduates often spent many years in anticipation of a well paid teaching position. In the meantime, they usually assisted their former teachers as tutors at their *alma mater*. Overall, education in *mádrasa*s was an arduous and time-consuming process, which demanded decades of selfless study and occasionally deprivation. In the course of their training, students were required to sacrifice not only their personal comforts but their family life as well, since only bachelors were allowed to reside in dorms attached to the *mádrasa*. The hardships and pressures of *mádrasa* education are aptly captured in the following advice to students by a renowned Hánafi jurist and theologian Abu Hafs al-Nasafí (d. 1142): "Be obedient and work diligently and do not become lazy. Thus you will turn to your Lord. And do not sleep at night for the best of mankind[27] only slept a little part of night."[28]

Students' stipends were often miniscule and insufficient to support a family anyway. Therefore, only the most determined individuals, fully invested in scholarship or having independent sources of income, could withstand the hardships of the long and arduous training necessary to obtain the status of a scholar. The high price of education that aspiring jurists and divines were expected to pay is conveyed by the following poetic lines: "How can you desire to become learned and skilled in argument except by labor? No gain of riches is possible without difficulties which you must take upon yourself. How can you expect to acquire learning without [sacrifice]?"[29]

Upon graduation, the former student's employment was far from guaranteed. As mentioned, he could spend years assisting his teacher in anticipation of the latter's retirement. Even after he had succeeded in obtaining an endowed teaching post with a decent salary, he was subject to the vagaries of funding, intrigues of his colleagues, and whims of the trustee-administrator. Some scholars had to accept teaching positions at several *mádrasa*s at the same time to provide for themselves and their families and to secure their future in case they would lose one of the jobs. Acute and acrimonious rivalries often flared up among competitors for the same prestigious teaching post. In this regard, their lives and careers were not dissimilar to those of their present-day colleagues.

Toward the end of the nineteenth century, the traditional *mádrasa*-based education in the Muslim world began to experience a steady decline under the strain of competition from modern institutions of higher learning that were imported from the West and Russia. Nevertheless, until today, many universities and colleges in the Muslim world have "faculties of the Shari'a and *fiqh*," which offer traditional Islamic disciplines in much the same way as the *mádrasa*s did in the premodern and early modern period. These educational outfits produce scholars who go on to become *fátwa*-givers (*muftis*), *mádrasa* instructors, mosque preachers, and judges. The latter's jurisdiction in most places is now confined strictly to the sphere of family and personal law. Many traditional centers of education have lost their former prestige (e.g., Bukhara and Samarqand in Central Asia, Konya in Turkey, and Nishapur in Iran); others have declined considerably, while still clinging to their former glory (e.g., Damascus in Syria). Still others have retained their status as the foremost seats of traditional Islamic learning (for instance, Cairo and Fez). In the meantime, new centers of religious learning have emerged in Saudi Arabia, Jordan, Pakistan, and Malaysia. They strive to attract students by recasting their educational strategies along the lines that are more consonant with the realities of the modern epoch. The vicissitudes of modern (and modernized) Islamic education will be discussed in the later chapters in this book.

Sufi Lodges

Learning and worship being closely related activities, it is only natural that both activities were pursued in ritually appropriate spaces, such as mosques or mosque-*mádrasa* complexes (see Figure 15.2). Another venue that brought together these two activities was Sufi lodges that began

Figure 15.2 The [al-]Azhar Mosque/Mádrasa Complex

Francesco Gasparetti: CC: Wikimedia Commons

to appear already in the ninth century. Initially a small retreat or hospice for ascetics and mystics, it gradually acquired a variety of educational, devotional, and social roles. Such institutions were known under different names in different parts of the Muslim world and in different epochs. The most common were *záwiya* (Arab., "corner"); *ribát* (Arab., "hospice" or "inn"); *khanaqá* (Persian, "hospice" or "convent"). Their functions varied from one locality to another. They could serve as inns, dining halls, prayer rooms, monasteries, and lecture halls, all in one. In some areas, such as Anatolia (Turkey) and North Africa, the functions of Sufi lodges largely overlapped with those of *mádrasa*s; they provided accommodations for Sufi brotherhoods, while also being centers of education and devotional practices.[30] Sufi lodges constituted a distinct feature of the Islamic religious, educational, and physical landscape (see Figure 15.3). Here, as in mosque-*mádrasa* complexes, the functions of education, edification, devotional practice, and collective worship were organically and inextricably combined. Supported by pious donations and endowment trusts, Sufi lodges provided room, board, and cash stipends to Sufis, who, in return, were expected to engage in reading the Qur'an and chanting Sufi litanies and mystical poetry to the accompaniment of musical instruments for the benefit of local communities and tribal groups that supported them.[31] In Mamluk Cairo (in the fourteenth and fifteenth centuries) and to some extent also in Anatolia and Africa, lodges housed Sufis, students of jurisprudence, and professional Qur'an reciters. In Cairo, Sufis were students and vice versa; they were supervised by a scholar of *fiqh* who was also a Sufi *shaykh*. Such an arrangement allowed "education and transmission of knowledge [to] reach ever deeper into the Muslim population of Cairo."[32] Unlike the majority of *mádrasa*s, which normally housed only professors and students belonging to one juridical school,[33] Egyptian Sufi lodges accepted students regardless of their juridical affiliation.[34]

The duties of the Sufi *shaykh* presiding over a Sufi lodge were similar to those of the abbot of a Christian monastery. He was required to protect his disciples (*murid*s) from harm, to instruct and admonish them in accordance with the level of their spiritual attainment, and to avoid the use

Figure 15.3 European Photograph of a Mádrasa and Sufi Lodge in Tlemcen, Algeria (Early 20th Century)
ND Pictures/Getty Images

of obscure language that might confuse them. The *shaykh* instructed his students step by step: After explaining to them the intricacies Qur'anic recitation, he proceeded to teach them the Sufi prayer formulas peculiar to his mystical brotherhood, as well as rules of collective devotional practices, especially *dhikr* or *sama'*.[35] In the process of the study, the *shaykh* and his disciples would assemble regularly to engage in these ritual activities, which infused their lives with a sense of camaraderie and belonging to the same spiritual tradition. Donors would occasionally stipulate the exact number of *dhikr* formulas and prayer sessions to be performed by the beneficiaries of their endowment funds. The donors could also ask the Sufis to pray for their (donors') souls at least once or twice a week in the hopes that the prayers of "holy men" would benefit them on the Judgment Day. The prayers and supplications of Sufis were believed by the populace to be a source of blessing to the Muslims living next to the lodge. Therefore, the latter would give their Sufi neighbors gifts in money and kind as compensation for their supplications and blessings. In times of drought, the locals would flock to the lodge and ask its inhabitants to pray for rain. If the Sufis' prayers were "answered," they would receive a certain percentage of the harvest in addition to the usual donations. These mutually beneficial relations between the inhabitants of Sufi lodges and the Muslim communities in which they were embedded are attested practically for every area of the Muslim world. One can describe these relations as an exchange of sorts: The spiritual benefits of Sufi blessings and prayers were remunerated by material gifts bestowed upon Sufis by their neighbors.

In rural areas and sparsely populated deserts, Sufi lodges were often the only centers of Islamic learning. Peasants and tribes living in the vicinity of the lodge sent their children there to learn the basics of Islam under the guidance of the *shaykh*, while also partaking of the latter's beneficial blessing (*báraka*). Due to their revered status, the *shaykh*s and their lieutenants were in a position to serve as arbitrators in conflicts between neighboring clans and tribes, as well as between rulers and their subjects. This role gave them real political clout, which they could use to rally their followers against an external military threat or the exactions of an oppressive ruler. Finally, lodges served as hostels for wayfarers and pilgrims, as well as kitchens for the poor. They often stored grain and other foodstuffs to be distributed at times of famine. It is often argued that Sufi lodges played an important, even critical, role in the dissemination of Islam among the non-Muslim populations of Anatolia, Africa, India, Indonesia, and Central Asia. In the absence of a centralized, state-controlled system of social welfare, Sufi lodges also served as an essential safety net for the poor and downtrodden. In addition to spiritual consolation, they provided food and accommodation for those who could not afford them.

Conclusions

As a renowned Western historian of Islamic civilization has pointed out, in premodern Islamic societies, "education was very widespread,"[36] when compared to the rest of the civilized world. Through the good services of *kuttáb* schools, which, as we have seen, functioned in practically every village not to mention towns and cities, gifted Muslim children acquired enough knowledge to pursue further studies at the *mádrasa* level, during which time they received stipends from a *waqf* endowment.[37] Even in the countryside, there was hardly a Muslim family in which at least one member could not read and write. In the urban setting, literacy was the rule rather than an exception. Knowledge was valued even by people who had only a bare modicum of it. Book culture flourished, and countless *mádrasa* halls, mosques, and Sufi lodges were abuzz with reading and scholarly discussion. Although, for a variety of reasons the premodern Muslim world did not develop a chartered, exterritorial institution along the lines of Western universities, it did produce a viable system of knowledge accumulation and transmission that assured its reproduction and continuity from one generation to another. In the Middle Ages and even later, this was no small achievement.

Questions to Ponder

1 Based on your knowledge of the history of Western education, what are the principal similarities and differences between it and its Muslim counterpart? In particular, in what ways is the premodern Western university different from or similar to the *mádrasa*?
2 What, in your view, is the closest Western analogue to the Sufi lodge (if any)?
3 Discuss the advantages and disadvantages of the curriculum and teaching methods in mosques, *mádrasa*s, and Sufi lodges.
4 Is the combination of learning and worship unique to Muslim societies? What impact did the venues of Muslim education have on students and why?

Summary

- Knowledge and learning in premodern Islamic societies hold a high status. Personal, face-to-face encounter between the teacher and his disciple(s) is the main method of knowledge transmission. Teaching venues range from mosques to *mádrasa*s.
- The transmitters and custodians of religious learning are the *'ulamá'* (sing. *'álim*) and the *fuqahá'* (sing. *faqíh*).
- Elementary education consists of the Qur'anic school (*kuttáb*) that plays an important role in reproduction of Islamic values, rituals, and norms.
- The emergence of religious colleges (*mádrasa*s) in the Muslim East (Iran and Iraq) under the Saljuk dynasty (in the eleventh–thirteenth centuries): the Saljuk vizier Nizám al-Mulk (d. 1092) and his Nizamíyya. *Mádrasas* proliferate throughout the Muslim world.
- *Waqf* (a charitable endowment or trust) is the material foundation of the *mádrasa* institution. The specificity of the Maliki school of law that disallows the donor to exercise control over the charitable fund once it is established is a major reason for the late appearance of *mádrasa*s in the Muslim West.
- Members of the ruling elite establish and support *mádrasa*s.
- *Mádrasa*-based education has its characteristic features, for example, the various categories of students and faculty and their career paths, as well as specific curricula and teaching methods.
- Sufi lodges (*záwiya*s, *ribát*s, and *khanaqá*s) are centers of learning and the dissemination of religious knowledge.
- Education in Sufi lodges combines Sufi spiritual and ascetic training with the study of Islamic law and creed. The role of the Sufi master (*shaykh*) as a disseminator of knowledge and as a dispenser of pious advice and *báraka*. The social functions of Sufi lodges include providing hostels for travelers, sites for negotiation and conflict resolution, refuges for the persecuted, and kitchens for the poor.

Notes

1 Jonathan Berkey, *The Transmission of Knowledge in Medieval Cairo*, Princeton University Press, Princeton, NJ, 1992, p. 3; the authenticity of this *hadíth* is doubted by many Muslim scholars.
2 Az-Zarnuji, *Ta'lim al-muta'allim tariq at-ta'allum: Instruction of the Student: The Method of Learning* (trans. G.E. von Grunebaum and Theodora M. Abel), King's Crown Press, New York, 1947, p. 21.

3 Az-Zarnuji, *Ta'lim al-muta'allim tariq at-ta'allum*, p. 13 et passim.

4 Michael Chamberlain, "The Production of Knowledge and the Reproduction of the A'yan in Medieval Damascus," in Nicole Grandin and Marc Gaborieau (eds.), *Madrasa: La transmission du savoir dans le monde musulman*, Arguments, Paris, 1997, p. 30.

5 Ibid., p. 34.

6 Az-Zarnuji, *Ta'lim al-muta'allim tariq at-ta'allum*, p. 16.

7 Ibid., p. 24.

8 George Makdisi, *The Rise of Colleges*, Edinburgh University Press, Edinburgh, 1981, pp. 9–10.

9 Az-Zarnuji, *Ta'lim al-muta'allim tariq at-ta'allum*, pp. 21–22.

10 Berkey, *The Transmission of Knowledge in Medieval Cairo*, p. 4.

11 Ibid., p. 5.

12 Chamberlain, "The Production of Knowledge and the Reproduction of the A'yan in Medieval Damascus," p. 49.

13 Makdisi, *The Rise of Colleges*, p. 19.

14 See Chapter 10, p. 154.

15 Marshall Hodgson, *The Venture of Islam*, University of Chicago Press, Chicago, 1974, vol. 2, p. 442.

16 Az-Zarnuji, *Ta'lim al-muta'allim tariq at-ta'allum*, p. 32.

17 Makdisi, *The Rise of Colleges*, pp. 12–17.

18 Berkey, *The Transmission of Knowledge in Medieval Cairo*, pp. 55–56.

19 Roy Mottahedeh, "The Transmission of Learning: The Role of the Islamic North-East," in Nicole Grandin and Marc Gaborieau (eds.), *Madrasa: La transmission du savoir dans le monde musulman*, Arguments, Paris, 1997, p. 62.

20 See Chapter 12, pp. 204–205.

21 George Makdisi, "Madrasa," *Encyclopaedia of Islam*, 2nd ed.; online edition: http://referenceworks.brillonline.com.

22 Berkey, *The Transmission of Knowledge in Medieval Cairo*, p. 46.

23 Makdisi, *The Rise of Colleges*, p. 238.

24 Patricia Crone, *Medieval Islamic Political Thought*, Edinburgh University Press, Edinburgh, 2004, pp. 306 and 312.

25 Chamberlain, "The Production of Knowledge and the Reproduction of the A'yan in Medieval Damascus," p. 39.

26 This term is roughly equivalent to the position of a present-day lecturer or teaching assistant. Devin Stewart, "The Doctorate of Islamic Law in Mamluk Egypt and Syria," in Joseph Lowry, Devin Stewart, and Shawkat Toorawa (eds.), *Law and Education in Medieval Islam*, Gibb Memorial Trust, Chippenham, UK, 2004, p. 63.

27 Meaning the Prophet.

28 Az-Zarnuji, *Ta'lim al-muta'allim tariq at-ta'allum*, p. 66.

29 Ibid., pp. 38–39; I have slightly changed the original translation.

30 Gary Leiser, "The Madrasah and the Islamization of Anatolia before the Ottomans," in Nicole Grandin and Marc Gaborieau (eds.), *Madrasa: La transmission du savoir dans le monde musulman*, Arguments, Paris, 1997, pp. 187–190.

31 Berkey, *The Transmission of Knowledge in Medieval Cairo*, p. 56.

32 Ibid., p. 58.

33 Leiser, "The Madrasah and the Islamization of Anatolia before the Ottomans," pp. 176–182; only the largest and best endowed *mádrasa*s housed all four Sunni schools of jurisprudence.

34 Leonor Fernandes, *The Evolution of a Sufi Institution in Mamluk Egypt: The khanqah*, K. Schwartz, Berlin, 1988, p. 110.

35 Makdisi, *The Rise of Colleges*, p. 216; for these Sufi terms, see Chapter 13.

36 Hodgson, *The Venture*, vol. 2, p. 118.

37 Ibid., p. 118.

Chapter 16

The Basic Beliefs and Practices of Islam

Islamic Life Cycle

Islamic Ethos and the Five Pillars

In the previous chapters, we have examined the rise and evolution of the principles of Islamic faith, which are collectively known as "Muslim doctrine" or "Muslim creed." Now we will try to find out how the general principles constituting the Muslim religious creed are manifested in the life and behavior of individual Muslims. Put differently, we will examine how the Muslims have internalized and implemented the major precepts of their religion. In academic literature, the practical realization of the tenets of a certain religious tradition by its followers is sometimes called "ethos."[1] Some scholars prefer to speak of "ritual," while having in mind basically the same thing. It is the ethos or ritual of the Muslims that is the subject matter of the present chapter.

Before describing how religious precepts shape the life of a practicing Muslim at its various stages, one should ask how Muslims themselves conceive of their faith and its practical implications. Speaking on their behalf, Muslim scholarship cites the five pillars of Islamic faith: the declaration of God's oneness and the prophetic mission of Muhammad; the performance of the five daily prayers; the fast of the month of Ramadán; the giving of alms; and visiting Mecca on a pilgrimage (*hajj*). The doctrine of the five pillars was formulated by Muslim scholars on the basis of the Prophet's instructions. It constitutes the core of Muslim identity, thought, and practice.

The Shaháda

The first pillar of Islam is a doctrinal statement, the remaining four being the practical requirements that flow from it. It is known as *shaháda*, which literally means "[bearing] testimony" or "witness." The *shaháda* consists of two parts. Its first part—*la iláha illa 'llah* ("there is no deity but God")—asserts the oneness of God; its second part—*Muhámmadun rasúl Allah* ("Muhammad is God's messenger")—confirms the status of Muhammad as the messenger of God to humankind. Although the phrase in its entirety is not mentioned in the Qur'an, its various iterations abound in the text of the Muslim sacred book. It is found, for example, in the so-called Throne verse of the Qur'an (2:255),[2] which says: "God, there is not God but He" (*la iláha illá húwa*). Various versions of the *shaháda*, including its canonical form, are also mentioned in the *hadíth*.[3]

The *shaháda* is sometimes seen as an Islamic equivalent of Judaism's *Shema* ("Hear O Israel, the Lord, our God is One Lord"), the repetition of which constitutes a daily religious duty of every practicing Jew.[4] Likewise, due to its centrality to the Muslim creed, the *shaháda* forms an essential part of every Muslim prayer or ritual practice. It is uttered many times a day by observant Muslims as a confirmation of their covenant with God, which can paraphrased as follows: "We do our part by acknowledging Your sovereignty and worshiping You; in return, we expect salvation in the next life that You have promised us."[5] The *shaháda*'s other function is to protect God's faithful servants, as confirmed by the Prophet in a *hadíth*: "God Most High says: '*La iláha illa 'llah* is My fortress, and he who enters My fortress is safe from My chastisement.'" By uttering the first part of the *shaháda,* the believer seeks divine protection from the thoughts of the enviers, haunting spirits, demons, demonic mates of evil, and all the hosts of the Devil.[6] Uttering the *shaháda* in the presence of three Muslim witnesses renders one a Muslim. Fathers whisper it in the ear of their newborn children—an act that symbolizes the induction of the latter into the ranks of the Muslim community. On their deathbed, Muslims are expected to utter the *shaháda* for the last time. It is also included in the prayer recited after their departure from this world. One can thus say that the *shaháda* accompanies Muslims throughout their lives. It should be noted that with time the Shi'ites have developed their own version of the *shaháda* that consists of three parts: After declaring the unity and oneness of God and Muhammad's prophethood, they add the phrase *wa-'Ali walí Allah,* that is, "and 'Ali is the friend of God." In this way the Shi'ites seek to demonstrate their distinctive identity with regard to the Sunni community, whose members considers this addition to be heresy.[7] When added to the call to prayer in a locale that has both Sunnis and Shi'ites, this addition might cause intercommunal strife.

The Prayer (Salát)

Once a person has acknowledged the uniqueness and sovereignty of God and the prophetic mission of Muhammad, he or she is obligated to fulfill the duties stipulated by the remaining four pillars of Islamic faith. Muslim girls and boys begin to pray when they turn nine or ten years of age, although some children start to pray earlier in imitation of their parents. The canonical or ritually prescribed prayer (*salát* or *namáz*),[8] as opposed to a free prayer or supplication, is incumbent on every Muslim. The canonical prayer serves as a potent and highly visible symbol of the believer's worship of and humility before God. No wonder, therefore, that it is featured in practically every documentary on Islam and the Muslims, as well as in oral, written, and visual accounts of Western visitors to Muslim countries. The sight of collectively praying Muslims prostrate in rows in a mosque has become part and parcel of the Western view of Islamic religion.

The importance of the canonical prayer is unequivocally stated in numerous passages from the Qur'an, often in conjunction with the other obligations incumbent on the faithful. In Q 2:43, they are enjoined "to be steadfast in prayer; [to] practice charity; and [to] bow down [their] heads with those who bow down in worship." Likewise, in Q 31:17, the Muslims are instructed to "perform the prayer and to command good and forbid evil." The faithful are portrayed as constantly "bowing in worship, prostrating, seeking bounty from God and good pleasure" (Q 48:29). In times of hardship, the faithful are encouraged to seek "help in patience and prayer" (Q 2:153), for "prayer forbids indecency and dishonor, and remembrance of God is the greatest thing [in life] without doubt" (Q 29:45). Already in the *kuttáb* school children learn that:

> [T]he most excellent of the ways of worship is the *salát,* since it is a pillar of faith, and includes within itself the invocation of God Most High and the declaration of His transcendence, and thanks to Him; the *salat* is the negation of immorality and of blameworthy and insolent behavior [that] purifies and strengthens the body.[9]

The preeminent importance of the canonical prayer for godly life is brought home in a famous saying of the Prophet, according to which, "Best of all works in the sight of God is the prayer-rite in its due time."[10]

The prayer is thus part and parcel of the devotional, social, and moral order sanctioned by God in his revelation to humankind. On a more personal level, it determines the rhythm of life of every observing Muslim, as he or she has to put aside his or her mundane preoccupations, no matter how urgent, to perform the duty of the canonical prayer five times a day. The Shi'ites are allowed to combine them into three. The importance of the canonical prayer was acknowledged by the Prophet's first successors. On their orders, numerous houses of prayer (mosques) were erected in

Muslim garrison towns in Syria, Iraq, Iran, and Egypt. From that time on, collective prayers in mosques or individual ones in private houses have become an essential element of Muslim life.[11]

The exact times, number, and other requirements of the canonical prayer are laid down in meticulous detail in *hadíth* collections (such as those of al-Bukhári and Muslim), as well as in juridical manuals. They occupy dozens of pages. While the Qur'an itself does not explicitly specify the number of canonical prayers required of every believer,[12] the *hadíth* put it at five. The famous legend of the Prophet's ascension to heaven, which is alluded to in the first two verses of *sura* 17 of the Qur'an and elaborated in numerous *hadíth*, relates that during his audience with God the latter commanded that Muhammad's followers should pray fifty times a day. Struck dumb by God's majesty, the Prophet humbly acceded to the divine order. On his way back to earth, he had met Moses, who persuaded him to renegotiate the number of prayers, for "your followers will not be able to bear with it."[13] Muhammad went back and pleaded with God to reduce the number. God, in his mercy, cut the number of prayers by half. Moses still considered this to be too heavy a burden. At his insistence, the Prophet made several more trips to God with the same request until God agreed to reduce the number of prayers to five. Despite Moses's protests, the Prophet accepted this number as final and conveyed it to his followers upon returning to Mecca.

The five prayers are to take place at stipulated times:

1   The dawn prayer to be completed between the daybreak and the rising of the sun; it requires two cycles of bodily postures and prostrations (*rak'a*s), which will be described below.
2   The midday or noon prayer to be performed from midday until afternoon; it requires four cycles of postures and prostrations.
3   The late afternoon prayer of four cycles to be performed between the noon prayer and the sunset prayer; it requires four cycles of postures and prostrations.
4   The sunset prayer to be performed after sunset and before dusk; it requires three cycles.
5   The evening or night prayer to be performed after darkness sets in; it requires four cycles.

The five separate prayers are incumbent upon all Sunni Muslims. The Shi'ites are allowed to join together the noon and afternoon prayers and the sunset and evening (night) ones. As a result, they may pray only three times a day, which is consistent with the verses 17–18 of *sura* 30 of the Qur'an.[14]

Each prayer time is announced by the call to the prayer, or *adhán* (see Figure 16.1). The use of the human voice to broadcast the call is unique to Islam (as opposed, for instance, to Christianity, which uses church bells or Buddhism, which uses gongs and two pieces of wood). A typical Sunni *adhán* consists of seven formulas, of which the sixth is a repetition of the first:[15]

1   *Allahu ákbar*: "God is most great/the greatest" (four times).
2   *Áshhadu an la iláha illa 'llah*: "I bear that there is no deity (god) but God (twice).
3   *Ashhadu anna Muhammadan rasúl 'llah:* "I bear witness that Muhammad is God's messenger" (twice).
4   *Hayya 'ala s-sala(t):* "Come to prayer" (twice).
5   *Hayya 'ala 'l-faláh:* "Come to salvation" (twice).
6   *Allahu ákbar:* "God is most great/the greatest" (twice).
7   *La ilaha illa 'llah:* "There is no deity (god) but God" (once).

There are slight variations in the articulation of the *adhán* from one Sunni legal school to another. For instance, Phrase 1 is repeated only twice by Malikis, while Phrases 2 and 3 are repeated in a louder voice by the followers of all Sunni schools, except the Hanafis. All four Sunni schools of law add the phrase "Prayer is better than sleep" before Phrase 1 of the morning prayer.

MUEZZINN PUBLIC.

MUEZZINN PARTICULIER.

Figure 16.1 A Muezzin Calls the Faithful to Worship

Wellcome Library/Wikimedia Commons

This phrase is believed to have been introduced by 'Umar, which explains why it is omitted from the Shi'ite *adhán*. On the other hand, the Shi'ite *adhán* contains the phrase *háyya 'ala khayr 'ámal* ("Come to the best of works!"), which is inserted between Phrases 5 and 6. If you hear an *adhán* with this additional formula, you can be sure that you are in a Shi'ite country. As mentioned in the section on the *shaháda*, the Shi'ite caller (*muezzin*) may also insert the phrase "'Ali is a friend of God" after Phrase 3. Unlike the previous one, this addition is not obligatory.[16]

On hearing the *adhán*, the believer is expected to repeat it verbatim except for Phrases 4 and 5, which are replaced by the phrase, "There is no strength no power but with/in God." He should then proceed to the mosque, if there is one in the vicinity. If there is no mosque, he is allowed perform the prayer at any place (in the field, in the street, on the shoulder of a road, on a boat, plane, and so on). Female Muslims are encouraged to perform the prayer in their houses, although they can also do this in a special section of the mosque. The preference for women to pray at home is often explained by the [male] expectation that they should be taking care of their household and children. Others say that praying women can be a distraction to praying men.

To perform the prayer, Muslims are required to be ritually clean. To this end, they have to make an ablution, as enjoined by verse 6 of *sura* 5 of the Qur'an: "O believers, when you stand up to pray, wash your faces, and your hands up to the elbows, and wipe your heads, and your feet, up to the ankles." Without ablution, the prayer is considered invalid under Shari'a. Here, too, there are differences between the Sunnis and the Shi'ites as to whether one should rub or wipe one's feet (the Shi'ites) or wash them (the Sunnis). Likewise, in the course of the Shi'ite ablution, water is allowed to run from the elbow to the palm, whereas the Sunni rite requires that it flow from the palm to the elbow. Finally, the Shi'ites perform their ablutions standing, whereas the Sunnis usually sit or squat.

Such minor differences may become crucial and even deadly at a time of sectarian strife. For instance, in premodern Yemen, Sunni callers to the prayer who resided in the areas controlled by Zaydi Shi'ites were occasionally required to add the Shi'ite formula to the prayer call. Those who failed to do so faced a severe punishment or even execution. At times of political and military turmoil, medieval Yemenis listened carefully to the wording of the *adhán* of the central mosque in order to determine which faction (Shi'ite or Sunni) was in power in the city. Likewise, a Shi'ite traveling incognito in a Sunni area could be exposed by making a Shi'ite-style ablution, in which case he or she could be imprisoned and interrogated as to his or her intentions. On occasion, such dissimulating Shi'ites could fall victim to mob violence.

To begin his prayer, the Muslim is required to face in the direction of Mecca (*qibla*). It is clearly marked by a vaulted recess in the wall of the mosque. Outside the mosque, it is up to the believer to properly identify the *qibla*. He can do so by asking the locals, or, if he is in a desert or open field, he can try to determine it by the position of the sun or stars. In modern times, traveling Muslims carry special timepieces that alert them when the time of the prayer comes; such timepieces are often equipped with a compass to help them identify the direction of Mecca. Before engaging in prayer, the worshipper is required to declare his or her intention to pray either mentally or loudly. This act is necessary to make sure that the praying person is paying attention to what he or she is about to do. Each prayer consists of two, three, or four cycles of bodily postures and prostrations accompanied by recitations of prayer formulas. As already mentioned, each cycle is called a *rak'a* (see Figure 16.2). After declaring his or her intention to perform the prayer, the worshipper proceeds to the prayer per se. Standing upright, male worshippers raise their hands to the ears with palms facing outward and say out loud: "God is most great/the greatest." They then recite the "Opening" *sura* (1) and at least three other short passages from the Qur'an and lean the upper part of their bodies at a right angle with their hands placed on the knees, while rendering praise to God. After that, they return to the upright position, saying the ritual phrases, "God hears him who praises Him" and "God is most great/the greatest." They

Tunis, Arabe en prière.   92.

Figure 16.2 European Photograph from the Late Nineteenth Century of a Tunisian Arab in Prayer
Eric Lernestal/Hallwyll Museum/Wikimedia Commons

then prostrate themselves on the floor, saying, "God is most great/the greatest" and "Praise be to my Lord, Most High!" For a few moments, their bodies should rest on their foreheads, the palms of both hands, both knees, and both feet. All these postures are shared by the Sunnis and the Shi'ites. The only difference is that the latter insist that the forehead be placed on dust, the earth, or on a small tablet of clay from one of the Shi'ite holy cities (Najaf, Kerbelá, or Mashhad). Sunni Muslims place their foreheads on the prayer rug or headscarf. According to an oft cited *hadíth*, it is in the lowly position of prostration that worshippers find themselves closest to God and, therefore, God is most likely to answer their prayers. After pausing in the prostrate position, the worshippers rise from it and sit on their heels, saying, "O my Lord, pardon me!" They then prostrate themselves once again, uttering, "God is most great/the greatest" and "Glory be to my Lord Most High!" The worshippers then stand up and repeat the prayer cycle. At the end of the second cycle, the worshippers do not stand up but sit on their heels, knees to the ground, and hands placed on the thighs. They declare God's greatness once again and pronounce an extended version of the *shaháda* that contains, in addition to the profession of faith, the blessings of God, the Prophet, and his companions. The Shi'ites add to the *shaháda* a phrase affirming 'Ali's special position as a friend of God. While reciting the *shaháda,* many Sunni Muslims often extend their forefingers and move them in circles as a symbolic declaration of God's oneness. This gesture is prohibited in Shi'ite Islam. Upon uttering the expanded *shaháda*, the worshippers stand up and perform one or two additional *rak'a*s (depending on the number of the cycles required by this particular prayer). At the end of the last *rak'a*, they remain seated. While in this seated position, they plead God to bestow blessings upon the Prophet and his family in the same way that he has bestowed them upon Abraham and his family. Finally, turning his head to the right and then to the left, they say: "Peace and God's blessings be upon you."[17] The double utterance of this phrase terminates the required (canonical) part of the prayer. The worshippers may then proceed to utter a prayer of supplication called *du'a.*

In addition to the five canonical prayers, there are several other types of prayers. The congregational prayer is performed at midday on Friday and is often called the Friday prayer. Its importance is attested by numerous *hadíth*, one of which declares it to be "worth twenty-five times the prayer performed at home or the market place."[18] It requires a minimal number of participants that varies from one legal school to another. It is obligatory for all male worshippers of a given locale and optional for women. Collective prayers are usually performed in large mosques, known as "congregational," in order to accommodate a large crowd of believers. Upon entering the mosque, Muslim men perform two *rak'a*s on their own. After the call to the prayer is broadcast, they stand in the courtyard of the mosque and listen to a short sermon (*khútba*) by the prayer-leader (*imam*) or preacher (*khatíb*). The sermon usually discusses the moral and ethical implications of a certain Qur'anic verse. The *imam* then descends from the stepped pulpit from which he has just pronounced the sermon and leads the worshippers in the prayer of two *rak'a*s, uttering the prayer formulas in a loud voice. Arranging themselves in rows behind the *imam*, the congregation follows his every movement. Traveling Muslims are allowed to shorten their prayers from four or three *rak'a*s to just two.[19]

There are other types of prayer, including the "prayer of fear," performed by a Muslim military detachment in anticipation of an imminent engagement with an enemy force; the prayer for rain; the prayer performed at the times of moon and sun eclipses; and two special prayers marking the two major Islamic festivals, namely the end of the month of fasting (Ramadán) and the end of the *hajj*. The Shi'ites have a large number of devotional prayers that are traced back to their *imam*s.[20] The prayer over a newly deceased occupies a special place in the Muslim ritual. It symbolizes the end of a Muslim's earthly life, which, as we remember, started with the utterance of the prayer call in the child's ear shortly after birth. Thus, as already mentioned, the prayer accompanies the believer from cradle to grave by tuning his or her entire life to the rhythm of the prayer ritual.

Unlike the other prayers just described, the prayer for the dead does not require the performance of *rak'a*s. The congregation gathers in rows behind the *imam* who stands upright facing the *qibla* with the body of the deceased laid crosswise in front of him. After saying "God is most great/the greatest" four times and reading the "Opening" *sura* of the Qur'an, the *imam* repeats the words of blessing said at the end of the canonical prayer, then offers a prayer for the deceased. He completes the prayer by asking God to bestow blessings upon the faithful. Although some scholars argue that this prayer should not be performed over the bodies of grave sinners or suicides, the scholarly consensus says that it is to be performed over all Muslims, except unredeemable heretics, highwaymen, and rebels.

Zakát

Zakát is an obligatory payment imposed on certain categories of property and income belonging to people of means. The Qur'an (2:177) describes it as one of the signs of true piety:

> It is not piety that you turn your faces to the East or to the West [in prayer]. Rather the pious person is someone who believes in God, and the Last Day, the angels and the Prophets, and who gives of one's substance, however cherished, to his kinsmen and orphans, the needy, travelers, beggars and slaves; and who perform the prayers and pay the *zakát*.

This verse not only links *zakát* to the other religious duties and beliefs incumbent on the Muslims but also outlines the categories of individuals entitled to receiving a portion of communal wealth accumulated through the collection of *zakát*. Some Muslim scholars have argued that in Mecca, where the first Muslims lived as a persecuted minority, *zakát* was not institutionalized. It was more or less a matter of one's personal conscience. However, after the first Muslim polity had been established at Medina, the collection of *zakát* was regularized to make it a religious duty alongside the other pillars of Islam. This is evident from Qur'anic verse 9:60, in which the giving of alms is designated by the word *sádaqa(t)*, roughly synonymous with *zakát*. The verse in question determines not only the legitimate categories of *zakát* recipients but also mentions certain unnamed individuals "who work to collect it." According to the Muslim legal theory, the Muslim's property and income are not religiously legal until they are "cleansed" by the payment of *zakát*, which etymologically means "purification." This function of *zakát* is based on the prophetic *hadíth* that tells believers, "God introduced *zakát* only to allow you [Muslims] to enjoy the remainder of your possessions with a clear conscience." Another *hadíth* asserts that the property on which *zakát* is levied is no longer considered to be a worldly treasure."[21] The concrete amounts due from various types of property are also specified in *hadíth*. Failure to pay *zakát* is considered to be a sign of hypocrisy, therefore the prayers of those remiss in its payment will not by accepted by God. Moreover, on the Day of Judgment they will be punished by being pursued by their hoarded treasures—pieces of silver and gold, which they concealed from their Muslim brethren, will turn into a fearsome serpent that will chase them, shouting mockingly, "I am your treasure." Those who have failed to render *zakát* from their livestock will be trampled and gored by the animals that were not "cleansed" by its rendition.[22] In like vein, "Everyone who does not submit the *zakát* imposed upon his possessions will have placed around his neck on the Day of Resurrection a slender, scurfy snake."[23]

After the payment of *zakát* was ordained by the Qur'an and *hadíth*, it fell to Muslim jurists to work out its concrete implications for various categories of Muslims. With time, it was agreed that *zakát* is due on property that is subject to growth either literally or virtually. Thus, livestock and commercial merchandise are prone to increase through natural growth and marketplace exchange respectively. The same is true of crops and minerals extracted from mines. To allow the property to grow, a one-year period is given to potential payers. In line with this general rule, all legal schools including Shi'ite agree that the alms should be levied on crops, livestock, gold, silver, and cash. The chief difference between the Shi'ites and the Sunnis is that the former render *zakát* to the representative(s) of the hidden *imam*, while the latter remit it to the state. In addition, the Shi'ites have to pay an annual tax of one-fifth that is levied on "net income, net increase in land holdings, stored gold, silver and jewelry, mined products, items taken from the sea and war booty." The proceeds of this tax go to the living descendants of the Prophet's family, orphans, the poor, and travelers.[24] As with the *zakát*, this tax is paid to the representatives of the hidden *imam*, that is, leading Shi'ite scholars. *Zakát* is due only on property that exceeds the minimal limits specified by jurists, for instance, five camels, nine sheep or goats, and so on. In the case of the livestock, *zakát* is paid in kind, for instance, one sheep or one goat from a herd of forty sheep or goats and so on. However, in the case of a flock of camels that consists of fewer than twenty-five animals, the alms can be paid in sheep or goats, not camels. The minimal amount of goats and sheep on which *zakát* is levied is set at forty. From this number, one ewe or one female goat is due.

As far as crops are concerned, there is a considerable disagreement among jurists over which of them are subject to the *zakát* tax. While the Twelver Shi'ites levy *zakát* only on wheat, barley, dates, and raisins, the Hánafis and Zaydi Shi'ites consider all agricultural produce to be liable to taxation. The other legal schools take a middle position by expanding the list of taxable crops, while excluding some from taxation. *Zakát* on gold and silver is due in kind, either in the raw form or in coins. The minimal amount is set at 85 grams of gold and 593 grams of silver with the rate of *zakát* set at 2.5 percent. Personal jewelry is exempt from taxation. The rate of *zakát* on minerals extracted from mines and buried treasures is also set at 2.5 percent, although the Shafi'i jurists are of opinion that the *zakát* on buried treasure of precious metals should be one-fifth (20 percent).[25] *Zakát* on merchandise and proceeds of trade, including land and slaves, is assessed at the same rate as gold and silver, namely, 2.5 percent. It is payable in cash.

We have already mentioned the categories of people which the Qur'an (9:60) designates as legitimate recipients of *zakát* alms. In the course of the development of Islamic legal theory, these categories received more precise definitions. They comprise the poor and indigent, orphans and widows, tax collectors, slaves who seek to purchase freedom but do not have sufficient funds, debtors, volunteers engaged in *jihád*, and travelers. While these categories are pretty straightforward, the Qur'anic reference to "those whose hearts are won over" has been an object of heated juridical debates among Muslim jurists. Some legal schools (such as the Shafi'is) defined them as new converts to Islam whose loyalty to their new religion is not yet proven or is in doubt. Other schools considered this category as being specific to the first Muslim community and no longer relevant in later times.

Today, as in the past, Muslim thinkers emphasize the beneficial socioreligious role that *zakát* has played in Muslim societies. They consider it to be an important bond between the givers and the recipients that, in theory at least, should enhance their sense of belonging to the same community of religious commitment. In an ideal Islamic society, the givers are supposed to derive satisfaction from fulfilling their obligation to God and less fortunate recipients. The latter's plight is alleviated by the knowledge that they are cared for by their Muslim brethren, which should instill in them a sense of fraternity and gratitude. In a similar vein, the payment of *zakát* is seen by Muslim theorists as an effective means of redistribution of wealth that contributes to the creation of "a cooperative environment" and that helps to "eliminate theft, vandalism, and other social ills."[26] In this respect, *zakát* plays the same role as a pious endowment (*waqf*) that, too, is supposed to serve the community's common good and to allay the inevitable inequities of human society. In real life, however, this ideal was often tarnished by the exactions and venality of tax collectors, by misappropriation of charitable funds by unscrupulous rulers and military commanders, and by the concealment of their income by taxpayers. The rulers, in particular, soon discovered that the rates of *zakát* were insufficient to fund their courts, army, and other state projects and that they had to levy non-Qur'anic taxes on their subjects, which the latter quite naturally resented. Overall, however, one cannot deny that in the absence of a comprehensive social security safety net sponsored by the state, the *zakát* tax has served its stated purpose by allaying the plight of the poor, infirm, or otherwise disadvantaged, who for one reason or the other were incapable of supporting themselves.

The Fast of Ramadán (Sawm, Uraza, Puasa)

That the practice of fasting is not unique to Islam is recognized by the Qur'an, which explicitly states that it was "prescribed for those before you" (2:183). In the Judeo-Christian scriptures, Moses, Elijah, and Jesus are mentioned as engaging in forty-day fasts in anticipation of an impending encounter with the divine.[27] In Judaism, it is practiced on the Day of Atonement (*yom kippur*), which is believed by many Western academics to be the most likely precursor of the Muslim fast. As far as Christianity is concerned, the Qur'an quotes Mary, mother of Jesus, as vowing "a fast to the All-Merciful" (God) (19:27). A few Western scholars have argued that the fast of Ramadán represents a cross of Jewish fast of the Day of Atonement (a one-time penitentiary fast) and the Christian Lent (a continuous, purifying fast).[28] Finally, Ramadán may also owe its existence, at least in part, to the "holy" or "sacred" months that had wide currency among the pre-Islamic Arabs and that were marked by a fast, among other practices.[29]

The Muslim tradition acknowledges that shortly after the Prophet's arrival in Yáthrib (Medina), he enjoined his followers to practice the 'Ashúra, namely fasting on the tenth day of the lunar month of Muhárram. Whether he did so in deference to the Jewish fast of the Atonement Day that is celebrated on the tenth day of the Hebrew month of Tishri or for some other reason is not quite clear. However, as Muhammad's relations with the Jews of Medina had grown strained because of their failure to recognize him as a monotheistic prophet, a new revelation ordained that the 'Ashúra fast be replaced by the fast of Ramadán. From that time on, the fast of the lunar month Ramadán has become one of the five pillars of Islam.

Not only does the Qur'an command its followers to fast during Ramadán, but it also provides a relatively detailed set of rules on how this command is to be observed and the categories of individuals who are exempt from it:

> O believers, prescribed to you is the fast as it was prescribed to those before you . . . for days numbered; and if any of you be sick, or if he be on a journey, then let him fast a similar number of days; and for those who cannot endure it, there is a redemption: the feeding of a poor man. . . . But to fast is better for you, if you but know it. The month of Ramadan, wherein the Qur'an was sent down to be a guidance to the people, and as clear guidance and discernment between right and wrong. So let those of you who are present at the month fast.[30]

The Qur'an explicates further rules of fasting, stipulating that eating, drinking, and having sexual intercourse during the daytime is strictly prohibited but becomes licit after the sunset and "until you can tell a white thread from a black one in the light of the coming dawn."[31] At that moment, the fast is to be resumed until the next nightfall. In other words, the fast of Ramadán is a daytime fast to be practiced by every able-bodied Muslim in full possession of his or her senses. Individuals who are sick, traveling, or nursing, and women who are pregnant or menstruating are exempt, although all of them are required to make up for the missed fasting days. Further details on fasting are supplied by the Prophet's *hadíth*. To these categories of individuals exempt from fasting was added that of fighters "in the way of God." The minimal distance of travel that absolves the believer from the obligation to fast was determined, and so were the polluting factors that invalidate one's fasting. They include—apart from eating, drinking, and having sexual intercourse—deliberate seminal emission, breaking an oath, manslaughter, and smoking. Even the swallowing of spittle was strongly discouraged. Infractions such as these require redemption or restitution by way of fasting one day for each day of the invalidated fasting.[32] Major deliberate infringements without extenuating circumstances require atonement that may involve the ransoming or liberation of a Muslim slave, two consecutive months of fasting (plus one day), or feeding a large group (up to sixty) of the poor.[33]

Most Sunni legal schools stipulate that the fasting person be a Muslim in full possession of his or her senses and mental abilities and capable of withstanding the hardships of abstention. Fasting women must be free from menstruation or bleeding caused by childbirth. Once these minimal requirements are met, the believer should declare his or her intention to practice abstinence either for the entire month or for the coming day (depending on the legal school). Apart from physical fasting, during the month of Ramadán, Muslims are encouraged to read the Qur'an, retire to the mosque for special prayers and supplications, and guard their tongues and minds against improper words and thoughts. These rules constitute the moral dimension of the Ramadán fast that, in the opinion of many Muslim scholars, is at least as important as abstinence from food, drink, and sex. This notion is based on the famous prophetic *hadíth*, according to which, "Five things break the fast of the faster—lying, backbiting, slander, ungodly oaths, and looking with passion [at other people]."[34] In Shi'ism, the declaration of the intention to begin fasting is not considered a necessary prerequisite for its validity, and the fast itself is slightly longer, since the Shi'ites break their fast only when the sun has completely set.[35]

A number of voluntary or supererogatory fasts are practiced by pious Muslims on certain days of the week (for instance, Mondays and Thursdays) or on certain days of some months (Rajab, Sha'ban, and so on). The Shi'ites have their own special fasting days that commemorate the pivotal points of the Shi'ite sacred history, such as the Prophet's designation of 'Ali as his successor at the Pond of Khumm (the eighteenth of Dhu 'l-Hijja) and the anniversary of al-Husayn's death at Kerbelá (the tenth day of Muhárram). However, these voluntary fasts are observed by a relatively small number of Muslims and will not be discussed here in detail.

The end of Ramadán is determined by the sighting of the new moon, which marks the beginning of the next (tenth) month of the lunar year named Shawwál. If the sky is obscured by clouds, the beginning of Shawwál is calculated as being thirty days after the beginning of Ramadán. It is marked by the so-called Festival of Breaking the Fast (*'id al-fitr*).[36] As with the other months of the lunar calendar, Ramadán comes eleven days earlier each year due to the difference between the length of the solar year (365 days) and its lunar counterpart (354 days). This being the case, Ramadán rotates, as it were, throughout the seasons of the solar year. Its end is marked by a special congregational prayer (attended mostly by men) that does not require the usual call. It starts after the sunrise, consists of two *rak'a*s, and is followed by a public sermon. After that, many Muslims make visits to cemeteries to pay tribute to their deceased relatives.

On the social plane, the end of Ramadán provides a welcome and much awaited occasion for celebration and social bonding: dressed in their finest clothes, Muslims visit each other to convey their greetings, exchange gifts, and have meals together. The celebration period lasts for three days. The special "festival charity" is contributed to by families of means for the benefit of the poor and needy. Although known officially as the "minor festival," it is in fact more popular with the Muslims than the so-called "Greater Festival" (*al-'id al-kabir*) marking the end of the pilgrimage to Mecca.[37] The self-imposed hardships and restrictions are now over. It is time for practicing Muslims to celebrate and enjoy life.

The spiritual benefits of the fast are discussed in great detail in many religious writings, including those of al-Ghazali, who dedicated a special chapter of his "Revivification of Religious Sciences" to the "mysteries of fasting." Quoting the Prophet, he asserts that the rewards of voluntary hunger equal the reward of the fighter for the sake of God and that "no one who has filled his stomach" will ever enter Paradise.[38] Al-Ghazali's insistence on the necessity of fasting and other types of abstinence is understandable in light of his fascination with Sufi frugality and asceticism, which he, as we remember, considered to be the surest way to attain piety in this life and salvation in the hereafter.[39] The social virtues of fasting are highlighted by the modern Pakistani thinker and politician Abu 'l-A'la Mawdúdi (d. 1979),[40] who stated that fasting "for a full month every year trains a man individually, and the Muslim community as a whole, in piety and self-restraint; [it] enables the society—rich and poor alike—to experience the pangs of hunger and prepares people to undergo any hardship to seek the pleasure of God."[41] No wonder, therefore, that public infringements of abstinence rules during Ramadán were (and to a lesser extent still are) viewed as an affront to the community's morality and, in some Muslim countries, can be punished by fines or flogging.

The Pilgrimage to Mecca (Hajj): Ritual Significance and Historical Roots

The pilgrimage to Mecca (*hajj*), the cradle and spiritual center of Islam, is the fifth and last pillar of the Muslim creed.[42] The *hajj* takes place during the second week of the twelfth month of the Muslim calendar Dhu 'l-Hijja, which literally means "that of the *hajj*." As with Ramadán and the other months of the Muslim lunar calendar, Dhu 'l-Hijja rotates throughout the seasons of the solar year. The *hajj* starts on the eighth and ends on the thirteenth day of Dhu 'l-Hijja. It culminates on the tenth day of the month of Dhu 'l-Hijja with the ritual slaughter of sacrificial animals by both the pilgrims and Muslims around the world. This event is known as the "Festival of the Sacrifice" or the "Greater Festival."

The performance of the *hajj* is explicitly commanded by the Qur'an,[43] which says:

> The first House established for the people was that at Bekka,[44] a place holy, and a guidance for all beings. Therein are clear signs—the station of Abraham and whosoever enters it is in security. It is the duty of all believers towards God to come to the House [that is, the Ka'ba] as a pilgrim, if he is able to make his way there.

Basing themselves on this verse, Muslim scholars argue that the *hajj* is required in each Muslim's lifetime but only if the pilgrim is a free adult and is both physically and financially capable. This last stipulation means that the believer should be in good health and have enough money to cover the expenses of the journey, while at the same time being able to provide for his or her dependents during his or her absence. Given this important condition, one can say that the *hajj* is the only pillar of Islam that is not absolutely obligatory. The *hajj* has always been an expensive venture, and the majority of pilgrims must save money for many years to cover the cost of the journey. Muslim scholars disapprove of borrowing money for this purpose because all debts must be paid before the *hajj* in order to make it valid. Those who are physically unable to make the journey may send a substitute, whose performance of the pilgrimage rites fulfills the Islamic duty of the sender but not his or her own. The schools of Islamic law generally agree that the pilgrimage of a child or of a slave who accompanies his master is considered a meritorious act but does not fulfill the obligation. It must be performed again after the boy has reached puberty or the slave has been manumitted. Some scholars insist that every woman must be accompanied by her husband or a close male relative. Others argue that a woman is obligated to go on a *hajj* even if she has no such guardian. Statistics show that only a small fraction of the world's Muslim population are able to make the pilgrimage during their lifetime.

The origins of the *hajj* go back to pre-Islamic times. Before Islam, many Arab tribes worshipped their idols and gods in Mecca and its vicinity. The *hajj* rituals were associated with various localities in and around Mecca and with the structure named "Ka'ba" ("cube"), which had been in existence well before the rise of Islam. The gods worshipped at Mecca before Islam were associated by the pagan Arabs with heavenly bodies, especially the Sun, Moon, and Venus. The pre-Islamic rituals centered on the Ka'ba included its circumambulation (i.e., circling around) by shaved pilgrims wrapped in a ritual white garment. The Plain of 'Arafat and Mount of Mercy, which lie outside Mecca, played a special role in these pagan rituals, as they do in their Islamic iterations. As we remember from Chapter 1, al-Quraysh, the native tribe of the Prophet, served as the custodians of the Meccan sanctuary. They organized and presided over the annual pilgrimage to the city by the Arab tribes of central and western Arabia.

Historically speaking, pilgrimages to a sanctuary and "standing" before God on the top of a sacred mountain are an old Semitic tradition that predates both Islam and Arab paganism. For instance, in Exodus 23:17 and 34:22, all male Israelites are commanded to appear before the Lord three times a year and to "stand upon the rock," which was identified with Mount Sinai. The Hebrew word "standing" (*hag*) may be at the origin of the Arabic *hajj*, especially since the "standing" on the Plain of 'Arafat before the Mount of Mercy constitutes the central part of the Muslim *hajj*. In short, most, if not all, of the principal stations and rituals of the *hajj* that we are about to describe were already in existence before Islam. The days of the *hajj* and the whole month during which it was performed were the season of peace: Tribal hostilities were suspended, and Arabs were not allowed to seek or exact revenge on their enemies.

Islam did not destroy the pre-Islamic pilgrimage rites. However, it thoroughly Islamized them. Thus, the Qur'an and the Muslim tradition came to depict the Ka'ba, the black cubic structure at the center of the holy city, as the first house of worship that was constructed by Adam and Eve to extinguish their guilt of eating of the tree of knowledge. Adam and Eve built it on a direct order from God, who instructed the couple to erect it opposite God's throne. According to the same tradition, Adam and Eve were the first dwellers of the Meccan sanctuary (*háram*). After their death, the Ka'ba and its sanctuary had fallen into disrepair, to be eventually completely destroyed by Noah's flood. It was restored by the resuscitator of monotheism, Abraham, and his elder son Ishmael (Isma'il)—an event that is mentioned in the Qur'an (2:125–128). These verses are understood by Muslims in such a way as to link the Israelite patriarch to the Meccan *háram*, thereby making it a potent symbol of monotheism that Abraham so vividly embodied. According to the Muslim tradition, the sacred history of monotheistic message came full circle after Muhammad had begun to receive revelations from God in and around the Meccan sanctuary. His prophetic mission reaffirmed the special status of Mecca and of its center, the Ka'ba, as the spiritual "navel of the universe" graced by divine presence. This is why the Qur'an calls the Meccan sanctuary the "House of God" (*bayt Allah*). Mecca's critical importance to Islamic faith is confirmed by the fact that it serves as the direction of the Muslim prayer and the site of the annual pilgrimage, which constitutes the fifth pillar of Islam. It is toward Mecca that the faces of the deceased are turned when their bodies are being placed in their graves. Nowadays, the Ka'ba is located at the center of the Sacred Mosque of Mecca. It is a cube-shaped building, whose four corners are oriented toward the four cardinal points. As it now stands, it is 15 meters (45 feet) high, 12 meters (36 feet) long, and 10.5 meters (31 feet) wide. The Ka'ba's walls are constructed of blue-gray granite blocks; their external surface is covered by *kiswa*, a black brocaded drape with Qura'nic verses inscribed in gold. The *kiswa* is replaced annually in anticipation of the pilgrimage season. Set into the eastern corner of the Ka'ba is the Black Stone, probably a meteorite, encased in a silver frame. If the Ka'ba can be seen as the focal point of the Meccan sanctuary, then the Black Stone is the focal point of the Ka'ba. Its importance is confirmed by the following *hadith*: "The Ka'ba or its eastern corner [in which the Black Stone is set] is God's right hand and with it He shakes the hand of His servants [when they kiss the Stone] as a man shakes the hand of his friend." Another *hadith* asserts that the Ka'ba will appear on the Day of Judgment to "testify in favor of those who have kissed it in truth."[45] A legend has it that when the Black Stone fell from heaven during the time of Adam and Eve, it was shiny white. With time it has grown black after absorbing the darkness and filth of human sins.

The rituals of the Islamic *hajj* were established by the prophet Muhammad himself during his Farewell Pilgrimage to Mecca in 632 (i.e., less than one year before his death). His last public preaching on the plain of 'Arafat confirmed the Abrahamic/monotheistic origins of the *hajj*, while also exhorting the Muslims to live in peace with one another. The Prophet's Farewell Pilgrimage is often seen as his last testament and instructions to his community. The rituals that the Prophet performed during his last visit to Mecca are usually interpreted as a recapitulation of the major stages of monotheism's sacred history: Abraham's (Ibrahim's) repulsion of Satan, who attempted to dissuade him from sacrificing his son; Hagar's desperate quest for water for her infant child Ishmael (Isma'il); Abraham's sacrifice of a ram, who was sent to him by God as a substitute for his son; and so on.

The significance of the *hajj* for the Muslim community as a whole and for its individual members is difficult to overestimate. It reaffirms each pilgrim's commitment to the sacred story of Islam and the values promulgated by God through the tongue of his last prophet. On a broader scale, it symbolizes the solidarity of all Muslims across the globe, as it attracts pilgrims from its every corner. This sense of solidarity comes to the fore during the ritual slaughter of animals by the pilgrims who are imitated by the members of the Muslim community worldwide on the morning of the tenth day of the month of Dhu 'I-Hijja.

The Major Stages and Rituals of the Hajj

What follows is just a general sketch. A detailed description of the ritual activities and their sequence can be found in special literature.[46] Upon arrival in the vicinity of Mecca, pilgrims enter the city's holy precincts through different gates. Non-Muslims are forbidden to advance beyond these points. Before crossing the border of the Meccan sanctuary, the pilgrim must assume the condition of *ihrám*, that is, the state of ritual purity and consecration. This word is derived from the same root as *háram*, meaning "holy" or "sacred." *Ihrám* is symbolized by a two-piece white cloth that male pilgrims are required to wear throughout the *hajj*. This seamless plain garment made of cotton is supposed to erase any distinctions pertaining to class, wealth, education, ethnicity, and so on that the pilgrims have in ordinary life. It stresses the equality of all believers before God on the Day of Judgment. Some scholars interpret the *ihrám* dress as a symbol of the shroud to be worn by resurrected human bodies on the Day of Judgment.

During the pilgrimage, all prayers are to be recited only in Arabic, the language of the revelation, although today pilgrims often make their prayers in their native tongues. Female pilgrims wear clothes that are native to their home countries. They cover their heads but not faces. Thus, it is sometimes argued that during the pilgrimage the *ihrám* garb of male pilgrims bears witness to Islam's unity and egalitarian message, whereas women, through the great variety of their national costumes, exemplify the diversity of Islam as a global community of faith.

Once the pilgrims have entered the state of *ihrám,* they are required to abide by certain rules associated with the Meccan sanctuary: They are forbidden to clip nails, cut hair, wear perfume, hunt, cut trees or bushes, argue with one another, and talk about the opposite sex. In the past, pilgrims were not permitted to wear shoes, although nowadays they usually wear sandals. Whereas women must keep their heads covered, men, on the contrary, must keep them uncovered. Throughout the *hajj* the pilgrims constantly recite the ritual phrase called *talbiyya*. It is derived from the Arabic word *labbayka*, which can be translated as, "Here I am, O my God, at Your service!"[47]

The pilgrims enter the sacred mosque of Mecca through the Gate of Peace and begin to perform the rites of the pilgrimage proper. These being rather complicated, foreign pilgrims are usually accompanied by specially trained local guides who lead them through the stages of the *hajj*. The rites begin with the circumambulation of the Ka'ba (*tawáf*), seven times in a counterclockwise direction. This ritual is performed three times: at the beginning, after the blood sacrifice, and before leaving Mecca at the end of the *hajj* (see Figure 16.3). Tradition holds that Abraham and Ishmael used to circle the Ka'ba in this manner and that Muhammad simply reinstated this rite. All rituals performed within the Meccan sanctuary are called *'úmra*.[48] If a pilgrim arrives off season, he or she can perform *'úmra* without performing the *hajj* itself[49] because it will not be valid anyway.

As mentioned, embedded in the eastern corner of the Ka'ba is the Black Stone. Cast from heaven by God, it symbolizes his covenant with Abraham and his son Ishmael. Those pilgrims who are able to get near enough kiss or touch it, as the Prophet used to do. After performing a prayer of two *rak'a*s at the Place of Abraham (Ibrahím) in the courtyard of the Sacred Mosque,[50] the pilgrims perform the ritual run (*sa'y*) between the two nearby hillocks, Safá and Márwa. This ritual commemorates the story of Abraham's slave-girl Hagar. When she was cast out of the house of Abraham at Sarah's insistence, she wandered in the wilderness with her infant son Ishmael (Isma'il) in search of sustenance and water. The legend has it that Ishmael kicked the ground, and a spring miraculously welled up from the spot where his heel struck the ground. This became the Well of Zámzam, whose water is considered to be blessed. Every pilgrim is expected to partake of it and make additional ablutions.[51] After running between Safá and Márwa seven times, the pilgrims proceed to perform the rituals of the *hajj* outside the Meccan sanctuary. They leave Mecca and travel to the little town of Mína, a few miles away. On the ninth day of Dhu 'l-Hijja, the pilgrims assemble there in front of the Mount of Mercy for the "standing at 'Arafat." It continues from noon to sundown and is believed to be the "heart" of the *hajj*. If a pilgrim fails to observe it, his or her whole pilgrimage is considered null and void. It is said that the pilgrims experience

Figure 16.3 Pilgrims on Their Way to Mecca (Western painting by Leon Belly [1827–1877])
Everett-Art/Shutterstock

a special closeness to God during this afternoon, while at the same time feeling themselves to be part of a world community as tens of thousands of other pilgrims around them share in the same unique experience.

After the sunset, the pilgrims set off on a hasty trip to Muzdalifa, an open plain on the way back to Mecca. On reaching Muzdalifa, they pray two prayers simultaneously (combining the sunset and night ones) and collect forty-nine pebbles for the ritual stoning of the Devil the next day. The stoning recollects the Devil's attempts to dissuade Abraham from sacrificing his son and Abraham's repulsion of his blandishments. The Devil is represented by the three stone pillars of the town of Mína.

On the tenth day of Dhu 'l-Hijja, the pilgrims, now encamped at Mína, slaughter sacrificial animals in commemoration of Abraham's sacrifice of the ram, which was provided in place of Ishmael after the old man's faith had been tested and found firm. Called the "Festival of the Sacrifice," this is an exciting event, which Muslims all over the world seek to take part in by slaughtering their own sacrificial animals and sharing their meat with their neighbors and the poor. The animals—sheep, goats, cows, and camels—are taken in hand, their heads pointing toward the Meccan sanctuary, whereupon a quick cut is made through the jugular vein and windpipe with the words, "In the name of God, the Merciful, the Compassionate." As mentioned, both at Mecca and elsewhere, the flesh of the sacrificed animal is partly eaten by the pilgrims and by Muslims around the world imitating them and partly distributed to others.

After the sacrifice is over, the pilgrims undergo the rite of deconsecrating, which involves a haircut. It marks the end of the state of consecration (*ihrám*), although sexual relations are still prohibited. At this point, the second round of circumambulations of the Ka'ba is performed. After the Festival of the Sacrifice, the celebration continues for three days and gives the pilgrims, still stationed in tents at Mína, a chance to socialize through collective prayers, visits, eating good things, and resting from the hardships of the *hajj*.

Conclusion

1   The rituals of the *hajj*, which probably have their origins back in the pagan pilgrimage around Mecca performed by the pagan Arab tribes, were Islamized by the Prophet and his successors by linking them with the life stories of Abraham (Ibrahim) and Ishmael (Isma'il) and, before them, Adam and Eve. According to the Islamic tradition that developed in the first centuries of Islam, Gabriel taught Adam and Eve how to perform prayers, whereupon they built a house of worship in expiation of their sins. After the house was destroyed by the great flood, Abraham and Ishmael rebuilt the shrine. Gradually, its monotheistic origins were forgotten by Arab tribes, which had reverted to paganism. They converted Abraham's house of worship into a pagan sanctuary. The prophet Muhammad restored the true and original meaning of the *hajj* after it had been obscured by pagan beliefs. By closely imitating Muhammad's ritual actions during his Farewell Pilgrimage, his followers have striven to achieve closeness to God and his Prophet ever since.

2   In the process of rededication of the pagan sanctuary to the God of Islamic monotheism, the complex rituals associated therewith were reimagined in such a way as to reflect the pivotal events of monotheism's sacred history, in particular the life stories of Abraham, Ishmael, and Hagar.

3   Some rituals of the *hajj* have a clear eschatological significance. Bidding farewell to their families and relatives by the pilgrims before embarking on journey to Mecca gives them a foretaste of being snatched from the loved ones at the time of death. Seeing "God's house" (Ka'ba) in this world implicitly prepares him to seeing God face-to-face on the Day of Judgment. Donning the *ihrám* reminds the pilgrims that on the Day of Resurrection they

will be wearing only a seamless white shroud to cover their nakedness. Circumambulating the Ka'ba may remind them of the angels circling God's throne and singing praises to God—an image that looms large in Islamic religious imagery. By touching the Black Stone, the pilgrims renew their allegiance to and covenant with God in imitation of the Prophet. Standing on the plain of 'Arafat almost naked and exposed to the elements impresses upon the pilgrims the gravity of the final reckoning at the end.

Visiting the Prophet's Tomb at Medina

After completing the *hajj*, many pilgrims undertake a journey to Islam's second greatest sanctuary, the tomb of the Prophet at Medina. It is a time-honored practice to stay there for ten days in order to perform fifty prayers. This trip is known as *ziyára* (literally, "visit"). The *ziyára* is not part of the *hajj* and is regarded as optional. Nevertheless, many pilgrims (about three-fourths, according to one estimation)[52] consider their *hajj* incomplete if they have not paid their respects to the founder of Islam. According to a famous prophetic *hadíth*, "Whosoever visits my tomb, my intercession will be granted to him."

Medina is located some 300 miles (450 kilometers) north of Mecca. While visiting the Prophet's tomb, pilgrims are not expected to perform the circumambulation of it as they do during their visit to the House of God in Mecca. Nor should they visit the tomb wearing the *ihrám* dress. Moreover, nowadays the authorities of the Kingdom of Saudi Arabia see to it that visitors do not kiss or touch it with the hand as they do with the Black Stone and the Ka'ba. The visitors enter the Prophet's mosque, which is covered by a splendid cupola, known as the "Green Dome," through the Gate of Peace. In the words of a European visitor to the city, this complex presents "a picture of the most striking beauty and magnificence."[53] Inside the mosque, a brass railing marks out the original home of the Prophet, where he was buried, and his private mosque. The Prophet's tomb is located in the southeast corner of the mosque, beneath the Green Dome. A famous *hadíth* says, "The space between my [Prophet's] house and my pulpit is one of the gardens of Paradise." The visitors perform a prayer of two prostrations in front of the tomb, followed by a supplication. They then file before the *qibla* wall of the mosque (facing south). While at the Prophet's tomb, they try to imagine themselves standing in front of the Prophet and greeting him in silence. Located next to the tomb are the graves of the two first caliphs, Abu Bakr and 'Umar. The pilgrims, if they are Sunnites, greet them too. The Shi'ites, who consider the first two caliphs to be usurpers, abstain from doing this. Instead, they visit the tombs of Fátima and of the second, fourth, fifth, and sixth *imam*s buried at one of Medina's cemeteries.[54] In the days that follow, the visitors usually spend much time in the Prophet's mosque reading the Qur'an. As in Mecca, they are often accompanied by special guides (usually native to the city), who instruct them in correct ways of honoring the Prophet and other heroes of early Islam buried in and around Medina.

Finally, it should be pointed out that the Shi'ites have their own pilgrimages to the tombs of their *imam*s outside Medina, namely, in Najaf ('Ali), Kerbelá (al-Husayn b. 'Ali), al-Kazimáyn (the seventh and ninth *imam*s), Mashhad (the eighth *imam*), and so on. These visits involve elaborate rituals that are described in special pilgrimage manuals. Each shrine has its own prayer of visitation associated with it.[55]

How Religion Shapes the Lives of Individual Muslims

Religion plays an important role in the Muslim rites of passage, that is, rituals that mark the transition of individual believers from one stage of their lives to another over time.[56] For instance, in Christian societies, the major milestones are birth, initiation, marriage, and death. They are associated with the religious rites of baptism, confirmation/anointment, church marriage, holiday celebrations, and death. The same is true of Islamic societies in which the transition of individual believers from one stage of life to another is marked by religiously sanctioned rituals.[57]

1   *Birth.* The entry of a newly born into the Muslim community is symbolically acknowledged by uttering the call to prayer (*adhán*) into its right ear. This ritual is based on the example of Muhammad, who is said to have done this on the occasion of the birth of his grandson al-Husayn, the future martyr of Kerbelá. Putting a small amount of chewed date flesh into the child's mouth is also believed to be based on a precedent established by the Prophet. The seventh day is the traditional time for naming. It is accompanied by the ceremony of animal sacrifice (two for a boy and one for a girl). The names given to the newly born often include an epithet or name of God, for instance 'Abdallah ("Servant of God"), 'Abd al-Ráhman ("Servant of the [All-]Merciful)," 'Abd al-Karím ("Servant of the [All-]Generous"), 'Abd al-Qádir ("Servant of the [All-]Powerful"), and so on. Some names hark back to the major personages of Islam's sacred history such as Muhammad, 'Ali, 'A'isha, Fátima, Khadíja, [al-]Hásan, [al-]Husayn, Abu Bakr, 'Umar, Khalid, and so on. Naturally, the names Abu Bakr and 'Umar would never be found among the Shi'ites (as well as that of 'A'isha or 'Uthman). Likewise, a Sunni family would hardly call its newly born 'Abd [al-]'Ali ("Servant of 'Ali"), 'Abd al-Husayn ("Servant of al-Husayn"), or 'Abd al-Máhdi ("Servant of the Máhdi")—names that are relatively common among the Shi'ites. Thus, an ostensibly innocuous process of naming a child often carries profound religious connotations, either dedicating the child to God or associating him with a hero of early Islam.

2   *Circumcision* is the removal of the boy's foreskin by a specially trained circumciser. It may take place either on the seventh day after the boy's birth or between ages three and nine. The former is recommendable (*mustahabb*). However, it may also be performed on a fourteen- or fifteen-year-old. Circumcision is not explicitly mentioned in the Qur'an but is sanctioned by numerous prophetic *hadíth*. According to one, "if the two circumcised parts have been in touch with one another, a major ablution (*ghusl*) is necessary."[58] This statement indicates that circumcision applies to both men and women, although opinions on this matter vary from one legal school to the other. The Maliki school does not view it as obligatory, whereas the Shafi'i one does. Furthermore, in the Middle Ages, the majority of Shafi'i jurists considered it to be equally obligatory for males and females.[59] The *hadíth* mention historical precedents justifying the practice. According to one tradition, Abraham (Ibrahim) was circumcised at the age of eighty, and the Prophet's younger companions requested to be circumcised when they were grown-ups. This is why, perhaps, a *hadíth* calls the Prophet "king of the circumcised." Based on these and other *hadíth*, the majority of Muslim scholars from all legal schools consider circumcision to be obligatory. They also agree that it must be performed on a boy before he reaches adulthood. The act of circumcision is accompanied by a recitation of the entire text of the Qur'an. On the eve of the event, a public celebration takes place at the boy's house, during which his parents receive gifts and congratulations. In return, they prepare a feast for friends, neighbors, and relatives. In some areas, on the day before the rite of circumcision is to be performed, boys from wealthy families, dressed in their best, are paraded through the streets on horseback accompanied by a crowd of relatives, friends, and musicians.[60] The operation used to be performed by a barber; nowadays it is usually done by medical specialists or certified barbers. Guests and relations are treated to a celebratory feast. Although not explicitly sanctioned by either the Qur'an or the Prophet's Sunna, female circumcision is performed in some parts of the Muslim world, especially in the Nile Valley. This rite is restricted to the women of the household and is concealed from the public. In the process, the

female genitalia are mutilated: a part or sometimes all of the external female genitalia (clitoris) is removed, allegedly in order to reduce woman's "desire for copulation." Clitoridectomy, as it is known among medical specialists, is not a universally accepted practice in the Islamic world. In fact, in most Muslim societies, the female circumcision is unknown.[61] Moreover, in the areas where it is practiced, for example in Egypt, female excision is not confined to the local Muslim communities but practiced by both Muslims and Christians (Copts) alike. Where this custom is practiced, its origins appear to be clearly pre-Islamic. According to some scholars, in traditional societies, it reflects the tension between the recognition by the local community of female sexual desire and the culturally constructed need to restrain it. For a boy, circumcision is an initiation ceremony that marks his transition from boyhood to puberty. After circumcision, the boy becomes a full-fledged member of the community of Islam with all the attendant obligations, although in principle he must pray, fast, and fulfill other religious obligations even without having undergone circumcision. On the social plane, the boundary of gender, which is still ambivalent in childhood, is rendered clear and unequivocal after circumcision. Having been sanctioned by prophetic *hadíth*, it serves as a vivid example of the way in which Islam puts its stamp on the natural stages of human life.

3   *Marriage and gender relations*. The Qur'an encourages and praises marriage and married life (e.g., Q 16:72 and 30:21). In a famous *hadíth*, the Prophet says: "O young people, whoever among you are able to marry, should marry, and whoever is not able to marry, is recommended to fast, as fast diminishes his sexual power." Marriage is thus enjoined on all able-bodied Muslims and considered a norm in Islamic society. Sexual intercourse is confined to marriage and bound by the norms of the Shari'a. According to these norms, fornication and adultery are punishable by either flogging or stoning. The former punishment is applied in the case of unmarried individuals, the latter in the case of married ones. To make sure no illicit activities become possible, any premarital contacts between bride and groom are discouraged, although in most societies they are allowed to enjoy each other's company in the presence of their relatives. Marriage payment (bride wealth) is advanced to the father of the bride by the groom or his father. The Islamic law has strict regulations concerning relations between sexes. Degrees of close blood relationship within which males and females may not marry are clearly defined in the Qur'an (4:23). Closely related individuals cannot be marriage partners, therefore they may associate socially with one another without public opprobrium. Conversely, a proper Muslim woman is not supposed to appear in public with a male who is not her close relative. If such a contact is necessary, she is expected to observe certain rules, namely, to be properly dressed (covered) and keep the door open so as to be observed by outsiders. In traditional Islamic societies, a female visiting an unrelated male (a doctor, lawyer, teacher, etc.) is usually accompanied by a relative. Such conventions are not usually observed by Muslims living in more secularized Muslim countries societies and in the West. In conservative Muslim societies, on the other hand, the rule of separation between the sexes applies to parties and other social events attended by unrelated Muslims. On such occasions, men and women often eat and enjoy themselves in separate rooms. In a more emancipated environment, women can mingle with men as long as they are properly dressed and behave modestly. Proper Muslim men do not normally inquire about female members of a nonkinsman's family. In marriage, strict division of social roles is maintained. A man has to provide for the family (according to a Qur'anic injunction), whereas the woman is responsible for the upbringing of children and keeping the household. The Qur'an allows a man to take up to four wives, on the condition that he is able to support them and treat them equally. As we shall see

in Chapters 18 and 21, the issue of male polygamy is not straightforward and is subject to a variety of interpretations. Divorce is easier for men. Muslim men are permitted to marry women from the People of the Book, whereas Muslim women are not allowed to marry non-Muslim men unless they convert to Islam. The marriage ceremony consists of writing and signing a contract between the partners on a day agreed upon by the sides. It is solemnized by a religious scholar or a judge (*qádi*). At the signing of the contract, the groom meets a male representative of the bride, who by signing the contract agrees to "give her away." The *Fátiha* chapter of the Qur'an is recited, which serves as the religious blessing for the newlyweds. Now they become legally married under the Shari'a law, and preparations begin for the wedding celebration. Marriage festivities vary widely from one geographical area to another. In Egypt, both the bride and the groom are bathed (separately) and have their hair done by a barber. A feast is then prepared by the family of the groom, which is usually accompanied by Qur'an recitation by a hired professional. The permissibility of using music and dancing during Muslim weddings is a debated issue and is decided by each individual family based on its understanding of propriety. Gifts are brought by the guests and names of the donors announced. Later, the bride and her family arrive. The bride is seated in a conspicuous place for everyone to see. Sweets, soft drinks, and food are served. Men often smoke water pipes. The celebration goes on until evening, at which time the groom finally retires to his wife's room, which she now takes in the house of the groom's father. Anthropologists sometimes interpret Muslim marriages as occasions to enhance the social cohesion of a local Muslim community. In any event, it is definitely an important rite of passage, in which Islam has a role to play.

4   *Death.* At the approach of death, the dying person should turn his or her head toward Mecca and say, "There's no deity but God." *Sura* 36 (*Ya Sin*) of the Qur'an is often recited to the dying person, then after his or her death, and at the funeral. It says, among other things (77–78), "Who will revive these bones when they have rotted? Say: He will revive them, Who produced them at the beginning, for He is the Knower of every station!" These Qur'anic phrases instill in the dying person hope for an eternal life to come. After death, an ablution is performed according to strict rites by a professional body washer. The body is then scented and wrapped in a plain grave cloth that completely enfolds the corpse. This is followed by a funeral procession and burial. Burial should take place on the same day but may not take place after sundown. The body is carried on a special litter to the cemetery. It is a communal obligation to follow the funeral procession, when one sees it, to the burial place. Upon arrival at the gravesite, the first *sura* of the Qur'an is recited. The *shaháda* is whispered into the ear of the deceased. The grave is four to six feet deep, with a shelf hollowed out on one side. The body is placed on the shelf with the head turned toward Mecca. Excessive mourning is discouraged; after all, the newly deceased is heading for a better world. The family of the deceased distributes gifts to the poor who assemble for that purpose at the grave. The special funeral prayer is recited that consists of the fourfold repetition of the phrase "God is the greatest" followed by a litany. On the next day, a reception is held at the house of the deceased, during which the entire text of the Qur'an is chanted by a hired reciter. The period of mourning lasts for three days. In many Muslim societies, the recitation of the entire Qur'an or its parts by professional reciters or members of the family of the deceased is also performed on the fortieth day after his or her death and repeated annually thereafter. Muslim martyrs require neither the ablution nor the funeral prayer. They are buried in their bloodied clothes that will serve as evidence of their special status on the Day of Judgment.

Conclusions

As we have seen, religious beliefs and obligations decisively shape the rhythm and trajectory of the life of Muslims residing in the Muslim world and in diaspora. As our brief discussion of the rites of passage in Muslim societies has shown, religion accompanies a believer throughout the course of his or her life—from cradle to grave. Many rites are culturally bound and differ from one society or legal school to another. However, the basics are the same throughout the Muslim world: the profession of the Muslim creed, the reading of the Qur'an, the performance of the canonical prayers, the payment of *zakát*, and the fast of Ramadán. Moreover, they are found in every locality where Muslims live outside the Muslim world. Every year, the *hajj* season brings together Muslims from all over the globe to take part in the rituals stipulated by the Qur'an and demonstrated by the Prophet during his Farewell Pilgrimage. In this way, the Five Pillars of Islam and the Muslim rites of passage serve as powerful and visible symbols of the distinctive Muslim identity. They give Muslims wherever they might live a sense of belonging to a global community of religious commitment.

Questions to Ponder

1   What is the significance of prostrating oneself before God? Discuss the various functions of the Muslim prayer.
2   What is the purpose(s) of self-imposed deprivation during the fast of Ramadán. Why is it sometimes called the "month of good works"?
3   Address the significance of the "rites of passage" in Muslim societies and compare them to those current in Western societies.
4   Discuss the symbolism and significance of the *hajj* rituals. How can their "pagan" origin be reconciled with their being the fifth pillar of Islam?
5   It is often argued that, unlike Christianity, which emphasizes the correct creed ("orthodoxy"), Islam is more concerned with the correct and regular performance of the religious duties by its followers ("orthopraxy"). After reading this chapter and the chapters that deal with theological and philosophical debates in Islam (i.e., Chapters 10 and 14), do you agree with this assessment? Substantiate your answer by evidence found in these three chapters.

Summary

*   The notions of "Islamic ethos" and "Islamic ritual." The practical realization and performance of the teachings of Islam by its followers: The Five Pillars of Islam.
*   The five canonical prayers (*saláts*) as the foundation of Islamic worship. Their timing, structure, and ritual formulas. Cycles of bodily postures and prostrations during the prayer (*rak'a*s). Prayers inside and outside the mosque.
*   Differences between Shi'ite and Sunni prayer rituals in regard to the *adhán*, ablutions, and placement of the forehead.
*   Sermons (*khútba*s) and collective prayers at congregational (Friday) mosques performed by *khatíb*s; their social and political significance.

- The giving of alms (*zakát*) and its social and religious significance. The taxable items: crops, livestock, gold, silver, cash, mines, and buried treasure. The Sunni–Shiʻite difference in matters of *zakát* collection.
- The fast of Ramadán (*sawm, urazá*) and its antecedents in other Middle Eastern religions.
- Voluntary or supererogatory fasts and special Shiʻite fasts.
- The spiritual and social benefits of fasting, according to al-Ghazali and Mawdúdi.
- The pilgrimage to Mecca (*hajj*) during the month of Dhu 'l-Hijja (eighth through the thirteenth). The ritual significance and historical roots of the Muslim pilgrimage.
- The Kaʻba as the "House of God" and the principal focus of religious devotion in Islam.
- The Prophet's "Farewell Pilgrimage" and his final sermon on the plain of ʻArafat in 632 are the precedent-setting events heeded and reenacted continuously by subsequent generations of Muslims.
- The major stages and rituals of the *hajj*: ritual consecration (*ihrám*), circling the Kaʻba (*tawáf*), drinking from the well of Zámzam, standing at Mount Mercy on the plain of ʻArafat, the animal sacrifice at Mína, and the ritual of deconsecrating.
- Pious visits (*ziyára*) to the Prophet's tomb at Medina and the graves of other Muslim heroes. The Shiʻite shrines in Arabia, Iraq, and Iran.
- The Muslim life cycle. How Islam leaves its imprint on the life trajectories of individual Muslims from cradle to grave (birth, the naming of newly born children, circumcision, marriage and marital life, and death).

Notes

1 Richard Martin, *Islamic Studies*, 2nd ed., Prentice Hall, Upper Saddle River, NJ, 1996.
2 For further instances, see Q 3:2; 28:70, and 59:22.
3 See, e.g., http://www.ahl-alquran.com/English/show_article.php?main_id=8374.
4 Constance Padwick, *Muslim Devotions: A Study of Prayer Manuals in Common Use*, S.P.C.K, London, 1961, p. 126.
5 Ibid., pp. 129–130.
6 Ibid., p. 130; for an illuminating discussion of the role of the Devil in Islamic theology see Peter Awn, *Satan's Tragedy and Redemption: Iblis in Sufi Psychology*, E. J. Brill, Leiden, 1983.
7 For the development of this precept and the polemic that surrounds it, see Joseph Eliash, "On the Genesis and Development of the Twelver-Shiʻi Three-Tenet *shahada*," in Gerald Hawting (ed.), *The Development of Islamic Ritual*, Ashgate-Variorum, Aldershot, UK, 2006, pp. 24–30.
8 The latter term is used in the Muslim East (Turkey, Iran, Central Asia, Russia, and China).
9 Padwick, *Muslim Devotions*, p. 6.
10 Ibid., p. 7.
11 Marshall Hodgson, *The Venture of Islam*, Chicago University Press, Chicago, 1974, vol. 1, p. 209.
12 It alludes only to the dawn, midday, and sunset prayers (see, for instance, Q 11:114; 17:78, and 30:17–18).
13 Ibrahim Abu Rabiʻ, "Salat," in John Esposito (ed.), *The Oxford Encyclopedia of the Modern Islamic World*, Oxford University Press, Oxford, 1995, vol. 3, p. 469.
14 Moojan Momen, *An Introduction to Shiʻi Islam*, Yale University Press, New Haven, CT, 1985, p. 178.
15 The following description is taken from the article "Adhan" in the electronic edition of the *Encyclopedia of Islam*, 2nd ed. (by Th. W. Jyunboll); online edition: http://referenceworks.brillonline.com.
16 Momen, *An Introduction to Shiʻi Islam*, p. 178.
17 Many Muslims believe that this phrase serves as a greeting to the two angels that accompany the faithful throughout their lives.
18 Muzammil Siddiqi and Tazim Kassam, "Salat," in Lindsay Jones (ed.), *Encyclopedia of Religion*, 2nd ed., Macmillan, Detroit, 2005, vol. 12, p. 8058; the same applies to every prayer performed in congregation rather than in the privacy of one's house.

19 As stipulated in the Qur'an, 4:101.

20 Momen, *An Introduction to Shi'i Islam*, p. 181.

21 Snouck Hurgronje, "On the Institution of *zakat*," in Gerald Hawting (ed.), *The Development of Islamic Ritual*, Ashgate-Variorum, Aldershot, UK, 2006, p. 191.

22 Aaron Zysow, "Zakat," *Encyclopaedia of Islam*, 2nd ed.; online edition: http://referenceworks.brillonline.com.

23 Gautier Juynboll, *Encyclopedia of Canonical Hadith*, E. J. Brill, Leiden, 2007, p. 597.

24 Momen, *An Introduction to Shi'i Islam*, p. 179.

25 Zysow, "Zakat."

26 Abdallah al-Sheikh, "Zakat," in John Esposito (ed.), *The Oxford Encyclopedia of the Modern Islamic World*, Oxford University Press, Oxford, 1995, vol. 4, pp. 367–368.

27 James Lindsay, *Daily Life in the Medieval Islamic World*, Greenwood Press, Westport, CT, 2005, p. 150.

28 Georges Vajda, "Fasting in Islam and Judaism," in Gerald Hawting (ed.), *The Development of Islamic Ritual*, Ashgate-Variorum, Aldershot, UK, 2006, pp. 133–149.

29 Shelomo D. Goitein, "Ramadan, the Month of Fasting," in Gerald Hawting (ed.), *The Development of Islamic Ritual*, Ashgate-Variorum, Aldershot, UK, 2006, pp. 151–171.

30 Q 2:183–185; 2:179–181, according to Arberry's translation.

31 Q 2:187; 2:183, according to Arberry's translation.

32 Zafar Ansari, "Sawm," in Lindsay Jones (ed.), *Encyclopedia of Religion*, 2nd ed., Macmillan, Detroit, 2005, vol. 12, p. 8141.

33 Ibid.

34 Lindsay, *Daily Life in the Medieval Islamic World*, p. 153.

35 Momen, *An Introduction to Shi'i Islam*, p. 179.

36 It is known as *urazá-bayrám* in the Muslim lands east of Iraq.

37 It will be discussed in the section that follows.

38 Al-Ghazali, *Abstinence in Islam* (trans. Caesar Farah), Biblioteca Islamica, Minneapolis, MN, 1992, p. 35.

39 William McNeill and Marilyn Waldman (eds.), *The Islamic World*, University of Chicago Press, Chicago and London, 1983, pp. 218–225.

40 His life and teachings are discussed in Chapter 22.

41 Ansari, "Sawm," p. 8141.

42 Some Muslim scholars consider *jihád* to be the sixth pillar, but this view is not generally accepted.

43 Q 3:90, according to Arberry's translation; Q 3:96–97, according to most other translations.

44 One of the names of Mecca, according to most Qur'an interpreters.

45 Hava Lazarus-Yafeh, "The Religious Dialectics of the *hadjdj*," in Gerald Hawting (ed.), *The Development of Islamic Ritual*, Ashgate-Variorum, Aldershot, UK, 2006, p. 275.

46 Bernard Lewis, Arent Wensinck and Jacques Jomier, "Hadjdj," in *Encyclopedia of Islam*, 2nd ed., online edition: http://referenceworks.brillonline.com; and Frederick Peters, *The Hajj*, Princeton University Press, Princeton, NJ, 1994.

47 Martin, *Islamic Studies*, pp. 185–186.

48 Sometimes translated as "minor pilgrimage."

49 Martin, *Islamic Studies*, pp. 186–188.

50 It is a small ornate shrine that commemorates the (re)establishment of the first place of worship by the Israelite patriarch. Martin, *Islamic Studies*, p. 188.

51 Lindsay, *Daily Life in the Medieval Islamic World*, p. 156 and Martin, *Islamic Studies*, p. 188.

52 Richard Winder, "al-Madina," in *Encyclopedia of Islam*, 2nd ed.; online edition: http://referenceworks.brillonline.com.

53 Ibid.

54 Ibid.

55 Momen, *An Introduction to Shi'i Islam*, p. 182.

56 Barbara Myerhoff, Linda Camino and Edith Turner, "Rites of Passage," in Lindsay Jones (ed.), *Encyclopedia of Religion*, 2nd ed., Macmillan, Detroit, 2005, vol. 11, p. 7796.

57 What follows is based on Martin, *Islamic Studies*, pp. 217–222 and Dale Eickelman, "Rites of Passage: Muslim Rites," in Lindsay Jones (ed.), *Encyclopedia of Religion*, Macmillan, Detroit, 2005, vol. 11, pp. 7824–7828.

58 This *hadīth* is mentioned by both al-Bukhari and Muslim; for the exact references, see Arent Wensinck, "Khitan," in *Encyclopedia of Islam*, 2nd ed.; online edition: http://referenceworks.brillonline.com.

59 Ibid., citing the famous Shafi'i jurist Yahya al-Nawawi (d. 1277).

60 Ibid.

61 Jonathan Berkey, "Circumcision Circumscribed: Female Excision and Cultural Accommodation in the Medieval Near East," *International Journal of Middle Eastern Studies*, vol. 28/1 (1996), pp. 19–38.

Chapter 17

Islamic Art and Religious Architecture (Mosque)

The Qur'an as the Focus of Devotion

The Qur'an constitutes the primary source and all-important focus of Muslim faith and devotion. Its message forms the very foundation of Islamic communal, cultural, and devotional life.[1] The entire worldview that we call "Islamic" evolved in response to the moral, ethical, aesthetical, and doctrinal precepts contained in the Muslim revelation. They are best summed up in the concept of *tawhid*, the emphatic assertion of God's absolute unity. From this assertion, as we have seen, spring all the other demands that God has imposed on his servants. As the principal and unrivalled source of Islamic doctrine and practice (even Islam's other major symbols, such as Mecca and the Ka'ba, are secondary, insofar as their significance is explained and conditioned by the Qur'anic text), the Qur'an demands that its followers pay undivided attention to its messages. Once the role of the Qur'an and the conduit to God has been accepted by the believers, they have begun to use it as means of worship:

> What one did with the Qur'an was not to peruse it but to worship by means of it; not to passively receive it but, in reciting it, to reaffirm it for oneself: the event of revelation was renewed every time one of the faithful, in the act or worship, relived the Qur'anic affirmations.[2]

In view of its centrality to Islamic faith and practice, the Qur'an can tolerate no rivalry from either human beings or physical objects that may potentially weaken or dissipate the worshipper's single-minded devotion to the one and only God of the Muslim scripture and to the moral and ethical imperatives that flow from it. The Qur'an's overriding importance for the Muslims has rendered them leery of any alternative mediators between God and human beings.

This single-minded preoccupation of Muslims with the Divine Word as the uncontested symbol of faith and the sole way to salvation stood in sharp contrast to most but not all pre-Islamic cultures of the Middle East. Here, we find a widespread use of images and representations that appeal to the human imagination by bringing into play symbolic correspondences among different objects. The figure of a beautiful woman could represent love and motherhood and, ultimately, also the source of life altogether. As such, it could easily become a symbol of a goddess of fertility or motherhood. The figure of a strong man might evoke military prowess, generative potency, and lordly authority. It could represent a god of war, fatherhood, or lordly power. These symbolic correspondences expressed in various figurative forms (from statues to paintings) were instrumental in developing, among certain groups of Middle Easterners, a mythical universe inhabited by minor and major deities that represented various social and natural powers. In placing themselves under their protection, these groups were able to make better sense of themselves, of the world around them, of the vicissitudes of their daily life, and, eventually, of death as well.

Not so in Muslim societies. In the light of the Qur'an's demand for the all-exclusive attention to its message, the imaginative life of the human spirit became religiously suspect. Representational art (sculpture and painting), poetry, music, and dance were particularly problematic from the viewpoint of the uncompromising monotheism advocated by the Qur'an.[3] Because such artistic pursuits appeal to human emotions and imagination, they may potentially lessen the believers' exclusive devotional focus on the Qur'an. Furthermore, seen from the Qur'anic perspective, these artistic objects and activities may appear to be subtle forms of idolatry. This perception inevitably had long-ranging religious implications, especially because Arabia's idol worshippers, as we remember, turned out to be the chief enemies of Islam and the Prophet at the initial stages of his mission. The Prophet was sent by God to abolish various Arabian gods and goddesses, as well as the idols representing them. The monotheism of the Qur'an demanded the sole medium of worship by the entire worshipping community. This attitude resembles the spirit of Protestantism that emphasizes the overriding importance of the text of the scriptures (the New Testament, in particular) to the exclusion of any other forms of worship, such as icons, incense burning, saints, relics, and huge, lavishly decorated cathedrals, all of which constitute part and parcel of both Catholic and Eastern Orthodox Christianity.

In Islam, this religious attitude, which academics often describe as "fear of symbols and images" or *iconophobia*,[4] predates European Protestantism. It was in evidence already among certain Christian sects of the Byzantine Empire. Whether they rejected icon worship under the influence of the Islamic ban of representational arts or, on the contrary, the Muslims were influenced by their Christian neighbors is still a subject of academic debate.[5] What is hardly in doubt is that the Islamic prohibition of realistic paintings and sculptures evolved gradually on the basis of similar attitudes in the other monotheistic religions of the Middle East. In short, there is nothing exclusively Islamic about the "fear of images": The Jewish communities of the Middle East had long before rejected them as a form of idolatry, whereas some Christians in the Byzantine Empire were also chary of using them, especially in their ritual practices.

Scriptural Evidence Against Figural Arts

Regardless of who influenced whom and when, there were important reasons for the iconophobic attitudes to take root in early Islam. Icons were a visible and ubiquitous symbol of Byzantine Christianity in the same way as sculptures and other representations of Iranian kings were a visible attribute of Sasanian imperial power. Since the latter was totally destroyed and the former drastically curtailed by the Arabs in the name of Islam, it was only natural that its triumphal leaders were eager to dissociate themselves from their imperial rivals on religious grounds. Rejecting all manner of figural arts, and of images of human beings in particular, was an effective and obvious way to do so. It fell to Muslim scholars to justify this rejection on the basis of the Qur'an and Sunna of the Prophet. Although Qur'anic evidence in this regard is rather scanty, one passage from the Muslim scripture condemns the worship of statues alongside games of chance, divination, and consumption of wine as "a crime, originating in Satan" (5:90–91). Another verse quotes Abraham who accuses his father of worshiping statues that represent pagan gods (6:74).[6] Similar evidence can be culled from the corpus of the Prophet's sayings. One *hadíth* asserts that "[a]ngels will not enter a house containing a bell, a picture or a dog." Another is even more damning. It asserts that on the Day of Judgment, those who claim that they can paint or fashion anything that looks like a living thing will be challenged by God to breathe life into their creatures and, after failing to do so, be condemned to torments in the hellfire.[7] This *hadíth* is usually understood by Muslim theologians in the light of the Qur'anic verse 39:62, in which God declares himself to be the sole creator and giver of life. The theologians argued that in trying to imitate him, human beings (in this case, artists and sculptors) encroach on God's sacrosanct prerogative to create and thus become liable to eternal punishment.[8] As already mentioned, Muslims (or at least the majority of Muslim scholars) adopted the attitude of hostility toward images that had prevailed among the Jews of the Middle East, who believed that "all figural imagery—in human and animal form—[be] ruled out in places of worship."[9] The more pious members of the Jewish communities sought to expel such imagery from public space altogether. Whether or not adopted in imitation of the Jewish rabbis or Christian iconoclasts, this iconophobic attitude has had a profound and long-lasting impact on the evolution of artistic tradition in Muslim societies, rendering it predominantly text oriented rather than image oriented. Despite the ban on figural art that the 'ulamá' endeavored to impose on their communities, it has persisted, quite vigorously, in the eastern areas of the premodern Muslim world, especially among the elites.[10] One can thus argue that the ban applied first and foremost to the presence of images in places of public worship (mosques), where it could distract the faithful from focusing on the fulfillment of their religious duties. At rulers' courts, it was often ignored, already by the Umayyads, who built sumptuous palaces richly decorated with mosaic pictures, statues, and engravings that depicted both humans and animals (and sometimes the rulers themselves).[11] The same openness to and enjoyment of figural arts can be found at Muslim courts and among intellectuals throughout Islamic history.[12]

How Did Artists Respond to the Restrictions?

Nevertheless, after the ban had become part of the religious dogma, it inevitably restricted artistic expression. The vast majority of Muslim artists was reluctant to openly violate the ban, either out of personal piety or out of fear of public backlash. They offered several positive ways to resolve the problem.

First, the artists aspired to make representation of natural objects, animals, and human beings extremely symbolic and unrealistic. In other words, they deliberately minimized any obvious correspondences between the images and the natural or living objects they depicted. It is in this sense that the Islamic arts are sometimes called "emblematic" or "symbolic." The images portrayed are usually two-dimensional and nonlifelike. They lack perspective. Nevertheless, even such stylized, flat images can still be appreciated by viewers and elicit their aesthetic and emotional responses.

The artists' second strategy in responding to the religious restrictions imposed on their creative work by the religious dogma was to use abstract design patterns that, in the West, have come to be known as "arabesque" (see Figure 17.1). The arabesque is a stylized interlacing of leaves and stems, which creates intricate networks of abstract forms. Once transposed onto a surface—be it parchment, paper, book cover, pottery, carpet, or wall—such abstract forms multiply themselves infinitely, becoming "an unending continuous pattern."[13] Vegetal design patterns are often intricately interwoven with geometrical figures: circles, triangles, squares, and other polygons. These intertwined figures constitute a complete and uninterrupted surface with no empty spaces. This is why the arabesque is described, in Western academic literature, as an art of "total space decoration" conditioned by the "fear of empty space."[14] The best samples of arabesque art "develop on several repeatedly intersecting levels, thus creating movement in depth."[15] Superimposed upon these two patterns (i.e., vegetal and geometric) are highly elaborate lines and stylized Arabic writing. The Arabic characters (often leafed or even flowered) intricately intertwine with the vegetal-geometrical patterns, forming a unique aesthetical whole.[16] Such text-and-design compositions had a dual impact on a viewer. They allowed him or her to appreciate the beautifully executed Arabic text, while at the same time admiring a no less splendid background on which it was inscribed.

The integration of stylized Arabic letters into the arabesque brings us to probably the most "Islamic" form of Islamic art, calligraphy. The art of Arabic writing or calligraphy developed in

Figure 17.1 An Arabesque Above the Entrance to Bibi-Khanym Mosque, Uzbekistan
David Holt/Flickr/Wikimedia Commons

the course of copying and transmitting the holy book of Islam. From its plain and often rather crude form, the Arabic writing gradually developed into a wide variety of calligraphic styles from a formal angular *kúfi* to a fluent cursive *náskhi*. These various scripts came to play an important, even critical role in the Muslim decorative arts and were often valued more highly than any other forms of artistic expression due to the sacred status of the Qur'anic text.[17] This is hardly surprising, because the Qur'an itself places great value on the notions of "writing," "reading," "pen," and "book." They figure prominently in the chapters (*sura*s) that are commonly believed to be the earliest revealed to the Prophet, namely, 96 and 68, as well as in later ones, such as 43, 44, 45, 46, and so on. The great value of writing is further confirmed by a *hadíth* that promises a place in Paradise to any person who can inscribe the word of God in a beautiful handwriting.[18] When superimposed on arabesque patterns, calligraphy served as an aesthetically sophisticated glorification of sacred phrases from the Qur'an and, somewhat less commonly, from the prophetic *hadíth*. A combination of arabesque patterns and beautiful calligraphy was employed to manufacture illuminated (i.e., beautifully adorned) copies of the sacred book. Production of such illuminated Qur'ans constituted a special branch of Islamic art.[19] The creative use of calligraphy and arabesque gradually expanded beyond the Qur'anic text to secular epic literature, as well as to various artifacts, from door handles and chalices to tiles and even drums.

In an illuminated manuscript, each page usually contains at least several lines of exquisite calligraphy with the remaining space devoted to delicately drawn arabesque patterns. Decorative framing bands and markings helped to turn text passages into a rich and elaborate composition. The finest decorations of all are the so-called carpet pages at the beginning of the books, whose extraordinary richness of color and detail makes them true artistic masterpieces. In the later periods, the calligraphic-cum-arabesque patterns just described often included stylized images of human beings, dragons, and groups of animals, all of which is a dramatic testimony to the relativity of the ban on figural art imposed by the custodians of Islamic orthodoxy.[20]

In trying to account for the predominance of arabesque art in premodern Muslim societies, Western scholars have sometimes argued that arabesque compositions symbolize "the infinite complexity and dynamism of existence, a perfect harmony of detail with detail and of part with whole." In such elaborate compositions "all the innumerable details are each felt equally precious, yet no one item stands to dominate the whole: the eye is fed with an infinitude of beauty."[21] According to other Western connoisseurs, the combination of order, symbolized by geometrical networks, and vigorous, vibrant growth, symbolized by vegetal and floral patterns, represents the dynamic relations between constancy and growth, between the immutable truths of the Qur'anic revelation and the seemingly unpredictable twists and turns of earthly existence.[22] One further argues that the arabesque art is a subtle allusion to a constant creative readjustment of purportedly unchangeable Qur'anic truths in response to changing times and conditions of human existence. Whether the Muslim artists who created arabesque patterns were indeed motivated by such philosophical and aesthetic considerations is a different story.

Western scholars and public at large have been particularly fascinated by the art of book illustration known as "miniature painting." It developed mainly in the eastern lands of Islam, where figurative arts had been well entrenched long before Islamization and where religious opposition to them was not as strong as in Arabia or the Maghrib. Illuminated manuscripts with miniature illustrations appeared rather late, in the eleventh and twelfth centuries, and flourished under the generous patronage of the Timurid, Ottoman, Safavid, and Mogul dynasties. Here we can provide only a very cursory description of this exquisite art, which deserves a far more detailed treatment.

The real blossom of the book miniature painting took place in Iran and Central Asia in the post-Mongol period, roughly between 1300 and 1600. It seems to have evolved under the strong influence of Chinese art and reached a high point during the age of the Timurids, descendants of the great Turkic military leader Timur Lang (Tamerlane, 1336–1405), who had conquered Central Asia, Iran, and some parts the Middle East. After his death, his empire was divided among his sons, who presided over an unprecedented cultural and artistic efflorescence in present-day Iran, Afghanistan, and Central Asia. This flowering of arts and crafts was so vivacious and robust that it is sometimes compared with the Italian Renaissance. By that time, the Persian language had already become the principal means of communication and artistic expression in the Muslim East.

The Iranian cultural renaissance found its most vivid and lasting expression in the profusion of book miniatures. To a lesser extent, it can also be observed in mural paintings from that period; however, the latter were more susceptible to the elements and physical decay, and, as a result, fewer samples of this art have come down to us. Exquisitely produced miniatures were used as illustrations for masterpieces of Persian epic tales and poetry, such as Firdowsi's "Book of Kings" (Shahname) and the great poetic compositions of Nizami, 'Attar, Rumi, Sa'di, Háfiz (or Hafez), Jami (eleventh–fifteenth centuries). Historical chronicles and world histories were also illustrated, as well as accounts of the Prophet's night journey and ascension to heaven alluded to at the beginning of *sura* 17 of the Qur'an. Of this large body of literary works, only various versions of the Prophet's night journey and ascension (*mi'raj-nama*) and the mystical poetry of 'Attar and Rumi can be described as "religious" in the full sense of this word. The rest deal almost exclusively with secular motifs, many of which predate Islam, such as the Persian epic novels "Book of Kings" and "Alexander [the Great] Romance" (Iskandarname).[23] Although composed in Islamic times, they depict the epic events of Ancient Iran and Asia Minor that predate Islam.

Book illustrators saw their task as aesthetically impressing the spectator through an intricate combination of colors, lines, stylized buildings, trees, as well as human and animal figures. The images in book miniatures were arranged in such a way as to convey the mood of agitation, drama, heroic daring, loving passion, or splendor. At the same time, they were not deliberately designed to "enlist the viewer's emotional participation in the scene illustrating a certain poetic work."[24] Nevertheless, the best samples of miniature painting succeed in involving "the viewer more immediately in the actions depicted."[25] In a typical Persian miniature, one usually does not find a single focus of interest: "The field tends to be broken up into many little vignettes handled with equal care; and every detail is presented with equal clarity."[26] To emphasize this specificity of a Persian book miniature, some Western scholars sometimes speak of the "decorative nature" of this art, whose foremost goal, in their view, was to impress the viewer with the elegance of detail and ornamentation. If we accept their analysis, then the painter would appear to us as first and foremost a skillful decorator, who was expected "to adorn beautifully both the leaves of an illuminated manuscript and the walls of a wealthy house."[27] The artifacts that these painters created display "a remarkable diversity of imagination, composition, draftsmanship, and color"[28] but are much less concerned with conveying the internal life and emotions of their subjects, although there have been some remarkable exceptions to this rule.[29]

Whereas, as already mentioned, most of the subjects of miniature painting were secular or didactic in character, we still find scenes with pronounced religious undertones, such as a public sermon at a mosque, a dervish dance, an itinerant Sufi, a judge listening to plaintiffs, a lesson at a religious school, the celebration of a religious festival, and so on. Also common were illustrations of Qur'anic stories, the colorful story of Joseph (Yusuf) in *sura* 12 being particularly popular with artists (see Figure 17.2).[30] Contrary to the widely held view that the Prophet was never portrayed by Muslim artists, we do see his images in book miniatures from the Timurid and Ottoman epochs (fourteenth–eighteenth centuries). Whereas he is usually depicted with his face veiled, occasionally his features are drawn in meticulous detail.[31] Such portraits usually appear in the manuscripts that describe the vicissitudes of his prophetic career, especially his birth, childhood, travels to Syria, marriage to Khadíja, participation in the restoration of the Ka'ba, and, of course, his miraculous ascension through seven heavens into the presence of God. Once again, we should bear in mind that the art of miniature painting was not confined to book pages. It was applied to a wide variety of objects from kitchen utensils, oil lamps, and pottery to murals and doors. In some cases, all these objects were decorated by the same artist.

To sum up, despite the dogmatic restrictions on the depiction of human beings and other living creatures, Muslim artists have found ways and means of exercising their creativity without incurring the rage of the pious. The number of artifacts they have produced over the centuries indicates that they were in great demand and highly valued by their patrons and customers. The presence of figural imagery, including portraits of the Prophet and his closest companions, in premodern and early modern Islamic culture is a vivid reminder of the dramatic disjuncture between religious norm and actual practice—a fact that is all too familiar to us from our own everyday experience. The ubiquitous presence of images is not dissimilar to the ubiquitous presence in premodern Islamic culture of the imagery of wine and its consumption, despite its prohibition in the Qur'an and the Prophet's Sunna as interpreted and applied by custodians of Islamic orthodoxy.[32] Bearing this discrepancy in mind should help us to avoid sweeping generalizations about Islam and the Muslims along the lines of "in Islam they never . . ." or "in Islam they always . . ." In the rich and variegated history of the Muslim world, we are always likely to find evidence to the contrary.

Figure 17.2 Yusef and Zuleykha

This said, the religiously motivated restrictions on figural imagery did have a profound impact on artistic expression in premodern Muslim societies. Somewhat paradoxically, its abstract character, unrealism, and propensity to pure visual effect anticipated certain avant-garde trends in modern Western art, which makes it even more fascinating.[33]

The Mosque: Architectural and Devotional Aspects

In a brief survey such as this one, it is impossible to address the vast topic of the rise and development of Islamic architectural art, except in a very cursory manner. Moreover, many architectural monuments in the Muslim world have only tangential relation to Islam as a religion, for instance, caliphal palaces, which were, after all, sites of the rulers' and their courts' pastimes, often unabashedly non-Islamic. Therefore, we will limit ourselves to the discussion of the most obviously religious of Islamic architectural monuments, the mosque.[34] In dealing with this subject, we will address not only the purely architectural aspects of this building but also the ritual behavior and religious personnel associated with it. This dual approach will allow us to see why the mosque is rightfully considered to be the most visible brick-and-mortar symbol and site of Muslim devotional and communal life.

The English word "mosque" is derived from the French *mosquée*, which in turn is borrowed from the Spanish *mezquita*. The Spanish word, in its turn, is taken directly from the Arabic *másjid*, which means "a place where one prostrates oneself [in worship]." The term predates Islam; it was known to the pagan Arabs of the Arabian Peninsula, who applied it to any place where a god or goddess was worshipped. Although the word *másjid* is frequently mentioned in the Qur'an, here it does not necessarily refer to a Muslim religious institution. For instance, in *sura* 18:21, the word "mosque" is mentioned in a context that definitely predates Islam. In *sura* 22:40, it is cited alongside other places of worship, namely, cloisters, churches, and oratories "wherein God's name is much mentioned." It may thus be argued that, for the first Muslims as for the pagan Arabs, the word *másjid* was a temple or a place of worship of any religion. Qur'an 17:1 refers to the Meccan sanctuary, which must have been "pagan" at that time, as the "Sacred Mosque" (*másjid harám*). The same verse mentions another mosque called the "Furthest Mosque" (*masjid áqsa*), which later came to be identified with the Temple Mount in Jerusalem, where the Dome of the Rock and the present al-Aqsa mosque now stand.

In Mecca, as we remember, the followers of the Prophet were a persecuted minority. Therefore, they had no special place of worship and performed their prayers in secret in the narrow alleys of their native town. Abu Bakr, the first caliph, who was a wealthy person, is said to have had a private place of prayer in the courtyard of his house. After Muhammad's following grew, they started to pray beside the Ka'ba, at that time still a pagan sanctuary. All this seems to indicate that, for the first Muslims at Mecca, the place of prayer was not that important. This attitude is further attested to by a famous *hadíth* that says that the Muslim's mosque is wherever he or she performs prayers. According to another *hadíth*, unlike the earlier prophets who had commanded their followers to worship God in specially designated places, that is, synagogues and churches, God gave Muhammad the whole world as a place of worship, so every site on which a Muslim prayer is performed is equally holy in the eyes of God (see Figure 17.3).

Nevertheless, following the Prophet's emigration to Medina, he ordered his followers to build a special structure where the Muslims would perform their prayers shielded from the bustle of everyday life. The Prophet himself is said to have laid the first stone in its foundation. Gradually, a few other mosques were built inside and outside the Muslim capital.

The first mosque in Medina was very simple: an unpaved roofless courtyard surrounded by a clay wall. Here the Prophet used to preach while leaning against a palm trunk. This was more than a simple place of worship. As the Muslim community grew into a Muslim state, the mosque in Medina came to serve as a center of administration and statesmanship, where decisions concern-

Figure 17.3 Tatar Muslims Praying in Kazan
A. Knysh

ing the internal and external state politics were debated, made, and announced to the public. The Muslims of Medina gathered there once a week, on Friday, to pray collectively and to listen to the Prophet's sermon. The collective prayer allowed individual Muslims to renew their loyalty to the community of Islam and to show their solidarity with their fellow believers. With time, the central mosque of a Muslim town or village came to be known as *másjid al-jámi'*, that is, the "mosque of assembly" or "congregational mosque." It was thus distinct from an ordinary street mosque (*másjid*), where prayers are performed by (mostly male) Muslims living nearby during the rest of the week. As described in Chapter 16, once a week, at around noon on Friday, all adult males are required to assemble in the central mosque of their city, town, or village to pray together and to hear a sermon.

Originally, the first Muslim mosque was an open quadrangle marked by a trench around it. Later on, mud-brick walls were erected around this open space, and later still the enclosure was covered by a roof that rested on crude columns made of palm trunks. The roof covered only the northern part of the courtyard. As mentioned, in that mosque the Prophet delivered his weekly sermons and dispensed justice. Initially, there were no specific rules as to what could and could not be done in the mosque. This distinguished the Muslim mosque from Jewish synagogues, Christian churches, or the Meccan temple, all of which had elaborate rituals of behavior associated with them. In Muslim societies, such rituals took some time to develop. Among them was the injunction to take off one's shoes on entering the mosque. Before offering a canonical prayer, visitors were now required to perform a cycle of ritual ablutions in a special room adjacent to the mosque. They were prohibited from spitting on the mosque's floor or from engaging in any inappropriate activities or small talk while there.

The mosque of Medina became the model for all later Islamic mosques. Its major elements can now be observed in every mosque, including the most modern ones. Their reproduction across time and space symbolizes the commitment of the Muslims of different epochs to the exemplary customs of the first community of Islam under the leadership of the Prophet. The communal prayer on Fridays requires a large space to accommodate numerous worshipers at the same time. Therefore, all mosques have a spacious square or rectangular courtyard and a covered sanctuary facing Mecca. The roof over the sanctuary is supported by rows of columns. The courtyard and the covered sanctuary constitute two basic features of a mosque. The focal point of sanctuary is called *mihráb*—a niche or recess in the wall that marks the direction of Mecca (*qibla*). The *mihráb* serves as the symbolic center or culmination of the mosque (somewhat similar to the altar in Western Christian churches or the iconostasis in Eastern Christianity). In large urban centers, it was often lavishly decorated with marble, carved calligraphic inscriptions, and fine ornaments. It was one of the typical objects of arabesque art. The *mihráb* is often flanked by elaborately designed colonnettes. To the right of the *mihráb* stands a stepped pulpit or *mínbar*. The preacher (*khatíb*) addresses his audience standing on the second step of the *mínbar*; he can occasionally use the step above it as his seat. After the sermon is over, he descends from the pulpit and leads the prayer facing the *mihráb*. His ritual postures are imitated by the entire congregation, who arrange themselves in parallel rows to pray behind him. *Mínbar*s are usually made of wood and elaborately encrusted with ivory, marble, or mother-of-pearl.

In later mosques, one often sees sumptuous domes set above the *mihráb* wall. Many mosques have a tall, tower-like structure known as the *minaret*. As mentioned in Chapter 16, in contrast to the Christian use of bells, in Muslim societies the faithful are called to prayer by human voice. Before the arrival of microphones, the call to the prayer was broadcast from the minaret by a specially delegated man known as *muezzin* (i.e., the enunciator of the call to prayer). The principal requirement for this position was and still is a beautiful voice, although nowadays the *muezzin* no longer has to climb up the minaret to recite the call. He can use a microphone installed in a special room to do so. However, minarets still have a function: They serve as platforms for the speakers through which the call to prayer is broadcast. As mentioned, all mosques have special facilities for ritual ablutions, preferably with running water. Many large congregational mosques have shallow pools for ablutions, which are often crowned by fountains. Some Muslim scholars have compared a beautifully decorated mosque courtyard to Paradise.[35] It is within the confines of the mosque that worshipping Muslims strive to achieve contact with their Lord, whom they hope to see with the naked eye in the afterlife. Prayer in the mosque can be seen as a preparation for this beatific vision promised to the faithful. This belief explains why later mosques are adorned by mosaic paintings, arabesques, and beautifully executed calligraphic inscriptions. Rulers spared no expense to construct sumptuously decorated mosques both out of personal piety and in order to demonstrate to their subjects their credentials as defenders and promoters of Islamic faith. In each area of the Muslim world, the architectural elements of the mosque reflect the specific features of the local artistic and architectural tradition. Thus, one can hear experts on architecture speak of an "Indian" mosque, a "North African" (Maghribi) mosque, of "Mamluk," "Mogul," "Ottoman," or "West African" mosques, and so on. Naturally, over time these geographical and dynastic architectural traditions have cross-pollinated, mutually enriching one another (see Figure 17.4).

The Friday or congregational mosque has played a particularly important role in the life of a Muslim community. In addition to being the center of Muslim devotional life, it is also a place where important public announcements and proclamations are made and believers gather at times of crisis—for instance, in order to support or denounce certain governmental policies, to mobilize

Figure 17.4 A Local Mosque in Upper Egypt (January 2010)
A. Knysh

resistance to an invading force, or to declare a holy war on a neighboring country or ruler. Furthermore, during the Friday service, the ruler's name is always mentioned in the sermon, so, in the past, when news took long to spread, believers would listen closely to the Friday sermon in order to know who is in charge and what to expect. As we discussed in Chapter 16, prior to the appearance of Muslim religious schools, mosques served as centers of education and forums for juridical and theological debates.

Throughout history, the mosque has served another important function, that of a shelter for the poor. Travelers and people without accommodation would occasionally sleep in the mosque. Today, as before, the mosque provides a space for Muslim men to rest, to socialize, to take time out from a busy day, and, of course, to perform the five daily prayers and read the Qur'an. It is permissible to consume food on the premises. During the last ten days of the month of Ramadán, pious Muslims keep nightly prayers and vigils in the mosque. As discussed in Chapter 16, mosques are supported by endowment funds assigned to them by rulers and wealthy members of the congregation. Some mosques were erected over or next to the graves of great heroes of early Islam, such as companions of the Prophet, his wife 'A'isha, his daughter Fátima, his cousin and son-in-law 'Ali, his grandsons al-Hásan and al-Husayn, as well as their descendants. Such commemorative structures are called "memorial mosques." A special mosque was built on the site of Khadíja's house in Mecca. It is called the Mosque of the Birthplace of Fátima. Some memorial mosques contain holy relics; for instance, the mosques of al-Husayn in Cairo and Damascus are believed to contain his head which, as we remember, was severed by the triumphal Umayyad military commander at Kerbelá, then sent as a trophy to the caliph Yazíd in Damascus. Mosques often form part of shrine complexes that may also contain a saint's tomb, a library, a cemetery, a Sufi lodge, a hostel, and a public bath.

Conclusions

The artistic tradition of Islam is characterized by a truly dizzying diversity of styles and techniques that are simply impossible to do justice to in a single chapter. Yet the tradition does exhibit certain common features that can be attributed to the specificity of Islamic religious dogma and practice. For instance, the religiously motivated uneasiness about representing living objects, especially humans, has given rise to recognizably "Islamic" artistic forms, which are found in many areas of the Muslim world. There is no doubt that the initially political, and later the juridical and confessional, unity of the Muslim world, which facilitated travel across the Muslim lands, has contributed to the exchange of creative ideas among Muslim artists and architects. At the same time, the exigencies of the Muslim ritual inevitably determined the uniformity of the principal elements of Islamic architecture, as exemplified by the mosque. Despite the outward diversity of architectural expression, the principal elements of the mosque remain the same across the Muslim world.

Questions to Ponder

1   Is Islamic art mere craftsmanship or a genuinely creative endeavor? Elaborate.
2   How can one explain the paradox of the prohibition of figural representation by Islamic theology, on the one hand, and the proliferation and flowering of the miniature art in certain Muslim societies, on the other?
3   What may be external influences (if any) on the ways in which nature, animals, and human beings are portrayed in Persian book miniatures?
4   Based on your knowledge of the Western figural art, what are the main differences between it and the Islamic artistic tradition?

Summary

*   The Qur'an constitutes the all-important focus of Muslim devotional life. As such, any potential rival objects of worship and devotion or alternative ways of communicating with God arouse the suspicion of the custodians of Islamic orthodoxy.
*   The overriding centrality of the Qur'an to Muslim devotional life is one reason for the iconophobic tendencies in Islam. The same tendencies are found in Judaism and some sects of Byzantine Christianity.
*   Scriptural evidence is marshaled by Muslim scholars to justify the ban on figural representation of human beings and other living objects. Fear of idolatry and the notion that the artist's work is an illicit encroachment on God's monopoly to create things seem to be the principal motivations behind the ban.
*   Muslim artists' response to the iconophobic restrictions is the emblematic, symbolic nature of the Islamic arts. Arabesque art is a ceaseless proliferation of abstract vegetal

- and geometrical patterns combined with Arabic calligraphy, the symbolism of which can be explained in various ways.
- Illuminated and calligraphically elaborate Qur'anic phrases can be seen as the quintessentially Islamic art.
- The art of the book miniature in the Muslim East blossomed during the post-Mongol period (roughly between 1300 and 1600). The principal features of miniature painting are a lack of perspective and one single focus of interest, the use of stylized, flat images, and a tendency toward ornamentation.
- Exquisite, carefully executed miniatures serve as illustrations of masterpieces of Persian epic tales and poetry, such as Firdowsi's *Book of Kings* (*Shahname*) and *The Alexander [the Great] Romance* (*Iskandarname*) by Nizamí and others, as well as the great poetic compositions of 'Attar, Rumi, Sa'di, Háfiz, and Jami.
- The concept of the "decorative nature" of the Persian miniature art. It privileges fine detail, elaborate workmanship, and ornamentation over conveying the internal life and emotions of the objects portrayed.
- The mosque is an architectural monument and symbol of Islam (functionality and artistry) and has its own scriptural and historical background.
- The main elements of the mosque are the courtyard with a sanctuary, the minaret, the stepped pulpit (*mínbar*), and the recess in the wall (*mihráb*) showing the direction toward Mecca. Mosque personnel are the caller to prayer (*muezzin*), the prayer leader (*imam*), and the Friday preacher (*khatíb*).
- Mosque is a shelter, a platform for public announcements, a place for study and meditation, and a site for private and collective worship.
- Types of mosques include the congregational/Friday mosque, the local or quarter mosque, and the memorial/commemorative mosques.

Notes

1 What follows is based on Marshall Hodgson's discussion of "the potency of the Qur'an" in his *Venture of Islam*, Chicago University Press, Chicago, 1974, vol. 1, pp. 366–369 and vol. 2, pp. 503–510.

2 Hodgson, *The Venture*, vol. 1, p. 367.

3 Ibid., p. 308.

4 Ibid., vol. 2, p. 502.

5 K.A.C. Cresswell, "The Lawfulness of Painting in Early Islam," in Jonathan Bloom (ed.), *Early Islamic Art and Architecture*, Ashgate-Variorum, Aldershot, UK, 2002, pp. 101–108; cf. Oleg Grabar, "The Umayyad Dome of the Rock in Jerusalem," in Jonathan Bloom (ed.), *Early Islamic Art and Architecture*, Ashgate-Variorum, Aldershot, UK, 2002, p. 250.

6 Richard Ettinghausen, Oleg Grabar and Marilyn Jenkins-Madina, *Islamic Art and Architecture*, Yale University Press, New Haven, CT, 2001, p. 6.

7 Cresswell, "The Lawfulness of Painting in Early Islam," pp. 165 and 162.

8 Ettinghausen et al., *Islamic Art and Architecture*, p. 6.

9 Hodgson, *The Venture*, vol. 2, p. 502.

10 Ibid., p. 511 and Eva Baer, "The Human Figure in Early Islamic Art," *Muqarnas*, vol. 16 (1999), pp. 32–41; for a recent attempt to question Islam's inherent iconophobia, see Shahab Ahmed, *What Is Islam? The Importance of Being Islamic*, Princeton University Press, Princeton, NJ, and Oxford, 2016, passim.

11 Robert Hillenbrand, "*La dolce vita* in Early Islamic Syria," in Jonathan Bloom (ed.), *Early Islamic Art and Architecture*, Ashgate-Variorum, Aldershot, UK, 2002, pp. 333–371; Ettinghausen et al., *Islamic Art and Architecture*, pp. 42–49.

12 For examples see Ahmed, *What Is Islam?* Chapter 1 et passim.

13 Ettinghausen et al., *Islamic Art and Architecture*, p. 66.

14 Hodgson, *The Venture*, vol. 2, 510.

15 Ettinghausen et al., *Islamic Art and Architecture*, p. 161.

16 Janine Sourdel-Thomine, "Khatt," in *Encyclopedia of Islam*, 2nd ed.; online edition: http://reference works.brillonline.com.

17 Ettinghausen et al., *Islamic Art and Architecture*, p. 73, and Sheila Blair and Jonathan Bloom, *The Art and Architecture of Islam: 1250–1800*, Yale University Press, New Haven, CT, 1994, p. 2.

18 Annemarie Schimmel, "Islamic Calligraphy," in Lindsay Jones (ed.), *Encyclopedia of Religions*, McMillan, Detroit, 2005, vol. 3, p. 1372.

19 Ettinghausen et al., *Islamic Art and Architecture*, pp. 73–78, and Blair and Bloom, *The Art and Architecture of Islam*, pp. 25, 102, 116, and so on.

20 Sourdel-Thomine, "Khatt"; Ettinghausen et al., *Islamic Art and Architecture*, p. 246.

21 Hodgson, *The Venture*, vol. 2, p. 510.

22 Richard Martin, *Islamic Studies: A History of Religions Approach*, 2nd ed., Prentice Hall, Upper Saddle River, NJ, 1996, p. 143.

23 Peter Jackson and Laurence Lockhart (eds.), *The Cambridge History of Iran*, Cambridge University Press, Cambridge, 1986, vol. 6, pp. 843–876 and Armand Abel, "Iskandar Nama," in *Encyclopedia of Islam*, 2nd ed.; online edition: http://referenceworks.brillonline.com.

24 Hodgson, *The Venture*, vol. 2, p. 512.

25 Blair and Bloom, *The Art and Architecture of Islam*, p. 58.

26 Hodgson, *The Venture*, vol. 2, p. 512.

27 Ibid., p. 513.

28 Blair and Bloom, *The Art and Architecture of Islam*, p. 168.

29 Baer, "The Human Figure in Early Islamic Art," pp. 35–36.

30 Blair and Bloom, *The Art and Architecture of Islam*, pp. 57–69 and Jackson and Lockhart (eds.), *The Cambridge History of Iran*, the illustrations between pp. 872–873.

31 Blair and Bloom, *The Art and Architecture of Islam*, p. 61 and Marie-Rose Seguy, *The Miraculous Journey of Mahomet*, G. Braziller, New York, 1977.

32 For an attempt at revision of the widely held stereotypes about Islam and the figural art, as well as Islam and wine, see Ahmed, *What Is Islam?*, passim.

33 Hodgson, *The Venture*, vol. 2, p. 507.

34 Some other architectural monuments of religious significance, namely the religious college and the Sufi lodge, have been discussed in Chapter 15.

35 Ettinghausen et al., *Islamic Art and Architecture*, p. 26.

Chapter 18

Women in Islamic Societies

The Controversial Topic

With the possible exception of so-called Islamic terrorism, it is difficult to find a subject that has generated more controversy in the modern Western media and public discourse than the status of women in Islamic societies. Seething with righteous indignation, many contemporary Western politicians, political commentators, members of the clergy, and media personalities have routinely denounced the "misogynist" (i.e., hostile to women) and "androcentric" (i.e., focused on and favorable to exclusively males) attitudes allegedly fostered by Islam. The widely held assumptions about "Islam's repression of women" can be occasionally used to justify hate crimes and verbal or media abuse directed at Muslim minorities in Western countries. Even more fatefully, such assumptions may become a pretext for Western aggression against Muslim countries, in the name, among other things, of "liberating" the "oppressed" female half of their population.[1] No wonder that Western invectives against the maltreatment of women by Muslim men in "the name of Islam" have provoked a backlash on the part of many Muslim intellectuals of both sexes. They have risen up to defend their religion against what they consider to be an anti-Muslim defamation campaign. Their goal, which for want of a better term can be described as "apologetic," is to prove that Islam's treatment of women is in fact much more humane than one found in the secularized liberal democracies of the West, not to mention women's alleged plight under communist rule.[2] These Muslim advocates are often assisted by those Western intellectuals who sympathize with Islam and the Muslims and who are eager to defend them against their critics, whom they accuse of being ignorant of the nuances of the Shari'a legislation about women.[3] Due to the emotionally and politically charged nature of the subject, debates over the status of women in Islam are often conducted "in tones of mutual animosity,"[4] which naturally has made it very difficult for the opposing parties to find a common ground.

In the heat of these modern-day debates the following factors are often forgotten:

1 Qur'an and *hadith* statements concerning women, which constitute the normative foundation for the subsequent codification of their status in Islamic societies, reflect the predominantly male-centered ethos of not just the relatively primitive Arabian society of Late Antiquity[5] but also that of the neighboring (arguably more culturally and socially advanced) societies of the Byzantine and Sasanian Empires.

2 Islam is not an independent actor that "oppresses" or "liberates" women but rather a conceptual and moral-ethical framework (or language) that concrete Muslim communities and individuals draw upon to interpret their life experiences and formulate their positions on certain vital issues of their daily existence.

3 The relative freedom and equality of Western women vis-à-vis Western men is a recent phenomenon that has organically emerged out of the socioeconomic and political conditions peculiar to Western societies—and that only after a protracted and acrimonious struggle between the advocates and opponents of female emancipation.[6]

Faced with such a politically and emotionally controversial issue, one is hard-pressed to furnish a balanced account of the vicissitudes of male–female relations in Islamic societies through the ages. Try as hard as one might, one is likely to end up being accused of advancing either a pro- or anti-Islamic agenda by one or both of the parties to the controversy. Another difficulty facing the investigator lies in the vast body of literature on the subject: It has been treated in hundreds of books and thousands of articles. To further complicate things, in both academic and popular accounts of the issue, religiously sanctioned norms regarding women and their relations with men are freely mixed with customary ethnographic practices that are either not directly endorsed by the foundational texts of Islam or, at times, openly contravene them.

Even a brief critical assessment of the vast literature on women in Islam and the methodologies employed by its authors would require a separate book. We shall therefore limit ourselves to a very brief survey of the question. Since our chief methodological principle in this book is to determine how ideas and phenomena have evolved in historical perspective and how they have engaged in dialogues with one another, we will begin by analyzing the normative Muslim sources in which attitudes toward women and gender were originally articulated. As usual, we begin with the Qur'an and *hadíth*.

Women in the Qur'an

The Qur'an's initial revelation was witnessed by Khadíja (d. 619), the Prophet's first wife and, according to many accounts, the first Muslim after the Prophet himself.[7] Although never explicitly mentioned in the Qur'an, she figures prominently in the *hadíth* corpus and the Prophet's biographies. Here "Khadíja the Pure" is portrayed as a paragon of chastity and staunch supporter of the Prophet "from the day they met to the day she died."[8] She is one of the four most virtuous women in the entire world who will be appointed as guides of and rulers over the female inhabitants of Paradise (the other three being the Pharaoh's wife Ásya,[9] Mary the mother of Jesus, and the Prophet's pious daughter Fátima).[10] As a reward for her invaluable services to the nascent Islamic religion, Khadíja will be one of the Prophet's wifely consorts in Paradise.[11]

While not necessarily mentioned in the Qur'an by their names, women are the subject of numerous Qur'anic verses. A whole chapter is named after women (*sura* 4). This long and complex chapter stipulates the divinely sanctioned rules regarding the proper relationships between free male and female Muslims (as well as free men and female slaves) in Islam. Another chapter of the Qur'an (19) is named after Mary (Maryam), the mother of Jesus. It describes episodes from Mary's life leading up to the birth of Jesus. Mary's story is recounted in numerous other passages of the Qur'an. Although Mary is the only woman who is mentioned by her name in the entire Qur'anic text, there are numerous other female personages in its historical and mythological narratives, such as the wife of Adam, the seductress of the prophet Joseph, the wife of Pharaoh, the Queen of Sheba, the wife of the Prophet's hostile relative Abu Láhab. Also mentioned are the wives of the prophets Noah, Lot, and Abraham. All these women are nameless in the Qur'an. They acquire their personal names in the later exegetical tradition— Eve (Hawwá), Zuláykha, Ásya, Bilqís (the Queen of Sheba), and so on. The wives of the Prophet are accorded special treatment in *sura* 33 that instructs them as to how they should behave themselves in public and in private. Again, none of the wives is mentioned by name. The names are supplied by the later accounts of the Prophet's life and the history of the first community of Islam.[12] The most renowned of them (apart from Khadíja) is 'A'isha, the daughter of the first caliph Abu Bakr, who is also sometimes included (by the Sunnis) into the cohort of the best women of all times.[13] 'A'isha is believed to be the subject of a long Qur'anic dispensation defending women against false accusations of adultery and threatening a painful punishment to individuals guilty thereof (Q 24:4–26).

The Qur'an clearly states that human beings are created in pairs (4:1) and are subject to the same religious obligations regardless of their gender. The basic equality of Muslim men and women in this respect is brought to the fore in the following passage (33:35):

> Men who surrender[14] to God and women who surrender to God, men who believe and women who believe, men who obey [God] and women who obey, men who speak the truth and women who speak the truth, men who persevere [in righteousness] and women who persevere, men who are humble and women who are humble, men who give alms and women who give alms, men who fast and women who fast, men who guard their modesty and women who guard [their modesty], and men who remember God much and women who remember God—for them God has prepared forgiveness and a mighty reward.

The equality of the religious duties imposed on both sexes implies the equality of reward in the hereafter. Indeed, the righteous Muslim men are promised the delights of Paradise in the company of their spouses (Q 36:55–56). "Those who did evil," in their turn, will be herded to Hell together with "their wives" (Q 37:22) to jointly suffer its horrors and torments. According to Q 7:22, both the first man and the first woman (not just the woman, as in the Judeo-Christian tradition) are equally responsible, after having been prompted by Satan, for violating God's prohibition to eat from the tree of knowledge—the event that caused their expulsion from Paradise.[15] At the same time, in addition to the many paradisiacal pleasures vividly depicted in the Qur'an, the righteous men are also promised the company of fabulous "wide-eyed (or black-eyed) maidens restraining their glances, as if they were hidden pearls" (Q 37:48–49 and 38:52). These are the famous "houries"—paradisiacal virgins "untouched before them [that is, the men of Paradise] by any man or jinn" (Q 55:56).[16] Since women are not promised an equivalent of men's reward, one can interpret such Qur'anic passages as implicitly privileging righteous men over righteous women.

This impression is reinforced by some other Qur'anic pronouncements that, if taken at face value, appear to treat Muslim women as being subordinate to their male guardians. For instance, in Q 2:223, women are described as "tillage" or a "field" that men can visit whenever they want. A few Qur'anic verses emphasize women's physical weakness and the need for male protection. In some passages they are mentioned alongside orphans, little children, and, possibly, men incapable of fighting (Q 2:2–3, 75, 98, 127). The inequality of women in social terms and their need of protection and maintenance are thrown into a sharp relief in Q 4:34: "Men are the managers (or sustainers) of women as God preferred one of them over another[17] because they [men] sustain them [women] from their wealth." This verse, like many Qur'anic pronouncements, allows for several different interpretations. It can be understood as an assertion of male superiority in the social and familial sphere or, alternatively, as men's obligation to provide material support to their womenfolk without necessarily privileging the former over the latter.[18] Naturally, in the final account, the truth lies in the eye of the beholder. This is not the only passage that may be interpreted as relegating Muslim women to a secondary position to men. The intellectual and judgmental capacities of women are called into doubt in Q 2:282, which asserts that in legal cases a woman's testimony is worth half that of a man. In other words, two women are required where one man would suffice (and no second man is available), so that "if one of them [women] errs the other will remind her."[19] Yet, at the same time, the Qur'an unequivocally declares the equality of compensation for male and female labor: "To the men a share of what they have earned and to the women a share of what they have earned" (Q 4:32; see also 3:195).

In terms of inheritance provisions, the Qur'an allows women to inherit from their relatives, but their share of inheritance "is usually half of that of a man of the same degree of kinship."[20] There is a certain logic to this dispensation (Q 4:7–20 and 175), for, after all, according to the aforementioned passage from the Qur'an, "men are managers/sustainers of women" and therefore should possess more resources to fulfill their obligations toward them. Offensive as this provision may appear to modern sensibilities steeped in the notions of gender equality, there is no doubt, however, that it has laid the groundwork for a relative independence of Muslim women from men in the economic sphere.[21] This independence constitutes a salient feature of Islamic legal dispensation as opposed to its Western counterparts that, in the Middle Ages and even later, denied women the right to inherit or own property. In sum, the provisions concerning witnessing and inheritance do give women a legal position, albeit a truncated one, "as she only counts as half the value of a man."[22]

Many Qur'anic verses are addressed to the Prophet's wives,[23] who constituted the female elite of the first Islamic community of Medina. Some verses seem to be addressed exclusively to them; others can be interpreted as being binding upon the entire female population of the Muslim community. In any event, the special status of the Prophet's wives is repeatedly and emphatically asserted (see Figure 18.1). Since they "are not like any other women" (Q 33:32) and, moreover,

Figure 18.1 The Prophet with His Womenfolk (The women with flaming halos are probably his daughter Fátima and his wives 'A'isha and Umm Salama)

are the "Mothers of the Faithful" (Q 33:6), they are entitled to respectful and honorable treatment. At the same time, they are subject to a special code of behavior: They should speak to strange male visitors only "from behind a curtain (*hijáb*)" (Q 33:53), stay in their houses, behave modestly in public and private, and in particular avoid "strutting about." As the Mothers of the Faithful, they are not allowed to remarry after the Prophet has divorced them or after his death (Q 33:6), for the Qur'an explicitly prohibits marriage with one's mother (Q 4:23). Indeed, none of the Prophet's wives remarried after he had died.[24] Their special status clearly established, the wives of the Prophet are threatened with "double chastisement" should they commit "a flagrant indecency" (Q 33:30–31). On the positive side, they are enjoined to "perform the prayer, pay the alms, and obey God and His messenger" (Q 33:33). The ideal women of the Prophet's household are ones "who have submitted to God, believing, penitent, devout, and given to fasting" (Q 66:5). The overall context of this verse may indicate that the Prophet's wives did not always live up to these high expectations and had to be reprimanded.[25] Nevertheless, the injunctions just quoted were apparently deemed to set the Prophet's womenfolk as a model for the rest of Muslim women to emulate.

In a few Qur'anic verses, the Prophet's wives are mentioned alongside other "believing women" of the community. For instance, verses 59–60 of *sura* 33 demand that not only the wives of the Prophet but also the Muslim women in general should "wrap themselves up in mantles" while in public. Likewise, Q 24:31 tells the "believing women" to "cast down their eyes, guard their private parts, and reveal not their adornment." The same verse then instructs all Muslim women to "cast their veils over their bosoms and reveal not their adornment" save to their husbands and close male relatives who cannot, by law, be their marriage partners. The degrees of kinship that allow unrestricted interaction between male and female relatives are carefully specified in the Qur'an (Q 33:55 and 4:26).

The Qur'an contains strict provisions for violations of the rules of sexual conduct. Fornication or adultery, if proven by the attestation of four witnesses, is punishable by the confinement of guilty women "to their houses until death takes them or God appoints for them a way" (Q 4:15). Another verse (Q 24:2), which the Muslim tradition considers to have been revealed later, prescribes one hundred lashes to each of the culprits. Although practiced in later times, punishing an adulterous couple by stoning to death is not explicitly commanded by the Qur'an. The Qur'anic verse to this effect was "remembered" by the second caliph 'Umar after the Prophet's death. However, even the caliph's towering stature was not enough to include it into the canonical text of the sacred book.[26] The punishment by stoning, therefore, is based exclusively on the Prophet's custom that, in turn, must have been derived from the ancient Jewish law.[27] Given the gravity of this transgression and its consequences, false accusations of adultery against married women are strongly and unequivocally condemned and punishable by flogging:

> And those who cast it [slander] upon women in wedlock, and then bring not four witnesses, scourge them with eighty lashes, and do not accept any testimony of theirs ever; those—they are the ungodly.
>
> (Q 24:4–5)

This verse is widely believed to have been revealed in response to the accusations of adultery brought up against 'A'isha by some of the Prophet's companions; it implicitly exonerates her of this sin and threatens her slanderers with a painful chastisement.[28] Note that the stipulation requiring four eye witnesses to attest to the crime makes it extremely difficult to prove, especially since, in accordance with a later juridical elaboration, the witnesses are required to unequivocally confirm the actual act of penetration: "Like a stick entering a kohl container." Nevertheless, as we shall see, in subsequent centuries, this provision was not strictly observed by male-dominated Muslim communities, and extrajudicial executions of women on a mere suspicion of adultery were not at all uncommon.

Muslim men are allowed to take up to four wives (Q 4:3) but only if they undertake to be "equitable" toward each of them. If not, they should take only one wife (Q 4:3 and 128). The equitability requirement is phrased in such a way as to imply an impossibility or near impossibility of polygamy in Islam. Muslim defenders of women's rights argue that the provision in question effectively precludes polygamous marriages, since the husband is simply incapable of treating all of his wives evenhandedly.[29] Other modern Muslim writers suggest that polygamy was historically conditioned by the shortage of men in the early Muslim community ("to control the excesses of the Arabs in the 7th century").[30] It is no longer valid due to the lack of similar conditions at present.[31] One verse (Q 4:24) may be interpreted as allowing for the possibility of temporary marriage, upon the termination of which men are encouraged to give their temporary partners "their wages appropriate." According to Sunni jurists, this verse was later abrogated by several other verses, as well as by the Prophet's explicit prohibition in a *hadíth*[32] and is thus no longer valid. Furthermore, this type of marriage was banned by the caliph 'Umar, who was known for his strict moral character and intolerance of any type of licentious behavior. According to one *hadíth*, 'Umar even prescribed stoning as punishment for the violators of this ban. It seems that it is precisely due to 'Umar's role in articulating and enforcing the ban of temporary marriage (*mut'a*) that it is considered legitimate by the Shi'ites. They continue to practice it today, thereby scandalizing the Sunnis.[33]

The Qur'an requires a marriage engagement to be sealed by the "knot of marriage" (Q 2:237), commonly understood as a marriage contract binding on both parties. Upon marriage, the bride is entitled to receive a bride-gift or bride-wealth (Q 4:4), which symbolizes her new status as a married woman and gives her a certain level of financial security. Contrary to the pre-Islamic Arabian custom, the Qur'an insists that the bride-gift or bride-wealth be rendered directly to the bride, not to her official guardian. This is another testimony to women's relative material independence under the Qur'anic legislature, as we have already pointed out in the case of inheritance and compensation for labor.

The Qur'an recognizes that not every man is capable of raising enough wealth to furnish a bride-gift. For such men, the Qur'an recommends marriage with their concubines who are described as "those whom your right hand owns." In other words, if a man cannot afford to pay the bride-wealth of a free woman (as stipulated in Q 4:4), he is allowed to take his "believing handmaids" as wives (Q 4:24–25). Here, as elsewhere (see, for instance, Q 24:32), the Qur'an unequivocally presents married life as a better alternative to celibacy, which accounts for the fact that even Muslim ascetics and mystics were and still are compelled to take wives (unlike, for example, Christian or Buddhist monks). A special dispensation prohibits men from forcing their slave-girls into prostitution (Q 24:33).

Divorce procedures have received considerable attention in the Qur'an. There is even a special chapter (Q 65) named after it, although it is also treated in other passages of the Muslim scripture, most importantly in Q 4:23–25; 2:228–232, 237–238. Such detailed provisions regarding divorce may indicate that they were relatively new to the Arabs of Muhammad's epoch and thus required a longer than usual explanation.[34] What is not in doubt is that these norms were aimed at improving women's lot by thwarting men's stratagems, such as, for instance, extorting the bride-wealth from their wives in exchange for divorce. The Qur'an also effectively protects the wives' and their children's right to be supported by their husbands after the divorce has been declared, facilitating the couple's reconciliation and, after everything else has failed, allowing the wife to purchase freedom from her unloved or abusive husband. These practical provisions are interspersed with strongly worded moral-ethical admonitions and invocations of God's wrath should the Qur'anic commands to this effect be violated.[35] This, in the opinion of some Muslim scholars, has created an even stronger incentive for Muslim men to treat their wives properly.[36]

In legal terms, women are granted the right to retain the entire amount of the bride-wealth given to them by their husbands upon marriage and the right to be supported by and remain in their husbands' households for three menstrual cycles, after the divorce has been declared. This is done in order to secure the future of the children[37] that may have been conceived prior to the declaration because men are always held responsible for the support of their offspring.[38] In general, however, the Qur'an strongly advocates for an amicable settlement between man and wife and enjoins husbands to treat their womenfolk kindly. It even contains a provision for a temporary interruption of marriage that can last up to four months, whereupon: "If they revert, God is All-Forgiving, All-Compassionate; but if they resolve on divorce, surely God is All-Hearing, All-Knowing" (Q 2:226–227). The Qur'an also ordains that upon the third declaration of the divorce formula by the husband,[39] the divorce becomes final: "A divorce is only permitted twice" (Q 2:229). Should the husband declare the divorce formula trice, he is no longer allowed to reconcile with his wife and take her back until she remarries and then divorces from her new husband. This provision was supposed to prevent frivolous divorces by husbands, for should a divorce become final, they were obligated to give back to their wives the entire amount of the bride-wealth (often quite substantial) and to provide full material support and lodging for them for three menstrual cycles.[40] Finally, in Q 66:5, the Prophet himself, apparently irritated by his wives' quarrels, threatens them with divorce and challenges them to choose between "the present life and its glitter" and "the last abode" (Q 33:28–29). The tradition has it that every wife chose the hereafter and stayed in his household.

This, in a nutshell, is what the Qur'an says about women and man–woman relations. As we have seen, Qur'anic references to the fair sex fall into three principal categories:

1   the pre-Islamic women of the Judeo-Christian scriptures: Eve; the lecherous wife of Joseph's master in the story of the prophet Joseph; Ásya the wife of Pharaoh;[41] the Queen of Sheba (Bilqís); Mary the mother of Jesus; as well as the wives of Noah, Abraham, and Lot;[42]
2   the wives of the Prophet and some unnamed women of Mecca and Medina, such as the wife of Muhammad's pagan nemesis Abu Láhab (*sura* 104), the main character of *sura* 58 ("She Who Disputes") and *sura* 60 ("The Woman Tested") and so on;
3   women in general as abstract objects of Qur'anic norms concerning gender roles, inheritance, family relations, proper manners in public and private, dress code, and so on (*sura* 4).

Women in *Hadíth* and *Fiqh*

It has often been argued that the generally "pro-female tone of the Qur'an is not replicated in the *hadíth* literature."[43] Indeed, the latter contains a number of statements, which, on the face of it, are disparaging, restricting, or condescending toward women. Thus, in a dream the Prophet is said to have looked into Paradise and saw that most of its inhabitants were the poor. He then looked into Hell only to see that most of its inhabitants were women.[44] In another *hadíth*, the Prophet is quoted as saying, "I have not left behind any temptation (or trial) more pernicious for men than women."[45] In a like vein, he remarked, "A people which have placed their affairs in the hands of a woman will never prosper."[46] In some prophetic *hadíth*, woman's primary purpose is described as being able to satisfy her husband's carnal desires. Should a woman spend even one night away from her husband's bed, "the angels will curse her until morning."[47] The presence of a woman may interrupt or even invalidate one's prayer (along with that of a black dog and a donkey).[48]

That sexual attraction between men and women may, under certain circumstances, disrupt the divinely established social and moral order was readily recognized by the Prophet. He instituted special precautions to keep it in check:

It is not permitted for a woman who believes in God and the Day of Judgment to travel on a journey of a day and a night if no respectable female chaperons are with her.[49]

If no female companions are available, the woman should be accompanied by her husband or a close male relative (*máhram*).[50] A number of *hadíth* requires that Muslim women protect themselves from indecent male gazes by speaking to men "from behind a veil" (*hijáb*)[51] or wearing a scarf or kerchief (*khimár*). If they fail to do so, their prayers will not be accepted by God.[52]

On the positive side, the Prophet is quoted as saying that the most delightful thing in this world is a virtuous woman.[53] He is also portrayed as visiting his mother's grave regularly and weeping profusely over it.[54] When asked about the person most deserving of love in this world, he says "mother" two times, relegating the father only to the third position. He is also quoted as saying that "paradise is at the mother's feet."[55] Such statements can be construed as an implicit reference to motherhood as woman's primary and most honorable role in Islamic society.

It is on the basis of these ambiguous and occasionally self-contradictory statements found in the Qur'an and *hadíth* that Islamic juridical norms pertaining to women and gender relations were formulated in subsequent centuries. Naturally, interpretations of Islam's foundational writings differed from one legal school to another and from one geographical region to another, conditioned as they were, often decisively, by local customs and perceptions of justice. It has sometimes been argued that the more cosmopolitan and pluralistic environment of the Iraqi garrison cities (namely, Kufa and Basra) was conducive to relatively liberal attitudes toward women in contrast to the patriarchal ones that prevailed in the more ethnically and culturally homogeneous milieu of the Arabian Peninsula. Thus, the Hánafi juridical school, which originated in Iraq, allows not only an adult woman but also a girl who has reached the age of puberty to arrange her own marriage, provided that her bridegroom is of an equal social stature and can furnish an adequate bride-wealth.[56] Although this ruling is based on an explicit statement of the Prophet,[57] the three other Sunni legal schools opine that a final decision in matters of marriage rests with the woman's father or male guardian.[58] In a similar vein, during the Umayyad period, the Hánafi school of Kufa allowed a repudiated wife full maintenance until she had completed three menstrual cycles.[59] Elsewhere, "she had the bare right to the shelter of the husband's roof,"[60] unless she was pregnant with child as a result of her terminated marriage.[61] These are just a couple of examples of how one and the same scriptural evidence can be interpreted differently by different legal scholars living under different social and cultural conditions.

Another example has to do with the marriage contract. The Hánafi legal school permits the bridegroom to stipulate that he should not take another wife or force his wife to leave her hometown. If he violates any of these conditions, the wife is given the right to dissolve the marriage.[62] The three other Sunni schools of law treat such stipulations as invalid or unenforceable.[63] Whereas the Hánafi school may appear to be more liberal on these two issues, its founder Abu Hanífa refused to dissolve a marriage unless the husband has been proven to be impotent or has some severe personal defects that make marital life impossible. In this respect, the Maliki school of law takes a more favorable approach to woman's rights by accepting as valid reasons for the marriage's dissolution the husband's desertion, failure to support her, cruelty, and maltreatment.[64] It is also more liberal in the case of a missing husband in that it allows his wife to remarry after four years, in contrast to the other legal schools, which stipulate that she is obligated to wait for the average life span of a person, namely up to eighty years.[65] The four schools also disagree as to whether a woman can serve as a judge, while being in agreement that, in accordance with Q 2:282, woman's testimony carries half the weight of that of a man.

Shi'ite law differs from its Sunni counterparts in points of detail. While Sunni legists allow the triple statement of the divorce formula to be made on one occasion (thereby making the divorce final and irrevocable), Shi'ite legal theory disallows this. It also requires the presence of two witnesses in order to make sure that the divorce formula was not uttered by the husband in the state of intoxication or rage.[66] Thus, the Twelver Shi'ite (Ja'fari) law seeks to "confine the husband's exercise of his power to repudiate [his wife] within the rigidly defined limits," whereas its Sunni counterparts generally give the husband free reign in matters of divorce.[67] In another important respect, the Twelver Shi'ite law is more generous to women than its Sunni counterpart. It concerns the shares of inheritance allocated to the survivors of the deceased. If, for instance, a deceased is survived by a daughter and a brother, Sunni law allocates half of the estate to each, whereas under Twelver Shi'ite law, the daughter receives the entire estate. Likewise, if a deceased is survived by the father, mother, and husband, under the Sunni law they receive one-third, one-sixth, and half respectively, whereas Shi'ite law mandates one-sixth, one-third, and half.[68] A more favorable treatment of women under the Twelver Shi'ite legal code is sometimes explained by the importance of the Prophet's daughter Fátima as a progenitor (with 'Ali) of the holy line of Shi'ite *imams*.[69]

It should now be abundantly clear that scriptural norms concerning women "are open to radically different interpretations" by (mostly male) Muslim legal scholars, who shared similar basic assumptions about what the proper relationships between the sexes in Islam should be.[70] We shall revisit the critical importance of the gender assumptions of the interpreters later on.

These, in a nutshell, are the scriptural foundations, as well as the subsequent juridical elaborations derived therefrom, that determined the status of Muslim women and their position in regard to men in Islamic societies until the onset of modernity and in some societies even later on. The exact ways in which these juridical discourses have impacted the lives of concrete women varied dramatically from one society and historical epoch to another. Attitudes toward Muslim women have been shaped, often decisively, by the pre-Islamic customs and traditions predominant in various Muslim communities. Oftentimes they could come into direct conflict with the scriptural regulations and their juridical elaborations just outlined. These local customs and traditions have proved to be so strongly entrenched in many Muslim societies that they may occasionally override or cancel explicit Qur'anic and juridical rulings. In some rare instances, especially in tribal, nomadic, and seminomadic societies, these local traditions can be relatively favorable to women.[71] Protected by tribal customary law (usually unwritten), tribal women would occasionally enjoy greater freedom compared to their Muslim sisters residing in an urban environment. For instance, they can freely mingle with their tribesmen, go uncovered, choose their husbands, have affairs with other men during a protracted absence of their husbands, and even have children out of wedlock without fear for their lives.[72] However, in the majority of cases, these unwritten local traditions and customs were detrimental to women. In many traditional Muslim societies, women were consistently denied inheritance (contrary to the explicit Qur'anic dispensations previously detailed) in preference to the male relatives of the deceased;[73] they were forcibly confined to harems—a practice not explicitly sanctioned by either the foundational texts of Islam or their juridical elaborations; given in marriage against their will to their paternal cousins to whom the patriarchal tradition grants the right of marital preemption; murdered by their male relatives or husbands without trial or investigation at a mere suspicion or rumor of marital infidelity; highly valued for their virginity to the detriment of divorced women and widows (despite the fact that of the Prophet's nine wives, only 'A'isha seems to have been virgin at the time of marriage); and so on.

Whether these attitudes have anything to do with Islam or are simply an inevitable consequence of the patriarchal, male-centered mind-set that has until recently prevailed in many Muslim majority societies is a complicated question. Readers should try to work it out for themselves on the basis of the evidence cited in this chapter and in the notes. In what follows, we will briefly outline some academic and semiacademic explanations of the progressive deterioration of the status of women in the Muslim world during the premodern and early modern epochs. These explanations are not the only game in town, as it were, but they are influential enough among academics and nonacademics alike to merit at least a cursory glance.

Theorizing the Muslim Woman

Some sympathetic scholars and advocates of women's rights in the West and in the Muslim world often argue that the Qur'anic injunctions about gender relations contain two mutually contradictory messages. On the one hand, as we have seen, they stipulate "the absolute moral and spiritual equality of men and women"[74] in insisting that men and women be held to the same standard of righteousness and virtue. In a similar vein, the "egalitarian" verses promise that women's and men's good deeds will have equal value in the eyes of God on the day of reckoning. Yet, at the same time, another group of Qur'anic statements seems to indicate that women have fewer rights compared to men in conjugal union and, to a lesser extent, in the social and economic sphere, thereby privileging men. In an attempt to address this apparent discrepancy in the Qur'anic messages, Leila Ahmed (b. 1940), an American scholar of Egyptian background, has pointed out that the former group of verses constitutes "the fundamental message of Islam," whereas the latter verses as well as the Prophet's "own practices, were ephemeral aspects of religion, relating only to that particular society at that historical moment."[75] Once this premise is granted, one can argue that the androcentric (pro-male) bias of later Islamic jurisprudence, theology, and social custom[76] was not inherent in the original Islamic message but was, in fact, accidental or even outright contrary to it.[77]

To substantiate her thesis, Leila Ahmed points out the relative freedom and respect that women enjoyed in the early Muslim community under the leadership of the Prophet and his immediate successors. During that period, female members of the community took an active part in the Muslim conquests and the first civil wars; they also enjoyed a high reputation as scholars, as well as considerable freedom in matters of marriage, divorce, and family life.[78] The fact that the bias against the female members of the *umma* became so deeply entrenched and pervasive in the subsequent period of Islam's history can be ascribed, on the one hand, to the "after-the-fact" scholastic elaborations and, on the other, to the predominant social and cultural practices of the age across the Mediterranean basin and beyond. Leila Ahmed argues that such elaborations and practices originated in a social and intellectual environment that was "far more negative for women than that in [Muhammad's] Arabia."[79] This misogynistic environment, so goes her argument, was inherited by the young Muslim polity from its defeated imperial predecessors, the Byzantine and Sasanian Empires, and went against the grain of the original Qur'anic message of gender equality.

Leila Ahmed further argues that alternative interpretations of Islam's foundational texts were possible and indeed found in the practices of some "heretical" Islamic sects and movements, such as the Sufis, the Kharijites, and the Qarmati Isma'ilis. The Kharijites, according to Leila Ahmed, "rejected concubinage and the marriage of nine-year-old girls (permitted by the orthodox)," whereas "the Qarmatis [also] banned polygamy and the veil."[80] Qarmati women and men freely socialized together,[81] and female Kharijites went into battle side by side with their male comrades.[82] The Sufis, in their turn, held a much more favorable view of women than mainstream Sunni and Shi'ite scholars and, on occasion, would place some female ascetics and mystics[83] above male Sufis in regard to piety and religious fervor.[84] In the later period, too, many women distinguished themselves as accomplished Sufi masters (*shaykha*s) and spiritual guides of renowned Sufis, including the great Arab-Spanish mystic Ibn 'Arabi (d. 1240).[85]

Yet, as Leila Ahmed herself recognizes, such favorable treatment of women remained marginal and was ultimately suppressed in favor of the androcentric and misogynistic culture that triumphed under the 'Abbásid dynasty. Once in place, it fell to the scholars loyal to the 'Abbásid rulers to find a religious justification of this state-sanctioned culture by selectively interpreting the often self-contradictory and inconclusive scriptural evidence. Leila Ahmed emphasizes the importance that male scholars of the 'Abbasid age assigned to the women-denigrating *hadíth* that may or may not have been authentic.[86] Even if they acted in good faith, the male scholars could not escape the predominant misogynist mentality of their age, which shaped their interpretations of Islam's foundational texts—often decisively. But exactly how and why did this mentality become predominant in Muslim societies?

According to Leila Ahmed, the 'Abbásids embraced the misogynistic mentality and cultural practices associated with their imperial predecessors. She argues, persuasively, that the societies of Christian Byzantium and the Zoroastrian Sasanian Empire on the eve of Islam furnish ample evidence of the veiling and seclusion of "honorable" (i.e., upper-class) women. Bad as things were for women in Byzantium,[87] they were worse still in Sasanian Iran, whose nobility maintained huge harems and freely loaned their wives to one another.[88] In striving to replicate the imperial grandeur of their predecessors, the 'Abbásid rulers adopted the same misogynistic (and essentially un-Islamic) stance toward the female half of their subjects:

> Keeping enormous harems of wives and concubines guarded by eunuchs became an accepted practice. The caliph al-Mutawakkil (r. 847–61) had four thousand concubines, Harun al-Rashid (r. 786–809) hundreds. Evidently, even the more moderately wealthy routinely acquired concubines; one young man, on receiving his inheritance, went on to purchase "a house, furniture, concubines and other objects."[89]

Another Arab scholar, Nabia Abbott, whom Leila Ahmed quotes profusely throughout her study, insists that the oppression of women under the 'Abbásid caliphs manifested itself in three institutions:

> Polygamy, concubinage, and seclusion of women. The seclusion of the harem affected the freeborn Arab woman to a greater extent than it did her captive or slave-born sister. The choicest women, free or slave, were imprisoned behind heavy curtains and locked doors, the strings and keys to which were entrusted into the hands of that pitiful creature—the eunuch. As the size of the harem grew, men indulged to satiety. Satiety within the individual harem meant boredom for the one man and neglect for the many women. Under these conditions . . . satisfaction by perverse and unnatural means crept into society, particularly its upper classes.[90]

According to Leila Ahmed, these three factors determined the plight of women in the 'Abbásid epoch. They persisted after the fall of the dynasty in 1258, setting the dominant pattern of gender relations in Muslim societies until the beginning of the twentieth century. Leila Ahmed was not alone in her condemnation of female seclusion. Sayyid Qutb (1906–1966), prominent member of the Muslim Brotherhood and a leading ideologist of modern Muslim political activism, writing in the middle of the twentieth century, argues that, whereas polygamy is permissible under the Muslim law, it "has nothing to do with harems, where large numbers of slave girls were 'gathered together in the palaces, and used as a means for animal-like sexual pleasure and in nights of debauchery.'"[91]

The deleterious impact of harem seclusion on men and women alike has been pointed out by Western historians with no apparent feminist axes to grind. Thus, the famous American scholar Marshall Hodgson (1922–1968) has the following to say on the issue:

> The whole atmosphere of servility and secrecy [in the harem], founded on the use of slave guards, was seriously alien to the Shar'i sense of human dignity. It could also be disastrous for a ruling class. The advice of women kept in seclusion was, in any case, not such as to inspire men with magnanimity, or even to curb them with practical good sense. Only an outstanding woman could rise above her status as to be of serious help to her husband. Worse . . . a typical secluded woman could not give her sons, in their formative early years, the experience and guidance which would enable them to profit most fully from their later years of apprenticeship

among the men. To the pampering that privileged children necessarily received from servants was too often added a petty and irresponsible direction from the mother.[92]

According to Hodgson, "The women's apartments . . . tended to be the center of intrigues: intrigues for the master's love . . . or for his respect (and monetary favors) or for his favoring of one's women's children over another's."[93] Even worse, "women deliberately kept ignorant" in the harem and generally unaware of the real world outside its walls could occasionally acquire considerable power over their husbands by means of harem intrigue. In such cases, their intrusive influence on state affairs could become truly detrimental not only for the ruling class but for society as a whole. Brought up in such an environment, princes inevitably fell prey to "the intrigues and rivalries of the women of the harem and the court eunuchs." Corroded by this unhealthy environment, the inmates of the harem would, by a quirk of fate, become kingmakers. While in this position, they would deliberately fashion the young monarch in such a way as to make him an obedient tool for their personal ambitions.[94]

This is not the place to dwell on the real or perceived horrors of the harem system.[95] Some aspects of life in harems may have been exaggerated by Western observers speaking from the perspective of present-day notions of gender equality and freedom from any type of bondage as an unalienable human right. For our purpose, it is more important to try to understand how this system came into being and why it has proved to be so persistent throughout the ages, coming to an end only in the first decades of the twentieth century. Marshall Hodgson offers his own explanation of the phenomenon of the harem (as well as the subjugated status of Muslim women in general), which does not necessarily contradict the thesis first advanced by Nabia Abbot and later refined by Leila Ahmed. Rather, his explanation may be seen as complementing theirs.

For Hodgson, as for Ahmed and Abbott, there is nothing inherently "Islamic" in the maltreatment, seclusion, and close supervision of women by men in the premodern and early modern societies of the Mediterranean basin and beyond.[96] In fact, he suggests that this attitude cuts across religious, cultural, and ethnic borders and can be observed throughout the vast swath of land and sea from Spain to Central Asia. The subjugated status of women in these societies, in Hodgson's view, is a natural consequence of the "cult of masculine honor" that has shaped local cultural practices. One element of this "cult" is the collective solidarity of all male members of a faction or clan in the face of a real or perceived attack on its "honor." This group solidarity has frequently manifested itself in "formal vengeance and feuding between families or factions," in which all "men of honor" belonging to a given faction or clan were required to participate, even when their personal honor was not directly at stake. The Montague–Capulet feud of Shakespeare's *Romeo and Juliet* in "fair Verona" (a Mediterranean city) immediately springs to mind. In Hodgson's explanation, the cult of masculine honor has had a lasting impact on the position of women in Mediterranean societies. Here, according to Hodgson, "a woman's 'honor', her shame, formed an important point in determining the honor of her man." Any attempt by outsiders to call in doubt a woman's chastity in public or even in private was (and still occasionally is) seen as an attack on the man's personal honor and social worth. Given this perception by society at large, it required of men drastic measures to shield their women from public gaze.[97]

Hodgson's thesis is not unique to him. The aforementioned peculiarity of the male ethos in Mediterranean societies and beyond has been registered by many observers. Speaking of the position of the Arab woman, a Western-trained anthropologist argues:

> In his [a man's] eyes she symbolizes his own virility: every thoughtless action [by an outsider] is interpreted by her strong protector as a challenge to his power, an outrage to his dignity. A whole mystique has grown up around the concept of honor which decrees that the modesty of the women whom he guards should be a sacred object. Any assault or attempted assault on their chastity is classed as murder and may be punished extremely severely.[98]

In a society that placed such a great premium on woman's chastity while simultaneously acknowledging her status as the primary symbol of her man's honor, "even the mention of a man's wife was regarded as indecorous," all the more so because women were "thought of as primarily objects of sexual pleasure."[99] Under such circumstances, even an apparently innocent joke about one's womenfolk could easily evolve into a full-fledged vendetta between two factions or clans,[100] since an assault on one member of a clan or faction demanded the participation of all "men of honor" belonging to them. To prevent this:

> The "honorable" woman was expected to be excluded from any sort of contact with possible sex partners other than her husband; the whole pattern of social life (especially in the upper classes) was geared to this exclusion.[101]

By "the pattern of social life," Hodgson apparently implied not only the social and cultural restrictions on woman's every movement or action but also the distinct spatial arrangements of Muslim cities in which the bland facades of houses conceal exquisitely decorated inner yards with delightful fountains, balconies, marble benches and recliners, and blossoming flowers and trees. Here the master of the house could enjoy the company of his womenfolk without the fear of exposing them to outsiders. Such wealthy households were small replicas of royal harems: They were divided into male and female quarters. Whenever male visitors appeared, the female half of the household retired to their part of the house, where they, in their turn, would receive female visitors (see Figure 18.2).

What has just been said applies almost exclusively to the women of the upper classes. Much as they would like to prevent their wives, daughters, and sisters from contact with potential sexual partners, men of lower social standing simply could not afford to keep their women permanently secluded and idle. In this respect, lower-class women enjoyed greater freedom (if also much less comfort) than their thoroughly secluded or even guarded upper-class counterparts (including the

Figure 18.2 A Young Muslim Woman Praying Inside a Mosque

slave-girls of upper-class men). Yet the rule of female chastity as the essential measure of man's honor would still apply in a remote village as well as in a craftsmen's quarter of a city or town. In such circles, in accordance with the unwritten law of honor, "brothers were expected . . . to kill a sister who had sex with the wrong man—sparing her husband."[102] In such cases, a rumor or innuendo was sufficient to warrant such an extrajudicial execution. No proof required by the Shari'a was necessary to justify it. Furthermore, in line with the patriarchal logic that prevailed in premodern and early modern Islamic societies, Shari'a courts and individual judges tended to treat the murderous relatives leniently. The judges would justify such lenient treatment by reference to the juridical consensus that it is legitimate to kill a married or even unmarried person caught red-handed in the act of adultery. However, if a later court trial determined that adultery had not taken place, the perpetrator(s) would be punished for murder. Nevertheless, a parent killing his or her child caught in the act of adultery has usually been absolved of the murder.[103]

Conclusions

After examining the scriptural evidence related to women and gender relations in Islam, it is difficult not to find it ambiguous and occasionally controversial. Some women and types of female behavior are highly praised in the Qur'an, while others are implicitly or explicitly condemned. Furthermore, it is not always clear to whom the Qur'an addressees its normative prescriptions: to the Prophet's wives only or to the Muslim women of the early *umma* in Medina or to all Muslim women regardless of the epoch and place their live in. In short, there is much ambiguity in the Qur'an that numerous *hadith*, circulated in the Prophet's name, apparently tried to dispel. As mentioned, the *hadith* in general are much less complimentary and lenient toward women than the Qur'an. The same is largely true of *fiqh*, differences among the Muslim schools of law notwithstanding.

In an effort to account for the subjugated status of the female half of the Muslim community in the Middle Ages, we have examined a theory that attributes the progressive deterioration of the status of women in medieval Islamic societies to external social and cultural factors, especially to the negative influence of the misogynist cultures of the Byzantine and Sasanian Empires whose lands and people were inherited by the Muslim state. Leila Ahmed, in particular, viewed the 'Abbasid dynasty, whose rulers emulated the kings of ancient Iran, as being responsible for introducing institutions and practices harmful to women, such as female slavery, harems, and polygamy.

Hodgson's theory, on the other hand, seeks to bring out the cultural and ethical reasons for the rise of what he calls the "harem system." He attributes it, in large part, to the "cult of masculine honor"—a sociocultural phenomenon that, according to Hodgson, was far from unique to Muslim societies.

Questions to Ponder

1   To what extent the institutions and practices described in this chapter are "Islamic" or "cultural"—that is, borrowed (inherited) from the previous societies and cultures of the region, then given an Islamic veneer by means of a selective interpretation of Islam's foundational texts?

2   This question inevitably brings up the broader issue of how one can separate "Islamic" beliefs and practices from "non-Islamic" ones and who (if anyone) should be the arbiter in such matters. Try to resolve this difficult issue by making use of the evidence provided in this and the previous chapters of this book.

Summary

- The status of women in Islamic societies is an object of heated debates and controversy. At the ideological underpinnings of these debates are Western attempts to "liberate" Muslim women from male oppression, which are perceived as attacks on Islam per se. Anti-Muslim rhetoric is countered by an apologetic response.
- Among the women in the Qur'an are Ásya, the Pharaoh's wife; Mary, the mother of Jesus; Eve (Hawwa); Zuláykha, the seductress of the prophet Joseph (Yusuf); Bilqís (the Queen of Sheba); and the wife of the Prophet's enemy, Abu Láhab.
- The wives of the Prophet are subjects of Qur'anic injunctions, including one that concerns false accusations of adultery (against 'A'isha). Qur'anic norms of proper behavior are incumbent upon Muslim women.
- There is a tension between Qur'anic verses asserting the equality of men and women in terms of their obligations toward God and those that seem to privilege men over women in the domestic, social, and economic spheres.
- The Prophet's wives are presented as Mothers of the Believers and as the models for other Muslim women to emulate.
- There are injunctions concerning adultery and polygamy, as well as an issue of temporary marriage (*mut'a*).
- Women are subject to regulations regarding marriage, divorce, and child care.
- Women, in the *hadíth* and *fiqh*, are subject to the variations in opinions among legal schools and between Sunni and Shi'ite jurisprudence in particular.
- There are contradictions between Islamic juridical theories and the patriarchal ethos and customs of some Muslim societies, as well as confusion between patriarchy and Islam. Patriarchy has an adverse effect on Muslim women.
- Some theoretical approaches to the status of women in Islamic societies are discussed. Nabia Abbott and Leila Ahmad argue that Muslim women are victims of the androcentric, patriarchal culture that has dominated Muslim societies since the early Middle Ages; the Muslim ruling elite inherited and internalized the misogynistic attitudes of their imperial predecessors, the Byzantine and Sasanian Empires. These misogynistic attitudes were appropriated and justified in Islamic terms by the Muslim scholars under the 'Abbasid dynasty to become the model and pattern for later generations to follow.
- Polygamy, female slavery, and seclusion in the harem are the three means of subjugating and disenfranchising women under the 'Abbásids and their successors.
- Marshall Hodgson's thesis concerns the emergence and persistence of the "harem system." It is the consequence of the so-called cult of masculine honor that was predominant in Mediterranean societies in the premodern epoch. The idea that a woman's chastity (shame) is the essential measure of her man's social worth led to the deliberate isolation of women from any possible contact with a potential sexual partner. The cult of masculine honor and interclan conflicts are symptomatic.
- Hodgson emphasizes, even exaggerates, the detrimental impact of the intrigue-ridden harem system on Muslim societies and the ruling classes in particular.
- The problem is that of separating "Islamic" norms from "patriarchal" customs responsible for the disenfranchisement and subjugation of Muslim women.

Notes

1 Lila Abu Lughod, *Do Muslim Women Need Saving?* Harvard University Press, Cambridge, MA, 2013, passim.

2 See, for instance, William Shepard (trans.), *Sayyid Qutb and Islamic Activism: A Translation and Critical Analysis of "Social Justice in Islam,"* E. J. Brill, Leiden, 1996, pp. 60–68; Amina Wadud, *Qur'an and Woman: Rereading the Sacred Text from a Woman's Perspective*, Oxford University Press, Oxford and New York, 1999; Olivier Carré, *Mysticism and Politics: A Critical Reading of* Fi Zilal al-Qur'an *by Sayyid Qutb (1906–1966)*, E. J. Brill, Leiden and Boston, 2003, Chapter 6 and pp. 281–289; and Abdessalam Yassine, *Winning the Modern World for Islam* (trans. from French by Martin Jenni), Justice and Spirituality Publishing, Iowa City, IA, 2000, pp. 93–99.

3 For a typical example, see John Esposito, *Islam: The Straight Path*, 5th ed., Oxford University Press, Oxford and New York, 2016, pp. 116–126, 274–278, et passim.

4 Barbara Stowasser, *Women in the Qur'an, Traditions, and Interpretation*, Oxford University Press, Oxford, 1994, p. 5.

5 Wiebke Walter, *Women in Islam*, Markus Wiener, Princeton, NJ, and New York, 1993, p. 47.

6 See, for instance, Leila Ahmed, *Women and Gender in Islam: Historical Roots of a Modern Debate*, Yale University Press, New Haven, CT, 1992, Chapter 8; cf. Nancy Hewitt (ed.), *A Companion to American Women's History*, Blackwell, Oxford, 2005.

7 Walter, *Women in Islam*, p. 34; and Barbara Stowasser, "Wives of the Prophet," in *Encyclopedia of the Qur'an*. General Editor: Jane Dammen McAuliffe; online edition: http://referenceworks.brillonline.com; some historians argue that 'Ali b. Abi Talib was the first to embrace Islam, see L. Veccia Vaglieri, "'Ali b. Abi Talib," in *Encyclopedia of Islam*, 2nd ed.; online edition: http://referenceworks.brillonline.com.

8 Stowasser, *Women in the Qur'an*, p. 59.

9 She corresponds to the Pharaoh's daughter of the Judeo-Christian canon.

10 Nicholas Awde (ed. and trans.), *Women in Islam: An Anthology from the Qur'an and Hadiths*, Hippocrene Books, New York, 2005, p. 144.

11 Stowasser, *Women in the Qur'an*, p. 80.

12 Stowasser, "Wives of the Prophet."

13 Stowasser, *Women in the Qur'an*, p. 80.

14 Or "submit themselves [to God]" (*muslim* masc.; *muslima* fem.).

15 Walter, *Women in Islam*, p. 51; these themes are explored in detail in Amina Wadud's *Qur'an and Woman*; see "Introduction" and Chapters 1–4.

16 For details, see Wadud, *Qur'an and Women*, pp. 54–57 (a Muslim perspective) and Stefan Wild, "Lost in Philology? The Virgins of Paradise and the Luxenberg Hypothesis," in Angelika Neuwirth, Nicolai Sinai, and Michael Marx (eds.), *The Qur'an in Context*, E. J. Brill, Leiden and Boston, 2010, pp. 625–648 (a Western academic perspective).

17 Or "God has preferred in bounty one of them over another." The exact meaning and translation of this verse have been the subject of a heated controversy among both Muslim and Western scholars.

18 Ruth Roded, "Women and the Qur'an," in *Encyclopedia of the Qur'an*. General Editor: Jane Dammen McAuliffe; online edition: http://referenceworks.brillonline.com; cf. Wadud, *Qur'an and Woman*, pp. 65–74.

19 Wadud, *Qur'an and Woman*, pp. 85–86.

20 Roded, "Women and the Qur'an"; for a Muslim perspective, see Wadud, *Qur'an and Woman*, pp. 87–88.

21 Wadud, *Qur'an and Woman*, ibid.

22 Joseph Chelhod, "Mar'a: Part 2, Section d: Arab Woman in Traditional Law," in *Encyclopedia of Islam*, 2nd ed.; online edition: http://referenceworks.brillonline.com.

23 Most reports agree that the Prophet had nine wives and several concubines who enjoyed the same status as wives; Stowasser, "Wives of the Prophet."

24 Ibid.

25 For details, see Stowasser, *Women in the Qur'an*, pp. 95–97.

26 Rudolph Peters, "Zina," in *Encyclopedia of Islam*, 2nd ed.; online edition: http://referenceworks.brillonline.com.

27 For the *hadíth* to this effect, see Gautier Juynboll, *Encyclopedia of Canonical Hadith*, E. J. Brill, Leiden and Boston, 2007, pp. 324 and 495; see also Alexander Knysh, "Multiple Areas of Influence," in Jane McAuliffe (ed.), *Cambridge Companion to the Qur'an*, Cambridge University Press, Cambridge, 2006, p. 218.

28 For details of the affair, see Stowasser, *Women in the Qur'an*, pp. 94–95.

29 Walter, *Women in Islam*, p. 57; for a Muslim perspective, see Wadud, *Qur'an and Women*, pp. 82–85.

30 Carré, *Mysticism and Politics*, p. 139.

31 For an eloquent argument to this effect, see Ahmed Souaiaia, *Contesting Justice: Women, Islam, Law, and Society*, SUNY Press, Albany, NY, 2008, pp. 42–57; cf. Wadud, *Qur'an and Women*, pp. 82–85.

32 "God has forbidden this [temporary marriage] to us up to the Day of Resurrection."

33 Moojan Momen, *An Introduction to Shi'i Islam*, Yale University Press, New Haven, CT, 1985, pp. 182–183; contrary to the opinion of many Sunnis, *mut'a* was still allowed by some Sunni judges under the Umayyads, e.g., in Egypt. Noel Coulson, *A History of Islamic Law*, Edinburgh University Press, Edinburgh, reprint, 1997, p. 31.

34 Josef Schacht and Aharon Layish, "Talak," in *Encyclopedia of Islam*, 2nd ed.; online edition: http://referenceworks.brillonline.com.

35 Wadud, *Qur'an and Women*, pp. 79–80.

36 Souaiaia, *Contesting Justice*, p. 36.

37 For rules pertaining to child care, see Q 2:223.

38 Wadud, *Qur'an and Women*, pp. 89–91; cf. Coulson, *A History of Islamic Law*, pp. 96–98.

39 Arabic, *taláq* ("[you are] set free").

40 Coulson, *A History of Islamic Law*, pp. 14–15.

41 In the traditional Biblical narrative it was Pharaoh's daughter, not his wife, who saved the child Moses by fishing him out of the river; see *Exodus*, Chapter 2.

42 For details see Stowasser, *Women in the Qur'an*, pp. 13–66.

43 Liyakat Takim, "Law: The Four Sunni Schools of Law," in *Encyclopedia of Women and Islamic Cultures*, E. J. Brill, Leiden; online edition: http:// http://referenceworks.brillonline.com.

44 Juynboll, *Encyclopedia of Canonical Hadith*, pp. 61, 542, and 622.

45 Ibid., p. 622.

46 Ibid., p. 177.

47 Ibid., p. 552.

48 Ibid., pp. 549 and 443.

49 Awde, *Women in Islam*, p. 103.

50 Ibid., p. 103 and Juynboll, *Encyclopedia of Canonical Hadith*, p. 21.

51 Juynboll, *Encyclopedia of Canonical Hadith*, pp. 165, 166, 194, 198, 202, 229, and so on; in the subsequent centuries, *hijáb* has come to be understood as any cover, such as headscarf, veil, shawl, or even a full face mask (*niqáb*), that protects sexually attractive parts of female body.

52 Ibid.

53 Walter, *Women in Islam*, p. 48.

54 Juynboll, *Encyclopedia of Canonical Hadith*, p. 429.

55 Walter, *Women in Islam*, p. 87.

56 Ibid., p. 55; Takim, "Law"; Coulson, *A History of Islamic Law*, p. 30 and 34–35.

57 Juynboll, *Encyclopedia of Canonical Hadith*, p. 316.

58 Walter, *Women in Islam*, p. 55.

59 In the Qur'an and *fiqh*, this period is called *'idda*; see Coulson, *A History of Islamic Law*, pp. 14–15 and 31.

60 Ibid., p. 31.

61 Ibid., pp. 95–96; this was the position of the Maliki school.

62 Ahmed, *Women and Gender in Islam*, p. 91.

63 Takim, "Law."

64 Coulson, *A History of Islamic Law*, p. 97.

65 Takim, "Law."

66 Momen, *An Introduction to Shi'i Islam*, p. 183 and Coulson, *A History of Islamic Law*, pp. 111–112.

67 Ibid., p. 112.

68 Souaiaia, *Contesting Justice*, p. 73.

69 Momen, *An Introduction to Shi'i Islam*, p. 183.

70 Ahmed, *Women and Gender in Islam*, p. 91.

71 Coulson, *A History of Islamic Law*, pp. 33–34.

72 Joseph Chelhod, "Mar'a: Part 2, Section c," in *Encyclopedia of Islam*, 2nd ed.; online edition: http://referenceworks.brillonline.com.

73 For the examples of both positive and negative influence of customary laws on the fortunes of women, see Coulson, *A History of Islamic Law*, pp. 135–138.

74 Ahmed, *Women and Gender in Islam*, p. 64.

75 Ibid., p. 66.

76 I will not discuss here the image of woman in secular literature and arts produced in the Muslim world over the centuries; generally speaking, this image reflects the same androcentric attitudes that one finds in Islamic religious discourses; see, for example, Nada Tomiche, "Mar'a," in *Encyclopedia of Islam*, 2nd ed.; online edition: http://referenceworks.brillonline.com.

77 It should be pointed out that toward the end of her academic career, Leila Ahmed seems to have changed at least some of her original views regarding Islam, Muslim women, and the practice of veiling; see Leila Ahmed, *A Quiet Revolution: The Veil's Resurgence, from the Middle East to America*, Yale University Press, New Haven, CT, 2013.

78 Ahmed, *Women and Gender in Islam*, pp. 69–77.

79 Ibid., p. 67.

80 Ibid., p. 66.

81 Ibid., p. 99.

82 Ibid., p. 71.

83 Such as Rábi'a al-'Adawiyya (d. 801), discussed in Chapter 13.

84 Ahmed, *Women and Gender in Islam*, pp. 96–97; see also Margaret Smith, *Rabi'a the Mystic and Her Fellow-Saints in Islam*, reprint, Cambridge University Press, Cambridge, 1984.

85 Ahmed, *Women and Gender in Islam*, p. 99.

86 Ibid., pp. 47, 67, and 88.

87 Ibid., pp. 25–29.

88 Ibid., pp. 17–24.

89 Ibid., p. 83, quoting Nabia Abbott (1897–1981).

90 Ibid., pp. 79–80, quoting Nabia Abbott.

91 Carré, *Mysticism and Politics*, pp. 139–140; quoting Qutb's commentary on the Qur'an.

92 Marshall Hodgson, *The Venture of Islam*, University of Chicago Press, Chicago, 1974, vol. 2, p. 144.

93 Ibid., p. 143.

94 Peter Holt, Ann Lambton and Bernard Lewis (eds.), *The Cambridge History of Islam*, vol. 1: *The Central Islamic Lands*, Cambridge University Press, Cambridge, 1970, pp. 424–425.

95 On the harem of the Ottoman sultans, see Leslie Peirce, *The Imperial Harem: Women and Sovereignty in the Ottoman Empire*, Oxford University Press, Oxford, 1993; for a fine pictorial survey, see Alev Lytle Croutier, *Harem: The World Behind the Veil*, Abbeville Publishers, New York, 1989.

96 Hodgson speaks of the "Irano-Mediterranean" cultural zone; *The Venture*, vol. 2, p. 140.

97 Hodgson, *The Venture*, vol. 2, p. 141.

98 Chelhod, "Mar'a: Part 2, Section c."

99 Hodgson, *The Venture*, vol. 2, p. 142.

100 Chelhod, "Mar'a: Part 2, Section d."

101 Hodgson, *The Venture*, vol. 2, p. 142.

102 Ibid.

103 Lama Abu-Odeh, "Honor: Crimes of, Overview," in *Encyclopedia of Women and Islamic Cultures*, E.J. Brill, Leiden and Boston; online edition: http://referenceworks.brillonline.com.

Chapter 19

Islam and the West

The Arab Conquests of Christian Lands

The age-old quarrel between Islam and Christianity or, to be more precise, between their followers is sometimes compared to the rivalry of two siblings competing for an inheritance. The inheritance is, in this case, Abrahamic monotheism, which each of the two religions claims to represent in its original purity. In a paradoxical way, Judaism, the forebear of the two rival siblings was, until recently, relegated to the periphery of this Muslim-Christian conflict,[1] and, on occasion, suffered blows from both of its descendants. This curious historical phenomenon can be explained by the fact that, by a quirk of historical fate, Judaism's monotheistic heirs managed to create and sustain powerful states that had the resources to field large armies. Followers of Judaism, on the other hand, were unable to reestablish their own polity until the mid-twentieth century. The Roman occupation and subsequent suppression of the Jewish state in Palestine in the first century left the Jews dispersed across the breadth and width of Africa and Eurasia, depriving them of any significant role in the military and political competition for the control of the Mediterranean basin and the lands adjacent to it.

The struggle between the Christians of Europe and the Muslims of the Middle East and North Africa started with the Arab conquests of 635–645. As we remember from Chapter 3, after the death of the founder of Islam (632), his followers in Arabia attacked the two great empires of the region, Byzantium and Persia (Iran), and managed to wrest large territories from them. By the mid-seventh century, the Sasanian Empire of Iran was absorbed in its entirety into the Abode of Islam (*dar al-islam*). The Byzantine Empire lost many of its territories—Syria, Egypt, Palestine, and, by 698, North Africa (Maghrib). Greek-speaking Byzantine Christians were forced to retreat to Anatolia (Turkey) and to start a long and grueling defensive war against their Muslim neighbors. During the century that followed, Constantinople, the capital of the Byzantine Empire in the Strait of Bosporus, suffered several major Muslim sieges, none of which was successful.

The Arab armies enjoyed greater success in the West. Using North Africa as their springboard, in 711–713 an Arab expeditionary force, supported by the newly converted Berber tribes,[2] overran the Iberian Peninsula.[3] After establishing themselves at the city of Cordova, they moved to the north, sweeping across the Pyrenees and deep into Gaul (Southern France) as far as Bordeaux. A contemporary Christian writer compared the Arab-Berber onslaught against the Frankish kingdoms of southern France with "a brush fire fanned by the winds."[4] The rapidly advancing "Saracens," as the Arabs were styled in medieval Christian chronicles, eventually encountered staunch resistance on the part of the local Frankish princes and their subjects. In 731, a large Arab military detachment was routed at Toulouse. In the following year, the historic Battle of Poitiers (Tours) took place in southern France. It was there that the army of the Frankish king Charles Martel (nicknamed "the Hammer"), assisted by his vassals, demolished a Muslim army led by the Umayyad governor of Spain, or "al-Andalus" as it called in Arabic sources. Despite these reversals, "the rhythm of holy war was unbroken," and the Muslim raids against the Christian population of France continued until

740, often with devastating consequences for the Frankish principalities of southwestern Europe.[5] After the death of Charles the Hammer in 741, Muslim incursions across the Pyrenees came to an end, although the Mediterranean remained a "Muslim lake" for many centuries.

European historians have consistently celebrated the defeat of the Arab-Berber army at Poitier (Tours) as a major turning point in Muslim–Christian confrontation. From the viewpoint of Christian chronicles of the age, this was the moment of truth, when a seemingly unstoppable Muslim onslaught was stemmed by a group of valiant defenders of Christian civilization led by the invincible Charles the Hammer.[6] Writing many centuries later, the influential British historian, free-thinker, and member of the British Parliament Edward Gibbon (1737–1794) aptly captured the common European perception of that fateful event in his groundbreaking book "The History of the Decline and Fall of the Roman Empire":

> A victorious line of march had been prolonged above a thousand miles from the rock of Gibraltar to the banks of the Loire [river]; the repetition of an equal space would have carried the Saracens to the confines of Poland and the Highlands of Scotland: the Rhine is not more impassable than the Nile or Euphrates, and the Arabian fleet might have sailed into the mouth of the Thames. Perhaps the interpretation of the Koran would now be taught in the schools of Oxford, and her pulpits might demonstrate to a circumcised people the sanctity and truth of the revelation of Mahomet.[7]

Another Western historian spoke of the Battle of Poitier as the moment when "the world's fate was played between the Franks and the Arabs."[8] Medieval Muslim chronicles, on the other hand, seem to have had a very different perspective of this event. The famous Muslim historian and geographer al-Mas'údi (d. 956) makes no mention of it, while his colleagues familiar with the event treat it as a relatively minor reversal, a bump "across the path of an unstoppable . . . advance blessed by Allah."[9] At the same time, Muslim sources acknowledge the heavy death toll suffered by the Muslim army in this battle by calling it "the Highway of the Martyrs" because it took place along an old Roman road. Nevertheless, unlike their European counterparts, Muslim chroniclers treated it as a relatively minor episode. An Egyptian historian of the Arab conquests who lived in the ninth century says:

> 'Ubayda [the governor of North Africa] had given authority over Spain to 'Abd al-Rahman ibn 'Abdallah al-'Akki. 'Abd al-Rahman was a worthy man who made expeditions against the Franks. They are the remotest of the enemies of Spain. He gained much booty and overcame them. . . . Then he went on another expedition, and he and his companions suffered martyrdom for Islam.[10]

Although no doubt a regrettable defeat at the hands of the infidel enemy, it happened too far from the heart of the Umayyad caliphate in Syria to present an immediate threat to the fortunes of the generally victorious Islamic state. In contrast to the rather terse and unemotional account of the Battle of Poitiers (Tours) just cited, Muslim historians have much more to tell us about the Arab attempts to conquer Constantinople, the heavily fortified capital of their still formidable Byzantine-Christian foe (see Figure 19.1). The hostilities around Constantinople lasted for years and required a much greater expenditure of Muslim life and treasure than the fateful military incursion into southern France.[11] The unsuccessful and bloody Muslim sieges of that city, organized and led by the caliphs themselves, are commemorated both in detailed historical accounts and in popular legend. As a Western scholar has cogently argued, in retrospect, it seems that Muslim historians perceived these events in a truer light than their Western counterparts. The Frankish force at Poitiers encountered little more than a large band of raiders that had ventured

Figure 19.1 The Fleet of the Romans Setting Ablaze an Enemy Fleet (Image from an illuminated manuscript, the Madrid Skylitzes)

Public Domain/Wikimedia Commons

far beyond their usual theater of operations. In France, the Muslim force's communication and supply lines were overextended, rendering it incapable of maintaining a sustained military effort in that remote area. The Christian Greeks of Byzantium, on the other hand, met and halted the forces of Islam while they were still fresh, strong, and based relatively close to the Byzantine border. Thus, it was the failure of the Muslim armies to conquer Constantinople, not the Frankish defeat of a relatively minor Arab army at Poitiers (Tours), that enabled Eastern and Western Christendom to survive the initial Muslim onslaught and to continue to resist Muslim attacks until the middle of the fifteenth century.[12]

Charles Martel's victory at Poitier (Tours) continues to loom large in the Western European imagination. From the viewpoint of Western historiography, not only did Charles the Hammer and his troops stem the tide of the seemingly unstoppable infidel invasion, they did so as *Europenses*—a name that was, for the first time, applied collectively to the victors in an early Western account of that battle. In other words, the joint resistance to the Muslim enemy helped the theretofore disunited subjects of Frankish kings and princes to forge a common identity, that of (West) European Christians.[13] This fact was to have long-ranging implications for the subsequent relations of the population of Western Europe with the outside world in general and with their Muslim neighbors to the south in particular.

In the East, Muslim attacks against neighboring Christian powers continued uninterrupted under the 'Abbásid caliphs, who relied on their Saljuk Turkic protectors for military support. The latter managed to conquer Anatolia (Turkey) from its Byzantine Christian rulers, forcing the area's Greek-speaking population to retreat to the Balkans throughout the eleventh and twelfth centuries.

The Beginnings of the Crusader Movement in Europe

The Muslim–Christian confrontation took an entirely new twist in the late eleventh century, when the crusader armies, which had arrived from Western Europe, succeeded in wresting Syria and Palestine from its Muslim rulers (mostly Turks). After a bloody and ruthless military campaign, the Crusaders seized Jerusalem in 1099. Their occupation of the Muslim principalities in southern Turkey, Syria, and Palestine (known collectively as the Levant) did not go unchallenged. In the first decades of the twelfth century, Muslim military rulers (*amírs*) of Syria and Egypt launched a holy war (*jihád*) against the crusader states along the East Mediterranean coast. By 1291, they managed to expel the last detachments of the Western intruders from the lands the latter had occupied almost two centuries prior. We shall discuss the Crusades in detail further on. In the subsequent centuries, the powerful Muslim Empire ruled by the dynasty of Ottoman Turks based in northwestern Anatolia waged a protracted and often successful warfare against its Christian nemesis up north. In 1453, the victorious Ottomans managed to capture Constantinople, putting an end to the once powerful Byzantine Empire. The Eastern Orthodox Christians lost their powerful defender and had to accept Muslim protection in return for the payment of a special poll tax. The fall of the Byzantine Empire laid the groundwork for the Ottoman advance in the Balkans and southeastern Europe. Meanwhile, Muslim states were gradually losing ground in the western Mediterranean. By the end of the thirteenth century, the Muslim presence in the Iberian Peninsula was reduced to a handful of small principalities surrounded by aggressive Catholic kingdoms. The last Muslim state in Spain Iberia, Granada, fell to the joint forces of the Spanish Catholic sovereigns Ferdinand and Isabella in 1492. Hostilities and commercial rivalry between the followers of the two Abrahamic religions continued unabated in the later centuries both in the Mediterranean basin and around the Indian Ocean, the latter triggered by the intrusion of the Portuguese Catholic Empire in the area in the early 1500s.

By the end of the eighteenth century, Western powers (including the Russian Empire), buoyed by their newly acquired technological and organizational superiority, began to gain the upper hand in the centuries-old confrontation with their Muslim opponents. One by one, Muslim states fell under Western sway. Some lost their independence completely to become European colonies; others had to accept their economical, political, and cultural dependency on the Western powers. The era of European colonial domination of Muslim lands was dawning. We shall discuss it in the chapters that follow.

God's Wars: The First Crusades and the Muslim Response

As long as the 'Abbásid caliphs in Baghdad remained strong and independent, they considered waging wars against the Byzantine Empire to be their primary religious duty, alongside conducting the Friday congregational prayer in the main mosque of Baghdad on special occasions and leading caravans of pilgrims to Mecca once a year. The caliphs viewed the Byzantine emperor, nicknamed "Tyrant," and his Christian subjects as the primary target of *jihád*.[14] This protracted, almost ritualized warfare took place along the Muslim–Byzantine frontier in northern Syria and southern Anatolia. Apart from the caliph's regular troops, the war attracted numerous volunteer "fighters for the faith" on both sides. In the end, the 'Abbásids proved to be victorious due in large part to the superior fighting skills of their Turkic protectors, the Saljuks. The military prowess of the mounted Saljuk warriors was readily recognized by Muslim scholars and statesmen, including al-Ghazali, who wrote:

> In this age of ours, from amongst the [various] kinds of human beings it is the Turks who possess force . . . If there should be an insurrection in any region of the earth against this resplendent state [the caliphate] there is not one among them [Turks] who on seeing strife beyond its frontiers would not fight in the way of God waging *jihad* against the infidels.[15]

Indeed, an able Saljuk military commander Alp Arslán not only succeeded in routing a large Byzantine army at Manzikert (in Eastern Turkey)[16] in 1071 but also took the Byzantine emperor Romanus IV prisoner. This victory led to the gradual evacuation of the Greek population from Anatolia to the Balkans. From that time on, the Christian population of Constantinople "could look across the Bosporus and see the land of the Turks."[17] Although undoubtedly a major triumph of the Muslim arms, by that time the Muslim borderland warfare against the Christian enemy had lost its original importance for both the caliphs and their provincial governors. They were much more concerned with internal sectarian strife within the Muslim world, in particular the prolonged conflict between the Sunni caliphate of Baghdad and its Shiʻite Fatimid rival in Cairo, as discussed in Chapter 12.

But if the Muslim preoccupation with the anti-Christian *jihád* was on the wane, the idea of the Christian holy war was just beginning to emerge. In Spain, the first half of the eleventh century witnessed the rise of the reconquest movement (Span. *reconquista*) led by the kings and princes of the northern Christian states of the Iberian Peninsula that had survived the Muslim conquests. The movement's goal was to expel the "Moors" (literally, "Blacks") from the Iberian Peninsula and make it once again a Christian land. In their endeavor, the forces of the Spanish royalty were supported by their Western European coreligionists in what was essentially the first European Crusade against the Muslim states of Iberia. In 1085, Toledo, a major cultural and religious center of Muslim Spain, fell to a victorious Christian army. In 1095, Sicily was conquered by another Christian force, and its Muslim population was forced to leave. From 1098, the Spaniards and Christian volunteers from Western Europe fighting against the "Moors" of al-Andalus were granted a remission of sins by the Catholic Church, which later equated their fighting with that of the crusaders in Syria and Palestine.[18]

Around the same time, we witness the first stirrings of another crusader movement in Western Europe. Unlike the Spanish Crusade, this one had the eastern lands of Islam in its sights. Desperate to regain the former Greek lands of Anatolia lost to the Saljuk Turks after 1071, the Byzantine emperor Alexius I (r. 1081–1118) appealed for help to his Western Christian brethren. The leaders of Western Catholic Christianity responded with enthusiasm. The popes of Rome in particular immediately acknowledged the benefits of a joint military action against an external enemy as a means of reasserting the authority of the Roman Catholic Church.[19] The moment was propitious for a number of reasons. Following a century of fratricidal warfare, Europe was teeming with armed men. Led by kings, princes, barons, and petty knights, they were fighting one another, wrecking havoc on the economy and social order of the land. The Catholic Church's desperate efforts to achieve reconciliation among the belligerents by instituting the "Peace of God" or, at the very least, the "Truce of God" had proved largely unsuccessful: The fratricidal bloodshed and rapine continued unabated.[20] Under these circumstances, drastic measures were needed to harness the bellicose energies of the European nobility and their private armies.

Emperor Alexius's appeal for help provided a common cause that the Catholic Church could now use to unite the militant and mutually hostile European noblemen and to channel their destructive energies outside Europe. In 1095, Pope Urban II publicly proclaimed a holy war against the "Saracens" at the Council of Clermont, in southern France. The war's stated goal went beyond the liberation of the Anatolian lands that the Saljuk Turks had recently wrested from the Byzantine Christians. The European Christians had not forgotten that many areas of the Muslim world comprised the lands that had once "belonged to Christendom." Now they wanted them back. So the Pope had no trouble justifying the impending war against the Muslims by the necessity to reconquer the Holy Land, the land of Christ and his apostles, for Christianity. He declared,

"Jerusalem, the holy city revered in the Scriptures, where Christ walked, preached, died and was resurrected," to be the ultimate object of what can be described as an armed pilgrimage to the Holy Land sanctioned and encouraged by the Catholic Church.[21] In his 1095 speech, Urban II made the following emotional appeal to his flock:

> They [the Muslim Turks] have completely destroyed some of God's churches and they have converted others to the uses of their own cult. They ruin the altars with filth and defilement. They circumcise Christians and smear the blood from the circumcision over the altars. . . They are pleased to kill others by cutting open their bellies, extracting the end of their intestines, and tying it to a stake. Then, with flogging, they drive their victims around the stake until, when their viscera have spilled out, they fall dead on the ground. They tie others, again, to stakes and shoot arrows at them; they seize others, stretch their necks, and try to see whether they can cut off their heads with a single blow of naked sword. And what shall I say about the shocking rape of women?[22]

Bishops and priests spread the Pope's inflammatory message far and wide, triggering an outburst of popular indignation at the alleged Muslim depredations in the Holy Land. Crowds of men—nobility, peasants, and townsfolk—hurried to enlist in crusader units by making a confession and an oath of allegiance to the cause of liberating the Holy Land from the infidel enemy in a ceremony known as the "taking of the cross." The slogan "God wills it!" rang out across the land.[23] The crusaders viewed themselves simultaneously as pilgrims, penitents, liberators of the Holy Land, and warriors for Christ.[24] To persuade those still hesitant about the necessity of warfare in the name of Christ, a thirteenth-century preacher argued: "But someone says, 'The Muslims have not hurt me at all. Why should I take the Cross against them?' But if he thought well about it, he would understand that the Muslims do great injury to every Christian."[25]

In the medieval papal propaganda, the presence of Muslims in the Holy land was depicted, somewhat incongruently, as an "existential" threat to every faithful Christian and his household. Nevertheless, the would-be "warriors of Christ" (*militia Christi*) found such argumentation persuasive. As an incentive, the Pope promised them protection of property at home, new lands in the East, plenary indulgencies for future sins, and a total remission of Church punishments for past sins. His audience must have heard this as a promise of absolution from sin and guarantee of salvation. Heady enthusiasm resulted. Motives behind this massive Christian military expedition to the Near East were complex and variegated: papal politics aimed at controlling Europe's secular rulers and nobility; Europe's demographic pressures; European inheritance laws under which only the eldest son could inherit, leaving his younger siblings without any means to support themselves other than plunder and fighting; pious zeal and idealism generated by the Pope's fiery appeal; as well as an unscrupulous calculation of their personal material advantages by some more pragmatically minded "pilgrims in arms." In other words, different people were driven by different motives: some by greed, others by desire to win glory and martyrdom in the battlefield, and still others by the hopes of securing a place in Paradise by vanquishing the enemies of Christian faith and returning the Holy Land to Christianity. There were probably also those who were motivated by the expectation of an impending apocalypse and the second coming of Christ, which had always been associated with the holy city of Jerusalem.[26]

Militarily speaking, the task of the crusaders was facilitated by the political fragmentation of the Muslim world, on the one hand, and, on the other, the control of the Mediterranean Sea by the fleets of Italian city-states Genoa and Venice. The process of Muslim political fragmentation was at its worst in Syria and Upper Iraq, where almost every important town had an independent military ruler, an *amír*. Most of the *amír*s were Turks from Central Asia, who, together with their tribal followers, had migrated to the Middle East and formed a sort of professional military class there.

Able and hardened warriors, the *amir*s were extremely jealous of one another and therefore unable to unite even in the face of the grave threat posed by the impending foreign invasion. When the crusading armies swept in upon their lands in the late eleventh century, the *amir*s could plan no unified defense. Each tried to hold out in his own fortified town in the hopes that the storm would blow over.[27] This was not to be. One by one, the Muslim cities of Syria and Palestine fell to the crusaders. In an apt remark of a British historian, the crusaders found themselves "charging through a gate which was already off its hinges."[28] In a stark contrast to the Muslim weakness and disunity, the crusaders showed themselves "to be strong and determined, vibrant with fanaticism and highly motivated to build structures of defense which would ensure their continuing presence in the Levant."[29]

As already mentioned, the First Crusade started in 1095 with the Pope's speech at Clermont and ended with the conquest and sack of Jerusalem by the crusader army in 1099. The crusader fighting units were a motley arrangement of Christian knights (nobles) and peasant and urban levies from France, England, and the Germanic lands. They arrived in Anatolia in several waves. The first wave of the crusader movement was led by fiery preachers and popular leaders such as Peter the Hermit and Walter Sansavoir ("Have-Nothing" or "Penny-less"). Ill-equipped and undisciplined, this avant-garde consisted mainly of poorly trained commoners inspired by the sermons of their priests and led by a relatively small group of petty nobles. The members of this "Peasants' Crusade," as it came to be known in Western chronicles, were eager to take on the Muslim enemy and refused to wait until the arrival of the more organized and disciplined troops of the crusading noblemen. Infused with pious zeal, they rushed unprepared into the enemy territory across the Strait of Bosporus, only to be mercilessly massacred by the cavalry of a Turkic *amir* in rural Anatolia.

The second wave of the Crusades consisted for the most part of European nobles and thus has come to be known as the "Barons' Crusade." This fighting force took much longer to assemble and equip, hence the delay in its arrival at the theatre of operations, which, as we have just seen, cost its "peasant" forerunner dearly. Much better organized, disciplined, and combat ready, the army of European noblemen waged a series of bloody battles in Anatolia and Syria against individual Turkic *amir*s, ensconced in their fortified cities. After much suffering and heavy losses, the crusader army managed to seize several important Muslim strongholds in Anatolia and Syria, including Edessa, Antioch, and Tripoli. In 1099, a joint force of the crusading barons besieged and conquered Jerusalem, putting its multiethnic and multiconfessional population to the sword. According to a Muslim chronicle, the conquerors killed "more than 70,000, a large number of them being imams, ulema, righteous men and ascetics."[30] The victorious crusaders looted Muslim sanctuaries, including the celebrated Dome of the Rock, taking booty "beyond counting."[31]

The Byzantine Empire benefited from the zeal and sacrifice of their warlike Western European brethren by regaining some of the territories it had lost to Central Asian Turkic tribes in Anatolia (see Map 19.1). Once this goal was successfully accomplished, the Byzantine emperor tried to bring the crusaders under his control. However, the latter refused to take orders from anyone except the Pope. Jealous of one another, the barons and princes of the First Crusade went about carving out independent fiefdoms for themselves in Anatolia and Syria. As a result, in the aftermath of the conquest, the crusader domains in Syria fragmented into a group of the so-called "Latin principalities,"[32] the Kingdom of Jerusalem being the largest of all. Ignoring the fate of the disunited Turkic *amir*s whom they had just defeated, crusader princes failed to form a strong centralized state. On the contrary, in their mutual feuding, some "warriors of Christ" had no compunctions about allying themselves with local Muslim rulers against their Christian rivals. Supported by the fleets of the Italian city-states, the crusaders were able to hold the major ports along the Mediterranean coast in Syria and Palestine, thereby securing supply routes and constant communication with their European homeland. In the decades that followed, Italian ships brought

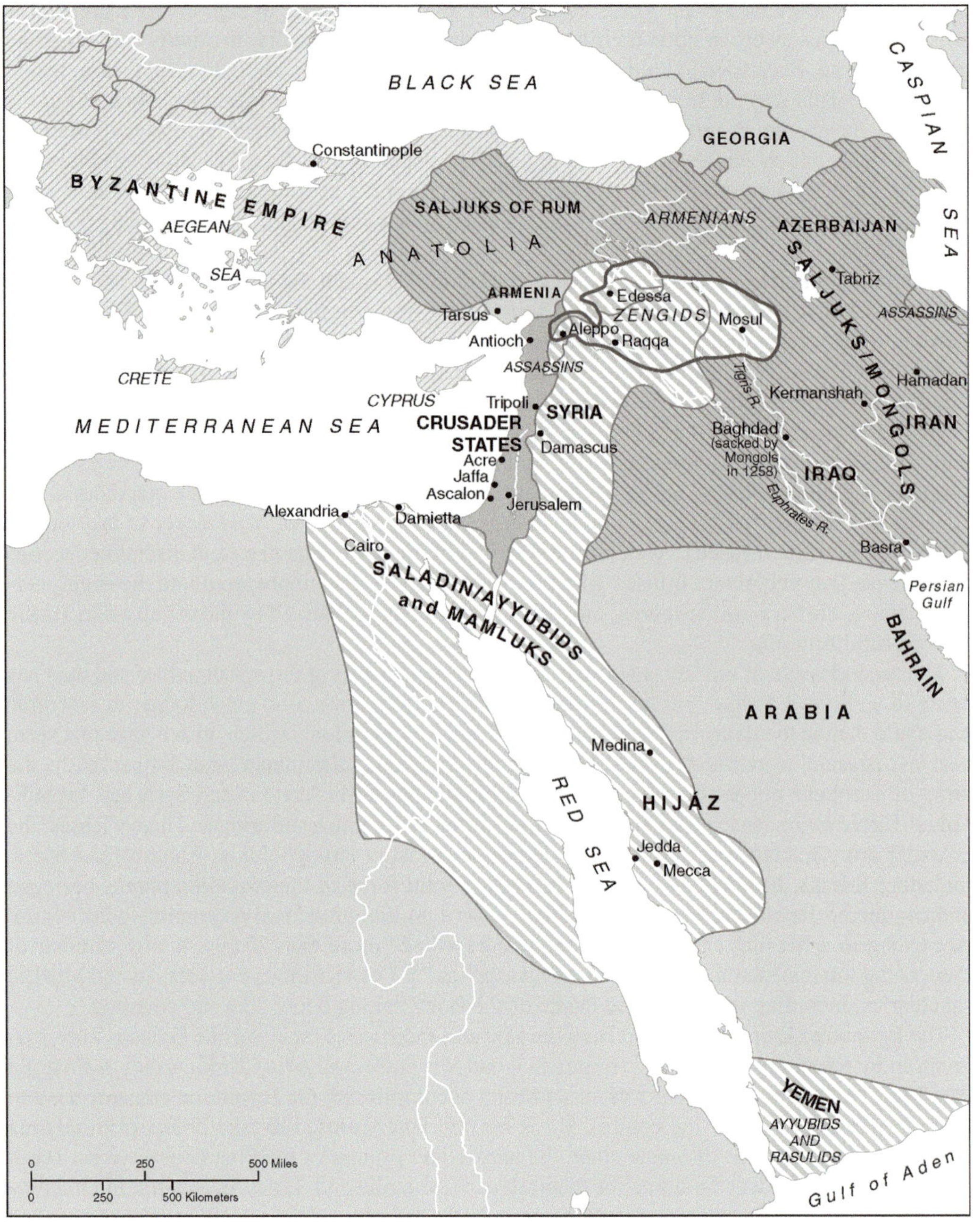

Map 19.1 The Middle East at the Time of the Crusades (eleventh–thirteenth centuries)

new detachments of crusading nobles and commoners inspired by the Pope's message of protecting the Holy Land from the Muslim enemy.

After the Christian conquest of Jerusalem in 1099, the region saw the emergence of the first military orders, in which "monastic discipline and martial skills were combined for the first time in the Christian world."[33] These institutions brought the idea of the Crusade to its logical conclusion by asserting the notion of "a knighthood dedicated to God."[34] Fiercely loyal to the idea of "new chivalry," the warrior monks of the Knights Templar (Templars)[35] and of the Hospital of St. John of Jerusalem (Hospitallers) proved to be a formidable and implacable enemy of Islam. Muslim warriors considered them to be "the most wicked of all the infidels"; if captured on the battlefield, the fighting monks were most likely to be executed.[36] In Europe itself, however, "the concept of members of a religious order . . . riding out to shed blood" did not receive universal acceptance. Writing in the first decade of the twelfth century, a French abbot raised the following objection to this combination of militancy and monasticism:

> It is useless attacking external enemies if we do not conquer those within ourselves . . . [F]irst purge our souls of vices, then the lands from the barbarians.[37]

Interestingly, similar misgivings about military action in the name of religion were expressed by Muslim Sufis, who viewed the internal, "greater *jihád*" against their lower souls and their carnal appetites to be superior to waging war against an external enemy in the so-called lesser *jihád*. Yet this was definitely a minority opinion on both sides. Voices of peace were drowned by war cries and the rattling of swords. St. Bernard, abbot of Clairvaux, who was one of the primary instigators of the Second Crusade (1146–1148), addressed the would-be crusaders as follows:

> Go forward then in security, knights, and drive off without fear the enemies of the Cross of Christ, certain that neither death nor life can separate you from the love of God which is Jesus Christ. . . . How glorious are those who return victorious from the battle! How happy are those who die as martyrs in the battle! Rejoice, courageous athlete, if you survive and are victor in the Lord; but rejoice and glory the more if you die and are joined to the Lord![38]

As a reward, fallen crusaders were "freed from both venal and mortal sins and from all enjoined penance, absolved from the penalties for sin in this world, from the penalties of purgatory in the next, secure from the torments of Gehenna, crowned with glory and honor in eternal beatitude."[39] Motivated and inspired in this way, the crusaders proved to be a formidable adversary. Their fighting units carried everything before them.

Despite their initial hostility to all things Muslim, many crusaders residing permanently in the East gradually became assimilated culturally and socially into local life. They made little contribution to it, though, with the possible exception of military architecture. On the other hand, their constant quarrels and duels of honor, in addition to their lack of elementary hygiene and medical skills, struck their Muslim opponents as well as local, "Oriental" Christians as crude and ridiculous. A Muslim observer recounted the following anecdote about the Frankish pastimes in Palestine:

> The cavaliers went out to exercise with lances. With them went out two decrepit, aged women whom they stationed at one end of the race course. At the other end of the field they left a pig which they had scalded and left on a rock. They then made the two aged women run a race while each one of them was accompanied by a detachment of horsemen urging her on. At the every step they took, the women would fall down and rise again, while the spectators would laugh. Finally, one of them got ahead of the other and won that pig for a prize.[40]

Satirical as this picture may appear, it definitely captures a typical Muslim revulsion at the crusader presence in their midst. In Muslim chronicles of the age, Frankish knights were depicted as cruel, uncultured brutes, incapable of any refined sentiment or intellectual discourse. Christian men were not the only object of condemnation and ridicule in Muslim accounts. Muslim writers of the age routinely accused Frankish women of promiscuity and loose sexual morals, going around unaccompanied by their male relatives or chaperons, and flirting with strange men oftentimes even in the presence of their husbands. This behavior was viewed by Muslim observers as a gross moral abomination. "[May] God protect us from the seductions of [their] sight," exclaimed one of them. At the same time, one cannot say that Muslim depictions of Frankish women were uniformly negative. Some Muslim writers were fascinated by their beauty ("A Frankish woman captivated me," confessed one of them), whereas others admired their martial skills ("They wear men's garb and they are prominent in the thick of the fray," mused another).[41]

The Muslims, for their part, took great pride in the skills of their doctors (who could be either Muslim or local, that is, "Oriental" Christian), which they compared favorably with what they considered to be the crude and primitive medicine of the Franks. Muslim sources provide vivid descriptions of how a simple amputation would result in the painful death of a patient at the hands of an ax-wielding Frankish quack. The same Frankish "doctor's" attempt to exorcise the devil out of a poor, sick woman would end in her quick and agonizing demise.[42]

On the other hand, the Frankish knights who had resided in the Levant for a long time were often fascinated by the refinement of local culture and occasionally strove to imitate it. Some European settlers even "went native," adopting elements of Muslim costume, way of life, and cuisine. A few even learned to speak Arabic.[43] Less open-minded newcomers from Europe often found the "Islamic" behavior and dress of the long-time European residents of the Holy Land to be disgusting and accused them of secretly converting to Islam. As one can expect, the Muslims felt much more affinity with the "Orientalized" Franks who had learned to respect their customs, while being more wary of the new arrivals, who were not only were ignorant of their way of life but also tried to forcibly convert them to Christianity.[44]

The Muslims Strike Back

By the mid-twelfth century, some farsighted Muslim rulers had begun to overcome their parochial quarrels and to form a unified front against the crusader states. The most prominent among them was *amír* Zengi, son of a Turkic slave officer in the service of the Saljuk dynasty, who became ruler of Mosul, in Upper Iraq, in 1127. An able general, Zengi managed to expand his domains and to muster enough resources to launch a concerted assault on the crusader positions in Anatolia and Syria. In 1144, he wrested Edessa from Frankish rule, an event that had long-ranging repercussions across Christian Europe. Zengi astutely sought to cultivate the Muslim *'ulamá'* in his domain with a view to securing their ideological support of his campaigns against the crusaders. The *'ulamá'* obliged by declaring Zengi to be the divinely appointed liberator of the Muslim lands and "tamer of the infidels and the polytheists."[45] Zengi's son Nur al-Din, who had received the city of Aleppo as his inheritance, proved to be even more successful than his father in his fight against the crusaders. Nur al-Din managed to recapture several major crusader strongholds in Syria and Palestine. Simultaneously with his war effort, Nur al-Din launched a vigorous propaganda campaign against the Frankish invaders, appealing to the religious sentiment of the Levantine Muslims. He presented his fight against the crusader states as part of an all-out, universal *jihád* against the vicious, infidel enemy. To bolster his Islamic credentials, he led a pious and frugal life and "founded numerous schools, mosques and Sufi convents."[46] His propaganda campaign against the Franks was not long in bearing fruit. In 1154, the population of Damascus expelled their Muslim ruler who had cooperated with the crusaders and invited Nur al-Din to take over the city and to lead them in their struggle against the crusaders.

Zengi's and Nur al-Din's victories prompted Pope Eugenius III to issue a bull calling upon Europe's nobility to "defend the eastern Church."[47] This papal call ushered in the Second Crusade (1146–1148). Led by the kings of Germany and France, it proved to be a military disaster. After losing thousands of knights in Anatolia, the remains of the crusader force departed for Europe, leaving Nur al-Din as strong as never before. After Nur al-Din's death in 1174, the leadership of the *jihád* passed on to his able lieutenant in Egypt, Saláh al-Din (Saladin), who had taken control of that rich country and put an end to Fatimid rule there in 1171. Like Nur al-Din, Saladin launched a vigorous propaganda of *jihád* against the Christian invaders. He abolished all religiously illegitimate taxes and spent large amounts of money on the construction of new mosques, libraries, *mádrasa*s, and Sufi lodges. His determination to banish the crusaders from the Muslim lands knew no limits, as his biographer and friend eagerly attested:

> The Holy War and the suffering involved in it weighed heavily on his heart and his whole being in every limb; he spoke of nothing else, thought only of equipment for the fight, was interested only in those who had taken up arms, had little sympathy with anyone who spoke of anything else or encouraged any other activity.[48]

Making use of Egypt's vast resources, Saladin started a well planned military campaign against the remaining crusader strongholds in the Levant. He managed to unify the Muslims of Syria, Palestine, and Egypt under his command and to create a powerful army able to take on his Frankish adversaries. To secure spiritual support for his war effort, Saladin cultivated cordial relations with several distant Muslim rulers, including the 'Abbásid caliph in Baghdad. Although by that time a mere figurehead, the caliph still symbolized Muslim unity that Saladin endeavored to recreate within his realm. Eventually, Saladin's efforts paid off handsomely. His army eliminated a major crusader force at the Battle of Hattín in Northern Palestine (see Figure 19.2). Building on this

Figure 19.2 Saladin and Guy de Lusignan After the Battle of Hattín in 1187
Said Tahsine/Public Domain/Wikimedia Commons

momentous victory, he managed to reconquer Jerusalem in 1187. After this victory, the crusader presence in the Holy Land was reduced to a few seaport towns. The loss of Jerusalem came as a great psychological blow to the Christian powers of Europe. Once again the Pope issued a call to the cross. A joint expedition of the kings of France and England managed to make significant gains by conquering the strategic port of Acre on the coast of the Mediterranean Sea. This conquest secured the Frankish presence in Palestine for another century. Richard the Lionheart's exploits in Palestine became the stuff of legend in medieval Europe.[49] Nevertheless, Jerusalem, the principal objective of the Third Crusade (1189–1192), remained in Muslim hands. Legends emphasize the differences in personalities between the English king Richard the Lionheart and Saladin. Richard's treacherous behavior (especially his massacre of the garrison of Acre in 1191 in violation of the promise of safe passage he had made to the defenders of the city) contrasted sharply with Saladin's magnanimity toward the vanquished enemy. In the words of a modern Western historian, Saladin's "moral superiority . . . was acknowledged in his own lifetime by his enemies, the Crusaders" and, in Europe, "his image. . . remained unsullied, even romanticized."[50]

After Saladin's death in 1193, his domains were divided among his relatives, who continued his *jihád* policies until 1250, when Saladin's dynasty was replaced, first in Egypt and later also in Syria, by the commanders of the slave soldier corps, known as Mamluks. It was a Mamluk general, the fearsome Baybars (d. 1277), and his immediate successors who made Saladin's dream come true by expelling the remaining crusaders from the Levant at the end of the thirteenth century. There were a number of later Crusades, including two led by the pious French king Louis IX (1214–1270), later canonized by the Catholic Church as St. Louis. Unlike the previous Crusades aimed at reconquering or protecting the Holy Land, king Louis's campaigns targeted North Africa, first Egypt and later Tunisia. Idealistic and chivalrous, he believed that, after conquering Egypt from its Muslim rulers, he would be able to exchange it for the Holy Land. This was not to be. Both his Crusades ended in disaster with St. Louis dying of a virulent disease in Tunis in 1270.[51]

In the meantime, a powerful Turkic dynasty emerged in northwestern Anatolia. Named after its founder Osman (Ottoman), his descendants set about conquering large swaths of the Balkan Peninsula from its Christian rulers. The Ottoman sultan Murád decisively defeated a Serbian army at the Battle of the Kosovo Field in 1389. When his successor set his sights on Hungary and Austria, a Crusade against the Ottoman Turks was declared in response to the plea from the Christian king of Hungary. Filled with chivalrous and religious zeal, the crusading European knights were confident of their victory. However, their lack of discipline and haughty disregard for their Muslim opponents proved to be their undoing. In September 1396, a joint force of the Hungarian king and of the French and German crusaders suffered a devastating defeat at the hands of the Ottoman army led by the sultan Bayazid I at the Battle of Nicopolis (Hungary). Eventually, the Ottomans managed to conquer the entire Balkan Peninsula, while also extending their rule to the Maghrib and the Middle East, including the Holy Land. The last Byzantine stronghold, Constantinople, fell to the army of the Ottoman sultan Mehmed II in 1453. With Ottoman military ascendancy undisputed, the hopes of recovering Jerusalem for Christendom faded. There were a number of later Crusades against the Ottomans around the Mediterranean and in the Balkans, but they were relatively minor events that lie outside the scope of this book.

The Legacy of the Crusades

For the medieval European Christians, the Crusades were acts of piety and penitence that intricately (and some would say incongruently) combined elements of military campaign and pilgrimage.[52] The Europeans viewed them as God's instrument in spreading Christian religious values, culture, and way of life. Initially successful, with time the Crusades lost their appeal to the populations of Western Europe, who no longer identified themselves first and foremost as loyal members of the body of Christ symbolized by the Papacy and the Catholic Church. By the mid-seventeenth century, European countries aligned themselves along political and dynastic lines rather than the Christian doctrines and papal authority that had played such a critical role in setting in motion the first crusades. As a result, the crusader ideals had lost their allure to the new generations of European rulers and nobility. Wars were now waged in the name of royal dynasties and territorial states associated with them rather than religion per se. Yet the powerful symbolism of holy war in the name of religion has persisted until today in both Europe and the Middle East.

In hindsight, it is easy for us to dismiss the Crusades as morally repugnant and intrinsically evil—a long act of intolerance and violence in the name of Christ. However, we should keep in mind that the infinitely more destructive and devastating wars in twentieth-century Europe were waged in the name of the political and social ideologies that the crusaders would probably have found pathetic, perhaps even ludicrous. Nor would the crusaders appreciate the pragmatic and ideological reasons behind the more recent military conflicts in the Muslim world instigated by the Western powers and their local allies. Should we, for a moment, step back and cast a dispassionate look at the wars waged in the name of either religion, the nation, or some broader geopolitical and economic objectives, we shall find out that, in any society, be it medieval or modern, people fight and sacrifice their lives for that which is most dear to them and that which, they believe, transcends their earthly existence. That is a fact of human nature that is not so changeable across time and space. One can put one's trust in the idea of liberating the Holy Land of an "infidel enemy" and restoring it to Christianity, Judaism, or Islam. In choosing this course of action, one can present one's actions as doing the will of God. Or one can set about spreading one's own values and principles in the name of freedom and democracy because one holds them to have universal value and applicability. Unfortunately, as history teaches us, regardless of the justification, the end result is likely to be the same: war, mayhem, and human suffering.

As we remember, in addition to the conquest of the Holy Land, the original aim of the crusaders was to help their fellow Christians of the Byzantine Empire as well as the Middle Eastern Christians who lived under Muslim rule. Ironically, after all the great sacrifices and bloodshed, this aim was not achieved. The sack of Constantinople by the marauding European knights of the Fourth Crusade in 1204 closed an iron door between the Catholic West and the Orthodox East. One can even argue that, as a result, the Byzantine Christians eventually preferred Ottoman Turkish rule to union with the Roman Papacy. The two churches parted ways and have not reconciled to this day. In the meantime, the lot of the Christian communities living under Muslim rule was not improved by the Crusades. In fact, it deteriorated drastically as they came to be seen by their Muslim overlords as the fifth column in the Abode of Islam, ever ready to join forces with the Frankish invaders. Persecutions and pogroms ensued, and various humiliating and onerous restrictions were imposed by Muslim rulers on their Christian subjects.

The Founder of Islam and His Message in the Eyes of His Followers and Through the Christian Looking Glass

After examining the political, military, and cultural aspects of the Muslim–Christian interaction during the premodern epoch, we should address their ramifications in modern times. The Prophet and his message, the Qur'an, being the fulcrum of Islamic faith, it is only natural that they have become a prominent theme of both Christian theological polemic and popular prejudice against Islam.

While the Qur'an and the Prophet himself never tire of insisting that he was but an ordinary human who was selected by God to deliver the last divine revelation to humankind—his main miracle, his status as the founder of the Muslim religion and later also the leader of the first Muslim polity in Medina, has rendered him, for his followers, a perfect human being. Indeed, according to the Muslim creed, Muhammad is the chosen one of God (*mústafa*), the praiseworthy (*áhmad*), and the best of all creatures (*khayr al-baríya*). Muslim poets have compared him to a cloud of mercy freely dispensing blessings on his followers.[53] Many other beautiful images of the Prophet abound in Muslim literature and folklore.[54] The Prophet being the exemplar, his every action and gesture should be imitated by pious Muslims. As we know, the affirmation of Muhammad's prophetic mission constitutes an essential part of the Islamic declaration of faith, the *shaháda*, alongside the proclamation of the unity and uniqueness of God. Therefore, any verbal attack on his dignity constitutes a grave offence against Islam that demands capital punishment for the culprit under the Shari'a law.

As a dramatic example of the Prophet's centrality to the Muslim faith and identity, one can cite the story of the so-called "martyrs of Cordova" in Islamic Spain. In the mid-ninth century, several dozen Spanish Christians living under Muslim rule were executed by the local Muslim authorities for publicly cursing and denigrating the Prophet.[55] It should be pointed out that the Muslim judges presiding over these cases of anti-Muslim blasphemy repeatedly asked the accused to retract their scandalous pronouncements. Nevertheless, the latter persisted, seeking martyrdom in the name of the Christian faith and duly received it. Although rare, such trials and occasional executions continued in the subsequent centuries (and not only against Christian culprits but Muslim heretics as well).

With time, the special place of the Prophet in Muslim piety came to be marked by a special holiday commemorating his birthday (*máwlid*)[56] and his miraculous night journey to Jerusalem, followed by his ascension through seven heavens into the presence of God.[57] Throughout the Middle Ages and beyond, miracle narratives about the Prophet gained wide circulation among the Muslim masses. Some of these stories were based on Qur'anic allusions, such as the aforementioned "night journey and ascension" (Q 17:1), the miracle of "the splitting of the moon" (Q 54:1), and the miracle of the opening of the Prophet's breast by the angels (Q 94:1–2). Much more numerous are the Prophet's miracles described in *hadíth* literature and in his biographies that began to appear from the mid-eighth century on. They portray Muhammad as a miracle worker on a par with the other major Biblical prophets: His washing water emanated blessings; his touch had rejuvenating and curing effects (for instance, he could milk a barren ewe); his companions occasionally observed a cloud hovering over his head to protect him from the intense heat of the Arabian sun; pebbles in his hand and the walls of his house greeted him; a shoulder of a lamb that was served to him for dinner warned him that it was poisoned by a Jewess; he was loved and missed by inanimate objects, for instance, the trunk of the tree against which he used to lean while preaching in Medina; animals loved him too—a cat saved him from a venomous snake, while a wolf and a lizard attested to his prophetic mission.[58] After his death, the mere act of blessing him was believed by his admirers to bring miraculous results, as numerous popular stories from different areas of the Muslim world eloquently attest.[59] The reverence and admiration for Muhammad was not confined to popular storytelling and folklore. In Muslim theological discourses, he is depicted as combining in his persona the character traits and functions of all previous prophets: He exemplified, simultaneously, the uncompromising monotheism of Abraham, the stern, warlike, and law-focused leadership of Moses, the gentle kindness and meekness of Jesus, and so on.

This is not how the prophet Muhammad was viewed by medieval European Christians. For them, his teaching, as well as the community of faith he founded, represented both a doctrinal challenge and a grave, almost existential danger. Their response was quite predictable. In the words of a contemporary Western scholar:

> Under the pressure of their [Christians'] sense of danger, whether real or imagined, a deformed image of their enemy's beliefs takes shape in men's minds. By misapprehension and misrepresentation, a notion of the ideas and beliefs of one society can pass into the accepted myths of another society, in a form so distorted that its relation to the original facts is sometimes barely discernable.[60]

Let us examine how medieval Christians perceived the prophet Muhammad and his message. His rapid rise to prominence and the subsequent political and military success of his followers called for an explanation. While Christian explanations were for the most part negative or hostile, they differed depending on the audiences to which they were addressed. Recent studies have shown that European Christian scholars had access to relatively accurate information about the Prophet's career and teachings. They acquired it from the Christians living under Muslim rule both in Islamic Spain and in the Muslim East, especially in Syria, Palestine, and Asia Minor.[61] In the eighth and ninth centuries, when the powerful Muslim armies were on Europe's doorstep, European reactions to Islam and its prophet were usually ones of fear and rejection. Among the Christian clergy (namely, monks, canons, and theologians), we find at least a modicum of knowledge about the Prophet's life and teaching. However, they consistently and deliberately distorted this knowledge to demonstrate to their audiences that Muhammad's life and actions were inconsistent with those of a true prophet. Hence the widely held image of Muhammad as either a clever and calculating imposter or a simpleton manipulated by some unscrupulous individuals in his entourage for their selfish ends. Because such individuals were routinely identified by Christian polemicists as unnamed Christian heretics who had found refuge in Arabia,[62] it was concluded that his teaching was nothing but an aberrant version of Christianity.

Also popular with the Christian polemicists was the "clever imposter" thesis, according to which Muhammad's initial goals had nothing to do with religion but were purely self-serving and mundane. After spending the first half his life in abject poverty and ignorance looking after other people's sheep and goats, he, by a stroke of luck, managed to marry a rich widow. This dramatic change of fortunes allegedly whetted his appetite for high social stature and leadership. He satisfied it by contriving a new religious teaching and presenting it to his followers as a divine revelation. By using his poetic skills, Muhammad managed to dupe the credulous Arabs into accepting him as their political leader. In this view, Muhammad's prophesy was nothing but the elaborate hoax of an unscrupulous charlatan.[63]

Such hostile depictions of Muhammad's prophetic career pervaded medieval Christian literature and, with time, acquired more and more fanciful and scandalous details. Some Christian authors described the Muslim prophet as a magician who enchanted a rich lady from a country named "Corozan." By marrying her, he came into the financial capital that he astutely used to entice his native tribe into accepting him as the leader. He then went about performing false miracles to convince his uncouth and gullible audience of the divine origin of his message. For instance, according to one polemical account, Muhammad trained a dove to eat a grain of corn from his ear, claiming that it was the Holy Ghost or an angel dictating divine revelations to him. A crafty manipulator, he also trained a bull to come in response to his call, "bearing the Book of Law bound to its horns."[64] Other anti-Muslim narratives depicted Muhammad as a renegade Christian priest or even as "a rogue cardinal," whose inordinate worldly ambitions drove him to apostatize and to establish a new heretical "church." In the majority of anti-Muslim treatises, the Prophet's humble origins are emphasized: He was originally a simple shepherd who rose to prominence either by a stroke of luck or by deceit.

As more information about Muhammad's prophetic career became available to Europeans through Muslim narratives or via Muslim–Christian encounters in Spain and the Middle East, the polemical ammunition of anti-Muslim polemicists—mostly Christian clergymen and monks—grew more varied and sophisticated. Muslim accounts that described the Prophet's agitated or depressed physical and psychological state at the time of his revelations were construed by his Christian detractors as evidence of his mental disease. The polemicists usually identified it as epilepsy, which effectively reduced Muhammad's revelations to the ravings of a madman. His military expeditions against the Arabian polytheists and Jews were held against him by Christian writers, who routinely described him as the "prophet of war" or the "prophet armed."[65] In attributing bellicose character traits to the Muslim prophet, his Christian critics sought to juxtapose his alleged propensity to violence with Jesus's meekness and pacifism. In their opinion, Muhammad's "militancy" was totally incompatible with the authentic prophetic mission as they understood it.

Muhammad's relationships with his wives and their number were widely exploited by Christian polemicists to impugn the Prophet's moral character. They accused him of promiscuity, lasciviousness, and an insatiable sexual appetite. Even the ostensibly positive religious precepts annunciated by the Muslim prophet became an object of Christian ridicule. Thus, the Qur'anic prohibition of alcohol was explained by his desire to punish himself for falling into a drunken stupor and thereby allowing his unruly followers to murder his Christian counselor who had dictated him his revelations. Similar derogatory stories were invented to explain the Qur'anic prohibition of the flesh of the swine.[66]

In the French *chansons de geste* (i.e., the French epic tales about the exploits of Charlemagne, composed in the twelfth–fourteenth centuries), the disparagement of Muhammad appears even cruder and evinces no concern whatsoever for historical fact. The famous French poem "The Song of Roland" ("Chanson de Roland") depicts in vivid detail the imaginary defeat of a "Saracen army" at the hands of the valiant warriors of the Frankish king Charlemagne. According to the poem, the Muslim fighters carried with them into battle an idol named "Mahumet" (or "Mahun"). When their army was routed by the Christian knights, they vented their frustration by throwing the idol into a ditch to be trampled by dogs and pigs.[67] The fact that the composition of "Chanson de Roland" coincides with the declaration of the First Crusade by Pope Urban II is hardly accidental. The poem was deliberately crafted to instill righteous indignation in the warriors of the cross by dehumanizing their Muslim adversary and by portraying Muhammad as a false god and Islam as polytheism. Inflammatory anti-Muslim rhetoric such as this helps to explain at least in part the savagery of the crusaders in the Holy Land. Faced with such a depraved and impious enemy, one could ill afford to be squeamish or magnanimous. Similar narratives, which depict Muhammad as either a god or an idol, were produced and circulated in growing quantities throughout the twelfth century. This was part of the Christian ideological warfare at the time of the Second and Third Crusades which, as we now know, were extremely bloody affairs and which were, for the most part unsuccessful, for the Christian "pilgrims in arms." In the heat of their life-and-death struggle against the Muslim enemy, the Christians of Western Europe had little concern for historical truth about Islam and its founder. As is often the case today as in the past, in times of war the opponent is reduced to a caricature.

The negative or outright slanderous images of Muhammad that were carefully assembled and disseminated in Europe by his Christian detractors during the age of the Crusades have proved extremely tenacious. Even the greatest minds of late medieval Europe were not immune from anti-Muslim bias. Thus, Dante Alighieri (d. 1321) considered the prophet of Islam to be a crafty usurper and sower of religious discord.[68] In his "Divine Comedy," he placed Muhammad and 'Ali into the ninth (and deepest) circle of Hell, where they were being lacerated by devils over and over again. For Dante, as for many of his European contemporaries, Muhammad was a vicious heresiarch, who introduced a schism into Christianity, thereby causing much bloodshed and mayhem. Hence the punishment assigned to him in the hereafter.

This is not to say that there were no attempts in medieval Europe to provide an alternative or at least more favorable image of the Prophet. The anonymous tale "Muhammad's Ladder" ("*Scala Mahomete*")—translated in the middle of the thirteenth century from Arabic into old Spanish at the order of Alfonso X the Wise, the learned king of Leon and Castile (r. 1252–1284)—accurately reproduces a traditional Muslim account of Muhammad's night journey and ascension through seven heavens into the presence of God. Brimming with fascinating details about the Prophet's encounters with the angels and prophets inhabiting the heavenly spheres, the tale contains no hostile criticism of Muhammad or his teaching. It proved to be quite popular in some circles of medieval European society and was translated into Latin and old French.

In modern times, we witness no dramatic change in the predominantly negative image of the prophet Muhammad that had formed during the European Middle Ages. Although Martin Luther considered the founder of Islam to be a lesser evil than the Catholic Pope,[69] he still viewed him as an instrument of the Devil. The majority of European authors who wrote about Muhammad in the seventeenth and nineteenth centuries repeat the already familiar medieval accusations against him as an imposter, a violent destroyer (the "prophet of murder"), and an immoral, lecherous man. At the same time, one can note a growing tendency on the part of European academics steeped in "Oriental" languages to pay much closer attention to the life and teachings of the Muslim prophet as they are depicted Muslim sources. This newly discovered interest among European "Oriental-ists" in Muhammad's historical personality was often stimulated by their efforts to provide accurate renditions of the Qur'an into European languages. Understanding its text required a considerable amount of contextual knowledge that could be found only in numerous Muslim commentaries on the sacred book of Islam and in Muslim biographies of Muhammad. The more open-minded European students of Islam were driven by a genuine desire to obtain accurate knowledge about Islam and its founder, even though it might contradict the deeply entrenched anti-Muslim stereotypes harking back to the Middle Ages. Others pursued more practical, ulterior goals. In particular, they wanted to gain a better understanding of Islamic religion in order to debate with its advocates more effectively and, with a little bit of luck, to convert them to Christianity. No wonder that the study of Islam flourished in the European clerical circles both on the European continent and in the Christian missions across the Middle East and South Asia that were established in the course of European colonization of these regions.

Nevertheless, even the most conscientious European scholars of Islam of the modern age exhibited ambiguity with regard to Islam and its prophet. On the one hand, they occasionally showed a deep appreciation of the Muslim religion, which they had developed in the course of their painstaking studies of its sources. On the other, they could not simply shake off the deeply ingrained anti-Muslim bias of European discourses about Islam and its founder. This ambivalence is aptly captured in the remarks of the famous British Arabist George Sale (1697–1736). In the introduction to his excellent (for his age) translation of the Qur'an published in 1734, he pays tribute to the negative Christian views of Islam current in his age:

> It is certainly one of the most convincing proofs that Mohammedanism was no other than a human invention, that it owed its progress and establishment almost entirely to the sword.[70]

Turning to the Prophet, Sale proceeds to argue that "Muhammad was, as the Arabs are by complexion, a great lover of women, as we are assured by his own confessions."[71] However, in the subsequent narrative, Sale qualifies his initial negative statements about the Prophet by arguing that his use of arms in self-defense "may perhaps be allowed" and that polygamy was part and parcel of social life in Arabia in his age and thus in no way unique to him. Countering the long-standing Christian view of Muhammad as an unscrupulous imposter, Sale expresses confidence that Muhammad was:

> [f]ully satisfied in his conscience on the truth of his grand point, the unity of God . . . all his other doctrines and institutions being rather accidental and unavoidable, than premeditated and designed.[72]

Placed in the historical context of the early eighteenth century, Sale's disclaimers represent what can be described as a diminution of prejudice by scholarship and an attempt by the European scholar to develop a certain level of empathy for Muhammad's "religious project." About the same time, we find the first biography of Muhammad in European literature to present him in a relatively positive light. Written by the Frenchman Boulainvillers (1658–1722), it portrayed him as a man of genius, a wise lawgiver, warrior, and statesman, whose teaching was characterized by justice, rationality, and tolerance. Such favorable depictions of the prophet of Islam by Europeans remained extremely rare, though. The writings of the founding fathers of the European Enlightenment demonstrate the same ambiguity about Muhammad's personality that we have already encountered in Sale's comments on Islam and its prophet. Thus, the great German philosopher Gottfried Leibniz (1646–1716) praised him for not deviating from what he considered the "natural religion," namely one that is in agreement with the natural disposition of human beings. Voltaire (1694–1778), who was partly influenced by Boulainvillers' positive image of Muhammad, makes contradictory statements about him. Voltaire used the story of the prophetic mission of Muhammad to disguise his condemnation of institutionalized religion as exemplified by the Catholic Church. In his famous tragedy "Fanaticism or the prophet Muhammad" (*Fanatisme, ou Mahomet le prophète*) Voltaire deliberately ignored the relatively accurate historical accounts (by that time already known to the educated European public) of the Prophet's biography, thereby implying that he had a different ax to grind than simply to slight the founder of Islam. Indeed, Voltaire's tragedy was closed after three performances in 1742; the censors quickly realized that the philosopher's intended target was not Muhammad or Islam but the authority of the Roman Catholic Church and its clergy. On the other hand, in his other writings, Voltaire pointed out Muhammad's sincerity and astute recognition of the weaknesses of human nature.[73] However, in the final account, Voltaire's deep-rooted suspicion of any organized religion as a deliberate deception of the masses by the clerics prevented him from revising the age-old negative perception of the Muslim prophet by the European public.

The nineteenth century added new nuances to Muhammad's portrait. The famous British (Scottish) philosopher and historian Thomas Carlyle (1795–1881), in his lecture "The Hero as Prophet. Mahomed" (1840), attested Muhammad's uprightness, justice, magnanimity, and personal modesty. His marriage to Khadíja, a woman much older than him, argued Carlyle, contradicted the accusation of sensuality routinely leveled at him by his European detractors. Carlyle also justified Muhammad's use of armed force to establish and defend his religion.[74] In the European and Russian poetry of that age, Muhammad was portrayed with great sympathy as a typical Romantic hero—a magnanimous and high-minded individual whom God had commissioned against his will to preach a rebirth of the human race through spirituality and justice. This is how he was seen by the great Russian poet Aleksandr Pushkin (1799–1837), who depicted Muhammad as a heroic figure commissioned by God to rescue his people from ignorance and misery. In a similar vein, the celebrated German poet and writer of the age Johann Wolfgang von Goethe (1749–1832) showed his admiration for Muhammad's genius and strength of character, which gave him power over his people. However, according to Goethe, with power came moral dilemmas, especially violence and the use of force, with which Muhammad had to wrestle throughout the rest of his prophetic mission.[75] Throughout the nineteenth century, European Romantics used Muhammad's image to explore what they considered the irresolvable conflict between a man of genius and the crowd. In short, each European writer shaped the Prophet's image according to his or her personal sociopolitical agenda. Detached from his Arabian and Islamic environment, Muhammad became a symbol of something or someone else. Thus, in a complete reversal of the old stereotypes regarding Muhammad's militancy and lasciviousness, the novel *Mohammed* written by the leftist German writer Friedrich Wolf (1888–1953) during World War I depicts Muhammad as a reclusive ascetic and advocate of nonviolence, who sought to achieve the fraternity of all humankind and to reconcile all nations.[76] Here the figure of the Muslim prophet is used in order to convey a pacifistic message at the time of a bloody European conflict.

The Scandinavian Caricatures of Muhammad and the Resurgence of Old Prejudices

How are these historical and cultural facts related to the recent scandal caused by the caricatures of the Prophet that appeared in a Scandinavian newspaper?[77] Some history might be of help in answering this question. First of all, we should remember that the earliest accounts of Muhammad's teaching and career were written by Christians who either lived under Muslim rule (in medieval Spain or the Levant and later also in Anatolia and the Balkans) or felt threatened by its impending imposition. No wonder that their portrayals of the Prophet were shaped by fear and loathing. These Christians found themselves confronted by an alien force that was animated and mobilized by a potent religious faith. Seen from this perspective, their tendency to demonize their fearsome Muslim opponent seems like a natural human reaction. Naturally, the founder of Islam, being the primary symbol of the hostile religion, was destined to bear the brunt of the fear and resentment felt by medieval European Christians. For them, casting aspersions on the Prophet's character was an effective way of discrediting Islamic religion and explaining to themselves "why they hate us."

After the Christian kingdoms and principalities bordering on the Muslim world had stemmed the Muslim advance and began to push it back, the negative stereotypes of the previous centuries became an offensive weapon, as medieval French and Spanish epic tales finely demonstrate. As in any ideological warfare, the enemy had to be disparaged and dehumanized. The image of Muhammad as a pagan idol or even a (false) god came in handy for the military leaders and ideologists of the *reconquista* and the First, Second, and Third Crusades. The absurdity of ascribing idolatrous beliefs to Islam, which emerged as an uncompromising rejection of Arab paganism, was conveniently ignored by Christian polemicists, as long as it served their ideological purpose. Fashioned under the condition of military confrontation, negative images of Islam and its prophet survived well into the modern epoch. While the idea of "Muslim idol-worship" was eventually abandoned due to its obvious inconsistency with Islam's emphasis on strict monotheism and divine transcendence, the less obvious negative stereotypes have persisted, especially during the period of the Ottoman domination of the Mediterranean and southeast Europe in the sixteenth and seventeenth centuries. As in the age of the early Muslim conquests, European Christian societies once again felt themselves threatened by a powerful and aggressive Muslim state. Several centuries of the Ottoman–European military and ideological confrontation "have scorched [historical] memory . . . indelibly."[78]

With the decline of Europe's principal nemesis, the Ottoman Empire, Western Europeans gradually began to lose their deeply held fear of Islam's military power. They could now step back to take a less prejudiced look at their Muslim opponent. Moreover, with the onset of colonialism, the European powers found themselves on the offensive and therefore in need of a more accurate picture of the beliefs and customs of the Muslims whom they sought to subjugate. Although the Age of Enlightenment produced a less biased view of Islam and its founder, the revision of Islam's and the Prophet's derogatory image by European intellectuals was still half-hearted and incomplete. The old negative stereotypes continued to weigh heavily on the minds of even the most emancipated European intellectuals, including those who specialized in the study of Islamic languages and religious beliefs (the so-called Orientalists).

Trite as it may sound, old prejudices do not die easily. The caricatures that appeared in the Danish newspaper *Jyllands-Posten* in September 2005 bear an eloquent testimony to this old wisdom. Consciously or not, the caricaturists reproduced the old polemical images dating back to the earlier stages of the Muslim–Christian confrontation. The caricatures published in Denmark and reprinted by a number of European newspapers portray the Muslim prophet as an uncouth shepherd obsessed with violence, bombs, warfare, women, and sex. Why did they appear in a European newspaper? Let us venture an explanation. Over the past few decades, the indigenous

Europeans have been acutely, even painfully aware of the growing number of Muslim immigrants in their midst. The most threatening aspect of this "peaceful occupation" of Europe by Muslim "aliens" was that they professed a different religion and adhered to a different culture. Their dress code and lifestyle were different, and so were their religious and moral-ethical values. No wonder that the newcomers often had a hard time seeing eye to eye with the members of their host societies. As a result of this cultural encounter, in the words of a Western scholar, "The phantasm of confessional peril has been resurrected in panicked predictions of a Muslim tide . . . engulfing what is still described in some quarters as Christian Europe."[79] To complicate things further, instead of "integrating" smoothly into Western societies by abandoning their religious and cultural codes, the exotic "aliens" expected those around them to respect them. Once again, the age-old enemy of "fortress Europe" was standing at its gate, albeit now unarmed but persistent in their demands for recognition. No wonder, therefore, that at least some Europeans have come to see the arrival of Muslims as a grave threat to their hard-won well-being and peace of mind, especially after the terrorist attacks of September 11, 2001 and the subsequent "Islamic" bombings and shootings in Britain and Spain (and more recently also in France, Denmark, and Belgium). In a typical Freudian scenario, the atavistic fear triggered by the specter of the old foe provoked an equally atavistic reaction. Deeply buried in the secret recesses of historical memories, the European anxieties over Islam sprang back to life. On one occasion, they transformed themselves into a series of caricatures mocking the Muslim prophet and his religion. Consciously or otherwise, they reproduced the hostile image of the Prophet and Islam that harks back to the European Middle Ages, as discussed earlier in this chapter. Using the notion of freedom of expression as a pretext, the authors of the caricatures struck at the enemy where it hurt most. The reply was not long in coming. On January 7, 2015, in Paris, four French caricaturists and seven of their coworkers paid with their lives for what they considered to be their right to express themselves freely and what their Muslim attackers interpreted as a gross blasphemy against the Prophet.[80] This explanation should, of course, be seen against the background of a broader picture. We live in an age when the overall geopolitical situation has been largely unfavorable to the Muslims. Wherever one looks, one finds Muslims who, rightly or wrongly, feel slighted, oppressed, and exploited by the West. The combination of the Muslim sense of being on the losing side of the postcommunist world order, faced as they are with the evermore self-confident, intrusive, and patronizing West, and the provocative cartoons published first in a provincial Danish newspaper and later in a French satirical weekly magazine has unleashed a whirlwind of anger among Muslims that has swept through the globe.

It is hardly surprising that the emotional outrage caused by the original "caricature scandal" played into the hands of the most radical fringes of Islamic/Islamist political activism. In April 2006, the late leader of al-Qaʻida Usáma b. (bin) Ládin (1957–2011) issued a legal ruling (*fátwa*) urging his fellow Muslims "to punish the crusader journalists who have committed horrible crimes against our Prophet Muhammad." "The *umma*," concluded Bin Ládin, "has reached consensus that he who offends or degrades the Messenger must be killed." The assassins of the French journalists, who had earlier pledged allegiance to al-Qaʻida, acted on Bin Ládin's *fátwa* despite the fact that he was no longer alive.[81]

Islamic Influences on European Culture

As we have seen, in the Middle Ages cultural exchange between the Muslim world and Europe was rather one-sided. Whereas they learned something from the Western invaders (for instance, the art of military fortification), by and large, the Muslims found very little in Frankish culture that they regarded as being worth learning and adopting. The Franks, on the other hand, were not totally averse to absorbing certain cultural practices, medical expertise, and scientific conceptions they encountered in the Middle East. For several centuries, the Abode of Islam served as a source of ideas for those Western European intellectuals who were eager to learn from Middle Easterners, despite their being predominantly Muslim and thus "infidel."[82] We have already mentioned the long-ranging influence of Muslim medical works on European medical science (especially those of Rhazes and Avicenna). The same applies to natural sciences, such as astronomy, mathematics, chemistry, and optics. In many instances, Islamic cultural and scientific influence was indirect. What was adopted was usually drastically transformed to fit local Western European conditions that were naturally quite distinct from those of the Middle East. While the Gothic arch was probably suggested by the corresponding "horseshoe" arches in Muslim buildings, the details of its construction were very different in a cathedral than they were in a mosque. Likewise, the romantic poetic tradition of traveling minstrels or troubadours[83] may have derived, at least in part, from the poetic and musical art of Islamic Spain. However, in the European context, it was drastically transformed to fit local social conventions and the predominant artistic tastes of the European nobility.[84]

As we already know, Arabic translations of Greek works on philosophy, medicine, natural sciences, and metaphysics were crucial in the revival of Greek sciences in the West. Commentaries on Aristotle's works by the great Muslim philosopher Ibn Rushd (Averroes) were studied at the first European universities in Latin translations up to the dawn of modernity. The prestige of Islamic learning among Christian scholars was very high. On the one hand, it posed a challenge to them as a product of the "infidel" culture. On the other, it served as an inspiration and motivation for them to try to outdo their Muslim counterparts. The massive presence of Arabic, Persian, and Turkish loanwords in European languages testifies to the wide range of Western arts and crafts in which Eastern influences were felt: orange, syrup, lemon, sugar, musk, muslin, guitar, lute, alcove, tariff, almanac, zenith, nadir, admiral, arsenal, amalgam, checkmate, sofa, mattress, cipher, and so on.[85] Particularly prominent, as one can see from the preceding list, were and still are astronomical terms and names of stars and constellations—a clear testimony to the flow of astronomical knowledge from the East to the West. Among other borrowings, mention should be made of numerous plants, vegetables, and flowers, but they deserve separate treatment.[86]

Yet at the same time, religious experience was rarely, if ever, shared or appreciated. As we have just seen, the overwhelming majority of Christian scholars who wrote about Islam repeated the most grotesque tales and stereotypes about the Muslim faith and its founder. These stereotypes have become deeply embedded in the Western psyche and may occasionally resurface even today, as has been shown in the previous section.

The Curious (and Inexplicable) Rise of the West

So why, one may ask, did Western Europe, at a certain stage of historical development, advance and the world of Islam fall behind? Over the past century and a half, this question has been raised by many Muslim thinkers, such as, for example, the Lebanese Shakib Arslan (1869–1946) in his book "Our Decline: Its Causes and Remedies."[87] There has been no shortage of explanations of the reasons for this "decline" in both the Muslim world and in the West. Thus, according to the great American scholar of Islam Marshall Hodgson, some modern Western writers have suggested that before the sixteenth century, the Muslim world was somehow "isolated," only to be brought into "the mainstream of history" by the Portuguese entry into the Indian Ocean around 1500. Hodgson dismisses this idea as patently incorrect, even ridiculous. If there was a mercantile and cultural "mainstream" at that age, it was the Portuguese Christians who were coming into it, not the Muslims.[88] The latter had already been in the very midst of it for centuries, engaged in trade and cultural exchange, and using sailing ships to spread Islamic beliefs and practices to the most remote areas of the world. Compared to the rather parochial culture of Christian Europe, which in the thirteenth and fourteenth centuries was, in Hodgson's estimation, still a backwater of the civilized world, Muslim civilization looked splendid and magnificent.

In the earlier period (the eighth--eleventh centuries), argues Hodgson, the overall cultural and economic superiority belonged to China, followed by India and the Muslim world, with Europe as a distant fourth. In the thirteenth--fifteenth centuries, Western European and Islamic societies were developing at roughly the same pace. At that time, we find what Hodgson calls "a three-cornered world": The Abode of Islam centered on the Indo-Persian and Mediterranean economic and cultural zones and North Africa; the Eastern cultural and economic complex in South and Southeast Asia and the Far East; and Western Europe. In that age, argues Hodgson, the Western European complex looked the least developed of the three but was growing steadily stronger until, in the sixteenth century, it began to compete on an equal footing with its rivals in the East. Prior to this, according to Hodgson, Europe was "a dark horse" in a race for global supremacy.[89] Its urban and cultural life was less advanced than that of its Eastern competitors. Its intellectual resources were less sophisticated and based, for the most part, on secondary material translated from Greek, Hebrew, and Arabic. By any standard, Europe's starting point in that global competition was much lower than that of its Eastern counterparts. This makes its subsequent cultural flowering and rapid economic and military development all the more striking. Yet even as Western Europe's ascendancy was beginning to make itself felt toward the late seventeenth century, the geographical and cultural horizons of Europe remained more limited than those of the Muslims. As Hodgson rightly points out, on the religious and cultural level, the works of the great Christian genius Thomas Aquinas (1225–1274) were being read from Spain to Hungary and from Sicily to Norway, whereas the great classics of Islamic literature, such as al-Bukhári (810–870), al-Tabári (838–923), Rumí (1207–1273), and Ibn 'Arabi (1165–1240), were perused from Spain to Sumatra and western China and from Yemen to the Volga region in present-day northern Russia. The sources and motives of Europe's strength and subsequent territorial and cultural expansion are, in the words of Hodgson, "the object of one of the most intriguing inquiries of world history."[90] Their long-ranging impact on Muslim societies will be examined in the chapters that follow.

Questions to Ponder

1 What factors prevented the Arab-Muslim armies from advancing beyond the Iberian Peninsula into southern France?
2 Draw up a list of factors that caused the rise of the crusader movement in Western Europe. Was any one cause (religious, social, demographic, etc.) decisive in motivating and launching the Crusades?
3 Consider the legacy of the Crusades in the modern world. Identify spheres of intellectual and cultural life in the Middle East and in the West in which the influence of the Crusades is still being felt most acutely?
4 Explain the reasons for the weakening and eventual downfall of the Byzantine Empire? Why, in the end, did the Christians of Western Europe fail to rescue it? Who or what was/were responsible?
5 Discuss the strategies adopted by European Christians in their ideological warfare against the Muslims. How did the Muslims respond to it?
6 How and why have Western perceptions of Islam and its prophet changed over time?
7 Discuss the factors that may have prevented Islamic civilization from successfully competing with Europe on the eve of the modern age. Who or what was responsible for the Muslim "decline"?

Summary

- The Arab-Islamic conquests of the Christian lands around the Mediterranean and the Christian resistance.
- The Muslim conquest of the Iberian Peninsula. Muslim attempts to advance northward are foiled. Charles Martel's victory over a Muslim army at the Battle of Poitier/Tours in southern France in 732 marks the end of westward expansion, while also helping the European Christians to forge the rudiments of a common (European) identity.
- The failure of the Arab-Muslim armies to capture Constantinople in the eighth century leads to a long stalemate along the Byzantine–Muslim border in northern Syria and southern Anatolia.
- The defeat of a Byzantine army by the Seljuks in Anatolia in 1071 opens the door to the colonization of Asia Minor by Central Asian Turkic tribes who have converted to Islam.
- Internecine warfare in medieval Europe and the papal attempts to put an end to it. The common enemy is found in the "Saracens." The proclamation of a holy war against the "Saracens" by Pope Urban II (1095) and the beginning of the crusader campaigns aimed at "liberating" the Holy Land.
- The ideological justification of the holy war by the Christian church authorities: Muslims are dangerous heretics who persecute the Christians under their rule and prevent European Christian pilgrims from visiting the sites of Jesus Christ's Passion in and around Jerusalem.
- The First Crusade and its participants: From the Peasants' Crusade to the Barons' Crusade. The reasons for the inability of Muslim rulers to offer an effective resistance to the Christian onslaught: They are mutually mistrustful and jealous, are militarily unprepared, and do not realize the magnitude and nature of the danger they are facing.
- The conquest and plunder of Jerusalem by the crusaders in 1099.
- The formation of the Latin principalities in the Levant (the east Mediterranean coast) leads to a clash of cultures and values in the Holy Land. The role of Christian monastic orders in sustaining the crusading zeal among the European expeditionary force. Muslim attitude toward the "warrior monks."
- The regrouping and consolidation of Muslim forces under the leadership the Zangid Turks of northern Iraq (r. 1127–1174). The declaration and methodical prosecution of a *jihád* against the Christian enemy by the Zangid *amír* Nur al-Din. Nur al-Din's propaganda campaign to promote *jihád* in an effort to unite Muslims with a view to expelling the Christian invaders from the Muslim territories.
- The rise of Saláh al-Din (Saladin) in Egypt and the success of the Muslim arms under his able generalship. Jerusalem retaken from the Christian king and his knights (1187).
- The later Crusades and Muslim response under the Mamluks and the Ottomans.
- The military, cultural, and geopolitical ramifications of the Crusades and their ideological reverberations today: Western colonial and postcolonial ventures in the Middle East and beyond are seen by both sides as a direct continuation of the medieval crusader movement.
- During the Middle Ages, the prophet Muhammad becomes the principal target of Christian ideological attacks against Islam and its followers. The repercussions of the medieval anti-Muslim polemic in today's world. The Danish and French "caricature scandals" have their consequences.
- Muslim influences on European science, culture, and theology/philosophy. Their nature and scope.
- The "sudden" rise of Europe in the seventeenth and eighteenth centuries and its consequences for the Muslim world.

Notes

1 Stephen O'Shea, *Sea of Faith: Islam and Christianity in the Medieval Mediterranean World*, Douglas and McIntyre, Vancouver and Toronto, 2006, p. 17.
2 The indigenous population of North Africa prior to the Arab conquest.
3 Present-day Spain and Portugal.
4 David Levering Lewis, *God's Crucible: Islam and the Making of Europe: 570 to 1215*, W.W. Norton, New York and London, 2008, p. 165.
5 Ibid., pp. 176–177.
6 Ibid., pp. 172–173.
7 Edward Gibbon, *The History of the Decline and Fall of the Roman Empire*, Allen Lane and Penguin Press, London, 1994, vol. 3, p. 336.
8 Lewis, *God's Crucible*, p. 173.
9 Ibid., p. 177.
10 Bernard Lewis, *The Muslim Discovery of Europe*, W. W. Norton, New York and London, 1982, p. 19.
11 Lewis, *God's Crucible*, p. 94.
12 Lewis, *The Muslim Discovery of Europe*, p. 20.
13 Lewis, *God's Crucible*, p. 172.
14 Marshall Hodgson, *The Venture of Islam*, Chicago University Press, Chicago, 1974, vol. 1, p. 292.
15 Carole Hillenbrand, *The Crusades: Islamic Perspectives*, Fitzroy Dearborn Publishers, Chicago and London, 1999, pp. 17–18.
16 This place is named "Malazgird" in Turkish sources.
17 Thomas Madden, *The New History of the Crusades*, Rowman & Littlefield, Lanham, MD, 2006, p. 5.
18 Jonathan Riley-Smith, *What Were the Crusades?* Ignatius Press, San Francisco, 2002, pp. 16–17.
19 Hillenbrand, *The Crusades*, p. 20.
20 Madden, *The New History of the Crusades*, p. 6.
21 Ibid., p. 8.
22 Ibid., pp. 8–9.
23 Ibid., p. 9.
24 Christopher Tyerman, *God's War: A New History of the Crusades*, Harvard University Press, Cambridge, MA, 2006, p. 65.
25 Riley-Smith, *What Were the Crusades?* p. 24.
26 For a helpful analysis of the numerous motives and forces behind the Crusades, see Norman Housley, *Contesting the Crusades*, Blackwell, Oxford, 2006, pp. 1–23.
27 Hodgson, *The Venture*, vol. 2, p. 264.
28 Riley-Smith, *What Were the Crusades?* p. 15.
29 Hillenbrand, *The Crusades*, p. 21; the Levant is one of the names of the eastern Mediterranean coast.
30 Donald Richards (trans.), *The Chronicle of Ibn al-Athir for the Crusading Period*, Ashgate, Aldershot, UK, 2006, p. 21.
31 Ibid., p. 22.
32 Named so because they used Latin as the language of communication and worship.
33 Madden, *The New History of the Crusades*, p. 47.
34 Ibid., p. 48.
35 Their headquarters was based on the site of the Jewish temple in Jerusalem, hence their name.
36 Hillenbrand, *The Crusades*, p. 335.
37 Tyerman, *God's War*, p. 256.
38 Riley-Smith, *What Were the Crusades?* p. 65.
39 Ibid., pp. 64–65.
40 Hillenbrand, *The Crusades*, p. 350.
41 Ibid., pp. 347–351.
42 Ibid., pp. 352–353.
43 Ibid., pp. 351–353.

44 Ibid., pp. 333–334 and 354–355.

45 Tyerman, *God's War*, p. 272.

46 Madden, *The New History of the Crusades*, p. 63.

47 Tyerman, *God's War*, p. 274.

48 Madden, *The New History of the Crusades*, p. 69.

49 See, for instance, James Reston, *Warriors of God: Richard the Lionheart and Saladin in the Third Crusade*, Doubleday, New York, 2001.

50 Hillenbrand, *The Crusades*, p. 195.

51 Tyerman, *God's War*, p. 812.

52 Riley-Smith, *What Were the Crusades?* p. 87.

53 Annemarie Schimmel, "Muhammad. 2. The Prophet in Popular Muslim Piety," in *Encyclopedia of Islam*, 2nd ed.; online edition: http://referenceworks.brillonline.com.

54 Ibid.

55 Albrecht Noth, "Muhammad. 3. The Prophet's Image in Europe and the West. A: The Image in the Latin Middle Ages," in *Encyclopedia of Islam*, 2nd ed.; online edition: http://referenceworks. brillonline.com.

56 Celebrated on the twelfth day of the Muslim lunar month Rabi' al-awwal.

57 See Chapter 2.

58 Noth, "Muhammad. 3."

59 See, e.g., Fritz Meier, *Essays on Islamic Piety and Mysticism*. Trans. and ed. by John O'Kane and Bernd Radtke, E. J. Brill, Leiden and Boston, 1999, pp. 549–588.

60 Norman Daniel, *Islam and the West*, Oneworld, Oxford, 1997, p. 12.

61 For details see Daniel, *Islam and the West*, pp. 35–130. What follows is partly based on Daniel's book and partly on Noth's "Muhammad.3."

62 This idea is based on *sura* 16, verse 105 of the Qur'an, which alludes to an unnamed man "teaching" him.

63 Noth, "Muhammad.3."

64 Daniel, *Islam and the West*, pp. 30–31 and 52.

65 Hodgson, *The Venture*, vol. 1, pp. 185–186.

66 Noth, "Muhammad.3."

67 Trude Ehlert, "Muhammad. B. The Image in Medieval Popular Texts and in Modern European Literature," in *Encyclopedia of Islam*, 2nd ed.; online edition: http://referenceworks.brillonline.com.

68 Ibid.

69 Ibid.

70 George Sale (trans.), *The Koran, Commonly Called the Alcoran of Mohommed*. Translated from the original Arabic. With explanatory notes, taken from the most approved commentators. O. Hodgson, London, 1838, p. 38.

71 Ibid., p. 31.

72 Ibid., p. 30.

73 Ehlert, "Muhammad. B."

74 Ibid.

75 Ibid.

76 Ibid.

77 For details, see Jytte Klausen, *The Cartoons That Shook the World*, Yale University Press, New Haven, CT, 2009.

78 O'Shea, *Sea of Faith*, p. 311.

79 Ibid., p. 311.

80 Alessandro Zagato (ed.), *The Event of Charlie Hebdo: Imaginaries of Freedom and Control*, Berghahn Books, New York, 2015, passim.

81 http://www.cnn.com/2015/01/13/world/kouachi-brothers-radicalization/.

82 Some doctors and scientists whom Europeans encountered in the Levant were members of various Eastern Christian churches, that is, Copts, Greeks, Armenians, Chaldeans, and so on. There were Jewish doctors as well.

83 Some Western scholars have derived this word, incorrectly it seems, from the Arabic verb *tariba*, "to sing," "to amuse"; or from *daraba*, "to strike" and, by extension, "to play a musical instrument"; see, e.g., Roger Boase, *The Origin and Meaning of Courtly Love*, Manchester University Press, Manchester, UK, 1977, pp. 62–74 and 131.

84 For details, see Roger Savory, *Introduction to Islamic Civilisation*, Cambridge University Press, Cambridge, 1976, Chapters 11 and 12.

85 Ibid., Chapter 11.

86 Ibid.

87 Translated by M.A. Shakoor, S. Muhammad Ashraf, Lahore, 1952.

88 Hodgson, *The Venture*, vol. 2, p. 331.

89 Ibid., p. 334.

90 Ibid., p. 335.

Chapter 20

Islam in the Gunpowder Empires
The World of Islam Faces Modernity and European Colonialism

The Gunpowder Empires

The period from the early sixteenth through the early eighteenth centuries witnessed the military and political ascendancy of three Muslim Empires: the Ottomans of Turkey, the Safavids of Iran, and the Moguls of India (see Map 20.1). There were, of course, other regional Muslim powers, such as the Shaybanids of Central Asia, the Sa'dids of Morocco, the Muslim dynasties of the Indonesian Archipelago, and so on. However, their influence on the areas beyond their immediate control was relatively minor compared to the wide reach of the three Muslim superpowers. In global terms, Muslim power achieved its peak in the sixteenth century not only in the lands once controlled by the 'Abbásid caliphate but also in the Indian Subcontinent, which the latter had never managed to conquer. The Muslim dominance began to decline in the eighteenth century. Whereas the Mogul and Safavid Empires in India, Iran, the Caucasus, and Central Asia disintegrated, the Ottomans had survived but were progressively losing control over their provinces in the Balkans, Arabia, the Middle East, and North Africa to eventually become, in the words of the Russian emperor Nicholas I (r. 1825–1855), "a sick man of Europe." As their names clearly indicate, these dynastic states were named after their founders' ancestors (the Great Moguls,[1] *shaykh* Safî al-Din, and Osman respectively). The complex political, economic, military, and social history of these empires lies outside the scope of this book. We shall therefore limit ourselves to a brief survey of the religious doctrines and institutions prevalent in these Muslim societies.

The Ottomans

The Ottoman Empire originated in central and western Anatolia (in present-day Turkey) in the mid-fourteenth century from a relatively small principality that derived its distinct cultural and religious identity from being a military outpost of Turkic-speaking Muslim fighters for religion (*ghazi*s) against the frontier forces of the Byzantine Empire. Taking advantage of the military weakness of its Christian and Muslim neighbors, the Ottoman principality gradually expanded its sway to the rest of Anatolia and to the Balkans to become a major regional power. By the first decade of the sixteenth century, it had accumulated enough military power to take on the Mamluk rulers of Syria and Egypt. The Ottomans' skillful use of the recently invented cannon gave them a critical advantage over the once invincible Mamluk cavalry. Following the defeat of the Mamluks by the Ottomans, the latter took control of Egypt in 1517. The Mamluk state became history. Under the later Ottoman sultans, the empire extended its rule to North Africa, the Middle East, Arabia, and the Balkans. Parts of Eastern Europe, especially the territories of present-day Romania, Bulgaria, the republics of former Yugoslavia, and Hungary also fell under its sway.

The doctrinal foundations of the Ottoman Empire rested on a complex intertwining of several cultural, religious, and military heritages: the Mongol-Turkic tradition of Genghis Khan (d. 1227)

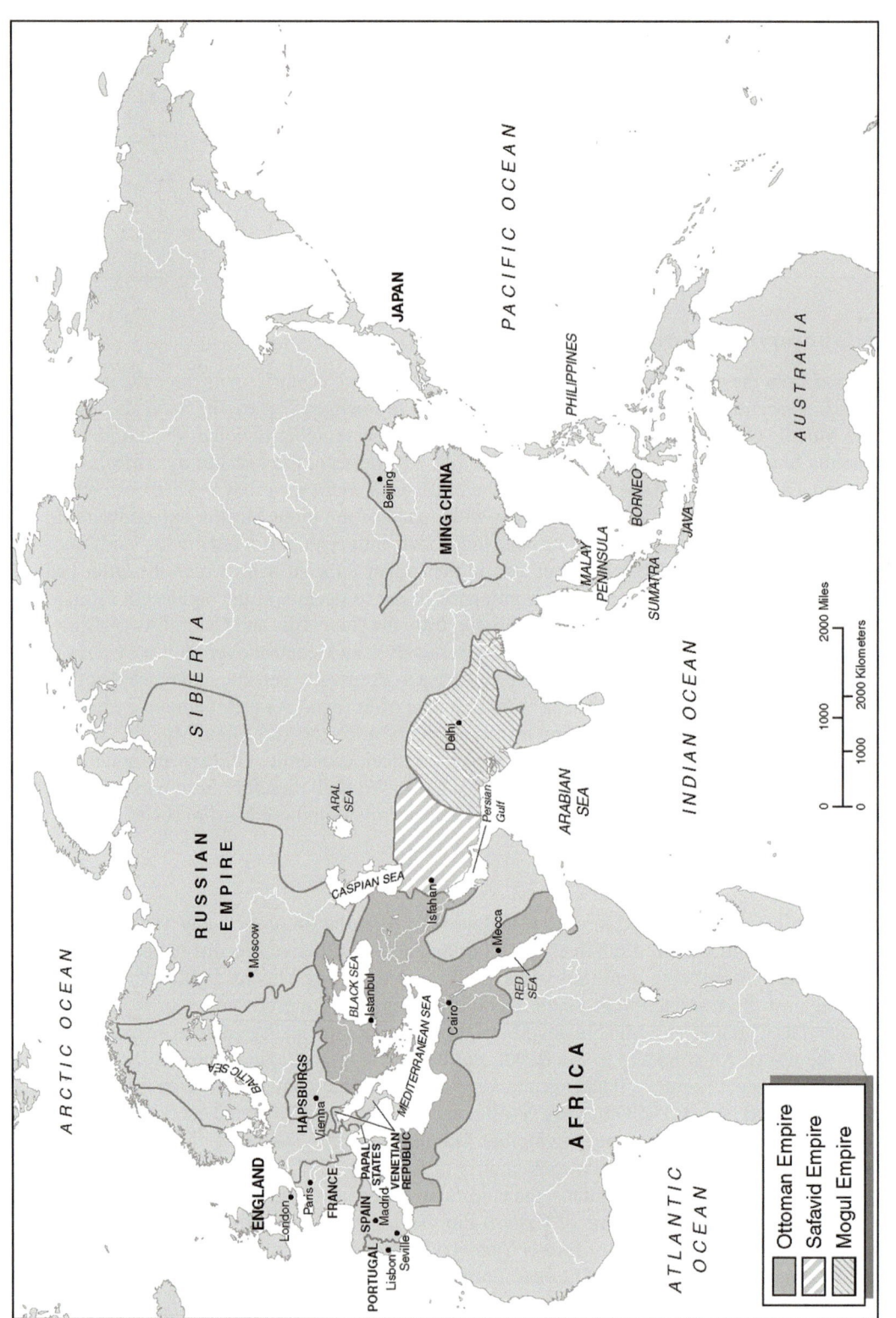

Map 20.1 The Age of the Gunpowder Empires: The Ottomans of the Middle East, Europe and North Africa; the Safavids of Persia/Iran; and the Moguls of India

and his successors, the Muslim *jihád*-oriented tradition of the frontier warriors (*ghazi*s) for the faith in Anatolia, and the Hánafi school of Islamic law that was shared by the overwhelming majority of Turkic-speaking Muslims. This combination of spiritual and legal traditions gave the Ottomans a distinct identity that served them well throughout their dominance of the Middle East, southeastern Europe, and North Africa in the sixteenth through the eighteenth centuries. The Otto-man sultans legitimized themselves simultaneously as promoters of the juridical and theological doctrines of Sunni Islam (as represented and interpreted by Sunni *'ulamá'*), as Islam's defenders against external enemies (be they the "heretical" Shi'ites of the Safavid Empire or the Christians of Byzantium and Western Europe), and, last but not least, as the restorers of the "Great Caliphate" established by the 'Abbásid dynasty.[2] As protectors of the two holy cities of Islam in Arabia, they enjoyed an additional ideological advantage over the other Muslim rulers of the age. Theirs was indeed a powerful and credible claim to Islamic legitimacy, as acknowledged by the ruler of Mecca, himself a vassal of the Ottoman Empire, in his letter to the Ottoman ruler, Suleiman the Magnificent (r. 1520–1566): "By conquering the countries of the Franks and of their likes, you are senior to us and to all the sultans of Islam."[3]

In 1453, the Ottoman sultan Mehmed II besieged and seized Constantinople, sounding the death knell for the Christian Byzantine Empire. From that time on, this city has come to be called by its Turkic name "Istanbul," allegedly coined by its conqueror.[4] Now it was, to quote a popular song, "Nobody's business but the Turks."[5] In the subsequent decades, the Ottomans managed to conquer the entire Balkan Peninsula, subjugating the local Christian princes and rendering them their tributaries and vassals. In addition to taxes in money and kind, the Ottomans imposed a special "children tax" (*devshirmé*) on their Christian subjects. The sons of Christian families col-lected under the *devshirmé* were converted to Islam, taught to speak Ottoman Turkish, trained in martial arts, and then conscripted into the Ottoman infantry. This infantry corps came to be known as the Janissaries, that is the "New Corps."

The sultans of the Ottoman Empire viewed themselves as worldwide defenders of Sunni Islam. Their principal geopolitical rival was the Safavid Empire, whose rulers and the majority of their subjects adhered to Twelver Shi'ism. The two empires engaged in a long series of wars in western Iran, the southern Caucasus, and Iraq. Despite tremendous losses in human life and materiel, neither power was able to defeat its opponent decisively. On the religious plane, each empire held its ground and derived its distinct identity from the version of Islam professed by the majority of its population—Hánafi Sunnism in the case of the Ottomans and Twelver Shi'ism in the case of the Safavids.

The Ottoman military expansion reached its peak during the reign of Sultan Suleiman the Magnificent, whose armies fought on many fronts and against a host of different enemies (see Fig-ure 20.1). In 1534, Sultan Suleiman dispatched a large army to restore Iraq to Ottoman rule. The lands of Iraq were of particular importance to the Ottoman sovereign, having once been the seat of the 'Abbásid caliphate of which the Ottoman sultans considered themselves to be the only legitimate heirs. In addition to political, economic, and military goals (such as securing access to the strategically and commercially important Persian Gulf), Suleiman's military campaigns in Iraq were driven by a religious agenda. Under the Safavids, Iraq's Sunni shrines were razed to the ground, and Sunni mosques were converted to Shi'ite places of worship. At the same time, the major Shi'ite shrines in Najaf, Kerbelá, Samarra, and Baghdad were restored, expanded, and lav-ishly endowed.[6] The Ottomans treated these actions as a major challenge to their prestige as protectors of Sunni Islam and were thus ready to go to great lengths in order expel the Safavid Shi'ites from the "'Abbasid domains" in Mesopotamia.

Suleiman's military campaigns were a success. In a symbolic gesture, after conquering Iraq and Baghdad, Suleiman ordered the demolition of the Shi'ite shrines and the restoration of Sunni holy places, shrines, and mosques. Iraq remained under Ottoman rule until 1624, when it was

Figure 20.1 Sultan Suleiman the Magnificent Hunting in Western Anatolia

reoccupied by the armies of the Safavid Shah 'Abbás, who, predictably, visited severe reprisals on Iraq's Sunnis, destroying their shrines and places of worship. Under the Ottoman sultan Murad IV (r. 1623–1640), Iraq was once again restored to Ottoman rule and remained in the Ottoman hands until World War I, when it was occupied by the British, who created the state that is now known as "Iraq" out of three Ottoman provinces: Mosul, Baghdad, and Basra.

The Ottoman wars against the Safavids over the control of the former 'Abbasid domains were motivated, at least in part by both religious and dynastic agendas. The same is true of the Ottomans' military campaigns against the Christian states of Europe. The Ottomans perceived them as a reen-actment of the centuries-old religious and military conflict that dated back to the Umayyad and 'Abbásid epochs. The difference now was that the major challenges to Ottoman power came not from the Byzantines or the crusaders but from the Portuguese on the high seas and from the Hungarians and the Habsburgs of southeastern Europe. Several Ottoman attempts to prevent the Portuguese from taking control of the Indian Ocean seafaring trade faltered due to their inferior naval capabilities. Nevertheless, the Ottomans were able to forestall the Portuguese attempts to desecrate the holy cities of Islam by attacking them from the sea. To prevent the Portuguese from landing in western Arabia, an Ottoman expeditionary force occupied Yemen in a campaign for which the Ottomans paid a very high price in lives and treasure. Nevertheless, their hold on that remote country with a fiercely independent population, both Sunni and Shi'ite, remained shaky.

The Ottomans were more successful in their struggle against the Habsburg dynasty of Austria. At one point (1529), the troops of Suleiman the Magnificent even managed to besiege its capital, Vienna, but were eventually forced to withdraw without occupying it.[7] The Ottomans were able to maintain a substantial naval presence in the Mediterranean basin until they lost the decisive naval battle of Lepanto in 1571 to a joint fleet of the Venetians and Spaniards. In 1629, another Ottoman siege of Vienna ended in failure, and in 1683–1699 the Ottomans suffered a series of major setbacks during their military campaigns against the Habsburg Empire and its European allies. As a result, they had to cede Hungary to Austria in 1699.

Under the generous patronage of Ottoman sultans, major cultural achievements were made in the fields of architecture, *belles lettres*, sciences, and the arts. The grandeur of Ottoman imperial architecture is still in evidence in the major cities of Anatolia and the Middle East. The skyline of Constantinople was transformed by the distinctive cupolas of richly decorated palaces and mosques. The giant libraries and religious colleges of the Ottoman capital housed millions of book manuscripts. The vast Ottoman realm was very diverse both ethnically and culturally. It spanned from North Africa to western Iran. Ottoman subjects came from a broad variety of ethnic, tribal, linguistic, and religious backgrounds. Its numerous ethnic and religious communities were granted a considerable degree of internal autonomy under the system of *millet* (variously translated as "religion," "confession," or "religious community"). The Ottoman *millet* system comprised such ethnic-confessional communities as Greeks, Serbs, Croats, Bosnians, Bulgarians, Armenians, Romanians, and Jews. Leaders of these religious communities were appointed by the sultan and made responsible for the collection of taxes that were then rendered to the Ottoman treasury. In return, the Ottomans' non-Muslim subjects were granted Ottoman military protection, while also enjoying considerable autonomy and freedom of worship within the confines of their respective *millet*s.

Religious sciences flourished. The Islamic law of the Hánafi legal school being the mainstay of the empire's social, domestic, and commercial life, the *'ulamá'* enjoyed great prestige and high social standing under Ottoman rule.[8] Joining their ranks required a long and arduous training and was made official only after a rigorous certification process. The Shari'a courts were fully integrated into the state's bureaucracy. In other words, the state-appointed and supported jurists were loyal servants of the imperial state. The *'ulamá'* class reproduced itself through a wide network of Islamic teaching institutions, especially Qur'anic schools, colleges (*mádrasas*), and Sufi monasteries. At the top of the complex hierarchy of religious officials stood the supreme *mufti* of the land or *shaykh al-Islam* (i.e., the "[Grand] Master of Islam"). Like the chief justice (*qádi*) of the empire, he was handpicked and appointed by the sultan himself.

An extensive network of Sufi institutions was overseen by the chief Sufi *shaykh* of the Ottoman state. Like the *'ulamá'*, the Sufi leaders also effectively became part and parcel of the imperial state apparatus. They lost their erstwhile independence from temporal rulers and, as a consequence, the ability to criticize their policies.[9] Heterodox communities and individuals perceived as "heretics" were mercilessly persecuted. The Shari'a was effectively confined to the sphere of family relations and personal status law. The sultan ruled on the basis of administrative precedents known collectively as *qanún* (from the Greek "canon"). It was, in essence, an Ottoman dynastic and administrative law that existed parallel to the religious law of the *'ulamá'* class. Sometimes

Ottoman judges would use the rulings of the *qanún* alongside those of the Shari'a. The wide implementation of the *qanún* by the sultan Suleiman and his continual introduction of ever new legal norms earned him the title of "Law-Giver."[10] Although all-powerful, the sultan was nevertheless careful to consult his religious officials to make sure that his edicts were not in conflict with the precepts of the Shari'a.[11] In this way, the Ottoman ruling elite succeeded in creating and maintaining a symbiosis of religion and dynastic rule that effectively legitimized their absolutist power over their subjects. It served the Ottomans in good stead for many centuries until the abolition of their empire by the Turkish secularist-nationalist government in 1924.

The Safavids

The Safavid dynasty (1501–1722) of Iran came to power on a wave of a popular religious revolt spearheaded by Turkic tribes of northwestern Iran (Iranian Azerbaijan). Nicknamed "Redheads" (*qizilbásh*), on account of their distinctive red headgear, the Turkic tribesmen were fierce and fearless warriors, who were motivated by their strongly held belief in the divinity or divine powers of their leaders. Under the leadership of Shah Isma'il (r. 1501–1524), they formed the military backbone of a popular messianic uprising of a Shi'ite inspiration. The Redheads' rebellion succeeded in dislodging Iran's Sunni rulers and bringing Shah Isma'il to power in the name of social justice and the "true religion." The self-abnegating loyalty of the Qizilbash to their leader rested in their belief in his direct descent from the hidden Shi'ite *imam*. At some point, they declared him to be the *máhdi* of the age who was divinely appointed and guided to revivify the spirit of the true Islam of 'Ali and his descendants. The Redheads expected Shah Isma'il to usher in an era of happiness, justice, and prosperity in this world and to assure them salvation in the hereafter. Such was their commitment to their semidivine leader that they reportedly would eat his fallen enemies raw in the battlefield. Infused with unshakable faith in Shah Isma'il's supernatural powers to protect them from enemy weapons, they would occasionally march unarmed into the battle. Their boundless zeal eventually paid off: Shah Isma'il's opponents were vanquished one after another.

However, after the triumph of the Redhead movement that had given Shah Isma'il full control over Iraq and Iran, the unbounded enthusiasm of his followers became a liability both for him and his successors at the head of the Safavid state. Once in power, the Safavid rulers were more interested in establishing a stable government and social order than in pursuing the millenarian dream of the overzealous Qizilbash. As a result, Shah Isma'il's heirs gradually rid themselves of their Turkic supporters whom they accused of "exaggerating" certain aspects of Shi'ite Islam. Instead, the Safavids began to vigorously promote a more moderate version of Shi'ism (that of the Twelvers), eventually adopting it as the official religion of the state. As Safavid rule had stabilized, rival Islamic factions and communities, especially Sunni ones, fell victim to Safavid persecution. Any departure from the Shi'ite orthodoxy as articulated by the Shi'ite scholarly establishment of the Safavid state was forcibly suppressed. To bolster the distinctive Shi'ite identity of the Safavid Empire, its rulers and the *'ulamá'* loyal to them deliberately encouraged the veneration of heroes and martyrs of the Shi'ite cause: 'Ali, Fátima, al-Hásan, al-Husayn, and their descendants, both male and female. The Shi'ite holy places and educational institutions at Kerbelá, Najaf, Qum, and Mashhad received generous donations from the Safavid state. The Shi'ite foundations of the Safavid Empire were highly visible in the public sphere. Shi'ite preachers cursed the first three caliphs from the pulpits of the mosques as usurpers of 'Ali's right to lead the nascent Muslim community. The anniversary of al-Husayn's tragic death at Kerbelá on the tenth day of the month of Muhárram was officially commemorated by passion plays and processions, during which participants subjected themselves to flagellation and mutilation in solidarity with the Shi'ite martyrs of old. Sermonizers in the mosques recounted in vivid detail the sufferings of al-Husayn, his family, and a handful of his loyal followers at Kerbelá, driving the captive audiences to tears.[12] The day of 'Ali's appointment as the Prophet's successor at the Pond of Khumm (the eighteenth day of the month Dhu 'l-Hijja) was declared a state holiday. Thus, Twelver Shi'ite Islam, originally the ideology of a persecuted minority, became the doctrinal foundation of the powerful Safavid state in the same way as the Sunni Islam of the Hánafi school was adopted by the Ottomans as the religious foundation of their vast empire.

The Safavid Empire reached its zenith under its most powerful ruler Shah 'Abbas (r. 1588–1629), who, in the words of a Western scholar, "does not suffer by comparison with the other great rulers of the age—Elisabeth I, Charles V, Suleiman the Magnificent and the Mughal Emperor Akbar."[13] Like his Ottoman counterparts, Shah 'Abbas was keen on legitimizing his absolutist rule by an elaborate religious symbolism. While the Ottoman sultan claimed to be the caliph of all Sunnis, "the Safavi monarch asserted his own position as spokesman of the Hidden Imam" and enforcer of the Twelver Shi'ite law and practice as formulated and applied by the leading scholars of his realm.[14] From his capital in Isfahan, in Central Iran, 'Abbas oversaw the ambitious program of state building and cultural florescence (see Figure 20.2). Arts, architecture, education, and crafts blossomed under the shah's benevolent patronage. As in the Ottoman Empire, generous royal donations supported the construction of sumptuous religious shrines, schools, colleges, mosques, libraries, and hospitals. Despite the differences in religious doctrine, the Safavid rulers' interactions with the *'ulamá'* class were quite similar to the relationships in the Ottoman empire. The leading scholars of the Safavid realm were coopted into the state hierarchy. On the top of the religious establishment stood the religious official called *sadr* ("the foremost," "the

Figure 20.2 The Safavid Emperor Abbas I (d. 1629) and a Courtier Offering Fruit and Drink

Persian School / Chehel Sotun, or 'The 40 Columns', Isfahan, Iran / Bridgeman Images supreme"). Appointed by the Safavid ruler, the *sadr* served as the supervisor of mosques, religious colleges, charitable endowments, and appointments to official religious posts. In other words, he was the indispensable intermediary between the dynastic state and the *'ulamá'* class. The *sadr* was also the guarantor of religious propriety at all levels of society and an untiring persecutor of heretics.[15] The *sadr*'s officials went around the country smashing jars of wine and shutting down houses of ill repute, taverns, and tobacco and coffee shops.[16] All manner of "frivolities" that they considered to be contrary to the moral code of Shi'ite Islam were vigorously exposed and persecuted. Under Shah Isma'il's successors, the office of the *sadr* gradually lost its original significance because the leading Shi'ite jurisprudents and theologians of the Safavid state had succeeded in reasserting their collective role as relatively independent stewards and interpreters of the Shi'ite law and doctrine. As a result, the functions of the *sadr* were limited to the supervision and management of pious endowments, whereas the *'ulamá'* class as a whole came to enjoy relative independence with regard to the Safavid court.

Building on Shah Isma'il's claim as the spokesman and embodiment of the hidden *imam*, his successors tried to blend the imperial ideas harking back to the pre-Islamic Iranian empires with the Shi'ite doctrine of the guiding role of an infallible and divinely inspired religious leader. The Safavids' goal was to position themselves as both spiritual and temporal sovereigns whose decrees should apply equally to religious and mundane matters.[17] This ambitious claim to the dual authority was not accepted by the majority of Shi'ite *'ulamá'*, who considered themselves to be the only rightful protectors and interpreters of the divine law as enunciated in the Qur'an and the teachings of the Shi'ite *imam*s. Tensions resulted. Following Shah 'Abbas's death in 1629, the *'ulamá'* grew increasingly reluctant to recognize the Safavid ruler as the infallible representative of the hidden *imam*. In their eyes, he was just an executor of the Shi'ite law that had to be explained and interpreted to him by its learned guardians, namely themselves. As for the hidden *imam*, his will was represented and executed collectively by the foremost Shi'ite scholars of the Safavid state, who, in turn, recognized the authority of the greatest among them. This supreme religious authority, named *shaykh al-Islam* (like his Sunni counterpart in the Ottoman Empire), was relatively independent of the state, increasingly seen as a temporal institution, in defining Shi'ite orthodoxy in matters of doctrine and practice.

With time, the Safavid state tacitly acknowledged the *shaykh al-islam*'s supremacy in religious matters and provided him with resources to enforce his vision of the correct Shi'ite faith. This meant not only allowing him to persecute Sunnis residing in the Safavid realm but also cracking down on all manner of Shi'ite "deviators." Among such "deviators" were popular Shi'ite Sufi orders that the supreme religious scholars of the Safavid state would occasionally condemn and declare to be beyond the pale of Shi'ite Islam.[18] After the destruction of the Safavid Empire by Afghan warlords in 1722, the notion of the imperial ruler as both spiritual and temporal guide was abandoned once and for all. As a result, the legal dualism of the Shari'a and the ruler's administrative law (*qanún*), which we have already observed in the context of the Ottoman Empire, became the order of the day in Shi'ite Iran as well.[19] The two legal codes were once again reunited only in the 1980s in the personality of *ayatollah* Khomeini, both the spiritual guide of the Iranian Shi'ites and the de facto political ruler of the Islamic Republic of Iran.

The Moguls

The third great Muslim dynasty of the age was founded in the sixteenth century in India by the descendants of the fearsome Mogul conqueror Genghis Khan (d. 1227). Its very name is derived from the Persian word for "Mongol." The rulers of the Mogul dynasty presided over a rich and ethnically diverse country divided between the Muslim minority and the Hindu majority. The Moguls, who were Muslims, faced the task of finding an accommodation with the Hindu population of the Indian Subcontinent without, however, alienating their Muslim subjects. That was not easy. Even at the peak of Mogul power, some Hindu-populated areas of India remained outside

Figure 20.3 Mogul Emperor Akbar (d. 1605) Receiving Two Jesuit Monks in His "House of Worship"

their reach. Several Mogul emperors tried to implement an "equal opportunity" policy by appoint-ing their Hindu subjects of noble extraction to positions of responsibility in the country's bureau-cracy and military. This policy inevitably created tensions between the empire's Muslim and Hindu subjects, as the former considered it to be contrary to the Muslim character of the state. In the end, each Mogul ruler had to resolve the dilemma to the best of his ability and imagination.

   The Mogul Empire reached the peak of its power under the emperor Akbar (r. 1556–1605), who managed to extend his rule to most areas of the Subcontinent (see Figure 20.3). Initially, Akbar cultivated good relations with the leading Muslim scholars of his realm by generously giving them land grants and endowing their religious establishments. To further appease them, he even imposed the poll tax on his non-Muslim subjects for a short time, which was an extraordinary measure given the predominantly Hindu composition of the country. In return, he expected the *'ulamá'* to recognize his position as the caliph of the Abode of Islam or at least of its eastern reach. In an attempt to bolster his religious credentials, Akbar took to personally leading the Friday prayer in imitation of the early caliphs of Islam.[20] Like the caliph al-Ma'mun before him, Akbar also attempted to convince the *'ulamá'* to acknowledge him as a just and competent Islamic ruler capable of serving as the ultimate recourse in matters of religious doctrine and practice, including judicial decisions.[21] This would render him the final arbiter in deciding which legal and doctrinal opinions of the *'ulamá'* should be applied in his realm.

Akbar's efforts yielded fruit. His courtiers duly declared him to be "the perfect man of the age" who alone was capable of leading each class of his subjects to perfection "according to its competence within the social hierarchy."[22] Furthermore, they compared his sovereign rule with "a radiance from the Incomparable Dispenser of Justice [God] and a ray of the sun, Illuminator of the Universe." Akbar's imperial residence was imagined by his courtiers as "the seat of the [universal] Caliphate." In claiming the role of the divinely inspired guide to salvation, Akbar seems to have underestimated the strength of the tradition of independence and self-sufficiency that was so dear to the Muslim learned class in his realm and elsewhere. In any case, some of its members refused to endorse the fulsome epithets bestowed upon the emperor by his overzealous courtiers. For them, he remained a temporal ruler who ascended the throne by a quirk of the inscrutable divine will.

Faced with the *'ulamá'*'s tacit but determined opposition to his claims to be the final arbiter in religious and juridical matters, Akbar decided to impose his will on his learned opponents by subjugating them to the supreme religious official (*sadr*), whom he would appoint or dismiss at his pleasure. The same course, as we already know, was taken by Akbar's imperial peers in Safavid Iran and Ottoman Turkey. Under the new policy, scholars, who had benefited from the land grants distributed and were supervised by the *sadr*, were required to present themselves at the emperor's court at least once.[23] Failure to do so would result in the revocation of their privileges, depriving them of income. This imperial condition was meant to demonstrate to the recalcitrant scholars that, in the final account, they were but disposable beneficiaries of the emperor's absolutist rule.

Akbar's religious policies later in his rule alienated the *'ulamá'* even further. In an effort to secure the loyalty of his non-Muslim subjects, Akbar attempted to introduce a universalist religion of sorts that, in his mind, would be acceptable to all intelligent individuals regardless of their original religious commitment. He dubbed his religious project "divine monotheism" or "divine religion" (*tawhíd or din-i ilahi*). Akbar's new religion was supposed to instill in its followers moral purity and high spirituality, while at the same time inculcating in them personal devotion to Akbar as the indispensable religious guide and protector of their religious freedom.[24] Akbar's followers were ranked according to four degrees of devotion, the fourth being the highest. Those who had attained it were considered to be the emperor's personal disciples (*murids*). Such an arrangement implied that Akbar was to be regarded by his subjects as their spiritual guide (*shaykh* or *pir*) in the same way as the Sufi *shaykh* is the spiritual preceptor and guide of his disciples.[25] Akbar considered this approach to be the best means to secure the loyalty of his multiethnic and religiously diverse subjects.

In an attempt to implement his concept of "peace for all" (*sulh-e kull*), Akbar financed the building of temples for various faiths and even suspended the death penalty for converts away from Islam.[26] He wanted to create an environment in which "thousands [would] find rest in the love of the king, and sectarian differences [would] not raise the dust of strife."[27] Akbar and his religious advisors preached that the truth could be found in all religions and that no one religion should claim a monopoly over it. To encourage an interfaith dialogue, in 1575 Akbar established the so-called House of Worship, which was designed to serve, among other things, as the venue for an open discussion of religious issues. Here learned representatives of major religious denominations of India (Sunni and Shi'ite Muslims, Hindus, Zoroastrians, as well as traveling Christians) were free to present and debate the advantages of their respective faiths. However, Akbar's universalist project eventually fell short of its goal. Despite his efforts to promote religious dialogue and mutual tolerance, the discussants remained stubbornly convinced of the superiority of their respective religious persuasions and scornful of the beliefs of their interlocutors.[28]

It is hardly surprising that Akbar's attempts to placate his non-Muslim subjects by promoting religious syncretism and abolishing the poll tax levied on them by the Muslim state were greeted with hostility by the *'ulamá'* class. They condemned the emperor's initiatives as a subtle attempt to dilute Islam by making it indistinguishable from Hinduism. In opposing Akbar's universalist project, the *'ulamá'* were driven in part by ulterior motives. Akbar's attempted reforms threatened to undermine their role as the sole custodians and interpreters of the religious law of the Mogul state. Were Akbar to succeed, they would have become one group of religious specialists among others, thereby forfeiting the privileged position they enjoyed in a state governed by a Muslim sovereign. The *'ulamá'* found such a prospect to be unappealing. No wonder that Akbar's initiatives were flatly rejected by several prominent Muslim leaders, including Ahmad Sirhindí (d. 1624), a respected *shaykh* of the Naqshbandi Sufi brotherhood who emphasized the necessity to preserve the Islamic character of the Mogul state and to keep its Hindu population in a subjugated position. Other Sufi thinkers, including a prince of the royal dynasty named Dara Shikóh (d. 1659), embraced Akbar's universalist vision and even encouraged the translation of the Hindu scriptures into Persian[29] in order to prove to India's Muslims the underlying consistency of Hinduism with Islam's monotheistic message.

Eventually, the communalist and exclusivist attitude advocated by Sirhindí triumphed over the universalistic and inclusivist one espoused by Akbar and Dara Shikóh. The triumph of the communalists inevitably led to the stiffening of the interconfessional boundaries, to the strengthening of anti-Hindu sentiments among India's Muslim minority, and, as a consequence, to religious strife. The last powerful Mogul emperor, Awrangzéb (r. 1658–1707), defeated his brother Dara Shikóh in the contest for the throne. He threw in his lot with the communalist *'ulamá'*, abandoned Akbar's universalistic experimentations, and forcibly reasserted the Islamic foundations of the Mogul Empire. His attempts to Islamize his Hindu subjects, including those previously loyal to the Mogul state, led to a series of bloody rebellions led by Hindu princes who had refused to forsake their faith. According to some historians of India, these upheavals exhausted the empire and rendered it incapable of effectively coping with both outside and inside problems. The subsequent emergence of independent Hindu principalities led to the progressive fragmentation of the empire into an assemblage of mutually hostile Indian and Muslim states. Their disunity prevented the former Mogul subjects from warding off the encroachments of the British East India Company and eventually invited the subjugation of the country by the British Raj.

Whether or not Awrangzéb's inflexible communalism was indeed the principal reason for the dissolution of the Mogul Empire (as some Western and Indian scholars have argued) is a moot point. What is clear is that the remarkable diversity of India's religious landscape gave rise to a wide array of syncretic religious faiths, of which the movement for spiritual rejuvenation launched by the mystic Kabír (d. 1518) and his intellectual successor Guru Nanák (d. 1538), known as "Sikhism," is the most dramatic example. Very often this religious syncretism evolved under the guise of monistic Sufism (along the lines of Ibn 'Arabi's doctrine of the unity of being), whose focus on the universality of human religious experience made it a convenient vehicle for interfaith dialogues and the formation of hybrid religious communities.

Conclusions

After briefly examining the fortunes of the Muslim gunpowder empires on the eve of European expansion, we can discern several major trends in their religious policies. Everywhere we notice a tension between the centralizing, absolutist aspirations of the imperial rulers and the religious scholars' determination to preserve their independence from the state. The scholars were particularly uncomfortable with rulers' attempts to establish themselves as the ultimate arbiters in religious matters as well as spiritual guides of their subjects. Such attempts went against the grain of the scholars' strongly held conviction that they were the only competent and legitimate interpreters of the divine law and guides of the masses to salvation. The tensions created by the mutually incompatible claims of the rulers and the scholars were usually resolved by a compromise in which the rulers would grant the scholars a certain autonomy in religious and juridical matters, while simultaneously seeking to secure their approval of political and fiscal measures pursued by the state. In the process, the scholars allowed the rulers to co-opt them into the state apparatus, thereby becoming executors of the monarch's will. The latter controlled them via the handpicked supreme religious functionary who served as mediator between the ruler's court and the scholarly establishment of a given realm. In short, this was a symbiosis of religious and temporal authority in which the level of scholars' independence varied from one state and ruler to another.

Of the three empires we have discussed, the populations of two (Ottoman and Safavid) were predominantly Muslim. However, in the case of the former, the percentage of non-Muslim population was almost equal to the Muslim one, especially in the northern provinces (namely, the Balkans and southeast Europe), which were predominantly Christian. Not so in the Mogul Empire. Here the vast Hindu majority was ruled by a Muslim minority. This situation called for creative solutions. Attempts on the part of some rulers (Akbar and Dara Shikóh) to introduce a universalist, supraconfessional model of religious coexistence ran into stiff opposition on the part of the communalistic 'ulamá', who advocated the preeminence of Islam and Muslims at all levels and in all spheres of Indian society. The 'ulamá' felt (rightly so, it seems) that their privileged position as the exponents and interpreters of the Islamic religious law and doctrine would be drastically undercut by Akbar's universalistic reforms aimed at accommodating his non-Muslim subjects. No wonder that the 'ulamá' staunchly supported Awrangzéb's attempts to restore Islamic communalism and suppress Hinduism with a view to reasserting the Islamic character of Mogul rule. In the end, the emperor's communalist policies led to an armed conflict between India's religious communities and, eventually, to the fragmentation of the once powerful state.

In the Ottoman Empire, the inevitable tension between the Muslim state and its non-Muslim subjects was resolved by the introduction of the system of religious and ethnic communities (millets), each of which was granted internal autonomy in return for the payment of the poll tax. Furthermore, under Ottoman rule, warriors recruited from the empire's non-Muslim subjects were integrated into the state structure and formed the very backbone of its military power.

In the Safavid Empire, the principal religious tension sprang from the presence in the country of the Shi'ite majority and the Sunni minority. The latter was seen by the state and the religious leaders loyal to it as a natural ally of the hostile Ottoman state, a "fifth column" of sorts. Here, as in the Ottoman Empire, the ruler (shah) sought to control the 'ulamá' class through the chief religious functionary of the state whom he personally appointed. In the end, however, the 'ulamá' succeeded in preserving a certain level of independence from the imperial court and were even able to secure its assistance in cracking down on what they considered to be "deviations" (such as, for instance, the teachings and practices of some popular Sufi orders) from the Shi'ite doctrines that they formulated and declared to be orthodox.

All three gunpowder empires were powerful geopolitical players capable of maintaining control, collectively, of a huge swath of land and sea from North Africa to the Himalayas. However, in the end, they proved to be helpless in the face of Europe's newly acquired technological and organizational strength.[30] The same applies to the lesser Muslim states of the modern age. Let us now examine how and why modernity became the root cause of European ascendancy and Muslim decline.

What Is Modernity?

Modernity is a global phenomenon that is usually associated with the rise in the seventeenth and early eighteenth centuries of the novel social, political, educational, and economic structures in the nation-states of Western Europe. Definitions of modernity abound and often contradict one another. Without going into too much detail, one can say that modernity's character is evident from the profound impact it had on the organization of human lives (including child care, marriage, education, and leisure), political participation, and productive activities. This impact manifests itself in fundamental changes in the makeup of the affected societies, as well as in predominant beliefs about economics, politics, social organization, and religious faith. These beliefs are embraced by the ruling elites and shared, to some extent, by the population at large. Modernity is not confined to any particular geographical zone. Once it has emerged in one area, it spreads across the globe, although its influence on different societies is different and often unique. What follows is a summary of the ways in which modernity has affected various spheres of human life:

- The condition of modernity in the economic sphere is characterized by rapid industrialization and explosive economic growth. This growth is accompanied by the expansion of banking systems, the quick flow of capital, and rampant consumerism cultivated by various means of mass communications. Science-based technology leads to a dramatic increase in the efficiency and productivity of human labor.
- The social sphere witnesses the increase in the socioeconomic and physical mobility of people and the emergence of new economic classes and professional organizations that often find themselves in opposition to or in open conflict with the old ones. Dramatic changes occur in the relations between the sexes and between the cities and the countryside (such as migration of the previously inert labor force to cities and the resultant urbanization). A faceless, impersonal bureaucratic rationalism becomes the principal way of organizing and administering human thought and activity in cities and in the countryside.
- The cultural field is drastically reshaped by the spread of the mass media, communication technologies, pop culture, and cross-cultural exchange.
- The political sphere witnesses the emergence of new patterns of popular organization and mobilization by means of political parties, trade unions, clubs, voluntary associations, and representative bodies.
- In the realm of intellectual life, the idea of progress becomes predominant; secular norms and ideologies are increasingly privileged over religious ones; and critical approaches to history, social and intellectual conventions, and received wisdom become widespread. Traditional authorities and concepts are consistently questioned and often found wanting.

Some sociologists have come up with what they call "five pillars of modernity":

1. Abstraction as manifested in an impersonal bureaucracy and technology;
2. Futurity, that is, the future, not the "glorious" past, is seen as the primary goal and orientation for human activity and imagination;
3. Individuation, that is, the separation of the individual from a collective entity, be it a village community or a town quarter; erosion of traditional institutions of social organization

and cohesion, such as tribe and other region- and kinship-based groups, guild, extended family, and so on;

4 Liberation of life; one sees one's own destiny not as predetermined by external forces or someone's dictate but, at least to some extent, as determined by one's own free choice; indirectly, one's exercise of free choice leads to liberation from dogma and received wisdom as well as to freedom of intellectual exploration and dissent;

5 In the spiritual and moral-ethical sphere, secular ideologies, not religion, become predominant; simultaneously, religion is increasingly pushed out of the public sphere into the sphere of individual's private life, leading to the marginalization of institutionalized religious structures; each person becomes his or her own judge on matters of truth and validity; the previously unshakable certainties of religious faith are called into doubt, and religious authority comes under scrutiny.

All or some of these characteristics were rife in the European societies throughout the nineteenth century. They could also be found in some Muslim societies of that age. However, in the Muslim world they were not given a chance to evolve gradually into new patterns of social organization and intellectual and economic production. The natural development of Muslim societies was interrupted by the aggressive intrusion into their lives of the better organized and technologically advanced societies of Western Europe and Russia that were eager to project their newly acquired power across the globe. The relentless military, cultural, and economic expansion of the European states turned out to be unstoppable. In the words of a famous American historian:

> The Europeans . . . had by 1800 reached a decisively higher level of *social power* than was to be found elsewhere . . . Individual Europeans might still be less intelligent, less courageous, less loyal than individuals elsewhere; but, when educated and organized in society, the Europeans were able to think and to act far more effectively, as members of a group, than members of any other societies.[31]

Aided by their superior technology, educational institutions, and organizational skills, the European powers and Russia embarked on the venture of global expansion and domination that is known as colonialism.

The Beginnings of European Colonial Expansion

Napoleon's arrival in Egypt in 1798, ostensibly to protect French merchants from local misrule, is often seen by scholars and laymen alike as the opening stage in the drama of the conquest and subjugation of the Muslim lands by the Europeans. In reality, Napoleon's military expedition was anticipated by the Portuguese and later Dutch intrusions into the predominantly Muslim territories around the Indian Ocean, which had gradually led to the Dutch colonization of the Indonesian and Malaysian Archipelago. The Dutch colonial venture in the East Indies started already in the seventeenth century and culminated in the nineteenth century with the creation of a commercial empire.[32] It required protection and management, and before long the Dutch turned their commercial presence in Southeast Asia into imperial rule pure and simple.

In Eurasia, Russia's southward advance had led to the annexation of the Muslim khanate of Crimea in 1774–1783.[33] It was followed by the Russian occupation of the predominantly Muslim lands of the Caucasus, which was completed in the first decades of the nineteenth century.[34] To assert their political control over the inhospitable and rugged mountainous terrain of the Northern Caucasus,[35] the Russians had to wage a protracted war against a number of local Muslim leaders who had declared a *jihád* against the Russian occupation. In 1859, the Russian victory over the forces of a Muslim resistance leader, *imam* Shamíl (d. 1871), led to a mass exodus of the local Muslim populations to the Ottoman Empire.[36] It was precipitated in part by the Muslims' desire to avoid living under infidel Christian rule. Within a few decades, the lands of the northwestern Caucasus, which had for centuries been predominantly Muslim, became predominantly Christian.[37]

This mass emigration of Muslims from the lands occupied by the Russian Empire was, however, an exception rather than rule. In most areas of the Muslim world, Muslims had to reconcile themselves to a life under European colonial domination no matter how intrusive and heavy-handed. When it became intolerable, anticolonial rebellions flared up. The nineteenth century witnessed a series of such rebellions, which were often waged in the name of a defensive *jihád*. Apart from the aforementioned rebellion of *imam* Shamíl, the most successful of them were led by charismatic religious leaders such as emir (*amír*) 'Abd al-Qadir of Algeria (against the French), the Mahdi of Sudan (against the British and Egyptians), the Sanusi *shaykh*s of Libya (against the Italians), and Muhammad 'Abdallah (aka the "Mad Mulla") of Somalia (against the British). The famous Sepoy Mutiny of 1857–1858 against the British Raj in India with the aim of restoring the rule of the Mogul emperor in Delhi also had Islamic underpinnings.

As already mentioned, in Western accounts of the European colonial expansion, its beginnings are routinely associated with Napoleon's conquest of Egypt. This is due in part to the French emperor's larger-than-life status as a major shaper of Europe's history at the turn of the nineteenth century.[38] Napoleon's interest in Egypt was determined by the larger geopolitical calculations of the French Empire. In bringing Egypt into the orbit of France's political and military control, Napoleon hoped to use it as a base of operations against his country's archenemy, the British Empire, which had already established its colonial presence in India and was anxious to safeguard the sea routes to its wealthy eastern colony. Napoleon also hoped to turn the fertile agrarian lands of the Nile Delta into a grain basket to feed the rapidly growing population of France. In other words, the invasion of Egypt by Napoleon's army was, from France's perspective, part of a greater geopolitical game in which Egypt was little more than a pawn. Nevertheless, the French took their task very seriously. Immediately upon the arrival of the French army in Egypt, its military superiority made itself felt. The Egyptian cavalry of slave soldiers, initially overconfident of their military prowess, turned out to be helpless against Napoleon's modern, better trained, better organized, and better equipped military force. The Egyptians suffered a crushing defeat at the Battle of the Pyramids in 1798, leaving the country at the conqueror's mercy. This was not a regular premodern conquest aimed at seizing booty and exploiting the subjugated territory without drastically affecting its way of life. Once in Egypt, the French officials began to set up hospitals, scientific laboratories, and up-to-date administrative structures, as if to demonstrate to the natives the superiority of their culture and organization. In other words, the French were engaged in social and cultural engineering on a grand scale. In addition to the cannon and materiel, the invading army brought with it French academic experts on Egyptian antiquities, natural scientists, as well as scholars specializing in the study of the Arabic language and Islam. In other words, this was as much an academic, cultural, and administrative venture as it was a military expedition. The upper-class natives looked on with awe and some with guarded admiration. One Egyptian scholar described his impressions as follows:

> If any of the Muslims came to them [the French] to look round they did not prevent him from entering their most cherished places . . . and if they found in him any appetite or desire for knowledge they showed their friendship and love for him, and they would bring out all kinds of pictures and maps, and animals and birds and plants, and histories of the ancients and of nations and tales of the prophets . . . I went to them often and they showed me all of that.[39]

We observe a similar pattern of colonizer–colonized interaction in practically all of the other European colonial ventures in the Muslim world. Wherever they went, the Europeans brought with them their superior organizational, industrial, and technological skills that were theretofore unknown to the locals and that the latter soon came to covet and try to imitate. The Europeans, in turn, viewed themselves as disseminators of a superior culture: a modern, progressive nation on a "civilizing mission" aimed at waking the "decaying" Muslim societies from their "intellectual stupor" and improving their lives by "rationalizing" their governance and educating their members in "new ways" of doing things. Assessing the validity of this self-serving image harbored by the Europeans lies outside the purview of this book. Nor should we busy ourselves verifying the Muslims' counterclaims that they were brutally conquered and subjugated by the "rapacious European imperialists." What happened, happened, and every reader should try to figure out for him- or herself who was right and who was wrong in that fateful encounter of civilizations, as well as whether the negative aspects of Western domination outweighed the technological, administrative, and social advantages (if any) that it had brought with it.

As Napoleon was "civilizing" Egypt, the British had consolidated their political and military control over India, which became the proverbial jewel in the British crown. To secure the safe passage of their steamers to India, the British occupied the port city of Aden (in present-day Yemen) in 1839 and set up a string of British protectorates along the eastern Arabian coast facing India.[40] While Napoleon's occupation of Egypt proved to be short-lived, the French did not abandon the idea of establishing colonies in Muslim lands. They now set their sights on North Africa, which lay just across the sea from southern France.

In 1830, a French army occupied Algeria and held it as a colony until 1962. Later on, another French expeditionary force occupied the eastern part of Morocco, leaving the rest of the country to the Spaniards to control and exploit. By the 1860s, the Russians had completed the conquest of the Caucasus and proceeded to subjugate the Muslim peoples of Central Asia, who became subjects of the Russian tsar as a result. The Dutch were now in full control of the Indonesian Archipelago, whose natural riches and population they exploited quite efficiently. The British held sway over the islands of present-day Malaysia and of Singapore. In the Far Fast, in the 1880s the Chinese state seized the territories of Eastern Turkestan, which were inhabited by the Turkic-speaking Uighur Muslims. From that time on, this region has been known by its Chinese name, Xinjiang.[41] It remains a Chinese province today. In 1882, Egypt fell under direct British rule that lasted until 1936. The British consul-general Lord Cromer, the actual ruler of the country, viewed his Egyptian subjects as "a backward race, needing to be protected and guided by Europeans for their own good as well as for the safety of the Europeans."[42] This patronizing attitude was shared by the overwhelming majority of European and Russian colonial officers who were convinced of the necessity (and even "nobility") of their "civilizing mission" in the Muslim lands. They were genuinely surprised and upset at any sign of the natives' resistance to their "benevolent" rule. As already mentioned, many areas of the Muslim world witnessed popular uprisings against the European "benefactors" waged under the banners of *jihád*. Most of them failed in the face of the colonial powers' military superiority and/or treachery on the part of Muslim elites co-opted by the colonizers.

Even those Muslim countries that remained formally independent fell into deep dependence on the Western powers and Russia, decisively shaping the economic and even political life of their subjects to the advantage of the colonizers. By availing themselves of their superior military and economic strength, the European powers set about liberating Christian communities of the Middle East from the "Muslim yoke." They actively assisted Greece in its war against the Ottoman Empire and helped the Greeks achieve political independence in 1829. By the late 1870s, the Ottomans had lost most of their territorial possessions in the Balkans and southeast Europe due, in considerable part, to Russia's aggressive foreign policy in the region. In the economic sphere, the Ottoman, Iranian, Indian, and Egyptian rulers were forced to grant sweeping trade concessions to European merchants, bankers, and industrialists operating within their countries, which effectively amounted to the forfeiture of their economic independence.[43]

Furthermore, in many formally independent Muslim countries, citizens of the European states and Russia were exempt from local jurisdiction and subject to their own courts that were set up by Western and Russian consulates. This arrangement gave the foreigners free hand in pursuing their activities as they saw fit without regard for local sensitivities, customs, or laws. Finally, to clearly define their spheres of influence vis-à-vis their imperial rivals, the Europeans set about drawing borders where they had not existed, sometimes quite arbitrarily. This mapping activity by the European powers was to have grave repercussions for the countries so mapped in the postcolonial epoch. In all, by the end of the nineteenth century wherever one looked, the Muslims were in retreat in the face of the superior military and economic power and organization of Europe and Russia.

Muslim Responses: Economic and Social

A detailed account of European conquests and domination of Muslim lands lies outside the scope of this book. What concerns us is the ways in which Muslim responded to this new situation and how individual Muslim rulers and thinkers tried to make sense of their plight in an effort to reverse it. By the second half of the nineteenth century, some forward-looking Muslim statesmen and intellectuals began to look for the root causes of their military, political, and social failures. Thus began a long process of soul-searching and self-reassessment in the face of the new challenges for the Muslims posed by modernity and Europe's political, economic, and military ascendancy.

It is only natural that the initial, almost semivisceral reaction of Muslim rulers to the new challenges was to try to rectify their military impotence vis-à-vis Europe's superior military might. Typical in this respect are the reforms of the able Egyptian ruler Muhammad 'Ali (r. 1805–1848), who set himself the task of creating a modern army on the European model. To this end, he hired Italian and French military advisors and gave them free reign in reforming the country's military establishment. An astute statesman, Muhammad 'Ali soon realized that a drastic reform of the army was impossible without instituting broader societal changes. Therefore, when sending a group of Egyptian Muslims to Europe for training, he decreed that some of them be educated as military officers, while others should acquire civilian professions as doctors, engineers, and civil administrators. To support the creation and maintenance of the new military, Muhammad 'Ali built roads, canals, modern Western-style teaching institutions, and printing presses, as well as factories to turn out uniforms and munitions for his modernized fighting force. His reorganization of state infrastructure and building projects required enormous investments. To fund them, he confiscated the lands of religious endowments and imposed heavy taxes on his subjects. Such measures inevitably undermined the economic position of the 'ulamá' class, which depended heavily on the income generated by charitable endowment properties. The Egyptian scholars found themselves deprived of their financial independence and had no choice but to turn to the state for financial support. As paid officials of the state, they were no longer able to effectively play their traditional role as intermediaries between the government and the common people. Rather, they were transformed into a category of paid government servants. Whereas the influence and independence of the traditional elites were severely curtailed by Muhammad 'Ali's reforms, there emerged a new elite of merchants who prospered as middlemen in Egypt's growing trade with European countries.[44] This new Egyptian elite also included Western-trained army officers, administrators, journalists, and engineers.[45]

In the religious sphere, Muhammad 'Ali placed the activities of the powerful and wealthy Egyptian Sufi orders under direct state control. From that point on, they were subject to state licensing and had to seek the state's permission to engage in any public activities or to appoint their leaders.[46] Inevitably, Muhammad 'Ali's heavy-handed implementation of his reformist plans aroused wide popular discontent. To suppress it, he had to rule as a dictator, relying on raw force to keep the indignation of the masses in check.

Cognizant of the high revenues generated by industrial production of goods, Muhammad 'Ali attempted to set up cotton, wool, and linen textile factories that would use locally grown long staple cotton and wool. This initiative came to naught due to the lack of technical skills among Egypt's workforce, the smallness of the country's market, and the stiff competition from cheaper and more attractive European goods.[47]

In the end, Muhammad 'Ali's enterprises failed, and the country was reduced to exporting raw cotton to Europe (primarily England), which effectively turned Egypt into a plantation economy. Western demand for cotton forced landowners to allocate more and more arable land to cultivate it. This led to a drastic reduction of productive lands and mass famine among the country's peasantry. As a result, Egypt became a net importer of foodstuffs and manufactured goods from the European continent. Under Muhammad 'Ali's successors, the country found itself deeply in debt. Matters came to a head in 1876, when Egypt was unable to meet its financial obligations to the European lenders and had to accept the joint French–British control of its banking system. Thus, what had begun as a relatively narrow-focus military reform turned into a major overhaul of all of the country's traditional structures from administration to industries, agriculture, and educational institutions. The rapid and often ruthless implementation of modernizing projects by Muslim autocrats like Muhammad 'Ali stretched the structures and resources of the affected societies to the breaking point. One observes the same picture over and over again throughout the Muslim world: in the Ottoman Empire, Iran, North Africa, and Russian Central Asia. Very often a mechanical, hasty, and shallow adoption of Western ways by the ruling class failed to improve efficiency or eliminate the bureaucratic corruption and red tape of the state apparatuses in Muslim societies undergoing reform. Dressed in Western clothes and sitting in European-style offices, Ottoman or Iranian officials remained as venal and inept as they were before the reforms. Many projects, such as, for instance, the establishment of a Western-style university in the Ottoman capital, stayed on paper.[48] Throughout, the implementation of modernizing projects by Muslim ruling elites resulted in a crushing financial burden that frequently necessitated surrender by their countries of economic or even political sovereignty to European banks, merchants, and corporations.[49]

As a rule, modernizing reforms were spontaneous and heavily dependent on the will of the sovereign. For instance, when Muhammad 'Ali died, some lines of his policy were abandoned by his successor, 'Abbas I (r. 1849–1854), only to be restored again under the next ruler, Sa'id (r. 1854–1863). As mentioned, the reforms were deeply resented by the masses because they usually went against the grain of their customs and traditions and resulted in wide-scale dislocation of the traditional social strata and in their loss of livelihood. Designed and implemented by a handful of Western or Western-trained advisors at the Muslim ruler's court, the reforms remained incomprehensible to the overwhelming majority of the population of the country. The latter remained immune to and resentful of Western influences on their lives. In the Ottoman and Iranian states, the new economic policies heavily favored merchants engaged in trade with Europe. The majority of these merchants were non-Muslims—Greeks, Armenians, Syrian Christians, Hindus, and Jews. As these West-oriented mercantile estates prospered, the previously powerful and influential groups were losing ground. With the introduction by the state administration of new, European-style legal codes and courts, Muslim jurists found themselves excluded from state legal practices and reduced to practicing only in the sphere of family and personal law. Traditional crafts suffered from the competition of cheap European manufactured goods, which impoverished the once prosperous artisan guilds.

One important consequence of the reforms implemented by Westernized ruling elites was the emergence in the Muslim world of dual societies—the prosperous mercantile, administrative, and professional classes that had benefited from Westernization, alongside the impoverished rural and urban populations that had lost their traditional sources of income and were unable to find their place in the new economic and social order promoted by the ruling classes. These two social groups were quite literally worlds apart. They wore different clothes, shopped at different stores, read different books (if they could read), and followed mutually incompatible values and tastes. The Westernized upper crust of society looked to Europe for ideas, fashions, and consumer goods, whereas the impoverished, uneducated, and downtrodden masses found solace and certainty in religion and in their time-tested local customs and traditions. The two populations living in the same state simply did not see eye to eye.

By the turn of the twentieth century, the major Western powers were competing with one another for the acquisition of new colonies, which became a European sport of sorts. As mentioned, in 1882, the British occupied Egypt. One year earlier, in 1881, the French had assumed direct control of Tunisia. In 1912, the sultan of Morocco was forced to sign an agreement accepting French protectorate. The country's western part was annexed by Spain. In the meantime, the French and the British extended their rule to the predominantly Muslim societies of West Africa. The recently unified Italy, too, was eager to flex its colonial muscle. In 1911, its military invaded the territory of present-day Libya and declared it Italy's colonial possession. By that time, Tsarist Russia had already been ruling Muslim Central Asia for several decades. These and other Muslim lands were now effectively being run by European and Russian colonial administrators, some of whom had good knowledge of the languages, cultures, and customs of local societies. Others had no such knowledge and learned "on the fly," as it were. Regardless of their personal intentions, their academic and administrative expertise became an effective tool of colonial domination over subjugated Muslim societies. Europe's and Russia's colonial expansion contributed to the development and flourishing of the academic discipline specializing in the study of "Oriental societies," that is, those that lay east of Europe. Commonly known as "Orientalism," this new branch of humanitarian knowledge attracted many ambitious young Europeans and Russians eager to pursue administrative careers in their countries' colonies. In this way, the colonial powers harnessed academic knowledge to their "civilizing missions" in the Muslim lands.[50]

In sum, the adoption by Muslim rulers of the military, technical, and administrative structures and practices of European societies failed to bridge the deep and growing divide between the modernized European states (and to a lesser extent the Russian Empire) and the Muslim world. Despite Muslim rulers' strenuous efforts to modernize their societies and to render them competitive with the West, their dependent position vis-à-vis the Western powers proved self-perpetuating.[51]

Questions to Ponder

1   Compare and contrast the religious politics of the Gunpowder Empires. How successful or otherwise were their attempts to co-opt religious scholars into the state apparatus? In what way was each empire's policy toward religion and its learned exponents different or similar? Why?

2   Consider the coexistence of the administrative dynastic law (*qanún*) and the Shari'a in the Ottoman Empire. What were the causes and implications?

3   Discuss the social, economic, and cultural impact of modernity on Muslim societies. What do you think were these societies' main weaknesses, and how did they affect Muslims' ability to respond to the new geopolitical challenges?

4   How was the status of the *'ulamá'* class affected by the drastic reforms implemented by the modernizing Muslim rulers of the nineteenth century? Do you see any similarities here to the vicissitudes of the Christian clergy in Western societies over the past two hundred years?

5   Address the phenomenon of "dual societies" in the Muslim world. Who and why were the beneficiaries and losers of the modernization projects launched by Muslim ruling elites? What, in your view, were the likely consequences of this bifurcation of Muslim societies?

Summary

- Why are they called the "Gunpowder Empires"—the Ottomans of Anatolia, North Africa, and the Middle East; the Safavids of Iraq and Iran; and the Moguls of India?
- The ideological foundations of the Ottoman state are the promotion of Hánafi Islam (and, to a lesser extent, Sufism and its institutions) and the defense of Sunnism against the Shi'ite rulers of the rival Safavid Empire of Iraq and Iran.
- Religious learning, along with the proliferation of *mádrasa*s and Sufi monasteries, flourishes across the Ottoman realm.
- The centralized hierarchical structure of the Ottoman religious establishment has the chief *mufti*, chief justice (*qádi*), and chief Sufi *shaykh* at the top—all appointed by the Ottoman sultan.
- The reign of the sultan Suleiman the Magnificent (1520–1566) is the highest point of Ottoman power and influence. The Ottoman campaigns in the name of Sunni Islam against the Safavid Shi'ite rulers of Iran are an instance of an intra-Muslim religious war.
- The religiously and ethnically diverse subjects of the Ottoman state are within the *millet* system accommodated by granting them internal religious and judicial autonomy.
- The Ottoman administrative law (*qanún*) and the Shari'a coexist—an instance of a symbiosis of the Islamic legal system and dynastic rule.
- The zealous "Redheads" (*qizilbásh*) of northern Iran/Azerbaijan are the driving force of the messianic revolution that brought to power Shah Isma'il (r. 1487–1524), the founder of the Safavid Empire centered in Iran.
- Shah Isma'il's successors abandon the original messianic claims and adopt a moderate version of Twelver Shi'ism as the religious foundation of the Safavid state. The ruling dynasty uses patronage of Shi'ite shrines, educational institutions, and the learned class as a way of bolstering its religious and political legitimacy.
- An impressive cultural and economic florescence occurs in Iran under Shah 'Abbas (r. 1588–1629), the greatest ruler of the Safavid dynasty. Isfahan becomes the new capital and symbol of Safavid material wealth and might.
- *Sadr*, the supreme religious official of the Safavid Empire, is appointed by the emperor. He serves as the mediator between the emperor and the Shi'ite religious establishment.
- The post emerges of *shaykh al-islam*, the supreme scholar (elected by the Shi'ite *'ulamá'* from among their own) and entrusted by his peers with defining and enforcing Shi'ite orthodoxy. Unlike the *sadr*, he enjoys relative independence vis-á-vis the emperor and the Safavid court.

- The Safavids gradually lose religious authority to the *'ulamá'*. The same process continues under the Safavids' successors, the Qajars (1794–1925).
- The Moguls (Moghuls) become the Sunni Muslim dynasty that govern the predominantly Hindu population of the northern areas of the Indian Subcontinent.
- The epoch of the emperor Akbar (r. 1565–1605) is the acme of Mogul power. With all the religious trappings of Akbar's rule, he is portrayed as a reflection of God's majesty, the caliph of the eastern part of the Muslim world, and the final recourse in matters of religious belief and practice.
- Akbar attempts to co-opt and subjugate the *'ulamá'* of India by imposing on them the authority of the supreme scholar of the Mogul realm (*sadr*), whom he himself handpicks for the post. Akbar uses material incentives to bring the *'ulamá'* under his personal control.
- Akbar experiments with a new religion ("divine monotheism" or "divine religion") . His universalistic concept is one of "peace for all" as a means of asserting his supremacy in matters of religious creed and practice and as a way to secure the loyalty of his Hindu and Muslim subjects.
- Communalist (anti-Hindu) reactions to Akbar's attempts to institute religious "universalism" and to "dilute" the importance of Sunni Islam eventually undermine the foundation of the Mogul state. *Shaykh* Ahmad Sirhindí (d. 1624) and the Naqshbandíyya brotherhood reject Akbar's religious experiments.
- Muslim communalism and exclusivity triumph over Akbar's universalistic agenda under the emperor Awrangzéb (r. 1658–1707). Eventually, the Moguls lose India to the British Raj.
- The phenomenon of modernity has long-ranging geopolitical implications.
- European colonial expansion begins during the second half of the eighteenth and throughout the nineteenth centuries. The French, British, Dutch and Russian Empires initiate an active and concerted military, economic, and cultural colonization of the Muslim lands.
- Muslim responses range from attempts to institute broad economic, social, and educational reforms to a defensive *jihád*.
- The failed reforms of Muhammad 'Ali in Egypt are typical of the response of the Muslim ruling elite to European domination.

Notes

1 They traced their ancestry back to the great Mongol conqueror Genghis Khan and his descendants.
2 Peter Holt, Ann Lambton, and Bernard Lewis (eds.), *The Cambridge History of Islam: Vol. 1. The Central Islamic Lands*, Cambridge University Press, Cambridge, 1970, pp. 320–323.
3 Ibid., p. 321.
4 According to some sources, it originally meant "Islam abounds" (*Islam-bol*).
5 For the full lyrics, see http://tmbw.net/wiki/Lyrics:Istanbul_(Not_Constantinople).
6 William Cleveland, *A History of the Modern Middle East*, Westview Press, Boulder, CO, 2000, p. 57.
7 Marshall Hodgson, *The Venture of Islam*, Chicago University Press, Chicago, 1974, vol. 3, pp. 114–115.
8 Ibid., p. 108.
9 Ibid., p. 111 and Holt, Lambton, and Lewis (eds.), *The Cambridge History*, vol. 1, pp. 302–303.
10 Hodgson, *The Venture*, vol. 3, p. 50.
11 Ibid., p. 109.

12 Ibid., p. 37.

13 Holt, Lambton, and Lewis (eds.), *The Cambridge History of Islam*, vol. 1, p. 421.

14 Hodgson, *The Venture*, vol. 3, p. 53.

15 Ibid., p. 52.

16 In some areas of the Muslim world, consumption of tobacco and coffee was considered to be contrary to the Shari'a prohibition of intoxicants.

17 Saïd Amir Arjomand, "The Salience of Political Ethic in the Spread of Persianate Islam," *Journal of Persianate Studies*, vol. 1 (2008), p. 37 and Saïd Amir Arjomand, *The Shadow of God and the Hidden Imam*, University of Chicago Press, Chicago, 1984, passim.

18 Alexander Knysh, *Islamic Mysticism: A Short History*, 2nd ed., E. J. Brill, Leiden and Boston, 2010, pp. 239–244.

19 Arjomand, "The Salience of Political Ethic in the Spread of Persianate Islam," p. 27.

20 Holt, Lambton, and Lewis (eds.), *The Cambridge History of Islam*, vol. 1, p. 62.

21 Hodgson, *The Venture*, vol. 3, p. 66.

22 Arjomand, "The Salience of Political Ethic in the Spread of Persianate Islam," p. 19.

23 Hodgson, *The Venture*, vol. 3, p. 65.

24 Ibid., p. 73.

25 Arjomand, "The Salience of Political Ethic in the Spread of Persianate Islam," p. 21.

26 Hodgson, *The Venture*, vol. 3, p. 72; under the Shari'a, apostasy is punishable by death.

27 Arjomand, "The Salience of Political Ethic in the Spread of Persianate Islam," p. 21.

28 Holt, Lambton, and Lewis (eds.), *The Cambridge History of Islam*, vol. 2, p. 62.

29 At that age, Persian was the language of high culture in India.

30 See, e.g., Hodgson, *The Venture,* vol. 1, pp. 50–53 and 97.

31 Hodgson, *The Venture*, vol. 3, p. 178.

32 Ira Lapidus, *A History of Islamic Societies*, Cambridge University Press, Cambridge, 1999, pp. 471–473.

33 Prior to that, the Russian tsars had conquered the Muslim lands along the Volga River and in Siberia, rendering them part and parcel of what was to become the Russian Empire.

34 Lapidus, *A History of Islamic Societies*, pp. 273–274.

35 Today's Dagestan, Chechnya, Ingushetia, and Circassia.

36 Moshe Gammer, *Muslim Resistance to the Tsar*, Frank Cass, London, 1994, passim.

37 See Alexander Knysh, "al-Kabk. 3: The Period 1800 to the Present Day," in *Encyclopedia of Islam*, 2nd ed.; online edition: http://referenceworks.brillonline.com.

38 For a lively account of Napoleon's expedition to Egypt, see Juan Cole, *Napoléon's Egypt: Invading the Middle East*, Palgrave Macmillan, New York, 2007.

39 Albert Hourani, *A History of the Arab Peoples*, Harvard University Press, Cambridge, MA, 1991, p. 266.

40 Ibid., p. 269.

41 Lapidus, *A History of Islamic Societies*, pp. 435–436.

42 Hodgson, *The Venture*, vol. 3, pp. 241–242.

43 Lapidus, *A History of Islamic Societies*, p. 364; Hodgson, *The Venture*, vol. 3, pp. 141–144 and 226–227; and Hourani, *A History of the Arab Peoples*, pp. 285–287.

44 Lapidus, *A History of Islamic Societies*, pp. 617–618.

45 Ibid., p. 619.

46 For details, see Frederick de Jong, *Turuq and Turuq-Linked Institutions in XIXth-Century Egypt*, E. J. Brill, Leiden, 1987.

47 Lapidus, *A History of Islamic Societies*, p. 616.

48 Hodgson, *The Venture*, vol. 3, p. 232.

49 Ibid., p. 235.

50 For an analysis of the role of academic and cultural Orientalism in the West's colonial ventures, see Edward Said, *Orientalism* [with a new preface by the author], Vintage Books, New York, 2003.

51 Hodgson, *The Venture*, vol. 3, p. 236.

Chapter 21

Renewal and Reform in Islam

The Emergence of Islamic Modernism and Reformism

Different Reformers and Different Reforms

As Muslim rulers responded to the growing political and domination of the Western powers by initiating social, economic, and cultural reforms of their societies, some Muslim intellectuals began to critically examine the theological and intellectual aspects of the Muslim predicament. Their line of thinking can be summarized as follows: Islam, which its followers viewed as the most perfect monotheistic religion predestined by God to succeed in this world,[1] obviously could not be blamed for the plight of the Muslim *umma* in recent times. By failing to live up to the original demands of their "perfected religion,"[2] it is the recent generations of Muslims who are to blame for its humiliation at the hands of the "infidel" European powers (see Map 21.1). The plight of Islam, according to the concerned Muslim thinkers, necessitated a drastic revision of current Muslim teachings and practices with a view to either restoring them to their original purity or bringing them in line with the exigencies of the modern age.

It is against this general social and intellectual background that we should consider the articulation of the concepts of "reform" (*isláh*) and "renewal" (*tajdíd*) by some critically minded Muslim scholars of the late nineteenth and early twentieth centuries. One should point out that the solutions offered by reform-minded scholars were not always approved by their peers. On the contrary, the former initially remained a tiny, if vocal and active minority within the much larger cohort of their conservative colleagues committed to the time-honored teachings and practices of their respective legal and theological traditions. The conservative scholars considered it beneath their dignity to revise their convictions and procedures in response to the Western challenge. For the most part, they preferred to advocate the status quo or to offer some minor, gradual adjustments to the traditions they represented. Their main concern was to preserve the integrity of their faith and not to dilute it too much with borrowed ideas and practices.

Finally, a third group of Muslim intellectuals advocated a drastic restructuring of Islamic societies to bring them in line with Western values, institutions, and laws. In their opinion, because Western ways of doing things had proved to be superior to the traditional Muslim ones, the former should be adopted by Muslim societies wholesale, as it were. Taking their cue from the Western notion of the wall of separation between church and state, they demanded that religion be removed from the public realm into the sphere of each person's private life. For the most part, these thinkers belonged to the newly emerging Westernized elites and did not have a solid grounding in traditional theology and jurisprudence. This circumstance made them vulnerable to the criticism of conservative, traditionally educated scholars who accused them of ignorance of nuances of Islamic legal theory and theology.

Naturally, these diverse intellectual positions produced disparate programs for religious, social, and cultural transformation. They can be categorized respectively as modernist, traditionalist/conservative, and secularist.[3]

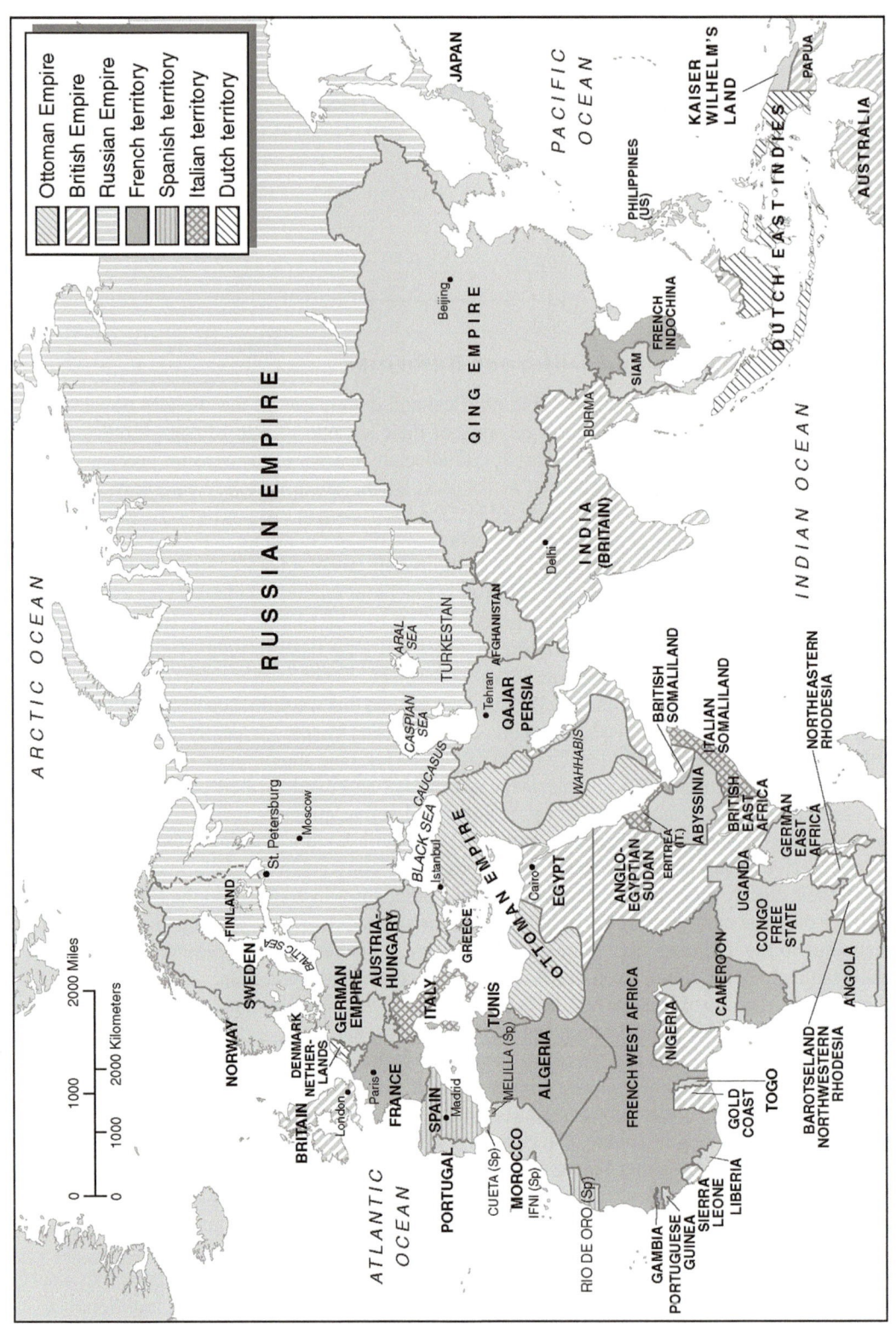

Map 21.1 European Colonial Expansion in the Muslim World in the Eighteenth and Nineteenth Centuries

The proponents of a modernist "improvement" (*isláh*) of Muslim life advocated a revivification of original Islamic precepts and practices with a view to purging it of what they regarded as idle superstitions, complacency, and intellectual stupor. In particular, they railed against blameworthy "innovations" (*bida'*; sing. *bid'a*) that had attached themselves to the pristine Islam of the Prophet and his immediate successors in the course of its long development. In the eyes of the Muslim modernists, such "accretions" as well as the lack of creative thinking among the recent generations of Muslims were the chief obstacles that had prevented Islam from successfully meeting the challenge posed by the resurgent West. To legitimize their reformist agendas, the modernists offered to return to the "original" or "authentic" teachings of Islam's scriptures as they understood them.

Here are a few examples of how the modernist thinkers attempted to justify their reformist agenda on scriptural grounds. Whereas the Qur'an and the Sunna contained numerous statements that could be interpreted as encouraging fatalistic submission to the inscrutable workings of the divine providence, the modernists would deliberately focus on those that enjoined the Muslims to actively reform or better themselves. One such passage is found in *sura* 11. It quotes the Qur'anic prophet Hud as saying (in verse 88): "I desire only to reform things (or set things right),[4] so far as I am able." The statement of the Qur'anic prophet was taken by the modernists as an unequivocal call upon the faithful to embrace social activism in order to improve the life of their communities. Given the plight of the Muslims in the face of Western technological and military superiority, the modernists/reformists interpreted this Qur'anic passage as encouragement for their coreligionists to change how they understood and practiced their religion.

To bring this idea home, the modernists would often quote another Qur'anic verse (8:53), according to which "God would never change the blessings with which He has graced a people unless they change their own selves." What was it if not God's appeal to his servants to reform themselves and their societies in response to the unprecedented challenges of the modern age?

Now, it should be pointed out that there was nothing particularly revolutionary about this call for reform of Islamic doctrines, institutions, and practices. In the premodern and early modern period, the Muslim community had never lacked individuals eager to initiate change, be it doctrinal or institutional, in order to "cleanse" the pristine faith and practice of the Prophet and his companions of all manner of "blameworthy innovations." The necessity of such a periodical reform of Islam is enshrined in a famous prophetic *hadíth* stating that, at the beginning of each Islamic century, God appoints a divinely guided "renewer" (*mujáddid*), who is entrusted with the task of restoring Islam to its former purity and glory. Among these renewers were such great scholars of the past as al-Ghazali (d. 1111; sixth Islamic century), Ibn Taymiyya (d. 1328; eighth century), Muhammad b. 'Abd al-Wahháb (d. 1792, eleventh century), and al-Shawkáni (d. 1834; twelfth century). These and other renewers left a rich legacy of reformist ideas that was eagerly tapped by later advocates of the Islamic reform, including Jamál al-Din al-Afgháni of Iran/Afghanistan (d. 1897), Muhammad 'Abdo of Egypt (d. 1905), Muhammad Rashíd Ridá (d. 1935) of Syria, Ibn Badís (d. 1940) of Algeria, and many others.

Although all these scholars agreed that the beliefs and practices of their coreligionists had to be reformed, they diverged over how to achieve this objective. Some advocated the restoration to their original purity of the beliefs and practices of the first community of Islam under the Prophet and his immediate successors. Others urged to bring Muslim life in conformity with the demands of the modern age by selectively borrowing Western technological and institutional achievements without, however, sacrificing the foundations of Islamic religion and culture. In all cases, the goal of the reformers was to purify Islam of "alien" elements and "superstitions," thereby restoring its former greatness.

The Fundamentalist Reform of Muhammad
b. 'Abd al-Wahhāb (d. 1792)

Whereas the role of Western political, military, and technological ascendancy in triggering movements for Islamic reform is hard to deny, the earliest such movement did not come in direct response to any immediate Western challenge. Rather, it was caused by local conditions, especially political fragmentation bordering on anarchy, a fierce competition for scarce resources among the Arab tribes of eastern Arabia, and the resultant demand of the local population for a state structure to impose order in the area. That popular demand was met by the formation of the Saudi-Wahhabi condominium.[5] It was only later that the presence in the Arabian Peninsula of the Ottoman Turks, who, as we know, were Sunni Muslims, became a factor in the vicissitudes of the reformist movement that had taken root there.[6]

Like scores of other reformist movements in Islam, the Saudi-Wahhabi one was launched in the name of cleansing Islam of "blameworthy innovations" and restoring it to its original purity.[7] This fundamentalist reform movement was initiated by the Arabian scholar Muhammad b. 'Abd al-Wahhāb, or Ibn 'Abd al-Wahhāb (d. 1791), as he is commonly called in Islamic chronicles. His legacy is still very much alive today in some areas of the Muslim world. Moreover, his following continues to grow in many Muslim countries, making the history of Ibn 'Abd al-Wahhāb's mission worthy of special mention.

Commonly referred to as "Wahhabism," this "puritanical" interpretation of Islam constitutes the ideological foundation of the Kingdom of Saudi Arabia and some Arab states of the Gulf region. Muslims who adhere to the teachings of Ibn 'Abd al-Wahhāb consider the term "Wahhabism" to be derogatory. They prefer to style themselves as "supporters of [the doctrine of] divine unity" (*muwahhidūn*) or "the adherents of the Prophet's Sunna and [communal] unity" (*ahl al-sunna wa 'l-jamá'a*).

Born in a family of religious scholars in an oasis in central Arabia, Muhammad b. 'Abd al-Wahhāb was schooled in the teachings of the Hanbali *mádhhab* of Sunni Islam. After mastering the basics of religious education, he pursued academic studies outside Arabia—in Iraq, Syria, Egypt, and western Iran. It appears that his exposure to various, often mutually hostile schools of thought within Islam convinced him that the Muslims had strayed from the path of the Prophet and his companions and had to be reeducated in the principles of "pure Islam," one that was free from "blameworthy innovations." From that moment on, the struggle against all manner of "innovations" became Ibn 'Abd al-Wahhāb's chief concern that eclipsed his other interests and preoccupations.[8] On returning from his travels, Ibn 'Abd al-Wahhāb settled in a village in eastern Arabia not far from the present capital of the Kingdom of Saudi Arabia, [al-]Riyadh. Around the mid-eighteenth century, his preaching of "pure Islam" attracted the attention of a local tribal chief of the Sa'ūd clan. Before long, Ibn 'Abd al-Wahhāb and the Sa'udi chief established a religiopolitical alliance aimed at eradicating what Ibn 'Abd al-Wahhāb branded as "vestiges of paganism" in the beliefs and practices of the local Muslims. In practical terms, this meant military conquest and the subsequent imposition of the "correct" Islam on the subjugated communities.

Ibn 'Abd al-Wahhāb's reformist program turned out to be too radical even for his colleagues who belonged to his own Hanbali school of law. They hastened to disown him and to declare him a "Kharijite" agitator due to his propensity to excommunicate and curse those Muslims who disagreed with his interpretation of Islam.[9] Unfazed, Ibn 'Abd al-Wahhāb continued his preaching in the name of the doctrine of divine oneness (*tawhíd*) and purifying Islam from all manner of harmful "aberrations." With time, Ibn 'Abd al-Wahhāb's teaching would become the official doctrine of the Sa'udi tribal state in eastern Arabia. Ibn 'Abd al-Wahhāb spent the rest of his life disseminating his ideas among the Bedouin communities of this area, commonly known as "Najd." After his death, his numerous descendants continued to spread his uncompromising interpretation of the doctrine of divine oneness with the robust military support of the Sa'úd clan.[10]

The doctrine of Ibn 'Abd al-Wahháb has some similarities with the teachings of the great Hanbali scholar Ibn Taymiyya (d. 1328),[11] who, in his own epoch, had distinguished himself as a relentless critic of "un-Islamic excesses," such as the adulation by the populace of Sufi masters, including visits to and worship at their tombs in the hopes of securing their blessing and intercession before God. Ibn 'Abd al-Wahháb took Ibn Taymiyya's message to the extreme by declaring any Muslim who adheres to such "illicit" forms of worship to be beyond the pale of Islam. In his words, "Believing in the [intercessory powers of] the pious is idolatry and whoever engages in this is an unbeliever."[12] Likewise, Ibn 'Abd al-Wahháb insisted that "touching the graves [of the pious] or visiting them with the intension of invoking the dead are not part of the religion of the Muslims."[13] With the support of the warlike Bedouin tribes loyal to the Sa'úd clan, Ibn 'Abd al-Wahháb launched a military and ideological campaign aimed at extirpating what he branded as the "pagan" practices of Arabian Muslims. Hundreds of saints' tombs and sacred sites across Arabia were desecrated or razed. Their visitors were threatened with severe punishment for violating the principle of divine oneness by seeking help from something or someone other than God. Taking a page from Ibn Taymiyya's book, Ibn 'Abd al-Wahháb excoriated all non-Sunni communities, including the Shi'ites, the Isma'ilis, the Zaydis, and so on.[14] For him, they were not only heretics but also apostates whose "blood was licit" to spill by the "true Muslims," that is, his followers. Ibn 'Abd al-Wahháb was also opposed to the teachings of the Sunni schools of law, speculative theology (*kalám*), and Sufism.[15] He condemned them as divisive "innovations" that had not existed during the lifetime of the Prophet but were introduced later by fallible human individuals:

> I am not calling you to the way of a Sufi or a *faqíh* or a *mutakállim* or one of the great *imam*s [of the past] . . . But I am calling you to God alone Who has no partners, and I am calling you to the Sunna of the Prophet which he bequeathed to the first and the last of his community.[16]

According to Ibn 'Abd al-Wahháb, "heretical innovations" had to be expunged from the faith and practice of the Muslim community in order to restore it to its erstwhile purity, glory, and power. The faithful should not follow blindly the fallible instructions of scholars and Sufi masters of old, no matter how distinguished. Rather, they must follow God's rulings as articulated in the Qur'an and the Sunna, bypassing the intervening juridical and pietistic traditions, which he dismissed as imperfect human products.[17] While practicing *bid'a* was, in Ibn 'Abd al-Wahháb's view, a serious violation of God's law, it did not necessarily render its practitioner an unbeliever. What made one an unbeliever was a willful and deliberate practical violation of the principle of God's oneness. Uttering the formula of divine oneness (*tawhíd*) alone was not, according to Ibn 'Abd al-Wahháb, enough to make someone a faithful Muslim. The words must always be supported by religiously sound acts of worship and behavior.[18] In this view, the worshipping and supplicating at saints' tombs and entertaining belief in their intercessory powers was not just *bid'a*. It was, in essence, an egregious manifestation of polytheism (*shirk*). As such, it must be redressed and its perpetrator punished. The same applies to submitting, sacrificing, and paying respect to someone or something other than God. Those guilty of this sin were, according Ibn 'Abd al-Wahháb, no better than the pagans of pre-Islamic Arabia who had rejected the Prophet's message of the one and only God. Hence his quarrel with Sufi masters, who, in his opinion, encouraged "pagan" practices by demanding the unquestioning obedience of their followers and, in so doing, positioning themselves as potential "idols" for the credulous populace.[19]

So strong was Ibn 'Abd al-Wahháb's aversion to all manner of *shirk* that he proclaimed those Muslims who refused to renounce it to be in the state of "ignorance" that had prevailed in Arabia on the eve of Islam. In a similar vein, he declared covert "idolaters" posing as Muslims to be apostates. Bearing in mind that apostasy is punishable by death under the Shari'a, this was a grave accusation indeed. Ibn 'Abd al-Wahháb considered himself to be the restorer of Islam's original purity and the reviver of the authentic beliefs of the practices of the "pious ancestors" (*sálaf sálih*), that is, the members of the first Muslim community at Medina. It is in this sense that one can designate him as "fundamentalist." Ibn 'Abd al-Wahháb demanded that his followers renounce obedience to rulers and religious authorities who did not act in accordance with his understanding of *tawhíd*. "*Tawhíd* was the citadel around which the people rallied, and the community that was held together by the presence of a ruler entitled to total obedience."[20] Inspired by his preaching of absolute and uncompromising *tawhíd*, Ibn 'Abd al-Wahháb's followers perceived themselves as a tiny faithful minority in a world corrupted by "paganism" and "idolatry."[21] It is with this idea in mind that Ibn 'Abd al-Wahháb and his supporters often quoted a *hadíth* in which the Prophet states that:

> Islam was born alone and will become alone again, as it was at its beginning. Happy are the solitary men. They will come to reform that which will be debased after my [the Prophet's] death.[22]

Ibn 'Abd al-Wahháb identified the "solitary men" mentioned by the Prophet as himself and his adherents. All other Muslims were declared to be in the state of sin, corruption, or outright apostasy. Naturally, this situation was intolerable for any true Muslim whom God had commanded to command good and forbid wrong.[23] It demanded immediate redress. No wonder that the proclamation of the Wahhabi theological creed had long-ranging political and military implications. Because, according to Ibn 'Abd al-Wahháb, words alone were not enough to prove one's faith; immediate and decisive actions were needed. The activist policy of enforcing "true Islam" started during Ibn 'Abd al-Wahháb's life and continued under his ideological successors and their Sa'udi supporters. The Wahhabi-Sa'udi religiopolitical alliance was intent on forcibly spreading the founder's teachings among the Bedouin tribes of Arabia and beyond. Infused with the righteous zeal, the Arabian tribes that had embraced the Wahhabi teaching launched a series of military attacks against neighboring countries, such as Iraq, Qatar, Oman, and Yemen. In 1802, Wahhabi levies devastated and plundered the Shi'ite sanctuaries of Lower Iraq, including the much revered tomb of the Shi'ite *imam* al-Husayn; in 1803, they seized Mecca and in 1805 overran Medina. While in the holy cities, the Wahhabis set about demolishing the tombs and mausoleums of the members of the Prophet's family and his successors. Domes over the birthplaces of Muhammad, 'Ali, Abu Bakr, and Khadíja were destroyed as the Muslim world looked on in horror. Even the Prophet's tomb did not escape the Wahhabis' iconoclastic rage. After overrunning Medina, the Wahhabi levies made an attempt to blow up the domed structure above it. The attempt failed.

To tighten up "loose morals" in their newly founded puritanical state, Wahhabi leaders prohibited the smoking of tobacco, the use of prayer beads, gambling, the celebration of the Prophet's birthday, and public Sufi gatherings and chants. Places of ill-repute and Sufi lodges were shut down, and any books that might lead good Muslims to polytheism, especially accounts of Sufi miracles, were put to the torch. The idea behind such drastic measures was to refocus the community's devotional life onto the mosque and the prayer. No alternative sites and means of worship were allowed in the Wahhabi realm. If they were found, they had to be suppressed, if necessary by force.[24] The study of Ibn 'Abd al-Wahhab's works was made compulsory in schools and study groups across eastern and central Arabia.

The Ottoman imperial authorities in Istanbul and Cairo were slow to recognize the gravity of the Wahhabi threat and to respond to it. Only in 1811 an Egyptian expeditionary force was dispatched to Arabia. Despite their religious fervor, the Wahhabi troops proved to be no match for the modernized and better equipped Egyptian military. In 1812–1813, the Egyptians expelled the Wahhabi forces from Mecca and Medina, and, in 1819, the Wahhabi headquarters in an Arabian oasis town was taken by storm and demolished. The leaders of the Wahhabiyya, including some four hundred of Muhammad b. ʿAbd al-Wahhab's descendants, were sent into exile or executed.

Nevertheless, soon after the Egyptian army had withdrawn, the chieftains of the Saʿud clan were able not only to rebuild their state but also to invade and conquer the lands of their Arabian neighbors. They moved their headquarters to the city of [al-]Riyadh that has remained the capital of the Saʿudi kingdom until today. Faced with the Wahhabi recrudescence, the Ottoman governor of Egypt, Muhammad ʿAli,[25] was again compelled to send another expeditionary force to suppress the movement. His efforts notwithstanding, the Wahhabi teachings and a small Saʿudi state built on their foundation survived the repeated Egyptian and Ottoman invasions. It was restored at the beginning of the twentieth century under the able leadership of king ʿAbd al-ʿAziz (d. 1953), better known as "Ibn Saʿud." In 1924–1925, Ibn Saʿud reconquered the Hijaz and the holy cities with the help of the British and his loyal Bedouin levies. As in the past, the war was waged in the name of purifying Islam of "blameworthy innovations." Ibn ʿAbd al-Wahhab's doctrine of *tawhid* became the official ideology of the new state, although with time his teaching was purged of its most radical and objectionable elements. Nevertheless, the principal points of Ibn ʿAbd al-Wahhab's religious creed, especially his overriding emphasis on the strict enforcement of *tawhid* and the concomitant rejection of anything smacking of polytheism (*shirk*), have remained unchanged until this day.[26]

In the second half of the twentieth century, the Wahhabi state managed to rehabilitate itself in the eyes of many Muslims by establishing numerous Islamic charities and schools, building mosques, funding various Islamic humanitarian causes, generously supporting the anti-Soviet *jihad* in Afghanistan, and organizing and hosting the annual *hajj* to Mecca. Yet the Wahhabis have failed to conciliate the Shiʿites of Iran, Iraq, and India, as well as numerous Sufi communities across the Muslim world.[27] Critics of Saudi Arabia in the West and the Muslim world consider it an authoritarian monarchy that is cunningly using Islam to stifle any opposition to its rule and to justify its grip on power. Many Western and Muslim commentators hold the Wahhabi religious establishment of the Kingdom of Saudi Arabia responsible for aiding and abetting militancy and terrorism in the name of Islam.[28] At the same time, many devout Muslims look to the Kingdom of Saudi Arabia as a beacon of the pure and unadulterated Islam of the Prophet and the first four caliphs and follow the authoritative rulings (*fatwa*s) of the country's conservative scholars.

The Modernist Reforms of al-Afghani and ʿAbdo

Ibn ʿAbd al-Wahhab's movement for the reformation of Muslim teachings and practices on the basis of his interpretation of the principle of *tawhid* unfolded within the context of a relatively socially backward and intellectually unsophisticated society of tribal Arabia. As such, it was in no need of—and actually lacked—a solid intellectual underpinning.[29] It would have hardly been appreciated by the reformer's uncouth tribal supporters anyway. On the other hand, the master plans for reforming the life of the *umma* that emerged in the more urbane environment of the core lands of Islam took on a more intellectually sophisticated shape. Furthermore, unlike Ibn ʿAbd al-Wahhab's teaching, which was based on and inspired almost exclusively by the Muslim scriptures and made no explicit references to Western ideas, the reformist agendas of the educated modernists of Egypt, Syria, Iran, Russia, and India were articulated in direct response to the political, military, administrative, and cultural ascendancy of Western powers. Typical in this regard is the reformist agenda formulated by the Iranian-born scholar Jamal al-Din al-Afghani.

Jamál al-Din al-Afgháni (d. 1897)

Although coming from a Shi'ite family of Iran, al-Afgháni chose to conceal his true origins out of concern that his Shi'ite upbringing might prevent the Sunni majority of the *umma* from accepting his demand that all Muslims should unify in the face of Western supremacy. To this end, he assumed the name "al-Afgháni" which implied that he was a Sunni Muslim.[30] Al-Afgháni's life can be seen as a series of journeys, first in quest of knowledge and later on a mission to disseminate among his coreligionists his message of the reform, rejuvenation, and unification of Muslim societies against the common threat of European colonialism. In the course of his travels, al-Afgháni acquired a solid mastery of Islamic theology and philosophy, which served him in good stead later in life.

While still in his teens, al-Afgháni left Iran for Afghanistan, where he became embroiled in local politics. He then traveled to India, where he gained firsthand experience of British rule. His criticism of British colonial rule in the Subcontinent attracted the hostile attention of the British authorities of India, as a result of which he had to emigrate to Cairo. During his long stay in the Egyptian capital, al-Afgháni won a relatively large following among local religious scholars and intelligentsia, some of whom were to become major lights in their respective fields of endeavor (education, administration, and politics). Among al-Afgháni's favorite students was the famous Egyptian scholar and journalist Muhammad 'Abdo, who was instrumental in keeping al-Afgháni's modernist agenda alive after his death. Following the failure of the 1882 Egyptian mutiny against British control of the country, in which al-Afgháni was indirectly implicated, he was banished from Egypt and settled in Paris. The French, who spared no effort to undermine the recently established British dominion over Egypt, seem to have taken him under their wing.

It is not clear who exactly funded al-Afgháni's short-lived but highly influential periodical "The Firmest Bond" (*al-'Urwa al-wuthqa*). Published in Arabic, it served as the mouthpiece of al-Afgháni's reformist program aimed at rejuvenating Muslim societies and rallying them around the common goal of ridding the Muslim world of infidel domination, especially that of the British. The latter goal was to be achieved by liberating the Muslims from their oppressive but ineffective rulers and the unification of the Muslim lands on the basis of the commonality of Muslim principles and vigorous prosecution of *jihád* against the Western colonial powers.[31] Collectively, these principles have come to be known as "pan-Islamism" (see Figure 21.1).[32]

Al-Afgháni edited "The Firmest Bond" together with his disciple Muhammad 'Abdo, who had joined his mentor in exile. Their contributions laid out foundations for a comprehensive reform of Muslim states aimed at empowering them against Western colonial encroachments. Al-Afgháni and 'Abdo's ideas proved too radical for Muslim rulers whom the reformers hoped to win over to their side in order to implement their ambitious religiopolitical projects. Copies of *The Firmest Bond* were prohibited from circulation in Turkey, Egypt, and India, and its publication was discontinued after eight months. Nevertheless, the periodical had a profound impact on many Muslim intellectuals who were dissatisfied with the subjugated status of their countries vis-à-vis the West and seeking ways to redress this humiliating dependency.

Al-Afgháni was more than just a vocal advocate of Islamic reform; he was also an active revolutionary who had no compunctions about using violence to achieve his goals. Some Western scholars argue that, in the end, al-Afgháni the revolutionary gained the upper hand over al-Afgháni the reformer.[33] Throughout his eventful life story, which reads like a thriller, al-Afgháni aspired to implement his ideas in real life by creating secret societies and converting Muslim rulers and high-ranking officials to his cause. He believed that his political acumen and rhetorical skills would enable him to manipulate the rulers and thus facilitate the achievement of his revolutionary ends. This was not to be. In the final account, the rulers' dynastic and personal interests proved to be at odds with al-Afgháni's pan-Islamic and revolutionary aspirations. This is hardly

Figure 21.1 Jamál al-Din al-Afgháni (d. 1897)
Yaquub Abd al-Aziiz Abul Ala Maududi/Public Domain/Wikimedia Commons

surprising because the rulers often represented the very forces of "obscurantism" and "impediment to progress and enlightenment" that al-Afgháni was determined to abolish.[34] In an age when there were no viable political parties and autocracy ruled supreme, al-Afgháni's preferred tactics were "assassinations, wars, intrigues or revolts."[35] This cloak-and-dagger approach to politics would hardly endear the reformer to Muslim autocrats, who felt that they may well end up as targets of his revolutionary plotting. Thus, al-Afgháni tried to convert to his cause the *amír* of Afghanistan, the leading political figures of Egypt, the Shah of Iran, and the Sultan of Ottoman Turkey, but to no avail. He was repeatedly expelled, placed under house arrest, imprisoned, or even threatened with execution. His only major revolutionary "success" was the assassination of the Iranian shah by one of his followers.

Other factors as well seemed to have soured al-Afgháni's relations with the Muslim ruling class. On the one hand, the monarchs were concerned that his vocal anti-Western invectives may offend the sensitivities of the Western powers on whose benevolence their regimes were so heavily dependent both economically and politically.[36] On the other, al-Afghání's appeals to the Muslim masses to rise and unite in the face of Western imperialism implicitly endangered the sovereigns' autocratic rule. Be this as it may, al-Afghání had no option but to court the rulers in order to convince them to initiate a comprehensive political, social, and military reform "from above." He was driven by the belief, which is still quite common among some Muslim thinkers, that it is possible to borrow selectively from the West only those elements that do not undermine the Muslims' religious and cultural identity, while empowering them militarily and politically.[37]

While al-Afghání had little success in winning over Muslim rulers, he was equally unsuccessful with their European counterparts. His persistent efforts to play one Western government against the other in order to liberate his fellow Muslims from the European imperial yoke bore no fruit. Al-Afghání ended his days in 1897 in Istanbul, where he was held under what amounted to house arrest on the orders of the Ottoman sultan.

Al-Afghání's adventures did not end with his death, though. His body was buried in an unmarked grave in one of Istanbul's cemeteries. A few decades later, al-Afghání's posthumous fame came to the attention of the American millionaire philanthropist Charles R. Crane (1858–1939), an Arabophile maverick. Crane ordered that al-Afghání's tomb—by that time neglected and forgotten—had to be found. He then provided funds to erect over it a monument to commemorate the Muslim thinker's intellectual and revolutionary legacy. In another bizarre quirk of fate, in 1944 al-Afghání's body was claimed by the Afghan government—after all, the thinker always maintained that he was an Afghan by birth. The Afghan authorities had his body exhumed and transported to the country's capital Kabul, where it was reburied with state honors. Whether or not these were indeed al-Afghání's remains,[38] this was a fitting end to al-Afghání's extraordinary life and political career.

Al-Afghání was an exceptional individual by any standard. A fiery orator versed in the major languages of Islam, he was able to win over to his cause many important intellectual and religious figures of the age. While, as we have seen, he was not very successful with Muslim and European rulers, many Muslim intellectuals found his fiery speeches and grand reformist projects to be persuasive. Some became his lifelong admirers and active proponents of his pan-Islamist and reformist agendas. Al-Afghání was particularly effective in front of live audiences. His written legacy, on the other hand, is rather modest. So, what were the main points of his masterplan for the transformation of the Muslim world in the face of European domination?

While in India and Egypt, al-Afghání had a chance to observe firsthand the impact of British colonialism on a Muslim society. He did not like what he saw. India's Muslims were forced to follow alien, non-Islamic laws and found themselves closely supervised and indoctrinated by the colonizer. Their Islamic identity was eroded by the wholesale imposition of Western-style education, social conventions, and culture by the British Raj. Like many Indian Muslim intellectuals, al-Afghání was impressed by the British technological, military, and economic superiority, as well as the administrative efficiency of colonial institutions. At the same time, he was deeply disturbed by the Muslims' subjugated status in British India and later also in Egypt. This subjugation to the foreign colonial master was, in his view, particularly intolerable in view of Islam's past intellectual excellence and political grandeur. Al-Afghání became an ardent advocate for Islamic resurgence:

> If someone says: "If the Islamic world is as you say, then why are the Muslims in such a sad condition?" I will answer: "When they were truly Muslims, they were what they were and the world bears witness to their excellence. As for the present, I will content myself with this holy text: 'Verily, God does not change the state of a people until they change themselves inwardly.'"[39]

Drastic measures were needed to rectify the plight of the Muslim world. According to al-Afghání, to liberate the *umma* from foreign dependence, it was essential that its members embrace the technological and scientific achievements of the West without, however, sacrificing the foundations of their faith and culture. A delicate balance had to be struck between the scientific exigencies of the modern age and the perennial truths of the Muslim religion. Contrary to the unfavorable view of Islam actively promoted by its European detractors, it was originally a religion of reason that encouraged scientific inquiry and artistic creativity. The West itself benefited greatly from Islamic scientific discoveries and artistic achievements. Therefore, Islam, if interpreted correctly, is by no means an obstacle to progress. Rather it is a natural vehicle for scientific and cultural advancement, and the true Muslims should never lose hope of restoring it to its original glory:

> Realizing that the Christian religion preceded the Muslim religion in the world, I cannot keep from hoping that Muhammadan society will succeed someday in breaking its bonds and marching resolutely in the path of civilization after the manner of Western society today. . . . No, I cannot admit that this hope be denied to Islam.[40]

In this passage, al-Afghání attempts to counter the claims of those Western scholars who insist that Islam is a backward, obscurantist religion incompatible with scientific progress. One should point out that in his defense of Islam, al-Afghání appeals to those of its aspects that were definitely not the ones emphasized and preached by more conservative Muslim scholars. Nor is it the Islam practiced by the Muslim masses. Rather, by underscoring the rationalist, enlightened, and science-oriented aspects of Islamic faith, al-Afghání consciously or unconsciously adopts the intellectual position of medieval Muslim philosophers, such as al-Farábi, Ibn Sina, and Ibn Rushd. As discussed in Chapter 14, these Muslim thinkers argued that while it was the task of the Muslim intellectual elite to pursue scientific investigations of general laws of nature unencumbered by the constraints of the religious dogma, the "unenlightened" masses should stick to the outward norms of the Shari'a, which was revealed to them so as to prevent them from succumbing to their unruly passions and irrational drives. For the common folk, going beyond the basic knowledge of God's oneness, existence, and commands would be a great strain beyond their intellectual abilities. Moreover, in trying to advance beyond Islam's basics, they are likely to "go off into discussions and speculations which prevent them from attending to their bodily acts and which . . . cause them to fall into opinions contrary to the good of society and inconsistent with the requirements of truth."[41] Even more seriously, such "discussions and speculations" may split the Muslim community into mutually hostile sects and factions. This would go against the grain of al-Afghání's cherished objective to unify all Muslims in the face of foreign domination. To achieve this objective, the Muslim masses should be instructed to take pride in Islam's great scientific achievements and be confident of the essential superiority of their faith over other religious creeds, especially Christianity. It was not necessary for them to delve into difficult scholastic and scientific issues on their own because this was the prerogative of the *umma*'s sophisticated intellectual elite. In short, in al-Afghání's teaching, the Islamic religion is transformed from a generally held religious faith and devotional practice into "an ideology of political use in uniting Muslims against the West."[42]

As just mentioned, al-Afghání's pragmatic view of revealed religion as a necessary check on the inherently violent and undisciplined human nature harks back to premodern *fálsafa*. Only now it was articulated against the background of the new geopolitical realities that were characterized by the subjugated status of Muslim nations due to the military, economic, and technological superiority of European powers. To challenge these unfavorable geopolitical realities, al-Afghání sought to press Islam into service by making it "into the mainspring of solidarity . . . on the same footing as other solidarity-producing beliefs."[43] This "instrumentalization" of religious faith became a distinctive hallmark of most programs of Islamic revival throughout the twentieth century.

Here is a brief outline of al-Afghání's major goals and methods to achieve them.[44] In adopting the old philosophical notion that the religion of the masses is inherently incompatible with the truths obtained through rational philosophical inquiry, al-Afghání used different levels of discourse while addressing different audiences. Since the overwhelming majority of his coreligionists were, in his opinion, incapable of grasping higher intellectual truths, they should be addressed in the only language they were able to understand, that of the allegories and myths of the Qur'anic revelation. To successfully meet the challenges of modernity, the masses should be persuaded that the desirable Western values and ideas were not original to Europe but could be discovered in the Qur'an and were in fact practiced by the earlier generations of Muslims at the time of Islam's prime. The promotion of this conviction became a favorite keynote of modernist reform agenda in the subsequent decades.[45]

When speaking to his intimate companions and, even more so, to European audiences, al-Afghání was much more frank. Some European intellectuals actually considered him a freethinker, if not a full-fledged heretic.[46] In his response (published in French) to a negative assessment of Islam by the renowned French intellectual Ernest Renan (1823–1892), he first admitted that:

> Religions, by whatever name they are called, resemble each other. No reconciliation is possible between these religions and philosophy. Religion imposes on man its faith and its belief, whereas philosophy frees him of it totally or in part. How could one therefore hope that they would agree with one another?[47]

Even more strikingly, al-Afghání makes no exception to Islam in this respect:

> It is permissible, however, to ask oneself why Arab civilization, after having thrown such a live light on the world, suddenly became extinguished; why this torch has not been relit since; and why the Arab world still remains buried in profound darkness? Here the responsibility of the Muslim religion appears complete. It is clear that wherever it became established, this religion tried to stifle the sciences and was marvelously served in its designs by despotism.[48]

No wonder that conservative Muslim scholars took a dim view of al-Afghání's ideas. For them, he was "a rebel against religion [who] came to believe that it was the enemy of science, reason and civilization."[49] In 1870, the chief religious official of the Ottoman Empire (*shaykh al-Islam*) expelled al-Afghání from Istanbul after he had given a bold talk about crafts and trade under Islam at the newly established Turkish University.[50] Following his death, his disciples 'Abdo and Rashíd Ridá went to great lengths to absolve him of accusations of heresy and unbelief. They have partly succeeded in this task. Al-Afghání's current image as an essentially orthodox Muslim thinker is largely the product of their prodigious efforts.

Since al-Afghání was ready to speak to every audience in the language they could understand, he inevitably found himself caught up in self-contradictions. His pan-Islamic agenda—that is, the idea that Islamic identity should transcend all other parochial identities, including nationalism, and that the Muslims of the world must rally against the West—did not prevent him from appealing to the growing nationalistic sentiment of Iranians, Egyptians, and Turks. How can these divergent aspirations be reconciled? Having witnessed in his lifetime the inexorable encroachment of European powers into Muslims lands (in Africa, Egypt, India, and Central Asia), al-Afghání became convinced that any ideology that would allow the Muslims to rise from their knees should be pressed into service. If this is pan-Islamism, fine; if this is nationalism—admittedly a Western import—this is fine as well. In line with this opportunistic attitude, al-Afghání was even eager to put up with the Westernization of Muslim societies, if it would improve their chances of ridding themselves of Western political domination. This idea of his, too, inevitably led to a contradiction, because embracing Western values and institutions, as we have seen, almost inevitably results in the loss by the Muslims of their Islamic identity (at least in its traditional sense), as well as a progressive secularization of Muslim societies. Al-Afghání strove to resolve this contradiction by claiming that Western technological and scientific advances, as well as efficient political and administrative structures, were in fact borrowed from Islamic civilization at its prime. It was, he insisted, the fault of later Muslim generations not to take advantage of the great legacy they had inherited from their forebears.[51] Thus, the principal task of the Muslims was to reappropriate the rationalist attitudes and scientific skills of their ancestors that had been "hijacked" by the European Christians. This should enable the *umma* to regain its erstwhile military and political strength and expel the Christian colonizers from the Muslim lands.

In sum, al-Afghání was primarily preoccupied with the "practical and political" aspects of Islam, "rather than its speculative and theological side."[52] He wanted to empower Muslim countries "here and now," either by means of a popular revolution or a powerful ruler's imposition of progressive reforms from above. In the end, however, al-Afghání efforts came to naught. His successors adopted a more gradualist approach to the tasks in hand, stressing a broad educational reform and a step-by-step adoption of modern ideas and technologies by Muslim societies. Foremost among them was Muhammad 'Abdo.

Muhammad 'Abdo (d. 1905)

Born in the Egyptian countryside of a humble family known for its learning and piety, Muhammad 'Abdo[53] studied reading and writing at home. His homeschooling experience gave him an outsider's perspective on the mechanical rote learning that had prevailed in Egypt's Qur'anic schools and mosques. His attempts to integrate himself into the traditional educational system, first in the Egyptian city of Tanta and later at the famous Islamic university al-Ázhar in Cairo, were unsuccessful. Already at that early stage, he became convinced of the necessity to drastically overhaul the educational process that was in use in Egyptian schools and colleges. In his autobiography, 'Abdo provides a damning assessment of the sorry state of Egyptian religious education:

> I spent a year and a half without understanding a single thing, because of the harmful character of the method of instruction; for the teachers were accustomed to use technical terms of grammar or jurisprudence which we did not understand, nor did they take any pains to explain their meaning to those who did not know it . . . .
>
> The teacher throws out what he knows, and what he does not know, without paying regard to the pupil and his capacity for understanding. But the majority of the students who do not understand, deceive themselves into supposing that they do understand something, so that they continue their studies until they have reached the age of manhood . . . and thereafter they are inflicted upon the people and become a calamity upon the public.[54]

Frustrated by the lack of progress in his studies, the young 'Abdo entered the Sufi path under on the advice of his pious uncle, who, in his words, "delivered me from the prison of ignorance." The young man adopted an ascetic lifestyle, spending nights in prayer, reciting Sufi *dhikr*, and wearing a rough woolen garment next to his body. Al-Afghani continued to engage in ascetic exercises even after he had settled in Cairo to study Islamic sciences at the al-Ázhar university.[55]

Around 1871, his Sufi master (*shaykh*) advised him to abandon his ascetic strictures and mystical meditations in order to spread the light of true religious learning among his fellow Muslims. It was around that time that he met the charismatic al-Afghání, who had recently arrived in Cairo from Istanbul. Al-Afghání's lively, unconventional lectures on theology, philosophy, jurisprudence, astronomy, and mysticism were like a breath of fresh air for the young man. 'Abdo described al-Afgháni's teaching method as follows:

> He would often explain the meaning of a point under discussion until it became clear to the understanding, then he would read the statement of the book and apply it to the point in question; if it was applicable, well; if not, he would point out what was lacking in it.[56]

'Abdo was captivated by al-Afgháni's critical and self-reflective approach to learning that was so different from the slavish acceptance of received wisdom by both pupils and teachers alike, which he observed firsthand in the classrooms of al-Ázhar University. In addition to the traditional Islamic sciences, al-Afgháni exposed his intellectually agile ward to the major Western philosophical theories and concepts of history by assigning him Arabic translations of European authors. 'Abdo's meeting with al-Afgháni transformed his entire life. He began to follow his teacher "like a shadow," and, after he had matured, he became al-Afgháni's principal collaborator in all of the latter's undertakings.

After receiving the formal degree of a religious scholar (*'álim*) from Ázhar University, 'Abdo embarked on a career of teacher and journalist. In 1879, his protest against the British intervention in Egypt's internal affairs led to his temporary expulsion from the country. One year later, he was pardoned by the liberal Egyptian prime minister Riyad Pasha, who appointed him as an editor and later editor-in-chief of Egypt's major official newspaper, "The Egyptian Events." This position gave 'Abdo the opportunity to take a direct part in shaping the country's public opinion. His contributions were often critical of government officials and demonstrated his abiding concern for the progress of the Egyptian nation. Unlike his revolutionary-minded mentor, 'Abdo was an advocate of gradual change in the customs, ideas, and behavior of his people. Such a change, according to 'Abdo, could not be accomplished by a ruler's decree and required a long time. Based on his adolescent experiences, he was convinced that no social progress was possible without a drastic improvement in education and the creation of a cohort of progressively minded religious scholars, who would then disseminate their ideas among the masses. 'Abdo's gradualist approach was tested in 1882, during an uprising of the Egyptian nationalist officers who were determined to "free the country from bondage to foreigners." Despite his aversion to using force in achieving political and social goals, 'Abdo took advantage of his position as censor and general director of the press of Egypt to support the rebellious officers.[57] After their uprising was quashed by the British, he was put on trial for treason and exiled to Syria. He resided in Beirut for some time[58] and then joined al-Afgháni in his Paris exile. As mentioned earlier, the two men launched the periodical entitled "The Firmest Bond." Its principal message to all Muslim peoples was "to unite on the basis of their common faith in order to resist the aggressions of their own rulers and those of foreign countries of another faith, and restore the lost glories of a united and victorious Islam." In one of his contributions 'Abdo stated:

> Islam is the one bond which unites Muslims of all countries and obliterates all traces of race and nationality. Its Divine Law regulates in detail the rights and duties of all, both rulers and subjects, and removes all racial distinctions and occasion for competition within the body of Islam . . . Islam does not concern itself only with the future life, as do other religions, but also deals sufficiently with this present life . . . The Muslim peoples were once united under one glorious empire, and their achievements in learning and philosophy and all sciences are still the boast of all Muslims. It is the duty incumbent upon all Muslims to aid in maintaining the authority of Islam and Islamic rule over all lands that have once been Muslim.[59]

"The Firmest Bond" was designed by their editors to furnish a comprehensive analysis of the weaknesses of Muslim societies. According to al-Afgháni and 'Abdo, the main causes of Islam's subjugated state lay in (a) the widespread ignorance or distorted understanding of the foundations of Islamic religion by the later generations of Muslims and (b) the wanton despotism and injustice of past and present Muslim rulers.[60] These weaknesses had eventually invited and facilitated foreign intervention into the affairs of Muslim countries and their loss of independence. In the words of 'Abdo:

> Today we see Muslim rulers giving free hand to foreigners to carry on the affairs of their states and even of their own houses, and fastening foreign rule upon their own necks. Europeans, greedy for Muslim lands, seek to destroy their religious unity and thus take advantage of the inner discord of Islam. Foreigners employed by Muslim governments . . . are not concerned for the honor of the state and its welfare, but look only for their pay and think only of their own interests. But the Muslim nations [too] today are not concerned about helping one another.[61]

'Abdo proceeded to accuse both Muslim rulers and scholars loyal to them of failing to unify their nations against the common threat. Thus, the blame did not lie exclusively at the door of the European states that ruled over most Muslim lands. Rather, the Muslims themselves were at fault. They were obligated to reform their societies in order to stand up to Western domination but were remiss in this task. "The only cure for these [Muslim] nations," wrote 'Abdo, "is to return to the rules of their religion and the practice of its requirements according to what it was in the beginning, in the days of the early Caliphs."[62]

For al-Afghāni, as we remember, the surest way to this goal was a radical transformation of Muslim societies from above or a popular uprising led by a charismatic, *máhdi*-like leader.[63] 'Abdo, on the other hand, wanted this goal to be achieved through a gradual and patient improvement of educational institutions and a measured inculcation in the Muslim youth of progressive, activist attitudes to life and work. In one of his treatises he wrote: "I had learned that [change] is a fruit which the nations gather from plantings which they themselves plant and nourish through long years. It is this planting which requires to be attended to now."[64]

As for "the matter of the government and the governed," it should, in 'Abdo's opinion, be abandoned "to the decision of fate."[65] This approach was different from that of his teacher who, as we remember, was eager to involve himself in state politics. In his administrative and educational activities following his return from exile, 'Abdo remained true to his gradualist, measured attitude to reform. Initially opposed to Ottoman dominion over Egypt, he later changed his mind and came to view the Ottoman dynasty as the Muslims' best hope for securing Egypt's independence from infidel rule (despite the Ottomans' obvious inability to do so). At the same time, he was not entirely averse to cooperating with the Egyptian government, now effectively "in the pocket" of the British Empire, as long as this cooperation helped to advance his reformist plans. 'Abdo's liberal and nonviolent agenda appealed to both the native Egyptian authorities and the British consul-general of the country Lord Cromer. He was given a number of high-ranking appointments in the Egyptian government, mostly in the judiciary, and served on a committee charged with the reform of the Ázhar University. Furthermore, in 1899, he became the chief *mufti* of Egypt. This was the highest office an Egyptian scholar could aspire to obtain because its holder was the supreme official interpreter of the Shari'a for the entire country, whose legal rulings (*fátwas*) were considered final and binding for all Egyptian Muslims.

This is not the place to detail 'Abdo's judicial and administrative accomplishments. Suffice it to say that until his death in 1905 he remained committed to his reformist and modernizing ideas. However, his attempts to reform first the Ázhar University and later the country's courts dealing with matters of personal status faltered. It should be pointed out that, in 'Abdo's age, both institutions were in a sorry state, ridden as they were by corruption, incompetence, petty corporate interests, and lack of accountability. Whereas 'Abdo's reforms were carefully thought through and admirably designed, their implementation ran into a stiff opposition on the part of conservative scholars who held on doggedly to the old ways and resented any change in the status quo as long as it was favorable to their personal and corporative interests. 'Abdo's attempts to overhaul the university curriculum by adding new subjects prompted his conservative peers to accuse him of seeking to convert al-Ázhar into "a school of philosophy and literary education" and, in so doing, to "extinguish the light of Islam."[66] His proposed reforms of the judicial system were favorably received at the top but never implemented due to the lack of political will and resources. As in the case of his mentor al-Afgháni, opposition to 'Abdo's reformist agenda often found expression in personal attacks on his religious credentials. His conservative critics among 'ulamá' found fault with "his association with Afghani, his interest in *fálsafa*, his advocacy of certain Mu'tazilite principles, his prohibition of traditional interpretation (*taqlíd*), his call for the study of modern sciences, his preference for the science of the Franks, and also letting his hair grow long (presumably like a [Sufi] dervish)."[67]

Referring to 'Abdo's West-induced liberalism, one of his former companions remarked that his head "was better [suited] for a [European] hat than a turban."[68] This observation seems to be all the more pertinent in the light of 'Abdo's *fátwas* giving permission to the Muslims of South Africa to wear European-style hats (as a concession to the prevailing custom of that society).[69] 'Abdo's liberal views are evident from his other legal rulings, which he issued in response to numerous requests not only from Egyptian Muslims but from those around the world as well. In one such ruling, contrary to the prevailing legal opinion, he allowed Muslims to consume the flesh of animals by Jews and Christians. In another, he made it lawful for Muslims to deposit their savings in Egyptian savings banks where they would draw interest. This ruling flew in the face of the famous Qur'anic prohibition of usury,[70] causing a major uproar among the country's conservative 'ulamá'.[71]

'Abdo's position on polygamy is yet another evidence of his liberal treatment of controversial religious issues. He argued that the Qur'anic permission for Muslim men to take more than one wife was predicated on the requirement that the husbands should treat their women equally in every respect—financially, physically, emotionally, and so on.[72] The Qur'an itself (4:129) expresses doubts as to whether husbands are able to remain impartial in dealing with their several wives. For 'Abdo, this scriptural doubt amounted to the effective ban of polygamous marriage because, in his opinion, even the Prophet himself was partial toward 'A'isha at the expense of his other wives.[73] While formally the Qur'anic permission to take multiple wives should be allowed to stand, 'Abdo suggested that the husband who intends to take a second wife be subject to a special examination by scholars of law to determine his ability to remain impartial toward both wives. This ruling effectively implied that polygamous marriages would not be authorized except in exceptional cases. For 'Abdo, polygamy made sense only during the first centuries of Islam and had since been superseded by new social sensitivities and moral values. He tried to show that polygamy was clearly detrimental to contemporary Egyptian society insofar as it bred animosities and hatred among wives and their offspring within a polygamous household.[74] Therefore, the frequency of polygamous marriages should be reduced to a minimum by setting legal obstacles for husbands intent on exercising their right to it.

This view logically springs from 'Abdo's general approach to the interpretation of the Shari'a. In his opinion, Islamic law contains some requirements (such as *shaháda*, prayer, fasting during Ramadán, almsgiving, and performing the *hajj*) that are immutable and not subject to reinterpretation. They constitute the very heart of Islam. Alongside them are those rules and norms that 'Abdo considered to pertain to "mundane matters." These, according to 'Abdo, are subject to change and reinterpretation to reflect the changing circumstances of the life of the *umma*. They include, among others, regulations regarding "divorce, polygamy, slavery and the like."[75] The task of reinterpreting them in accordance with the demands of the new age devolves upon the leading scholars of the community. The latter should accomplish it by abandoning blind dependence on prior legal authorities (*taqlíd*) and embracing a free and independent investigation of legal and moral issues at hand, in order to bring their legislative activity in line with new social circumstances (*ijtihád*) as they evolve. The notion of a dynamic relation between the immutable/essential and changeable/nonessential aspects of the Muslim revelation has proved highly influential among later Muslim reformers to become an important part of Islamic reformist agendas until today.

Let us now briefly outline the major points of 'Abdo's religious program, bearing in mind that many of his ideas had a profound impact on Muslims well beyond Egypt. These points still figure prominently in the programs of Islamic/Islamist political parties as well as individual and collective blueprints for the reform of Islam and Muslim societies. 'Abdo's religious creed is expounded in a relatively short treatise entitled "The Message of Divine Oneness" (*Risalat al-tawhíd*).[76] Its lucid, accessible style is indicative of the author's desire to reach out to Muslims of all social classes, not just the theologically proficient scholarly elite.[77] At the outset, 'Abdo declares the purpose of his creed to be:

> The correction of the articles of belief and the removal of the mistakes which have crept into them through misunderstanding of the basic texts of the religion, in order that, once the beliefs have been made free of harmful innovations, the activities of Muslims may, as a result, be made free from disorder and confusion, the conditions of individual Muslims be improved, their understanding enlightened by the true sciences, both religious and secular, and wholesome traits of character developed.[78]

To rectify the current plight of the *umma*, 'Abdo urged its members to return to the Qur'an as the only true foundation of their religion because "to attempt reform by means of a culture or philosophy that is not religious in character would require the erection of a new structure, for which neither materials nor workmen are available."[79] According to 'Abdo, the Islamic doctrine and practice, shorn of harmful accretions such as the blind adherence to prior authorities (*taqlíd*) and despotism, should become the primary framework for a comprehensive reform of Islamic societies aimed at bringing them in harmony with the exigencies of the modern age. To succeed in this difficult undertaking, the Muslims must unite around the authentic teachings of the Qur'an and the Prophet. Anything that stands in the way of their unity should be brushed aside, especially "the matters that they [Muslims] have added to it [Islam], perhaps derived from some other religion."[80] Among these, 'Abdo singles out the cult of "God's friends," or "saints," which, he suggests, was borrowed by Muslims from Catholic Christianity and which, in his opinion, distracts the Muslims from the urgent task of rebuilding their lives on authentic Islamic principles. On the doctrinal plane, he condemns the fruitless debates over the divine predestination and human free will, as well as over the nature of God's unique essence and its relationship with multiple divine attributes. 'Abdo dismisses the former issue as "an attempt to pry into the secrets of Destiny, which we have been forbidden to plunge into." Wrangling over the latter issue is not conducive to the improvement of Muslim life and therefore should be abandoned. Those who continue to engage in such useless discussions are directly responsible for the creation of the "divisions and sects" that have weakened the originally unified and powerful *umma*.[81] In short, "it is sufficient," argues 'Abdo, "to know that God possesses these attributes. Anything beyond that He has concealed within His own knowledge, and it is not possible for our reason to attain to it. For this reason, the Qur'an and previous books only direct attention to that which has been created."[82]

The Qur'an being concerned primarily with mundane matters, the Muslims too should focus their attention on the acquisition of knowledge of the "here and now" and, in so doing, to appreciate better the perfection of God's creative design. This was exactly the view maintained by the Muslim philosophers of the classical age of Islam who, in 'Abdo's words, devoted themselves to "the discovery of the secrets which are concealed in the bosom of the universe."[83] Furthermore, according to 'Abdo, neither philosophy nor any other sciences related to the empirical world "should be mixed up with questions of religion." This being said, he still considers Islam to be preeminently a religion of reason whose former greatness depended on the Muslims' determination to exercise their rational faculties and logic. As long as Muslims had applied their collective intellectual power to the proper object (i.e., nature, not God), Islam was triumphant. However, after the free exercise of reason (*ijtihád*) had been abandoned by later generations of Muslims in favor of the blind adherence to authoritative precedents (*taqlíd*), the political and economic fortunes of the Muslim world suffered a precipitous decline. To prove his point, 'Abdo invokes numerous Qur'anic passages which, in his opinion, confirm the lack of conflict between revelation and scientific enquiry. In fact, he argues, the Qur'an foretold many recent scientific discoveries. To conclude his argument, 'Abdo has the following to say:

> The light of this Glorious Book which has been followed by science whithersoever it has gone, East or West, must once more return to full manifestation; and this Book will rend the veils of error, and it will return again to its original place in the hearts of the Muslims, and will find a resting place there. And science will follow it, since science is its true friend, which associates with it only, and depends upon it alone.[84]

'Abdo's progressive reformist ideas have acquired great fame and influence in the Muslim world and beyond due, in large part, to the efforts of his Syrian disciple, Muhammad Rashíd Ridá.

Muhammad Rashíd Ridá (d. 1935) and *al-Manár*

Although often viewed as 'Abdo's primary intellectual heir and promoter of 'Abdo's ideas, Muhammad Rashíd Ridá was definitely his own man. In his capacity as editor-in-chief of the main mouthpiece of reformist Islam, the periodical "The Beacon" or "The Lighthouse" (*al-Manár*), he was able to present his teacher's views to the reading public in accordance with his own understanding of them. On most issues, he took a more conservative stance than his liberally minded teacher. At the same time, 'Abdo's towering stature as reformer and modernizer of Islam definitely gave his student's writings greater credibility with "The Beacon's" world-wide readership.

Born in a rural Syrian family known for its Islamic learning and piety (in this regard, his background is similar to that of his teacher), Rashíd Ridá was initially exposed to reformist ideas through local scholars. A critical turning point in his life came after his acquaintance with an issue of "The Firmest Bond," the Arabic-language periodical that was coedited and published by al-Aghfani and 'Abdo in Paris. Rashíd Ridá devoured every issue of the periodical he could find and enthusiastically embraced its advocacy for a comprehensive reform and modernization of Muslim societies.[85] He made every effort to make the acquaintance of the two editors of "The Firmest Bond," but succeeded in meeting only one of them, 'Abdo, during the latter's visit to Syria. Impressed by 'Abdo's personality and ideas even further, Rashíd Ridá eventually joined him in Cairo. It was Rashíd Ridá who persuaded 'Abdo to launch an Egyptian periodical dedicated to the dissemination of reformist ideas across the Muslim world. 'Abdo and Rashíd Ridá edited the new journal named "The Beacon" in partnership. However, the younger and more energetic Rashíd Ridá was definitely the heart and soul of this momentous reformist enterprise.

Today it is a widely accepted fact that the introduction and dissemination of the printed word have been instrumental in paving the way for change in modern Europe, beginning with the Reformation to the French and Russian Revolutions and beyond. The same is true of the Muslim world, although here changes, driven by a wide dissemination of printed books, pamphlets, magazines, and newspapers, took longer to evolve. For the Middle East at the turn of the twentieth century, mass print was still a relatively new phenomenon, so the fact that Rashíd Ridá realized its power to effect change is evidence of both his perspicacity and his foresight. The social and cultural realities of the modern age required new ways of doing things.

Rashíd Ridá's *al-Manár* came to serve as the major forum and vehicle for Islamic reform. Its issues circulated well beyond Egypt, reaching as far as the Malaysian Archipelago, Singapore, India, North and South Africa, and even some European countries. Initially addressed to a liberal, cultured minority, it reached out to the broader circle of Muslim intelligentsia representing various professions and social classes. The publication of "The Beacon" started in 1898 and ended in 1940, five years after Rashíd Ridá's death. Ideas originally articulated in this periodical have been the stock-in-trade of Islamic reformist movements ever since.

A prolific writer and active organizer of all manner of Islamic societies and congresses, it is difficult to give justice to Rashíd Ridá's rich and variegated intellectual legacy in a short survey such as this. We will outline only the principal points of his reform program, bearing in mind that they were often restatements and elaborations of the reformist ideas and goals discussed earlier in this chapter. This applies not only to the legacy of al-Afghání and 'Abdo but also to that of Muhammad b. 'Abd al-Wahháb, whose ideas Rashíd Ridá found congenial.

"The Beacon" was Rashíd Ridá's brainchild and source of popularity: "[I]nto it he poured his reflections on the spiritual life, his explanations of doctrine, his endless polemics in attack and defense, all the news that came to him from the corners of the Muslim world, his thoughts on world politics, and the great commentary on the Qur'an . . . based on 'Abduh's lectures and writings, carried farther by 'Abduh's disciple but never finished."[86] Apart from the editorship of "The Beacon," Rashíd Ridá pursued a variety of religious and social projects, such as, for instance, the founding of a school for Muslim missionaries to counter the spread of Christian missions throughout the Muslim world. He also attended and took an active part in two global Muslim congresses in Mecca in 1926 and in Jerusalem in 1931. They were part of his master plan to unify all Muslims in the face of the Western domination of Muslim lands.[87]

Rashíd Ridá's overall vision of the Muslim world and its current condition was shaped by the ideas of al-Afghání and 'Abdo. Later in life, he embraced the doctrine of Ibn 'Abd al-Wahháb, by then the official ideology of the recently created Saudi kingdom in Arabia. Although initially critical of Wahhabi radicalism, he eventually embraced its call for the purification of Islam by all means necessary. This must have happened as a result of his disillusionment with the events in Turkey that led to the dissolution of the Ottoman caliphate and the establishment of the secular nation-state by Kemal Ataturk in 1924. For Rashíd Ridá, Wahhabism and the Saudi state were now the only hopes for restoring Islam to its original purity and for unifying the Muslims in the face of European colonialism.

In general, the restoration of Muslim economic and military power constitutes the capstone of Rashíd Ridá's reform program. The *umma*'s loss of its erstwhile strength was, in his view, the logical result of Muslims being neglectful of the original precepts of their religion. The primeval, uncorrupted Islam contained all that was necessary to meet the challenges of modernity: Consultation of the masses by their rulers (contrary to the prevailing authoritarianism of later Muslim dynasties), technical and scientific acumen (after all, Europe learned its sciences from the Muslim world in the Middle Ages), social activism, commitment to economic development and prosperity, brotherhood and cooperation of all in matters of common concern, and, perhaps most importantly, unity of religious doctrine and statecraft. These were, in Rashíd Ridá's view, the characteristic features of Islam under the Prophet and his immediate successors. It was practiced by the first generations of Muslims (*sálaf*; lit. "ancestors" or "forebears") only to become gradually obscured by harmful innovations and borrowings from other religions. One such innovation was a blind fanatical loyalty of Muslims to a legal or theological school. The other was a slavish and unquestioning acceptance by present-day Muslims of precedents established by earlier authorities (*taqlíd*). As a result of such innovations, Muslims, according to Rashíd Ridá, lost their unity, on the one hand, and the creative and dynamic spirit of Islam's "pious ancestors," on the other.[88]

Among other factors contributing to Muslim disunity, Rashíd Ridá mentions Sufi orders and their practices (such as collective *dhikr*s and celebrations of the birthdays of various Sufi saints). They often "enlist more enthusiasm on the part of the people than do the true religious forms."[89] Furthermore, in Rashíd Ridá's opinion, ignorant Muslims are often blindly loyal to Sufi *shaykh*s whom they wrongly regard as intercessors, miracle workers, and dispensers of divine blessing. As a result, the *shaykh*s acquire, in the eyes of their followers a near divine status. To make matters worse, to preserve their influence on the masses, the *shaykh*s irresponsibly teach them that Islam is a religion of passive submission and introspection. This teaching, according to Rashíd Ridá, is totally incompatible with the activist message of Islam as practiced by its founders. For it was precisely religious enthusiasm and activism that empowered the "pious forebears" to bring half of the civilized world under Muslim sway. Rashíd Ridá's condemnation of Sufism is much more stringent than that of 'Abdo, who, after all, was himself a practicing Sufi earlier in his life. Rashíd Ridá went so far as to denounce some forms of Islamic mysticism as a Zoroastrian plot to "corrupt the [primeval] religion of the Arabs."[90]

To counter the misguided teachings and practices of Sufism and other deviant Muslim sects, Rashíd Ridá presents the correct Islam of the Prophet and his companions as a religion of reason, social activism, mutual cooperation, and creativity. This Islam, unlike its distorted interpretations of the recent centuries, is fully compatible with the demands of the modern age. Rashíd Ridá lays the blame for Islam's current plight at the door of the conservative and complacent *'ulamá'*, who had neglected their duty to guide the Muslim masses along the straight path of the Prophet and his companions. A new, forward-looking cohort of Muslim scholars should be brought up and educated in ways more consistent with the exigencies of the *umma*'s existence in the modern age. These progressive scholars should put aside senseless bickering over petty points of religious law and doctrine to formulate, in consultation with one another, a straightforward activist creed that would rally Muslims around the common cause of restoring Islam to its original purity and strength. The ultimate goal of this religious restoration is to lay the groundwork for the creation of a powerful and unified caliphate. Its ruler will be elected by a special electoral council of the leading scholars of the Muslim community. He will not oppress his subjects but rather serve as the chief executor of the precepts of the Qur'an and the Prophet's Sunna on the basis of advice given to him by the enlightened *'ulamá'*.

The exact territory where Rashíd Ridá wanted this caliphate to be established changed with the changing political realities of the Middle East. As mentioned, at the outset, he thought of a reformed Ottoman caliphate cemented by the strategic religiopolitical alliance between the Turks and the Arabs. However, after Kemal Ataturk and his followers (whom Rashíd Ridá considered infidels) had abolished the Ottoman caliphate in 1924, he turned his attention to Arabia, most of which was now firmly under the control of the Saudi ruling family. Rashíd Ridá entertained some other possible locations for the caliphate, but in the end his dreams and actions failed to bring fruit. As Muslims were increasingly identifying themselves with their respective nation-states (admittedly imposed upon them by the Europeans), nationalism became a powerful means of mass mobilization and identity making that Muslim reformers had no choice but to reckon with. At some point, nationalism and some other secular ideologies imported from the West (such as, liberalism, socialism, and communism) seem to have become, as it were, the only game in town. However, as we shall see in the chapters that follow, this seemingly plausible assumption has eventually turned out to be wrong.

By Way of Conclusion: A Summary of the Major Precepts of Islamic Reform

- Muslims must return to the original principles of Muslim faith. Islam in its entirety is contained in the Qur'an. Faithfulness to the authentic Qur'anic teachings will assure Islam's eventual triumph as the greatest global force in the same way it had assured its ascendancy after it was promulgated by the Prophet to the Arabs. The Qur'an is the supreme source of correct creed and the ultimate guide to pious living. However, in order for it to serve as the foundation of a just social order in this world and the guarantor of salvation in the hereafter, it should be properly interpreted by the religious scholars and practiced by the rest of the *umma*. Allegorical interpretations of the Qur'an by the Sufis, Shi'ites, and Isma'ilis, who claimed to have discovered its hidden, secret meaning, are false and must be condemned. They are either senseless innovations or importations from other religions that do nothing but confuse the believers. Sound interpretations of the Islamic scriptures should emphasize the moral and ethical values contained therein and instruct their followers as to how they can be implemented in real life.

- The Custom (*sunna*) of the Prophet constitutes the second major source of the true, authentic Islam. The Prophet's Sunna clarifies the meaning and practical implications of the Qur'anic message, especially because the Qur'an itself (4:80) clearly states that "whoever obeys the Messenger has obeyed God." Some later Muslim reformers, however, would occasionally downplay the role of *hadith* in light of the doubts about their authenticity voiced by some Western scholars of Islam and Muslim history.

- The exemplary ways of the pious forebears of Islam (*sálaf salih*), led by the Prophet, should be studied carefully by all modern-day Muslims. Unlike the later generations of Muslims, which were prone to innovations and deviations, the members of the first Muslim community benefited from the direct guidance of the Prophet and were thus immune to error. The emphasis that the reformers placed on the example set by the first Muslims is reflected in the common name of their movement—*salafiyya*, meaning, "followers of the pious ancestors [of Islam]." According to the *salafiyya*, later generations of Muslims have strayed from the "straight path" of Islam[91] by adopting all manner of blameworthy innovations, such as the cult of saints; preoccupation with Sufi chants and dances; belief in sorcery, magic, the healing power of amulets; and so on. Therefore, the exemplary, unerring ways of the pious ancestors of Islam must be restored and meticulously emulated by latter-day Muslims.

- Apart from rejecting innovations in worship and belief (as just outlined), the reformed Muslim community should also declare war on the evil habits and practices proscribed by the Qur'an and the Prophet's Sunna (such as gambling, alcohol, immodest behavior and dress, charging banking interest, submitting to human-made laws, and so on). This measure should stem the erosion of Muslim morals under the corruptive influence of the West.

- A comprehensive legal reform is necessary to achieve the uniformity of Islamic legal theory and practice. This reform involves a drastic revision of the obsolete legal traditions that are based on faulty human reasoning and discretion of individual jurists, not on the foundational sources of Islam. A blind, unquestioning imitation of earlier legal precedents (*taqlíd*) by both Muslim scholars and Muslims at large should be discouraged. Mindless conformity to antiquated practices and authorities is a major cause of the decline of the Muslim world and of its resultant inability to successfully compete with the West. It breeds passivity and mindless repetition of outdated formulas and practices. Furthermore, a blind, unquestioning adherence to the various legal schools leads to mutual hostility among their partisans, causing disunity and strife within the *umma* and, as a consequence, its weakening.

- This slavish imitation of earlier legal authorities and precedents should be replaced by an independent investigation of legal issues (*ijtihád*) by a qualified and enlightened Muslim jurist (*mujtáhid*). Ideally, every educated Muslim should "exert himself/herself"[92] in order to grasp the authentic meaning and ultimate intent of the foundational sources of Islam. Once a correct understanding of the scriptures has been obtained through *ijtihád*, it should be used to resolve the problems faced by the *mujtáhid* and his community. Whereas the fundamentals of religion (that is, its principal dogmas, ritual practices, rules of worship, and canonical prohibitions) cannot be arbitrarily reinterpreted, it is the duty of each Muslim to seek to understand what the Qur'anic revelation and the Sunna of the Prophet mean for him or her personally at any given moment in time. By availing themselves of *ijtihád* Muslims can respond adequately and expeditiously to the ever changing times and conditions of their existence. Failure to exercise *ijtihád* results in the stagnation and decline of Muslim societies. *Ijtihád* is a professional duty of the learned leaders of the community because its fruits are essential for its strength and prosperity. However, conclusions of the *mujtáhid*s, no matter how distinguished and respected, must never be at odds with the spirit and letter of the Qur'an and the Sunna.
- In matters pertaining to the well-being and direction of the entire community, its leading scholars are allowed to form a consultative body (*shúra*) that is granted the authority to articulate religiously sound decisions concerning the problems faced by the community.
- In the modern age, the *umma* has found itself threatened by Western (Christian) values and institutions. It must defend itself ideologically and, if necessary, militarily by waging *jihád* against the aggressor. In addition to encouraging military training of Muslims, special missionary schools should be established to counter the insidious influence of Christian missions in the Muslim world. Traditional religious education should be combined with the study of modern sciences in the spirit of the Prophet's injunction to seek knowledge wherever it can be found ("even in China").
- Islam is a liberal and liberating religion. Its central message frees the faithful from the worship of human-made objects, institutions, and individuals that are nothing but "pagan idols" that Islam was sent to destroy. In the social and economic sphere, the Islamic doctrine of the omnipotence and uncontested sovereignty of God is the sole guarantor of the equality of all believers.
- Islam is a moderate, middle-of-the-way religion[93] that is consistent with human nature, while also liberating it from slavish dependence on uncontrolled passions and irrational drives.
- Islam is totally consistent with the demands of logic. Essentially a rational religion encouraging scientific exploration, it does not, however, neglect the spiritual needs of its followers. It appeals to both human emotions and the human intellect. When it is interpreted correctly, it is a religion conducive to technological and scientific progress.

These, in a nutshell, are the principal points of Muslim reformism and revivalism that will be reappearing in various guises and formulations throughout the last chapters of this book.

Questions to Ponder

1   Consider various paths of Islamic reform: from a fundamentalist restoration of the pure and unadulterated Islam of the first Muslim community to a modernist (modernizing) re-reading of the Islamic tradition with a view to instituting a comprehensive social, political, and intellectual reform of Islamic societies. Assess the strengths and weaknesses of each path. Which path, if any, is more feasible and practicable under the present geopolitical conditions? Why? Can you suggest any alternative ways to achieve the goals set by the reformers examined in this chapter?

2   To what extent are Islamic modernism and reformism knee-jerk reactions to the challenges posed by Western colonialism and modernity or, on the contrary, natural (and thus inevitable) internal developments of the societies in question? In other words, could Islamic modernism and reformism have emerged irrespective of the challenges posed by the military, political, and economic ascendancy of the West and Russia?

3   Examine the ideological challenges presented to Islam and its learned custodians by Western ideologies, such as liberalism, socialism/Marxism, scientism, and nationalism. How did Muslim intellectuals respond to these challenges? Were their responses effective or ineffective? Why?

Summary

- In response to the military, economic, and political domination of Western Europe and Russia, Muslim thinkers advocate the necessity to "reform" (*isláh*) and "renew" (*tajdíd*) the life of Muslim societies. Scriptural evidence is cited by the reformers to justify the drastic reforms that they propose (e.g., Qur'an 8:53).
- Various approaches are taken to the task of purifying Islam of "alien" elements and restoring it to its former glory and might.
- The conservative reform of the Hanbali scholar Muhammad b. 'Abd al-Wahháb (1703–1792) in Arabia becomes possible thanks to his alliance with the tribal chiefs of the Sa'úd family in eastern Arabia.
- Ibn 'Abd al-Wahháb proposes to restore the doctrine of the absolute oneness of God (*tawhíd*) by cleansing the beliefs and practices of his coreligionists of all manner of "heretical innovations" (*bid'a*). He uses the military resources of the Bedouins loyal to the Sa'úd family to advance his religious agenda.
- Among the practices condemned by Ibn 'Abd al-Wahháb as "vestiges of paganism" are such sinful behaviors as gambling, fornication, wine drinking, smoking tobacco; visits to the tombs of the friends of God; placing one's trust in sorcery, amulets, and magic; seeking assistance from or making offerings for anyone or anything but God; and so on.
- The Wahhabis occupy the central and northern parts of the Arabian Peninsula, sack Mecca and Medina, and raze its revered cemeteries and mausoleums. They also attack and rob the Shi'ite sanctuaries in Iraq.
- The radicalism of the followers of Ibn 'Abd al-Wahháb causes their opponents to compare them to the Kharijites of early Muslim history who, like the Wahhabis, excommunicated Muslims who disagreed with them and declared their property and lives to be "licit" to the "true believers."
- During the nineteenth and twentieth centuries the Wahhabi state, repeatedly defeated, resurfaces with a vengeance with the help from the British during the first two decades of the twentieth century. The Kingdom of Saudi Arabia is established by 'Abd al-'Aziz b. Sa'ud in 1924–1925 to become the bastion of conservative Islam. It gains popularity among the Muslims by using its oil wealth to fund all manner of Islamic causes and charities worldwide, most notably the anti-Soviet *jihád* in Afghanistan in 1979–1989.
- A different type of reform takes shape in Egypt: al-Afgháni (d. 1897) and 'Abdo (d. 1905) become the harbingers of Islamic modernism.

- These two thinkers conduct a critical analyses of the plight of the *umma* in the colonial age and propose programs for Islamic revival. However, they differ in the ways their reformist agendas should be implemented: Al-Afghâni's attempts to institute reforms "from above" by winning over Muslim rulers to his cause or plotting revolutions, whereas 'Abdo's emphasizes the need for a gradual reform of Muslim education with a view to transforming the passive Muslim mind-set and attitude to life. The goal is to bring them in line with the demands of the new epoch.

- Al-Afghâni has an affinity with the intellectual elitism of medieval Islamic philosophers. Philosophical theories are for the elite, and prophetic religion is for the masses. Islam should be used as a means of rallying the populations of the Muslim countries for the defense of the *umma* against European colonial expansion into their territories.

- 'Abdo consistently points out that scientific and socioeconomic progress is fully compatible with the original precepts of Islam as practiced by the Prophet and his companions. He rejects "blind imitation" (*taqlíd*) in favor of a creative interpretation and implementation of the "spirit" of the divine revelation (*ijtihád*) by enlightened Muslim thinkers. 'Abdo is critical of doctrinal and juridical dogmatism, political despotism, and "Sufi superstitions," seeing them as the major impediments to the modernization and rejuvenation of Muslim societies.

- The Salafi reform program is the product of 'Abdo's disciple Rashíd Ridá (d. 1935), whose journal "The Beacon" (*al-Manár*) plays a major role in disseminating reformist ideas across the Muslim world. Among other things, Rashíd Ridá offers a modernist interpretation of the Qur'an.

- Much more stridently than 'Abdo, Rashíd Ridá rejects Sufi teachings and practices as "idle superstitions"; he considers Sufi *shaykh*s to be charlatans and manipulators of the ignorant masses. At the same time, he blames the inaction of *'ulamá'* for the plight of Islam and the impotence of the *umma* in the face of European domination.

- Rashíd Ridá sympathizes with the Wahhabi movement and the Sa'úd ruling family of Arabia following the abolition of the Ottoman caliphate by Ataturk in 1924. He sees in the Saudi puritanism the potential for launching a pan-Islamic movement that should forestall the splitting of the *umma* into competing nation-states. Once united, the *umma* will be able to reassert its independence of the European powers.

- The principal articles of the modernizing reform program emerge. The Muslims must embrace the activist and dynamic Islam of the pious founders (*sálaf*) of the *umma*, namely, the Prophet and his companions. They need to go back to the primary sources of Islam, namely the Qur'an and the Sunna, bypassing the debilitating "accretions" and "innovations" of the later centuries. Islam, if understood and practiced correctly, contains all that is necessary to restore the *umma* to its erstwhile glory and might.

Notes

1 Marshall Hodgson, *The Venture of Islam*, Chicago University Press, Chicago, 1974, vol. 1, p. 71, quoting Q 3:110.
2 Q 5:3.
3 Simon Wood, *Christian Criticisms, Islamic Proofs: Rashid Rida's Modernist Defense of Islam*, Oneworld, Oxford, 2008, pp. 18–23.
4 Arab. *isláh*.
5 Michael Crawford, *Ibn 'Abd al-Wahhab*, Oneworld, London, 2014, pp. 90–91.
6 Ibid., p. 106.

7 Ibid., pp. 14 and 137–138.

8 Ibid., pp. 54–58.

9 Ibid., pp. 61–65.

10 Crawford, *Ibn 'Abd al-Wahhab*, Chapters 3 and 4.

11 Ibid., pp. 23 and 50–51.

12 Esther Peskes, "The Wahhabiyya and Sufism in the Eighteenth Century," in Frederick de Jong and Berndt Radtke (eds.), *Islamic Mysticism Contested*, E. J. Brill, Leiden and Boston, 1999, p. 151; see also Crawford, *Ibn 'Abd al-Wahhab*, pp. 57–58, 83–86.

13 Peskes, "The Wahhabiyya," p. 151.

14 Crawford, *Ibn 'Abd al-Wahhab*, pp. 25–26, 46, 86–88.

15 Ibid., pp. 31 and 83–86.

16 Peskes, "The Wahhabiyya," p. 151; cf. Crawford, *Ibn 'Abd al-Wahhab*, pp. 50–51.

17 Crawford, *Ibn 'Abd al-Wahhab*, pp. 54 and 56.

18 Ibid., pp. 54–58.

19 Ibid., p. 85.

20 Ibid., p. 97.

21 Ibid., pp. 92–94 and 97–98.

22 Arent Wensinck, *A Handbook of Early Muhammadan Tradition*, E. J. Brill, Leiden, 1971, p. 114.

23 Crawford, *Ibn 'Abd al-Wahhab*, pp. 94–96.

24 Esther Peskes, "Wahhabiyya," in *Encyclopedia of Islam*, 2nd ed.; online edition: http://referenceworks.brillonline.com.

25 His efforts to modernize Egypt were discussed in Chapter 20.

26 Crawford, *Ibn 'Abd al-Wahhab*, Chapter 9.

27 Peskes, "Wahhabiyya."

28 Crawford, *Ibn 'Abd al-Wahhab*, pp. 125–126 and Chapter 9.

29 Ibid., Chapter 4.

30 With an exception of a small Shi'ite minority in the central mountains of Afghanistan, the country's population is predominantly Sunni.

31 Nikki Keddie, *Sayyid Jamal ad-Din "al-Afghani": A Political Biography*, University of California Press, Berkeley, 1972, pp. 133–142.

32 Azmi Özcan (ed.), *Pan-Islamism: Indian Muslims, the Ottomans and Britain, 1877–1924*, E. J. Brill, Leiden and Boston, 1997, passim.

33 Keddie, *Sayyid Jamal ad-Din*, pp. 140–142.

34 Nikki Keddie, *An Islamic Response to Imperialism*, University of California Press, Berkeley, 1968, p. 40.

35 Ibid., p. 33.

36 Ibid. and Keddie, *Sayyid Jamal ad-Din*, p. 115.

37 Rudi Matthee, "Jamal al-Din al-Afghani and the Egyptian National Debate," in M. Ikram Chaghatai (ed.), *Jamal al-Din al-Afghani: An Apostle of Islamic Resurgence*, Sang-e-Meel Publications, Lahore, 2005, p. 346.

38 Elie Kedourie, *Afghani and Abduh*, 2nd ed., Frank Cass, London and Portland, OR, 1997, p. 63.

39 Keddie, *An Islamic Response*, p. 173, quoting the Qur'an 8:53.

40 Keddie, *An Islamic Response*, p. 183.

41 Ibid., pp. 49–50.

42 Ibid., p. 35.

43 Sylvia Haim (ed.), *Arab Nationalism*, University of California Press, Berkeley, 1962, p. 15.

44 This outline is based on Keddie, *An Islamic Response*, pp. 36–45.

45 Nikki Keddie, "Sayyid Jamal al-Din 'al-Afghani'," in Ali Rahnema (ed.), *Pioneers of Islamic Revival*, Zed Books, Atlantic Highlands, New Jersey, 1994, p. 27.

46 Kedourie, *Afghani and Abduh*, pp. 41–43.

47 Charles Kurzman (ed.), *Modernist Islam (1840–1940): A Textbook*, Oxford University Press, Oxford, 2002, p. 110.

48 Keddie, *An Islamic Response*, p. 187.

49 Kedourie, *Afghani and Abduh*, p. 46.

50 Charles Adams, *Islam and Modernism in Egypt*, reprint, Routledge, London and New York, 2000, p. 6.

51 Keddie, *An Islamic Response*, pp. 42–44.
52 Ibid., p. 41.
53 His last name is also spelled 'Abduh or 'Abdu.
54 Adams, *Islam and Modernism in Egypt*, pp. 21–22.
55 Ibid., pp. 32–33.
56 Ibid., p. 34.
57 Ibid., pp. 53–54.
58 At that time, the present-day country of Lebanon was not yet established; what is now Lebanon was part of so-called Greater Syria (al-Sha'm).
59 Adams, *Islam and Modernism in Egypt*, p. 59.
60 Anke von Kügelgen, "Abduh, Muhammad," in *Encyclopedia of Islam*, E. J. Brill, Leiden, 3rd ed.; online edition: http://referenceworks.brillonline.com.
61 Adams, *Islam and Modernism in Egypt*, pp. 59–60.
62 Ibid., p. 60.
63 Keddie, *Sayyid Jamal ad-Din*, p. 142.
64 Adams, *Islam and Modernism in Egypt*, pp. 64–65.
65 Ibid., p. 63.
66 Kügelgen, "Abduh, Muhammad."
67 Kedourie, *Afghani and Abduh*, p. 12.
68 Ibid.
69 Kügelgen, "Abduh, Muhammad."
70 Q 3:130; 3:125 in Arberry's translation.
71 Adams, *Islamic and Modernism in Egypt*, p. 80.
72 For the concrete Qur'anic verses on which the permission and the restriction are based, see Chapter 18.
73 Jacque Jomier, *Le commentraire coranique du Manâr*, G.-P. Maisonneuve, Paris, 1954, p. 181.
74 Ibid., pp. 179–180.
75 Adams, *Islam and Modernism in Egypt*, p. 175.
76 For an electronic copy of the Arabic text see https://archive.org/details/risalataltawhid00muamuoft.
77 Adams, *Islam and Modernism in Egypt*, p. 114.
78 Ibid., p. 110.
79 Ibid., p. 110.
80 Ibid., p. 173.
81 Ibid., p. 116.
82 Ibid., p. 119.
83 Ibid., p. 125.
84 Ibid., p. 143.
85 Albert Hourani, *Arabic Thought in the Liberal Age, 1798–1939*, Oxford University Press, Oxford, 1970, p. 226.
86 Ibid., pp. 226–227.
87 For details, see Martin Kramer, *Islam Assembled*, Columbia University Press, New York, 1986.
88 Adams, *Islam and Modernism*, pp. 190–191.
89 Ibid., p. 188.
90 Hourani, *Arabic Thought in the Liberal Age*, p. 232.
91 Q 1:6.
92 The initial meaning of the Arabic root *jahada* is "to strive," "to exert oneself." The word *ijtihád* is derived from this root and can thus be translated as "striving" or "self-exertion."
93 See, e.g., Q 2:143

Chapter 22

Islam as a Political Force and Vehicle of Opposition

Major Stages of the Movement for Reform and Renewal of Islam

The previous chapter focused on the plans for reform and renewal of Islam that were developed by a number of enlightened Muslim thinkers active in the late nineteenth-early twentieth centuries. Although their goals had some things in common, these plans were distinct from those that animated the conservative reform movement of Ibn 'Abd al-Wahháb and his Saudi supporters in Arabia in the second half of the eighteenth–early nineteenth centuries. These, plans, events, and thinkers can be seen as representing the formative period of Islamic reformism, during which its foundational principles were articulated by a handful of concerned Muslim intellectuals. Some were inspired by al-Afghani's modernist agenda, others by the desire to restore the original purity of Islam as it was professed and practiced by the first Muslim community under the leadership of the Prophet and his companions. The reformers sought to implement their ideas either from above by winning rulers over to their cause (as was the case with al-Afghani and Ibn 'Abd al-Wahháb) or by instituting broad social and educational reforms and reaching out to like-minded Muslims via the printed word (as was the case with 'Abdo and Rashíd Ridá). Whereas the Wahhabi-Saudi alliance proved successful in the end, the Egyptian modernizers failed to establish a broad popular base of support for their project or to institutionalize it. Nevertheless, their ideas survived to inspire those who came in their wake, both in Egypt and elsewhere. Moreover, in the second half of the twentieth century and for reasons that will be discussed further on, the reformist agenda laid down by 'Abdo and Rashíd Ridá acquired a much broader following among different classes of Muslim societies. This period can be designated as one of the coming of age and popularization of Muslim movements for reform and renewal. It is characterized by their deeper involvement in the political and social life of their societies. Some investigators associate this period with the emergence of what is currently being called, accurately or otherwise, as "Islamism" or "political Islam."

The Complicated Issue of Terminology

Designations such as these bring up the issue of terminology over which both Western and Muslim scholars of Islamic religion have spilled much ink of late.[1] Without going too deep into these academic debates, a word of warning is in order. The movements and individuals who have appealed to Islam and Islamic values and concepts in order to justify their political and social actions have been given different names by different observers. Such names often reflect the designator's personal attitude toward the movement(s) in question. In other words, the names given to such movements are not neutral but evaluative. Whereas they often capture an important aspect of the movement in question, they may also obscure another that may be no less significant for assessing it. One result of the process of naming is that the movement thus named may appear uncomplicated and unidirectional. Its internal diversity, contradictions, and complexity are "lost in translation," as it were. This may come in handy for media coverage of various manifestations of Islamic activism, when time is limited and all that matters is catchy sound-bites. However, to the more demanding inquirer, this name-dropping may appear to be too simplistic or even outright misleading. Here are some of the terms that are commonly applied to movements, individuals, and organizations that claim to act in the name of Islam.

The most common of these terms, widely used by both specialists and media commentators in the West and elsewhere, is "Islamic fundamentalism" or, less frequently, "Islamism." One cannot deny that the term "Islamic fundamentalism" does capture an important aspect of the phenomenon in question. In the previous chapter, we repeatedly emphasized that the founding fathers of the Muslim reform and renewal movement al-Afghání, 'Abdo, and Rashíd Ridá, not to mention Ibn 'Abd al-Wahháb, consistently called the Muslims to return to Islam's original truths as enunciated in the Qur'an and the Sunna of the Prophet and as practiced by the first generation of Muslims (*sálaf*). This return implied the rejection by latter-day Muslims of the theological and juridical elaborations of the postprophetic age as "human-made products." As such, they did not carry the same authority as the foundational sources and, moreover, could be outright misleading. They had to be downplayed or even abandoned altogether, whereas the primary sources of Islamic faith are to be restored to their rightful place as the sole legitimate foundations of Islamic life and governance. It is with this particular sense in mind that one can call various groups advocating for this approach to Islamic reform "fundamentalists" (*salafiyya*). However, if we consider closely the case of the three Egypt-based reformers described in the previous chapter, we will find out that the changes they proposed went far beyond a simple "return to the fundamentals." Objectively speaking, as we have seen, they attempted to modernize Islam. This measure inevitably implied a selective borrowing of Western technological and institutional achievements in order to enable the Muslims to counter Europe's global dominance. Seen from this perspective, they can be rightfully defined as "modernizers," despite the fact that they consistently packaged their modernizing ideas to their audiences as "return" to the "forgotten" or "obscured" fundamentals of the primeval Islam of its pious forebears (*sálaf sálih*). As we have seen, Ibn 'Abd al-Wahháb can also be called "reformer," albeit one who wanted to reform Islamic faith and practice without modernizing, not to mention Westernizing, the life of his coreligionists. This is why in the previous chapter we defined his program as one of "conservative reform." So all of these individuals were, to some extent, "reformers" and "fundamentalists." However, each envisioned reform on his own terms, as the deep difference between Ibn 'Abd al-Wahháb of Arabia and the three Egypt-based reformers makes abundantly clear.

Now, in their efforts to implement their ideas in real life, these reformers and those who came in their wake considered generally held religious beliefs to be a means to certain ends that we would commonly consider to be political. For instance, they definitely intended to use Islam as a tool to liberate the Muslims from Western domination or as a means of restoring the Muslim character of their societies by compelling their political rulers to implement the norms of the Shari'a. If we admit that their objectives are political, then such reform-minded individuals can indeed be called proponents of one or the other version of "political Islam." Finally, those reformers who availed themselves of Islamic precepts (such as, for example, *jihád*, *ijtihád*, struggle against "blameworthy innovations," or "commanding right and forbidding wrong") to recruit followers and then to attack their ideological opponents (be they governments, groups, or individuals) by using armed force can be dubbed "Islamic radicals" or "Islamic militants." In the end, the precise definition of political, social, and military activism in the name of Islam is in the eye of the beholder. It largely depends on whether one is its target, supporter, or outside observer. What is obvious to any impartial student of Islam and recent Muslim history is that this kind of activism, or "Islamic resurgence" as it is often dubbed in media reportage, has been a universal phenomenon from the 1920s up until today.

The Latest Stages of the Evolution of Islamic Activism

The evolution of Islamic or Islamist movements, if we accept the latter term, from the 1970s until today can be classified into several stages. Following the Soviet invasion of Afghanistan in 1979 and the Iranian revolution of 1978–1979, Islamic activism entered a new era. It is characterized by the fragmentation of Islamic/Islamist movements into a motley array of attitudes from Islamic liberalism and active participation of Islamic/Islamist parties in the political life of their countries to the uncompromising militancy of global *jihadism* á la Bin Ládin and the Islamic State in Iraq and Syria, as well as that of their supporters worldwide.[2] These latest manifestations of Islamic activism will be discussed in the last chapter of this book.

In the meantime, a general observation is in order. Political activism and militancy in the name of religions are not unique to Islam. It is found in most institutionalized religions, including Christianity, Judaism, Hinduism, and even peace-loving Buddhism, as the tumultuous events around the procession of the Olympic torch in 2008 finely demonstrated.[3] However, it is its Islamic/Islamist form that has caught the attention of the global media and public at large. This is, in large part due to its association with such dramatic events as the Soviet–Afghan War, the Iranian Revolution, the Iran–Iraq War, the First Gulf War, the terrorist attacks orchestrated by al-Qa'ida in the name of global *jihád*, the "Islamic/Islamist" unrest in Pakistan and Indonesia, the political brinksmanship of the Islamic Republic of Iran, the rise of the militant Islamic courts and Islamic youth movements in Somalia, and, of course, the U.S.-led wars in Afghanistan and Iraq. Add to this list the rise and expansion of the Islamic State in Iraq and Syria (ISIS) and its numerous "franchises" in 2014–2016, and any further explanation becomes superfluous. In all these and some other events, Islam has figured prominently at least on the rhetorical level, which means so much for the media and the public at large. In other words, these dramatic political, social, and military developments have been consistently explained in religious terms. For example, they have been presented to the public as a conflict between two interpretations of Islam (Sunni versus Shi'ite), between Islam and the secular state, or as a "perennial" confrontation between Judeo-Christian and Islamic civilizations. It should be pointed out that such explanations have been advanced by both insiders (Muslims) and outsiders (non-Muslims).

We will leave the outsiders (mostly Westerners) and their rhetoric aside for the moment to focus on why and how the insiders (i.e., the Muslims) have availed themselves of Islam as a means of mass mobilization and an idiom (and occasionally *the* idiom) for expressing their political, social, and cultural aspirations and frustrations. In the rest of this chapter, we will examine several concrete cases from Egypt, India/Pakistan, and Iran that, in our view, are emblematic of Islamic/Islamist political and social activism as a whole.

Hasan al-Banna (d. 1949) and the Muslim Brotherhood

Hasan al-Banna's early career is typical of Islamic/Islamist leaders. He combined a solid background in traditional Islamic sciences with modern education, which he acquired at a Western-style teachers' college.[4] Like 'Abdo, he initially joined a Sufi brotherhood.[5] He was impressed by its austere ways that "forbade men to wear gold, encouraged women to dress modestly, and restricted conduct at tombs [of God's friends] to acts and words sanctioned by scripture."[6] He was even more impressed by the strong emotional bonds between the master and his disciples that were cultivated within the Sufi brotherhood that he joined.[7] For al-Banna, life within the Sufi community became a blueprint for ties of loyalty and commitment between the leader and his followers that he sought to recreate in the organization that he was bound to establish.[8] No wonder that some pious exercises of the Muslim Brotherhood are patterned on Sufi meditation techniques. Al-Banna also adopted (and adapted) the organizational structure of a Sufi *taríqa*—individual

Figure 22.1 Hamas Supporters in the West Bank Carrying a Portrait of the Founder of the Muslim Brotherhood Hasan al-Banna on December 14, 2012

SAIF DAHLAH/AFP/Getty Images

cells/communities answering to and governed by a supreme master. Thus, one can describe al-Banna's Muslim Brotherhood as a modernized and politicized Sufi order (see Figure 22.1).[9]

Al-Banna was less satisfied with the Sufi otherworldly orientation and focus on the internal life of the human spirit at the expense of social engagement. A natural born "mover and shaker," he chose the career of a schoolteacher in order to be in the thick of people's everyday life and to disseminate among them what he considered to be the pure and unadulterated Islam of its pious founders (*sálaf*).[10] Why was education so important to al-Banna? It should be remembered that Egyptian society had been under British occupation from 1882 to 1922 and remained a British dependent until 1955, when the last British detachment left the Suez Canal zone. No wonder that the country's life had become thoroughly permeated by European influences. The British established in Egypt a constitutional monarchy with a parliament, elections, and vocal and competitive political parties of nationalist slant.[11] By the 1920s, the Egyptian political elite embraced a secular nationalist ideology to such an extent as to argue that the Egyptian people should look for their roots in the country's pharaonic past, bypassing its Muslim identity.[12] Taking their cue from the Western notion of separation between church and state, secularized Egyptian intellectuals considered religion to be part of the person's private life that had no place in the public sphere. Social and cultural life, at least in the country's major cities, came to be dominated by European fashions, ideas, and institutions that the Egyptian upper class regarded as being superior to the local traditions and culture and that it aspired to imitate. Wealthy neighborhoods in Cairo boasted Western-style restaurants, cinemas, nightclubs, and theaters.[13] This rampant Westernization was considered by many pious Egyptians to be a source of moral decay. Al-Banna expressed their feelings in the following poignant passage:

> Indiscriminate mixing of the sexes has led to debauchery. Women have lost their Muslim virtues by their immodest participation in the partying and dancing which marks so many of the official and unofficial functions. Why? Because "European women do it and we want to be like Europe in all respects!"[14]

It is in this context that that one understands al-Banna's famous remarks about two types of Western imperialism: "external," which had imposed its "immoral" civilization on the Egyptian people by raw military force, and "internal," which was a result of the mindless imitation by some highly positioned Egyptians of European lifestyle, fashions, and values. Their infatuation with things European, according to al-Banna, made them oblivious to their Muslim identity and pride.[15] The "moral defeat" of Egypt's upper classes, argued al-Banna, resulted in widespread corruption, administrative inefficiency, abuse of authority, loss of confidence in law, and a futile, petty bickering among the country's political parties.[16] In the final analysis, al-Banna viewed the spread of Western education, laws, customs, and cultural values in the Muslim lands as far more pernicious than Europe's political and military domination. In his opinion, it threatened to corrupt the very soul of the Muslim *umma* by depriving it of its faith and Islamic identity.

According to Hasan al-Banna, the only way to forestall the wave of corruptive Western influences was to revive Egypt's Muslim identity and to reunite religion, politics, and culture which, contrary to Western models, were inseparable during the golden age of Islam. In al-Banna's famous words, "Islam is dogma and worship, fatherland and nationality, religion and state, spirituality and action, Qur'an and sword."[17] Egypt should return to Islam and become an Islamic nation once again. Loyalty to any other ideology including nationalism, liberalism, or communism amounted to surrender to the West.[18] For al-Banna, as for many Islamic/Islamist thinkers today, "Islam is the answer." He argued passionately that "Islam is the complete constitution of the world, and it should order [human] life in this world and in the world to come."[19] However, this needed to be the authentic Qur'anic Islam of the first Muslim community, not the distorted, human-made Islam of the later generations.[20]

To uncover the correct Islam, al-Banna undertook a critical analysis of Islamic history. Like his reformist forerunners, al-Banna believed that things had started to go wrong for the Muslim *umma* following the age of the rightly guided successors to the Prophet (caliphs) when political power was usurped by the Umayyad dynasty. Its unscrupulous and mundane rulers replaced the liberal, open and just social and political order of the original *umma* with a despotic "kingship." Aided and abetted by docile and venal scholars, the 'Abbásids pushed state despotism to the limit. In the end, the misrule of the two dynasties led to the disintegration of the once all-powerful Muslim state. Tribalism and factionalism reared their ugly heads as they became a means for the ruler to cling to power by implementing a divide-and-rule policy. From that time on, the fortunes of the *umma* had been going downhill despite temporary Muslim successes under Persian, Mamluk, and Ottoman dynasties.

The great military might wielded by these Muslim empires notwithstanding, their rulers were oblivious of the liberal, communal, and consultative spirit of the original Islam of the Prophet and his companions. Again, the corrupt Muslim scholars failed to advise them and to guide them on the straight path. Despotism and misrule had prevailed in the Muslim world until it finally fell prey to a resurgent Europe. Thus, the poisonous combination of rulers' despotism and scholars' inaptitude and docility led to what al-Banna portrayed as the catastrophe that had befallen the Abode of Islam in the recent decades.[21] The only way for the Muslims to be rescued from their plight is to restore the Qur'an and the Sunna of the Prophet to their rightful place in Muslim society and to use them as the only foundations of everyday life and governance.

In the perfect Muslim society envisioned by al-Banna, the ruler should be accountable to both God and the people. Like the rightly guided caliphs of the golden age of Islam, he would be a simple servant of his community, first among equals. He would exercise his executive powers in consultation with the community as a whole. Each member of the community should have the right to offer advice (and if necessary admonition) to the ruler, and the latter, as a faithful servant of God, would have the obligation to heed this advice. Al-Banna's ideal Muslim community should act as one man because brotherhood and cooperation among the believers was the trademark of the original Islam of the Prophet and his companions.[22] Once the Islamic order is made prevalent in a country or region, all things that divide Muslims, such as rival political parties, theological or legal schools, should be banished from the public sphere. The same applies to all Western ideologies, be it capitalism, communism, or Nazism.[23] In the long term, al-Banna advocated the restoration of the caliphate that would unite all Muslims regardless of their nationality under the aegis of Islam. In the short term, he prudently suggested that Egyptian society be gradually [re-]Islamized through grassroots action and propaganda of the correct Islamic faith and morals among the masses that, in his view, had been betrayed by the official *'ulamá'*.[24]

To achieve his short-term and long-term objectives, in 1928 al-Banna created the religiopolitical movement that has come to be known as the Muslim Brotherhood or the Muslim Brethren.[25] In its founding manifesto, al-Banna declared:

> The action is ours, the success is God's! Let us pledge our obedience to God, through which we shall be the soldiers of the mission of Islam, a message that embraces the life of our country and the strength of the Muslim nation. . . We are brothers in the service of Islam, we are the Muslim Brothers.[26]

Al-Banna then outlined the major goals of the movement and the principal stages of their implementation:

> Our duty as Muslim Brothers is to work for the reform of ourselves, of hearts and souls by joining them to God the All-High; then to organize our society to be fit for the victorious community which commands the good and forbids evil-doing, then from the community will arise the good [Islamic] state.[27]

The activists of the Brotherhood "went to the masses." They recruited followers in secondary schools and universities, in the mosques and the military barracks. The Brotherhood's primary constituency consisted of students, civil servants, teachers, shopkeepers, artisans, recent migrants from the countryside, soldiers, and police. Once recruited, the new brother took an oath of loyalty and joined the so-called "family" of like-minded "brothers" and "sisters." From that moment onward, the "brothers" and "sisters" in faith were obligated to take part in the "family's" activities, such as communal worship, meditation, discussion groups, social outings, and regular meetings to discuss internal matters. Not only would the members of such a "family" help each other in financial and other difficulties, but they were also expected to engage in charitable activities and support disadvantaged individuals and households in their neighborhood.[28] This popular outreach definitely added to the Brotherhood's popularity and recruitment capacity. Regardless, there is little doubt that the "brothers and sisters" of the society were genuinely concerned with the improvement of the lives of their fellow Muslims. The Brotherhood's "families" established and maintained dispensaries and charitable funds to support the needy; its educated members offered free classes to the illiterate; those of them in the medical profession provided free treatment to the sick. This was done in the name of social justice and care for the needy, which, according to al-Banna, were part and parcel of the true, Qur'anic Islam.

In this way, al-Banna and his comrades were able to create a broad popular social movement or "civil society" (*mujtama' madani*),[29] of which he became the supreme guide. Al-Banna referred to the now numerous members of his organization as "battalions of salvation for this nation afflicted by calamity" and "troops of God whose 'armament' was their Islamic morality."[30] Before long, cells of the Muslim Brotherhood mushroomed throughout the country, especially in urban centers. Disciplined and loyal to the supreme guide, they constituted a formidable social force. In certain respects, al-Banna's Brotherhood resembled the contemporary Communist Party of Egypt, which also had a hierarchical structure with an enlightened, activist avant-garde presiding over a network of local cells that were glued together by a strict party discipline. The only major difference was ideology—Islamic/Islamist in the case of the Brotherhood and atheistic/Marxist in the case of the Communist Party of Egypt. It is a cruel irony that both movements fell victim to state persecution under the nationalist regime of Jamál 'Abd al-Násir, better known in the West as Gamal Abdel Nasser (d. 1970).[31]

Although al-Banna advocated a peaceful and gradual transition to an Islamic state, his organization gradually acquired a military wing known as "Secret Apparatus." Well organized, trained, and armed, it was capable of striking back with violence if attacked. Usually, its violence came in response to repressive actions on the part of the state authorities, which were fearful of the movement's popularity and internal strength. The Secret Apparatus and the Brotherhood as a whole became convenient scapegoats in all acts of antigovernment violence whether real or deliberately staged by the ruling regime to justify repressive measures against its political opponents.[32]

The Brotherhood became a target for government repression, first under the Egyptian parliamentary monarchy (before 1952) and later also under Nasser's authoritarian rule (1952–1970). When in 1948 the organization was shut down by a government decree on charges of sedition and terrorist activities, al-Banna lost his ability to control its members. In retaliation for the closure of the Brotherhood and the persecution and torture of its members, a young member of the Secret Apparatus assassinated the Egyptian prime minister. Although al-Banna hastened to denounce this and other acts of violence against the state targets, his days were numbered. He was assassinated by undercover agents of Egypt's secret police in February 1949.[33]

On the international arena, volunteer detachments of the Muslim Brotherhood took part in the Palestinian revolt of 1943 and in the Arab–Israeli War of 1948. They were motivated by the sense of Muslim solidarity that has been a prominent feature of Islamic/Islamist political activism ever since. The Brothers' participation in the Arab–Israeli hostilities, however, failed to change the outcome of both conflicts, which were disastrous for the Arabs. The Brotherhood was more successful in waging a guerilla war against the British occupation of the Suez Canal zone that eventually forced the British to evacuate (1955).

Following the revolution of Egypt's so-called Free Officers in 1952, the Brotherhood reemerged as an important player on Egypt's political scene. Initially, they supported the Officers in the hopes that the latter would embrace their idea of making Egypt an Islamic country governed by the Shari'a. Indeed the new government showed its goodwill to the organization by meting out long prison sentences to the secret service officers who had assassinated Hasan al-Banna.[34] Obviously, the Free Officers and the Brotherhood shared much in common, especially the awareness of the numerous social ills of Egyptian society that needed redress. Both were eager to empower the country's masses by providing free education and expanding considerably state support to the poor. Both wanted a fairer distribution of wealth and upward mobility for the lower classes. However, before long, relations between the new rulers and the Brothers soured. The leadership of the Brotherhood wanted to provide religious guidance to what was essentially a secular nationalist regime. Furthermore, the Brothers expected the new regime to implement an all-encompassing Islamic reform of all aspects of the country's life. The new regime's primary goal, on the other hand, was to not take advice from anyone but to consolidate its grip on power and to detect and crush any incipient opposition to its rule. A bitter power struggle ensued in which the Brotherhood lost to the former Free Officer and now Egypt's president, Gamal Abdel Nasser. For the ambitious and authoritarian Nasser, the Brotherhood was but a dangerous rival, so he soon found a pretext to suppress it. In the fall of 1954, following an attempt on his life by an alleged Muslim brother, Nasser ordered the dissolution of the Brotherhood and the arrest of thousands of its members. Some were tortured in prison, and six members of the society's Consultative Council were hanged.[35]

The Reform Agenda of Sayyid Qutb (d. 1966)

Among the Muslim Brothers imprisoned in 1954 was Sayyid Qutb. A former secular intellectual and prolific writer, he embraced the Brotherhood's Islamic/Islamist agenda later in his life to become the organization's most authoritative and eloquent spokesman. The reach of his popularity extended beyond the membership of the Brotherhood proper. Qutb's passionate advocacy of Islam as the only legitimate foundation of the Egyptian state had brought him nationwide and even international fame. He was to pay dearly for his popularity, spending ten years (1954–1964) in Nasser's jail. Qutb's imprisonment and ill health did not prevent him from completing his widely popular commentary on the Qur'an ("In the Shade of the Qur'an") and a short but even more influential book "Milestones." The latter has become a true Islamist catechism and remains so today. Building on the foundations established by al-Banna and his Egyptian predecessors, Qutb made several critical contributions to the Islamic/Islamist assessment of the state of Islam in the modern world that will be addressed in what follows. It should be pointed out that Qutb did not represent the position of the entire Muslim Brotherhood, some of whose leading members bowed to the state repression and sought accommodation with Nasser's regime.

After having been part of Nasser's inner circle in the aftermath of the revolution of 1952, Qutb realized that the would-be president of Egypt had no intention of assisting the Brotherhood in constructing a truly Islamic state. Nasser was, above all, interested in consolidating his personal power in the name of anti-imperialist struggle and pan-Arab nationalism. Furthermore, he accepted financial and military support from the "godless" Communist regime of the Soviet Union and even began speaking of "Arab Socialism" (yet another "human-made" doctrine, according to Qutb) as his ideology of choice.[36] Although the two men parted ways on ideological grounds, Nasser remained jealous and resentful of Qutb's wide-ranging influence on the hearts and minds of Egyptian Muslims. So he made sure that his popular Islamist rival would be confined to a prison cell for the rest of his life. His personal feelings apart, Nasser was well aware that the social base of the Muslim Brotherhood of which Qutb was the informal leader was much broader than that of the Free Officers' military regime and thus could be easily mobilized against it. This consideration sealed Qutb's fate.

Qutb's prison experiences, which included psychological pressure and torture, seems to have radicalized his original view of the situation in Egypt and in the Muslim world as a whole. He became the mouthpiece of those Muslim brothers who had refused to cooperate with Egypt's new rulers and who were doomed to share their leader's tragic fate as a consequence. For Qutb and his fellow prisoners, Nasser's nationalist regime was but a modern-day reincarnation of the pagan society of Arabia in the age of pre-Islamic "ignorance" (*jahilíyya*). Like the pagan (*jahili*)[37] leaders of Arabian tribes before Islam, the secularized and Westernized ruling class of Egypt was godless, oppressive, and inherently opposed to humankind's natural disposition to serve God and God alone. Built on faulty human-made laws, the Egyptian state allowed "one man's lordship over another"[38] and, to boot, was incapable of securing social justice for all of its members. Nasser's regime had no respect for the right of every person to be free from tyranny and oppression, which, according to Qutb, was possible only under the rule of the divinely revealed law, the Shari'a. Qutb did not limit himself to the condemnation of the anti-Islamic, "pagan" character of Nasser's regime. He went further, arguing:

> The *jahili* society is any society other than the Muslim society; and if we want a more specific definition, we may say that any society is a *jahili* society which does not dedicate itself to submission to God alone, in its beliefs and ideas, in its observances of worship, and in its legal regulations. According to this definition, *all* societies existing in the world today are *jahili*.[39]

As one can see, the state of "paganism" and "godlessness," according to Qutb, was not unique to the *umma*. It was shared by Muslim and non-Muslim societies alike, at least in his age. Societies could be Jewish, Christian, secular, Communist, liberal or authoritarian, but this did not change their inherently godless nature. Nevertheless, according to Qutb, the Muslim societies were more at fault because they had allowed the superior values of their religion to lapse, thereby "selling out" to the "pagan" civilization of the West. They were Muslim only in name. At a closer look, they were as wicked, decadent, and oblivious of God's explicit commands as were the Westerners whom they had been trying to imitate without much success. The rulers of formerly Muslim societies, who had mindlessly embraced Western values and doctrines alien to the true Islam, were but "apostates." Having abandoned Islam, they deserved to be punished by death as required by the Shari'a. The "infidel" rulers and their regimes were thus legitimate targets of *jihád* in the same way as the pagan enemies of Islam in Arabia were legitimate targets of the Prophet's holy war. Qutb defined *jihád* as "[A] movement to wipe out tyranny and to introduce true freedom to mankind." Its ultimate objective is to establish "the sovereignty of God and His Lordship throughout the world," to put an end to "man's arrogance and selfishness," and to implement "the rule of the Divine Shari'a in human affairs."[40]

Mistaken are those Muslim thinkers who, like 'Abdo and Rashíd Ridá, had tried to reduce the Qur'anic demand for Muslims to pursue *jihád* to "the defense of the 'homeland of Islam.'" Their narrow understanding of *jihád* diminishes the global outreach of God's writ, which is obligatory for Muslims at all times, in all places, and under any conditions. Implementing God's will on the global scale was, for Qutb, much more important than the protection of one's "homeland."[41] Furthermore, the idea of "defensive *jihád*," advanced by some pro-Western Muslim thinkers, was, in Qutb's mind, nothing but a concession to the Western vilification of Islam as a religion inherently prone to violence. This vilification, of course, was nothing but wanton hypocrisy on the part of the West, which itself had no compunctions about forcibly subjugating Muslims and stealing their wealth. Despite the formal independence of Muslim countries, Western governments, according to Qutb, continued to exercise control over the Muslim world through the ruling "apostates" and "renegades" who had nothing Islamic about them except their names. Therefore, *jihád* must be prosecuted everywhere and incessantly in order to defeat those who resist the implementation of God's law—the only legitimate power, ideology, and social system to the exclusion of any other "powers and orders that seduce and mislead the believers."[42]

For Qutb, Islam was the only harmonious and equitable social order and moral way of life. As such, it needed neither justification nor apology:

> In Islam the individual and the group are not enemies . . . [A]n individual does not prescribe for the group how to act, and the group does not prescribe for the individual how to act. They are both subject to the law of God that takes care of both of them.[43]

Only those Muslim "hypocrites" who had succumbed to the allure of Western "paganism" (*jahilīyya*) felt themselves compelled to defend their religion before its Western detractors. To expose their servile submission to the authority of the West, Qutb launched into an eloquent tirade that captures the essence of his attitude toward Western civilization as a whole. Because his statement is based on his direct encounter with Western (American) society and culture, it merits to be reproduced in full:

> During my stay in the United States,[44] there were some people . . . who used to argue with us—with us few who were considered to be on the side of Islam. Some of us took the position of defense and justification. I, on the other hand, took the position of attacking the Western *Jahilīyya*, its shaky religious beliefs, its social and economic modes, and its immoralities. [I told them]: "Look at these concepts of the Trinity, Original Sin and Redemption, which are agreeable neither to reason nor to conscience. Look at this capitalism with its monopolies, its usury and whatever else is in it; at this individual freedom, devoid of human sympathy and responsibility for relatives except under the force of law; at this materialistic attitude which deadens the spirit; at this behavior, like animals, which you call 'Free mixing of the sexes'; at this vulgarity which you call 'Emancipation of women'; at these unfair and cumbersome laws of marriage and divorce, which are contrary to the demands of practical life. [And now look at] Islam, with its logic, beauty, humanity and happiness, which reaches the horizons to which man but does not reach. It is a practical way of life and its solutions are based on the foundation of the wholesome nature of man." These were the realities which we encountered [in America]. These facts, when seen in the light of Islam, made American people blush. Yet, there are people—exponents of Islam—who are defeated before this filth . . . to the extent that they search for resemblances to Islam among this rubbish heap of the West, and also among the evil and dirty materialism of the East.[45]

Elsewhere Qutb undertakes a painstaking critique of the status of women in Western societies. While Islam has bestowed the spiritual and material rights and dignity upon Muslim women, the West has reduced them to sexual objects whose feminine charms have become, in Qutb's phrase, but a commodity in the workplace or in public interaction.[46] It is therefore particularly ridiculous that Muslim women should aspire to imitate their Western counterparts, argues Qutb. He bitterly bemoans the "extreme," "back-breaking" pressure put upon the Muslim women of his age by the seductive, if false, Western concept of emancipation and urges them to remain true to their Islamic values and moral code. He concludes by saying that, unlike Western feminism, Islamic teachings are in full harmony with feminine nature in that they do not require the fair sex to perform the social and productive functions that God has allotted exclusively to men.[47]

After examining the immorality and viciousness of the "pagan condition" which, in his opinion, has engulfed the entire world, Qutb calls his audience to come out of its darkness and misery into the light of true Islam in order to enjoy its blessings, serenity, and harmony.[48] For him, the traditional Islamic concepts of the "Abode of Islam" (i.e., territories ruled by Muslims), as opposed to the "Abode of War" (i.e., territories ruled by non-Muslims), have no concrete geographical location. Qutb divides the whole world, including his native Egypt, into the realms of Islam—namely, the Society of the Muslim Brothers—and that of "paganism" (*jahilíyya*)—namely Egypt's "godless," Westernized state and its backers. For Qutb, you can be considered a true Muslim only if you unconditionally accept God's absolute sovereignty (*hakimíyya*) over your own life and that of society as a whole. If, on the other hand, you submit yourself to the rule of anyone or anything else, be it a despotic regime, a dictator, a human-made constitution, or a humanly elected parliament, you are nothing but "polytheist." In this case, you may be considered by true Muslims to be a legitimate target of *jihád*, especially if you actively resist the execution of God's will as enshrined in the holy book of Islam.

As long as "polytheism" and "ignorance" remain prevalent, a small vanguard of true believers should psychologically insulate themselves from the *jahili* society around them until they are strong enough in their faith and numbers to launch a *jihád* aimed at bringing "pagans" under the rule of God.[49] Until that time, the vanguard of the faithful should avoid any association with "a political system from which it could expect nothing."[50]

Today, Qutb's powerful message continues to animate Islamic parties, movements, and even entire countries. A much revered figure among Islamists, his works are being avidly studied either in the original Arabic or in translation across the Muslim world. In 1984, the postal service of the Islamic Republic of Iran issued a postage stamp depicting Sayyid Qutb behind bars either in his prison cell or in the military court that condemned him to death.[51] This was no small honor to be bestowed by a predominantly Shi'ite country upon a Sunni thinker. Qutb is held in high regard in the countries whose religious establishments share at least some of his ideas, especially in Saudi Arabia, Sudan, Pakistan, and Afghanistan under the Taliban. His legacy is very much alive among militant groups active in Somalia, West Africa, the Philippines, Central Asia, Yemen, Syria, and Iraq.

Sayyid Qutb's analysis of the plight of Muslim societies and the radical means he proposed to redress it did not go unchallenged. His insistence on establishing an Islamic state "here and now" was dismissed as impracticable by some more realistic members of his own Muslim Brotherhood. Invoking the intransigence and zealotry of the Kharijite movement in early Islam, respected Egyptian scholars affiliated with the Ázhar University have accused Qutb of espousing a modern-day reincarnation of Kharijite "extremism" (*ghuluww*).[52] Nevertheless, his passionate and eloquent advocacy for social justice, freedom from oppression, and high moral standards under a truly Islamic order, combined with his martyrdom at the hands of the "godless" regime of Gamal Abdel Nasser, have made him a true hero of Islamic/Islamist movements worldwide. It is worth mentioning that Sayyid Qutb's brother, Muhammad Qutb (d. 2014), who had emigrated to Saudi Arabia, was a religious mentor of Usáma Bin Ládin.

After Qutb: The Islamization of Egyptian Society in the 1970s and 1980s

Driven underground by Nasser's repressions, the Society of Muslim Brothers managed to preserve itself against all odds. It was given a powerful shot in the arm by Egypt's humiliating defeat by Israel in the Six-Day War of 1967. This catastrophic event for the Egyptian state seriously undermined Nasser's legitimacy, as well as the secular nationalist and socialist ideals he had so vigorously promoted. Disillusioned and disheartened, Egyptian Muslims embarked on a new round of soul-searching and reassessment of their ideological orientations. Because the secular-nationalist ideas constituting the foundation of Nasser's regime had failed to deliver, many Egyptians started to look to Islam for solutions for the country's social and economic problems.[53]

The vacuum created by the implosion of the nationalist ideology promoted under Nasser's rule was filled with alternative ideologies. In Egypt, as well as in some other Arab countries affected by the 1967 war (e.g., Jordan), such ideological alternatives could be provided by only two political forces: the leftists (Communists and Socialists) or the Muslim Brothers. Both groups had suffered persecutions under Nasser, and their most active members had served time in the regime's prisons or in hard labor camps. Following Nasser's death, the secular leftist ideology (with some elements of nationalism) continued to inspire college students and industrial workers.[54] However, so-called Arab Socialism had little appeal to the rural population of Egypt, including recent rural migrants to the country's major cities, whose deep-seated religiosity prevented them from embracing the "godless" doctrines of Marx, Engels, and Lenin. As a consequence, these segments of the Egyptian population turned to the Islamic/Islamist solutions proposed by the Muslim Brotherhood.

Egypt's new rulers were quick to grasp the dual challenge to their authority posed by leftists and Islamists. They made a conscious choice between "the two evils," giving preference to the latter. After Nasser's death in 1970, his successor President Anwar Sadat gradually abandoned the late leader's socialist ideas in favor of free market and Western-style capitalism. In the ideological sphere, Sadat decided to cultivate the Muslim Brotherhood to empower it against his leftist critics, who were particularly active among college students and industrial workers. In line with his new policy, Sadat ordered the release of numerous members of the Muslim Brotherhood imprisoned by Nasser's secret police. Restrictions on the society's activities were lifted, and its activists given free hand in propagating their ideas on the university campuses, in the mosques, at professional schools, and even in army barracks. Sadat's measures paid off. By the mid-1970s, socialist and leftist rhetoric was out of vogue, and Islam became the preferred frame of reference and code of behavior among Egypt's petty bourgeoisie, civil servants, army corps, and students. Public space, too, was thoroughly (re-)Islamized. The most visible symbols of this ideological and cultural reorientation were veils, gloves, and long free-flowing dresses worn by women. Men took to sporting beards and wearing traditional loose ankle-length garments (*djellaba*s).[55]

Sadat's government actively supported Islamic/Islamist student organizations in an effort to woo them away from the leftist groups. Sadat, a former Free Officer and secular nationalist, quickly reinvented himself as a "Believer-President."[56] The government-controlled media routinely portrayed him in prayer, and his public speeches were generously peppered with Qur'anic quotations and references to Islamic history.[57] The 1973 Egyptian–Israeli War was waged under Islamic slogans and portrayed by the Egyptian media as a special form of *jihád*. Its relatively favorable outcome for the Egyptian side was attributed to divine help (in contrast to the devastating defeat of 1967 under Nasser's secular nationalist rule).[58] The wealthier members of the Brotherhood were satisfied by Sadat's pro-Islamic gestures and efforts to suppress "godless Socialism" and accepted his one-party rule. For some time it seemed that Sadat's gamble paid off handsomely. However, contrary to his calculations, the campaign to Islamize the country eventually proved to be his undoing.

Despite the religious trappings of Sadat's regime, not every Egyptian Muslim was convinced by its commitment to Islamic values. Quite the opposite, many believed that he used Islam as a simple façade for his authoritarian rule. The "open-door" economic policy instituted by Sadat in contradistinction to Nasser's socialism benefited only a handful of already wealthy individuals with close ties to the regime. The result was a rampant inequality between the rich and the poor. The abject poverty of the lower classes was further aggravated by Egypt's demographic explosion of the early 1970s. With the leftist (or for that matter any other) ideology effectively banished from the public sphere in favor of the ruling party's Egyptian nationalism with religious trappings,

Islam became practically the only means for the disenfranchised classes to express their dissatisfaction with the economic and social status quo.

Seen against this ideological and social background, it becomes clear why various Islamic/Islamist groups outside Egypt's official religious establishment were so eager to explore the practical implications of Qutb's radical philosophy previously outlined. One such group has come to be known as *al-Takfīr wa 'l-Hijra*, a phrase that can be translated as "Excommunication and Emigration."[59] Its leader, Shukri Mustafa (d. 1977), a former Muslim brother and agronomist by profession, pushed Qutb's ideas to the limit. Qutb seems to have implied that whereas the incumbent Egyptian rulers (namely, Nasser and his officials) were indeed "apostates," whose "blood was licit" under the Shari'a, their subjects were nominally Muslims, albeit ones who had been coerced into "unbelief" by the "godless regime." This being the case, social contacts with them were permissible, and they could not be legitimately declared targets of *jihād*. Shukri Mustafa went further. Not only did he consider all present states and regimes to be un-Islamic (which was the position of Qutb as well), but he also declared all Muslims who were not part of his movement to be apostates or even infidels. For Shukri Mustafa, Egypt was "an abode of unbelief," "because of 'un-Islamic' ways of [both] the government and society."[60] By refusing to fight for God's sovereignty and bowing to Sadat's "infidel rule," Egypt's Muslims, in his view, had abandoned their religious duty to practice Islam and were thus unbelievers like their rulers. Seen from this vantage point, Sadat himself was a modern-day reincarnation of the godless and arrogant Pharaoh of the Qur'an, whereas his obedient subjects were unbelievers by association.

Shukri Mustafa insisted that the Qur'an should be the only source of divine guidance. The entire corpus of Islamic jurisprudence, being a product of fallible human thinking, should be declared invalid and discarded.[61] Its learned custodians, the *'ulamá'*, were thus effectively delegitimized and their guidance rejected. Shukri Mustafa viewed them as simple pawns of Egypt's "godless regime." The same applied to the other classes of Egyptian society that cooperated with the state authorities.

Shukri Mustafa's teaching had long-ranging practical implications. First, because the true Egyptian Muslim could not live a religiously sound life under the country's *jahili* law amidst "apostates and infidels," he or she had to emigrate (*hijra*) from the "godless" society in the same way as the Prophet and his closest followers emigrated from Mecca to Medina. Second, anyone who deserted Shukri Mustafa's group automatically became an apostate whose "blood is licit" for his former comrades. In real life, Shukri Mustafa's exclusivist principles found their expression not just in the psychological (per Qutb) but also in the physical isolation of his followers from the rest of Egyptian society. The leaders of Excommunication and Emigration ordered the rank-and-file members of the movement to reside in communal apartments in city suburbs or in the countryside. They were discouraged from having any interaction with Muslims outside their community. Some went even further by withdrawing into the mountains and caves of Upper (i.e., southern) Egypt to reduce to a minimum any contact with outsiders. Those who resided in urban centers and villages refused to pray in the official mosques for fear of "pollution."[62] To maintain the purity of the movement, members of Excommunication and Emigration arranged their own, internal marriages without the payment of the customary bride-wealth, which they regarded as an un-Islamic "innovation."[63] Shukri Mustafa's teaching was a pure utopia—an attempt to "achieve a perfect state of sociopolitical being without even a remotely realistic account of the current situation nor a strategy of achieving such a state."[64] From the perspective of the academic discipline called "religious studies," his movement falls on the borderline of a sect or a cult, whose members blindly and mindlessly follow their leader who promises them salvation from a corrupt and ungodly world and eternal bliss in the hereafter.[65] Seeing that he unconditionally rejected Muslim jurisprudence and theology, the Egyptian religious establishment denounced Shukri Mustafa as an out-and-out heretic and a new age "Kharijite." In his teaching, the spirit of Kharijite exclusivity and intolerance of other viewpoints, which had characterized Qutb's intellectual position, reached its most extreme form.

The Egyptian authorities initially considered Shukri Mustafa's movement to be inwardly oriented and thus harmless. However, in 1976–1977, they arrested some of its members as part of the government's overall crackdown on "religious extremism." To secure the release of their comrades, the group abducted their erstwhile critic and former Minister of Pious Endowments, *shaykh* al-Dhahabi. When their demands for the release of their comrades were not met by the government, they murdered him. Throughout the trial that followed, Shukri Mustafa and his soulmates remained defiant. Shukri Mustafa's flat denial of the authenticity of the famous *hadíth*, according to which the Muslim *umma* collectively cannot agree on an error, created a public furor.[66] This denial was a logical consequence of his exclusivist claim to represent the true Islam of the Qur'an, which relegated all Muslims who had refused to join his movement to the position of misguided heretics or even apostates. According to Shukri Mustafa's logic, their collective opinion had no religious legitimacy. In other words, they had "agreed on an error," by accusing him and his followers of deviating from true Islam. Shukri Mustafa claimed to be the leader of the handful of the faithful who were chosen by God to be saved from the hellfire. All the rest were but apostates and infidels destined to hell.

Shukri Mustafa's treatment of other burning issues of the day was no less controversial. When asked about the Israeli–Palestinian conflict, he denied that the Palestinians were engaged in an Islamic holy war. Even if (re)conquered by Egypt from Israel, Palestine, in his view, would still not be considered a land governed by Islamic law. Therefore, as Palestine's potential liberators, the Egyptians should first convert to "the true Islam," implement God's rule in their own land, and only then begin to spread it beyond the country's borders.[67] The trial, conducted as a public show, ended with the execution of Shukri Mustafa and four of his followers directly implicated in the murder of the Minister of Pious Endowments.[68] As a result, Excommunication and Emigration was effectively wiped out from the political scene. Its disappearance, however, did not spell the end of radical Islamism in Egypt.

Even by the most strident Islamic/Islamist standards, Shukri Mustafa's group was a maverick. The overwhelming majority of Islamic/Islamist movements, either cultivated by Sadat's regime or opposed to its rule, viewed the liberation of Palestine as an important part of their religiopolitical agenda. No wonder that the Islamists were stunned and deeply offended by Sadat's visit to Jerusalem in November 1977 to initiate a peace treaty with the Israeli government. Most of Egypt's Islamist leaders hurried to voice their outrage at the president's policy of capitulation before the "Zionist foe." They grew ever more vocal following Sadat's "shameful" signing of the peace treaty with Israel in 1979. The president's belated crackdown on the country's Islamists (as well as other oppositional forces in Egypt) failed to achieve its goals. On October 6, 1981, Sadat was assassinated during a military parade. His assassin, a military officer, declared that he had just killed Pharaoh—the Qur'anic embodiment of arrogance, godlessness, and wanton oppression.[69]

The assassin belonged to the militant Jihad Organization, some of whose members had been implicated in an earlier attempt to overthrow Sadat's regime in an armed coup. The Jihad Organization was a relatively broad-based movement that represented all the major professional classes of Egyptian society: civil servants, small-time traders, the military, university students, professors, radio and television workers.[70] The members were bound by strict discipline, staunchly loyal to their leaders, the *amir*s, and ready to face martyrdom "in the path of God."[71] Unlike the maverick "Excommunication and Emigration," which regarded all Egyptian Muslims as unbelievers due to their acceptance of human-made laws and Sadat's "infidel" rule, the leaders of the Jihad Organization did not consider Egypt's society to be responsible for the regime's transgressions against God's will. Rather, the Muslim community of Egypt was a victim deliberately kept from living according to God's laws by its "impious" rulers.[72] In his famous tract, "The Missing Obligation," the chief ideologist of the group Muhammad al-Faraj (al-Farag),[73] makes no bones about it:

> The rulers of these days are apostate. They have been brought up at the tables of colonialism, no matter whether of the crusading, the communist or the Zionist variety. They are Muslim only in name, even if they pray, fast, and pretend that they are Muslims.[74]

Taking his cue from Sayyid Qutb's idea of "divine sovereignty" (*hakimiyya*),[75] al-Faraj proposes the following course of action:

> [We] have to establish the Rule of God's Religion in our country first, and to make the Word of God supreme . . . There is no doubt that the first battlefield for jihad is the extermination of these infidel leaders and to replace them by a complete Islamic Order. From here we should start.[76]

Two things are worth pointing out here. First, the title of al-Faraj's pamphlet forefronts *jihád* as a major obligation of Muslims, implying that they have somehow neglected or forgotten it. Al-Faraj calls upon the faithful to restore it to its rightful place as a key religious principle of Islam (alongside the Five Pillars); as such, it must be implemented by all believers subject to "infidel" rule. Second, al-Faraj was an electrical engineer by profession. Who, one might ask, gave him the right to reinterpret the Muslim tradition in such a drastic way? Al-Faraj had a ready answer to this question. In his view, by being effectively state employees and fulfilling the rulers' every whim, the official religious establishment of Egypt and especially the *'ulamá'* associated with the Ázhar University, had forfeited its right to interpret God's will and to lead the community of the faithful to salvation. In the absence of sound religious guidance and authority, *jihád* becomes the personal obligation of every believer and the only realistic way to establish an Islamic state.[77] The goal of fighting the "near enemy" should take precedence over all other considerations, including the liberation of Palestine from the "Zionist foe." The latter objective can be achieved only under the banner of Islam, which illegitimate, "apostate" regimes are not qualified to do. We will revisit this issue in Chapter 24, while discussing the recent reorientation of some Islamic/Islamist groups toward fighting the "far enemy," that is, the United States and its allies.

The rejection of the official religious authority voiced by al-Faraj was shared by the other members of the Jihad Organization. In prison interviews, they mockingly described the official *'ulamá'* of al-Ázhar as "pulpit parrots" in cahoots with the ruling "apostates."[78] The official scholars' failure to provide sound religious guidance to the country's Muslims, according to al-Faraj, entitled him, an electrical engineer, to step forward as interpreter of God's will and admonisher of his fellow Muslims. Al-Faraj's condemnation of Sadat for Egypt's ills was final and unequivocal. For Sadat, having been one of those "apostates of Islam fed at the tables of imperialism and Zionism,"[79] the sentence was death, according to God's law.

Thus, contrary to Sadat's expectations, the Islamic/Islamist forces that he had emancipated after Nasser's demise became the proverbial genie out of a bottle. The Jihad Organization was one of several radical Islamic/Islamist groups that have been active in Egypt over the past thirty years. Even though their members were occasionally allowed by the regime to stand in the elections, they were denied the status of regular political parties. The Muslim Brotherhood won the presidential election after the fall of president Mubarak's regime in June 2012 but was outlawed one year later as a result of the military coup engineered by the Egyptian military. One wonders how did Islamic/Islamist parties fare elsewhere? Let us examine Pakistan, whose Islamic/Islamist parties have taken an active part in the country's political life since its inception in 1947. The case of the Islamic Group (*jama'át-i Islamí*) movement, founded by the influential Indo-Pakistani Muslim thinker Abu A'la Mawdúdi (Maudoodi), is particularly pertinent and instructive.

The Revivalist Islam of Mawdúdi (d. 1979) and Jama'át-i Islamí

As with the Egypt-based Muslim activists described earlier in this chapter, Mawdúdi's movement came in response to Western colonialism. What sets him apart from his Egyptian counterparts is the unique confessional and political environment of the Indian Subcontinent in the decades preceding independence from the British Raj. Of special importance is the fateful partition of this vast country into India and Pakistan in August 1947. Mawdúdi's plan for the revival of Islam and Muslim life in the Subcontinent was shaped by the specificity of Muslim–Indian experience under British colonial rule in the first decades of the twentieth century. With the British Empire in decline, many Indian Muslims were apprehensive of their fate after the impending withdrawal of the British. On the one hand, they were nostalgic for the past glory of the Muslim state in the Subcontinent under Mogul rule. On the other, they were worried about their fate as a minority under the governance of the Hindu-dominated ruling Congress Party. In the final account, their abiding fear of being subjugated by or fully absorbed into the Hindu majority led to the country's partition into the predominantly Hindu and Muslim parts in 1947.

Mawdúdi's philosophy was a religious response to the anxieties and aspirations of the Indian Muslims in his age. It stood in stark contrast to the generally secularist attitudes of the founders of modern Pakistan and contributed in significant ways to the progressive Islamization of the country's life in the decades following its separation from India.[80] Mawdúdi apparently considered himself the reviver of Islam of his age. His task was, in his own words, "to comprehend the fundamental principles of Religion, judge contemporary culture and its trends from the Islamic viewpoint, and determine the changes to be effected in the existing patterns of social life."[81] Mawdúdi spent his entire life doing just that. Here we shall focus primarily on the doctrinal aspects of Mawdúdi's masterplan for the revivification of Islam in India. The details of his and his movement's involvement in Pakistani politics constitute a separate subject that we shall touch upon only cursorily.

An offspring of a renowned family of Muslim scholars whose ancestors had occupied high positions in the Mogul state bureaucracy, Mawdúdi was brought up in a traditional Islamic environment "carefully insulated from western culture and the English language."[82] Under the guidance of his father, a pious lawyer from Delhi, Mawdúdi learned to look back nostalgically on the past glory of the Indian Muslim community, while also recognizing the precarious position of the Indian Muslims under British rule. In his later writings, Mawdúdi attributed the sorry state of the Indian Muslim community in the first decades of the twentieth century not so much to the Western military and political domination, as to what he described as "the fall of Islam." This "fall," in turn, was a direct result of the failure on the part of individual Muslims and their leaders to implement the original principles of their religion. Mawdúdi saw his vocation as a Muslim scholar and public intellectual in resuscitating the dormant energies of Islamic faith with a view to mobilizing India's Muslims around clearly articulated and achievable sociopolitical goals. In Mawdúdi's mind, this mobilization was necessary in order to help India's Muslim community to counter the corroding influences of alien ideological systems (both religious and secular) and to improve the fortunes of Islam in the Subcontinent. To achieve these goals, Mawdúdi launched what he described as a "three-pronged offensive" aimed at (1) destroying "the ideological foundations of Western culture" by showing their inferiority to the Muslim doctrine; (2) elucidating to the masses the principles of the authentic, activist Islam; (3) offering "practical Islamic solutions of important problems [to] which previously even observant Muslims could see no alternative but to follow the West."[83]

Central to Mawdúdi's blueprint for Islamic revival was the idea of absolute submission to God (*islám*), which, in his view, was implemented by the Muslim *umma* under the Prophet and his immediate successors. However, contrary to the traditional (especially Sufi) interpretations of this idea, which implied resigning oneself to one's divinely predetermined fate, Mawdúdi spoke of "*active* submission" that would result in establishing a truly Islamic social and political order. In practice, this meant focusing on social action rather than dreaming idly of salvation in the hereafter. "We believe in cash, not in credit," wrote Mawdúdi in one of his poems, "so why narrate to us the story of paradise?"[84] The down-to-earth, businesslike approach advocated by the Indian thinker was to lead to the creation of an authentic Islamic state. It stood in opposition to the more traditional, inward-oriented interpretation of Islam that emphasized personal faith and pious behavior as the surest way for the believer to achieve otherworldly bliss. Political and social action here and now became, in Mawdúdi's teaching, the quintessential manifestation of Islamic faith. All alternative expressions of Islamic faith, including philosophy, mysticism, literature, the arts, and cultural habits, were dismissed as "foreign borrowings" on which the Muslims had frivolously squandered their creative energies while being forgetful of their immediate, mundane needs.[85]

To rectify this pitiful situation, Mawdúdi offered what can be described as a sociopolitical and activist reading of the Qur'an. He consistently used the Muslim scripture as the chief reservoir of practical solutions to the maladies and imperfections of the current social and political order in the Muslim world. In his view, God's commands should be the only sound foundation of governance and socioeconomic life of the *umma*. Implementing them in real life should heal Muslim societies of their numerous ills and abiding anxieties. God would never reward the faithful for the mere profession of Muslim faith; they would be rewarded only for actively executing its principles.[86] Earlier in this chapter, we mentioned the instrumentalization of religious faith by several prominent Muslim reformers and modernizers. In Mawdúdi's reformist philosophy, this line of thinking and action reached its consummate expression. His attempts to reduce Islam to the role of a sociopolitical blueprint for the creation and successful functioning of an Islamic state did not go unopposed. A number of traditionally minded Pakistani scholars accused the reformer of completely denuding Islam of its devotional, spiritual, and emotional aspects. In the opinion of his critics, Mawdúdi's purely pragmatic, instrumental approach to Islam was but innovation or even heresy. His followers, on the contrary, viewed him as a reviver of Islam at the time of its decline and weakness.

How exactly did Mawdúdi want to establish an Islamic state that would function in concert with God's will? As a first step, he suggested mounting a comprehensive Islamic "revolution" because the revolutionary spirit is an inherent part of correct Islam:

> Islam is a revolutionary ideology and a revolutionary practice, which aims at destroying the social order of the world totally and rebuilding it from scratch . . . and Jihad denotes the revolutionary struggle.[87]

On the face of it, this statement sounds quite radical because in the Western mentality the word "revolution" is closely associated with violence. However, behind Mawdúdi's revolutionary rhetoric hides a gradualist, evolutionary approach to change. "We desire," wrote Mawdúdi, "no demonstrations or agitations, no flag waving, slogans and the like . . ." Rather, he said, addressing his followers, "You must kindle the light of Islam in your hearts, and change those around you."[88] A sudden, abrupt change of the old social order, according to Mawdúdi, was likely to be short-lived. Contrary to his revolutionary talk, he, in fact, wanted to follow in the footsteps of the

Prophet, whose "patience and pacifism" he highly praised and valued. In line with his, in its essence, evolutionary approach to change, Mawdúdi rejected violent, militant interpretations of *jihád*. The latter should by no means denote "a crazed faith, . . . blood-shot eyes, shouting *Allahu akbar* [God is the greatest], decapitating an unbeliever wherever you see one, cutting off heads while invoking *La ilaha illa-llah* [there is no god but God]."[89]

To reiterate, according to Mawdúdi, the correct Islamic order was to be built gradually by means of education and a patient preaching of the true Islam of the Prophet and his companions among the masses. As the first step, Mawdúdi called for the Islamization of the public sphere by encouraging followers to take an active part in elections, parliamentary politics, and public relations campaigns and debates. As regards changes in Muslim life, he advised modernization without Westernization, arguing that "even a bulldozer and computer would be 'Islamic' if used in the path of God." Mawdúdi pointed out that, in and of themselves, technical innovations are "pure" and "licit." It is only their "misuse" by Westerners to achieve their godless ends that renders them "impure" and "suspect" in the eyes of the Muslims.[90] When adopted by the members of the *umma* to advance God's cause, they become totally licit and even desirable.

As already mentioned, Mawdúdi's ultimate goal was to [re-]create a powerful Islamic state on the Indian Subcontinent. Islamic teachings, in his view, were uniquely suited for this task because of what he considered to be their political implications. Unlike Christianity, he argued, Islam "makes no distinction between the spiritual and the secular life";[91] therefore, in a truly Islamic state, politics is to be rendered sacred, whereas in non-Muslim societies, it is regarded as something profane and irrelevant to religious faith.[92]

How did the Indian thinker define the character of the Muslim state he proposed to found? According to Mawdúdi, it "would be democratic because its leadership would be duly elected and bound by the writ of divine law." The fact that it is built on the principles of the Shari'a would make it distinct from both communist dictatorship and Western parliamentary democracy, which rest on human-made ideological premises. In such a state, there will be no need for persuasion, divisive debates, or coercion because its citizens will voluntarily follow the revealed law in order to avoid punishment in the hereafter. Mawdúdi described this state as "democratic caliphate" or "theo-democracy."[93] Built on Islamic foundations, it will not grant equal rights to its non-Muslim citizens. They will have to submit themselves to the "protection" (*dhimma*) stipulated in the Shari'a. The same applies to Muslim women, who should observe the restrictions imposed on them in the holy books of Islam and *fiqh* literature. In this respect, Mawdúdi's "Islamic democracy" differs from that of the West, in which men and women are placed on an equal footing. This factor did not trouble Mawdúdi too much because he rejected a blind imitation of Western values by Muslims as being contrary to human nature and divinely revealed order of things.

The Islamic state, according to Mawdúdi, will be governed by an *amír* ("commander"), who is to be elected on the basis of the precedents established under the four rightly guided caliphs who succeeded the Prophet at the *umma*'s helm. The *amír* will govern in consultation with the leading scholars and intellectuals of the community, all of whom are bound by the injunctions of the Qur'an and the Prophet's Sunna. The reliance of the state officials on Islam's foundational texts, in Mawdúdi's mind, was supposed to prevent any discord within the community. All branches of power must resolve potential conflicts among them by referring to the precedents and commands found in the sacred books of Islam and the history of the first Muslim community.[94] The economic policies of the Islamic state are determined by the Shari'a rules, with the prohibition of usury and the collection of the "poor" tax (*zakát*) strictly enforced. Otherwise, Mawdúdi's economic program is rather vague. It seems that he was of the opinion that all economic problems would resolve themselves once the correct Islam had been internalized and implemented by every citizen of the Islamic state.

Unlike the Egyptian Muslim Brotherhood, Mawdúdi did not seek to achieve his goals by creating a broadly based popular movement. The establishment of the Islamic state, according to Mawdúdi, could be realized only by a concerted political action of a relatively small but highly motivated group of pious intellectual leaders fully devoted to the vision of correct Islam that he advocated. To this end, in 1941 he founded a political movement named "Islamic Community" or "Islamic Group" (*Jama 'át-i Islamí*). He wanted it to be a vanguard of the movement for Islamic revival that would steer the Muslims of India in the direction of a righteous commonwealth based on the will of God and the custom of his Prophet.[95] From the outset, the movement was quite elitist. Its members were recruited from among students, professionals, and civil servants in the hopes that those of them in positions of power would become conduits and implementers of its revivalist ideology "from the top." As mentioned, despite his vocal revolutionary rhetoric Mawdúdi did not condone the use of violence to achieve his goals. The Islamic revolution he envisioned had to be accomplished gradually through the education of the masses in the principles of true Islam and implementation of modernizing reforms by his movement's enlightened leaders. The *Jama 'át-i Islamí* under the leadership of its founder and his successors set as the movement's primary objective the preservation of "the place of Islam in society and politics while it trains a vanguard Islamic elite to oversee the revival of Islam on a national level."[96]

Each time the movement's leaders felt that the Islamic character of Pakistani society was threatened or compromised, they used all means at their disposal to forestall this unwelcome development. To this end, they would resort to inciting their constituencies to demonstrate against government reforms. They were also eager to put pressure on the Pakistani government through the parliament or through the media outlets they controlled. The *Jama 'át-i Islamí* is largely responsible for preserving the Islamic character of Pakistan's constitution (against the opposition of secular nationalists) and keeping rigid boundaries between Islamic orthodoxy (Sunnism) and some religious movements that they felt had strayed from it, such as, for instance, the Ahmadiyya of Qadiyan, the Sikhs, and so on. The movement has stridently criticized and opposed Pakistan's secular leaders and used its political clout to scuttle their economic and social reforms by declaring them to be "un-Islamic." The movement's heyday came in 1977, when the secular nationalist regime of premier Zulfiqar Bhutto (d. 1979; father of the famous female politician Benazir Bhutto, assassinated in 2007) was overthrown by a military coup led by the army general Ziau 'l-Haq (d. 1988). Under his rule, which derived its legitimacy from promoting Islamic values and institutions, the *Jama 'át-i Islamí* "became a major political and ideological force close to the center of power."[97] For the first time in his life, Mawdúdi felt that his dream of an Islamic state was close to becoming a reality. However, he did not live to see Ziau 'l-Haq's Islamist experiment come to fruition. He died in a clinic in Buffalo, New York, on September 22, 1979.[98]

After the founder's death, the leaders of the *Jama 'át-i Islamí* continued to cultivate close relations with Ziau 'l-Haq's military regime. In recognition of their loyalty, the regime appointed them to key government offices, thereby enabling them to play an active role in the progressive "Islamization of the country, as well as in articulating state policy, especially concerning the Afghan war."[99] The *Jama 'át-i Islamí* strongly supported the Afghan *jihád* against the Soviets and is believed to have been involved in Pakistan's undeclared war against India in Kashmir. In the late 1990s, U.S. intelligence agencies suspected the movement of maintaining close ties with al-Qa'ida and the Taliban both before and after their defeat by the coalition forces in 2002.[100] The *Jama 'át-i Islamí*'s close association with the increasingly unpopular and authoritarian regime of Ziau 'l-Haq took a heavy toll on its popularity. Since the general's death in 1988, it has been making only a rather modest showing in Pakistan's national elections and had to work in coalition with the country's other Islamic parties, even though they might disagree with their political and religious agendas. Nevertheless, the movement's following among Pakistani students and intelligentsia and its penetration of the state bureaucracy continue to assure it an influence that is disproportionate to its size and presence in Pakistan's elected bodies. The *Jama'át-i Islamí*'s relative success in implementing its revivalist agenda is conditioned by "the power of discipline and organization rather than the power of numbers."[101] The movement's struggle to keep Islam at the center of Pakistan's political, social, and cultural life is likely to continue in the years to come.

Some Comparative Observations

The vicissitudes of the two Islamic/Islamist movements we have discussed so far demonstrate different possible patterns of interaction between Islamic activists and the state. In the case of the Muslim Brotherhood, we are dealing with a movement with a broad popular base active at the grassroots level (through charities, dispensaries, provision of services and education, and so on). Bound by a rigid discipline and fully loyal to their leaders, its members are intent on achieving a gradual transition of Egypt to an Islamic state governed by Qur'anic principles and the exemplary ways of the "pious ancestors" of Islam. Initially apolitical and prone to cooperating with state authorities, it gradually developed a militant wing in response to state repression. The Brotherhood's doctrine served as an ideological alternative first to the liberal secularism and nationalism of Egypt's parliamentary monarchy and later on to the pan-Arabism and socialism of Nasser's military regime. The Brotherhood's persecution under both led to its split into a moderate wing that was still willing to cooperate with state authorities and an assemblage of radical groups embittered by their own prison experiences or by the sufferings of their comrades at the hands of the regimes' secret police. Embracing Qutb's sharp division of the world into the righteous minority and the herd of "godless renegades," some semi-clandestine splinter groups of the movement embarked on the path of antigovernment agitation and, eventually, armed struggle and terrorism. Their militant actions inevitably led to further repressions, resulting in a vicious cycle of violence and retribution. Still, the Brotherhood's moderate elements eventually found a tacit accommodation with the regime of President Mubarak in exchange for its agreement to pay public tribute to Islamic values and symbols. In the final account, such an accommodation, however, was reached on the regime's terms. As the regime weakened in the winter of 2011, the Brotherhood and its Islamist allies seized the opportunity to come to power through the ballot box, only to be thwarted by the Egyptian military in July 2013. At present, the future of the Brotherhood in the country remains dim.

In Mawdúdi's *Jama'át-i Islamí*, we find a movement whose primary raison d'être was to participate in the country's political life in order to preserve its Islamic character and, in the long term, steering Pakistani society in the direction of an Islamic state. In contrast to the Muslim Brotherhood and other popular Islamic/Islamist movements, the *Jama'át-i Islamí* did not attempt to attract a mass following. Created as a vanguard party of the Leninist type, it targeted pious intellectuals, professionals, and students in the hopes of winning them over to its revivalist agenda. Once on board, they were supposed to become conduits of Mawdúdi's ideas to the public at large. In other words, the movement's highly educated and pious membership was to effect change from above by using their positions in the state administration, elected bodies, legal profession, and educational facilities. Despite Mawdúdi's revolutionary rhetoric, the transition of Pakistan to a truly Islamic state (as he envisioned it) was to be instituted gradually through education and the wide dissemination of Mawdúdi's revivalist agenda among the Pakistani Muslims. Initially opposed to both the secular nationalism of the ruling elite and the traditionalist Islam of the *'ulamá'* class, in the course of its active involvement in Pakistan's political life, the *Jama'át-i Islamí* learned to cooperate with its political rivals without, however, compromising its basic goals. Its flexibility has assured its survival in the tumultuous and fickle atmosphere of Pakistani politics.

In the end, both the Muslim Brotherhood and the *Jama'át-i Islamí* have failed to seize political power and use it to construct an Islamic state. We will now consider an Islamist movement that has succeeded in attaining this goal.

Ayatollah Khomeini (d. 1989) and the Iranian Revolution

The Iranian Revolution of 1978–1979 is definitely one of the major turning points of the twentieth century that some scholars have compared to its Russian counterpart of 1917,[102] despite the obvious differences between the two.[103] It has received much media and academic coverage in the West following the seizure in November of 1979 of the U.S. Embassy in Teheran and the taking of its personnel hostage by the Islamic Revolutionary Guard.[104] Both the Islamic revolution and the hostage-taking crisis were intimately associated with the figure of Ayatollah Khomeini, who is often viewed as their principal instigator and mastermind. The Iranian Islamic revolution is a complex and multifaceted social, political, and ideological event that cannot be done justice in this chapter. We will focus on Khomeini's justification of revolutionary action in the name of Islam and some of the reasons for his success in capturing political power in Iran, in contrast to the failure of the other Islamic/Islamist movements to achieve this goal, as just discussed.

Khomeini is often portrayed as a charismatic religious leader who astutely used religious rhetoric to unify the Shi'ite masses of Iran around the idea of Islamic revolution and then to overthrow the pro-Western regime of the Shah Muhammad Reza Pahlavi (d. 1980). Some observers have seen the cause of Khomeini's success in his ability to combine his high position in the conservative religious hierarchy of Shi'ite Iran with his role as a popular spokesman for the disenfranchised elements of the Iranian nation who gave voice to their grievances and aspirations.[105] Others have emphasized the historical specificity of Shi'ite Iran that facilitated Khomeini's rise to power, especially the relative economic and ideological independence of the country's religious establishment from the monarchical state, as well as the pervasive influence of Shi'ite clerics on the Iranian masses, who looked to them for guidance and instruction.[106] Finally, some experts have drawn attention to Khomeini's creative reinterpretation of the tenets of Shi'ite Islam that inspired a broad popular following, which was combined with his ability to channel the masses' revolutionary zeal toward concrete political and social ends, while at the same time outsmarting his political and religious rivals.[107] All such analyses have some truth to them as they highlight one or the other aspect of Khomeini's complex personality and its interaction with the no less complex phenomenon of the Iranian Revolution. Let us now examine the personality, teachings, and sociohistorical context of this Muslim leader to ascertain for ourselves the validity of the aforementioned analyses.

Khomeini was born in 1902 in a small village in central Iran. His father was a religious scholar who was killed by bandits when Khomeini was just seven months of age. Brought up by his mother and aunt, Khomeini then followed the usual path of a Shi'ite jurist and theologian, studying religious sciences first in Arak (near Isfahan) and later on in the holy city of Qumm (Qomm), a major seat of Shi'ite religious learning in Iran to this day. In the course of his studies there, Khomeini developed close ties to the major religious luminaries of the age, some of whom became his mentors. Several of them bore the honorary title of *ayatollah* ("sign of God"), which indicated their supreme position in the Twelver Shi'ite clerical hierarchy. After two decades of arduous study, Khomeini joined their ranks (see Figure 22.2).

In the early stages of his scholarly career, Khomeini became fascinated with the Iranian version of Islamic mysticism, whose roots stretched back to the mystical school of Ibn 'Arabi (d. 1240)[108] and his Shi'ite interpreters. Ibn 'Arabi's ideas had a profound impact on Khomeini's personality, as attested to by his own writings and the testimonies of his friends and family. His study of mystical philosophy may have contributed to his perception of himself as a representative of the hidden *imam* of the Shi'ites and a divinely inspired exponent of the hidden, inward aspect of Muhammad's prophetic mission revelation.[109] This fact would explain Khomeini's unshakable faith in his

Figure 22.2 Ayatollah Khomeini and Child
Public Domain/Wikimedia Commons

infallibility first as a religious scholar and later also as the political leader and spiritual guide of the entire Iranian nation. Young Khomeini's fascination with Islamic mystical philosophy did not go unnoticed by his peers and seniors, who looked down upon it as an almost heretical pursuit unbecoming to a licensed Shi'ite jurist (*mujtáhid*).[110] Because of their disapproval, Khomeini kept his mystical propensities to himself. However, as time went by, he became preoccupied with much more immediate and urgent concerns that put an end to his exploration of Sufi philosophy. These concerns had to do with what the young jurist and preacher perceived to be the Iranian state's forsaking of its Islamic identity due to the secularizing efforts of its ruling class and the resultant "erosion" of society's Islamic morals and way of life. To such pressing concerns an abstract mystical philosophy was of little relevance, so it took a backseat to Khomeini's involvement in Iranian politics.

Khomeini was now fully devoted to exposing and condemning what he considered to be the ethical, moral, and economic ills of Iranian society and its ruling class. His position as a preacher and authoritative jurisprudent entitled him to publicly pass judgment on the burning issues of the day. His overarching goal was to restore Islam to its rightful place in Iranian society and to cure the Iranian Muslims of their economic, moral, and social woes. Due to his active political stance and extensive public preaching, first in Qumm and later in exile, Khomeini emerged as the chief ideologist and architect of the Islamic Revolution in Iran. To understand why his preaching fell on a fertile soil, we should briefly consider the transformation of Iranian society throughout the 1930s–1960s.

This transformation was rapid and tumultuous. After having been divided into spheres of influence between the two imperial powers Britain and Russia, in 1921 Iran finally managed to gain independence from its unwanted European "managers" as a result of a military coup led by the ambitious army officer named Reza Khan. His goal was to create a strong, modern, and independent state that could withstand any future encroachments on its sovereignty by Western powers. A strong-willed military man, Reza Khan embarked on the task of industrializing and modernizing Iran's conservative, diverse, and tradition-bound society with ruthless determination. To achieve his goals, he did not hesitate to grab authoritarian powers by having himself crowned as *shah* (king) of Iran in 1926.

Relying on Iran's newly equipped army and numerous civil servants and bureaucrats, Reza Shah, as he now titled himself, launched a series of sweeping reforms aimed at integrating Iran into the modern world and making it a major regional power. The ruler envisioned Iran as a secular state with a strong modern army, advanced industry, and developed infrastructure run by a Western-style administrative apparatus. A strong believer in secularism (in that respect, he seems to have consciously followed in the footsteps of Turkey's Kemal Ataturk),[111] Reza Shah did his utmost to isolate religion from politics. In the process, he marginalized Iran's large and influential clerical class, which he considered to be an obstacle to the country's transition to modernity.[112] In an effort to forge a new national identity for his country, Reza Shah consistently downplayed its Islamic legacy, while at the same time emphasizing its pre-Islamic, imperial past. For him, the Islamic period of Iran's history was but an unfortunate interlude between the fall of the once all-powerful Persian monarchy and its restoration under his rule. This, of course, was a direct challenge to the Shi'ite *'ulamá'*, who derived their legitimacy, income, and authority from being stewards and interpreters of the Islamic law and theology in their Shi'ite versions. Reza Shah missed no opportunity to humiliate the country's clerical establishment. For instance, he ordered men of religion to replace their turbans and free-flowing costumes with European-style hats and suits. As a final affront to their Islamic sensitivities, he mandated the unveiling of Iranian women. No less devastating to the Shi'ite religious class was Reza Shah's ban on religious instruction (including the study of the Qur'an) in state schools and his decree that replaced religious courts with secular ones subject to his Ministry of Justice. He also brought the administration of formerly independent religious endowments under state control, thereby drastically curtailing the financial independence of the clerical class. A man of great ruthlessness and brutal strength, he had no compunctions about publicly beating those highest-ranking religious officials who were, in his view, resistant to his drastic secularization of the country.[113]

While the majority of the country's population initially supported Reza Shah's drive to reassert Iran's sovereignty and national pride after decades of colonial dependence, his authoritarian methods eventually alienated many of his subjects from the Western-oriented, secular regime that he endeavored to construct. In the countryside and among the urban classes of the bazaar, attachment to Shi'ite Islam and its learned exponents remained strong. Many Iranians were appalled by the ruler's attempts to force secularization from above and by his mistreatment of the religious scholars, whom they deeply revered. They breathed a sigh of relief when his rule came to an abrupt end. At the outbreak of World War II, Reza Shah made an ill conceived decision to side with Nazi Germany against Iran's former imperial masters Britain and Russia (now the USSR). In retaliation, the military units of these two powers invaded Iran and removed Reza Shah from power in 1941.

It is important to point out that, despite Reza Shah's overt anticlerical policies throughout his rule, the Shi'ite religious establishment based in Shi'ism's holy cities of Qumm and Mashhad remained for the most part passive, even docile. This was to change only well into the reign of Reza Shah's son, Muhammad Reza Shah, who succeeded his father on Iran's throne. The new ruler continued his father's policies, albeit under vastly different geopolitical circumstances. They were marked by the growing involvement of the United States in the Middle East and its politics. In the young, Swiss-educated shah, the United States found a loyal ally who was eager to forge close military, economic, and cultural ties with the new world superpower.

In return, the U.S. government helped the shah to defeat his internal opponents, thereby keeping him in power. Most notably, in 1953, the Central Intelligence Agency (CIA) engineered the coup to overthrow the popular prime minister Mohammad Mosaddegh (Mossadeq), who was intent on nationalizing Iran's oil industry and reducing the shah's role to that of a ceremonial constitutional monarch.[114]

With his grip on power secure and unchallenged, Muhammad Reza Shah resumed his father's drive to modernize Iranian society. This entailed an even deeper secularization of the country's life by means of curtailing the influence of its powerful clergy and substantially increasing cultural and economic cooperation with the West. The shah's reformist ambitions were funded by Iran's oil wealth, now the chief source of revenues for the state treasury. As the shah's reforms took root, the structure of Iranian society underwent profound changes. A deep divide opened up between the relatively small pro-Western elite of professionals, civil servants, and private contractors that had benefited from the country's integration into the world markets and from Iran's oil wealth, on the one hand, and the traditional social classes, on the other hand, that were either unaffected or adversely affected by the drastic changes in the country's economic and cultural orientation. Left behind by the rapid pace of economic and cultural transformation and frustrated in their attempts to maintain their living standards, the rural and urban lower classes turned for help to their traditional spiritual guides, the Shiʻite ʻulamáʼ. In 1962 the shah launched the ambitious White Revolution, aimed at setting Iranian society on the path of modernization once and for all. The revolution's agenda included the spread of literacy in rural areas through a state-supported literacy corps, votes for women, privatization of some key industries, and a sweeping land reform. These measures were undertaken against the background of the further expansion of the army and secret police through American military aid and the tightening of state control over all spheres of the country's life.[115]

Opposition to the shah's reforms and autocratic rule came from different quarters. On the one side of Iran's political spectrum were Marxist parties, which advocated state control and collective ownership of the country's major industries and equal distribution of wealth under the benevolent supervision of a socialist state to be modeled on the Soviet Union that supported the leftists. On the other was Iran's clerical class. Disgusted by the shah's heavy reliance on Western institutions, values, and financial and military aid and threatened economically and socially by his drastic reforms of land usage and education, the Shiʻite ʻulamáʼ stood to lose the most. Yet they did not present a unified front. Whereas some continued to adhere to the religious establishment's traditional principle of nonresistance to the temporal government, others became active critics of the shah and the newly emerging Westernized elite engendered by the country's modernization. The most radical of these critics called for the removal of the shah's "corrupt" and "immoral" regime in order to replace it with a just and benevolent Islamic state. They found an eloquent and persuasive spokesman in Ayatollah Khomeini.

Khomeini's Doctrine of the Government of the Jurist

An accomplished theologian and jurist, Khomeini justified the necessity of removing the shah from power by arguments from Islam's foundational sources and sacred history. On occasion, he also availed himself of rational logic to prove his case.[116] Drawing on the ideas of some leftist Shiʻite thinkers who emphasized the revolutionary character of Shiʻite Islam as opposed to the "passive servility" of Sunnism, he asserted that "Islam is the religion of militant individuals who are committed to truth and justice."[117] Under the oppressive conditions of the shah's rule, the goal of such "committed" individuals was to launch an all-out campaign against the imperialist control of the country and internal corruption. Khomeini juxtaposed his revolutionary vision of Islam with that of "the servants of imperialism," who insisted that Islam is "not a comprehensive religion providing for every aspect of human life." Much more than just "rules of ritual purity after menstruation and parturition,"[118] Islam, according to Khomeini, "instituted laws and practices for all human affairs and laid down injunctions for individuals extending from even before the embryo until after he is placed into the tomb."[119] In short, interpretations of Islam that reduced it to a sum total of regulations pertaining to personal piety and family matters were, according to Khomeini, deliberately disseminated among the Muslim masses to prevent them from gaining freedom from local oppressors and dependence on Western imperialism. Islam, in Khomeini's opinion, was the essential means of empowering Muslims to create an Islamic government "that will assure their happiness and allow them to live lives worthy of human beings."[120]

Khomeini viewed the substitution of the Shari'a by the shah for foreign, human-made laws as the root of all societal and economic ills in Iran: "They [Iran's rulers] have removed all judicial processes and political laws of Islam and replaced them with European importations, thus diminishing the scope of Islam and ousting it from Islamic society."[121]

The Shari'a, according to Khomeini, should be reinstituted immediately and unconditionally as the only law of the land. But this alone would not be enough. Its ordinances were to be strictly enforced. In the Prophet's age, he was the executor of God's law. Had he not assumed this executive function, Islam would not have survived against all odds as either a religion or a polity. Under the Prophet and his only legitimate successor 'Ali, there was no separation between religion and statesmanship, between Islam's moral injunctions and people's everyday life. The fact that they became separate in his own day was, in Khomeini's view, part of the "imperialist" plot to subjugate the Muslim world. To rectify the situation, Khomeini declared it every Muslim's religious duty to strive to establish an Islamic government that would be responsible for implementing the provisions of the divine law encompassing all spheres of Muslims' communal and private life.[122]

This government, according to Khomeini:

> [Is] neither tyrannical nor absolute, but constitutional. It is not constitutional in the current sense of the word, namely based on the approval of laws in accordance with the opinion of the majority. It is constitutional in the sense that the rulers are subject to a certain set of conditions in governing and administering the country, conditions that are set forth in the Noble Qur'an and the Sunna of the Most Noble Messenger.[123]

In such a government, argued Khomeini, "sovereignty belongs to God alone and law is His decree and command."[124] The question then arose as to who was competent to head this Islamic government? For Khomeini, natural intelligence and administrative ability were not sufficient qualifications for the Muslim ruler. He must also possess "knowledge of law and justice" and be personally sinless and pious. In Khomeini's interpretation, this individual must first and foremost be an expert on Islamic law or jurist (*faqíh*; pl. *fuqahá'*). Although inferior with respect to spiritual virtues to the Prophet and the caliph 'Ali (both of whom are, according to the Shi'ite tradition, "the best of humankind"), the best qualified jurist of the modern epoch should still be able to exercise his duties as ruler, namely, levying and collecting taxes, appointing governors, equipping and mobilizing armies, and taking care of the welfare of the Muslims.[125] Therefore, concluded Khomeini:

> [I]t is necessary that the *fuqaha'* proceed, collectively or individually, to establish a government in order to implement the laws of Islam and protect its territory. If this task falls within the capacities of a single person, it is personally incumbent on him to fulfill it; otherwise, it is a duty that devolves upon the *fuqaha'* as a whole.[126]

Khomeini's analysis of the condition of Iranian society and its implications for Iran's clerical class were nothing short of revolutionary. In a remarkable departure from the tradition of noninvolvement in politics and aloofness from temporal authorities on the part of Iran's Shi'ite scholars, Khomeini called upon them to initiate a revolutionary action aimed at overthrowing the incumbent ruler and replacing him with the "government or governance of the jurist" (*vilayát-i faqíh*). Thus, in Khomeini's doctrine, the spiritual authority of the Shi'ite divines was boldly joined with the temporal power of the absolute ruler, resulting in what can be described as the Shi'ite equivalent of a "papal monarchy."[127]

Now, Khomeini's radical redefinition of the role of Shi'ite jurists in Iranian society was determined by a combination of factors, most importantly, the drastic modernization and secularization policies pursued by the Iranian monarchy throughout the 1930s–1970s. As mentioned, these policies threatened the vested interests of traditional classes of Iranian society (especially the Shi'ite clergy and small-time traders and craftsmen associated with the bazaar), which led to their alienation from the modernizing and Westernizing regime. Khomeini's vocal denunciation of the shah's autocratic rule and secularizing reforms, as well as his public pronouncements against the country's subservience to the American *diktat* and against the erosion of Islamic moral standards, struck a chord with many discontented elements of Iranian society. Although their aspirations may have been diverse, they were united in their rejection of the shah's rule. Khomeini's stark juxtaposition of the "arrogant" Westernized elite with the "disinherited" masses was readily understood and appreciated by the Iranian public at large. His use of a dramatic religious imagery and rhetoric to describe the plight of the "disinherited" and "downtrodden" masses appealed to both their religious sentiments and life experiences. Particularly effective with the masses was his strong emphasis on the revolutionary potential of Shi'ite Islam in a country that had for many centuries derived its distinct identity from its Shi'ite faith. The fact that Khomeini fell victim to the shah's persecution and had to live in exile gave him the aura of a persecuted Shi'ite hero not dissimilar to that of the *imam*s under the Umayyads and 'Abbasids. In the end, Khomeini's major achievement consisted in consolidating all social forces discontented by the shah's rule and directing their revolutionary zeal against the regime. When the Iranian "disinherited" and "downtrodden" rose up in rebellion to set up an Islamic state, the "arrogant" secular regime of the shah quickly crumbled into dust.

Once in power, Khomeini set about silencing his critics among the country's apolitical clergy who argued that by arrogating the sacred title of *imam*, he had effectively encroached on the prerogative of the hidden *imam* and *máhdi* to liberate the entire world from injustice at a divinely appointed time. He also cracked down on those of his colleagues who considered his "governance of the jurist" thesis to be a dangerous innovation and who wanted to restrict the influence of the high-ranking clergymen on the country's politics out of fear that power might corrupt them. On the political plane, Khomeini's larger-than-life status as the leader and spiritual guide of the nation allowed him to marginalize or muzzle his former allies from among secular liberal intellectuals and leftist parties. In a strange paradox, as a result of his astute political moves, Khomeini acquired the same unrestricted, autocratic powers that the shah had once enjoyed. Khomeini availed himself of his vast powers as the ruling *faqíh* to form a government obedient to his will and to confiscate the property of the ruling family and the Westernized magnates associated with it. The confiscated property was declared "war booty."

Faced with the exigencies of day-to-day rule in a vast and complex country, Khomeini pushed his concept of "governance of the jurist" even further by giving himself the right to overrule not just the decisions of the Iranian parliament but also the injunctions of the Shari'a itself, such as prayer, fasting, and performing the *hajj*. He presented this unprecedented authority as a temporary measure that was necessary to preserve and protect the well-being of the Islamic state.[128] In this way, Khomeini made himself the sole legitimate interpreter and executor of the will of God, in full compliance with his theory of the (absolute) governance of the jurist outlined in his theological writings. While seeking to drive his community to "a state of perfection," Khomeini remained a pragmatist. As the chief legislator of the Islamic Republic, he constantly emphasized "the importance of taking into account the requirement of time and space."[129] His recognition of the need for adaptability and flexibility[130] found an expression in his allowing things and behavior that the traditional Shi'ite law strictly prohibited, such as contraception, chess playing, and trade in musical instruments,[131] "provided they [were] not used for corrupt purposes."[132] Furthermore, Khomeini permitted the use of the principle of "public interest" (*maslaha*) in legislative acts that was looked down upon by more conservative Shi'ite jurists due to its close association with Sunni jurisprudence. To recognize the important role of Iranian women in the success of the Islamic Revolution and in the new society it created, Iran's supreme leader granted them certain freedoms. Thus, to the dismay of many of his conservative colleagues among the *fuqahá'*, he decreed that women could appear on radio and television. When the indignant *fuqahá'* protested, his response was:

> I feel it necessary to express my despair about your understanding of the divine injunctions and of the [Shi'ite] traditions . . . The way you interpret the traditions, the new civilization should be destroyed and the people should live in shackles or live forever in the desert.[133]

As in many other similar encounters, his towering authority carried the day. Some contemporary Shi'ite scholars refer to Khomeini's example to justify their own liberal positions on such issues as human rights, gender relations, political participation, democracy, and so on.[134]

His occasional liberal gestures notwithstanding, the supreme leader of the Islamic Republic ruled the country with an iron fist and brooked no opposition. To curtail the independence and insubordination of the parliament, he granted extraordinary powers to various clerical supervisory bodies (such as the Council of the Guardians) to the extent that they were allowed to veto any parliamentary decision they considered to be in violation of Shari'a norms.[135] In this way, Khomeini hoped to preserve the Islamic character of the regime from being eroded by party politics. Khomeini built well. Almost three decades after his death, his legacy lives on in the institutions, social conventions, and ideology of the Islamic Republic of Iran.

Conclusions

The success of the Islamic/Islamist revolutionary movement initiated by Ayatollah Khomeini stands in sharp contrast to the failure of numerous other Islamic/Islamist projects worldwide. Unlike the Sudanese military dictatorship behind a Shari'a facade or the conservative monarchies of the Gulf states that rely on Islam for their legitimization, Iran is the only country that has adopted and implemented Islamic/Islamist ideology as a result of a successful popular revolution against a secular, Westernized regime. If we compare Khomeini to Hasan al-Banna, Qutb, and Mawdúdi, we will see that one important factor sets him apart from them. Being intellectuals with modern education, al-Banna, Qutb, and Mawdúdi received no formal theological training and were thus vulnerable to the attacks of traditionally minded scholars who could and did impugn them on account of their lack of knowledge of the Islamic sciences. This lack of knowledge, according to the critics, rendered the three aforementioned reformers prone to "heretical" interpretations of Islam.[136] Not so with Ayatollah Khomeini. Himself a member of the *fuqahá'* class, he was immune to such criticisms, which may explain, at least in part, his success in mobilizing the discontented Iranian masses against the shah's secularist regime. It is true that his revolutionary (re)interpretation of the tenets of Shi'ite Islam was challenged by some of his peers. However, in the end, his populist advocacy for the "disinherited" and "downtrodden" under the shah's "ungodly" regime enabled him to overcome the objections of his learned critics and to establish himself as the sole legitimate interpreter and executor of the divine will. Khomeini's success may have been facilitated by the unique position of Iran's Shi'ite clergy vis-à-vis both temporal authorities and society at large that does not have obvious parallels in the Sunni world.

Questions to Ponder

1   Address ideological, social, and political factors behind the rise and growth of political activism in the name of Islam.
2   Why did Islamic/Islamist slogans and ideology prove so attractive to various social groups and classes of Muslim societies throughout the twentieth century?
3   The proliferation and popularity of Islamic movements and parties are sometimes explained in academic studies by the desire of Muslim laboring masses, bourgeoisie, and intelligentsia to restrict or balance the overwhelming and often arbitrary power of the secular nation state. Is there any truth to this explanation?
4   What other examples of Islamic/Islamic movements can you name (apart from the ones discussed in the chapter)? Address the causes of their success or failures.

Summary

- There are three principal stages of the movement for the reform and rejuvenation of Islam. Its study is hampered by a problem with terminology ("political Islam," "Islamic fundamentalism," "Islamism," "Islamic reformism," "Islamic modernism," etc.) Each term captures one aspect of the phenomenon at hand while obscuring other, no less important aspects.
- Political and social action in the name of Islam is led by Hasan al-Banna (d. 1949) and the Muslim Brotherhood of Egypt.
- The major goals of the Muslim Brotherhood are the Islamization of Egyptian society and the building of an Islamic state based on the Qur'an and the Sunna. The principal stages of their implementation are envisioned by its founder.
- The structure and internal organization of the Brotherhood focus on charitable and educational work among the Muslim masses.
- The Brotherhood's relations with state authorities vary before and after the antimonarchical revolution of 1952.
- The movement is radicalized as a consequence of the ruthless crackdown on its activities and activists by President Nasser (d. 1970) in an effort to secure his monopoly on political power and to prevent Islam from becoming a vehicle and ideology of opposition to his military regime.
- A radical Islamist program is initiated by Sayyid Qutb (d. 1966). According to Qutb, the pre-Islamic "ignorance," "idolatry," and "paganism" (*jahiliyya*) of Arabia on the eve of Islam have become the predominant state of affairs across the Muslim world, including Egypt. For Qutb, God is the only legitimate and just sovereign and legislator over his human servants. Therefore, human-made laws are imperfect, faulty, and invalid and should be abandoned in favor of God's rule (*hakimiyya*). Failing this,

Muslims are doomed to worship the "false idols" of parliamentary democracy, capitalism, nationalism, liberalism, socialism, communism, and the like.

- Qutb has a long-ranging influence on the political practice and ideology of Islamic/Islamist movements up to the present.
- Egyptian society undergoes a gradual Islamization in the 1970s. The state's fear of leftist opposition prompts it to support Islamic/Islamist movements in the hopes of using them to counterbalance the influence of the leftist forces on the masses. A broad popular disappointment with the results of Nasser's Arab nationalist project and flirtation with Socialism compels young Egyptians to seek solutions in activist interpretations of Islam.
- Sadat attempts rapprochement with the Islamists, with unexpected consequences.
- "The jinni is out of a bottle" with the emergence of Shukri Mustafa and his Excommunication and Emigration (*al-takfīr wa 'l-hijra*) and al-Faraj (al-Farag) and his Jihad Organization.
- Al-Faraj's "neglected principle" (i.e., *jihád*) becomes a rallying cry for Islamists of all stripes. The assassination of President Sadat in 1981 leads to the suppression of the Brotherhood.
- While formally banned and recently outlawed by the Egyptian military, the Brotherhood remains a major force in Egypt's political life to this day.
- The Indo-Pakistani thinker Mawdúdi (d. 1979) is the chief defender of the rights of Indian Muslims. His goal is to establish an Islamic state on the Indian Subcontinent and to preserve the Muslim character of Indian society. The creation of the Islamic Group (*Jama'át-i Islamí*) is part of Mawdúdi's strategy to achieve this goal.
- According to Mawdúdi's "holistic" approach to Islamic religion, Islam "makes no distinction between the spiritual and the secular life"; therefore, any attempt to separate politics from the revelation is a concession to the "erroneous" Western idea of the separation of church and state. All political actions should be based on the Qur'an and the Sunna and geared to the advancement of Islam as devotional tradition, a political and social system, and a way of life.
- Mawdúdi proposes to cultivate an Islamist vanguard of devoted followers in order to implement his plans through a series of gradual reforms of Indo-Pakistani society. The fortunes of Mawdúdi's Islamic Community rise under the dictatorship of general Ziau 'l-Haq (d. 1988). Although not as popular as it once was, the Community continues to work to keep Islam at the center of Pakistan's political, social, and cultural life.
- Al-Banna's Muslim Brotherhood and Mawdúdi's Islamic Community have their similarities and differences. The former is a popular grassroots movement actively involved in the provision of services for the poor and needy; the latter is a relatively elitist movement of the educated middle classes intent on Islamizing society "from above."
- Ayatollah Khomeini (d. 1989) is a scholar and religious leader.
- Iranian society is rapidly Westernized and modernized under Shah Reza (r. 1921–1941) and his son Muhammad Reza (r. 1941–1979). The rulers' policy consists of the deliberate marginalization and disenfranchisement of the traditional Shi'ite *'ulamá'* in favor of Westernized, secular-minded intellectuals. Despite the efforts of the secular state, the *'ulamá'* continue to enjoy support and prestige among the traditional social classes of Iran. The shah's White Revolution becomes a major source of popular discontent among the classes left behind in the course of change.

- In an ideological justification of the necessity of clerical rule, Khomeini advances the doctrine of "the government/governance of the jurist" (*vilayát-i faqíh*). He uses the widespread public disgruntlement of the time to justify the necessity of overthrowing the "impious" Iranian monarchy and instituting a religious republic led by the country's Shi'ite scholars.
- Clerical rule is consolidated under the new revolutionary Islamic regime. Khomeini's relative adaptability and flexibility in matters of public concern do not prevent him from granting the Shi'ite clergy almost unrestricted control over all aspects of the country's life.

Notes

1 See, e.g., Richard Martin and Abbas Barzegar (eds.), *Islamism: Contested Perspectives on Political Islam*, Stanford University Press, Stanford, CA, 2010.
2 Especially in Somalia, Yemen, the Maghrib, West Africa, and Afghanistan.
3 See, e.g., http://www.nytimes.com/2008/04/10/world/asia/10tibet.html?pagewanted=print&_r=0; and http://www.reuters.com/article/us-olympics-torch-china-idUSPEK6593920080407.
4 Gudrun Krämer, *Hasan al-Banna*, Oneworld, Oxford, 2010, Chapter 1.
5 Ibid., pp. 10–16.
6 David Commins, "Hasan al-Banna (1906–1949)," in Ali Rahnema (ed.), *Pioneers of Islamic Revival*, Zed Books, Atlantic Highlands, New Jersey, 1994, p. 129.
7 It was called al-Hasafíyya, a branch of the popular Shadhilíyya *taríqa*; Krämer, *Hasan al-Banna*, pp. 13–14.
8 Ibid., p. 16.
9 Ibid., the very title of the supreme leader of the Brotherhood, *múrshid*, is Sufi in its origin.
10 Ibid., p. 25.
11 Commins, "Hasan al-Banna (1906–1949)," p. 127 and Krämer, *Hasan al-Banna*, p. 28.
12 Krämer, *Hasan al-Banna*, p. 105.
13 Commins, "Hasan al-Banna (1906–1949)," p. 128; cf. Krämer, *Hasan al-Banna*, pp. 93–96 et passim.
14 Richard Mitchell, *The Society of the Muslim Brothers*, Oxford University Press, Oxford, 1993, p. 223.
15 Ibid., p. 218.
16 Ibid., p. 219 and Krämer, *Hasan al-Banna*, pp. 38–39 and 114.
17 Gilbert Delanoue, "al-Ikhwan al-muslimun," in *Encyclopedia of Islam*, 2nd ed.; online edition: http://referenceworks.brillonline.com.
18 Krämer, *Hasan al-Banna*, pp. 92 and 112–116.
19 David Sagiv, *Fundamentalism and Intellectuals in Egypt, 1973–1993*, Frank Cass, London, 1995, p. 63 and Krämer, *Hasan al-Banna*, pp. 112–113.
20 Krämer, *Hasan al-Banna*, pp. 28 and 103.
21 Mitchell, *The Society of the Muslim Brothers*, pp. 210–211.
22 Commins, "Hasan al-Banna (1906–1949)," p. 135.
23 Ibid., p. 138 and Krämer, *Hasan al-Banna*, p. 92.
24 Krämer, *Hasan al-Banna*, p. 60.
25 The latter translation is more accurate, but the former is more commonly used in Western literature.
26 Olivier Carré, *Mysticism and Politics: A Critical Reading of Fi Zilal al-Qur'an by Sayyid Qutb (1906–1966)*, E.J. Brill, Leiden and Boston, 2003, p. 3.
27 Sami Zubaida, *Islam, the People and the State*, I.B. Tauris, London, 1993, p. 33.
28 For details, see Krämer, *Hasan al-Banna*, Chapter 3.
29 Ibid., p. 113.
30 Mitchell, *The Society of the Muslim Brothers*, p. 207.

31 Krämer, *Hasan al-Banna*, p. 122.

32 Ibid., pp. 79–81.

33 Mitchell, *The Society of the Muslim Brothers*, p. 71 and Krämer, *Hasan al-Banna*, pp. 79–81.

34 Krämer, *Hasan al-Banna*, pp. 121–122.

35 Mitchell, *The Society of the Muslim Brothers*, p. 160.

36 For details, see P. J. Vatikiotis, "Ishtirakiyya: 2. The Arab Lands," in *Encyclopaedia of Islam*, 2nd ed.; online edition: http://referenceworks.brillonline.com.

37 In Qutb's writings, this term carries a panoply of negative connotations: not just "pagan," "barbaric," "anti-Islamic," and "godless," but also "vicious," "wicked," and "lawless"; see Johannes Jansen, *The Dual Nature of Islamic Fundamentalism*, Hurst and Co., London, 1997, p. 51.

38 Sayyid Qutb, *Milestones*, Mother Mosque Foundation, Cedar Rapids, IA, n.d., p. 46.

39 Ibid., p. 80.

40 Ibid., pp. 61–62.

41 Ibid., p. 71.

42 Carré, *Mysticism and Politics*, p. 246.

43 Jansen, *The Dual Nature of Islamic Fundamentalism*, p. 53.

44 Qutb spent two years in the United States (1948–1950) on an educational exchange mission as an official of the Egyptian Ministry of Education.

45 Qutb, *Milestones*, pp. 138–139; "the materialism of the East" refers to Soviet Communism.

46 William Shepard, *Sayyid Qutb and Islamic Activism*, E.J. Brill, Leiden and Boston, 1996, pp. 61–66.

47 Qutb, *Milestones*, p. 139.

48 Ibid., p. 140.

49 Zubaida, *Islam*, p. 52.

50 Gilles Kepel, *Jihad: The Trail of Political Islam*, Belknap Press, Cambridge, MA, 2002, p. 36.

51 Carré, *Mysticism and Politics*, p. 9.

52 Ibid., p. 247.

53 Saad Eddin Ibrahim, "Anatomy of Egypt's Militant Islamic Groups: Methodological Note and Preliminary Findings," *International Journal of Middle East Studies*, vol. 12 (1980), p. 425.

54 Kepel, *Jihad*, p. 63.

55 Ibid., p. 82.

56 Dale Eickelman and James Piscatori, *Muslim Politics*, Princeton University Press, Princeton, NJ, 1996, p. 12.

57 John Esposito, *Islam: The Straight Path*, 5th ed., Oxford University Press, Oxford, 2016, p. 203.

58 Kepel, *Jihad*, p. 63.

59 Esposito, *Islam*, p. 203; a more accurate translation would be "declaring [other Muslims] to be unbelievers and emigrating [from the infidel society]," but it is too long and cumbersome to be of use.

60 Eickelman and Piscatori, *Muslim Politics*, p. 12.

61 Jansen, *The Dual Nature of Islamic Fundamentalism*, p. 93.

62 Ibrahim, "Anatomy of Egypt's Militant Islamic Groups," p. 427.

63 Zubaida, *Islam*, p. 54.

64 Ibid., p. 55.

65 Jansen, *The Dual Nature of Islamic Fundamentalism*, p. 89; cf. Jonathan Smith, *Imagining Religion: From Babylon to Jonestown*, University of Chicago Press, Chicago, 1988, Chapter 7.

66 Jansen, *The Dual Nature of Islamic Fundamentalism,* pp. 76–77.

67 Ibid., p. 85.

68 Ibid., pp. 90–91.

69 Esposito, *Islam*, p. 204.

70 Ibid., pp. 203–205.

71 Ibrahim, "Anatomy of Egypt's Militant Islamic Groups," pp. 436–437 and 441.

72 Ibid., p. 431.

73 The name in parentheses shows the Egyptian vernacular pronunciation.

74 Fawaz Gerges, *The Far Enemy: Why Jihad Went Global*, 2nd ed., Cambridge University Press, Cambridge, 2009, p. 10.

75 This term implies one's denial of any authority other than the Qur'an and the Prophet's Sunna and living one's life in complete accordance with them.

76 Roxanne Euben and Muhammad Qasim Zaman (eds.), *Princeton Readings in Islamist Thought*, Princeton University Press, Princeton, NJ and Oxford, 2010, p. 337.

77 Gerges, *The Far Enemy*, p. 10.

78 Ibrahim, "Anatomy of Egypt's Militant Islamic Groups," p. 434.

79 Kepel, *Jihad*, p. 86.

80 F. C. R. Robinson, "Mawdudi, Sayyid Abu 'l-A'la," in *Encyclopedia of Islam*, 2nd ed.; online edition: http://referenceworks.brillonline.com; cf. Kepel, *Jihad*, pp. 33–34.

81 John Esposito and John Voll, *Makers of Contemporary Islam*, Oxford University Press, Oxford, 2001, p. 127.

82 Robinson, "Mawdudi."

83 Seyyed Vali Reza Nasr, *Mawdudi and the Making of Islamic Revivalism*, Oxford University Press, Oxford, 1996, p. 55.

84 Ibid., p. 57.

85 Ibid., p. 59.

86 Ibid., p. 67.

87 Ibid., p. 70.

88 Ibid., pp. 71–72.

89 Ibid., p. 74.

90 Ibid., pp. 52–53.

91 Ibid., p. 80.

92 Ibid., p. 81.

93 Seyyid Vali Reza Nasr, "Mawdudi and the Jama'at-i Islami," in Ali Rahnema (ed.), *Pioneers of Islamic Revival*, Zed Books, London and New Jersey, 1994, p. 108.

94 Nasr, *Mawdudi*, pp. 93–96.

95 Kepel, *Jihad*, pp. 34–35.

96 Nasr, "Mawdudi and the Jama'at-Islami," p. 113.

97 Ibid., p. 118.

98 Nasr, *Mawdudi*, p. 46.

99 Nasr, "Mawdudi and the Jama'at-i Islami," pp. 118–119.

100 Steven Emerson, *Jihad Incorporated*, Prometheus Books, Amherst, NY, 2006, pp. 287–290.

101 Nasr, "Mawdudi and the Jama'at-i Islami," p. 120.

102 See, e.g., Ghoncheh Tazmini, *Revolution and Reform in Russia and Iran: Modernisation and Politics in Revolutionary States*, I. B. Tauris, London and New York, 2012.

103 The latter was launched under atheistic (Marxist-Leninist) slogans, whereas the former was waged in the name of the creation of a theocratic Islamic state.

104 This crisis lasted for 444 days until January of 1981.

105 See, for instance, Kepel, *Jihad*, p. 37.

106 Said Amir Arjomand, *The Shadow of God and the Hidden Imam*, University of Chicago Press, Chicago, 1984, pp. 264–270.

107 Vanessa Martin, *Creating an Islamic State: Khomeini and the Making of a New Iran*, I.B. Tauris, London, 2000, pp. 197–204 and Said Amir Arjomand, *The Turban for the Crown: The Islamic Revolution in Iran*, Oxford University Press, Oxford, 1988, pp. 100–102.

108 On him see Chapter 13, pp. 233–234.

109 Baqer Moin, "Khomeini's Search for Perfection: Theory and Reality," in Ali Rahnema (ed.), *Pioneers of Islamic Revival*, Zed Books, London and New Jersey, 1994, pp. 72–73; Alexander Knysh, "*Irfan* Revisited: Khomeini and the Legacy of Islamic Mystical Philosophy," *Middle East Journal*, vol. 46 (Autumn 1992), pp. 631–653.

110 Moin, "Khomeini's Search for Perfection," p. 77.

111 Arjomand, *The Turban for the Crown*, p. 82.

112 Martin, *Creating an Islamic State*, p. 9.

113 Arjomand, *The Turban*, pp. 81–83.

114 Martin, *Creating an Islamic State*, p. 18.
115 Ibid., pp. 20–21.
116 Zubaida, *Islam*, p. 16.
117 Hamid Algar (trans.), *Islam and Revolution: Writings and Declarations of Imam Khomeini*, Mizan Press, Berkeley, CA, 1981, p. 28.
118 Ibid.
119 Ibid., p. 30.
120 Ibid., p. 28.
121 Ibid., p. 35.
122 Ibid., pp. 36–39 and 42–43.
123 Ibid., p. 55.
124 Ibid., p. 56.
125 Ibid., p. 62.
126 Ibid., p. 64.
127 Arjomand, *The Turban*, pp. 75–76.
128 Moin, "Khomeini's Search for Perfection," p. 93; cf. Algar (trans.), *Islam*, pp. 75–76.
129 Shireen Hunter (ed.), *Reformist Voices of Islam: Mediating Islam and Modernity*, M.E. Sharpe, Armonk, NY, 2009, p. 58.
130 Martin, *Creating an Islamic State*, p. 199.
131 Moin, "Khomeini's Search for Perfection," p. 94.
132 Hunter (ed.), *Reformist Voices of Islam*, p. 58.
133 Charles Kurzman (ed.), *Liberal Islam: A Sourcebook*, Oxford University Press, Oxford, 1998, p. 25. This quotation contains a subtle allusion to the desert lifestyle of the Arab Bedouins (= Sunnis), which is implicitly juxtaposed with the more culturally sophisticated society of Shi'ite Iran.
134 Hunter (ed.), *Reformist Voices of Islam*, p. 59.
135 Saïd Amir Arjomand, "Khumayni," in *Encyclopedia of Islam*, 2nd ed.; online edition: http://reference works.brillonline.com.
136 Kepel, *Jihad*, p. 37

Chapter 23

Islam Reinterpreted

Major Trends in Islamic Thought Today

In Quest of Liberal Islam

In their preoccupation with Islamic "militancy," "extremism," "fundamentalism," "jihadism," and so on, Western pundits, political scientists, and policy makers have until recently paid scant attention to a truly astounding variety of (re)interpretations of Islam over the past few decades.[1] The preoccupation of Western experts with the "violent and irrational" aspects of modern-day Islamic/Islamist ideology, especially with its forceful rejection of Western political, cultural, and economic values and institutions, is understandable.[2] It is determined by the high visibility of extremist versions of Islamic theory and practice that captivates the imagination of the Western public at large anxious to know "why they hate us."[3] Hence, the consistent academic and media foregrounding, in Western societies,[4] of the extremist, militant aspects of contemporary movements acting on behalf and in the name of Islam.[5] A major downside of this Western fixation on "Islamic militancy" is that the richness and diversity of the Muslim intellectual life in the recent decades have been all but ignored. Hence the widespread Western perception of Islam as being uniformly and irrevocably hostile to Western values, institutions, and lifestyles—a religion allegedly impervious to change, "stuck" in the Middle Ages, and incompatible with, or unwilling to embrace, modernity, change, and progress.[6] The dramatic and tragic events of the past four decades, especially several wars in the Middle East, North Africa, and Afghanistan, the Arab–Israeli conflict, the confrontation between India and Pakistan over Kashmir, and acts of terrorism in the name of Islam the world over, have done little to change this deeply ingrained Western perception of Islam and the Muslims. If anything, these events have reinforced it. At the same time, they have prompted many Western politicians and experts employed by various Western think tanks to initiate a pragmatic quest for a "good Islam," namely one that is friendly to the West, shares its values, appreciates its freedoms and institutions, and thus can be used to offset the influence of "radical" ("militant," "fundamentalist," "jihadist," etc.) teachings on the Muslims both at home and abroad.[7] This quest is, of course, a purely utilitarian, political exercise that we should leave to those better trained to pursue. Our goal here is to dispassionately examine the latest trends in the interpretation of Islamic legacy by Muslim intellectuals residing both in the East and in the West. Our examination will focus on the question whether one is justified to speak about "liberal" ("progressive," "moderate") Islam, and, if yes, how compatible or otherwise it is with Western values and theories of social and cultural development. We have to be very selective in our choice of evidence due to the constraints of space, while at the same time making rather broad generalizations on this relatively slim factual basis. This caveat is important to keep in mind.

Before embarking on our journey through the intellectual landscape of latter-day Islam, it should be pointed out that many of the concepts advanced by today's Muslim intellectuals are already familiar to us from the previous chapter. They are often but elaborations of the reformist and modernizing interpretations of Islam initiated by al-Afgháni, 'Abdo, and their followers in the first half of the twentieth century. Yet these recent elaborations bear an unmistakable imprint of our postmodern epoch in their choice of themes, language, and accents. Furthermore, today's intellectual descendants of the founding fathers of Islamic modernism and reformism are much more conversant with Western philosophical ideas, languages, and ethical and cultural assumptions than their intellectual forerunners of the late nineteenth to early twentieth centuries. This should not come as a surprise to us, for many present-day interpreters of Islam have received their doctoral degrees from Western universities in the West or Western-style institutions of higher learning in their own countries.

Standard Western definitions of liberalism depict it as tolerance of views differing from one's own. They also stress that liberalism advocates democratic or republican forms of government with a special focus on reform. Finally, liberalism is defined as struggle for and defense of collective and personal freedoms, such as freedom of speech, religious faith, and association. Let us examine to what extent these values are present in the theories of those Muslim thinkers who are commonly considered to be "liberal" or "moderate." Unlike secular liberals in Muslim-majority countries who have fully embraced Western values and institutions and who seek to relegate Islam to the sphere of private devotion, liberal-minded Islamists want Islam to remain at the forefront of social, political, and cultural life in their respective countries. Furthermore, they also see Islam as the final recourse and frame of reference in matters of dispute over the future of their societies. In other words, contrary to the secularists who are inspired almost exclusively by Western philosophical and social theories in advocating their positions, liberal-minded Muslims make extensive and creative use of Islam's foundational texts (the Qur'an and the Sunna) and the events of early Muslim history. Finally, they employ traditional Islamic forms of debate.[8] Their overriding commitment to the Islamic tradition has occasionally caused their secular critics to call into doubt their liberal credentials.[9]

The Principal Themes of Islamic Liberalism

To begin with, let us outline the principal themes that have animated Islamic/Islamist liberal discourses over the past few decades. They include:

- the nature and necessity of the Islamic state;
- the place in Muslim society of Islamic religious and political movements and their relationship with the secular, Westernized state;
- Islam and modernity (can Islam be modernized and how?); Islamic intellectual, political and cultural heritage and its relevance or otherwise to the burning problems of the modern age;
- democratic forms of government and their compatibility with the Shari'a;
- the rights of women and non-Muslim minorities in contemporary Muslim countries;
- Islam's attitude toward pluralism of opinions, freedom of thought, and religious tolerance;
- ways to renew/revive Islamic societies and to achieve social and economic progress;
- the scope and application of the Shari'a in Muslim societies and Muslim diasporas worldwide;
- the role of traditional *'ulamá'*;
- Islam's attitude to different social classes, in particular, issues of social inequality, poverty, equitable distribution of wealth, and so on;
- the viability or otherwise of Islamic economics and Islamic banking.

By necessity, we will be able provide only a very cursory treatment of the ways in which these issues are addressed by various Muslim thinkers. Some of their approaches, as we shall see, are usually seen as liberal either in their own countries or in the West or both. Others are not but only if we keep sticking closely to the Western definition of the word.

To begin with, the majority of Muslims intellectuals today are not afraid to offer critical assessments, often quite poignant, of the problems of their own societies. In fact, they view a healthy dose of self-criticism as an essential part of their intellectual mission to reform or revive Islam. At the same time, they are at least as eager to criticize the faults and weaknesses of Western societies and cultures in order to determine what their own societies can and cannot borrow from the West.[10] Muslim intellectuals address the themes just enumerated from a broad variety of intellectual perspectives. What unites them is their constant invocation of the authority of the Qur'an and the Sunna of the Prophet.[11] While they seem to agree that the Islamic revelation is not an immutable set of norms and practices but requires continual reinterpretation, they differ as to how exactly Islam's sacred texts are to be engaged. What follows is a brief summary of some of the approaches current among liberal and not so liberal Muslim thinkers today.

Liberal-minded Muslim thinkers tend to argue that in and of themselves the scriptures are liberal;[12] however, they have been interpreted illiberally by the prior generations of Muslim scholars due to the prevailing illiberal (or outright despotic) political and social conditions of their societies. The liberals then hasten to add that all of the democratic and liberal values praised by the Westerners today were already present in the Muslim scriptures, albeit under different names.[13] Thus, the central Qur'anic notion of God's absolute sovereignty equals (and predates) the Western notion of "natural law"; the statements in the Qur'an and the Sunna as to what Muslims and non-Muslims should or should not do to others and themselves correspond to (and predate) the Western concept of "human rights"; the ancient Islamic requirement that leaders of the Muslim community should consult (*shúra*) one another and their constituencies regarding matters of governance anticipates the Western idea of "democracy" and "parliament"; and so on.[14] In line with this idea, the Muslim liberals demand that modern Muslims revive these liberal concepts and practices of the Muslim scriptures and Muslim history after they have been neglected or obfuscated by the previous generations. Once restored to their rightful place, Muslim societies will be rejuvenated and empowered in their struggle for independence from the West.

In a similar vein, modern Muslim liberals argue that because the divine law of Islam is silent on certain issues, it is up to Muslims to investigate the underlying intentions of the divinely revealed texts and to "derive rulings from them to fill the space for which there is no authoritative textual evidence."[15] This approach can be described as the "silent Shari'a" theory. As one of its proponents has put it,

> If Islam does not "mention" something, this indicates one of two things: either that it is not stated anywhere in the traditional sources or that Muslims have never practiced it throughout their history. In the first case, . . . it is permitted. The only exception to this rule is the subject of worship . . .[16] In the second case, . . . [it] is only natural that Muslims should respond to changes and developments at all times and in all circumstances [by reinterpreting their scriptures].[17]

The concept of the "silent Shari'a" may have long-ranging ideological and political implications. Thus, according to a liberal-minded Egyptian scholar 'Ali 'Abd al-Ráziq (d. 1966), the revelation contains no explicit and detailed provisions for Islamic government, state, politics, and "the aims of kings and commanders";[18] therefore, he argues: "There is nothing in the Islamic *shari'a* that compels one to bind religion to a state-setting. The *shari'a* does not deal with any specific form of government."[19] 'Abd al-Ráziq's conclusion resonates with the idea of separation of religion and state governance, which, as we have observed in Chapter 22, was a bane to politically minded Muslim thinkers such as al-Banna, Qutb, Mawdúdi, and Khomeini.

Interpretations such as those just cited have drawn the criticism of conservative scholars and some Muslim activists who insist that the sacred texts be understood and implemented literally, because the messages that they contain are eternal and unchangeable. To counter this criticism, liberal Muslims would often quote the Prophet's saying, according to which: "The Qur'an is malleable, capable of many types of interpretation. Interpret it, therefore, according to the best possible type."[20] They would also point out that the plurality of opinions and interpretations of the revelation is a blessing for the Muslim community, according to another widely cited prophetic *hadíth*. Interpretative pluralism has been advocated by no less authority than Yusuf al-Qaradawi,[21] a leading Sunni religious thinker of today, who said:

> My worst fear for the Islamic Movement is that it opposes the free thinkers among its children and closes the door to renewal and *ijtihád*, confining itself to only one type of thinking that does not accept any other viewpoints . . . The end result will be for the movement to lose the creative minds among its ranks and eventually to fall prey to stagnation.[22]

The idea of the revelation as a living and constantly evolving reality in need of continual reinterpretation is thrown into a sharp relief in the following statement of a Muslim academic from Australia,

> I am [not] rejecting the heritage of *tafsir* and *fiqh* . . . I do not [however] accept the idea that somehow Muslims in the past reached the zenith of intellectual achievement in the area of *tafsir* and *fiqh*. In my view, Muslims are engaged in the process of refinement, improvement, change and addition to the existing body of knowledge. This also means that new approaches will be continuously developed as time passes and as the needs of the community change.[23]

The Australian scholar then goes a step further, arguing that one does not have to be a religious scholar versed in Arabic and the tradition of Qur'an interpretation (*tafsír*) to seek an understanding of the Qur'an:

> [All] Muslims have an equal right to understand the Scripture according to their ability and skill. Whether the text is read in Arabic or in translation, aiming at some understanding of God's word is not a sin; on the contrary, it reflects obedience to the Qur'anic command to think and reflect on its meanings.[24]

Statements such as these are quite common in the contemporary Muslim discourse. They aptly capture what can be described as the democratization of the understanding of the Muslim Scripture that has grown prominent over the past few decades both in the Muslim countries and in the Muslim diasporic communities in the West.[25] Whereas in the past, the prerogative of elucidating and applying God's commands to concrete cases of law and conscience belonged exclusively to the class of learned professions, the *'ulamá'*, with the spread of mass education and means of mass communication, this scholarly monopoly has begun to erode.[26] Empowered by modern education and the ubiquitous spread of information technologies, previously disenfranchised, illiterate, or marginal groups in Muslim societies have now gained direct access to Islam's sacred texts to begin to interpret them in accordance with their own life experiences, social conditions, political preferences, and moral-ethical convictions.

In so doing, they no longer feel bound by the age-old interpretative traditions of the *'ulamá'* class. Indeed, nowadays, interpreters of the Qur'an and the Sunna can be found among secularly educated professionals, academics, students, politicians, civil servants, and, increasingly, Muslim women of various social and educational backgrounds. Naturally, their interpretations differ significantly from the exegetical traditions carefully assembled and preserved by the multiple generations of premodern *'ulamá'*. As one Western scholar has persuasively argued:

> The present "revolution" in thinking about Islam is not a complete break with the past. However, the rise in educational levels and the multiple channels of communication have created an unprecedented opportunity for people to talk back to authorities, both religious and political, and to invest conventional forms with new meanings and contexts.[27]

One consequence of this popularization of thinking about Islam's fundamentals, is the fragmentation of the field of religious authority throughout the Muslim world and in Muslim communities in non-Muslim countries.[28] What this means is that traditionally educated and trained *'ulamá'* no longer have the exclusive right to define the "orthodox" Muslim position on certain controversial or obscure issues of the day. Their voices have become just one in a much larger chorus speaking on behalf of Islam. Some of the alternative, nontraditional voices are male, others female. Some advocate liberal agendas aimed at "Islamizing modernity" or "modernizing Islam" by emancipating Muslim women, granting basic human rights to the Muslims of all classes, ensuring more equitable distribution of wealth, and creating vibrant pluralistic and democratic societies with leaders fully accountable to their constituencies.

In their attempt to reformulate Islam, Muslim liberals face a stiff opposition not only from traditionally trained *'ulamá'* but also from those Islamic/Islamist groups that assert their distinctive identity and ideology in opposition to the West and its values. Such groups have grown ever more numerous and influential over the past decades in large part due to the generous ideological and material support they receive from the conservative states of the Gulf, especially Saudi Arabia. They advocate a return to the authenticity and pristine purity of early Islam as represented by its "pious ancestors" (*sálaf sálih*), namely the Prophet and his companions and successors at the head of the *umma*.

Often characterized as "fundamentalist," these groups are determined to build an Islamic state in which the sovereignty of God will be the foundation of social life. Once this goal is achieved, they hope to rid themselves of dependence on the West and its institutions and ideologies. Outside the Gulf region, Muslim activists of a "fundamentalist" slant are often closely surveilled or suppressed by secular governments because they consider the Islamists to be the major threat to their rule. As a result of state repression, these Islamic/Islamist oppositional groups tend to grow more and more radical and uncompromising. Some have recourse to terrorism and violence against their secularized persecutors, whom they treat as apostates and unbelievers on the payroll of the domineering and manipulative Western powers. As mentioned earlier, it is the radical voices of such Islamic/Islamist groups that have received the lion's share of media attention in the West, leaving more liberal and moderate voices of Islam in the shade. In the rest of this chapter, we will shed light on some major Muslim thinkers of recent time, bearing in mind that their ideas may not necessarily appear "liberal" when judged by Western criteria.

The Geopolitical Roots of Liberal Islam

Before discussing individual Muslim thinkers who espouse various types of liberalism, we should revisit the general historical and (geo)political circumstances that gave rise to political and social activism in the names of Islam during the last quarter of the twentieth century. As the previous chapter has shown, the first half of that century witnessed the vigorous rise of nationalist movements across the entire width and breadth of the Muslim world. Under the influence of Western nationalist ideologies that had arrived on the heels of European colonialism, Muslims embarked on the quest for a national identity. As a result, they soon came too perceive themselves first and foremost as Moroccans, Tunisians, Egyptians, Syrians, Jordanians, Iraqis, Malaysians, Indonesians, Tatars, Uzbeks, Pakistanis, and so on. Although their "Muslim-ness" was definitely part and parcel of this newly discovered national identity, it was now overshadowed by the Muslims' allegiance to their territorial nation-states with their distinctive national languages, cultural practices, mythologies, and symbolisms. These new nation-states and their ideological premises were modeled on those of their European colonial masters.[29]

Whereas in the nineteenth century, resistance to European colonial encroachments on the Muslim lands was usually waged under Islamic slogans (such as a defensive *jihád*), in the twentieth it took the form of movements for national liberation led by Western-educated and secularized local elites (both military and civilian). They waged their struggle against European powers that had subjugated them in the name of their respective nations rather than Islam. There were, of course, a number of deviations from this pattern, e.g., in the Indian Subcontinent, where the deep religious divisions between the Hindus and the Muslims (despite their common ethnic roots) led to the breakup of the country and the formation in 1948 of two states in the aftermath of the British evacuation. In ethnically diverse Pakistan, Islam has become an all-important unifying factor and critical element of the new country's national identity. In the rest of the Muslim world, the ethnic-nationalism pattern of state- and identity-building has been dominant.

With the end of the colonial era in the 1940s–1960s, the secularized elements of local societies (often of military background), which had spearheaded the struggle for national independence, found themselves in power following the withdrawal of European colonizers. Thus began the era of the domination of Muslim countries by Westernized secular elites that derived their legitimacy from their leading role in anticolonial resistance and liberation movements of the colonial era. However, as time went on, these nationalist leaders grew increasingly authoritarian, corrupt, and unable to deliver on their earlier promises of justice and prosperity. They no longer enjoyed the broad popular support that had brought them to power after the collapse of the European colonial order. In their effort to hold on to power, the secular regimes began to suppress any signs of opposition to their rule either from the right or from the left. As we have seen in the previous chapter, the principal sources of opposition to Nasser's secular nationalist rule came from the country's communists, on the one hand, and from Islamists, represented by the Muslim Brotherhood, on the other.

By the time of his death in 1970, Nasser's nationalist pan-Arab policies and ideology were largely discredited as a result of Egypt's economic and social woes and, even more importantly, the country's defeat by Israel in 1967. The intellectual void left by the collapse of secular nationalism had to be filled with a new ideology. With leftist movements weakened by Nasser's persecutions and, to boot, ideologically unpopular in a country still deeply committed to its Islamic roots, the Muslim Brotherhood and related Islamic/Islamist movements gained a wide popular support.

How could their newfound popularity be explained in sociological terms? It has sometimes been argued that Islamic/Islamist ideology was adopted by the state-employed petty bourgeoisie, the underemployed and underpaid intelligentsia, and the growing student population. All these social groups hoped to restrict the practically unlimited powers of authoritarian nationalist regimes such as Nasser's in Egypt or Assad's in Syria.[30] Because the nationalists derived their identity from the promise of a Western-style modernization of their respective societies and espoused secular ideas borrowed from the West, it was only natural that their opponents would turn to religious doctrines and values, declaring them to be the only authentic and appropriate ones for their countries. In the case of Egypt, this ideological reorientation led to the re-Islamization of Egyptian society, in the course of which protests against state policies and authoritarian rule were increasingly couched in the rhetoric of either "Islamic modernity" or, alternatively, a return to the glorious epoch of the Prophet and his companions. The same is true of many other

Muslim societies from North Africa in the West to Eurasia, India, and the Indonesian Archipelago in the East. Secularism having been the primary ideological foundation of the nation-state, it was, together other Western "isms," targeted for criticism by the leaders of the increasingly vocal Islamic/Islamist movements of the 1970s–1980s.

The Antisecularist Critique of Ráshid al-Ghannúshi (b. 1941)

Typical in this regard is the criticism of Western-style secularism by the renowned contemporary Tunisian intellectual Ráshid al-Ghannúshi (Rachid Ghannouchi). The leader of a popular Islamic movement in Tunisia in the late 1980s, his party was banned by the country's secular regime from participating in the electoral process. Al-Ghannúshi fell victim to his popularity. The regime sentenced him to death in absentia for plotting terrorist acts against the state. He returned to Tunisia on January 30, 2011, after spending twenty-two years in exile in London as a political refugee.[31] It is hardly surprising that there was no love lost between al-Ghannúshi and his country's secularist and Westernized rulers.

In one of his writings, al-Ghannúshi argues that "secularism came to us on the back of a tank, and it has remained under its protection ever since."[32] Al-Ghannúshi then proceeds to draw a parallel between the secular ideology of the former colonial master (in this case, France) and that of its indigenous successors, the secularized and Westernized ruling elite of his native Tunisia. He finds many similarities. However, at some points the similarities end, for, according to al-Ghannúshi, whereas "modernity, secularism, and democracy in the West have freed the intellect of people by granting them authority," in the Muslim world these concepts have been usurped by "dictators," such as Nasser of Egypt, Assad of Syria, Bourguiba of Tunisia,[33] Atatürk of Turkey, and the Shah of Iran, who used them to stay in power and quell opposition to their authoritarian rule.[34] Al-Ghannúshi calls upon Muslim intelligentsia to embrace the positive and liberating aspects of Western modernity, while bemoaning the fact that, in the Muslim world, modernity has been hijacked by "a tiny class of indigenous Westernized intellectuals" who alone have benefited from its material advantages, leaving the rest of society to linger in ignorance, misery, and squalor. Because the Westernized elite has routinely sent "their children to the schools of the West," local educational institutions suffered a steep decline. In short, according to al-Ghannúshi, in the hands of the Westernized Tunisian rulers, modernity has become a convenient "tool" of manipulation and an "elite privilege."[35] In the process, al-Ghannúshi himself and the vast majority of the country's population came:

> to feel like strangers in our own country. We had been educated as Muslims and Arabs, while we could see that the country had been totally molded in the French cultural identity. For us the doors to any further education were closed since the university was completely Westernized. At that time, those wanting to continue their studies in Arabic had to go to the Middle East.[36]

In al-Ghannúshi's view, the secular, Francophone education imposed on their subjects by the secularized and Westernized regimes of North Africa "effectively robs the people of a sense of their own cultural identity and history, contributes to their dislocation, makes them dependent on foreign culture/identity, and undermines indigenous cultural and belief systems."[37]

Faced with this dire situation, al-Ghannúshi urges Muslim intellectuals to join forces in devising a truly Islamic educational system that is capable of effectively dealing with the challenges of the modern world. The education provided by this system should be rational and unencumbered by irrelevancies of traditional Islamic theology, such as fruitless debates over the status of divine attributes or the created-versus-eternal nature of the universe. These issues, according to al-Ghannúshi, are totally useless to Muslims in their task to successfully meet the challenges of the modern world.[38] All such "ideological fossils" should be, according to al-Ghannúshi, relegated to the "museum Islam" of the stick-in-the-mud *'ulamá'* who take refuge in the past from the pressing exigencies of modern civilization.

Although modernity, in al-Ghannúshi's view, is an essential precondition for social, economic, and cultural progress of humankind, he insists that it should be "indigenous and homegrown," not imported wholesale from the West. Only such modernity is capable of infusing all levels and classes of society with a truly democratic, creative spirit and of improving the lot of all its members, not just the privileged few.[39] Cultivating this indigenous modernity, in al-Ghannúshi's opinion, is the main task of the Islamic/Islamist movement in Tunisia and other Muslim countries. The goal of achieving political power takes backseat to this immediate, pressing objective. According to al-Ghannúshi: "The Islamic movement must not have the government as its first priority . . . A bigger achievement would be if the people would love Islam and its leaders."[40]

This position effectively implies that the Islamic/Islamist movement advocated by al-Ghannúshi renounces violence as a political tool. In his view, the movement should strive to achieve its goals by democratic means, especially since the Qur'an enjoins rulers to "consult" (*shúra*) the most respected and competent representatives of their constituencies and holds the ruling class answerable to their subjects for any injustice they might perpetrate. This being the case, "the Muslims will find nothing in their religion to oppose [Western] democracy." Therefore, the Muslims should "re-establish their own modern *shúra*-based system of government . . . bound by a set of divine guidelines."[41] Al-Ghannúshi considers liberal and democratic forms of government, which are prevalent in the West, to be an indispensable precondition for the success of the Islamic/Islamist movement across the Muslim world. In his opinion, "it is preferable [for Muslims] to live in a secular state where there is freedom than in a country where the *shari'a* is the official law but where freedom does not exist."[42] This last statement apparently contains a veiled criticism of the authoritarian "rule of the mullahs" in Iran; the undemocratic, monarchical regimes of the Gulf "wrapped in *shari'a* mantles"; and, possibly, the Kingdom of Morocco as well. Whether religious or secular, when faced with opposition, illiberal, authoritarian regimes almost instinctively react by resorting to repression. By suspending democratic processes to stay in power, the secular rulers of Algeria and Tunisia, in the words of al-Ghannúshi, have forced "the Islamic movements to lose faith in democracy and resort to violence."[43]

As mentioned, al-Ghannúshi's criticism of the Westernized ruling class of his native Tunisia, as well as the electoral success of the Islamic/Islamist movement he headed, did not endear him to the powers-that-be. Imprisoned and harassed by the Tunisian regime, he emigrated to England in 1989. The Jasmine Revolution in Tunisia in the winter of 2010–2011 swept aside the regime that had persecuted al-Ghannúshi, propelling him to the forefront of events in his country. The democratic elections saw the victory of a coalition of the Islamist Ennahda Movement with the center-left Congress for the Republic and the left-leaning Ettakatol as junior partners. As president of the Ennahda Movement, he was again actively engaged in the politics of his native country and was awarded the 2012 Chatham House Prize for "the successful compromises achieved during Tunisia's democratic transition." However, he was not part the Tunisian National Dialogue Quartet that has recently steered the country toward the peaceful resolution of the country's numerous problems and political rivalries—an achievement that was recognized internationally by the award to the Quartet of the 2015 Nobel Peace prize.[44] In fact, he actively opposed the political settlement brokered by the other political players, albeit unsuccessfully.[45]

Like al-Ghannúshi, who has spent twenty-two years in exile in Europe, the influential Iranian thinker Abdul-Karim Soroush (b. 1945) was also expelled from his native country.

Liberal Trends in Shi'ite Islam: Soroúsh and Bazargán

A pharmacologist and philosopher educated in Iran and England in the 1970s, Soroúsh distinguished himself as a vocal critic of Iranian leftist and Marxist thought (see Figure 23.1). Upon his return from England to Iran shortly after the Islamic revolution of 1979, he was appointed to high positions in the administration of the new Islamic regime, including the Advisory Council of the Cultural Revolution in Tehran. For some time, he was even regarded as the Islamic Republic's "premier ideologue,"[46] overseeing, among other things, "the purification of universities and the rewriting of school books."[47] In the late 1980s through the early 1990s, Soroúsh devoted himself to a drastic reexamination of such sensitive topics as the role of religion and clergy in Iranian society and state politics, the relationship between religion per se and its understanding by its followers, as well as the relations between Iran and the West. His conclusions often departed radically from the state ideology of the Islamic Republic of Iran. Soroúsh's innovative approach to Islam won him an avid audience among some liberally minded Iranians (especially students), while at the same time triggering a vocal and occasionally violent condemnation of his views on the part of some conservative elements of Iranian society. In the mid-1990s, while touring Iranian universities with lectures, he and his listeners were attacked by a conservative student group. In the aftermath of that episode, he received death threats and had to withdraw from public lecturing.[48] Soroúsh benefited from the liberalization of Iran's public life under President Mohammad Khatamí (1997–2005) and was even allowed to respond to his conservative detractors.[49] However, faced with the growing domination of religious hardliners in Iranian politics and intellectual discourse, he was forced to leave the country. Since 2000, he has held several teaching positions at major American universities, including Harvard, Princeton, Yale, Columbia, Georgetown, and Chicago.

Figure 23.1 Abdul-Karim Soroúsh
Scott Peterson/Hutton Archive/Getty Images

Whereas the majority of modern Muslim thinkers we have discussed so far sought to "restore" or "reform" Islam, Soroúsh takes a different path. For him, the religious truth that was revealed to the prophet Muhammad is immutable and cannot be changed. What can and must be adjusted is "human understanding" of its principles. The goal of this adjustment is to reconcile the human understanding of religion (*ma'rifat-i dini*)[50] with the transformations of human beings' material existence.[51] Moreover, any objection to this adjustment should be dismissed as a senseless tribute to prior, outdated understandings that have lost their validity under new historical circumstances. According to Soroúsh, religion and human understanding of it differ in the following ways:

- Revealed religion itself is true and free from contradictions, but human understanding of religion may not be so.
- Religion is perfect and comprehensive, but the human interpretation of religion is by its very nature imperfect and incomplete.
- Religion is divine, but its interpretation is thoroughly human, age-bound, and this-worldly.[52]

Seen from this perspective, concludes Soroúsh, "just as no understanding of nature is ever complete and is enriched by new scientific works and the arrival of competing views and historical developments, so are understandings of religion."[53] This thesis allows for an infinite variety of understandings of any given religion by its followers living under different historical conditions. In the case of Islam, instead of the one and only "straight path" (Q 1:7) to the religious truth, there are multiple understandings of the latter by different classes and generations of Muslims.[54] Furthermore, according to Soroúsh, like any branch of human knowledge, each understanding of religion inevitably combines correct insights with errors, misunderstandings, and dubious hypotheses.[55] As human understanding of religion progresses, these erroneous presuppositions are discarded, only to be replaced by new ones that, too, inevitably contain both truths and delusions. Hence, there can be no final or conclusive understanding of religion. Rather, Soroúsh sees it as an open-ended, perpetual process, similar to any branch of human knowledge.[56]

Coming from a man of science, this analogy between religion and the scientific quest for truth seems logical, if unconventional. However, seen from the perspective of Iran's religious officials, Soroúsh's ideas were not just some sort of theological heresy. They were an indirect attack on their right to govern the country as the sole legitimate representatives of Twelver Shi'ism, the country's official ideology. For Soroúsh, the assumption of political governance by Iran's clerical class had effectively transformed the open-ended and contestable process of understanding and interpreting religion into a set of rigidly fixed and immutable dogmas. As a consequence of this transformation, religion had become an ideology claiming absolute and uncontestable truth. As such, it could be used by interested parties as a potent instrument of both political and intellectual domination.[57] Clad in a religious garb, this human-made ideology of power had become an impediment to both a free pursuit of knowledge and efficient governance. A society based on the free allegiance of its members to the divinely revealed moral and ethical norms was surreptitiously transformed into an ideology-based regime that restricted the right to interpret and implement these norms to a handful of officially authorized religious bureaucrats. The dynamic process of the understanding of religion by its followers, according to Soroúsh, was thus replaced by an array of rigid dogmatic propositions that is used as a stick to beat down any intellectual or political dissent.

It goes without saying that Soroúsh's distinction between religion and religious knowledge flies in the face of Khomeini's doctrine of the "governance of the jurist" (*vilayát-i faqíh*) that, as we now know, forcibly asserts the ruling jurist's competence to declare what the religious truth is, while simultaneously implying his uncontested spiritual and political authority over his subjects. Whereas Soroúsh does not rule out that a competent *faqíh* can be part of the state administration, he should be subject to criticism and removal by the people in the same way as any secular government official is.[58] This proposition logically flows from Soroúsh's claim that no individual is capable of arriving at a perfect and finite understanding of religion. Therefore, the *faqíh* is as prone to error as any other human being. Moreover, according to Soroúsh, the juridical and theological knowledge possessed by the *fiqh* is hardly sufficient to make him an effective political leader under the condition of modernity. Modern methods of government presuppose a good mastery of such sciences as economics, sociology, statistics, and public administration.[59] Therefore, narrowly trained religious specialists with little knowledge of the modern world are not in a position to interfere with state governance.

On the issue of Islam and democracy, Soroúsh emphasizes that the two do not contradict each other and that the democratization of a society does not automatically presuppose its "de-religion-ization."[60] Soroúsh has promoted the idea of "religious democracy," that is, a society where democratic institutions coexist with and are being reinforced by the deep religious commitment of its members. The religious commitment is essential because by their very nature human beings are weak and susceptible to temptation, even predation. Therefore, Soroúsh admits that the ruler's primary obligation is to protect the sanctity of religion, if it is professed by the country's majority. However, if the government imposes on its citizens a particular official interpretation of religion (which, according to Soroúsh, is as imperfect and fallible as any human knowledge) and then sets out to persecute those who disagree with it, that government loses its mandate to rule. To Soroúsh, a truly pious and religiously committed government should protect religion only because the majority of its subjects believe it to be the essential guarantor of a just and ethical social order and of the spiritual well-being of the believers. Hence, if a government defends human rights, it thereby protects the religion of its citizens and the ethical and moral foundations of their lives. In Soroúsh's view, religion is inextricably intertwined with both democracy and human rights because its final goal is to secure the happiness and well-being of the faithful. Any violation of human freedom and human rights in the name of religion or any other human-made ideology inevitably leads to injustice, oppression, and misery, which is the opposite of religion's essential goal.[61] In the final analysis, the path to religious democracy is predicated on the protection of religious pluralism and human rights; one is impossible without the other.[62]

It should be pointed out that in the recent years, Soroúsh has reinvented himself as a secular thinker, arguing, for instance, that Shi'ite Islam's notions of the infallibility of the *imam*s is essentially authoritarian and not conducive to democracy. He has also averred that "the Qur'an was the product of Muhammad's thoughts and feeling rather than revelation from God" and that the Prophet's revelatory experiences were akin to poetic inspiration.[63] These statements have aroused much controversy. Even his former admirers are now accusing Soroúsh of being a heretic and atheist. Nevertheless, his pioneering role in the articulation of an alternative Islamic discourse in Iran can hardly be contested.[64]

A similar liberal discourse can be found in the writings of Mahdi (Mehdi) Bazargán (d. 1995), a French-trained engineer and self-taught scholar of Islam, who had led a peaceful opposition to the rule of the shah of Iran. After the shah was overthrown by the Islamic revolution and fled the country in 1979, *ayatollah* Khomeini appointed Bazargán as the first prime minister of the revolutionary government. A moderate, conscientious, and pragmatic politician, Bazargán's rule was undermined by the radical elements of the Islamic/Islamist revolutionary movement who accused him of being too "soft" on the Americans and Iranian liberals. After some ten months in office (February–November 1979), his position as the head of the Islamic government became untenable, and he had no choice but to submit his resignation.[65] Afterwards, he became head of the "Freedom Movement" that challenged the legality of clerical rule in Iran. His criticism of Khomeini's doctrine of the "governance of the jurist" aroused the ire of the regime's conservative clerics. Reviled and humiliated, "he lived in a sort of political limbo until his death."[66]

Like Soroúsh, Bazargán experienced firsthand what happens when self-righteous religious dogmatism is extended into the sphere of state politics and everyday governance. Whereas one of the primary functions of religion is to serve as a guarantee against despotism, if misused, it can lead to "stagnation, corruption, and eventually even unbelief."[67] To demonstrate his point, Bazargán examined the history of Western civilization with special reference to the role of official religious authorities. As a result of his examination, Bazargán arrived at the conclusion that Western societies were able to achieve democracy, individual liberties, and scientific progress only after they had thrown off "the rigidity, stagnation, tyranny of the Catholic clergy."[68] Bazargán's findings are summed up in the following damning assessment of clerical rule in any human society.

> Democracy, science, investigation, expertise, and erudition seem to be the necessary results of denouncing religion and the religious scholars, while the acceptance of the sovereignty of God and the stewardship on earth of the church or religious scholars would [inevitably] lead to tyranny, enslavement, inquisition and violence.[69]

Citing his analysis of the detrimental role of the Catholic Christian church in premodern European societies, Bazargán posited the separation of church and state as a precondition for a just and harmonious political and social order. This helps to explain his staunch opposition to Khomeini's doctrine of the "governance of the jurist," which he likened to the despotism of the Catholic Church and its meddling in mundane affairs.

However radical his critique of religious authorities may appear, Bazargán was not opposed to religion as such. For him, religion's original goal was to liberate the people from "false gods, the darkness, and the tyrants." Quoting the Qur'anic injunction not to impose Islam on the unbelievers by force (Q 2:256; cf. 10:99–100 and 33:43–48), Bazargán proposed that any violence in the name of religion was illegitimate from the viewpoint of "God's religion."[70] The Prophet himself was commanded to spread his message by means of persuasion, not force. This was, in Bazargán's view, the original message revealed to the Prophet. The Prophet's Islam had nothing to do with "the religion born of human illusion and ill-intent," namely one that was liable to be used by individuals claiming religious authority to hold on to power and persecute those who dared to disagree with them.[71] Human beings, according to Bazargán, should be given the freedom to choose their faith and face the consequences of their choice in the afterlife. "Freedom," in Bazargán's words, "is God's gift to His steward on earth, humankind. Whoever takes away this freedom is guilty of the greatest treason against humankind."[72] Unlike Sunni Islam, in which, beginning with the Umayyads, the authoritarian state dominated religion by appointing hand-picked religious functionaries to the positions of power, the learned exponents of Shi'ism for many centuries were independent of state authorities and concerned themselves primarily with education, moral guidance, scholarship, and legal rulings on certain difficult points of Shi'ite jurisprudence .

This situation, according to Bazargán, changed dramatically in the 1960s and 1970s, when religious scholars and students became politically active in opposing the shah's regime. Their activism culminated in their seizure of political power after the revolution of 1979. The adoption of Khomeini's doctrine of the "governance of the jurist" as the paramount principle of the constitution of the Islamic Republic of Iran led to the establishment of absolute clerical control over the country's administration, executive powers, and politics.[73] This development, in Bazargán's view, undermined "one of the basic principles of the Shi'a, namely, the more or less democratic way of choosing one's own religious authority" by the individual believer.[74] Now, the clerical establishment of the Islamic Republic of Iran has arrogated the right to foist upon the oppressed population religious executives who wielded unprecedented (and unrestricted) legislative and executive powers.[75] The rigid enforcement of the official dogma by the clerical authorities of postevolutionary Iran, in Bazargán's opinion, goes against the grain of the teachings of the Prophet and the Shi'ite *imam*s, both of whom allowed "difference of opinion in the realm of the tenets of religion, let alone in administrative and governmental issues." Moreover, classical Shi'ite theology and jurisprudence actively encouraged a free independent investigation (*ijtihád*) by qualified believers of various controversial issues faced by the Shi'ite community, whereas the ruling clerics of Iran implicitly or explicitly disallow it.[76]

While the ideas of Bazargán and Soroúsh have apparently found traction among some members of Iranian society (mostly students and liberal intelligentsia), in the end, they failed to make a significant dent in the formidable edifice of official Iranian ideology that derives its legitimacy from the revolutionary ideas of Imam Khomeini. Given its continual strength, it seems likely that the reassessment and readjustment of Khomeini's legacy along more liberal lines will come from within the official clerical establishment of the Islamic Republic. This scenario is even more likely given the presence in Iran of a few liberal-minded *ayatollah*s who are eager to reconsider the more objectionable aspects of clerical rule. Due to space constraints, it is impossible to discuss their ideas here.[77]

Dreaming of an Islamic State: Al-Ghazáli and Yassine

Although carefully couched in religious language and imagery, Bazargán's and Soroúsh's critiques of the harmful impact of clerical rule on Iranian society places them in the camp of Muslim secular liberals. This is evident from the fact that they seek to confine Islam to the sphere of the individual's spiritual life and to treat it primarily as a glorious cultural legacy, as well as a means to pursue one's personal freedom of conscience in the face of the repressive policies of an authoritarian regime. It is hardly accidental that both Iranian thinkers are fond of quoting Persian Sufi poets (alongside the Prophet and *imam* 'Ali), whom they regard as model freethinkers and advocates for the right to spiritual and intellectual freedom for every believer.[78]

The liberal ideas of the Shi'ite thinkers we have just discussed, however, are not shared by the vast majority of contemporary Islamic/Islamist leaders, both Sunni and Shi'ite. They continue to insist on the necessity to maintain the primacy of religious precepts and ideals in all spheres of human life, be it politics, economics, ethics, or culture. For them, any attempt to divorce Islam from the social, political, and cultural life of a given society effectively amounts to the abandonment of the teachings of the Prophet and his companions. What both liberal and not-so-liberal Muslim thinkers today agree on is that the religious doctrines and practices prevalent in their societies are in need of a critical reassessment. This reassessment, they believe, is necessary to lay the groundwork for a comprehensive reform aimed at bringing all spheres of society in line with what they consider to be "primeval" Islamic norms rather than their later reinterpretations.

In the process of reevaluating the state of affairs in their respective societies, Islamic/Islamist intellectuals pay special attention to religious education and the role of *'ulamá'* in guiding their communities along the right path. They are so preoccupied with these two issues because they consider the lack of proper religious education and sound moral guidance in their communities to be the main reason for the decline of Islam's erstwhile strength and glory in modern times.

One of the leading proponents of this reassessment of Muslim faith and practice is the famous Egyptian scholar and preacher Muhammad al-Ghazáli (d. 1996), a namesake of the great medieval Muslim theologian, mystic, and critic of *fálsafa*, whose legacy was discussed earlier in this book. A member of the Egyptian Muslim Brotherhood, al-Ghazáli's numerous books, public sermons and lectures have won him a large following both inside and outside Egypt. His followers come from a variety of social backgrounds from city slums and villages to middle-class neighborhoods across the Muslim world and beyond. Along with his admirer and student, the Qatar-based scholar

Yusuf al-Qaradawi (b. 1926, in Egypt),[79] al-Ghazáli is often considered to be one of the most authoritative and influential Sunni thinkers of the second half of the twentieth century.[80] Therefore, his ideas warrant a closer look.

Al-Ghazáli's works are dedicated to a critical analysis of contemporary Muslim intellectual, social, and cultural life and institutions. In his words:

> Some [Muslims] prefer that I discuss the points of weakness in other societies. To my mind, this is self-deceit, and an attempt at satisfying a lying ignorance. The naïve feeling that we are better than others engenders this. And this is a costly loss of consciousness.[81]

Al-Ghazáli's scathing criticism of the ills of contemporary Islamic societies is not an end in itself. It is aimed at laying the groundwork for a sweeping reform of the status quo in which Islam is assigned the primary role. Coming from the ranks of formally trained *ulamá* (he was a graduate of the renowned al-Ázhar University in Cairo), al-Ghazáli is acutely aware of the shortcomings of his learned colleagues and does not mince words in laying them bare. Although himself a religious functionary in Nasser's Egypt, al-Ghazáli is sharply critical of the learned backers of Sadat's and Mubarak's regimes, calling them the "dogs of Hell-fire."[82] Like Hasan al-Banna, whom he counts among his teachers, al-Ghazáli accuses the official *'ulamá'* of the Egyptian state of selling out to the ruling secular elite and neglecting their duty to guide the country's masses on the path to salvation.[83] In his words, while "the high-ranking thieves who have stolen [the reigns] of power enjoy themselves," they are aided and abetted by a crowd of the learned "incense-burners and traders in the Divine Law."[84] Even those scholars who are not catering to the needs of the secularized and Westernized elite of Egypt have lost touch with reality. Preoccupied with legal, theological, and ritual minutia of scholastic learning, they have forgotten that Islam is an all-comprehensive system that comprises such critical aspects of modern life as trade, economics, politics, and social relations.[85] Like Mawdúdi and Qutb, al-Ghazáli is of the opinion that the Qur'an provides the indispensable guidance to human beings in their relations with their Maker, the state, one another, and the world as a whole. Thus, Islam is the only guarantor of a just and morally sound social and political order. Instead of delving into scholastic trivia, the *'ulamá'* should study closely what the Qur'an says concerning social justice, politics, and economics.[86]

It is largely due to the narrow-minded interpretation of Islam by the *'ulamá'* that it has lost its former vibrancy and dynamism and, as a consequence, its attractiveness to modern men and women. "If I were a European or American," asks al-Ghazáli rhetorically, "would I consider embracing Islam?" "No, I do not think so," he answers, for the Islam as it is taught and practiced in this age, in his view, holds little appeal to the Westerners because it is irrelevant to their social, political, cultural, and spiritual aspirations. Despite the liberal, even permissive message of the primeval Islam of the Qur'an and the Prophet, its dogmatic interpretation by the stick-in-the-mud men of religion has rendered it an impediment to the social, political, and economic progress of Muslim societies. No wonder, argues al-Ghazáli, that today the Westerners are much more interested in learning about Arab oil then they are about the Arabic Qur'an.[87] In a remarkably candid statement about Islam's inferior position in the modern world, al-Ghazáli says:

> Number-wise, the Muslim *umma* is one fifth of the world population. [Yet] it is absent from the fields of [human] knowledge and production . . . [It is ruled by] feudal and pharaonic governments. Its people are in constant search for sustenance, and its art revolves around pure pleasure and ways to attain it. Its religious-minded people are preoccupied with mental garbage. . . . As for the developed world, it worships itself and spares no effort to enslave the backward nations, the Muslims included.[88]

The weakness of the Muslim world compared with the powerful, domineering, and selfish West is, according to al-Ghazáli, determined by both internal and external factors. Internally, its former strength has been sapped by centuries of despotic rule by authoritarian sultans and tribal warlords, who were aided and abetted by sycophantic scholars. As the Muslim world fell under the sway of European colonialism, there emerged a class of the Westernized newly rich, who began to govern Muslim societies on behalf of their colonial masters. This, according to al-Ghazáli, was true during the period of the direct colonial occupation of the Muslim world by Western powers, and this remains true today, with the only difference that Western dominance is now exerted in a more subtle and covert way. Fully dependent on the economic, administrative, and technological aid of the West, the native ruling class has turned its back on the original Islamic values.

The abyss between the secular-minded, Western-educated rulers and their semiliterate and downtrodden subjects has never been wider. The only thing they have in common is their neglect of the principles of pure Islam as taught and practiced by the Prophet and his companions. The Westernized ruling class looks to the West for guidance, assistance, entertainment, and fashions; it has no interest whatsoever in restoring Islam to its original glory. The impoverished and downtrodden masses, betrayed as they are by their religious leaders, are floundering in the darkness, ignorant about the true precepts of their religion.[89] Hence, the steep decline of Muslim societies in the recent two centuries and their resultant inability to resist the imposition of alien political rule, social mores, and culture.

A man of a rather humble social background, al-Ghazáli raises his voice against the social inequities and economic exploitation he observes around him. The chasm between the rich (whom al-Ghazáli dubs the "leisured class") and the poor has grown all but unbridgeable. The two classes reside in completely different worlds and espouse mutually incompatible ideas and values. In his rejection of the excesses of both capitalism and socialism, al-Ghazáli appeals to the authority of the Qur'an, which, in his view, consistently defends the disadvantaged members of the *umma* from the exactions of the rich and powerful. In the final analysis, he leans more toward socialism, at least in its ideal form, as being on the side of the laboring and downtrodden masses.[90]

The crushing burden of authoritarian rule, according to al-Ghazáli, had effectively ruptured the social fabric of Muslim societies on the eve of the modern epoch, rendering them incapable of standing up to outside threats. In his words, not only did "internal colonialism" precede the "external one," but it facilitated the triumph of the latter.[91] In the end, al-Ghazáli argues, the agents of both colonialisms have colluded to keep the Muslim masses in check by denying them access to the pristine founts of their faith. Therefore, he concludes:

> Before they can comprehend Islam and promote its cause, the masses of the Muslim Middle East are in need of gigantic efforts to improve their ethical and material levels. That is to say, the human value [of those Muslim masses] must be restored first . . . Without taking this step, the efforts of the reformers would become like waves of water pouring on desert sand, waiting in vain to bear fruit.[92]

Who are these reformers? Al-Ghazáli identifies them as the most broad-minded, conscientious, and forward-looking *'ulamá'* of the Muslim community, who combine expertise in the Muslim scriptures with a profound and accurate understanding of the conditions of the modern world, its scientific achievements, and the challenges it faces. A religious scholar who has learned by heart the text of the Qur'an but is ignorant of how to apply and interpret its messages in accordance with the changing conditions of modern life is disqualified from properly guiding the Muslim masses.[93] Al-Ghazáli bemoans the fact that the majority of graduates of the al-Ázhar University has fallen into this category, whereas those capable of providing proper guidance to their coreligionists are few and far between. He attributes this deplorable situation to the stifling and corrupt atmosphere of Islamic religious institutions in his native Egypt and beyond.[94] This outdated educational system breeds scholars who are more interested in their personal well-being and comfort than in advancing the cause of Islam. In al-Ghazáli's words:

> The service of God and Mammon cannot be combined . . . It requires a really deranged mind to bring these opposites together in any system of human life. Such must be the minds of those Azharites[95] who grow fat while Islam grows thin, and repose in comfort, while [Muslims] suffer in anguish. These deceivers have devised devilish means for escaping the genuine duties of Islam. They are more sly than those hashish smugglers who escape justice and the police.[96]

According to al-Ghazáli, the corrupt scholars are not the only cause of the plight of religious education in Egypt and other Muslim countries. The secular governments of Muslim states are equally culpable because they routinely allocate the most prestigious and highly paid offices in the state administration to the graduates of secular institutions, while denying them to individuals with religious education.[97] In al-Ghazáli's view, the deplorable bias of the state apparatus toward secular educated employees accounts in large part for the failure of religious educational institutions to recruit the best lights of society who would be intellectually and morally equipped to deal with the challenges of the modern age. Graduates of religious colleges are steeped in tedious and irrelevant juridical and ritual minutia, while lacking even a basic background in "secular sciences." The intellectual vacuum left by the drastic decline of education and intellectual production in leading Muslim universities such as al-Ázhar is filled by aggressive but intellectually shallow demagogues who profess hostility to the West, while also accusing their own governments of being "infidel," "apostate," or "un-Islamic."[98]

Nowhere is the influence of these "retrograde and closed-minded" demagogues more detrimental to the well-being of the Muslim community than in the sphere of gender relations. Al-Ghazáli boldly raises his voice against the denigration of women by the Muslim fundamentalists. He scathingly derides their obsession with such petty, irrelevant issues, as insistence that shaking hands with a woman annuls one's ritual purity or that gazing at a woman's face leads to idolatry.[99] Al-Ghazáli argues that these obsolete, antediluvian attitudes not only are contrary to the egalitarian spirit of the modern age but also contradict the Qur'anic commandments that, in his opinion, forcefully assert the equality of both sexes before God. Nowhere in the Qur'an, according to al-Ghazáli, can one find passages that prohibit women from seeking jobs or education outside their households. By denying them equal rights with Muslim men in the professional sphere and confining them to their households, patriarchal interpretations of the Shari'a effectively bar one-half of the Muslim population from participating in the construction of a truly Islamic social, political, economic, and moral order. The subjugated status of Muslim women is, in al-Ghazáli's mind, a major cause of Muslim weakness in comparison to the societies that grant equal rights to their male and female members.[100]

In all, al-Ghazáli considers any doctrine or school of thought in Islam that preaches passivity, complacency, or resignation to one's fate to be contrary to the creative and activist spirit of primeval Islam. It is against this background that we should view his sharp denunciation of Sufism as the philosophy of "doomsayers and defeatists." According to al-Ghazáli, the "infection" of Sufism's fatalistic and passive attitudes has insidiously invaded the originally healthy body of the Muslim *umma*, sapping its former strength and activism.[101] "The moribund ideas," writes al-Ghazáli, "that Sufism has spread among later generations have corrupted Muslim attitudes toward human life as laid down in the Qur'an; they have corrupted both the practical actions of the Muslims and their understanding of their religion."[102] In its essence, Sufism is nothing but a borrowing from Christian monasticism; it has rendered "the Muslims the hindermost nation [on earth]," "doomed them to enslavement," and "destined them to humiliation, inequity, and ignominy."[103]

As an alternative to the defeatist flight from the world propounded by Sufi *shaykh*s or to the narrow-mindedness and pettifogging casuistry of official *'ulamá'*, al-Ghazáli offers a new systematic theology that makes full use of Islam's original liberalism in mundane and religious matters. It rests on the following principles extracted from the Qur'an and the Sunna:

- avoidance of harm under any circumstances;
- prevention of unnecessary distress and difficulty;
- intolerance of false pretexts and expediencies;
- putting the prevention of harm before the bringing about of benefits;
- allowing necessities to trump prohibitions;
- opting for a lesser evil;
- passing judgment on the basis of commonality (between two cases);
- treating that which leads to or facilitates the illicit as being illicit itself.[104]

These, in al-Ghazáli's mind, are the principles of Shari'a that make Islam the most flexible and humane religion ever revealed to humankind. The fact that these original precepts have now been rendered a dead letter at the hands of their narrow-minded custodians, the *'ulamá'*, does not detract from their inherent validity. Once implemented, the new systematic theology proposed by al-Ghazáli is bound to cleanse the *umma* of the stifling layers of dogma or from ascetic withdrawal from this world, thereby releasing its creative energies and potentialities. In this way, the fatalistic and defeatist attitudes of the previous generations will be thwarted, and young Muslims will acquire an activist, enlightened, and progressive worldview and the diligent work ethic associated with it.[105] Armed with these newly acquired strengths, a vigorous, reformed cohort of Muslims will embark on the construction of a just and prosperous Islamic state.

Whereas al-Ghazáli sees Sufism as a major obstacle on the path of Islamic reform, the influential Moroccan thinker Abdessalam Yassine/'Abd al-Salám Yasín (d. 2012)[106] considers Sufi spirituality to be an indispensable means of reviving the *umma* and creating a worldwide Islamic state (or caliphate) (see Figure 23.2). His plan for achieving a spiritual rejuvenation of the *umma* is based on the Sufi doctrine of the "greater *jihád*"—that is, a person's spiritual struggle against the drives and passions of his or her lower soul and intellectual delusions with the goal of becoming a faithful servant of God and God alone. Availing himself of the widely accepted tripartite division of Islam,[107] Yassine argues:

> *Islam* is an ascent, not a stationary state. The first rung is that of the practicing Muslim [who is] attentive to fulfilling the obligations the Law prescribes to every Muslim. The second rung is that of *iman*,[108] where worship and moral rectitude are on a par. The third degree, *ihsan*,[109] is the springboard for the great spiritual journey and its infinite space. A spiritual guide is needed for the highest degree, since the path is long and the way is full of snares.[110]

In an indirect way, Yassine, a former Sufi master turned politician,[111] positions himself as this indispensable "spiritual guide" of his fellow Muslims in Morocco and beyond. He recognizes that the cultivation of what he calls "Godly Personality"[112] will be a long and arduous educational process. If successful, the reward will be great: the critical mass of spiritually enlightened individuals will be raised ready for the important tasks ahead. Unlike the rest of modern-day Muslims, the individuals endowed with Godly Personality will rid themselves of the slavish adherence to "Western, secular modes of thinking" or of blind trust in the powers

Figure 23.2 Abdessalam Yassine (d. 2012)

ABDELHAK SENNA/AFP/Getty Images

of human reason. Instead they will acquire "an identity based on Islamic literary and historical heritage."[113] This "God's Army," as Yassine dubs this enlightened Muslim vanguard,[114] is destined to launch the revivification of the *umma* and the construction of a just Islamic society. Through a patient reeducation of the masses and proper organization, the "God's Army" will lay the foundation for a much-needed resurgence of the authentic Islamic values.[115] The resurgence itself does not have to be violent. However, should state authorities resort to repression, the goals of the resurgence will be achieved through acts of civil disobedience or general strikes—for obvious reasons Yassine is vague on this point.[116] Yassine is sharply critical of "young Muslims who are left to their own devices, read Mawdudi and Qutb," then start to see *jahilíyya* in "the mother who does not pray, the uncle who drinks alcohol, and the sister who dresses immodestly."[117] Acts of violence occasionally perpetrated by the misguided youth against the secular state are senseless or outright counterproductive because they lead to state suppression of freedom of expression and action. Change should start from within the soul of the individual believer through his or her recommitment to the precepts of the pure Islam of the Prophet and his companions.[118] Through patient inculcation and dissemination, this godly mind-set will gradually encompass the entire *umma*. After the objective of Yassine's resurgence has been achieved and the sovereignty of God and his word established:

> Everyone . . . will have to take part in working toward restoration. Since Islam is not a doctrine of vengeance and settling accounts, all who were seeking meaning in their lives in the form of an outdated good citizenship or archaic patriotism will be offered the opportunity to prove, by their actions, that they are not carry-overs from an order that is dead and gone, and that their turnabout is not motivated by complacency and opportunism.[119]

In the newly (re)created Islamic society, the leaders of the "peaceful uprising" will not seek to impose their will on the citizens because the will of God will be the only law of the land. Officials will be appointed and promoted based on their commitment to the Islamic/Islamist cause and the well-being of the community. Their fear of God and righteousness will not allow them to become corrupt. All government and economic structures will be rebuilt on new, Islamic foundations. Unlike the secular *ancien régime*, they will be characterized by transparency, accountability, and material equity.[120] The Qur'anic notion of *shúra* (Q 42:38), understood as "mutual consultation," will form the principal foundation of public policy. By putting it into practice, the Muslims will "break the yoke of docile vassalage to imported modern norms," such as democracy, which in modern Islamic societies has often served as a cover of fraud and oppression perpetrated by the ruling class.[121] Luxury will be discouraged as un-Islamic; wealth distributed justly and evenly among the members of the *umma*; exploitation reduced to a minimum because, in the words of Yassine, "material exploitation entails religious exploitation."[122] In this respect, there are clear parallels between Yassine's socioeconomic agenda and that of Imam Khomeini. Indeed, Yassine even uses the same Qur'anic terms to designate the oppressors and the oppressed (*mustakbirun* and *mustad'afun*, respectively).[123] Naturally, the "oppressors" will have no place in the just Islamic society envisioned by the Moroccan thinker.

Yassine's advocacy for the creation of a truly Islamic society through the reeducation of the masses, organized public action, and engagement in politics is not confined to Morocco. He sees it as being applicable on the global scale. For him, the construction of a true and just Islamic polity, promised to the Muslims in a prophetic *hadíth*, is essential. If successful, it will be "a means to deliver God's message to humankind by setting a resplendent example of virtue and morality."[124] On the international plane, Yassine dreams of "a union of Muslim countries"[125] "to counterbalance Western hegemony"[126] and to harness the powers and opportunities of modernity to Islamic causes. This is why he repeatedly refers to his project as the "Islamization of modernity."[127] Its goal is to create a modernity on Islamic terms that would be free from the dehumanizing aspects characteristic of the imported, Western-style modernity upheld by the secular ruling elite of Muslim societies.

Yassine's masterplan for Islamic reform is rooted in his unshakable conviction of the superiority of Islamic religion over all other religious and philosophical systems. He is particularly disturbed by what he considers to be the misplaced faith of both Westerners and some Muslims in the power of science, rationalism, and individualistic self-sufficiency. He is particularly critical of Darwinism that, in his words, "has the effrontery of presenting itself as a science" and using "the skeletons of primates in order to shore up [its] doctrines."[128] He juxtaposes the "bestial thesis" of Darwinism with the "tranquility and sweetness of faith" that rests on the Muslim believer's "contentment with God, his obedience to Him and his loyalty to the *sunna* of God's Messenger."[129] Yassine condemns Darwin's theory of evolution for the rampant immorality he observes in Western societies:

> If men and women were nothing but apes passing through this life without direction or meaning—it would be an insufferable injustice to refuse them the right to cull life's desirable fruits to the maximum. Woman would then be man's paradise, her body the object of legitimate masculine coveting.[130]

As a result, argues Yassine, women in Western and Communist societies have become mere sex objects for men, which promotes promiscuity and moral chaos. Islam, on the other hand, has protected the dignity of Muslim women by granting them a panoply of rights, such as:

> To choose their husbands, not to accept a suitor without conditions (including the condition of not marrying a second woman), to ask for divorce, to work and assume social and professional responsibilities, and to dispose freely and independently of their income.[131]

At the same time, Yassine recognizes that, in real life, the Muslim woman may be oppressed by men. This is, he argues, the consequence of her being unaware of her basic rights under Islam. "Stunned by illiteracy and weighted down by unjust macho traditions," she silently suffers oppression and negligence at the hands of her menfolk.[132] The plight of the Muslim woman makes the Islamic "uprising" even more pressing. Informed of her rights and liberated from the shackles of un-Islamic customs by the "decisive hand of the Islamic government," the Muslim woman will become a valuable and productive member of the new Islamic order.[133]

Yassine's eldest daughter Nadia (b. 1958) can be cited as a vivid example of his emancipatory agenda for Muslim women. Being the founder of the women's division of her father's Islamist movement in Morocco, she has become its most eloquent and visible representative. Building on her father's ideas, Nadia has stridently denounced terrorism in the name of Islam and become a vocal advocate for the "internal *jihád*" against the base traits of the human character with the aim of achieving a comprehensive spiritual rejuvenation of the *umma*, not a battlefield victory.[134] On the political plane, Nadia has been a great supporter of the Qur'anic principle of "mutual consultation" (*shúra*; Q 42:38) that, in her view, was successfully implemented by the first Muslim community of Medina. This principle, argues Nadia, was the decisive factor behind its participatory and egalitarian character of the first Muslim state that was "extinguished by the rise of the Umayyad dynasty."[135]

While being strongly opposed to Western-style feminism, Nadia has embraced its Islamic version, which she views as a necessary means to restore "inalienable rights that Muslim societies have underhandedly and systematically confiscated from women more than they have from men."[136] To this end, she encourages Muslim women to make use of the "instruments of classical theology" and engage the Islamic scriptures directly through intellectual self-exertion (*ijtihád*).[137] This effort will result in a gradual restoration of women's rights under Islam, which were suppressed by the patriarchal-minded male elite. In Nadia's opinion, the liberation of Muslim women from oppressive patriarchal practices is inextricably tied to the spiritual rejuvenation of Muslim communities promoted by her father. This idea is brought to the fore in the following passage from her writings:

> When spirituality embraces the heart of a Muslim . . . he will consider his fellow Muslim woman not as a baby-making machine, or a lieutenant of Satan, or a commodity or sex target. He will see her as a fully-fledged citizen and full-time partner in the management of societal concerns.[138]

Conclusions

Our survey of liberal and reformist ideas advanced by some Muslim thinkers is far from exhaustive. Many more voices deserve to be heard but have been omitted due to considerations of space. Nevertheless, we hope that our narrative has captured the principal points of the agendas promoted by reform- and liberal-minded Muslim intellectuals today.

Scholars of Islam have often argued that Muslim reformist and liberal thought has evolved in response to the challenges posed by Western-style modernity and the West's economic and political domination of the globe that was facilitated by it.[139] Consciously or not, the thinkers we have discussed endeavor to create Islamic alternatives to Western modernity in the hopes of enabling their societies to compete with the West on an equal footing. Some do this openly, others implicitly. For instance, Muhammad al-Ghazáli's ideas contain no direct reference to modernity as such. And yet he consistently advocates the necessity of a broad sociopolitical reform of Egyptian society with a view to releasing its dormant creative energies and making its values and institutions compatible with the exigencies of modern life. On the other hand, al-Ghannúshi and the Yassines speak explicitly about the pressing need to forge an Islamic version of modernity that would be free from what they consider to be objectionable aspects of its Western counterpart. For all these thinkers, the positive aspects of modern life and governance are not Western products. Deeply imbedded in the authentic Islam of its founding fathers, they need not be borrowed or invented from scratch, only restored.

The ideas of Bazargán and Soroúsh evolved in response to the events of the Islamic Revolution of 1979 and, in particular, the authoritarian rule of the Shiʻite clerical class that ensued. Their principal goal is to demonstrate the detrimental consequences of mixing statesmanship and religious ideology and to bring out and implement the humanistic and liberating potential of Islamic faith.

Overall, the experiences of the Muslim liberal thinkers we have discussed are quite diverse. While Bazargán and Soroúsh were, at some point, part of the ruling elite, Abdessalam Yassine and his daughter have been in permanent opposition to the Moroccan monarchy that has subjected them to persecution and harassment.[140] Despite his vocal criticism of the inequities of the Egyptian regime and its learned backers, the official *'ulamá'* of al-Ázhar, al-Ghazáli has stayed away from active involvement in state politics. Finally, al-Ghannúshi's critique of Tunisia's secularist regime and his advocacy of the Islamic/Islamist movement opposed to it has forced him into exile. Nevertheless, despite their vastly different life experiences and political programs, these liberal Muslim thinkers are unified in their dissatisfaction with the status quo in their societies and share the common goal of reforming them on an Islamic basis. The other characteristic they have in common is their belief in Islamic democracy and aversion to violence in the name of religion. This sets them apart from the proponents of *jihád*, whose ideas and practices will be the subject of the last chapter of this book.

Questions to Ponder

1 The Islamic/Islamist thinkers discussed in this chapter offer some serious criticisms of Western versions of modernity. Why? Do you think the alternatives they offer are viable or practicable under current geopolitical conditions?

2 Western scholars have pointed out that the reformist programs of reformist and liberal thinkers often gain considerably fewer followers than those of their more radical, fundamentalist counterparts. If this is indeed the case, why?

3 Consider how the thinkers we have discussed deal with the issue of democracy and its compatibility (or incompatibility) with the foundational principles of Islamic religion. Do you find their arguments convincing? Explain.

4 How do some of the thinkers we have discussed approach the status of women in Islamic societies? What measures do they propose to improve the lot of women? Do you find these measures feasible and practicable? Elaborate.

Summary

- Media hype over "militant Islam" and "Islamic terrorism" obscures the complexity of Islamic/Islamist thought today.
- Liberal trends in contemporary Islamic/Islamist thought are elaborations of the ideas articulated by the founding fathers of Islamic reformism and modernism (al-Afgháni, 'Abdo, and, to a lesser extent, Rashíd Ridá).

- To what extent are these trends "liberal" in the Western sense of the word? Is it possible to speak about "liberalism" in Islam, bearing in mind the concept's rootedness in Western political thought?
- The major themes of Islamic liberalism today are the nature and necessity of an Islamic state, Islam and modernity, Islam and Western civilization, what Muslims can and cannot borrow from the West (and, if the former, to what extent), the compatibility of democracy and Shari'a legislation, the scope and application of Shari'a in modern Muslim societies, the rights of women and non-Muslim minorities, ways and means of reforming Muslim societies, the equitable distribution of wealth and Islamic economics, and the role of religious scholars (*'ulamá*) in reforming the *umma*.
- Liberal interpretations of the Muslim Scripture emerge. The Qur'an and the Sunna contain everything that is necessary to build a just, morally upright, and prosperous society. Progressive Western ideas and institutions, including parliamentary/consultative democracy and the quest for scientific knowledge, can be found in the Islamic revelation and early Islamic history.
- How should one read and interpret the Qur'an and the Sunna in today's world? According to the concept of the "silent Qur'an," if the sacred texts of Islam happen to be silent on certain burning issues of modern life, Muslims have the right to fill in the gaps by using their understanding of what is appropriate and beneficial for them under the current historical conditions. Thus, the understanding of the will of God by his human servants is an evolving and dynamic process that will and should continue as long as the *umma* exists.
- As the foundational texts of Islam have opened up to a wide range of interpretations by a new crop of interpreters (women, scientists, secular professionals, students, etc.), the *'ulamá* have lost their erstwhile monopoly on determining the meaning and implications of these texts for the *umma*.
- This popularization of the exegetical and legal field in Islam leads to the fragmentation of religious authority across the Muslim world. In Sunni Islam, in particular, there is no one individual or center of authority whose interpretations of Islam's tenets are recognized as final and binding by the entire *umma*.
- The geopolitical roots of Islamic liberalism can be found in colonialism and national liberation movements. The resurgence of newfound nationalist aspirations across the Muslim world is followed by the modernization and Westernization of newly independent states in Africa, the Middle East, and South and Southeast Asia. This phenomenon, in turn, is followed by the ubiquitous failure of nation-building projects and the broad popular disillusionment with nationalism and other Western ideologies, resulting in the global resurgence of Islamic/Islamist ideologies. The new generations of Muslims see their Islamic faith and identity as a way to challenge the social, economic, and political status quo in their countries.
- Liberal antisecularism in Islamic garb is embodied in Ráshid al-Ghannúshi (Rachid Ghannouchi) of Tunisia (b. 1941). Al-Ghannúshi attempts to articulate a notion of "Islamic modernity" that would keep Islam at the center of the political and social life of Muslim nations, while allowing them to take advantage of Western technological and scientific achievements.
- Liberal trends in Shi'ite Islam are reflected in the work of Soroúsh (b. 1945) and Bazargán (d. 1995). Critical is the distinction between the revealed religion (eternal and immutable) and its human understanding (changeable and adjustable to new existential conditions).

- Shi'ism is a liberal and democratic version of Islam in contradistinction to the authoritarian tendencies of Sunnism that was, from the outset, co-opted and instrumentalized by the despotic dynastic state.
- Soroúsh and Bazargán reject Khomeini's doctrine of the "governance of the jurist" as being contrary to the liberal spirit of Islam in general and Shi'ite Islam in particular.
- Al-Ghazáli (d. 1996) of Egypt and Yassine (d. 2012) of Morocco explore the plight of Islam in their respective societies and ways to revive it.
- In al-Ghazáli's program of a broad sociopolitical reform of Egyptian society, the view is to release its dormant creative energies and make its values and institutions compatible with the exigencies of modern life. He sees Islam as a just religion that defends and secures the rights of the downtrodden.
- Al-Ghazáli critiques the Egyptian scholarly establishment for being remiss in its duty to guide Egyptian society along the straight path. The inactivity and venality of the *'ulamá'* and many centuries of despotic dynastic rule have sapped the creative energies of Islam and rendered it the religion of the losers.
- Al-Ghazáli's recipe for the revival of Islam is the rejection of outdated dogmatism, the reform of religious education, the emancipation of women, creative and flexible interpretation, and application of the Shari'a.
- Yassine proposes a project of "Islamizing modernity" and of the spiritual rejuvenation of the *umma*. He criticizes Western secular ideologies, especially Darwinism and nationalism, as well as the West's lack of a "moral compass." Yassine is equally critical of Islamic/Islamist radicals who are quick to excommunicate and attack their fellow Muslims for the slightest of sins.
- Yassine describes the model Islamic state and ways to implement it. His emphasis is on the spiritual rejuvenation of the *umma* through an "internal *jihád*" that inculcates in its practitioners a "Godly Personality" and prepares them for leading the *umma* to an eventual triumph of Islam over the forces of barren secularism, nihilism, and immorality.
- Yassine's daughter Nadia (b. 1958) is a popular religious leader who advocates, as a way of rejuvenating Muslim societies, the creative reinterpretation of Islam (*ijtihád*) and the empowering of Muslim women over against the oppressive patriarchal customs of the past.

Notes

1 Ibrahim Abu-Rabi', *Contemporary Arab Thought*, Pluto Press, London and Sterling, VA, 2004, p. 16.
2 Shireen Hunter, "Preface," in Shireen Hunter (ed.), *Reformist Voices of Islam: Mediating Islam and Modernity*, M.E. Sharpe, Armonk, NY, 2009, p. xix.
3 Yvonne Haddad, *Islamists and the Challenge of Pluralism*, Center for Contemporary Arab Studies, Georgetown University, Washington, DC, 1995, p. 4.
4 My definition of "Western societies" in this context includes not only the U.S. and Western European ones but also those of Eastern Europe and Russia.
5 See, for example, Laurent Murawiec, *The Mind of Jihad*, Cambridge University Press, Cambridge, 2008, pp. 5–58, 324–325 et passim.
6 For a typical example, see Ayaan Hirsi Ali, *Heretic: Why Islam Needs a Reformation Now*, Harper, New York, 2015; for a comparative analysis of the status of Islam in the modern word with special reference to political uses of Islam by various Muslim groups, see Michael Cook, *Ancient Religions, Modern Politics: The Islamic Case in Comparative Perspective*, Princeton University Press, Princeton, NJ and Oxford, 2014.

7 For some typical examples, see an article in *Time Magazine* (July 22, 2009) tellingly titled "Can Sufism Diffuse Terrorism," http://www.time.com/time/world/article/0,8599,1912091,00.html?artId=1912091? contType=article?chn=world; see also a *New York Times* article (October 14, 2009) on a Sufi-oriented religious college in South Yemen: http://www.nytimes.com/2009/10/15/world/middleeast/15yemen. html?_r=4; for an academic study of the "good Sufi Islam," see Mark Sedgwick, "Sufis as 'Good Muslims, '" in Lloyd Ridgeon (ed.), *Sufis and Salafis in the Contemporary Age*, Bloomsbury Academics, London and New York, 2015, pp. 105–118.

8 Charles Kurzman, "Introduction," in Charles Kurzman (ed.), *Liberal Islam: A Sourcebook*, Oxford University Press, Oxford, 1998, p. 5 and Abu-Rabi', *Contemporary Arab Thought*, pp. 15–16 and 64–65.

9 See, for example, Bassam Tibi, *Political Islam, World Politics and Europe*, Routledge, London and New York, 2008, p. 246, note 34.

10 Hunter (ed.), *Reformist Voices of Islam*, pp. 12–13.

11 Shi'ite scholars, in addition, rely heavily on the traditions traced back to the Shi'ite *imams*.

12 Charles Kurzman (ed.), *Liberal Islam: A Sourcebook*, Oxford University Press, Oxford, 1998, p. 14.

13 Leonard Binder, *Islamic Liberalism: A Critique of Development Ideologies*, University of Chicago Press, Chicago and London, 1988, pp. 243–244.

14 Ridwan al-Sayyid, "Contemporary Muslim Thought and Human Rights," *Islamochristiana*, vol. 2 (1995), p. 30; Gudrun Krämer, "Techniques and Values: Contemporary Muslim Debates on Islam and Democracy," in Gema Martín Muños (ed.), *Islam, Modernism and the West*, I. B. Tauris, London and New York, 1999, pp. 174–175; Abdessalam Yassine, *Winning the World for Islam* (trans. Martin Jenni), Justice and Spirituality Publishing, Iowa City, IA, 2000, pp. 158–161.

15 Gudrun Krämer, "Drawing Boundaries: Yusuf al-Qaradawi on Apostasy," in Gudrun Krämer and Sabine Schmidtke (eds.), *Speaking for Islam: Religious Authorities in Muslim Societies*, E. J. Brill, Leiden and Boston, 2006, p. 205.

16 Namely, the Five Pillars of Islam or "acts of worship" ('*ibadát*).

17 Kurzman, *Liberal Islam*, pp. 14–15.

18 Ibid., p. 36.

19 Ibid., p. 15; see also Binder, *Islamic Liberalism*, p. 243.

20 Mahmoud Ayoub, *The Qur'an and Its Interpreters*, SUNY Press, Albany, NY, 1984, p. 23.

21 Born in Egypt in 1926, he has maintained close ties with the country's Muslim Brotherhood throughout his long career, although he has repeatedly declined offers to become its "supreme guide." Since 1961, he has resided in the Gulf state of Qatar; see Krämer, "Drawing Boundaries," pp. 188–189.

22 Kurzman, *Liberal Islam*, p. 17.

23 Abdullah Saeed, *Interpreting the Qur'an: Towards a Contemporary Approach*, Routledge, London, 2006, p. 5.

24 Ibid., p. 22.

25 Ibid., p. 21.

26 Dale Eickelman, "Inside the Islamic Reformation," in Barry Rubin (ed.), *Revolutionaries and Reformers: Contemporary Islamist Movements in the Middle East*, SUNY Press, Albany, NY, 2003, pp. 203–204.

27 Dale Eickelman, "Foreword," in trans. and ed. by Andreas Christmann, *The Qur'an, Morality and Critical Reason: The Essential Muhammad Shahrur*, E. J. Brill, Leiden, 2009, p. x.

28 Dale Eickelman and James Piscatori, *Muslim Politics*, Princeton University Press, Princeton, NJ, 1996, p. 131.

29 To reiterate, the notion of "European" comprises the Russian Empire, a major colonial power of the age.

30 Binder, *Islamic Liberalism*, pp. 16–17.

31 Abdel Bari Atwan, *The Secret History of al Qaeda*, updated edition, University of California Press, Berkeley and Los Angeles, 2008, p. 243; see also Yahia Zoubir, Review of Azzam Tamimi, *Rachid Ghannouchi: A Democrat Within Islamism*, Oxford University Press, Oxford, 2001 in *Review of Middle East Studies*, vol. 43/1 (Summer 2009), p.104.

32 Abu-Rabi', *Contemporary Arab Thought*, p. 203.

33 The late president of Tunisia who died in 2000 after having ruled the country uncontested for thirty years (1956–1987); see John Esposito and John Voll, *Makers of Contemporary Islam*, Oxford University Press, Oxford, 2001, p. 92.

34 Abu-Rabi', *Contemporary Arab Thought*, p. 210.

35 Ibid., p. 209.
36 Esposito and Voll, *Makers of Contemporary Islam*, p. 98.
37 Ibid., p. 112.
38 Abu-Rabi', *Contemporary Arab Thought*, p. 208 and Esposito and Voll, *Makers of Contemporary Islam*, p. 112.
39 Abu-Rabi', *Contemporary Arab Thought*, pp. 208–209.
40 Ibid., p. 207.
41 Tamimi, *Rachid Ghannouchi*, p. 91.
42 Voll and Esposito, *Makers*, p. 114.
43 Ibid.
44 http://www.theguardian.com/world/2015/oct/09/who-are-the-tunisia-national-dialogue-quartet-nobel-peace-prize-winner.
45 Sarah Chayes, "How a Leftist Labor Union Helped Force Tunisia's Political Settlement," Carnegie Endowment for International Peace, March 27, 2014; online: http://carnegieendowment.org/2014/03/27/how-leftist-labor-union-helped-force-tunisia-s-political-settlement-pub-55143.
46 Voll and Esposito, *Makers*, pp. 151–153.
47 Hunter (ed.), *Reformist Voices of Islam*, p. 77.
48 Kurzman, *Liberal Islam*, p. 244.
49 Esposito and Voll, *Makers*, pp. 151 and 173–174.
50 Also translated as "science of religion" or "knowledge of religion."
51 Voll and Esposito, *Makers*, p. 153.
52 Kurzman, *Liberal Islam*, pp. 245–246.
53 Hunter (ed.), *Reformist Voices of Islam*, p. 78.
54 Ibid., p. 78.
55 Kurzman, *Liberal Islam*, p. 247.
56 Ibid., p. 251.
57 Esposito and Voll, *Makers*, p. 156 and Hunter (ed.), *Reformist Voices of Islam*, p. 80.
58 Esposito and Voll, *Makers*, pp. 159–160 and Hunter (ed.), *Reformist Voices of Islam*, p. 79.
59 Esposito and Voll, *Makers of Contemporary Islam*, p. 159.
60 Hunter (ed.), *Reformist Voices of Islam*, p.79.
61 Esposito and Voll, *Makers of Contemporary Islam*, p. 161.
62 Kurzman, *Liberal Islam*, p. 251.
63 Hunter (ed.), *Reformist Voices of Islam*, p. 80.
64 Ibid., p. 80.
65 Ibid., p. 49.
66 Kurzman, *Liberal Islam*, p. 73.
67 Hunter (ed.), *Reformist Voices of Islam*, pp. 48–49.
68 Kurzman, *Liberal Islam*, p. 74.
69 Ibid., p. 75.
70 Ibid., p. 76.
71 Ibid.
72 Ibid., p. 77.
73 Hunter (ed.), *Reformist Voices of Islam*, p. 49.
74 Bazargán refers here to the right of every Shi'ite Muslim to choose any respected scholar as his or her primary guide in matters of conscience and religious practice; for details, see Chapter 11, p. XXX.
75 Katajun Amirpur, "A Doctrine in the Making? *Vilayat-e faqih* in Post-Revolutionary Iran," in Gudrun Kramer and Sabine Schmidtke (eds.), *Speaking for Islam: Religious Authorities in Muslim Societies*, E. J. Brill, Leiden and Boston, 2006, p. 224.
76 Kurzman, *Liberal Islam*, p. 79.
77 For a survey of their discourses, see Hunter (ed.), *Reformist Voices*, pp. 58–77.
78 See, for instance, Kurzman, *Liberal Islam*, pp. 82 and 251; cf. Esposito and Voll, *Makers*, p. 158.
79 On him, see note 21.
80 Gilles Kepel, *Jihad: The Trail of Political Islam*, Belknap Press, Cambridge, MA, 2002, p. 287.
81 Abu Rabi', *Contemporary Arab Thought*, p. 223.

82 Ibid., pp. 223 and 229.
83 Muhammad al-Ghazáli, *Kayfa nafham al-Islam* (*How Do We Understand Islam?*), Nahdat Misr, Cairo, 2005, p. 21.
84 Ibid., p. 5.
85 Ibid., p. 23.
86 Abu Rabi', *Contemporary Arab Thought*, p. 226.
87 Al-Ghazáli, *Kayfa nafham al-Islam*, pp. 9–10.
88 Abu Rabi', *Contemporary Arab Thought*, p. 230.
89 Al-Ghazáli, *Kayfa nafham al-Islam*, pp. 6–7.
90 Muhammad al-Ghazáli, *Al-Islam al-muftara 'alayh*, online edition: www.al-mostafa.com; p. 3.
91 Abu Rabi', *Contemporary Arab Thought*, p. 232.
92 Ibid., p. 233.
93 Al-Ghazáli, *Kayfa nafham al-Islam*, pp. 21–22.
94 Ibid., p. 20.
95 Namely, the faculty and students of the al-Ázhar University in Cairo.
96 Abu Rabi', *Contemporary Arab Thought*, p. 235.
97 Ibid., p. 237.
98 Ibid., pp. 238–239.
99 Ibid., pp. 239–240.
100 Ibid., p. 240.
101 Al-Ghazáli, *Kayfa nafham al-Islam*, p. 33.
102 Ibid., p. 40.
103 Ibid., p. 41.
104 Al-Ghazáli, *Al-Islam al-muftara 'alayh*, pp. 100–101.
105 Abu Rabi', *Contemporary Arab Thought*, pp. 226–227.
106 Born in Marrakesh (Morocco) in 1928, he worked as a teacher and a school inspector for the Ministry of Education. He joined the Moroccan Sufi brotherhood Boutchichiyya but later parted ways with it over the refusal of its leadership to engage more directly in the country's politics; see Aissa Kadri (ed.), *Parcours d'intellectuels maghrébins*, Karthala, Paris, 1999, pp. 129–164.
107 See the *hadíth* of Gabriel discussed in Chapter 6.
108 Meaning "faith."
109 Literally, "making something beautiful or good"; hence, "perfection."
110 Yassine, *Winning the World for Islam*, pp. 111–112.
111 He was head of the influential Justice and Spirituality movement that has taken an active part in Morocco's political life.
112 David Bienert, "The Concept of *jihad* in the Writings of Abdessalam Yassine," an unpublished MPhil thesis, Oxford, Worcester College, 2007; http://users.ox.ac.uk/~metheses/Bienert%20Thesis.pdf, p. 16.
113 Ibid., p. 47.
114 Ibid., pp. 79, 81, et passim.
115 Ibid., p. 78.
116 He spent a decade and a half under house arrest, accused of sedition against the Moroccan monarchy.
117 Bienert, "The Concept of *jihad* in the Writings of Abdessalam Yassine," p. 38.
118 Yassine, *Winning the World for Islam*, pp. 105–106.
119 Ibid., p. 146.
120 Bienert, "The Concept of *jihad* in the Writings of Abdessalam Yassine," pp. 81–82.
121 Yassine, *Winning the World for Islam*, p. 159.
122 Bienert, "The Concept of *jihad* in the Writings of Abdessalam Yassine," p. 83.
123 Ibid., p. 83.
124 Ibid., p. 104.
125 Yassine, *Winning the World for Islam*, p. 149.
126 Bienert, "The Concept of *jihad* in the Writings of Abdessalam Yassine," p. 102.
127 Yassine, *Winning the World for Islam*, p. ix.
128 Ibid., p. 63.

129 Abdessalam Yassine, *The Muslim Mind on Trial: Divine Revelation Versus Secular Rationalism*, Justice and Spirituality Publishing, Iowa City, IA, 2003, p. 31.

130 Yassine, *Winning the World for Islam*, p. 95.

131 Ibid., p. 94.

132 Ibid., p. 93.

133 Ibid., pp. 94–95.

134 Roxanne Euben and Muhammad Qasim Zaman (eds.), *Princeton Readings in Islamist Thought: Texts and Contexts from al-Banna to Bin Ladin*, Princeton University Press, Princeton, NJ, 2009, p. 307.

135 Euben and Zaman (eds.), *Princeton Readings in Islamist Thought*, pp. 307–308.

136 Ibid., p. 309.

137 Ibid.

138 Ibid., p. 310.

139 Hunter (ed.), *Reformist Voices*, pp. 9–10.

140 Euben and Zaman (eds.), *Princeton Readings in Islamist Thought*, pp. 302–303 and 305.

Chapter 24

The Ideology and Practice
of Globalized Jihadism

As has been pointed out in the previous chapter, over the past few decades, the world media have been focused on Islamic/Islamist "militancy," occasionally to the point of obsession. One consequence of this overriding media focus on the "blood and gore" associated (rightly or wrongly) with so-called radical or jihadist movements in the modern Muslim world is that the less dramatic (and more thoughtful) manifestations of Islamic faith have received short shrift in Western media coverage and academic literature. In Chapter 23 of this book, we have attempted to rectify this misbalance by providing an overview of various reformist, self-reflective, and nonviolent trends in contemporary Islamic/Islamist thought. Whether or not one classifies them as "liberal" remains an open question, as has been shown.

In this chapter, we will address militant activism in the name of Islam as professed and practiced by some Islamic/Islamist groups both in the Muslim world and in the West. We will pay special attention to what is now routinely described as "jihadism"—a global war waged by certain groups of Muslims in defense of Islam against its real or imagined enemies.[1] Hundreds of books, popular essays, op-eds, and academic and journalistic articles on the subject have appeared since the tragic events of September 11, 2001—a highly symbolic event aimed at demonstrating to the world that the proponents of "global *jihád*" represented by al-Qa'ida meant business.[2] Overnight, this organization and its leaders Usáma bin Ládin (1957–2011) and Áyman al-Zawáhiri (b. 1951) gained worldwide notoriety. In addition to hundreds of academic studies and journalistic accounts, they have become the protagonists of dozens of film documentaries aimed at exposing what their producers have often described as the "roots of Muslim rage."[3] Some are unapologetically biased; others do their best to remain neutral and objective. However, regardless of the intensions of the authors, such films and publications inevitably reflect their deeply held and not always evident personal convictions and intellectual and cultural backgrounds of their authors. Only rarely does one find a deliberate attempt on the part of the author or filmmaker to furnish a dispassionate and evenhanded analysis of the phenomenon of "global jihadism." Unfortunately, such rare attempts are routinely drowned out by the aggressively anti-Muslim and biased discourses that have dominated Western discussions of the phenomenon in question since the mid-1990s and even more so after the events of September 11, 2001, and the rise in 2014 of the Islamic State (IS) in Syria and Iraq.

Naturally, our own analysis of what is commonly dubbed in the Western media as "militant," "radical," or "jihadist" Islamism cannot be free from biases and ready-made presuppositions. To minimize their influence, we have avoided blanket and ideologically driven generalizations about this controversial phenomenon. Instead, by quoting extensively from the statements of the leading spokespersons of jihadi movements, we have left it to the readers to form their own opinion of their motives and goals as well as their likely outcomes under the current geopolitical conditions. In addition, we have used what we consider to be relatively evenhanded academic studies of the agendas and practices of militancy under the banner of Islam. What follows is but a brief summary of the evolution and current status of jihadi Islamism that, by necessity, dispenses with many important nuances and details. They can be found in the literature cited in the footnotes.

The Afghan War, 'Abdallah 'Azzám, and the Rise of Transnational Jihadism

As mentioned in the previous chapter, the Islamic resurgence of the 1970s–1980s came on the heels of the broad popular disillusionment with the results of reformist projects launched by the Westernized elites of Muslim countries in the name of modernization and sovereign nation-building. Within a couple of decades, the heady enthusiasm generated by the liberation of Muslim countries from the direct or indirect colonial rule of Western powers gave way to a deep skepticism of the Muslim masses over the effectiveness of the much-touted modernization and nation-building projects. While the newly independent states of the Muslim world (as well as the Third World as a whole) could boast some undeniable achievements (such as the introduction of mass literacy and universal health care, improved social mobility, the creation of local industries, a relative emancipation of women, etc.), the popular expectations of quick economic prosperity and social solidarity in the name of nationalism were dashed by the inherent weaknesses of developing economies and ubiquitous corruption among the members of society's upper echelons. Formally independent, Muslim countries remained heavily reliant on the West in the economic sphere. On the political and social levels, their progress was debilitated by the harsh realities of authoritarian rule exerted by the secularized and often militarized ruling elite. Its representatives proved to be the principal beneficiaries of the reforms they initiated, with the vast majority of population left out to linger in poverty and misery with no say in the matters of domestic and foreign policies of their countries.

The ills of Muslim societies across the globe in the postcolonial epoch was further aggravated by the demographic explosion of the second half of the twentieth century. The rapid growth of population stretched the already meager resources of many Muslim countries to the breaking point. Social upheavals resulted. To keep the popular discontent in check, the ruling classes tightened their stranglehold on power by using the military and security agencies at its disposal to suppress voices of dissent. In many cases, freedom of expression and association was drastically curtailed, even in comparison with the period of European colonial rule.

Blessed with rich oil resources, the Arab countries of the Gulf after World War II found themselves controlled by monarchic or princely dynasties that by their very nature were averse to any change, not to mention transition to democratic forms of governance. To shore up their legitimacy, these regimes have availed themselves of the most conservative forms of Islam. Somewhat paradoxically, not to say ironically, they have remained totally dependent on their new patron, the United States, for their external and internal security and politics. This strange symbiosis was a direct consequence of the United States' own dependence on these countries' oil resources, which has often caused the White House and the Congress to turn a blind eye to the undemocratic policies and institutions of their oil-rich Muslim clients.[4] Some researchers have even argued, rightly or wrongly, that at least these clients were direct creatures of American oil corporations that had no compunctions about allying themselves with the most conservative local regimes as long as they guaranteed the internal stability of their countries and, as a consequence, the uninterrupted flow of oil to the West.[5] As for the Muslim countries with large populations and little or no oil or other valuable natural resources, not only did the modernization projects launched by their secular elites fail to empower them in the face of the domineering West, but they in fact rendered them more dependent on the technical, administrative, and financial assistance and expertise of the Western powers. This phenomenon is commonly known as "neocolonialism."

It is therefore only natural that in their quest for social justice and relief from state oppression, the disenchanted masses of semimodernized Muslim societies turned to their primordial ideologies among which Islam was the most obvious, if not the only choice.[6] We have already discussed the rapid Islamization of the public sphere in Egypt in the aftermath of the Arab–Israeli War of 1967.[7] As we have seen, not only did the autocratic military rulers of Egypt after Nasser allow it to unfold, but they, in fact, actively promoted it in the hopes of undermining leftist groups, which they viewed as the greater evil compared to the as yet poorly organized Islamic/Islamist movements. Although personally secular-minded and thoroughly Westernized, Sadat pragmatically calculated that he would be able to keep the re-Islamization of Egyptian society under control by casting himself as a "Believer President." Wittingly or not, Sadat and his peers in other Muslim countries followed in the footsteps of the premodern and early modern Muslim emperors and sultans who had legitimized their rule by presenting themselves as indispensable protectors and enforcers of the Shari'a.[8]

However, the calculative autocrats were soon up for an unpleasant surprise as they discovered that Islamic/Islamist forces they had promoted refused to play the parts assigned to them by the secular state. Secular government being a bane for leaders of Islamic/Islamist movements, they openly and boldly challenged it as "un-Islamic." Secular parties promoting it, including the rulers themselves, were accused of violating Islamic norms because they had failed to institute a social, political, and economic order consistent Muslim precepts and values. Some critics went as far as to call for the abolition of secular state structures and laws so that they could be replaced by an Islamic polity governed by the Shari'a.[9]

Throughout the 1970s, Islamic/Islamist opposition to the rule of secularized nationalist elites grew stronger and more assertive. The clash between the two political forces became inevitable, especially in the aftermath of the 1978–1979 Iranian revolution, which, despite its pronounced Shi'ite character, galvanized Sunni Islamic/Islamist revolutionaries across the Muslim world.[10] Luckily for the secular regimes, at the very end of 1979, the aging communist leadership of the Soviet Union made the fateful decision to invade Afghanistan in an attempt to install a friendly secular regime there. The reasons for this decision are complex and should not detain us here. What matters is that the occupation of an area of the Abode of Islam (*dar al-islam*) by an atheist non-Muslim power sent shock waves across the breadth and width of the Muslim world. Many influential Muslim scholars hurried to declare Afghanistan the land of a defensive *jihád* against the "infidel" invader[11] and urged Muslim youth to join the Afghans in their resistance against the Soviets and Soviet allies in the region.[12]

The Palestinian professor of Islamic theology and law named 'Abdallah 'Azzám (d. 1989) became the principal harbinger of the Afghan *jihád* against the Soviets.[13] Whereas he was not the first to present "war in the path of God"[14] as an individual duty of every true Muslim,[15] his main contribution to modern Islamist political theory was to redirect the focus of *jihád* from the Muslim secular regimes to Islam's non-Muslim enemies outside the Muslim world. This was a radical move by any standard that has been decisively shaping the vicissitudes of political and militant movements in the name of Islam to this day. Contrary to Sayyd Qutb's idea that the primary objective of Islamic/Islamist movements was to overthrow tyrannical secular regimes at home,[16] 'Azzám called upon Muslims worldwide to take arms against any foreign aggressor occupying Muslim lands. In his widely disseminated 1984 declaration "The Defense of Muslim Territories Constitutes the First Individual Duty," 'Azzám states:

> The Ancients and the Moderns,[17] all the jurists and hadith scholars, at all times during the Islamic era, have agreed that, if a portion of Islamic territory is invaded, jihad becomes an individual duty for all Muslim men and women. Children can go to fight without their parents' permission,[18] and a wife can go without that of her husband.[19]

To explain the reticence of some Muslims to join the *jihád* against the infidel Soviet aggressor, 'Azzám quotes a prophetic *hadíth* that predicts that Muslims' love of life and fear of death will become the main source of weakness of the Muslim community.[20] For 'Azzám, only those capable of overcoming the basic instinct for self-preservation can be considered true Muslims, the rest being nothing but "flagrant cowards" undeserving of the name.[21] Simultaneously, 'Azzám condemns those Muslim scholars who have viewed *jihád* as a collective duty, that is, a war effort organized and prosecuted by a Muslim ruler or an Islamic state. According to 'Azzám—and here he follows the opinion of the Egyptian Islamist al-Faraj mentioned in Chapter 22 of this book—*jihád* is definitely an individual, personal duty incumbent upon every faithful Muslim.[22] Those believers who for one reason or another abstain from fighting the infidel invader and accede to life under infidel rule are, in 'Azzám's view, mortal sinners:

> I believe that every Muslim on earth bears the responsibility of abandoning jihad and the sin of abandoning the gun. Every Muslim who passes away without a gun in his hand faces Allah with the sin of abandoning fighting. Now, jihad is compulsory upon each and every Muslim except those who are exempt,[23] and by definition a compulsory act is an act that brings [divine] reward and punishment.[24]

Thus, for 'Azzám, *jihád* becomes "the sole operative criterion on which a Muslim should judge his faith."[25] Although 'Azzám acknowledges that there are other geographical areas where Muslims are suffering under an infidel yoke and are thus in need of liberation, he declares Afghanistan to be the principal battleground of *jihád*. In explaining why the Afghan *jihád* should take priority over other worthy causes, he cites the Afghan resistance as being consistently and uncompromisingly Islamic in its makeup and aspirations.[26] Even 'Azzám's native Palestine takes a backseat to the Afghan *jihád* against the atheist Soviet invaders. In his view, victory in Afghanistan is even more urgent because it would make that country the "solid base" (*qa'ida súlba*) "from which to launch the reconquest of other Muslim territories," including "Palestine, Bukhara, Lebanon, Chad, Eritrea, Somalia, the Philippines, Tashkent, and Andalusia."[27] According to some scholars, it is 'Azzám's reference to the "solid base" in this passage that may have given name to the movement later to be known as "al-Qa'ida."[28] Be this as it may, in 'Azzám's *fátwas*, the widely held Islamist idea that "the road to Jerusalem passes through [the liberation of] Cairo"[29] is abandoned in favor of an all-out international *jihád* against the "far enemy." Instead of fighting their own regimes, the *mujahideen* ("*jihád* fighters") should now rally for an international *jihád* against the Soviet Union and its Afghan allies.[30]

In 'Azzám's writings and speeches, *jihád* has acquired a truly cosmic role. In the same way as the Prophet's *jihád* against the Meccan pagans led to the strengthening and consolidation of the first Muslim community in Medina, the anti-Soviet *jihád* in Afghanistan should become a means of unifying the world's Muslims around the ultimate goal of establishing a universal Islamic caliphate.[31] This goal has to be achieved by a holy alliance of dedicated *jihád* fighters and religious scholars, both of whom form the bedrock of the Muslim community:

> The life of the Muslim *umma* [community] is solely dependent on the ink of its scholars and the blood of its martyrs. What is more beautiful than the writing of the *umma*'s history with both the ink of a scholar and his blood, such that the map of Islamic history becomes colored with two lines: one of them black—that is what the scholar wrote with the ink of his pen—and the other one red—what the martyr wrote with his blood? And [is there] something more beautiful than when the blood is one and the pen is one, so that the hand of the scholar, which expends and moves the pen, is the same as the hand that expends its blood and moves the *umma*?[32]

'Azzám is acutely aware of the high price to be paid by the *umma*'s vanguard of scholars and fighters to secure the eventual triumph of Islam:

> History does not write its lines except with blood. Glory does not build its lofty edifices except with skulls. Honor and respect cannot be established except on a foundation of cripples and corpses. Empires, distinguished peoples, states, and societies cannot be established except with examples. Indeed, those who think that they can change reality or change societies without blood, sacrifices, and invalids—without pure innocent souls—do not understand the essence of this *din* [Islam], and they do not know the method of the best of Messengers [Muhammad].[33]

Given the critical importance of *jihád* for the fortunes of the *umma*, its neglect by the faithful, according to 'Azzám, equals the forfeiture by them of the Five Pillars of Islam.[34] Like any warfare, *jihád* demands sacrifices. Quoting a prophetic *hadíth*, 'Azzám praises martyrdom for the sake of Islam:

> The martyr is granted . . . special favors by God: He is forgiven his sins with the first drop of his blood, he sees his place in Paradise, he is clothed in the raiment of faith, he is wedded with seventy-two wives from among the beautiful maidens of paradise, he is saved from the punishment of the grave, he is protected from the Great Terror (of the Day of Judgment), on his head is placed a crown of dignity, one jewel of which is better than this world and all it contains, and he is granted intercession for seventy people of his household.[35]

'Azzám's eloquent *fátwas* and dramatic exhortations in speech and writing energized thousands of Muslim volunteers who flocked to the border areas between Pakistan and Afghanistan to defend Islam from the infidel invaders and to seek martyrdom "in the path of God." On arrival, they would receive a crash course of military training, weapons, and ammunition, then cross the border to join Afghan guerilla units. Some returned after a few days "in the field"; others stayed. The former were usually rich Saudis or citizens of the Gulf states who arrived on so-called "*jihád* tours" in search of photo opportunities and in order to experience "firsthand" the heroic atmosphere of a Muslim holy war.[36] In a caustic remark of one Western observer: "Their tour was organized so that they could step inside Afghanistan, get photographed discharging a gun, and promptly return home as a hero of Afghanistan."[37]

The more committed group, usually young pious Muslims of modest means, were driven by a sincere and high-minded aspiration to help their fellow Muslims in their unequal struggle against the Soviet Army. They were ready to sacrifice their lives for the noble cause of reintegrating Afghanistan into the Abode of Islam. Among such religiously motivated enthusiasts were those who had served prison sentences in their own countries for taking part in *jihád* against the "near enemy," that is, their countries' secular rulers. The latter were only too happy to see these "trouble-makers" "vanish into the mountains of Afghanistan."[38] In this way, the belligerent energies of the most radical Islamists were diverted from their home fronts toward the "far enemy" in Afghanistan.

The organization Islamic Jihad, headed by the Egyptian surgeon Áyman al-Zawáhiri (b. 1951), exemplifies this trend in the evolution of Islamic/Islamist movements. After fighting a losing battle against the regimes of Presidents Sadat and Mubarak, he and his comrades-in-arms made their way to Afghanistan, where they joined the local resistance against the Soviets and their Afghan allies to eventually become part of the global, transnational *jihád* against the West embodied by al-Qa'ida.[39] The effectiveness of these foreign fighters, many of whom hailed from various

Arab countries, is a moot issue. Some Western scholars argue that they had little impact on the actual military operations against the Soviet Army that were conducted for the most part by Afghan guerilla units lavishly supplied and equipped by the United States, Saudi Arabia, and Pakistan.[40]

This was not how the foreign *mujahideen* themselves perceived their role. In their eyes, their war effort was crucial for the eventual expulsion of the Soviet Army from Afghanistan.[41] Moreover, they were convinced that "they [had] destroyed a superpower by faith alone, and argued that the same fate would lie ahead for the only remaining superpower."[42] In support of their claims, leaders of the foreign *mujahideen* in Afghanistan produced a rich array of miracle stories about their heroic exploits during the Afghan *jihád*. 'Azzám led the way by composing a special treatise glorifying their superhuman feats of valor and steadfastness. In his and similar narratives, the bodies of fallen *mujahideen* are depicted as not being subject to decomposition: Long after their physical death, they continue to emanate a sweet smell; as the Prophet's army during the Battle of Badr, the *mujahideen* receive angelic or divine reinforcement on the battlefield; dogs do not bark at their passing, and rain covers their tracks as they return from a mission; reading the Qur'an or holding its copy miraculously protects them from enemy bullets and bombs.[43] Widely disseminated via audio- and videotapes, and more recently also through the Internet, such stories have already become the stuff of jihadist mythology, They continue to inspire young Muslims worldwide in their eagerness to defend Islam against its adversaries, although today al-Qa'ida, built in large part on 'Azzám's ideas of universal *jihád*, has a serious rival in the Islamic State of Syria and Iraq.[44]

Whatever military impact the foreign volunteers may have had on the war in Afghanistan, there is no reason to doubt that in the course of their fighting against the Soviet Army they formed strong bonds of friendship and camaraderie. These bonds were to serve the *mujahideen* in good stead in the subsequent decades. A French political scientist has argued that:

> For the international jihadists, the journey to Peshawar[45] was above all an initiation, a socialization of Islamist networks; thereafter, for some of them, it turned into a radicalization process, as they came into contact with militants who were much more extreme than [even] their Saudi sponsors.[46]

Indeed, the *mujahideen*'s entire world outlook was often decisively shaped by their residence in Afghan training camps. According to a Western observer:

> In the artificial setting of the camps, a semblance of equality and fraternity can easily be approximated for the duration of the training. The trainees live in a communal setting, where their normal life responsibilities are suspended and mutual care is encouraged. The camps re-create the ideals of the mythical *umma* and give concrete life to the virtual community hinted at on the Internet. The camps generate an esprit de corps for this ideal *umma*, for which the graduate mujahed might be willing to sacrifice his life.[47]

It was during the Afghan *jihád* that the beginnings of al-Qa'ida ("foundation" or "base") as a global network of militant Islamist cells were formed. Some Western experts on terrorism[48] have derived its name from the computer "database" (*qá'idat al-ma'lumát*) of Muslim volunteers that was created and maintained by Usáma bin Ládin and his mentor 'Abdallah 'Azzám at their "Bureau of Services"[49] in Peshawar on the Afghan–Pakistani border. Whether or not this etymology is accurate, it is a fact that the name and address of every new volunteer were entered into that database, which was thus to become, literally, the "base" or "foundation" (*qa'ida*) of 'Azzám's and Usáma bin Ládin's organization.[50] Initially, practically all of its members were so-called "Afghan Arabs," that is, those Arab volunteers who at one point or the other had taken part in the Afghan *jihád* against the Soviet Army and the Afghan communist regime.[51] Their war effort was generously supported by Saudi Arabia, the United States, and Pakistan. Saudi Arabia, in particular, became "a ferrying port and station for Arab veterans and jihadis," whose government "provided a 75% discount on airline tickets for young Muslims wishing to join jihad" in Afghanistan.[52] The U.S. assistance, for the most part indirect, was funneled by the CIA through the Pakistani intelligence agency, ISID.[53]

Changing the Target and Means: al-Qa'ida, Usáma bin Ládin, and Áyman al-Zawáhiri

'Azzám's idea of the global as opposed to local *jihád* resonated with the aspirations of many young Arab Muslims throughout the 1980s. Among them was the pious Saudi millionaire Usáma bin Ládin (Bin Ládin). Born in 1957 to one of the richest families of Saudi Arabia, he sacrificed the comforts of his privileged position in order to rescue his fellow Muslims in Afghanistan from the horrors of infidel rule. Unassuming, soft-spoken, and pious, Bin Ládin's sacrifice of his privileged status and single-minded commitment to the Afghan cause were duly appreciated by both the Afghan guerillas and the foreign *mujahideen*. Many of the latter eventually pledged allegiance to him and became his loyal foot soldiers.[54] Hailing, for the most part but not exclusively, from the Arab world, by 1988 they had formed the core of al-Qa'ida.

Among Bin Ládin's closest associates was the aforementioned Áyman al-Zawáhiri, leader of Egypt's Islamic Jihad. A surgeon by profession, he played a prominent part in the Islamists' struggle against Egypt's "godless" regime, was arrested on charges of conspiracy and treason after the assassination of President Sadat, and spent three years in prison, where he was reportedly subjected to harsh interrogations and tortures.[55] As was the case with many other Islamists incarcerated by the regime, al-Zawáhiri's prison experiences radicalized his political views. Released in 1984, he became obsessed with revenge for the tortures he had suffered at the hands of President Mubarak's "apostate" government. His other goal was to eventually make Egypt an Islamic state ruled by the Shari'a. Motivated by these two goals, al-Zawáhiri traveled to Afghanistan in the hopes of gaining military experience and recruiting new members for his underground organization.[56] The Egyptian secret service agencies were probably happy to see him leave the country. Be this as it may, at that stage, al-Zawáhiri's objectives appear to have been thoroughly local and consistent with his famous slogan that "the road to Jerusalem passes through [the liberation of] Cairo."[57] In other words, al-Zawáhiri and his fellow leaders of other Egyptian militant groups were still convinced that "confronting the Egyptian regime superseded everything else, including confronting Israel and the United States."[58] Only after Egypt had been "liberated" from its "apostate" rulers could the country's Islamic/Islamist operative units turn their attention to international causes, such as Palestine, Kashmir, Somalia, the Philippines, and so on. In line with this idea, while fighting in Afghanistan, volunteers from Arab countries and South Asia were getting ready to wage war against their "impious" regimes back home. As mentioned, in their struggle against the Soviet Union and the Afghan communists, foreign and Afghan *mujahideen* were actively assisted by the United States, Saudi Arabia, and Pakistan.[59] This is hardly surprising, because, in the words of one researcher: "They had a common enemy and a vested interest in joint coordination and collaboration, at least until the Russians[60] folded their military tents and hurried back home in disgrace."[61]

A number of the leaders of the Afghan *mujahideen* (including 'Azzám and al-Zawáhiri) visited the United States in the 1980s to fund-raise for Islamist causes in general and for the Afghan *jihád* in particular.[62] This "marriage of convenience" between the United States and the Afghan *mujahideen* had lost its actuality following the withdrawal of Soviet troops from Afghanistan in 1989 and came to an end completely after the dissolution of the Soviet Union in 1991.

Figure 24.1 Usáma bin Ládin and His Deputy Ayman al-Zawáhiri at an Undisclosed Location in Afghanistan
Courtesy of Wikimedia Commons

By the time al-Zawáhiri befriended Bin Ládin, the latter had already embraced 'Azzám's idea of global *jihád* (see Figure 24.1). It seems that it also began to appeal to al-Zawáhiri, eventually causing him to reassess his strategic priorities.[63] Whereas it is not quite clear who of the two men influenced whom,[64] al-Zawáhiri's change of heart certainly did not happen overnight; he himself and his Islamic Jihad remained committed to fighting the Egyptian regime after the withdrawal of the Soviet Army from Afghanistan in 1989. It seems likely that al-Zawáhiri's eventual adoption of the idea of global *jihád* against the "far enemy" was prompted, in part, by the disastrous actions of his organization in 1997 in Egypt and the decision of his former comrades from the Islamic Group (*al-Jamá'a [al-Gama'a] al-Islamiyya*), the most influential Islamist movement in Egypt at that time, to abandon their armed struggle against the ruling regime in order to participate in the country's political processes.[65] Frustrated by what he viewed as the betrayal of the Islamist cause by his former confederates, al-Zawáhiri left Egypt for Afghanistan to join al-Qa'ida.[66]

As al-Zawáhiri was trying to rebuild his Islamic Jihad Organization in Egypt (for the most part unsuccessfully), Bin Ládin had already launched his own version of global *jihád* by ordering attacks on American and Western targets in Yemen, Saudi Arabia, and East Africa. After al-Zawáhiri had rejoined Bin Ládin in Afghanistan in 1997, it was only a matter of time that they found a common understanding as to what the primary target of the jihadist movement represented by al-Qa'ida should be. With the Soviet Union no longer in existence, many veterans of the Afghan *jihád* turned their attention to their former supporter, the United States and its Western allies. Their line of thinking had some logic to it: Since the United States had for decades aided and abetted the corrupt and oppressive regimes dominant in many Muslim countries, it was, by association, the enemy of the Islamic/Islamist movements seeking to overthrow these regimes.

The United States' unwavering support of Israel in its repression of the Palestinians was another major grievance cited by the *mujahideen* as a justification of their battle against the sole super-power still standing. The generous financial and ideological support lent by the CIA to the Afghan resistance against the Soviet invasion was now conveniently forgotten.[67]

February 26, 1998, marks a critical turning point in al-Zawáhiri's redefinition of the primary objective of *jihád*. Together with Bin Ládin and a few other jihadist leaders, and contrary to his previous conviction that *jihád* should be directed against the "near enemy" at home, al-Zawáhiri signed a communiqué that declared the creation of The World Front for Jihad against Jews and Crusaders.[68] Citing the presence of American troops on the sacred land of the Arabian Peninsula, the authors of the communiqué accused the United States of "plundering its [Peninsula's] riches, dictating to its rulers, humiliating its people, terrorizing its neighbors."[69] With the sacred lands of Islam under infidel occupation, *jihád* against the foreign invader was to become an individual duty of every Muslim:

> Killing Americans and their allies—civilians and military—is an individual duty for every Muslim who can carry it out in any country where it is possible, in order to liberate al-Aqsa Mosque[70] and the holy sanctuary[71] from their grip, and to the point that their armies leave all Muslim territory, defeated and unable to threaten any Muslim.[72] This is in accordance with the words of God Almighty,[73] "And fight the pagans . . . until there is no more tumult or oppression, and justice and faith in God prevail."[74]

To prove that they meant business, the leaders of al-Qa'ida planned and executed two simultaneous attacks on U.S. embassies in East Africa, killing 224 people, most of whom were not Americans.[75] The U.S. retaliatory attacks ordered by President Clinton failed to destroy the organization. Following the 1998 American missile strike at an al-Qa'ida camp in Afghanistan that missed its targets, al-Zawáhiri coolly remarked that the holy war had just begun.[76] The American attacks only reinforced al-Qa'ida's determination to deliver a painful blow to the only remaining superpower on the face of the earth at the time. Ignoring the harsh criticism leveled at the leaders of al-Qa'ida by some of their former comrades who continued to believe that their primary objective was to overthrow the "impious" regimes at home,[77] Bin Ládin, al-Zawáhiri, and their confederates devoted the next three years to preparing a surprise attack on the United States. The underlying purpose of the Afghan *jihád* was now drastically reassessed. Contrary to his former conviction that the aim of the holy war in Afghanistan was to prime the *mujahideen* for taking on the Egyptian regime at home, in his famous manifesto "Knights Under the Prophet's Banner," al-Zawáhiri declared: "The jihad [in Afghanistan] was a training course of the utmost importance to prepare Muslim mujahedeen to wage their awaited battle against the superpower that now has the sole dominance over the globe, namely, the United States."[78]

This idea was fully shared by Bin Ládin, for whom "exacting revenge on the Americans and inflicting massive civilian casualties"[79] became a near obsession. He justified it by citing the deep trauma he had experienced in 1982 during an Israeli bombardment of Beirut, when he saw:

> Blood and severed limbs, women and children sprawled everywhere. Houses destroyed along with their occupants and high-rises demolished. . . As I looked at those demolished towers in Lebanon, it entered my mind that we should punish the oppressor in kind and that we should destroy towers in America.[80]

Writing a few months after the events of September 11, 2001, al-Zawáhiri took a less personal and more pragmatic approach to the matter. He condoned al-Qa'ida's attack on America by the fact that "the Judeo-Christian alliance, led by the United States, will not allow any Muslim force to attain power in any Muslim country." Hence, according to al-Qaʻida's "Number Two" at that time,[81] attempts to establish an Islamic state in any given Muslim country were doomed to failure as long as the U.S. government was ready and willing to deploy its political and military clout against Islamic/Islamist oppositional movements. "This is," concluded al-Zawáhiri, "why we must move the battle to the enemy's territory, to burn the hands of those who have set fire to our countries."[82] Adding a concrete practical dimension to his general conclusion, al-Zawáhiri suggested that:

> It is always possible to track an American or a Jew, to kill him with a bullet or a knife, a simple explosion device, or a blow with an iron rod. Setting fire to their property with a Molotov cocktail is not difficult. With a means available, small groups can spread terror among Americans and Jews.[83]

To justify the recourse to indiscriminate violence that he so vigorously promoted, al-Zawáhiri argued that:

> The West, led by the US, which is under the influence of Jews, does not know the language of ethics, morality and legitimate rights. They only know the language of interests backed by brute military force. Therefore, if we wish to have a dialogue with them and make them aware of our rights, we must talk to them in a language they understand.[84]

This sentiment was echoed in Bin Ládin's "Message to the American People" (October 2004), in which he said, reminiscing about his Beirut experiences:

> It was as if a crocodile had seized a helpless child, who could not but scream. Tell me: Does the crocodile understand any language other than that of force . . .[?] And that day, I realized that killing innocent women and children is a deliberate American policy.[85]

With the Muslim community under siege worldwide, the leaders of the transnational *jihád* movement argued that any means of self-defense, including "martyrdom operations," were allowed in order to "inflict maximum casualties on the enemy at the least cost for the *mujahideen*."[86] In this epic struggle for the survival of the *umma*, no holds are barred. In fact, proponents of transnational *jihád* insisted that acts of terror against infidels were explicitly commanded by the Qur'anic verse 8:60 that says:

> Against them make ready your strength to the utmost of your power, including steeds of war, to strike terror into [the hearts of] the enemies of God and your enemies, and others besides, whom you may not know, but whom God doth know. Whatever ye shall spend in the cause of God, shall be repaid unto you, and ye shall not be treated unjustly.[87]

This passage, and especially the phrase about "striking terror into [the hearts of] the enemies," has been widely used by jihadists as a proof text for the permissibility of terrorizing the enemy bent on harming Islam and the Muslim community. Thus, the Syrian Islamist Abu Musʻab al-Súri (b. 1958), whom some Western experts on terrorism have dubbed "architect of global jihad," provided the following commentary on the implications of this Qur'anic passage for today's *mujahideen*:

> The verse is clear in its text and unambiguous in its meaning . . . *"Make ready"* means train for combat. *"Against them"* means against your enemies. *"Your strength to the utmost of your power, including steeds of war"* is the shooting, riding and weapons . . . *"The enemies*

of God and your enemies": They are the ones whom the act of terror is intended for. *"And others besides"*: Means the ones who support and help them, or the ones who wait in ambush in order to attack you. When they witness your terror against the assailants, your resistance, and self-defense, they will "be terrorized" and frightened, and deterred from attacking, without you even knowing about their determination to attack.[88]

Seen from this vantage point, concluded Abu Mus'ab al-Súri:

> Yes, we are terrorists towards God's enemies. We have already struck terror in them, and we have made them tremble in their holes, in spite of the hundreds of thousands of agents in their security agencies, praise God, and this happened after they [had] terrorized the countries and humankind . . . From this follows that terrorism has been commanded in God's book, and in situations where the Mujahidun are repelling their enemy and the enemy's terror through a defensive jihad. This is one of the most important religious duties. In fact, there is no duty more obligatory than this, except believing that God is one, as established by Islamic jurists and clerics.[89]

The idea of "terror for terror" reappeared regularly in Bin Ládin's "messages to the world." He often quoted medieval commentaries on the Qur'an to argue, "If unbelievers were to kill our children and women, then we should not feel ashamed to do the same to them, mainly to deter them from trying to kill our children and women again."[90]

The Doctrine of "Amity and Enmity"

Even at a time when hostilities are not being actively pursued by either side, the true Muslims should practice what al-Zawáhiri and other Islamist ideologists call "amity and enmity" (*al-walá' wa 'l-bará'*), that is, being friendly and forgiving toward like-minded Muslims, while dissociating themselves decisively from and maintaining hostility toward unbelievers, apostates, and miscreants. Citing a Qur'anic verse that depicts Abraham as separating himself resolutely from his idolatrous tribesmen once and for all (60:4), Islamist ideologists have elevated this newly found principle to the status of the essential prerequisite for the correct profession and practice of the Muslim creed. Without the implementation of the amity and enmity principle, so the argument goes, the creed of Islam is but a dead letter.[91] Consequently:

> Islam is defined . . . not only by the willingness to fight, but also by the polarities of love and hatred: love for anything or anybody defined as Islam and Muslim, and hatred for their opposites or opponents . . . [This principle] enables radical Muslims to assert control over the definitions of who is and who is not a Muslim and . . . forces those who would wish to challenge that control into silence or into being categorized as "non-Muslims."[92]

In view of its overriding importance for jihadist ideology, al-Zawáhiri even declared the principle of "amity and enmity" to be an "essential pillar" of Islam alongside *jihád*.[93] On the practical level, the implementation of this principle means prohibiting "true Muslims" from engaging in any transaction or collaboration with "unbelievers," be they Westerners or their Muslim "lackeys." Both are proclaimed to be off-limits for "true Muslims" who wish to preserve the purity of their faith. Al-Zawáhiri considers helping infidels in their oppression of other Muslims (for instance, the invitation of American troops by the rulers of Saudi Arabia during the First Gulf War or the tacit permission by the Pakistani, Afghani, and Yemeni governments for the American military to assassinate *mujahideen* by means of special operation units, air raids, and drones, etc.) to be particularly repugnant.[94]

Islamic governments that want to be faithful to the principle of amity and enmity, according to al-Zawáhiri and several other theorists of global *jihád*, should never appoint unbelievers to important administrative positions, never sign or honor contracts with them, and never respect their laws or values. Even seemingly innocent daily interactions with unbelievers are to be avoided, to the extent of "not having tea or coffee with them."[95] In al-Zawáhiri's view, *jihád* is the only proper interaction of the faithful with "unbelievers who seize Muslim land," "apostates governing Muslim lands," "hypocrites who sow doubt," and "those who ally themselves with the unbelievers."[96] This statement conveniently summarizes the main categories of people against whom the enmity of true Muslims should be directed. As for the objects of amity, al-Zawáhiri argues, they are "true Muslims" who are always helping one another in their unequal struggle against the unbelievers and their Muslim collaborators. According to Al-Zawáhiri, refusal or failure to do so constitutes a mortal sin.[97]

Al-Zawáhiri's interpretation of the principle of amity and enmity[98] has fallen upon fertile ground. Many of today's jihadist spokespersons elevate it to the rank of *jihád* itself. Or, to be more precise, they regard it as an indispensable prerequisite for launching a worldwide revolution aimed at the establishment of "a pure Islamic system" and making "God's word" triumph over human-made laws, values, constitutions, and systems of government.[99] As proof of the legitimacy of this strategic goal, jihadist leaders are fond of quoting the Qur'anic verse (8:39) that urges the believers to "Fight them [the unbelievers], so that sedition might end and the only religion will be that of God."[100]

In a world shaped by the concept of amity and enmity, as understood by al-Zawáhiri and other jihadist scholars, there is no place for shade or doubt. It is starkly divided into the realm of:

> A dark image, filled with idolatry, infidelity, sedition, injustice, outrage, and immorality, which covers most of the world. Muslims there live a marginal life full of submissiveness and subordination . . . The other image is a bright one, radiant with rays of light, faith, true religion, piety, and virtue, under whose protection the unitarian[101] *mujahid* youth—who have not become accustomed to a life of humiliation and submissiveness—are prominent.[102]

The Self-Sacrificing Revolutionary Vanguard: Between Marxism and Islamism

The preceding quotation, from the strategic manual of a military commander (*amír*) of "al-Qa'ida in the Arabian Peninsula,"[103] implies the existence of an elect group of Muslim fighters who are destined by God to spearhead the epic battle against the "impious" world of the "dark image." This belief is shared by the majority of jihadists. Thus, Usáma bin Ládin and his closest followers assert that "[t]he first men to answer the call to arms, leaving behind them worldly preoccupations to undertake *jihad*, make up the [Muslim] community elite."[104] To justify this idea on scriptural grounds, Bin Ládin cites a *hadíth* in which the Prophet is quoted as saying: "I declare obligatory upon you five things; God has commanded me to do so. They are: organization [*jamá'a*], the listening and obeying,[105] and making *hijra*[106] and making *jihad* [for the sake of] God."[107]

In Bin Ládin's interpretation, the five actions prescribed by this *hadíth* not only supplement the Five Pillars of Islam but, in fact, are the most pressing duty of the revolutionary vanguard of the *umma*. Therefore, in response to the prophetic instruction, the select few should muster up the courage to step forward and shoulder the burden of fighting at a time when the ordinary believers do not dare to take arms against the superior enemy force. Organized into fighting units bound by sincere faith (*jama'át*), they should follow the orders of their commanders and plunge themselves impetuously into the unequal battle with the infidel adversary. In an act of almost suicidal courage, these self-sacrificing bands of fighters for religion absolve their less committed or more timid fellow Muslims from losing their lives and property in defending the global *umma* and its values.[108] Looking back on Islamic history, we find a similar self-sacrificing, uncompromising attitude among the Kharijite opponents of 'Ali b. Abi Talib and the Umayyad state. Indeed, the jihadists' critics both inside and outside the Muslim world have routinely drawn parallels between these two factions.[109]

Building on 'Azzám's recommendation to maintain the alliance between pen and sword in the service of Islam, the new generation of *jihádi* ideologists has argued that "one can only acquire a true understanding of the world and become part of the 'victorious group' (*al-tá'ifa al-mansúra*) if one contributes materially to Islamic resistance and even more so if one actively participates in the *jihad*."[110] In other words, being proficient in religious scholarship alone is insufficient for salvation in the hereafter unless one's religious knowledge is accompanied by actions in this world of which *jihád* is by far the most meritorious one.[111] This idea, too, can be traced back to the early Islamic debates around the nature of faith, namely whether a verbal declaration of faith is enough to make someone a believer or whether it requires that he or she demonstrate belief by acts of righteousness.[112]

The doctrine of a universal and permanent *jihád* places religious faith above any natural human attachments, including the natural human instinct for self-preservation. In the words of a Saudi jihadist: "They [the *mujahideen*] sell their land, and leave their wives and children and money, and they will trample on all forms of opulence and comfort [to achieve their goals]."[113]

Because only a limited number of Muslims can live up to such demanding standards of piety and self-sacrifice, the fully committed *mujahideen* perceive themselves as "strangers" in the world engulfed in injustice, avarice, depravity, and cowardice.[114] They often draw a parallel between themselves and the "stranger(s)" mentioned in a famous prophetic *hadíth*, according to which: "Islam began as a stranger, and it would revert to its [old position of] being one. So, [give] good tidings [of salvation] to the strangers."[115] The special status of today's jihadi "strangers" vis-á-vis the rest of the Muslim community rests "on the moral authority of self-sacrifice" and "a privileged access to truth," which they acquire in the course of their struggles against Islam's internal and external enemies.[116] By denying themselves the good things of this world, as well as the comforts and affections of family life and by deliberately seeking martyrdom "in the path of God," these self-professed "strangers" are bound to achieve personal salvation and redeem the *umma* from its plight. They may be less proficient than professional *'ulamá'* in the niceties of jurisprudence and theology, but in return for their self-abnegating readiness to give their lives for the triumph of Islam, God has bestowed on them the superior religious status and authority about which the *'ulamá'* who refuse to participate in *jihád* can only dream.[117]

This cult of revolutionary struggle waged by a self-sacrificing vanguard of fighters eager to redress the wrongs of this world and rebuild it on new, more just and moral foundations rings familiar. It inevitably invites comparisons with similar concepts found in Marxism-Leninism. Such comparisons indeed abound in recent scholarship on the subject. Sociologists and historians present today's *mujahideen* as a religiously inspired analogue to the world-liberating proletarian vanguard of classical Marxism. Seen from this perspective, the militant Islamism of the last two and a half decades may indeed appear as a somewhat paradoxical reincarnation of European radical leftism, on the one hand, and an Islamic/Islamist version of today's antiglobalism and third-worldism, on the other.[118] The revolutionary aspirations and practices of these movements are indeed quite similar, and "many radical [Muslim] preachers mix the Koran with almost Marxist statements."[119] Their denunciation of the injustices of the current world order has fallen on fertile soil, as many young Muslims in poor neighborhoods and slums "find in radical Islam a way to recast and rationalise their sense of exclusion and uprootedness."[120]

Tempting as such comparisons may appear, one should not downplay the cardinal differences between Marxism-Leninism and Islamism. Thus, the Islamists' exclusivist focus on religious identity and their unshakable faith in absolute divine sovereignty over the world and its human inhabitants are incompatible with the universalistic and atheistic message of classical Marxism that portrays revolutionary masses regardless of their religious or ethnic background as the sole, self-sufficient agent and shaper of historical processes. Marxists-Leninists of various shades do not recognize God's sovereignty in any shape or form, nor do they believe in the afterlife. Rather they strive to build a just and harmonious world on the basis of the universal socioeconomic laws discovered by Marx and Engels in which religion has absolutely no role to play. Moreover, whereas Marxism-Leninism has grown organically from certain strands of European religious, political, and social thought, radical Islamist groups, such as the Islamic State in Iraq and Syria[121] want to dissociate themselves unequivocally and emphatically from the West as the dictator of the rules, institutions, and values that, in their view, have resulted in Islam's decline and subjugation in the modern epoch. Driven by this perception of the role of Western ideologies, al-Qaʿida and the Islamic State want to rebuild the world on their own, purely Islamic terms. In this alternative world envisioned by the builders of the Islamic state (caliphate), Islam will determine what should be considered licit (*halál*) and what should not (*harám*). The Western powers, the UN, or any other international bodies will have no say in such matters. In a similar vein, the builders of the Islamic state do not care a bit about Western liberal sensitivities or standards, and they are eager to show this disregard to the entire world. When they commit horrific acts of violence or destruction in Syria, Iraq, Europe, and beyond, which are immediately translated across the world via the TV and the Internet, they do not do so randomly, out of sheer viciousness or irrational anger. Rather, these acts are carefully orchestrated and staged to foreground the irrevocable contradiction between Islamic norms as the Islamist builders of the caliphate understand them and the "tamed," "domesticated" Islam that, they believe, the manipulative Western governments want to promote among both their Muslim citizens and the Muslims worldwide. The builders of the Islamist caliphate want the world to know that they have rejected this "sugarcoated" Islam of Muslim liberals in favor of the authentic, nonsentimental, and self-assertive Islam that, they believe, led Muslims to great victories in the past. In other words, the actions of the individuals who have joined the Islamic State in Iraq and Syria are aimed at demonstrating their overriding commitment to a total and unapologetic moral-ethical revolution (pointed backward) for the consumption of the transnational community of Muslims, especially those disenchanted with their own personal lives and prospects, as well as with the position of Islam on the global stage generally. To sum up, if we are to view Marxism-Leninism with its belief in the communist utopia as a religious faith of sorts, then a comparison between its ideology and that of jihadi Islamism may not appear so far-fetched.[122]

As with radical Marxism, there is an apparent disjuncture between the purely local aspirations and grievances of concrete Muslim communities and the grand plans for achieving universal justice and winning the world for Islam espoused by the Islamist revolutionary vanguard. For the overwhelming majority of Muslims, the idea of (re)constructing a grand but entirely mythic worldwide caliphate does not hold much appeal. They are much more preoccupied with quite concrete and all too familiar economical-social injustices and oppressive political conditions they are facing on a daily basis. This is why, prior to 1991, al-Qaʿida's attempts to internationalize what were essentially internal, local conflicts between Islamist movements and their governments had been unsuccessful.[123] Only when external, non-Muslim powers entered the political scene did the project of global *jihád* get a shot in the arm. Since that time, al-Qaʿida has benefited tremendously from, initially, the deployment of U.S. troops in the Arabian Peninsula during the First Gulf War (1991), and later from the U.S. occupation of Afghanistan and Iraq (2001 and 2003). The Russian repression of the Chechens' bid for independence under Islamic slogans in 1994–1996 and the war in Bosnia between the Christian Serbs and the Muslim Bosnians in 1992–1995 were also grist for the mill of al-Qaʿida's propaganda machine. These and other conflicts involving Muslims allowed al-Qaʻida and its followers across the Muslim world to portray Islam and its community as being under attack by the arrogant Christian or infidel powers. In so doing, the leaders of the jihadist movement managed to attract a considerable number of pious, idealistic young Muslims to the idea of a universal *jihád* in defense of Islam. As it has turned out, this was exactly al-Qaʻida's strategy from the outset.

Al-Qaʻida's Strategy and Its Consequences

One of the world's leading experts on al-Qaʻida and its local "franchises" across the globe has suggested:

> Al Qaeda is unique in the history of radical organizations. It is the first to have such a significant global constituency, due to the two factors—the diaspora of Muslims throughout the world and, even more critically, the Internet. Any Muslim anywhere in the world can immediately be part of the electronic *umma*[124] whose *jihadi* wing is fronted by al Qaeda first and foremost.[125]

According to the organization's manifesto "al-Qaeda's Strategy to the Year 2020," the goals of the organization are to be achieved in five stages.[126] During the first stage, al-Qaʻida's goal was to provoke the "ponderous American elephant" into invading parts of the Muslim world. This task was accomplished as a result of the September 11, 2001 attacks, which prompted the United States to invade Afghanistan and Iraq. These invasions, according to al-Qaʻida's strategists, were supposed to pave the way for the second stage, during which another "giant elephant," the entire Muslim *umma*, was to be awakened from its "slumber" by the "American aggression." In the words of a jihadi strategist: "The purpose of [the 9/11 attacks] was to awaken the Islamic nation, which has been drugged, put to sleep and been absent from the confrontation, in order to put it face to face with her duty of jihad."[127]

The awakening of the *umma* would lead to a global clash of the "two giants." At that juncture, al-Qaʻida's vanguard of mujahideen would militarily engage the infidel aggressor and declare a global *jihád*. The devout Muslims from all corners of the world would pour into the hotbeds of military conflict between Muslims and unbelievers to fulfil their duty of defending Islam. According to this scenario, we should now be witnessing the unfolding of the third stage in the course of which the expeditionary forces of the United States and its allies in the Middle East and beyond become weakened and demoralized through a protracted war of attrition against the *umma*. During the fourth stage, al-Qaʻida would transform itself from a territorial entity into a global network of semi-independent franchises, whose commanders (*amírs*) would "have full autonomy in planning, choice of targets and tactics, giving the organization an immense flexibility while ensuring an ideological and strategic cohesion."[128] This process would be facilitated by the active use of the Internet to broadcast the message of the all-out, universal *jihád*. In the fifth and final stage, al-Qaʻida's strategists envision the United States to have become stretched beyond its capacities after having fought wars on many fronts simultaneously, while also trying to protect its population and industries from terrorist attacks. Preoccupied, on top of all this, with protecting its access to Middle Eastern oil and defending its principal ally, Israel, from being savaged by the awakened *umma*, the United States would be on a "mission impossible." In the minds of al-Qaʻida's strategists, these multiple challenges would eventually weaken the Americans' political will, demoralize its military, ruin its financial system, and exhaust its economy. In the end, the world's last superpower will go the way of the Soviet Union.[129] After the United States has withdrawn from the Muslim world to "lick its wounds," al-Qaʻida and its sister organizations would overthrow the despotic pro-Western regimes in the Arab lands and beyond, instituting a new international polity, the caliphate. The leadership of this polity would then actively prosecute a worldwide *jihád* against the "nonbelievers" with a view to making "God's word" triumph on the global scale.[130]

Some of al-Qaʻida's strategic goals have indeed been achieved. For instance, it has succeeded in bringing "large numbers of US soldiers onto Muslim soil," thereby generating "the widespread hatred of America" across the Muslim world and substantially expanding al-Qaʻida's recruitment base.[131] On the other hand, there is no doubt that the al-Qaʻida leaders have overestimated the depth and breadth of the expected Muslim indignation at the U.S. occupation of the Muslim lands. While insurgencies in Iraq and Afghanistan were extremely ferocious and bloody, they have triggered neither major popular uprisings against the American troops in the region nor the collapse of the Muslim governments cooperating with the United States in its so-called War on Terror. On the contrary, the United States was able to find allies among the populations of the countries it occupied and beyond (e.g., in Yemen) in order to use them against the local militant groups loyal to al-Qaʻida. The goal of "milking America dry" economically and militarily has not been fulfilled either. The American losses of life and materiel, although substantial, have not been on the scale predicted by the al-Qaʻida strategists.

Al-Qaʻida, on the other hand, has paid dearly for its partial successes. In overplaying the "Shiʻite card" in Iraq (often with a wanton disregard for the consequences of its military operations for Iraqi civilians), al-Qaʻida's local branch led my Abu Musʻab al-Zarqáwi (d. 2006) alienated, at least for a while, its erstwhile supporters among the country's Sunnis. Although al-Zarqáwi was killed in an American airstrike, his followers continued his policy of ruthless extermination of Shiʻites in Iraq and later on in Syria as well. As a result, al-Qaʻida, whose leadership had originally been opposed to indiscriminate attacks on the Shiʻites, witnessed the emergence of a formidable rival, the Islamic State of Iraq and Syria that not only does not take orders from the al-Qaʻida leadership based in Afghanistan and Pakistan but also has effectively contested its erstwhile monopoly on global *jihád*. Many military commanders loyal to al-Qaʻida were killed by the Islamic States' operatives in Syria, Iraq, and Afghanistan. A tit-for-tat war ensued that has been more detrimental to al-Qaʻida and its franchises than to the Islamic State and its local branches. A handful of surviving al-Qaʻida leaders remain in hiding, constantly on the run and thus incapable of effectively directing the actions of its *mujahideen* worldwide. Major national Muslim movements (such as those in Palestine, Uzbekistan, Kashmir, Xinjiang, Tajikistan, the Philippines, and the Northern Caucasus) have lost international support and credibility due, in large part, to their alleged or real association with al-Qaʻida's terrorist tactics. The Taliban regime of Afghanistan, al-Qaʻida's staunch onetime supporter, has been severely weakened by the Western coalition forces. Its remnants in Afghanistan and Pakistan, although occasionally successful, remain under attack from the air and on the ground. Across the globe, Islamist movements and parties, both peaceful and militant, are worse off as a result of al-Qaʻida's actions. Their leaders are imprisoned as "terrorists," their channels of financing have been severed, and their activities are being closely monitored by security and police agencies. Muslim minorities in the United States, Europe, Russia, and China are mistrusted and mistreated by both their governments and their fellow citizens as potential al-Qaʻida operatives or sympathizers.[132] Some of the organization's former allies have renounced violence and now hold al-Qaʻida responsible for discrediting and distorting the original Islamic/Islamist ideals.[133] In the final account, al-Qaʻida's cherished desire to mobilize the *umma* around the banner of global *jihád* and to establish an international Islamic state in the Middle East and South Asia remains but a dream. Although a similar dream is now being pursued by al-Qaʻida's former splinter group and present-day nemesis, the Islamic State in Iraq and Syria, the prospects of this neo-jihadist project, too, remain gloomy.

Instead of a Conclusion: Does the Islamist Project Have a Future?

Some influential Western scholars have argued that "political Islam" in general and militant Islamism in particular had reached its highest point already during and shortly after the Soviet–Afghan War. Since that time, the scholars argue, "political Islam" has suffered a progressive decline, losing much of its erstwhile appeal to the Muslim masses.[134] If this is indeed the case, the Islamist project does not seem to have any future. Its financial and human resources have been depleted; its strategic goals are unattainable, despite some recent successes in Syria and Iraq; and, worse still, it has failed to enlist the level of support among the Muslim masses its leaders had hoped for. While there is some truth to such academic predictions of the eventual "failure of political Islam," they should be treated with a grain of salt, so to say. As long as Islam continues to generate loyalty and emotional responses among its followers, as long as Muslims worldwide continue to face injustices and oppression, either real or perceived, and as long as foreign policy of the major international powers such as the United States, the European Union, China, and Russia continues to be a source of frustration for Muslims the world over, both jihadist and non-jihadist Islamism, as an ideology and an organizational framework, will remain relevant and active. The exact forms and strategies of various strands of Islamist movement will, of course, change in response to changing local circumstances and geopolitical realities. For example, the present leaders of jihadist Islamists have been placing more and more emphasis on the propaganda and dissemination of its ideologies in the hope of expanding their recruitment base and making it truly global. If anything, they have succeeded in creating a virtual Islamist utopia that has little to do with the realities on the ground but that has a powerful appeal to Muslim youth worldwide.[135] Some movements have made a good-faith effort to integrate peacefully into their countries' political processes.[136] When and where such attempts have been thwarted by authoritarian military rulers (the Muslim Brotherhood in Egypt being the most dramatic example), expect a resurgence of violent jihadism. In sum, temporary or permanent changes in tactics notwithstanding, it is likely that Islamic/Islamist movements are here to stay for the observable future. Whether their actions will take violent or peaceful forms depends in great part on the political choices of those currently in power in the Muslim world, as well as on international politics of the Western powers led by the United States. Should the incumbent state authorities (and their Western allies) decide to rely on brutal suppression as Jamál 'Abd al-Násir (Nasser) once did, they are bound to perpetuate the vicious circle of a tit-for-tat violence as discussed in Chapter 22. If, on the other hand, the incumbent rulers decide to abandon their zero-sum mentality and accept Islamism as a legitimate oppositional force and interlocutor, its leaders may well respond by shedding their more radical ideas to transform themselves into a regular political party "with an Islamic character."[137] This is exactly what happened in the past to some branches of the Muslim Brotherhood in Jordan, Tunisia, and Egypt,[138] although more recently we have seen some dramatic reversals by ruling elites of this accommodating attitude. Such fluctuations in state policies toward Islamic/Islamist parties and movements are likely to continue in the foreseeable future. The actions of the parties and movements, in their turn, will be shaped by such fluctuations. In any event, it seems that the news of the death and failure of "political Islam" has been greatly exaggerated by some Western observers.

Conclusions

On September 11, 2001, the whole world shuddered at the news of the deadly suicide attacks on the New York Twin Towers and the Pentagon. The Western public demanded explanations, and an army of experts, pundits, and commentators rushed to oblige. On the conservative, right-wing side of the political spectrum, the most common explanation was to emphasize the inherently violent nature of Islam as a religious faith and to hold its scriptures, teachings, and practices responsible for the tragedy. Right-wing TV broadcasts and radio talk shows attributed "Islamic terrorism" to the Muslims' "natural propensity to violence" as manifested in their alleged commitment to the global *jihad* against the "infidels." Left-wing political commentators and some Muslim activists, on the other hand, flatly rejected such religion-based explanations, pointing instead to U.S. policies in the Middle East as the root cause of anti-American and anti-Western sentiment throughout the Muslim world. In and of itself, they argued, Islam was a religion of peace, reason, and tolerance; it was simply "hijacked" by a few crazed "bad guys" who illegitimately arrogated some randomly and incompetently chosen Islamic tenets to justify their acts of senseless violence against civilian populations of Western states. Analysts steeped in modern history spoke of the heavy price that the West and Russia had to pay for their ruthless colonization and exploitation of the Muslim world in the nineteenth and twentieth centuries. They suggested that militant movements in the name of Islam were motivated by the abiding resentment that many Muslims still feel over their colonial past and, even more pertinently, their neocolonial present. The political borders randomly drawn by the Europeans across the Middle East, North Africa, Central Asia, and beyond were also routinely invoked as a major source of Muslim troubles and discontent today. Some commentators went further back in history to conjure up the trauma that Europe's medieval Crusades left on the Muslim collective psyche and the desire on the part of some radically minded Muslims to redeem themselves by punishing the descendants of the crusaders for the misdeeds of their ancestors. Still others drew their audiences' attention to the rampant inequalities of the current global order, shaped and dominated as it is by the unchallenged and unbridled Western powers and their rapacious corporations. In short, such left-leaning commentators presented (and still do) the Western neocolonial domination over the Muslim lands today as the chief cause of the tragedy of September 11, 2001, and of its subsequent replays, on a smaller scale, in terrorist attacks against "soft" targets in Europe, Russia, the Middle East, Africa, and South Asia.

Seen through the prism of this left-wing analysis, militant actions of certain Islamic/Islamist groups are but a revolt of the "wretched of the earth"[139] against the club of the wealthy capitalist nations that have cynically exploited to their exclusive advantage the material benefits of globalization. Finally, a group of historians and political scientists who wanted to account for the events of September 11, 2001 tended to present have presented violence in the name of Islam as an unexpected consequence of the Cold War. In their view, in trying to defeat the Soviet Union, the United States and its allies in the region unwittingly brought up a generation of hardened Muslim fighters who eventually turned their arms against their erstwhile benefactors. All of the explanations just mentioned may have some truth to them as they highlight one or the other aspect, often quite important, of the complex phenomenon at hand. They continue to inform Western academic perceptions of the events of September 11, 2012 and their aftermath until today.

In the introduction to this book, we pointed out that the exact ways in which Islam is understood and practiced by its followers are shaped decisively by the sociopolitical and cultural conditions of the societies in which they happen live. In the absence of a centralized ecclesiastic authority that would once and for all declare a certain Islamic dogma to be the only correct one, while condemning competing interpretations as "heresies," the Muslims will continue to draw vastly dissimilar conclusions from the same foundational texts and from these texts' theological and juridical elaborations produced in the course of Islam's long evolution. This means that any claims to express or represent the only true, authentic, and ever relevant essence of Islam made in either good faith or with pragmatic political goals in mind should be seen for what they are—one of the numerous, if not countless possible interpretations of Islam's immensely rich and variegated legacy. For every group of Muslims who have drawn militant conclusions from their engagement with the Muslim tradition by setting on the path of war against either the "near" or the "far enemy," one can always find another group that has taken a diametrically opposed path. Who, then, can be the impartial judge of the respective faithfulness of such groups to the fundamental tenets of the Islamic religion? To avoid the predicament of passing judgment on this fraught matter, it seems more productive to examine the respective sociopolitical environments and personal inclinations of the members of each group in order to find out the objective and subjective factors that have caused them to choose one path and not the other. If this book has helped the reader to realize the astounding richness of the Islamic tradition and the endless variety of paths it offers to its followers to pursue, then its goal has been achieved.

Questions to Ponder

1   Enumerate some social, political, and cultural factors that may have been responsible for the survival and continual relevance of Islamic/Islamist movements (either violent or peaceful) in the modern world. In a similar vein, what is it about Islamic/Islamist religiopolitical agendas that make them so attractive to Muslims of vastly diverse backgrounds?
2   Give a few examples of religion-based parties in the Western political arena, especially in the United States and Europe. How different or similar are they to Islamic parties and movements discussed in the last two chapters of this book?
3   Consider the origins of al-Qaʻida in the Afghan *jihád* against the Soviet army and the rise of radical Islamism in Egypt under Sadat and Mubarak. Both movements are often cited by political scientists as typical illustrations of the "law of unintended consequences" (alongside the U.S. invasion of Iraq that has become a *cause célèbre* for jihadists of all stripes). With the benefit of hindsight, do you think their emergence was inevitable and logical? Who was responsible and why?
4   How serious are the recent splits in the ranks of the *mujahideen*, and what are their causes? Is unity possible in principle?

Summary

- The Western media conducts extensive (and often inaccurate) coverage of militancy in the name of Islam.
- The political, economic, and social problems faced by Muslim societies in the post-colonial era are at the root of the rise and rapid expansion of oppositional movements under Islamic/Islamist banners.
- Neocolonialism (understood as Western political, economic, and cultural domination and the West's interference in the affairs of Muslim states) is perceived by many Muslims as the chief reason for the plight of Muslim societies in the modern world. This results in the spread of anti-Western sentiments among many Muslims who have not benefitted from the Westernization and modernization of their societies.
- As nationalist projects fail and secular nationalist governments grow more oppressive, Islam becomes the last recourse for the disenchanted and victimized masses. Secular rulers of Muslim countries make attempts to harness this Islamic/Islamist resurgence

- and use it for their political ends, both domestically and internationally. As they often underestimate the depth and strength of the Islamic/Islamist movements they cultivate, their efforts backfire, resulting in the proverbial "jinni out of the bottle."
- The Soviet occupation of Afghanistan in 1979 and the Iranian revolution in the same year become the critical turning points in the evolution of Islamic/Islamist movements worldwide.
- 'Abdallah 'Azzám (d. 1989) becomes the principal harbinger of the Afghan *jihád* against the Soviets and the early advocate of the global *jihád* against anti-Muslim forces wherever they may be. The ultimate goal of the supporters of the idea of global *jihád* is to liberate Muslim lands from infidel domination and to establish a just and harmonious Islamic state.
- According to 'Azzám, the vanguard of the *umma*, which consists of *jihád*-minded scholars and *jihád* foot soldiers (*mujahideen*), is the essential driving force behind the global *jihád*. The jihadist ethos and mythology emerge, with its emphasis on sacrifice and martyrdom "in the path of God."
- With 'Azzám's and Usáma bin Ládin's (1957–2011) initiation of the Bureau of Services at Peshawar, Pakistan, al-Qa'ida comes into existence.
- Ayman al-Zawáhiri's (b. 1951) life story shows a curious evolution from an Egyptian Islamist with a local agenda to a transnational jihadist and Bin Ládin's right-hand man and, after the latter's death, the leader of al-Qa'ida.
- The World Front for Jihad Against Jews and Crusaders is created in 1998, and al-Qa'ida's all-out war against the United States is initiated. Bin Ládin and his followers use terror tactics in an effort to force the United States to withdraw from the Middle East or to invade Muslims lands and become embroiled in an epic struggle against the *umma* as a whole.
- Al-Qa'ida leadership justifies the indiscriminate use of violence against the "far enemy" and the use of terrorism against civilian populations.
- The doctrine of amity and enmity (*al-wala' wa 'l-bara'*) plays a significant role in drawing a sharp borderline between the jihadists (the "true Muslims") and their enemies, be they Westerners or their Muslim "lackeys."
- The jihadist leaders of al-Qa'ida portray themselves and their followers as a self-sacrificing revolutionary vanguard of the *umma*. In this respect, al-Qa'ida and more recently the Islamic State in Iraq and Syria show some affinity with the theory and practice of Marxism-Leninism. In particular, the jihadist vanguard parallels the world-liberating proletarian vanguard of classical Marxism. Both Marxism and jihadism are prone to utopian thinking. The possible reasons behind the anti-Western rhetoric and actions of the jihadists in Iraq and Syria lend some credence to the overall validity of comparisons between international jihadism and Marxism-Leninism.
- There is a disjuncture between the purely local aspirations and grievances of concrete Muslim communities and the grand plans of the jihadist leadership to bring about Islam's universal dominance by establishing an international Islamist caliphate.
- Al-Qa'ida's long-term strategy is to embroil the United States in a global conflict with the Muslim world with a view to uniting the Muslims in a life-and-death struggle against the aggressor and eventually taking control of the newly unified *umma* and establishing an international caliphate.
- This strategy for al-Qa'ida itself and global jihadism as a whole has its geopolitical consequences. As the United States and its allies strike back, the jihadist movement becomes fragmented into a loose assemblage of fighting units and "sleeper cells." The

jihadists' principal goal is to inflict as much damage as possible on their infidel enemies in retaliation for their losses. The grievances and sufferings of the Muslims worldwide are used by al-Qaʻida and its "franchises," including its current nemesis, the Islamic State in Iraq and Syria, to justify their *jihád* and acts of terror against both the "far" and the "near" enemies and to recruit new members. These are the international dimensions and propaganda strategies of al-Qaʻida and the Islamic State.

- The Islamic/Islamist project faces a dubious future but is likely to continue in one form or the other, in any of several possible scenarios.

Notes

1 In what follows the terms "global *jihad*/jihadism" and "transnational *jihad*/jihadism" are used interchangeably.
2 For some typical examples, see Jason Burke, *Al-Qaeda: Casting the Shadow of Terror*, I.B. Tauris, London and New York, 2003; Richard Clarke, *Against All Enemies: Inside America's War on Terror*, Free Press, New York, 2004; Jonathan Schanzer, *Al-Qaeda's Armies: Middle East Affiliate Groups and the Next Generation of Terror*, Specialist Press International, New York, 2005; Steven Emerson, *Jihad Incorporated*, Prometheus Books, Amherst, NY, 2006; Christopher Ankersen and Michael O'Leary (eds.), *Understanding Global Terror*, Polity Press, Malden, MA, 2007; David Bukay, *From Muhammad to Bin Laden*, Transaction Publishers, New Brunswick and London, 2008; Laurent Murawiec, *The Mind of Jihad*, Cambridge University Press, Cambridge, 2008; David Springer, James Regens and David Edger, *Islamic Radicalism and Global Jihad*, Georgetown University Press, Washington, DC, 2009.
3 *In Search of Bin Laden*, a Frontline coproduction with New York Times and RainMedia Inc., 2001; *In Search of al-Qaeda*, a Frontline coproduction with RainMedia Inc., WGHB Boston, 2002; *Campaign Against Terror*, produced and directed by Mark Anderson and Greg Barker, A Brook Lapping Production, WGHB, Boston, 2002; *Obsession: Radical Islam's War Against the West*, produced and directed by Peter Mier, Raphael Shore, Wayne Kopping, and others, Clarion Fund, New York, 2006; *God's Muslim Warriors*, produced and directed by Christina Amanpour, a CNN documentary, August 2007; "The 9/11 Decade: A Special Three-Part Series Taking an In-Depth Look at the Post 9/11 'War on Terror'": http://www.aljazeera.com/programmes/aljazeeraworld/2011/10/2011102075124103401.html; "Al Qaeda Informant," a new film documentary produced by Al Jazeera: http://topdocumentaryfilms.com/al-qaeda-informant/.
4 Timothy Mitchell, "McJihad: Islam in the U.S. Global Order," *Social Text*, vol. 73/4 (Winter 2002), p. 1.
5 Ibid., pp. 4–5, 7–11, et passim.
6 Tribalism is another "primeval ideology" that may occasionally experience resurgence as a consequence of the collapse or discredit of secular and nationalist models of development; see, for example, Paul Dresch, *Tribes, Government and History in Yemen*, Clarendon Press, Oxford, 1989, passim.
7 See Chapter 22.
8 See Chapter 20.
9 Marc Sageman, *Understanding Terror Networks*, University of Philadelphia Press, Philadelphia, 2004, pp. 26–28.
10 Ibid., p. 30.
11 Many Western and Eastern observers have tended to conflate the former Soviet Union with Russia and to present the Soviet Army as predominantly Russian in its ethnic composition; see, for example, Fawaz Gerges, *The Far Enemy*, 2nd ed., Cambridge University Press, Cambridge, 2009, pp. 12–14, 80–87, et passim. This is inaccurate because the occupation of Afghanistan was a typical *Soviet* venture with the strategic decision to invade that country made by the multiethnic Communist Party Politburo in the name of "Communist internationalism." The Soviet expeditionary force in Afghanistan was ethnically diverse, reflecting the motley ethnic composition of the former Soviet Union.

12 Abdel Bari Atwan, *The Secret History of al Qaeda*, updated edition, University of California Press, Berkeley and Los Angeles, CA, 2008, p. 74 and Gilles Kepel, *Jihad: The Trail of Political Islam*, Belknap Press, Cambridge, MA, 2002, pp. 138–140; Gilles Kepel and Jean-Pierre Milelli (eds.), *Al Qaeda in Its Own Words* (trans. Pascale Ghazaleh), Belknap Press, Cambridge, MA, and London, 2008, pp. 41–46, 91–95, 106–109, et passim.

13 For a recent account of his life and work, see Bernard Rougier, "Azzam, 'Abdallah," in *Encyclopedia of Islam*, 3rd ed.; online edition: http://referenceworks.brillonline.com.

14 Q 4:95, 9:81, 49:15, et passim.

15 This ideological step had already been taken by the ideologists of Egypt's Islamist militant groups responsible for the assassination of President Sadat; see Chapter 22 and Kepel and Milelli (eds.), *Al Qaeda in Its Own Words*, p. 98.

16 See Chapter 22 and Gerges, *The Far Enemy*, pp. 4–9.

17 Namely, Muslim authorities of the past and present epochs.

18 As opposed to the situation when *jihád* is the collective duty executed by the Muslim ruler and his military force.

19 Kepel and Milelli (eds.), *Al Qaeda in Its Own Words*, p. 103.

20 Ibid., p. 106.

21 Ibid., p. 104.

22 Kepel, *Jihad*, p. 146.

23 Here he lists the blind, terminally ill, lame, oppressed as well as those who are somehow incapable of making their way to the battlefield; see David Cook, *Understanding Jihad*, University of California Press, Berkeley, CA, 2005, p. 130.

24 Cook, *Understanding Jihad*, p. 130.

25 Ibid., p. 131.

26 Kepel and Milelli (eds.), *Al Qaeda in Its Own Words*, p. 108 and Brynar Lia, *Architect of Global Jihad: The Life of al-Qaida Strategist Abu Mus'ab al-Suri*, Columbia University Press, New York, 2008, pp. 73–74.

27 Kepel and Milelli (eds.), *Al Qaeda in Its Own Words*, p. 107.

28 Ibid., p. 100, 118–119, and 140–143; Kepel, *Jihad*, p. 147; Gerges, *The Far Enemy*, p. 136; Sageman, *Understanding Terror Networks*, p. 36.

29 This was the title of a 1995 article by Ayman al-Zawáhiri, who was to become Usáma bin Ládin's ideologist and right-hand man; see Montasser al-Zayyat, *The Road to al-Qaeda: The Story of Bin Laden's Right-Hand Man* (trans. Ahmed Fekry), Pluto Press, London and Sterling, VA, 2002, p. 62 and Gerges, *The Far Enemy*, p. 11; the idea of the primacy of the "near enemy" can be traced back to the Egyptian Islamists Sayyid Qutb and 'Abd al-Salam Farag (Faraj); see Gerges, *The Far Enemy*, pp. 10–12.

30 Gerges, *The Far Enemy*, pp. 135–136 and Lia, *Architect of Global Jihad*, pp. 72–73.

31 Gerges, *The Far Enemy*, p. 49.

32 Cook, *Understanding Jihad*, p. 129; I have slightly modified Cook's translation of this passage.

33 Cook, *Understanding Jihad*, p. 129.

34 Kepel and Milelli (eds.), *Al Qaeda in Its Own Words*, p. 117.

35 Ibid., p. 119.

36 Kepel, *Jihad*, p. 148.

37 Sageman, *Understanding Terror Networks*, p. 58.

38 Kepel, *Jihad*, p. 148.

39 Atwan, *The Secret History of al Qaeda*, pp. 75–85.

40 Kepel, *Jihad*, p. 147 and Sageman, *Understanding Terror Networks*, pp. 58–59.

41 As attested by Bin Ládin himself; see Kepel and Milelli (eds.), *Al Qaeda in Its Own Words*, pp. 41–46.

42 Sageman, *Understanding Terror Networks*, p. 59.

43 Cook, *Understanding Jihad*, pp. 153–154.

44 An accurate and balanced account of this new Islamist movement is yet to written; those publications that have already appeared are usually superficial and lack academic rigor; for a typical example, see Michael Weiss and Hassan Hassan, *Isis: Inside the Army of Terror*, Regan Arts, New York, 2015.

45 The capital of the North West Frontier province of Pakistan, which served as headquarters of the Afghan resistance movement during the Soviet occupation of Afghanistan.

46 Kepel, *Jihad*, p. 148.

47 Sageman, *Understanding Terror Networks*, p. 163.

48 See, for instance, Kepel, *Jihad*, p. 315 and Kepel and Milelli (eds.), *Al Qaeda in Its Own Words*, pp. 7, 19 and 35.

49 An organization whose goal was "to facilitate the arrival of Arab volunteers and to coordinate the distribution of recruits to the various battlefields, training camps" in support of the Afghan *jihád*; see Kepel and Milelli (eds.), *Al Qaeda in Its Own Words*, p. 93 and Lia, *Architect of Global Jihad*, pp. 71–72.

50 Atwan, *The Secret History of al Qaeda*, p. 44 and Kepel, *Jihad*, p. 315.

51 The largest contingents of volunteer fighters hailed from Saudi Arabia, Yemen, Egypt, Algeria, Syria, and Palestine; see Lia, *Architect of Global Jihad*, p. 74.

52 Gerges, *The Far Enemy*, p. 69.

53 "Inter-Services Intelligence Directorate"; Sageman, *Understanding Terror Networks*, pp. 56–57.

54 Kepel and Milelli (eds.), *Al Qaeda in Its Own Words*, p. 20 and Atwan, *The Secret History of al Qaeda*, pp. 43–44.

55 Al-Zayyat, *The Road to al-Qaeda*, p. 31 and Kepel and Milelli (eds.), *Al Qaeda in Its Own Words*, p. 152.

56 Al-Zayyat, *The Road to al-Qaeda*, pp. 33–34; Kepel and Milelli (eds.), *Al Qaeda in Its Own Words*, p. 154; Sageman, *Understanding Terror Networks*, pp. 34–35.

57 See note 29.

58 Gerges, *The Far Enemy*, p. 11 and al-Zayyat, *The Road to al-Qaeda*, p. 62.

59 Atwan, *The Secret History of al Qaeda*, pp. 44 and 58.

60 See note 11.

61 Gerges, *The Far Enemy*, p. 14.

62 Atwan, *The Secret History of al Qaeda*, pp. 76–77 and Rougier, "'Abdallah 'Azzam."

63 According to an alternative explanation, the idea of *jihád* against "the far enemy" originated among the Egyptian jihadists in Bin Ládin's inner circle; see Sageman, *Understanding Terror Networks*, pp. 54–59.

64 Ibid., p. 44.

65 In that year, al-Zawáhiri's organization was implicated in the massacre of fifty-eight foreign tourists and four Egyptians at a popular tourist site of Luxor in Upper (southern) Egypt; although al-Zawáhiri later praised it as a major "offensive against the enemies of Islam," the Egyptian public at large disagreed with his assessment as the attack struck at the very heart of Egypt's tourist industry, the major source of the country's economic well-being. As a result, the Islamic Jihad and its militant sister movements found themselves deeply unpopular, which appears to have been the main reason for al-Zawáhiri's departure for Afghanistan; see Atwan, *The Secret History of al Qaeda*, p. 78 and Gerges, *The Far Enemy*, p. 153.

66 Al-Zayyat, *The Road to al-Qaeda*, pp. 73–90.

67 Gerges, *The Far Enemy*, p. 14.

68 Kepel and Milelli (eds.), *Al Qaeda in Its Own Words*, p. 158 and Atwan, *The Secret History of al Qaeda*, p. 79.

69 Kepel and Milelli (eds.), *Al Qaeda in Its Own Words*, pp. 53–54.

70 An Islamic sanctuary in Jerusalem on the top of the Temple Mount.

71 The Muslim shrine complex on the top of the Temple Mount.

72 Atwan, *The Secret History of al Qaeda*, p. 55.

73 Q 2:193.

74 Kepel and Milelli (eds.), *Al Qaeda in Its Own Words*, p. 55; see also Cook, *Understanding Jihad*, pp. 174–175.

75 Atwan, *The Secret History of al Qaeda*, p. 79.

76 Gerges, *The Far Enemy*, p. 184.

77 Sageman, *Understanding Terror Networks*, p. 47.

78 Gerges, *The Far Enemy*, p. 13.

79 Ibid., p. 184.

80 Atwan, *The Secret History of al Qaeda*, pp. 11–12.

81 After the death of Bin Ládin in 2011, Ayman al-Zawáhiri became head of the al-Qa'ida; he is currently in hiding in the border area between Afghanistan and Pakistan.

82 Kepel and Milelli (eds.), *Al Qaeda in Its Own Words*, p. 202.

83 Ibid., p. 198 and Atwan, *The Secret History of al Qaeda*, p. 83.

84 Atwan, *The Secret History of al Qaeda*, p. 84.

85 Kepel and Milelli (eds.), *Al Qaeda in Its Own Words*, p. 72.

86 Atwan, *The Secret History of al Qaeda*, p. 84.

87 Lia, *Architect of Global Jihad*, pp. 466–467.

88 Ibid., pp. 385–386.

89 Ibid., p. 387.

90 Bruce Lawrence (ed.), *Messages to the World: The Statements of Osama Bin Laden*, Verso, London, 2005, pp. 118–119 and 39.

91 Joas Wagemakers, "A Purist Jihadi-Salafi: The Ideology of Abu Muhammad al-Maqdisi," *British Journal of Middle Eastern Studies*, vol. 36/2 (August 2009), pp. 288–289 and 293; idem, *A Quietist Jihadi: The Ideology and Influence of Abu Muhammad al-Maqdisi*, Cambridge University Press, Cambridge, 2012, Part III.

92 Cook, *Understanding Jihad*, p. 141.

93 Kepel and Milelli (eds.), *Al Qaeda in Its Own Words*, pp. 231–233.

94 Ibid., p. 218 and Wagemakers, "A Purist Jihadi-Salafi," p. 287.

95 Kepel and Milelli (eds.), *Al Qaeda in Its Own Words*, pp. 212–216 and Wagemakers, "A Purist Jihadi-Salafi," p. 287.

96 Kepel and Milelli (eds.), *Al Qaeda in Its Own Words*, pp. 219–225.

97 Ibid., pp. 222–225.

98 He was not alone in advancing this principle and explicating its practical implications; for its interpretation by the renowned Jordanian-Palestinian scholar Abu Muhammad al-Maqdisi (b. 1959), see Wagemakers, *A Quietist Jihadi*, Part III.

99 Norman Cigar (trans.), *Al-Qa'ida's Doctrine for Insurgency: 'Abd Al-'Aziz Al-Muqrin's A Practical Guide for Guerilla War*, Potomac Books, Washington, DC, 2009, p. 16 and Roel Meijer, "Yusuf al-'Uyairi and the Making of a Revolutionary Salafi Praxis," *Die Welt des Islams*, vol. 47/3–4 (2007), pp. 426 and 441–446.

100 Cook, *Understanding Islam*, p. 161.

101 Namely, those who profess divine unity and oneness (*tawhid*).

102 Cigar (trans.), *Al-Qa'ida's Doctrine*, pp. 15–16.

103 'Abd al-'Aziz al-Muqrin, who was killed by Saudi security forces in June 2004.

104 Kepel and Milelli (eds.), *Al Qaeda in Its Own Words*, p. 34.

105 That is, "listening" to the command of a military and/or religious leader and "obeying" it.

106 That is, withdrawing from an "impious" society to one of "true believers."

107 Kepel and Milelli (eds.), *Al Qaeda in Its Own Words*, p. 33.

108 Ibid., pp. 34–35.

109 Ibid., pp. 339–340, note 68; Murawiec, *The Mind of Jihad*, pp. 51, 96, 115–116; Kepel, *Jihad*, p. 85; Springer, Regens and Edger (eds.), *Islamic Radicalism and Global Jihad*, p. 231; Nelly Lahoud, *The Jihadis' Path to Self-Destruction*, Hurst, London, 2010, passim; for the historical Kharijites, see Chapter 7.

110 Meijer, "Yusuf al-'Uyairi and the Making of a Revolutionary Salafi Praxis," p. 442.

111 Ibid., pp. 442–443.

112 See Chapter 10.

113 Meijer, "Yusuf al-'Uyairi and the Making of a Revolutionary Salafi Praxis," p. 444.

114 See, for instance, http://www.islamictreasure.com/788-glad-tidings-to-the-strangers-ghuraba/.

115 Lia, *Architect of Global Jihad*, p. 251; I have modified the translation according to a more common version of the *hadith*.

116 Meijer, "Yusuf al-'Uyairi and the Making of a Revolutionary Salafi Praxis," p. 444.

117 Alexander Knysh, "Islam and Arabic as the Rhetoric of Insurgency: The Case of the Caucasus Emirate," *Studies in Conflict and Terrorism*, vol. 35/4 (2012), pp. 315–337, esp. p. 326.

118 See, for instance, Olivier Roy, *Globalized Islam: The Search for a New Ummah*, Columbia University Press, New York, 2004, pp. 43, 45–50, 59, et passim; Gerges, *The Far Enemy*, pp. 117 and 297; Murawiec, *The Mind of Jihad*, pp. 77, 145–147, 276–294, 309–313, et passim; Meijer, "Yusuf al-'Uyairi and the Making of a Revolutionary Salafi Praxis," pp. 443–444.

119 Roy, *Globalized Islam*, p. 324.

120 Ibid.; given the overall context of Roy's study, this statement seems to apply primarily to the disenfranchised and impoverished Muslim youth of European megalopolises.

121 Also known under its Arabic acronym "Da'ish," namely *al-Dawla al-Islammiyya fi al-'Iraq wa-al-Sha'm*. The word "Syria" (Arab. al-Sha'm) stands for "Greater Syria" that includes today's Palestine, Israel, Jordan, Syria, Lebanon, and parts of southwest Turkey. It is sometimes rendered into European languages as "Levant."

122 See, e.g., Richard King, *Orientalism and Religion: Post-Colonial Theory, India and "the Mystic East,"* Routledge, London and New York, 1999, pp. 13–14.

123 Gerges, *The Far Enemy*, pp. 26–27, 30–31, 114–115, 118, 294 et passim.

124 As analyzed in detail in Roy's *Globalized Islam*.

125 Atwan, *The Secret History of al Qaeda*, p. 220.

126 What follows is a summary of this document based on Atwan, *The Secret History of al Qaeda*, pp. 221–222.

127 Lia, *Architect of Global Jihad*, p. 315.

128 Atwan, *The Secret History of al Qaeda*, p. 222; this strategy was refined by the jihadist intellectual Abu Mus'ab al-Súri (b. 1958), who was arrested by Pakistani intelligence agents in October 2005 and who is now in U.S. custody. In particular, he advocated the creation of "phantom organizations consisting of self-sufficient cells acting independently of any central command"; see Lia, *Architect of Global Jihad*, p. 6.

129 Lia, *Architect of Global Jihad*, pp. 368–370.

130 Atwan, *The Secret History of al Qaeda*, p. 222.

131 Ibid., p. 221.

132 Roy, *Globalized Islam*, p. 325.

133 Al-Zayyat, *The Road to al-Qaeda*, pp. 93–102 and Gerges, *The Far Enemy*, pp. 284–305.

134 See, for instance, Oliver Roy, *The Failure of Political Islam* (trans. Carol Volk), Harvard University Press, Cambridge, MA, 1994, passim and idem, *Globalized Islam*, pp. 321–325; Kepel, *Jihad*, pp. 366–376.

135 The glossy image of "the virtual jihad state" has been actively promoted by the online English-language journal *Dabiq*, published by the Islamic State in Iraq and Syria; originally freely available online, it has now been censored by major Internet service providers.

136 Roy, *Globalized Islam*, p. 325.

137 Augustus Richard Norton, "Thwarted Politics: The Case of Egypt's Hizb al-Wasat," in Robert Hefner (ed.), *Remaking Muslim Politics: Pluralism, Contestation, Democratization*, Princeton University Press, Princeton, NJ, 2005, pp. 133–160 and 156–158 in particular.

138 For similar developments in Saudi Arabia see, Gwenn Okruhlik, "Empowering Civility Through Nationalism: Reformist Islam and Belonging in Saudi Arabia," in Hefner (ed.), *Remaking*, pp. 188–212.

139 To use the title of the book by Franz Fanon (1925–1961), one of the twentieth century's most important theorist of revolution, colonialism, and racial difference.

Bibliography

Abrahamov, Binyamin. *Islamic Theology: Traditionalism and Rationalism*. Edinburgh University Press, Edinburgh, 1998.

Abu Lughod, Lila. *Do Muslim Women Need Saving?* Harvard University Press, Cambridge MA, 2013.

Abu Rabi', Ibrahim. *Contemporary Arab Thought*. Pluto Press, London and Sterling, VA, 2004.

———. "Salat," in Esposito, John (ed.). *The Oxford Encyclopedia of the Modern Islamic World*. Oxford University Press, Oxford, 1995, vol. 3, pp. 469–473.

Adams, Charles. *Islam and Modernism in Egypt*. Reprint, Routledge, London and New York, 2000.

Adamson, Peter. "al-Kindi," in Adamson, Peter and Taylor, Richard (eds.). *The Cambridge Companion to Arabic Philosophy*. Cambridge University Press, Cambridge, 2004, pp. 32–51.

Adamson, Peter and Taylor, Richard (eds.). *The Cambridge Companion to Arabic Philosophy*. Cambridge University Press, Cambridge, 2004.

Agha, Saleh Said. *The Revolution that Toppled the Umayyads*. E.J. Brill, Leiden, 2003.

Ahmed, Leila. *A Quiet Revolution: The Veil's Resurgence, from the Middle East to America*. Yale University Press, New Haven, CT, 2013.

———. *Women and Gender in Islam: Historical Roots of a Modern Debate*. Yale University Press, New Haven, CT, 1992.

Ahmed, Shahab. *What Is Islam? The Importance of Being Islamic*. Princeton University Press, Princeton and Oxford, 2016.

Algar, Hamid (trans.). *Islam and Revolution: Writings and Declarations of Imam Khomeini*. Mizan Press, Berkeley, CA, 1981.

Alikberov, Alikber. *Epokha klassicheskogo islama na Kavkaze (The Epoch of Classical Islam in the Caucasus)*. Nauka, Moscow, 2003.

Amir-Moezzi, Mohammad. *The Divine Guide in Early Shi'ism*, trans. by David Speight. SUNY Press, Albany, NY, 1994.

Amirpur, Katajun. "A Doctrine in the Making? *Vilayat-e faqih* in Post-Revolutionary Iran" in Krämer, Gudrun and Schmidtke, Sabine (eds.). *Speaking for Islam: Religious Authorities in Muslim Societies*. E.J. Brill, Leiden and Boston, 2006, pp. 218–240.

Ankersen, Christopher and O'Leary, Michael (eds.). *Understanding Global Terror*. Polity Press, Malden, MA, 2007.

Ansari, Zafar. "Sawm," *Encyclopedia of Religion*. 2nd ed. Macmillan Reference, Detroit, 2005, vol. 12, p. 8141.

Arberry, Arthur J. (trans.). *Muslim Saints and Mystics*. Arcana, London and New York, 1990.

———. *Sufism: An Account of the Mystics of Islam*. George Allen and Unwin, London, 1950.

——— (trans.). *The Doctrine of the Sufis*. Reprint, Cambridge University Press, Cambridge, 1991.

———. *The Koran Interpreted*. Touchstone, New York, 1996.

Arjomand, Said Amir. "The Crisis of the Imamate and the Institution of Occultation in Twelver Shi'ism," in Kohlberg, Etan (ed.). *Shi'ism*. Ashgate-Variorum, Aldershot, UK, 2003, vol. 33, pp. 109–133.

———. "The Salience of Political Ethic in the Spread of Persianate Islam," *Journal of Persianate Studies*, vol. 1 (2008), pp. 5–29.

———. *The Shadow of God and the Hidden Imam*. University of Chicago Press, Chicago, IL, 1984.

———. *The Turban for the Crown: The Islamic Revolution in Iran*. Oxford University Press, Oxford, 1988.

Asad, Muhammad (trans.). *The Message of the Qur'an*. Dar al-Andalus, London Gibraltar, 1980.

Atwan, Abdel Bari. *The Secret History of al Qaeda*. Updated ed. University of California Press, Berkeley and Los Angeles, CA, 2008.

Awde, Nicholas (ed. and trans.). *Women in Islam: An Anthology from the Qur'an and Hadiths*. Hippocrene Books, New York, 2005.

Awn, Peter. *Satan's Tragedy and Redemption: Iblis in Sufi Psychology*. E.J. Brill, Leiden, 1983.

Ayoub, Mahmoud. *The Qur'an and Its Interpreters*. SUNY Press, Albany, NY, 1984.

Baer, Eva. "The Human Figure in Early Islamic Art," *Muqarnas*, vol. 16 (1999), pp. 32–41.

Banani, Amin and Hovannisian, Richard et al. (eds.). *Poetry and Mysticism in Islam*. Cambridge University Press, Cambridge, 1994.

Bar-Asher, Meir. *Scripture and Exegesis in Early Imami Shiism*. E.J. Brill, Leiden, 1999.

Barlas, Asma. "Women's Readings of the Qur'an," in McAuliffe, Jane (ed.). *The Cambridge Companion to the Qur'an*. Cambridge University Press, Cambridge, 2006, pp. 255–272.

Bashear, Suliman. "Riding Beasts on Divine Missions: An Examination of the Ass and Camel Traditions," *Journal of Semitic Studies*, vol. 37 (1991), pp. 37–75.

Bayhom-Daou, Tamima. *Shaykh Mufid*. Oneword, Oxford, 2005.

Bell, Richard. *The Origin of Islam in Its Christian Environment*. Cass, London, reprint, 1968.

Berkey, Jonathan. "Circumcision Circumscribed: Female Excision and Cultural Accommodation in the Medieval Near East," *International Journal of Middle East Studies*, vol. 28, no. 1 (1996), pp. 19–38.

———. *The Formation of Islam*. Cambridge University Press, Cambridge, 2003.

———. *The Transmission of Knowledge in Medieval Cairo*. Princeton University Press, Princeton, NJ, 1992.

Bienert, David. "The Concept of *jihad* in the Writings of Abdessalam Yassine," unpublished MPhil thesis. Oxford, Worcester College, 2007. Available online at http://users.ox.ac.uk/~metheses/Bienert%20Thesis.pdf.

Binder, Leonard. *Islamic Liberalism: A Critique of Development Ideologies*. University of Chicago Press, Chicago and London, 1988.

Blair, Sheila and Bloom, Jonathan. *The Art and Architecture of Islam: 1250–1800*. Yale University Press, New Haven, CT, 1994.

Blankenship, Khalid Y. *The End of the Jihâd State*. SUNY Press, Albany, NY, 1994.

Bloom, Jonathan (ed.). *Early Islamic Art and Architecture*. Ashgate-Variorum, Aldershot, UK, 2002.

Boase, Roger. *The Origin and Meaning of Courtly Love*. Manchester University Press, Manchester, 1977.

Bobrick, Benson. *The Caliph's Splendor: Islam and the West in the Golden Age of Baghdad*. Simon and Schuster, New York, 2012.

Bonner, Michael. *Jihad in Islamic History: Doctrines and Practice*. Princeton University Press, Princeton, NJ, 2006.

Böwering, Gerhard (ed.). *The Minor Qur'an Commentary of Abu 'Abd al-Rahman Muhammad b. al-Husayn al-Sulami (d. 412/1021)*. Dar al-Machreq, Beirut, 1995.

———. *The Mystical Vision of Existence in Classical Islam*. Walter de Gruyter, Berlin, 1980.

Brown, John. *The Darvishes or Oriental Mysticism*, ed. by H. A. Rose. Frank Cass, London, 1968.

Bukay, David. *From Muhammad to Bin Laden*. Transaction Publishers, New Brunswick and London, 2008.

Bulliet, Richard. *The Camel and the Wheel*. Columbia University Press, New York, 1990.

Burke, Jason. *Al-Qaeda: Casting the Shadow of Terror*. I.B. Tauris, London and New York, 2003.

Burton, John. *An Introduction to the Hadith*. Edinburgh University Press, Edinburgh, 1994.

Carré, Olivier. *Mysticism and Politics: A Critical Reading of Fi Zilal al-Qur'an by Sayyid Qutb (1906–1966)*. E. J. Brill, Leiden and Boston, 2003.

Chabbi, Jacqueline. "Réflexions sur le soufisme iranien primitif," *Journal Asiatique*, vol. 266, no. 1–2 (1978), pp. 37–55.

Chaghatai, M. Ikram (ed.). *Jamal al-Din al-Afghani: An Apostle of Islamic Resurgence*. Sang-e-Meel Publications, Lahore, 2005.

Chamberlain, Michael. "The Production of Knowledge and the Reproduction of the A'yan in Medieval Damascus," in Grandin, Nicole and Gaborieau, Marc (eds.). *Madrasa: La transmission du savoir dans le monde musulman*. Arguments, Paris, 1997, pp. 1–36.

Chittick, William. "Ibn 'Arabi and His School," in Nasr, Sayyed H. (ed.). *Islamic Spirituality: Manifestations*. Crossroad, New York, 1991, pp. 49–79.

————. *In Search of the Lost Heart: Explorations in Islamic Thought*. SUNY Press, Albany, NY, 2012.

————. "Rumi and *wahdat al-wujud*," in Banani, Amin and Hovannisian, Richard et al. (eds.). *Poetry and Mysticism in Islam*. Cambridge University Press, Cambridge, 1994, pp. 77–79.

———— (ed.). *The Inner Journey*. Morning Light Press, Sandpoint, ID, 2007.

————. *The Sufi Path of Knowledge*. SUNY Press, Albany, NY, 1989.

Choueiri, Youssef (ed.). *A Companion for the History of the Middle East*. Blackwell, Oxford, 2005.

Christmann, Andreas (trans. and ed.). *The Qur'an, Morality and Critical Reason: The Essential Muhammad Shahrur*. E.J. Brill, Leiden, 2009.

Cigar, Norman (trans.). *Al-Qa'ida's Doctrine for Insurgency: 'Abd Al-'Aziz Al-Muqrin's* A Practical Guide for Guerilla War. Potomac Books, Washington, DC, 2009.

Clarke, Richard. *Against All Enemies: Inside America's War on Terror*. Free Press, New York, 2004.

Cleveland, William. *A History of the Modern Middle East*. Westview Press, Boulder, CO, 2000.

Cole, Juan. *Napoléon's Egypt: Invading the Middle East*. Palgrave Macmillan, New York, 2007.

Commins, David. "Hasan al-Banna (1906–1949)," in Rahnema, Ali (ed.). *Pioneers of Islamic Revival*. Zed Books, London and New Jersey, 1994, pp. 125–153.

Cook, David. *Understanding Jihad*. University of California Press, Berkeley, CA, 2005.

Cook, Michael. *Ancient Religions, Modern Politics: The Islamic Case in Comparative Perspective*. Princeton University Press, Princeton, NJ and Oxford, 2014.

————. *Commanding Right and Forbidding Wrong in Islamic Thought*. Cambridge University Press, Cambridge, 2000.

Corbin, Henry. *Creative Imagination in the Sufism of Ibn 'Arabi*. Princeton University Press, Princeton, NJ, 1969.

Cornell, Vincent. *Realm of the Saint*. University of Texas Press, Austin, TX, 1998.

Coulson, Noel. *A History of Islamic Law*. Edinburgh University Press, Edinburgh, 1997.

Crawford, Michael. *Ibn 'Abd al-Wahhab*. Oneworld, London, 2014.

Cresswell, K. A. C. "The Lawfulness of Painting in Early Islam," in Bloom, Jonathan (ed.). *Early Islamic Art and Architecture*. Ashgate-Variorum, Aldershot, UK, 2002, pp. 101–108.

Crone, Patricia. *Meccan Trade and the Rise of Islam*. Princeton University Press, Princeton, NJ, 1987.

————. *Medieval Islamic Political Thought*. Edinburgh University Press, Edinburgh, 2004.

————. *Pre-Industrial Societies: Anatomy of the Pre-Modern World*. Oneworld, Oxford, 2003.

Crone, Patricia and Hinds, Martin. *God's Caliph: Religious Authority in the First Centuries of Islam*. Cambridge University Press, Cambridge, 1986.

Croutier, Alev Lytle. *Harem: The World Behind the Veil*. Abbeville Publishers, New York, 1989.

Daftary, Farhad. *Ismailis in Medieval Muslim Societies*. I.B. Tauris, London and New York, 2005.

————. "The Earliest Isma'ilis," in Kohlberg, Etan (ed.). *Shi'ism*. Ashgate-Variorum, Aldershot, UK, 2003, pp. 235–266.

————. *The Isma'ilis: Their History and Doctrines*. Cambridge University Press, Cambridge, 1990.

Daniel, Norman. *Islam and the West*. Oneworld, Oxford, 1997.

Denny, Frederick. *An Introduction to Islam*. 3rd ed. Pearson and Prentice Hall, Upper Saddle River, NJ, 2006.

Donner, Fred. *The Early Islamic Conquests*. Princeton University Press, Princeton, NJ, 1981.

Dresch, Paul. *Tribes, Government and History in Yemen*. Clarendon Press, Oxford, 1989.

Eickelman, Dale. "Foreword," in Christmann, Andreas (trans. and ed.). *The Qur'an, Morality and Critical Reason: The Essential Muhammad Shahrur*. E.J. Brill, Leiden, 2009, pp. vii–xii.

————. "Inside the Islamic Reformation," in Rubin, Barry (ed.). *Revolutionaries and Reformers: Contemporary Islamist Movements in the Middle East*. SUNY Press, Albany, NY, 2003, pp. 203–206.

————. "Rites of Passage: Muslim Rites," *Encyclopedia of Religion*. Macmillan Reference, Detroit, 2005, vol. 11, pp. 7824–7828.

Eickelman, Dale and Piscatori, James. *Muslim Politics*. Princeton University Press, Princeton, NJ, 1996.

El-Bizri, Nader. "God: Essence and Attributes," in Winter, Tim (ed.). *The Cambridge Companion to Classical Islamic Theology*. Cambridge University Press, Cambridge, 2008, pp. 121–140.

Eliash, Joseph. "On the Genesis and Development of the Twelver-Shi'i Three-Tenet *shahada*," in Hawting, Gerald (ed.). *The Development of Islamic Ritual*. Ashgate-Variorum, Aldershot, UK, 2006, pp. 24–30.

Emerson, Steven. *Jihad Incorporated*. Prometheus Books, Amherst, NY, 2006.

Encyclopaedia of Islam. 2nd ed., 12 vols. E.J. Brill, Leiden, 1960–2009 and the online edition at http://www.brillonline.nl.

Encyclopedia of the Quran. 6 vols. E.J. Brill, Leiden, 2001–2006 and the online edition at http://www.brillonline.nl.

Encyclopedia of Religion. 2nd ed., 15 vols. Macmillan Reference, Detroit, 2005.

Encyclopedia of Women and Islamic Cultures. 6 vols. E.J. Brill, Leiden, 2003–2007, and the online edition at http://www.brillonline.nl.

Ernst, Carl. *Eternal Garden: Mysticism, History, and Politics at a South Asian Sufi Center*. SUNY Press, Albany, NY, 1992.

———. *The Shambhala Guide to Sufism*. Shambhala Publications, Boston, MA, 1997.

Esposito, John. *Islam: The Straight Path*. 5th ed. Oxford University Press, Oxford and New York, 2016.

———. *The Oxford Encyclopedia of the Modern Islamic World*. Oxford University Press, Oxford, 1995.

Esposito, John and Voll, John. *Makers of Contemporary Islam*. Oxford University Press, Oxford, 2001.

Ettinghausen, Richard, Grabar, Oleg and Jenkins-Madina, Marilyn. *Islamic Art and Architecture*. Yale University Press, New Haven, CT, 2001.

Euben, Roxanne and Zaman, Muhammad Qasim (eds.). *Princeton Readings in Islamist Thought: Texts and Contexts from al-Banna to Bin Ladin*. Princeton University Press, Princeton, NJ, 2009.

Fakhry, Majid. *A History of Islamic Philosophy*. 3rd ed. Columbia University Press, New York, 2004.

———. "Ibn Rushd," *Encyclopedia of Religion*. Macmillan Reference, Detroit, 2005, vol. 6, p. 4272.

Fernandes, Leonor. *The Evolution of a Sufi Institution in Mamluk Egypt: The khanqah*. K. Schwartz, Berlin, 1988.

Firestone, Reuven. *Jihad: The Origin of Holy War in Islam*. Oxford University Press, Oxford, 1999.

Fisher, Greg (ed.). *Arabs and Empires Before Islam*. Oxford University Press, Oxford, 2015.

Frank, Richard. *Beings and Their Attributes*. SUNY Press, Albany, NY, 1978.

Frye, Richard. *Ibn Fadlan's Journey to Russia*. 2nd ed. Markus Wiener, Princeton, NJ, 2006.

Fueck, Johann. "The Role of Traditionalism in Islam," in Swartz, Merlin (trans. and ed.). *Studies on Islam*. Oxford University Press, Oxford, 1981, pp. 99–122.

Gammer, Moshe. *Muslim Resistance to the Tsar*. Frank Cass, London, 1994.

Geaves, Ron, Dressler, Markus and Klinkhammer, Gritt (eds.). *Sufis in Western Society*, Routledge, London and New York, 2009.

Gerges, Fawaz. *The Far Enemy: Why Jihad Went Global*. 2nd ed. Cambridge University Press, Cambridge, 2009.

Gibbon, Edward. *The History of the Decline and Fall of the Roman Empire*. 3 vols. Allen Lane/The Penguin Press, London, 1994.

Al-Ghazali, Muhammad (d. 1111). *Abstinence in Islam,* trans. by Caesar Farah. Biblioteca Islamica, Minneapolis, 1992.

———. *The Alchemy of Happiness*. Ashraf, Lahore, 1964.

Al-Ghazáli, Muhammad (d. 1986). *Kayfa nafham al-Islam* ("How Do We Understand Islam?"). Nahdat Misr, Cairo, 2005.

Goitein, Shelomo D. "Ramadan, the Month of Fasting," in Hawting, Gerald (ed.). *The Development of Islamic Ritual*. Ashgate-Variorum, Aldershot, UK, 2006, pp. 151–171.

Grabar, Oleg. "The Umayyad Dome of the Rock in Jerusalem," in Bloom, Jonathan (ed.). *Early Islamic Art and Architecture*, Ashgate-Variorum, Aldershot, UK, 2002, pp. 223–256.

Graham, William. *Divine Word and Prophetic Word in Early Islam*. Mouton, The Hague, 1977.

Grandin, Nicole and Gaborieau, Marc (eds.). *Madrasa: La transmission du savoir dans le monde musulman*. Arguments, Paris, 1997.

Guillaume, Alfred (trans.). *The Life of Muhammad*. Oxford University Press, Oxford and Karachi, 1982.

Gurnah, Abdulrazak (ed.). *The Cambridge Companion to Salman Rushdie*. Cambridge University Press, Cambridge, 2007.

Haddad, Yvonne. *Islamists and the Challenge of Pluralism*. Center for Contemporary Arab Studies, Georgetown University, Washington, DC, 1995.

Haim, Sylvia (ed.). *Arab Nationalism*. University of California Press, Berkeley, CA, 1962.

Hallaq, Wael. *A History of Islamic Legal Theories*. Cambridge University Press, Cambridge, 1997.

———. "On Orientalism, Self-Consciousness and History," *Islamic Law and Society*, vol. 18 (2011), pp. 387–439.

———. *Shari'a: Theory, Practice, Transformations*. Cambridge University Press, Cambridge, 2009.

Halm, Heinz. *Shiism*. Edinburgh University Press, Edinburgh, 1991.

———. *Shi'ism*. 2nd ed., trans. by J. Watson and M. Hill. Columbia University Press, New York, 2004.

———. *The Empire of the Mahdi: The Rise of the Fatimids*, trans. by Michael Bonner. E.J. Brill, Leiden, 1996.

———. *The Fatimids and Their Traditions of Learning*. I.B. Tauris, London, 1997.

Hawting, Gerald R. (ed.). *The Development of Islamic Ritual*. Ashgate-Variorum, Aldershot, UK, 2006.

———. *The First Dynasty of Islam*. Southern Illinois University Press, Carbondale and Edwardsville, 1987.

Haykel, Bernard. *Revival and Reform in Islam: The Legacy of Muhammad al-Shawkani*. Cambridge University Press, Cambridge, 2003.

Heath, Peter. *Allegory and Philosophy in Avicenna (Ibn Sina)*. University of Pennsylvania Press, Philadelphia, 1992.

Heck, Gene. *Islam, Inc.: An Early Business History*. Kind Faisal Center for Research and Islamic Studies, Riyadh, 2004.

Heer, Nicholas (ed.). *The Precious Pearl: al-Jami's al-Durrah al-fakhirah*. SUNY Press, Albany, NY, 1979.

Hefner, Robert (ed.). *Remaking Muslim Politics: Pluralism, Contestation, Democratization*. Princeton University Press, Princeton, NJ, 2005.

Hewitt, Nancy (ed.). *A Companion to American Women's History*. Blackwell, Oxford, 2005.

Hillenbrand, Carole. *The Crusades: Islamic Perspectives*. Fitzroy Dearborn Publishers, Chicago and London, 1999.

Hillenbrand, Robert. "*La dolce vita* in Early Islamic Syria," in Bloom, Jonathan (ed.). *Early Islamic Art and Architecture*. Ashgate-Variorum, Aldershot, UK, 2002, pp. 333–371.

Hirsi Ali, Ayaan. *Heretic: Why Islam Needs a Reformation Now*. Harper, New York, 2015.

Hirtenstein, Stephen and Tiernan, Michael (eds.). *Muhyiddin Ibn 'Arabi: A Commemorative Volume*. Element, Brisbane, 1993.

Hodgson, Marshall. *The Venture of Islam*. 3 vols. The University of Chicago Press, Chicago, 1974.

Holt, Peter, Lambton, Ann and Lewis, Bernard (eds.). *The Cambridge History of Islam*. Vol. 1. *The Central Islamic Lands*. Cambridge University Press, Cambridge, 1970.

Hourani, Albert. *A History of the Arab Peoples*. Harvard University Press, Cambridge, MA, 1991.

———. *Arabic Thought in the Liberal Age, 1798–1939*. Oxford University Press, Oxford, 1970.

Housley, Norman. *Contesting the Crusades*. Blackwell, Oxford, 2006.

Hovannisian, Richard and Sabagh, Georges (eds.). *The Persian Presence in the Islamic World*. Cambridge University Press, Cambridge, 1998.

Hunter, Shireen (ed.). *Reformist Voices of Islam: Mediating Islam and Modernity*. M.E. Sharpe, Armonk, NY, 2009.

Hurgronje, Snouck. "On the Institution of *zakat*," in Hawting, Gerald (ed.). *The Development of Islamic Ritual*. Ashgate-Variorum, Aldershot, UK, 2006, pp. 239–261.

Hurvitz, Nimrod. *The Formation of Hanbalism*. Routledge and Curzon, Oxon and New York, 2002.

Hussain, Jassim. *The Occultation of the Twelfth Imam*. The Muhammadi Trust, London, 1982.

Ibn Khaldún. *The Muqaddimah: An Introduction to History*. 3 vols., trans. by Frantz Rosenthal. Columbia University Press, New York, 1958.

Ibrahim, Saad Eddin. "Anatomy of Egypt's Militant Islamic Groups: Methodological Note and Preliminary Findings," *International Journal of Middle East Studies*, vol. 12 (1980), pp. 423–453.

Isutsu, Toshihiko. *Ethico-Religious Concepts in the Qur'an*. McGill University Press, Montreal, 1966.

Jackson, Peter and Lockhart, Laurence (eds.). *The Cambridge History of Iran*. Cambridge University Press, Cambridge, 1986.

Jansen, Johannes. *The Dual Nature of Islamic Fundamentalism*. Hurst and Co., London, 1997.

———. *The Interpretation of the Koran in Modern Egypt*. E.J. Brill, Leiden, 1974.

Jomier, Jacque. *Le commentaire coranique du Manâr*. G.-P. Maisonneuve, Paris, 1954.

de Jong, Frederick. *Turuq and Turuq-linked Institutions in Nineteenth-century Egypt.* E.J. Brill, Leiden, 1978.

de Jong, Frederick and Radtke, Bernd (eds.). *Islamic Mysticism Contested.* E.J. Brill, Leiden, 1999.

Judd, Steven. *Religious Scholars and the Umayyads.* Routledge, London and New York, 2014.

―――. "The Third *Fitna*: Orthodoxy, Heresy and Coercion in Late Umayyad History," unpublished Ph.D. dissertation, University of Michigan, Ann Arbor, 1997.

Juynboll, Gautier. *Encyclopedia of Canonical Hadith.* E.J. Brill, Leiden, 2007.

Kadri, Aissa (ed.). *Parcours d'intellectuels maghrébins.* Karthala, Paris, 1999.

Karamustafa, Ahmet. *God's Unruly Friends.* University of Utah Press, Salt Lake City, UT, 1994.

Keddie, Nikki. *An Islamic Response to Imperialism.* University of California Press, Berkeley, CA, 1983.

―――. *Sayyid Jamal ad-Din "al-Afghani": A Political Biography.* University of California Press, Berkeley, CA, 1972.

―――. "Sayyid Jamal al-Din 'al-Afghani,' " in Rahnema, Ali (ed.). *Pioneers of Islamic Revival.* Zed Books, London and New Jersey, 1994, pp. 11–29.

Kedourie, Elie. *Afghani and Abduh.* 2nd ed. Frank Cass, London and Portland, OR, 1997.

Kennedy, Hugh. *The Prophet and the Age of the Caliphates.* Longman, London and New York, 1986.

Kepel, Gilles. *Jihad: The Trail of Political Islam.* The Belknap Press, Cambridge, MA, 2002.

Kepel, Gilles and Milelli, Jean-Pierre (eds.). *Al Qaeda in Its Own Words*, trans. by Pascale Ghalaleh. Belknap Press, Cambridge, MA and London, 2008.

Khalidi, Tarif. *Classical Arab Islam: The Culture and Heritage of the Golden Age.* Darwin Press, Princeton, NJ, 1985.

King, Richard. *Orientalism and Religion: Post-colonial Theory, India and "the Mystic East."* Routledge, London and New York, 1999.

Klausen, Jytte. *The Cartoons that Shook the World.* Yale University Press, New Haven, CT, 2009.

Klemm, Verena. "The Four *sufara'* of the Twelfth Imam: On the Formative Period of the Twelver Shi'a," in Kohlberg, Etan (ed.). *Shi'ism.* Ashgate-Variorum, Aldershot, UK, 2003, pp. 135–152.

Knysh, Alexander. "A Clear and Present Danger: 'Wahhabism' as a Rhetorical Foil," *Die Welt des Islams*, vol. 44, no. 1 (2004), pp. 3–26.

―――― (trans.). *Al-Qushayri's Epistle on Sufism.* Garnet Publishing, Reading, UK, 2007.

―――. "Contextualizing the Sufi-Salafi Conflict (from the Northern Caucasus to Hadramawt)," *Middle Eastern Studies*, vol. 43, no.4 (2007), pp. 503–530.

―――. "Historiography of Sufi Studies in the West," in Choueiri, Youssef (ed.). *A Companion for the History of the Middle East.* Blackwell, Oxford, 2005, pp. 106–131.

―――. *Ibn 'Arabi in the Later Islamic Tradition.* SUNY Press, Albany, NY, 1999.

―――. " *'Irfan* Revisited: Khomeini and the Legacy of Islamic Mystical Philosophy," *Middle East Journal*, vol. 46 (Autumn 1992), pp. 631–653.

―――――. "Islam and Arabic as the Rhetoric of Insurgency: The Case of the Caucasus Emirate," *Studies in Conflict and Terrorism*, vol. 35, no. 4 (2012), pp. 315–337.

―――. *Islamic Mysticism: A Short History.* 2nd ed. E.J. Brill, Leiden and Boston, 2010.

―――. "Multiple Areas of Influence," in McAuliffe, Jane (ed.). *Cambridge Companion to the Qur'an.* Cambridge University Press, Cambridge, 2006, pp. 211–233.

―――. "The *tariqa* on a Landcruiser: The Resurgence of Sufism in Yemen," *Middle East Journal*, vol. 55, no. 3 (2001), pp. 399–414.

Kohlberg, Etan. "From Imamiyya to Ithna 'Ashariyya," *Bulletin of the School of Oriental and African Studies*, vol. 39 (1976), pp. 521–534.

―――(ed.). *Shi'ism.* Ashgate-Variorum, Aldershot, UK, 2003.

Kraemer, Joel. *Humanism in the Renaissance of Islam: The Cultural Revival during the Buyid Age.* E.J. Brill, Leiden, 1992.

Kramer, Martin. *Islam Assembled.* Columbia University Press, New York, 1986.

Krämer, Gudrun. "Drawing Boundaries: Yusuf al-Qaradawi on Apostasy," in Krämer, Gudrun and Schmidtke, Sabine (eds.). *Speaking for Islam: Religious Authorities in Muslim Societies.* E.J. Brill, Leiden and Boston, 2006, pp. 181–217.

―――. *Hasan al-Banna.* Oneworld, Oxford, 2010.

————. "Techniques and Values: Contemporary Muslim Debates on Islam and Democracy," in Martín Muños, Gema (ed.). *Islam, Modernism and the West*. I.B. Tauris, London and New York, 1999, pp. 174–190.

Krämer, Gudrun and Schmidtke, Sabine (eds.). *Speaking for Islam: Religious Authorities in Muslim Societies*. E.J. Brill, Leiden and Boston, 2006.

al-Kulayni (or al-Kulini). *Al-Usul al-Kafi*. 7 vols. Matba'at al-Haydari, Tehran, 1955.

Küng, Hans. *Islam: Past, Present and Future*, trans. by John Bowden. Oneworld, Oxford, 2007.

Kurzman, Charles (ed.). *Liberal Islam: A Sourcebook*. Oxford University Press, Oxford, 1998.

————. *Modernist Islam (1840–1940): A Textbook*. Oxford University Press, Oxford, 2002.

Landolt, Hermann. "Al-Ghazali and Religionswissenschaft," *Asiatische Studien*, vol. 55, no. 1 (1991), pp. 19–72.

Lapidus, Ira. *A History of Islamic Societies*. Cambridge University Press, Cambridge, 1999.

Lawrence, Bruce (ed.). *Messages to the World: The Statements of Osama Bin Laden*. Verso, London, 2005.

Lawson, Todd (ed.). *Reason and Inspiration in Islam*. I.B. Tauris, London and New York, 2005.

Lazarus-Yafeh, Hava. "The Religious Dialectics of the *hadjdj*," in Hawting, Gerald (ed.). *The Development of Islamic Ritual*. Ashgate-Variorum, Aldershot, UK, 2006, pp. 263–283.

Leaman, Oliver. *An Introduction to Classical Islamic Philosophy*. Cambridge University Press, Cambridge, 2002.

Leiser, Gary. "The Madrasah and the Islamization of Anatolia before the Ottomans," in Lowry, Joseph, Stewart, Devin and Toorawa, Shawkat (eds.). *Law and Education in Medieval Islam*. Gibb Memorial Trust, Chippenham, UK, 2004, pp. 174–191.

Levering Lewis, David. *God's Crucible: Islam and the Making of Europe 570 to 1215*. W.W. Norton, New York and London, 2008.

Levtzion, Nehemia and Voll, John (eds.). *Eighteenth-Century Renewal and Reform in Islam*. Syracuse University Press, Syracuse, NY, 1987.

Lewis, Bernard. *The Muslim Discovery of Europe*. W.W. Norton, New York and London, 1982.

Lia, Brynar. *Architect of Global Jihad: The Life of al-Qaida Strategist Abu Mus'ab al-Suri*. Columbia University Press, New York, 2008.

Lindsay, James. *Daily Life in the Medieval Islamic World*. Greenwood Press, Westport, CT, 2005.

Lowry, Joseph, Stewart, Devin and Toorawa, Shawkat (eds.). *Law and Education in Medieval Islam*. Gibb Memorial Trust, Chippenham, UK, 2004.

Madden, Thomas. *The New History of the Crusades*. Rowman and Littlefield Publishers, Lanham, 2006.

Madelung, Wilferd. *The Succession to Muhammad: A Study of the Early Caliphate*. Cambridge University Press, Cambridge, 1997.

Makdisi, George. *The Rise of Colleges*. Edinburgh University Press, Edinburgh, 1981.

Marmura, Michael. "Falsafah," in *Encyclopedia of Religion*. 2nd ed. Macmillan Reference, Detroit, 2005, vol. 5, p. 2970–2978.

Martín Muños, Gema (ed.). *Islam, Modernism and the West*. I.B. Tauris, London and New York, 1999.

Martin, Richard. *Islamic Studies: A History of Religions Approach*. 2nd ed. Prentice Hall, Upper Saddle River, NJ, 1996.

Martin, Richard and Barzegar, Abbas (eds.). *Islamism: Contested Perspectives on Political Islam*. Stanford University Press, Stanford, CA, 2010.

Martin, Richard and Woodward, Mark. *Defenders of Reason in Islam*. Oneworld, Oxford, 1997.

Martin, Vanessa. *Creating an Islamic State: Khomeini and the Making of a New Iran*. I.B. Tauris, London, 2000.

Massignon, Louis. "La legende 'De Tribus Impostoribus' et ses origins islamiques," in Moubarac, Youakim (ed.). *Opera Minora*. Presses universitaires de France, Paris, 1969, vol. 1, pp. 82–84.

Matthee, Rudi. "Jamal al-Din al-Afghani and the Egyptian National Debate," in Chaghatai, M. Ikram (ed.). *Jamal al-Din al-Afghani: An Apostle of Islamic Resurgence*. Sang-e-Meel Publications, Lahore, 2005, pp. 325–348.

McAuliffe, Jane (ed.). *Cambridge Companion to the Qur'an*. Cambridge University Press, Cambridge, 2006.

McGinnis, Jon and Reisman, David (ed., trans. and annotation). *Classical Arabic Philosophy*. Hackett Publishing Company, Indianapolis, 2007.

McNeill, William and Waldman, Marilyn (eds.). *The Islamic World.* University of Chicago Press, Chicago and London, 1983.

Meier, Fritz. *Essays on Islamic Piety and Mysticism*, trans. and ed. by O'Kane, John and Radtke, Bernd. E.J. Brill, Leiden and Boston, 1999.

Meijer, Roel. "Yusuf al-'Uyairi and the Making of a Revolutionary Salafi Praxis," *Die Welt des Islams*, vol. 47, nos. 3–4 (2007), pp. 422–459.

Melchert, Christopher. *The Formation of the Sunni Schools of Law, 9th–10th centuries C.E.* E.J. Brill, Leiden, 1997.

Mitchell, Richard. *The Society of the Muslim Brothers.* Oxford University Press, Oxford, 1993.

Mitchell, Timothy. "McJihad: Islam in the U.S. Global Order," *Social Text*, vol. 73, no. 4 (Winter 2002), pp. 1–18.

Moin, Baqer. "Khomeini's Search for Perfection: Theory and Reality," in Rahnema, Ali (ed.). *Pioneers of Islamic Revival.* Zed Books, London and New Jersey, 1994, pp. 64–97.

Momen, Moojan. *An Introduction to Shi'i Islam.* Yale University Press, New Haven, CT, 1985.

Morris, James. "How to study the *Futuhat*," in Hirtenstein, Stephen and Tiernan, Michael (eds.). *Muhyiddin Ibn 'Arabi: A Commemorative Volume.* Element, Brisbane, 1993, pp. 73–89.

Mottahedeh, Roy. "The Transmission of Learning: The Role of the Islamic North-East," in Grandin, Nicole and Gaborieau, Marc (eds.). *Madrasa: La transmission du savoir dans le monde musulman.* Arguments, Paris, 1997, pp. 63–72.

Murata, Sachiko and Chittick, William. *The Vision of Islam.* Paragon House, New York, 1994.

Murawiec, Laurent. *The Mind of Jihad.* Cambridge University Press, Cambridge, 2008.

Myerhoff, Barbara, Camino, Linda and Turner, Edith. "Rites of Passage," in *Encyclopedia of Religion.* 2nd ed. Macmillan Reference, Detroit, 2005, vol. 11, pp. 7796–7800.

Nagel, Tilman. *The History of Islamic Theology*, trans. by Thomas Thornton. Markus Wiener Publishers, Princeton, NJ, 2000.

Nasr, Sayyed H. (ed.). *Islamic Spirituality: Manifestations.* Crossroad, New York, 1991.

Nasr, Seyyed Vali Reza. "Mawdudi and the Jama'at-i Islami," in Rahnema, Ali (ed.). *Pioneers of Islamic Revival.* Zed Books, London and New Jersey, 1994, pp. 98–124.

———. *Mawdudi and the Making of Islamic Revivalism.* Oxford University Press, Oxford, 1996.

Nicholson, Reynold (ed.). *The Kitab al-luma' fi 'l-tasawwuf of Abu Nasr Abdallah ibn Ali al-Sarraj.* E. J Brill, Leiden and London, 1914.

Norton, Augustus Richard. "Thwarted Politics: The Case of Egypt's Hizb al-Wasat," in Hefner, Robert (ed.). *Remaking Muslim Politics: Pluralism, Contestation, Democratization.* Princeton University Press, Princeton, NJ, 2005, pp. 133–160.

Okruhlik, Gwenn. "Empowering Civility through Nationalism: Reformist Islam and Belonging in Saudi Arabia," in Hefner, Robert (ed.). *Remaking Muslim Politics: Pluralism, Contestation, Democratization.* Princeton University Press, Princeton, NJ, 2005, pp. 188–212.

O'Shea, Stephen. *Sea of Faith: Islam and Christianity in the Medieval Mediterranean World.* Douglas and McIntyre, Vancouver and Toronto, 2006.

Özcan, Azmi (ed.). *Pan-Islamism: Indian Muslims, the Ottomans and Britain. 1877–1924.* E.J. Brill, Leiden and Boston, 1997.

Padwick, Constance. *Muslim Devotions: A Study of Prayer Manuals in Common Use.* SPCK, London, 1961.

Paret, Rudi. *Der Koran: Kommentar und Konkordanz.* Verlag W. Kohlhammer, Stuttgart, 1971.

Peirce, Leslie. *The Imperial Harem: Women and Sovereignty in the Ottoman Empire.* Oxford University Press, Oxford, 1993.

Peskes, Esther. "The Wahhabiyya and Sufism in the Eighteenth Century," in de Jong, Frederick and Radtke, Bernd (eds.). *Islamic Mysticism Contested.* E.J. Brill, Leiden, 1999, pp. 145–161.

Peters, Frederick. *The Hajj.* Princeton University Press, Princeton, NJ, 1994.

Pourjavady, Nasrollah. "Opposition to Sufism in Twelver Shiism" in de Jong, Frederick and Radtke, Bernd (eds.). *Islamic Mysticism Contested.* E.J. Brill, Leiden and Boston, 1999, pp. 614–623.

Powers, David. "The Exegetical Genre *nasikh al-Qur'an wa mansukhuhu*," in Rippin, Andrew (ed.). *Approaches to the History of the Interpretation of the Qur'an.* Clarendon Press, Oxford, 1988, pp. 117–138.

Qutb, Sayyid. *Milestones.* The Mother Mosque Foundation, Cedar Rapids, IA (no date).

Radtke, Bernd. "Theologen und Mystiker in Hurasan und Transoxanien," *Zeitschrift der Deutschen Morgenländischen Gesellschaft*, vol. 136, no. 1 (1986), pp. 536–569.

Rahman, Fazlur. *Major Themes of the Qur'an*. 2nd ed. Bibliotheca Islamica, Minneapolis, MN, 1989.

Rahnema, Ali (ed.). *Pioneers of Islamic Revival*. Zed Books, London and New Jersey, 1994.

Reinert, Benedict. *Die Lehre vom tawakkul in der klassischen Sufik*. Walter de Gruyter, Berlin, 1968.

Reston, James. *Warriors of God: Richard the Lionheart and Saladin in the Third Crusade*. Doubleday, New York, 2001.

Reynolds, Gabriel Said. *The Qur'an and Its Biblical Subtext*. Routledge, New York, 2010.

Richards, Donald (trans.). *The Chronicle of Ibn al-Athir for the Crusading Period*. Ashgate, Aldershot, UK, 2006.

Riley-Smith, Jonathan. *What Were the Crusades?* Ignatius Press, San Francisco, 2002.

Rippin, Andrew (ed.). *Approaches to the History of the Interpretation of the Qur'an*. Clarendon Press, Oxford, 1988.

———. *Muslims: Their Religious Beliefs and Practices*. Routledge, London and New York, 1990.

——— (ed.). *The Blackwell Companion to the Qur'an*. Blackwell, Oxford, 2006.

Roy, Olivier. *Globalized Islam: The Search for a New Ummah*. Columbia University Press, New York, 2004.

———. *The Failure of Political Islam*, trans. by Carol Volk. Harvard University Press, Cambridge, MA, 1994.

Rubin, Barry (ed.). *Revolutionaries and Reformers: Contemporary Islamist Movements in the Middle East*. SUNY Press, Albany, NY, 2003.

Sachedina, Abdulaziz. *The Just Ruler in Shi'ite Islam*. Oxford University Press, Oxford, 1988.

Saeed, Abdullah. *Interpreting the Qur'an: Towards a Contemporary Approach*. Routledge, London, 2006.

Sageman, Marc. *Understanding Terror Networks*. University of Pennsylvania Press, Philadelphia, PA, 2004.

Sagiv, David. *Fundamentalism and Intellectuals in Egypt, 1973–1993*. Frank Cass, London, 1995.

Sale, George (trans.). *The Koran, Commonly Called the Alcoran of Mohommed*. O. Hodgson, London, 1838.

Saunders, John Joseph. *A History of Medieval Islam*. Reprint. Routledge, London and New York, 1990.

Savory, Roger. *Introduction to Islamic Civilisation*. Cambridge University Press, Cambridge, 1976.

Schanzer, Jonathan. *Al-Qaeda's Armies: Middle East Affiliate Groups and the Next Generation of Terror*. Specialist Press International, New York, 2005.

Schimmel, Annemarie. "Islamic Calligraphy," in *Encyclopedia of Religions*. Macmillan Reference, Detroit, 2005, vol. 3, pp. 1372–1373.

———. *Mystical Dimensions of Islam*. University of North Carolina, Chapel Hill, NC, 1975.

Schmidtke, Sabine. "Theological Rationalism in the Medieval World of Islam," *al-'Usur al-Wusta*, vol. 20, no. 1 (2008), pp. 17–28.

Sedgwick, Mark. "Sufis as 'Good Muslims,'" in Ridgeon, Lloyd (ed.). *Sufis and Salafis in the Contemporary Age*. Bloomsbury Academics, London and New York, 2015, pp. 105–118.

Seguy, Marie-Rose. *The Miraculous Journey of Mahomet*. G. Braziller, New York, 1977.

Sells, Michael. *Approaching the Qur'an: The Early Revelations*. White Cloud Press, Ashland, OR, 1999.

Shahid, Irfan. *Byzantium and the Arabs in the Sixth Century*. 2 vols. Dumbarton Oaks Research Library and Collection, Washington, DC, 1995.

Sharon, Moshe. *Revolt: The Social and Military Aspects of the 'Abbasid Revolution*. The Hebrew University Press, Jerusalem, 1990.

al-Sheikh, Abdallah. "Zakat," in *The Oxford Encyclopedia of the Modern Islamic World*. Oxford University Press, Oxford, 1995, vol. 4, pp. 366–370.

Shepard, William (trans.). *Sayyid Qutb and Islamic Activism: A Translation and Critical Analysis of "Social Justice in Islam."* E.J. Brill, Leiden, 1996.

Siddiqi, Muzammil and Kassam, Tazim. "Salat," in *Encyclopedia of Religion*. 2nd ed. Macmillan Reference, Detroit, 2005, vol. 12, pp. 8054–8058.

Smith, Jonathan. *Imagining Religion: From Babylon to Jonestown*. University of Chicago Press, Chicago, IL, 1988.

Smith, Margaret. *Rabi'a the Mystic and Her Fellow-Saints in Islam*. Reprint. Cambridge University Press, Cambridge, 1984.

———. *Studies in Early Mysticism in the Near and Middle East*. 2nd ed. Oneworld, Oxford, 1995.

Souaiaia, Ahmed. *Contesting Justice: Women, Islam, Law, and Society*. SUNY Press, Albany, NY, 2008.

Spellberg, Denise. *Politics, Gender and the Islamic Past: The Legacy of 'A'isha bint Abi Bakr*. Columbia University Press, New York, 1994.

Springer, David, Regens, James and Edger, David. *Islamic Radicalism and Global Jihad*. Georgetown University Press, Washington, DC, 2009.

Steigerwald, Diana. "Isma'ili *ta'wil*," in Rippin, Andrew (ed.). *The Blackwell Companion to the Qur'an*, Blackwell, Oxford, 2006, pp. 386–400.

Stewart, Devin. "The Doctorate of Islamic Law in Mamluk Egypt and Syria," in Lowry, Joseph, Stewart, Devin and Toorawa, Shawkat (eds.). *Law and Education in Medieval Islam*. Gibb Memorial Trust, Chippenham, UK, 2004, pp. 45–90.

Stowasser, Barbara. *Women in the Qur'an, Traditions, and Interpretation*. Oxford University Press, Oxford, 1994.

Strenski, Ivan. *Thinking about Religion*. Blackwell Publishing, Oxford, 2006.

Stroumsa, Sarah. *Freethinkers of Medieval Islam*. E.J. Brill, Leiden, 1999.

Swartz, Merlin (trans. and ed.). *Studies on Islam*. Oxford University Press, Oxford, 1981.

al-Tabari, Muhammad b. Jarir. *The History of al-Tabari*. Vol. 16. *The Community Divided*, trans. and annotated by Adrian Brockett. SUNY Press, Albany, NY, 1997.

———. *The History of al-Tabari*. Vol. 17. *The First Civil War*, trans. and annotated by G. R. Hawting. SUNY Press, Albany, NY, 1996.

———. *The History of al-Tabari*. Vol. 22. *The Marwanid Restoration*, trans. and annotated by Everett Rowson. SUNY Press, Albany, NY, 1989.

———. *The History of al-Tabari*. Vol. 27. *The 'Abbasid Revolution*, trans. and annotated by John Williams. SUNY Press, Albany, NY, 1985.

———. *The History of al-Tabari*. Vol. 32. *Reunification of the 'Abbasid Caliphate*, trans. and annotated by C.E. Bosworth. SUNY Press, Albany, NY, 1987.

Takim, Liyakat. *The Heirs to the Prophet: Charisma and Religious Authority in Shi'ite Islam*. SUNY Press, Albany, NY, 2006.

Tamimi, Azzam. *Rachid Ghannouchi: A Democrat within Islamism*. Oxford University Press, Oxford, 2001.

Tazmini, Ghoncheh. *Revolution and Reform in Russia and Iran: Modernisation and Politics in Revolutionary States*. I.B. Tauris, London and New York, 2012.

Tibi, Bassam. *Political Islam, World Politics and Europe*. Routledge, London and New York, 2008.

Traboulsi, Samer. "The Queen Was Actually a Man," *Arabica*, vol. 50, no. 1 (2003), pp. 96–108.

Trimingham, James S. *Sufi Orders in Islam*. 2nd ed. Oxford University Press, Oxford, 1998.

Turner, John. *Inquisition in Early Islam: The Competition for Political and Religious Authority in the Abbasid Empire*. I.B. Tauris, London and New York, 2013.

Tyerman, Christopher. *God's War: A New History of the Crusades*. Harvard University Press, Cambridge, MA, 2006.

Vajda, Georges. "Fasting in Islam and Judaism," in Hawting, Gerald (ed.). *The Development of Islamic Ritual*. Ashgate-Variorum, Aldershot, UK, 2006, pp. 133–149.

Van Bruinessen, Martin and Howell, Julia Day (eds.). *Sufism and the 'Modern' in Islam*. I.B. Tauris, London and New York, 2013.

Van den Bos, Matthijs. *Mystic Regimes: Sufism and State in Iran*. E.J. Brill, Leiden, 2002.

Van Ess, Josef. *Theologie und Gesellschaft im 2. und 3 Jahrhundert Hidschra*. 6 vols. Walter de Gruyter, Berlin and New York, 1991–1995.

Versteegh, Kees. *The Arabic Language*. Columbia University Press, New York, 1997.

Vööbus, Arthur. *Syriac and Arabic Documents Regarding Legislation Relevant to Syrian Asceticism*. Estonian Theological Society in Exile, Stockholm, 1960.

Wadud, Amina. *Qur'an and Woman: Rereading the Sacred Text from a Woman's Perspective*. Oxford University Press, Oxford and New York, 1999.

Wagemakers, Joas. "A Purist Jihadi-Salafi: The Ideology of Abu Muhammad al-Maqdisi," *British Journal of Middle Eastern Studies*, vol. 36, no. 2 (August 2009), pp. 281–297.

———. *A Quietist Jihadi: The Ideology and Influence of Abu Muhammad al-Maqdisi*. Cambridge University Press, Cambridge, 2012.

Waki' b. al-Jarrah. *Kitab al-zuhd.* ed. by al-Faryawani, 'Abd al-Rahman. 2 vols., 2nd ed. Dar al-Sumay'i, Riyadh, 1994.

Walker, Paul. "Philosophy of Religion in al-Farabi, Ibn Sina and Ibn Tufayl," in Lawson, Todd (ed.). *Reason and Inspiration in Islam.* I.B. Tauris, London and New York, 2005, pp. 85–101.

Walter, Wiebke. *Women in Islam.* Markus Wiener, Princeton and New York, 1993.

Watt, Montgomery. *Faith and Practice of al-Ghazali.* Allen and Unwin, London, 1953.

———. *Islamic Philosophy and Theology.* Edinburgh University Press, Edinburgh, 1985.

———. *The Formative Period of Islamic Thought.* Oneworld, Oxford, 1998.

Watt, Montgomery and Bell, Richard. *Introduction to the Qur'an.* Edinburgh University Press, Edinburgh, 1994.

Weismann, Itzchak. *The Naqshbandiyya.* Routledge, London and New York, 2007.

Weiss, Bernard. *The Spirit of Islamic Law.* University of Georgia Press, Athens and London, 1998.

Weiss, Michael and Hassan, Hassan. *Isis: Inside the Army of Terror.* Regan Arts, New York, 2015.

Wensinck, Arent. *A Handbook of Early Muhammadan Tradition.* E.J. Brill, Leiden, 1971.

Wild, Stefan. "Lost in Philology? The Virgins of Paradise and the Luxenberg Hypothesis," in Neuwirth, Angelika, Sinai, Nicolai and Marx, Michael (eds.). *The Qur'an in Context.* E.J. Brill, Leiden and Boston, 2010, pp. 625–648.

Winter, Tim (ed.). *The Cambridge Companion to Classical Islamic Theology.* Cambridge University Press, Cambridge, 2008.

Wolfson, Harry. *The Philosophy of the Kalam.* Harvard University Press, Harvard, MA and London, 1976.

Wood, Simon. *Christian Criticisms, Islamic Proofs: Rashid Rida's Modernist Defense of Islam.* Oneworld, Oxford, 2008.

Yassine, Abdessalam. *The Muslim Mind on Trial: Divine Revelation versus Secular Rationalism.* Justice and Spirituality Publishing, Iowa City, IA, 2003.

———. *Winning the Modern World for Islam*, trans. from French by Martin Jenni. Justice and Spirituality Publishing, Iowa City, IA, 2000.

Zagato, Alessandro (ed.). *The Event of Charlie Hebdo: Imaginaries of Freedom and Control.* Berghahn Books, New York, 2015.

Az-Zarnuji. *Ta'lim al-muta'allim tariq at-ta'allum: Instructions of the Student: The Method of Learning*, trans. by G. E. von Grunebaum and Theodora M. Abel. King's Crown Press, New York, 1947.

al-Zayyat, Montasser. *The Road to al-Qaeda: The Story of Bin Laden's Right-Hand Man*, trans. by Ahmed Fekry. Pluto Press, London and Sterling, VA, 2002.

Zubaida, Sami. *Islam, the People and the State.* I.B. Tauris, London, 1993.

Index

Aaron 42, 199

'Abbas I, Shah 239, 370, 373–4, 384

'Abbas (uncle of the Prophet) 110, 120, 121, 127

'Abbásids 114, 120–1, 123–5, 127–8, 132–3, 136, 144, 151, 154, 159, 167–8, 171–4, 177–9, 181–2, 185–6, 193–5, 197, 199–201, 203, 205, 207–8, 211, 213–14, 221, 223–4, 227, 251, 261, 278, 332–3, 336, 343–4, 351, 367, 369–70, 373–4, 419, 440; Abu Muslim and 122–4; agents of 128; 'Alids and 125, 168, 172; caliphs 120, 124, 128, 168, 174, 177–8, 181, 197, 199, 211, 278, 343–4, 369; cause (religio-political) 121, 123–4; clan 120, 121; dynasty 53, 66, 70, 124, 144, 171, 173, 186, 369; epoch 119, 167, 333, 370; fall of 124; family 120–1; government 128, 168; Hashimiyya and 120, 125; historiography 70, 119, 120, 127; justice under 144; *mádrasa* 278; *mawáli* and 125; propaganda (*da'wa*) and 121–2 (*see also da'wa*); rebels 123; revolution 118–22, 124, 127, 167, 172; scholars ('*ulamá'*) and 128; Shi'ite imamate under 125, 172–5; sources of discontent with 119–20; state 124–5, 127, 151, 159, 161, 201, 214; status of women under 332–3, 336; theological underpinnings of 118–19; third *fitna* and, beginning of 120–2; triumph of 123–4; usurper(s) 124, 171, 193, 199; victors 123, 125, 132; vizier(s) under 128, 144

Abbot, Nabia 333–4

'Abd al-'Aziz ("Ibn Sa'úd") 395

'Abdallah b. 'Abbas 120, 121, 127

'Abdallah b. al-Mubarak 223

'Abdallah b. al-Zubayr 65–9, 82; caliphate of 66–8; Marwánids and 68–9; Mukhtár and 67–8

'Abdallah b. Ja'far al-Sádiq 176, 193

'Abdallah b. Mas'ud 82

'Abdallah b. Maymún al-Qaddáh ("The Cataract Remover") 195, 199–200

'Abdallah, Muhammad of Somalia ("Mad Mulla") 381

'Abdallah/'Ubaydallah (Sa'íd) the Fatimid *máhdi* 199–202, 210, 212; *see also* Fatimids; *máhdi/qá'im*

'Abd al-Majíd (Fatimid caliph) 211

'Abd al-Malik 67, 69–70, 152; Umayyad rule under, consolidation of 69–70

'Abd al-Muttálib 19

'Abd al-Qadir al-Jilani 234

'Abd al-Qadir, *amír* 241, 381

'Abd al-Rahman (Umayyad prince) 123

'Abd al-Rahman al-'Akki (governor of al-Andalus) 342

'Abd al-Rahman b. 'Awf *see* 'Awf, 'Abd al-Rahman b.

'Abd al-Ráziq, 'Ali 450

'Abdán (brother-in-law of Qármat) 200, 212

'Abdo, Muhammad 391, 396, 401–6, 423; al-Afgháni and 401–4, 406, 407, 423, 448; modernist reforms of 401–6, 448 (divorce 404; education, reform of 403–4; legal rulings (*fátwas*) 403, 404; liberal attitude 404; points of religious program 405–6; polygamous marriage 404; Rashíd Ridá and 406–7; slavery 404; Sufi path 401)

Abel 199

ability to work miracles (*karamát*) 237

Abode of Islam 71, 108, 112, 197, 341, 353, 361–2, 376, 420, 425, 429, 477, 479; Islamic concepts of 425

Abode of War 108, 425

Abraham 8, 23–4, 29, 35, 84, 199, 291, 296–300, 302, 310, 324, 329, 354, 485; Abrahamic monotheism 35, 298, 341; Muslim 29; *see also* Ibrahim

abrogation theory (*naskh*) 138

absolute justice ('*adl*) 156

absolute unity (*tawhíd*) 156, 392–3

absolutist rule 144, 373, 376

Abu 'Abdallah al-Shi'i 200, 201

Abu 'Ali al-Jubbá'i *see* al-Jubbá'i, Abu 'Ali

Abu Bakr (the first caliph) 22, 24, 29, 35, 40–4, 47, 54, 56, 63, 66, 81–2, 92, 95, 109, 167, 169, 179, 184–5, 228, 301–2, 316, 324, 394; and collection of the Qur'an 81

Abu Hanífa 101, 139–40, 274–5, 330

Abu Háshim (son of Muhammad b. al-Hanafiyya) 110–11, 121–2, 125

Abu Háshim al-Jubbá'i *see* al-Jubbá'i, Abu Háshim

Abu Hurayra (*hadíth* transmitter) 95–7

Abu Jahl 28

Abu 'l-'Abbás (first 'Abbasid caliph) 123–4
Abu Láhab ("Flame Man") 24, 324, 329
Abu 'l-Fadl the Zoroastrian 213
Abu Músa al-Ash'ari 63
Abu Mus'ab al-Súri 484–5
Abu Múslim 122–4
Abu Sa'íd al-Jannábi see al-Jannábi, Abu Sa'íd
Abu Sálama 123–4
Abu Sufyán 31, 34, 60, 65
Abu Sulayman al-Darani 223
Abu Táhir see al-Jannábi, Abu Táhir
Abu Tálib 19, 23
Abu 'Ubayda 46
Abu Yazíd (Man of the Donkey) 202
Abu Yúsuf (Hanafi *faqíh*) 133, 139
Abyssinia 11, 15, 23; Yemen invasion by 16;
    see also Ethiopia
acquisition of actions (*kasb*) 163
Acre 207, 352
Adam 24, 100, 150, 169, 199, 222, 297–8, 300, 324
Adam and Eve 297–8, 300
Adamic religion 213
Aden 382
adhán 288–90, 302; see also five daily prayers
adherents of *Hadíth see* Hadith party
'*adl* (divine justice) see absolute justice
adultery 31, 134, 303, 324, 327, 336
Advisory Council of the Cultural Revolution 456
"Afghan Arabs" 481
Afghan guerilla units 479–80
Afghan *jihád* 433, 477–9, 482
Africa 210, 214, 240, 282–3, 341, 400, 492
Africans (Sudanis) in the service of the Fatimids 207
agent (*wakíl*) in Twelver Shi'ism 174
age of enlightenment 220, 248, 358–9
age of ignorance 26; see also *jahilíyya*
Agha (or Aga) Khan ("Supreme Commander") of
    the Nizari Isma'ilis 198, 210
ahl al-bayt (people of the Prophet's house) 20,
    109, 121
ahl al-dhimma 44
ahl al-hadíth (adherents/followers of *hadíth*) 97,
    140, 158; see also Hadith folk; Isma'ilis
ahl al-haqq ("people of the Truth") 193
ahl al-sunna wa 'l-jamá'a (People of the Prophet's
    Sunna and Consensus/Community) 111–12, 392;
    Shi'ites and 112; see also Hadith folk; Sunnis
Ahmed, Leila 332–4, 336
Ahrar, 'Ubaydallah 232
'A'isha (Mother of the Faithful) 29–31, 35, 55,
    57–9, 66, 95–7, 134, 138, 324, 326–7, 331, 404;
    hostility toward 'Ali b. Abi Talib 57–9
Akbar (Mogul emperor) 373, 375–8
al-'Ádid (Fatimid caliph) 211
al-Áfdal (Fatimid vizier) 207–8, 211
al-Afghání, Jamál al-Din 391, 395–401, 415;
    'Abdo and 395–6, 400–8, 415–17, 423, 448;
    advocacy of Islamic resurgence 396, 398–9;

British colonization of the Muslim world 396;
    despotism 400, 403; 1882 Egyptian rebellion
    396; Islamic reform 396–401; *jihád* against
    the Western colonial powers 396; mastery of
    Islamic theology 396; negative assessment
    of Islam in his age 396; pan-Islamism 396,
    400; revolutionary tactics 396–7; scientific
    discoveries 399–401, 406; Western imperialism
    398; Westernization of Muslim societies 400
al-Ámir (Fatimid caliph) 211
al-Amín (son of the caliph Harún al-Rashíd)
    160, 173
al-'amma see general populace
Alamút 207, 209–11
al-Andalus 131, 139, 232, 265, 341, 345, 478; *see
    also* Iberian Peninsula; Spain
al-Ash'ari, Abu 'l-Hasan 156, 161–3
al-Ash'ari, Abu Músa see Abu Músa al-Ash'ari
al-'Ashúra (commemorative holiday in Shi'ism) 179
al-Awzá'i (Syrian jurist) 101, 139
al-Ázhar university 204, 425, 429, 461, 463, 468
al-'Azíz (Fatimid caliph) 204–5
al-Badr, Muhammad (Zaydi *imam*) 186
al-Balkhi, Shaqíq 223
al-Banna, Hasan 417–22, 461; see also Islamic
    activism
al-Báqir, Muhammad (fifth *imam* of Shi'ism) 99,
    172, 183–5
al-Barbahári 163
al-Basri, al-Hásan 151–2, 154, 157, 222, 228, 275
al-Bistámi, Abu Yazíd 224, 226
al-Bukhári 98, 288, 362
alcohol 55, 82, 134, 142, 356, 409, 465
Alcoran see Qur'an (*al-qur'án*)
al-Daráni, Abu Sulaymán 223
al-Dárazi, Anushtekín (founder of Druze
    community) 206
al-Dhahabi, Shaykh 428
"Alexander [the Great] Romance" (Iskandarname) 313
Alexandria 48, 207
Alexius I (Byzantine emperor) 345
al-Fadl, 'Ali b. 200
al-Farábi, Abu Nasr 254–6, 258; cosmology 255;
    happiness 255; revelation and prophethood
    255–6; virtuos city 255–6; see also *fálsafa*
al-Faraj (al-Farag) Muhammad 429, 478
al-Fátiha 78
Alfonso X the Wise 356
Algeria 108, 200–2, 243, 282, 382, 455
al-Ghannúshi, Ráshid 454–5, 467–8
al-Ghazali, Muhammad (d. 1111) 228–9, 260, 261–5,
    278, 295, 296, 344, 391; criticism of *fálsafa* by
    261–5, 267, 268
al-Ghazáli, Muhammad (d. 1986) 460–4, 467, 468
al-Hádi, 'Ali ("The Guide to the Truth") see 'Ali
    al-Hádi
al-Háfiz (Fatimid caliph) 211, 212
al-Hajjáj 69

al-Hákim (Fatimid caliph) 204–7; Druzes and 206–7
al-Halláj 224, 225–6, 230, 232
al-Hásan (elder son of 'Ali) 64–5, 66, 109
al-Hasan al-'Askari (eleventh *imam* of Twelver Shi'ism) 174–5
al-Husayn (younger son of 'Ali) 65–8, 109, 125, 168, 171, 176, 179, 184–5, 201, 204, 301, 302, 319, 372, 394; death of 66, 68
al-Husayn b. Numayr, Umayyad military commander 67
al-Husayni, Karim 210
'Ali al-Hádi (tenth *imam* of Twelver Shi'ism) 174
'Ali b. Abi Talib (the Prophet's cousin and son-in-law) 19, 22, 31, 43, 53–5, 57–68, 92, 95, 99–100, 106, 108–14, 118, 120–2, 158, 167–71, 176, 176, 179, 183, 195, 199–200, 203–5, 214, 239, 287, 289, 291, 295, 302, 319, 331, 356, 372–3, 394, 439, 460, 487; accession of 57; 'A'isha and 57; Battle of Camel and 57–9; Battle of Siffin and 61–3; caliphate of, final years of 64; death of 64; ideal leader 64; imamate 109; Kharijites and 63–4, 487; legatee of the Prophet 58, 109, 439; Mu'awiya and 60, 64
'Ali b. al-Fadl *see* al-Fadl, 'Ali b.
'Ali b. Músa al-Ridá (eighth *imam* of Twelver Shi'ism) 173
'Alids 61, 67, 120, 124–5, 168, 172–3, 204; agents of 173; authority 121, 125; caliphs 179, 184; candidates 109–11, 125, 127; family 122, 168, 179, 186, 200, 201; *imam(s)* 99, 124, 125, 168, 169, 170, 183–4, 331; loyalism 71, 167; movement 109, 111, 114, 121, 125, 167, 199; party (*[al-]shi'a*) 61, 108, 122, 127, 167, 173; rebellions of 67–8, 125, 172–3; sacred (divine) knowledge of 169, 172, 173, 174, 176, 177, 203, 239, 264–5
'Ali–Fátima lineage 125, 143, 168, 171, 176, 183, 186, 193, 199, 200, 201, 203, 204, 214, 239, 331
Alighieri, Dante 356
al-Isbahani, Abu Nu'aym 228
'Ali's family 68, 99, 118, 120–1, 123, 124–5, 167–9, 172, 179, 185, 194, 199, 203, 204, 214, 372
'Ali's party (*al-shi'a* or *shi'at 'Ali*) 61, 108, 109–11, 167–8; *see also* Shi'ites
'Ali Zayn al-'Abidín (fourth *imam* of Twelver Shi'ism) 66
al-jabr (compulsion) *see* compulsion
al-Jamá'a [al-Gamá'a] al-Islamiyya 482
al-Jamáli, Badr (Fatimid general) 207
al-Jannábi, Abu Sa'íd 200, 212
al-Jannábi, Abu Táhir 212–14
al-Jubbá'i, Abu 'Ali 156, 161, 162
al-Jubbá'i, Abu Háshim 156
al-Junayd 224–7, 234
al-Káfi 99; *see also* al-Kulayni
al-Kalabádhi, Abu Bakr 228

al-Kázim, Músa (seventh *imam* of Twlever Shi'ism) 173, 175, 193
al-khassa (God's elect [Shi'ite] servants) 178
al-Kindi 251–2; *see also fálsafa*
al-Kulayni 99, 175
al-Lat 11, 24, 83
All-Compassionate (*al-rahím*) 79, 81
All-Forgiving (*al-ghafúr*) 79, 83
All-Glorious (*al-jalíl*) 83
All-Hearing (*al-samí'*) 79
All-Knowing (*al-'alím*) 79
All-Merciful (*al-rahmán*) 79, 81, 83
All-Wise (*al-hakím*) 79
al-mafdúl (inferior *imam*) 185
al-Mákki, Abu Tálib 228
al-Ma'mún (caliph) 150, 160, 251, 376
al-Manár ("The Beacon" or "The Lighthouse") *see* "Beacon, The"
al-Mansúr, Abu Ja'far ("The Victor") 124, 128
al-Matúridi 163
alms (*zakát*) 155, 292–3, 305
al-Mufíd, al-Shaykh 181–2
al-Muhásibi, al-Hárith 224
al-Mu'ízz (Fatimid caliph) 202–4
al-Mulk, Fakhr 263
al-Mulk, Nizám 208, 261–3, 278
al-Múntazar, Muhammad "The Awaited" 175; *see also* hidden *imam*
al-múrji'a ("postponers") 153
al-Múrtada, al-Sharíf 182
al-Must'áli (Fatimid caliph) 207, 211
al-Mustánsir ('Abbásid caliph) 278
al-Mustánsir (Fatimid caliph) 203, 207, 211, 278; succession of, crisis over 207–11
al-Mutawakkil (caliph) 161, 174, 333
al-Muwátta' 139
al-Nasá'i 98
al-Násir, Jamál 'Abd 421, 491; *see also* Gamal Abdel Nasser
al-Núri, Abu 'l-Husayn 225
Alp Arslán 345
al-Qa'ida 360, 417, 433, 475, 479–84, 486, 488–90; Afghan *mujahideen* and 480–1; "amity and enmity" 485–6; bombings in Britain and Spain inspired by 360; cells of 480, 489, 494; etymology of 480; rivalry with Islamic State in Syria and Iraq 489; self-sacrificing revolutionary vanguard 486–9; strategy and its consequences 489–90; use of local grievances by 488–9; *see also* global *jihád*; terrorism
al-qá'im 100, 173, 193; *see also máhdi/qá'im*
al-Qaradawi, Yusuf 461
al-Qúnawi, Sadr al-Din 232
al-Qushayri, 'Abd al-Karím 228, 232
al-rahím 79, 81
al-rahmán 79, 81
al-Rashíd, Harún 128, 133, 139, 150, 159–60, 173, 333

al-Razi, Abu Bakr 253–4; *see also fálsafa*
al-ridá (the agreed upon from the Prophet's family)
 120, 121
[al-]Riyadh 392
al-sálaf al-sálih see "pious ancestors/forebears
 [of Islam]"
al-Samarri, 'Ali ibn Muhammad 176
al-samí' 79
al-Sarráj, Abu Nasr 227
al-Shafi'i, Muhammad 97–8, 140–3
al-shari'a 101, 131, 213, 455
al-Shawkani 238, 391
al-Shaybáni 139–40
al-Shibli 225
al-shúra/shúra 50, 52, 53, 57, 59, 60, 63, 65, 67, 410
al-Sijistáni, Abu Dawúd 98
al-Suhrawardi, Abu Hafs 'Umar 234
al-Súlami, Abu 'Abd al-Rahman 228
al-Tabari 24, 83, 88, 138, 362
al-Takfír wa 'l-Hijra 427
al-Taqí, Muhammad "The God-Fearing" (the ninth
 imam of Twelver Shi'ism) 173
al-tawwábún 67
al-Táyyib (Fatimid caliph) 211
al-Tháqafi, Mukhtár see Mukhtár, rebellion of
al-Tírmidhi 98
al-Tusi, Muhammad 99, 182
al-'Uzza 11, 83
al-Zarqáwi, Abu Mus'ab 490
al-Zawáhiri, Áyman 479, 481–4
al-Zubayr 53, 58, 65
ambassador (safír) in Twelver Shi'ism 174
amír (military commander or ruler) 34, 60, 144,
 177, 187, 201, 346–7, 350, 381, 432, 486, 489
amír al-mu'minín ("commander of the faithful")
 42, 63–4, 69, 118; see also caliph
amity and enmity 485–6
'Amr b. al-'As 48, 55, 60, 61, 63, 64
'Amri family of Twelver Shi'ites 175–6
analogical reasoning or analogy (qiyás) 140,
 142–3, 181
Ánas b. Malik (hadíth transmitter) 95, 97
Anatolia 46, 48–9, 139, 231, 232, 282–3, 341,
 343–5, 347, 350, 352, 359
Angel Gabriel (Jibril) 21–2, 24–5, 32, 76, 92, 94,
 100, 300
Anglo-Afghan war 210
ansár (helpers of the Prophet at Medina) 26, 27,
 40, 55, 57, 67
anthropomorphism 155, 162, 185
anti-Muslim polemical treatises 355
anticolonial resistance 380–2
Antioch 46, 347
anti-Soviet jihád 395, 433, 478, 479–81
anti-Umayyad propaganda campaign 119, 121–2;
 see also 'Abbásids, propaganda (da'wa)
anti-Umayyad revolts see "third fitna, the"
apostates 429

'Aqíl (elder brother of 'Ali b. Abi Talib) 195
'aql (reason) 143, 181
Aquinas, Thomas 258, 362
Arab conquests 40–2, 341–2; Egypt 48; Iraq 46–8
 (Sasanid Empire 48–9); Syria and Palestine
 44–6; 'Umar 42, 44, 46–9; 'Uthman 49–50
Arab-dominated state (under Umayyads) 106
Arabesque 311–13, 318; see also figural arts
Arabia 7–16, 19, 23, 32–5, 40–2, 44, 47, 58, 64–5,
 67–8, 93, 106, 108, 124, 131–2, 143, 173–4,
 184, 194–5, 199–200, 212, 297, 332, 355,
 367, 371, 392–5, 407–8, 425; see also Arabian
 Peninsula
"Arabia Felix" 8
Arabian Peninsula (jazírat al-'árab) 7–16;
 Arabs 8–11; Bedouin tribes 9–15, 32–4, 40,
 108; geography 7; Mecca 11–15; religious
 communities 15–16
Arabian society: Christianity 15–16; customary
 law 331; fairs 10–11, 24, 237; Judaism 15–16,
 26, 150, 294, 341, 353, 417; pagans 14–15, 23,
 27–9, 33, 42, 82, 132, 393, 478; tribal paganism/
 polytheism 13, 16, 19, 22, 26–7, 131
Arabic language 15, 23, 77, 79, 265, 268, 276, 280,
 381, 406
Arab–Israeli conflict (war) 421, 448, 477
Arab Muslims 46, 68, 106, 481
Arab paganism 13, 297, 359
Arabs 8–11; divisions 8; origin 8; South Arabian
 kingdoms 8
Arab Socialism 422, 426
Arab tribal poetry 10–11
Arab tribes 10–11, 16, 24, 31, 33–4, 42–4, 49, 67,
 79, 83, 105–6, 119, 296–7, 300, 392
Aramaic (Syriac) literature 150, 251
argumentation 150–1, 154, 164, 181, 249, 263–5,
 346; see also kalám
Aristotle 154, 250–1, 253–4, 259, 265, 268, 361
Armenia 48, 82
Arslan, Shakib 361
art and religious architecture 310–20; see also
 calligraphy; figural arts; miniature painting;
 mosque
articles of faith 150
Árwa bint Ahmad 212; see also Sulayhid dynasty
ascetic(s) 222–4, 282
ascetic-mystical movement 220, 222, 224, 227;
 see also Sufism
Ash'arism 161–3, 249; Hadith party and 163;
 Maturidism and 163, 249; as theological "middle
 way" 161–3
ashráf/sharíf ("noblemen"; descendents of 'Ali and
 Fátima) 174
'Áskar Múrkam 195
assassins (hashíshiyya or hashishiyyún) 201, 208–9,
 211, 360; see also fidá'is
Ásya (wife of the Pharaoh) 324
Ataturk, Kemal 407–8, 437, 454

atonement 29, 294–5
attacks on the New York Twin Towers and
  Pentagon 491
attacks on U.S. embassies in East Africa 483
'Attar, Farid al-Din 230, 232, 313
authenticated (*muwáththaq*) *hadíth* 99
Averroes 265; *see also* Ibn Rushd
Avicenna 256; *see also* Ibn Sina
'Awf, 'Abd al-Rahman b. 53
Awrangzéb (Mogul emperor) 377, 378
Aws (Arabian tribe) 24, 26
Axum (Abyssinia) 11
ayat (Qur'anic verse) 79
Ayatollah ("sign of God") 435
Ayyúb, Saláh al-Din b. (Saladin) *see* Saláh al-Din
  b. Ayyúb
Ayyubid dynasty 278
Azerbaijan 82, 210, 372
'Azzám, 'Abdallah 476–81

Baghdad 66, 125, 128, 150, 154, 158, 160, 161,
  172–4, 177–82, 194, 200, 202–3, 211, 213–14,
  223–5, 227–9, 236, 251, 253–4, 261–2, 278,
  344–5, 351, 369–70
Baghdad school of Sufism 224–7, 228
Bahrain 15, 200, 212–14; Qarmati state in, rise
  of 212–14
Balkans 236, 343–5, 359, 367, 369, 378, 382
Banu Háshim 15, 19, 23–4; Quraysh tribe and 11,
  15, 19, 23, 24; *see also* Hashimites/Hashimiyya
Banu Makhzúm 19
Banu Umáyya 19; *see also* Umayyads
baqa' 225
báraka (blessing) 283
Barjawán 205
Baron's Crusade 347
basmala (bismi 'lláhi 'l-rahmán al-rahím) 79–80
Basra 48, 58, 68, 82, 108, 151, 154, 156–7, 161,
  195, 212, 222, 224, 226–7, 330, 370
Basran mosque 154
bátin ("hidden"; "esoteric" [aspect of revelation])
  111, 196, 199
Batriyya Zaydis 185
Battle of Badr 27–8
Battle of Hattín 351
Battle of Jalúla 48
Battle of Kosovo Field 352
Battle of Lepanto 371
Battle of Nicopolis 352
Battle of Poitiers 341–2
Battle of the Bridge 47
Battle of the Camel 57–9, 65
Battle of the Ditch 32
Battle of the Pyramids 381
Battle of Úhud 31–2, 40, 60, 135
bay'a (oath of allegiance) 33–4
Bayazid I 352
Baybars (Mamluk sultan) 210, 352

Bayqara, Husayn 232
Bazargán, Mahdi (Mehdi) 458–60, 468
"Beacon, The" (*al-Manár*) 406–7
Bedouin tribes (Bedouins) 9–10, 13–14, 16, 32, 47,
  58, 65, 196; camel 9–10; Christianity 15–16; diet
  10; group affiliation 10; Ka'ba ("Cube") 13–14;
  mobility 9–10; Muhammad and 40; nomadic
  9–10; seminomadic 9–10; social structures 10;
  warfare and raiding 10
"Bee" (name of a Qur'anic *sura*) 78
believer (*mu'min*) 157
beneficial blessing *see báraka*
bequest of the imamate (*nass*) 109
berber tribe(s)/berbers 144, 196, 200–2, 207
"Bezels of Wisdom" 232
Bhutto, Benazir 433
Bhutto, Zulfiqar 433
bid'a 159, 163, 224, 391, 393; *see also* innovation
Bihbahaní ("Sufi-Killer") 239
Bilqís 324, 329
Bin Ládin (b. Ládin), Usáma 360, 417, 425,
  475, 480–6
birth *see* Islamic life cycle
Bishr al-Hafi 224
bismi 'lláhi 'l-rahmán al-rahím see basmala
Black Stone 213–14, 297–9, 301
Bóhras (merchants or traders) 212; *see also*
  Táyyibi-Isma'ili community in Yemen and India
Bonaventure 268
Book of God 61–4, 121; *see also* Qur'an
  (*al-qur'án*)
"Book of Kings" (Shahname) 313
Boulainvillers 358
"Breaths of Divine Intimacy" 232
bride-money (bride gift/wealth) 135, 142, 303, 328,
  329, 330, 427; *see also* marriage and gender
  relations; women in Islamic societies
Britain 210, 360, 436, 437
British East India Company 377
British Empire 381, 403, 430
British Raj 203, 387, 381, 398, 430
Buddhism 241, 288, 417
Bukhara 98, 185, 206, 228, 256–7, 281, 478
bureaucratic corruption 384
Buyids 178–80, 194; family 178, 179
Byzantine Christians 61, 341, 345, 353
Byzantine Empire 46, 48, 310, 341, 344, 347, 353,
  367, 369; coins 70; emperor(s) 10, 15–16, 46,
  48, 70–1, 128, 344–5, 347; social structure 10

Cairo 48, 202, 204, 206–7, 214, 278, 281–2, 319,
  345, 394, 396, 401, 406, 419, 461, 478, 481
caliph (*khalífa*) and caliphate (*khiláfa*) 33, 34, 40,
  42, 46, 49, 53–8, 60–1, 63–71, 81–2, 92, 94–6,
  98–9, 105–6, 109, 114, 118–25, 128, 132, 137,
  144, 150–61, 167–8, 170–4, 177–9, 181–5,
  194–5, 197, 199–208, 211–14, 222–4, 225, 227,
  251, 274–5, 277–8, 301, 316, 320, 324, 327–8,

333, 342–5, 351, 367, 369, 372–3, 376, 395, 403, 407–8, 419–20, 432, 439, 464, 478, 488, 490; 'Abbásids 120–8, 148, 133, 136, 144, 148, 167–8, 171, 172, 174, 178, 182, 202, 203, 251, 333; 'Abdallah b. al-Zubayr 66–9; 'Ali b. Abi Talib 57–64; 'Alids 168, 179, 184; Fatimids 202–7 (collapse of 211); Mu'awiya ("Son of the Liver-Eater") 64–5; rightly guided 40–2; Sunnis 167, 168, 178, 203

caller or summoner in Isma'ilism (*dá'i*) *see dá'i*

calligraphy 311–13; calligraphic-cum-arabesque patterns 313; carpet pages 312; styles 311; *see also* art and religious architecture

call to prayer *see adhán*

camel 9–10, 33, 57–60, 65, 69, 88, 95, 136, 201, 213, 279, 293, 300

"Canon of Medicine" (Ibn Sina) 258

capitalism 420, 424, 426, 462

"caricature scandal" 360

Carmathians 200, 205, 206; *see also* Qarmatis

carpet pages 312

Caspian Sea 178, 184–5

"Cataract Remover, The" (al-Qaddáh) *see* 'Abdallah b. Maymún al-Qaddáh

Catholic Church 353, 358, 405

Catholic clergy 459

Catholic kingdoms 344; *see also* Al-Andalus; Spain

Caucasus 380, 382

causality 162, 249, 252, 254

Central Asia 42, 49, 71, 98, 121–2, 139, 163, 194–5, 199, 210, 223, 228, 236, 238, 254, 278, 281, 283, 313, 334, 346–7, 367, 382, 384–5, 400, 425, 492

Central Intelligence Agency (CIA) 438, 481, 483

"Chanson de Roland" 357

charitable endowment or trust (*waqf*) 278–9, 283, 293

Charlemagne 356

chief of Arabian tribe (*shaykh*) 10

chiliasm 171; *see also* millennialism

Chishtiyya 236

Christ 15, 83, 92, 345–7, 349, 353; *see also* Jesus ('Isa)

Christian Church 53, 131

Christian Church of St. John 70

Christian clergy 355, 385

Christian Copts 48, 205

Christian Emperor of Byzantium 16

Christian holy book *see* Gospel

Christianity 15–16, 19, 46–8, 53, 70, 150, 268, 294, 310, 318, 341, 345–6, 350, 353, 355–7, 399, 405, 417, 432; Bedouin tribes (Bedouins) 15–16; Islam and 52, 341 (quarrel and rivalry between 341, 344)

Christian monasticism 241, 348, 349, 463

Christian monk(s) 19, 83, 209, 221, 328, 349, 355, 375

Christian mysticism 220

Christian Neoplatonists 250

Christian polemical literature 355

Christian polemicists 355–6, 359

Christians 15, 23, 35, 42, 46, 61, 78, 83, 88, 92, 132, 134, 150, 158, 203, 205, 303, 310, 341, 343–6, 349, 352–6, 359, 361, 369, 377, 384, 401, 404

Cilicia 48

circumcision 302–4; boys 302; female 302–3

"clear Arabic language" 79

client clans 10

"clients" of Arabs (*mawáli/máwla*) 68, 71, 105–6, 119, 122, 125

Clinton, Bill 483

"Clouds, The" 122

Cold War, consequence of 492

collective prayers and formulas of *dhikr* 236, 283

college (*mádrasa*) 274, 277; *see also* mádrasa

commander in chief (*amír*) *see amír*

commander of the faithful (*amír al-mu'minín*) *see amír al-mu'minín*

communism 408, 419, 420

community welfare (*máslaha*) 143, 441

companions of the Prophet 53, 58, 82, 96, 99, 158, 178–9, 205, 319

compulsion (*al-jabr*) 112

concubines *see* women in Islamic societies

confusion (*hayra*) 174–5

Conrad, Marquis 209

consensus (*ijmá'/jama'a*) 111–12, 114, 115, 139, 142–3, 154, 181, 336, 360

conservative reform of Muhammad b. 'Abd al-Wahhab 415–16

"Consideration of the Disputed Reports" 182

Constantinople 11, 15, 46, 48, 49, 194, 341–5, 352–3, 369, 371

consultative or electoral council (*al-shúra*) 50, 53–4, 57, 58, 60, 63, 65, 67, 167, 410, 450, 455, 466–7

conversion to Christianity 16

Coran *see* Qur'an (*al-qur'án*)

Cordova 202, 265–6, 341, 354

correct faith 159, 183

Council of Clermont 345

courts for redress of wrongs (*mazálim*) 144

Crane, Charles R. 398

creed 88, 94, 286

Crimea 380

Cromer, Lord 382, 403

Crusader chronicles 208

Crusaders 208–9, 211, 344–7, 349–53, 356, 363, 371, 483, 492

Crusades *see* West and Islam

Ctesiphon 46–8, 125

cult of "friends of God" (*awliyá'*) 237–8, 241, 405; *see also* walaya

custom of the Prophet (*súnnat al-nabí*) 71, 82, 92, 97; *see also* Sunna (custom) of the Prophet

Cyrenaica 202

dahr (Time) 13
dá'i (Isma 'ili missionary or summoner) 195–7, 200–5, 207, 212, 214
dá'i mútlaq 212
Damascus 46, 60, 64, 66–7, 70, 82, 254, 278, 281, 319, 350
dar al-'ilm 180
Darwinism 466
date juice (*nabídh*) 142
Da'údis 212; *see also* Fatimids
"Daughters of God" 23, 83
David (Qur'anic prophet) 84
da'wa 121–3, 194–7, 205, 207–8, 211, 212
Daylam/Daylaman 178, 184, 207–8
Day of Atonement (*yom kippur*) 294
Day of Judgment 22, 28, 83, 150, 153, 157, 159, 162, 203, 292, 297–8, 300, 304, 310, 329, 479
Day of the Cave 179
Day of the Covenant 222; *see also* Sufism
"Days of the Arabs" 10
"Deliverance from Error" (al-Ghazali) 229, 261
Delta of the Nile 48
democracy and Islam 458
demographic explosion in the Muslim world 426, 476
Denmark 359
despotism 400, 403, 405, 419–20, 459
Devil, the 287, 298, 300, 350, 356–7; *see also* Iblís; Satan
devotees (*fidá'is*) 208
devshirmé 369
Dhahabiyya 238
dhikr 236, 237, 283, 401; *see also* recollection of God
Dhu 'l-Hijja *see* five pillars of Islam; *hajj*
Dhu 'l-Nun al-Misri 223
Dhu Nuwás (Yemeni king) 15, 16
"Diamond" (nickname of a Fatimid general) 202
dietary prohibitions 26, 275
din (religion) 94, 479
din 'Ali (religion of 'Ali) 58
Dirar b. 'Amr 151
dirhams 47, 142, 276
discernment *see* Qur'an (*al-qur'án*)
divide and rule policy 419
"Divine Comedy" (Dante) 356; *see also* Alighieri, Dante
divine decree (*qadar*) 152
divinely guided leader (*máhdi* or *qá'im*) 171, 193–203, 205
divine path (*shari'a*) 101
divorce 93, 96, 98–9, 101, 134–5, 304, 327–32, 404, 424, 460, 466; *see also* *taláq*
diwán (register) 44
doctrine of occultation, political and social aspects of 177
"dogs of hellfire" 461
Dome of the Rock 70, 316, 347
dress code 98, 221, 235, 329, 350, 360

Druze religion 206–7
dual truth theory 268; *see also* Ibn Rushd
Durúz see Druze religion
Dutch 380, 382
Dyophysitist creed 46

Eastern Orthodox Christians 344
ecstatic trance (*wajd*) 234
education *see* *kuttáb*; *mádrasa*
Egypt 46, 48–9, 54–5, 60, 64, 67, 69, 71, 78, 105–6, 118, 123, 140, 194–5, 197, 200–12, 213–15, 221, 223, 236, 264–5, 278, 282, 288, 303–4, 319, 332, 341–2, 344, 351–2, 367, 380–5, 391–2, 394–8, 400–7, 415–23, 425–30, 433–4, 150, 453–64, 460–3, 467–8, 477–9, 481–3, 491; Arab conquest of 46; Fatimid conquest of 202–4; "godless regime of" 481
Egyptian Copts 49
"Egyptian Events, The" 402
Egyptian Muslims 383, 403–4, 422, 425, 428
Egyptian mutineers 55, 60, 118
Egyptian notables 204
electoral council (*shúra*) *see* consultative or electoral council
elementary education: *kuttáb* 275–7, 279, 283, 287 (Arabic calligraphy 276; learning religious duties 276; reciting Qur'anic *súras* 275)
"emigrants" 26, 27, 40, 132
emigration or migration 26–9, 101; *see also* *hijra*
Emperor of Constantinople 15
"Empty Place" *see* Rub' al-Khali
Enoch or Elijah *see* Idris
epic tales 10–11, 313, 356, 359
"Epistle on Sufism" (al-Qushayri) 228
"erotic mysticism" 223
esoteric or interior meaning of revelation (*bátin*) *see* *bátin*
Ethiopia 11, 15, 23
European ascendancy, cause of 378, 380, 381
European colonial expansion 380–3; Battle of the Pyramids *see* Battle of the Pyramids; Dutch colonization *see* Dutch; resistance to 380–1; Russian conquest 380; Sepoy Mutiny 381; social and cultural engineering 381
European Romantics 358
European-style legal codes 101, 133, 136, 384
Eve (Hawwá) 324
evildoer (*fásiq*) 153
exaggerators (in Shi 'ism) 206
"Excommunication and Emigration" *see* al-Takfir wa 'l-Hijra
exegesis 96, 99, 233, 275, 279
exemplary custom (*sunna*) *see* Sunna (custom) of the Prophet; *súnnat al-nabí*
exoteric or external aspect of revelation (*záhir*) *see* *záhir*
extremist Shi'ism 205–6
Ezra 83–4

"fair" (*hásan*) *hadíth* 99
fálsafa 248–51, 254, 256–8, 261, 264, 266–8, 399, 404, 460; al-Farábi 254–6, 258; al-Ghazali's cricicism of 261–5; al-Kindi 251–2; al-Razi, Abu Bakr 253–4; Aristotelian philosophy and 260, 268; beginnings of 251; definition of 248–9; doctrine of salvation 265; elitism of 256, 267–9, 399; fossilization of Islamic philosophical thinking 264; Gnostic tradition 260; Greek roots of 248, 251, 265; Ibn Rushd (Averroes) 265–8; Ibn Sina (Avicenna) 256–61; *kalám* and 248–50, 252; Neoplatonic doctrine (theory) of emanation and 197–8, 250, 251, 254–5, 259; Neoplatonism 250–1, 260; opposition to 266, 269; practical usefulness of 249, 399; prophetic guidance and 256; revelation and 256, 258, 259, 263, 264, 266–7
family of the Prophet 19, 110, 326–7; *see also ahl al-bayt*; wives of the Prophet
fana' 225, 230, 232; *see also* Sufism
Fanatisme, ou Mahomet le prophète 358
faqíh/fuqahá' 101, 136–8, 140, 142, 144, 145, 181, 225, 275, 393, 439, 440–1, 457–8
"Farewell Pilgrimage" 34, 298, 300, 305
fásiq (evildoer) *see* evildoer
fast of Ramadán *see* Ramadán fasting
fatalism and fatalists 13, 163, 223
Fátima (the Prophet's daughter) 66, 67, 120, 168
Fatimid Isma'ilism 207, 214
Fatimids 194, 199–207, 214; army 202, 205, 207; caliphate 194, 202–7, 214, 345 (fall of 211); consolidation of power of 202–4; dynasty 204, 211; Egypt, conquest of 202–4, 214; family 205, 211; florescence of learning under 204–5; Háfizi-Táyyibi split 211–12; *imam* 199, 203, 211, 214; judge 205, 211; *máhdi* 199–202, 205; mission (*da'wa*) 207, 211, 212; name of 200; power 202; Qarmati split from 199–200, 213, 214; rise of 197, 200–2; schism(s) 205, 207, 211, 212; state 197, 200, 201, 203, 204, 206, 207, 211; *see also* Isma'ilis
fátwa (legal ruling) 83, 144, 360, 395, 403
fátwa-givers (*muftis*) 281; *see also muftis*
Festival of Breaking the Fast (*'id al-fitr*) 295
Festival of the Sacrifice (*'id al-adha*) 296, 300
fidá'is 208–11; *see also* assassins; devotees
figural arts: disjuncture between norm and practice 314; iconophobia 310; miniature painting 313–16; patronage of 313; religious restrictions on artistic expression 310–11, 314; text-and-design compositions 311; total space decoration 311; vegetal pattern 311, 313; worship of idols and 310–11; *see also* art and religious architecture; calligraphy
fiqh 101, 136, 140, 143–4, 151, 156, 164, 274, 280–2, 336, 432, 451, 458
"Firmest Bond, The" 396, 402, 406
First Crusade 345–9, 356, 359

First Gulf War 417, 485, 488
fitna ("trial"; "temptation") 53, 55, 58, 66, 105, 111, 118
five daily prayers 44, 76, 286–92, 319
five pillars of Islam 286–301, 404; Fast of Ramadán (*sawm*) 29, 294–6 ('Ashúra and 29, 294; end of 295; fasting women 294, 295; festival charity 295; "minor festival" 295; moral dimension of 295; public infringements of 296; rules of fasting 94, 294–5; Shi'ism 295; special congregational prayer 295); Pilgrimage to Mecca (*hajj*) 286, 296–301 ('Arafat, plane of 297, 298; Black Stone 297, 301; Dhu 'l-Hijja 296, 298, 300; dress of consecration (*ihrám*) 298, 300, 301; Festival of the Sacrifice 296, 298, 299, 300; forty-nine pebbles for the ritual stoning 300; Ka'ba 297, 299, 300; major stages and rituals 298–300; Mína 299–300; Mount of Mercy 297, 298; Muhammad and 298; origins of 296–7; rite of deconsecrating 300; ritual run (*sa'y*) 299; ritual slaughter of animals 298; significance 298–300; stoning the Devil 300; *talbiyya* 298; *tawáf* 299; *úmra* 299; Well of Zámzam 299; women 296, 298); Prayer (*salát*) 287–92 (*adhán* (call to prayer) 288–9, 290; for the dead 292; *khútba* (sermon) 291; *qibla* (direction of prayer) *see qibla*; Shi'ite 287, 288–9, 290, 291; supplication 291; *see also* five daily prayers); *Shaháda* 286–7, 289, 291; *Zakát* 292–4 (on gold and silver 293; recepients of 293; *sádaqa(t)* 292; taxable crops 293)
five pillars of modernity 379–80
"Flame Man" *see* Abu Láhab
foreign *mujahideen* 480–1; *see also mujahideen*
Fourth Crusade 353
France 119, 210, 258, 341–3, 345, 347, 350, 352, 360, 381–2, 454
French Empire 381, 382
Friday prayer 44, 55, 291, 376
friend(s) of God (*walí*; pl. *awliya'*) 223, 241; *see also walaya*
Fudayl b. 'Iyad 223
fundamentalism 416, 448
fundamentalist(s) 394, 448, 452
fuqahá' see faqíh/fuqahá
Fustat 48, 64, 82; *see also* Cairo

Gabriel *see* Angel Gabriel (Jibril)
Gamal Abdel Nasser 421–2, 426
Garden of Death 41, 81
Gaul (France) 119, 341
general [non-Shi'ite] populace (*al-'amma*) 178
"Generations of the Sufis" 228
Genghis Khan 367, 374
Ghadír Khumm 168, 179, 204
Ghassan tribe 16
ghayba 171, 173
ghazis 367, 369

ghoul (*ghul*) 12
"Gifts of Mystical Knowledge" 234
Gilan 184
global *jihád* 475, 482, 483, 490, 498; Afghanistan as principal battleground of 477–8, 480–1; concept of amity and enmity 485–6; parallels with Marxism 486–9; redefinition of objectives 483; rejection of Western values and Islamic liberalism 488; self-sacrificing vanguard of 486–7; targets of 482–3; terrorizing enemy 484–5; *see also* al-Qaʻida; *mujahideen*
global jihadism 417, 475; *see also* al-Qaʻida; transnational jihadism
global supremacy, race for 362
gnosis (*maʻrifa*) *see* Sufi knowledge
Gnosticism 197, 233, 241
God (*Allah*) 14, 15, 20, 22–3, 26–9, 34–5, 77–82, 83–4, 112, 154–60, 162–3, 232
goddesses 11–14, 83, 310
Godhead 156, 205
godless 112, 432, 434–7, 444, 489
"Godly Personality" 464
God's argument (*hujja*) 173
God's elect servants (*al-khassa*) *see* al-Khassa
God the creator 14, 20, 206, 232, 310
Goethe, Johann 358
Golden Age of Islam, The 128, 419
Gospel (*Injíl*) 76, 79, 86, 92, 134, 199
government (governance) of the jurist (*vilayat-i faqíh*) 438–41, 457
grape wine (*khamr*) 142
grave sinner 153–4, 157, 162–3
Greater Festival *see* Festival of the Sacrifice
Greater Occultation (in Twelver Shiʻism) 176, 177, 187
Greater Zab 123
Greek logic 150, 154, 164, 252
Greeks 382
Greek wisdom 150, 249, 251, 256
guerilla war 421
Gujarat 212
Gunpowder Empires 367–79; Moguls 374–7 (Akbar, image of 376; British Raj 377; descendants of Genghis Khan 374; Hindus under 374–8; "peace for all" 376–7; peak of power 375; poll tax 376, 377; religious policies and reforms 376–7; social hierarchy 376; *'ulama'* and 376–7; universalism and communalism 377, 378); Ottomans 367–72 (abolition of empire 372; anti-Christian *jihád* 368; cultural achievements 371; *devshirmé* 369; doctrinal foundations 367–8; Indian Ocean seafaring trade and 371; *millet* system 371, 378; The New Corps 369; Portuguese and 371; Safavids and 369–70; Shariʻa courts under 371; struggle against Habsburg dynasty 371); Safavids 372–4 (educational institutions 372; Ottomans and 369, 373; promotion of Twelver Shiʻism

372–3; Redhead movement 372, 374; religious orthodoxy 372, 374; royal donations 372; *Sadr* 374; Shah Ismaʻil 372; *shaykh al-islam's* supremacy 374; *'ulama'* and 373–4)
Guru Nanák 377

Habsburgs 371
Hadíth 86, 92–101, 112, 133–4, 137, 140–3, 153, 155–63, 168–9, 175, 181–4, 221, 263, 265, 274–6, 278–80, 286, 288, 291–2, 294–5, 297, 301–3, 310, 312, 316, 323–4, 328–30, 332, 336, 354, 391, 394, 409, 428, 451, 466, 477, 479, 486–7; adherents of 140–2, 153, 155, 157, 159; arrangement of 97; authentic or sound (*sahíh*) 98, 99, 141, 143; canonical collections of 98, 99; clarification of Qurʼanic commandments in 93, 140–2; creed 158–62; definition of 92; fabricated 96; importance of 93, 98, 140–3, 159; as "Islamic tradition" 92; as "Muslim Gospel" 92; sacred or holy 100; science of 96, 141, 143; as second revelation 98, 140, 159; Shiʻite 92, 98–100; six collections of 98; and Sunna (custom) of the Prophet 93, 140, 142; transmission and collection of 95–6, 142; two main parts of 96; types of 93–5, 98–9, 100; writing down of 96–8
Hadith folk 97, 143, 158, 159, 160, 161, 162, 163, 264; *see also ahl al-hadíth*; Hadith party
Hadith party (*ahl al-hadíth*) 153, 155, 156, 157, 158–63; *see also* Ahl al-hadíth; Hadith folk
Hadíth qúdsi 100
Háfiz (Hafez) (Persian poet) 313
Háfizi-Táyyibi split *see* Fatimids
Hafsa (daughter of caliph ʻUmar) 81
Hagar 8, 298–300
Hagareni 8
hajj 29, 33, 34, 44, 71, 120, 128, 213, 286, 291, 296–300, 301, 305, 395, 404, 440; Adam and Eve 297; ceremonies/rituals 213, 296, 297–9; etymology 297; Ishmael/Ismaʻil 297; Quraysh and 297; standing on the Plain of ʻArafat 297; *'úmra* 299; women 296, 298; *see also* "Farewell Pilgrimage"; five pillars of Islam; Mecca; pilgrimage rites
Halakhá 131
Hamza (the Prophet's uncle) 31, 60
Hamza b. ʻAli (leader of the Druze) 206
Hánafi juridical (legal) school 101, 139, 140, 142, 143, 205, 228, 275, 280, 330, 369, 371, 373
Hánafi Muʻtazilite 158
Hánafi Sunnism 369
Hanafites/Hanafis 163, 288, 293
Hanbali school of law 101, 139, 143, 228, 234, 275, 392; *see also mádhhab*
Hanbalism 163, 392
Hanbalites 158, 162–3, 393
haníf see "spontaneous" monotheists
Hanifa tribe 67, 110, 120

520 Index

"Happy Arabia" 8

háram 15, 297; *see also hajj*; Mecca

harem system 333–4, 336

Harún al-Rashíd *see* al-Rashíd, Harún

Hasan II (Nizári *imam*) 210

Hasanid(s) 172–3, 186

Hashimites/Hashimiyya 11, 15, 53, 57, 110–11, 120, 125, 140, 168

hashísh 208

hashishiyún see assassins

hashíshiyya see assassins

hashish smugglers 463

hayra ("confusion" [in Shi 'ite Islam]) *see* confusion

headscarf (*khimár*) 330; *see also hijáb*

"Healing of the Soul" (Ibn Sina) 258

Hebrew Bible 76

Hell 22, 24, 87–8, 108, 150, 152, 154, 157, 162–3, 256, 310, 325, 329, 356, 428, 461

Hellenistic Gnosticism 197

Hellenistic philosophy 229, 251

"helpers" of the Prophet 105, 132; *see also ansár*

Heraclius (Byzantine emperor) 46, 48

heresy 53, 144, 161, 223, 225, 264, 265, 287, 400, 431, 457

He Who Is Not Visited by a Faqíh 181

hidden *imam* 175–6, 179, 181–3, 193–5, 293, 372–4, 435, 440; *see also* al-Múntazar, Muhammad; *máhdi/qá'im*

Highway of the Martyrs 342

hijáb 30, 327, 330; *see also* headscarf; veil

Hijáz 8, 11, 31–3, 58, 65–6, 68–9, 83, 125, 172, 203, 162, 395; Arabs of 8; trade 11

híjra 26–9, 66, 108, 427; *see also* emigration

Himyarite civilization 8

Hindus 212, 377, 384, 453

Hishám (Umayyad caliph) 119, 184

"History of the Decline and Fall of the Roman Empire, The" 342

hobgoblins 12

Hodgson, Marshall 333–5, 336, 361–2

Holy Land 345, 346, 348, 350, 352, 353, 356

Hospitallers 349

hostels for wayfarers and pilgrims *see* Sufi lodge

"House of God" (*bayt Allah*) 196, 297, 301

"House of Wisdom" 150, 204, 211, 251, 274

howdah 58

Húbal (Meccan idol) 12

[al-]Hudaybiyya 33, 34

Hudhayfa (military commander) 82

hújja 173, 197, 199, 200, 209, 212

Hulagú-khan 210

human free will, doctrine of *see* Qadarites

Hungary 352, 362, 367, 371

hypocrite(s) (*munáfiq*; *munáfiqún*) 26, 27, 29, 31, 32, 78, 154, 424, 486

'ibadát (acts of worship) 101

Iberian Peninsula 42, 71, 123, 341, 344–5

Iblís 160

Ibn al-Mubárak *see* 'Abdallah b. al-Mubárak

Ibn 'Arabi 232–4, 377, 435

Ibn Babawayh 99, 180–2, 188

Ibn Badís (Algerian reformer) 391

Ibn Bájja (Andalusian philosopher) 256

Ibn Hánbal 101, 143, 160–1; inquisition of 160–1

Ibn Háwshab 200

Ibn Khaldún 150

Ibn Mája 98

Ibn Múljam 64

Ibn Rushd 265–8, 361, 399; allegorical interpretation of the Qur'an 268; Aristotle, commentator of 265–6, 268, 361; rebuttal of al-Ghazali 267–8; revealed religion and philosophical wisdom 266–7; search for happiness 267, 268

Ibn Sina 253, 256–61, 263, 399; medicine, study of 258; philosophical reasoning, types of 258; prophethood and philosophy 259–61; resurrection of bodies 260; types of existence 259; wine's prohibition 258; *see also fálsafa*

Ibn Taymiyya 234, 391, 393

Ibn Tufáyl 265

Ibn Ubáyy 29, 31

Ibrahim 8, 122–3, 125, 223, 299, 300–2; *see also* Abraham

Ibrahim b. Ad'ham 223

Ibrahim b. Muhammad, *imam* of the 'Abbasids 122, 123

iconophobia *see* figural arts

'idda (waiting period for women) 135

"idle superstitions" (in Sufism) 220, 241, 391

Idris (Enoch or Elijah) 24, 84

'ifríts 12

ignorance 88, 394; *see also jahilíyya*; paganism; pre-Islamic ignorance

ijáza (license to teach) 235, 280

ijmá' (juridical consensus) *see* consensus

ijtihád 143, 181, 405–6, 410, 416, 451, 460, 467

illiterate *see ummi*

'ilm (knowledge) 109, 111, 121, 169, 172, 173, 174, 177, 183; 'Alids, possessors of 109, 110, 111, 114, 121, 169, 173, 174, 176, 177, 183–4

imam(s) 63, 66, 68, 81, 99–101, 106, 109–12, 120–5, 138, 143, 167–79, 181–7, 193–200, 203–5, 210–15, 239, 265, 277, 291–3, 301, 331, 347, 372–4, 381, 440, 458, 460; 'Alids 168, 169, 170–8, 183–4; definition 106; Fatimids 202–7, 211; hidden 175–7, 179, 181–3, 194–5, 210, 293, 373–4, 435, 440; Isma'ilis (*bátiniyya*) 193–5; Kharijites 106, 108, 112, 187; Muhammad b. al-Hanafiyya 67–8; Nizári-Isma'ilis (*al-nizáriyya*) 209–10; occultation of 182, 203; Shi'ites 66, 92, 99, 109, 133, 143, 167–79, 187, 194, 203; Sunnis 112; tombs of 301; Zaydis 184–6

Imamis or Imamites 167; *see also* Twelver Shi'ites

"Incoherence of the Philosophers, The" 261, 263
India 71, 119, 139, 199–200, 204, 210–12, 215,
  236, 283, 362, 367–8, 374, 377, 381–2, 395–6,
  398, 400, 407, 417, 430, 433, 448, 454
Indian Isma'ilis 210, 212
Indian Ocean 7–8, 212, 344, 361, 371, 380
Indian Subcontinent 210, 367, 430
India vs. Pakistan, Kashmir issue 433, 448
Indonesian Archipelago 367, 382, 454
Injíl 86; see also Gospel
innovation (bid'a) 101, 135, 151, 391–3, 395, 427;
  see also bid'a
inquisition (míhna) 160–1; see also Ibn Hánbal
insurgencies in Iraq and Afghanistan 490
"Intentions of the Philosophers, The" 261
interactions (mu'amalát) 101
interior aspect of revelation (bátin) see bátin
interlopers 109, 170
intermediate position 157, 162
interpretation (ijtihád) see ijtihád
"intoxicated" Sufism 225; see also al-Hallaj;
  "sober" Sufism
intoxicating beverages 134–5; see also grape wine
Iran 11, 15, 34, 42, 46–9, 65, 67–9, 98, 108, 121–2,
  139, 168, 173–4, 178, 182, 184–5, 194–6,
  198–200, 204, 207–10, 212, 215, 220, 223,
  229–30, 232, 238–9, 253, 258, 261, 278, 281,
  313, 333, 336, 341, 367, 371–4, 376, 384, 397, 417,
  425, 435, 435–41, 454–60; caravan trade with 8
Iranian revolution 239, 417, 435–41, 477; Council
  of the Guardians 441; historical background of
  436–8; Khomeini's doctrine of the government
  of jurist 438–41; liberation of "disinherited"
  and "downtrodden" 440, 441; Mosaddegh
  (Mosaddeq) 438; role of Iran's clerical class
  (fuqahá') in 437–41; seizure of U.S. embassy
  in Tehran 435; White Revolution 438
Iraq 42, 46–50, 63–9, 71, 82, 105, 108–9, 121–5,
  133, 139–40, 168, 173–5, 177–8, 184, 194–5,
  199–200, 204, 207–8, 212, 214, 221, 223–4,
  227–8, 236, 288, 330, 346, 350, 369–70, 372,
  392, 394–5, 417, 425, 475, 480, 488–91
irjá' (postponement of judgement) 153
'Isa 34, 86; see also Christ; Jesus
Isaac (Is'haq) 84
Is'haq see Isaac
Ishmael (Isma'il) 8, 29, 35, 84, 199, 297–300
ISID–Pakistani intelligence agency 481
Iskandarname see "Alexander [the Great]
  Romance"
islah see reform (isláh) and renewal (tajdíd);
  reformist agenda
Islam and Christianity 53, 341; Abrahamic legacy
  341; conflict between 341–2
Islamic activism: Hasan al-Banna and Muslim
  Brotherhood 417–22, 461 (brotherhood and
  cooperation 420–1; charitable activities 421;
  criticism of despotism 418–19; Egyptian

parliamentary monarchy 421, 434; free officers
  and 421–2; going to the masses 420; restoration
  of the caliphate 420; Secret Apparatus 421;
  supreme guide 421; Western ideologies 420;
  Westernization 418–19); Iranian revolution 435–41
  (see also Khomeini, Ayatollah); Islamization
  of Egyptian society 425–30 (anti-Israeli jihád
  427; assassination of Sadat 428; bride-wealth
  427; cultural reorientation 426; demographic
  explosion 426; divine sovereignty 429; Egypt
  as "abode of unbelief" 427; godless doctrines
  of Marx, Engels and Lenin 426; Israeli–
  Palestinian conflict 428; Jihad Organization
  428–9; "Missing Obligation" 429; peace treaty
  with Israel 429; Sadat's "godless regime" 427;
  Shukri Mustafa and "Excommunication and
  Emigration" 427–8; Six-Day War of 1967 425;
  "Zionist foe" 428); militancy of 428–9, 475;
  reform agenda of Sayyid Qutb 422–5 (anti-
  Western rhetoric 423–4; hakimíyya 425, 429;
  jahilíyya and godlessness 423–5, 465; jihád
  423–4; Kharijite instansigence and zealotry 425;
  Qur'an commentary 422; radical philosophy
  427; Western feminism 424; Western vilification
  of Islam 423; women's dignity under Islam 424);
  revivalist Islam of Mawdúdi 430–4 ("active
  submission" 431; democratic caliphate 432;
  economic program 432; Hindu-dominated
  ruling Congress Party 430; Indian-Muslim
  experience under British colonial rule 430;
  instrumentalization of religious faith 431;
  Islamic democracy 432; Islamic revival program
  of 430–1; Jama'at-i Islami movement 430, 433–4;
  jihád 432; Pakistan's separation from India
  430; religious response to anxieties of India's
  Muslims 430; revolution, concept of 431; status
  of women 432); Soviet invasion of Afghanistan
  and 416; stages of 416–17
Islamic culture 71, 151, 229, 314; see also art and
  religious architecture
Islamic faith 98, 101, 148, 286–7, 297, 309, 318,
  353, 399, 416, 420, 430–1, 468, 475
Islamic fundamentalism 416
Islamic identity 76, 398, 400–1, 419, 436
Islamic influences on European culture 360–1;
  buildings 314, 361; medical works 253, 361
Islamic Jihad Organization 481–2
Islamic jurisprudence 99, 132, 137, 139, 140–3,
  248, 274, 275, 280, 282, 332, 389, 401, 402,
  427, 428; see also fiqh; Islamic legal theory;
  jurisprudence (fiqh)
Islamic justice 108
Islamic law 31, 101, 131–6, 142–4, 161, 203,
  205, 213, 223, 241, 261, 296, 303, 369, 371,
  404, 428, 437, 439; 'Abbásids, parallel system
  of justice under 144; abrogation theory in 138;
  al-Sháfi'i, role in formation 140–3; Arabian
  paganism and 131–2; articulation of 132–3, 144;

European legal codes and 133; *fiqh/fuqahá'*, role of in 136–7, 143–5; four roots of 141–3; *ijtihád* 143, 410; judges (*qádis*) role of 133–4, 137; later developments in 143; *mádhhab* (method) of 139; major stages of evolution of 131–4; *muftis*, role of in 137–8; Qur'anic roots of 134–6, 138–9 (on divorce 135; on homicide, punishments for 136; on inheritance 135–6; on marriage 135); regional schools of 133, 139–40, 143, 145; Sunni version of 133; Twelver Shiʻi version of 133, 143, 145, 174, 178, 180–2
Islamic legal theory 131–8, 140–3, 227, 293, 389, 409; *see also* Islamic jurisprudence; Islamic law; jurisprudence (*fiqh*)
Islamic legitimacy 53, 65, 124, 369
Islamic liberalism: criticism of contemporary Muslim societies 461–2; criticism of government of the jurist 457–8; geopolitical roots of 452–4; Islamic economics and banking 449; Islamizing modernity 466–8; natural law 450; popularization of thinking about Islam 452; principal themes of 449–52; Qur'an's liberal message 461; rights of women 449, 463, 466–7; role of *'ulama'* 449, 452, 457–60, 461–3, 468; scholastic trivia 461; scope and application of the Shariʻa 449; *shúra* 450, 455, 466, 467; "silent" Shariʻa 450; Sufism and 463–4; *tafsír* 451; two types of religion 457; Westernized ruling class, criticism of 454–5, 462; *see also* liberal Islam
Islamic life cycle 286, 301–4
Islamic militancy 241, 448; *see also* global jihadism; jihadism
Islamic militants 416; *see also* jihadism; *mujahideen*
Islamic modernism and reformism 389
Islamic (Muslim) polity 26, 27, 31, 34, 44, 50, 292, 332, 353, 466, 477, 490
Islamic mysticism (Sufism) 151, 220, 226, 408, 435; *see also* ascetic-mystical movement; Sufism
Islamic orthodoxy, custodians of 313–14
Islamic radicals 416; *see also* jihadism; *mujahideen*
Islamic reform, major concepts of 409–10, 415; *ijtihád* 405–6; *jihád* 410; meaning and practical implications of the Qur'anic message 406; rejection of *taqlíd* 405–6; return to the roots/fundamentals 391, 393–4; *salafiyya* 407; *shúra* 410
Islamic renaissance 178
Islamic revelation 151, 164, 196, 248, 450
Islamic revolution 435–6, 441, 456, 458, 468; *see also* Iranian revolution
Islamic Revolutionary Guard 435
Islamic science 138, 151, 401–2, 417, 441
Islamic Spain (al-Andalus) 139; *see also* Iberian Peninsula; Spain
Islamic speculative/discursive theology 151; *see also* Islamic theological reasoning; Islamic theology

Islamic State (IS) in Syria and Iraq 475, 488, 490
Islamic terrorism 323, 492; *see also* terrorism
Islamic theological reasoning 148–51, 141; acquisition of actions (*kasb*) 163; anthropomorphism 155, 159, 162; apologetic goals of 150; beginnings of 112–14, 150, 164; divine oneness 156, 162; divine predestination *vs.* human free will 151–3, 160, 162; faith, problem of 150, 153–4, 162; Greek methods of 150, 248; postponement, doctrine of 153, 157; *see also kalám*
Islamic theology 100, 114, 148–53, 154, 158, 161, 164, 178, 181, 182, 228, 229, 233, 248–50, 252, 260, 332, 389, 393, 396, 401, 428, 437, 454, 467, 477, 487; *see also kalám*
Islamic tradition xv, 2, 83, 92, 193, 279, 300, 449, 493
Islamism 415–16, 428, 475, 486–8, 491
Islamist revolutionary vanguard 488
Islamization 313, 425, 430, 432, 433, 477
island (*jazíra*) 7, 197
Ismaʻil *see* Ishmael
Ismaʻil b. Jaʻfar al-Sádiq 172, 176, 193, 194; *see also* Ismaʻilis
Ismaʻili-Fatimid state in North Africa 201, 264
Ismaʻili-Nizari community 207–9
Ismaʻilis (*bátiniyya*; *ahl al-haqq*) 167, 177, 193–7, 199–200, 203–4, 207–8, 210–11, 214, 250, 264, 332, 393, 409; al-Ghazali's attack on 264–5; assassins 201, 208–9, 211; beliefs 212; caliphate 186, 202–7, 211; cause 201, 215; cells 194–5, 197, 199; and Christianity 195; communities 196–7, 199, 200, 208; cosmology 197–9; *daʻis* 196–7, 199–202, 212, 214, 215; *daʻwa* 194, 195, 196, 203, 205; doctrine 193–4, 195–9, 201, 203, 214, 264; enclaves 194; hidden meaning of revelation, belief in 193, 196, 199; *hujja* 197, 199, 212; *imam* of 172, 193, 194, 195, 196; intellectual leaders 196, 199, 203, 214; law 204; message 194, 199; missionaries 195–7; movement 193–200, 205, 215; origin of 195; recruitment strategy 196–7; revolution 195–7, 212–14, 215; speaking and silent prophets 198–9; *ta'wíl* 196; true religion 193–4, 196, 199, 213
Ismaʻilism 172, 193, 264; *see also* Ismaʻilis (*bátiniyya*)
Ismaʻil, Muhammad b. (son of Ismaʻil b. Jaʻfar al-Sádiq) 195, 199, 210, 212
Ismaʻil, Shah 372
isnád 96
Isolationists 145; *see also* Muʻtazilites
Israel 207, 425, 428, 453, 481, 483, 489
Israeli bombardment of Beirut 483
istihsán (personal preference) 143
istisláh (consideration of human interest) 143
Italian Renaissance 313

Jabrite-Qadarite debate 112–14
Jabrites 112

Ja'far al-Sádiq (sixth imam of the Shi'ites) 99–101, 109, 123, 125, 133, 138, 143, 172–3, 176, 185, 193, 194, 198
Ja'fari school of *fiqh* 101, 133, 143, 330; *see also* Shi'ites, jurisprudence
jahilíyya 26, 88, 423–5, 465; *see also* ignorance; paganism
Jama'at-i Islami (Islamic group) 430, 433–4; *see also* Islamic activism
Jami, 'Abd al-Rahman 230, 232, 313
Jarúdiyya 184–5
Jasmine Revolution in Tunisia 455
Javád Nurbakhsh 239
Jawhar ("Diamond"; Fatimid general) 202
jazíra ("island" in Isma'ili network) 197
jazírat al-'árab see Arabian Peninsula
Jerusalem 24, 29, 46, 70, 209, 316, 344, 346–9, 352, 354, 407, 428, 478, 481
Jesus ('Isa) 34, 86, 324
Jewish Halakhá (law) 101, 131
Jews 8, 15, 23, 27–9, 32–3, 34, 47, 83, 86, 132, 158, 205, 294, 311, 341, 355, 371, 384, 404, 483–4; Yáthrib (Medina) of 15, 26, 28, 29, 32, 134
jihád 61, 71, 108, 182, 221, 223, 293, 296, 344, 350–1, 352, 380–2, 395–6, 410, 416–17, 423, 425–9, 431–3, 453, 464, 467–8, 475, 477–90, 492; defensive 423, 477; external and internal 223, 349, 464, 467; personal duty 478; proponents of 477; use of terror 484–5; *see also* global jihádism
jihadism 417, 448, 475, 491; *see also* transnational jihadism
Jihad Organization 428–9
jihád tours 479
jinn and *'ifríts* 12, 84, 100
jizya (poll-tax levied on non-Muslims) 44, 46
John the Baptist (Yahya) 23–4, 84
Jordan 34, 120, 122, 281, 426, 491
Joseph/Yusuf (prophet), story of 182, 314, 324, 329
Judaism 15, 16, 19, 26, 70, 131, 150, 294, 341, 353; Arabian 15 (Christianity and 15; Medina (Yáthrib) 15; sectarian 15; Yemen 15, 16); Islam and 341; *Shema* 286
Judeo-Christian alliance 483
Judeo-Christian scriptures 19, 24, 83–4, 100, 294, 329
judges (*qádis*) 70, 128
Judgment Day 22, 80, 83, 87–8, 157, 196, 252, 260, 279, 283
juridical revolution in Arabia 132
jurisprudence (*fiqh*) *see fiqh*; Islamic jurisprudence
Jyllands-Posten 359

Ka'b, Ubayy b. *see* Ubayy b. Ka'b
Ka'ba ("cube") 13, 14, 19, 29, 35, 67, 69, 83, 196, 213, 296–7, 299–301, 309, 314, 316; Bedouin

tribes (Bedouins) 14; bombardment of 67; direction of prayer 29; *hajj* 297; Lord (*rabb*) 14
Kabír (poet) 377
káfir 157
káhins 13; *see also* soothsayers
Kairouan 201
kalám 150–1, 154, 160–1, 163–4, 181, 249–50, 252, 261, 264, 393; *see also* Ash'arism; *fálsafa*; Mu'tazilism
Karbalá/Kerbelá 65–7, 171, 174, 179, 184, 204, 291, 295, 301–2, 320, 369, 372
Karkh 180, 182, 224
Karramiyya 223, 227
kasb see acquisition of actions
khábar/akhbár (Shi'ite *hadíth*) 99; *see also* news
Khadíja 19, 22–3, 30, 66, 314, 324, 358, 394
Khálid (son of caliph Yazíd) 67
Khálid b. al-Walíd 31, 40, 41, 46, 47
khalwa (seclusion; retreat in Sufism) 237
khamr see grape wine
Khan, Reza 437
khanaqá see Sufi lodge
Kharijism 108
"Kharijite agitator" 392
Kharijites (*khawárij*) 63–4, 71, 106, 108–9, 111, 112, 114, 118, 120, 143, 153, 186, 202, 425, 428, 487; Ibadis and 186
Khazraj (tribe) 24, 26
khirqa (Sufi robe) 235
Khomeini, Ayatollah 83, 374, 435–42, 450, 457–60, 466; governance of jurist 438–41; legislator of Islamic Republic 441; member of the *fuqaha'* class 435, 441; mystical propensities of 435–6; principle of public interest *(máslaha)* 441
khums (tax) 176
Khurasán 98, 119–24, 223, 227–8, 238, 263
khurúj (marching out) 63
khútba see five pillars of Islam
kings (*mulúk*; sing. *málik*) 119, 178
knowledge ('*ilm*) 109, 111, 114, 125, 239
Koran *see* Qur'an (*al-qur'án*)
Kubrawiyya 236
Kufa 48, 55, 58, 61, 63, 64, 65, 66, 67, 68, 69, 82, 108, 109, 111, 120, 123, 139, 174, 184, 212–14, 224, 276, 330
Kutáma 201–2
Kutayfát (Fatimid vizier) 211
kuttáb 275–6, 279, 287; *see also mádrasa*

last supper 86
"Latin principalities" 347
law in Islam and Judaism 131
Law of Islam (*al-shari'a*) 199, 450; *see also* Shari'a
leader (*imám*) 29; *see also* imam(s)
learned men (*rijál*) in Shi'ism 174, 176–7, 182–3
Lebanon 207, 478, 483

legacy of the Crusades 352; Byzantine Empire 341, 344, 347, 353; Christian religious values 352; infidel enemy 223, 342, 346, 350, 353; Papacy and the Catholic Church 353
legal method *see mádhhab*
legal ruling (*fátwa*) *see fátwa; fiqh*
Leibniz, Gottfried 358
Lepanto 371
"Lesser Occultation, The" 176; *see also ghayba*
Levant 208–10, 344, 347, 350–2, 359; *see also* Palestine; Syria
"Leveled Path, The" (*al-Muwátta'*) 139
liberal Islam 448–68; antisecularism 454–5, 464–7; conceptions of Islamic state 460–7; conservative *'ulama'* and 452, 455, 463–4; criticism of clerical rule 458–60; definition of 448–9; democracy 458; de-religionization of government 457–60; geopolitical roots of 452–4; "Godly Personality" in 464; *ijtihád* 460; liberal trends in Shi'ite Islam 456–60; major representatives of 454–67; women's rights in 452, 463, 466–7; *see also* Islamic liberalism
liberalism, definitions of 449
license to teach (*ijáza*) *see ijáza*
light (*nur*) 169
"Living, Son of the Awake (Hayy b. Yaqzan), The" 265
Lord (*rabb*) 14, 83
"Lord of the Divine Messengers, The" 81
Louis IX (king of France) 352
love (or erotic) mysticism 222, 223, 225; *see also* al-Hallaj; "intoxicated" Sufism
Luke (evangelist) 92
Luther, Martin 357

mádhhab (legal method or path) 139, 143, 392; *see also* Islamic jurisprudence (*fiqh*); Islamic legal theory; *mádrasa*
"Mad Mulla" 381
mádrasa 204, 274–5, 277–81, 283, 371; decline of 281; economic foundations of 278–9; foreign sciences in 274; *mádrasa*s of Baghdad 278; Maliki school of law and 278–9; methods and curricula of 279–81; patrons of 278–9; pedagogy at 279–80; personnel of 277, 279–81; *see also* college; *kuttáb*
Maghrib 201, 232, 236, 278, 313, 318, 341, 352
Magnus, Albertus 268
máhdi-like leader 403
Mahdi of Sudan 381
máhdi/qá'im 68, 171, 172, 193–203, 205, 213–14; al-Hasan al-'Askari 175; Isma'il b. Ja'far al-Sádiq 193; Khomeini and 440; Muhammad al-Múntazar ("The Awaited") 175; Muhammad al-Nafs al-Zakiyya 125; Muhammad b. al-Hanafiyya 68, 111; Muhammad b. Isma'il 193, 195, 199, 200, 212; Muhammad Nurbakhsh 238; Músa al-Kázim 173; Sa'íd (alias 'Abdallah

or 'Ubaydallah) 195, 200, 212 (*see also* Fatimids; Isma'ilis); Shah Isma'il 372
mádhi-ship 200, 201, 212
mahr see bride-money
máhram (close male relative) 330
Maker 94, 112, 177, 232, 250, 267, 461
Makhzumis (Banu Makhzúm) 15
máktab see kuttáb
Malamatiyya 223, 227, 228
Malaysia 210, 281, 382
Málik b. Ánas (founder of the Maliki school of law) 101, 139–40
Maliki legal theory 140–1
Maliki school of law 139–40, 142, 143, 265, 266, 275, 278, 288, 302, 330
Malikiyya 139; *see also* Maliki school of law
Mamluks 210, 278, 352, 367
Manát (Arabian goddess) 11, 83
Manichaens 47
Man of the Donkey *see* Abu Yazíd
"Man with the Birthmark" 201
"Man with the She-Camel" 200–1
Marib Dam 8
ma'rifa see Sufi knowledge (gnosis)
ma'rifat-i dini 457
marja'-i taqlid 183
Mark (evangelist) 92
marriage and gender relations 303–4, 328–9, 335–6; marriage contract 304, 328, 330; marriage payment (bride-wealth) 303, 328, 330; norms of propriety 303, 327; norms of Shari'a 303, 336; weddings 304; *see also* Islamic life cycle
Martel, Charles (Frankish king) 341–3
"Martyrs of Cordova" 354
Ma'ruf al-Karkhi 224
Marwán (secretary of 'Uthman and caliph) 55, 58, 65, 67, 69
Marwán II (caliph) 123
Marwánids 67, 69
Marw/Merv 49, 122
Marx 426, 488
Marxism and Islamism 486–9
Mary (Maryam) 34, 86, 324, 329
Maryam *see* Mary
masáhif see Qur'an (*al-qur'án*), scrolls of
Mashhad (Meshhed) 229
Masíh 86
máslaha (common good) *see* community welfare
master–disciple bond (in Sufism) 234
matn 96
Matthew (evangelist) 92
Maturidites 158, 163
Maturidite school of theology 249
mawáli/máwla see "clients" of Arabs
Mawdúdi, Abu 'l-A'la 296, 430–4, 441, 461, 465
Mawlawiyya (Sufi order) 230–1
máwlid (birthday of the Prophet) 354

mazálim (courts for redress of wrongs) *see* courts for redress of wrongs
Mecca 8, 11–16, 19, 20, 24–9, 31, 40, 44, 57, 60, 67, 76, 81–3, 94, 108, 120, 132, 140, 169, 179, 196, 203, 212–14, 232, 286, 290, 292, 295–301, 304, 309, 318–19, 329, 344, 369, 394–5, 407, 427; Battle of the Ditch 32; Battle of Úhud 31–2; caravan trade 8; geography 7–8; *hajj* 296–300; Muhammad 20–6, 33–5; oath of allegiance 33; religious center 11–15; sanctuary 12, 14–15, 29, 33–4, 40, 66–7, 297, 316; trade hub 11; Treaty of Hudaybiyya 34
Meccan emigrants to Medina 27; *see also ansár*
Meccan pagans 23, 27, 42, 478
Meccan period 27, 78
"Meccan Revelations" 232
Medina (Yáthrib) 24, 26–35, 40–4, 55–60, 63, 65–7; agriculture of 8; Aws tribe 24, 26; Banu Qaynuqa‘ 28; Battle of Badr 27–8; Battle of the Ditch 32; Battle of Úhud 31–2; geography 8; hypocrites 26–7, 29, 32; Judaism 15, 16, 19, 26; Khazraj tribe 24, 26; legal system 132; Meccan "emigrants" 26; Nakhla raid 28; *umma* 26–8, 33; visit to the tomb of the Prophet 301; Wahhabi conquest of 394
Medinan helpers 26, 40, 105, 132; *see also ansár*
Medinan period 26, 79, 134
Medinan state 108
meditation 19, 221, 229, 232, 234, 242, 255, 262, 264, 401, 417, 421
Mediterranean basin 8, 55, 332, 443, 341, 371
Mehmed II, Ottoman sultan 369
memorial mosques 175, 319
"Memorial of [Sufi] Saints" 230
Mesopotamia 369
"Message of Divine Oneness, The" 405
messenger of God (*rasúl [Allah]*) 23, 27, 29, 86, 93; *see also* Muhammad, the prophet of Islam
Messiah (*masíh*) 86, 203
míhna 160; *see also* Ibn Hánbal
"Milestones" (Qutb) 422
military commander (*amír*) *see amír*
millennialism 203; *see also chiliasm*
millet system 371
mínbar 318
miniature painting 313–16
ministers (viziers) 144, 179, 207
minstrels 361
"Missing Obligation, The" 429; *see also* al-Faraj (al-Farag) Muhammad
mission (*da‘wa*) in Isma‘ilism *see da‘wa*
Mistansiríyya 278; *see also mádrasa*
modernist reformation (*isláh*) 391, 399; *see also* reformist agenda
modernity 379–80; bureaucratic rationalism 379; colonialism 380; economic growth 379; five pillars of 379–80; industrialization 379; production of social power 380

Moguls 367, 374–7; *see also* Gunpowder Empires
monastic discipline and martial skills 348
Mongol army 210
monophysitism 15, 46, 48
monotheism 16, 23, 297, 298, 300, 310, 354, 376
monotheism of Abraham 23, 354
Montferrat 209
month of fasting (Ramadán) 78, 291; *see also* Ramadán fasting
Morocco 200, 201, 202, 266, 267, 282, 385, 455, 464, 466, 467
Moses 24, 35, 84, 199, 288, 294, 354
mosque (*másjid*): architectural and devotional aspects 316–20; center of administration and statesmanship 316–17, 318–19; communal prayer on Fridays 318; congregational (Friday) mosque (*másjid al-jámi‘*) 317, 318; courtyard 318; "Dome of the Rock" 70, 316, 347; education at 274, 277–8, 281, 318; five daily prayers 319; Furthest Mosque 316; memorial mosques 320; *mihráb* 318; *minaret* 318; *mínbar* 318; mosque-*mádrasa* complex 278, 281; *muezzin* 318; preacher (*khatíb*) 318; *qibla* 318; Ramadán vigils in 319; Sacred Mosque 316; shelter for the poor 319
Mosque of the Umayyads 70
Mother of the Faithful *see* ‘A’isha
Mothers of the Faithful 326–7; *see also* women in Islamic societies
mu‘amalát see interactions
Mu‘awiya II 67
Mu‘awiya b. Abi Sufyan 48, 119; caliph 64–5, 118; death of 65; governor of Syria 54, 60; rise of 100; son of the Prophet's enemy 49, 60; struggle with ‘Ali 60–3, 118
Mudari 8
muezzin see mosque
mufti(s) 137–8; *see also fatwa*; *fatwa*-givers
muhájirún see "emigrants"
Muhammad, the prophet of Islam: ascension to heaven and night journey of 24, 85, 288, 313, 354; background 19–20; Banú Háshim 15, 19, 23–4; Battle of the Ditch 32; Battle of Úhud 31–2; Bedouin tribes and 32–3; birthday of *see máwlid*; caravan trade 8; caricatures of 359–60; Christian views of 353–7, 359; emigration (*híjra*) 26–9; *jihád* against Meccan pagans 478; legislator 132, 134, 139, 140; Mecca 19–25; Medina 26–35; messenger of God (*rasúl Allah*) 23, 27, 29, 76, 86, 93; miracles of 94, 95, 354; mortal 86, 353; Mount Hirá 20; public preaching 22–5, 132; revelations of 20, 132; romantic portrayal of 358; Tabúk 34; Western stereotypes about 357–60, 361; wives of 326–7, 355
Muhammad ‘Ali 383, 384, 395
Muhammad al-Nafs al-Zakiyya, "Muhammad the Pure Soul" 172, 173

Muhammad al-Taqí (ninth *imam* of Twelver Shi'ism) 173
Muhammad b. 'Abd Wahháb 407; fundamentalist (conservative) reform of 392–5, 415; gambling 394; manifestation(s) of polytheism (*shirk*) 393; "pious ancestors" 394; prohibited the smoking of tobacco 394; religio-political alliance with the Sa'úd family 393, 408; *tawhíd* 392–5
Muhammad b. al-Hanafiyya 67–8, 110, 111, 120, 125, 127
Muhammad b. 'Ali the 'Abbasid 121–2
Muhammad b. Isma'il (son of Isma'il b. Ja'far al-Sádiq) 193–5, 199, 200, 212; *see also* Isma'ilis
Muhárram (*al-'Ashúra*) 29, 66, 179, 294, 295, 372
Mu'izz al-Dawla ("Glorifier of the State") 178
mujahideen (*jihád* fighters) 478, 480, 487–90; "strangers" in this world 487; *see also* foreign *mujahideen*
mujtáhid 143, 410, 436
Mukhtár, rebellion of 67–8
mu'min see believer
munáfiq (hypocrite) *see* hypocrite(s)
muqatila (Arab warriors) 44
murid (pl. *muridun*) Sufi disciple 223, 228, 234, 236, 282, 376
Músa al-Kázim *see* al-Kázim, Músa
musánnaf 97
Musaylima ("false prophet") 41, 82
Muslim [b. al-Hajjáj] 98
Muslim Brotherhood 333, 417–22, 426, 429, 433–4, 453, 460, 491; *see also* al-Banna, Hasan
Muslim–Christian confrontation 342, 343, 359; *see also* Crusades
Muslim college *see mádrasa*
Muslim creed *see* creed
Muslim dogma 148, 151
Muslim modernism 391
Muslim polity *see* Islamic (Muslim) polity
Muslim reform and renewal movement 416
Muslim world, dual societies in 385
músnad 97
Mustafa, Shukri 427–8
mut'a see women in Islamic societies
mutakállim (pl. *mutakállimún*) 151, 181, 248, 249, 393; *see also* kalám
Mu'tazilism 151, 154–8, 181, 182, 185; emergence of 154–5
Mu'tazilite creed 156–7; *see also* al-Jubbá'i, Abu 'Ali; al-Jubbá'i, Abu Háshim
Mu'tazilites 154–8, 182
muwáththaq hadíth see authenticated (*muwáththaq*) *hadíth*
"mystical brotherhoods" 283; *see also* Sufism
mystical poetry chanting (*sama'*) 228, 234; *see also* Sufi lodges
Mzab region of Algeria 143

nabídh see date juice; intoxicating beverages
Nahrawán canal 64
Na'ila (wife of caliph 'Uthmán) 60
Najaf 179, 182, 291, 301, 369, 372
Nakhla (oasis) 28
Napoleon 380–2
Naqshband, Baha' al-Din 232
Naqshbandíyya 232, 236, 377
naskh see abrogation theory
nass 109
nátiq 198
názar 154
Nazism 420
neocolonialism 476
Neoplatonic cosmology 198
Neoplatonic doctrine of emanation 197–8, 250–1
Neoplatonic metaphysics 233
Neoplatonic philosophy 241, 250–1
Neoplatonists 250
"neo-Sufi" movements 220
Nestorian Christianity 47
news (*khábar/akhbár*) *see khábar/akhbár*
New Testament 78, 310
"Niche for the Lights" 229
Nihawánd 49
Nile Valley 381
Ni'matullahiyya 238–9
Nizami 313
Nizamíyya 279; *see also mádrasa*
Nizár *see* Nizári-Isma'ilis (*al-nizáriyya*); Sabáh, Hasan-i
Nizári-Isma'ilis (*al-nizáriyya*) 207–10, 215; community 207–8, 210; creed 209–10; *fidá'is* (assassins) 208–9, 210, 211; *imams* 209–10; movement 208; rise of 207–8; state 210, 211; *see also* Sabáh, Hasan-i
Noah 8, 199, 297, 324, 329
noblemen (*ashráf/sharíf*) *see ashráf/sharíf*
nomadic and seminomadic tribes 9–10
nomadic Bedouin tribes 9; *see also* Bedouin tribes
non-'Alid caliphs 184
non-'Alid dynasty 124
non-Arab converts to Islam (*mawáli/máwla*) 50, 106, 73, 106
non-Arab Muslims 71, 276
nondenominational Sufism 242; *see also* "neo-Sufi" movements
non-Muslims 49, 108, 158, 298, 384, 417, 425, 450, 485
North Africa 42, 71, 98, 139, 143, 173, 186, 194, 195, 196, 197, 199, 200, 201, 202, 203, 212, 214, 232, 236, 264, 265, 278, 279, 282, 318, 341, 342, 352, 362, 367, 368, 369, 371, 378, 382, 384, 448, 454, 492; *see also* Maghrib
"Nourishment for Hearts, The" 228
Nufúd desert 7
nur 169
Nur al-Din Zengi (Zangi) *see* Zangi, Nur al-Din

Nurbakhsh, Javád 239
Nurbakhshiyya 238

oath of allegiance *see bay'a*
occultation (*ghayba*) 110, 171, 176–8, 187, 203;
    see also Greater Occultation
Old Man of the Mountain *see* Sinán, Rashíd al-Din
Olympic torch 2008 417
Oman 15, 108, 143, 186, 394
"On First Philosophy" 262
"Opening," the (*al-Fátiha*) 78
oppressors 184, 439, 466
"Oriental" Christians 349
Orientalists and Orientalism 357, 359, 385
Oriental societies 385
"Ornament of Saints, The" 228
orthodoxy 53, 119, 150, 228, 313, 372, 473
Osman (founder of Ottoman dynasty) 367
Ottoman Empire (caliphate) 359, 367, 403, 407,
    408; *see also* Gunpowder Empires
Ottoman–European military and ideological
    confrontation 359
"Our Decline: Its Causes and Remedies" 361

paganism 13, 16, 297, 359, 392, 394, 423–5;
    Mecca, center of 11–14; *see also jahilíyya*
Pahlavi, Muhammad Reza 435; *see also* Iranian
    revolution
Pakistan 210, 281, 296, 417, 425, 430–4, 448,
    453, 479, 480, 481, 485, 490; *see also* India *vs.*
    Pakistan, Kashmir issue
Palestine 15, 54, 123, 202, 341, 343, 344, 345, 347,
    349, 350, 351, 352, 355, 428, 429, 478, 481,
    490; Arab conquests of 44–6; *see also* Syria
Palestinian revolt 421
Palmyra 11
pan-Arabism 434
"papal monarchy" 440
paradise 87–8, 152, 157, 162, 256, 301, 318, 324–5,
    329, 346, 431, 479
Party of 'Ali *see* Shi'ites
"peace for all" (*sulh-e kull*) 376
Peasants' Crusade 347
penitents (*al-tawwábún*) 67
"people of hell" 108
"people of paradise" 108
People of the [Prophet's] House (*ahl al-bayt*) *see
    ahl al-bayt*
"People of the Prophet's Custom and Community/
    Consensus" (*ahl al-sunna wa 'l-jamá'a*) 111–12
"people of the Truth" (*ahl al-haqq*) 193
Peripatetic (Aristotelian) philosophical thought 267
Persia (Iran), caravan trade 8
Persians 121–2
personal opinion/discretion (*ra'y*) 141, 143; *see
    also ra'y*
Peshawar 480
Pharaoh 427, 438

Pharaoh's administration 175
philosophers (*falásifa*), social profiles of 256,
    268–9; *see also fálsafa*
pilgrimage rites 34, 296–9; *see also hajj*
"pious ancestors/forebears [of Islam]" (*al-sálaf
    al-sálih*) 394, 408, 409, 416, 418, 434, 452;
    see also Salafism and Salafis
plantation economy 384
Plato 250–1
Poitier (Tours) 341–3
political Islam 415–16, 491; proponents of 416
poll-tax *see jizya*
polygamy 135, 304, 328–9, 332–3, 336,
    357, 404
Pond of Khumm (*Ghadír Khumm*) 168
poor tax *see zakát*
Pope 345–6, 352, 357
Portuguese 344, 361, 371
Postmodern Western art 316
postponement doctrine (*irjá'*) 153–4
postponers (*al-múrji'a*) 153
praiseworthy (*áhmad*) 353; *see also* Muhammad,
    the prophet of Islam
prayer *see* five pillars of Islam
prayer-leader (*imam*) 106, 321
prayer of supplication (*du'a*) 291
prayers during Ramadán (*tarawíh*) 201
preacher *see* mosque
predestinarians 112, 114; *see also* Jabrites
pre-Islamic Arabia 131, 328, 393
pre-Islamic cultures of the Middle East 309
pre-Islamic ignorance (*jahilíyya*) 26, 88, 423; *see
    also* ignorance; *jahilíyya*
primeval [divine] decree (*qadar*) 152
pro-'Alid movement (party) 114, 121, 123, 125,
    127, 153, 167, 171–3, 193
pro-'Alid propaganda campaign 114, 121
pro-'Alid sentiment 114, 121, 125
proof (*hújja*) 209; *see also hújja*
prophetic custom 132; *see also* Sunna (custom) of
    the Prophet
prophetic *hadíth* 92–100, 140, 142, 168, 181, 183,
    194, 263, 265, 292, 295, 301–3, 312, 329, 391,
    466, 477, 479, 487; *see also* Sunna (custom) of
    the Prophet
Prophet of Islam 199, 274, 356; *see also*
    Muhammad, the prophet of Islam
"prophet of war" or "prophet armed" 355
Prophet's custom (*sunna*) *see* Sunna (custom) of
    the Prophet
Prophet's encounters with the angels 356
Prophet's helpers *see ansár*
Prophet's house (*ahl al-bayt*) *see ahl al-bayt*
Prophet's tomb 301
Protestantism 310
proto-Sunnis 167
punishment stories 84–5
Pushkin, Aleksandr 358

qadar see divine decree
Qadarites 153
Qadiríyya (Sufi order) 236
qádis 70, 101, 125; *see also* judges
Qajars of Iran 245, 387
qanún 371–2
Qármat, Hamdán 200
Qarmati-Fatimid split 199–200, 205, 214
Qarmati rebellion 212–13
Qarmatis (*qarámita*) 200, 205, 212–14; leaders 200, 212–14; *máhdi* 213, 214; revolt 212–14, 215; state in Bahrain 212, 213, 214
Qayrawán (Kairouan) 201
qeryana 77
qibla 290, 292, 301, 318
qiyás (reasoning by analogy) 140, 142–3, 181
qizilbásh 372; *see also* Gunpowder Empires, Safavids
Queen of Sheba 79, 324, 329
Qumm (Qomm) 174, 181, 238, 435, 436, 437
Qur'an (*al-qur'án*): Abraham/Ibrahim in *see* Abraham; allusions to 'Alid *imams* in 111, 183–4; *basmala* in 79, 80; central themes of 83–4, 88; collection of 81–3; created or uncreated 148, 159, 160; creedal statements in 88; disputation, object of 148–9; errors of the Jews and the Christians 78, 83–4; esoteric and exoteric aspects 111, 172, 183, 196, 227, 233; female behavior 326–8, 347; as focus of devotion 309–10; as foundation of Muslim faith and identity 44, 76, 89, 148, 183, 309–10; God in 83–4, 148, 155–7, 161–3; as "guidance to the people" 76; Hell in 87–8; hypocrites in 26, 27; illuminated manuscripts of 312; interpretation of 88–9, 183–4, 196, 451; Jesus and Mary 86, 324; Judgement Day 23, 87–8; language of 79–80; legal norms and rules in 134–8, 324–9; liturgical use 78; Muhammad as messenger in 86; as Muslim law 134; and Muslim tradition 22, 28, 78, 88; mysterious letters in 80–1; name and structure of 77–9; Paradise in 87; prophets and messengers in 83, 84–6; recitation of 279, 282; as revelation 76–7; rhyming prose of 79; as sacred book 76–7, 89; "Satanic verses" in 83; scrolls of 61; Shi'ite views of 183–4, 196; sociopolitical reading of 152; "stoning verse" 82, 327; and Sunna of the Prophet 183; and Thorah and Gospel 76, 92; Throne verse of 286; translation of 357; 'Uthmanic text of 82, 92, 96, 183
Qur'anic allusions 183
Qur'anic message 83–8, 148
Qur'anic narrative 76–9, 152
Qur'anic principle of "mutual consultation" 466–7; *see also al-shúra*
Qur'anic prohibitions 26, 93, 155, 275, 464
Qur'anic punishments for homicide 136
Qur'anic revelations 20, 23, 27–9, 32, 44, 76, 80, 132, 138, 263, 355–6

Qur'anic text 77, 79, 81–4, 88–9, 92, 148, 160–1, 184, 309, 312, 324
Qur'anic verses (exegesis) 96
Qur'an-reciters (*qurrá'*) 62
Quraysh tribe 11, 15, 19, 23, 24, 47, 55, 112, 120–1, 132; Muhammad and 19–20; trade caravans 11; values 15, 26; *see also* Banu Háshim; Battle of the Ditch; Battle of Úhud; Bedouin tribes; Mecca, sanctuary
Qutb, Muhammad (brother of Sayyid Qutb) 425
Qutb, Sayyid 333, 422–5, 465; *see also* Islamic activism
qu'úd ("sitting still") 184

rabb see Lord (*rabb*)
Rábi'a al-'Adawiyya 223
Radical Islamic (Islamist) movements 417, 428; *see also* global jihádism; jihadism
radicalism 109, 114, 215, 407
radicalization process 480
radical Marxism 488
Rafida (derogatory term for Twelver Shi'ites) 194
raids 10, 29, 34, 44, 212–13, 341
rak'a (prayer posture) 288, 290–2; *see also* five pillars of Islam
Ramadán 29, 78, 94, 122, 155, 201, 204–5, 294–6, 305, 319, 404
Ramadán fasting 29, 94, 204, 294–6
Raqqa (city) 61
rasúl see messenger of God
rationalist theology 151, 164, 249; *see also kalám*
raw cotton export 384
ra'y (legal opinion of a jurist) 141, 143
Rayy 49, 174, 181, 253
reason (*'aql*) *see 'aql*
reasoning (*názar*) 154
reasoning by analogy (*qiyás*) 142, 181
recollection (remembrance) of God (*dhikr*) 226, 234, 236, 283
reconquest movement (*reconquista*) in Spain 345
redeemer (*al-máhdi*) 68, 176, 193, 199–200; *see also máhdi/qá'im*
"Refinement of Legal Rulings, The" (*Tahdhíb al-ahkám*) 182
reform (*isláh*) and renewal (*tajdíd*) 389–91
reformist agenda 409–10
reform-minded critics of Sufism 393
"Register of the Arabs" (poetry) 10
"Religion of 'Ali" (*din 'Ali*) 58
"Religion of Muhammad" 58
religious judges *see* judges
reminder *see* Qur'an (*al-qur'án*)
Renan, Ernest 400
renegades 168, 171, 423–4
renewal *see* reform (*isláh*) and renewal (*tajdíd*)
restorer of religion (*mujáddid*) 263; *see also* reform (*isláh*) and renewal (*tajdíd*)
retreat or seclusion (*khalwa*) 234, 237

revelation *see* Qur'an (*al-qur'án*)
"Revivification of Religious Sciences, The" 229, 263
Reza Khan (Reza Shah) 437
Rhazes *see* al-Razi, Abu Bakr
ribat wa-jihad 221; *see also* Sufi institutions; Sufism
Richard the Lionheart (king) 352
Ridá, Muhammad Rashíd 391, 406–8; *al-Manár* 406–7; caliphate 408; condemnation of Sufism 408; mass mobilization 408; missionary school 407; mutual cooperation 407; reform program 407, 423; secular ideologies 408; social activism 407–8; *taqlíd* 408; use of printed word 406–7; Wahhabism and 407
ridda (Wars of Apostasy) 40–1
Rifa'íyya 236
rightly guided caliphs 40–9, 158, 420, 432
rights of passage *see* Islamic life cycle
rijál 174, 177, 182, 183, 184, 187; *see also* learned men (in Twelver Shi'ism)
riser (*al-qá'im*) 100, 173, 193, 196; *see also máhdi*
Roman Catholic Church 345, 346, 353, 358; *see also* Catholic Church
Romeo and Juliet 334
Rub' al-Khali (Empty Place) 7
Rukn al-Dawla 181
Rumi, Jalal al-Din 230, 244, 313
Rushdie, Salman 83
Russia 236, 242, 281, 344, 358, 362, 380, 381, 382, 383, 384, 385, 395, 406, 435, 436, 437, 481, 488, 490, 491, 492

Sabaean civilization 8
Sabaean (South Semitic) language 8
Sabáh, Hasan-i 207–10, 215
Sadat 426, 428, 429, 477
Sa'd b. Abi Waqqas 47, 48, 53
sadr 373, 374, 376
Safavid Empire 210, 372–4; *see also* Gunpowder Empires
Safavid rulers 186, 372–4
Safí al-Din, *shaykh* 367
safir see ambassador
sahih see sound (*sahih*) *hadíth*
Sahl al-Tustari 226–7, 228
Sa'íd *see* 'Abdallah/'Ubaydallah (Sa'íd)
Saladin (Saláh al-Din b. Ayyúb) 207, 209, 211, 351–2
Salafism and Salafis (*salafiyya*) 241, 409, 416
Saláh al-Din b. Ayyúb *see* Saladin
Salamiyya 195, 200
Sale, George 357, 358
Saljuk dynasty 208, 261, 350
Saljuk Turks 203, 344–5
salvific knowledge 187, 275
Samarra 174–5, 177, 369
sámit 198

Saracens 8, 341–2, 345
Sari al-Saqati 224
Sasanian coins 70
Sasanian/Sasanid Empire 42; Arab conquests 42, 46, 48–9; emperors 119; social structure 10; women in 323, 332–3, 336; Zoroastrian communities 15
Satan 77; *see also* Devil; Iblís
"Satanic verses" 82, 83, 88
"Satanic Verses" (Rushdie) 83
Saudi Arabia 14, 15, 242, 281, 301, 392, 394, 395, 425, 452, 480, 481, 482, 485
Sa'udis 408
Scala Mahomete 356
Scandinavian caricatures of Muhammad 359–60
schools of Islamic law 101, 137; *see also mádhhab*; *mádrasa*; Shari'a
schools of theology 158, 228; *see also* Islamic theology; *kalám*
scripture and divine law, study of 274
Second Crusade 349, 350, 356
secularization of education 220
self-imposed deprivations 221
Sem (Shem) 8
seminomadic Bedouin tribes 9–10
semitic linguistic group 8
separation *see* Qur'an (*al-qur'án*)
Sepoy mutiny 381
sermon *see* five pillars of Islam; *khútba* (sermon)
Seveners 167, 193; *see also* Isma'ilis
"Shade of the Qur'an, In the" 422
Shadhiliyya 236
"Shadow" (name of the 'Abbásid flag) 122
Shadow of God on Earth 178
Shafi'i legal school 140–3, 163
Shafi'i Mu'tazilite 158
shaháda (profession of faith) 86, 286–7, 289, 291, 354, 404; *see also* five pillars of Islam
Shahname 313
Shah of Iran 437–8
Shamanism 241
Shamíl 381
Shams-i Tabriz 230
Shari'a 101–2, 134, 136–7, 144, 168, 171, 186, 196, 199, 210, 213, 229, 234, 242, 304, 323, 326, 336, 354, 371–2, 394, 399, 403–4, 416, 422–3, 427, 439, 440–1, 449–50, 463–4, 477, 481; capital punishment under 354; definition 101; democracy and 469; emergence of 101, 144; and Halakhá 101, 131; precepts of 101, 144, 372; scope of 101, 134, 136; two major components of 101; unifying force 144; *see also* Islamic law; "silent Shari'a"
Shawwál (month) 94, 295
shaykh (spiritual mentor or master in Sufism) 223–4, 230, 234–7, 241–2, 371, 376–7, 401
shaykh (tribal leader) 10
shaykh al-Islam 371, 374, 400

shaykh al-tá'ifa 182
Shem (Sem) *see* Sem
shi'a 61, 127, 180–1, 459
Shi'at 'Ali 61, 108, 167; *see also* 'Ali's party
   (*al-shi'a* or *shi'at 'Ali*); Shi'ites
Shi'ism 66, 137, 167, 171, 172, 178–82, 186–7,
   207–11, 238, 264, 295, 369, 437, 457; factions
   of 167; revolutionary character of 438–9; *see
   also* 'Ali's party (*al-shi'a* or *shi'at 'Ali*); Shi'ites
Shi'ite century 178–80
Shi'ites xv, 19, 64, 66, 92, 98, 99, 109, 110, 112,
   133, 143, 149, 157, 160, 167–84, 193, 195,
   199, 204, 205, 210, 221, 239, 302, 395; absence
   of the *imam* 176–8, 194, 203; *ayatollah* 435;
   caliph 179; call to prayer 287; doctrine and
   creed 125, 153, 167, 170, 172, 176–7, 181,
   287, 288–9, 290, 295; *faqíh* 181, 439–40; *fiqh*
   143, 293, 328; *hadíth* 98–100, 143, 168, 183;
   holiday (*Ghadír Khumm*) 179, 204; *imams* 125,
   158, 167–79, 183, 185, 187, 193, 203, 239, 301,
   435; Islam, vision of 143, 171–2, 178, 187;
   jurisprudence 133, 144, 174, 178, 180–3, 293,
   295; *kalám* and 151, 164, 181; legal school
   (Ja'fari) 101, 133, 143, 330; *mujtáhids* 143, 181,
   410; *rijál*, guiding role of 182–3, 184; scripture,
   attitude toward 183; *shaháda* 287; "source of
   emulation" (*marja'-i taqlid*) 183; sources 143;
   and Sufis 239, 264, 409; and Sunnis 144, 145,
   167, 178, 182, 287, 291, 293, 301, 369, 393,
   490; temporary marriage (*mut'a*) 328; theology
   164, 174, 178, 180–3; *'ulama'* 437–8; *vilayát-i
   faqíh* 440; *see also* Shi'ism
Shikóh, Dara 377
shirk (polytheism) 393, 394, 395
Siffín, Battle of 61–3
Siger of Brabant 268
Sikhism 377
silent prophet (*sámit*) 198
"silent Shari'a" 450
silsila see spiritual genealogy [in Sufism]
Simon Peter 199
Sinán, Rashíd al-Din ("Old Man of the
   Mountain") 208
Singapore 210, 382, 407
síra (biography of the Prophet) 88
Sirhindí, Ahmad 377
sitting still (*qu'úd*) 184
Six-Day War 425
"Six Mothers" 98
slaves 10, 11, 23, 96, 108, 214, 292, 324;
   see also women in Islamic societies, slave-girls
"sober" Sufism 225, 234
social activism 391, 407–8, 417, 452
socialism 426
Solomon 79
soothsayers (*káhins*) 13, 131
Soroúsh, Abdul-Karim 455–8
"sound" (*sahíh*) *hadíth* 96, 98–9, 101

"source of emulation" (*marja'-i taqlid*) 183
South Arabian kingdoms 8–9; agriculture 8;
   collapse 8–9; settled civilization 9; trade 8
South Semitic language 8
Soviet–Afghan war 491; *see also* Afghan *jihád*
Soviet Union 422
Spain 123, 139, 202, 232, 265, 266, 279, 334, 341,
   342, 344, 345, 354, 355, 359, 360, 361, 362, 385
speaking prophet (*nátiq*) 198–9
speculative theology 150, 154; *see also* kalám;
   rationalist theology
speech (*kalám*) 150–1
spirits (*jinn* and *'ifríts*) 12
spiritual chivalry (*futuwwa*) 222
"spiritual concerts" in Sufism (*sama'*) 228, 234
spiritual genealogy in Sufism (*silsila*) 220, 225, 236
"spontaneous" monotheists (*hanífs*) 19
"stoning verse" 82, 138, 328
"suckling verse" 138
Sudanese military dictatorship 441
Suez Canal zone 418, 421; British occupation of 421
Sufi institutions 220, 229, 234–7, 242, 281–3; *see
   also taríqa*
Sufi knowledge (or gnosis) 224, 229, 230, 239, 265
Sufi litanies (*awrad*) 234, 236
Sufi lodge (*zawiya*) 229, 234, 281–3
Sufi miracles (*karamát*) 228, 237, 241
Sufi music 230, 231, 234, 241
Sufi orders *see* Sufi institutions
Sufi path to God 224, 229, 232, 234, 262; stations
   and states of 223, 228; *see also taríqa*
Sufi "psychology" 224
Sufi robe (*khirqa*) 235
Sufis 81, 100, 221, 222, 264–5, 409; spiritual elite
   (*khassa*) 227, 265; and state authorities 241
Sufi science 224–5, 227, 228
Sufi *shaykh*, duties of 282; *see also* shaykh
   (spiritual mentor or master in Sufism)
Sufi shrines 237–8, 283
Sufism (ascetic mystical movement in Islam)
   151, 220–43; al-Ghazali's advocacy of 262–5;
   beginnings of 221; classical age of 225; criticism
   of 234, 238, 241; economic foundations of 220,
   283; esoteric aspects 229, 230, 265; and friends
   of God 237–8; *hadíth qúdsi* 100; ideals and goals
   221–2; literature 220, 222, 223, 224, 227–32
   (couplet poems (*mathnawí*) 230; hagiography
   238); metaphysics 232–3; morals and values
   229, 296; *nafs* (base, animal soul) 222; Qur'an
   and 81, 88–9, 221, 222, 227, 228, 234; revival
   of 220; Shi'ism and 238–9; "unveilings" 234; in
   the West 241–2; *see also taríqa*
Sufi tradition 220, 229, 232; maturity of 229;
   systematization of 227–8, 232
Sufyanids 66
Suhrawardíyya 236
súhuf 81, 96
Sulayhid dynasty 212

Sulaymánis 212
Suleiman (Sulaymán) the Magnificent 369, 371, 372, 373
sultán 187
sultanate 143, 208
Sultan Walad (Sultan Veled) 230
súnan 98
sunna 23, 86, 92, 97–8, 111, 148, 159, 171, 409, 466
Sunna (custom) of the Prophet 71, 82, 86, 91–2, 96–9, 101, 112–15, 121, 132–4, 136–44, 148, 151, 154–5, 159, 164, 172, 213, 227, 233, 248, 274, 302, 310, 314, 391–3, 408–10, 416, 420, 432, 439, 449–51, 464; authority of 111, 159; second source of Islamic faith and practice 98, 101, 148, 183
súnnat al-nabí 31, 91; *see also* Sunna (custom) of the Prophet
Sunni Mu'tazilites 185
Sunnis 92, 167, 168, 175, 193, 287, 288–9, 490; caliphate 154, 168, 211, 373; community 111–14, 157; creed 143, 148, 167, 177, 194, 289; dynasty 185, 202–3; elite 112, 115, 179; *fiqh* 136–8, 293; *hadíth* 98–9; historians 205; Islam of 97–8, 101, 127, 133, 137, 143–4, 154, 203, 228–9, 263–4, 369, 373, 392, 459, 477 (vision of 111–15, 127, 171–2, 178); legal schools 133, 143, 288, 290, 295, 330; majority 115, 153, 154, 168, 170–1, 173, 193, 396; pragmatism 112, 114–15, 186; sources 140–3; today 115; *umma* 153, 157, 229
"Sunnisation of Zaydism, The" 186
Sunni scholars (*'ulama'*) 186, 229
Sunnism 98, 127, 264, 369, 433; Shi'ite creed in opposition to 125, 143, 167, 168, 171, 178, 179, 181, 193, 204, 289, 291, 293, 328, 438
Sunni theology 186, 229
supernatural beings 12
supporters of *hadíth see* Hadith party
súras 78–82, 275–6, 312
swift justice 144
Switzerland 210
Sword of God 40
"sword verse" 138
syllogistic reasoning 154, 268
symbolic interpretation 183; *see also tafsír*
Syria 11, 19, 31, 40, 47, 48, 58, 60, 61, 63, 64, 67, 69, 71, 82, 105, 106, 119, 121, 122, 133, 139, 140, 168, 195, 199, 200, 201, 202, 205, 207, 208, 209, 210, 211, 212, 214, 220, 221, 223, 254, 262, 264, 281, 288, 341, 342, 343, 344, 345, 346, 347, 350, 351, 352, 367, 391, 392, 395, 402, 406, 417, 425, 453, 454, 475, 480, 488, 490, 491; Arab conquests of 40, 44–6, 47, 48; caravan trade 11, 28, 33, 314; and Palestine 42, 46, 51, 54, 67, 214, 345, 347, 351, 355; *see also* Levant; Palestine
Syrian *fidá'is* 208
Syrian *hujja* 209, 212

Tabaristán 185
Tabúk 34
tafsír 88–9, 459; *see also* Qur'an (*al-qur'án*)
Tahdhíb al-ahkám 99
Tahert 202
Ta'if 11, 24, 34
tajwíd (Qur'an recitation) 279
taláq (divorce) 126; *see also* divorce
Talha 53, 58
Taliban 425, 433, 490
taqlíd 404, 405, 406, 409
tarawíh 201
taríq ("method" of a Sufi master) 234
taríqa (Sufi brotherhood or order; pl. *túruq*) 220, 234, 236, 242; rise and spread of 234–7; and state authorities 236; *see also* Sufism
tasáwwuf 221, 224; *see also* ascetic-mystical movement; Sufi science; Sufism
tawakkul 223; *see also* ascetic-mystical movement; Sufism
tawhíd 156, 160, 252, 309, 392, 394, 395; *see also* absolute unity
ta'wíl 196, 268
Táyyibi-Isma'ili community in Yemen and India 198, 211–12
Táyyibi supreme missionary (*dá'i mútlaq*) 212
Teacher of the Shi'ite Community (*shaykh al-tá'ifa*) 182
Templars 349
Temple Mount 70, 316
temporary marriage (*mut'a*) 328
Ten Commandments 88
terror for terror, idea of 485
terrorism 241, 323, 396, 434, 448, 452, 467, 480, 484–5; *see also* Islamic terrorism; jihadism
"That Which is Essential (or Basic) in Sufism" 227
theology *see* Islamic theology
Third Crusade 352, 359
third *fitna*, the 120–1
Throne verse of the Qur'an 286
Tigris River 224
Tijaníyya 243
Time (*dahr*) *see* dahr
Timurids 313
Timur Lang/Tamerlane 313
Torah 76, 134, 199
tragedy of September 11, 2001 492
translation activity under al-Ma'mun 150
transmission of Islamic learning 274–83; *kuttáb* 275–7, 279; *mádrasa* 274, 277–8; mosque 274, 275; Sufi lodge 281–3
transnational jihadism 476
trial/temptation (*fitna*) *see fitna*
tribal chief (*shaykh*) 10
tribal laws 131
tribesmen 10, 13, 19, 23
troubadours 361
true religion (*din al-haqq*) 196

Tunisia 201, 352, 385, 454, 455, 468, 491
Turkish slave guards 174
Turks 144, 203, 207
Tus 173, 182, 229, 261, 263
Twelver Imamism 158
Twelver Shi'ism 167, 172–9, 180–3, 184, 187, 211, 373
Twelver Shi'ite law 181–3, 331, 373; see also Ja'fari school of fiqh
Twelver Shi'ite Mu'tazilite 158
Twelver Shi'ites (Twelvers) 133, 143, 157, 167, 172, 176–7, 180–4, 187, 193, 194, 199, 203, 372; see also Shi'ites
tyrants 182, 187, 459

'Ubaydallah see 'Abdallah/'Ubaydallah (Sa'íd)
'Ubaydallah b. Ziyád (governor of Iraq) 66, 67, 68
Ubayy b. Ka'b 82
Úhud 31–2, 40, 60, 135
'ulamá' 128, 144, 161, 225, 229, 233, 275, 350, 468
'Umar b. 'Abd al-'Aziz ('Umar II) 70, 71, 119
'Umar b. al-Khattab 54, 92, 94, 138; appointment of [al-]shúra 53, 57, 58, 60; assassination of 49; and collection of the Qur'an 81; Commander of the Faithful 42; leadership 40, 42, 44, 49–50, 54, 55; legislator 44, 82, 132, 138, 327, 328; organization of conquests 42–4, 47, 48, 49
'Umar II see 'Umar b. 'Abd al-'Aziz
Umayyad clan 15, 31, 54, 57, 60, 64, 65, 105, 167
Umayyad dynasty in Spain 123
Umayyad Empire 71
Umayyads 15, 53, 54, 55, 60, 66, 67, 68, 69, 70, 71, 127, 132, 133, 150, 221, 311, 342, 419, 440; 'Ali's party and 64, 66, 109–11; appointment of judges by 70, 128, 132; authoritarian rule of 69–71, 136, 167, 459, 467; internecine struggle 119; Kharijites and 106, 108–9, 114; "kings" (mulúk) 119, 311; legislators 132, 139; legitimacy of 70, 71, 112, 118–19, 127, 152, 153; loyalists of 111–12, 153; mawáli and 105, 106, 119, 122; opposition to 105–6, 108, 109, 111, 113, 114, 118, 119, 121, 122, 123; overthrow of 120, 123–4, 132, 139; perpetual conquest, policy of 119; representatives (vicegerents) of God 118; theological debates under 112–14; "usurpers" 119, 171, 419, 440; victims of 'Abbasid terror 123
umma 15, 27, 33, 57, 58, 63, 70, 157, 395, 396, 398, 399, 401, 404, 405, 406, 452, 465, 466, 478; after the Prophet 40; defeat 32; formation of 26; islám 26; jihád and 478–80; kufr 26; leadership of 63, 66, 99, 167; military successes 28–9; moral values 26
úmmi 23
unbeliever (káfir) 157
unity of existence, doctrine of 234; see also Ibn 'Arabi
"Unveiling of That Which Is Hidden, The" 228

Urban II 345, 356
U.S. intelligence agencies 433
U.S. occupation of Afghanistan and Iraq 488
usurpers 119, 168, 171, 182, 184, 185, 199, 372
'Uthman 60, 153, 182, 185; Arab conquests 49; collection of the Qur'an 82, 96, 183; election of 53, 182; grievances against 54–6, 105; murder of 56, 118, 153; shirt of 60

veil (hijáb) 30, 327
Victor, The 124
Vienna 371
vilayat-i faqíh see government (governance) of the jurist
vizier(s) 144, 203, 207, 211
Volga region 139, 236, 362
Voltaire 358
voluntary fasts 295
voluntary military service (ribat wa-jihad) 221

wahdat al-wujud see Ibn 'Arabi; unity of existence, doctrine of
Wahhábis 241, 392, 394, 395
Wahhábism 392, 395, 407; see also Muhammad b. 'Abd Wahháb
waiting period for women ('idda) see 'idda
wakíl 174
walaya or wilaya (friendship with God or sainthood in Sufism) 222–3; see also cult of "friends of God"; friend(s) of God
Walíd b. 'Abd al-Malik 69
Walíd II (Umayyad caliph) 119
waqf endowment see charitable endowment or trust
Waqqás, Sa'd b. Abi 47–8, 53
Wáraqa 19, 22
warning prophets 84
warriors for faith (mujahidún) 214
warriors of Christ (militia Christi) 346
wars of apostasy see ridda
wasí (legatee) 58
Wásil b. 'Atá 151, 154, 157
Way of the Prophet 29; see also Sunna (custom) of the Prophet
"weak" (da'íf) hadíth 96, 99
wedding see marriage and gender relations
West and Islam (the Muslim world) 341–62; Arab conquests 341; colonial expansion of Europe and Russia 380–3; Constantinople 342, 343, 344; Crusades 343–53, 356 (acts of piety and penitence 346, 352; composition of 347; Franks in Palestine 349–50; Jerusalem 347–9, 352; "Latin principalities" 347, 350; Louis IX (St. Louis) 352; Mamluks 352; monastic orders and 348–9; motives of 346, 353; Ottoman Turks 352; papacy and 345–6, 353; political fragmentation of the Muslim word and 346–7; reconquista 345, 359; Saladin 351–2); cultural exchange between

360–1; image of the prophet Muhammad in
353–60, 361; rise of the West 361–2
Western consumerism 241
Western domination 389
Western education 398, 419
Western imperialism 439
Western media 448, 452, 475
Western scholars (scholarship) 19, 27, 77, 79, 81,
82, 150, 160, 161, 177, 180, 241, 262, 294, 313,
314, 396, 399, 409, 480, 491
Western technological and military superiority 391
whirling dervishes see Mawlawíyya
White Revolution 438; see also Iranian revolution
wisdom see Qur'an (al-qur'án)
wives of the Prophet 29–30, 324–5, 336
women in Islamic societies 135, 303–4, 323–36;
'A'isha 324, 327; Ásya 324, 329; Bilqís 324,
329; controversial topic 323–4; Eve (Hawwá)
324; Fátima 324; in Hadíth and fiqh 329–31
(divorce 330–1; hijáb 330; legal schools 330–1;
máhram 330; marital duties 329; marriage
contract 304, 330; missing husband 330;
motherhood 330; paternal cousins 331; stoning
for adultery 327; tribal customary law 331;
triple statement of the divorce formula 330;
unfavorable treatment of women 329–30, 332,
336; virginity 331); Khadíja 324; male-centered
ethos of Arabian society 323, 330; male–female
relations 324, 327, 329, 330, 331, 332–6;
Mary (Maryam) 324, 329; patriarchal mind-set
331, 336; pre-Islamic customs and traditions
331, 333, 336; in the Qur'an 135, 303, 324–9
(adultery 324, 327; bride-gift/wealth 135, 328,
329; celibacy 328; concubines 328; degrees of
kinship 327; divorce 135, 328, 329; equality
of religious duties 325–6; four wives 135, 328;
hijáb 30, 327, 330; inheritance provisions 135–6,
326; intellectual and judgmental capacities 325;
marriage contract 328; polygamy 135, 303,
328; prostitution 71, 328; right to be supported
328–9; slave-girls 328; social and economic
inequality 326; temporary marriage (mut'a)
328); Sayyid Qutb's views of 424; theorizing the
Muslim woman 332–6 (adultery, punishment of
336; androcentric and misogynistic culture of
'Abbásid society 332–3; class factor of gender
relations 335–6; concubinage 333; equality of
sexes as the fundamental message of Islam 332;
female chastity 334–6; freedom and respect 332;
harem 333–5, 336; Kharijites 332; maltreatment
323, 330, 334; masculine honor 334–5;
Mediterranean culture(s) 334–5, 336; misogynist
attitudes 323, 331; moral and spiritual equality
332; objects of sexual pleasure 335; polygamy

303, 332, 333, 336; Qarmatis 332; seclusion
333–4; slave-girl(s) 8, 110, 299, 324, 328, 333,
336; Sufis 332; veil 332, 333); Zuláykha 324
"wool-people" or "wool-wearers" see Sufis
World War I 358, 370
World War II 437, 476
worship ('ibadát) 101

Xinjiang 382

Yahya see John the Baptist
Yahya al-Hádi ila 'l-haqq ("Yahya Who Leads on
the Path of Truth") 186
Yamáma 41, 81
Yamani: Arabs 8; language 8
Yassine, Abdessalam 464–7
Yassine, Nadia 467
Yazdagird III 48, 49
Yazíd (caliph and son of Mu'awiya) 65, 66–7
Yemen 7, 15, 16, 33, 236, 278, 290, 362, 371,
394, 425, 482, 485, 490; British colonization
of 382; Isma'ilism in 194, 200, 201, 204, 211,
212, 215; Judaism in 15, 16; Marib Dam 8;
Ottoman occupation of 371; Zaydism in 143,
167, 184–7, 290; Zoroastrian communities
in 15

Zagros Mountains 47–9
záhir (external; exoteric) 111, 143, 196, 199
Záhiri school of Baghdad 143
zakát tax 33, 40–1, 293–4; see also five pillars
of Islam
Zangi (Zengi) Nur al-Din 211, 350
Zangids (Zengids) 209
záwiya see Sufi institutions; Sufi lodge
Zayd b. 'Ali (founder of Zaydism) 123, 184
Zayd b. Thabit 81–2
Zaydi [Shi'ite] Mu'tazilite 158
Zaydis 109, 167–8, 177, 184–7, 194, 393; doctrine
184–5; dynasty 186; imam 184–7; Yemen 143,
185–6; see also Zayd b. 'Ali
Zaydi Shi'ites 133, 167, 178, 184, 187, 290, 293;
see also Yemen; Zaydis
Zaydism 143, 158, 179, 184–7
Zengi see Zangi (Zengi) Nur al-Din
Ziau 'l-Haq 433
Zionism 429
Zirids 202
ziyára(t) (pious visit; local pilgrimage) 237; to the
Prophet's tomb 301
Zoroastrian 15, 47, 49, 213, 333, 408
Zoroastrianism 16, 47, 49, 122, 150; Persians 16,
47, 49
Zuláykha 324